A Global Encyclopedia of Historical Writing

GARLAND REFERENCE LIBRARY OF THE HUMANITIES (VOL. 1809)

A Global Encyclopedia of Historical Writing

Volume II
K–Z

Editor
D.R. Woolf

Managing Editor
Kathryn M. Brammall

Editorial Assistant
Greg Bak

Advisory Editors
Peter Burke
John Flint
Georg G. Iggers
Donald R. Kelley
F.J. Levy
D.L. McMullen
Peter Novick
Karen Offen
Anthony Reid
Kenneth Sacks
Judith P. Zinsser

GARLAND PUBLISHING, INC.
A member of the Taylor & Francis Group
New York & London, 1998

Library of Congress Cataloging-in-Publication Data

A global encyclopedia of historical writing / editor, D.R. Woolf ;
     managing editor, Kathryn M. Brammall ; editorial assistant, Greg Bak
   ; advisory editors, Peter Burke . . . [et al.].
          v.   cm. — (Garland reference library of the humanities ; vol.
     1809)
          Includes bibliographical references and index.
          ISBN 0-8153-1514-7 (v. 1 : alk. paper)
          1. Historiography.   2. Historians.   I. Woolf, D. R. (Daniel R.)
     II. Series.
     D13.G47   1998
     907'.2—dc21   97-42982
                                                                                    CIP

Cover art: Antique map, World / Seutter 1730
Cover design: Lawrence Wolfson Design, New York

Printed on acid-free, 250-year-life paper
Manufactured in the United States of America

Contents

A Global Encyclopedia of Historical Writing

Volume II
K–Z

K

Kagwa, Sir Apolo, (1869–1927)

Baganda "protonationalist," prime minister *(katikkiro),* and writer. Kagwa was born in 1869 into a Baganda aristocratic family, and had some Western education as provided by the missions. Initiated early into politics, Kagwa rose rapidly in the royal service of King Mutesa, becoming the *katikkiro* in 1889. Between 1897 and 1914 Kagwa ruled Buganda as a regent and negotiated the Agreement of 1900 with Britain, which guaranteed for Buganda some degree of autonomy under colonial rule. He was knighted in 1902. Besides Kagwa's profound but controversial political accomplishments, he found time to engage in historical writing. Although he wrote in *Luganda* (the language of the Baganda people), his works provided the first attempt at ethnohistory of a people to be done by any East African. Kagwa's efforts resulted in the publication of many books, most of which have been translated into English. Out of these works, two remain very significant: *The Kings of Buganda* (1901) and *The Customs of the Baganda* (1909). While *The Kings of Buganda* attempted to demonstrate that the precolonial political system of the Kingdom of Buganda had already exhibited outstanding capacity for good and effective government, *The Customs* stressed the need to preserve the continuity as well as the self-respect of the Baganda people in an era of rapid and humiliating change occasioned by European imperialism. Based mainly on the record of the oral traditions of the kingdom and particularly events of his own time, it was clear that the purpose of these works was to legitimize the extraordinary degree of autonomy claimed by the Baganda in the Agreement of 1900 with the British. Kagwa's writings, by their clarity and elegance, helped to establish Luganda as a language in which an educated elite could express complex ideas. More widely significant for historical studies in the future was the way in which Kagwa's writings demonstrated that some African societies had highly complex historical memories, hitherto orally transmitted, which could form a basis of "oral documents" for the reconstruction of precolonial history in Africa.

Apollos O. Nwauwa

Texts

The Customs of the Baganda. Ed. May
   Mandelbaum Edel; trans. Ernest B. Kalibala.
   New York: Columbia University Press, 1934.
The Kings of Buganda. Ed. and trans. M.S.M.
   Kiwanuka. Nairobi: East African Publishing
   House, 1971.

References

Mukasa, Ham. *Sir Apolo Kagwa Discovers Britain.*
   Ed. Taban lo Liyong. London: Heinemann,
   1975.
Wrigley, C.C. "Apolo Kagwa: Katikkiro of
   Buganda." In *Leadership in 19th Century
   Africa: Essays from Tarikh,* ed. Obaro Ikime.
   London: Longman, 1974, 116–127.

Kaizuka Shigeki (1904–1987)

Japanese historian of China. Born in Tokyo, Kaizuka graduated from Kyoto Imperial University before joining its affiliated Institute of Oriental Culture. He served as the director of the institute, renamed as the Research Institute of Humanistic Sciences, between 1949 and 1955, retiring from it in 1968. Kaizuka's main area of interest was the ancient Shang, and he was among the first to use systematically the inscriptions on oracle bones and bronze vessels for the study of its history. Kaizuka published, in addition to a number of books on ancient Chinese history and culture, several edited collections of oracle bone inscriptions.

John Lee

Texts

Kaizuka Shigeki chosakushō [Collected Works of Kaizuka Shigeki]. 10 vols. Tokyo: Chūō Kōron Sha, 1976–1978.

Kalista, Zdeněk (1900–1982)

Czech historian, poet, and translator. A promising docent at the University of Prague in his early career, his progress was impeded by his imprisonment from 1950 to 1960 and subsequent discrimination by Communist authorities; he nevertheless managed to produce or edit over twenty books and numerous articles, some in *samizdat* fashion. (*Samizdat* was a practice of self-publishing common in Communist countries, whereby an author, denied access to regular, government-controlled presses, allowed multiple typewritten copies of his or her work to circulate in typewritten form.) In 1991, in recognition of his fortitude and his achievements, he was posthumously awarded one of the highest decorations of then Czechoslovakia by President Václav Havel.

Kalista belonged to a group of Czech intellectuals who tried, largely successfully, to rehabilitate the baroque as a positive period in Czech culture and history, in contrast to previous writers, who had viewed it mostly negatively. The list of his major works in this field starts with a brilliant monograph on the making of a perfect baroque cavalier, *Mládí Humprechta Jana Černína z Chudenic* [The Youth of Humprecht Jan Černín z Chudenic] (1932); reaches its pinnacle in his panoramic overview of Czech literary baroque, *České baroko* [Czech Baroque] (1941); and ends with a passionate summation of his many insights into this phenomenon in his *Tvář baroka* [The Face of the Baroque] (1982), which he had to dictate to his friends owing to the loss of his eyesight in the last years of his life. A special place among his works belongs to *Česká barokní gotika a její žďárské ohnisko* [Czech Baroque Gothic and Its Focal Point in Žďár] (1970), a study of a unique type of Czech architecture that had tried to unite, with admirable results, Gothic and baroque structures and forms. A talented poet, he also published several volumes of poetry and numerous translations of historical and literary works from several languages.

Josef Anderle

Texts

Česká barokní gotika a její žďárské ohnisko. Brno: Blok, 1970.
České baroko. Prague: Evropský literární klub, 1941.
Mládí Humprechta Jana Černína z Chudenic. Prague: Nákladem vlastním, 1932.
Tvář baroka. Munich: Edice Arkýř, 1982.

References

Kalista, Zdeněk. *Cesty historikovy* [The Ways of a Historian]. Praha: Václav Petr, 1947.
"Zdenek Kalista." In František Kutnar. *Přehledné dějiny českého a slovenského dějepisectví* [General History of Czech and Slovak Historiography]. Prague: Státní pedagogické nakladatelství, 1977, vol. 2, 319–322.

al-Ḳalḳashandī, Abu 'l-'Abbās Aḥmad ibn 'Abdallāh (1355–1418)

Mamlūk official and author. al-Ḳalḳashandī was born in Ḳalḳashanda in the Egyptian delta. He served in various capacities during the second Mamlūk period (1382–1517) but achieved prominence as secretary of the chancery. He completed the *Ṣubḥ al-a'shā fī ṣinā'at al-inshā* '[The Morning Light in Chancery Art], an encyclopedic manual for chancery scribes during the Mamlūk period, in 1412. Based on the author's own observations and experiences and containing a host of treaties and documents, it offers historians a treasure of information on Islamic history, especially on Fatimid Egypt (969–1172) and the Mamlūk period. It contains, among other things, detailed expositions on the practical and theoretical training of the scribe; geography and topography; the Caliphate; Egypt's districts and their boundaries, cities, organization, administration, climate, crops, and finances; language arts; the Prophetic Traditions; the economy; and correspondence between provinces.

Mahmood Ibrahim

Texts

Ṣubḥ al-a'sha fī kitabat al-inshā'. Trans. Luis Seco de Lucena (into Spanish). Valencia: Anubar Ediciones, 1975.
Ṣubḥ al-a'shā fī ṣinā'at al-inshā'. Cairo: al-Mu'assasas al-Misriyya al-'Amma li 'tta'lif wa 'ttarjama wa 'ttiba'a wa 'nnashr, 1964.
Faharis ṣubḥ al-A'sha [Indices]. Ed. Muḥammad Qandil al-Baqli. Cairo: 'Alam al-Kutub, 1972.

References

Bjorkman, W. *Beiträge zur Geschichte der Staatskanzlei im islamischen Ägyten* [Contributions to the History of the Chancellory in Islamic Egypt]. Hamburg: Friederichsen, De Gruyter and Co., 1928.
Little, Donald. *History and Historiography of the*

Mamluks. London: Variorum Reprints, 1986.

Popper, William. *Egypt and Syria under the Circassian Sultans, 1382–1468.* University of California Series in Semitic Philology, vols. 15–16. New York: AMS Press, 1977.

Kampuchean Historiography

See CAMBODIAN HISTORIOGRAPHY.

Kang Youwei [K'ang Yu-wei] (1858–1927)

Chinese philosopher and leader of the reform movement in the late Qing dynasty. Born in Nanhai in Guangdong province, Kang grew up in a family with Confucian classical learning. Although he earned his status in modern history mainly because of his leading role in the "Hundred Days' Reforms" in 1898, throughout his life his central aim was to initiate reform in the political, economic, and intellectual spheres of traditional China. The decisive commitment of his scholarly life lay in his pursuit of the "New Text" tradition in Confucian scholarship. In painting Confucius as a reformer, he tried to revive Confucianism by dissociating it from a rigid, state-sponsored orthodoxy. In his work, Kang laid the groundwork for a theory of historical progress based on the New Text concept of the Three Ages, wherein society advanced from an earlier age of "disorder" through an age of "minor tranquillity," that in turn anticipated the future era of a global "great peace." In *Datong shu* [Grand Unity] (1901–1902), Kang described his vision of a utopian world that reflected what he conceived to be the best of revised Confucianism and various international traditions, sciences, and technologies.

Shao Dongfang

Texts

Kang Youwei quanji [Completed Works of Kang Youwei]. Ed. Jiang Yihua and Wu Gengliang. Shanghai: Shanghai renmin chubanshe, 1987–1995.

Tang T'ung Shu: The One World Philosophy of K'ang Yu-wei. Trans. Lawrence G. Thompson. London: Allen and Unwin, 1958.

References

Hsiao Kung-ch'üan. *A Modern China and a New World: K'ang Yu-wei, Reformer and Utopian, 1858–1927.* Seattle: University of Washington Press, 1975.

Lo Jung-pang, ed. *K'ang Yu-wei: A Biography and a Symposium.* Tucson: University of Arizona Press, 1967.

Kann, Robert A. (1906–1981)

Austro-American historian. Born into a Viennese professional family, Kann received a law degree from Vienna University in 1930. After almost a decade of law practice he emigrated to the United States in 1938. There he joined Princeton's Institute for Advanced Study before obtaining his doctorate in history from Columbia University. From 1946 until his retirement in 1976 he taught at Rutgers University and as a visiting professor at Columbia, Princeton, and Vienna. Kann's studies of the structure of the Habsburg monarchy and the legacies of its constituent nationalities earned him a place among the world's foremost scholars on Eastern Europe. Besides dealing with political history and the complexities of ethnicity, his research embraced the study of the area's intellectual traditions and the issues revolving around the emergence of the successor states after World War I. His academic eminence was recognized by the receipt of Prize for Humanities of the City of Vienna and membership in the Austrian Academy of Science.

William O. Oldson

Texts

A History of the Habsburg Empire, 1526–1918. Berkeley: University of California Press, 1977.

The Multinational Empire, Nationalism and National Reform in the Habsburg Monarchy, 1848–1918. New York: Octagon Books, 1970.

Das Nationalitätenproblem der Habsburgermonarchie [The Problem of Nationalism in the Habsburg Monarchy]. Second ed. Graz: H. Böhlau, 1964.

A Study in Austrian Intellectual History, from Late Baroque to Romanticism. New York: Octagon, 1973.

References

Obituary. *New York Times.* September 2, 1981, A18.

Kantorowicz, Ernst Hartwig (1895–1963)

German historian of the Middle Ages. Kantorowicz began his career as a devotee and member of the inner circle of the poet Stefan George. A fierce nationalist with strong literary talents, he was asked to write a biography of Emperor Frederick II. When his *Kaiser Friedrich der Zweite* finally appeared in 1927, it created a huge debate among those who extolled it for its rich literary virtues and those who decried it as a biased, unscholarly treatment of the controversial ruler. The original biography having

K

been published without footnotes or citations, Kantorowicz responded to criticism in 1931 by publishing an *Erganzungsband*, rich with annotations and commentaries on the original text. The author slowly gained recognition as a historian and serious academic. Jewish by birth, Kantorowicz soon found himself forced out of his university position by the Nazi regime, and eventually out of Germany itself. He spent a year at Oxford, then taught for a time at Berkeley until the dispute over the loyalty oaths demanded of California professors convinced him to settle at Princeton. His interdisciplinary approach and broad-ranging interests manifested themselves in two monographs and some fifty articles, notes, and reviews. In 1957 he published his most famous book, *The King's Two Bodies*, a rich melding of traditional archival, artistic, literary, and legal sources into a complex and multilayered, if at times esoteric, study of the ideas and symbols of medieval kingship. The work has had a lasting impact on studies of medieval and early modern political thought.

Krista Kesselring

Texts

Ernst Hartwig Kantorowicz: Geschichtsschreiber [Selections]. Vienna: Turia & Kant, 1992.
Frederick the Second, 1194–1250. Trans. E.O. Lorimer. London: Constable, 1931.
The King's Two Bodies. Princeton, NJ: Princeton University Press, 1957.
Selected Studies. Locust Valley, NY: J.J. Augustin, 1965.

References

Abulafia, D. "Kantorowicz and Frederick II." *History* 62 (1977): 193–210.
Baethgen, Friedrich. "Ernst Hartwig Kantorowicz." *Deutsches Archiv für Erforschung des Mittelalters* 21 (1964): 1–14.
Malkiel, Y. "Ernst H. Kantorowicz." In *On Four Modern Humanists: Hofmannsthal, Gundolf, Curtius, Kantorowicz,* ed. A.R. Evans. Princeton, NJ: Princeton University Press, 1970.

Karamzin, Nikolai Mikhailovich (1766–1826)

Russian historian, journalist, and novelist. Born a nobleman, Karamzin became a successful journalist. In 1803, Emperor Alexander I appointed him official historian of the Russian Empire. He wrote a twelve-volume *History of the Russian State,* which ended at the Time of Troubles with the author's death. His view of history was a mixture of Enlightenment views and feudal ideology. A firm nationalist, he identified the history of Russia with the state and autocracy. He defended serfdom as an inalienable part of the society. He criticized Peter I for importing foreign ways and praised Catherine II for subordinating the Poles to Moscow. He used many new historical sources and was a proponent of the "Normanist theory" of the origin of Kievan Rus' (the ducal state within what is now Ukraine and which existed from the ninth to the thirteenth centuries). His work was popular with the educated public because of its high standards of scholarship and informal, readable style. His conservative views were the basis for much of official nineteenth-century Russian historiography.

Elizabeth V. Haigh

Texts

Istoriia gosudarstva Rossiiskogo [History of the Russian State]. 12 vols. St. Petersburg: N. Grecha, 1818–1829.
Karamzin's Memoir on Ancient and Medieval Russia. Trans. and by Richard Pipes. Cambridge, MA: Harvard University Press, 1959.

References

Black, J.L. *Essays on Karamzin: Russian Man-of-Letters, Political Thinker, Historian, 1766–1826.* The Hague and Paris: Mouton, 1975.
———. *Nicholas Karamzin and Russian Society in the Nineteenth Century: A Study in Russian Political and Historical Thought.* Toronto: University of Toronto Press, 1975.

Kareev, Nikolai Ivanovich (1850–1931)

Russian historian and sociologist. Kareev was the author of a groundbreaking study of prerevolutionary France and preeminent academic representative of the Russian "subjective school" of sociology. Kareev's 1879 work *The Peasantry and the Peasant Question in France* transformed the analysis of the *ancien regime* peasantry. Utilizing new archival sources—particularly peasant *cahiers*—Kareev rejected the juridical discussion of the peasantry and established that feudal obligations were resurgent in the prerevolutionary epoch. He contradicted Alexis de Tocqueville's interpretation that the Revolution was unnecessary. The work was translated into French, elicited approval from Marx and Engels, and helped establish *l'école russe,* which reflected Russian social anxiety in the intensive study of *ancien regime* France. He authored numerous works on French, European, and Polish history. Kareev also wrote extensively on the philosophy of history. He attempted to reconcile Comtean sociological objectivism with Russian populist ethical voluntarism, allotting to sociology the elaboration of laws of human social behavior. He bridged the gap to social engagement by applying elements of subjective sociology to the historical process. His analysis led to the discussion of ideographic versus nomothetic historical phenomena (roughly speaking, those that are unique, and those that may be grouped together or explained by laws), significantly predating Heinrich Rickert's work, and to insightful critiques of Marxism. Kareev's death coincided with the purge of historians in Stalin's USSR.

T. Sanders

Texts

Istoriki frantsuzskoi revoliutsii [History of the French Revolution]. Leningrad: Izd-vo "Kolos," 1924–1925.

Les paysans et la question paysanne en France dans le dernier quartier du XVIIIᵉ Siècle [The Peasants and the Peasant Question in France during the Last Quarter of the Eighteenth Century]. Paris: V. Giard & E. Briere, 1899.

"Les travaux russes sur l'époque de la révolution française depuis six ans" [Russian Work on the French Revolutionary Era in the Past Six Years]. *Bulletin de la societé d'histoire moderne,* Third Series, 10 (1912): 81–91

References

Hecker, Julius F. *Russian Sociology: A Contribution to the History of Sociological Thought.* Studies in History, Economics, and Public Law Edited by the Faculty of Political Science of Columbia University, vol. 67, no. 161. New York: Columbia University Press, 1915.

Veber, Boris, G. "Nikolai Ivanovich Kareev." In *The Modern Encyclopedia of Russian and Soviet History.* Vol. 16, ed. Joseph L. Wieczynki. Gulf Breeze, FL: Academic International Press, 1980.

Vucinich, Alexander. *Social Thought in Tsarist Russia: The Quest for a General Science of Society, 1861–1917.* Chicago: University of Chicago Press, 1976.

Ka'ti, Maḥmūd bin al-Hādjdj al-Mutawakkil (d. 1593)

Arab historian and author of *Ta'rīkh al-fattāsh* [History of the Searcher]. The little that is known about his life is contained in *Ta'rīkh al-fattāsh* and in al-Sa'dī's *Ta'rīkh al-Sūdān* (ca. 1655). Most probably Ka'ti was born during the reign of

Askia al-hadjdj Muḥammad I (1493–1528). He is mentioned as the Kadi (Judge) of Tindirma in 1588. *Ta'rīkh al-fattāsh,* a work on the history of Timbuktu, was completed in the later seventeenth century, after Ka'ti's death, but the text was corrupted in the nineteenth century to justify Aḥmadu Lobbo's claim as the spiritual successor of Askia Muḥammad. Modern scholarship has raised questions about the authorship of the work. Elias N. Saad believes that the first part of the text was written in 1519 by Maḥmud bin Umar Aqit; N. Levtzion, however, rejects this thesis. The chronicle has also been associated with Ka'ti's son Ismail, who inherited both his father's historical interests and his judgeship, and is believed to have revised the chronicle from his father's notes. Maḥmud Ka'ti's grandson, Ibn al-Mukhtar Qunbulu is also mentioned as a possible author. The corrupted text has been edited and translated into French by O. Houdas and M. Delafosse.

Hootan Shambayati

Texts

Tarikh el-fettach, ou, Chronique du chercheur, pour servir à l'histoire des villes, des armées et des principaux personnages du Tekrour. Trans. into French O. Houdas and M. Delafosse. Paris: E. Leroux, 1913.

References

Levtzion, N. "A Seventeenth Century Chronicle by Ibn al-Mukhtar: A Critical Study of Tarikh al-fattash." *Bulletin of the School of Oriental and African Studies* 34 (1971): 571–593.

Saad, Elias N. *Social History of Timbuktu.* Cambridge, Eng.: Cambridge University Press, 1983.

Katō Shigeshi (1880–1946)

Japanese economic historian of China. Born in Matsue, Japan, Katō graduated from Tokyo University in 1906. As professor at Keiō, and then at Tokyo, Katō became the pioneering scholar of Chinese economic history in modern Japan. He wrote prolifically on commerce, currency, and urbanization in the Han, Tang, and Song periods, but achieved prominence with his two-volume *Tōsō Jidai ni okeru Kingin no Kenkyū* [Studies on Gold and Silver in the Tang and Song Periods] (1925–1926). The quality of the book's empirical evidence and critical analysis made it a seminal work in the field and brought Katō a doctoral degree and a historiographical prize. Other major publications include *Shina Keizaishi Gaisetsu*

[Outline of Chinese Economic History] (1944) and annotated translations of some of the dynastic records. His most important writings appeared in *Shina Keizaishi Kōshō* [Observations on Chinese Economic History] (1949).

Janet E. Hunter

Texts

Tōsō Jidai ni okeru Kingin no Kenkyū. Tokyo: Tōyō Bunko, 1925–1926.
Shina Keizaishi Gaisetsu. Tokyo: Kōbundō, 1944.
Shina Keizaishi Kōshō. Tokyo: Tōyō Bunko, 1952–1953.

References

Enoki Kazuo. "Katō Shigeshi Hakase Shōden [Brief Biography of Dr. Katō Shigeshi]." In *Shina Keizaishi Kōshō*, vol. 2. Tokyo: Tōyō Bunko, 1952–1953.
Fairbank, J.K., et al. *Japanese Studies of Modern China.* Cambridge, MA: Harvard University Press, 1971.

Ke Shaomin [K'o Shao-min] (1850–1933)

Chinese historian. Ke was a late Qing scholar-official, known for his compilation of histories of the Qing (Manchu, 1644–1911) and Yuan (Mongol, 1260–1368) dynasties written during the early republic. Born in Liaoxian, Shandong province, Ke won the *jinshi* degree in 1886 and served in various posts as an educational official until the fall of the dynasty. In 1914 he joined the Qing History Bureau and was responsible for completing parts of the history of the Qing (Manchu) dynasty, *Qing shigao* [Draft Qing History], which appeared in 1928. For some fifty years, Ke's main attention was devoted to studying Chinese and foreign materials related to the Yuan dynasty whose official history, the *Yuanshi* [Yuan History], had been hastily produced early in the Ming era and was generally known to contain many errors. Ke's efforts resulted in the monumental *Xin Yuanshi* [New Yuan History] (1922), a work especially well received in Japan for the quality of its *zhi* (monograph) sections. It was formally designated by the republican government as one of the "Standard Histories" *(zhengshi),* thus increasing the number of Standard Histories from twenty-four to twenty-five. Ke responded to somewhat less favorable appraisals from contemporary Chinese scholars, who quite correctly pointed out errors in his work, in *Xin Yuanshi kaozheng* [Evidential Basis for the New History of the Yuan Dynasty], published in 1935.

Albert Feuerwerker

Texts

Xin Yuanshi. 60 vols. Taibei: Ehr shih wu shih pien kan kuan, 1956 (facsimile of Tianjing: Tuigengtang, 1922 ed.).

References

Liu Yicheng. "Ke Shaomin." *Guoshiguan guankan* [Journal of the Institute of National History] 1 (1948): 89–92.

Kelly [Kelly-Gadol], Joan (1928–1982)

Marxist-influenced feminist and Renaissance historian. A graduate of St. John's University, she received her M.A. and Ph.D. (1963) from Columbia University. Her study of Leon Battista Alberti became the standard work on that Renaissance humanist. She was a professor at the City University of New York's Graduate Center and a founder of their women's studies program. She codirected the M.A. program in women's history at Sarah Lawrence with Gerda Lerner and was mentor to many of the leading women's historians in the United States. She is best known for her 1977 essay "Did Women Have a Renaissance?" in which she proved that liberating eras for men were not necessarily liberating for women and called into question the universality of traditional historical periodization. Her subsequent essays called for consideration of "gender," or "the social relationships of the sexes," as a significant analytical category in all history.

Susan A. Stussy

Texts

Bibliography in the History of European Women. Fifth ed. Bronxville, NY: Sarah Lawrence, 1982.
Leon Battista Alberti: Universal Man of the Early Renaissance. Chicago: University of Chicago Press, 1969 [Published as Joan Gadol].
"The Unity of the Renaissance: Humanism, Natural Science and Art." In *From the Renaissance to the Counter-Reformation: Essays in Honor of Garrett Mattingly,* ed. Charles H. Carter. New York: Random House, 1965.
Women, History, and Theory: The Essays of Joan Kelly. Chicago: University of Chicago Press, 1984.

References

Zinsser, Judith P. *History and Feminism: A Glass Half Full.* New York: Twayne, 1993.

Keyser, Rudolph (1803–1864)

Norwegian historian. The son of a Lutheran bishop and one of three brothers at the new University of Oslo, Keyser taught history there from 1828 to 1862. He trained the next generation of Norwegian historians, including Peter Andreas Munch (1820–1863). Norway achieved self-government in 1814, bringing the need to establish a national cultural identity after four centuries of Danish rule. Keyser was the first professional historian to accept that challenge. In *Nordmændenes Herkomst og Folke-Slægtskab* [Origins and Tribal Kinship of the Norwegians] (1839), he argued that Scandinavia was populated from the northeast around 300–400 B.C. by Nordic peoples who had subdued the earlier Germanic Goths. In *Den norske Kirkes Historie under Katholicismen* [History of the Norwegian Church under Catholicism] (1856–1858), Keyser argued that Norwegian society was a patriarchal democracy of allodial landowners until warlord kings arose during the Viking Age, leading to a golden age (A.D.1000–1150) of balance between the powers of monarch and people. Then the swelling power of the church upset the balance, leading to civil war, national stagnation, and collapse for centuries, until the seeds of national renewal bore fruit in 1814.

J.R. Christianson

Texts

Norges Historie. 2 vols. Christiania: P.T. Mallings, 1866–1870.
Den norske Kirkes Historie under Katholicismen. 2 vols. Christiania, Denmark: C. Tonsberg, 1856–1858.
The Private Life of the Old Northmen. Trans. M.R. Barnard. London: Chapman and Hall, 1868.

References

Dahl, Ottar. *Norsk historieforskning i 19. og 20. århundre* [Norwegian Historical Writing in the Nineteenth and Twentieth Centuries]. Oslo: Universitetsforlaget, 1970.

Khʷāndamīr, Ghiyath al-Dīn Muḥammad (1475–1535)

Persian Timurid official and author. Khʷāndamīr was born to a well-connected family of scholar-officials who served the Timurids in eastern Iran. In 1500, he joined the service of Mīrzā Badi' al-Zamān and was in Herat when the Ozbeks attacked the city in 1506. He negotiated its surrender on behalf of the inhabitants and was still there when the Safawids occupied it in 1510. Later, he traveled to Agra, India, and served Bābur, founder of the Mughals. Khʷāndamīr was a voluminous writer, but his most valuable work is *Habibu al-Siyar* [Beloved Biographies], which he completed in 1520. The work contains a general history from the pre-Islamic period up to the end of the Safavid Shah Isma'il's reign (1502–1524). This book is of immense value for the period from 1470 onward because he recounts the events he witnessed firsthand. Of these, three were historical developments of particular importance: the collapse of the Timurids, the rise and expansion of Safavid power, and the rise of the Mughals, all of which are amply documented in his book.

Mahmood Ibrahim

Texts

Habibu al-Siyar. Ed. Jalaluddin Huma'i. Tehran: Kitabfurushi-i Khayyam, 1983.

References

Browne, E.G. *A History of Persian Literature under Tartar Dominion, (A.D. 1265–1502).* Cambridge, Eng.: Cambridge University Press, 1920.
Jackson, Peter, and Laurence Lockhart, eds. *The Timurid and Safavid Periods.* Cambridge History of Iran, vol. 6. Cambridge, Eng.: Cambridge University Press, 1986.

Kida Sadakichi [Teikichi] (1871–1939)

Japanese historian and ethnographer. Kida was born in Kagoshima and graduated from Tokyo Imperial University, where he specialized in ancient Japanese history. He worked for the ministry of education and taught at Kyoto and Tohoku universities. His works include studies of early Japanese society; some of the first treatises on Japan's outcasts; and theoretical essays on history and ethnography. He is best remembered, however, for a controversy that erupted in 1911 surrounding a Japanese history textbook he had helped to author in 1904. At issue was the text's treatment of the era of the northern and southern courts (1336–1392). Although, as Kida pointed out, there was in fact no official policy regarding which line was to be regarded as legitimate, Kida was accused of desecrating the national polity for mentioning the two courts and thereby suggesting that the imperial authority was divisible. Within months, the controversy had occasioned a national political crisis, which forced Kida from his position and prompted a hasty revision of the text to eliminate any reference to the northern line.

Thomas Keirstead

Texts

Kida Sadakichi chosakushu [Collected Works]. Tokyo: Heibonsha, 1979–1982.

References

Varley, H. Paul. *Imperial Restoration in Medieval Japan.* New York: Columbia University Press, 1971.

Kiernan, Victor Gordon (b. 1913)

English historian and essayist. Kiernan was born in Ashton-on-Mersey and educated at Manchester Grammar School, subsequently studying history at Cambridge University, where he became a fellow of Trinity College. During World War II he taught in India before returning to Cambridge and then moving to a lectureship at the University of Edinburgh. He remained there, eventually becoming professor of modern history until his retirement in 1977. An original member of the Communist Party Historians' Group (1946–1956), Kiernan left the Party in 1959 but remained a socialist and Marxist. Against the grain of modern scholarly specialization, Kiernan's historiography has been global in nature, encompassing every region, every period, and every field. His greatest contributions have been to the study of modern European nation-state formation and imperialism and colonialism, and even these have ranged from matters political, diplomatic, and military, to questions of economy, society, and culture. Exploring the totality of the imperial and colonial experiences, Kiernan not only examined the impact Europeans had upon the peoples whom they conquered and ruled, he also pioneered the study of the impact that those experiences have had upon Europeans themselves. In addition, Kiernan has translated Urdu and Hindi works for English publication and has written many historical and literary essays for popular periodicals, addressing contemporary issues.

Harvey J. Kaye

Texts

America, the New Imperialism: From White Settlement to World Hegemony. London: Zed Press, 1978.

British Diplomacy in China, 1880–1885. Cambridge, Eng.: Cambridge University Press, 1939.

The Duel in European History: Honour and the Reign of Aristocracy. Oxford: Oxford University Press, 1988.

European Empires from Conquest to Collapse, 1815–1960. Leicester: Leicester University Press and Fontana Books, 1982.

History, Classes, and Nation-States: Selected Writings of V.G. Kiernan. Ed. Harvey J. Kaye. Cambridge, Eng.: Polity Press; New York: Blackwell, 1988.

Imperialism and Its Contradictions. Ed. Harvey J. Kaye. New York: Routledge, 1995.

The Lords of Human Kind; Black Man, Yellow Man, and White Man in an Age of Empire. Boston, Little, Brown, 1969.

Marxism and Imperialism. London: Edward Arnold, 1974.

The Revolution of 1854 in Spanish History. Oxford: Clarendon Press, 1966.

State and Society in Europe, 1550–1650. Oxford: Blackwell, 1980.

Tobacco: A History. London: Hutchinson Radius, 1991.

References

Edwards, Owen Dudley, ed. *History and Humanism: Essays in Honour of V.G. Kiernan.* Edinburgh: Edinburgh University Press, 1977.

Kaye, Harvey J. *The Education of Desire: Marxists and the Writing of History.* New York: Routledge, 1992.

Kim Pu-sik (1075–1151)

A scholar-official of late Koryŏ Korea. Kim played a part in the internal struggles that afflicted the Koryŏ dynasty in the mid-twelfth century, but he is best known as compiler of the *Samguk sagi,* a history of the Korean peninsula from earliest times through the end of the tenth century. Composed in 1145, in the fashion of Chinese histories such as the *Shiji* and the *Hanshu,* the work combines historical annals, treatises on such topics as rituals and music, and biographies of notable figures. It is an important product of the rise of Confucianism—and its emphasis on history—at the Koryŏ court. Based on sources (no longer extant) from the Silla kingdom, Kim's compilation is widely regarded as the best source for the history of the peninsula during the period that saw the formation of the first Korean kingdoms. It is also a valuable source of information about early Japan and its interactions with the Korean peninsula.

Thomas Keirstead

Texts

Samguk sagi. Seoul: Yanghungyak, 1983.
Sankoku shiki. Tokyo: Heibonsha, 1980.

Kitabatake Chikafusa (1293–1354)

Japanese scholar, court official, and military leader. Kitabatake served the activist emperor Godaigo and prevailed upon that emperor, forced into abdication by the Ashikaga shōgun, to leave Kyoto with the imperial regalia and establish the rival southern court. Kitabatake campaigned in the long dynastic struggle that ensued, writing an historical account, *Jinnō Shōtōki* [Record of the Legitimate Line of Divine Sovereigns], to instruct Godaigo's heir in good government through the appointment of meritorious officials. Kitabatake invoked the divinity of Japan's origins in arguing that the emperor's involvement in politics put the unbroken descent line at risk. This, and the southern court's legitimacy, remained issues for debate into the twentieth century.

Rosemary Gray Trott

Texts

A Chronicle of Gods and Sovereigns: Jinnō Shōtōki of Kitabatake Chikafusa. Trans. H. Paul Varley. New York: Columbia University Press, 1980.

References

Brownlee, John S. *Political Thought in Japanese Historical Writing from Kojiki (712) to Tokushi Yoron (1712).* Waterloo, Ont. Canada: Wilfrid Laurier University Press, 1991.

Robinson, G.W., and W.G. Beasley. "Japanese Historical Writing in the Eleventh to Fourteenth Centuries." In *Historians of China and Japan,* ed. W.G. Beasley and E.G. Pulleyblank. London: Oxford University Press, 1961, 241–244.

Klapisch-Zuber, Christiane (b. 1936)

French historian. Although deeply influenced by historians of the Annales school, Klapisch-Zuber, currently director of studies at the École des Hautes Études en Sciences Sociales in Paris, has created her own approach to the social history of the Italian Renaissance. Devoting most of her studies to decoding the society of Renaissance Florence and its norms, she moves easily from textual to quantitative studies, and from ethnology to art history in the quest for understanding the texture of social relations, ritual, and behavior. Her major publications include *Les Toscans et leurs familles* (1978), coauthored with David Herlihy. This analysis of fifteenth-century Tuscan society is based on the tax declarations of 1427, which the authors mined with historical imagi-nation and methodological sophistication. Her most important essays to date are collected in *Women, Family, and Ritual in Renaissance Italy* (1985). They are based on quantitative sources and on Florentine *ricordanze,* the family memoirs written by fathers and meant for their progeny. Klapisch-Zuber sheds much new light on family customs and rituals and especially on the role of women.

Elisabeth G. Gleason

Texts

And David Herlihy. *Tuscans and Their Families: A Study of the Florentine Catasto of 1427.* New Haven, CT: Yale University Press, 1985.

Women, Family, and Ritual in Renaissance Italy. Chicago: University of Chicago Press, 1985.

Kliuchevskii, Vasili Osipovich (1841–1911)

Historian of Russia. Born the son of a village priest, Kliuchevskii studied in Moscow University under S.M. Solov'ev. He became a popular professor there and a full member of the Academy of Sciences. Along with Solov'ev, he is one of the most influential historians in Russian scholarship and a major figure in the development of Russian historiography. The Solov'ev–Kliuchevskii thesis was that the colonization of new land was the central fact of Russian history. Kliuchevskii adopted an "imperialistic" approach to the subject, stressing the continuity of Russian history from the Kievan period and largely ignoring other nationalities associated with Russian history. He thereby played a major role in establishing the structure and periodization of Russian history for subsequent generations. Something of a pioneer in the field of social and economic history, he also studied the origin of serfdom, the evolution of the *zemsky sobor* (the general assembly of the Muscovite state from the mid-sixteenth to late seventeenth centuries), church–state relations, and the boyar *duma* (the council of old Russian nobles).

Elizabeth V. Haigh

Texts

A History of Russia. Trans. by C.J. Hogarth. 5 vols. London: J.M. Dent; New York: E.P. Dutton, 1911–1931.

References

Hrumenuk, Stanley. *Russian Historiography in Russian Writings, 1815 to the Present.* Ann Arbor, MI: University Microfilms, 1979.

Kluit, Adriaan (1735–1807)

Dutch historian and scholar of constitutional law. Born in Dordrecht, Kluit was initially active as preceptor and rector at various Latin schools, before becoming a professor of rhetoric at the Atheneum Illustre in Middelburg. In 1778 he became professor of antiquities and the history of the state treaties of the republic, a position which he held in Leiden until his death, with an interruption of seven years, during which time he was suspended for his Orangist opinions. With his unfinished *Historia critica comitatus Hollandiae et Zeelandiae* [A Critical History of the Counties of Holland and Zeeland] (1777–1782), he played an important role in the development of the study of the Middle Ages and its auxiliary sciences. In his principal work, the *Historie der Hollandsche staatsregering* [History of the State Government of Holland] (1802–1805), using his extensive legal knowledge, he attacked the republican and democratic theories concerning political sovereignty in the republic.

Jo Tollebeek

Texts

Historia critica comitatus Hollandiae et Zeelandiae ab antiquissimis inde deducta temporibus [A Critical History of the Counties of Holland and Zeeland from Antiquity through the Ages]. 4 vols. Middelburg: P. Gillissen (and Son) and J. de Winter, 1777–1782.
Historie der Hollandsche staatsregering, tot aan het jaar 1795 [History of the State Government of Holland, up to the Year 1795]. 5 vols. Amsterdam: Brave, 1802–1805.

References

Hugenholtz, F.W.N. "Adriaan Kluit en het onderwijs in de mediaevistiek [Adrian Kluit and the Teaching of Medievalism]." In *Geschiedschrijving in Nederland* [Historical Writing in the Netherlands], ed. P.A.M. Geurts and A.E.M. Janssen. The Hague: Martinus Nijhoff, 1981, vol. 1, 142–162.
Leeb, I.L. *The Ideological Origins of the Batavian Revolution. History and Politics in the Dutch Republic 1747–1800.* The Hague: Martinus Nijhoff, 1973.

Knowles, Dom David [Michael Clive David Knowles] (1896–1974)

English historian of medieval monasticism. Knowles joined the Benedictine community at Downside at the age of eighteen. He studied at Cambridge from 1919 to 1922, where he developed a love for classical literature and Greek philosophy that would shape much of his future writing. His early works ranged widely in interest, including in 1926 a study of the American Civil War. Soon thereafter he began publishing an important series of "Essays in Monastic History" in the *Downside Review* (1931–1934). This series culminated in his *Monastic Order in England* (1940). Quickly acclaimed as a historical masterpiece for its emphasis on intellectual history, and still regarded as a watershed in the study of monastic history, this book propelled Knowles to an academic career at Cambridge. He had left Downside in 1939 after a failed attempt to create a new monastic order. Though he was formally reconciled with his order in 1952, he was given permission to live outside the monastery and pursue his academic work. Having succeeded Z.N. Brooke as professor of medieval history at Cambridge, Knowles would later hold the Regius professorship and the presidency of the Royal Historical Society (1956–1960). He retired in 1963, with a long list of significant articles and monographs to his credit.

Krista Kesselring

Texts

Bare Ruined Choirs: The Dissolution of the English Monasteries. Cambridge, Eng.: Cambridge University Press, 1976.
The English Mystical Tradition. New York: Harper, 1961.
The Evolution of Medieval Thought. Baltimore, MD: Helicon Press, 1962.
Great Historical Enterprises. London: Nelson, 1963.
The Monastic Order in England: A History of Its Development from the Times of St. Dunstan to the Fourth Lateran Council, 943–1216. Cambridge, Eng: Cambridge University Press, 1940.
The Religious Orders in England. 3 vols. Cambridge, Eng.: Cambridge University Press, 1948–1959.

References

Brooke, C.N.L. *David Knowles Remembered.* Cambridge, Eng.: Cambridge University Press, 1991.
Morey, A. *David Knowles: A Memoir.* London: Darton, Longman & Todd, 1979.

K'o Shao-min

See KE SHAOMIN.

Kogălniceanu, Mihail (1817–1891)

Romanian historian, and statesman. Kogălniceanu was born in Iaşi and studied in both France and Germany. He contributed actively to the promotion of Romanian national culture, advocating national literature and nationalist sentiment in a literary review, *Dacia literară* [Literary Dacia] (1840). He also participated in the most important events in the construction of modern Romania: the revolution of 1848; the unification of Moldavia and Wallachia (1859), when he became prime minister and achieved many important reforms; and the independence of Romania (1877), when he held office as foreign minister. He died in Paris.

Before being absorbed in the political struggle, Kogălniceanu had already made an important historiographical contribution although the number of his works was not great. In 1837 in Berlin, he published the first volume of a synthesis of his country's history, the *Histoire de la Valachie, de la Moldavie et des Valaques transdanubiens* [History of the Wallachians, Moldavians and the Transdanubian Wallachians]. The aim of this work was to make the Romanian past better known in western Europe, while at the same time establishing his modern, nationalist view of the country's past. His inaugural lecture in Iaşi in 1843 on Romanian history won him great popularity, and it was while teaching there that he developed his historical thought, which strongly emphasized the importance of the national past. He also edited the first Romanian academic journal devoted to history, *Arhiva românească* [Romanian Archive] which appeared in two volumes in 1840 and 1845, and a three-volume edition of ancient Moldavian chronicles.

S. Lemny

Texts

Histoire de la Dacie, des Valaques transdanubiens et de la Valachie. New ed. Berlin: B. Behr, 1854.
Opere [Works]. Ed. D. Simonescu. Vol. 2, ed. Alexandru Zub. Bucharest: Editura Academiei Republicii Socialiste România, 1975.

References

Jelavich, Barbara. "Mihail Kogălniceanu: Historian As Foreign Minister." In *Historians As Nation-Builders: Central and South-East Europe,* ed. Dennis Deletant and Harry Hanak. Basingstoke: Macmillan, 1988, 87–105.
Zub, Alexandru. *Mihail Kogălniceanu istoric* [Kogălniceanu As Historian]. Iaşi: Junimea, 1974.

Kohn, Hans (1891–1971)

German-speaking émigré and U.S. historian of nationalism. Kohn was born in Prague, served in the Austro-Hungarian army and the Czech Legion during and after World War I, and completed his scholarly education at the German University in Prague. From 1920 on he lived in Paris, London, and Jerusalem, working as an independent researcher and publicist. In 1933 he moved to the United States, taking up a series of academic positions. From 1949 until his death he was professor of history at City College, New York. Kohn's central European Jewish background, his commitment to Zionism, and the rise of totalitarianism had a decisive impact on his intellectual development and historiographical contribution. His scholarly work focused on the intellectual history of political ideas in the modern world, and in particular on various forms of nationalism. In his early writings he dealt with the history of Zionism and Judaism. Kohn's reputation rested principally on *The Idea of Nationalism* (1944), in which he traced the intellectual origins of European nationalism. He continued to examine the history of nationalism in a great variety of countries in both the Western and non-Western world. In *The Mind of Germany* (1960) Kohn elaborated the thesis of a German *Sonderweg*, Germany's alienation from Western civilization and its culmination in the rise of national socialism. Kohn remained strongly committed to liberal nationalism, which was compatible with the basic principles and the heritage of the Enlightenment.

Georgi Verbeeck

Texts

A History of Nationalism in the East. New York: Harcourt Brace, 1929.
The Idea of Nationalism: A Study in Its Origins and Background. New York: Macmillan, 1944.
The Mind of Germany: The Education of a Nation. New York: Scribner, 1960.
Nationalism in the Soviet Union. London: G. Routledge, 1933.

References

Epstein, Catherine. *A Past Renewed: A Catalog of German-Speaking Refugee Historians in the United States after 1933.* Cambridge, Eng., New York, and Melbourne: Cambridge University Press, 1993.
Lehmann, Hartmut, and James J. Sheehan, eds. *An Interrupted Past: German-Speaking Refugee Historians in the United States after 1933.* Cambridge, Eng., New York, and Melbourne: Cambridge University Press, 1991.

K

Wolf, Ken. "Hans Kohn's Liberal Nationalism: The Historian As Prophet." *Journal of the History of Ideas* 37 (1976): 651–672.

Koht, Halvdan (1873–1965)

Norwegian historian. Probably his country's most famous historian, Koht was professor of history at the University of Oslo from 1910 to 1935. He served as Norway's foreign minister from 1935 to 1941 in a Social Democratic government. Koht is best known for his work on Norwegian history, above all for *Norsk Bondereising* (1926), a study of peasant uprisings from the Middle Ages to 1814, and for his biography of Henrik Ibsen (1931). However, Koht also published studies of European history (the revolutions of 1848), American history (the genesis of its independence), and the philosophy of history (*Drivmakter in historia,* 1959). Koht was sympathetic to Marxism, but he was not himself a Marxist. He interpreted history in terms of class conflict, but he rejected determinism. He was particularly interested in the relation between society and individuals and ideas such as nationalism, socialism, and democracy. With his interests in both comparison and individualism he belongs to a distinctive Norwegian tradition.

Peter Burke

Texts

The American Spirit in Europe. Philadelphia: University of Pennsylvania Press, 1949.
Drivmakter in historia. Oslo: H. Aschehoug, 1959.
Driving Forces in History. Trans. (of *Drivmakter*) by Einar Haugen. Cambridge, MA: Harvard University Press, 1964.
Norsk Bondereising. Oslo: H. Aschehoug (W. Nygaard), 1926.

References

Skard, Sigmund. *Mennesket Halvdan Koht* [Halvdan Koht the Man]. Oslo: Norske Samlaget, 1982.

Kong Qiu

See CONFUCIUS.

Konopczyński, Władysław (1882–1952)

Polish historian and editor of sources. Konopczyński was born in Warsaw and was connected with the Jagiellonian University from 1911. Politically active, he was affiliated with the right-wing National Democratic Party and served as a deputy from 1922 to 1927. He initiated the publication of the *Polish Bibliographical Dictionary,* of which he was also the editor (1931–1949). Opposed to Marxism and to Communist rule, he was persecuted by the authorities after World War II. He died at Młynik. Konopczyński was renowned for his unrivaled knowledge of archival sources, with which he had become acquainted while touring European archives prior to World War I. As an eminent student of the constitutional and political history of Poland in the seventeenth and eighteenth centuries, he became famous for several works. These include *Geneza i ustanowienie Rady Nieustającej* [The Genesis and Establishment of the Permanent Council] (1917); *Przyczyny upadku Polski* [Reasons for the Fall of Poland] (1918); *Dzieje Polski Nowożytnej 1506–1795* [History of Modern Poland 1506–1795] (1936–1938); *Konfederacja barska* [The Confederation of Bar] (1936–1938); and *Kwestia bałtycka* [Baltic Affairs] (1947). His historical writings were marked by psychologism, intuitionism, and personalism, but Konopczyński was not fond of historiographical novelties and chose rather to follow traditional methodological models.

Ewa Domańska

Texts

Brief Outline of Polish History. Geneva: Atar, 1919.
Dzieje Polski Nowożytnej [History of Modern Poland]. Vols. I, II. Warsaw: Instytut Wydawniczy PAX, 1986.
Geneza i ustanowienie Rady Nieustającej. Cracow: Akademia Umiejetnosci, 1917.
Konfederacja barska. Second ed. 2 vols. Warsaw: Volumen, 1991.

References

Maternicki, Jerzy. "Władysław Konopczyński i jego synteza dziejów Polski nowożytnej. [Konopczyński's Synthesis of the History of Modern Poland]." In Konopczyński, *Dzieje Polski Nowożytnej* [History of Modern Poland], vol. I. Warsaw: Instytut Wydawniczy PAX, 1986, 5–61.

Kordatos, Yiannis (1891–1961)

Greek Marxist historian and pioneer of the communist movement in Greece. Born at Zagora on Mount Pilion in Thessaly, Kordatos was exposed to socialist thinking during his secondary education in Smyrna and in Volos, where he also came in touch with the local workers' organizations. He studied in the law school of the University of Athens and from

1917 he became actively involved in the social-ist movement and a contributor to the socialist (later communist) newspaper *Rizospastis*. In 1918 Kordatos was among the founding members of the Socialist Workers' Party of Greece (SEKE), which subsequently became the Communist Party of Greece. Between 1922 and 1924 he was elected SEKE's general secretary, but he spent most of this time in prison. He withdrew from the Party in October 1924 because of his disagreement with the Party's line on the "Macedonian Question." Kordatos spent the rest of his life as an indepen-dent communist intellectual, often publicly criti-cizing the Communist Party. During the German occupation of Greece (1941–1944), he was in-volved in the resistance organization National Lib-eration Front (EAM). He died in Athens.

Kordatos wrote on all periods and aspects of Greek history. His work has been criticized by other Marxist scholars for a mechanistic applica-tion of Marxist categories, and it presents many problems concerning factual accuracy and respect for evidence. It nevertheless represents a major turning point in twentieth-century Greek histori-ography not only as the fountainhead of a long tradition of Marxist historical writing but also as a corpus of social history marked by a pronounced critical perspective on the conventional truths and ideological taboos of nationalist academic histori-ography. Kordatos's major historiographical con-tribution has been his view of the Greek war of independence of the 1820s as a class struggle in which the bourgeoisie played a leading part. This view was offensive both to nationalist idealism and to other Marxist interpretations, which stressed the role played by the popular and agrarian masses in the revolution. In other writings, Kordatos sub-jected the teachings of Christianity to historical criticism, stressed the social functions of religion, pointed to the socioeconomic construction of nations, and insisted on the social character of cultural conflicts.

Paschalis M. Kitromilides

Texts
I koinoniki simasia tis Ellinikis Epanastaseos tou 1821 [The Social Significance of the Greek Revolution of 1821]. Athens: G. Vassiliou, 1924.
Istoria tis neoteris Elladas [History of Modern Greece]. 5 vols. Athens: Eikostos Aionas, 1957–1958.
Istoria tis Vyzantinis aftokratorias [History of the Byzantine Empire]. 2 vols. Athens: Eikostos Aionas, 1959–1960.

Istoria tou ellinikou ergatikou kinimatos [History of the Greek Labor Movement]. Athens: P.D. Karavakos, 1931.
Rhigas Pheraios kai i Valkaniki Omospondia [Rhigas Pheraios and Balkan Federalism]. Athens: Zacharopoulos, 1945.

References
Mexis, D.N. *O istorikos Yiannis Kordatos kai to ergo tou* [The Historian Yiannis Kordatos and His Work]. Athens: Boukoumanis, 1975.

K

Korean Historiography

The writing of history by and about the Korean people and state, from earliest times to the present. There are three dominant schools of thought that form the basis of Korean historiography. The first school is influenced by the Chinese dynastic idea of history with its Confucian historiographic per-spective. It views history as cyclical and morally didactic. It recognizes the process of change as much in the life of state and society as it does in the life of an individual. However, the change is understood within ancestral tradition and in the context of an enduring quality or continuum in the Chinese civi-lization. In terms of the style and methods of writ-ing, this school was conscious of the dynastic tradi-tion of the Chinese Empire, which Korea emulates as its closest neighbor. This school is best represented by the standard history *(chŏngsa)* of premodern, dynastic Korea, comparable to the Chinese Standard Histories or *Zhengshi*.

The second school is distinct from but not necessarily exclusive of the first school. It consists of a nativistic conception of Korean identity as both a state and a race. While acknowledging the Chinese dynastic view of history, it asserts that Korean his-tory is unique and distinct from Chinese history. It identifies and defends Korean particularism with its own myths, geography, and sociopolitical character-istics. Its predominant approach is an emphasis on the continuity of Korean tradition.

If the above two approaches characterize pre-modern Korean historiography, the third school belongs to the modern period, when the hermit kingdom was encroached upon by the Western nation-states. This school accepts the modern Western progressive-linear perspective of history, often with a great admiration for the industrial and capitalistic West and equally with a tone of disdain to Korea's "feudalistic" past. If this school seeks objective, if not scientific, and universalistic law to explain the human past, as the Confucian school attempted to do in a different manner, it also accepts the Western idea of a particularistic and nationalistic historical perspective by incorporating traditional nativistic thought on Korean identity. Thus it may be argued that modern Korean historiography is not so much an antithesis as a synthesis of the premodern historiography. As Korea became a victim of Western imperialism and Japanese colonialism in particular, this school developed in parallel with the growth of anticolonialism, anti-imperialism, and nationalism in modern Korea. Among European liberal and progressive ideologies, Marxism played a significant role in explaining the tension between particularism and universalism in historical development. Overall, this school contributed to the historical perspective that views modern Korea as discontinuous from the premodern period, holding that permanent and revolutionary changes have occurred in modern, industrializing Korea, changes marked by a break with the "undemocratic" Korean past.

A traditional Korean state compiled the official history of a dynasty with Confucian historiographic perspectives in a manner consistent with the Chinese classics. Such a history constituted an orthodox history in the form of dynastic annals (*sillok*) that record, chronologically, the major events of each reign. The earliest extant work of this kind is *Samguk Sagi* [History of the Three Kingdoms] by Kim Pu-sik in 1145. It used both Chinese and Korean references: the *Sanguozhi* [Chronicle of the Three Kingdoms]; the *Houhanshou* or Annals of the Later Han Dynasty; and now-lost pre-Koryŏ documents, such as *Samhan Kogi* [Ancient Record of the Three Kingdoms], *Haedong Kogi* [Ancient Record of Korea], and *Silla Kogi* [Ancient Record of Silla] to record the history of the Silla (ca. 57 B.C.–A.D. 935), Koguryŏ (ca. 37 B.C.–A.D. 668), and Paekche (ca. 18 B.C.–A.D. 660) kingdoms. Silla is recorded as the oldest kingdom of the three, with its founder, Pak Hyŏkkŏse, born of a large egg and with light radiated (*pak* or *palk*), like the sun, from his body. Although Silla was the youngest in terms of its development of a state, Kim Pu-sik regarded it as the most significant and legitimate kingdom, undoubtedly because of its victory over the other two and its tributary relationship to Tang China. It also records that ancient Korea was founded by Kija, a Chinese prince who was said to be enfeoffed (invested with a feudal estate) by the Chou emperor Wu, thus supporting the Chinese origin of the Korean state.

Koryŏsa [The History of Koryŏ] chronicles the history of the Koryŏ dynasty (918–1391) that succeeded the unified Silla. It was completed in 1451 by a group of Confucian scholar-officials led by Kim Chong-sŏ, Yi Sŏn-je, and Chŏng In-ji in the Office for Annals Compilation (*ch'unch'ugwan*) in the early Chosŏn dynasty. It records major events of each reign and compiles encyclopedic information on political, social, economic, cultural, and geographical subjects of the dynasty, as well as biographies of diverse people, all taken from the annals and other sources, many of which have since been lost. Accompanying the *Koryŏsa* is *Koryŏsa chŏryo* [Essentials of Koryŏ History], which was completed in 1452, providing a chronological description of each reign; not always a summary of the *Koryŏsa*, it often adds new information not found in its predecessor.

The Chosŏn dynasty compiled and published the *Chosŏn Wangjo Sillok* [Annals of the Dynasty of Chosŏn] of each reign, altogether twenty-five reigns in 888 volumes over 472 years, until the reign of King Ch'ŏlchong (d. 1863). The *Sillok* was based on historical documents that were compiled by court historians in the Bureau of State Records, who had access to both government and private records that were considered relevant. The actual writing of the *Sillok* was done by officials in the ad hoc Office of the Veritable Records (*sillok ch'ŏng*) of a given reign, comprising some seventy-eight officials from various offices led by the State Council, Royal Secretariat, and Censorial Organs. When the final draft was approved, it was printed and kept in the repositories located in the capital, Seoul, as well as Ch'ungju, Chŏnju, and Sŏngju in remote mountainous regions in the countryside for safekeeping. The *Sillok* were kept out of the public view, inaccessible even to the king. Nevertheless, historical writing and editing created controversies and became subject to factional struggle after the seventeenth century. The revised versions were published three times (although the originals were kept intact) for the reigns of kings Sŏnjo, Hyŏnjong, and Kyŏngjong, in order to provide views in support of an opposing court faction that later came into power.

Other writings that support the orthodox history are records of important offices, such as the *Sŭngjŏngwŏn Ilgi* [Daily Records of the Royal Secretariat] and the *Pibyŏnsa tŭngnok* [Record of Border Defense Council], as well as the *Ilsŏngnok* [Royal Annals], including the monarch's daily activities, edicts, correspondence, and so forth. The Daily Records of the Royal Secretariat were compiled in principle in one volume per month, recording all the royal edicts and events that took place. The Japanese Hideyoshi invasion destroyed the early records before the seventeenth century, but records from 1623 to 1894 remained largely intact despite the fires that struck the Royal Secretariat compound in 1744 and 1888. The Record of the Border Defense Council deals with the discussions at the highest level of officials in the Office of the Border Defense, which was the military and political council that became the highest organ shortly after the Japanese invasion of 1591 to 1598. Two-hundred-seventy-three volumes from 1617 to 1892 are extant. The Royal Annals comprises 2,329 volumes recording the daily activities of the monarchy from 1760 to 1910. In 1829, Yu Tong-ye, a son of the Royal Librarian Yu Tŭk-kong, cataloged the entire collection under such headings as astronomy, ancestral rites, audiences, royal grants, official appointments, remonstrances, civil service examinations, punishments, and the like. The basic ideas that lay behind the dynastic history reveal the Confucian belief that the Korean rulers strove to bring about harmonious relations between heaven and people as just and benevolent kings of China's loyal vassal state.

The Confucian dynastic view of history did not prevent Koreans from developing a nativistic view of their own identity. Korean particularism was evident in *Samguk Yusa* [The Memorabilia of the Three Kingdoms] written by the monk Iryŏn (1206–1289). According to this text, ancient Korea was founded by Tan'gun, a contemporary of the sage kings Yao and Shun in China, who was divine in origin born of the heavenly father named Hwanung and a bear-turned-woman. His reign lasted for 1,908 years until he became a mountain spirit, at which time Kija came from China to rule Korea. Complementing the orthodox history, the non-official, so-called field history *(yasa)* and supplementary history *(pyŏlsa)* were compiled in great volumes during the Chosŏn period. For example, *Tongguk t'onggam* [Comprehensive Mirror of the Eastern Kingdom] completed by Sŏ Kŏ-jŏng and others in 1484 describes Tan'gun's reign, along with Kija's, and evaluates the history of the fourteen centuries from Pak Hyŏkkŏse of Silla to King Kongyang of Koryŏ. The late Chosŏn historian An Chŏng-bok represents the so-called *sirhak* (that is, practical learning) scholars' interest in studying and analyzing all the available historical evidence to reform the state and society in accordance with their Confucian visions. In 1778, he wrote the *Tongsa kangmok* [Essence of Korean History] in an effort to understand the nature of Korean civilization. Numerous works were published from the mid-Chosŏn period by officials and nonofficials on specific subjects ranging from

the history of factionalism, to geography, rituals, clans, family, local region, and foreign invasions. Remarkably, the interest of these books in Korean identity did not diminish their sense of identity with the universalistic view of the Confucian world order. Traditional Korea achieved stability and harmony so effectively that the Chosŏn dynasty became the longest Confucian dynasty in the world.

Beginning in the second half of the nineteenth century, Korean historiography changed greatly, due largely to the challenges to Korea's traditional thought and institutions presented by western Europeans and by the similarly Westernizing influence of Meiji Japan. It proved a painful process for Koreans to understand and accept the Western idea of an equal and individualistic nation-state. As imperialism threatened the independence and sovereignty of Korea, Korean elites who studied the West rewrote Korean history with a nationalistic and progressive historiographic perspective. To name a few representative historians, Sin Ch'ae-ho (1880–1936) wrote extensively and critically on ancient and early modern Korean historiography. He rejected the cyclical view of history and attempted to find evidence of strong Korean identity as a nation and historical progress toward the liberation and equality of its people, as shown in his works, such as *Chosŏn Sanggosa* [History of Korean Antiquity], published in 1931, and numerous writings in the *Tanjae Sin Ch'ae-ho Chŏnjip* [Complete Collection of Sin Ch'ae-ho's Writings].

Similarly Ch'oe Nam-sŏn (1890–1957) wrote *Chosŏn yŏksa* [Korean History] in 1946, followed by *Chosŏn sangsik mundap* [Questions and Answers on the Common Knowledge of Korea] (1946) and numerous articles collected in the *Yuktang Ch'oe Nam-sŏn Chŏnjip* [Complete Collection of Ch'oe Nam-son's Writings]. He divided Korean history into four progressive stages: the ancient *(sanggo)* period from Tan'gun to the fall of Silla; the medieval period *(chunggo)* of the Koryŏ dynasty; the early modern period *(kŭnse)* from the founding of the Chosŏn dynasty to the rise of Tonghak (eastern learning) movement of the late nineteenth century; and the recent period *(ch'oegŭmse)* from the rule of Taewŏngun to the Korean enlightenment and the Japanese occupation of Korea. Like Sin Ch'ae-ho, he was an ardent nationalist who was imprisoned for his writings and activities by the Japanese colonial authority. He was committed to the preservation of Korean historical records, as well as to national independence, and exerted a great influence on the development of modern historiography in South Korea since 1948.

Paek Nam-un (1895–1974) applied the Marxist view of historical dialectic materialism to the analysis of Korean history. He was interested in the periodization of Korean social and economic progress over time. He published *Chosŏn sahoe-kyŏngjesa* [Social and Economic History of Korea] in 1933 and *Chosŏn ponggŏn sahoe kyŏngjesa: Sang* [Economic History of Korean Feudalistic Society, Part I] in 1937. After the establishment of the Democratic People's Republic of Korea (North Korea), he served in important government positions, such as minister of education and director of the Korean Academy, until he vanished in the early 1960s.

The Marxist idea of universal and scientific law, along with the Western idea of nationalism, influenced Korean historiography of the twentieth century. Both Marxist and nationalistic views of history were and still are influential in contemporary Korea because of their antifeudalism, anticolonialism, and anti-imperialism. Their emphasis of change over continuity is marked by the social and economic realities of a rapidly industrializing Korea. The division of Korea into two opposing nations has reinforced the importance of nationalism based on the common history, language, and people for the eventual reunification of the two states. Since the liberation of Korea in 1945, Korean historians have successfully refuted the Japanese colonialist historiography that viewed Korean history as backward, nondevelopmental, and toadyish. They have documented the dynamic and progressive historical changes in Korea's past. However, in doing so, they have de-emphasized the value of a continuous Korean history, if not ignored it altogether, in the name of change. A more balanced view of Korean history may have to await a time when the Korean people have achieved national reunification and secured the ability to interact with the world as a single nation.

Fujiya Kawashima

References

Eckert, Carter J., Ki-baek Lee, Young-ick Lew, Michael Robinson, and Edward W. Wagner. *Korea Old and New: A History.* Cambridge, MA: Harvard University Press, 1990.

Ki-baik Lee. *A New History of Korea.* Trans. Edward W. Wagner with Edward J. Shultz. Cambridge, MA: Harvard University Press, 1984.

Koryŏ Taehakkyo Minjok Munhwa Yŏn'guso. *Hanguk Tosŏ Haeje* [Annotated Bibliography of Korean Books]. Seoul: Koryŏ [Korea] University Press, 1971.

Itō Abito, Ōmura Masuo, Kajimura Hideki, and Takeda Sachio, eds. *Chōsen O Shiru Jiten* [Dictionary of Information about Korea]. Tokyo: Heibonsha, 1986.

Koselleck, Reinhart (b. 1923)

German philosopher of intellectual history and language. Koselleck is notable for a number of theoretical contributions to recent German historiography. The principal theorist of *Begriffsgeschichte* (the history of concepts, conceptual history), he is also responsible, as its surviving editor, for completing *Basic Concepts in German Political and Social Language.* This multiauthored work, already a classic, covers in its seven thousand pages more than a hundred concepts crucial to modern German political and social discourses.

Two of Koselleck's books are available in English translation. *Vergangene Zukunft* (Frankfurt, 1979) has been translated by Keith Tribe as *Futures Past* (1985). *Futures Past* is a collection of essays, some stating Koselleck's theory of *Begriffsgeschichte,* while others raise metatheoretical questions about the necessary conditions and the temporal horizons of historical writing. *Critique and Crisis,* an earlier book first published in German in 1959, is a brilliant but controversial indictment of the Enlightenment as responsible for modern utopianism, the confusion of politics with morality, obsession with the direction of history, and the arrogance of intellectuals who criticize all practices and beliefs.

Koselleck's thought was shaped by the dominant philosophies of Heidelberg, where he studied after World War II: those of Friedrich Nietzsche, Edmund Husserl, Martin Heidegger, and Hans-Georg Gadamer. Interpretation and hermeneutics were held by these thinkers to be at the heart of history, no less than of philosophy. Koselleck's later thesis about the political consequences of a society's expectations, prognoses, and historical horizons stems from his earlier engagement with Heidegger and Gadamer. Gadamer's influence is no less evident in Koselleck's insistence that *Begriffsgeschichte* be carried on through the analysis of texts in terms of the author's self-understanding, as well as the spatial and temporal horizons bounding thought.

Because his final work as a student was directed by the founder of German social history, Werner Conze, Koselleck moved away from Heidegger and Gadamer, whose concerns with language were primarily ontological. Recently Koselleck has condemned Heidegger and Gadamer for having failed to account for the work actually done by historians. (See the talk given at Heidelberg by Koselleck on the occasion of Gadamer's 85th birthday, along with Gadamer's rejoinder: *"Hermeneutik und Historik,"* in *Sitzungsberichte der Heidelberger Akademie der Wissenschaften. Philosophisch-historische Klasse,* 1987, Bericht 1.)

Koselleck's own synthesis combined conceptual with structural social history. At Conze's insistence, he did not confine himself to the history of concepts, already prominent in *Critique and Crisis,* but combined conceptual with social, legal, and administrative history. The result was *Prussia between Reform and Revolution,* a groundbreaking book dealing with the Prussian General Code as the embodiment of a social theory applied from above. Reconceptualizing the legal and economic bases of citizenship, birth was replaced by property; group membership by individual rights. This exemplary study in administration, social change, and legal history provided Koselleck with rich materials for his new synthesis of conceptual and social history. Thus beginning with a hermeneutic style of historical enquiry, which stressed the conceptual apparatus, horizons, and self-understandings of historical actors, Koselleck went on to develop a historical semantics related to structural continuities and changes in government, society, and the economy.

Koselleck argues that the central concepts of political and social language of German-speaking Europe before the French and industrial revolutions were transformed during the period Koselleck calls the *Sattelzeit.* Not only did political and social concepts shift their meaning at an ever accelerating speed, but four other key changes occurred as well: (1) the insertion of such concepts into one or another philosophy, or horizon of history, set out teleologically, such as the theory of progress or other secular eschatologies. Hence Koselleck's hypothesis that concepts vary, not only according to their semantic field, but also according to the temporal assumptions built into them; (2) democratization of political and social vocabularies, which prior to this period, had been specialized and relatively restricted to elite strata; (3) the growing extent to which concepts were so phrased as to make them easy to incorporate into ideologies; (4) the politicization of concepts. As revolution, war, and economic change destroyed the social groupings, regional units, and constitutional identifications of Old Regime Europe, political and social concepts became increasingly used as weapons among antagonistic classes, strata, and movements seeking power.

Connecting Koselleck's writing on historiography to *Basic Concepts in German Political and Social Language* is the central hypothesis investigated in both: that in modern European societies between about the middle of the eighteenth and nineteenth centuries, the *Sattelzeit,* there occurred a crucial shift in the conception of time. This involved a reorientation toward the future, that is, a general expectation of not just progress, but the successful resolution of all other previously intractable political and social problems, including emancipation from previous forms of domination.

Melvin Richter

See also BEGRIFFSGESCHICHTE.

Texts

Critique and Crisis: Enlightenment and the Pathogenesis of Modern Society. Oxford and New York: Berg, 1988.

Futures Past: On the Semantics of Historical Time. Trans. Keith Tribe. Cambridge, MA: MIT Press, 1985.

Preussen zwischen Reform und Revolution: Allgemeines Landrecht, Verwaltung, und soziale Bewegung von 1791–1848 [Prussia between Reform and Revolution: The General Code, Administration, and Social Movements from 1791 to 1848]. Second ed. Munich: Klett-Cotta im Deutschen Taschenbuch Verlag, 1989.

References

Carr, David. Review Essay on *Futures Past. History and Theory* 26 (1987): 198–204.

Motzkin, Gabriel. "On Koselleck's Intuition of Time in History." In *Begriffsgeschichte,* ed. Hartmut Lehmann and Melvin Richter. German Historical Institute (Washington, DC), Occasional Paper. New York and Oxford: Berg Publishers, 1996.

Richter, Melvin. *The History of Political and Social Concepts: A Critical Introduction.* New York: Oxford University Press, 1995.

Kossmann, Ernst Heinrich (b. 1922)

Dutch historian. Kossmann was born in Leiden. After having taught for several years as a lecturer at the University of Leiden, he was appointed in 1957 as reader and later as professor of Dutch history and institutions at University College, London. In 1966 he was appointed to the chair of modern history in Groningen. Initially, Kossmann's historical interests focused on the history of political theory under the *ancien régime*. Inspired by the work of, among others, Friedrich Meinecke and Paul Hazard, he has published since 1960 a great number of essays in the field of intellectual history. His principal work, however, remains *De Lage Landen* [The Low Countries] (1976, expanded edition 1986), a parallel history of the Netherlands and Belgium in the period from 1780 to 1980. In this work, he explicitly distanced himself from the teleological perspective which had long dominated the national historiographies of the Netherlands and Belgium: Kossmann's attitude was one of detached amazement at both the transience and the continuity of the Low Countries' history.

Jo Tollebeek

Texts

The Low Countries 1780–1940. Oxford: Clarendon Press, 1978.
Politieke theorie en geschiedenis: Verspreide opstellen en voordrachten [Political Theory and History: Uncollected Essays and Lectures]. Amsterdam: Bert Bakker, 1987.
Vergankelijkheid en continuïteit: Opstellen over geschiedenis [Transience and Continuity: Essays on History]. Amsterdam: Bert Bakker, 1995.

References

Blaas, P.B.M. "E.H. Kossmann en de intellectuele geschiedenis [E.H. Kossmann and Intellectual History]." *Ons Erfdeel* 30 (1987): 353–360.
Wesseling, H.L. "Kossmanns meesterwerk [Kossmann's Masterwork]." In his *Onder historici: Opstellen over geschiedenis en geschiedschrijving* [Among Historians: Essays on History and Historical Writing]. Amsterdam: Bert Bakker, 1995, 152–160.

Krantz, Albert (ca. 1450–1517)

German historian. Born in Hamburg, he became rector of the University of Rostock in 1482. Krantz's career included service as canon of the cathedral in Hamburg and diplomatic assignments for the Hanseatic League of commercial cities and for the king of Denmark and the duke of Holstein. A competent humanist scholar, he wrote histories of the Vandals (1519), the Saxons (1520), Sweden and Denmark (1545), and a church history of Saxony (1548). All of his major works appeared in print after his death. His writings are available only in scarce sixteenth-century Latin and German editions.

James Edward McGoldrick

Texts

Ecclesiastica historia, sive Metropolis. Basel: Ioannem Oporinum, ca. 1568.
Regnorum aquilonarium, Daniae, Sueciae, Norvagiae, chronica. Frankfurt am Main: Haeredes Andreae Wecheli, ca. 1583.
Saxonia. Cologne: J. Soter, c. 1520.
Vandaliae & Saxoniae Alberti Cranzii continuatio. Wittenberg: J. Cratonis, 1586.

References

Roden, Ferdinand. *Albert Krantz als Syndikus von Lübeck und Hamburg* [Albert Krantz As City Administrator in Lübeck and Hamburg]. Marburg: J.A. Koch, 1910.

Krishnaswami Aiyangar, Sakkotai (1871–1947)

Indian historian of south India who made a major contribution to the development of south Indian history. He was educated in science at Central College, Bangalore, and taught mathematics, before receiving his M.A. in 1899. He served as lecturer in history at Central College from 1900 and filled the first chair in Indian history and archaeology at the University of Madras in 1914. His *Ancient India* (1911), *The Beginnings of South Indian History* (1918), and *South India and Her Muhammadan Invaders* (1921) helped to establish the basic outlines of south Indian history. In *Some Contributions of South India to Indian Culture* (1923) he wrote of the distinctive devotional tradition *(bhakti)* of the south and its special administrative forms. Aiyangar also served for many years as editor of a number of scholarly journals such as *Quarterly Journal, Indian Antiquary,* and the *Journal of Indian History.* He received the Campbell Gold Medal from the Bombay branch for the Royal Asiatic Society for his lifetime contributions.

Roger D. Long

Texts

Ancient India. London: Luzac, 1911.
The Beginnings of South Indian History. Madras: Modern Printing Works, 1918.
Evolution of Hindu Administrative Institutions in South India. Madras: University of Madras Press, 1931.
Some Contributions of South India to Indian Culture. Calcutta: University of Calcutta Press, 1923.
Sources of Vijayanagar History. Madras: University of Madras Press, 1931.
South India and Her Muhammadan Invaders. London: Oxford University Press, 1921.

References
Dr. S. Krishnaswami Aiyangar Commemoration Volume. Madras: S.K.A. Commemoration Committee, 1936.

Krom, Nicolaas Johannes (1883–1945)

Dutch archaeologist of Indonesia. Krom trained in European archaeology at Leiden University, obtaining his doctorate in 1908. He was appointed in 1910 as head of the Commission of Archaeological Investigation in Java and Madura and was instrumental in having the Commission transformed into a full Archaeological Service in 1913. He oversaw the excavation and inventorying of Hindu–Buddhist monuments in the Indies, especially Borobudur in Central Java, and took a conservative attitude toward reconstructing ruined structures. After his return to the Netherlands for health reasons in 1915, he continued to write, becoming professor of archaeology and ancient history of the Netherlands Indies at Leiden in 1919. His pioneering work on Hindu-Javanese history (1926) was the first to assemble and interpret new archaeological data in an analytical framework, though it was later criticized both for overemphasizing the Indian impact on Indonesia and for uncritical reliance on early Javanese texts such as the *Nāgarakṛtāgama* (the text now known as the *Désawarṇana*).

Robert Cribb

Texts
Hindoe-Javaansche Geschiedenis [Hindu-Javanese History]. Second ed. The Hague: Nijhoff, 1931.

References
Hall, D.G.E., ed. *Historians of South East Asia.* London: Oxford University Press, 1961.

Kromer, Marcin (1512–1589)

Polish diplomat, bishop of Warmia, historian, and polemicist on behalf of the Counter Reformation. Kromer was born in Biecz and served as secretary to Archbishop Piotr Gamrat and to Cardinal Stanisław Hosius. He died in Lidzbark. When working in the royal chancellery he ordered and listed the most important royal archives in Cracow. He became famous for the translation and publication (1545–1552) of six homilies of the church father John Chrysostom, discovered in a codex in Bologna. Kromer was active in political and diplomatic life (numerous legations). He was one of the most important figures in the Polish Counter Reformation and an active participant in the anti-Protestant campaign through his apologetic and polemical writings. His major work, intended for a foreign readership, is his history of Poland from legendary times to 1506: *De origine et rebus gestis Polonorum libri XXX* [The Origin and Acts of the Poles in Thirty Books] (Basel, 1555). While it was intended as a revision of the earlier history by Jan Długosz, it was in many ways superior. Kromer referred to more than one hundred documents, including the chronicle of Gallus Anonymus, whose nationality he identified. He made known abroad his theory of the Sarmatian origin of the Slavs. In addition to *De origine,* he contributed a geographical and political description of Poland: *Polonia* [Poland] (1577).

Ewa Domańska

Texts
Polska czyli o położeniu, ludności, obyczajach, urzędach i sprawach publicznych Królestwa Polskiego księgi dwie [Poland; or, The Location, Peoples, Customs, Officials and Commonwealth of the Kingdom of Poland, in Two Books]. Przekład Stefana Kazikowskiego, wstęp i opracowanie Romana Marchwińskiego. Olsztyn, Poland: Pojezierze, 1984.

References
Starnawski Jerzy "O dwu historycznych dziełach Marcina Kromera" [On Two Historical Works by Marcin Kromer]. In *Odrodzenie: Czasy—ludzie—książki* [Renaissance: Age—People—Books]. Łódź: Wydawnictwo Uniwersytetu Łódzkiego, 1991, 86–103.

Ku Chieh-kang

See GU JIEGANG.

Ku Yen-wu

See GU YANWU.

Ku Ying-t'ai

See GU YINGTAI.

Kuhn, Thomas Samuel (1922–1996)

American historian of science. Educated at Harvard, where he received his Ph.D. in 1949, Kuhn began his academic life as a student of physics but soon developed a passion for the history of science. His illustrious career commenced at Harvard (1948–1956), from where he moved to University of California, Berkeley (1956–1964), Princeton (1964–1979), and finally the Massachusetts Institute of Technology.

Kuhn's greatest historiographical impact came in the wake of the publication of *The Structure of Scientific Revolutions* (1962), a work that at once challenged established opinions regarding how scientific understanding has "progressed" throughout history and questioned whether the scientific revolution of the early modern era deserved the name at all. Traditional historiography had viewed the history of science as a story that recounted the inevitable (and natural) development of modern scientific knowledge out of a primitive or flawed understanding of the physical world. Progress was marked as scientists formulated neutral theories and tested them against available data, gradually increasing the sophistication of these theories by accommodating seemingly contradictory evidence. Science and its practitioners were, from this perspective, above all, objective and their findings disinterested and "true."

Kuhn's *Structure* suggested a radically different historical picture. Scientists were, he proclaimed, as affected by the intellectual, social, cultural, political, and religious milieu in which they lived as the rest of the population. As a consequence, even the most objective scientific investigators operate within a "paradigm" controlled by traditions and perceptions that have proven useful in organizing the social experiences of the community. These traditions survive and adapt as scientists explore their world but collapse when one or more of the investigators realizes that inconsistencies can no longer be accommodated. At that time a revolution occurs (scientific or otherwise) in the sense that the old paradigm is abandoned in favor of another, more inclusive, set of socially constructed principles. We are left therefore with a world in which scientific knowledge is subjective and which unfailing progress becomes an elusive ideal, or at least a matter of small steps made by "normal science," the daily work of research scientists that is determined and limited by the prevailing paradigm. Historical development for Kuhn and those who follow his lead is a more ambivalent term than for earlier historians of science, because it has become a contextualized subject. Historians can no longer point to an uninterrupted march toward modern, objective scientific knowledge because the actors alleged to have participated in this march have been placed back in their historical, often unscientific, environments. Scientists like Newton and Darwin are, in the wake of Kuhn, men who were defined by their historical community even as they rose above it. Outside the history of science, many historians and social theorists have attempted to use Kuhn's "paradigm" to explain intellectual change in other areas of knowledge, including history at large.

Kathryn M. Brammall

Texts

The Copernican Revolution: Planetary Astronomy in the Development of Western Thought. Second ed. Cambridge, MA: Harvard University Press, 1959.

The Essential Tension: Selected Studies in Scientific Tradition and Change. Chicago: University of Chicago Press, 1977.

The Structure of Scientific Revolutions. Second ed. enlarged. Chicago: University of Chicago Press, 1964.

References

Andersson, Gunnar. *Criticism and the History of Science: Kuhn's, Lakatos's, and Feyrabend's Criticisms of Critical Rationalism.* Leiden and New York: E.J. Brill, 1994.

Cohen, H. Floris. *The Scientific Revolution: A Historiographical Inquiry.* Chicago: University of Chicago Press, 1994.

Gutting, Gary, ed. *Paradigms and Revolutions: Appraisals and Applications of Thomas Kuhn's Philosophy of Science.* Notre Dame: University of Notre Dame Press, 1980.

Hollinger, David A. "T.S. Kuhn's Theory of Science and Its Implications for History." In his *In the American Province: Studies in the History and Historiography of Ideas.* Bloomington: Indiana University Press, 1985, 105–129.

Kula, Witold (1916–1988)

Polish economic historian. Kula was born in Warsaw and obtained a Ph.D. from Warsaw University (1939). He was appointed professor in 1950 and in 1970 became doctor *honoris causa* at Besançon University in France. He also served on several occasions as directeur d'études of the École des Hautes Études en Sciences Sociales in Paris. From 1970 until his death he was affiliated with many prestigious associations including the Polish Academy of Sciences, the International Association of Economic History, the Comité International pour la Métrologie Historique, and the Polish Historical Association. Kula's main research areas were interdisciplinary and included investigation into the transition from feudalism to capitalism and the history of social structures. He was also interested in the methodology of history, historical metrology, and historical microanalysis. Kula's works, translated into many European languages, presented a Marxist analysis of his subjects and often stirred polemic and provoked discussions.

Jolanta T. Pękacz

Texts

An Economic Theory of the Feudal System: Towards a Model of the Polish Economy, 1500– 1800. Trans. Lawrence Garner. London: NLB, 1976.

Measures and Men. Trans. R. Szreter. Princeton, NJ: Princeton University Press, 1986.

Problemy i metody historii gospodarczej [Problems and Methods of Economic History]. Warsaw: PWN, 1963.

Rozwój gospodarczy Polski XVI-XVIII w [Economic Development of Poland]. Warsaw: PWN, 1993.

Wokół historii [Around the History]. Warsaw: PWN, 1988.

References

Bianco, Marta Herling. "Una storia per comprendere il presente: L'opera di Witold Kula" [History As a Means of Understanding the Present: The Work of Witold Kula]. *Passato e Presente* 10 (1986): 95–126.

Cataluccio, Francesco M. "Witold Kula: Uno storico atipico [Witold Kula: An Atypical Historian]." *Societa e Storia* 11.42 (1988): 973–978.

Elżbieta Kaczyńska, "Witold Kula (18 IV 1916– 12 II 1988)." *Kwartalnik Historyczny* 95.3 (1988): 300–305.

Kulturgeschichte

German for "cultural history," a form of historical writing prevalent in nineteenth-century Germany that stressed the importance of nonpolitical phenomena such as literature, science, customs, and technology for historical change. *Kulturgeschichte* denoted a variety of methodologies, but all shared a basic opposition to a historiography restricted to the deeds of kings and generals.

The first works of *Kulturgeschichte* date from the end of the Enlightenment and were written under the influence of Voltaire's *Essai sur les moeurs et l'esprit des nations* [Essay on the Manners and the Spirit of Nations] (1756). J.C. Adelung's (1732–1806) *Versuch einer Geschichte der Cultur des menschlichen Geschlechts* [Attempt at a History of the Culture of the Human Race] (1782) described the progressive maturation of the human race from primitive origins to an enlightened state of civilization, focusing on the contributions of commerce, literature, religion, and science.

During the nineteenth century, another tradition of *Kulturgeschichte* emerged that was widely popular with the middle tier of academics who formed the ranks of Germany's historical and antiquarian associations. This kind of *Kulturgeschichte* recounted customs and practices drawn from local history. Such efforts were often anecdotal and dilettantish and earned the contempt of professional historians, who dismissed *Kulturgeschichte* as a "science of old pots."

After mid-century, *Kulturgeschichte* rose in status, thanks largely to contributions by nonhistorians. The anthropologist Gustav Klemm's (1802–1867) *Allgemeine Cultur-Geschichte der Menschheit* [Universal Cultural History of Mankind] (1843–1852) stressed the significance of material conditions and technology for the development of human history. The folklorist Wilhelm Heinrich Riehl (1823–1897) drew on extensive field work to produce a "natural history" of the German people in the 1850s as well as detailed studies of individual regions such as the Palatinate. The novelist Gustav Freytag (1816–1895), in his popular *Bilder aus der deutschen Vergangenheit* [Scenes from the German Past] (1859–1867), offered a series of historical portraits that related the history of the German "folk-soul" from antiquity to 1848. After German unification in 1871, hard-nosed but widely popular cultural histories appeared by the geographer Friedrich von Hellwald (1842–1892) and the politician and Gymnasium teacher Julius Lippert (1839–1909). Inspired by Darwin and Spencer, these *Kulturgeschichten* traced the rise of human civilization from its beginnings in prehistory, identifying the instinct for self-preservation and work as the motors of progress.

Among university historians, two figures stand out. In his *Kultur der Renaissance in Italien* [Civilization of the Renaissance in Italy] (1860), the Swiss historian Jacob Burckhardt (1818–1897) drew on typical personalities and phenomena from the Italian Renaissance in order to illustrate the individualistic spirit of that age. Burckhardt restricted *Kultur* to creations of the human spirit; these included poetry, satire, and festivals, but also the state. For his twelve-volume *Deutsche Geschichte* [German History] (1891–1909), the Leipzig historian Karl Lamprecht (1856–1915) synthesized elements of economic history and folk psychology into a system of five "culture ages." His stress on material factors and his search for laws of historical development constituted a challenge to the Rankean school, which had traditionally maintained the primacy of the state and the sovereignty of the individual. In the ensuing controversy (1891–1898), Lamprecht was thoroughly discredited, although his legacy lived on among a circle of scholars at the Institut für Kultur- und Universalgeschichte in Leipzig. For most of the twentieth century, the term *Kulturgeschichte* has referred primarily to encyclopedic surveys of world civilization, regional histories, or to popular works about past manners, customs, and clothing.

Until recently, modern American "cultural history" worked exclusively from the Burckhardtian tradition, focusing on works of high culture. In recent years, however, American cultural historians have turned their attention to popular culture and material culture. They have also begun to view culture as a symbolic system encompassing all levels of society. Such approaches parallel aspects of Lamprecht's *Kulturgeschichte,* although they do not reflect his broader interest in discovering laws of development in human history.

George S. Williamson

See also CULTURAL HISTORY; ENLIGHTENMENT HISTORIOGRAPHY; GERMAN HISTORICAL THOUGHT.

Texts

Adelung, Johann Christoph. *Versuch einer Geschichte der Cultur des menschlichen Geschlechts* [Attempt at a History of the Culture of the Human Race]. Leipzig: Hertel, 1782.

Burckhardt, Jacob *The Culture of the Renaissance in Italy.* Trans. S.G.C. Middlemore. New York: Modern Library, 1954.

Freytag, Gustav. *Bilder aus der deutschen Vergangenheit* [Pictures from the German Past]. 4 vols. Leipzig: Hirzel, 1859–1867.

Hellwald, Friedrich Anton Heller von. *Culturgeschichte in ihrer natürlichen Entwicklung bis zur Gegenwart* [Cultural History in Its Natural Evolution to the Present]. Augsburg, Ger.: Lampart and Co., 1874.

Klemm, Gustav. *Allgemeine Cultur-Geschichte der Menschheit* [Universal Cultural History of Mankind]. 10 vols. Leipzig: B.G. Teubner, 1843–1852.

Lamprecht, Karl. *Deutsche Geschichte* [German History]. 12 vols. in 13. Berlin: Gärtner, 1891–1909.

Lippert, Julius. *Kulturgeschichte der Menscheit in ihrem organischen Aufbau* [Cultural History of Mankind in Its Organic Structure]. 2 vols. Stuttgart: Enke, 1886–1887.

Riehl, Wilhelm Heinrich. *Die Naturgeschichte des Volkes als Grundlage einer deutschen Sozial-Politik* [The Natural History of the Common People As the Basis for German Social Policy]. 4 vols. Stuttgart: Cotta, 1854–1869.

References

Chickering, Roger. *Karl Lamprecht: A German Academic Life.* Atlantic Highlands, NJ: Humanities Press, 1993.

Hartmann, Volker. *Die Deutsche Kulturgeschichtsschreibung von ihren Anfängen bis Wilhelm Heinrich Riehl* [German Cultural History Writing from Its Beginnings to Wilhelm Heinrich Riehl]. Ph.D. dissertation, Marburg University, 1971.

Smith, Woodruff. *Politics and the Sciences of Culture in Germany, 1840–1920.* Oxford: Oxford University Press, 1992.

Kulturpessimismus

Term in German intellectual history referring to a cultural critique that expresses deep anxiety about the viability of traditional European culture in the face of technology, mass society, the end of aristocracy, and other aspects of the modern world. The high point of *Kulturpessimismus,* famously translated by Fritz Stern as "cultural despair," was reached at the end of the nineteenth and early twentieth centuries in Germany, but the ideas can be traced to German romanticism and live on, in various forms, in late-twentieth-century thought. Cultural despair emerges in German thought as a result of a series of philosophical contrasts: culture/nature, culture/civilization, and community/society. German romanticism, influenced by Rousseau's philosophy of alienation, tended to denigrate culture/society (not yet differentiated) as artificial, and elevated nature as authentic. By the middle of the nineteenth century, the difference between culture and civilization, already enunciated by Kant, came to designate the "higher" German education, the "deep soul" and "eternal values" of post-Goethe classicism, while civilization referred to the technical, mechanical, and utilitarian aspects of a crass and commercial society, which one would supposedly find in France, England, and the United States. Culture, in this model of thinking, always refers to a value in itself, while civilization is always a means to an end. This model could also be assimilated to the sociological distinction between "community" *(gemeinschaft)* and "society," *(gesellschaft)* made by the German sociologist Ferdinand Tönnies, that referred to the supposedly organic organization of traditional European towns and farm communities, under assault by the urbanization and industrialization of modern cities. While the right-wing conservatives of the nineteenth century attacked modern civilization, their version of *Kultur* itself was the object of a sustained critique by Friedrich Nietzsche, who lambasted their philistinism. Nietzsche measured culture by aesthetic standards and by the measure to which it contributed to enhancing life, thereby adding a Darwinist element to the evaluation of culture. Oswald Spengler followed Nietzsche in this vein, but treated historical cultures as if they were literally biological organisms with cycles of birth and death. In his most famous book, *The Decline of the West,* he interpreted European society as being in the last stages of cultural death. Martin Heidegger's philosophy is also a history of decline from an original Greek epiphany to modern forgetting and the domination of technological thinking. Many of the ideas of *Kulturpessimismus* were discredited after World War II because they were seen as having given sustenance to the amorphous brew of Nazi ideology. But a pervasive discomfort with modern civilization still shapes the philosophy of cultural conservatism as well as certain strands of environmentalism, feminism, and some leftist critiques of capitalism.

Elliot Neaman

See also DECLINE, IDEA OF; *KULTURGESCHICHTE;* NIETZSCHE, FRIEDRICH; SPENGLER, OSWALD.

Texts

Nietzsche, Friedrich. *Untimely Meditations.* Trans. R.J. Hollingdale. Cambridge, Eng.: Cambridge University Press, 1983.
Spengler, Oswald. *The Decline of the West.* Trans. Charles F. Atkinson. New York: Knopf, 1926.

References

Mosse, George. *The Crisis of German Ideology.* New York: Schocken, 1964.
Stern, Fritz. *The Politics of Cultural Despair.* Berkeley: University of California Press, 1961.

Kume Kunitake (1839–1931)

A pioneer scholar of ancient documents, and the first modern victim of Japanese government suppression of scholarship. A member of the Bureau of Historiography, Kume was concurrently appointed professor at Bunka College, later Tokyo Imperial University, in 1888. The Japanese were influenced by Ludwig Riess (1861–1928), who introduced Rankean scientific historical methods into their country. Along with his colleagues, Kume attacked many traditional beliefs about history. An 1890 article on ancient Shinto, associated with the imperial house, provoked wide criticism and personal threats. In 1892 Kume was dismissed from the university and retracted the article. Postwar scholars have called this government oppression, but neither Kume nor his colleagues viewed him as a victim of censorship. Citing political and personal reasons for the incident, he believed that Japanese scholarship was developing freely. Moving to Waseda University, he developed the study of ancient documents. His *Nihon Kodai Shi* [History of Ancient Japan] (1907) became the standard work on that subject. A 1907 work on the Nara period was censored in 1926, but Kume's faith in academic freedom remained unshaken.

John S. Brownlee

Texts

Kume Kunitake Rekishi Chosaku Shū [Collected Historical Works of Kume Kunitake]. Ed. Ōkubo Toshiaki. 6 vols. Tokyo: Yoshikawa Kōbunkan, 1989–1991.

References

Mehl, Margaret. "Scholarship and Ideology in Conflict: The Kume Affair, 1892." *Monumenta Nipponica* 48 (1993): 337–357.

Kung Tzu-chen

See GONG ZIZHEN.

Kuo Sung-t'ao

See GUO SONGTAO.

Kurd ʿAlī, Muḥammad Farīd (1876–1953)

Syrian journalist and historian. Born of a Kurdish father and a Circassian mother, Kurd ʿAlī learned French at an early age, allowing him to complement his early education in Arabic–Islamic sciences with knowledge of Western, particularly French, civilization and literature. He spent the years from 1901 to 1908 (with a brief intermission during which he returned to Damascus) in Cairo where he attended the lectures of Muḥammad ʿAbduh at al-Azhar and collaborated with Egyptian intellectuals. At the end of 1908, he traveled to France where he stayed for a year studying French

K

culture and civilization. In 1919, he founded the Arab Academy in Damascus. He also served two terms as the minister of public education. His career in journalism began in 1897, when he joined the staff of *al-Shām*, the first Arabic newspaper in Damascus, and established an association with the Egyptian journal *al-Muktataf*. In Cairo, he founded and edited the review *al-Muktabas,* which was moved to Damascus in 1908 and continued publication until 1914. In 1913, he visited Italy where he compiled most of the material for his major work on the history of Syria, *Khitat al-Shām* (1925), a work known both for its content and for its methodology. In addition to *Khitat al-Shām,* Kurd ʿAlī wrote numerous articles and books, and edited a variety of classic historical and literary texts.

Hootan Shambayati

Texts
Khitat al-Shām. Second ed. 6 vols. Beirut: Dar al-ʾIlm lil-Malayin, 1969–1972.
Memoirs, a Selection. Trans. Khalil Totah. Washington, DC: American Council of Learned Societies, 1954.

References
Alusi, Jamal al-Din. *Muhammad Kurd ʿAli.* Baghdad: Dar al-jumhuriyah, 1966.
Ayalon, Ami. *The Press in the Arab Middle East.* New York: Oxford University Press, 1995.
Hermann, Rainer. *Kulturkrise und konservative Erneuerung: Muhammad Kurd ʿAli (1876–1953) und das geistige Leben im Damaskus zu Beginn des 20. Jahrhunderts* [Cultural Crisis and Conservative Revival: Muhammad Kurd ʿAlī (1876–1953) and Intellectual Life in Damascus at the Beginning of the Twentieth Century]. Frankfurt am Main and New York: Peter Lang, 1990.

Kuriyama Senbō (1671–1706)

Japanese Confucian scholar and historian of the Mito school. Born near Kyoto in 1671, at the age of eighteen Kuriyama wrote a book entitled *Hōken taiki* in which he gave an account of Japanese history in the second half of the twelfth century. In 1697 he was appointed the head of the Shōkōkan, the research institute established by Tokugawa Mitsukuni to compile the *Dai Nihon shi* [History of Great Japan]. This was a massive research project, which aimed at describing Japanese history from the accession of the legendary Emperor

Jimmu up until the reign of Emperor Komatsu (1382–1412). Although the work as a whole was not completed until 1906, the major part dealing with the lives of the emperors, important ministers, and other eminent people was finished in 1709, just three years after Kuriyama's death. The editors of the *Dai Nihon shi* were greatly concerned with historical accuracy and in this regard their research established an unprecedentedly high standard. The real significance of the work, however, lay in its concern to show the proper relationship between ruler and subject and the consequent impetus it gave to the loyalist movement that led to the Meiji Restoration of 1868.

Graham Squires

Texts
Dai Nihon shi. Tokyo: Yoshikawa Kobunkan, 1911.

References
Brownlee, John S. *Political Thought in Japanese Historical Writing: From Kojiki (712) to Tokushi Yoron (1712).* Waterloo, Ont., Canada: Wilfrid Laurier University Press, 1991.

Kuroita Katsumi (1874–1946)

Japan's leading scholar of ancient history from the 1920s to the 1940s. An 1896 graduate of Tokyo Imperial University, Kuroita helped Taguchi Ukicki (1855–1905) compile the sixty-volume *Kokushi Taikei* [Compendium of Japanese History]; he later undertook a revision and the series is now usually identified with Kuroita. He joined the Historiographical Institute of Tokyo Imperial University in 1901, becoming a professor in 1919. His *Kokushi no Kenkyū* [Research in Japanese History] (1908, revised 1913 and 1931) succeeded Kume Kunitake's *Nihon Kodai Shi* [History of Ancient Japan] (1907) as the standard work. From the 1920s, rationalism and nationalism contended with each other in Kuroita's mind, with nationalism winning. By 1935 he seldom expressed scholarly reservations about the founding myths. He was a member of the committee to compile *Kokutai no Hongi* [Cardinal Principles of the National Essence, 1937], which affirmed the myths. Crippled by a stroke in 1936, he participated little, but did not repudiate the results. By 1940 there remained little trace of scientific history in his work. Despite his affirmation of imperial truths, two works were censored in 1941 for disturbing the public peace.

John S. Brownlee

Texts

Kuroita Katsumi: Kyoshin Bunshū [Collected
Works of Kuroita Katsumi]. 8 vols. Tokyo:
Yoshikawa Kōbunkan, 1934. (Kyoshin was
Kuroita's pen name, meaning "straight from
the heart".)

References

Matsushima Ei'ichi. "Kuroita Katsumi." In *Nihon
no Rekishika* [Japanese Historians], ed.
Nagahara Keiji and Kano Masanao. Tokyo:
Nihon Hyōron Sha, 1976.

Kuwabara Jitsuzō (1870–1931)

Japanese historian of China. Kuwabara was one
of a group of sinologists trained at Tokyo Imperial
University by Shiratori Kurakichi in the field of
Tōyōshi (oriental history). A graduate in *Kangaku*
(classical sinology), he brought skills in close philological investigation to the new conceptions of
scientific research on Chinese history and culture
introduced at Tokyo University by Ludwig Riess
(1861–1928), a disciple of Ranke. In 1898 Kuwabara
published his *Intermediate History of the Orient,* a
comprehensive account of the history of China
and its relations with other Asian and Central
Asian peoples. Designed to counterbalance Western
histories, it became an influential school text. As
a professor at the University of Kyoto, Kuwabara
wrote widely on Chinese foreign relations as well as
on such curious subjects as eunuchs and cannibalism.

Rosemary Gray Trott

Texts

"On P'u Shou-keng . . . with a General Sketch
of Trade of the Arabs in China." *Memoirs of
the Research Department of the Tōyō Bunko*
2 (1928): 1–79; 7 (1935): 1–104.

References

Fogel, Joshua A. *Politics and Sinology: The Case
of Naitō Konan (1866–1934).* Cambridge,
MA: Harvard University Press, 1984.

L

La Popelinière, Henri Lancelot Voisin, Sieur de (1541–1608)

Noble Huguenot, soldier, and author of the first known history of historical writing. La Popelinière was born in eastern Poitou, received a classical education, and, after 1562, left his legal studies at the University of Toulouse to become an officer of Huguenot forces in the religious wars. His history of the war, *La vraye et entière histoire de ces derniers troubles* [The True and Complete History of the Recent Troubles] (1571; republished in 1581 as *Histoire de France*) looked to the more distant past and many aspects of political, social, and cultural life as sources to an objective understanding of the conflict. In three works that were published together in 1599—the *Histoire des histoires* [History of Histories], the *Idée de l'historie accomplie* [Idea of Perfect History], and the *Dessein de l'histoire nouvelle des françois* [Plan for a New History of the French]—he emphasized the need for a history that maintained verisimilitude and completeness in the representation of the past. He criticized all past historiography, proposed a new theory of "perfect history," and offered ways of applying his new method. More systematically than previous humanist historians, he delineated four stages of the growth of historiography: the natural, or mythic; the poetic; the continuous, or chronicler; and the analytical and persuasive stages. He rejected short-term explanations of events and argued for the long-term continuity of political and cultural structures. His works were influential and helped open the way to secular historical explanations that were free of theological sidetracks and mythic notions, such as the inseparable destiny of the monarchy and Catholicism or the Trojan origins of kingdoms.

Lawrence M. Bryant

Texts
L'Histoire des histoires, avec l'idée de l'histoire accomplie: Plus le dessein de l'histoire nouvelle des françois. Paris: Fayard, 1989.

References
Huppert, George. *The Idea of Perfect History: Historical Erudition and Historical Philosophy in Renaissance France.* Urbana: University of Illinois Press, 1970.

Kelley, Donald R. "History As a Calling: The Case of la Popelinière." In *Renaissance Studies in Honor of Hans Baron,* ed. Anthony Molho and Julius Kirshner. DeKalb: Northern Illinois University Press, 1971: 773–789.

Schiffman, Zachary Sayre. "An Anatomy of Historical Revolution in Renaissance France." *Renaissance Quarterly* 42 (1989): 507–533.

Labor History

Branch of historical study concerned with the organization, communities, experience, beliefs, and behavior of workers. The origins of labor history in the nineteenth century owed much to Marx's insistence on the primacy of social and economic struggle between classes as the motor of historical change, as it allowed a clear distinction to be drawn between the radical political movements of his time—containing, but rarely led by, workers—and more truly proletarian organizations such as unions and cooperatives that merited discrete research. Yet Marxism, while pointing out the need to study labor organizations, contained within it a controversial thesis about the historical role of trade unions, seeing them as essential to the formation of an initial, industrial, class consciousness, yet unable to discharge their full historical importance unless they became instruments of the creation of a politicized and revolutionary class consciousness among their members. Thus, Marx and his followers on the one hand stressed the importance of the study of formal working-class institutions, yet assessed them on criteria relating to their success or failure in a function for which they were rarely created. Given the actual history of many labor organizations in the West, most Marxist labor historiography has been concerned with explaining how and why trade unionism in advanced industrial countries has failed to live up to its potential role as, in Engels's words, "schools of war" between the proletariat and the bourgeoisie and why narrow trade union "economism" has rarely developed further into broad-ranging political goals.

Marx himself identified from the 1860s onward a process whereby a "labor aristocracy" of skilled, unionized workers was split from the mass of the proletariat and integrated into the values and outlook of the capitalist class. Later writers such as Lenin added to this analysis a tendency of union officials to become a self-serving bureaucracy, and, with the emergence of the New Imperialism in these decades, identified a source of wealth for capitalist economies to provide workers with sufficient social reforms to keep them reconciled to the prevailing system. In general, then, Marxist labor historiography in the late nineteenth and early twentieth centuries reveals a preoccupation with the description and analysis of the inherent inertia of formal labor organizations, and their tendency to concentrate on short-term goals of immediate material advantage at the expense of a longer-term, politicized strategy of class struggle.

English Fabian historians such as Sidney and Beatrice Webb and G.D.H. Cole rejected the Marxist dynamic, substituting instead an analysis of labor organizations that concentrated on their slowly evolving maturity into the increasingly powerful, effective, yet moderate representatives of workers in British society. Class struggle was played down, and the pragmatic sensibility and organizational skills of the leaders of British trade unionism were highlighted. Such an approach tended to be Whiggish to a high degree: forms of labor organization in the past, such as Luddism, that did not lead to those of the present were dismissed or condemned, and, overall, the focus was placed upon the nonrevolutionary, bureaucratic responses of labor to the historical changes in the British economy. For the Fabians, the achievement of socialism would come about through a gradual evolution led by state-employed technocrats and professionals, a process in which tightly organized and competently led trade unions would play a key, although subordinate role.

In the United States, the Wisconsin school led by J.R. Commons provided, in the first third of the twentieth century, the dominant analysis of the history of American labor. In certain respects, the works of Commons and his associates, such as R.T. Ely and S. Perlman, may be said to stand Marx on his head: the history of nineteenth-century American labor in their paradigm is one of a slow learning process whereby radical political aims became gradually divorced from the labor movement and a purely "business unionism" developed, which accepted and worked within the capitalist system. American labor, according to the Commons school, developed not class consciousness, but job conciousness. In doing so, organizations like the American Federation of Labor performed valuable functions, by limiting the concentration of wealth and by forming an important element of stability in social relations in a period of massive economic change. Thus, that pragmatic outlook identified by Marxist historians as fatal to the long-term interests of workers was given triumphalist treatment by the Wisconsin school. Unions had, in a sense, saved the democratic spirit of America during its difficult passage from a commercial and agrarian to an industrial society. American labor historiography of the Commons school was consistent with the dominant themes of American history, which stressed its "exceptionalism," compounded of the presence of the frontier, its strong liberal tradition, its high geographic mobility, and its diverse ethnic makeup. All these factors made the construction of a class view of society by either union leaders or political radicals both extraordinarily difficult and irrelevant to the conditions of American society. So strong was the Commons approach until after World War II that even Marxist labor historians like Philip Foner accepted its basic categories, but refused to applaud the victory of accommodation over radicalism.

Despite some fundamental, indeed antagonistic, differences in interpretation, labor historians before the 1960s shared many common approaches, asked many similar questions, and utilized much the same range of sources. The first similarity was the tendency to concentrate upon organizational, narrative history built from trade union, party, and government archives, to the exclusion of less structured aspects of workers' lives such as communities and community practices, belief systems, or family life. The second was a reading of the history of labor that was—and not only among Marxists—teleological to an extreme: labor was expected to develop along a certain path according to a certain dynamic, which led to an often ahistorical treatment of the many diverse forms of labor organization that workers have constructed to confront different problems in many different contexts. Finally, there was a concentration on the political repercussions of the developing social and economic consciousness of workers.

The creation of a new type of labor history during the last several decades is inseparable from two interrelated trends: the general explosion of social history in all its facets in the recent past, and the emergence of the New Left in the 1960s with its strongly culturalist, communitarian, and antihierarchical outlook. The new labor history that emerged as a subset of these developments throughout the West shared some common characteristics. It was concerned to place collective forms of political and industrial action within a much wider communal and historical context, by relating them to the existing cultural values, customs, and experiences of the people involved. It rejected the view that the history of workers could be entirely subsumed into the development of the labor movement, especially a labor movement traveling along a preconceived trajectory, and thus it paid a great deal more attention to the impact of grassroots behavior and outlook on working-class history than had previously been the case. The new labor historians were also by and large much more suspicious of the state and of nongovernmental bureaucracies than the older ones. The regulatory and administrative achievements of the emerging welfare state, assessed positively by the Fabians in England and the Commons school in the United States, were interpreted by the New Left in Gramscian terms as successful attempts to coopt, channel, and thus defuse the inherently oppositional culture and behavior of the ordinary workers.

In Britain, E.P. Thompson presented a strong and extremely influential challenge to both the traditional Marxist and the Fabian analyses of the emergence of the English working class. Thompson's working class was less the product of the process of industrialization than it was the purposeful and creative response of the laboring poor themselves. Thompson argued the need to see the workers of Britain as a series of communities equipped with a long history of oppositional traditions, such as religious dissent, a jealously guarded notion of ancient liberties, and a host of long-established workshop and craft customs, buttressed by a moral reading of the purpose of economic activity. It was these traditions and values that provided the English workers with the tools to construct modes of resistance to exploitation and that were refashioned and recombined to produce the peculiarly English version of class consciousness. While older labor history was concerned with reading the present into the past, Thompson was concerned with placing the reactions of workers to the new market and industrial relations of the early nineteenth century in their own historical context, as rational responses that needed to be understood in their own terms before the larger development of a self-created class consciousness could be uncovered. In the United States, Herbert Gutman undertook a similar task by concentrating on the role that ethnicity, religious culture, and social ideals played in shaping both the lives of American workers, and by extension, American society, in the era of industrialization. Overall, such work insisted that the history of labor in its political and organizational aspects had first to be refracted through the lens of social and cultural experience as it was lived by ordinary workers.

Such an agenda was an open-ended one that has led since the 1960s to an undeniable invigoration in the writing of labor history, but which has also brought to the subdiscipline some methodological and theoretical quandaries. In insisting on the primacy of the social and cultural history of labor over the political history of the labor movement, these scholars opened the field to the investigation of such diverse aspects as the roles played by family structure, household economy, religion and ethnicity, gender, leisure, popular culture, and a host of other factors in the development of working-class communities and organizations. Some major steps forward in our understanding of the topic have resulted: for example, it is now clear how important it is to recognize the role that concepts of masculinity played in the very notion of the working class that developed in the West, with the additional factor of white, preferably northern European, ethnicity in the United States. Even in the more traditional investigatory realm of workshop and factory, much recent British labor history, by Gareth Stedman Jones, Ross McKibbin, Patrick Joyce, and others, has focused on the role that rhetoric, language, and other cultural constructs play in defining areas of conflict or reciprocity, exclusion, or recognition. Far from being peripheral topics, such factors are now seen to be essential to any complete understanding of working-class communities and the organizations that they developed to protect and extend their interests.

While historical writing undeniably benefits from such diversified input and cross-fertilization, there is also something to be said for the maintenance of a fairly well defined and limited subdiscipline with its own methodological approaches and identifiable hypotheses. Indeed, the very diversity in labor historiography in the past thirty years has, either through design or accident, prevented the creation of any recognizable larger theory of labor comparable to the European Marxist, the Wisconsin, or the Fabian schools. It has seemed to some labor historians, given the expansion of the boundaries of the field, that labor history itself is in danger of being subsumed or swallowed up in the much more amorphous field of social history. There is also a danger that the social history of labor will never be reconnected to the older history of the labor movement, leading to the disappearance of labor history per se.

Although such problems are real enough, obituaries for labor history would be premature. The complexity and diversity of working-class organizations and communities revealed by the new labor history should be regarded as a challenge rather than an obstacle. Furthermore, in many areas of historical study, the application of the approaches of both the older and the newer labor historians still offer great scope. This is true of the preindustrial period as a whole: it is even truer of the entire non-Western world, where such research is only beginning, with the work of scholars such as Sharon Stichter and Jane Parpart. Given the evident importance of labor to the development of societies, it is likely that the topic will continue to attract both further research and further debate.

Michael Childs

See also BUSINESS HISTORY; CAPITALISM; CLASS; GENDER; HISTORY WORKSHOP; MARXISM AND HISTORIOGRAPHY; RADICAL HISTORY.

Texts

Commons, John R., et. al. *History of Labor in the United States.* 4 vols. New York: Augustus Kelley, 1966.

Thompson, E.P. *The Making of the English Working Class.* Harmondsworth: Penguin Books, 1968.

Webb, Sidney, and Beatrice Webb. *The History of Trade Unionism.* Revised ed. London: Longmans, 1926.

References

Baron, Ava, ed. *Work Engendered: Toward a New History of American Labor.* Ithaca, NY: Cornell University Press, 1991.

Van der Linden, Marcel, ed. "The End of Labor History?" *International Review of Social History,* vol. 38, supplement I (1993).

Labriola, Antonio (1843–1904)

Italian philosopher of history. Labriola was introduced to Hegel's philosophy in 1861, while at the University of Naples, the center of Hegelianism in Italy. His interest in Hegel led to a study of Marx and to the rejection of the positivism, scientism, and naturalism that were then dominant in European intellectual circles. Labriola refused to be ensnared in a closed philosophical system and conceived of historical materialism as a philosophy with practical social implications. After securing a teaching position at the University of Rome (1874), Labriola moved increasingly to the political left; by 1887, he was an avowed socialist and began to introduce Marxist thought into Italy. When the Italian Socialist Party was formed in 1892, however, Labriola refused to join because of its positivist theoretical stance. It was Labriola, along with Benedetto Croce, who did more than anyone else to disseminate Marxism in Italy around the turn of the century.

Stanislao G. Pugliese

Texts

Opere. Ed. Franco Sbarberi. Naples: Rossi, 1972.

Essays on the Materialistic Conception of History. Trans. C.H. Kerr. Chicago: C.H. Kerr, 1904.

Socialism and Philosophy. Trans. E. Untermann. Chicago: C.H. Kerr, 1912.

References

Centi, Beatrice. *Antonio Labriola.* Bari: Dedalo, 1984.

Sbarberi, Franco. *Ordinamento politico e societa nel marxismo di Antonio Labriola* [Political and Social Order in the Marxism of Labriola]. Milan: F. Angeli, 1986.

Labrousse, Ernest (1895–1988)

French economic historian. Trained in both history and economics, Labrousse began his career as a scholar of the eighteenth century and the French Revolution, studying under Alphonse Aulard in the 1910s. Following the publication of his two most important works, *Esquisse du mouvement des prix et des revenues* [Sketch of the Movement of Prices and Incomes] (1933) and *La crise de l'économie française* [The Crisis of the French Economy] (1944), Labrousse was appointed to a lectureship at the Sorbonne. He remained an active socialist for most of his career, editing *L'Humanité* until 1924 and the *Revue Socialiste* from its foundation in 1946 until 1954. Labrousse's influence on French historiography is due in large part to his supervision of graduate students, whom he trained in the social and economic history of both the modern and early modern periods.

Labrousse is responsible for introducing quantitative techniques to the Annales school. His rigorous use of statistical methods and his discussion of long- and short-term economic cycles influenced colleagues and a generation of students. *Esquisse* and *La crise* linked *annaliste* concerns about long-term structures with the traditional political history of the French Revolution. They argued the case for an economic crisis of the 1780s as a necessary condition for revolution in 1789. After those studies, Labrousse produced further general works on the relationship between economic trends, social structures, and political movements.

Carol E. Harrison

Texts

La crise de l'économie française. Paris: Presses Universitaires de France, 1944.

Esquisse du mouvement des prix et des revenues. Paris: Librarie Dalloz, 1933.

And Fernand Braudel, eds. *Histoire économique et sociale de la France* [Economic and Social History of France]. 4 vols. Paris: Presses Universitaires de France, 1982.

References

Grenier, Jean-Yves, and Bernard Lepetit. "L'expérience historique à propos de C.-E. Labrousse [Historical Experience: on C.E. Labrousse]." *Annales: Economies, Sociétés, Civilisations* 44 (1989): 1337–1360.

Renouvin, Pierre. "Ernest Labrousse." In *Historians of Modern Europe,* ed. H.A. Schmitt. Baton Rouge: Louisiana State University Press, 1971.

Lafuente y Zamalloa, Modesto (1806–1866)

Spanish historian and liberal politician. Lafuente began his career writing political satire: *Viajes de Fray Gerundio* [Voyages of Friar Gerundio] (intermittently from 1837 to 1856) and *Teatro social del siglo XIX* [Social Theater of the Nineteenth Century] (1847). Lafuente was a member of the Cortes and an active supporter of the moderate progressives led by General O'Donnell. In 1850 he began the publication of his *Historia general de España* [General History of Spain]. This work, appearing in thirty volumes between 1850 and 1867, was a continuation of an earlier history written in the seventeenth century by the Jesuit priest Juan de Mariana. Lafuente's work was Spain's great national history of the nineteenth century, written for a popular audience and addressing such interests as how the Spanish nation was formed and how one could explain Spain's greatness and subsequent decline. Above all, Lafuente sought to vindicate nineteenth-century Spanish liberalism through a biased liberal interpretation of Spanish history that, for example, praised the medieval municipal *fueros* and the Constitution of 1812 while condemning the Inquisition, the Habsburgs, and Ferdinand VII. Lafuente's liberal and nationalistic interpretation of Spanish history remained popular in Spain well into the twentieth century.

George L. Vásquez

Texts

Historia general de España. 30 vols. Madrid: Establecimiento Tipográfico Mellado, 1850–1867.

Teatro social del siglo XIX. 2 vols. Madrid: Establecimiento Tipográfico Mellado, 1846.

Viajes de Fray Gerundio. 2 vols. Madrid: Establecimiento Tipográfico Mellado, 1842–1843.

References

Cirujano Marín, Paloma, et al. *Historiografía y nacionalismo español: 1834–1868* [Spanish Historiography and Nationalism: 1834–1868]. Madrid: Consejo Superior de Investigaciones Científicas, 1985.

Lamb, Martha Joanna Reade [née Nash] (1829–1893)

Writer and historian. Born in Plainfield, Massachusetts, Martha Nash married Charles A. Lamb in 1852. In 1866, the couple moved to New York City, where she remained until her death. It was in New York that Martha Lamb began her authorial career in earnest. She wrote on a wide variety of topics in a number of different styles. Her early works consisted of several children's books and a romantic, adult novel, *Spicey* (1873), using the Chicago fire as a background. She edited a collection of poetry entitled *The Christmas Basket* in 1882. From 1883 to 1893, she served as an editor of and contributor to the *Magazine of American History,* the only periodical then devoted to American history. As a historian, Lamb is most well-known for her *History of the City of New York* (1877–1896). Although she was untrained in historical methodology, her book is noted for its solid scholarship combined with a popular writing style. Lamb also edited or wrote other histories, including *The Homes of America* (1879) and *Wall Street in History* (1883). Her history of Wall Street was reprinted in 1992.

Judith Boyce DeMark

Texts
History of the City of New York: Its Origin, Rise, and Progress. 3 vols. New York: A.S. Barnes, 1877–1896.
Ed. *The Homes of America.* New York: D. Appleton, 1879.
Wall Street in History. New York: Funk & Wagnalls, 1883.

References
Lyman, Susan Elizabeth. *Lady Historian, Martha J. Lamb.* Northampton, MA: Smith College Library, 1969.

Lambarde, William (1536–1601)
English antiquary, legal scholar, and royal official. Lambarde was the eldest son of John Lambarde, of Lambert, Draper, and Alderman of London, and his wife, Juliana Horne. He was thrice married, and had three sons and a daughter by his second wife, Sylvestra Deane. He died at his manor of Westcombe, East Greenwich. Educated at Lincoln's Inn (1556), Lambarde was a distinguished justice of the peace, chancery official, and keeper of the records in the Tower of London. The question of whether he was the outspoken member of Parliament in 1566 and author of *Notes on the Procedures and Privileges of the House of Commons* (1584) remains controversial, but on balance the evidence is in his favor. Lambarde was a product of the Elizabethan historical renaissance and devout Protestantism; he is considered to be the paradigmatic legal antiquary of the common law tradition. His principal historical work was the *Archaionomia* of 1568, the influential edition and paraphrase of Anglo-Saxon laws. The chorographical *Perambulation of Kent* (1576) was the first county history to be published; his wide-ranging topographical researches in and around the years 1567–1577 (abandoned owing to William Camden's work on *Britannia*) were

eventually published in 1730 as *Dictionarium Angliae Topographicum et Historicum* [Topographical and Historical Dictionary of England]. The monumental *Archeion* (a draft of which was completed about 1577 and the final version finished in 1591) is the authoritative study of the history and functions of England's central legal institutions. Lambarde was an astute and influential commentator upon his own society and its historical evolution.

J.D. Alsop

Texts
Archeion; or, A Discourse upon the High Courts of Justice in England. Ed. C.H. McIlwain and P.L. Ward. Cambridge, MA.: Harvard University Press, 1957.
A Perambulation of Kent. London: n.p., 1826.

References
Alsop, J.D., and W.M. Stevens. "William Lambarde and the Elizabethan Polity." *Studies in Medieval and Renaissance History* 8 (1987): 233–265.
Prest, Wilfrid. "William Lambarde, Elizabethan Law Reform, and Early Stuart Politics." *Historical Journal* 34 (1995): 464–480.
Warnicke, Retha M. *William Lambarde, Elizabethan Antiquary.* London: Phillimore, 1973.

Lambros, Spyridon (1851–1919)
Greek historian, university professor, and prime minister. Lambros was born in Corfu, the son of the distinguished numismatist Paul Lambros. He graduated from the University of Athens in 1871. Between 1872 and 1875 he pursued postgraduate work at Berlin and Leipzig under Ernst Curtius and Theodor Mommsen. In 1873 he was awarded his doctorate by the University of Leipzig. Between 1875 and 1877 he traveled extensively in several European countries in order to examine Greek manuscripts and collect archival evidence on medieval and modern Greek history. Upon his return to Greece in 1878 Lambros was appointed to a lectureship on Greek history at the University of Athens, where he introduced for the first time the teaching of paleography. In 1887 he became an associate professor and from 1890 to 1917 occupied the chair of world history. He was a founder of the literary association Parnassos in 1865, of the Historical and Ethnological Society of Greece in 1882, and in the 1890s he was involved in the irredentist National Society, which was largely responsible for the outbreak of the Greek–Turkish

war of 1897. Amidst a major political crisis over Greece's involvement in World War I, which led to the resignation of elected prime minister Venizelos, King Constantine on September 27, 1916, appointed Lambros to the premiership, which he kept until April 21, 1917. In August 1917 Lambros was tried in a special political tribunal for his actions as prime minister, he was condemned and exiled to the islands of Hydra and Skopelos until March 1919, four months before his death.

Lambros's significance as a historian lies both in his having given Greek historical writing an analytical orientation, and in his promotion of the systematic collection of source material on medieval and modern Greek history. The products of his paleographical researches were published, with critical annotations, in the twenty-one volumes of his journal *Neos Ellinomnimon* (1904–1927) and in his four-volume collection on the Peloponnese in the Paleologean period (1912–1930). His major scholarly achievement was a two-volume catalog of Greek manuscripts in the monastic libraries of Mount Athos (1895–1900), a task that he accomplished while Athos was still under Ottoman rule. His album of 395 Byzantine imperial portraits (1930) was also a pioneering work in the use of visual evidence in historical writing. In addition to his critical editions of sources, Lambros produced a six-volume illustrated synthesis of the history of Greece from earliest times to 1453 (1886–1908) and many other shorter works, as well as translations of works on Greek history by major European historians.

Paschalis M. Kitromilides

Texts

A Catalogue of the Greek Manuscripts on Mount Athos. 2 vols. Cambridge, Eng.: Cambridge University Press, 1895–1900.
Palaiologeia kai Peloponnisiaka [Paleologan and Peloponnesian matters]. 4 vols. Athens: Committee for the Publication of Sp. Lambros' Works, 1912–1930.

References

Charitakis, G. [A Bibliography of the Works of Lambros]. *Neos Ellinomnimon* 14 (1920): 145–260.
Skias, A.N. "Spiridon P. Lambros." *Neos Ellinomnimon* 14 (1920): 115–139.

Lammens, Henri (1862–1937)

Belgian Jesuit and historian of Islam. Born in Ghent, Lammens arrived in Beirut in 1877. After a year at the Beirut Jesuit College he joined the monastery of Mount Lebanon. In 1886 he returned to the college as an instructor of Arabic, leaving this position in 1891 only to return again six years later. In 1900, he became the editor of the Jesuit newspaper *al-Bashir*, which he had previously edited briefly in 1894. He returned to the college a third time in 1903, on this occasion as an instructor of geography and history. In 1907, he was appointed as a professor at the newly established School of Oriental Studies within the Beirut Jesuit College, and in 1927, he became the editor of the Jesuit journal *al-Mashriq*. Lammens is best known for his systematic study of the historical personality and prophetic career of Muḥammad based on the Arabic biographies of the prophet (*sira*). In "Qoran et tradition; comment fut compose la vie de Mahomet" (1910) Lammens argued that it was possible to reconstruct the life and the career of the prophet based on the *sira*. He also wrote extensively on the history of Syria, pre-Islamic Arabia, and the Ummayads. Lammens's works suffer from his strong hostility to Arabs and Islam. Equal to his disdain for Islam was his love for Syria. His *La Syrie, précis historique* [Syria: A Brief History] (1921) was written with the encouragement of the French Mandatory authorities (the ruling power established after World War I). In it Lammens develops the concept of the Syrian nation as a Christian nation that had fallen victim to Islam. Consequently, the French emerge as natural allies of Syria against both the Turks and the Arabs.

Hootan Shambayati

Texts

L'Arabie occidentale avant l'hegire. Beirut: Imprimerie Catholique, 1928.
Études sur le regne du Calife Omaiyade Mo'awia Ier [Studies on the Reign of Caliph Ommayad Mo'awia I]. Paris: Geuthner, 1908.
Études sur le siècle des Omayyades [Studies on the Century of the Ummayads]. Beirut: Imprimerie Catholique, 1930.
Islam: Beliefs and Institutions. Trans. E. Denison Ross. New York: Dutton, 1926.
La Syrie, précis historique. 2 vols. Beirut: Imprimerie Catholique, 1921.

References

Salibi, K.S. "Islam and Syria in the Writings of Henri Lammens." In *Historians of the Middle East*, ed. Bernard Lewis and P.M. Holt. London: Oxford University Press, 1962, 330–342.

Lamprecht, Karl Gotthard (1856–1915)

German medievalist and historian of social psychological types, who challenged the historicist orthodoxy of his time. Lamprecht was born at Jessen in Saxony. Like many stars of the German cultural firmament, he attended the famous Schulpforta classical secondary school. Thereafter he studied at the universities of Göttingen, Leipzig, and Munich. Beginning his teaching career at Bonn in 1881, he later taught at Marburg and Leipzig. During his long tenure at Leipzig, Lamprecht argued for a new kind of cultural history based on his own psychological typology of collective mentalities at a time when German history was only beginning to move beyond the study of high politics. In 1891 his ideas incited a *Methodenstreit* (battle over methodology) that persisted until his death. His detractors accused him of the closely related heresies of scientism or positivism. Although this controversy was almost exclusively intramural, his multivolume *German History* (1891–1911) was intended for a wider audience. Trained in economic and art history as well as political history, Lamprecht was strongly influenced by new disciplines of the nineteenth century such as psychology, biology, and sociology. In dozens of articles and essays, Lamprecht insisted that general laws of psychological development could be discovered, through which each nation passed in the course of its history and by which nations could be compared. The disclosure of these laws would lay the foundation for a comparative universal history of mankind.

Thomas E Willey

Texts

Ausgewählte Schriften zur Wirtschafts-und Kulturgeschichte und zur Theorie der Geschichtswissenschaft [Selected Writings on Economic and Cultural History and on the Theory of Historiography]. Aalen, Germany: Scientia, 1974.
What Is History? New York: Macmillan, 1905.

References

Cassirer, Ernst, "Karl Lamprecht." In *The Problem of Historical Knowledge*. New Haven, CT: Yale University Press, 1950, 281–294.
Chickering, Roger. *Karl Lamprecht: A German Academic Life (1856–1915)*. Atlantic Highlands, NJ: Humanities Press, 1993.
Weintraub, Karl J. "Karl Lamprecht." In *Visions of Culture*. Chicago: University of Chicago Press, 1966, 161–208.

Lang, John Dunmore (1799–1878)

Scottish Presbyterian clergyman, politician, and emigration publicist. Lang was born at Greenock and educated at the University of Glasgow before emigrating to New South Wales as a missionary in 1822. During numerous visits to Britain, he tirelessly advocated emigration to the Australian colonies and enjoyed a long political career in eastern Australia as a constitutional reformer and republican. In addition to the publication of numerous political pamphlets and church writings, often vituperative and controversial, Lang's reputation rests on his longer descriptive emigration works and, principally, upon his *Historical and Statistical Account of New South Wales* (1834), a two-volume work that ran to three further editions (1837, 1852, 1875). A full account of the colony from the convict period, progressively updated to include the era of responsible government, Lang's *Historical Account* attracted criticism from London reviewers, who considered it excessively autobiographical and sectarian. With the publication of the second edition, Lang was given the opportunity of stating his views on the failure of the convict system before the Molesworth Committee on transportation. Despite its flaws and Lang's unwillingness to modify his judgments, the *Historical Account* remained the most influential and important work of its kind for most of the nineteenth century.

Denis Cryle

Texts

Historical Account of the Separation of Victoria from New South Wales. Sydney: J.L. Sherriff, 1870.
An Historical and Statistical Account of New South Wales: Both As a Penal Settlement and As a British Colony. 2 vols. London: Cochrane and McCrone, 1834.
John Dunmore Lang: Chiefly Autobiographical, 1799 to 1878: Cleric, Writer, Traveller, Statesman, Pioneer of Democracy in Australia. Ed. Archibald Gilchrist. Melbourne: Jedgarom Publications, 1951.

References

Baker, D.W.A. *Days of Wrath: A Life of John Dunmore Lang*. Melbourne: Melbourne University Press, 1985.
Barton, G.B. *Literature in New South Wales*. Sydney: Government Printer, 1866, 124–130.

Langlois, Charles-Victor (1863–1929)

French medievalist, historian, and bibliographer. Langlois was born in Rouen and schooled at the

École des Chartes. After becoming an archivist-paleographer, he received a doctorate in history from the Sorbonne in 1887. He taught at Douai (1885), Montpellier (1886), and, from 1888, at the Sorbonne, where he remained until 1913. Langlois then became director of the Archives Nationales, where he supervised the acquisition of the Rohan mansion and the publication of archival catalogs. In 1917, he was elected to the Académie des Inscriptions et Belles-Lettres. At the Sorbonne, Langlois taught paleography, bibliography, diplomatic, historiography, and medieval history, thereby promoting the need for greater technical preparation of university students. His scholarship reflected his mastery of a scientific approach to history; whereas publications such as *Manuel de bibliographie historique* [Manual of Historical Bibliography] (1896) focused on technical methodology, other works were historical, including his analysis of the Capetian kings from 1226 to 1328 (1901). Langlois's efforts in medieval social history, such as *La Société française au XIIIᵉ siècle d'après dix romans d'aventure* [French Society in the Thirteenth Century According to Ten Adventure Novels] (1904), also received wide acclaim.

Bonnie Effros

Texts

With Charles Seignobos. *Introduction to the Study of History*. Trans. G.G. Berry. Westport, CT: Greenwood Press, 1979.
Manuel de bibliographie historique. 2 vols. Graz: Akademische Druck- und Verlaganstalt, 1968.
Saint Louis, Philippe le Bel, les derniers Capétiens directs: 1226–1328. Paris: J. Tallandier, 1978.
La Société française au XIIIᵉ siècle d'après dix romans d'aventure. Third ed. Paris: Hachette, 1911.

References

Keylor, William R. *Academy and Community: The Foundation of the French Historical Profession*. Cambridge, MA: Harvard University Press, 1975.
Leguay, Pierre. *Universitaires d'aujourd'hui* [Academics of Today]. Paris: Bernard Grasset, Éditeur, 1912.

Las Casas, Bartolomé de (1484–1566)

Spanish missionary and historian. Las Casas was born in Seville and went in 1502 to the island of Hispaniola, from which he participated in the conquest of Cuba. In 1514, he denounced the conquerors' treatment of the Indians, beginning his life-long struggle in support of the Indians' rights. In 1520, he attempted the peaceful conversion of the natives in Venezuela, and himself entered the Dominican order two years later; he helped to establish missions in Guatemala in 1537. Returning to Spain for a time, he wrote and in 1542 read publicly his *Brevísima relación de la destrucción de las Indias* [The Devastation of the Indies: A Brief Account], a highly polemical work, and one that had an influence on imperial policy toward the new colonies. In 1544, Las Casas came back to the Indies as Bishop of Chiapas, but was recalled in 1547 as a result of disagreements with other colonists. Resuming his writing, he produced in 1550 a further polemical piece, this time directed against the doctrine that a war against the Indians could be "just." He resigned his bishopric in 1550 and published the *Brevísima relación* two years later, together with a number of other treatises. He was accused of treason in Spain and Spanish America, but Protestant Europe used his work as a weapon against Catholic Spain's domination of the New World. Las Casas is best known for two other books, the *Apologética historia de las Indias* [Apologetic History of the Indies], which argued for the rationality of the Indians, and the *Historia de las Indias* [History of the Indies], in which he recounted the story of Spanish colonization from 1492 to 1520. This latter work, on which rests his reputation as a historian, was based on manuscript archival sources and contemporary historical literature, as well as on Las Casas's personal experiences and acquaintances.

Carlos Pérez

Texts

The Devastation of the Indies: A Brief Account. Trans. Herma Briffault. Baltimore, MD: Johns Hopkins University Press, 1992.
History of the Indies. Ed. and trans. A. Collard. New York: Harper and Row, 1971.

References

Friede, Juan, and Benjamin Keen, eds. *Bartolomé de Las Casas in History: Toward an Understanding of the Man and His Work*. DeKalb: Northern Illinois University Press. 1971.
Hanke, Lewis. *Bartolomé de Las Casas: Historian*. Gainesville: University of Florida Press, 1952.

Latin American Historiography (excluding Mexico and Brazil)—Writing on the precolonial and colonial periods from the sixteenth century to the present day

The Sixteenth Century

The expansion of Spain into the American continent in the sixteenth century modified the traditional way in which Europeans wrote history. The dominance of political history, which had prevailed since the time of Thucydides, gave way to a much broader historiographical vision—one that encompassed the totality of civilization. The Spanish chroniclers of the era of discovery and conquest, often eyewitnesses to the events that they described in the manner of Herodotus, expanded the scope of historical writing while innovating its methodology. They combined ethnography and geography with history—something that had been done only rarely in the West since the Ionic historians of the fifth and sixth centuries B.C.

The chroniclers sensed from the outset their uniqueness—that their comprehensive accounts of the manners and customs of new civilizations transcended conventional European historical experience. Francisco López de Gómara, author of the *Historia general de las Indias* [General History of the Indies] (1522), recognized this truth when he heralded the Spanish discovery of the New World rather than the revival of letters in Italy "as the advent of a new epoch in the history of humanity." Not only did this Spanish humanist regard the discovery of America as the greatest event since Creation but he also regarded the Indian question as a challenge to traditional historiography.

The main historiographical question confronted by these early chroniclers, which would hold sway until the middle of the seventeenth century, dealt with the issue of the justice of Spanish conquest and dominion in the New World. Two historiographical schools emerged that battled over these questions: the imperial tradition of conquest history and its opponents, the patriotic tradition. The imperial school, as David Brading has shown, "began with Gonzalo Fernández Oviedo, reached an early climax in Francisco López Gómara, and was finally consolidated by Antonio de Herrera." The individual who had triggered this historiographical and ideological controversy was the sixteenth-century Dominican Friar, Bartolomé de Las Casas. In his most notorious tract, *Brevísima relación de la destrucción de las Indias* [A Short Account of the Destruction of the Indies] (1542), Las Casas argued that the Indians should be regarded as human and entitled to the basic rights of humankind. Furthermore, he attacked the Spanish atrocities in the New World and questioned the very legitimacy of Spanish dominion. It was this inflammatory diatribe, later translated into Dutch and English, that gave birth to the "Black Legend"—Hispanophobic propaganda used to denigrate Spain's accomplishments in the Old and New Worlds.

The first important work on the Incas was Pedro de Cieza de León's *La crónica del Perú* [The Chronicle of Peru] (1552). Unfortunately, only the introductory portion of this work was published, which detailed the travels of the author from Panama to Potosí. Here the Spanish humanist marveled over Inca architecture and government while lamenting the depopulation and destruction suffered at the hands of the Spaniards. In 1564, little more than a decade later, Bartolomé de Las Casas's *Los tesoros del Perú* [The Treasures of Peru] was published. In this polemical tract, Las Casas—the "Apostle of the Indies"—questioned the legitimacy of Spanish rule while at the same time defending the right of the Indians to rebel. However, the principal source of contemporary knowledge of the Incas was José de Acosta's *Historia natural y moral de las Indias* [Natural and Moral History of the Indies] (1590). Acosta too was sympathetic toward the Incas, although in an earlier work, *De procuranda Indorum Salute* [Preaching the Gospel in the Indies] (1588), the Jesuit referred to the Indians as barbarians, "who had to be governed by force and fear." Here Acosta put forward his celebrated thesis regarding the three classes of barbarians in descending order of civilization: first came the Chinese, Japanese, and East Indians; then the Incas and Aztecs; and finally savages such as the inhabitants of the Amazon. What distinguished the Incas were their fixed settlements and forms of religion and government and a modicum of historical memory. What kept them from the first rank, however, was that they did not possess an alphabet and so had no written documents. Nevertheless, despite Acosta's defense of the Indians against the charge that they were "brutish, unintelligent people," he wrote in his *Moral and Natural History* that Satan ruled in the Americas and that his power "pervaded all Indian society, corrupting morality and perverting religion."

The Spanish imperial school of historical writing, known in Peru as the Toledan school (so called because it supported uncritically the sixteenth-century Viceroy Francisco de Toledo's efforts to restore Spanish dynastic absolutism in

Peru) was best represented by Pedro Sarmiento de Gamboa. He published his *Historia indica* [History of the Incas] in 1572. Here he echoed the leading chroniclers of the conquest and civil wars—Agustín de Zárate and Diego Fernández—affirming the tyranny of the Inca empire and the havoc caused by constant warfare, rebellion, and civil war. Sarmiento justified the Spanish conquest as it represented a liberating force against Inca tyranny while being the agent of Christian evangelization. The zenith of the imperial school's influence came in 1577 when Philip II "prohibited all further inquiry into native religion and history and ordered the colonial authorities to confiscate all manuscripts dealing with such topics" (Brading, 1991, 143).

The patriotic school was best represented in Peru by Las Casas's two principal Andean disciples: the Indian Felipe Guamán Poma de Ayala and the mestizo Garcilaso de la Vega, El Inca. Guamán Poma's *Nueva coronica y buen gobierno* [New Chronicle and Good Government] was written between 1567 and 1615 as two letters to the king of Spain. The manuscript was lost and only unearthed in the Royal Library of Copenhagen in 1908 by a German scholar and made available in a facsimile edition in 1936 by the Ethnographical Institute of Paris. Guamán Poma's purpose was to bring to the attention of the Spanish king "the great merits and the sufferings under Spanish rule of the Peruvian people." The manuscript covers the three phases of Andean history: pre-Columbian times, the conquest, and the subjugation of the Indians under Spanish rule. Guamán Poma offered a defense of the provincial Indian nobility of which he was a member. His innovative prescription for remedying Peru's ills was to separate the Indians from the Spaniards, leaving the governance of the former in the hands of the *caciques,* or Indian leaders. Although Guamán Poma advocated a token Westernization of the Indian nobility, his work represents a yearning for the golden age of the Incas prior to the arrival of the Spaniards. By far the most authentic aspect of his work were the more than three hundred and fifty illustrations that accompany the text. These depicted the dress and customs of the Incas, making Guamán Poma's chronicle an indispensable primary source for modern Andeanists.

Garcilaso de la Vega's history of the Inca empire and of the early years of Spanish rule appeared in two separate works: *Comentarios reales de los Incas* [Royal Commentaries of the Incas] (1608) and *Historial general del Perú* [General History of Peru] (1616). The author's purpose was not to discredit the conquest but to attack the imperial regime introduced by Philip II and his proconsuls. In doing this he sought to rehabilitate the Incas who had prepared the Andean world for Christian evangelization. Following Las Casas's example, Garcilaso emphasized the monotheistic aspects of Inca religion. The fundamental premise of his panegyric was that the Incas governed their great empire in accordance with the dictates of natural law. Unlike Guamán Poma, Garcilaso called for "the creation of a Holy Inca Empire, based on the marriage of conquerors and Inca noblewomen, governed by a mestizo encomendero class, Christian in religion, ruling a native peasantry in accordance with the principles of Inca legislation" (Brading, 1986, 22). According to Arnold Toynbee, Garcilaso's *The Royal Commentaries* constitutes "one of the prime sources of our knowledge of the pre-Columbian civilization of the Andean World." It became the foremost classic of colonial Spanish literature and still remains the point of departure for anyone studying the Inca world.

The Seventeenth Century

Many more historians and chroniclers wrote about the Peruvian viceroyalty in the seventeenth century than previously, but none of the works was truly memorable. Nevertheless, a wealth of information concerning colonial institutions and the customs and daily activities of the mixed population found its way into print. For the first time, a greater number of native-born historians than Spaniards was writing about every facet of colonial life and publishing many of their works in Lima rather than in Europe. The majority of the historians were Jesuits although there were always a few Dominicans and Augustinians as well. The nonreligious historians tended to be minor colonial civil servants, working as *oidores* or members of various *Audiencias*. In addition, histories were being written not only about Peru but also about the provincial regions such as La Plata, Chile, Santa Fé (Colombia), and Tierra Firme (Venezuela).

One of the most important historians of the seventeenth century was Antonio Rodríguez de León Pinelo. Born in Lima, he was the first historian of the New World to research archives not only in the viceroyalties of Peru and New Spain but also in Madrid and Simancas. His *Discurso sobre la importancia, forma y disposición dela recopilación de las leyes de Indias* [Discourse on the Importance, Form and Organization of the Digest of the Laws of the Indies] (1623) was a gargantuan work of legal erudition containing more than five hundred royal letters patent and 300,000 decisions—

it ran to some 120,000 pages in length. His bibliography on New World themes was first published in 1629 and was unsurpassed during the colonial period. The Spanish crown rewarded León Pinelo with lucrative appointments on the Council of the Indies and in the Casa de Contratación as well as with the coveted position of chronicler of the Indies.

Another important early-seventeenth-century work was that of the Spanish jurist, Juan Solórzano Pereira, who published a description of Spanish colonial government in two volumes in Latin, *De Indiarum jure* [On the Laws of the Indies] in 1629 and 1639, respectively. The Spanish translation, *Política indiana* [Politics of the Indies] was published in 1648 and became the standard handbook for government officials in Spain and in the colonies. It provided a digest of colonial laws and decrees as well as detailed descriptions of the geography, the Indians, and the civil and religious organization of Spanish America. An early institutional history was written by Pedro Antonio de la Calancha y Benavides on the history of the Augustinian Order from 1551. Published in two parts (1638 and 1653), the *Crónica moralizada del orden de San Agustín en el Perú con sucesos ejemplares en esta monarquía* [The Moral Chronicle of the Order of Saint Augustine in Peru with Exemplary Events of this Monarchy] provided important insight into the civil and religious government of Peru and contained an excellent natural history of the Pacific coast of South America. In 1646 another native-born historian published the first general history of Chile. Alonso de Ovalle del Manzano's *Histórica relación del reyno de Chile y de las misiones y ministerios que exercita en él la Compañía de Jesús* [The Historical Account of the Kingdom of Chile and of the Missions and Ministries Carried Out by the Company of Jesus] was published simultaneously in Spanish and Italian in 1646. Although he focused on the activities of the Jesuits in Chile, Ovalle—like the majority of his contemporaries—described the physical geography, the natural history, and the customs of the people. Another important history was Fernando Montesinos's two-volume work *Ophir de España o annales peruanas* [Ophir in Spain or the Peruvian Annals] published in 1650. Here the Spanish Jesuit claimed that Peru was the Ophir of Solomon and that it was originally colonized by Jews. More interesting to the twentieth-century historian is his long account of a famous *auto da fé* (public burning) carried out in Lima on January 23, 1639; this is the first history of the Inquisition in the viceroyalty of Peru. Bernabé Cobo de Peralta wrote a *Historia del Nuevo Mundo* [History of the

New World], completed in 1653 but not published until it appeared at Sevilla in four volumes between 1890 and 1895; he was also the author of the first full-length account of the founding of Lima. While serving as a member of the Audiencia of Lima, the Spanish-born Jesuit, Diego Andrés de Rocha wrote his *Tratado único y singular del origen de los indios occidentales del Perú, México, Santa Fé y Chile* [The Unique and Singular Treatise on the Origins of the Western Indians of Peru, Mexico, Santa Fe, and Chile] (1681). It was a highly imaginative attempt to prove that the Indians of the New World were descended from the lost Ten Tribes of Israel. The value of his work, however, stems from the fact that he traveled widely throughout the viceroyalty of Peru, studying the Indians and their customs. The most detailed description of Lima in the seventeenth century, which listed churches, convents, and religious corporation, was the history of the Dominicans in the Spanish colonies published by the Peruvian Dominican, Juan de Meléndez, in three volumes (1681–1682). This work, *Tesoros verdaderos de los yndios en la historia de la gran provincia de San Juan Bautista del Perú de el orden de Predicadores* [Real Treasures of the Indians in the History of the Great Province of Saint John the Baptist of Peru of the Preaching Order], provided much original information not found in other chronicles. Another very useful history of the Audiencia of Nueva Granada (present-day Colombia) was published in 1688 by Colombian-born, Jesuit-educated, Lucas Fernández de Piedrahita. Although conceived in two parts, only the first part of the *Historia general de las conquistas del Nuevo Reino de Granada* [General History of the Conquests of the New Kingdom of Granada] appeared, which took the narrative to the year 1563. It is particularly useful for its excellent account of the history and customs of the Chibcha Indians.

Eighteenth Century

Historical works about Spanish America during the eighteenth century fall into two general categories. There are the conventional histories, which deal with particular institutions or with a century or more of colonial history. These works were sometimes written by European scholars who never visited the New World, but who relied heavily on secondary sources, and who lacked the intimacy of the sixteenth-century chroniclers. Until the expulsion of the Jesuit Order from the Spanish colonies in 1767, much of the historiographical output of the southern hemisphere was the product of Jesuit scholars. However, the number of lay writers increased steadily and became an overwhelming majority during the second half of the eighteenth century. Many of these writers held important positions in the Spanish colonial administration, from governor of Louisiana, to captain-general of Tierra Firme, to president of the first Constitutional Congress of Peru. The second type of writers were famous international travelers who cannot technically be considered historians but whose works are invaluable sources for the histories that would be written in the future.

José Antonio de Oviedo y Baños published a history of the conquest of Nueva Granada to the end of the sixteenth century in 1723. He made a great effort in his *Historia de la conquista y población de la provincia de Venezuela* [History of the Conquest and Population of the Province of Venezuela] to be accurate and justified his work as an attempt to preserve the facts found in decaying manuscripts in the archives of Caracas and Bogotá. An important contribution was made by Dionisio de Alcedo Ugarte y Herrera who published four treatises on various aspects of colonial history, including one on the commerce of Peru. He also published a three-volume work in 1749 entitled *Historiadores primitivos de las Indias Occidentales* [Early Historians of the West Indies], which was a collection of source materials on Spanish colonial history including original chronicles, journals, and biographical sketches. The most enduring work, however, was written by Jorge Juan and Antonio de Ulloa, two Spanish scientists and engineers, who were sent by the Spanish king to join a French scientific expedition to measure the circumference of the earth at the equator at Quito. Their extended trip to South America resulted in three important works. The first, entitled *Noticias americanas* [American Notices] (1772) was a study of colonial society in the viceroyalty of Peru, which included many recommendations for needed governmental and church reforms. The second work, *Noticias secretas de América* [Secret Information on Spanish America], written in 1740, remained in manuscript until 1826 when an English merchant in Cádiz unearthed it and had it published. The original title given by its principal author, Ulloa, translates as *Discourse and Political Reflections on the Present State of the Peruvian Realms*. It was intended as a confidential report for the king and his ministers which may account for the eighty or so years that it remained unpublished. According to Irving A. Leonard, "the work was a devastating account of the evils of the colonial regime in Peru, including the venality of officialdom, the tyranny of local magistrates, the heartless exploitation of the Indian population, the depravity of the clergy, and the abiding antipathies of the American-born Spaniards and the European Spaniards for each other" (Leonard, 1964, 12–13). Together with the writings of Bartolomé de Las Casas, it is regarded as "the most damaging denigration of Spain's rule in the New World" (Leonard, 1964, 13). Their third collaborative work, *Relación histórica del viage a la América Meridional* [A Voyage to South America], appeared in five volumes in 1748 and 1749; an English abridgment of this was prepared by John Adams in 1802. This work described every facet of life in the viceroyalty of Peru and reported on the scientific investigations of Charles Marie de la Condamine. A Spaniard who wrote extensively on Paraguay was the Jesuit, Pedro Lozano. He is remembered for three important works: one on the history of the Jesuits in Paraguay; a second on the history of the conquest of Paraguay, Río de la Plata, and Tucumán; and a third on the revolt of the comuneros in Paraguay. Only the first work, *Historia de la Compañía de Jesús en la provincia del Paraguay* [History of the Company of Jesus in the Province of Paraguay] (2 vols., 1754–1755), was published during his lifetime. The other two appeared in print only at the end of the nineteenth century. Lozano is also remembered for writing a detailed account of the great earthquake at Lima on October 28, 1746, which the French writer Voltaire would describe in his *Candide*. The chief work on Chile was written by Juan Ignacio Molina y González, a sixth-generation Chilean creole. His work entitled *Saggio sulla storia naturale de Chile* [The Geographical, Natural, and Civil History of Chile] (1782) is important not only for his observations on geography, natural history, and political events but because of the inclusion of a list of Chilean writers who might have been lost to historians otherwise. Finally, there is the notable Peruvian Enlightenment figure, José Hipolito Unanue, who—in addition to his many governmental posts and pedagogical endeavors—was a prolific writer and the founder of *El Mercurio Peruano*. His best-known historical work, *Guía política, eclesiástica y militar del virreinato del Perú* [Political, Ecclesiastical, and Military Guide to the Viceroyalty of Peru] was a collection of his treatises on political and economic subjects, which appeared in five volumes from 1793 to 1798.

Excluding the work of Juan and Ulloa, three travel accounts of Spanish-speaking South America stand out. These are Louis Amedée François Frezier's *Relation du voyage de la Mer du Sud aux côtes du Chily et du Perou* [A Voyage to the South Seas along the Coasts of Chile and Peru] (1716), Thomas

L

Falkner's *A Description of Patagonia, and the Adjoining Parts of South America* (1774), and Alexander von Humboldt's *Voyagae aux regions equinoxiales de nouveau continent* [Personal Narrative of Travels to the Equinoctial Regions of the New Continent during the Years 1799–1804] (1814–1819). Frezier provided a detailed account of the conditions of the viceroyalty of Peru in its southern regions. He was one of the earliest writers to describe the Inca *quipus*—knotted strings used for statistical records. Although his description of Lima was enthusiastic, he scorned the religious superstition evident in the processions of religious flagellants. An able observer, he made mention of the bitter rivalry between Creoles and "peninsulars" a century before the independence movement. Thomas Falkner provided the classic description of the Patagonian and Pampa Indians of Argentina. Falkner spent thirty-five years in the southern reaches of the hemisphere. He was a keen observer of the natural habitat of the region and traveled extensively, venturing as far as the Straits of Magellan and the Falkland Islands. He included a grammar and vocabulary of the Patagonian language in his work. Alexander von Humboldt's *Voyage aux regions equinoxiales de nouveau continent* [Personal Narrative of Travels] (1814–1819) is the account of his 1,500-mile journey up the Orinoco, across the grasslands of the Llanos, to the rain forests of Guiana. In this work, as well as in another travel journal entitled *Vues des cordilères et monuments des peuples indigènes de l'Amerique* [Views of the Mountain Ranges and Monuments of the Indigenous Peoples of America] (1810), Humboldt, a famous German natural scientist, expounded on his theories of climatic determinism, which explained the stunted development of primitive civilization in the New World and of Asian intervention in the Americas. If the Incas and their counterparts in the central Mexican Valley and in the Yucatan Peninsula had reached a higher level of development than the Amazonian tribesmen, he believed, even their civilization was precluded from further progress. This was so because it was plagued by the despotism and barbarity of their social institutions. According to Humboldt, "if tropical savagery derived from degeneration caused by the environmental pressure, highland civilization sprang from Asian missionaries blessed with a culture that precluded any genuine flowering of the human spirit" (Brading, 1991, 525).

The Nineteenth Century

As Juan Maiguashca's survey of modern Latin American historiography demonstrates in the next entry in this encyclopedia, the writing of history became very popular in nineteenth-century South America. With few exceptions—Diego Barros Araña in Chile and Carlos Wiese in Peru who were both history professors at major universities—history remained the preserve of amateurs. The historians of note preferred careers in public office or private enterprise to pedagogical and scholarly pursuits; there were renowned military officers, distinguished diplomats, and successful newspaper editors and booksellers. One major change was the almost total disappearance of religious figures writing history, although even here there remains the odd exception, such as Federico González Suárez, an Ecuadorean Jesuit who later became Archbishop of Quito.

Most of these historians ignored pre-Columbian and colonial history in favor of writing on the independence and early-nineteenth-century periods. These historians wrote primarily from a liberal political viewpoint. This meant that their works were characterized by a marked Hispanophobia, which denigrated everything having to do with Spain and, most especially, the colonial experience. This widespread denunciation of Spanish colonial policies contributed to the already established Black Legend of Spanish barbarism in the New World. Those who did write on the colonial period tended to emphasize the cultural and psychological impact that Spanish subjugation had on the postcolonial society. Very few historians had a hemispheric perspective; most were nationalistic in their philosophies and concentrated their research on their respective countries. One significant exception was the Uruguayan, Andrés Lamas, who stressed the uniformity of the independence movements throughout Latin America by pointing to the similarity of the conquests and the colonial experiences.

Nineteenth-century Spanish American historians preferred writing narrative general histories that were largely devoid of conceptual analysis while being well researched. Many, like Andrés Bello (the Venezuelan author of a famous article on how to write history), believed that the historian should do extensive research in primary documents and avoid philosophical generalizations; these historians felt obliged not only to comb their respective national and regional archives but to go to Spain to work at the Archives of Simancas as well as at the Archives of the Indies in Seville. Toward the end of the century one can see the growing influence of positivism in the writing of history, which meant a departure from traditional political and military history and the application of the theories of social evolution to the study of the historical process.

The Chilean historian José Toribio Medina is generally regarded as the foremost nineteenth-century colonial scholar. This is due to his Herculean accomplishment of publishing seventy-eight volumes on biography and history, which have themselves become primary sources for the writing of colonial Latin America history. Using the archives in Spain and in the Vatican, he gathered data for the study of the Araucanian Indians, the history of the colonial press in Chile and several other Latin American countries, and the Inquisition in America. His most significant works are *Historia de la literatura colonial de Chile* [History of the Colonial Literature of Chile] (1882), in three volumes, and *Colección de documentos inéditos para la historia de Chile desde el viaje de Magallanes hasta la batalla de Maipo (1518–1818)* [Collection of Unpublished Documents for the History of Chile from the Voyage of Magellan to the Battle of Maipo, 1518–1818] (1888–1902), in thirty volumes.

Most historians who wrote about the colonial period of the nineteenth century did so only as an introduction to their general histories, wherein they traced the origins of the subsequent independence movements of the early nineteenth century. These surveys provided an unbalanced treatment of the colonial period in contrast to the section on the wars of independence. This was certainly the case with the Venezuelan Rafael María's Baralt's *Resumen de la historia de Venezuela* [Outline of the History of Venezuela] (1841). Exceptions to this rule, however, were provided by the Chilean Diego Barros Araña and the Ecuadorean González Suárez. The latter's work, *Historia general de la república del Ecuador* [General History of the Republic of Ecuador] (7 vols., 1890–1903), for example, traced the development of Ecuador's indigenous population using archaeological as well as documentary evidence and criticized the Dominican Order for excesses committed during the colonial period.

One of the few monographs written exclusively on the colonial period during this century was Javier Prado y Ugarteche's *El estado social del Perú durante la dominación española* [The Social Conditions of Peru during the Spanish Domination] (1894). Written by a Peruvian professor of the history of philosophy, Prado's positivist history gave a favorable interpretation of Spanish rule and argued that Peruvians could not avoid the legacy of three hundred years of colonial history. His professor at the University of San Marcos, Carlos Wiese, had instilled in him the importance of researching both the pre-Columbian and the colonial eras—something that few nineteenth- and twentieth-century South American historians were prepared to do. Wiese's *Historia y civilización del Perú* [History and Civilization of Peru] (1891) demonstrated how archaeology could be linked with history and was unique in devoting attention to Inca and Hispanic colonial regional history.

Another South American historian who focused on the colonial period and especially on Native Americans under Spanish rule was the Venezuelan, Arístides Rojas. The latter's *Estudios indígenas: Contribucción a la historia antigua de Venezuela* [Indigenous Studies: A Contribution to the Ancient History of Venezuela] (1878) showed how profoundly Rojas had been influenced by Humboldt. Indeed, prior to writing his history he retraced Humboldt's route through the Venezuelan outback. Rojas was one of the first South American historians to insist that the scientific knowledge of pre-Hispanic populations was a prerequisite to the understanding of subsequent history of any Latin American nation. He became an early champion of the Indian population of Venezuela and argued in his text in favor of educating the native Indians.

The Twentieth Century
The twentieth century has witnessed a veritable renaissance in historical writing on colonial Latin America. No longer can we speak of this field, as Lucien Febvre did in 1929, as a "new frontier." In the United States alone, there are two historical journals dedicated exclusively to colonial Latin American history. Indeed, one of the principal historiographical developments of this century has been the preeminent role played by historians based in the United States. This trend, which began in the nineteenth century with the groundbreaking works of William H. Prescott, Hubert H. Bancroft, and Charles F. Lummis, gathered momentum with the publication of Edward G. Bourne's *Spain in America* (1904). Bourne's work offered a new interpretation of Spanish colonial policies and practices, which questioned the Black Legend by offering a positive assessment of the early Spanish experience in the New World. This interpretation was further strengthened by Herbert E. Bolton's positive assessment of Spanish colonization in the Spanish Borderlands.

The next generation of U.S. revisionist historians, writing during the interwar years, further corrected the bias of the Black Legend tradition. They also prepared solid monographs on administrative and political topics that also dealt with social, economic, and cultural subjects. The most important work produced by these post-1920s revisionists was Lesley Byrd Simpson's *The Encomienda in New Spain* (1929). Its chief weakness, however, was that it assessed Spanish colonial administration from the Spanish point of view while totally ignoring the interests of the Indians. Simpson's history epitomized the "white man's burden" defense of Spanish colonialism by stating that "the great empires of the past have been built upon slave labor or upon coerced labor of some sort."

In 1964 Charles Gibson's *The Aztecs under Spanish Rule* pointed to the direction that postwar colonial historiography was taking: switching the focus from colonial elites to the indigenous populations, applying a multidisciplinary approach—especially combining anthropology and sociology with history and questioning the Hispanophile bias of the revisionist literature of the interwar period. These new trends took hold first in the writing of colonial Mexican history. An analogous shift amongst historians of the pre-Columbian and early colonial years of Spanish South America took place with the publication of John Hemming's *The Conquest of the Incas* (1970). Hemming's purpose was to refute many misconceptions about the decline of the Inca empire and to attempt to look at the conquest of Peru not only from the viewpoint of the victors but of the vanquished as well. Praising Prescott for his "immortal narrative," Hemming was determined to provide a more complete account by exploring social conditions in post-conquest Peru, especially the integration of the Incas into Spanish society.

Following Hemming's prize-winning account of the fall of the Inca empire was the publication, over the next two decades, of numerous monographs, which explored previously ignored subjects or even familiar ones using, however, the new criteria mentioned above. In 1972 James Lockhart's *The Men of Cajamarca* offered a collective biography of the men who accompanied Pizarro to Peru and demonstrated that "every stratum of Spanish society and every region of the Spanish mainland was represented in force." In 1980 Mark A. Burkholder's *Politics of a Colonial Career: José Baquíjano and the Audiencia of Lima* examined eighteenth-century Bourbon administrative and political reforms from the viewpoint of a single career-seeker who epitomized "the discrimination and frustration that plagued native sons in particular as their personal goals conflicted with royal policy." Two years later, Steve J. Stern's *Peru's Indian Peoples and the Challenge of Spanish Conquest: Huamanga to 1640* accomplished for the Incas what Gibson's work had for the Aztecs. Stern's

avowed purpose was to tell "how conquest transformed vigorous native peoples of the Andean sierra into an inferior caste of 'Indians' subordinated to Spanish colonizers." A second work on the impact of the conquest on Andean society followed in 1984, written by Karen Spalding. In *Huarochirí: An Andean Society under Inca and Spanish Rule,* Spalding presented a full-scale interpretation of the process of change in Andean society from pre-Inca times to the late eighteenth century. The new emphasis was on the indigenous population and the stratagems it adopted to resist Spanish pressure.

In 1983 Luis Martín's *Daughters of the Conquistadores* examined the role played by women during the early years of the Spanish colonization of Peru. Although Martín looked only at upper class Hispanic women, and an equal treatment for lower-class Hispanic, Indian, and black women is still unavailable, he provided the first full-scale study of Hispanic women in colonial Peru. Finally, Sabine MacCormack's pioneer work entitled *Religion in the Andes* (1991) should be mentioned as a prime example of the union of anthropology and history in the effort to reconstruct and understand Andean religion in early colonial Peru. MacCormack succeeds in her work in providing us with a framework where the voices of Andean people "can be heard speaking about the divine powers of their majestic land."

Historical writing in the Spanish-speaking world in the last century has taken a different path than that described above. In Spain the emphasis has been on writing multivolume histories on the colonial period linking the history of metropolitan Spain with its colonies. Although the portion devoted to the Americas has always been significantly less than on Spain, new interpretations regarding social and economic developments make these works valuable to the North American specialist. The best of these multiauthored general histories is the five-volume *Historia social y económica de España y de América* [Social and Economic History of Spain and America] (1957–1959) edited by Jaime Vicens Vives, the disseminator of the Annales school of historiography in Spain. Another impressive multiauthored work is the fourteen-volume *Historia de América* [History of America] (1940) edited by the Argentine historian, Ricardo Levene.

In the New World, and specifically in Peru, the focus was much more specific. Some general trends have included the resuscitation and reinterpretation of El Inca, Garcilaso de la Vega's historical output, the study of the Andean Indian from a multidisciplinary point of view, and the reexamination of various colonial institutions and Indian revolts. The list of twentieth-century Garcilasistas reads like a *Who's Who* of distinguished contemporary Peruvian historians including José de la Riva-Agüero, Raúl Porras Barrenechea, and Aurelio Miró Quesada. The revival of Inca studies in the pre-Columbian period has also attracted first-rate historians and sociologists. Beginning with Luis E. Valcárcel's *Altiplano andino: Período indígena* [The Andean High Plateau: The Indigenous Period] (1953) to María Rostworowski de Diez Canseco's *Historia del Tahuantinsuyu* [History of the Inca Empire] (1988), Andeanists no longer need rely solely on sixteenth-century Spanish accounts to portray the Inca world in a multidimensional fashion. Studies focusing on institutions, regional history, and native rebellions include Guillermo Lohmann Villena's *El corregidor de indios en el Perú bajo los Austrias* [The Viceroyalty of the Indians in Peru under the Habsburgs] (1957), Carlos Daniel Valcárcel's *Túpac Amaru: Precursor de la Independencia* [Túpac Amaru: Precursor of Independence] (1977), and José Tamayo Herrera's three-volume *Historia general del Qosqo* [General History of Cuzco] (1992). What is apparent is that the renaissance in colonial studies continues strong at the end of the century on both sides of the Atlantic and in both halves of the hemisphere.

George L. Vásquez

See also EUROPEAN EXPANSION, CHRONICLERS AND HISTORIANS OF; INDIGENOUS HISTORIOGRAPHY; LATIN AMERICAN HISTORIOGRAPHY—NATIONAL PERIOD; MEXICAN HISTORIOGRAPHY; WOMEN'S HISTORY, LATIN AMERICA.

Texts

Burkholder, Mark A. *Politics of a Colonial Career: José Baquíjano and the Audiencia of Lima.* Second ed. Wilmington, DE: Scholarly Resources Inc., 1990.

Cieza de León, Pedro de. *The Incas.* Trans. Harriet de Onis. Norman: University of Oklahoma Press, 1959.

Cobo, Bernabé. *Inca Religion and Customs.* Ed. and trans. Roland Hamilton. Austin: University of Texas Press, 1990.

Garcilaso de la Vega, El Inca. *Royal Commentaries of the Incas and General History of Peru.* Trans. Harold V. Livermore. Austin: University of Texas Press, 1987.

Guamán Poma de Ayala, Felipe. *Letter to a King: A Peruvian Chief's Account of Life under the Incas and under Spanish Rule.* Ed. and trans. Christopher Dilke. New York: E.P. Dutton, 1978.

Hemming, John. *The Conquest of the Incas.* San Diego: Harcourt Brace Jovanovich, 1970.

Humboldt, Alexander von. *Cartas Americanas* [American Letters]. Caracas: Biblioteca Ayacucho, 1980.

Juan, Jorge. *Discourse and Political Reflections on the Kingdom of Peru.* Ed. and trans. John J. TePaske and Besse A. Clement. Norman: University of Oklahoma Press, 1978.

———, and Antonio de Ulloa. *A Voyage to South America.* Abrid. and trans. John Adams. New York: Alfred A. Knopf, 1964.

Las Casas, Bartolomé de. *A Short Account of the Destruction of the Indies.* Trans. Nigel Griffin. New York: Penguin Books, 1992.

Lockhart, James. *The Men of Cajamarca: A Social and Biographical Study of the First Conquerors of Peru.* Austin: University of Texas Press, 1972.

MacCormack, Sabine. *Religion in the Andes: Vision and Imagination in Early Colonial Peru.* Princeton, NJ: Princeton University Press, 1991.

Martín, Luis. *Daughters of the Conquistadores: Women of the Viceroyalty of Peru.* Albuquerque: University of New Mexico Press, 1983.

Mendiburú, Manuel de. *Diccionario histórico biográfico del Perú* [Dictionary of Peruvian History and Biography]. 11 vols. Lima: Imprenta Enrique Palacios, 1931–1934.

Miró Quesada, Aurelio. *El Inca Garcilaso* [The Inca Garcilaso]. Lima: Pontificia Universidad Católica del Perú, Fondo Editorial, 1994.

Montesinos, Fernando. *Memorias antiguas historiales del Perú* [Historical Reports of Peru]. Ed. and trans. Philip Ainsworth Means. London: Hakluyt Society, 1920.

Oviedo y Baños, José de. *The Conquest and Settlement of Venezuela.* Trans. Jeannette Johnson Varner. Berkeley: University of California Press, 1987.

Rostworowski de Diez Canseco, María. *Historia del Tahuantinsuyu* [History of the Inca Empire]. Fourth ed. Lima: Instituto de Estudios Políticos, 1992.

Tamayo Herrera, José. *Historia general del Qosqo: Una historia regional desde el período lítico hasta el año 2000* [General History of Cuzco: A Regional History from the Stone Age until the Year 2000]. Cuzco, Peru: Editorial Mercantil, 1992.

Spalding, Karen. *Huarochirí: An Andean Society under Inca and Spanish Rule.* Stanford, CA: Stanford University Press, 1984.

L

Stern, Steve J. *Peru's Indian Peoples and the Challenge of Spanish Conquest: Huamanga to 1640*. Madison: University of Wisconsin Press, 1982.

Valcárcel, Carlos Daniel. *Túpac Amaru: Precursor de la Independencia* [Túpac Amaru: Precursor of Independence]. Lima: Universidad Nacional Mayor de San Marcos, Dirección Universitaria de Biblioteca y Publicaciones, 1977.

References

Brading, David A. *The First America: The Spanish Monarchy, Creole Patriots, and the Liberal State, 1492–1867*. Cambridge, Eng.: Cambridge University Press, 1991.

———. "The Incas and the Renaissance: The Royal Commentaries of Inca Garcilaso de la Vega." *Journal of Latin American Studies* 18 (1986): 1–23.

Chaunu, Pierre. *Las grandes lineas de la producción histórica en América Latina (1950–1962)* [Major Trends in Historical Writing in Latin America]. Caracas: Escuela de Historia, Facultad de Humanidades y Educación, Universidad Central de Venezuela, 1965.

Esteve Barba, Francisco. *Historiografía indiana* [New World Historiography]. Madrid: Editorial Gredos, 1964.

Feliú Cruz, Guillermo. *Historiografía colonial de Chile* [Colonial Historiography of Chile]. Santiago: Fondo Histórico y Bibliográfico José Toribio Medina, 1958.

Gibson, Charles. "The Colonial Period in Latin American History." In *Latin American History: Essays on Its Study and Teaching*. ed. Howard F. Cline. Vol. 2. Austin: University of Texas Press, 1967, 598–611.

Halperín Donghi, Tulio. "The State of Latin American History." In *Changing Perspectives in Latin American Studies: Insights from Six Disciplines,* ed. Christopher Mitchell. Stanford, CA: Stanford University Press, 1988, 13–62.

Keen, Benjamin. "Main Currents in United States Writings on Colonial Spanish America, 1884–1984." *Hispanic American Historical Review* 65 (1985): 657–682.

Leonard, Irving A. *Books of the Brave: Being an Account of Books and of Men in the Spanish Conquest and Settlement of the Sixteenth-Century New World*. Berkeley: University of California Press, 1992.

Riva-Agüero, José de la. *La historia en el Perú.* [History in Peru]. Vol. IV of *Obras Completas de José de la Riva-Agüero.* Lima: Pontificia Universidad Católica del Perú, 1965.

Stern, Steve J. "Latin America's Colonial History. Invitation to an Agenda." *Latin American Perspectives* 12 (1985): 3–16.

TePaske, John. "Spanish America: The Colonial Period." In *Latin American Scholarship since World War II: Trends in History, Political Science, Literature, Geography, and Economics,* ed. Roberto Esquenazi-Mayo and Michael C. Meyer. Lincoln: University of Nebraska Press, 1971, 5–19.

Wilgus, A. Curtis. *The Historiography of Latin America: A Guide to Historical Writing, 1500–1800*. Metuchen, NJ: Scarecrow Press, 1975.

Zavala, Silvio. "A General View of the Colonial History of the New World." *American Historical Review* 66 (1961): 913–929.

Latin American Historiography (excluding Mexico and Brazil)—The National Period, 1820–1990

A large body of literature covering the processes of independence of the Spanish colonies in the Americas and their organization as independent nation-states in the nineteenth and twentieth centuries. These works were produced in three stages: the liberal (1820s–1900s), the revisionist (1900s–1930s) and the academic (1930s–1990s).

Liberal Historiography, 1820s–1900s.

The historiography on the national period by nineteenth-century historians was written mostly from a liberal perspective that, as the century wore on, experienced changes giving rise to three types of liberal history: "constitutional liberalism," "romantic liberalism," and "positivism."

Influenced by the Enlightenment and the American and French revolutions, the first group of liberal historians, the constitutionalists (1820s–1850s), conceived of the process of independence and that of national formation in Latin America as the logical consequence of the expansion of European history. Moreover, being advocates of republicanism, they highlighted the role of constitutions in the postcolonial order because they believed that these legal instruments had the power to safeguard individual liberty, promote social harmony, and advance material progress. Representatives of this kind of history are the Colombian J.M. Restrepo, the Guatemalan A. Marure, the Venezuelan R.M. Baralt, the Ecuadorian P.F. Cevallos, the Peruvian M.F. Paz-Soldán, the Chilean L.M. Amunátegui, and the Argentinian Bartolomé Mitre.

Beginning in the 1830s, the process of national formation fell into disarray almost everywhere in Latin America. According to the second group of liberal historians, the romantics (1850s–1880s), this was because constitutions alone were not sufficient to usher in the republican era and because the authoritarian and hierarchical values of the colonial period were still very much alive. In their opinion, however, there was room for optimism. Whereas the constitutional historians had conceived of Latin American history as an extension of that of Europe, the romantics, borrowing from thinkers such as Johann Gottfried Herder, Augustin Thierry, and Jules Michelet, viewed it instead as the unfolding of individual Latin American nations guided by the "spirit of the people." This spirit, which manifested itself in different ways in different countries, was characterized everywhere by a budding democratic republican ethos. According to the romantics, democratic republicanism had already found expression in forceful political and military leaders. It was only a question of time before it replaced the values and even the customs of the colonial period. Examples of romantic historians are the Argentinian V.F. López, the Chileans J.V. Lastarria and B. Vicuña Mackenna, and the Cuban J.A. Saco.

The last type of liberal historians, the positivists (1880s–1900s), appeared toward the end of the century. Impressed by the economic growth that took place in Latin America at this time, they became intensely interested in the economic and social aspects of the process of national formation. Following European thinkers like Auguste Comte, Herbert Spencer, Henry Thomas Buckle, and Hippolyte-Adolphe Taine, the positivists elaborated a new kind of liberal history. For them, the Latin American economic boom was an indication that this part of the world was evolving, albeit at some distance, in the same direction as western Europe, that is, from a "military" to an "industrial–scientific" stage. Because of this, they argued, the task of the positivist historian was to discover the "laws" that governed this process so that "scientific politicians" could use this knowledge in order to bring about "order and progress" and thus consolidate the new nation-states. The best representatives of this school of history are the Chileans D. Barros Araña and V. Letelier, the Bolivian G. René-Moreno, the Argentinians A. Saldías and E. Quesada, the Peruvian J. Prado y Ugarteche, and the Venezuelan J. Gil Fortoul.

Revisionist Historiography, 1900s–1930s

Liberal historiography in its various forms lost momentum at the beginning of the twentieth century. The most salient factors behind this decline were the following. American interventions in Central America and the Caribbean at this time, combined with the carnage of World War I, did much to diminish the admiration Latin Americans had for the United States, England, and France, the birthplaces of liberalism. Simultaneously, the Catholic Church experienced a renewal, and its influence in Latin America grew significantly. Last but not least, the Mexican revolution demonstrated the vitality of the Latin American Indian and rural masses. Influenced by these circumstances, a new generation of Latin American historians began to question the validity of the liberal interpretations of the national period. Accusing the liberal historians of having seen Latin America through the distorting lenses of European theories, the revisionists proclaimed the need to reexamine the history of the subcontinent, this time from an internal perspective.

There were various kinds of "revisionist" historians depending on how they conceived this perspective. The most conspicuous among them was a group of conservative intellectuals such as the Uruguayan L. Herrera, the Peruvian J. de la Riva Agüero, and the Chileans A. Edwards and F. Encina. In their opinion, the adoption of liberalism and the abandonment of the colonial-Hispanic tradition during the nineteenth century had been responsible for the difficulties Latin Americans had experienced in organizing themselves as new nations. Far from being an obstacle to national formation, the colonial-Hispanic tradition was the only solid foundation Latin Americans could really build upon. For another group of revisionist historians, among which figured prominently the Bolivian A. Arguedas and the Venezuelan L. Vallenilla Lanz, the "European bias" of the liberal historians had prevented them from understanding the most important feature of the Latin American historical experience, that is, the extensive racial mixture that had taken place throughout the colonial period and the nineteenth century. This phenomenon, they argued, had eroded European values and customs in Latin America, particularly among the lower classes. This explained why the Latin American masses had not contributed to an orderly transition from colony to nation and why, as a result, authoritarian and clientelistic political systems had arisen throughout the subcontinent. A third type of revisionists, on the other hand, thought of race mixture in positive terms.

For authors like the Argentinian R. Rojas and the Peruvian R. Porras Barrenechea, racial and cultural syncretism had produced a new and vibrant civilization in Latin America. Failure to understand this phenomenon had driven nineteenth-century historians to seek inspiration abroad.

Academic Historiography, 1930s–1990s

While the revisionist debates raged, Latin American history as an institution finally came of age. From the 1880s onward archives were opened to the public; documentary collections, bibliographies, and journals began to appear; and national academies and research centers were organized. Moreover, history as a discipline found its place in a number of Latin American universities. Lastly, the institutional base of Latin American history became internationalized. A crucial dimension of this process was the foundation in the United States of the *Hispanic American Historical Review* in 1918 and of the *Handbook of Latin American Studies* in 1936, two publications that are regarded today as a sine qua non for historical research everywhere. Most of this organizational effort can be traced to a group of historians who were contemporaries of the revisionists but who, unlike them, were far more interested in institution building than in what they considered mere ideological debates. Thus, by the 1930s there had emerged a small but energetic community of scholars in Latin America and the United States, devoted to the idea of producing "academically" sound history.

Since then the historiography of the national period has gone through two stages. During the first, which lasted until the 1950s, the brand-new professionals produced works rich in scholarly apparatus and cautious in interpretation. The most important among these historians are the Argentinians R. Levene, E. Ravignani, and R.R. Caillet-Bois, the Paraguayan E. Cardozo, the Chilean G. Feliú Cruz, the Bolivian H. Vázquez-Machicado, the Peruvian J. Basadre, and the Americans C.H. Haring, M. Burgin, and A.P. Whitaker.

During the second stage, which began in the 1960s and is still with us today, a new generation has taken over the writing of Latin American history. Far more numerous than in the past, the new team of professionals is to be found not only in Latin American and U.S. history departments and research centers but also in English, French, Spanish, Italian, Canadian, German, Swedish, Russian, and Japanese institutions. In methodological terms, they have experimented with a wide variety of approaches, the most important among which are the modernity, Marxist, Annales, and dependency

paradigms. The last of these approaches, the dependency paradigm, was formulated in Latin America and has been influential on North American, European, and Third World historical writing. As for topics of research, in the 1960s and 1970s the academic historians concentrated mainly on economic history, but since then they have widened their concerns to include social, cultural, environmental, feminist, and other kinds of history. Besides specialized research, they have also given attention to global interpretations of the national period. Of all this output the most important has been the monographic work of hundreds of scholars from a wide variety of countries. Thanks to this literature we have gained a better understanding of the complex process of national formation in Latin America, particularly from the 1880s to the present. As for the early national period (1810–1880), long seen as difficult to study because of the political and social disorder prevailing at the time, it is only very recently that it has finally become the object of intense scrutiny.

Juan Maiguashca

See also ANNALES SCHOOL; BRAZILIAN HISTORIOGRAPHY; LATIN AMERICAN HISTORIOGRAPHY—WRITING ON THE PRECOLONIAL AND COLONIAL PERIODS FROM THE SIXTEENTH CENTURY TO THE PRESENT DAY; MEXICAN HISTORIOGRAPHY; WOMEN'S HISTORY—LATIN AMERICAN.

Texts

Liberal historians; Constitutional Liberalism.
Gil Fortoul, José. *Historia Constitucional de Venezuela* [The Constitutional History of Venezuela]. Fifth ed. Caracas: Sales, 1964.
Mitre, Bartolomé. *Historia de Belgrano y de la Independencia Argentina* [History of Belgrano and Argentine Independence]. Fourth ed. Buenos Aires: F. Lajouane, 1887.
Vicuña Mackenna, Benjamin. *Los Jirondinos Chilenos* [The Chilean Girondins]. Ed. Cristian Gazmuri. Santiago: Editorial Universitaria, 1989.

Revisionist historians.
Arguedas, Alcides. *Historia general de Bolivia: El proceso de la nacionalidad, 1809–1921* [A General History of Bolivia: The National Process, 1809–1921]. La Paz: Arno hermanos, 1922.
Edwards, Alberto. *La fronda aristocrática en Chile* [The Aristocratic Rebellion in Chile]. Santiago: Ediciones Ercilla, 1936.

Rojas, Ricardo. *Eurindia: Ensayo de estética fundado en la experiencia histórica de las culturas americanas* [Eurindia: Aesthetic Essay Based on the Historical Experience of the American Cultures]. Buenos Aires: Libreria "La Facultad," J. Roldan, 1924.

Academic historians.
Basadre, Jorgé. *Historia de la República del Perú* [History of the Republic of Peru]. Fifth expanded ed. 11 vols. Lima: Editorial "Historia," 1962–1964.
Levene, Ricardo. *Historia de la Nación Argentina* [History of the Argentinian Nation]. 7 vols. Buenos Aires: Impr. de la Universidad, 1936–1949.

References
Acevedo, Edberto Oscar. *Manual de Historiografía Hispanoamericana Contemporánea* [A Handbook of Contemporary Hispanic American Historiography]. Mendoza: Universidad Nacional de Cuyo, 1992.

Lattimore, Owen (1900–1989)

American traveler and historian of Inner Asia. Raised in China, Lattimore attended high school in England. From 1926 to 1937 he traveled and researched first in Xinjiang and then Manchuria and Inner Mongolia. In 1941 and 1942, he served as adviser to Chiang Kai-shek. After World War II, Lattimore created a pioneering research unit on Inner Asia at Johns Hopkins University. The McCarthy era damaged Lattimore's American career and in 1963 he founded a Mongolian studies program at Leeds University in England. Methodologically based in anthropology and geography, Lattimore's influential early works, particularly *Inner Asian Frontiers of China* (1940), sought to explain the dynamics of China's relations with Inner Asia as a recurring cycle of nomadic–sedentary conflict and coexistence.

Christopher Pratt Atwood

Texts
Inner Asian Frontiers of China. Oxford: Oxford University Press, 1988.
Mongols of Manchuria. New York: The John Day Co., 1934.
Nomads and Commissars: Mongolia Revisited. New York: Oxford University Press, 1962.
Studies in Frontier History: Collected Papers, 1928–1958. London: Oxford University Press, 1962.

References
Cotton, James. *Asian Frontier Nationalism: Owen Lattimore and the American Policy Debate.* Manchester: University of Manchester Press, 1989.
Newman, Robert P. *Owen Lattimore and the "Loss" of China.* Berkeley: University of California Press, 1992.

Latvian Historiography

Historical writing produced in Latvia, one of the Baltic republics in northeastern Europe, especially after 1918 when the country acquired independence from the Russian Empire. Until that time, historical writing in and about the so-called Baltic provinces (Livland, Courland, Estland) had been done by Baltic Germans, the traditional dominant nationality group of the area; and to a lesser extent by Imperial Russian historians and commentators. Starting with the 1860s, the Latvian "national awakening" called for history about Latvians written by Latvians, but the call was not answered until around the turn of the century when a few histories (e.g., those by Jānis Krodznieks and Kārlis Landers) portrayed Latvians as a colonized and oppressed people. The founding of the University of Latvia and of a National Archival Administration in 1919 gave to Latvian historical writing an institutional base within which training of a new generation of historians could take place; and the possibility of growth was further enhanced by the founding in 1936 of a Latvian Institute of History with its own quarterly journal. These developments were interrupted by World War II, however, during which time Latvia was occupied by and incorporated into the Soviet Union (1940–1941), then included within the eastern territories of the German Third Reich (1941–1945), and finally, in 1945, reincorporated into the USSR. During this turmoil, a number of historians of the interwar period were deported to Siberia by Soviet authorities and many others—such as Arvēds Švabe and Edgars Dunsdorfs—became refugees; some resumed their work as historians in Sweden, Australia, Germany, and North America. In the period from 1945 to 1989, historical writing by Latvians about Latvia had two distinct branches. On the one hand, the work of the historians in the Institute of History of the Academy of Sciences of the Latvian Soviet Socialist Republic, the Institute of Party History, and the University of Latvia, was strictly controlled by the Latvian Communist Party and had to demonstrate not only the inevitability of communism in Latvia but also the benefits derived by Latvians from living in close proximity to Russians. On the other hand, the émigré Latvian historians, when they wrote on Latvian topics, envisaged themselves to be continuing the work of the interwar period of independence, and, in spite of having virtually no access to the archives in Latvia, still produced a considerable literature, notably a ten-volume general history of Latvia (the so-called Daugava series), published in Sweden. Since the 1991 collapse of the Soviet Union, and Latvia's regaining of independence, the division between Latvian historians working inside and outside of Latvia has been virtually eliminated, as those living elsewhere now have access to Latvian archives and as the historians in Latvia are able to write without the interpretations imposed on them by the Communist Party and the larger Soviet historical establishment.

Andrejs Plakans

See also ESTONIAN HISTORIOGRAPHY; LITHUANIAN HISTORIOGRAPHY.

References

Plakans, Andrejs. *The Latvians: A Short History.* Stanford, CA: Hoover Institution Press, 1995.

Strods, Heinrichs. "Die Geschichtswissenschaft Lettlands in den Jahren 1945–1990 [The Historical Sciences in Latvia in the Years 1945–1990.]" *Acta Baltica* 28 (1991): 9–17.

Lavisse, Ernest (1842–1922)

Historian and educational reformer. A scholarship student from a modest background, Lavisse pursued a distinguished career as scholar and teacher. He was an instructor at (1876) and later director of the École Normale Supérieure (1904) and for many years held a chair in history at the Sorbonne, to which he was appointed in 1888. He was elected to the Académie française in 1893. Lavisse had a profound influence on the teaching of history at all levels of education during the Third French Republic. His early work was in German history, an interest inspired by Germany's military victory over France in 1871. He wrote studies of the rise of Brandenberg-Prussia, and of imperial Germany, as well as biographies of Frederick the Great. Critics argue that he studied Germany primarily to understand its historic rivalry with France and that his unstated objective as a historian was to account for France's recent defeat and so to use lessons learned to help restore its national stature. As a student in Germany during the 1870s, Lavisse was impressed with the research seminar in history inaugurated by Leopold von Ranke and later introduced this institution into French higher education.

Despite the recognition he received for his historical scholarship and his commitment to scientific research, scholars credit Lavisse with neither methodological nor interpretative originality, but rather with a capacity for clear and effective generalization. He is accordingly best known for his editorship of three vast projects of synthesis during his mature years: the first dealing with the rise of Europe (1892–1901), the successors with the history of France to the Revolution (1903–1911) and in the contemporary age (1921–1922). These served students as the standard introduction to French history during the Third Republic.

These histories for a learned audience notwithstanding, Lavisse probably exercised a more lasting influence upon the attitudes of the French toward their past through his textbooks in French history, which for some four decades provided children in the public schools with their first (and for many only) exposure to their national history. A moralist about French national identity, Lavisse designed these primers to inculcate in French youth a pride in country and a sensitivity to the obligations of good citizenship.

While not a politician, Lavisse worked closely with leaders of the Third Republic to reform public education at all levels. He played a key role in the integration of various schools of higher education in Paris into a single university, and he was responsible for refashioning the requirements for the professional training of historians. Seemingly the quintessential republican reformer, he never completely relinquished his early Bonapartist sympathies (he had served as tutor to a Bonapartist prince in the last years of the Second Empire) and for some biographers his nationalism always overshadowed his republicanism, particularly after World War I in his vindictive attitude toward Germany in defeat.

Patrick Hutton

Texts

Histoire de France contemporaine depuis la Révolution jusqu'à la paix de 1919 [History of Modern France, from the Revolution to the Peace of 1919]. 10 vols. Paris: Hachette, 1920–1922.

(ed.) *Histoire de France depuis les origines jusqu'à la Révolution* [History of France from its Origins to the Revolution]. 9 vols. Paris: Hachette, 1903–1911. Paris: Hachette, 1900–1911.

Histoire générale du IVᵉ siècle à nos jours [General History from the Fourth Century to Our Day]. 12 vols. Paris: Colin, 1892–1901.

References

Lach, Donald. "Ernest Lavisse." In *Essays in Modern European Historiography,* ed. S. William Halperin. Chicago: University of Chicago Press, 1970, 143–159.

Nora, Pierre. "Ernest Lavisse: Son rôle dans la formation du sentiment national [Ernest Lavisse: His Role in the Formation of National Sentiment]." *Revue historique* 228 (1962): 73–106.

———. "L'Histoire de France de Lavisse." In *Les Lieux de mémoire* [The Places of Memory], ed. Pierre Nora. Paris: Gallimard, 1986, vol. 2, 317–375.

Law and History

The fortunes of law and history were linked from earliest times in the sense that law, too, depended on memory and on written form that would distinguish it from mere custom. "[T]he most important part of anything is its beginning," declared the Roman jurisconsult Gaius; and it was on these grounds that Pomponius proposed to "account for the origin and development of [civil] law itself" in his study *Of the Origin of Law.* This work, placed in the first title of Justinian's authoritative *Digest* of classical jurisprudence, became itself the subject of later commentary and of derivative efforts to explore the origins (and in this sense the causes) of law.

Medieval commentaries on Roman law were at least inadvertently historical; and distinctions were made between "ancient," "middle," and "modern" interpreters of texts that from the twelfth century were taught in the universities and adapted to the commercial, social, and political problems of life in late medieval Europe. Canon law, modeled on civil law, displayed similar patterns of development and accumulated similar layers of commentary for pedagogical and practical objectives. European customary law, including English common law, went through its own parallel and often overlapping development, proceeding from oral to written forms as lawyers and imperial, royal, and civil governments employed it for their own secular purposes.

The rise of legal history in the Renaissance was based in part on humanist scholarship, for which Roman law was one of the most prized aspects of the classical heritage and which envisioned (as in the work of François Baudouin) a methodological "alliance between history and jurisprudence"—which relied on similar procedures of authentication and proof—for the benefit of both. For Jean Bodin the old Roman category of the "law of nations" *(jus gentium)* became a new field of the universal history of the comparative "history of nations," which involved questions of climate, social customs, and national origins. "The best part of universal law lies in history," he remarked—and, it might be suggested, vice versa.

In early modern times legal history, according to such scholars, involved not only applying the methods of humanist philology to legal texts but also tracing these various legal traditions, for practical as well as commemorative purposes, and debating the provenance and cultural meaning of European legal and social institutions. Was feudalism, for example, Roman or Germanic in origin and thus in character? More invidiously termed, should European legal institutions follow the grasping and despotic nature of the Romans and their legacy as expressed in civil and canon law or rather the free and open customs of the Germans and Anglo-Saxons? Such debates between Romanists and Germanists have shaped the interpretation of political, institutional, and social history down to present times.

For historiography the value of legal history has been that it has extended horizons beyond the *histoire événementielle* of politics and war to social and economic relations and has included private as well as public matters. The history of law has necessarily confronted questions of national character, social structure and change, and cultural difference; and to this extent it has inspired specialized lines of inquiry into these areas of historical study. The study of French provincial customs undertaken by sixteenth-century jurists like Charles Dumoulin and François Hotman for juridical purposes has been carried on by modern scholars like Marc Bloch and Emmanuel Leroy Ladurie for purposes of social history. Similar scholarly continuities can be seen in other countries—in England, for example, between the efforts of legal scholars like Henry Spelman and John Selden in the seventeenth century to apply criticism to the myths of "immemorial" common law and, more recently, Frederic Maitland and his school; and in Germany between the Renaissance commentators and the work of Friedrich von Savigny and the Historical School of Law, which tried to place the Roman and Germanic legal traditions in perspective.

L

The study of the history of law led naturally to larger questions of social development, and it is significant that the modern "four-stage" theory of historical progress was first formulated in this connection, most notably in Adam Smith's early lectures on jurisprudence. This theory, which posited progress through the ages of gathering, of fishing and hunting, and of settlements and commercial activity underlying the shift from "barbarism" to full "civilization," was reflected in and largely documented by the laws of particular nations; and it was taken over not only by Marx and other social theorists but also by later historians of culture.

Legal history was a subject of scholarly publication from the sixteenth century, but it was in the nineteenth century that the subject achieved disciplinary status, flourishing especially in Germany under the aegis of the Historical School, which identified law with the spirit, values, and destiny of the nation. In other European countries, too, the history of law was pursued in connection first with the romantic fascination with the national past, and the collection of its legal records, and then with the scientific history, which proposed to give an objective account of legal and institutional development on the basis of a critical study of these sources.

Legal history has remained curiously separated from the study of history proper, partly because it has often been segregated into law schools and partly because social historians have distrusted the official provenance and legalistic character of the records. This helped to explain, in Maitland's famous lament, "Why the History of English law [was] not written" and, also, why social history, especially French and English (with some important exceptions, especially in the area of criminal law, witchcraft, and marriage), has persisted in an empirical mode and has not made full use of legal sources. Yet law remains an aspect of social and cultural memory, a product of human behavior, organization, and ideals, which not only represents the accumulated materials and forms of historical experience but suggests models for historical method and interpretation. And the relationship is mutual, for "History should be illuminated by law," as Montesquieu put it, "and laws by history."

Donald R. Kelley

See also LEGAL HISTORY; MOS GALLICUS AND MOS ITALICUS; PHILOLOGY.

References

Grossi, Paolo, ed. *Quaderni fiorentini per la storia del pensiero giuridico moderno* (periodical published in Milan since 1972).

Hammerstein, Notker. *Jus und Historie: Ein Beitrag zur Geschichte des historischen Denkens an deutschen Universitäten im späten 17. und im 18. Jahrhundert.* [Law and History: A History of Historical Thought in the German Universities in the Seventeenth and Eighteenth Centuries]. Göttingen: Vandenhoeck and Rupprecht, 1973.

Kelley, Donald R. *Foundations of Modern Historical Scholarship: Language, Law, and History in the French Renaissance.* New York: Columbia University Press, 1970.

———. *The Human Measure: Social Thought and the Western Legal Tradition.* Cambridge, MA: Harvard University Press, 1990.

Paradisi, Bruno. *Apologia della storia giuridica* [Defense of Legal History]. Bologna: Il Mulino, 1973.

Stein, Peter. *Legal Evolution: The Story of an Idea.* Cambridge, Eng.: Cambridge University Press, 1980.

Ullmann, Walter. *Law and Politics in the Middle Ages: An Introduction to the Sources of Medieval Political Ideas.* Ithaca, NY: Cornell University Press, 1975.

Le Goff, Jacques (b. 1924)

French medievalist. Le Goff's name has been associated with the new school of social history and of the study of *mentalités* in France since the 1970s. Educated at the École Normale Supérieure and in the faculty of letters in Paris, he taught medieval history at Lille before becoming professor (1960) and director of studies in the sixth section of the École Pratique des Hautes Études. From 1972 to 1977 he was director of the École des Hautes Études en Sciences Sociales. Since 1967 he has been on the board of the journal *Annales: Économies, Sociétés, Civilisations,* devoted to the New History method, combining a study of material culture, economic and social structures, and popular culture. Le Goff has applied this method to the study of social life and religious thought in the high Middle Ages. In *Pour un autre moyen âge* (1978), he discusses the changing notion of time and profit among merchants following the introduction of municipal clocks, which allowed standard timekeeping to replace the monastic system of bells marking the natural daily cycle. *La naissance du purgatoire* (1981), a controversial study, traces the shift from a two-tier to a three-tier ordering of reality in the high Middle Ages (reflected, for instance, in the three orders of society) and its impact on the perceptions of the next world, with purgatory emerging as a third and distinct place from heaven and hell. In all his work, Le Goff has drawn upon a variety of disciplines to describe and explain not merely the ideas of the literate few but the mentalities of the mass of medieval people.

Monica Sandor

Texts

The Birth of Purgatory. Trans. Arthur Goldhammer. Chicago: University of Chicago Press, 1983.

History and Memory. Trans. Steven Rendall and Elizabeth Claman. New York: Columbia University Press, 1992.

The Medieval Imagination. Trans. Arthur Goldhammer. Chicago: University of Chicago Press, 1985.

Time, Work and Culture in the Middle Ages. Trans. Arthur Goldhammer. Chicago: University of Chicago Press, 1980.

Your Money or Your Life. Trans. Patricia Ranum. New York: Zone, 1988.

Le Quy Don (ca. 1726–1784)

Vietnamese historian. Le Quy Don was born in the Duyen Ha district of what is the modern-day Thai Binh province. After passing an examination in 1752, he held many posts in the government, including the head of the Historical Board of the Kingdom. Despite his position, however, his *Le Trieu Thong Su* [Complete History of the Le Dynasty], also known as *Dai Viet Thong Su* [Complete History of Dai Viet], was a vehicle for his own views on Vietnamese historiography of the late Le dynasty, rather than an official history. For the first time in Vietnamese history, it presented Le history as a series of biographies of the emperors and other important figures, rather than as a chronicle. It covers more than one hundred years and ten emperors of the Le dynasty. Another historical writing by Le Quy Don, *Phu Bien Tap Luc* [Miscellaneous Records of Pacification in the Border Area], included many details obtained from the documents of the Nguyen southern regime in the eighteenth century. It is the major source for studying that period in Vietnamese history. Among his many other works two are of encyclopedic scope—*Van Dai Loai Ngu* and *Kien Van Tieu Luc*. He is remembered as one of the most prominent scholars in early Vietnamese historical writing.

Li Tana

Texts

Le Quy Don Toan Tap [A Complete Collection of Le Quy Don's Works]. 3 vols. Hanoi: Khoa hoc xa hoi, 1977.

References

Duiker, William. *Historical Dictionary of Vietnam.* Metuchen, NJ, and London: Scarecrow Press, 1989, 91.

Nguyen Huyen Anh. *Viet Nam Danh Nhan Tu Dien* [Dictionary of the Famous People in Vietnam]. Saigon: Khai Tri, 1967, 140–141.

Tran Van Giap. *Tim Hieu Kho Sach Han-Nom* [Understanding the Chinese and Nom Collections]. Vol. 1. Hanoi: Van Hoa, 1984, 110–121; 379–384 (entries on *Le Trieu Thong Su* and *Phu Bien Tap Luc*).

Le Roy Ladurie, Emmanuel (b. 1929)

French social historian. Although born into a conservative Catholic family in Normandy, Le Roy Ladurie would become a specialist on the history of southern France and, for seven years, a member of the Communist Party. While at the École Normale Supérieure (1949–1952), he dedicated himself to a teaching career and joined the Party. He developed a strong interest in the economic and social history of Languedoc when he took a post in Montpellier. After extensive archival research conducted under the direction of Fernand Braudel, he produced an impressive dissertation on the region in 1966. He then entered the ranks of university professors before arriving at the prestigious Collège de France and serving as director of the Bibliothèque Nationale from 1987 to 1994. A leading member of the Annales school, Le Roy Ladurie became an eminent authority on early modern France. His dissertation on Languedoc embodied the "total history" that the Annales school advocated. It carefully examined the physical environment in which peasants lived and toiled and analyzed the changing movements of population, climate fluctuations, agricultural production, and alternating periods of prosperity and poverty over three centuries. His most lively and popular work, *Montaillou,* explored a medieval mountain village investigated for heresy by the Inquisition. Other books focused on social conflict in a sixteenth-century town and the deeper meaning of peasant folktales. Many of these writings illustrated his concept of "history that stands still," the long-term stability of population and productivity characteristic of medieval and early modern history. Le Roy Ladurie's substantial output and imaginative reconstructions earned him an international reputation.

James Friguglietti

Texts

Carnival in Romans. Trans. Mary Feeney. New York: Braziller, 1979.

Montaillou: The Promised Land of Error. Trans. Barbara Bray. New York: Braziller, 1978.
The Peasants of Languedoc. Trans. John Day. Urbana: University of Illinois Press, 1974.

References

Le Roy Ladurie, Emmanuel. *Paris-Montpellier. P.C.-P.S.U. 1945–1953.* Paris: Gallimard, 1982.

Lecky, William Edward Hartpole (1838–1903)

Irish essayist, politician, and historian of Great Britain. Lecky was born in Newton Park, county Dublin, and educated at Trinity College, Dublin. As an undergraduate he was much influenced by the historical writings of H.T. Buckle. Like many historians of the nineteenth century, Lecky held no formal academic appointment through most of his career, publishing his works as a private scholar. He was offered the Regius professorship in modern history at Oxford in 1892, which he declined. He did, however, receive honorary degrees from several universities, and after his death, a chair in history was endowed by his widow at Trinity College, Dublin, where his papers were later deposited. Lecky was also a member of the French Institute and a founding member of the British Academy. For a decade before his death he served as member of Parliament for Dublin University, and was designated privy councillor in 1897, all the while serving as a leader of the Unionist position for Ireland. In the tradition of his countryman Edmund Burke, Lecky feared democracy and opposed extension of the franchise; he presented the major address at Trinity College marking the centenary of Burke's death in 1897. Lecky wrote philosophical and political treatises on subjects such as the histories of rationalism and of European morals and a two-volume study, *Democracy and Liberty* (1896; rev. ed. 1899). As J.A. Froude had covered the sixteenth century and Samuel R. Gardiner the seventeenth with multivolume histories of England, so Lecky carried on for the eighteenth century, producing a history consisting of seven volumes devoted to England and five on Ireland. He was praised for balanced perspectives, for the coverage of the American Revolution, and even for his coverage of Irish history, despite his emotional attachment, but not for original research and creativity. His emphasis throughout the history was on politics, religion, and material matters.

Eugene L. Rasor

Texts

Historical and Political Essays. Freeport, NY: Books for Libraries Press, 1970.
History of England in the Eighteenth Century. 8 vols. New York: D. Appleton, 1878–1890.
History of European Morals from Augustus to Charlemagne. 2 vols. New York: D. Appleton, 1869.
A Victorian Historian: Private Letters of W.E.H. Lecky, 1859–1878. Ed. H. Montgomery Hyde. London: Home, 1947.

References

Auchmuty, James J. *Lecky: A Biographical and Critical Essay.* London: Longman, 1945.
Lecky, Elisabeth van Dedem. *A Memoir of the Right Hon. William Edward Hartpole Lecky, M.P., Litt.D., Member of the French Institute and the British Academy, by His Wife.* New York: Longman, 1909.
McCartney, Donal. *W.E.H. Lecky: Historian and Politician, 1838–1903.* Dublin: Lilliput, 1993.
McDermott, Frank C. *Taking the Long Perspective: Democracy and Terrorism in Ireland: The Writings of W.E.H. Lecky and After.* Dublin: Glendale, 1991.

Lefebvre, Georges (1874–1959)

French historian. Born in Lille, the son of a bookkeeper, he rose through the state school system with scholarship assistance. He then entered the academic world, teaching at a succession of lycées. Specializing in the history of the Revolution, Lefebvre completed his doctoral dissertation examining the peasants of his native Nord Department only in 1924. Thereafter, he taught at the university level and attained a chair at the Sorbonne by 1937. Even after retiring in 1945, he continued to publish extensively. Lefebvre's modest social origins and Marxist sympathies led him to view history "from below." His considerable output, based on patient archival research, centered on France's rural population. Lefebvre believed that an autonomous rural revolution had taken place beginning in 1789, with most peasants seeking to abolish manorial dues and church tithes, but eager to defend their own traditional gleaning and grazing rights. He also studied collective behavior, seeing in popular mentality a combination of fear and punitive will responsible for provoking the Great Fear, the September Massacres, and the Terror.

James Friguglietti

Texts

The French Revolution. Trans. Elizabeth Moss Evanson, John Hall Stewart, and James Friguglietti. 2 vols. New York: Columbia University Press, 1962–1964.

References

Cobb, Richard. "Georges Lefebvre." In his *A Second Identity.* London: Oxford University Press, 1969, 84–100.

Legal History

In a strict sense, the branch of history concerned with law and its relationship to the rest of human life. Lawyers, however, have tended to produce internal, decontextualized, Whiggish accounts of the development of legal doctrine and institutions. These also purport to be "legal history."

Arnaldo Momigliano once spoke of a distinction between "historians' history" and "jurists' history." The distinction has existed for hundreds of years because of the different questions that the two professions put to legal texts. To be sure, humanist jurists in the Renaissance, Giambattista Vico in the eighteenth century, and proponents of historical jurisprudence in the nineteenth, were important contributors to the construction of modern historical consciousness; for English-speaking historians, a lawyer, F.W. Maitland, is (in G.R. Elton's words) the "patron saint" of their profession. All the same, lawyers primarily have been interested in the past for the light it throws on the present.

"Jurists' history" typically involves tracing the pedigree of modern legal forms, with scant attention to social setting or effect, as if law were a self-contained universe. The pseudohistoricity of English common law particularly encourages common lawyers to treat the past in terms of notions of significance derived from the present. (In this respect, again in Elton's words, the "Whig interpretation" of English history "was really lawyers' interpretation.") But the phenomenon occurs in other legal systems as well. Hence the debate in Italy at one time about whether Roman law should be taught in terms of modern categories, to make it useable; or, more recently, in Germany, about how much the study of pan-European legal history should focus on its relevance to the construction of a new *ius commune,* a common body of European private law.

Nonetheless, the differences between "lawyers' history" and history are diminishing. Thirty years ago, Momigliano observed that, at least in the field of ancient law, books produced by jurists were no longer distinguishable from those by "'pure' historians"—the result, he thought, of general recognition that law is not a self-contained autonomous activity, but rather "a systematization of social relations at a given level." It followed that legal history could not be a distinct branch of study, but must rather be a part of general (and, in a broad sense, social) history.

Nowadays, with respect to other periods as well, self-contained "legal history" is increasingly regarded as obsolete; there is unease on all sides when problems of legal history are treated in traditional lawyers' terms. But instead of legal history having been absorbed by social history, in a reaction against social functionalism, it is more and more viewed as an independent branch of history posing its own special questions about how law is generated and experienced.

Diverse influences—including the ideas of Karl Marx, Max Weber, Emile Durkheim, and Marc Bloch—have contributed to the recognition that meaningful legal history must be more than the internal history of legal doctrine. In the United States, despite precursors, the move (beginning in the 1950s) to extend legal history to include attention to interactions between law and society is largely associated with the "Wisconsin school" founded by J. Willard Hurst. Lawrence M. Friedman's survey, *A History of American Law* (1973), encapsulates the Hurstian approach in its master image of law as a "mirror of society." Law, in this view, is a dependent variable, and the central problem of legal history is to identify the exogenous factors that cause legal change. Unorthodox in its day, it became the prevailing paradigm, at least in the United States.

During the past two decades, legal history again has been transformed both in the United States and elsewhere. It not only has grown exponentially; it has been affected by the same "postmodern" ferment, excitement, and disarray that have characterized history in general. No single paradigm dominates the field, but there has been on the whole what Michael Grossberg calls "a flight from functionalism," a widespread perception that law cannot adequately be treated simply as a reflection of something else, whether of social "needs," economic relations, or interest-group politics. Law is seen to be (to some extent) "relatively autonomous," having a history of its own, yet so closely "imbricated" (in E.P. Thompson's phrase) with other human activities, so tightly woven into the texture of social life, that it is hard to draw sharp lines between legal and extralegal or "social reality."

Related developments emphasize the intricate ways in which law intersects with other normative systems prevalent in particular communities and subgroups. In part this is an outgrowth of the use in social history of legal records as a source of evidence about previously marginalized populations. Going on to ask how law was understood and used by those who experienced it has led to fascinating questions about the interaction of law and other normative systems (legal and nonlegal, moral and customary). Normative pluralism is also, of course, a basic fact in the history of colonial and postcolonial regimes where imposed or transplanted law interacts with indigenous customs and the legal culture of successive waves of immigrants—although this has been obscured by a tendency to present the legal history of the United States in terms of the unimpeded spread of English "common law." It has been a recurrent feature as well in the history of both English and European law, although similarly obscured by depictions of national legal development as a uniform process of centralization and formalization.

In various ways, then, both law and experience with law are coming to be seen as involving, at any given time, complex and chaotic interactions between a host of diverse and fluid normative systems. The outstanding problem, as in history generally, is to represent the chaos both accurately and coherently.

Edward M. Wise

See also LAW AND HISTORY.

References

Elton, G.R. *F.W. Maitland.* London: Weidenfeld and Nicolson, 1985.

Friedman, Lawrence M. *A History of American Law.* Second ed. New York: Simon and Schuster, 1985.

Gordon, Robert W. "Historicism in Legal Scholarship." *Yale Law Journal* 90 (1981): 1017–1056.

Grossberg, Michael. "Social History Update: 'Fighting Faiths' and the Challenges of Legal History." *Social History* 25 (1991): 191–201.

Hall, Kermit, ed. *Main Themes in United States Constitutional and Legal History.* New York and London: Garland Publishing, 1987.

Knafla, Louis A., and Susan W.S. Binnie. "Introduction. Beyond the State: Law and Legal Pluralism in the Making of Modern Societies." In *Law, Society, and the State: Essays in Modern Legal History,* ed. Knafla and Binnie. Toronto: University of Toronto Press, 1995, 3–33.

Momigliano, Arnaldo. "The Consequences of New Trends in the History of Ancient Law." In his *Studies in Historiography.* London: Weidenfeld and Nicolson, 1966, 239–256.

Schulze, Reiner. "European Legal History—A New Field of Research in Germany." *Journal of Legal History* 13 (1992): 270–295.

Sugarman, David, and G.R. Rubin. "Towards a New History of Law and Material Society in England, 1750–1914." In *Law, Economy and Society, 1750–1914: Essays in the History of English Law,* ed. G.R. Rubin and David Sugarman. Abingdon: Professional Books, 1984, 1–123.

Leibniz, Gottfried Wilhelm (1646–1716)

Philosopher, scientist, and mathematician. Leibniz was Germany's most important pre-Enlightenment thinker. Much of his scientific work prepared the way for the scientific revolution of the eighteenth century. His philosophical work only deals indirectly with the practice of history, which remained secondary. His most important work of history, the *Imperial Annals of the House of Brunswick* (1703–1716), was written late in life and was conceived of within traditional bounds of early "universal history." It was concerned more with the study of chronology and genealogies, rather than the problems of interpretation and explanation. Of greater influence for the development of historiography was Leibniz's concept of "monadology." He argued that the world was governed by a system of monads, which were unique, self-contained individualities that operated within a broader, universal whole. Leibniz's monadology, therefore, prefigured the historicists' emphasis on the individual character of historical phenomena and the relationship between particular and the whole.

John R. Hinde

Texts

Leibniz: Political Writings. Trans. P. Riley. Second ed. Cambridge, Eng.: Cambridge University Press, 1988.

Sämtliche Schriften und Briefe [Collected Works and Letters]. Ed. Deutsche Akademie der Wissenschaft. Darmstadt: O. Reiche, 1923– .

References

Mates, Benson. *The Philosophy of Leibniz.* New York: Oxford University Press, 1986.

Leland, John (ca. 1506–1552)

English antiquarian, topographer, and cleric. Born in London, Leland attended St. Paul's School before matriculating at Christ's College, Cambridge, where he received his B.A. in 1522, and then embarked on further study at Oxford and Paris. By 1530 he was working as a librarian for Henry VIII and in 1533 began his antiquarian studies (although he was never officially given the title of King's Antiquary with which he is often credited). Leland planned a massive antiquarian work to be entitled "The History and Antiquities of This Nation" and between 1534 and 1543 he traveled throughout England gathering materials for this work. Although he was a Protestant, Leland was appalled by the destruction of the monastic libraries that occurred as a result of the dissolution of the monasteries in the late 1530s, and in 1545 he proposed that Henry VIII establish a national library to preserve monastic books. Meanwhile he continued to labor on his great project but by 1547 he had become insane, and died five years later with his work unfinished. Leland's reputation is based on two works that were first edited and published by Thomas Hearne in the early eighteenth century: the *Itinerary* (1710–1712) and the *De Rebus Britannicis Collectanea* (1715). The first work was a topographical and antiquarian study of England and Wales based on Leland's journeys, while the second was a detailed bibliographic study of monastic books that Leland observed or collected. Both books represent pioneering advances in antiquarian and topographic studies and were influential among antiquaries, in manuscript form, long before Hearne's editions rendered them available to a wider readership.

Ronald H. Fritze

Texts

Leland's Itinerary in England and Wales. Ed. Lucy Toulmin Smith. Rev. ed. 5 vols. Fontwell, Sussex: Centaur; Carbondale: University of Southern Illinois Press, 1964.
De Rebus Britannicis Collectanea. Ed. T. Hearne. 6 vols. Oxford: for the author at the Sheldonian Theatre, 1715.

References

Levy, F.J. *Tudor Historical Thought.* San Marino, CA: Huntington Library, 1967.
McKisack, May. *Medieval History in the Tudor Age.* Oxford: Oxford University Press, 1971.

Lelewel, Joachim (1786–1861)

Polish politician and historian. Born in Warsaw, Lelewel studied at the University of Vilna (Wilno) and later taught there, combining the professions of politician, historian, librarian, geographer, and numismatist. Appointed professor of history and librarian at the University of Warsaw in 1818, he returned to Vilna in 1821 as professor of history; there, his lectures on Polish history enjoyed great popularity. Nationalism of any kind raised the ire of the Russian authorities, who stripped Lelewel of his position in 1824. Lelewel then went once more to Warsaw, where he was elected to the Diet in 1829 and participated in the revolution of 1830. He served in the government but was forced to flee after its suppression. He reached Paris in 1831, but was expelled from France at the request of the Russian ambassador in 1833. In Brussels, where he spent most of his remaining years, he made a meager living by his writings and by giving courses in modern history at the newly founded university. A true polyhistor, Lelewel's production was prodigious by any standard. He wrote on subjects as diverse as Scandinavian literature, numismatics, medieval history, and Arabic geography. His works on Polish history are a model for the minutely scrupulous and critical study of documentary sources. They were collected and published in twenty volumes under the title *Poland, Her History and Affairs Surveyed* (in Polish) at Poznan (1853–1876), a collection that includes his autobiography. One of his most important publications was his five-volume opus *La géographie au moyen âge* (1852–1857), for which he furnished an *Atlas* (1849) of fifty plates that he engraved himself. The overpowering scope and breadth of Lelewel's publications do not entirely compensate for his sometimes careless and plodding narrative style. These faults by no means diminish Lelewel's importance as a pioneer in many fields, including the national history of Poland and the history of geography and cartography.

Andrew Colin Gow

Texts

Dzieje Polski potocznym sposobem opowiedziane [Polish History]. Warsaw: Panstwowe Wydawnictwo Naukowe, 1961.
Joachim Lelewel: Textes choisis [Selected Works]. Ed. T. Wysokinska. Brussels: Centre International Lelewel, 1986.

References

Rose, W.J. "Lelewel As Historian." *Slavonic and East European Review* 15 (1936–1937): 649–662.
Serejski, M.H. "Joachim Lelewel, 1786–1861." *Acta Poloniae Historica* 6 (1962): 35–54.

Lenin, Vladimir Ilich (1870–1924)

Russian philosopher, revolutionary, and politician. Lenin was born in Simbirsk (Ulianovsk), the son of a school teacher and the younger brother of a revolutionary, Alexander, who was executed for attempted regicide against Alexander III in 1887. After graduating from St. Petersburg University in law in 1891, he suffered imprisonment and banishment to Siberia and eventual exile to Switzerland for revolutionary activities. A founder of the Communist (Bolshevik) Party and Communist International, he led the Russian Revolution of November 1917 and Soviet Russia until his death. In the creation of his revolutionary ideology, Lenin adapted classical Marxism to Russian history in numerous works such as *Razvitiia kapitalizma v Rossii* [The Development of Capitalism in Russia] (1899) and *Gosudarstvo I Revolutsiia* [State and Revolution] (1917), and like M.N. Pokrovskii, Lenin stressed materialism over objectivism in his historical outlook. In *Imperialism, the Highest State of Capitalism* (1916) he saw World War I as being brought about by the inherent excesses and competitiveness of nationalism, capitalism, and imperialism and as preceded by intense class struggle. With his own extensive philosophical–historical writings and as the head of the Communist Party and the Soviet government he laid many of the foundations and set many of the directions for the official Soviet state historiography that persisted until the demise of the Soviet Union in 1991.

Dennis Reinhartz

Texts

Collected Works. 45 vols. Moscow: Foreign Languages Publishing House, 1960–1970.

References

Fischer, Louis. *The Life of Lenin.* New York: Harper & Row, 1965.

Mazour, Anatole G. *The Writing of History in the Soviet Union.* Stanford, CA: Hoover Institution Press, 1971.

Shub, David. *Lenin.* Baltimore, MD: Penguin, 1967.

Shteppa, Konstantin F. *Russian Historians and the Soviet State.* New Brunswick, NJ: Rutgers University Press, 1962.

Volkogonov, Dmitrii A. *Lenin: A New Biography.* New York: Free Press, 1994.

Lerner, Gerda (b. 1920)

Women's historian. Lerner was born in Vienna and came to the United States during the Nazi occupation. After raising a family, she returned to college and then received a graduate degree in history from Columbia University. She was a professor at Sarah Lawrence College and then at the University of Wisconsin–Madison, where she founded the graduate programs in women's history. She served as president of the Organization of American Historians in 1979. Lerner's first book, published in 1967, was a biography of the Grimké sisters that emphasized the links between abolitionism and the struggle for women's rights. Lerner then turned to editing primary source collections on American women's history. A book of documents on black women's history emphasized such new themes as black resistance to slavery, black women's struggles to obtain educations after the Civil War, and the overwhelming importance of black female employment in the lives of individual blacks and the black community. A book on the entire female experience in America emphasized organizing documents in ways that reflected female experience rather than male categories—for example, the book started with the self and family and only later considered women's public lives. The book's sections were organized around the female life cycle rather than more familiar male patterns of historiography. Lerner's insights on the importance of gender in history were applied to teaching in a pamphlet published in 1981, *Teaching Women's History.* Lerner's most ambitious work has been a two-volume study of women and their condition starting with the ancient world of Mesopotamia and ending with mid-nineteenth-century America and Western Europe. The first volume, *The Creation of Patriarchy,* deals with the origins and causes of female subordination, placing great emphasis on the influence lost by women with the advent of male deities. The sequel, entitled *The Creation of Feminist Consciousness,* details women's struggles to achieve equal status with men through such means as reconceptualizing religion to include women, proving their capacity for intellectual activity, and upgrading images and ideas surrounding motherhood.

Barbara A. McGowan

Texts

Ed. *Black Women in White America.* New York: Pantheon, 1972.

The Creation of Feminist Consciousness. New York: Oxford University Press, 1993.

The Creation of Patriarchy. New York: Oxford University Press, 1986.

Ed. *The Female Experience: An American Documentary.* Indianapolis, IN: Bobbs-Merrill, 1977.

The Grimké Sisters from South Carolina. New York: Schocken Books, 1971.

The Majority Finds Its Past: Placing Women in History. New York: Oxford University Press, 1979.
Teaching Women's History. Washington: American Historical Association, 1981.

Reference
Zinsser, Judith P. *History and Feminism: A Glass Half Full.* New York: Twayne, 1994.

Leur, Jacob Cornelis van (1908–1942)
Dutch historian of Indonesia. Van Leur completed a doctoral thesis on early Asian trade at Leiden University in 1934, before departing for the Netherlands Indies as a colonial official. He continued writing, but in 1940 he joined the Dutch navy and was aboard the *USS Houston* when it was sunk after the Battle of the Java Sea in February 1942. Using Weberian analytical categories, van Leur argued that external influences—Hindu–Buddhist and Islamic—had been much less significant in Indonesian history than previously argued, describing them as a "thin and flaking glaze" over strong indigenous cultures. He also criticized the prevalent tendency to view Indonesian history "from the deck of the ship, the ramparts of the fortress, the high gallery of the trading house" by placing Europeans at the center of analysis as soon as they appeared in the region. His work became widely known outside the Netherlands only after translation and publication as *Indonesian Trade and Society* in 1955, when it made a major contribution to the movement for writing Indonesia-centric history.

Robert Cribb

Texts
Indonesian Trade and Society: Essays in Asian Social and Economic History. Second ed. The Hague: Van Hoeve, 1967.

References
Soedjatmoko et al., eds. *An Introduction to Indonesian Historiography.* Ithaca, NY: Cornell University Press, 1965.

Levene, Ricardo (1885–1959)
Argentine historian and university administrator. Levene became professor of history at the University of La Plata in 1919. Here he founded the Faculty of Humanities and Education and became its dean. In 1920 he created chairs in Argentine and Latin American history. He later became president of the university and was responsible for expanding its curriculum.

Levene's focus on comparative history led to his editorship of the fourteen-volume *Historia de América* [History of America]. An early publication was a two-volume survey, *Lecciones de historia argentina* [Lessons of Argentine History] (1913). This textbook "may well have been used by more students of history than any other history textbook in Latin America," according to Joseph R. Barager. During the 1920s Levene published three monographs that secured his reputation as Argentina's leading historian. These works transcended traditional political history and dealt with economic and judicial questions as well. His major work was the impressive ten-volume *Historia de la nación argentina* [History of the Argentine Nation] which he edited between 1936 and 1942, and to which he contributed several chapters. In his most controversial book, *Las indias no eran colonias* [The Indies Were Not Colonies] (1951), he argued that Spain's American possessions were not mere colonies but "ultramarine kingdoms" under the Castilian crown.

George L. Vásquez

Texts
Ed. *Historia de América.* 14 vols. Buenos Aires: W.M. Jackson, 1940.
Ed. *Historia de la nación argentina.* 10 vols. Buenos Aires: Librería y Editorial "El Ateneo," 1936–1942.
Las indias no eran colonias. Madrid: Espasa-Calpe, 1973.

References
Barager, Joseph R. "The Historiography of the Río de la Plata Area Since 1830." *Hispanic American Historical Review* 39 (1959): 603–605.
Mariluz Urquijo, José M. "Ricardo Levene, 1885–1959." *Hispanic American Historical Review* 39 (1959): 643–646.

Lévi-Provençal, Evariste (1894–1956)
French historian of premodern North Africa and Islamic Spain. Lévi-Provençal was born and educated in Algiers. There, he acquired his expertise in Arabic and textual analysis, the fields in which he made his most significant academic contribution. After World War I, during which he went to Morocco to work in the Bureaux des affaires Indigènes, he joined the Institut des Hautes-Études Marocaines. In 1923 he began to catalog the Arabic manuscripts in the Escorial Library where he edited and translated many manuscripts that

L

remain indispensable for the field. The publication of the multivolume *Histoire de l'Espagne musulmane* [History of Muslim Spain] made him the leading authority on Islamic Spain. After World War II, he moved to Paris to occupy a chair especially created for him at the Sorbonne, where he also served as the director of l'Institut d'Études Islamiques and the Centre d'Études de l'Orient Musulman. He founded the journal *Arabica* and directed the French edition of the *Encyclopedia of Islam* contributing more than ninety entries to it. He left an indelible mark on Islamic/Arabic studies with nearly three hundred publications (not including book reviews) encompassing a variety of fields.

Mahmood Ibrahim

Texts

Histoire de l'Espagne musulmane. 3 vols. Paris: G.-P. Maissonneuve, 1950–1953.

References

Études d'orientalisme dédiées à la mémoire de Lévi-Provençal [Studies in Orientalism in Memory of Lévi-Provençal]. Paris: G.-P. Maisonneuve et Larose, 1962.

Levillier, Roberto (1886–1969)

French-born Argentine diplomat and historian. After completing his legal studies, Levillier did research in Seville's Archives of the Indies, publishing several compilations of documents on Argentina's colonial history. In 1918 he entered the Argentine diplomatic service and served for twenty-four years. As minister to Peru he gathered the material that found its way into his most important work, *Nueva crónica de la conquista de Tucumán* [New Chronicle of the Conquest of Tucumán], published in three volumes in 1926, 1930, and 1932. Other works on the colonial period include a monograph published in 1933 on the early Spanish conquistadores, a detailed three-volume biography (1935–1942) of Francisco de Toledo, and a two-volume work on the Incas, which appeared in 1942. His later work included several monographs on colonial Argentina as well as a two-volume study on the voyages of Americo Vespucci. He also worked on a forty-volume collection of sources on Argentine history sponsored by the Argentine congressional library. He wrote primarily on the colonial period, but unlike many of his nineteenth-century predecessors he acknowledged that Latin America's Spanish heritage had been a beneficial influence in shaping colonial civilization.

George L. Vásquez

Texts

Americo Vespucio. Madrid: Ediciones Cultura Hispanica, 1966.

Don Francisco de Toledo, supremo organizador del Peru: Su vida, su obra (1515–1582) [Don Francisco de Toledo, Supreme Governor of Peru: His Life, His Work (1515–1582)]. 3 vols. Madrid: Espasa-Calpe, 1935–1942.

Nueva crónica de la conquista de Tucumán. 3 vols. Buenos Aires: Editorial "Nosotros," 1926–1932.

References

Caillet-Bois, Ricardo R. "Roberto Levillier (1886–1969)." *Revista de historia de América* 71 (1971): 156–160.

Thomas, Jack Ray. *Biographical Dictionary of Latin American Historians and Historiography.* Westport, CT: Greenwood Press, 1984, 234–235.

Lewis, Bernard (b. 1916)

Historian of the Middle East. Lewis was born in London, earned his Ph.D. at the University of London in 1939 and, after serving in the British Army, became professor of the history of the Near and Middle East at the School of Oriental and African Studies (SOAS) in 1949. There he stayed until 1974, when he moved to Princeton. He retired in 1986. Lewis's numerous publications reflect his broad interests in Islamic and Middle Eastern History. In addition to several survey books, his published work has focused on four topics: Ismāʿīlī Shiʿism; Jews in Muslim lands; nationalism; and historiography. One work has aged especially well: *The Emergence of Modern Turkey,* first published in 1961, marks something of a watershed in the historiography of modern Turkey, and if the notions of modernization that underpin it are now open to some criticism, the breadth of sources, command of detail, and narrative coherence are much less so. Lewis had previously written *The Arabs in History* (1950), an admirably succinct overview of Islamic history that served as the introduction to the subject for a generation of Islamicists. In the latter part of his career Lewis has proved himself no cloistered scholar: much of his work, now written for a wide audience, has addressed timely (and occasionally controversial) issues such as the Islamic "resurgence," Zionism, and the Arab/Israeli conflict.

Chase F. Robinson

Texts

The Arabs in History. London: Hutchinson, 1950.

The Emergence of Modern Turkey. London: Oxford University Press, 1961.

History—Remembered, Recovered, Invented. Princeton, NJ: Princeton University Press, 1975.

Race and Slavery in the Middle East. Oxford: Oxford University Press, 1990.

Li Ch'ing

See LI QING.

Li Dao [Li Tao] (1115–1184)

Chinese historian during the Song period. Li passed the highest civil service examination and subsequently served in the government, while spending many years writing history. He was a prolific author, producing seventy-one works in a total of 3,211 *chüan* (volumes), the most important of which was *Xu zi zhi tong jian chang bian* [Long Draft of a Continuation of the Comprehensive Mirror for Aid in Governing].

In A.D. 1084, Sima Guang [Ssu-ma Kuang] had completed his monumental work *Zi zhi tong jian* [Comprehensive Mirror As an Aid to Government], which covers 1,326 years of Chinese history chronologically, from 403 B.C. to A.D. 959. Upon its completion that work had received high praise in the academic world and had inspired several imitators and continuators. Li Dao's *Xu zi zhi tong jian chang bian* was among the latter, and it closely imitated the form and style of the *Comprehensive Mirror,* which it continued into the period of the Song dynasty (A.D. 960–1127).

Li Dao spent forty years compiling his voluminous *Long Draft.* It covers, in 980 *chüan,* 168 years of history, including the reigns of all nine Song emperors. Li collected material from a wide range of sources. Besides official records, such as *shi lu* (veritable records) and *guo shi* (national history), he consulted several hundred privately compiled sources, including tombstone epitaphs. The data he collected were kept systematically in his filing system, which itself deserves to be remarked on. Li had ten cabinets, each of which had twenty drawers. The two hundred drawers were organized in chronological order, with the years marked. Every item of data collected was filed in the drawers according to its date.

One of the features of his work which Li Dao borrowed from Sima Guang was the latter's *kao-yi* section (the critical investigation of the various accounts of an event). On each event, and its various versions, Sima Guang had listed all the different items of evidence, made his selection of one of them, and gave the reason for his choice. Li Dao adopted this practice in his work, which was completed in A.D. 1182 and constitutes an indispensable source for the history of the Song dynasty. It attracted much attention from contemporaries and, like Sima Guang's work earlier, was itself copied by many people. During the process of its transmission, however, several portions were lost, leaving us today with only 520 *chüan.*

Tao Tien-yi

Texts

Xu zi zhi tong jian chang bian. Taibei: Shijia shuju, 1964.

References

Wang Deyi. *Li Dao fu zi nian pu* [A Chronological Biography of Li Dao and His Father]. Taibei: Zhongguo xueshu zhu zuo jiang zhu wei yuan hui, 1965.

Yang Jialuo. "Li dao zhu shu kao [Bibliographical Essay on Li Dao's Literary Works]." In *Xu zi zhi tong jian chang bian,* vol. 3. Taibei: Shi jia shuju, 1964.

Li Dazhao [Li Ta-chao] (1889–1927)

Librarian and professor at Peking University (Beida) and a founder of the Chinese Communist Party. Born in Leting, in Hebei province, Li graduated from the Beiyang School of Law and Government in 1913 and, from 1913 to 1916, studied at Waseda University in Tokyo. He was an active nationalist and reformist political writer and editor from the time he arrived in Japan, and continued in that role when he returned to China—for example as an editor of the influential *Xin Qingnian* [New Youth]. In 1918 Li became head of the Beida library and in 1920 he was appointed a professor of history and political science. Li was a founding member of the Chinese Communist Party in 1921, and coordinated its activities in north China until his arrest and execution by the warlord Zhang Zuolin. Not a professional historian, most of Li's writings were topical pieces that appeared in magazines and newspapers. He did, however, compose a number of essays discussing dialectical and historical materialism and their application to China's history, such as *Shixue yaolun* [Essentials of Historiography] (1924). His chiliastic vision of history had a large influence on some of his students, including the young Mao Zedong, who worked for a time as a clerk in the Beida library.

Albert Feuerwerker

Texts

Huang Sung-k'ang, ed. *Li Ta-chao and the Impact of Marxism on Modern Chinese Thinking.* The Hague: Mouton, 1965. (Selections of Li's works in English and Chinese.)

Li Dazhao xuanji [Selected works of Li Dazhao]. Beijing: Renmin, 1962.

References

Meisner, Maurice J. *Li Ta-chao and the Origins of Chinese Marxism.* Cambridge, MA: Harvard University Press, 1967.

Li Qing [Li Ch'ing] (1602–1683)

Chinese historian. Li came from Jiangsu in the south and served in the government in the late years of the Ming dynasty (1368–1644), but was very hostile to the rule of the Manchus, whose Qing dynasty was established in 1644. With the fall of Jiangsu to the Manchus in 1645, he went into retirement, devoting himself entirely to historical and other scholarship and refusing any further office. His main works are commentaries on the standard histories. His *Ershiyi shi tongyi* [Similarities and Differences in the Twenty-One Histories] was ordered destroyed in 1787 by Emperor Qianlong (1735–1796) who believed it to be anti-Manchu. His longest surviving work, the *Nanbei shi hezhu* [Comments on the Southern and Northern Histories] concerns the Standard Histories of the period from 386 to 589 known as the "northern and southern dynasties."

Colin Mackerras

Texts

No easily accessible text of Li's work survives.

Li Ta-chao

See Li Dazhao.

Li Tao

See Li Dao.

Li Yanshou [Li Yen-shou] (ca. 612–ca. 678)

The Tang dynasty historian Li Yanshou is primarily known for his compilation of *Nanshi* [History of the Southern Dynasties, 420–589] and *Beishi* [History of the Northern Dynasties, 386–618]. He began to work in the Historical Archive in 629, his task being to edit and polish source materials. This gave him privileged access to both first-hand materials and completed histories of the previous dynasties. *Nanshi* and *Beishi* were written on the basis of his father's unfinished drafts and Li's own research. Although completed on Li's own initiative rather than by imperial order, the two histories were recognized as the official history of the northern and southern dynasties. Both being comprehensive histories, *Nanshi* and *Beishi* were modeled after Sima Qian's *Shiji* [Records of the Historian]. Prior to Li's two histories, the northern and southern dynasties recognized their own regimes only and were typically ignorant and derogatory in writing about their rivals. Li's two histories offered a more impartial and balanced account of each of the two dynasties, and thus made most earlier histories on the same period obsolete.

Yuet Keung Lo

Texts

Beishi. 10 vols. Beijing: Zhonghua shuju, 1974.

Xin jiaoben Nanshi fu suoyin [New Critical Edition of the History of the Northern Dynasties with Indices]. 3 vols. Taibei: Dingwen shuju, 1991.

References

Li Yanshou. "Autobiography." In his *Beishi*. 10 vols. Beijing: Zhonghua shuju, 1975.

Li Zongye. *Zhongguo lishi yaoji jieshao* [Introduction to Major Works of Chinese History]. Shanghai: Shanghai Guji chubanshe, 1982.

Li Yen-shou

See Li Yanshou.

Liang Ch'i-ch'ao

See Liang Qichao.

Liang Qichao [Liang Ch'i-ch'ao] (1893–1929)

Chinese historian. A pioneer of modern Chinese historical scholarship, Liang was born near Canton, Guangdong province. He was a major leader of the Hundred Days Reform (1898). A prominent thinker and a prolific writer, Liang saw the importance of history in facilitating political renewal in China. In his *Xin shixue* [New History] (1902), Liang advocated a "revolution in history" by abolishing the practice of the writing of dynastic histories. To promote a collective identity among Chinese, Liang argued that the "new history" should include the different social sectors in China and depict the evolutionary path of the nation. Over the next twenty years, Liang illustrated the concept of new history by writing on world history, Chinese historical heroes, early Chinese thinkers, and Qing [Ch'ing] (1644–1911) intellectual history. In his later life, Liang was concerned about making history scientific. In his *Zhongguo lishi yanjiu fa* [The Methods of Studying Chinese History] (1921–1922) and its supplement (1926–1927), Liang discussed the textual, philological, and quantitative methods that would make history more accurate.

Tze-ki Hon

Texts

Intellectual Trends in the Ch'ing Period. Trans. Immanuel C.Y. Hsu. Cambridge, MA: Harvard University Press, 1959.

References

Chang, Hao. *Liang Ch'i-ch'ao and Intellectual Transition in China, 1890–07.* Cambridge, MA: Harvard University Press, 1971.

Liang Yusheng [Liang Yü-sheng] (1745–1819)

Chinese historian and textual critic. A native of Qiantang in Zhejiang province, Liang was born into a wealthy family celebrated for successive generations of scholarly prestige, but had himself little interest in the civil service examinations. After giving up any aspirations for a career in the bureaucracy, Liang devoted his energy to historical research and textual criticism. He spent twenty years completing a textual analysis of the problems of composition, discrepancies, variations, and authenticity in Sima Qian's *Shiji* [The Records of the Historian] entitled *Shiji zhiyi* [Casting Doubts on *The Records of the Historian*] (1787). Liang's work has been regarded as one of the most valuable studies on *Shiji*. He also made a study of the *Gujin renbiao* [Prominent Figures of Ancient and Modern Times] section of *Han Shu* [History of the Former Han Dynasty], which he brought together under the title *Renbiao kao* [The Investigation of Prominent Ancient Figures] (1786). His other books on ancient history and texts include *Lüzi jiaopu* [Additions and Corrections to Mr. Lü's Annals] (1788), *Yuanhao kao* [The Table of Chinese Reign Titles] (1793) and *Pieji* [Miscellaneous Notes] (1796). His historically based textual criticism was rooted in hard facts and involved the meticulous verification of data based on rigorous standards of precision.

Shao Dongfang

Texts

Reibiao kao. Beijing: Zhonghua shuju, 1982.
Shiji zhiyi. Beijing: Zhonghua shuju, 1981.

References

Elman, Benjamin A. *From Philosophy to Philology: Intellectual and Social Aspects of Change in Late Imperial China.* Cambridge, MA: Harvard University Press, 1984.
Liang Chi-chao. *Intellectual Trends in the Ch'ing Period.* Trans. Immanuel C.Y. Hsu. Cambridge, MA: Harvard University Press, 1959.

Liao Ping [Liao P'ing] (1852–1932)

Chinese writer and historian. Born in Sichuan province, Liao, upon the recommendation of Zhang Zhidong (1837–1909), studied with Wang Kaiyun (1832–1916), who was then a leading advocate for the New Text Classics. In 1888, Liao wrote *Zhisheng pian* [Knowing the Sage] and *Piliu pian* [Disbelieving Liu Xin], arguing that all Old Text Classics were forgeries; this had a great impact on Kang Youwei's work on New Text Confucianism. A year later, Liao attained the *Jinshi* and became a professor at several provincial colleges. He lost his teaching position after the 1898 Reform movement, because of his scholarly connection with Kang Youwei, but resumed his teaching career at a number of Beijing colleges in the 1910s and 1920s. He retired to his hometown in Sichuan in 1924. In addition to the aforementioned books, Liao (also known by the courtesy name Liuyi) published other works on the classics, history, geography, and historical geography and edited *Liuyi-guan congshu* [Book Series of the House of Liuyi].

Q. Edward Wang

Texts

Dili bianzheng buzheng [A Supplementary Study of the Examination on Geography]. Taibei: Qiwen shushe, 1981.
Liao Ping xueshu lunzhu xuanji [Liao Ping's Selected Scholarly Works]. Chengdu: Bashu shushe, 1989.

References

Han Yu-shan. *Elements of Chinese Historiography.* Hollywood, CA: W.M. Hawley, 1953, 135.
Li Yaoxian. *Liao Ping yu jindai Jingxue* [Liao Ping and Modern Classical Studies]. Chengdu: Sichuan renmin chubanshe, 1987.
Liang Ch'i-ch'ao. *Intellectual Trends in the Ch'ing Period.* Trans. Immanuel C.Y. Hsu. Cambridge, MA: Harvard University Press, 1959.
Liao Youping. *Liao Jiping* [Liao's "style" name or *zi*, adopted at manhood] *nianpu* [A Chronological Biography of Liao Ping]. Chengdu: Bashu shushe, 1985.

Liebermann, Felix (1851–1925)

German historian. The son of a wealthy Berlin merchant, Liebermann quit the business world after working two years for a firm in Manchester (1871–1873), choosing instead to study history at Göttingen under Georg Waitz and Reinhold Pauli. A specialist in English medieval history, Liebermann was a tireless editor of medieval texts. Soon after his promotion he worked with Pauli on the edition of English sources for the *Monumenta Germaniae Historica.* Liebermann is best known for his three-volume edition of English legal sources, which covered the Anglo-Saxons and the period of the Norman conquest, *Die Gesetze der Angelsachsen* [The Laws of the Anglo-Saxons] (1898–1916), and his numerous articles on Anglo-Saxon history. This work contained unparalleled documentation of interest to scholars from all fields and earned him international respect. Although he was a private scholar and never held an academic appointment, he was awarded honorary degrees by both the universities of Oxford and Cambridge. His extensive contacts in Britain came to an end with the outbreak of the First World War.

John R. Hinde

Texts

The Law of England at the Norman Conquest. Columbus, OH: F.J. Heer, 1932.
The National Assembly in the Anglo-Saxon Period. Halle: J. Niemeyer, 1913.

References

Thompson, J.W. *A History of Historical Writing.* 2 vols. New York: Macmillan, 1942.

Lingard, John (1771–1851)

English Roman Catholic historian. Born to an old but humble Catholic family in Winchester, Lingard was sent to the English College in Douai, France, in 1782. He returned to England during the revolution and in 1795 became vice president of Crookhall College, near Durham. Subsequently, in 1808, he became vice president of Ushaw College, also in county Durham, which post he retained until 1811, when he retired to a mission at Hornby, Lancashire, remaining there until his death, save for two visits to Rome in 1817 and 1825. In 1821 Pope Pius VII awarded him with a triple degree of doctor in divinity, civil, and canon law. Despite his scholarly contributions and degrees his orthodoxy was questioned at home and in Italy.

Lingard's main contributions as a historian are *Antiquities of the Anglo-Saxon Church* (1806) and his eight-volume *History of England* (1819–1830), the latter of which won him international renown. Although his principal motivation was the defense of the Catholic religion, Lingard's work was sufficiently impartial to be read by Protestants as well. Working for most of his long historiographic career from the relative isolation of Hornby, he mastered several languages including Anglo-Saxon, Hebrew, Spanish, Italian, and Greek. Lingard prided himself on his extensive use of primary sources and was the first scholar to use transcripts from the Vatican Archives. His history had gone through five editions by the time of his death.

Lorraine Gallant

Texts

Antiquities of the Anglo-Saxon Church. Newcastle: Edward Walker, 1800.
The History of England. 8 vols. London: J. Mawman, 1819–1830.

References

Ausubel, Herman, J.B. Brebner, and E.M. Hunt, eds. *Some Modern Historians of Britain.* New York: Dryden Press, 1951.
Kenyon, John. *The History Men: The Historical Profession in England since the Renaissance.* London: Weidenfeld and Nicolson, 1983.
Peardon, Thomas. *The Transition in English Historical Writing, 1760–1830.* New York: AMC Press, 1966.
Shea, Donald F. *The English Ranke: John Lingard.* New York: Humanities Press, 1969.

Literary Theory, Uses of in Historiography

The pervasiveness of postmodernist/poststructuralist assumptions in the human sciences is manifest in the current "linguistic turn" in historiography. This preoccupation with language—the virtual textualization of reality—has made the search for the past more complicated and the truth claims of historians more dubious. Building on hermeneutics and the metaphysical and linguistic skepticism of Jacques Derrida and other champions of "deconstruction," the New History challenges the "modernist" methodological credo of objective and disinterested reason, the universality of truth, the accessibility of "documents" that mirror past reality, and patterns of meaning and development over time that can be captured in overarching narratives. Quite to the contrary, since the "turn," the past has become more an array of obfuscating texts that must be deciphered than social and intellectual realities that can be encountered directly or reconstituted objectively. And the study of history is moving closer to, if not becoming synonymous with, the study of literature. Literary "works," eschewed by modernists for more reality-mirroring evidence, acquire equal status with "documents." Both are approached as "texts" that must be treated with skepticism and linguistic ingenuity.

This deepening symbiosis between literary and historical studies has spawned what Jean Howard has called "a new historical literary criticism." The prominence of literary theory in historiography has produced a new set of assumptions, for instance: human nature is a construct, not an essence; language is opaque and self-referential; the historian, a product of his or her own history and language context, can comprehend the past ("the other") only through a biased lens; and, as Hayden White has argued, the past ultimately is more constructed than discovered. Nor, after Michel Foucault is history formulated best as a continuous narrative from past to present. It is rather a "dialogue" between two historical "moments" or an "intervention" of the present into the past.

The best we can hope for, according to Stephen J. Greenblatt, is "resonance" between present and particular settings in the past. This he finds in the paradigmlessness—and the consequent need to "fashion" ourselves—that we in the late-twentieth-century West share with the denizens of Greenblatt's central period of interest, the English Renaissance. Greenblatt's ingenious, anthropologically driven, literary historicism reveals the "social presence to the world of the literary text and the social presence of the world in the literary text." In a different light, and from the perspective of nineteenth-century intellectual history, Dominick LaCapra approaches as "texts" materials ranging from novels to archival records and, like the historian of political thought, J.G.A. Pocock, sees them as events in the history of language. Yet, LaCapra warns against the urge to "over-contextualize" and thus reduce texts to "mere documents." Equally important are their "worklike" qualities through which they add to and subtract from "reality" and speak to the historian directly as a "reader."

Paul A. Fideler

See also ESSENTIALISM; LITERATURE AND HISTORY; NEW HISTORICISM; POSTMODERNISM; STRUCTURALISM.

Texts

Derrida, Jacques. *Of Grammatology.* Trans. Gayatri Chakravorty Spivak. Baltimore, MD: Johns Hopkins University Press, 1977.
Foucault, Michel. *The Order of Things.* New York: Random House, 1970.
Greenblatt, Stephen J. *Renaissance Self-Fashioning, from More to Shakespeare.* Chicago: University of Chicago Press, 1980.
LaCapra, Dominick. "History, Language, and Reading: Waiting for Crillon." *American Historical Review* 100 (1995): 799–828.
———. *Rethinking Intellectual History: Texts, Contexts, Language.* Ithaca, NY: Cornell University Press, 1983.
Pocock, J.G.A. "Languages and Their Implications: The Transformation of the Study of Political Thought." In his *Politics, Language and Time.* New York: Atheneum, 1971.

References

Jean E. Howard, "The New Historicism in Renaissance Studies." In *Renaissance Historicism,* ed. Arthur F. Kinney and Dan S. Collins. Amherst, MA: University of Massachusetts Press, 1987.
Rosenau, Pauline Marie. *Post-Modernism and the Social Sciences: Insights, Inroads, and Intrusions.* Princeton, NJ: Princeton University Press, 1992.
Taylor, Charles. *Human Agency and Language: Philosophical Papers.* Cambridge, Eng.: Cambridge University Press, 1985.
Toews, John E. "Intellectual History after the Linguistic Turn: The Autonomy of Meaning and the Irreducibility of Experience." *American Historical Review* 92 (1987): 879–907.

Literature and History

Relations between the "fictional" or "imaginative" genres of writing and history as a "factual" genre. Various cultures have at different times either seen a close relation between historical writing and literature or fought hard to press a distinction between them. In the West, history has had a disciplinary identity apart from literature (and particularly the study of rhetoric or of law) for a relatively short period of time. This is in contrast to the importance granted to state-sponsored historical writing—which nonetheless possessed a literary quality—in other parts of the world, most notably China.

Various ancient theorists of history wrote comments about history's place within or outside literature. For the Greeks, for whom ἱστορια *(historia)* was really an "enquiry" rather than a form of writing specifically about the past, the principal distinctions of genre were made in Aristotle's *Poetics* and elaborated by later writers such as Lucian of Samosata. Aristotle did not see history as a major branch of literature, nor did many of his successors. Roman society saw a somewhat closer relation, as measured in the highly rhetorical quality of such authors as Livy and Sallust. Medieval writers, many of whom followed Aristotle or his scholastic and Arabic interpreters, were of divided opinions. Most held literature, in the sense of poetry and drama, in relatively low esteem, written as it often was in a vernacular language and without high purpose. History, in contrast, if not as important a genre as grammar or logic, was at least an important branch of rhetoric, and one that, cast as universal history, placed the story of mankind, arranged annalistically, within a universal providential framework. It should be noted, however, that recent scholarship on medieval chronicles has pointed to the strong influence of literary models, in particular romance, on the writers of chronicles, many of which could be called, in Nancy F. Partner's words, "serious entertainments"; the vernacular histories of a writer like Froissart were without question intended to amuse the fancy as much as to illuminate or teach.

During the Renaissance, the relationship between history and literature grew closer in the work of highly polished rhetoricians such as Bruni, while at the same time it was subverted from two different ends; first, by those antiquaries or philologists who, beginning with Flavio Biondo, wrote in a nonnarrative fashion about physical artifacts, landscape, and architectural remains surviving from antiquity and the Middle Ages, often composing their tracts in a fact-oriented and unliterary style; and second, by poets such as the Englishman Sir Philip Sidney who, building on Aristotle's old analysis, made a case for the intellectual and ethical superiority of poetry to history, on the grounds that the former dealt with the world as it should be, the ideal (hence placing it closer to philosophy than most earlier writers would have conceded), and the latter, history, merely with the temporal and particular. The vogue at the end of the sixteenth and beginning of the seventeenth century for *artes historicae,* manuals delimiting the varieties of historical genre, bespeaks a continued anxiety and uncertainty about the relations of imagination and research, of the literary and historical, rather than the firm embracing of the factual for which it has often been mistaken. Francis Bacon, whose *Advancement of Learning* (1605) is a well-known example of this genre, simply associated history with the faculty of memory and with facts (akin to the study of the natural world) and poetry with the imagination.

The period from the later seventeenth century through the Enlightenment and into the early nineteenth century saw the rapid growth of public interest in history, which was widely read as a form of literature across Europe and its colonies. Although the nineteenth century would return to the distinction between the literary (imaginative) and historical (factual), particularly in the writings of Ranke and his French and American disciples, historical writing in fact maintained a highly literary quality; no one could read the works of Tocqueville or Michelet, or even those of Ranke himself, and not be struck by the literary aspects of their prose. And with some writers, for example, Thomas Macaulay or the Americans Francis Parkman and William Prescott, the literary style is so strong as to give the author's work an enduring attractiveness and readability even today, whatever its biases or factual inaccuracies. By this time, too, the rising popular genre of historical fiction—a branch of the dominant eighteenth- and nineteenth-century genre of imaginative literature, the novel—had supplanted the chivalric romances of the medieval and Renaissance era, or the court romances of the French classical era; heroes and heroines were now regularly placed within temporally specific settings (as for example in the novels of Sir Walter Scott) rather than timeless and thoroughly imaginative arcadian realms.

The twentieth century, until relatively recently, formalized the distinction between literature and history, as evident in the fact that these subjects are taught by different academic departments which, in the United States, for instance, are sometimes even in different faculties (where there is such a division between the humanities and the social sciences), and in the existence of a proliferating number of journals in each discipline, most of which have had little overlap. In the last two decades, however, factors such as the impact of postmodernism and the New Historicism have intruded to weaken the distinction once again, with historians beginning to acknowledge more openly the literary and imaginative aspects of what they do, and literary scholars also beginning to include noncanonical works, such as historical documents, within their studies as an ancillary to classic literary texts. The rise of the new cultural history, for which both elite and popular literatures (ballads, dime novels, and newspapers, for instance) of past societies provide an essential source, has also contributed to the greater presence of the literary work in historical research. Interdisciplinary graduate and undergraduate programs, and scholarly societies focused on a period or country rather than on a discipline, have provided an institutional framework for this noticeable rewarming of relations between Clio and her literary sisters.

D.R. Woolf

See also ARS HISTORICA; CULTURAL HISTORY; NARRATIVE, IN HISTORICAL WRITING; NEW HISTORICISM; POSTMODERNISM; ROMANTICISM.

References

Bann, Stephen. *Romanticism and the Rise of History.* New York: Twayne, 1995.

Beasley, Faith. *Revising Memory: Women's Fiction and Memoirs in Seventeenth-Century France.* New Brunswick, NJ: Rutgers University Press, 1990.

Braudy, Leo. *Narrative Form in History and Fiction: Hume, Fielding and Gibbon.* Princeton, NJ: Princeton University Press, 1970.

Bremner, R.H., ed. *Essays on History and Literature.* Columbus: Ohio State University Press, 1966.

Cadenhead, I.E., ed. *Literature and History.* Tulsa, OK: University of Tulsa Press, 1970.

Kellner, Hans. *Language and Historical Representation: Getting the Story Crooked.* Madison: University of Wisconsin Press, 1989.

Partner, Nancy F. *Serious Entertainments: The Writing of History in Twelfth-Century England.* Chicago: University of Chicago Press, 1977.

Schulze, Leonard. *Literature and History.* Lanham, MD: University Press of America, 1983.

Stone, Lawrence. *The Past and the Present Revisited.* London and New York: Routledge and Kegan Paul, 1987.

White, Hayden. *Metahistory: The Historical Imagination in Nineteenth-Century Europe.* Baltimore, MD: Johns Hopkins University Press, 1973.

Wright, Neil. *History and Literature in Late Antiquity and the Early Medieval West.* Aldershot, Eng.: Variorum, 1995.

Lithuanian Historiography

L

Historical writing by and about the Lithuanian people, from earliest times to the present. The first information concerning Lithuanian history may be found in eleventh-century Latin chronicles. For Lithuanian chronicles proper—written in Chancellery Slavonic rather than Lithuanian—one must await the fifteenth and sixteenth centuries, which produced such works as the *Letopisets Litovskii* [Chronicle of Lithuania] (ca. 1420) and *Kronika Bychotvsa* [Chronicle of Bychoviets] (after 1550).

Augustine Rotundus or Mielecki (ca. 1520–1582), can be considered the first true historian of Lithuania, the author of the *Chronica sive historia Lithuaniae* [Chronicle or History of Lithuania] (1569) and the *Epitome principum Lithuaniae* [Compendium of Lithuanian Princes] (1576). The first printed history, however, was Maciej or Matthew Stryjkowski's *Kronika Polska, Litewska, Zmudzka i wszystkiej Rusi* [Chronicle of Poland, Lithuania, Samogitia, and Russia] (1582). Alexander Guagnini (1538–1614) published two works: *Sarmatiae Europeae Descriptio* [Description of European Sarmatia] (1578) and *Kronika Sarmacyey Europeyskiey* [Chronicle of European Sarmatia] (1611), providing geographical and historical descriptions of Poland, Lithuania, and Prussia. Albert Kojalowicz-Wijuk (1609–1677) wrote a two-volume history of Lithuania, the *Historiae Litvanae* (1650–1659). This work was made more accessible in western Europe by the German scholar August Ludwig Schlözer (1735–1809), who summarized it as *Geschichte von Litauen, als einem eigenen Groszfuerstentume, bis zum Jahr 1569* [History of Lithuania As an Independent Grand Duchy, to the Year 1569]. An important historical source published by Matthew Dogiel (1715–1760) in his edition of the *Codex diplomaticus Regni Poloniae at Magni Ducatus Lithuaniae* [Diplomatic Book of the Kings of Poland and Grand Dukes of Lithuania] (1758). Perhaps the greatest work on Lithuanian history to appear over the ensuing century was the great Polish historian Joachim Lelewel's (1786–1861) *Dzieje Litwy i Rusi az do unji z Polska* [History of Lithuania and Rus' until the Union with Poland] (1839; French translation 1861).

Lelewel's history was important, but was not the only work of note to appear in the nineteenth century—the era of critical historiography in Lithuania as elsewhere. Further surveys of Lithuanian history and numerous editions of source material continued to be issued from European presses. Ignacy Danilowicz (1787–1843), for instance, edited *Skarbiec diplomatow*, a two-volume collection of historical documents for the period up to the sixteenth century (1860–1862). Jozef Jaroszewicz (1793–1860), wrote an extensive history of Lithuania in three volumes, entitled *Obraz Litwy pod wzgledem jej oswiaty i cywilizacji* (1844–1845). To this group of critical historical works also belongs *Zemajtiu wiskupiste* [Bishopric of Samogitia] (2 vols., 1848) by Bishop Motiejus Valancius (1801–1875).

A romantic–didactic approach to historiography emerged at the University of Vilnius in the first third of the nineteenth century. Theodor Narbutt (1784–1862) wrote a nine-volume history of the Lithuanian nation, *Dzieje narodu litewskiego* (1835–1841), up to the time of Sigismund Augustus (1572). Simonas Daukantas (1793–1864), the first author to write a history in Lithuanian, describes the character of ancient Lithuanians and Samogitians in his *Budas senoves lietuviu kalnenu ir zemaiciu* [Character of the Old Lithuanian Highlanders and Lowlanders] (1845). He also wrote a number of other works: *Darbai senuju lietuviu ir zemaiciu* [Deeds of Ancient Lithuanians and Samogitians] (1822); *Istorija zemaitiska* [Samogitian History] (1838); and *Pasakojimas apie veikalus lietuviu tautos senoveje* [What Lithuanians Did in the Past] (1850).

Throughout the nineteenth century, Lithuania was officially referred to as the Northwestern Territory ("Severo-Zapadnyi Krai") of the Russian Empire. Under this rubric the Russian Archaeographic Commission published several collections of historical documents dealing with Lithuanian history, including, among others: *Zapadnorusskie letopisi* [West Russian Chronicles] (1907); *Akty otnosiashchiessia k historii Juzhnoi i Zapadnoi Rossii* [Documents Pertaining to the History of South and West Russia] (15 vols., 1863–1892); *Akty otnosiashchiesia k istorii Zapadnoi Rossii* [Documents Pertaining to the History of West Russia] (5 vols., 1846–1853); and *Litovskaia Metrika* [The Lithuanian Register] (4 vols., 1903–1905). In the tradition of German record publications such as the *Monumenta Germaniae Historica,* Augustin Theiner (1804–1874) edited *Vetera Monumenta Poloniae et Lithuaniae . . . ex Tabularis Vaticanis* [Ancient Documents of Poland and Lithuania, extracted from the Vatican Archives] (4 vols., 1860–1864), which included many documents concerning Lithuania. Despite their tendentiousness, between 1885 and 1915 Russian historians (Mitrofan Dovnar-Zapolskii, Mikhail Koialovich, Fedor I. Leontovich, Matvei K. Liubavskii, Nikolai A. Maksimeiko, Joannikii A. Malinovskii, and Mikhail F. Vladimirskii-Budanov among others) also produced valuable and often objective studies on the political, social, legal, and economic aspects of Lithuania's past.

Studies written by Polish historians (Feliks Koneczny, Ludwik Kolankowski, Anatol Lewicki, Antoni Prochaska, Stanislaw Smolka, Kazimierz Stadnicki) around the turn of the century were, in contrast to Russian-authored works, generally devoted to the rulers of Lithuania-Poland. Other Polish historians dealt with topics such as the governing elite (Adam Boniecki, W. Semkowicz, and Jozef Wolff), the legal/social system (Stanislaw Kutrzeba), education (Michael Balinski, Jozef Lukaszewicz, Stanislaw Rostowski, and Josef Bielinski), Lithuania's Christianization (Wladislaw Abraham and Jan Fijalek), and union with Poland (Oskar Halecki). Antoni Prochaska edited a collection of documents from the time of Vytautas, the *Codex epistolaris Vitoldi* (1882). In 1848, Edward Raczynski published *Codex diplomaticus Lithuaniae, 1253–1433.* Jozef Ignacy Kraszewski's *Litwa* [Lithuania] appeared in two volumes published in 1847 and 1850, respectively.

The period of independent Lithuanian statehood (1918–1940) was too short to create its own school of Lithuanian history. The main historians of this period included Antanas Alekna (1872–1930) who wrote Lithuanian history textbooks, but also authored a monograph about an earlier historian, Bishop Motiejus Valancius (1922), and a *History of the Lithuanian Catholic Church* (1930). Alekna's exact contemporary, Jonas Totoraitis (1872–1941) published *Suduvos Suvalkijos Istorija* [History of Southern Lithuania] in 1938. Narrower spans of time and specific topics were also studied. Ignas Jonynas (1884–1954) researched the political history of the thirteenth to sixteenth centuries while Ivan I. Lappo (1861–1944) investigated legal systems and sixteenth-century relations between Lithuania and Poland; his *1588 metu Lietuvos Statutas* [Lithuanian Code of Laws of 1588] (3 parts, 1934–1938) is particularly important. Of a somewhat younger generation that survived World War II, Augustinas Janulaitis (1878–1950) wrote about the history of Lithuania's legal system, and Konstantinas Jablonskis (1892–1960) compiled lists of inventories from the sixteenth and seventeenth centuries (*Lietuvos inventoriai,* 1934 and 1962).

A new generation of historians had joined research and university teaching staffs before the war. Paulius Slezas (1902–1938) edited a monograph on *Vytautas Didysis* [Vytautas the Great] in 1930. Adolfas Sapoka (1906–1961) edited the monograph *Jogaila* (1935). Moreover, studies by individual authors dealt with a variety of Lithuanian rulers from Mindaugas to Svitrigaila. Juozas Stakauskas (1900–1972) wrote *Lietuva ir Vakaru*

Europa XIII amziuje [Lithuania and Western Europe in the Thirteenth Century] (1934). Juozas Jakstas (1900–1989) studied Kings Vytenis's and Gediminas's relations with the Teutonic Order in his *Vokieciu Ordinas ir Lietuva Vytenio ir Gedimino metais* (1945–1936). Perhaps most significant was Adolfas Sapoka's *Lietuvos istorija* [History of Lithuania] (1936), which remains after sixty years the only definitive history of Lithuania.

Not all the historical writing of the prewar and immediate postwar periods was concerned with politics. A number of historians paid attention to social history. In 1940 Konstantinas Avizonis (1909–1960) published *Bajorai valsybiniame Lietuvos gyvenime Vazu laikais* [Nobility in the Lithuanian Government under the Vasas]. Zenonas Ivinskis (1908–1971) researched Lithuania's peasant class in *Geschichte des Bauernstandes in Litauen*, 1933. Ivinskis, whose last work, *Lietuvos istorija iki Vytauto Didziojo mirties* [The History of Lithuania until the Death of Vytautas the Great] was published posthumously in 1978, is widely deemed to have been the leading modern Lithuanian historian.

A number of Polish and German authors enriched Lithuanian historiography between the world wars. Henryk Paskiewicz, for example, published the first volume of his *Jagiellonowie i Moskwa* [The Jagellonians and Moscow] in 1932 and *O Genezie i Wartosci Krewa* [About the Origin and Value of Krivas] in 1938. Henryk Łowmiański (1898–1984) wrote *Studja nad poczatkami spoleczenstwa i panstwa litewskiego* [Studies about the Beginning of the Lithuanian State and Society] (2 vols., 1931–1932). Ludwik Kolankowski's (1882–1956) *Dzieje Wielkiego Ksiestwa Litewskiego I* [History of the Grand Duchy of Lithuania] appeared in 1930, as did the German historian Josef Pfitzner (1901–1945) in his *Grossfürst Witold von Litauen als Staatsman* [Prince Witold of Lithuania As Statesman].

When the Soviet Union seized Lithuania in 1944, most historians fled to the West, where they continued to produce scholarly works. Among the publications of the exiles, one should include the historical entries in *Lietuviu Enciklopedija* [Lithuanian Encyclopedia] (37 vols., 1953–1985) and in the English-language *Encyclopedia Lituanica* (6 vols., 1970–1978), as well as studies in a number of periodicals: *Proceedings of the Lithuanian Catholic Academy of Arts and Sciences* (Rome); *Lietuviu Tautos Praeitis* (Chicago); *Proceedings of the Institute of Lithuanian Studies* (Chicago); and *Lituanus* (Chicago). A number of new surveys of Lithuanian history also appeared in the first

quarter-century after the war, such as Constantine R. Jurgela's *History of the Lithuanian Nation* (1948) and the multiauthored *Lithuania: 700 years* (1969), in which J. Puzinas, J. Jakstas, A. Gerutis, and other authors collaborated to produce a synoptic overview of Lithuania's history from prehistoric times to World War II. Also notable are Petras Klimas's *Ghillebert de Lannoy in Medieval Lithuania* (1945), V. Daugirdaite-Sruogiene's *Lietuvos istorija-Lietuva amziu sukury* [Lithuania in the Whirlpool of Centuries] (1956), and Martynas Senprusiu Anysas's *Pruthenorum gentaes kovos del laisves su Vokieciu Riteriu Ordinu nuo 1230 iki 1283 metu* [The Old Prussians and Their Wars against the Teutonic Order . . .] (1968). Most recently, reports of Lithuania's bishops to the Holy See have been published as *Relationes status diocesium in Magno Ducatu Lituaniae* (vol. I, 1971); Patricia Kennedy Grimsted's *Lithuanian Metrica in Moscow and Warsaw: Reconstructing the Archive of the Grand Duchy of Lithuania* appeared in 1984; and Jonas Dainauskas's *Lietuvos bei lietuviu krikstas ir 1387–ji metai* [The Baptism of Lithuania and Lithuanians and the Year 1387] was published in 1991. Further important research on the medieval Baltic can be found in William Urban's *Baltic Crusade* (1975) and his separate study, *The Samogitian Crusade* (1989).

As in other parts of the Eastern Bloc (for instance Poland, Romania, and Bulgaria), conditions in Soviet-occupied Lithuania after World War II were not conducive to the production of objective historical writing. The *History of the Lithuanian SSR* (Lietuvos TSR Istorija, 3 vols., 1957–1965) is a prime example of Soviet-inspired historical misinterpretation. On the other hand, the period did produce a number of noteworthy collections of historical sources. *Lietuvos valstieciu ir miestieciu gincai su dvaru valdytojais* (1959–1962) contains many documents generated by litigations between peasants and landlords; Bronius Dundulis's *Lietuvos kova del valstybinio savarankiskumo XV amziuje* [The Lithuanian Struggle for Sovereignty in the Fifteenth Century] (1968); Jerzy Ochmanski's *Historia Litwy* [History of Lithuania] (1967–1990); Vladimir Pasuto's *Lietuvos valstybes susidarymas* [Formation of the Lithuanian State] (1971), and *Lietuvos TSR Istorijos saltiniai, I* [The Sources of the History of Lithuanian SSR, vol. I] (1955) are also significant.

J. Dainauskas and J. Rackauskas

See also ESTONIAN HISTORIOGRAPHY; LATVIAN HISTORIOGRAPHY; POLISH HISTORIOGRAPHY.

References

Encyclopedia Lituanica, vol. I–VI. Boston: Lithuanian Encyclopedia Press/Juozas Kapočius, 1970–1978.

Gerutis, Albertas, ed. *Lithuania. 700 Years.* Second ed. New York: Manyland Books, 1969.

Kennedy-Grimsted, Patricia, ed. *The Lithuanian Metrica.* Cambridge, MA: Harvard University Press, 1984.

Urban, William L. *The Baltic Crusade.* Second ed. Chicago: Lithuanian Research and Studies Center, 1994.

Litta, Count Pompeo (1781–1852)

Soldier, statesman, and genealogist. Filled with ardor for the constitution of the Cisalpine Republic and inspired by the glories of Napoleon's armies, Litta enrolled as a simple soldier in the imperial army in 1804. The Milanese patrician served at the battles of Ulm, Austerlitz, and Wagram (1806), where he earned the rank of captain. He later commanded an artillery corps. At the close of the Napoleonic wars, Litta immersed himself in the study of history, numismatics, and belles lettres. After years of travel and research, he published the first folios of his masterpiece of genealogical scholarship, *Famiglie Celebri Italiane* [Famous Italian Families] (1819). During the revolution of 1848, Litta held the post of minister of war in the provisional Lombard government. A scrupulous philologist and a balanced judge of character (the only animus that he demonstrates in his writing is directed at poets of the Baroque era), Litta composed pithy biographies for members of 113 of the peninsula's ecclesiastical, military, and political dynasties. The eleven volumes of the *Famiglie Celebri Italiane* bequeathed enough material to future Italianists to furnish numerous studies of the Italian aristocracy from the Renaissance to the Risorgimento. Later editions of the *Famiglie Celebri Italiane* contained genealogies composed by other aristocratic genealogists, most notably Count Luigi Passerini.

Edward Michalik

Texts

Famiglie Celebri Italiane. 11 vols. Milan: P.E. Giusti, 1819–1872.

References

Hoefer, M. (Jean Chrétien Ferdinand). *Nouvelle biographie générale depuis les temps les plus reculés jusqu'à 1850–1860* [A New Biographical Dictionary from Antiquity to the 1850s and 1860s]. Vols. 31–32. Copenhagen: Rosenkilde et Bagger, 1963–1969.

Mario, Jessie White. *The Birth of Modern Italy.* London: T. Fisher Unwin, 1909.

Liu Chia-ho

See Liu Jiahe.

Liu Chih-chi or Liu Tzu-hsüan

See Liu Zhiji.

Liu Hsu

See Liu Xu.

Liu I Cheng

See Liu Yizheng.

Liu Jiahe [Liu Chia-ho] (b. 1928)

Modern Chinese historian. Born in Liuhe in Jiangsu province, Liu was brought up in an atmosphere of traditional learning. During the 1940s he studied under two noted scholars, Tang Junyi and Qian Mu. After graduating from Furen Catholic University, Liu began a lengthy academic career at Beijing Normal University. Recognized as one of China's prominent authorities in ancient history, his long-term research interests have covered ancient China, India, and Greece. His research on the last resulted in the monograph *Lun heluoshi zhidu* [On Helotry] (1957). His major publications on India, *Yindu zaoqi fojiao de zhongxing zhidu guan* [The Indian Caste System Reflected in Early Buddhist Texts] (1963) and *Gudai yindu de tudi guanxi* [The Land System of Ancient India] (1964), are historiographically significant as the first works to make use of Buddhist texts, particularly the *Tripitaka,* to study ancient India. Liu's reputation rests principally on his ability to synthesize the study of ancient Chinese civilization with that of other contemporary cultures. His *Shijieshi gudaishi bian* [A History of the Ancient World] (1994) reveals this ability to take such a comparative approach to the subject and has been praised as a groundbreaking study of ancient history as a coherent whole in East and West. In a similar vein, his recent *Gudai zhongguo yu shijie* [Ancient China and the World] (1995) is a major contribution to the study of ancient civilizations, especially, but not only, that of his own country.

Shao Dongfang

Texts

Gudai zhongguo yu shiji. Wuhan: Wuhan chubanshe, 1995.

Shijieshi gudaishi bian. Beijing: Gaodeng jiaoyu chubanshe, 1994.

References

Bai Shouyi. *Zhongguo tongshi* [A General History of China]. Shanghai: Shanghai renmin chubanshe, 1994, vols. 1 and 3.

Croizier, Ralph. "World History in the People's Republic of China." *Journal of World History* 1 (1990): 151–169.

Liu Wenqi [Liu Wen-chi] (1789–1856)

Chinese historian and classical scholar. Born in Jiangsu province, after earning the *Xiucai* degree Liu was elected in 1819 to the Imperial Academy as a senior licentiate, where he spent most of his later life teaching and studying. Although he failed to obtain a higher degree, Liu's erudition in the classics was well known at the time. As a result, he was often employed by men of wealth to assist in their scholarly activities. Liu's own major achievement was his critical study of the *Chunqiu Zuozhuan* [Zuo Commentary on the Spring and Autumn Annals]. Liu was displeased with the existing commentary and other exegetic works on the classic *Chunqiu,* including Du Yu's (A.D. 222–284) exegesis, which was long regarded as the authoritative interpretation. He decided to write a new book, which he planned to entitle *Zuozhuan jiuzhu shuzheng* [A Study of the Old Commentaries on the Zuozhuan], to be based on a thorough examination of every extant work of commentary and on his own knowledge of the original text. Liu therefore became the first Qing scholar to initiate the modern critical study of the *Zuozhuan;* although he failed to complete his labors before he died, the work was continued by his son. In addition, Liu wrote some other books, including one on the canal system in Yangzhou and another on the territories of the feudal lords in the late Qin Dynasty; he also left notes on his readings.

Q. Edward Wang

Texts

Chuhan zhuhou jiangyou zhi [Biographical Studies of the Princes and Generals of the Former Han]. Taibei: Guangwen shuju, 1978.

Jiutangshu jiaokanji [Annotations of the Old Tang History]. Taibei: Zhengzhong shuju, 1971.

References

Han Yu-shan. *Elements of Chinese Historiography.* Hollywood, CA: W.M. Hawley, 1955, 135–136.

Liang Ch'i-ch'ao. *Intellectual Trends in the Ch'ing Period.* Trans. Immanuel C.Y. Hsu. Cambridge, MA: Harvard University Press 1959.

Liu Xu [Liu Hsu] (888–947)

Chinese statesman and historian during the Five Dynasties period (907–960). Liu held a variety of official positions in both the Later Tang and Later Jin dynasties. In 941 there came the order to compose the *Tang shu* [Tang History], later known as the *Jiu Tangshu* [Old Tang History] in order to distinguish it from the *Xiu Tangshu* [New Tang History] compiled in the Song dynasty. The actual compilers, according to most Chinese scholars and the English historian Denis Twitchett, were Zhao Ying, Zhang Zhaoyuan, Jia Wei, Wang Shen, and Zhao Xi. In 945, when the *Old Tang History* was completed, Liu was serving as both chief minister and director of the Historiographical Office at the court, and it was in this latter capacity that he presented the *Tang shu* to the throne, along with his memorial. Consequently his name was recorded as the principal compiler.

Q. Edward Wang

Texts

Jiu Tangshu [Old Tang History]. 16 vols. Beijing: Zhonghua shuju, 1975.

References

Twitchett, Denis. *The Writing of Official History under the T'ang.* Cambridge, Eng.: Cambridge University Press, 1992.

Wang Gungwu. "Some Comments on the Later Standard Histories." In *Essays on the Sources for Chinese History,* ed. Donald D. Leslie, Colin Mackerras, and Wang Gungwu. Canberra: Australian National University Press, 1973, 53–63.

Liu Yizheng [Liu I Cheng] (1879–1956)

Chinese cultural historian. Born to a poor family of teachers in Jiangsu province, Liu was known to literary circles through his precocious poetic and calligraphic talents. Under the direction of the classicist–historian Miao Quansun (1844–1919), Liu wrote one of the first history textbooks in modern China, *Lidai shilue* [Brief History of Dynasties] (1902). From 1916 to 1925, Liu taught at Nanjing's Southeastern University *(Dongnan daxue)* where he founded the *Xue heng* [Critical Review] in collaboration with Mi Guangdi (1890–1945) and Wu Mi (1894–1977). In contrast to the 1920s wish to Westernize China, the *Xue heng* group glorified the Chinese cultural and literary tradition. In his *Zhongguo wenhua shi* [Chinese Cultural History] (1932), Liu furthered the *Xue heng* view by identifying the distinctive trajectory of Chinese development through a historical narrative of China from early antiquity to modern times. Liu reiterated the uniqueness of China in his *Guoshi yaoyi* [The Essential Elements of National History] (1948).

Tze-ki Hon

Texts
Guoshi yaoyi. Shanghai: Zhonghua shuchu, 1948.
Zhongguo wenhua shi. Shanghai: Zhongguo dai baike quanshu chubanshe, 1983.

References
Schneider, Laurence. "National Essence and the New Intelligentsia." In *The Limits of Change: Essays on Conservative Alternatives in Republican China,* ed. Charlotte Furth. Cambridge, MA: Harvard University Press, 1976, 57–89.

Liu Zhiji [Liu Chih-chi] (661–721)
Chinese historiographer, historian, and scholar-official. He was involved in the writing of some dozen works and took part in debates over Confucian texts. His most important work is the *Shitong* [Generalities on History], which was completed in 710. It is a critical discussion, and to some extent analysis, of the nature of history as it had been practiced in China up to Liu's time. It is clearly a landmark work in being not only history but also historical theory, the first treatise on the writing of history ever written in Chinese. It discusses the various categories of history of ancient times, and focuses on two: chronicles *(biannian)* and the annals-and-biography *(jizhuan),* which had already become the model for the Standard Histories. It also considers issues like the function of history. Liu saw history as a register of change. His work is replete with Confucian moralism, and he clearly subscribed to the view then prevalent that history teaches lessons for the present. Liu's work has a good deal to say about style, as well as content, and places a considerable emphasis on conciseness. Liu Zhiji and his *Generalities on History* have been enormously influential among traditional Chinese historians.

Colin Mackerras

Texts
Shitong jianji [Annotated Generalities on History]. Annotations by Cheng Qianfan. Beijing: Zhonghua shuju, 1980.

References
Hung, William. "A T'ang Historiographer's Letter of Resignation." *Harvard Journal of Asiatic Studies* 29 (1969): 5–52.
Pulleyblank, E.G. "Chinese Historical Criticism: Liu Chih-chi and Ssu-ma Kuang." In *Historians of China and Japan.* ed. W.G. Beasley and E.G. Pulleyblank. London: Oxford University Press, 1961, 135–166.

Livy [Titus Livius] (59/64 B.C.–A.D. 17)
Roman historian. Livy was born in Patavium (Padua), in northern Italy. His family was of Italian stock and probably wealthy. Little is known of his early life. As a young man, he moved to Rome where he spent the rest of his adult life researching and writing on Rome's past. Livy became a member of the circle of the Emperor Augustus, with whom he established a lifelong friendship. In ca. 27 B.C. Livy began publishing in segments his history of Rome entitled *Ab Urbe Condita* [From the Founding of the City]. This history, of which less than one-third still survives, contained 142 books covering the years from Rome's earliest times to the year 9 B.C. Books 1 through 10 (Rome's earliest history to 293 B.C.) are extant as are books 21 through 45 (219 B.C. to 167 B.C.). An epitome of Livy's complete history was made during the first century A.D.: books 37 through 40 and 48 through 55 are extant. Further, abstracts *(Periochae)* of each book also exist for all but two of the 142 books. Livy's purpose in writing is to tell not only of Rome's rise to power and the noble achievements of its citizens, but also of the republic's moral and political decline.

His history is especially noted for its prose style and literary artistry, and it is our most important source for much of early Roman history. Yet Livy was sometimes uncritical in his use of earlier written histories, and his treatment of military matters, geography, and practical politics was at times flawed. The publication of his work brought Livy immediate fame throughout the empire, and his history became the standard source for later Roman historians writing on the Roman Republic. Livy was much admired by Renaissance scholars.

Ralph F. Gallucci

Texts

Livy: From the Founding of the City. Trans. B.O. Foster, E.T. Sage, and A.C. Schlesinger. 14 vols. Cambridge, MA: Harvard University Press/Loeb Classical Library, 1919–1959.

References

Luce, T.J. *Livy: The Composition of His History.* Princeton, NJ: Princeton University Press, 1977.

Ogilvie, R.M. *A Commentary on Livy: Books 1– 5.* Revised ed. Oxford: Clarendon Press, 1984.

Lo Chen-yü

See Luo Zhenyu.

Local History

The study of the history of particular places as opposed to countries. Geography, as classical authors from as early as Herodotus recognized, has always been intimately tied to history. Indeed, ancient authors such as Pausanias, Pliny, and Herodotus himself tended to subordinate time to place, while later classical authors such as Livy and Tacitus, who wrote narrative histories, nevertheless recognized that geography could play a role in historical events. During the Renaissance, scholars such as Flavio Biondo and William Camden practiced a form of historical antiquarianism that looks like a near ancestor of modern local history, beginning with a place and exploring its people and historical events rather than the other way around as a narrative historian might. The English genres "chorography" and "topography," which have Chinese equivalents in the *dili* (local geographical treatises) and *fangzhi* (local gazetteers), were heavily historical, despite their organization along spatial lines. This permitted early practitioners to include much detail on local life and customs that would have been deemed unworthy of formal, narrative historiography with its fixation on great men and events. In some ways, local history has thus always been more open to representing nonelite experience, and to relaying facts from outside the realm of politics, than mainstream historiography.

It was precisely the secondary status of antiquarianism, closely associated with local study, that relegated local history to a subordinate role from the seventeenth to the nineteenth century. As early modern and eighteenth-century writers emphasized politics and religion in their accounts, so their nineteenth-century successors stressed the growth of the state. And since the general trend of European politics from the end of the Thirty Years' War was also toward greater unification of small territories into larger ones, culminating in the nation-states of the last century, there was at first little support for an academic form of local history. There were of course some conspicuous exceptions: Justus Möser's study of Osnabrück is now properly regarded as a gem of early German historicism, despite its focus on a single community, and the early founders of the Victoria County History in England, a series that has yet to be completed, established local study as once again a respectable and deeply learned form of research into the past.

In the past hundred years, local history has come into its own, both as an amateur pursuit closely linked to rural and urban antiquarianism, and to the study of history through architecture and landscape. Where the nineteenth century emphasized the study of records and other documents generated by and deposited within centralized institutions (the Public Record Office in London, the *Archives* in Paris, or the various state archives of the constituent parts of Germany and Italy), recent historiography, with its thrust toward the social and generally nonpolitical, has made intensive use of local sources and often made particular tiny areas the subject of investigation. The subjects of such explorations can vary widely. The European *microstoria* consists of close scrutiny or "total history" of a particular town, manor, seignory, or parish; the "English" school of local history, established by W.G. Hoskins and his disciples, applies similar methods to reconstruct and quantify aspects of life in the past in particular places. The French Annales school has similarly turned in recent years from broad national and global patterns to the locality, Emmanuel Le Roy Ladurie's reconstruction of life in a medieval Cathar village, *Montaillou,* being a celebrated instance. One recent good example is Marjorie Keniston Mackintosh's recent studies of the tiny manor Havering, in medieval and Tudor Essex; another is John Demos's reconstruction of family life in Plymouth colony during the colonial period, *A Little Commonwealth.* In the United States scholars have used state and urban archives to construct intensive analyses of the histories of cities, towns, and agricultural regions. Doctoral theses in history often now focus on particular towns or villages as a way of providing an exhaustively documented monograph on a particular area that is nevertheless manageable within a short period.

D.R. Woolf

See also ANTIQUARIANISM; ATLASES—HISTORICAL; CHINESE HISTORIOGRAPHY—LOCAL GAZETTEERS *(FANGZHI);* HISTORICAL GEOGRAPHY; MICROHISTORY; RURAL HISTORY; URBAN HISTORY.

References
Douch, Robert. *Local History and the Teacher.* London: Routledge, 1967.
Finnegan, Ruth, and Michael Drake, eds. *Sources and Methods for Family and Community Historians.* Cambridge, Eng.: Cambridge University Press (for the Open University), 1994.
Hey, David. *The Oxford Companion to Local and Family History.* Oxford, Eng., and New York: Oxford University Press, 1996.
Hoskins, W.G. *Local History in England.* Third ed. London and New York: Longman, 1984.
Pearson, Lionel. *The Local Historians of Attica.* Second ed. Westport, CT: Greenwood Press, 1972.
Thompson, Enid T. *Local History Collections: A Manual for Librarians.* Nashville, TN: American Association for State and Local History, 1978.
Tiller, Kate. *English Local History.* Stroud, Eng.: Alan Sutton, 1992.

Lodge, Sir Richard (1855–1936)

English diplomatic historian. Lodge was born at Penkhull, Staffordshire, and was educated at Horncastle Grammar School, Christ Hospital, London, and Balliol College, Oxford. He became a fellow of Brasenose College, Oxford, in 1878. He later took up professorships first at Glasgow University in 1894 and then at the University of Edinburgh, where he remained until his retirement in 1923. Lodge believed that universities had an obligation to prepare students for their civic duties and that in this process, history was of integral importance. His conviction that the dynamics of the historical process must be sought in the political domain permeated all his early works, most notably *The Student's Modern Europe* (1885), *Richelieu* (1896), and *The History of England from the Restoration to the Death of William III* (1910). Lodge made his major contributions in the area of diplomatic history. Here his reputation rests principally on two works: *Great Britain and Prussia in the Eighteenth Century* (1923), an authoritative

account of Anglo-Prussian relations incorporating substantial archival research, and *Studies in Eighteenth Century Diplomacy, 1740–1748* (1930). This last is perhaps his best book and still commands respect today; its insights and erudition made it a model for subsequent historians of British foreign policy, and it has shaped the lines of future research in the genre.

Karl Schweizer

Texts
Great Britain and Prussia in the Eighteenth Century. Oxford: Clarendon Press, 1923.
The History of England from the Restoration to the Death of William III. London and New York: Longmans, Green, 1910.
History of Modern Europe. New York: Harper and Bros., 1887.
Studies in Eighteenth-Century Diplomacy, 1740–1748. London: J. Murray, 1930.

References
Lodge, Margaret. *Sir Richard Lodge: A Biography.* London: Blackwood and Sons, 1946.

Logic and Historical Enquiry

The relations of logic, in application and in conception, to the methods of the historian. If there is logic in stories, there is logic in the stories told about history. And how could there not be? Even when the event is a surprising one, we are led to think of it as something that we can infer from a sufficiently full description of the situation and of the motives of the people present there. On a grander scale, many have thought of history on the whole as a story about a problem put to humankind, which reaches resolution only at the end of history—after every nation has been given a chance to hear the Gospel, reached Judgment Day, and the children of light have ascended to salvation; *or,* after the class struggle has been reduced to a polarized opposition between two classes, the Revolution, with an enlightened proletariat completing the quest for fully rational social institutions. They will be fully rational because they bring in democratic economic planning where opposed classes and interests have argued in a logically irreconcilable way from different premises. Skeptics about these grand narratives need not be skeptics about logic supplying rational tests for the arguments that lead generals, politicians, citizens, farmers, or capitalists to decide how they will act. The arguments may be logically defective as well as irresponsibly ignorant. However, even if they are well informed and logically adequate for each individual agent, the actions that they lead to may combine socially to produce unexpected and paradoxical consequences. Here and elsewhere logic can be called upon to specify important features of historical events. People deliberate about interpretations of the Constitution and about other policies; and present specifiable arguments sometimes valid, sometimes invalid, for adopting one policy as the rule rather than another. In these cases, and in less deliberated cases, too, a good deal of historical change involves changes in specifiable social rules, like the changes from the rules of the Middle Ages governing work on manors and in guilds to the rules allowing under capitalism for fluid labor markets and freedom to introduce new technologies. A suitably conceived logic of rules comes into play to formulate the rules *ex ante* and the rules *ex post* and, as well, the rules that may be invoked to justify changing from one to the other. Such a logic must give due weight to the difficulty that people face in quandaries—situations in which they feel bound by rules that prohibit every line of action feasible—without letting the surrounding system of rules appear to be in such disarray as to license every line of action. This will be no ordinary logic. It will have a dimension that cannot be reduced to the truth or falsity of the propositions that figure as ingredients of rule-formulas. It will keep close company with late-twentieth-century developments in logic that allow logic to face contradictions and go on working while the contradictions are resolved. But then it will fit under Hegel's description of the dialectic as exhibiting what no ordinary logic can, the orderly movement of history from contradiction to contradiction. It will also justify in part Marxist claims for the dialectic. It is reasonable to identify Marxists' contradictions with quandaries in the logic of rules; and to represent details of the large changes from feudalism to capitalism and from capitalism to socialism as changes forced on people by quandaries. The quandaries arise from the incursion of new social practices into social institutions (systems of rules) that cannot logically accommodate them unless changes in the rules occur. Thus, surprisingly, a more sophisticated logic, which fits more easily into accounts of history, does not discredit the dialectic, but does something to vindicate it.

David Braybrooke

See also PHILOSOPHY OF HISTORY—ANALYTICAL.

References

Braybrooke, David, Bryson Brown, and Peter K. Schotch. *Logic on the Track of Social Change.* Oxford: The Clarendon Press, 1995.

Carr, David. *Time, Narrative, and History.* Bloomington: Indiana University Press, 1986.

Elster, Jon. *Logic and Society.* New York: John Wiley, 1978.

Löwith, Karl. *Meaning in History.* Chicago: University of Chicago Press, 1949.

L

Lomonosov, Mikhail Vasil'evich (1711–1765)

Russian scientist, writer, and historian. Of humble origins, Lomonosov rose to become the embodiment of mid-eighteenth-century Russian enlightenment. In addition to his significant contributions in the fields of physics, chemistry, geology, and mineralogy, Lomonosov played a critical role in the development of a Russian literary language through his poems, odes, and orations and his publication of the first Russian grammar. In 1751, Lomonosov received an assignment from Empress Elizabeth to write in his distinctive literary style a comprehensive history of Russia. The result was his *Drevniaia rossiiskaia istoriia* [Ancient Russian History] published a year after his death. The first part of a planned four-volume work, Lomonosov's history covers the period up to the death of Iaroslav the Wise in 1054. While in large measure a literary embellishment of the Kievan Primary Chronicles, Lomonosov's history focused particular attention on the problem of the origins of the Slavic peoples and the establishment of the Kievan state. A passionate opponent of the "Norman" (that is, Scandinavian) theory of the origins of Kievan Rus', which he regarded as demeaning to Russian national pride, Lomonosov strove in his historical writings to prove the Slavic origins of the Kievan princely dynasty. In comparison with contemporaries such as Vasilii Nikitich Tatishchev (1686–1750) and Gerhard Friedrich Müller (1705–1783), Lomonosov was lacking both in his mastery of sources and his critical methods, but later scholars have given him credit for his insights into the formation of ethnicity. Lomonosov's attempt to produce a literary narrative of Russian history marked the start of a "rhetorical orientation," which would be continued by lesser eighteenth-century historians and reach its apogee in the work of Nikolai Mikhailovich Karamzin (1766–1826) in the early nineteenth century.

Nathaniel Knight

Texts

Drevniaia rossiiskaia istoriia ot nachala rossiiskogo naroda do konchiny velikogo kniazia Iaroslava Pervogo ili do 1054 goda, sochinennaia Mikhailom Lomonosovym [Ancient Russian History from the Origin of the Russian People to the Death of the Grand Duke Iaroslav the First or until the year 1054, Composed by Mikhail Lomonsov]. St. Petersburg: Imperial Academy of Sciences, 1766.

Polnoe sobranie sochinenii [Complete Works]. 11 vols. Moscow: Izdatel'stvo Akademii nauk SSSR, 1950–1983.

References

Menshutkin, Boris Nikolaevich. *Russia's Lomonosov: Chemist, Courtier, Physicist, Poet.* Trans. Jeanette Eyre Thal and Edward J. Webster. Princeton, NJ: Princeton University Press, 1952.

Miliukov, Pavel Nikolaevich. *Glavnye techeniia russkoi istoriograficheskoi mysli* [Main Trends in Russian Historiographical Thought]. Second ed. Moscow: I.N. Kushnerev, 1898.

Pavlova, Galina Evgen'evna and Aleksandr Sergeevich Fedorov. *Mikhail Vasil'evich Lomonosov: His Life and Work.* Trans. Arthur Aksenov. Ed. Richard Hainsworth. Moscow: Mir Publishers, 1984.

Rubinstein, N.L. *Russkaia istoriografiia* [Russian Historiography]. Moscow: Gospolitizdat, 1941, 86–92.

Lopes de Castanheda, Fernão (ca. 1500–1559)

Portuguese historian. Very little is known of the life of Lopes de Castanheda, the author of the *Historia do Descobrimento & conquista da India pelos Portugueses,* the first history of the Portuguese discovery and conquest of India. He was born in Santarém, though the year is uncertain, and entered the Dominican order while still young. He was the son of the first Portuguese judge of Goa and went with his father to India in 1528. He remained approximately ten years, but it is not known with any exactitude when he returned to Portugal. Sick and poor, the only job available to him was as a beadle and guard in the College of Arts of the University of Coimbra, where he eventually died. He spent twenty years writing his history, which is divided into ten books. Only books one to eight, published between 1551 and 1561, have survived; the first book was translated into French and Spanish after its initial printing in Portuguese.

Carlos Pérez

Texts

Historia do Descobrimento & Conquista da India pelos Portugueses [History of the Discovery and Conquest of India by the Portuguese]. Ed. M. Lopes de Almeida. 2 vols. Porto, Portugal: Lello, 1979.

References

Bell, Aubrey F.G. *Portuguese Literature.* Oxford: Clarendon Press, 1922, 190–191.

Lopez, Roberto Sabatino (1910–1986)

Italian-born American medieval and renaissance economic historian. Lopez was born in Genoa and studied medieval history at the University of Milan, where he received the doctorate in letters in 1932. After having taught in Italy, he moved to America in 1939 and entered the graduate school of the University of Wisconsin, from which he received a Ph.D. in 1942. His teaching career in America started as lecturer at Brooklyn College in 1943 and ended as Sterling professor of history at Yale University. After having served at Yale from 1946 to 1981, he died in New Haven, Connecticut. His publications include sixteen books and more than one hundred articles on a variety of topics in medieval Europe, especially the Genoese economy and Mediterranean trade. His major contribution was the thesis of "the commercial revolution of the Middle Ages." Lopez rejected older notions of the economic stagnation before the Renaissance and successfully demonstrated that Europe had experienced a great commercial expansion during the period between 950 and 1350.

Hiroshi Takayama

Texts

The Birth of Europe. London: Phoenix House, 1967.

The Commercial Revolution of the Middle Ages, 950–1350. Revised ed. New York: Cambridge University Press, 1975.

The Shape of Medieval Monetary History. London: Variorum, 1986.

The Three Ages of the Italian Renaissance. Charlottesville: University Press of Virginia, 1970.

References

Lewis, Archibald R., Jaroslav Pelikan, and David Herlihy. "Robert Sabatino Lopez." *Speculum* 63 (1988): 763–765.

Munro, John H. "Economic Depression and the Arts in the Fifteenth-Century Low Countries." *Renaissance and Reformation* 7 (1983): 235–250.

Lorenz, Ottokar (1832–1904)

Austrian historian, politician, and publicist. Lorenz was born in Bohemia and taught at the university of Vienna from 1860 to 1885, and then at Jena until his death. Although he was a great admirer of Ranke, he scorned the belief in historical objectivity and disapproved of the trend toward specialization of the discipline. Lorenz was initially an opponent of the German historical school and a supporter of the principles of a multinational Austrian state as a counterweight to Prussian hegemony in central Europe. His first major work, *Deutsche Geschichte im dreizehnten und vierzehnten Jahrhundert* [German History in the Thirteenth and Fourteenth Centuries] (1863–1867) was directed not only against the principles of the nation-state, but also against the *"kleindeutsch"* school of historical thought, which advocated Prussian domination of Germany. Shortly after the establishment of the Austro-Hungarian dual monarchy, his passion for Austria waned. In light of the weakened Austrian central state, he began to view the "small-German" Prussian program as the best possible, given the changed political circumstances.

John R. Hinde

Texts

Deutsche Geschichte im dreizehnten und vierzehnten Jahrhundert. 2 vols. Vienna: W. Braunmuller, 1863–1867.
Kaiser Wilhelm und die Begrundung des Reiches [Kaiser Wilhelm and the Foundation of the Empire]. Jena, Germany: G. Fischer, 1902.

References

Srbik, Heinrich Ritter von. *Geist und Geschichte* [Mind and History]. 2 Vols. Munich: F. Bruckmann, 1950.

Lot, Ferdinand (1866–1952)

French historian and archivist. Lot was born in suburban Paris and later studied at the École des Chartes. In 1890, he found work at the Bibliothèque de l'Arsenal and then as the assistant librarian at the University of Paris (1893). From 1900, Lot taught at the École Pratique des Hautes Études. He received his doctorate at Nancy in 1903, and from 1909 lectured at the Sorbonne, becoming its professor of medieval history in 1920. He was elected to the Académie des Inscriptions et Belles-Lettres in 1924 and retired in 1939, continuing his research until his death. Lot's work on the late Carolingian kings began under the tutelage of Alfred Giry (d.1899). With his own student, Louis Halphen (d.1950), Lot wrote the first volume of *Le règne de Charles le Chauve* [The Reign of Charles the Bald] (1909), and later directed the series *Diplomata Karolinorum* [Carolingian Diplomatic Documents] (1936–1940). Lot's interest in the origins of France led him to late antique as well as early British sources. His *La fin du monde antique et le début du Moyen Age* [The End of the Ancient World and the Beginnings of the Middle Ages] (1928) challenged the Pirenne thesis, suggesting a more subtle process of economic stagnation. Texts such as his *Les invasions germaniques* [The Germanic Invasions] (1935) popularized medieval history among a more general audience.

Bonnie Effros

See also PIRENNE, HENRI.

Texts

Ed. *Diplomata Karolinorum.* 7 vols. Paris: H. Didier, 1936–1940.
The End of the Ancient World and the Beginnings of the Middle Ages. Trans. Philip and Mariette Leon. New York: Harper, 1961.
Les invasions germaniques. Paris: Payot, 1945.
Recherches sur la population et la superficie des cités remontant à la periode gallo-romaine [Research on the Population and Topography of Cities from the Gallo-Roman Epoch]. 3 vols. Paris: Librairie Honoré Champion, 1969–1970.
and Louis Halphen. *Le règne de Charles le Chauve.* Geneva: Slatkine Reprints, 1975.

References

Merlin, Alfred. *Notice sur la vie et les travaux de M. Ferdinand Lot.* Paris: Académie des Inscriptions et Belles-Lettres, 1956.
Perrin, Charles-Edmond. *Un historien français Ferdinand Lot 1866–1952.* Travaux d'histoire éthico-politique, vol. 15. Geneva: Librairie Droz, 1968.
Recueil des travaux historiques de Ferdinand Lot [Collected Historical Works of Ferdinand Lot]. 3 vols. Geneva: Librairie Droz, 1908–1973.

Lovejoy, Arthur Oncken (1873–1962)

American philosopher and historian. Born in Berlin, Germany, Lovejoy completed his B.A. at the University of California at Berkeley and his M.A. at Harvard University by 1897. After further study and a series of short academic appointments in philosophy, he moved to the Johns Hopkins

University in 1910, where he taught until his retirement in 1938. He remained in Baltimore and continued as an active scholar until his death. Lovejoy began the modern study of the history of ideas as a distinct subdiscipline of history—the pursuit of relatively few, but protean, "unit-ideas" that in various combinations and at different times form philosophical systems and schools of thought. It was especially important, in his view, to expose the semantic "confusions" and authorial "waverings" in the use of unit-ideas and to explain the "pathos," or affective appeal, of certain combinations of ideas. In his masterpiece, *The Great Chain of Being* (1936), Lovejoy traced the "chain of being"—together with its core ideas of plenitude, gradation, and continuity—from its Platonic roots to its decline early in the nineteenth century. Lovejoy demonstrated in *Essays in the History of Ideas* (1948) how changing uses of "pride," "nature," "perfectibility," and other unit-ideas contributed to the onset of romanticism. Lovejoy consistently advocated scholarly collaboration across disciplinary boundaries and in 1940 was a founder of the *Journal of the History of Ideas,* which remains the most important vehicle for articles in intellectual history today, although much of it in forms that Lovejoy himself could not possibly have anticipated.

Paul A. Fideler

Texts

Essays in the History of Ideas. Baltimore: Johns Hopkins University Press, 1948.

The Great Chain of Being: A Study of the History of an Idea. Cambridge, MA: Harvard University Press, 1936.

And George Boas. *Primitivism and Related Ideas in Antiquity.* Baltimore, MD: Johns Hopkins University Press, 1935.

Reflections on Human Nature. Baltimore, MD: Johns Hopkins University Press, 1961.

The Revolt against Dualism: An Inquiry Concerning the Existence of Ideas. LaSalle, IL: Open Court Publishing Company, 1930.

The Thirteen Pragmatisms and Other Essays. Baltimore, MD: Johns Hopkins University Press, 1963.

References

Kelley, Donald R., ed. *The History of Ideas: Canon and Variations.* Rochester, NY: Rochester University Press, 1990.

Wilson, Daniel J. *Arthur O. Lovejoy: An Annotated Bibliography.* New York: Garland, 1982.

———. *Arthur O. Lovejoy and the Quest for Intelligibility.* Chapel Hill: University of North Carolina Press, 1980.

Special issue on Lovejoy and his work. *Journal of the History of Ideas* 48, no. 2 (April–June 1987).

Luo Zhenyu [Lo Chen-yü] (1866–1940)

Chinese archaeologist and historian. The son of a merchant, Luo Zhenyu was born in Huaian in Jiangsu province. Assigned to the Board of Education in 1905, he began a multifaceted career in the collection, compilation, and publication of ancient Chinese texts. As a Manchu loyalist, after the Revolution of 1911 Luo went to Japan where he completed many of his works on ancient inscriptions. Luo's loyalty to the Manchus convinced him to help create Manchukuo, a puppet regime established by the Japanese in 1932. He served the deposed emperor Puyi until he retired in 1938, when he continued his pursuit of China's antiquities. In addition to his various fragments of research, his best works consisted of archaeological and historical studies. Luo's most important contributions included several edited collections of ancient inscriptions and graphs, which can be divided into six groups: Shang oracle inscriptions; Han and Jin wooden documents; Dunhuang manuscripts; Qing imperial archives; stone and bronze inscriptions; and Chinese paleography. Luo was among the most productive scholars in modern China; no student of ancient China can fail to derive great advantage from his works.

Shao Dongfang

Texts

Luo Xuetang xiansheng quanji [Complete Works of Luo Zhenyu]. Seventh series. Taibei: Wenhuan chuban gongsi, 1968–1970 (series 1–3); Taibei: Dadong shuju, 1972, 1973, 1976 (series 4–7).

References

Bonner, Joey. *Wang Kuo-wei: An Intellectual Biography.* Cambridge, MA: Harvard University Press, 1986.

Luo Jizu. *Yongfeng xiangren xingnianlu* [A Chronological Biography of Luo Zhenyu]. Nanjing: Jiangsu renmin chubanshe, 1980.

Lussan, Marguerite de (1682–1758)

Translator, novelist, and historian. An illegitimate daughter of Thomas of Savoy, Marguerite was considered both compassionate and mannish, charming aristocrats despite her reputation for irritability and gluttony; she died from acute gastritis. Urged by Huet, Bishop of Avranches, to study religion, Lussan later turned to writing. Her first novel was dedicated to Langlade de la Serre, playwright, adviser, lover, and her permanent guest. Her most popular work was *Anecdotes de la cour de Philippe-August* [Anecdotes from the Court of Philip Augustus], consisting of royal "histories" furnished with trivialities. Her *Annales galantes de la cour de Henri II* [Love Stories from the Court of Henry II] involved brother–sister love. Prudhomme recognized Lussan's credentials as a historian, but also noted her carelessness. On the other hand, some of her works were historically more solid. Her *Vie de Louis Balbe-Berton de Crillon* [Life of Crillon], for example, was researched using archival sources in Sardinia, Quiers, and Turin.In this work Lussan attributed Henry of Navarre's victory over the League to personality, polemic, and politics.

Barbara Sher Tinsley

Texts

Annales galantes de la cour de Henri II.
Amsterdam: J. Desbordes, 1749.
Anecdotes de la cour de Philippe-August. 3 vols.
Amsterdam: Pauli, 1733.

Anecdotes de la cour de François Ier [Anecdotes of the Court of Francis I]. 3 vols. London: Jean Nours, 1748.
Marie d'Angleterre [Mary Tudor (daughter of Henry VII and briefly wife, 1514–1515, to Louis XII of France)]. Amsterdam: J. Desbordes, 1749.
Vie de Louis Balbe-Berton de Crillon, surnomme le Brave. Paris: Pissot, 1758.

References

Haac, Oscar A. "Un chef-d'oeuvre du roman personnel: Le récit de Calemane dans *L'Histoire de la Comtesse de Gondez* de Lussan [A Masterpiece of the Intimate Novel: The Narrative of Calemane in *The History of the Countess of Gondez* of Lussan]." *Saggi e ricerche di letteratura francese* 9 (1968): 186–206.
Rustin, J. "Amour, magie et vertu, 'Les Veillées de Thessalie' de Lussan [Love, Magic and Virtue, 'The *Thessalian Evenings* of Lussan']." *Bulletin de la Faculté des Lettres, Strasbourg* 41 (1962–63): 287–302.

L

M

Ma Duanlin [Ma Tuan-lin] (1254–1325)

Chinese historian. Born in Jiangxi province, Ma Duanlin's career as an official was cut short by the Mongol conquest of China in 1276. Only late in his life did he reemerge in public office as a director of studies. Loyal to the defunct Song dynasty, he redirected his lifelong passion into the writing of *Wenxian tongkao* [General Study of the Literary Remains], China's best-known institutional history. Ma Duanlin intended his history to serve as a moral guide to statecraft; it is divided into twenty-four thematic examinations of Chinese history, each richly documented and critically examined up to the author's period. In seeking to understand the changes, flaws, and strengths of the past and the present Mongol age, Ma Duanlin was assisted by his father Ma Tingluan, who had accumulated an intimate and profound knowledge of the functions and developments of government during his long tenure as chief minister. Ma's analyses extended beyond institutions (for example, taxation, government, and monopolies) into other topics such as astronomy and geography. The section on foreign countries attracted the most attention from late-nineteenth-century Western sinologists, who translated some chapters. Three successive sequels to *Wenxian tongkao* by later historians update the coverage to 1370, 1747, and 1921, respectively.

Jennifer W. Jay

Texts

Wenxian tongkao [General Study of the Literary Remains]. Shanghai: Shangwu yinshu guan, 1936.
Ethnographie des Peuples Etrangers à la Chine: Ouvrage Composé au XVIII siècle de Notre Ere, par Ma Touan-lin [The Ethnography of Foreign Peoples in China: A Work Composed in the Eighteenth [*sic*] Century of Our Era, by Ma Duanlin]. Trans. d'Hervey Saint-Denys (into French). Geneva: H. Georg, 1876–1883.
"Problemes Géographiques: Les Peuples Etrangers chez les Historiens Chinois." Trans. G. Schlegel. *T'oung Pao* 3 (1892); 4 (1893); 10 (1899).

References

Chan, Hok-lam. "'Comprehensiveness' (T'ung) and 'Change' in Ma Tuan-lin's Historical Thought." In *Yuan Thought: Chinese Thought and Religion under the Mongols,* ed. Hok-lam Chan et al. New York: Columbia University Press, 1982, 27–87.

Ma Huan (fl. 1413–1451)

Chinese Muslim interpreter and author who, over the period 1413–1433, accompanied Chinese naval forces on expeditions that ventured as far as the Arabian peninsula. His prominence derives from authorship of the *Ying-yai Sheng-lan* [Wonderful Views of the Ocean's Shores], which comprises accounts of the various places visited on these voyages. Little is known of Ma Huan's early years, but by 1413 he was obviously sufficiently well-versed in Arabic to be appointed as an interpreter/translator on a naval expedition led by the eunuch admiral Zheng He, which was to take him as far as Hormuz. His notes from this voyages were combined with observations from two subsequent expeditions in which he participated to form the basis of *Ying-yai Sheng-lan*. The latest recorded date we have for Ma Huan is 1451, which is also the likely date of the first printing of his work. While the Chinese literati have never considered *Ying-yai Sheng-lan* to be a great literary work, over the last century its importance as one of the few detailed accounts of the port polities of Southeast, South, and West Asia during the early fifteenth century has been increasingly recognized by scholars. The various extant versions of the work were collated in an annotated edition by Feng Cheng-jun in 1935, and that text has recently been made more widely available through an extensively annotated English translation by J.V.G. Mills.

Geoff Wade

Texts

Ma Huan: Ying-yai Sheng-lan: The Overall Survey of the Ocean's Shores [1433]. Ed. Feng Cheng-jun [Feng Ch'eng-Chun]; trans. J.V.G. Mills. Cambridge, Eng.: Cambridge University Press, 1970.

References

Duyvendak, J.J.L. *Ma Huan Re-examined.* Amsterdam: Noord-Hollandsche uitgeversmaatschappij, 1933.

Wang Gungwu. "Ma Huan." In *Dictionary of Ming Biography 1368–1644,* ed. L. Carrington Goodrich and Fang Chaoying. New York: Columbia University Press, 1976, 1026–1027.

Ma Su (1621–1673)

Scholar of Chinese history of the ancient pre-Han period. Ma received his *jinshi* (doctoral) degree in 1659. As a young man, he compiled the *Zuozhuan shiwen,* a detailed study of early China in twelve chapters plus an eight-chapter addendum, the material of which was ordered in chronological fashion. He continued his studies in this field, finally producing his *I-shih* in 1658, a remarkable 160-chapter encyclopedic history from the earliest times to the fall of the Qin dynasty. He divided the work into five section: Antiquity, the first Three Dynasties, the Spring and Autumn period, the Warring States era, and Addendum *(Wailu).* The latter consisted of treatises including those on geography, economy, and official organizations and genealogical charts, tables, and diagrams to assist in the interpretations of the previous sections. Ma's employment of a wide selection of source material, in poems from the classic *Shijing,* in his discussion of Confucian and other philosophic schools, and in his treatment of rituals, institutions, and bureaucracy, make the *I shih* an extraordinarily rich work on the classical period of Chinese history and earned him the eponym "Ma Sandai" or "Three Dynasties Ma."

Carney T. Fisher

Texts

I shih. 2 vols. Yangzhou shi: Jiangsu Guangling guji ke yinshe, 1990.

References

Hummel, Arthur, ed. *Eminent Chinese of the Ch'ing Period (1644–1912).* New York: Paragon Book Gallery, 1970.

Ma Tuan-lin

See MA DUANLIN.

Mabillon, Jean (1632–1707)

French historian of Benedictine monasticism and founder of diplomatic. Mabillon was born in Champagne and joined the monastic order of the Congregation of Saint-Maur at Rheims in 1654. Summoned to Paris in 1664 to assist Luc d'Achery, the librarian of Saint-Germain-des-Prés, he collaborated with Maurist scholars editing manuscripts and writing Benedictine history. In recognition of his contributions to the analysis of medieval documents, Mabillon was invited to join the Académie Royale des Médailles et des Inscriptions in 1701. He died at Saint-Germain-des-Prés. Mabillon's achievements followed extensive travels in western Europe for manuscripts integral to the Maurist edition of the works of St. Bernard (1667), *Acta Sanctorum Ordinis Sancti Benedicti* [Deeds of the Saints of the Order of St. Benedict] (1668–1701), *Vetera Analecta* [Ancient Analects] (1675–1685), and *Annales Ordinis Sancti Benedicti* [Annals of the Order of St. Benedict] (1703–1739). His most influential work was *De re diplomatica* [Regarding Diplomatic] (1681), a methodological treatise on the authentication of medieval charters. Defending Maurist scholarship against Protestant and Jesuit criticism, Mabillon exonerated the reputation of Benedictine archives and methodology.

Bonnie Effros

See also BOLLANDISTS AND MAURISTS.

Texts

Ed. *Acta Sanctorum Ordinis Sancti Benedicti.* 9 vols. Paris: Louis Billaine, 1668–1701.

Annales Ordinis Sancti Benedicti. 6 vols. Lucca, Italy: L. Venturini, 1739–1745.

De re diplomatica Libri VI. Rome: Bibliopola, 1965.

Ed. *Life and Works of Saint Bernard, Abbot of Clairvaux.* Trans. Samuel J. Eales. 4 vols. London: J. Hodges, 1889–1896.

And Michel Germain. *Museum Italicum*. 2 vols. Rome: Bibliopola, 1971.

Ed. *Vetera Analecta*. 4 vols. Farnborough, Eng.: Gregg, 1967.

References

Barret-Kriegel, Blandine. *Jean Mabillon*. Paris: Presses universitaires de France, 1988.

Knowles, David. *Great Historical Enterprises: Problems in Monastic History*. London: Thomas Nelson and Sons Ltd., 1963.

Tassin, René-Prosper. *Histoire littéraire de la Congrégation de Saint-Maur* [Literary History of the Congregation of Saint-Maur]. Paris: Chez Humblot, Libraire, 1770.

Macaulay, Catharine Sawbridge (1731–1791)

English historian and radical. Macaulay (the surname is that of her first husband) was born in Wye, Kent, and educated privately, developing an early passion for Greek and Roman history. She wrote against Hobbes and Burke, campaigned on behalf of authorial copyright and American rebellion, and became the first English radical to visit America after its independence in 1784. She died at Binfield, Berkshire. The first published English woman historian, Macaulay's reputation rests on her *History of England* (1763–1783), which covered the period from 1603 to the Glorious Revolution. She conceived the *History* as a successor to Paul de Rapin-Thoyras's *Histoire d'Angleterre*, partly as a Whig counterblast to David Hume's *History of England*. She was the first historian to make extensive use of the English pamphlet literature of the mid-seventeenth century. Her passionate republicanism shaped every aspect of the *History*, including its sympathy for the Long Parliament, the Commonwealth, and the execution of King Charles I, as well as its hostility toward Oliver Cromwell. She interrupted composition of her major work to write the epistolary *History of England from the Revolution to the Present Time* (1778), of which she only completed one volume, ending in 1733.

David Armitage

Texts

History of England from the Accession of James I to That of the Brunswick Line. 8 vols. London: J. Nourse, 1763–1783.

History of England from the Revolution to the Present Time, in a Series of Letters to the Reverend Doctor Wilson. Bath: R. Cruttwell, 1778.

References

Hill, Bridget. *The Republican Virago: The Life and Times of Catharine Macaulay, Historian*. Oxford: Oxford University Press, 1992.

Minuti, Rolando. "Il problema storico della libertà inglese nella cultura radicale dell'età di Giorgio III: Catharine Macaulay e la Rivoluzione puritana [The Historical Problem of English Liberty in Radical Culture in the Time of George III: Catharine Macaulay and the Puritan Revolution]." *Rivista Storica Italiana* 98 (1986): 793–860.

Macaulay, Thomas Babington (1800–1859)

English historian, essayist, and politician. Macaulay was born in Leicestershire in 1800 into a prosperous and literary family and began his studies at Trinity College, Cambridge, in 1818; by the mid-1820s, Macaulay had been admitted to the practice of law and began to publish essays in prominent journals such as the *Edinburgh Review* on topics such as the character and thought of Francis Bacon, poetry, philosophy, and various historical episodes. In 1830 he entered the House of Commons and soon found himself involved in the debates leading up to the passage of the Reform Act of 1832. Between 1834 and 1838 Macaulay lived in India where he served on the Supreme Council of India; returning to London in 1838, he again took a seat in Parliament. During the 1840s Macaulay expended additional efforts on his literary projects, such as his *Lays of Ancient Rome* (1842). In 1850, owing to health problems, Macaulay withdrew from politics and dedicated himself to writing. He died in 1859. Macaulay's reputation as the premier narrative English historian of the century and as the preeminent advocate of the "Whig Interpretation of History" is based on his *History of England from the Accession of James II*. He intended the *History* to cover the period from 1688 to 1820, but by the time of his death, his five-volume work had reached only 1702. Macaulay argued that the modern history of England was the record of human progress, and that the realignment of the nation's political processes reflected values that were inherent in the English character. Macaulay's *History* was read widely throughout the English-speaking world and remains a classic of English historical writing.

William T. Walker

Texts

The Complete Works of Lord Macaulay. Ed. W.A. Madden. 12 vols. New York: AMS Press, 1980.

M

History of England from the Accession of James II. Ed. C.H. Firth. 6 vols. New York: AMS Press, 1968.

References

Clive, John. *Macaulay: The Shaping of the Historian.* New York: Knopf, 1974.

Millgate, Jane. *Macaulay.* London: Routledge, 1973.

Burrow, J.W. *A Liberal Descent: Victorian Historians and the English Past.* Cambridge, Eng.: Cambridge University Press, 1981.

Machiavelli, Niccolò (1469–1527)

Renaissance political thinker and historian. Machiavelli was born in Florence into a moderately prosperous family. He received a conventional schooling at first but soon studied Latin with a teacher who was both a priest and a lawyer, in whose company he read Cicero, Boethius, and many other ancient authors. He was only nine years old when the Pazzi conspiracy to assassinate Lorenzo de' Medici, the de facto ruler of Florence, came close to succeeding (an act that would feature prominently in his later history of Florence). His father's indebtedness forced him to cut short his legal training, but did not inhibit his progress through the ranks of Florentine civil servants. His official career culminated in his appointment as secretary and second chancellor to the Florentine republic. This occurred in the aftermath of the Medici expulsion of 1494 and in the aftermath of the fall of Savonarola, during a time of great instability in Florence and Italy generally. In his official role he undertook missions to Louis XII of France and Emperor Maximilian I and accompanied the warrior-pope Julius II in 1503 on his campaigns. He also organized the military force that captured Florence's long-time satellite, Pisa, in 1509. After the defeat of Florentine forces at Prato in 1512, the Medici were restored to power. Machiavelli lost his position and after being briefly imprisoned and tortured, retired to his farm near San Casciano. He spent the remainder of his life in writing, his aspirations to return to power proving unsuccessful until the Medici were once again expelled in 1527. He died later that year following a brief return to public life.

Machiavelli's contribution to historical thought came in two forms. The first comprises his most famous works. *Il Principe* [The Prince] (1516) was a guidebook for would-be rulers, widely read and generally excoriated for its apparent encouragement of duplicity and naked force, but revered in political theory since the later seventeenth century. The *Discorsi* [Discourses on the First Decade of Livy] (1513–1521), which Machiavelli began before writing *Il Principe* but took several years to complete, was a more measured and detailed consideration of the stability of different types of government (more favorable than *Il Principe* to republican institutions), which took the form of an extended commentary on Livy and which was shaped by a reading of the ancient historian of Rome, Polybius. Throughout both these works, Machiavelli drew heavily on historical example, both ancient and recent, in advancing his political theories. Both works are concerned with matters of which he had direct experience: the instability of all governments including the changeable Florentine regime; the need for citizen armies in place of the mercenary forces traditionally relied upon by many city-states; the conduct of diplomacy; and the successful, albeit ruthless, exercise of power. His tendency to draw conclusions from widely disparate historical examples was criticized by his younger contemporary and fellow Florentine historian, Francesco Guicciardini, who was more skeptical of the applicability of cases drawn from the past and their usefulness as a guide to action in the present.

Although not himself a humanist (in the sense of a writer in Latin on the subject of antiquity and its texts), his exposure to the ancients, and to the humanist values that had dominated Florentine intellectual life for over a century, gave him a profound interest in and sense of history. He wrote—in the vernacular Tuscan of his day, rather than in the more highly favored Neo-Ciceronian Latin favored by other humanist historians of his era—a full-length work of narrative history of Florence, the *Istorie Fiorentine*, ending with the death of Lorenzo de' Medici in 1492, the event that signaled the end of several decades of political stability in Florence. This was commissioned by Cardinal Giulio de' Medici in 1520 and Machiavelli, eager to restore his fortunes by ingratiating himself with the restored Medici government, completed it in 1525; it was first published, at Florence and Rome, in 1532. The *History* recounts the story of Florence's rise to power from ancient Roman times, but concentrates on the fifteenth century. Because Machiavelli, as a former diplomat, was preoccupied with foreign affairs, much non-Florentine history is also covered in the book. The last quarter of the work is taken up with the career of Lorenzo, and includes one of Machiavelli's most famous set pieces, Lorenzo's speech after the suppression of the Pazzi conspiracy, a typical exercise in humanist oratory reminiscent of the speech to Athens of Thucydides' Pericles. Although not regarded as a reliable authority for late-fifteenth-century politics, the *History* is nonetheless an important work, an early attempt to integrate the lessons of politics into a vision of the civic and peninsular past written for a wider audience than the Latin histories of the fifteenth century.

D.R. Woolf

Texts

History of Florence and of the Affairs of Italy from the Earliest Times to the Death of Lorenzo the Magnificent. Introduction by Felix Gilbert. New York: Harper, 1960.

Opere [Works]. Ed. Mario Bonfantini. Milan: Ricciardi: 1954.

The Portable Machiavelli. Ed. and trans. Peter Bondanella and Mark Musa. New York: Viking, 1979.

References

de Grazia, Sebastian. *Machiavelli in Hell.* Princeton, NJ: Princeton University Press, 1989.

Gilbert, Felix. *Machiavelli and Guicciardini: Politics and History in Sixteenth-Century Florence.* Princeton, NJ: Princeton University Press, 1965.

Hulliung, Mark. *Citizen Machiavelli.* Princeton, NJ: Princeton University Press, 1983.

Ridolfi, Roberto. *The Life of Niccolò Machiavelli.* Trans. Cecil Grayson. Chicago: University of Chicago Press, 1963.

Mackintosh, Sir James (1765–1832)

British historian and essayist. Mackintosh was born in the county of Inverness, Scotland. He took a medical degree at the University of Edinburgh in 1787 and soon thereafter studied law in London. His dominant interests, however, were literature, philosophy, and politics. In 1812 he was elected a member of Parliament for the Scottish county of Nairn and was returned to a new Parliament in 1819 for Knaresborough, which he represented up to the time of his death. A reformer, he advocated broadening the representation of Parliament and reducing drastically the excessively large number of crimes that were punishable by death. An early critic of Edmund Burke, Mackintosh's lengthy pamphlet *Vindiciae Gallicae* (1791) was a defense of the French Revolution. His inclination for and knowledge of English history led in late life to two works. *The History of England* (1830–1831) had reached the fourteenth year of Queen Elizabeth's

reign (1572), when Mackintosh died in London, and was continued by W. Wallace; a complete edition was published in 1853; the work emphasized political and legal institutions, illustrating England's singular distinction in its advancement toward liberty. The work of a Whig apologist, Mackintosh's *History of the Revolution in England in 1688* examined the reign of James II and the causes of the Revolution; it had reached page 358 at Mackintosh's death and was completed, up to the settlement of the crown, by the editor (and was posthumously published in 1834). Mackintosh's valuable essays included such subjects as ethical philosophy, the rights and duties of nations, and contemporary European political developments.

Bernard Hirschhorn

Texts

The History of England: From the Earliest Times to the Final Establishment of the Reformation. Ed. R.J. Mackintosh. New ed. London: Longman et al., 1853.

History of the Revolution in England in 1688. London: Longman et al., 1834.

The Miscellaneous Works of the Right Honourable Sir James Mackintosh. London: Longman, Brown, Green, 1846.

References

Bulwer, Sir Henry Lytton. "Mackintosh: The Man of Promise." In his *Historical Characters.* Leipzig: Bernhard Tauchnitz, 1868.

Mackintosh, Robert James, ed. *Memoirs of the Life of the Right Honourable Sir James Mackintosh.* Boston: Little, Brown and Co., 1853.

Madox, Thomas (1666–1727)

English historian and antiquary. Neither a university graduate nor called to the bar, Madox nonetheless was among the foremost scholars of his age, a member of the Society of Antiquaries and, from 1714, Historiographer Royal. Under the patronage of Lord Somers he assembled *Formulare anglicanum* (1702) a collection of nearly eight hundred charters, carefully annotated, illustrating the development of English law from William I to Henry VIII. His second published work, *The History and Antiquities of the Exchequer of the Kings of England* (1711) pioneered the study of the exchequer, greatly illuminating medieval financial administration. Madox's rigorous standards of accuracy, attention to detail, and outstanding scholarly abilities render these works of enduring value almost three hundred years later. Two further works of his were published, one posthumously. Although *Firma Burgi* (1722) on medieval urban history, and *Baronia Anglica* (1736) on feudal tenures, are works of great erudition neither has remained as vital as his two previous publications. He was in the process of compiling a comprehensive history of medieval England when he died. The ninety-three volumes of transcripts which he compiled over his lifetime, now in the possession of the British Library, attest to the tremendous scope of his interests and industry.

Greg Bak

Texts

Firma Burgi, or An Historical Essay Concerning the Cities, Towns and Buroughs of England.. London: W. Bowyer, 1726.

Formulare anglicanum, or A Collection of Ancient Charters and Instruments of Divers Kinds. London: J. Tonson and R. Knaplock, 1702.

The History and Antiquities of the Exchequer of the Kings of England. Second ed. New York: A.M. Kelley, 1969.

References

Douglas, David C. *English Scholars 1660–1730.* Second ed. London: Eyre and Spottiswoode, 1951, chapter 11.

Maffei, Raffaele, called "Il Volterrano" (1456–1537)

Humanist and historian at the Roman curia. Maffei belonged to an important family of Volterra boasting a number of prominent curial officials and scholars. One brother, Antonio, was executed for his involvement in the 1478 Pazzi conspiracy against the Medici; another, Mario, became influential under the Medici popes. Maffei was the author of many learned works in the history of classical antiquity, ecclesiastical history, theology, and moral philosophy. A student of the Byzantine philosopher George of Trebizond, he translated a number of Greek authors, among them Procopius. Maffei's major work is the *Commentariorum urbanorum libri octo et triginta* [Thirty-Eight Books of Refined Commentaries], one of the earliest Renaissance encyclopedias. The work is divided into three parts, called, respectively, *geographia, anthropologia,* and *philologia.* Historical geography on the model of the earlier antiquary Flavio Biondo is included in the first section, lives of great men are found in the second, while the third comprises such diverse fields as biology, grammar, and law.

William J. Connell

Texts

Commentariorum urbanorum libri octo et triginta. Rome: Besicken, 1508.

References

D'Amico, John F. *Papal Humanism in Renaissance Rome: Humanists and Churchmen on the Eve of the Reformation.* Baltimore, MD: Johns Hopkins University Press, 1983.

Falconcini, Benedetto. *Vita del nobil' uomo e buon servo di Dio Raffaello Maffei, detto il Volterrano* [The Life of the Noble Man and Good Servant of God Raffaello Maffei, called Il Volterranno]. Rome: Komarek, 1722.

Paschini, Pio. "Una famiglia di curiali: I Maffei di Volterra [A Curial Family: The Maffei of Volterra]." *Rivista di storia dell chiesa in Italia* [Review of the History of the Church in Italy] 7 (1953): 337–376.

Magdeburg Centuriators

Sixteenth-century Lutheran historians and theologians, authors of the *Magdeburg Centuries* (1559–1574). The first history of the Christian church from a Protestant perspective, the *Ecclesiastical History . . . by Studious and Pious Men in the City of Magdeburg* takes its popular name from two features. In the mid-1500s, Magdeburg was a bastion of loyalty to principles associated with Luther, in particular the doctrine that no liturgical tradition has neutral value for salvation. In this position Magdeburg theologians opposed fellow Lutherans who allowed Catholic practices imposed by imperial decree. The leading Magdeburg evangelical was Matthias Flacius Illyricus (1520–1575), who advocated resistance to the Holy Roman Empire as strongly as he resisted theological compromise. The *Centuries* was written by a team of clergy under Flacius in this polemical spirit. As its name indicates, the work is organized into hundred-year periods, from the origins of Christianity to 1400. It chronicles the decline of the church under Roman Catholicism, and defends Protestantism by identifying it with the pure Christianity of antiquity. The accumulation of doctrines and practices over time is depicted as progressive corruption, and the historical record of the Roman church is regarded as self-serving fabrication. Dismissed by many for its polemics, the *Centuries* nevertheless continued to influence opinion and stimulate questions about objectivity in religious history; it was one of the most widely read ecclesiastical histories of the Reformation and Counter-Reformation eras.

Ralph Keen

Texts

*Ecclesiastica historia, integram ecclesiae Christi
ideam . . . complectens.* Basel: Johannes
Oporinus, 1559–1574.

References

Massner, Joachim. *Kirchliche Überlieferung und
Autorität im Flaciuskreis* [Ecclesiastical Tra-
dition and Authority in the Flacian Circle].
Berlin and Hamburg: Lutherisches
Verlagshaus, 1964.

Scheible, Heinz. *Die Entstehung der Magdeburger
Zenturien* [Origins of the Magdeburg Cen-
turies]. Gütersloh: Gerd Mohn, 1966.

Magnus, Olaus (1490–1557)

Swedish prelate and scholar. After university
studies between 1510 and 1517 at different
German universities, Olaus Magnus traveled to
Norrland and Norway. He embarked on a clerical career and was employed by King Gustav Vasa
at diplomatic missions and in trade negotiations.
As both a Swedish patriot and an opponent of the
Reformation, he came into conflict with the king,
and in 1527 Magnus went into exile together
with his brother, Johannes, archbishop of Uppsala,
with whom he traveled to Rome in 1541. Olaus
Magnus succeeded his brother in 1544 as titular
archbishop of Sweden, an office he was never actually able to take up in his homeland. He tried in
vain to interest the Pope and the Emperor Charles
V in winning Sweden back to the Roman Church.
To this end, also, he organized a printing house in
St. Bridget's House in Rome, and from 1550, he
published St. Bridget's legends, together with his
brother's and his own publications.

Magnus's chief work, *Historia de gentibus
septentrionalibus* [History of the Nordic People]
was published in 1555; not a narrative history,
it described manners, customs, and the natural
world. Passages on exotic elements such as curiosities and miracles are intermixed with descriptions of folklife, trade, and natural resources.
Throughout this work Magnus's patriotic and
Roman Catholic views are discernible, not least in
its thinly veiled attacks on the Lutherans. The
Historia is illustrated with woodcuts and written
in a simple metaphorical prose. These features,
combined with its content, made the work more
popular than his brother Johannes's *Historia de
omnibus Gothorum Svenonumque regibus* [History
of the Gothic and Swedish Kings] (1554). On the
other hand, Magnus did not write his book for a
popular readership but rather for the Swedish
aristocracy and the European elite. His work is a
fürstenspiegel—a mirror of princes—within which
can be found frequent and continuing allusions to
contemporary events in Gustav Vasa's Sweden.
Published in many editions and translated into
several languages, the *Historia,* together with the
historical work of Johannes Magnus, formed the
basis of European knowledge of Sweden for the
following century. It remains today an important
source for late-medieval and sixteenth-century
Swedish culture and history.

Jens E. Olesen

Texts

*A Compendious History of the Goths, Svvedes &
Vandals, and Other Northern Nations.* London: Humphrey Mosely et al., 1658. (A
seventeenth-century English translation.)

Historia de gentibus septentrionalibus. Rome: n.p.,
1555.

Historia om de nordiska folken. Ed. John Granlund.
4 vols. Stockholm: Gidlund, 1976. (A modern Swedish translation with commentaries).

References

Johannesson, Kurt. *The Renaissance of the Goths
in Sixteenth-Century Sweden: Johannes and
Olaus Magnus As Politicians and Historians.*
Ed. and trans. James Larson. Berkeley: University of California Press, 1991.

Mahan, Alfred Thayer (1840–1914)

American naval officer, theorist, and historian.
Mahan was born at West Point, where his father was a professor of engineering at the United
States Military Academy. Mahan graduated second in the Class of 1859 from the United States
Naval Academy. Following duty on land and sea,
including appointment as president of the Naval
War College, Mahan retired in 1896 from active
service. He died in Washington, DC. An arrogant
loner who had no love for the sea, Mahan found
solace through the study of history. His academic
preparation for assignment in 1885 to the faculty
of the newly established Naval War College provided the foundation for the thesis that would gain
Mahan worldwide recognition. His central idea,
that command of the sea and national power had
been inextricably intertwined throughout human
history, was presented in *The Influence of Sea Power
upon History* (1890) and fueled the growing flames
of imperialism and naval expansionism then en-
gulfing the Western world. He later became a
prolific writer of potboilers that proffered his

M

opinions on contemporary issues. Even so, he was elected president of the American Historical Association in 1902. Mahan then used this platform to espouse his support of subordinationist methodology for writing history. The war that erupted on the European continent only months before his death was in no small fashion a direct result of Mahan's theory.

William E. Fischer Jr.

Texts

The Influence of Sea Power upon History, 1600–1783. Boston: Little, Brown, 1890.

The Influence of Sea Power upon the French Revolution and Empire, 1793–1812. 2 vols. Boston: Little, Brown, 1892.

Letters and Papers of Alfred Thayer Mahan. 3 vols. Ed. Robert Seager II and Doris D. Maguire. Annapolis: Naval Institute Press, 1975.

Mahan on Naval Warfare: Selections from the Writing of Rear Admiral Alfred T. Mahan. Ed. Allan Westcott. Boston: Little, Brown, 1941.

References

Hattendorff, John B., and Lynn C. Hattendorff. *A Bibliography of the Works of Alfred Thayer Mahan.* Newport: Naval War College Press, 1986.

Seager, Robert II. "Biography of a Biographer: Alfred Thayer Mahan." In *Changing Interpretations and New Sources in Naval History,* Ed. Robert W. Love Jr. New York: Garland, 1980.

Maior, Petru (ca. 1761–1821)

Romanian historian. Maior was born in Târgu-Mureş in Transylvania, but the precise place and date of his birth remain matters of controversy. He completed a theological education at Rome (1774–1779) and Vienna (1779–1780) before returning to his native land where he became a teacher and a prominent member of the Greek-Catholic Church. In 1809 he settled at Buda where he lived until his death. Maior was the major representative in Transylvania of the late-eighteenth-century Romanian Enlightenment. His interests and knowledge were encyclopedic—he wrote or translated books in such diverse fields as religion, science, and the languages. He was also a staunch defender of Romanian interests. These views can be seen in his political memoirs from 1791, when he was an active contributor to politics.

In 1813 Maior published a history of the Romanian church which was clearly influenced by the Catholic Enlightenment and by Gallicanism. But his reputation as a historian rests on the *Istoria pentru începutul românilor în Dachia* [The History of the Origins of the Romanians in Dacia], which was first published at Buda in 1812. This book was a study of Romanian history from the Roman era up to the Magyar invasion of the tenth century; in it, Maior upholds the thesis of the "pure romanity" of Romanians and their uninterrupted continuity as the occupants of Transylvania. The *Istoria* proved an important contribution to the foundation of modern Romanian historiography, and also became a source of later nationalist ideology.

S. Lemny

Texts

Istoria pentru începutul românilor în Dacia. Ed. Florea Fugariu. 2 vols. Bucharest: Albatros, 1971.

References

Hitchins, Keith. *The Rumanian National Movement in Transylvania, 1780–1849.* Cambridge, MA: Harvard University Press, 1969, 86–94.

Maitland, Frederic William (1850–1906)

English legal historian. Maitland, arguably the finest English medieval historian ever to have lived, was born in Gloucestershire and was educated at Eton and Trinity College Cambridge, where he studied philosophy under Henry Sidgwick until 1872. At Lincoln's Inn (one of London's "inns" in which common lawyers were trained), he was called to the bar in 1876, where he spent eight unsatisfying years as a conveyancer. In 1885 he returned to Cambridge to take up a readership in English law, and three years later was elected Downing professor of the laws of England, a title he held for the rest of his life. In 1886, he was instrumental in founding the Selden Society (named for the great seventeenth-century historian and jurist, John Selden, 1584–1654), which was dedicated to publishing the records of English law; he became its first literary director. Maitland's health was increasingly poor, and he found it necessary to winter in the Canary Islands. In 1906, while sailing there, he contracted pneumonia and died at the age of 56.

Maitland's influence on both medieval and other venues of history has been tremendous. He was extremely prolific, writing eight major studies in twenty-two years, translating another, editing by himself or in collaboration at least seventeen works, and writing over sixty-nine articles. His work and method provided a standard and model for his successors to follow. Maitland was first and foremost accurate and open; not only did he take care to define with skill the dry technicalities of the medieval common law, but he never mistook speculation for fact. His method was often comparative and exhibited his wide range of knowledge. His focus in much of his work was on the words of his sources: their deeper meaning, their semantic development over time and in courts. But his view of language was not two-dimensional; the words he studied had been used by people to convey meaning to their contemporaries, and it was that three-dimensional vision that set him apart from other historians. His study of Law French (the language of medieval common law), which constituted the introduction to his first yearbooks (*Year Books 1 & 2 Edward II* [1903]), has been reprinted in the *Cambridge History of English Literature* and is still the place to begin work on that arcane dialect. His technical expertise and clarity of vision opened up for him the general concepts of the common law in different phases of its development. To Maitland, the common law was an ever-changing guide to its society. Escaping from the anachronism that beset lawyers' history, Maitland also avoided many of the dogmatisms that afflicted contemporary historical work. He displayed none of the nationalistic chauvinism toward foreigners ranging in his chosen English field; his correspondence is filled with encouragement to American and German legal historians at work on the English common law. Maitland's style, while idiosyncratic, allows the claim that he was the best English historical writer of the last two centuries. Working more from the level of the word, rather than the sentence or paragraph, Maitland filled his prose with metaphors and vivid illustrations not only to give life to the results of his analysis but also to imply its certainty. Finally, Maitland endures because of his tremendous foresight: historians who work on medieval England very often find that Maitland has preceded them not only in asking the right questions but in supplying the answers.

In his specific field of medieval English law, Maitland is responsible for much of the current understanding of the twelfth and thirteenth centuries. For example, it is to his *History of English Law* (1895), his most important work, that the acceptance of the twelfth and thirteenth centuries as the formative period of the common law can be traced. It was also Maitland's idea, spelled out in the *History* and elsewhere, to analyze medieval society in terms of its tenures. Perhaps his single most important thesis, argued in *Records of the Parliament Holden at Westminster* or *Memoranda de Parliamento* as it is generally known (1893), was that the medieval parliament was not a political assembly, but at its heart a court of law. Finally, Maitland invented the art of backtracking from Domesday Book in order to describe late Anglo-Saxon society (*Domesday Book and Beyond* [1887]). Because of his achievements, Maitland is considered by some to be the progenitor of modern historical method in the English-speaking world.

Bruce R. O'Brien

Texts

Collected Papers of Frederic William Maitland. Ed. H.A.L. Fisher. 3 vols. Cambridge, Eng.: Cambridge University Press, 1911.

The Constitutional History of England: A Course of Lectures. Holmes Beach, FL: Gaunt, 1993.

Domesday Book and Beyond: Three Essays in the Early History of England. Cambridge, Eng.: Cambridge University Press, 1987.

Frederic William Maitland, Historian: Selections from His Writings. Ed. R.L. Schuyler. Berkeley: University of California Press, 1960.

and F. Pollock. *History of English Law before the Time of Edward I.* Second ed. 2 vols. Cambridge, Eng.: Cambridge University Press, 1968.

Ed. *Records of the Parliament Holden at Westminster on the Twenty-Eight day of February, in the Thirty-Third Year of the Reign of King Edward the First* (A.D. 1305). Wiesbaden: Kraus Reprint, 1964.

References

Elton, G.R. *F. W. Maitland.* London: Weidenfeld and Nicolson, 1985.

Fifoot, C.H.S. *Frederic William Maitland.* Cambridge, MA: Harvard University Press, 1971.

Malay Historical Writing

Texts of a historical nature in traditional Malay prose and poetry, presumably written under courtly patronage from the seventeenth century onward and generally prior to the twentieth century. Given the existence of epigraphic material as well as textual and philological considerations, an older historiographical tradition can be assumed, but there is no immediate manuscript evidence available that predates the wider presence of Islam from the fifteenth century onward. Most of the presumably earlier texts known to us today are preserved in sometimes incomplete nineteenth-century library copies of manuscripts, and their true age and history of transmission are rarely clear. While the original authors of many historical texts are known, some authors remain as anonymous as most of the later scribes and copyists who molded their adaptations of existing texts to the specific needs and demands of their royal employers. There is a suggestion that Malay historiography is centered on the Malay peninsula and northern Sumatra, however, the texts known originate from all parts of the Malay world, that is, from those regions of Southeast Asia that are also referred to as Nusantara—the present Brunei Darussalam, various parts of western and eastern Indonesia, Malaysia, Patani in southern Thailand, parts of the southern Philippines and Singapore—which for centuries have recognized Malay as the language of Islamic teaching, diplomatics, international diplomacy, and commerce. Significant Malay historical texts have also been discovered recently in modern-day Sri Lanka.

Traditional Malay texts are usually written in Jawi, the Malay version of the Arabic script, and some of the historical texts can be found not only in several manuscript copies but also in more than one textual version. Many of these texts had no titles of their own, and if they did, they were frequently dismissed by Western scholars who gave them their own misleading labels. The distinction between prose *(hikayat)* and poetry *(syair)* is more a question of style than of substance, since any form of historical narrative can be expressed in either or both literary genre, as for example in the nineteenth-century *Silsilah Melayu dan Bugis dan segala keturunannya* [Genealogy of the Malay and Buginese and All Their Descendants] by Raja Ahmad and Raja Ali Haji bin Ahmad. A certain preference may be observed in the *syair* for the eulogy of individual rulers, such as the anonymous *Syair Sultan Maulana* [Poem for Sultan Maulana], which has been edited as *The Battle of Junk Ceylon,* or the description of contemporary events and single incidents, such as the *Syair Singapura terbakar* [Poem of Singapore Burning] by Abdullah Munsyi or the *Syair Perang Mengkasar* [Poem of the Macassar War] by Encik Amin. Nevertheless there were exceptions, such as the still unpublished anonymous epic *Syair Awang Semaun* [Poem of Awang Semaun], which relates the mythical and early history of the sultans of Brunei Darussalam.

To date, much of Malay historical writing remains in manuscript form and is not readily accessible. Only a few texts have been published and even fewer have been edited philologically in a critical manner. The accessible examples of Malay historiography differ so much in nature as to render dangerous any generalizations based on the partial evidence of single manuscripts or, more commonly, philologically unreliable editions.

Looking at the evidence of the manuscripts, a distinction can be made between texts with a clear concept of historiography and texts of a historical nature. The amount of Malay historical writing that meets the standards of historicity conventionally deemed appropriate by Western or Islamic scholarship is rather limited. The body of textual sources, which is full of historical material but whose conceptual terms of reference are less clear to us, is much larger.

A clear Islamic concept of historiography is most lucidly applied by two writers, the seventeenth-century Indian theologian and moralist Nuruddin ar-Raniri and the nineteenth-century Bugis-Malay theologian and scholar Raja Ali Haji who was a member of the elite that controlled the old sultanate of Johor. Court-centered as are all traditional Malay historians, they maintain nevertheless a separate identity and gain independent strength from their theological point of departure. Syeikh Nuruddin ar-Raniri composed a brief history of the north Sumatran state of Aceh with a particular emphasis on the reign of his royal patron, Sultan Iskandar Thani. This history is part of his much larger, encyclopedic mirror-of-conduct, the *Bustan'us-Salatin* [Garden of Kings]. Raja Ali Haji, who came from a family interested in letters, is best known for his *Tuhfat al-Nafis* [The Precious Gift]. Inspired by al-Ghazali, his is a history of various Malay sultanates and their involvement with the Buginese mercenaries and adventurers who by the nineteenth century had taken control of most Malay states. Unlike any Malay historian before him, Raja Ali Haji states explicitly that he bases his own synthesis on a range of other sources, most of which he identifies. Like other Malay writers, however, Raja Ali Haji did not see a historical text as something inviolate, and he encourages future readers to correct all his mistakes and add to the narrative where deemed necessary.

Other Malay historical writing tends to have a courtly and dynastic focus. It covers, albeit unevenly and rarely containing all the elements listed below, the history of almost all Malay states of the last few centuries. From their mythical and legendary origins in a distant past to the time of writing, it changes its emphasis with the narrative of more recent happenings of the seventeenth, eighteenth, and nineteenth centuries. A dynastic myth of origin, which traces the lineage of each ruling house to some shared suprahuman, heavenly origins located within the Malay cosmos, may feature a princess borne by foam or stepping out of a bamboo shoot and may well include Alexander the Great (Iskandar Zulkarnain), mythical founder of many dynasties in the Islamic world. Rum (the second Rome) or Constantinople, the See of the Caliph, may feature prominently as the place from which other ancestors hail. There may be lists of names of rulers; royal events, commands, utterances, journeys, and deeds may be mentioned without any further background information; persons may be referred to whose true identity, full name(s), and status remain unexplained. Many texts comprise folkloristic and legendary elements specific to traditions of a particular region and to local topography; some will deal extensively with the country's seemingly miraculous conversion to Islam, while others hardly mention it.

With rare exception, the historical writing is parochial; it is focused exclusively on the history of one state, which normally is synonymous with that of one particular royal house. Very few texts acknowledge the existence of other textual sources, although in many cases it is obvious that we are facing competing traditions. Few texts have a chronology, and most lack any dates at all. The incompleteness of some manuscripts aside, Malay historical writing is selective and seemingly eclectic, as if these texts were mere referential notes for those already in the know. To name but one example, hardly any text mentions the arrival and presence of the Europeans in the Malay world. Questions of causality do not feature explicitly in the historical writing, although these texts may serve as a mirror and reminder to further generations. The *Sulalat'us-Salatin* [Genealogy of Kings] by Tun Seri Lanang, a prime minister of Johor about whom nothing is known, may serve as the example here; it is not only the most famous of all Malay historical texts, but also one of the more problematic, since it has come to us in three main versions and many more manuscript copies. In a sense it displays all the strengths and weaknesses of Malay historical texts perceived by readers trained in a Western tradition. It is better known as *Sejarah Melayu* [Malay Annals], a misnomer allocated by Eurocentric scholarship. Despite the edition of two other manuscripts of the *Sulalat'us-Salatin,* it is usually quoted in its most hybrid form, which is also the one still used in Malaysian schools and combines several versions into one text.

Together with the anonymous *Hikayat Raja Pasai* [The Story of the King(s) of Pasai], Tun Seri Lanang's *Sulalat'us-Salatin* covers the history of the earliest Islamic Malay sultanates known from perhaps the thirteenth century onward. Its particular focus is the history of the golden age of Malay rule, the fifteenth century, and the most famous of all Malay sultanates, the sultanate of Melaka (Malacca). The narration, while seemingly relating the story of the reign of the sultans of Melaka until the conquest of Melaka by the Portuguese in 1511 and beyond, deals with a core issue of Malay statehood and historiography, the relationship between ruler and ruled. It favors the holders of the hereditary and powerful office of *bendahara,* or prime minister who, as the supreme representative of the people, was linked by marriage to the sultan's family and who by way of a sacred covenant, which went back to the mythical origins of Malay statehood, had surrendered the people to the sultan's sovereignty or *daulat,* the violation of which was vilified in the concept of treason or *durhaka.* The *Sulalat'us-Salatin* has almost all of the ingredients of a historical text listed above, but exceeds most other texts by the color, liveliness, and fullness of its narrative. Once said to date from the sixteenth century—the *Sulalat'us-Salatin,* like so many other texts, has no original colophon—it is now believed to have originated from a mere list of kings, as found elsewhere, and to have been composed in its short version only at the beginning of the seventeenth century; have been extended in the eighteenth century into a long version, linking the history of Melaka with that of its successor Johor; only to be enlarged again in the nineteenth century, when Siak made competing claims on the succession to the aura of the rulers of Melaka in a text also referred as the *Hikayat Siak* [Story of Siak] or *Hikayat Raja Akil* [Story of Raja Akil]. It seems therefore no coincidence that the eighteenth- and nineteenth-century Johor texts, known as the *Hikayat Negeri Johor* [Story of the State of Johor] and the *Peringatan Sejarah Negeri Johor* [Notes on the Story of the State of Johor]— yet another European title for a rather incomplete text whose bias is nevertheless obvious—take up their account literally at the point when the long version of the *Sulalat'us-Salatin* ends.

While at least part of the narrative of Tun Seri Lanang's *Sulalat'us-Salatin* finds support in other, local and nonindigenous sources, hardly anything can be verified by conventional means in the anonymous, so-called Kedah Annals or *Hikayat Merong Mahawangsa* [The Story of Merong Mahawangsa], whose original title was also *Sulalat'us-Salatin.* This text has fascinated researchers conditioned by Western models of thinking from the colonial administrator to the postcolonial receptionist. It is a composite text of three parts that purports to relate the origins and early history of Kedah in the northwest of the Malay peninsula, which for centuries had a close relationship with Siam, but which developed its ethnic and religious identity as a Malay state. The first part deals with the earliest history of Kedah, the colonization, cultivation, and civilization of a new territory and the acquisition of a citizenry by rulers who made the transformation from tribal, cannibalistic chiefs to Hindu and Buddhist kings. The text shows the symbiotic relationship with Siam, which is rationalized as the result of royal marriage. With the increasing despotism and irrationality of its ruler, the ground is laid for a change. The second part narrates the arrival and acceptance of Islam through the exemplary journey and teaching of one Syeikh Abdullah. This part is didactic, too, and in its detailed description of un-Islamic habits and customs and their revision by the Syeikh, it provides a vivid picture of the transformation of the country from Tantrism through Sufism into an Islamic state. All this is condensed into the reign of only a few rulers who really stand out among the others mentioned in these two parts of the text. The third and final part provides a list of kings updated into the nineteenth century when our known version was last copied. This is a complex text that is a significant witness of historical, cultural, social, and political processes of change.

E. Ulrich Kratz

See also BUGIS AND MAKASSAR (IN SULAWESI) HISTORIOGRAPHY; INDONESIAN HISTORIOGRAPHY.

Texts

Brown, C.C. "The Malay Annals Translated from Raffles MS 18." *Journal of the Malayan Branch of the Royal Asiatic Society* 25, nos. 2 and 3 (1953): 1–276

Entji' Amin. "Sja'ir Perang Mengkasar." Ed. and trans. C. Skinner. Verhandelingen van het KITLV, 40. The Hague: Martinus Nijhoff, 1963.

Hill, A.A. ed. *Hikayat Raja Pasai. Journal of the Malayan Branch Royal Asiatic Society* 33, no. 2 (1960): 1–215.

Ismail Hussein, and Kalthum Ibrahim. *Bibliografi sastera Melayu tradisi* [A Bibliography of Traditional Malay Literature]. Bangi: Perpustakaan Cabang IBKKM, 1990.

Kathirithamby-Wells, J., and Muhammad Yusoff Hashim, eds. *The Syair Mukomuko: Some Historical Aspects of a Nineteenth Century Sumatran Chronicle.* Malaysian Branch of the Royal Asiatic Society, Monograph 13. Kuala Lumpur: MBRAS, 1985.

Raja Ali Haji. *The Precious Gift.* Ed. and trans. Virginia Matheson and Barbara Watson Andaya. Kuala Lumpur: Oxford University Press, 1982.

Skinner, C., ed. *The Battle for Junk Ceylon.* Bibliotheca Indonesica, 25. Dordrecht: Foris Publications, 1985.

Teeuw, A., and D.K. Wyatt., eds. *Hikayat Patani—the story of Patani.* Bibliotheca Indonesica, 5. The Hague: Martinus Nijhoff, 1970.

References

Andaya, Barbara Watson. *Perak: The Abode of Grace.* Kuala Lumpur: Oxford University Press, 1979.

Andaya, Leonard Y. *The Kingdom of Johor 1641–1728.* Kuala Lumpur: Oxford University Press, 1975.

Bastin, J., and R. Roolvink. *Malayan and Indonesian Studies.* Oxford: Clarendon Press, 1964.

Bottoms, J.C. "Some Malay Historical Sources: A Bibliographical Note." In *An Introduction to Indonesian Historiography,* ed. Soedjatmoko et al. (eds.). Ithaca, NY: Cornell University Press, 1965, 156–193.

Brakel, L.F. "Dichtung und Wahrheit, Some Notes on the Development of the Study of Indonesian historiography." *Archipel* 20 (1980): 35–44.

Hall, D.G.E., ed. *Historians of Southeast Asia.* London: Oxford University Press, 1961.

Hussainmiya, B.A. *Lost Cousins: The Malays of Sri Lanka.* Bangi: Institut Bahasa, Kesusasteraan dan Kebudayaan Melayu, 1987.

Kratz, E.U. "The Concept of Durhaka in the Hikayat Hang Tuah." *South East Asia Research* 1 (1993): 68–97.

———. "The Editing of Malay Manuscripts and Textual Criticism." *Bijdragen tot de Taal-, Land- en Volkenkunde* 137, nos. 2 and 3 (1981): 229–243.

Maier, H.M.J. *In the Center of Authority: The Malay Hikayat Merong Mahawangsa.* Ithaca, NY: Southeast Asia Program, Cornell University, 1988.

Matheson, Virginia. "Questions Arising from a Nineteenth Century Riau Syair." *RIMA* 17 (1983): 1–61.

———. "The Writing of Malay History in Lingga and Riau." *Tenggara* 21/22 (1988): 19–27.

Muhammad Yusoff Hashim. *Pensejarahan Melayu* [Malay Historiography]. Kuala Lumpur: Dewan Bahasa dan Pustaka, 1992.

Roolvink, R. "The Variant Versions of the Malay Annals." *Bijdragen KITLV* 123, no. 3 (1967): 301–324.

Siti Hawa Haji Salleh. "Sastera Sejarah [Historical Literature]." In *Kesusasteraan Melayu tradisional* [Traditional Malay Literature], Zalila Sharif and Jamilah Haji Ahmad. Kuala Lumpur: Dewan Bahasa dan Pustaka, 1993, 280–347.

Mâle, Emile (1862–1954)

French art historian. Mâle completely transformed the studies of Christian iconography in France at the end of the nineteenth century and his insights in the field were of such significance that a chair at the Sorbonne was created for him in 1906. Until the publication of his doctoral dissertation, *Religious Art in France in the Thirteenth-Century* (1898), the "new" science of iconography, born in the polemical climate of the Counter Reformation, was in France the exclusive domain of members of the Catholic clergy and devout scholars. It still kept its normative orientation: setting the rules for religious representations and indicating doctrinal errors made by artists. For Mâle however, the figurative monuments of the Middle Ages in France were the sites of a specific expression of faith and religious feelings, and the intrinsic meaning of these monuments could not be disclosed without analyzing their particular historical, geographical, and intellectual backgrounds. His method was intuitive, demanding a thorough knowledge of artistic imagery and related written sources within a strictly delimited historical period. Together with his German contemporary, Aby Warburg, Mâle was among the first to establish vital links between artistic imagery, religion, myths, and poetry in their relations with the culture of a period.

Carol Doyon

Texts

Religious Art in France: The Late Middle Ages: A Study of Medieval Iconography and Its Sources. Princeton, NJ: Princeton University Press, 1986.

Religious Art in France: The Thirteenth Century: A Study of Medieval Iconography and Its Sources. Princeton: Princeton University Press, 1984.

Religious Art in France: The Twelfth Century: A Study of the Origins of Medieval Iconography. Princeton, NJ: Princeton University Press, 1978.

References

Grodecki, Louis. *Le Moyen-Age retrouvé: De l'an mil à l'an 1200* [The Middle Ages Recovered: 1000–1200]. Paris: Flammarion, 1986.

Schmitt, Jean-Claude. *La Raison des gestes dans l'Occident médiéval* [The Sense of Gesture in the Medieval West]. Paris: Gallimard, 1990.

Wirth, Jean. *L'Image médiévale, naissance et développements (VIᵉ-XVᵉ siècle)* [The Medieval Image, Its Birth and Development, Sixth to Fifteenth Centuries]. Paris: Méridiens Klincksieck, 1989.

Małowist, Marian (1909–1988)

Social and economic medieval and early modern European historian of Polish nationality. Małowist was born in Łódź and attended Warsaw University where he obtained a Ph.D. (1934) in economic history. After some years as a lecturer, he became a professor at the same institution in 1952. In 1958 he was appointed an editor of *Acta Poloniae Historica.* He was also an honorary member of the Polish Historical Society and the English Historical Association, as well as a member of the Hansischer Geschichtsverein, Commission d'Histoire Maritime. He investigated a vast array of economic and social problems and infused into his work an understanding of how the European trade affected north, south, east, and west differently. For example, he examined the unequal division of economic and social structures between northern and southern Europe; the economic role of East-Central Europe; and the early phase of colonialism from the African as well as European perspective. He also analyzed the economic histories of the Mongol Empire and Poland.

Jolanta T. Pękacz

Texts

Europa a Afryka Zachodnia w dobie wczesnej ekspansji kolonialnej [Europe and Western Africa during the Early Colonial Expansion]. Warsaw: PWN, 1969.

Croissance et régression en Europe XIV-XVII s [Growth and Recession in Sixteenth and Seventeenth Century Europe]. Paris: A. Colin, 1972.

M

Wschód a Zachód Europy w XIII-XVI wieku: Konfrontacja struktur społeczno- gospodarczych [The East and West of Europe in the Thirteenth to Sixteenth Centuries: The Confrontation of Social and Economic Structures]. Warsaw: PWN, 1973.

with Iza Bieżuńska-Małowist. *Niewolnictwo* [The Slavery]. Warsaw: Czytelnik, 1987.

References

Adamczyk, Jacek, and Krzysztof Kowalewski. "Bibliografia prac Profesora Mariana Małowist za lata 1971–1988 [A Bibliography of Małowist]." *Przegląd Historyczny* 80 (1989): 647–649.

Kąkolewski, Igor, and Krzysztof Olendzki. "Strefa południka 20: Mit czy rzeczywistość? Wokól problematyki badań porównawczych Mariana Małowista nad historią Europy środkowowschodniej [The Zone of the 20th Meridian: Myth or Reality? Problems Connected with the Comparative Research of Marian Małowist Relating to the History of East-Central Europe]." *Przegląd Historyczny* 81 (1990): 301–311.

Samsonowicz, Henryk. "Marian Małowist (19 XII 1909–30 VIII 1988)." *Kwartalnik Historyczny* 95 (1988): 297–300.

———. "Mariana Małowista pisarstwo historyczne [The Historiography of Marian Małowist]." *Historyka* 20 (1990): 51–56.

Mályusz, Elemér (1898–1989)

Hungarian historian. Mályusz studied in Budapest and worked from 1922 to 1930 as an archivist at the Hungarian National Archives. In 1930 he was appointed professor of medieval Hungarian history at Szeged, moving in 1934 to a professorial post in Budapest. He was obliged to retire in 1945 owing to his conservative political views, but between 1954 and 1968 was a member of the Institute of History in the Hungarian Academy of Sciences. Mályusz's research interests covered nearly the whole span of Hungarian history; his most outstanding works dealt with Hungarian social, political, and intellectual history during the fifteenth and eighteenth centuries. He initiated a number of research projects on the genesis and social transmission of Hungarian national identity and is regarded as among the founders of Hungarian ethnohistory.

Attila Pók

Texts

Egyházi társadalom a középkori Magyarországon [Church Society in Medieval Hungary]. Budapest: Akadémiai Kiadó, 1971.

Geschichte des ungarischen Volkstums von der Landnahme bis zum Ausgang des Mittelalters. Budapest: Pannonia Verlag, 1940.

Kaiser Sigismund in Ungarn 1387–1437 [Emperor Sigismund's Reign in Hungary 1387–1437]. Trans. A. Szmodits into German. Budapest: Akadémiai Kiadó, 1990.

Királyi kancellária és krónikaírás a középkori Magyarországon [The Royal Chancellery and the Writing of Chronicles in Medieval Hungary]. Budapest: Akadémiai Kiadó, 1973.

Sándor Lipót főherceg nádor iratai, (1790–1795) [The Papers of Palatine Archduke Alexander Leopold, 1790–1795]. Budapest: Magyar Történelmi Társulat, 1926.

A türelmi rendelet II: József és a magyar protestantizmus [The Tolerance Edict: Joseph II and Hungarian Protestantism]. Budapest: Magyar Protestáns Irodalmi Társaság, 1939.

Turóc megye kialakulása [The Formation of Turóc County]. Budapest: Budavár Tudományos Társaság, 1922.

Ed. *Zsigmond-kori oklevéltár* [Documents on the Sigismund-Period]. 2 vols. Budapest: Akadémiai Kiadó, 1951–1958.

References

Jakó, Zsigmond. "Mályusz Elemér." *Magyar Tudomány* [Hungarian Scholarship] 97 (1990): 100–102.

Soós, István. "Mályusz Elemér." *Levéltári Szemle* [Archival Review] 40 (1990): 106–108.

Mandrou, Robert Louis Réné (1921–1984)

French historian. Mandrou was born in Paris and educated at the universities of Lyon and Paris, where he also taught. Mandrou chaired studies of Histoire Sociale des Mentalités at the Sorbonne and served as secretary for the influential journal *Annales: Économies—Sociétés—Civilisations.* He died in Paris. Mandrou's work emphasized French intellectual history, one of his most reprinted texts being a collaboration with Georges Duby, *Histoire de la civilisation française: Moyen age—XVIe siècle* [History of French Civilization: Middle Ages—Sixteenth Century] (1958); the second volume of this work appeared in 1976 and dealt with the period from the seventeenth to the twentieth century. Mandrou's *Introduction to Modern*

France, 1500–1640: An Essay in Historical Psychology (1961) provided a synthesis of French cultural and spiritual life. Mandrou wanted to answer his mentor Lucien Febvre's appeal for historical studies of mentalities; in following this path, his *From Humanism to Science, 1480–1700* (1973) analyzed intellectuals' changing roles in history. Class conflict also became a frequent theme in Mandrou's works.

Elizabeth D. Schafer

Texts

De la culture populaire aux XVIIᵉ et XVIIIᵉ siècles: La Bibliothèque bleue de Troyes [Popular Culture in the Seventeenth and Eighteenth Centuries: The Bibliothèque bleue of Troyes]. Paris: Stock, 1964.

From Humanism to Science, 1480–1720. Atlantic Highlands, NJ: Humanities Press, 1979.

An Introduction to Modern France: An Essay in Historical Psychology. Trans. R.E. Hallmark. New York: Holmes and Meier, 1975.

Louis XIV en son temps, 1661–1715 [Louis XIV and His Times]. Second ed. Paris: Presses universitaires de France, 1973.

Magistrats et sorciers en France au XVIIᵉ siècle, une analyse de psychologie historique [Magistrates and Sorcerers in Seventeenth-Century France: An Analysis in Historical Psychology]. Paris: Plon, 1968.

References

Le Roy Ladurie, Emmanuel. *The Mind and Method of the Historian.* Trans. Siân Reynolds and Ben Reynolds. Chicago: University of Chicago Press, 1981.

Manetho (fl. 275 B.C.)

Egyptian priest. Manetho was a priest of the cult of Serapis at Heliopolis who possibly dedicated his work(s) to Ptolemy II. Although many works were attributed to him, only a history of Egypt *(Aegyptiaca)* and unnamed cultic writings referred to by Plutarch *(On Isis and Osiris)* are presently credited to him. Although the *Aegyptiaca* is no longer extant, excerpts were preserved by Josephus *(Contra Apion I)* along with other spurious passages. An epitome was made at an early date in the form of lists of dynasties and kingdoms with short notes on kings and events. This was in part preserved primarily by Africanus *(Chronicle)* and Eusebius *(Ecclesiastical History)*. The original makeup of the *Aegyptiaca* appears to have also contained narratives.

Mark W. Chavalas

Texts

Manetho. Trans. W.G. Waddell. Cambridge, MA: Harvard University Press/Loeb Classical Library, 1980.

References

Helck, H.W. *Untersuchungen zu Manetho und den ägyptischen Königslisten* [Explorations in Manetho and the Egyptian King-Lists]. Berlin: Akademie Verlay, 1956.

Redford, D.B. *Pharaonic King-Lists, Annals, and Day-Books: A Contribution to the Study of the Egyptian Sense of History.* Mississauga: Benben Publications, 1986.

Stern, M. ed. *Greek and Latin Authors on Jews and Judaism.* 3 vols. Jerusalem: Israeli Academy of Sciences and Humanities, 1974–1984, I, 62–86.

Manetti, Giannozzo (1396–1459)

Renaissance humanist and historian. Manetti served first the Florentine republic (in a variety of diplomatic and political positions) and, later, Pope Nicholas V and King Alfonso the Magnanimous of Aragon. Owing to his advocacy of a republican alliance with Venice, Manetti was subjected to punitive taxation by partisans of Cosimo de' Medici. In 1453, he chose exile over bankruptcy, fleeing Florence for Rome, and then Naples, where he died. Interested chiefly in moral philosophy, Manetti was a student of the humanist Ambrogio Traversari (d. 1438) and a friend of Leonardo Bruni. Manetti's historical works include biographies of Nicholas V, Dante, Petrarch, Boccaccio, and Niccolò Niccoli (the Florentine antiquary of the early fifteenth century), as well as the parallel lives of Socrates and Seneca. A three-book history of Pistoia, the *Chronicon Pistoriense,* was a small-scale response to the *Historiae Florentini Populi Libri XII* by Bruni, whose funeral elegy Manetti wrote.

William J. Connell

Texts

Chronicon Pistoriense, in *Rerum italicarum scriptores.* Ed. L.A. Muratori. Vol. 19. Milan: tip. Societatis Palatinae, 1731, cols. 985–1076.

Vitae Socratis et Senecae [Lives of Socrates and Seneca]. Ed. A. De Petris. Florence: Olschki, 1979.

References

Cochrane, Eric. *Historians and Historiography in the Italian Renaissance.* Chicago: University of Chicago Press, 1981, 26–27; 408–409.

Mansi, Giovanni Domenico (1692–1769)

Italian ecclesiastical historian and archbishop. Mansi was born into a wealthy and noble family that had settled in Lucca in A.D. 964. As a professor of moral philosophy, he traveled extensively throughout Europe, visiting the great libraries in Naples, Vienna, and the Vatican. As a young man, he entered a religious order, taught at the University of Naples, and was named archbishop of Lucca by Pope Clement XIII in 1765. Mansi was charged with editing Diderot's *Encyclopedia* to conform with Catholic theology. By 1758, he had completed a review of the first three volumes, but in the next two years, as he was working on volumes four to seven, political and religious protests flared over the work. Mansi's "corrections" were deemed insufficient, and he was forced to abandon the project after a conflict with the pope. In addition to his collection of the writings of Pius II, he is best known for his edition (in thirty-one volumes) of the texts of the sacred councils of the Catholic Church from the first to the eighteenth century. His *Carmen elegiacum de vita sua* [Elegiacal Song on His Own Life] (1762) is an autobiography in poetic form of 216 verses.

Stanislao G. Pugliese

Texts

Sacrorum conciliorum nova et amplissima collectio. 31 vols. Paris: H. Welter, 1900–1927.

References

Carmen elegiacum de vita sua. Ed. Aldo Marsili. Lucca: M. Pacini Fazzi, 1984.

Mao Tse-tung

See MAO ZEDONG.

Mao Zedong [Mao Tse-tung] (1893–1976)

Political and ideological leader of the Chinese Communist Party (CCP), founder of the People's Republic of China (PRC) in 1949. Mao was born in Shaoshan, Hunan province, into a well-off peasant family. Exposed to the rapid political and cultural changes sweeping China during his years at the Hunan First Normal School, from which he graduated in 1918, early on Mao turned to radical political activity. He was a founding member of the CCP in 1921 and a prominent but controversial activist during the "United Front" with the Guomindang (Kuomintang) between 1923 and 1927 and after. Only in 1935, in the course of the "Long March," did Mao gain effective control over the CCP. During the next decade, in the CCP's Yan'an capital in northwest China, Mao constructed a version of China's past with himself and the CCP as the ultimate agents of history that was instrumental in mobilizing and motivating the revolutionary movement that defeated Chiang Kai-shek's Guomindang in the civil war of 1946 to 1949. The writings that assert this almost millenarian vision are not, of course, academic history; but they would have an enormous influence on the study of history in the PRC until Mao's death (see the entry for Shang Yue). The "sinification of Marxism" that they accomplish was the basis for Mao's claim to equal status with Marx and Lenin as a Marxist theorist, as in the once omnipresent mantra "Marxism-Leninism and the thought of Mao Zedong" in PRC discourse.

Mao Zedong's principal historical statements include: "Strategic Problems of China's Revolutionary War" (1936); "The Chinese Revolution and the Chinese Communist Party" (1939); "On New Democracy" (1940); "Talks at the Yenan Forum on Art and Literature" (1942); "On Coalition Government" (1945); and "On the People's Democratic Dictatorship" (1949). There is, as yet, no complete collection available of Mao's writings and speeches, but several efforts are underway to remedy that lacuna. The *Selected Works,* incomplete and sometimes bowdlerized, contain most of the items above.

Albert Feuerwerker

Texts

Selected Works of Mao Tse-tung. 5 vols. Peking: Foreign Languages Press, 1961–1965, 1977.

References

Apter, David E., and Tony Saich. *Revolutionary Discourse in Mao's Republic.* Cambridge, MA: Harvard University Press, 1994.

Schram, Stuart R. *The Thought of Mao Tse-tung.* Cambridge, Eng., and New York: Cambridge University Press, 1989.

Marāṭhā Historiography

Historical chronicles and biographies, called *bakhars,* written in the Marāṭhī language of western India. The Marāṭhā kings and their brahman ministers, the peshwās, ruled western and central India from the late seventeenth century until being conquered by the British in 1817. During this period writers in Marāṭhī used both the successes and failures of Marāṭhā political and military policy to illustrate a Marāṭhā and Hindu national consciousness and also to provide moral lessons on the qualities of leadership.

Kinds of historical writing in Marāṭhī prose date to the thirteenth century and the earliest period of the language's development. At this time the subject matter generally consisted of stories about noted religious figures and their disciples. Nevertheless, this early literature does possess an attention to realistic detail and chronological accuracy. In addition to religious biography, another source for the Marāṭhā historical tradition is a genealogical and biographical literature *(kaiphiyat)* maintained by important families and lineages in western India. The Marāṭhā historical tradition can also be seen preserved in examples of a village bardic literature *(povāḍe)* that recite the deeds of the Marāṭhā people. The life of the Marāṭhā king Shivājī (1627–1680) and his struggles against the Mughal emperor Aurangzeb provided the first important political subject for Maratha chroniclers. Kriṣṇājī Anant Sabhāsad's *Sabhāsadī bakhar* (1697) is perhaps the most notable example this first phase of Marāṭhī historical writing. The life of Shivājī contains the seeds of Marāṭhā nationalism, which is understood in terms of the struggle of Hindus against Muslim domination.

Marāṭhā expansion into central and northern India in the eighteenth century provided much material for *bakhar* writers. In particular, the Marāṭhā defeat at the battle of Pānipat in 1761, when Marāṭhā northward expansion was stopped by the intervention of the Afghans, provided a key event for the chroniclers. The *Bhāusāheb bakhar* (ascribed to the otherwise unknown Kriṣṇājī Shyamrāo) is a narrative of seemingly invincible success cruelly stopped by the personal failings and intrigues of the Marāṭhās and their allies. A central place is given to the character and actions of the Marāṭhā general Sadāshivrāo "Bhāusāheb," who died at Pānipat. Chronicle writing continued until the end of Marāṭhā rule and on into the first decades of British rule in western India. Thus, authors working in the traditional *bakhar* form, such as Kriṣṇājī Vināyak Sohinī in the *Peshvyāṃcī bakhar,* summarized the period of independent Marāṭhā rule while attempting to account for the British conquest. Marāṭhā historiography provided much of the substance of the first European accounts of the Marāṭhās, in particular James Grant Duff's *History of the Mahrattas* (1826).

Laurence W. Preston

Texts

The Decade of Panipat (1751–1761). Trans. Ian Raeside. Bombay: Popular Prakashan, 1984.

Śiva Chhatrapati, Being a Translation of Sabhāsad Bakhar with Extracts from Chiṭṇis and Śvadigvijaya. Trans. Surendranath Sen. Calcutta: University of Calcutta, 1920.

References

Tulpule, Shankar Gopal. *Classical Marāṭhī Literature, from the Beginning to A.D. 1818.* Wiesbaden: Otto Harrassowitz, 1979.

Marcks, Erich (1861–1938)

German historian. Born in Magdeburg, Marcks taught at Freiburg, Leipzig, Heidelberg, Hamburg, Munich, and finally in Berlin, where he died. Marcks's historical writings were particularly strong at penetrating the psychology of historical figures. His essays were also well known for their polish and intellectual acumen, but he was uncompromisingly partisan from a conservative point of view. His historical works attempted to give a classical Goethean gloss to the new self-consciousness of German nationalism in the age of Bismarck and Treitschke. He was an avowed opponent of the Weimar Republic and supported Alfred Hugenberg's anti-Semitic and chauvinist German National People's Party.

Elliot Neaman

Texts

Bismarck. Stuttgart: Cotta, 1909–1939.
Bismarck und die deutsche Revolution [Bismarck and the German Revolution]. Stuttgart: Deutsche Verlagsanstalt, 1939.
Deutsche Geschichte von 1806–1871 [German History from 1806–1871]. Stuttgart: Deutsche Verlagsanstalt, 1936.
Gaspard von Coligny. Stuttgart: Deutsche Verlagsanstalt, 1925.
Männer und Zeiten [Men and Their Times]. Leipzig: Quelle & Meyer, 1911.

References

Iggers, Georg G. *The German Conception of History.* Second ed. Middletown, CT: Wesleyan University Press, 1983.

Marczali, Henrik (1856–1940)

Hungarian positivist historian. Marczali studied in Budapest, Berlin, Paris, and Vienna, and in 1895 was appointed professor of history at the Péter Pázmány University in Budapest. During his tenure, he contributed to the modernization of historical studies at the university. Obliged to retire from his

M

chair in 1924 because of his alleged sympathies for the Hungarian Soviet Republic of 1919, he lived under trying financial circumstances until his death. Marczali's uniquely broad research interests cover nearly the whole span of Hungarian history from the first settlements in the Carpathian Basin to the early nineteenth century. His most original works deal with Hungary in the eighteenth century and offer a comprehensive picture of all major social, economic, political, and cultural developments based on a thorough knowledge of the primary sources. He also edited a large, twelve-volume *Universal History* (1898–1905), of which he himself wrote the six volumes covering the period from the sixteenth century to his own times. In addition, he penned a wide range of journalistic works.

Attila Pók

Texts
Az 1790–91. Országgyűlés [The Diet of 1790–91]. 2 vols. Budapest: Magyar Tudományos Akadémia Könyvkiadó Vállalata, 1907.
Hungary in the Eighteenth Century. Cambridge, Eng.: Cambridge University Press, 1910.
A magyar történet kútfői az Árpádok korában [Sources of Hungarian History during the Age of the Árpád Dynasty]. Budapest: Franklin T., 1880.
Ed., with Dávid Angyal and Sándor Mika. *A magyar történet kútfőinek kézikönyve* [A Manual on the Sources of Hungarian History]. Budapest: Atheneum, 1901.
Magyarország története II. József korában [A History of Hungary during the Time of Joseph II]. 3 vols. Budapest: Magyar Tudományos Akadémia Könyvkiadó Vállalata, 1881–1888.
Ungarisches Verfassungsrecht [Hungarian Constitutional Law]. Tübingen: J.C.B. Mohr (P. Siebeck), 1910.

References
Péter Gunst, ed. *Henrik Marczali.* Budapest: Gondolat, 1982.

Marianus Scotus (ca. 1028–1082/83)
Irish monk and chronicler. Marianus was born in Ireland and entered Mag Bile monastery there in 1052. Thrown out of Mag Bile in 1056, Marianus joined the Irish monks at St. Martin's Abbey in Cologne, moving to Fulda in 1058. Ordained priest in 1059, Marianus went to St. Martin's monastery in Mainz ten years later. He wrote a universal chronicle from Creation to 1082, which Robert of Losinga, bishop of Hereford (1079–1095),

carried with him to England. There it was used by later chroniclers, particularly Sigebert of Gembloux and Worcester monks. Marianus's chronicle is a good source of information concerning Anglo-Saxon, Scottish, and Irish events; the extensive Irish monastic community in Germany; saints' lives and miracles; and Irish words, names, and place-names.

Christopher M. Bellitto

Texts
Patrologia Latina. Ed. J.-P. Migne. Vol. 147. Paris: Garnier, 1853, cols. 623–802.

References
Brett, Martin. "The Use of Universal Chronicle at Worcester." In *L'historiographie médiévale en Europe* [Medieval Historiography in Europe], ed. Jean-Philippe Genet. Paris: CNRS, 1991, 277–285.
Von den Brincken, Anna-Dorothea. "Marianus Scottus: Unter besonderer Berücksichtigung der nicht veröffentlichen Teile seiner Chronik [Marianus Scotus: With Particular Attention to the Unpublished Part of His Chronicle]." *Deutsches Archiv für Erforschung des Mittelalters* 17 (1961): 191–238.

Marsden, William (1754–1836)
British colonial administrator and orientalist. Born in Ireland, Marsden received a classical education in Dublin and was preparing to enter Trinity College when, at the suggestion of his eldest brother, a writer with the East India Company at Bencoolen in Sumatra, he obtained an appointment from the company. From 1771 until 1779, he was subsecretary and then principal secretary to the British government in Sumatra. In 1770 he left Sumatra and established an East India agency in London with his brother. In London, Marsden joined many learned societies, most prominently the Royal Society of which he was at various times treasurer, vice president, and acting president. In 1795 Marsden accepted the post of second secretary of the admiralty. He retired in 1807, shortly before he married Elizabeth Wray. In 1823 he published *Numismata Orientalia,* a description of his collection of oriental coins. Following his death from an apoplectic attack, his widow edited his autobiography and had it privately printed. Marsden's major work, the *History of Sumatra,* was first published in 1784, then again in 1811, and it was translated into German and French. His scientific interests are apparent in this work, which starts with an exhaustive natural history of the island

before moving onto anthropology, politics, and linguistics. Marsden wrote his *History* against earlier fantastical accounts of the island. It received enthusiastic reviews praising its scientific detachment and sobriety. In it Marsden privileged the unspectacular Rejang tribe over other tribes such as the cannibalistic Batak people. He considered the Rejang to be the "original Sumatrans," least tainted by later-introduced Malay and Javanese customs. His concern with the ancient and the original, especially the origins of language, continues in his later works, such as his *Dictionary of the Malayan Language* (1812).

Mary C. Quilty

Texts

A Brief Memoir of the Life and Writings of the Late William Marsden, Written by Himself with Notes from His Correspondence. London: J.L. Cox & Son, 1838.

The History of Sumatra: Containing an Account of the Government, Laws, Customs, and Manners of the Native Inhabitants, with a Description of the Natural Productions and a Relation of the Ancient Political State of That Island. Kuala Lumpur: Oxford University Press, 1975.

Miscellaneous Works of William Marsden. London: J.L. Cox and Son, 1834.

References

Bastin, John. "English Sources for the Modern Period of Indonesian History." In *An Introduction to Indonesian Historiography*, ed. Soedjatmoko et al. Ithaca, NY: Cornell University Press, 1965, 252–271.

Boon, James. *Affinities and Extremes: Criss-crossing the Bittersweet Ethnology of East Indies History, Hindu-Balinese Culture and Indo-European Allure.* Chicago: University of Chicago Press, 1990.

Quilty, Mary. "Textual Empires: A Reading of Early British Histories of Southeast Asia." Ph.D. thesis, University of Melbourne, 1992.

Martini, Martino (1614–1661)

Italian polymath and Jesuit missionary to China. Martini rendered the greatest service to his order on a mission to Rome when he secured from Alexander VII in 1556 a decree that favored provisionally the Jesuit position on the Rites Controversy, that is, a position that accepted many Chinese ceremonies (and honors) as civil and political rather than religious in nature. If the continuing Rites Controversy led to a general expansion of European knowledge of China, Martini made more specific contributions to that increase of information. Initially presented in the form of letters, his accounts of the Manchu conquest of Ming China, which he both witnessed and accepted, and his research in ancient Chinese sources established his reputation as a historian. Although not without errors, his *Novus Atlas Sinensis* [A New Atlas of China] (1654), based upon Chinese sources and his own travels, was an even greater contribution to European knowledge of the Middle Kingdom.

John F. Laffey

Texts

Bellum Tartaricum, or The Conquest of the Great and Most Renowned Empire of China, by the Invasion of the Tartars. London: John Crook, 1654.

Novus Atlas Sinensis. Amsterdam: Johannes Blaeu, 1654.

References

Allan, C.W. *Jesuits at the Court of Peking.* Arlington, VA: University Publications of America, 1975.

Rowbotham, A.H. *Missionary and Mandarin: The Jesuits at the Court of China.* New York: Russell & Russell, 1966.

Martyrology

Form of historical writing presenting accounts of deaths of victims of religious persecution. The term "martyr" derives from the Greek for "witness": true Christian martyrdom could only be sealed with testimony culminating with death of the martyr. A martyrology is, then, a collection of testimonies or witnessings, of and for a particular doctrine during a time of persecution, although its compilation is not necessarily contemporaneous. Tertullian claimed that "the blood of the martyrs is the seed of the Church," and in stating this, he implicitly identifies the significant role that martyrological accounts and compilations play in the establishment of a church. It is from the martyrs, through the martyrologies, that the Christian faith established its identity and created its history.

The earliest-known Christian martyrologies, such as the "Syriac Breviary" (fourth-century), cataloged those who fulfilled these requirements. The first martyrologies were essentially calendars documenting local martyrs in the order of their feasts, identifying a specific day for commemoration, and in some instances, including a brief description of their martyrdom. The purpose and composition of many of the later martyrologies, however, went beyond merely recounting instances of persecution or establishing feasts. These placed their martyrs within a historical framework, providing context and commentary.

The functions of the later martyrologies range from the inspirational and commemorative, to the didactic and exemplary, to the dogmatic and polemical. Hence, they disseminated particular messages and instructions to their readers through commentary and the examples provided by the martyrs. Within the narrative accounts and the literary reconstruction of the martyrs' words and experiences lay the virtues, doctrine, and values held by the oppressed group: the textualized martyrs become the "physical" embodiment of the (once) persecuted movement. The martyrs' accounts are pasteurized and stereotyped through the incorporation of dogma, myth, and propaganda to legitimate and support the cause of the (once) persecuted faction. The historical martyrology is thus a major source for understanding both the context of religious persecutions and the movements themselves.

A well-known and very influential history-cum-martyrology is that of Eusebius of Caesarea, the *Ecclesiastical History* (early fourth century), written at a time when the early Church was bringing to a close its struggle against oppression, but was continuing to wage war on heresy. In effect, it documents the rise of the Christian Church, its martyrs and persecution, and the political context out of which it arose. This type of model differs from that of the preceding martyrologies: it brings to light the problematic relationship between politics and religion, and between earthly and divine institutions. This new model of ecclesiastical history and martyrology illustrates the perception of the inherent connection between religious and political factors during a time of persecution. Essentially, this work established a new form in the historiography of persecution—one which would be revived in the sixteenth century.

The martyrologies of the medieval period, such as those of Bede (eighth century) and Usuard (ninth century), borrowed from Eusebius, and simultaneously added scriptures, legend, and the writings of the church fathers, expanding and universalizing the local martyrologies of the early Church. These are known as the "historical martyrologies." Composed during a time not of persecution, but of ascension and consolidation, they lack the defensive tone of Eusebius, and instead focus on the didactic, exemplary, and historic, rather than on the political and polemical.

These works, together with Jacobus de Voragine's *Legenda Sanctorum* [Golden Legend] (thirteenth century), form the basis of the modern Roman martyrology.

During the politico-religious conflicts of the sixteenth century, the historical martyrology underwent a kind of renaissance and renewed politicization, producing no less than eight major Protestant works, most in multiple editions, and in both the vernacular and Latin: Jacques Lefèvre d'Etaples's *Agones martyrium meni ianuarii* (1529); Ludwig Rabe's *Der heiligen aus erwohlten Gottes Zeugen Bekennen und Martyren* (1552); John Foxe's *Acts and Monuments* (1554); Jean Crespin's *Le Livre des Martyrs* (1554); Matthias Flacius Illyricus's *Catalogus testium veritatis* (1556); Adrian Cornelis van Haemstede's *De Gheschiedenisse ende den doodt der vromer Martelaren* (1559); Heinrich Pantaleone's *Martyrum historia* (1563); and Antoine de la Roche Chandieu's *Histoire des persecutions de l'Eglise de Paris* (1563). These works drew on the methods and models of earlier histories and martyrologies, such as those by Eusebius and Jacobus de Voragine, while also borrowing freely from each other. In drawing on the early Christian tradition, and in many instances including the accounts of early Christian martyrs, these editor-authors attempted to establish a continuum and association between the early Church and the fledgling "reformed" faith(s). In so doing, they presented themselves as the true descendants of the original Christians, especially under the auspices of "persecution marks the true church of God" to which Crespin refers in the first line of the preface to his first edition.

Unlike the martyrologies of the medieval period, these works were written in an environment of persecution and oppression; as such, the propagandist element in the sixteenth-century compilations is much more pronounced. The instances of persecution and martyrdom are set in a highly polemical, historical, and political context. The martyrologists used and often included transcriptions of trial records, eyewitness accounts, epistolary and personal letters, propagandist pamphlets, and other literary sources, including contemporary histories, to create the martyrological narratives and their settings. Interspersed between and included within the accounts are commentaries on the nature, origins, and general history of the persecution as well as that of the movement itself. And embedded deeply within the entire martyrology is the polemical stance of the various movements. Hence, in its very essence, the sixteenth-century martyrology is a work of propaganda.

Like the early Christian church, the Protestant movements struggled against both oppression and heresy, so their martyrologies not only depicted persecution, but defined doctrine against those espousing heretical beliefs. And, like Eusebius, they defined their martyrs as those testifying in blood for the "true" faith: a martyr can only be considered as such if he or she dies upholding the correct doctrine. All others were "false" martyrs. During this period of the proliferation of different Protestant martyrologies, Calvinist and Lutheran works distinguished Anabaptist martyrs as heretical, while also combating the "superstitions and lies" of the Roman Church. The Catholic anti-martyrologies similarly struck out at all the martyrs of the reformed faiths as "false." Although creating the impression of widespread persecution was essential to the developing churches, it was even more important to include only those who testified correctly and would convey the proper doctrine.

From its conception, the Christian martyrology documented instances of persecution, and identified those who testified for their faith with both their words and blood. Combined with commentary and history, the martyrology developed into a powerful vehicle for the transmission of a movement's values, doctrine, and propaganda. Not only did they document the "rise" of a faith through the accumulation of "witnesses," but they also aided in the establishment of orthodoxy and established the models for resistance during periods of persecution and establishment of Christian faiths.

Nikki Shepardson

See also ECCLESIASTICAL HISTORY; HAGIOGRAPHY.

References

Delehaye, H. *Les Passions des martyrs et les genres litteraires* [The Passions of the Martyrs and Literary Genres]. Second ed. Brussels: Subsidia Hagiographica, 1966.

Frend, W.H.C. *Martyrdom and Persecution in the Early Church.* Oxford: Blackwell, 1965.

Knott, John Ray. *Discourses of Martyrdom in English Literature, 1563–1694.* Cambridge, Eng.: Cambridge University Press, 1993.

Kolb, Robert. *For All the Saints.* Macon, GA: Mercer University Press, 1989.

Verheyden, Alphonse. *Le Martyrologe Protestant des Pays-Bas du Sud au XVI siècle* [Protestant Martyrology in the Southern Low Countries in the Sixteenth Century]. Brussels: Editions de la Librairie des éclaireurs unionistes, 1960.

Maruyama Masao (1914–1996)

Japanese historian of East Asian, and especially Japanese, political thought. Maruyama spent his childhood in Tokyo, where he was exposed to some of the foremost critical journalists of the 1920s. Educated at the elite First Higher School and in the Law Faculty of Tokyo Imperial University, he remained there as a graduate assistant, assistant professor, and finally professor of East Asian political thought, retiring from the university in 1971. Maruyama's intellectual maturation coincided with the final, harrowing crisis of the Japanese empire; and in a fundamental sense his historical vocation has consisted of an attempt to grapple with the deeper intellectual and psychological causes of the tragedy of Japanese modernization in its imperial phase. Maruyama's major works, *Nihon seiji shisōshi kenkyū* [Studies in the Intellectual History of Tokugawa Japan] (1952), *Nihon no shisō* [Japanese Thought] (1961), and *Gendai seiji no shisō to kōdō* [Thought and Behavior in Modern Japanese Politics] (1969) treat the role of nature and invention in Tokugawa political thought, the psychological mechanisms of ultranationalism and "Japanese fascism," and the basic structures of Japanese historical, political, and ethical thought; his analyses have entered the vocabulary, indeed the grammar, of scholarly discourse in and about Japan.

Andrew E. Barshay

Texts

Maruyama Masao shū [Collected Works of Maruyama Masao]. 17 vols. Tokyo: Iwanami Shoten, 1995–1997.

Studies in the Intellectual History of Tokugawa Japan. Trans. Mikiso Hane. Tokyo and Princeton, NJ: Princeton University Press, 1979.

Thought and Behaviour in Modern Japanese Politics. Ed. Ivan Morris. New York: Oxford University Press, 1969.

References

Barshay, Andrew E. "Imagining Democracy in Postwar Japan: Reflections on Maruyama Masao and Modernism." *Journal of Japanese Studies* 18 (1992): 365–406.

Sasakura Hideo. *Maruyama Masao ron nōto* [Maruyama Masao: Notes toward a Study]. Tokyo: Misuzu Shobō, 1988.

Marx, Karl (1818–1883)

German political philosopher, historian, social theorist, and revolutionary. Born in Trier, Marx was from a Jewish middle-class family that had converted to Protestantism. While attending the University of Berlin, he was influenced by the philosopher Georg Wilhelm Friedrich Hegel, participated in the liberal and reformist Young Hegelian movement, and began his career as a political activist by editing the liberal newspaper, *Rheinische Zeitung*. After the newspaper was shut down by the government, Marx emigrated first to Brussels and then to Paris (1843), where he became a revolutionary communist. It was in Paris that he met Friedrich Engels, who became his lifelong friend and collaborator. To escape the reactionary political climate on the European continent following the suppression of the 1848 revolutions, Marx moved again, this time to London, where he lived until his death. In England, Marx continued his career as a revolutionary activist and thinker, helping to found in 1864 the International, the first international socialist organization, producing his unfinished, three-volume masterpiece of economic analysis, *Capital* (1867–1894), and writing numerous shorter works of contemporary political and historical analysis.

Marx's materialist theory of history, "historical materialism," has had a profound impact on modern historiography. Never systematically articulated, it was developed in several works, beginning with *The German Ideology* (1845–1846). For Marx, and Engels, history was progressive, proceeded by a series of class struggles, and consisted of historical epochs defined by their dominant mode of production. Those they identified included slave, feudal, capitalist, and (the yet to emerge) communist. Modes of production consisted of two components: productive forces (tools and materials at a particular stage of development) and the social relations of production (economic class relations, which historically were inherently unequal and exploitative). As the forces of production developed, they eventually were hindered by the existing production relations, and their progress depended on the emergence of new relations that only become dominant following a period of revolutionary turmoil. Marx's test case was the collapse of feudalism and the birth of industrial capitalism, which he and Engels described in *The Communist Manifesto* (1848). This interpretation gave rise to modern historiographical debates on both the transition from feudalism to capitalism and the significance of the French and English revolutions. More generally, in the preface to *A Critique of Political Economy* (1859), Marx articulated his view of society in terms of "base" and "superstructure." Here productive relations (the base) were the real foundation on which politics

and ideology (the superstructure) were built. One of Marx's most influential and controversial ideas, it has been extensively debated by Marxists, not least because both he and Engels gave different accounts of it. Where, in the version cited above, the superstructure was completely dependent on the base, elsewhere they seemed to suggest that it had a causal impact of its own.

Dennis Dworkin

See also ENGELS, FRIEDRICH; MARXISM AND HISTORIOGRAPHY.

Texts
The Marx-Engels Reader. Ed. Robert C. Tucker. New York: W.W. Norton and Co., 1972.

References
Cohen, Gerald A. *Karl Marx's Theory of History: A Defence.* Oxford: Oxford University Press, 1978.
McLellan, David. *Karl Marx: His Life and Thought.* London: MacMillan, 1974.

Marxism and Historiography

The use by historians of Marxist and Marxian theories. When Karl Marx died in 1883, he left behind scattered reflections on his philosophy of history and several examples of his historical method, including *The Communist Manifesto* (1848), *The Class Struggles in France* (1850), and *The 18th Brumaire of Louis Bonaparte* (1852). It was Friedrich Engels, Marx's friend and collaborator, who embarked upon the task of systematically presenting Marx's views and who can be credited with transforming Marx's thought into "Marxism." Where his efforts to define Marx's philosophy as "dialectical materialism" (a term never used by Marx himself) inaugurated the first stage in the development of a Marxist orthodoxy, Engels's reflections on his friend's historical method constituted a critique of just such a process. He was concerned with a growing tendency to simplify Marx's views and took pains to clarify them. In a famous letter to Joseph Bloch (1890), Engels asserted that Marx had never meant (as some had assumed) that economic relations alone provided the key to understanding concrete historical situations. While they might constitute "the *ultimately* determining element in history," it was also the case that the "superstructure"—constitutions, juridical forms, philosophical theories, and religious views—also influenced historical outcomes. Engels's concern that historical materialism, rigidly applied, "would be easier than the solution of a simple equation to the first degree" proved to be prophetic, as the fate of intellectual life under Stalinism so vividly proved. But in western Europe and the United States (where Marxism was a minority current), an alternative tradition emerged that resisted this ossification, and, following Engels, viewed Marxism as a guide to historical study rather than as a substitute for it. This Marxist tradition has had a major impact on the writing of history in the twentieth century and has become part of the mainstream of historical thought in the West: it has been important for both the history of radical intellectual culture and academic historiography.

Arguably the first and most visible instance of the impact of Marxism on historiography was its role in shaping the social interpretation of the French Revolution. Developed in tandem with the establishment of the Third French Republic in the late nineteenth century, the social interpretation viewed the French revolutionary turmoil as a "bourgeois revolution," a class conflict in which the capitalist bourgeoisie supplanted the old nobility and aristocracy and established republican institutions. Developed by liberal, republican, and socialist historians—including Alphonse Aulard, Jean Jaurès, and Albert Mathiez—it was compatible with and indebted to Marx's picture of capitalist development rather than seeking to advance historical materialism per se. A major landmark in this tradition was the work of George Lefebvre, who saw the revolution as a whole as being bourgeois, but recognized that it advanced by a series of smaller revolts: aristocratic, bourgeois, peasant, and sans-coulotte. His pioneering work on the role of the peasants in the Revolution, culminating in *The Great Fear* (1932), represented a milestone in the developing field of "history from below." Lefebvre's student and intellectual successor, Albert Soboul, extended this tradition of people's history in his work on the sans-culottes, while openly acknowledging that his theoretical position was Marxist, something from which his predecessor had refrained.

By the 1960s, the social interpretation dominated French revolutionary historiography, championed by Marxist and non-Marxist historians alike. Since that time, however, it has come under increasing attack: if historians have not reached a consensus on an alternative model, they have increasingly become disenchanted with the Marxist version. This process commenced with Alfred Cobban's attack on Marxist theory in *The Social Interpretation of the French Revolution* (1964), wherein he argued that the bourgeoisie made the

Revolution, but that they were not a capitalist class. It has been extended by historians like François Furet, who argued that politics could not be reduced to economic interests, and revived Alexis de Tocqueville's argument that the most far-reaching consequence of the French revolutionary events was accelerated state centralization. Rather than view the transformation as a conflict between the bourgeoisie and the aristocracy, the new revisionism has tended to view prerevolutionary France as dominated by a single elite drawn from both groups and to see successive waves of revolution as movements of national revival.

In Great Britain, the impact of Marxism on historical writing came later than in France, but it tended to be more theoretically ambitious. Indeed, whereas in France the most creative theoretical work connected to Marxism tended to be in philosophy—for instance, Louis Althusser and Jean Paul Sartre—in Britain it frequently came from the field of history. A pivotal moment in the creation of a Marxist tradition of historical scholarship in Great Britain was the Communist Party's Historians' Group, which was active between 1946 and 1957. The group included several important social and economic historians: Maurice Dobb (somewhat older than the rest), Christopher Hill, Rodney Hilton, Eric Hobsbawm, Victor Kiernan, George Rudé, John Saville, and Dorothy and Edward Thompson. In spite of crippling illusions about Stalin's regime and the nature of their own party, the group openly debated Marxist theory, critically examined historical issues central to the study of British history, and, in conjunction with a few sympathetic non-Marxist historians, launched the social history journal *Past & Present* in 1952. In the aftermath of the crisis in international communism in 1956–1957, culminating in the Soviet invasion of Hungary, the great majority of the historians denounced Stalinism and orthodox Marxism, left the Party, and helped launch the British New Left.

The British Marxist historians have had a major effect on the development of social and cultural history in both Britain and the United States. Here it is possible to distinguish two dimensions of their work that have had widespread consequences. One of the group's major concerns was the transition from feudalism to capitalism. Dobb's *Studies in the Development of Capitalism* (1946) was the central text: it provided the historians with a basic draft of early modern English historical development, represented a historical argument about the development of capitalism more generally, and provoked an international debate that included prominent Marxist economists and historians from Europe, North America, and Asia. The two major interlocutors in the debate were Dobb and the American economist Paul Sweezy. Dobb's explanation for the decline of feudalism closely followed Marx's own. Like other modes of production, feudalism was threatened by *internal* instability, the conflict between the forces and the relations of production. Feudal lords' efforts to extract increasing amounts of the surplus from the peasantry eventually produced intensified class struggle in the form of the fourteenth-century crisis. Capitalism appeared only after feudalism had already reached an advanced state of decay. Sweezy's account of the "transition" was indebted to the Belgian historian, Henri Pirenne. Sweezy believed that feudal decline was caused by *external* forces: the revival of international commerce and trade and the growth of medieval towns in the twelfth and thirteenth centuries. These same forces were responsible for the growing division of labor, the spread of wage labor, and the birth of capitalism.

The "transition debate" raised challenging questions about the nature of the epochal transition from feudalism to capitalism, but, because it was launched by Marxist academics at the height of the Cold War, it had little effect beyond radical intellectual circles. In contrast, the work of Robert Brenner, an American historian of early modern Europe, provoked a much wider discussion, including responses from Guy Bois, J.P. Cooper, Emmanuel Le Roy Ladurie, and M.M. Postan. Brenner's work, notably "Agrarian Class Structure and Economic Development in Pre-Industrial Europe" (1976), represented a highly sophisticated renewal and extension of Dobb's original position (as well as a rejection of Sweezy's critique). For Brenner, the development of feudalism in Europe was inseparable from the class conflicts that were *intrinsic* to it as a mode of production. Its decline in western Europe (as well as its intensification in central and eastern Europe) was dependent on the ability of peasants in a particular place to resist landlords' efforts at maintaining or intensifying feudal obligations. Brenner's inclination to see historical change within the framework of structurally determined class relations was in sharp contrast to the demographic models of Le Roy Ladurie and Postan, which analyzed feudal and early modern development in the context of the tension between population and resources. Le Roy Ladurie, in particular, argued for a Malthusian historical approach whereby food shortages, plagues, and wars were viewed as the inescapable result of population growth beyond the means of subsistence. He once stated that Malthus had come too late, meaning that a Malthusian perspective was better fitted to explain backward agrarian societies than industrial ones.

The second influential dimension of the work of the British Marxist historians, originating during the days of the Historians' Group, was their contribution to "history from below" or "history from the bottom up." There was nothing specifically Marxist about emphasizing the role of the popular classes in history, but the historians framed their analysis within the context of a wider class struggle, and implicitly made the claim that the view at the bottom of society (unlike the top) was free from mystification. Hilton's writings on medieval peasant uprisings in works like *Bond Men Made Free: Medieval Peasant Movements and the English Rising of 1381* (1973), Hill's recovery of the radical fringe of the English revolution in *The World Turned Upside Down* (1972), and Hobsbawm's analysis of preindustrial forms of resistance in *Primitive Rebels* (1959) and *Bandits* (1969) provided exemplary models for what became known as the "new social history." However, by far the most central work of the genre was E.P. Thompson's *The Making of the English Working Class* (1963), arguably the most important work of social history written in English since World War II. Thompson's book was an alternative to an older tradition in labor history, which viewed early working-class agitation as a precursor to the Labour party and the trade unions and which was more interested in the leaders than the grassroots of the movement. Most important, it was written in opposition to two approaches that, in his view, denied working-class people "human agency." It was opposed to structural functionalist sociology, which Thompson believed reduced the working class to a "thing," a component of the social structure. It was likewise antagonistic to orthodox Marxists, whom he portrayed as perceiving the working class exclusively from the point of view of productive relations. In a famous formulation, Thompson argued that creation of the working class was a historical and cultural process founded on evolving experience and consciousness: it made itself as much as it was made.

For the rising generation of young radical scholars and their older associates, whose sympathies lay with the grassroots, student, and countercultural movements of the 1960s, the book's celebration of working people's spontaneous forms of protest had a remarkable appeal. This was enhanced by Thompson's own practice as a radical and a scholar. The book was not the product of an academic environment: Thompson wrote it as an adult education teacher of working-class students. In Britain, Thompson's book, and the tradition to which it belonged, were a major inspiration for the History Workshop, founded at Ruskin College, Oxford University in 1966. A group of socialist and feminist historians (created in large part because of the efforts of Raphael Samuel), it played a central role in spreading the new social history, particularly through *History Workshop: A Journal of Socialist and Feminist Historians* launched in 1976. In the 1970s, workshop historians celebrated the lives of the popular classes by extending Thompson's method to capture smaller slices of regional and local history and the rhythms of working-class daily life. Yet in aiming their investigations at such a microscopic level, they tended to lose sight of the national political context, a critique made by Thompson himself. The group was also important because of its connection with the new socialist feminist history in Britain. Sheila Rowbotham's writings on the history of British socialist feminism and women in revolutionary movements, Catherine Hall's research on early-nineteenth-century middle-class gender relationships, Sally Alexander's work on working-class women in nineteenth-century London, and Barbara Taylor's recovery of the feminist dimension of the early socialist movement collectively contributed to establishing a tradition of socialist feminist historiography. Of these, perhaps the most important in the initial stage was Rowbotham, who in *Women, Resistance and Revolution* (1972) and *Hidden from History* (1973) attempted to achieve for women what Thompson had accomplished for the working class, while simultaneously recognizing that many women had been oppressed because of both their gender and their class.

Thompson's *Making of the English Working Class* was not only influential on historians in Britain, but was also enthusiastically received by new left, feminist, and radical historians in the United States. Never, in fact, has a work in European history affected American historians so deeply or so immediately. Of the numerous social historians who fell under Thompson's influence, perhaps the most important was Herbert Gutman, whose *Work, Culture and Society in Industrializing America* (1977) was written in opposition to the dominant, economistic modes of labor history: their stress on trade unionism excluded many working people, and their institutional emphasis separated workers from their subcultures and from the national culture as a whole. Following Thompson, Gutman saw working people as authors of their own history; and he viewed working-class history from the point of view of the institutions, beliefs, traditions, and ideas that American workers (many of whom were recent immigrants) created and re-created in their adaptation to the harsh realities of the new industrial system. But however inspired Gutman might have been by Thompson's historical approach, his adaptation proved to be selective, particularly his avoidance of the class struggle motif, which was so crucial to the latter's world view. For David Brody, Gutman's work represented a "strategic retreat" from Thompson's basic position; and David Montgomery criticized its inclination to treat political power as a tangential dimension. There were certainly American social historians who saw working-class history through the perspective of class struggle—for instance, Alan Dawley in his study of the skilled working class, *Class and Community: The Industrial Revolution in Lynn* (1976). Yet by the end of the seventies, a growing chorus of radical critics voiced political concerns about the American disciples of Thompson and the state of social history in the United States more generally. Among those critics who voiced this more general concern were Eugene Genovese and Elizabeth Fox-Genovese, who argued that there was a "political crisis of social history"—a phrase that served as the title for an article they wrote in 1976.

In part, the appeal of Thompson's work was his commitment to a Marxist theoretical tradition freed of Stalinist dogmatism and economism. His efforts at reviving and renewing creative Marxist thinking was part of a wider movement on both sides of the Atlantic to recast Marxism in more contemporary terms, while reviving submerged and suppressed traditions within Marxist thought. Two of the most influential Marxist theorists in this context were the founder of the Italian Communist Party, Antonio Gramsci, and the French structuralist philosopher, Louis Althusser, both contributors to the "Western Marxist" tradition. Gramsci's attempt to understand the historical and structural underpinnings of modern society in western Europe resulted in his abandonment of Marxist orthodoxy and his development of a sophisticated and complex understanding of the dynamics of political and ideological struggles. He came to understand that bourgeois rule in the West was achieved not through coercion, but through consent or "hegemony," and that political causes in the modern age were lost and won on the cultural and ideological battlefield.

M

Although writing mostly in the 1920s, Gramsci was virtually unknown to leftist historians (outside of Italy) until the 1960s and 1970s. His notion of "hegemony" was highly influential both because it was theoretically compelling and because it articulated what many were saying already. In Britain, Gramsci's ideas influenced the direction of both radical historiography and the developing field of cultural studies, including the work of Thompson, Raymond Williams, and Stuart Hall. In the United States, one of the earliest and most famous applications of a Gramscian approach was Eugene Genovese's *Roll, Jordan, Roll: The World the Slaves Made* (1972). For Genovese, the slaveholding society of the Old South was rooted in the cultural hegemony of the slaveholders, their paternalistic ideology establishing both the potential and limits for a semiautonomous slave culture of resistance. He acknowledged that this society was rooted in class antagonisms, and accepted that it was ultimately based on coercion, but he believed that it consisted of a web of reciprocal obligations and customary rights, much like the relationship between lord and serf in feudal Europe. Another notable use of "hegemony" in a work by an American historian was T.J. Jackson Lears's *No Place of Grace: Antimodernism and the Transformation of American Culture, 1880–1920* (1981). Lears argued that the dominant classes in late-nineteenth- and early twentieth-century America were deeply conflicted about the "overcivilized" modern world; and he viewed antimodernism as both a protest against bourgeois values and ultimately the means by which these values were stitched back together. The result was a renewed cultural hegemony that smoothed the transition to twentieth-century corporate capitalism and consumer culture.

In contrast to radical historians' widespread acknowledgment of Gramsci's importance, the reception of Althusser's ideas proved more controversial. Like other Western Marxists, Althusser criticized the economic reductionism of the base/superstructure model. But where Gramsci sought new ways to confront historical complexity, Althusser suggested that the problem with Marxism was that it was not theoretical enough: it was contaminated by empiricist and humanist assumptions; it needed to be established as a science (something that Marx himself had only barely achieved). Althusserian "theoretical practice" viewed history as a series of modes of production fraught with intrinsic structural conflicts. Far from being the makers of history, human agents were the vehicle through which these deeper structural movements played themselves out. In Althusser's

schema, the relations of production defined the basic parameters of the social formation but (following Engels) only in the last instance: in practice, social formations consisted of semiautonomous levels—the economic, the political, and the ideological. In a pivotal essay, "On Ideology and Ideological State Apparatuses" (1971), Althusser argued that ideology and the state could act independently from the economic infrastructure, but ultimately were the arena in which capitalist social relations were reproduced, a functionalist interpretation that minimized both human agency and class struggle. But he also stressed the "unconscious," or "forms" of ideological practices, and, following the psychoanalyst Jacques Lacan, saw individuals' perception of their autonomy resulting from their interpellation by ideological discourses. This latter view gave an autonomy to language, discourse, and representations that seemed to point beyond Marxism altogether.

Althusser had less influence than Gramsci on the actual writing of history: his interest was in deep structures rather than concrete history; he had little respect for the historians' enterprise, which (for him) was mired in ideology—imaginary representations of the real conditions of existence. Yet he raised important questions about the epistemological status of historical knowledge and forced radical historians to reflect upon their all but universal assumption that they produced an objective account of people's experiences. In Britain, such issues gave rise to a major debate in the pages of *History Workshop* in 1978–1979. It was initiated by the historian Richard Johnson of the Centre for Contemporary Cultural Studies at the University of Birmingham, who put forward an Althusserian critique of the writings of both Thompson and Genovese. Johnson rejected their culturalism—their tendency to minimize the impact of productive relations on cultural processes—and criticized them for being unreflective about the problems involved in producing historical knowledge. In "The Poverty of Theory" (1978), Thompson responded to such criticism with a polemical tour de force, denouncing Althusser's theoretical practice for being "idealist" and self-confirming. For Thompson, Althusser conflated the ideology of empiricism with the empirical mode of thought and distorted the real process of history by ignoring the contribution of consciousness, experience, and human agency. Yet if Thompson's polemic was persuasive, his portrayal of what historians did (or thought that they did) was, if anything, conventional and ignored the epistemological issues that they faced.

The thought of Gramsci and Althusser rejuvenated discussions in Marxist historical theory, but also underscored its limitations as a conceptual framework. By the 1980s, Marxism (as Victor Kiernan observed) was not unlike the Ptolemaic system before the Copernican revolution: it was able to incorporate the growing body of new evidence only at the expense of theoretical coherence. In addition, it was under attack on several overlapping theoretical fronts: poststructuralists attacked its claims to objectivity and its aspiration to understand the social world as a totality; feminists criticized its reduction of gender to class and rejected its exclusive preoccupation with the public sphere, and postmodernists found its attachment to the working class to be politically nostalgic. Meanwhile, there emerged an interdisciplinary approach partially indebted to the field of cultural studies, which, though originating in Marxism itself, took a "linguistic turn," asserting that language and discourse played constitutive roles in society that could not be reduced to material interests. This more textual approach created problems not only for Marxism, but for the social history paradigm more generally. Two social historians who emerged as defenders of a linguistic and cultural approach were Gareth Stedman Jones and Joan Scott. In *The Languages of Class* (1984), Jones challenged the prevailing notion that Chartism could be understood exclusively in terms of the material interests of the early working class, arguing that existing discursive formations played pivotal roles in shaping Chartist consciousness. In *Gender and the Politics of History* (1988), Scott argued that feminist historians must produce their own historical narratives independent of social historians like Thompson. The discursive practice of social history, though claiming to be about the class experience in general, was constructed in gendered terms that marginalized working-class women as subjects. Most importantly, she rejected the idea that historians could ever recover the "experience" of women, claiming that there was nothing beyond the representation of gender in discourse.

As the end of the twentieth century approaches, then, the future of Marxism is an open question. It has been largely discredited as an alternative to capitalism. It has run into troubled waters in its effort to keep pace with a rapidly changing world. Here Marxism is no different than other classical social theories, whether derived from Emile Durkheim, or Max Weber, or others. But what is not in doubt is the richness of its legacy to the field of history. While it has never been dominant, many of the strides made by social and cultural

historians and several of the major historiographical debates of this century would have been unthinkable without it.

Dennis Dworkin

See also CAPITALISM; CLASS; DIALECTIC; ENGELS, FRIEDRICH; FRENCH REVOLUTION; GENDER; INDUSTRIAL REVOLUTION; MARX, KARL; RADICAL HISTORY (UNITED STATES).

Texts

Aston, T.H., and C.H.E. Philipin, eds. *The Brenner Debate: Agrarian Class Structure and Economic Development in Pre-Industrial Europe.* Cambridge, Eng.: Cambridge University Press, 1985.

Dobb, Maurice. *Studies in the Development of Capitalism.* London: Routledge and Kegan Paul, 1946.

Genovese, Eugene D. *Roll, Jordan, Roll: The World the Slaves Made.* New York: Random House, 1972.

Gutman, Herbert G. *Work, Culture, and Society in Industrializing America.* New York: Random House, 1976.

Hilton, Rodney, ed. *The Transition from Feudalism to Capitalism.* London: Verso, 1976.

Scott, Joan Wallach. *Gender and the Politics of History.* New York: Columbia University Press, 1988.

Thompson, E.P. *The Making of the English Working Class.* Revised ed. Harmondsworth: Penguin, 1968.

References

Comninel, George C. *Rethinking the French Revolution: Marxism and the Revisionist Challenge.* London: Verso, 1987.

Dworkin, Dennis. *Cultural Marxism in Postwar Britain: History of the New Left, and the Origins of Cultural Studies.* Durham, NC: Duke University Press, 1997.

Kaye, Harvey J. *The British Marxist Historians: An Introductory Analysis.* Cambridge, Eng.: Polity Press, 1984.

Tyrrell, Ian. *The Absent Marx: Class Analysis and Liberal History in Twentieth-Century America.* Greenwood, CT: Greenwood Press, 1986.

Maspero, Henri (1883–1945)

French sinologist. Born in Paris, Maspero was the son of a renowned Egyptologist. Maspero became professor at the École française de l'Extrême Orient in 1911, and in 1920 at the Collège de France.

He died at Buchenwald in 1945. Maspero authored many works on all aspects of Southeast Asian society including its languages, history, and religions. His *China in Antiquity* (1927) employed a philological method to scrutinize ancient Chinese civilization from its origins to the third century B.C. Although published before the discovery of archaeological remains of ancient China, his history endures for its meticulous research and its concentration on the mythological, religious, and ritualistic aspects of Chinese society. This was followed by *Histoire et Institutions de la Chine ancienne* [History and Institutions of Ancient China] (1967), covering antiquity and the First Empire, and by *Taoism and Chinese Religion* (1981). *Taoism,* which emphasized popular religious practices, is the first comprehensive study of the religious traditions of ancient China. Maspero was a pioneer in Western sinology. At the time he was writing, his knowledge of every feature of Chinese civilization was unsurpassed. He introduced the *Taoist Canon,* the *Tao Tsung* to the Western world. His research forms the basis of current scholarship in this field, and his works remain classics in Western sinology.

Leigh Whaley

Texts

China in Antiquity. Trans. Frank A. Kierman Jr. Amherst: University of Massachusetts Press, 1978.
Histoire et institutions de la Chine ancienne. Paris: Presses universitaires de France, 1967.
Taoism and Chinese Religion. Trans. Frank A. Kierman Jr. Amherst: University of Massachusetts Press, 1981.

References

Notice sur la vie et les travaux de M. Henri Maspero [Notice on the Life and Works of Henri Maspero]. Paris: Institut de France, 1951.

Mas'ūdī, Abu'l Ḥasan 'Ali bin al-Ḥusayn (ca. 893–956)

Arab historian. Born in Baghdad into a family originally from Kufa, Mas'ūdī's profession is not known, but the autobiographical sketches contained in his writings suggest that he traveled widely in the Islamic world, as far as Egypt and India. Similarly, not much is known about his religious beliefs, although he is clearly sympathetic to the Shiite branch of Islam. Thirty-six works are attributed to Mas'ūdī, only two of which

have survived: the *Murūdj al-dhahab* [Meadows of Gold] and the *Kitāb al-Tanbīh wa al-ishrāf.* The *Murūdj al-dhahab* was written in 943, when Mas'ūdī was in Cairo, and was revised in 947 and again in 956 by the author himself. The only version that has survived, however, is the original recension of 943, which has been edited and published in the original Arabic, in five volumes (Beirut, 1966–1974). The first part of the *Murūdj* contains the history of the then known world, Islamic and non-Islamic, up to the time of Muḥammad. The variety of subjects covered is a testimony to the broadness and the depth of Mas'ūdī's intellectual interests. The second part is the history of the Islamic world from the time of the prophet Muḥammad to the reign of the Caliph al-Muti, and includes individual chapters on the life and times of the first four righteous caliphs and Umayyad and 'Abbāsid leaders. Mas'ūdī's other surviving book is the *Kitāb al-Tanbīh wa al-ishrāf.* Written in 955–56, the *Tanbīh* is believed to be Mas'ūdī's last work and follows a plan similar to that of *Murudj,* but expands on many of the points raised in his earlier works.

Hootan Shambayati

Texts

Kitāb al-Tanbīh wa-al-ishrāf. Second ed. Leiden: Brill, 1967.
The Meadows of Gold. Ed. and trans. Paul Lunde and Caroline Stone. London and New York: Kegan Paul International, 1989.

References

Khalidi, Tarif. *Arabic Historical Thought in the Classical Period.* Cambridge, Eng.: Cambridge University Press, 1994.
———. *Islamic Historiography: The Histories of Ma'sudi.* Albany: State University of New York Press, 1975.

Material Culture

See CULTURAL HISTORY; MUSEUMS.

Materialism

In philosophy, the conviction that everything is matter or matter-dependent. Historical materialism holds that the ultimate causes of all important events are economic and that economic changes cause the bigger social, political, and cultural changes. Marx is usually credited with inventing historical materialism. Although historical materialism and the ensuing historiographic discipline of economic history were developed initially by Marxists, modern-day historical materialism does not imply acceptance of the Marxist theory of history and can be based just as easily on "neo-classical" or "bourgeois" economics.

Marxist historical materialism holds that the development of the means of production determines the relations of production, class distinction, and the relations between those who own and those who labor with the means of production. The political and legal superstructure perpetuates class structure and privileges, and social consciousness legitimizes it. Historical change is caused by changes in the foundational productive forces necessitating corresponding social, political, and ideological changes.

Criticism of historical materialism contends that it does not account for economic changes that originate within the innovative and entrepreneurial human consciousness. In response, Frankfurt school historical materialists have revised the theory to include knowledge, information, and ideology among the means of production.

Aviezer Tucker

See also CLASS; DIALECTIC; MARXISM AND HISTORIOGRAPHY.

References

Cohen, Gerald A. *Karl Marx's Theory of History: A Defense.* Oxford: Oxford University Press, 1978.

Shaw, William H. *Marx's Theory of History.* Stanford, CA: Stanford University Press, 1978.

Mathiez, Albert (1874–1932)

French historian and educator. Born in Franche Comté into a modest peasant family, he nonetheless received an excellent education. Three years spent at the École Normale Supérieure (1894–1897) prepared him well for the teaching profession. By 1904 he had completed his doctoral dissertation, which carefully examined two revolutionary cults. Professor first at the University of Dijon, and then at the University of Besançon, Mathiez in 1926 became a lecturer at the Sorbonne. He sought but never attained the chair of the history of the French Revolution long held by his rival Alphonse Aulard. He died of a stroke while teaching a class. Mathiez made extensive use of archival documents in producing his numerous publications. Initially he studied the political and religious achievements of the Revolution and, af-

ter the First World War, its economic and social consequences. A Socialist, and during the early 1920s a Communist, he infused his work with a strong Marxist interpretation. Most of his career was devoted to defending Maximilien Robespierre, whose personal integrity and democratic principles he greatly admired. By the volume of his writings and his forceful style, Mathiez exerted a profound influence over the study of the French revolutionary period.

James Friguglietti

Texts

The French Revolution. Trans. Catherine Alison Phillips. New York: Knopf, 1931.

References

Friguglietti, James. *Albert Mathiez, historien révolutionnaire (1874–1932)* [Albert Mathiez, Revolutionary Historian (1874–1932)]. Paris: Société des études robespierristes, 1974.

Mattingly, Garrett (1900–1962)

American historian of sixteenth-century Anglo-Spanish relations. After receiving his Ph.D. from Harvard University (1935), Mattingly taught at Northwestern (1926–1928) and Long Island (1928–1942) universities before serving in the U.S. navy during World War II. He became professor of European history at Columbia University in 1948, remaining there until his death. Noted for his lucid prose and talent for writing narrative history, Mattingly's works were scholarly yet became popular among the general public. His first book, *Catherine of Aragon* (1941), eschewed personal anecdotes for the broader political and international issues that encompassed her life. Well-versed in the Spanish archives, he helped edit many of those that pertain to England during this period. His *Renaissance Diplomacy* (1955) traced the origins of modern diplomacy to the fifteenth century and the Italian city-states. *The Armada* (1959), his most popular work, was almost a novel in form; it brought to life major figures and events in a compelling manner and was the first treatment that attempted to place that event within a European, rather than strictly English, context. He also published a controversial article in 1958 arguing that Machiavelli's *Prince* was really a satire since the Italian political thinker had elsewhere rejected those very principles that have become associated with his name.

Ben Lowe

Texts

The Armada. Boston: Houghton Mifflin, 1959.
Catherine of Aragon. Boston: Little, Brown, 1941.
"Machiavelli's *Prince:* Political Science or Political Satire?" *American Scholar* 27 (1958): 482–491.
Renaissance Diplomacy. Boston: Houghton Mifflin, 1955.

References

Carter, Charles H., ed. *From the Renaissance to the Counter-Reformation: Essays in Honor of Garrett Mattingly.* New York: Random House, 1965.
Fernandez-Armesto, Felipe. *The Spanish Armada: The Experience of War in 1588.* Oxford: Oxford University Press, 1988.

Maurists

See BOLLANDISTS AND MAURISTS.

Mazrui, Ali Al'amin (b. 1933)

African political scientist, essayist, and historian. Born in Kenya and educated at the universities of Manchester, Columbia, and Oxford, Mazrui started teaching politics at Makerere University, Uganda in 1963. Having taught at the University of Michigan from 1974 to 1991, he is now Albert Schweitzer professor and director of the Institute of Global Cultural Studies at the State University of New York, Binghamton. Since 1965 he has also held many visiting posts in Africa and the United States. His preeminence among contemporary African scholars derives from his prolific production (including over twenty books) and from his provocative treatment of widely divergent African and global issues. Specifically historical writing comprises a minor part of his output. However, like all his work, it stimulates through synthesis and insight rather than archival discovery, revolving loosely around the interaction of politics and culture in twentieth-century Africa. *The African Condition* (1980) scrutinizes postcolonial leadership. *Nationalism* (1984) examines nation-building. *The Africans* (1986) surveys how Africa's complex cultural heritage has met the challenges and opportunities posed by Western imperialism.

P.S. Zachernuk

Texts

Ed. *Africa since 1935.* Vol. 8 of *UNESCO General History of Africa.* Berkeley: University of California, 1993.

The African Condition: A Political Diagnosis. London: Heinemann, 1980.
The Africans: A Triple Heritage. New York: Little, Brown, 1986.
And M. Tidy. *Nationalism and New States in Africa.* London: Heinemann, 1984.

McFarlane, Kenneth Bruce (1903–1966)

British medieval historian. McFarlane took a first-class degree in history at Exeter College, Oxford, in 1925; he was elected official fellow and tutor in 1928 and later appointed university reader in medieval history. He died in Oxford. McFarlane was a counterintuitive, revisionist, and scrupulous historian. Although he never authored a full-length monograph, his various essays and short studies, many published posthumously, have had a lasting influence on the historiography of late medieval England. Because of the dearth of information about individuals, McFarlane was convinced that the province of the medieval historian was "the growth of social organization, of civilization, of ideas." He was influenced early by both Karl Marx and the literary historian A.L. Rowse, and consequently he never made strong distinctions among political, constitutional, and social history. In his many lectures, McFarlane extended his views on "bastard feudalism" and on fiscal and contractual obligation. Far from a sign of corruption, though, these arrangements provided paths of mobility to the ambitious "middling sort" and a check on the natural bent to conflict among the magnates. In a different vein, his brief book on *John Wycliffe and the Beginnings of English Nonconformity* (1952) demonstrated that the biographer must be "destructive," to free the subject from earlier "repainting" and "varnish." In McFarlane's interpretation, Wycliffe emerges as more a protean force than a man, and the prosecuting bishops "humane, hesitant, almost squeamish." Thus English nonconformity was born and survived.

Paul A. Fideler

Texts

England in the Fifteenth Century. Ed. G.L. Harriss. London: Hambledon Press, 1981.
John Wycliffe and the Beginnings of English Nonconformity. London: English University Press, Ltd., 1952.
Lancastrian Kings and Lollard Knights. Oxford: Clarendon Press, 1972.
The Nobility of Later Medieval England. Oxford: Clarendon Press, 1973.

The Wars of the Roses. (Raleigh Lecture on History); *Proceedings of the British Academy* 50 (1964).

References

Britnell, R.H., and A.J. Pollard. *The McFarlane Legacy: Studies in Late Medieval Politics and Society.* London: Alan Sutton, 1995.

Mead, Kate Campbell Hurd (1867–1941)

Physician and historian of medicine. Born in Danville, Quebec, Canada, Mead received her M.D. from Woman's Medical College of Pennsylvania in 1888 and continued her studies at a variety of medical centers. She became the medical director of Bryn Mawr in 1890 and in 1891 founded the Evening Dispensary for Working Women and Girls in Baltimore. She established her medical practice in Middletown, Connecticut, in 1893 and remained in practice until 1925. She died of a heart attack in Haddam, Connecticut, during a brush fire on her estate. Mead is best known for her work *A History of Women in Medicine* (1938). The book was a wide-ranging chronicle of women's participation in medicine, far more comprehensive than earlier efforts. Extremely detailed, the book incorporated literary references, mythology, and archaeological evidence, as well as secondary and primary sources in Spanish, French, German, and English. Apart from her discussion of classical antiquity, the work is largely confined to Britain, France, and Italy. Mead had previously published *Medical Women of America* (1933), while her extensive papers, held at the Schlesinger Library, include notes prepared for subsequent volumes.

Peter L. Twohig

Texts

A History of Women in Medicine from the Earliest Times to the Beginning of the Nineteenth Century. Haddam, CT: The Haddam Press, 1938.

Medical Women of America: A Short History of the Pioneer Medical Women of America and of a Few of Their Colleagues in England. New York: Froben Press, 1933.

References

Bass, Elizabeth. "Kate Campbell Hurd Mead, M.D." *Journal of the American Medical Women's Association* 11 (1956): 155.

Lovejoy, Esther P. "Kate Campbell Hurd-Mead (1867–1941)." *Bulletin of the History of Medicine* 10 (1941): 314–317.

Medicine, Historiography of

Medical history as a branch of historical writing. Long before professional historians began to study the history of medicine, medicine's past was of critical consequence to medical practitioners and professors, eager to immortalize dead forebears for the instruction of students and to erect a pedigree for their art. Past heroes long enjoyed present authority. The humanist physicians of the sixteenth and seventeenth centuries treated the oeuvres of medicine's founding fathers, notably Hippocrates and Galen, as canonical, living founts of wisdom rather than mere objects of antiquarian curiosity.

The first significant attempt to construct a full narrative of medicine's rise was *Histoire de la médecine d'ou l'on voit l'origine et le progrès de l'art* (1696) by Daniel Leclerc, professor of medicine in Geneva. It was followed by the derivative *History of Physick* (1725–1726) by the London physician, John Freind. Freind's survey of Greco-Roman and medieval medicine was structured with half an eye to contemporary debates concerning the medical applications of Newtonian mechanical philosophy: the past could still determine current controversies.

As with political history, in the history of medicine the Enlightenment and, even more so, the nineteenth century mark the scholarly watershed. Historians began to insist that the past was truly distinct from the present. Study of long-dead medical theorists and their musty tomes gradually ceased to be definitive of medical thinking itself and turned into a scholarly passion, or pastime, in its own right. The first history of medicine in this "modern" mode was Kurt Sprengel's (1766–1833) *Versuch einer pragmatischen Geschichte der Arzneikunde* [An Attempt at a Practical History of Medical Knowledge] (1792), which aimed to steer a middle course between lofty philosophical interpretation and pedantic antiquarianism. In the nineteenth century, German scholarship led the field. In his *Lehrbuch der Geschichte der Medizin und der Volkskrankheit* [Textbook on the History of Medicine and Human Diseases] (1845), Heinrich Haeser (1811–1884) produced the first professed textbook of medical history—a work giving consideration to historical epidemiology as well as to the biographies of physicians. The first periodical devoted exclusively to medical history, the German-language *Janus,* was founded in 1846—it lasted a mere two years!—and the first chair in the history of medicine was created in Vienna in 1850.

Attention began to be devoted to producing authoritative editions of major texts. Nineteenth-century scholars created many of the editions of the classic authors still in use. Galen's works were edited in Leipzig between 1823 and 1833, while between 1839 and 1861 the French philological scholar, Emile Littré (1801–1881), edited Hippocrates. From 1844, the Sydenham Society dedicated itself to publishing a series of English translations of Greek, Latin, and Arabic medical classics. Alongside the creation of a canon of classical medical texts, book collecting became prestigious. Sir William Osler (1849–1919) built up a celebrated personal library, now preserved in Montreal, and, most spectacularly, Sir Henry Wellcome (1853–1936) channeled profits from his pharmaceutical business into an enormous collection of medical books, manuscripts, paintings, and artifacts, that was later to form the core of the Wellcome Institute for the History of Medicine in London. Among historians of medicine, the pivotal figure was Karl Sudhoff (1853–1938), professor of the history of medicine at Leipzig from 1905 to 1925 and director of the first institute of the history of medicine, which became the model for medical historians the world over. Sudhoff set particular store by manuscript research. Under his direction, *Sudhoffs Archiv,* the first enduring journal of the history of medicine, was set up and essential reference works compiled, notably the *Biographisches Lexikon der hervorragenden Arzte* [Biographical Dictionary of Eminent Physicians] by August Hirsch (1817–1894) and Julius Pagel (1851–1912), which began to appear in 1884 and took fifty years to complete.

Sudhoff's successor at Leipzig, the Swiss, Henry Sigerist (1891–1957), broadened the intellectual vision of medical history and, as a committed admirer of the Soviet Union, developed a more socially oriented vision of medical history. In 1932 Sigerist was appointed head of the new Institute for the History of Medicine at the Johns Hopkins University, Baltimore. From 1933 under his guidance, the *Bulletin of the History of Medicine* began to appear, and the American Association for the History of Medicine was founded.

Until recently the bulk of writings in the history of medicine have been "in-house": written by doctors, for doctors, and about doctors. This tendency to treat medical history as the contributions of physicians and scientists to the progress of medical knowledge and surgical techniques has come under attack during the last generation as being unacceptably Whiggish. Many historians of medicine today stress the dangers of anachronism, insisting that earlier physicians and medical belief-systems must be understood within their own contexts rather than evaluated in terms of their contribution to the triumphs of modern medicine. They also seek to widen the vision, paying greater attention to the history of patients and not just practitioners, to lay wisdom and popular forms of healing, to medical institutions and the paramedical professions, and to the social and political ramifications of medical knowledge.

Roy Porter

References

Brieger, G.H. "The Historiography of Medicine." In *Companion Encyclopedia of the History of Medicine,* ed. W.F. Bynum and Roy Porter. London: Routledge, 1993, 24–44.

Webster, Charles. "The Historiography of Medicine." In *Information Sources in the History of Science and Medicine,* ed. P. Corsi and P. Weindling. London and Boston: Butterworth Scientific, 1983, 29–43.

Meinecke, Friedrich (1862–1954)

German historian. Meinecke studied at the universities of Berlin and Bonn and received his scholarly education from leading representatives of the classical German historical school, such as J.G. Droysen, Heinrich von Sybel, Heinrich von Treitschke, and Harry Bresslau. Meinecke held a chair at the universities of Strasbourg, Freiburg im Breisgau, and Berlin. As editor of the leading German historical journal, the *Historische Zeitschrift,* from 1893, he engaged in a bitter controversy over Karl Lamprecht's conception of a new paradigm of historical scholarship. Meinecke's work was closely interwoven with his political opinions, which rejected both radical reforms and totalitarianism. Under Nazi rule he was eased out of his editorial position in 1935 but continued to write. In 1948 he became the first rector of the newly established Free University of Berlin. Meinecke is generally regarded as one of the most influential historians of his generation in Germany. His work concentrated on the history of political ideas, the history of Prussia, and the philosophy of history. In his *Weltbürgertum und Nationalstaat* [Cosmopolitanism and the National State] (1907), he elaborated his central thesis that a unique symbiosis of power politics and culture had characterized the nation building of Germany and established its superiority over Western democracies. In *Die Entstehung des Historismus* [The Origins of Historicism; later translated into English as *Historism*] (1936), he analyzed the interrelation between the German conception of history and politics and explored the problem of historical relativism. *Die deutsche*

Katastrophe [The German Catastrophe] (1946) examined the impact of national socialism. He strongly advocated the idea that the Third Reich was merely an accident in German history, rather than the outcome of national traditions. Meinecke's *Ideengeschichte,* or history of ideas, had considerable impact on a postwar generation of students of German history, who started to investigate the roots of the failure of democracy in Germany.

Georgi Verbeeck

Texts

The Age of German Liberation, 1795–1815. Ed. P. Paret; trans. P. Paret and H. Fischer. Berkeley: University of California Press, 1977.

Historism: The Rise of a New Historical Outlook. Trans. J.E. Anderson. Second ed., Trans. revised by H.D. Schmidt. London: Routledge and Kegan Paul, 1972.

Machiavellism: The Doctrine of Raison d'Etat and Its Place in Modern History. Trans. Douglas Scott. New Haven, CT: Yale University Press, 1957.

References

Iggers, Georg G. *The German Conception of History: The National Tradition of Historical Thought from Herder to the Present.* Middletown, CT: Wesleyan University Press, 1968.

Pois, Robert A. *Friedrich Meinecke and German Politics in the Twentieth Century.* Berkeley and Los Angeles: University of California Press, 1972.

Ringer, Fritz K. *The Decline of the German Mandarins: The German Academic Community 1890–1933.* Cambridge, MA: Harvard University Press, 1969.

Memoirs
See AUTOBIOGRAPHY.

Memory and History
Modern interest in the relationship of memory to history may be considered in three historiographical contexts: nineteenth-century historicism, twentieth-century postmodernism, and recent testimonies about the Holocaust.

Nineteenth-Century Historicism
Historicists tended to emphasize the interplay between memory and history. From Jules Michelet to R.G. Collingwood, collective memory was the inspiring source of historical understanding. Often sympathizing with the political traditions they studied, historicists regarded history as a more accurate rendering of memory's insights. They studied history so as to re-create in the present the past as it had originally been imagined. In evoking the images in which the world was once conceived, they taught, the historian can reenter the mental universe of historical actors and so recover the presence of those actors' past. The early historicists' ambition to resurrect the imagination of the past in present memory (Michelet), however, was chastened by their later followers who acknowledged the reconstructive nature of integrating images of the past into the present historical imagination (Benedetto Croce, Wilhelm Dilthey). R.G. Collingwood, a late exemplar of historicism, further limited such reconstruction to the reasoning processes of historical actors. Recently some historians have dismissed memory's claims upon history altogether. While memory might provide the raw data of history, they contend, the historian corrects memory's distortions by reconstructing the past on the basis of the documentary record. While such evidence might be regarded as relics of once living memory, the historian has no reason to believe that the presence of the past can any longer be evoked from them.

Late-Twentieth-Century Postmodernism
Postmodernists accept this opposition between memory and history. But rather than dismissing the value of memory because of its distortions, they have made these the subject of historical enquiry. They inventory memory's representations as a basis for explaining the ways in which they had been used to legitimize particular conceptions of the past. Taking their cue from the work on collective memory of the French sociologist Maurice Halbwachs early in this century, these historians have focused on the way collective memory frames the interests, subject matter, and interpretations through which the past is enshrined in tradition. So reconceived, the postmodern formulation of the memory/history problem has redirected attention from the nature of recollection to the politics of memory. These historians study representations of the past (its imagery as well as its discourse) as signatures of the power of those who formulated and publicized them.

The postmodern interest in the politics of memory reflects the temper of our times in its weakening identification with the traditions of the modern age. It has inspired studies that deconstruct the myths, rituals, modes of publicity, and conventions of discourse "invented" to sustain particular traditions. Noteworthy are studies of the politics of commemoration, through which particular persons have been cast in idealized images and particular events have been consecrated as places of memory. Their purpose is to show how public memory is continually revised to suit present needs. In effect, the postmodernists' focus on the politics of memory discredits what the historicists saw as their raison d'être: the validation of the traditions in which public values have been preserved. Important recent studies in this genre have been written by Pierre Nora for France, Michael Kammen for the United States, and Yael Zerubavel for Israel.

Contemporary Historiographical Issues Relating to Living Testimonies of the Holocaust

The historicist conception of memory has nonetheless presented itself again today in a different guise as a response to efforts to use the authority of historical interpretation to deny the claims of living memory, notably those of the survivors of the Holocaust. The controversy over the efforts of "revisionist" historians to downplay Nazi atrocities against European Jewry highlights the peril of detaching history's interests completely from the recollections of living memory, thereby severing all conscious ties between past and present realities. Were the past to be equated with its imaginary representations, historians of the Holocaust contend, then historians would be abandoning their quest to uncover the reality of the past and the basis for choosing one historical interpretation over another would be reduced to the controversies of present politics. While living memory may be an unreliable basis for historical interpretation, its testimony, however provisional, provides existential verification of the reality of the past.

Historicists and postmodernists tend to focus on the opposing sides of memory's dynamic operations: the repetition of well-remembered imagery versus the recollection of images that have been forgotten. The former evokes the past, the latter reconstructs it. While historians may tend to favor one or the other, historical thinking invariably mimicks memory's dynamic movement between received tradition and recollective reconstruction and so can never completely escape its claims.

Patrick Hutton

See also AUTOBIOGRAPHY; HISTORICISM; HOLOCAUST, HISTORIOGRAPHY OF THE; POSTMODERNISM.

Texts

Collingwood, R.G. *The Idea of History*. Oxford: Oxford University Press, 1946.
Halbwachs, Maurice. *The Collective Memory*. Trans. Francis Ditter. New York: Harper & Row, 1950.
Hobsbawm, Eric, and Terence Ranger, eds. *The Invention of Tradition*. Cambridge, Eng.: Cambridge University Press, 1983.
Kammen, Michael. *Mystic Chords of Memory*. New York: Knopf, 1991.
Nora, Pierre, ed. *Les Lieux de mémoire* [The Places of Memory]. 3 vols. Paris: Gallimard, 1984–1992.
Vidal-Naquet, Pierre. *Assassins of Memory*. Trans. Jeffrey Mehlman. New York: Columbia University Press, 1992.
Zerubavel, Yael. *Recovered Roots*. Chicago: University of Chicago Press, 1995.

References

Friedlander, Saul, ed. *Probing the Limits of Representation*. Cambridge, MA: Harvard University Press, 1992.
Hutton, Patrick. *History As an Art of Memory*. Hanover, NH: University Press of New England, 1993.
Le Goff, Jacques. *History and Memory*. Trans. Steven Rendall and Elizabeth Claman. New York: Columbia University Press, 1992.

Menéndez Pelayo, Marcelino (1856–1912)

Spanish literary and intellectual historian. Menéndez Pelayo taught literature at the University of Madrid and became director of the National Library. His principal works—*La ciencia Española* [Spanish Science] (1876), *Historia de los heterodoxos españoles* [History of Spanish Heterodox Thinkers] (1880), and *Historia de las ideas estéticas en España* [History of Aesthetic Ideas in Spain] (1883)—were all written during his twenties. They reveal a sometimes intemperate defender of Spanish culture and an apologist for Catholicism. Menéndez Pelayo expressed his ideas on history in his inaugural address to the Real Academia de la Historia in 1883. Here he criticized Hegel for not appreciating "the aesthetic character of history" and disagreed with Aristotle's dictum that history was less profound than poetry. For Menéndez Pelayo the functions of the historian and the poet were the same: "to discover the universal in the mundane." He stressed the importance of writing "internal" history especially in terms of the history of ideas. He praised the ancient historians because they were both subjective and great stylists. Menéndez Pelayo inspired the Catholic ultraconservatives of twentieth-century Spain who regarded liberal historiography as anathema.

George L. Vásquez

Texts

Historia de las ideas estéticas en España. 5 vols. Santander: Aldus, S.A. de Artes Gráficas, 1940–1947.

Historia de los heterodoxos españoles. 8 vols. Santander: Aldus, S.A. de Artes Gráficas, 1946–1948.

La ciencia Española. Third ed. Madrid: Imp. A. Pérez Dubrull, 1887–1888.

References

Palacio Atard, Vicente. *Menéndez Pelayo y la historia de España* [Menéndez Pelayo and the History of Spain]. Valladolid: Universidad de Valladolid, Colección estudios y documentos, 1956.

Menéndez Pidal, Ramón (1869–1968)

Spanish historian. Menéndez Pidal was born in La Coruña, Spain. In 1892, he completed his doctoral thesis at Madrid University on *El Conde Lucanor* [Count Lucanor]. The following year, his study on the *Cantar de Mio Cid* [Romance of the Cid] demonstrated his interest in medieval Spanish history. In 1896, he published *La Leyenda de los Infantes de Lara* [The Legend of the Princes of Lara], in which he argued that Spanish traditional ballads had originated in earlier epic poems. In 1899, Menéndez Pidal joined the faculty of the University of Madrid where, from 1910 to 1936, he directed the Center for Historical Studies. In 1901, he was elected to the Royal Spanish Academy and became its director in 1925. In 1929, he published *La España del Cid* [The Cid and His Spain], which used both archival sources and literary texts to enhance historical understanding of medieval Spain. Forced into exile after 1936 by the Spanish Civil War he published *La idea imperial de Carlos V* (1937) [The Imperial Idea of Charles V] an essay that argued that Charles V had expanded the notion of empire by constructing an ideal and universal Christian unity in Europe and the Americas. On Menéndez Pidal's return to Spain in 1939, the Franco regime abolished the center and revoked his directorship of the academy. In 1947, he published *Los españoles en la historia* [The Spaniards in Their History], which examined the Spanish national character and emphasized Castile's

importance in the historical construction of Spain. At the end of that year, the academy reinstated his directorship. He died six years later in Chamartin. Menéndez Pidal's most polemical work, published in 1963, was *El Padre Las Casas: Su doble personalidad* [Father Las Casas: His Double Personality], a controversial rethinking of the place of Las Casas in Spanish colonial history that argued against the traditional view of Las Casas as a progressive and sympathetic writer.

Carlos Pérez

Texts

The Cid and His Spain. Trans. Harold Sunderland. London: John Murray, 1934.

El imperio hispánico y los cinco reinos [The Spanish Empire and the Five Kingdoms]. Madrid: Instituto de Estudios Políticos, 1950.

El Padre Las Casas: Su doble personalidad. Madrid: Espasa-Calpe, 1963.

Romancéro hispánico [Spanish Romances]. 2 vols. Madrid: Espasa-Calpe, 1953.

The Spaniards in Their History. Trans. Walter Starkie. New York: Norton, 1950.

References

Hess, Steven. *Ramón Menéndez Pidal.* Boston: Twayne, 1982.

Smith, C. *Ramón Menéndez Pidal, 1869–1968.* London: Hispanic and Luso Brazilian Councils, 1970.

Mentalities [French: *mentalités*]

A concept in intellectual and cultural history widely employed toward the end of understanding and explaining apparently alien or at least "unmodern" behavior in past cultures. The idea of different mentalities or modes of thought was shared by a number of eighteenth-century thinkers, from Vico to Montesquieu, who explained the medieval custom of the judicial ordeal by "the way of thought of our ancestors." All the same, it was only in the twentieth century that the history of "collective mentalities" developed as a specific approach to the past, above all in France. Marc Bloch's *The Royal Touch* (1923) and Lucien Febvre's *The Problem of Unbelief in the Sixteenth Century: The Religion of Rabelais* (1942) are classics of the genre, although their example was not commonly followed until the 1960s. Contrast and comparison may help define the history of mentalities closely. It differs from the "history of ideas" of Arthur O. Lovejoy and his followers because it focuses on unspoken assumptions, attitudes, and habits of thought rather than on consciously formulated concepts, and because it is concerned with all social groups rather than with philosophers and other intellectuals. It differs from the "ideology" of the Marxists by placing less emphasis on social "class" and by making no assumptions about "false consciousness," economic determinism, or the manipulation of "the masses" by elites. The stress on "collective" mentalities runs counter to the individualist tradition, a point that may explain the continuing reluctance of many British historians to follow the foreign model of what many still call "the history of *mentalités*." On the other hand, the history of mentalities has much in common with "historical psychology" (a phrase used by Bloch and Febvre), and also with historical anthropology, for anthropologists since Durkheim have concerned themselves with modes of thought and "collective representations." In the 1980s and 1990s, the term "mentality" has been falling out of use among French historians, but the new history of the imagination *(l'imaginaire social),* despite its greater emphasis on images, has much in common with its predecessor.

Peter Burke

See also ANNALES SCHOOL; ANTHROPOLOGY AND HISTORY; CLASS; CULTURAL HISTORY; IDEAS, HISTORY OF; SOCIAL HISTORY; SOCIOLOGY AND HISTORY.

References

Burke, Peter. *History and Social Theory.* Oxford, Eng.: Polity, 1992.

Vovelle, Michel. *Ideologies and Mentalities.* Trans. Eamon O'Flaherty. Cambridge, Eng.: Polity, 1990.

Merton, Robert King (b. 1910)

American sociologist of science. Born in Philadelphia, Merton graduated from Temple University (1931) and pursued graduate studies at Harvard University (Ph.D., 1936). His distinguished career at Columbia University spanned more than four decades (1941–1984); he remains (1997) Emeritus professor of sociology. A pioneer in the sociology of science, he studied the interaction of cultural values (Puritanism and Pietism), technological innovations, and social institutions in the development of science in seventeenth-century England. First published in 1938, but largely ignored, Merton's *Science, Technology & Society in Seventeenth Century England* was subsequently reissued and is sometimes regarded as having contributed to the

later reformulation of the history of science by Thomas S. Kuhn and others. He also contributed to historiography with his concise explanations of such sociological concepts as status and role, manifest and latent functions, anomie, reference groups, self-fulfilling prophecy, structural and functional analysis, middle range theories, and the paradox of unintended consequences.

Ross Evans Paulson

Texts

Science, Technology & Society in Seventeenth Century England. New York: Howard Fertig, 1970.

Social Theory and Social Structure. Enlarged ed. New York: Free Press, 1968.

References

Coser, Lewis, ed. *The Idea of Social Structure: Papers in Honor of Robert K. Merton.* New York: Harcourt Brace Jovanovich, 1975.

Sztompka, Piotr. *Robert K. Merton: An Intellectual Profile.* London: Macmillan, 1986.

Mexican Historiography

Historical writing in and about Mexico since the Spanish conquest. History in Mexico has played a central role in creating a sense of national identity and as such has often been politically contentious. To this day history textbooks for schools are the object of controversy. These debates derive not merely from the conservative-radical divide, they also reflect differing approaches to the three great periods into which the Mexican past is divided: the cycle of native civilization, the centuries of Spanish rule (1521–1821), and the revolutions of the nation-state. Although the geographical boundaries of Mesoamerica, New Spain, and the Mexican United States differed considerably, in all three periods the cultural and political heartland has been the Valley of Mexico. But the degree to which a national history can be fabricated out of these geographical continuities is open to question. In any case, for much of its development, native civilization can only be approached through a study of its material artifacts. For Mayan cities, however, the recent deciphering of glyphs has uncovered the dynastic history of the classic period (A.D. 250–900). A more ample narrative can be written of the Mexica (the native peoples of the region) since the foundation of Mexico-Tenochtitlan in 1325. The Spanish conquerors, Hernán Cortés and Bernal Díaz del Castillo wrote lively accounts of the city, its temples, and final siege in 1521. The Franciscan and Dominican missionaries thereafter studied

Indian languages, religion, and culture and composed chronicles based on questioning native elders and record-keepers. Indeed, Bernardino de Sahagún (1499–1590) presented his encyclopedic survey in parallel columns of Nahuatl and Spanish accompanied by lavish illustration. From the 1570s onward, acculturated native and mestizo chroniclers wrote accounts of their respective peoples, the most notable the history of Texcoco by Fernando de Alva Ixtlilxóchitl (1578–1650). This cycle of historiography culminated with the publication of *Monarquía indiana* (1615) in which Juan de Torquemada (ca. 1564–1624) incorporated not merely the researches of his Franciscan predecessors but also a wealth of data from other chroniclers, including material from Bartolomé de las Casas's celebrated defense of the American Indians. In this monumental work, Torquemada openly challenged the imperial historians of Spain who adopted a scornful view of native cultural capacity. When the exiled Mexican Jesuit, Francisco Javier Clavijero (1731–1787) published his *Historia Antígua de México* (1780–1781), in order to combat the denigration of Aztec civilization launched by the enlightened historians William Robertson and Guillaume Raynal, he simply condensed and rewrote Torquemada's work in neoclassic prose.

The three centuries of Pax Hispanica did not produce dramatic events for the style of narrative history then in fashion. Once the conquest was over, it was the missionary activity of the mendicant orders that attracted the pen of numerous chroniclers. The Franciscans, Toribio de Benevente and Jeronimo de Mendieta, both framed exuberant accounts of the "spiritual conquest," but it was left to Torquemada to appropriate their manuscripts for his great work. It was thus only with the Insurgency of 1810 against Spanish rule that Mexico experienced the battles and political debate that offered materials for a generation of historians. The most notable was Carlos María de Bustamente (1774–1848) who interpreted the insurgency as a campaign waged by the Mexican people to regain their independence, a view that installed the Aztec empire as the foundation of the nation. Thereafter, Bustamante chronicled the disorders of the republic, which culminated in the American invasion of 1846–1848 and the loss of national territory. His nationalist vision was sharply criticized first by Liberal historians and then by Lucás Alamán (1792–1853), whose *Historia de Méjico* (1849–1852) resumed this cycle of historiography, contrasting the prosperity of the colony with the ruinous state of Mexico in 1850. The bitter civil wars caused by the Liberal assault on the Catholic Church, 1855–1867, provoked a second flurry of narratives, which were resumed in *Mexico a través de los siglos* (1884–1889), an all-encompassing national history, edited by Vicente Riva Palacio (1832–1896). Its Liberal triumphalism, however, was attacked by Francisco Bulnes (1847–1924) whose *El Verdadero Juárez* (1904) caused such scandal that Justo Sierra (1848–1912), the leading historian of the epoch, replied with his *Benito Juárez* (1906), a magisterial portrayal of nineteenth-century Mexico written from the Liberal viewpoint.

The Mexican Revolution of 1910–1920 generated many novels and memoirs, the best written by Martín Luis Guzman and José Vasconcelos, but it did not immediately elicit any significant historical narratives, in part because the country remained disturbed until 1940. It was Frank Tannenbaum (1893–1969) who, in *The Mexican Agrarian Revolution* (1929), defined the movement as essentially Indian and agrarian. In part, he was indebted to Manuel Gamio (1893–1960) whose *La población del valle de Teotihuacan* (1922) insisted on the historical continuity of Indian culture in Mexico. It was only after World War II that Mexican history was professionalized and became, at the same time, the object of European and North American interest. The extent of the demographic catastrophe occasioned by the Spanish conquest was demonstrated by Sherburne Cook and Woodrow Borah in a series of monographs. The rise of the great estate was narrated by Francois Chevalier and the mendicant churches of the sixteenth century were presented by George Kubler as a paradigm of acculturation. In his *Historia Moderna de México* (1955–1963), Daniel Cosío Villegas (1898–1976), the founder of *Historia mexicana* (1951–), reinterpreted the period 1867–1910. Other Mexican scholars of that generation include Silvio Zavala and Edmundo O'Gorman, whose works deal with the colonial period. Only since the 1970s has it been possible to write of the Mexican Revolution with any degree of impartiality. At present, Mexican history is cultivated by many scholars, remains contentious, and is still central to any sense of cultural identity. It is also a fascinating object of study for many foreign historians.

D.A. Brading

See also INDIGENOUS HISTORIOGRAPHY; LATIN AMERICAN HISTORIOGRAPHY.

References

Memorias del Simposio de Historiografia Mexicanista. Mexico City: Proceedings of the Symposium in Mexican Historiography, 1990.

Brading, D.A. *The First America: The Spanish monarchy, Creole patriots and the Liberal State 1492–1967.* Cambridge, Eng.: Cambridge University Press, 1991.

"México e Hispanoamérica: Una reflexión historiográfica en el Quinto centenario [Mexico and Hispanic America: Reflections on the Fifth Centenary]." *Historia Mexicana,* 166–167 (1992–1993).

Griffin, Charles C., ed. *Latin America. A Guide to the Historical Literature.* Austin: University of Texas Press, 1971.

Meyer, Eduard (1855–1930)

German ancient historian. Born in Hamburg, Meyer studied at Bonn and Leipzig; he subsequently taught at Leipzig, Breslau, and Berlin. He pioneered the scientific study of ancient near eastern, especially Egyptian, history, as well as Greek and Roman history, beginning with his famous *Geschichte des Altertums* [History of Antiquity] in 1884, which remains the most ambitious attempt to synthesize classical and near eastern history. He also directed his efforts toward the study of slavery in antiquity (*Die Sklaverei in Altertum,* 1898). He lectured (1909–1910) in the United States, took a strong pro-German viewpoint during World War I, and headed the University of Berlin in 1919–1920. A major publication of this period was *Caesars Monarchie und das Principat des Pompeius* [Caesar's Monarchy and the Principate of Pompey]. (1918).

Stephen A. Stertz

Texts

Caesars Monarchie und das Principat des Pompeius. Stuttgart and Berlin: Cotta, 1918.

Geschichte des Altertums. 5 vols. Stuttgart: Cotta, 1884–1902.

Die Sklaverei in Altertum. Stuttgart: Cotta, 1898.

References

Christ, Karl. *Von Gibbon zu Rostovzeff* [From Gibbon to Rostovzeff]. Darmstadt, Germany: Wissenschaftliche Buchgesellschaft, 1972, 286–333.

Mézeray [or Mézerai] François Eudes de (1610–1683)

French historian. Born near Argentan, Mézeray studied at the University of Caen before going to Paris, where he sought to make a career for himself as a poet and translator (despite a brief episode as a *commissaire des armées* in 1635). Attracting the interest of Cardinal Richelieu, Mézeray was appointed royal historiographer in 1643. In the same year, his *Histoire de France* began to appear. This work was widely read, although it earned the disapproval of the French academy for its popular style. Mézeray's later work, the *Abrégé chronologique* [Abridged Chronology] (1668), was too politically audacious for the government of Louis XIV, whose minister Colbert revoked Mézeray's pension and suspended his appointment. Mézeray's career illustrates the transition from humanist to Enlightenment traditions of historical writing, the bare political and military chronology of the early works eventually being supplemented by greater attention to social and cultural developments as well as broader reference to historical sources.

Ian Germani

Texts

A General Chronological History of France. Trans. J. Bultee. London: T. Basset et al., 1683.

Histoire de France, depuis Faramond jusqu'à maintenant. Revised ed. Paris: D. Thierry, 1685.

References

Evans, Wilfred Hugo. *L'Historien Mézeray et la conception de l'histoire en France au XVIIᵉ siècle* [The Historian Mézeray and the Idea of History in Seventeenth-Century France]. Paris: J. Gamber, 1930.

Lefler, Phyllis. "From Humanist to Enlightenment Historiography: A Case Study of François Eudes de Mézeray." *French Historical Studies* 10 (1978): 416–438.

Ranum, Orest. *Artisans of Glory: Writers and Historical Thought in Seventeenth-Century France.* Chapel Hill: University of North Carolina Press, 1980.

Michelet, Jules (1798–1874)

French romantic historian and philosopher of history. Michelet was born in humble circumstances and acquired a keen interest in the past, and a sensitivity to its physical remains, as a child. He spent the early part of his career as professor of ancient history at the École Normale Supérieure, subsequently becoming keeper of the national archives and professor at the Collège de France (1838). His dislike of the government of King Louis-Philippe turned him to the subject of French revolutionary history. He was banned from teaching under the July Monarchy and, on refusing allegiance to Napoleon III, deprived of all his positions, spending the rest of his life in retirement. Michelet's metahistorical approach explored new areas of historical writing. Swept along with the great revolutionary changes, he continually redefined the historian's task and the meaning of the history of France. After translating Giambattista Vico's *Scienza nuova* he became convinced of the necessity of writing a history that balanced the concepts of change and continuity. Influenced by J.G. Herder's idea of the *Volk* [People], he also embraced Vico's belief in the active part that humans play in the making of history. This further alienated him from the Catholic conception of history current in his time. In Michelet's view, the Revolution was the incarnation of justice. In the 1840s his ideas began to follow a more radical, republican, and democratic agenda. Changes in his historical and political ideas paralleled his personal experience, and he developed an early psychohistorical approach. Michelet's tombstone carries the epitaph, "history is a resurrection"; he was able to relive the fate of historical actors through his own "descent" and to understand the past by a careful, microscopic study of details rendered in vivid colors. Michelet's intense love for France was heralded in his popular book *Le Peuple*. A good example of "social romantic" nationalism, its thesis is that the fraternity of the people, the sacrifice of artisans (especially women) and traditional relations of equality, rather than church, king, or nobility, had brought true liberty to France; the nation had to reconcile its differences between all classes, develop a greater love for nature (through science) and the land, and revive the family as a basic social unit. Although Michelet has been faulted for his lack of attention to primary sources, there is lasting value in his study of common people and the human psyche in history.

John B. Roney

Texts

History of France. Trans. G.H. Smith. 2 vols. New York: P. Appleton, 1847.
History of the French Revolution. Ed. Gordon Wright; trans. Charles Cocks. Chicago: University of Chicago Press, 1967.
Joan of Arc. Trans. Albert Guerard. Ann Arbor: University of Michigan Press, 1982.
The People. Trans. John P. McKay. Urbana: University of Illinois Press, 1973.

References

Barthes, Roland. *Michelet*. Trans. Richard Howard. Oxford: Basil Blackwell, 1987.
Fauquet, Eric. *Michelet, ou La gloire du professeur d'histoire* [Michelet, or the Glory of a Professor of History]. Paris: Les Éditions du Cerf, 1990.
Febvre, Lucien. *Michelet et la Renaissance*. Paris: Flammarion, 1992.
Kippur, Stephen. *Jules Michelet: A Study of Mind and Sensibility*. Albany, NY: SUNY, 1981.
Mitzman Arthur. *Michelet, Historian: Rebirth and Romanticism in Nineteenth-Century France*. New Haven, CT: Yale University Press, 1990.
Orr, Linda. *Jules Michelet: Nature, History, and Language*. Ithaca, NY: Cornell UP, 1976.

Microhistory or *Microstoria*

A historical method that isolates the beliefs or social interactions of individuals or small groups in order to uncover more general patterns obscured by other methods. Microhistory first appeared as an identifiable historical movement in Italy between 1976 and 1983 in the journal *Quaderni Storici* and the *microstorie* series of books published by Giulio Einaudi in Turin. Similar tendencies could be found among historians in France and the United States at about the same time, but they lacked the theoretical underpinnings and systematic publishing program enjoyed by the Italian practitioners of *microstoria*. In many respects, however, microhistory's fascination with the particular merely reasserts a historiographical tradition that stretches back to antiquity.

Deeply influenced by social and cultural anthropology, the microhistorians of the 1970s were reacting to the then dominant quantitative serial history that analyzed through statistical methods large social groups over long periods of time, uncovering the deep structures of family life in an entire region, a particular class over several centuries, or the capitalist world system. The quantitative history of the French Annales school, the Cambridge Population Group, and American cliometricians reduced individuals to the few characteristics that could be represented in numerical form, usually economic or demographic ones. The microhistorians, in contrast, wanted to recapture a fuller picture of individual experiences and choices. In place of numerical data derived from thousands of similar sources, such as tax records or censuses, microhistorians concentrated on a few revealing documents, such as the transcripts of trials or inquisitorial proceedings that recorded the actual words of participants. Rather than analyzing persistent structural continuities (the *longue durée*), they wrote narrations limited to the time span of a single life and spotlighted abrupt changes. Most microhistorians also attempted to give a voice to persons whose low social status, illiteracy, or unconventional ideas made them otherwise lost to history. These early microhistorians were, thus, rejecting the perceived ethnocentricity of modernization theory and striving to rewrite history from below.

According to theorists such as Carlo Ginzburg, Eduardo Grendi, Carlo Poni, and Giovanni Levi, all of whom were associated with *Quaderni Storici, microstoria* has two distinguishing principles. The first reduces the scale of historical research to identifiable individuals: the fundamental unit of analysis becomes the "name" since a name marks individuality and a name can be traced through a wide variety of records. By following names, microhistorians can reconstruct networks of social relationships and determine the actual significance of various kinds of social ties and interactions: those determined by gender, household, family, community, class, faction, occupation, belief, or ideology. The goal is to create a history in which the vital relationships, constraints, and decisions faced by identifiable persons in actual historical situations would emerge. Some microhistorians refer to this objective as the history of "real life" or of "lived experience."

The second principle explicates an alternative standard of historical proof called the "evidential" or sometimes the "conjectural paradigm." It is this aspect of microhistory, most famously associated with the work of Carlo Ginzburg, that has provoked the most controversy. The evidential paradigm suggests that the evidence appropriate for a "science of the particular" must be different from what would be acceptable in a normal scientific endeavor that is devoted to establishing generally applicable laws derived from quantifiable investigations. The microhistorian employs a method similar to the detective's search for clues, which serve as signs that indicate the presence of something that is otherwise hidden. For example, a detective finds fingerprints useful not because they reveal general principles of human nature but because each finger differs from every other. The presence of a print at the scene of a crime allows the police to identify the only person who could have left the idiosyncratic print. Likewise, the microhistorian uses isolated bits of evidence to identify the distinctive behaviors or beliefs of a particular historical person or group. The microhistorian might argue that the testimony of a single talkative defendant is more revealing of the

nature of heretical beliefs than the statistical analysis of a thousand heresy trials, in which the accused are classified according to the standard social categories of age, gender, class, and occupation. A verbal slip or misunderstanding might tell more about a person's worldview than repeated stereotypical statements. The evidential paradigm has also been applied to the study of celebrated personages, such as Galileo, whose trial Pietro Redondi reinterpreted by emphasizing a few obscure, previously ignored documents that did not fit into the pattern apparent in the bulk of the evidence.

Microhistory has typically been devoted to cultural or social history, although there are some notable examples of economic and political microhistories. Many of the cultural microhistories have concentrated on the relationships and influences among various cultural levels: literate and nonliterate, written and oral, learned and popular. These often employ rigorous philological methods to reconstruct the meaning of a particular utterance or text in its original context and attempt to avoid anachronisms by assuming that past ways of thinking were very unlike those of the present. Social microhistories carefully reconstruct the constituents of a social group, such as a community or feuding faction, and sometimes apply the concept of the "normal exception," which isolates for study persons whose behavior is exceptional according to the norms of their own society, such as rebels, heretics, and criminals. The normal exception permits historians to show how certain kinds of transgressions against authority may be abnormal to the dominant group but normal behavior for those on the periphery of society; it opens up history to include a wide range of human experience; and it reveals how the prosecution of certain categories of belief and behavior serves as a commentary on the values of the master groups in society. Economic microhistories, especially those of Eduardo Grendi, have uncovered the overwhelming influence of cultural and social factors in economic decisions, and political microhistory has greatly expanded the realm of politics beyond the actions of elites and official institutions.

Microhistory can perhaps be best understood as an effort to sharpen the focus of history rather than to limit its aims, and its most significant consequence has been to expand the range of historical study into many previously obscure or unrecognized areas of human behavior and thought. The most effective microhistories have been based on well-documented cases involving individuals whose experiences or thoughts appear to be revealing of more widespread social practices.

For example, Carlo Ginzburg has investigated the case of a heretic miller in the sixteenth century to gain access to the cosmology of peasants, which was transmitted through oral means and therefore invisible to normal historical methods; Giovanni Levi uncovered the vital social networks of a cluster of communities by tracing the career of an exorcist; and Eduardo Grendi has reinterpreted the cultural significance of money by looking at the activities of counterfeiters.

By making historians sensitive to the nuances of power and to the changes of voice in documents, microhistory offers great rewards. It allows scholars to uncover disjunctures between what those who created documents thought was necessary to record and what the scholar wants to know, and it indicates gaps between what the educated jurist, for example, meant when he asked questions and what the bewildered defendant understood in answering.

A common criticism of the movement is that it has yet to demonstrate the significance of the various microhistories for broader historical trends and that it risks trivializing the past. Others have accused the microhistorians of historical relativism, classifying the genre as an example of the postmodern loss of faith in grand systems and in the ability to reconstruct a coherent story of the past. In response, defenders of the genre have pointed out that the best examples are widely comparative and deeply invested in questions of theory and values. Several of the most noted microhistorians have also pursued sweeping macrohistorical projects and do not see microhistory as a substitute for but a supplement to grander schemes. Microhistory has been especially useful for testing generalizations and for opening new directions of research.

Edward Muir

See also ANNALES SCHOOL; ANTHROPOLOGY AND HISTORY; CULTURAL HISTORY; ETHNOHISTORY; MODERNIZATION THEORY.

Texts

Ginzburg, Carlo. *The Cheese and the Worms: The Cosmos of a Sixteenth-Century Miller.* Baltimore, MD: Johns Hopkins University Press, 1980.
———. *The Enigma of Piero: Piero della Francesca: The Baptism, the Arezzo Cycle, the Flagellation.* London: Verso, 1985.
Grendi, Edoardo. "Counterfeit Coins and Monetary Exchange Structures in the Republic of Genoa during the Sixteenth and Seventeenth Centuries." In *History from Crime,* ed. Edward Muir and Guido Ruggiero. Baltimore, MD: Johns Hopkins University Press, 1994, 170–205.
Levi, Giovanni. *Inheriting Power: The Story of an Exorcist.* Chicago: University of Chicago Press, 1988.
Redondi, Pietro. *Galileo Heretic.* Princeton, NJ: Princeton University Press, 1987.

References

Ginzburg, Carlo. "Clues: Roots of an Evidential Paradigm." In his *Clues, Myths, and the Historical Method.* Baltimore, MD: Johns Hopkins University Press, 1989, 96–125.
Levi, Giovanni. "On Micro-History." In *New Perspectives on Historical Writing,* ed. Peter Burke. University Park: Pennsylvania State University Press, 1992, 93–113.
Muir, Edward, and Ruggiero, Guido, eds. *Microhistory and the Lost Peoples of Europe.* Baltimore, MD: Johns Hopkins University Press, 1991.

Migne, Jacques-Paul (1800–1875)

French editor and publisher of Latin and Greek texts. Educated at the seminary of Orleans, Migne served as a parish priest for nine years until 1833, when he moved to Paris to become a religious journalist. Three years later he founded a publishing house, the Ateliers Catholiques, with which he hoped to create a two thousand–volume *Bibliothèque universelle du clerge.* Migne sought to create a library of inexpensive, accessible, republished Catholic texts that would rival the *Bibliothèque nationale* in size and scope and rekindle interest in Catholic teachings. The fire that destroyed the Ateliers in 1868 effectively ended Migne's publishing career, but not before some 1,100 texts and collections had been produced. He is best remembered by historians today for his two monumental collections of *Patrologia.* The first, the *Patrologia Latina,* was produced between 1844 and 1855. Its 218 volumes contain the works of the Latin fathers of the Church, ranging chronologically from the writings of Tertullian to those of Pope Innocent III. The second set, the *Patrologia Graeca,* came off the presses between 1857 and 1866. It includes 166 volumes of the Greek fathers, accompanied in many cases by Latin translations. The energetic, tenacious, and abstemious abbé enlisted the help of the patristic scholar, and later Vatican librarian, Jean-Baptiste Pitra, in the preparation of these collections. Although many of the individual works have been reedited since Migne's time, the two *Patrologiae* remain the standard edition for much of the religious Latin and Greek literature of the patristic and medieval periods.

Krista Kesselring

Texts

Patrologiae Cursus Completus . . . Series Graeca. 162 vols., index vol. 162 by F. Cavallera. Paris: Migne, 1857–1912.
Patrologiae Cursus Completus . . . Series Latina. 221 vols., including 4 vols. of indices. Paris: Migne, 1844–1864.

References

Bloch, R. Howard. *God's Plagiarist: Being an Account of the Fabulous Industry and Irregular Commerce of the Abbé Migne.* Chicago: University of Chicago Press, 1994.
Sheppard, L.C. "The Abbé Jacques-Paul Migne." *American Benedictine Review* 7 (1956–1957): 112–128.

Mignet, François-Auguste-Marie-Alexis (1796–1884)

French historian, journalist, archivist, and academician. Mignet was born in Aix-en-Provence, son of a locksmith. He attended the law school of Aix where he began a lifelong friendship with Adolphe Thiers. Moving to Paris, he became a journalist for the *Courrier français* and protested against Charles X in 1830. The July Monarchy made Mignet director of the Archives of the Ministry of Foreign Affairs. He was devoted to the Académie des sciences morales et politiques, particularly after losing his archival post in 1848, until his death. Mignet's reputation as a historian rests principally on his *Histoire de la révolution française depuis 1789 jusqu'en 1814* (1824), the first survey by a noncontemporary, which defends the Revolution's advancement of liberty. His insistence on logic has been stigmatized as "historical fatalism," whereas he saw history as the key to establishing human sciences. Mignet's rigor and detached style contributed to the preeminence of historical writing in the nineteenth century.

William S. Cormack

Texts

Antonio Perez and Philip II. Trans. C. Cocks. London: Longman, Brown, Green, and Longmans, 1846.
The History of Mary, Queen of Scots. Trans. Andrew R. Scobie. London: R. Bentley and Son, 1851.

History of the French Revolution from 1789 to 1814. London: Bell, 1919.

References

Knibiehler, Yvonne. *Naissance des sciences humaines: Mignet et l'histoire philosophique au XIXᵉ siècle* [The Birth of the Human Sciences: Mignet and Philosophical History in the Nineteenth Century]. Paris: Flammarion, 1973.
Mellon, Stanley *The Political Uses of History: A Study of the Historians of the French Restoration.* Stanford, CA: Stanford University Press, 1958.

Mikami Sanji (1865–1939)

Japanese historian. Mikami was the most influential prewar Japanese historian among the first generation of Tokyo Imperial University graduates to be trained in the scientific method. In 1895 the Japanese government reorganized the Historiographical Institute at the university under strict rules in an effort to avoid public controversy. Mikami became the director of the institute from 1899 to 1919, during which time he guided the development of academic historiography. A devoted public servant, he gave his full attention to the institute, and his own works consequently had to await posthumous publication. His *Edo Jidai Shi* [History of the Edo Period] (1944) is a masterpiece of research and elegant narrative. Having been criticized in the 1911 southern–northern courts textbook controversy, Mikami distinguished between education, which was designed to teach the people through invigorating myths, and scholarship, which sought truth. He advanced this view in the 1935 Education Reform Council and in the committee established to compile *Kokutai no Hongi* [Cardinal Principles of the National Essence] (1937). Mikami headed the Commission of Inquiry into the Historical Sites Related to Emperor Jinmu, celebrating the 2,600th anniversary of Emperor Jinmu in 1940. Mikami did not believe that 600 B.C. was the true founding date of the empire, but he withheld his reservations. He never showed apprehension that the distinction between education and scholarship was being erased in favor of education.

John S. Brownlee

Texts

Edo Jidai Shi. 2 vols. Tokyo: Kōdansha Gakugei Bunko [Kōdansha Scholarly Library], 1992.

Military History, Historiography of

Historical writing on warfare and other military matters. Hans Delbrück has observed that military history begins with the history of man but that the military historian should start "where the source materials begin to provide a full and valid glimpse into the events."

Ancient Period.

Herodotus of Halicarnassus (ca. 484–ca. 420 B.C.), often called the father of history, was also the first military historian. His *Persian War* covers the struggle between the Greeks and the Persians to the fall of Sestos (478 B.C.). His history is told with a pro-Athenian bias, and his knowledge of warfare is at best rudimentary. Herodotus recognized the principles of historical criticism, but he applied them unsatisfactorily and sporadically. Thucydides (ca. 460–ca. 400 B.C.), an Athenian general, was the first critical historian. His work, *The History of the Peloponnesian War,* can be divided into two parts. The first ends with the peace of Nicias (421 B.C.). The second was intended to continue the conflict to the fall of Athens (404 B.C.), but ended in 411. Influenced by the Sophists, Thucydides was the first to introduce a standard of accuracy and an ideal of historical research. His approach produced a rationalistic history.

Thucydides' work was continued by the soldier-historian, Xenophon (ca. 430–354 B.C.). Xenophon joined the "ten thousand" that supported Cyrus the Younger against his brother Artaxerxes II (404–364 B.C.). The Greeks won the battle of Cunaxa (401 B.C.), but Cyrus was killed and the Greeks had to fight their way back. Xenophon was elected leader and later wrote the *Anabasis,* an account of the expedition. This work had a great influence on Alexander. On his return, Xenophon fought for Sparta against both Athens and Thebes. Later he wrote the *Hellenica,* which continues the work of Thucydides to the death of Epaminondas at Mantinaea (362 B.C.). As a critical historian Xenophon was inferior to Thucydides.

Aeneas Tacticus (fl. 360 B.C.) pioneered the content and form of military treatises. The influence of Aeneas was paramount among Greek, Roman, and Byzantine writers. Unfortunately only one work, *How the Besieged Ought Best to Resist,* survives. His contemporary in China, Sun Tzu, wrote *Ping Fa* [The Art of War], a work of a more conceptual type, which has had a wider and more enduring influence. Its general precepts are as applicable today as they were when *Ping Fa* was written.

From the rise of Philip of Macedon to the Diadochi and Epigoni, the military texts are preserved only by later derivative writers. It is not until the second century that the history of Polybius of Megalopolis (ca. 198–117 B.C.) restores military history to the quality of Thucydides. Polybius, an experienced cavalry commander, wrote a history, which has not completely survived, covering the period from 264 to 146 B.C. Like Thucydides, Polybius held that accuracy was the fundamental duty of the historian. Finally, among the Greeks, Diodorus Siculus (first century B.C.) wrote an incompletely preserved universal history, *The Library of History,* that ends with the year 60/59 B.C. The most important section covers the period from 323 to 262 B.C., drawing on the soldier-historian Hieronymus of Cardia.

The first extant Roman historian was Sallust (86–35 B.C.). His principal works that have survived are the *Bellum Catilinarium,* a description of Cataline's conspiracy (63–62 B.C.), and the *Bellum Jugurthinum,* which covers the war with Jugurtha (111–106 B.C.). Caius Julius Caesar (100–44 B.C.) wrote two historical works in the form of a personal memoir. *De Bello Gallico* covers his campaigns in 58–52 B.C. for the conquest of Gaul in seven books with an eighth added by Aulus Hirtius. The *De Bello Civili* deals with the civil war but was never completed. Both works were written to defend his actions. Titus Livius (59 B.C.–A.D. 17) wrote *Ab Urbe Condita* from the foundation of Rome to the death of Drusus (9 B.C.) in 142 books of which only 35 survive. He provides the only military account of the period. His work is far inferior to that of Polybius.

In the period of the empire, the foremost Latin historian is Tacitus (ca. A.D. 56–120). His works, *Agricola,* the *Annals,* and the *Histories* are the most important. The former deals with the campaigns of his father-in-law. The *Histories* are mostly lost, except the part that covers A.D. 69–70, but the *Annals* is more completely preserved. The last historian of this period was Ammianus Marcellinus (A.D. 330–400). A soldier-historian, his history sought to continue Tacitus from 96 to 378. Only the part relating to his own period survives. For the military historian they are of considerable interest, especially for his description of artillery.

Among the later ancient historians that wrote in Greek, Arrian (ca. 85–ca. 175) was the most prolific. A former general he wrote the *Anabasis* of Alexander based on contemporary authorities and the *Ta meta Alexandrou,* which covered Alexander's successors, but is fragmentary. Appian of Alexandria (ca. 90–ca. 165) wrote a history of

Rome of which half survives including the Spanish, Punic, Illyrian, Syrian, Mithridatic, and the civil wars. In addition to these works there are several military manuals of some interest: Asclepiodotus's work, *Tactica,* written during the first century B.C.; Onasander's *On Generalship,* from the reign of Claudius (A.D. 41–54); Frontinus's *Stratagems* (A.D. 84–96); Aelian's *Tactical Theory* (A.D. 98–117); and Vegetius's *De re militari* (A.D. 378–395).

The Middle Ages (A.D. 400–1500)

In the Middle Ages the most important writers for military history are found in the Byzantine east. The first is Procopius of Caesarea who was adviser and secretary to the famous general Belisarius during his campaigns against the Vandals, Ostrogoths, and Persians. His *History of the Wars* covered the reign of Justinian (527–565) to the year 553. Agathias's *On the Reign of Justinian* continued Procopius's history to 558, and Menander Protector extended the coverage of the period to 582. The imperial secretary Theophylakt Symokatta added the reign of Maurice (582–602).

A bleak period followed from the seventh to the tenth century with only chronicles and military manuals. Among the latter are the *Anonymous Byzantini* (late sixth century), the *Strategikon* of Maurice (ca. 700), the *Tactica* of Leo the Wise (ca. 900), *Para paradromo polemou* of Nicephorus Phocas (963–969), the *Anonymous Vári* (eleventh century), the *Strategikon* of Kekaumenos (eleventh century), and the *Tactica* of Nicephorus Ouranos (eleventh century).

In the tenth century renewed interest in the historical works of Herodotus, Thucydides, Xenophon, and Polybius revived the writing of history. Leo the Deacon, a contemporary of Basil II (976–1025), left the *Historiae* in ten books, dominated by the campaigns of Romanus II, Nicephorus Phocas, and John Tzimisces against the Arabs, Bulgars, and Russians during 959–976.

Contemporaneously with the Byzantines, the Arab writer al-Balādhurī's (ca. 829) *Futūh al-Buldān* [Conquest of Countries] offers the most useful account of the earliest Arab expansion; Al-Ṭabarī's (838–923) *Taʾrīkh* [History] covers the period immediately following with al-Yaʿqūbī (ca. 897) and al-Masūdī (ca. 893–956). Finally, Ibn al-Athīr's (1160–1232) *al-Kāmil fī al-taʾrīkh* [Universal History] gives the best Moslem account of the later crusades.

During the period of the Comneni and Angeli in the Byzantine east, Nicephorus Bryennius, who was influenced by Xenophon, wrote a history from 1070 to 1079. His wife, Anna Comnena (1083–

1153/4) continued his work in the *Alexiad.* Influenced by Thucydides and Polybius, this biography covers the reign of her father Alexius I and the First Crusade. John Cinnamus wrote a history of the reigns of John and Manuel Comnenus (1118–1176), following the examples of Herodotus, Xenophon, and Procopius. Niketas Choniates completed this period with a history covering the years from 1118 to 1206. It includes an eyewitness account of the capture of Constantinople in 1204 during the Fourth Crusade. The empire of Nicaea and the early Paleologi are covered by George Akropolites whose history begins with 1203 and ends with the recapture of Constantinople in 1261. His history was continued to the year 1307 by George Pachymeres, who includes an account of Roger de Flor's Catalan expedition.

The rest of the Paleologian period falls into two groups. The first includes Nicephorus Gregoras and John Cantacuzenos. The former renders a graphic and reliable account of the period, 1204 to 1359. The latter is apologetic, beginning with the accession of Andronicus III in 1320 and ending with the author's abdication as emperor in 1356. The second group consists of historians who wrote after the fall of Constantinople and supplement each other. The first is George Phrantzes, a high official and friend of the imperial family, whose history covers the time from 1258 to 1478 and includes an eyewitness account of the siege of Constantinople. A second is Laonikos Chalkokondyles (ca. 1423–ca. 1490) who used Herodotus and Thucydides as models to write a history from 1298 to 1464. The pro-Genoese Ducas provides the most detailed account from 1341 to 1462. Last is Critobulus (Greek: Kritoboulos) of Imbros, who left a eulogistic account of Mohammed II's reign from 1451 to 1467.

In Japan during the thirteenth century, the anonymous *Heike monogatarai* [The Tale of Heike] is the first of the distinctive "war tales" *(gunkai monogatarai),* which highlight the period 1192–1600, when the shōgunate and the samurai dominated Japanese cultural, political, and social life.

In the West, while chronicles provide valuable materials on military affairs, it is not until the twelfth century that historians reemerge. The first is Otto of Freising (ca. 1112–1158) who participated in the campaigns of his half brother Conrad III against the Guelphs and on the Second Crusade. Otto wrote the *Gesta Friderici* about his uncle Frederick Barbarossa. With his death in 1158, the history was continued by Rahewin. Later in the century, Geoffrey of Villehardouin (ca. 1150–ca. 1213) wrote the *Conquest of Constantinople,* covering the period from 1198 to 1212 as a military memoir. The reign of Louis IX (1228–1270) was covered by Jean de Joinville (ca. 1224–1317) in his *Histoire de Saint Louis*. For the Hundred Years' War there is the *Chronique* of Jean Froissart (1337–ca. 1404) in four books covering the events from 1325 to 1400. Froissart also includes contemporary conflicts in of Flanders, Scotland, and Spain. At the end of the fourteenth century the most significant military historian was Philippe de Commynes (ca. 1447–1511) who wrote a *Memoir* in eight books that covers the events from 1484–1498. It is important for the wars of Louis XI and Charles VII, including the Italian invasion of 1494–1495.

Modern Period

The modern period of military historiography begins with the Florentine Niccolò Machiavelli (1469–1527). His works established the foundations on which modern military thought is based. The *Art of War* is influenced by Frontinus, and Vegetius must be used with his other works, the *Prince,* the *Discourses,* and the *History of Florence,* to grasp his military thinking.

The first modern theorist to make a comprehensive analysis of war in all its ramifications was Raimondo Montecuccoli (1609–1680), the Habsburg general and historian. In a literary career that spanned some thirty years he sought axioms that would make the conduct of war predictable. Montecuccoli's works were widely read until the French Revolution. This period also witnessed the advancement of science into warfare. Advances in artillery made sieges more important than battles, and battles frequently resulted from protracted sieges. Works on military technology became more important. None enjoyed more influence and prestige than the writings of Sébastien le Prestre de Vauban (1633–1707). Vauban's publications on siegecraft and on the science of fortification made him one of the most influential military writers. His influence continued into the eighteenth century and remained undiminished even into the Napoleonic period.

Frederick the Great's writings over a period of forty years describe the actual warfare of his time. Among them are his *Principes généraux de la guerre* [General Principles of War], *Testament militaire* [Military Testament], *Elements de castramétrie et de tactique* [Elements of Logistics and Tactics] and *L'art de la guerre* [The Art of War]. These works show that he was a product of his age. He had a strong belief in limited warfare. In spirit he conceived the idea of blitzkrieg but within the confines of the thinking of his age. On the other hand, his

contemporary Maurice de Saxe (1696–1750) was a forerunner in many areas, as his *Reveries* attest. They evince a deep insight into tactics and leadership. In the field of tactics he scorned the use of entrenchments and was the first modern general to advocate the pursuit of a defeated enemy. In organization Saxe was to be a progenitor of the modern divisional unit. Finally, Saxe's advocacy of conscription antedated all previous ideas on this subject.

The comte de Guibert's (1743–1790) *Essai général de Tactique* brought him instant fame. It called for a new kind of army based on a citizen force and advocated a war of movement to enable an army to live off the land and enjoy greater flexibility in action. The supreme synthesizer of all that came before him was Napoleon Bonaparte (1789–1821). This can only be grasped from a careful study of his vast correspondence and his memoirs, dictated while in exile. Napoleon had a paramount influence on military thinkers in the nineteenth century. The first was Baron Antoine Henri de Jomini (1779–1869). A prolific writer his greatest theoretical work is the *Art of War* in two volumes. Jomini accepted war as an integral part of history and sought to demonstrate that there are fundamental principles in all operations of war. In the history of military thought he clarified the basic concepts of military science and defined the sphere of strategy in warfare. His contemporary was Carl von Clausewitz (1780–1831), who sought to discover the universal nature of war by using a comprehensive analysis of the strategy, operations, and tactics of the Napoleonic wars and their eighteenth-century background. His principle work, *On War,* in eight books, was left unfinished but nonetheless became a classic that influenced military thinkers into the twentieth century.

In Germany it had a profound role in establishing the Prusso-German school. The foremost figure of this school was Helmut von Moltke (1800–1891) who shaped the Prussian army and was the architect of victories of the Seven Weeks War and the Franco-Prussian War. A prolific writer, von Moltke was influenced by Clausewitz, but also drew from his own personal experiences and the study of military history, which he regarded as an indispensable tool. He rejected Clausewitz's views that strategy was a science with general principles. Instead, he sought to find ways to conduct war successfully.

The first to use the scientific methods of Leopold von Ranke in military history was the prolific writer Hans Delbrück (1848–1929). His *History of the Art of War within the Framework of Political*

History stands as a monumental work. Covering the period from the Persian War to the Napoleonic wars, it is a valuable source of information to the military historian and theorist.

In the United States Francis Parkman (1823–1893) established the foundations for the study of the American military past. His principle work, *France and England in North America,* in nine volumes, was written as a historical narrative in the grand literary tradition. A later contemporary was the prolific Theodore Ayrault Dodge (1824–1909), who focused on the art of war as exemplified by the great captains of history. Through a meticulous use of the sources, along with personal visits to the battle sites, his works included the military biographies of Alexander the Great (1890), Hannibal (1891), Caesar (1892), Gustavus Adolphus (1895), and Napoleon (4 vols., 1904–1907). Following in the tradition of von Moltke was Alfred Thayer Mahan (1840–1914). Both historian and theorist, Mahan's reputation rested on two works, *The Influence of Sea Power on History, 1660–1783* and *The Influence of Sea Power on the French Revolution and Empire, 1793–1812.* Mahan was the first theorist of sea power.

In England, the dean of military historians was Sir Charles William Chadwick Oman (1860–1946). Oman's greatest works are the two-volume *Art of War in the Middle Ages* (1924); the seven-volume *History of the Peninsular War* (1902–1930); and *The Art of War in the Sixteenth Century* (1937). After World War I, one of the most important military historians was the military theoretician, Major-General John Frederick Charles Fuller (1876–1966). Fuller was one of the founders of modern armored warfare, and he wrote more than thirty books on all aspects of warfare. His most comprehensive work is the three-volume *Military History of the Western World* (1954–1956) in which he analyzed Western warfare from its beginnings to World War II. A younger contemporary was the military historian and strategist Basil Henry Liddell Hart (1895–1970). Like Fuller, he advocated mechanized warfare. Over a period of four decades, Liddell Hart wrote on a wide range of military subjects, including biographies (Scipio Africanus, Sherman, Foch, and T.E. Lawrence), theory *(The Ghost of Napoleon* and *Strategy—The Indirect Approach),* and great conflicts *(The Real War* and *History of the Second World War).* Of these the most important is his *Strategy—the Indirect Approach,* which appeared in six successive editions between 1929 and 1967.

In the 1980s and 1990s outstanding new interpretative and theoretical work has been done by Martin van Creveld, Trevor N. Dupuy, Sir Michael Howard, Donald Kagan, John Keegan, and Peter Paret. These works have had and are having a wide influence outside of the confines of narrow military specializations.

Norman Tobias

References (Arranged by Period)

Ancient
Cambridge Ancient History. 12 vols. Cambridge, Eng.: Cambridge University Press, 1923–1954.
Pauly's Real Encyclopädie der klassichen Altertumswissenschaft. Ed. G. Wissowa. 49 vols. in 58. Stuttgart: J.B. Metzler, 1894–1980.

Middle Ages
Cambridge Medieval History. 8 vols. Cambridge, Eng.: Cambridge University Press, 1911–1936.
Contamine, Philippe. *War in the Middle Ages.* Trans. Michael Jones. London: Basil Blackwell, 1984.
Dain, Alphonse. "Les Stratégistes Byzantins." *Travaux et Mémoires* 2 (1967): 317–390.
Dennis, George T. *Maurice's Strategikon.* Philadelphia: University of Pennsylvania Press, 1984.
Dennis, George T. *Three Byzantine Military Treatises.* Washington, DC: Dumbarton Oaks Press, 1985.
Hunger, Hans. *Die hochsprachliche profane Literatur der Byzantiner.* 2 vols. Munich: C.H. Beck, 1978.
Manitius, Max. *Geschichte der lateinischen Literatur des Mittelalters.* Munich: C.H. Beck, 1911.
Oman, Charles. *History of the Art of War in the Middle Ages.* Second ed. 2 vols. London: Basil Blackwell, 1924.
Pohler, Johann. *Bibliotheca historico-militaris. Systematische Übersicht der Erscheinungen aller Sprachen auf dem Gebiete der Geschichte der Kriege und Kriegswissenschaft seit Erfindung der Buchdruckerkunst bis zum Schluss des Jahres 1880.* 4 vols. Cassel, Leipzig: Akademie der Wissenschaften, 1890–1899.

Modern
Gat, Azar. *Military Thought in the Nineteenth Century.* Oxford: Clarendon Press, 1992.
Jähns, Max. *Geschichte der Kriegswissenschaften.* 3 vols. Munich and Leipzig: Akademie der Wissenschaften, 1889–1891.

Montross, Lynn. *War through the Ages.* New York and London: Harper and Brothers, 1944.

Paret, Peter, ed. *Makers of Modern Strategy from Machiavelli to the Nuclear Age.* Princeton, NJ: Princeton University Press, 1986.

Ropp, Theodore. *War in the Modern Age.* Durham, NC: Duke University Press, 1959.

Miliukov, Pavel Nikolaevich (1859–1943)

Russian historian and politician. Miliukov was born in Moscow and eventually studied history and the humanities under such notables as V.O. Kliuchevskii and S.M. Solov'ev at Moscow University, completing an M.A. thesis that was published in 1892 as *Gosudarstvennoe khoziaistvo Rossii v pervoi chetverti XVIII stoletiia I reforma Petra Velikago* [The Financial Administration of Russia in the First Quarter of the Eighteenth Century and the Reform of Peter the Great]. A founder of the liberal Russian Constitutional Democratic Party ("Kadets"), he was dismissed from his lectureship at Moscow University in 1895 for his political activities. Miliukov's *Glavnyia techeniia russkoi istoricheskoi mysli* [Chief Currents of Russian Historical Thought] (1895) was a major work, but completed only to P.I. Chaadaev (1794–1856). His three-volume *Ocherki po istorii russkoi kultury* [Studies in the History of Russian Culture] (1896–1903), reflecting Kliuchevskii's influence, traced the natural evolution of ideas and institutions in Russia and was eventually severely challenged by M.N. Pokrovskii's deterministic economic materialism in 1923. He was a kadet leader in the Third and Fourth Dumas and the minister of Foreign Affairs in the Provisional Government until May 1917. After fleeing the Bolsheviks into exile in London and finally Paris he published numerous significant historical works, many of which, such as *Istoriia vtoroi russkoi revoliutsii* [A History of the Second Russian Revolution] (1921–1923) and *Rossia na perelome* [Russia's Catastrophe] (1927), were partially based on his own experiences. At the time of his death in Paris, he supported the Soviet Union against Nazi Germany.

Dennis Reinhartz

Texts

With C. Seignobos and L. Eisenmann. *History of Russia.* Trans. C. Markmann. 3 vols. New York: Funk and Wagnalls, 1968.

Outlines of Russian Culture. Ed. Michael

Karpovich; trans. Valentine Ughet and Eleanor Davis. 3 vols. Philadelphia: University of Pennsylvania Press, 1942.

Russia and Its Crisis. New York: Collier, 1962.

Russia To-day and To-morrow. New York: The Macmillan Company, 1922.

References

Mazour, Anatoly G. *Modern Russian Historiography.* Revised ed. Westport, CT: Greenwood Press, 1975.

Shteppa, Konstantin F. *Russian Historians and the Soviet State.* New Brunswick, NJ: Rutgers University Press, 1962.

Mill, James (1773–1836)

Scottish radical and utilitarian political philosopher, economist, and historian of British India. Mill was born in Scotland and studied divinity and philosophy at the University of Edinburgh in the 1790s under Dugald Stewart. He subsequently moved to London where he met Jeremy Bentham (1748–1832), whose close friend and political collaborator he was until the philosopher's death. After beginning his career as a journalist, Mill published a *History of British India,* in four volumes (1817). This influential work, which earned him public acclaim and a position in the administration of the East India Company in London, was the first history to connect the coming of British dominion in India to the secular course of Indian history and to propound an analytic view of the importance and purposes of Great Britain as an Indian power. Mill was far from holding that form of admiration for Indian civilization born with the rise of eighteenth-century British orientalism. In his view, the British government should have played the role of an absolute reforming ruler, replacing the inept oriental despots. The measures suggested by English utilitarian reformers with regard to land taxation and the judicial system in Britain should, he felt, have been applied also in India, even allowing for certain variations arising from differences in the local situation.

Guido Abbattista

Texts

The History of British India. Ed. H.H. Wilson. 10 vols. London: James Maden, Piper, Stephenson and Spence, 1858.

The History of British India. Abrid. ed. Ed. W. Thomas. Chicago: University of Chicago Press, 1974.

References

Abbattista, Guido. *James Mill e il problema indiano: Gli intellettuali britanici e la conquista dell'India* [James Mill and the Indian Problem: The British Intellectual and the Conquest of India]. Milan: Giuffré, 1979.

Forbes, Duncan. "James Mill and India." *Cambridge Historical Journal* 5 (1951–1952): 19–33.

Majeed, Javed. *Ungoverned Imaginings: James Mill's History of British India and Orientalism.* Oxford: Clarendon Press, 1992.

Stokes, Eric. *The English Utilitarians and India.* Oxford: Oxford University Press, 1959.

Millar, John (1735–1801)

Scottish historian and law professor. Millar was born in Shotts, Lanarkshire. He was educated at Glasgow University, where he attended Adam Smith's lectures on moral philosophy and became acquainted with David Hume; he became professor of law there in 1761. He supported American independence, parliamentary reform, abolition of the slave trade, and the French Revolution. He left Scotland only twice, to visit England in 1774 and 1792, and died at Millheugh, outside Glasgow. In his *Origin of the Distinction of Ranks* (1771), which he called an enquiry into "the natural history of mankind," Millar was the most notable exponent of the "four-stages theory," a consistently materialist account of human development from the simplicity of the hunter-gatherer to the sophistication of the commercial citizen. He attributed this progress to the satisfaction of needs, which inspires human inventiveness and propels evolutionary progress from rudeness to civilization. In the *Historical View of the English Government* (1787), which he left uncompleted at his death, he similarly traced the "natural growth" of English liberty and institutions not to deliberate foresight but rather to contingent developments designed to remedy immediate wants.

David Armitage

Texts

An Historical View of the English Government from the Settlement of the Saxons in Britain to the Accession of the House of Stewart. Second ed. London: A. Strahan, 1790.

The Origin of the Distinction of Ranks. In *John Millar of Glasgow 1735–1801: His Life and Thought and His Contributions to Sociological Analysis,* William C. Lehmann. Cambridge, Eng.: Cambridge University Press, 1960, 175–322.

References

Lehmann, William C. *John Millar of Glasgow 1735–1801: His Life and Thought and His Contributions to Sociological Analysis.* Cambridge, Eng.: Cambridge University Press, 1960.

Meek, Ronald. *Social Science and the Ignoble Savage.* Cambridge, Eng.: Cambridge University Press, 1976.

Millenarianism

A form of apocalyptic eschatology that looks for the realization of God's Kingdom within history. Although this term is often used to cover virtually any charismatic, messianic, utopian, or restorative outlook, it refers more strictly to the belief of some Christians that the savior will return, either literally or in spirit, to overcome his enemies and to establish an earthly reign of righteousness. As part of the larger complex of Judeo-Christian eschatology, millenarian ideas have been of crucial importance in the evolution of Western attitudes toward time and history.

Christian millenarianism is grounded above all on Revelation 20, which refers to a thousand-year period ("mille anni") when Satan will be bound and Christ will reign. The most literal forms of belief based on this passage are sometimes termed "chiliasm" (from the Greek *chilias,* a thousand). But the thousand-year figure is frequently taken metaphorically; the millennium may be understood as an incalculably long time, or conversely as a very brief burst of earthly glory. While millenarianism is often difficult to distinguish clearly from other forms of prophetic and apocalyptic thought, its core feature is the belief that the Last Judgment, the end of time, and the establishment of the eternal Kingdom will come only at the end of this period of historical triumph.

Such notions were common in early Christianity, which inherited Jewish hopes for a messianic kingdom, and were espoused by several prominent early Christian theologians. Gradually, however, this and other forms of apocalyptic expectation lost favor among church leaders. Augustine of Hippo (d. 430) worked to play down the historical significance of the Last Things, interpreting the millennium figuratively as the indeterminate period between the first and second advents. Reflecting this Augustinian view, medieval world-chronicles generally assumed a providential, but nonmillenarian, pattern for history. Yet hope for a historical victory of good over evil remained a strong undercurrent among Christian thinkers. The notion that the ages of the world corresponded to the six days of creation—accepted by Augustine himself—led easily to the idea of a seventh, "Sabbatical" age. From the twelfth century on, prophecies of a final spiritual flowering proliferated as part of a general revival of apocalyptic thinking. The trinitarian scheme of history introduced by Joachim of Fiore (d. 1202) was millenarian only in a broad sense, for Joachim conceived the coming new age less as the triumph of the Gospel message than as the breakthrough of the Holy Spirit. In subsequent eras, however, Joachimite visions became so interwoven with more traditional forms of millenarianism that the various threads are almost indistinguishable.

In the late Middle Ages, millenarian schemes helped inspire heretical opposition to the church and to feudal social structures. But the traditional tendency to view millenarianism mainly in connection with social radicalism and revolutionary movements is misleading. The millenarian outlook is inherently neither revolutionary nor quietist; the coming golden age could imply the need to resist or destroy the existing order, but it could just as easily suggest a providential role for powerful rulers, groups, or institutions (papacy, empire, king, nation, the elect, the converted, the enlightened, etc.).

Despite the formal rejection of explicit millenarianism by leading Protestant and Catholic reformers, hopes for a final spiritual fulfillment within history supplied a sense of divine sanction and purpose for emerging religious, social, and political interests in the early modern age. Among groups and movements as varied as Puritans migrating to the New World, Mennonite communities struggling for survival, proponents of kingly absolutism, and Jesuits missionaries in Asia, history was commonly interpreted as a divine plan in which truth and justice—variously conceived—would inevitably triumph.

Millenarianism takes form not only in visions of sudden, radical, and divinely effected transformation, but also in more gradualist conceptions of spiritual progress and triumph. The former type has come to be called "premillennialism"; here the second advent precedes and initiates the earthly kingdom. The latter, gradualist forms are typically termed "postmillennialism," for here Christ will not literally reappear until the Last Judgment itself, at the very end of history. But there is no rigid divide between these views. Hence again, while it is true that individuals and groups who have felt oppressed by sociopolitical structures have often tended to adopt premillennial hopes, it is dangerous to generalize about therelationship of millenarian forms to radicalism or activism.

Indeed, beyond its association with the Judeo-Christian conceptions of apocalyptic conflict and a unique, unidirectional unfolding of time toward an end, millenarianism has few if any definite historiographical implications. It is compatible both with perceptions of breakdown and with faith in history's forward march. Many, perhaps most, secularized forms of progressive, reformative, or revolutionary ideology have roots in Christian millenarianism and are justifiably regarded as its motley offspring. Enlightenment visions of progress and human perfectibility surely owed much to this source. Hegelian philosophy, with its concept of history as the progressive self-realization of Spirit, arguably derived from millenarianism. The connections between Marxism and Christian eschatology have often been noted, as have the twisted uses of inherited prophetic themes in the Nazi "Thousand-year Reich." Scholars also commonly recognize that nineteenth- and early-twentieth-century views of the providential, world-historical role of the American nation had a millenarian aspect. The apocalyptic atmosphere of the cold war era favored the more sensational scenarios of premillenialism, as have growing fears of ecological and demographic disaster. As cold war tensions eased, some intellectuals speculated that the waning of ideological conflict was bringing an end to world-historical strife generally and the promise of a virtual millennium.

While traditional millenarian views have long since disappeared from professional historical writing, various apocalyptic, utopian, and New Age assumptions are closer to the main stream of postmodern culture than is generally admitted. Indeed, beneath the veneer of rationality projected in much contemporary public discourse lies a surging quest for meaning—both personal and historical—that may well take shape in new and immensely powerful visions of worldly hope as we enter the dawn of the third millennium A.D.

Robin B. Barnes

See also CHRISTIANITY, VIEWS OF HISTORY IN; FOUR EMPIRES; PERIODIZATION; RELIGIONS, HISTORY OF; TIME.

References

Cohn, Norman. *The Pursuit of the Millennium: Revolutionary Messianism in Medieval and Reformation Europe and Its Bearing on Modern Totalitarian Movements.* New York: Harper, 1961.

McGinn, Bernard. *Visions of the End: Apocalyptic Traditions in the Middle Ages.* New York: Columbia University Press, 1979.

Tuveson, Ernest. *Millennium and Utopia: A Study in the Background of the Idea of Progress.* Berkeley: University of California Press, 1949.

———. *Redeemer Nation: The Idea of America's Millennial Role.* Chicago: University of Chicago Press, 1968.

Miller, Perry (1905–1963)

U.S. historian of colonial America. Miller was born and raised in Chicago, where he attended the University of Chicago for his undergraduate and graduate studies. He moved to Cambridge, Massachusetts, where he taught at Harvard University throughout his entire career, until his premature death. Although an agnostic, Miller nevertheless took religious ideas more seriously than earlier twentieth-century historians and revitalized the field of Puritan studies. His major insights into the Puritans were set forth in *Orthodoxy in Massachusetts, 1630–1650, The New England Mind: The Seventeenth Century, The New England Mind: From Colony to Province;* and in a collection of essays, *Errand into the Wilderness.* Criticized for overemphasizing the departures Puritans made from the Calvinist tradition and for not paying sufficient emphasis to diversity within Puritan thought, his reconstruction of early New England intellectual life still shapes scholarly discourse at the end of the twentieth century. In all, Miller published six books and three volumes of essays and edited sixteen volumes of texts on subjects ranging from the seventeenth through the nineteenth centuries, all displaying his characteristic insistence on taking ideas seriously and his awareness of the ironic elements in history.

Francis J. Bremer

Texts

Errand into the Wilderness. Cambridge, MA.: Harvard University Press, 1956.

Jonathan Edwards. New York: Sloane, 1949.

The New England Mind: From Colony to Province. Cambridge, MA: Harvard University Press, 1953.

The New England Mind: The Seventeenth Century. New York: Macmillan, 1939.

Orthodoxy in Massachusetts, 1630–1650: A Genetic Study. Cambridge, MA: Harvard University Press, 1933.

Roger Williams: His Contribution to the American Tradition. Indianapolis, IN: Bobbs-Merrill, 1953.

References

Harvard Review 2 (1964): special issue dedicated to Miller.

Middlekauff, Robert. "Perry Miller." In *Pastmasters: Some Essays on American Historians,* ed. Marcus Cunliffe and Robin W. Winks. New York: Harper & Row, 1969, 167–190.

Mink, Louis Otto, Jr. (1921–1983)

A leading developer of the narrative philosophy of history and professor at Wesleyan University in Connecticut. Mink attempted to mediate between rhetorical relativism and historiographic realism. An early critical Collingwoodian, Mink argued for the autonomy of historical understanding. Historiographic narratives do not *reduplicate* the past but *construct* it. Historical narratives displace each other, rather than fit together as subplots of universal history. "Narrative histories should be aggregative, insofar as they are histories, but cannot be, insofar as they are narratives." Mink wished to avoid the relativist implications of this position, acknowledging the commonsense ideal of historiography as "what really happened." It seemed impossible to compare the truth value of narratives because narratives are not built of the same events. Mink died before he was able to resolve this tension between truth and narrativity.

Aviezer Tucker

Texts

Historical Understanding. Ed. Brian Fay, Eugene O. Golob, and Richard T. Vann. Middletown, CT: Wesleyan University Press, 1987.

References

Vann, Richard T. "Louis Mink's Linguistic Turn." *History and Theory* 26 (1987): 1–14.

Mitre, Bartolomé (1821–1906)

Argentine historian. Mitre was born in Buenos Aires. His family moved to the Patagonian frontier, but returned to Buenos Aires in 1831. He entered the Military College of Montevideo in 1836 and participated in a number of military campaigns. After the Uruguayan government expelled him and the rest of the Argentine community from that country he went to Bolivia, where he edited the newspaper *La Epoca* [The Age] and headed the Military College. In 1848, he was exiled to Chile and then expelled once again, this time to Peru.

Returning to Argentina, Mitre participated in the struggles that overthrew the Argentine *caudillo* Juan Manuel de Rosas in 1852. Subsequently, he held numerous military and political posts, culminating in 1862 with his election as the first constitutional president of Argentina. Mitre left the presidency in 1868, but continued to participate in Argentina's political life. He also continued his journalistic interests, founding and editing the newspaper *La Nación* [The Nation]. During his active political life, Mitre had conducted research for his notable biographies of Manuel Belgrano and José de San Martín. He utilized biography, the historical genre in which he worked, as a means to foster nationalism through the lives of great men. In spite of his journalistic background, he was a strong believer in the use of primary sources and made extensive use of them to buttress his accounts. His works were based, however, not only on documents but also on personal interviews. His *Historia de Belgrano y de la independencia argentina* [History of Belgrano and the Independence of Argentina] went through four editions, the final and definitive recension being published in 1887. His *Historia de San Martín y de la emancipación sudamericana* [History of San Martín and South American Independence] was first published in 1887, and the second edition was published in 1890. These two biographies are a triumph of scholarly research and documentation.

Carlos Pérez

Texts

Historia de Belgrano y de la independencia argentina. Fourth ed. (reprinted). Buenos Aires: Editorial Universitaria de Buenos Aires, 1967–1968
Historia de San Martín y de la emancipación sudamericana. Second ed. 3 vols. Buenos Aires: Editorial Universitaria de Buenos Aires, 1968.
Obras completas [Complete Works]. 18 vols. Buenos Aires: Leonardo Impresora, 1938–.

References

Burns, E. Bradford. "Bartolomé Mitre: The Historian As Novelist, the Novel As History." *Revista Interamericana de Bibliografía/ Review of Inter-american Bibliography* 32 (1982): 155–167.
Jeffrey, William H. *Mitre and Argentina.* New York: Library Publishers, 1952.
Robinson, John L. *Bartolomé Mitre: Historian of the Americas.* Washington, DC: University Press of America, 1982.

Modernization Theory

One of the most influential paradigms of the social sciences, modernization theory has had a powerful although often indirect influence on historical writing, particularly with respect to the development of non-Western societies. Beginning in the late nineteenth century, European intellectuals sought the meaning of European "modernity" by contrasting it with the "traditionalism" of their own past and with the societies brought to Western attention through colonial conquest (for example, Emile Durkheim). The rationalism of the West—scientific, legal-bureaucratic, and economic—became the central thesis in a dialectic of contrast with "traditional" cultures. Max Weber, for example, elucidated his hypothesis on the economic implications of the Protestant ethic by describing the fetters placed on capitalism by the ethics of Hinduism and Confucianism.

Evolutionist assumptions affected the application of the modernization paradigm to non-Western societies. The ideal types of the modern/ traditional contrast—*gesellschaft* over *gemeinschaft,* achievement over ascription, universalism over particularism, market economics over gift exchange, scientific rationalism over traditional religious precepts, individualism over group identity—implied a historical trajectory, indicating that the Western transition to modernity could be repeated elsewhere. Indigenous attempts at modernization that followed Western models, as in Japan and Turkey, seemed to affirm these assumptions.

After 1945, modernization theory became closely identified with an optimistic American vision of global progress. From this perspective, market economics were the foundation on which modernization had been achieved in the West and could be attained elsewhere. Advocates of a capitalist ascendancy through what Walter Rostow called "stages of economic growth" made explicit the cold war implications of modernization theory by dismissing socialist alternatives. The optimistic view that the spread of capitalism would make possible Western-style advances in developing societies faced two challenges. One came from economic historians who argued that global capitalism, far from "developing" Latin America, Africa, and most of Asia, had marginalized these areas on the "periphery" of the world market. For "dependency" theorists such as Immanuel Wallerstein, capitalism was the root cause of persistent poverty in these areas, not a pathway leading toward modernization.

Another critique came from scholars who observed that the pressures of modernization led to the breakdown of traditional institutions and mores without adequate replacement by modern ones. While such dislocations might be seen as temporary and "transitional" (Daniel Lerner) they might also be viewed as an enduring consequence of culture conflict. There was an enormous gap between the aspirations and the abilities of non-Western societies that sought to emulate a foreign model of modernization, according to Theodore H. von Laue.

The basic polarity on which modernization theory rests, the divide between the "modern" and the "traditional," has more recently come into question. "Tradition" has been shown to be a flexible language of social discourse. Traditions can be adapted to new circumstances, and even "invented" to provide historical charters to legitimate present political practice (Hobsbawm and Ranger). While the assumptions of modernization theory have spread broadly and deeply, and therefore continue to influence historical writing, the concept is no longer frequently used by either social scientists or theoretically reflective historians.

Kenneth R. Curtis

See also SOCIOLOGY AND HISTORY; WORLD HISTORY; WORLD SYSTEMS THEORY.

Texts

Durkheim, Emile. *The Division of Labor in Society.* New York: Free Press, 1984.

Hobsbawm, Eric, and Terence Ranger, eds. *The Invention of Tradition.* New York: Cambridge University Press, 1983.

Lerner, Daniel. *The Passing of Traditional Society: Modernizing the Middle East.* New York: Free Press, 1958.

Rostow, W.W. *The Stages of Economic Growth: A Non-Communist Manifesto.* Third ed. New York: Cambridge University Press, 1990.

Von Laue, Theodore H. *The World Revolution of Westernization: The Twentieth Century in Global Perspective.* New York: Oxford University Press, 1987.

Wallerstein, Immanuel. *The Modern World-System.* Vol. 1: *Capitalist Agriculture and the Origins of the European World-Economy in the Sixteenth Century.* New York: Academic Press, 1974. Vol. 2: *Mercantilism and the Consolidation of the European World-Economy, 1600–1750.* New York: Academic Press, 1980. Vol. 3: *The Second Era of Great Expansion of the Capitalist World-Economy, 1730–1840s.* San Diego: Academic Press, 1989.

Weber, Max. *The Sociology of Religion.* Boston: Beacon Press, 1963.

References

Apter, David. *Rethinking Development: Modernization, Dependency and Postmodern Politics.* Newbury Park, CA: Sage Publications, 1987.

Momigliano, Arnaldo Dante (1908–1987)

Italian ancient historian. Momigliano was born at Caraglio and studied at the universities of Turin and Rome under Gaetano de Sanctis. He taught at Rome and was made professor of Roman history at Turin in 1936, a position he lost in 1938 owing to the racial policies of the fascist government. Thereafter he came to England, researching at Oxford during World War II. Restored to his chair in Italy after the war, he nevertheless remained in England, taking posts at the University of Bristol. In 1951 he became professor of ancient history at University College, London, and from 1964 was also professor at the Scuola Normale Superiore in Pisa. He was made an honorary Knight of the British Empire in 1974, and died in London. Momigliano's vast output ranged over early Greek, Hellenistic, and Roman history and ancient and modern historiography. He eschewed massive works, producing short books and enormous numbers of articles. His first book, *La composizione della storia di Tucidide* [The Composition of Thucydides' History] (1930), was rapidly followed by *Prime Linee di storia della tradizione maccabaica* [Outlines of the History of the Maccabean Tradition] (1931), in which work his Hellenistic and Jewish interests are manifest. He produced two full-blown biographies, *Claudius* and *Filippo il Macedone* (both 1934), while *The Development of Greek Biography* (1971) discusses the history of this genre in antiquity. With *Alien Wisdom* (1975) he returned to the Hellenistic world, treating Greek attitudes to the intellectual achievements of non-Greek cultures. The *Contributi alla storia degli studi classici e del mondo antico* [Contributions to the History of Classical Studies and the Ancient World] (1955–1992), in nine installments (a tenth is forthcoming), is a collection of Momigliano's articles on numerous subjects.

Richard Fowler

Texts

Alien Wisdom. Cambridge, Eng.: Cambridge University Press, 1975.

The Classical Foundations of Modern Historiography. Berkeley: University of California Press, 1990.

Contributi alla storia degli studi classici e del mondo antico. Rome: Storia e Letteratura, 1955–1992.

The Development of Greek Biography. Second ed. Cambridge, MA: Harvard University Press, 1993.
Studies in Historiography. New York: Harper and Row, 1966.

References
Nippel, Wilfried. "Arnaldo Momigliano (1908–1987)." *Storia della storiografia,* 14 (1988): 3–7.
Phillips, Mark Salber. "Reconsiderations on History and Antiquarianism: Arnaldo Momigliano and the Historiography of Eighteen-Century Britain." *Journal of the History of Ideas* 57 (1996); 296–316.
[Various authors]. Special number of *Rivisti Storici Italiana* 100, no. 2 (1988) with several articles on Momigliano.

Mommsen, Theodor (1817–1903)
German historian of Rome. Born in Schleswig, the son of a pastor, he studied law at Kiel and then inscriptions in Italy with a Danish government fellowship. Returning in 1848, he became professor of Roman law at Leipzig, but was dismissed after three years for his liberal political opinions. He moved to Zürich (1852), then Breslau (1854), and finally Berlin (1858), where he finished his career as professor of ancient history. Undoubtedly the most famous and influential modern historian of Rome, and the only one to receive the Nobel Prize for Literature (1902), Mommsen was equally successful in writing specialized works of scholarship and analytical narrative history for a more general public. His specialized works include the *Corpus of Latin Inscriptions* and definitive works on Roman constitutional and criminal law. His more general reputation is based on his four-volume *History of Rome* (1854–1856 and 1885), which was shaped by the liberal views born of his own political experience. His commitment to publishing all kinds of technical documentary evidence decisively influenced the organization of research in Roman history.

Catherine Rubincam

Texts
Corpus Juris Civilis. 3 vols. Berlin: Weidmann, 1877.
The History of Rome. Trans. W.P. Dickson. 4 vols. London: J.M. Dent, 1929.
The Provinces of the Roman Empire, from Caesar to Diocletian. Trans. W.P. Dickson. 2 vols. New York: Scribner's, 1887.

References
Guilland, Antoine. *Modern Germany and Her Historians.* London: Jarrold and Sons, 1915.

M

Monastic History
See CHRONICLES, MEDIEVAL.

Mongolian Historiography
Historiographical tradition among ethnic Mongols from the thirteenth century to the present. Mongolian historiography falls into four major periods. The tradition began in the thirteenth century with works centered on the deeds and sayings of Chinggis Khan (usually known in the West as Genghiz or Genghis Khan) and his immediate successors. From the late sixteenth century to 1911, a vast number of chronicles of strongly stereotyped character appeared, centering on the Chinggisid nobility and the Buddhist church. In late-nineteenth-century Inner Mongolia, interest in Chinese sources initiated a new focus on the historical Chinggis Khan as a heroic figure, a trend that after Mongolia's independence in 1911 merged with a spate of revolutionary reminiscences and biographies to form a new nationalist historiography. After World War II, under communist influence, these writings gave way to the Marxist–Leninist historiography that endured until 1989.

Mongolian historiography begins with its best-known work, the *Secret History of the Mongols* (1228 or 1240). The *Secret History* recounts the genealogy of Chinggis Khan, the life and campaigns of the great conqueror, and the positions awarded to his followers. An epilogue, possibly added subsequently, gives an incomplete account of Chinggis Khan's successor Ögedei. Largely written in prose, with shorter or longer passages of alliterative verse, the *Secret History* describes the rise of Chinggis Khan in vivid and often unflattering detail. This vividness and the martial theme have led some commentators to see the *Secret History* as Mongolia's archetypal epic, although it has no close affinity to the existing traditions of Mongolian oral epic. While some have denied the reliability of the *Secret History,* it is usually conceded to be a valuable, albeit partisan, account written not long after the events it describes. Although the *Secret History* is the only Mongolian historical work to have survived intact from the thirteenth century, other works certainly existed.

No writings have survived from the period between the Mongols' expulsion from China in 1368 and the large-scale conversion to Buddhism in the late sixteenth century, yet thirteenth-century texts, including the *Secret History of the Mongols,* were certainly preserved among the Mongols. In the seventeenth century a large number of chronicles, such as Lubsangdanjin's *Altan Tobchi* [Golden Chronicle] (c. 1635) and Sagang Sechen's *Erdeni-yin Tobchi* [Jeweled Chronicle] (1662), appeared. This genre, immensely popular in Mongolia, and of which new examples were being produced up to the early twentieth century, followed a set three-part format. The first part, largely worthless as a historical source but of intellectual historical interest, interweaves legend and history to portray Chinggis Khan as the heaven-destined sovereign of Mongolia. The second part, containing valuable historical information, recounts the fifteenth-century wars between Chinggis Khan's descendants and the Oirad Mongolian usurpers and the reestablishment of true Chinggisid rule under Dayun Khaan (ca. 1461–1543). The third part contains genealogies tracing the descent of the Mongolian nobility back to Chinggis Khan, his brothers, and his comrades. Buddhist influences figure strongly in all of these chronicles. Thus, they traced the ancestry of Chinggis Khan through the early Tibetan emperors back to the earliest mythical Buddhist monarchs of India.

By the close of the seventeenth century, Mongolian monks also began to write histories of Buddhism in Tibetan language closely following Tibetan models, but adding information on the history of Buddhism in Mongolia. Examples of this genre subsequently also appeared in Mongolian language. Other historical genres in this period include biographies of both lay rulers and Buddhist clerics, annotated genealogies of local nobility, and histories of famous monasteries. The Oirad or Kalmyk Mongols of Xinjiang and European Russia and the Buriats of southern Siberia also had their own distinctive, non-Chinggisid, chronicle traditions. Viewed as historical sources, these minor genres are often more reliable and detailed than the general family and religious histories.

Although all of Mongolia came under the control of the Manchu Qing dynasty during the course of the seventeenth century, Chinese historiography at first had negligible influence on that of the Mongols. The Inner Mongolian historian, Rashipungsug, in his *Bolor Erikhe* [Crystal Rosary] (1775) was the first Mongolian historian to be significantly influenced by Chinese historical writing. He still followed the basic structure of the Mongolian chronicle tradition but used Chinese histories in Manchu translation to fill in data particularly about the Mongol emperors in China. At the same time, Rashipungsug was the first Mongolian historian to notice and challenge the anti-Mongol and anti-Buddhist attitudes typical of Chinese sources. In 1871, another Inner Mongolian, Injannashi, used Chinese sources virtually to rewrite the history of Chinggis Khan in his *Khökhe Sudur* [Blue Chronicle]. Injannashi presented Chinggis Khan largely as a Chinese dynastic founder, rather than as a Buddhist world monarch, and prefaced his history with a violent critique of both the decadent nobility and the obscurantist Buddhist clergy. By implication, he viewed all of Mongolian history after the world empire as profoundly anticlimactic, a view that would become prevalent in the early twentieth century.

In 1911, Outer Mongolia declared its independence, while Inner Mongolia came under the new Republic of China. In the social and political turmoil that engulfed both regions from then until 1950, the hereditary nobility and the Buddhist church were both swept away and with them the historiographical traditions they had favored. In independent Mongolia, contact with Russified Buriat Mongols resulted in increased familiarity with romanticized Western accounts of Chinggis Khan. After the Soviet-supported 1921 revolution, the government of the Mongolian People's Republic encouraged historical research, emphasizing the world empire and the use of European and Chinese sources. The revolutionary events also spawned a large body of biography and contemporary history, much of it penned by government officials and strongly nationalist and anti-aristocratic in tone, yet still without any serious Marxist content. In Inner Mongolia under China, little contemporary history appeared, but the new glorification of Chinggis Khan as a secular martial hero appealed strongly to the nationalist youth of the time. Under the Japanese occupation from 1931 to 1945, Inner Mongolian publishers produced the first printed editions of Injannashi's *Khökhe Sudur* and Rashipungsug's *Bolor Erikhe,* among others. An important development in both Inner Mongolia and Mongolia proper was the rediscovery, by way of European, Chinese, and Japanese scholarship, of the original *Secret History* text.

By around 1950, independent Mongolia had completed its transformation into a Soviet satellite state and abandoned the traditional Mongolian script for the Cyrillic, while Inner Mongolia had come under the People's Republic of China. In independent Mongolia, the government followed Soviet pressure and criticized adulation of Chinggis Khan, turning the focus of history writing instead toward socioeconomic topics. In 1955 a team of Soviet and Mongolian scholars produced *The History of the Mongolian People's Republic,* the first comprehensive history of Mongolia from prehistory to the contemporary period. While the application of simplified Marxist ideas was heavy-handed and at times wildly tendentious, the focus on modes and relations of production, class conflict, and international trade did break important new ground. Detailed monographic research on the period between 1368 and 1911 was another positive feature of Mongolian Marxist historiography. Similar comprehensive histories of Inner Mongolia appeared soon after, in both Chinese and Mongolian languages. Although the Sino-Soviet split produced intense polemics on the role of Chinggis Khan and the relation of China to the Mongols, the basic historical approaches of Marxism–Leninism and nationalism remained unchallenged in both areas until 1989.

History writing has always occupied a fundamental place in Mongolian culture. From the seventeenth century at least, Mongolian intellectual life has been strongly didactic, nationally conscious, this-worldly, and filiopietistic, so it is not surprising that history has served as the major vehicle for literate Mongols to reflect upon their world. Yet little of this tradition is known outside Mongolia. While a few of the major premodern histories, particularly the *Secret History,* have been widely studied and translated, a vast number of valuable works, particularly in the minor genres, remain either unpublished or unutilized. The Marxist–Leninist historiography has likewise produced many indispensable monographs based on Mongolia's rich archival material, but their results still await comprehensive conceptual rethinking.

Christopher Pratt Atwood

See also CENTRAL ASIAN HISTORIOGRAPHY.

Texts

Bawden, C.R. *The Mongol Chronicle Altan Tobci.* Wiesbaden: Otto Harrassowitz, 1955.

Damchø Gyatsho Dharmatâla. *Rosary of White Lotuses.* Trans. Piotr Klafkowski. Wiesbaden: Otto Harrassowitz, 1987.

History of the Mongolian People's Republic. Moscow: Nauka Publishing House, 1973.

Mongolian Heroes of the Twentieth Century. Ed. and trans. Urgunge Onon. New York: AMS Press, 1976.

"Secret History of the Mongols." Trans. Igor de Rachewiltz. Serialized in *Papers on Far Eastern History* 4 (Sept. 1971)—33 (March 1986).

References

Bira, Sh. *Mongolian Historical Literature of the XVII–XIX Centuries Written in Tibetan.* Trans. Stanley N. Frye. Bloomington, IN: Mongolia Society and Tibet Society, 1970.

Halkovic, Stephen A., Jr. *The Mongols of the West.* Bloomington, IN: Research Institute for Inner Asian Studies, 1985.

Hangin, John Gombojab. *Köke Sudur (The Blue Chronicle).* Wiesbaden: Otto Harrassowitz, 1973.

Heissig, Walther. *Die Familien- und Kirchengeschichtsschreibung der Mongolen* [The Family- and Church-Historical Writings of the Mongols]. 2 vols. Wiesbaden: Otto Harrassowitz, 1959.

M

Monstrelet, Enguerrand de (ca. 1390–1453)

Burgundian official and historian. Monstrelet heard firsthand accounts of the important events of his day, including the meeting between the Duke of Burgundy and Joan of Arc, while holding civil and church posts. He wrote a two-volume French *Chronique* of the Hundred Years' War and French civil war from 1400–1444. Monstrelet complemented Jean Froissart by picking up where he left off and provided a French counterpoint to Jean de Wavrin's English perspective of the Hundred Years' War. He is considered more historian than mere chronicler because he was fairly impartial despite his service to both church and state. He distilled multiple accounts of events, avoided legends, and covered political and religious events in addition to the central military encounters of the wars. Moreover, he included many of the letters and treaties he used as sources.

Christopher M. Bellitto

Texts

Contemporary Chronicles of the Hundred Years War. Ed. and trans. Peter E. Thompson. London: The Folio Society, 1966, 17–20, 257–338.

The Chronicles of Enguerrand de Monstrelet. Trans. Thomas Johnes. 2 vols. London: George Routledge and Sons, 1884.

References

Thompson, James Westfall. *A History of Historical Writing.* Gloucester, MA: Peter Smith, 1967, 381–383.

Montesquieu, Charles-Louis de Secondat, Baron De La Brède et de (1689–1755)

French man of letters and political philosopher. Born near Bordeaux, he studied law at the University of Bordeaux, becoming an advocate in 1708. In 1716 he inherited the judicial post of *Président à mortier* in the Bordeaux Parlement; he sold it in 1726, and from 1728 to 1731 traveled throughout Europe, staying in England for two years. He returned to France, and until his death, divided his time between Paris and his estate near Bordeaux. During his life, Montesquieu published three major works: *Lettres Persanes* [Persian Letters] (1721); *Considérations sur les causes de la grandeur des Romains et de leur décadence* [Considerations on the Causes of the Greatness of the Romans and Their Decline] (1734); and *L'Esprit des lois* [The Spirit of the Laws] (1748). Montesquieu introduced a historical and sociological approach to the study of the legal structures of states. He wrote no sustained philosophy of history; however, in *Considérations* he argues that history is determined neither by fortune nor providence, but by "general causes." General causes are divided into two groups: physical (such as climate or terrain) and moral (such as political structures and religion). The interrelation of these causes he calls "the spirit of the laws," and in *L'Esprit des lois* he uses this concept to explain the existing laws of states as well as any changes to those laws. Primary among the general causes are the "natures" and "principles" of governments. Breaking with traditional Aristotelian classification, Montesquieu divides the natures of government into three—republics, monarchies and despotisms—to which correspond three animating principles: virtue, honor, and fear. Virtuous republics belong primarily in the ancient world, monarchies in contemporary Europe, and despotisms in the non-European world. Montesquieu's discussions of feudalism, commerce, climate, and the separation of powers were all deeply influential for eighteenth-century historical scholarship.

Neil G. Robertson

Texts

Considerations on the Causes of the Greatness of the Romans and Their Decline. Trans. David Lowenthal. New York: Free Press, 1965.

Persian Letters. Trans. C.J. Betts. Harmondsworth: Penguin, 1973.

The Spirit of the Laws. Ed. and trans. Anne M. Cohler, Basia Carolyn Miller, and Harold Samuel Stone. Cambridge, Eng.: Cambridge University Press, 1989.

References

Althusser, Louis. *Montesquieu, Rousseau, Marx: Politics and History.* Trans. Ben Brewster. London: Verso, 1982.

Carrithers, David. "Montesquieu's Philosophy of History." *Journal of the History of Ideas* 47 (1986): 61–80.

Shackleton, Robert. *Montesquieu: A Critical Biography.* Oxford: Oxford University Press, 1961.

Montfaucon, Bernard de (1655–1741)

French philologist and paleographer of the Greek church fathers and historian of French antiquities. Montfaucon was born near Narbonne into a noble family. After a failed army career, he entered the Benedictine Congregation of Saint-Maur in Toulouse (1676). His studies in philosophy, theology, and Greek at the abbey of Grasse earned him a place at Saint-Germain-des-Prés in 1687. In recognition of his achievements in Greek and scholarship on French antiquities, the Académie Royale des Inscriptions et Belles Lettres honored Montfaucon in 1719. He died at Saint-Germain-des-Prés. Montfaucon rendered the Greek church fathers accessible to Western scholars with editions and translations of unprecedented accuracy. Collaborating with Maurists Antoine Pouget and Jacques Lopin, he composed *Analecta Graeca* [Greek Analects] (1688) and edited Athanasius of Alexandria's works (1698). Following research in Italy, he edited and translated writings of Origen (1713) and John Chrysostom (1718–1738), and cataloged related manuscripts in *Palaeographia Graeca* [Greek Paleography] (1708) and *Bibliotheca Bibliothecarum Manuscriptorum Nova* [New Catalog of Manuscript Libraries] (1739). Montfaucon also investigated classical monuments in *Diarium Italicum* [Italian Diary] (1702) and royal ceremonial and symbolism in *Les monumens de la Monarchie françoise* [Monuments of the French Monarchy] (1729–1733).

Bonnie Effros

Texts

Analecta Graeca. 4 vols. Paris: Edmund Martin et al., 1688.

The Antiquities of Italy. Trans. John Henley. London: J. Darby, 1725.

Antiquity Explained and Represented in Sculptures and *The Supplement to Antiquity Explained.* Trans. David Humphreys. 3 vols. New York: Garland, 1976.

Bibliotheca Bibliothecarum Manuscriptorum Nova. 2 vols. Paris: Briasson, 1739.

A Collection of Regal and Ecclesiastical Antiquities of France. 2 vols. London: W. Innys et al., 1750.

Palaeographia Graeca. Reprint ed. Farnborough: Gregg, 1970.

Ed. *Sancti Patris Nostri Joannis Chrysostomi Archiepiscopi Constantinopolitani Opera Omnia* [All of the Works of Our Holy Father John Chrysostom, Patriarch of Constantinople]. Revised ed. 13 vols. Paris: Gaume Fratres, 1834–1839.

References

Knowles, David. *Great Historical Enterprises: Problems in Monastic History.* London: Thomas Nelson and Sons Ltd, 1963.

Tassin, René-Prosper. *Histoire littéraire de la Congrégation de Saint-Maur* [Literary History of the Congregation of Saint-Maur]. Paris: Chez Humblot, Libraire, 1770.

Texts

Beyond Equality: Labor and the Radical Republicans, 1862–1872. New York: Random House, 1967.

Citizen Worker: The Experience in the United States with Democracy and the Free Market during the Nineteenth Century. Cambridge, Eng.: Cambridge University Press, 1993.

The Fall of the House of Labor. Cambridge, Eng.: Cambridge University Press, 1987.

Workers Control in America. Cambridge, Eng.: Cambridge University Press, 1979.

References

Buhle, Paul. *Marxism in the United States.* London: Verso, 1987.

"David Montgomery," in *Visions of History: Interviews,* by MARHO, the Mid-Atlantic Radical Historians Organization. New York: Pantheon, 1983.

Montgomery, David (b. 1927)

American historian. The outstanding U.S. labor historian during the last third of the twentieth century, Montgomery was raised in Pennsylvania, served in the army at Los Alamos, worked as machinist, and then became a professor of history at the University of Pittsburgh and Yale University. Montgomery has changed fundamentally the ways in which scholars approach working-class history. Through his own work and that of his many students, he has illuminated the shifting nature of the production process and the subtle day-to-day activities of working people themselves. His work also predicted, and in a variety of ways has consolidated, a broad turn of younger U.S. history scholars toward Marxist methodology. A union activist (and Communist) through much of the 1950s, Montgomery began graduate school after being blacklisted. His dissertation, revised and published as *Beyond Equality,* carefully analyzed the growing class divisions that doomed the greatest radical-tinged political coalition since the American revolution. His subsequent studies offered the closest studies of workplace life published hitherto, demonstrating widespread "mutual support" among varied groups of workers and the perpetual search for more democratic control of the production base; treated the role of the state in redefining the possibilities of workplace democracy; and drew the story back to its origins in the struggle of workers for meaningful citizenship in a polity warped by capitalism.

Paul M. Buhle

More, Sir Thomas (1477/78–1535)

English lawyer, statesman, and humanist. Educated in London and at Canterbury Hall, Oxford, More then studied the law at New Inn and Lincoln's Inn. Although he briefly contemplated a career in the church, More remained in the world of public affairs and enjoyed a successful practice at the bar before entering Parliament in 1504. Having entered the service of Henry VIII (r. 1509–1547), he became a privy councillor and favorite of the king, earning several high-ranking official appointments. He succeeded Cardinal Thomas Wolsey as Lord Chancellor in 1529 but resigned the office in 1532 because of his disagreement with Henry's ecclesiastical policies and the king's divorce from Catherine of Aragon. Steadfast in his opposition to the Reformation, More refused to swear to the Act of Succession or to any such measure that bestowed ecclesiastical supremacy on the crown. Together with Bishop John Fisher, he was imprisoned in 1535, tried for treason, and beheaded in July of that year. He was canonized in 1935, marking the fourth centenary of his martyrdom.

A friend and associate of John Colet, William Grocyn, Desiderius Erasmus, and other English and continental humanists, More authored a large corpus of English and Latin works on a wide range of subjects in a variety of styles. Many of his works were recognized as exemplary humanist scholarship during his lifetime and after. His reputation as a historian rests on his history of King Richard III (r. 1483–1485), of which two versions exist, one written in English and the other in Latin. Neither of the versions was completed or published in More's lifetime. The differences between the histories are sufficient to establish that neither is simply the translation of the other, but the thematic and substantial similarities of the two works permit them to be considered as a unit. More's account of Richard III is noteworthy for a number of reasons. At a time when most writing on the past was in the disjointed style of chronicles and annals, More wrote flowing narratives in beautiful prose; and while chronicles present lists of not necessarily related events, More carefully established causal relations, often making the character and motivations of individuals decisive. Although the history's dark portrait of Richard III helped define that king as a royal archdemon for several centuries, it may have been intended by its author as a lesson on the consequences of tyranny, instructive to both the reigning monarch and the people around him.

Greg Bak

Texts

Historia Richardi Tertii. Ed. Daniel Kinney
In *The Complete Works of St. Thomas More.* New Haven, CT: Yale University Press, 1963– , vol. 15.

The History of King Richard the Third and *Historia Regis Angliae Eius Nominis Tertii.* Ed. Richard S. Sylvester. In *The Complete Works of St. Thomas More.* New Haven, CT: Yale University Press, 1963– , vol. 2.

References

Donno, Elizabeth Story. "Thomas More and Richard III." *Renaissance Quarterly* 35 (1982): 401–447.

Geritz, Albert J. "Recent Studies in More (1977–1990)." *English Literary Renaissance* 22 (1992): 112–140.

Levy, F.J. *Tudor Historical Thought.* San Marino, CA: Huntington Library, 1967.

Morga, Antonio de (1559–1636)

Spanish historian of the Philippines. Born in Seville, Morga graduated from the University of Salamanca in 1574 and was granted a doctorate in canon law in 1578. He taught in Osuna and then returned to Salamanca, where he graduated in civil law. In 1580, Morga entered government service as a lawyer and at the age of thirty-five was appointed by King Philip II as lieutenant to the governor (and therefore the second in command) in the

Philippines. This marked the beginning of forty-three years of colonial service. He left Spain with his family in 1594 and arrived the next year in Manila. Morga served in the Philippines until 1603, when he was transferred to Mexico. Six years later, while in Mexico, he published his *Sucesos de las Islas Filipinas* [History of the Philippines], the original title of which was *Descubrimiento, conquista, pacificacion, y poblacion de las Islas Philippinas.* This was the only Spanish history of the Philippines written by a lay person to be published before 1887. While some of the material is based on personal experiences, Morga also relied on earlier writers and on eyewitness accounts. Although it is written in the third person and states its purpose as being the provision of information regarding the Philippines, the sixth and seventh chapters of Morga's work appear to be an apologia for his performance in battle against the Dutch leader Van Noort. Morga's book is valuable for its depiction of the Spanish community in Manila and its detailed account of the evolution of the city. Perhaps more valuable, however, is his description of the indigenous population. He devotes almost a third of his book to this subject, providing a rich source for linguistic, social, ethnographic, and other studies of the indigenous population during the early Spanish period.

Damon L. Woods

Texts

The Philippine Islands, Moluccas, Siam, Cambodia, Japan, and China, at the Close of the Sixteenth Century. Trans. Henry E.J. Stanley. London: Hakluyt Society, 1868.

Sucesos de Las Islas Filipinas. Ed. and trans. J.S. Cummins. Cambridge, Eng.: Hakluyt Society/Cambridge University Press, 1971.

References

Phelan, John Leddy. *The Kingdom of Quito in the Seventeenth Century.* Madison: University of Wisconsin Press, 1967.

Boxer, C.R. "Some Aspects of Spanish Historical Writing on the Philippines." In *Historians of South East Asia.* ed. D.G.E. Hall. London: Oxford University Press, 1961, 200–212.

Morgan, Edmund Sears (b. 1916)

American historian. Morgan was born in Minneapolis, Minnesota, but spent much of his youth in Cambridge, Massachusetts. He received his B.A. and Ph.D. from Harvard University, where he studied for a time under Perry Miller. Morgan taught at Brown University and at Yale. At a time when the discipline was increasingly characterized by narrow specialization, he was distinctive among colonialists for his wide range of interests, while his graceful style and strong narrative emphasis made his work easily accessible to nonspecialists as well as professionals. His biography of John Winthrop, *The Puritan Dilemma,* along with *The Puritan Family, Roger Williams: The Church and the State* and *Visible Saints* helped establish him as one of the foremost interpreters of early New England. *Virginians at Home* and *American Slavery, American Freedom* offered new insights into the early Chesapeake, while *The Gentle Puritan, The Stamp Act Crisis,* and *The Birth of the Republic* demonstrate his equal mastery of the revolutionary century.

Francis J. Bremer

Texts

American Slavery, American Freedom: The Ordeal of Colonial Virginia. New York: Norton, 1975.

The Birth of the Republic, 1763–1789. Chicago: University of Chicago Press, 1956.

Inventing the People: The Rise of Popular Sovereignty in England and America. New York: Norton, 1988.

The Meaning of Independence: John Adams, George Washington, and Thomas Jefferson. Charlottesville: University of Virginia Press, 1976.

The Puritan Dilemma: The Story of John Winthrop. Boston: Little, Brown, 1958.

The Puritan Family: Religion and Domestic Relations in Seventeenth-Century New England. Rev. and enl. ed. New York: Harper & Row, 1966.

Roger Williams: The Church and the State. New York: Harcourt, Brace & World, 1967.

With Helen M. Morgan. *The Stamp Act Crisis: Prologue to Revolution.* Chapel Hill: University of North Carolina Press, 1953.

Virginians at Home: Family Life in the Eighteenth Century. Williamsburg, VA: Colonial Williamsburg, 1952.

Visible Saints: The History of a Puritan Idea. New York: New York University Press, 1963.

Morison, Samuel Eliot (1887–1976)

American historian. Born in Boston of Puritan ancestry, Morison was attracted to the history of New England and to the sea. A graduate of Harvard, he spent most of his career as a member of the Harvard faculty, interrupted by visiting appointments such as his tenure as the first Harmsworth professor of American history at Oxford University (1922). Morison's early work

focused on colonial New England and included *Builders of the Bay Colony,* a three-volume history of early Harvard, and *The Puritan Pronaos.* His maritime studies began with *The Maritime History of Massachusetts;* included his first major success, the two volume *Admiral of the Ocean Sea: A Life of Christopher Columbus;* continued with the official *History of United States Naval Operations in World War II* in fifteen volumes; and concluded with two volumes on *The European Discovery of America.* Morison was his country's leading exponent of history as a literary art, and received two Pulitzer prizes and numerous other awards for his more than forty volumes. He was strongly influenced by Francis Parkman not only in his approach to narrative but in his insistence on using personal exploration of historical sites to enhance his understanding.

Francis J. Bremer

Texts

Admiral of the Ocean Sea: A Life of Christopher Columbus. 2 vols. Boston: Little, Brown, 1942.

Builders of the Bay Colony. Boston and New York: Houghton Mifflin, 1930.

The European Discovery of America: The Northern Voyages, A.D. 500–1600. New York: Oxford University Press, 1971.

The European Discovery of America: The Southern Voyages, A.D. 1492–1616. New York: Oxford University Press, 1974.

Harrison Gray Otis, 1765–1848: The Urbane Federalist. Boston: Houghton Mifflin, 1969.

History of United States Naval Operations in World War II. 15 vols. Boston: Atlantic/ Little, Brown, 1947–1962.

The Puritan Pronaos: Studies in the Intellectual Life of New England in the Seventeenth Century. New York: New York University Press, 1936.

References

Pfitzer, Gregory M. *Samuel Eliot Morison's Historical World: In Search of a New Parkman.* Boston: Northeastern University Press, 1991.

Mos Gallicus and Mos Italicus

Methods of studying Roman law. Medieval jurisprudence originated with the work of the "glossators," who commented on the surviving text of Roman law, Justinian's *Corpus juris civilis.* They regarded this text as providing an internally consistent and universally valid body of civil law, whose principles

M

only needed logical exposition and clarification. Their commentaries on Roman law became the basis of legal education and juridical opinion.

In the fourteenth century, this logical analysis of Roman legal terminology was supplanted by a freer analysis, designed to apply the principles of the *Corpus juris* to a widening range of contemporary legal problems. This movement, sometimes referred to as the "post-glossators," originated in the tumultuous world of the Italian city-states. Its most famous practitioner, Bartolus of Sassoferrato (1314–1357), worked directly from the text of the *Corpus juris,* defining its terms as suited his purposes. His approach provided a new basis for legal education, eventually becoming known as the *mos italicus,* or "Italian manner" of teaching Roman law.

By the beginning of the sixteenth century, humanist philologists began to study the text of the *Corpus juris,* maintaining, in contrast to Bartolus, that it had to be restored to its classical purity before its principles could be understood for contemporary application. The Frenchman Guillaume Budé (1468–1540) made the first substantial study of the text. His style of philological analysis was incorporated into the legal curriculum by an Italian sojourning in France, Andrea Alciato (1492–1550), who established the law school at Bourges as the center for what became known as the *mos gallicus,* or "French manner" of studying Roman law. Ironically, philological analysis of the *Corpus juris* soon revealed that Roman law was not universal law but rather the law of a specific past society. The *mos gallicus* thus initiated the historical study of law.

Zachary S. Schiffman

See also LAW AND HISTORY; PHILOLOGY; RENAISSANCE, HISTORIOGRAPHY DURING.

References

Franklin, Julian H. *Jean Bodin and the Sixteenth-Century Revolution in the Methodology of Law and History.* New York: Columbia University Press, 1963.

Gilmore, Myron P. *Humanists and Jurists.* Cambridge, MA: Harvard University Press, 1963.

Kelley, Donald R. *Foundations of Modern Historical Scholarship.* New York: Columbia University Press, 1970.

Mos Italicus

See MOS GALLICUS AND MOS ITALICUS.

Möser, Justus (1720–1794)

German politician, administrator, and historian. An important figure of the German Enlightenment, Möser dominated the political and cultural life of his hometown of Osnabrück during the second half of the eighteenth century. Möser was involved from an early age in the administration of the prince-bishopric of Osnabrück and wrote extensively on political, social, and economic reform. His many essays were published in book form in 1774 as *Patriotische Phantasien* [Patriotic Fantasies]. Möser began to write history late in life. His best-known study, the *History of Osnabrück,* which he began in 1765, was a significant transitional work in the development of historicism. With this work, Möser broke in many respects with the traditional universalism of the Enlightenment, emphasizing locality, the uniqueness of historical phenomena, and the rationality of the historical process.

John R. Hinde

Texts

Justus Mösers Sämtliche Werke: Historisch-kritische Ausgabe [The Complete Works of Justus Möser in a Critical-Historical Edition]. 14 vols. Oldenburg, Berlin, and Hamburg: G. Stalling, 1944–1990.

References

Knudsen, Jonathan B. *Justus Möser and the German Enlightenment.* Cambridge, Eng.: Cambridge University Press, 1986.

Meinecke, Friedrich. *Historism: The Rise of a New Historical Outlook.* Trans. J.E. Anderson. Second ed. Trans. revised by H.D. Schmidt. London: Routledge and Kegan Paul, 1972.

Mosheim, Johann Lorenz von (1694/95–1755)

German church historian and theologian. Mosheim was born in Lübeck. After his studies in Kiel, he graduated as Magister Artium in 1718 and in 1719 became a teacher in the philosophical faculty. There he lectured on logic and metaphysics and studied theology. In 1723 Mosheim became professor at the University of Helmstedt. He rose rapidly to the most important positions within the school and within the church system of Braunschweig (Brunswick). In 1734–1735 he drew up the statutes of the theological faculty in Göttingen, and in 1747 he attained a chair of theology and the office of chancellor at that university. Mosheim's literary work covers a broad spectrum. Most important are his historical works, which mediated between Pietism and Lutheran Orthodoxy and prepared the way for the historiography of the Enlightenment: the *Institutiones historiae ecclesiasticae antiquae et recentioris* (1739) is a survey of church history, while in the *Versuch einer unparteiischen und gründlichen Ketzergeschichte* [Attempt at an Impartial and Complete History of Heresy] (1746) he tried to portray diverse heretical groups in an unprejudiced way. He interpreted the church first of all as a human community with its own laws and rules, examining its history from a pragmatic rather than ideological point of view. He emphasized the importance of the independence of the historian, a critical attitude toward the evidence, and the use of primary sources. In his interpretation he saw the Reformation as the dawn of a new ethos and intellectual milieu and as the process from which further progress began; accordingly, he rejected the Protestant idea of the decline of civilization.

Thomas Fuchs

Texts

Geschichte der Kirchenverbesserung im sechszehnten Jahrhundert [History of the Reformation of the Church in the Sixteenth Century]. Ed. J.A.C. von Einem. Leipzig: C.F. Weygand, 1773.
Institutes of Ecclesiastical History, Ancient and Modern. Trans. J. Murdock. New York: R. Carter & Brothers, 1881.
Versuch einer unpartheyischen und gründlichen Ketzergeschichte. Second ed. Helmstedt: C.F. Weygand, 1748.

References

Meinhold, P. *Geschichte der kirchlichen Historiographie* [History of Ecclesiastical Historiography]. Vol. 2. Freiburg und München: Karl Alber, 1967.
Stroup, J. "Protestant Church Historians in the German Enlightenment." In *Aufklärung und Geschichte: Studien zur deutschen Geschichtswissenschaft im 18. Jahrhundert* [Enlightenment and History: Studies in German Historical Thought in the Eighteenth Century], ed. H.E. Bödeker, et al. Göttingen: Vandenhoeck & Ruprecht, 1986, 169–192.

Motley, John Lothrop (1814–1877)

American historian and diplomat. Motley was born in Dorchester, Massachusetts. Following graduation from Harvard University in 1831 he attended the University of Göttingen where he became a close friend with his fellow student Otto von Bismarck. In 1841 he accepted a short-lived appointment as secretary to the United States legation in St. Petersburg. With his reputation as a European diplomatic historian established by *The Rise of the Dutch Republic,* Motley subsequently served as minister to Vienna (1861–1867) and then London (1869–1870), where he was unjustly dismissed from his post. Indignant over the episode, he maintained residence in England until his death at Kingston Russell, near Dorchester. Deterministic in outlook, Motley's early writings were romantic narratives of great men dominating great events. *The Rise of the Dutch Republic* reflected such an approach and gained much of its initial success through a symbolism of liberty and union that destined the United States to civil warfare. Yet, his determinism later waned as he turned increasingly toward the use of sources from multiple archives to construct his narration. As such, Motley's methodology helped American historical writing gain recognition within an emerging international profession.

William E. Fischer Jr.

Texts

The Complete Works of John L. Motley. 17 vols. New York: Society of English and French Literature, 1900.
History of the United Netherlands. 4 vols. New York: Harper and Brothers, 1861–1868.
The Life and Death of John of Barneveld, Advocate of Holland: With a View of the Primary Causes and Movements of the Thirty Years' War. 2 vols. New York: Harper and Brothers, 1874.
The Rise of the Dutch Republic: A History. 3 vols. New York: Harper and Brothers, 1855.

References

Higby, Chester Penn, and B.T. Schantz, eds. *John Lothrop Motley, Representative Selections, with Introduction, Bibliography and Notes.* New York: American Book Company, 1939.
Levin, David. *History As Romantic Art—Bancroft, Prescott, Motley and Parkman.* Stanford, CA: Stanford University Press, 1959.

Motoori Norinaga (1730–1801)

Japanese National Learning *(Kokugaku)* scholar of the Edo period. Born into a merchant family, Motoori practiced medicine for a living. Considering himself a disciple of the *Kokugaku* scholar Kamo Mabuchi (1697–1769), Motoori

M

was a seminal figure in the National Learning movement that strove to formulate a philosophical cosmology based on a Japanese tradition untainted by Chinese or other foreign influences. *Kokugaku* emphasized the importance of Shinto and of research into Japan's own literature in order to find the roots of Japanese tradition. Historiographically, Motoori's name is associated particularly with an analysis and annotated translation of the *Kojiki* (a history compiled in 712 and the oldest surviving Japanese book), which he attempted to establish as a basic Shinto scripture. Motoori personally had an absolute religious faith in the native Shinto *kami* of Japan. In interpreting *Genji Monogatari,* he saw this Heian novel as the embodiment of the aesthetic term *mono no aware,* which referred to human sensitivity. Motoori believed sensitivity was one of the most important qualities native to the Japanese, a view that conflicted with the rationalist thought of contemporary Zhu Xi [Chu Hsi] Confucian scholars. His thought had a profound influence on subsequent Japanese perceptions of their country's past.

A. Hamish Ion

Texts

Gyoju gaigen. Tsu: Yamagataya, 1796.
Ed. *Kojiki.* Tokyo: Kaizosha, 1939.
Motoori Norinaga sekinin henshu Ishikawa Jun. Tokyo: Chuo Koronsha, 1970.

References

Maruyama Masao. *Studies in the Intellectual History of Tokugawa Japan.* Trans. Mikiso Hane. Tokyo: University of Tokyo Press, 1974.
Matsumoto Shigeru. *Motoori Norinaga, 1730–1801.* Cambridge, MA: Harvard University Press, 1970.
Tsunoda Ryusaku, William Theodore de Bary, and Donald Keene, eds. *Sources of Japanese Tradition.* New York and London: Columbia University Press, 1958.

Mousnier, Roland (1907–1993)

French historian. Roland Mousnier was a long-time professor of history at the Sorbonne. While other historians—particularly those in the Annales school like Fernand Braudel, Emmanuel Le Roy Ladurie, and Pierre Goubert—made their mark in social history, Mousnier established his reputation with *La Venalité des offices,* an institutional study of the venal office system in seventeenth-century France. As a result, Mousnier was destined to be an outsider to the Annales school, but was no less influential for it. In the 1960s Mousnier did move into comparative and social history to study peasant rebellions, and he criticized the Soviet historian, Boris Porshnev, for overemphasizing class tensions in the peasant revolts of the seventeenth century. He was equally critical of the quantitative social history of historians such as François Furet and Adeline Daumard in his *Social Hierarchies.* This led to his own redefinition of early modern society, which he saw not as a class society, but as a "society of orders." This view was most fully explained in his *Institutions of France under the Absolute Monarchy.*

Mack P. Holt

Texts

The Assassination of Henry IV. Trans. Joan Spencer. London: Faber and Faber, 1973.
The Institutions of France under the Absolute Monarchy, 1598–1789. Trans. Arthur Goldhammer. 2 vols. Chicago: University of Chicago Press, 1979–1983.
Peasant Uprisings in Seventeenth-Century France, Russia and China. Trans. Brian Pearce London: George Allen and Unwin, 1971.
Social Hierarchies, 1450 to the Present. Trans. P. Evans. New York: Harper and Row, 1971.
La Venalité des offices sous Henri IV et Louis XIII [Venality of Offices under Henri IV and Louis XIII]. Second ed. Paris: Presses Universitaires de France, 1971.

Mumford, Lewis (1895–1986)

A self-trained and immensely popular historian of architecture and urban life at large, Mumford was the illegitimate son of a Manhattan housemaid and a prominent Jewish businessman's nephew. Mumford taught at several colleges and lectured widely for decades. But he was best known for his essays and his proliferation of volumes on the changing quality of life in civilization. Mumford developed his early ideas in the radical milieu of the 1910s, among friends like Waldo Frank, Van Wyck Brooks, and the later Communist novelist, Mike Gold. Disillusioned with the U.S. role in World War I, he sought to comprehend the roots of a damaged American culture. The *Story of Utopias* and *The Golden Day* examined the early-nineteenth-century promise and the intellectual efflorescence in the "American Renaissance." *Sticks and Stones,* one of the first widely read histories of American architecture, carried the same message, the hopes of the New England village and the failures of the imperial city arising out of the new wealth created in the later nineteenth century. By the 1930s, Mumford's "Skylines" column in the *New Yorker* had won him a wide readership. *Technics and Civilization* and *Culture and the Cities* established his critique of technology and its uses in day-to-day life. His narrative for the documentary film, *The City*, became one of the most popular attractions of the 1939 World's Fair. After World War II, he wrote eloquently against the arms race and the needless devastation of urban life and of the natural environment generally. A new series of synthetic studies, beginning with *The City in History*, restated his main themes and won him a National Book Award in 1961.

Paul M. Buhle

Texts

The City and History: Its Origins, Its Transformations, and Its Prospects. New York: Harcourt, Brace and World, 1961.

The Culture of Cities. New York: Harcourt, Brace, 1938.

Findings and Keepings: Analects for an Autobiography. New York: Harcourt, Brace, Jovanovich, 1975.

The Golden Day: A Study in American Experience and Culture. New York: Boni and Liveright, 1926.

Sticks and Stones: A Study of American Architecture and Civilization. New York: Dover, 1955.

The Story of Utopias. New York: Boni and Liveright, 1922.

Technics and Civilization. New York: Harcourt, Brace, 1934.

References

Hughes, Thomas P., and Agatha C. Hughes, eds. *Lewis Mumford: Public Intellectual.* New York: Oxford University Press, 1990.

Miller, Donald L. *Lewis Mumford: A Life.* New York: Weidenfeld & Nicholson, 1989.

Münedjdjim Bashî [Muneccimbashi], Darwish Aḥmed Dede bin Luṭf Allāh (1631–1702)

Turkish historian. Born in Selanik, Münedjdjim Bashî was trained in astronomy and astrology and was appointed chief astrologer at the court of Sultan Meḥemmed IV in 1667 and 1668. Although he was a member of the sultan's inner circle, he was exiled to Egypt a decade later. After several years' stay in Egypt, he went to Mecca where he was appointed as the head of the local Sufi lodge. He lived in Medina from 1693, returning in 1700 to Mecca, where he is buried. Münedjdjim Bashî is the author of a number of works on religion, mysticism, geometry, and music. He wrote sufi poetry under the pen name *Ashik* (lover). His most important work is *Djāmiʿ al-duwal,* a general history of the world in Arabic. The first part of the work deals with the life of Muḥammad and is followed by the history of non-Islamic and Islamic dynasties, ending with the history of the Ottoman dynasty down to 1678. In compiling his general history, Münedjdjim Bashî relied on a number of earlier sources, some of which have since been lost. In the early eighteenth century the Turkish poet Ahmed Nedīm (1681–1730) translated the original Arabic text into Turkish under the title *Ṣaḥāʾif al-akhbār.*

Hootan Shambayati

Texts

Tertip ettiki Sahaif al-akhbar. 3 vols. Istanbul: Matbaa-yi Amire, 1868/69.

References

Khalidi, Tarif. *Arabic Historical Thought in the Classical Period.* Cambridge, Eng.: Cambridge University Press, 1994.

Rosenthal, Franz. *A History of Muslim Historiography.* Second ed. Leiden: E.J. Brill, 1968.

Muratori, Ludovico Antonio (1672–1750)

Italian man of letters, antiquarian, librarian, and historian of medieval Italy. A native of Vignola, Muratori took his training in civil and canon law at Modena, and entered the priesthood, but spent most of his life as librarian to the dukes of Modena. From here he conducted an extensive correspondence and frequent travels, reaching out across the Italian peninsula for archival materials from the medieval and early modern period, and preparing critical documentary collections modeled on the French Maurists. His early published work consisted of four volumes of classical texts (*Anecdota*, 1697–1698, 1713), polemical texts related to land disputes between Modena and the papal state, and biographical studies of Italian authors. More significantly, he collected and published Latin and vernacular chronicles from medieval and Renaissance Italy in the twenty-eight-volume *Rerum italicarum scriptores* [The Writers of Italian History] (1723–1751), a series generally known simply as *RIS;* this would be expanded to thirty-four multipart volumes in the twentieth century. Muratori then began publishing the more analytical *Antiquitates italicae medii aevi*

[Italian Antiquities of the Middle Ages] (1738–1742), a six-volume collection of documents arranged thematically in support of seventy-five dissertations on medieval Italian social, legal, and political life. His last extended work was a chronological history of Italy, the *Annali d'Italia* [Annals of Italy], whose twelve volumes encompassed peninsular history from A.D. 1 to 1749.

Nicholas Terpstra

Texts

Annali d'Italia. Revised and extended ed. 40 vols. Florence: Leonardo Marchini, 1827.
Antiquitates italicae medii aevi. 6 vols. Milan: Societas palatinae, 1738–1742.
Ed. *Rerum italicarum scriptores*. Milan: Societas palatinae, 1723–1751.

References

Bertelli, S. *Erudizione e storia in Ludovico Antonio Muratori* [Erudition and History in Ludovico Antonio Muratori]. Naples: Nella sede del Istituto, 1960.
Knowles, David. *Great Historical Enterprises*. London and New York: Nelson, 1964.

Museums

If it is a human characteristic to collect, it is the Greeks who taught us to measure and systematize our collections. Thus the museum in its most basic form is a collection, and it is its curators who measure, order, and define the contents. Moreover, the Greeks and their descendants cataloged these things for a purpose: to serve the needs of rulers with archives and libraries, to inspire the faithful with relics, to entertain the leisure class with animals for sport and with exotica for its amusement. These diverse roots lead to common themes that define museums: to collect, identify, and organize a collection for an "essentially educational or aesthetic purpose." This last quote is from the accreditation standards set forth by the American Association of Museums (AAM). The AAM includes within its purview museums of art and archaeology, science of all branches, aquaria, zoos, observatories, and botanical gardens as well as museums and agencies with historical related and natural history collections.

The first museum was established in Alexandria by Ptolemy I Soter in the third century B.C. as a sort of institute for advanced study supported by a significant library. The idea of collecting things for the purpose of study probably is derived from Aristotle and his efforts to develop taxonomies and classifications systems for them. The first modern European museums (other than art collections) were founded in the seventeenth century and consisted principally of collections of material for botanical gardens or specimens preserved for study. The British Museum was founded in 1753 "to collect all arts and sciences." It initially allowed a very limited public access.

The artist, Charles Willson Peale, gets credit for the first American museum established as an institution for the *public* and for profit. His museum founded in 1786 was located in Philadelphia with branches in New York and Baltimore. It housed specimens of natural history, historical memorabilia, and portraits. Peale's sons tried to carry on the enterprise but most of the collection ultimately went to Phineas T. Barnum and Moses Kimball of Boston. Most of Barnum's collection was burned in various fires in the mid-nineteenth century; Kimball's artifacts ended up at Harvard's Peabody Museum. Peale and subsequently Barnum understood the appeal of a "cabinets of curiosities"; the most notable exhibit at the Peale museum was a mastodon skeleton from Ulster County, New York. It earned more than eighteen hundred dollars in one year from fifty-cent admissions.

The maintenance of libraries and archives and scholarly publication were and are the principal mission of the early American historical societies. Specifically the American Philosophical [1769], the Massachusetts [1791], the East India Marine [1799], the New York Historical [1804], and the American Antiquarian [1812] societies were founded for just that purpose. The archives of these institutions were collected primarily from private bequests, and often art and artifacts with some historical association were included in these bequests, so that today, some of these institutions have valuable material collections as well as well-endowed libraries.

The State Historical Society of Wisconsin was the first historical society to gain tax support. Lyman Draper (1854–1887) and Reuben Gold Thwaites (1887–1913) were the pioneer directors of the society building a notable library and archive, and along the way collecting and preserving Wisconsin's material culture so that today the society runs a major indoor museum, a major outdoor museum—Old World Wisconsin—and five historic houses and sites. The Wisconsin society has served as a model for others in the country.

The most significant indoor history museum in the United States is the Smithsonian Institution, located in the National Mall, which today is a complex of art museums, history and anthropology museums, a natural history museum, and an air and space museum, with branch museums elsewhere in Washington and New York.

George Washington's Mount Vernon was founded as a house museum by Ann Pamela Cunningham and opened to the public in 1860. Following in that tradition, many local societies have taken over older buildings in the community and restored them; or they have furnished rooms within their institutions as period rooms. Period rooms themselves cover a wide range: some showcase antiques and decorative arts, some are functional kitchens, some are shops.

Outdoor museums also cover a broad range. The idea of the outdoor (or folk) museum originated with Artur Hazelius who founded Skansen with a collection of farmsteads, buildings, and craft activities moved to an island outside of Stockholm. Outdoor museums attempt to re-create settings and lifestyles using architecture and furnishings, craft activities, and costumed docents to explain particular ethnic environments at a given time and place. Greenfield Village (near Detroit) and Old Sturbridge Village in Massachusetts both owe their conception to Skansen. Some outdoor museums are totally restored historic districts like Colonial Williamsburg; some combine the restoration of building facades with total restoration of a few buildings like Strawbery Banke in Portsmouth, New Hampshire. An outdoor museum is distinguished from a theme park by the seriousness and integrity of its research for historic interpretation and its willingness to tackle more controversial historical subjects.

The public role of the museum is threefold: interpretation of the collection by way of exhibits, the publication of catalogs, and education through a range of public programs for all age groups within the community. Research-based interpretation has a special meaning in history museums. Freeman Tilden of the National Park Service defined it as: "An educational activity which aims to reveal meanings and relationships through the use of original objects, by firsthand experience, and by illustrative media, rather than simply to communicate factual information." Any methodology that achieves this end is acceptable ranging from the employ of costumed human actors to high-tech emulations and robotics.

To meet the demands of a growing clientele, history museums have collaborated with the American Association of State and Local History and the American Association of Museums to establish and meet professional standards. Various university programs provide public history curricula to train the new professional public historians, ensuring the continuing development of quality programs in the public interest. There are some five thousand museums in the United States today, the vast majority being history museums of one sort or another. The visitation of these museums is far greater than the readership of any history book and rivals television as a source of historical knowledge for the American public.

Elizabeth Hitz

References

Alexander, Edward P. *Museums in Motion.* Nashville, TN: American Association for State and Local History, 1979.

Burkaw, G. Ellis. *Introduction to Museum Work.* Second ed. Nashville: American Association of State and Local History, 1983.

Hooper-Greenhill, Eilean. *Museums and the Shaping of Knowledge.* London and New York: Routledge, 1992.

Tilden, Freeman. *Interpreting Our Heritage.* Chapel Hill: University of North Carolina Press, 1957, 1967, 1977.

Tolles, Bryant E., Jr., ed. *Leadership for the Future.* Nashville, TN: American Association for State and Local History, 1991.

Mutafchiev, Petŭr (1883–1943)

Bulgarian historian. Born in Bozhentsi, Mutafchiev studied geography and history with Vasil Zlatarski in Sofia. From 1910 to 1920, he ran the medieval section of the Sofia National Museum, and from 1920 to 1923, while residing in Munich, he specialized Byzantine history. After his return to Sofia, he was appointed a professor of Eastern European and Byzantine history. Mutafchiev dealt mainly with the political history of medieval Bulgaria and with the problems of feudal land ownership in Byzantium. He also wrote a number of studies on historical geography and on the history of the Dobrudja, engaging in polemic with his Romanian colleague Nicolae Iorga. Mutafchiev was the first Bulgarian historian who consistently studied Bulgarian history within a wider European framework. Although originally a Marxist, his major work *History of the Bulgarian people,* the scope of which is limited to the Middle Ages, fairly reflects the "idealistic" approach to history and the nationalist positions to which he adhered.

R. Detrez

Texts

Istoriya na bûlgarskiya narod, 681–1323 [History of the Bulgarian people, 681–1323]. Ed. Vasil Gyuzelev. Sofia: Bulgarian Academy of Sciences, 1986.

Izbrani proizvedeniya [Selected works]. Ed. Dimitûr Angelov. 2 vols. Sofia: Nauka i izkustvo, 1973.

Myth and History

The relationship between the mythical or legendary past and the documentable past as studied by historians. Myth is in some ways the mother of history, but the child's relationship to the parent has been both nurturing and at times highly quarrelsome. Early societies made what sense they could of their pasts through myth, and particularly through aetiological myth (pertaining to the origins or founding of a particular city or people) in which gods and demigods were held to have played a major role in the foundation of a society or regime.

The earliest annals or king-lists of Mesopotamia provide examples of historical writing where the mythological and historical blend together in such a manner, for instance the ancient record, from the city of Lagash, that traces the origins of a boundary dispute to the adjudication of Enlil, ruler of all the gods. The Greek epics, the *Iliad* and *Odyssey,* build a fictional and legendary story upon a kernel of historical truth, and the Greek mythographer, Hesiod, contributed to this mode of thinking by humanizing many of the gods. The Hebrew scriptures similarly take what was probably a historical exodus and mythologize it. Indigenous peoples such as the Incas, the Aztecs, Hawaiians and Fijian Islanders, and many tribes in Africa all developed origin myths closely connected to their sense of the history and genealogy of their institutions.

Among writers of history, myth and legend has always had its critics. In the Middle Ages, forms of literature such as the *chansons* and the sagas variously integrate historical events with stories of gods and heroes, but there were those at the same time who rejected such a mixture of fact and fancy. The medieval chronicler William of Newburgh (1136–ca. 1198), for instance, was skeptical of the apparently invented series of British kings in Geoffrey of Monmouth's *British History,* and Renaissance scholars like Polydore Vergil and Etienne Pasquier were highly suspicious of myths of national origin, such as the foundation of Britain by a race of giants led by Albion, who in turn were defeated by Brutus, a grandson of Aeneas

the Trojan, or the analogous French myths that attributed the founding of the Gauls to Francion, another Trojan refugee, while placing the creation of the French monarchy in the hands of a later legendary king, Pharamond. By 1600, many historians were choosing the path of cautious skepticism and did not commit themselves in print either for or against such myths and legends, which died hard, particularly when national identities and pride were involved.

At the same time that historians and antiquaries were beginning to find fault with myths from an evidentiary point of view, others were recognizing that myth had played an important role in the evolution of social consciousness. Francis Bacon referred to his "Idols of the tribe and cave," including myth, which needed to be dispensed with in his own time (since they stood in the way of his project for the "advancement of learning"), but he conceded that they had played a useful intellectual role in the past. The Frenchman Henri de La Popeliniere traced the emergence of history from the era of myths and legends to his own day. The most sophisticated critique of myth, which saw it as an essential part of primitive thinking, came from Giambattista Vico's *New Science* at the start of the eighteenth century, in which Vico distinguished society according to ages not of gold, silver, bronze, and iron (as the poets since Hesiod had) but of gods, heroes, and men, according to the modes of thought that applied. Those skeptical of myth were able to use a kind of early form of anthropological thinking to turn the gods and heroes into real people rather than dispensing with them altogether: many Renaissance and early Enlightenment thinkers, for instance, continued to think in terms of single inventors of things (the wheel, fire, letters) as god-heroes (such as Jupiter, Daedalus, Prometheus, or Cadmus) based on real persons; this intellectual process of adapting myth into a revised historiography is called "euhemerism," after an ancient Greek mythographer, Euhemerus (fl. 300 B.C.) who believed that mythologies arose out of the deification of men.

In modern times, historians have become particularly critical of myth. Nineteenth-century archivally oriented historians fought bitterly to discredit several long-standing myths—Bishop William Stubbs's discrediting of the belief that Britain had first been made Christian by a fictitious first-century king named Lucius is a good example. But other myths and legends were created in their stead, as colonial and newly independent societies generated their own quasihistorical accounts of the past, albeit principally involving flesh and blood historical figures rather than gods. The story of George Washington chopping down his cherry tree would be a case in point: whether the event actually happened is of little significance because it has didactic value and speaks to the wish to ascribe greater than normal virtue to the United States' first leader. What matters is that this story has acquired mythic proportions in the American national sense of identity. An even broader example would be the myth of the rugged frontiersman settling a savage wilderness and civilizing a nation: although it has elements of truth, it has turned figures like Daniel Boone and Davy Crockett into folk heroes, thereby providing the emotive underpinnings for more scholarly work, as for instance in the frontier thesis of F.J. Turner. In the twentieth century, we have constructed mythologies surrounding a variety of historical figures and events; to concede this is by no means to admit the absurd claims of those who would challenge the historicity of events such as the Holocaust. It is merely to acknowledge that myth will always be with history, and that historical writing, popular and academic, derives much of its persuasive force from myth: the trick for the modern student is to be able to tell the difference between the two, and to recognize varying degrees of the fictional and legendary in the "facts" of historical accounts.

D.R. Woolf

See also LITERATURE AND HISTORY; SAGAS.

References

Brown, Donald. *Hierarchy, History, and Human Nature: The Social Origins of Historical Consciousness.* Tucson: University of Arizona Press, 1988.

Butterfield, Herbert. *The Origins of History.* London: Eyre Methuen, 1981.

Carpenter, Rhys. *Folk Tale, Fiction and Saga in the Homeric Epics.* Berkeley: University of California Press, 1962.

Ferguson, Arthur B. *Utter Antiquity.* Durham, NC: Duke University Press, 1993.

McNeill, William H. *Mythistory and Other Essays.* Chicago: University of Chicago Press, 1986.

Sahlins, Marshall. *Islands of History.* Chicago: University of Chicago Press, 1985.

Strenski, Ivan. *Four Theories of Myth in Twentieth-Century History: Cassirer, Eliade, Levi-Strauss, and Malinowski.* Iowa City: University of Iowa Press, 1987.

Urton, Gary. *The History of a Myth: Pacariqtambo and the Origin of the Inkas.* Austin: University of Texas Press, 1990.

M

N

Nāgarakṛtāgama
See DEŚAWARṆANA.

Naima, Mustafa (1655–1716)

Ottoman historian and author of *Annals of the Turkish Empire from 1591 to 1659 of the Christian era.* A native of Aleppo, Naima migrated early in life to Istanbul where he entered the secretarial profession and filled a succession of positions, especially in the finance bureaus. With the encouragement of one of his later patrons Amca-zade Hüseyn Pasha (Grand Vizier 1697–1702) he began to compose a history of the Ottoman dynasty during the previous century relying mostly on the (now lost) work of an Ottoman scholar named Şarih al-Menar-zade Ahmed Efendi (d. 1647) and heavily influenced also by the chronicle of Katib Çelebi. He never fulfilled his intention to write a history of his own times. While giving principal weight in his history to the opinions expressed by the contemporary authorities on whom he mostly relied, Naima added his own critical assessments, and his history represents something of a departure from "traditional" historiography, which tended to display somewhat unidimensional and rhetorical versions of past events. The *Tarih-i Naima,* as it is known, remains the most cited and authoritative source for the history of the Ottoman empire in the first six decades of the seventeenth century.

Rhoads Murphey

Texts

Annals of the Turkish Empire from 1591 to 1659 of the Christian era. Trans. Charles Fraser. London: Oriental translation fund, 1832. [Note: this translation presents select passages from vols. 1 & 2 of the 1864 ed., ending with the rule of Ahmed I (r. 1603–1617)].

Tarih-i Naima (Rawdat al-Husayn fi khulasat akhbar al-khafiqayn). 2 vols. Istanbul: n.p., 1734; 6 vols. Istanbul: n.p., 1864–1866

References

Thomas, Lewis V. *A Study of Naima.* New York: New York University Press, 1972.

Naitō Konan (1866–1934)

Japanese historian of East Asia. He was born Naitō Torajirō in Akita, to a samurai family with an extended history of service to the Nambu clan. After extensive home-study, he traveled to Tokyo to work with the leading Buddhist historian, Ouchi Seiran, editing the Journal *Meikyō shinshi;* he also began his extensive writing career at this time by contributing numerous articles as a journalist-scholar to the burgeoning newspaper and journal industry. He began his studies with a focus on nativism *(Kokugaku)* but shifted to continental studies, especially China, after a fire destroyed his library in 1899. He became a lecturer at Kyoto Imperial University in 1907 and was appointed a professor there in 1909. In that same year he began his seminar on East Asian history, which operated continuously until his death in 1934. He is widely recognized as an independent thinker, an incomparable scholar, and a trailblazer. A central tenet of his philosophy of history was his theory of shifting cultural centers. He demonstrated how the center of East Asian *(tōyō)* culture constantly moved to new areas; this allowed for the identification of new periods. His periodization of China's past has become a standard, although not uncriticized, model for premodern systems in general. His emphasis upon the emergence of the lower classes as a key historical force also contributed to a significant rethinking of East

Asian history. By identifying an essential "East Asian culture" and history, he could also posit Japan's crucial role as the next step in this history.

James Edward Ketelaar

Texts
Shinshinaron [New Thesis on China]. Tokyo: Hakubundō, 1924.

References
Tanaka, Stefan. *Japan's Orient: Rendering Pasts into History*. Berkeley: University of California Press, 1993.

Namier, Sir Lewis Bernstein (1888–1960)

Polish-born British historian. Namier studied briefly at Lvov and Lausanne before going to Balliol College, Oxford, in 1908. He eventually became a naturalized British subject and held the chair of modern history at the University of Manchester from 1931 to 1953. He was knighted in 1952. Namier produced two distinct bodies of work. The first, on the structure of English politics under George III and in America during the Revolutionary War, focused on the House of Commons, king, cabinet, parliament, and monarchy during the rise of the party system. The second, a series of European studies, comprised such topics as nationalism, the Habsburg Empire, the revolutions of 1848, and the dynamics of Europe's final "decay" with the rise of Hitler. Namier revolutionized Anglo-American scholarship in his Georgian studies, which embodied his ideas on the nature of history and political action. Skeptical of ascribing agency to ideas, he focused on the "morphology of human affairs." For Namier, "structure" signified the complex matrix of social institutions giving purpose and meaning to human life. He rejected the Whig interpretation of history, regarding the past as an "intelligible disorder." He took pride in digging below ideology to the bedrock of "interests." Critics said he took men and the mind out of history. Namier accepted that ideas shaped actions and he filled his books with brilliant portraits. But he denied that party cant revealed political purpose, or that great men made history. His concern was with men taken in aggregates, and he described the interests and passions that mobilized them to actions that were often destructive of what they said they wished to preserve: the order of society under law, which secured to persons moral validity and liberty.

Arthur J. Slavin

Texts
Avenues of History. London, Hamish Hamilton, 1952.
Diplomatic Prelude, 1938–1939. London: Macmillan, 1948.
1848: The Revolution of the Intellectuals. London: G. Cumberlege, 1944.
England in the Age of the American Revolution. Second ed. London: Macmillan 1961.
Europe in Decay: A Study in Disintegration, 1936–1940. London: Macmillan, 1950.
Ed. *The House of Commons, 1754–1790*. 3 vols. London and New York: Oxford University Press for the History of Parliament Trust, 1964.
In the Nazi Era. London: Macmillan, 1952.
The Structure of Politics at the Accession of George III. London: Macmillan, 1929.

References
Kenyon, J.P. *The History Men*. London: Weidenfeld and Nicolson, 1983.

Nanni, Giovanni [Annius of Viterbo] (ca. 1432–1502)

Italian antiquary, historian, and forger. A Dominican friar, born in Viterbo, Nanni was, at various times, a Latin teacher, an astrologer, and the court theologian to Pope Alexander VI. A proud supporter of his own city's history and anxious to push its origins back as far as possible into the remote classical past, Nanni's *Antiquitatum Variarum Volumina XVII* [Seventeen Volumes of Various Antiquities] (1498), was one of the most successful forgeries of all time. The *Antiquitates* contained what were allegedly the translations of several long-lost classical histories. Despite being crude forgeries, they were accepted as authentic by most readers. They were popular because they provided textual proof for the foundational myths of the world's major nations. In fact, the *Antiquitates* was the only source of information on many non-European peoples. While conclusively proved to be a fraudulent in 1583 by Joseph Scaliger, Nanni's pseudohistories continued to be popular sources well into the eighteenth century.

Keith Robinson

Texts
Annio da Viterbo: Documentie recherche. Rome: Consiglio nazionale delle richerche, 1981.
Auctores vetustissimi. Venice: Bernardinus Venetus de Vitalibus, 1498.

Commentarium super opera diversorum auctorum de antiquitatibus loquentium [Commentary on Works by Various Authors Referring to Antiquities]. Rome: Eucharius Silber, 1498.

References

Grafton, Anthony. *Forgers and Critics: Creativity and Duplicity in Western Scholarship.* Princeton, NJ: Princeton University Press, 1990.

Ligota, C. "Annius of Viterbo and Historical Method." *Journal of the Warburg and Courtauld Institutes* 50 (1987): 44–56.

Tigerstedt, E.N. "Ioannes Annius and *Graecia Mendax.*" In *Classical, Mediaeval, and Renaissance Studies in Honor of Berthold Louis Ullman,* ed. Charles Henderson Jr. Rome: Edizioni di storia e letteratura, 1964, 293–310.

Weiss, Roberto. *The Renaissance Discovery of Classical Antiquity.* Second ed. Oxford: Basil Blackwell, 1988.

Narrative, in Historical Writing

The view of history as a story or storylike account (Latin: *narrare,* to tell or relate). Most historiography prior to that with scientific aspirations conformed to this pattern. Indeed, in all cultures, early historiography began with grand narratives—the epics—such as Homer's *Iliad.* They lacked a concept of continuous time for connecting the distant past with the present and had gods, goddesses, heroes, and heroines rather than people of the daily life as important actors. Recited over and over with the flexibility of oral accounts, the epics made transparent fundamental features of the human condition, thus, teaching and entertaining simultaneously. While reverently preserved, the epic yielded its predominant place in the world of the Greek city-states to the historical prose narrative that reflected the increasing human control over the world. The new narrative reflected the new time concept in the city-states, diminished the role of gods, and replaced heroes with prominent humans (radically so, in the new genre of the biographical narrative). The histories of Herodotus and Thucydides shaped influential patterns for subsequent historical narratives: descriptive narratives (Herodotus's ethnographic sections and Thucydides' report on the plague), dramatic and event-oriented narratives (accounts of wars and politics), and nonconforming elements (such as speeches, designed to explain ideals and contexts in a nonabstract manner). In the absence of mythical explanations for long series of historical events (such as the one for the Trojan War: the judgment of Paris, the subsequent abduction of Helen, and the resulting war), human ideals and motives began to serve as elements for constructing those governing stories of which individual events were subplots. Herodotus viewed and thus explained the war of the Greeks against the Persians as the struggle of freedom against despotism, and Thucydides spoke of long-range causes (interests of sea and land powers competing for supremacy) that overarched immediate or incidental causes. Classical narrative history became closely linked to the increasingly elaborate enterprise of rhetoric, particularly in the reflections on the historian's practice. Concerned with a clear distance to the fictional narrative, the authors of historical narratives took seriously their obligation to tell what actually had occurred and not what could have been. Cicero, although allowing for some distortion in order to persuade, stressed the importance of such truthfulness for history to function as the proper teacher of life *(magistra vitae).* Lucian of Samosata (second century A.D.) gave practical advice on how to begin a historical narrative, how to arrange the material, what to leave out, how properly to proportion the parts, and how to choose the right words as well as how to fit them artfully together.

Medieval historical narratives were much beholden to classical historiography, although they created new narrative forms—the chronicle and the *gesta* (deeds). Stylistically, a simple writing style *(sermo humilis)* was considered to be appropriate for the Christian writer. With divine providence guiding history toward its fulfillment, the medieval historian needed not to construct overall meanings; a fact expressed in the preference for paratactical writing (the narrative linkage through "and" and "then," for example) over causal phrases. The revival of classical learning in the Renaissance brought a corresponding strengthening of classical rhetorical influences on historical narratives visible in the striving for an elegant and pure classical Latin and a resurgence of interest in quasi-empirical overall explanatory constructs linking the story elements (as with, for instance, Leonardo Bruni's connection of civic freedom and a state's prosperity). A renewed interest in the theory and methods of narrative history brought forth a substantial sixteenth-century body of works on the *ars historica.* The term *ars* refers here to an endeavor that has clear and sufficient rules for its practice. Heavily influenced by such ancient rhetoricians as Cicero and Aulus Gellius, the Italian *trattatisti* (writers of tracts) elaborated on the rules for history writing, emphasizing that the historical narrative must both teach and delight. Without the latter—helped by elegant figures of speech, dramatic episodes, and colorful words—the former was ineffective. The "nude" narrative had no impact on the reader, while the properly crafted narrative was seen as so powerful that its account of the affairs of state must be kept away from common people and the young. Some *trattatisti,* aware of the complexities of the selection from a mass of material for the narrative, made a rather modern distinction between a "true" and a "truthful" account (with the designation "true" solely reserved for the biblical account).

Narrative histories in a traditional mode (as the story of persons and events), although never absent from western historiography, found their most serious competitor in the historiography that built its accounts not in conformance with rules and ideals of rhetoric but patterned them in the image of the emerging sciences. Here the accent in history writing shifted to representing the past as accurately as possible by the assembly of documented elements of past reality and connecting them by forces (in past reality and in the text) that were accessible to empirical enquiry. This development reached back to the erudite and legal historians of the 1500s and 1600s, who were minimally concerned with beauty of language and grace of style for the purpose of persuasion.

Nineteenth-century historiography formed a transition with its grand traditional narrative histories (Jules Michelet, Thomas Babington Macaulay, and George Bancroft), its histories with a vast philosophical sweep (Georg Wilhelm Friedrich Hegel and Karl Marx) yet still based on a grand narrative plot, and the works in the vein of the new German *Geschichtswissenschaft* pioneered by Leopold von Ranke and its historicist epigones. But from the 1890s, historians, who took their precepts from positivist philosophy and the natural sciences, engaged in a strenuous effort to cleanse historiography of all traces of rhetoric and literary aspirations—both of which were now seen as mere embellishments that were unnecessary, even harmful to a scientific historiography. The future was to belong to the monograph, stylistically unadorned, devoid of story plot, dealing with forces beyond the individual, and using causal explanations; all preferably put in a precise technical language, intended as a perfectly neutral medium in representing the past.

After 1960, there emerged, in opposition to history as a part of a positivist unified scientific theory and to subsequent structural histories, a conscious reaffirmation of the narrative backed up by a systematic theory that was equidistant from scientism and traditional rhetoric: narrativism. It aimed to establish the narrative as the proper cognitive instrument for the representation of the past; the one that most faithfully reflected the contingent order of human life rather than lawlike causal explanations. In the focus of narrativist theory stood the complex relationship between the author's consciousness and its contextual links, the structures of language, and objective past reality.

In the 1960s, narrativist theoreticians searched for those arguments that gave the narrative form links to past reality the greatest possible certainty (William Gallie; William Walsh). Subsequently, narrativists found the accessibility of objective reality less certain, although they still asserted a significant element of pretheoretical experience of life (Paul Ricoeur, David Carr). But, in the 1970s, the emphasis shifted decisively away from the reconstructive activity of the historian toward an autonomous role for language. The latter appeared first as the "deep verbal structures" in Hayden White's works (such as dominant tropes). A mediating position appeared in the so-called contextualism (J.G.A. Pocock) and *Begriffsgeschichte* (Reinhart Koselleck), with their delicate balance between rational agents and the constitutive force of language. Then, in poststructuralism or deconstructionism, language itself became the reality from which must be banned hegemonical, oppressive discourses (with associated institutions, for Michel Foucault) and in which language was ever-shifting, self-referential, and shaped by the free play of signifiers (words) that derived their meanings solely from the differences from each other rather than from any reference beyond the language (Jacques Derrida). From such texts meta- or master-narratives (Jacques-François Lyotard)—as the totality-constituting meanings—were to be banned, because of their hegemonical and oppressive hold on the elements of the narratives. At that point, the borders between the fictional and historical narratives became completely blurred. Yet in the world of practicing historians, important elements of traditional narratives survived, even finding a new appreciation in historiographies formerly hostile to them (such as the Annales school).

Ernst Breisach

See also ARS HISTORICA; LITERATURE AND HISTORY; MYTH AND HISTORY; PHILOSOPHY OF HISTORY—ANALYTICAL; POSTMODERNISM; SCIENTIFIC HISTORY.

References

Ankersmit, F.R. *Narrative Logic: A Semantic Analysis of the Historians's Language.* Boston: Martinus Nijhoff, 1983.

Cameron, Averil, ed. *The History As Text: The Writing of Ancient History.* Chapel Hill: University of North Carolina, 1989.

Canary, Robert, and Henry Kozicki. *The Writing of History: Literary Form and Historical Understanding.* Madison: University of Wisconsin Press, 1978.

Carr, David. *Time, Narrative, and History.* Bloomington: Indiana University Press, 1986.

Danto, Arthur C. *Narration and Knowledge.* New York: Columbia University Press, 1985.

Gossman, Lionel. *Between History and Literature.* Cambridge, MA: Harvard University Press, 1990.

Kellner, Hans. *Language and Historical Representation: Getting the Story Crooked.* Madison: University of Wisconsin Press, 1989.

Ricoeur, Paul. *Time and Narrative.* Trans. K. McLaughlin and D. Pellauer. 3 vols. Chicago: University of Chicago Press, 1983–1985.

Stone, Lawrence. "The Revival of the Narrative: Reflections on a New, Old History." *Past and Present* 85 (1979): 3–24.

Vance, Eugene. *From Topic to Tale: Logic and Narrativity in the Middle Ages.* Minneapolis: University of Minnesota Press, 1987.

White, Hayden. *The Content of the Form: Narrative Discourse and Historical Representation.* Baltimore: Johns Hopkins University Press, 1987.

Naruszewicz, Adam (1733–1796)

Polish historian, poet, bishop of Smolensk and then of Lutsk. Adam Naruszewicz was born in Pinskie, near Lahiczyn. He lectured in Vilna Academy and then in the Jesuit College in Warsaw. A Jesuit until the abolition of the order, he became a secular priest. In 1778 he was appointed the bishop of Smolensk, and in 1790 of Lutsk. As a poet, Naruszewicz was one of the founders of the Polish Enlightenment. Closely associated with King Stanislaus Augustus Poniatowski, he became interested in history under the king's influence. He died in Janów Podlaski on July 8, 1796. In his *Memorial wzgledem pisania historii narodowej* [Memorandum on the Writing of National History] (1775), Naruszewicz presented his methodological background, defining the history of the nation as the history of the whole society, including all estates, and postulated a critical approach to historical sources. His *Historia narodu polskiego* [A History of the Polish Nation] (vols. 2–6 1780–1786; vol. 1 1824) is considered to be the first scholarly representation of Polish history. Naruszewicz was a representative of the idea of monarchism. He is known to have collected source material, the so-called *Teki Naruszewicza* [Naruszewicz's Portfolios].

Ewa Domańska

Texts

Historia narodu polskiego [A History of the Polish Nation]. 6 vols. Warsaw: Nakl. Tow. Królewskiego Warszawskiego, 1803–1824.

References

Grabski, Andrzej Feliks. "Synteza historyczna Adama Naruszewicza [Adam Naruszewicz's Historical Synthesis]." In his *Myśl historyczna polskiego Oświecenia* [Historical Thought in the Polish Enlightenment]. Warsaw: PWN, 1976, 160–184.

Rutkowska N. *Bishop A. Naruszewicz and His History of the Polish Nation.* Washington, DC: Catholic University of America Press, 1941.

National Character

The composite of mental traits and behavior patterns that defines a nationality. The notion of national character, a subspecies of the idea of social character, stems from the premise that nations possess distinctive personalities that condition the behavior of their members. The idea of social character springs from the commonsense observation of shared customs within human groups. We take for granted, for instance, the possible existence of common thought and behavior patterns among members of social classes or religious denominations. The basis of the notion of *national* character is this same existence of like manners. As an explicit concept, "national character" had to await the seventeenth- and eighteenth-century rise of the modern ideas of "character" (the "aggregate of the distinctive features of any thing"—*Oxford English Dictionary*), and "nation" (in the double sense of territorial state and ethnic group). These ideas were linked by such eighteenth-century authors as Montesquieu (who spoke of *diverses caractères des nations*) and Rousseau (who declared "each people has, or ought to have, its own character"). In his essay "Of National Characters" (1748), David Hume affirmed that "each nation has a peculiar set of manners" that may be a basis for prediction regarding its members' conduct, though he warned against generalizations that "admit of no exception."

Especially important in the idea's diffusion was the philosopher J.G. von Herder, who translated the French expression *esprit des nations* into the German *Volksgeist*. By this he understood an intangible essence, or folk spirit, manifest in distinctive national traits such as language, folk custom, and folk music. The idea was influential in nineteenth-century ethnography and social science generally. "Nation" was the key organizing concept of nineteenth- and early-twentieth-century historiography, and the related notion of national character was a cornerstone of much scholarship. Leopold von Ranke, for instance, presumed that relations between nations were determined by their "peculiar character." The concept itself was seldom examined; it was unclear if national character was something fixed and immutable, a result of divine will or heredity, or a product of environment and subject to change. In the late nineteenth century the concept was colored by social Darwinian and racialist theory, and became associated with ethnic stereotyping. Following World War I, for example, the U.S. Army launched an ill-fated project—replete with cultural and racial bias—to classify the characters of foreign nations as a predictive aid to American policy. As racialism fell into discredit, especially following full disclosure of the fruits of Nazi racism in 1945, the concept of national character began to fall into disrepute. Yet the work of leading historians of nationalism such as Carlton J.H. Hayes and Hans Kohn continued to reflect cautious acceptance of the idea, so long as it was seen as a product of cultural conditioning rather than heredity. Recent work in social history, with its stress on the array of behavior patterns that may distinguish groups *within the nation* (classes, genders, subcultures), has further undermined the notion of unified national character, and some authorities now repudiate the idea. Yet national distinctiveness remains a theme of interest to historians worldwide, and the tradition of acceptance is still encountered. For the United States, David Potter's judgment of 1954 still merits reflection: "Among the more prominent American historical writers, there is hardly one who does not, either occasionally or constantly, explicitly or implicitly, invoke the idea of an American national character." Ironically, some authors who renounce the *word* still employ the *notion* behind it. Lately the idea has resurfaced in the guise of such surrogate concepts as "ethnicity" and national "identity."

Harry Ritter

See also ETHNICITY AND NATIONAL ORIGINS; NATIONALISM.

References

Anderson, Benedict. *Imagined Communities: Reflections on the Origins and Spread of Nationalism.* Revised ed. London and New York: Verso, 1991.

Farrar, L.L., Jr. "Porous Vessels: A Critique of the Nation, Nationalism and National Character As Analytical Concepts." *History of European Ideas* 10 (1989): 705–720.

Hartshorne, Thomas L. *The Distorted Image: Changing Conceptions of the American Character since Turner.* Cleveland, OH: Press of Case Western Reserve University, 1968.

National Origins

See ETHNICITY AND NATIONAL ORIGINS.

Nationalism

Political idea with implications for historical writing and a subject of historical research. Three sets of questions appear fundamental in the research on nationalism: When did it originate? What has been its historical meaning? How and why did it spread the world over? Until the 1920s, nationalism was not a subject of systematic historical research. The first distinguished approach (exemplified by Hans Kohn and Carlton Hayes) viewed nationalism as an idea—based on the notions of rationalism, progress, citizenship, and democracy—originating in the West as the political expression of the bourgeoisie. In this view, nationalism later spread to the more backward eastern Europe and Asia, where an organic mode of nationalism based on the ancient *Volk* developed political forms of authoritarianism and totalitarianism. The advantage of this approach lies in viewing the nation as "a state of mind" (Kohn). But its problems are also evident. It was Eurocentric, for it viewed nationalism in the West as the original to which all nationalisms must be measured. It ignored the social history of nationalism by exploring it mainly among the works of intellectuals. And, in the wake of Nazism, it condemned nationalism as a historical aberration, instead of explaining why millions are ready to die for their nation.

A new interpretation developed beginning in the 1950s, based on modernization theories (Karl Deutsch, Miroslav Hroch, Eugen Weber). This approach views nationalism not as a product of an idea, but as an unavoidable outcome of modernity, as a belief produced by the cultural, economic, and technological transformation into and of modernity. It emphasizes the process by which social and economic change pulled people from local to national institutions and worldviews, and how the common experience of communication, education, military conscription, and the market developed in them a sense of national belonging. The strengths of this approach contain also its weaknesses: while focusing on the social and economic production of national belongings, it neglects to interpret their cultural origins and meaning; while viewing nationalism as an outcome of modernization, it also views national belongings as a fixed process from traditional into modern identity.

In the last two decades the most influential method of interpreting nationalism has viewed the nation, in an anthropological key, as an invented cultural artifact (Ernest Gellner, Eric Hobsbawm). In an influential interpretation, Benedict Anderson argued that the nation is not a predetermined historical force but a modern "imagined community" of people who share a past and a future with conationals they will never meet, who cherish national landscapes they will never visit, and who believe in the "horizontal comradeship" of the national community in spite of its inherent inequality.

The cultural (like the modernization) approach studies nationalism without condemnation, as a genuine historical phenomenon by which people from all walks of life transform their notions of history, territory, and association. It avoids (unlike the modernization approach) the teleological view of nationalism as the progression from a traditional to a modern identity that obliterates other identities that exist in the nation; it sees nationalism instead as a process by which people simultaneously repudiate and reclaim the past. It emphasizes (1) the unique success of national identity to represent the nation while accommodating the particularity of other identities that exist in it such as regional and ethnic identities and (2) the contested political struggle over the making of national identity. Thus recent research explores gender, race, regional, and religious issues in the making of nations. Historians explore the symbolism and social engineering of nationalism by analyzing the representation, social practice, and political meaning of artifacts such as monuments, museums, and celebrations.

This approach is not without problems, however. It shares with the modernization approach the idea that nationalism is a worldview rooted in modernity. While viewing national ideology and political movements as modern phenomena, Anthony Smith argued that modern nations owe to premodern ethnic communities, whose identity

resided in a "'myth-symbol' complex" that endures for centuries and thus conditions the modern nation. Another problem concerns the fundamental topic of the relations between the origins and spread of nationalism. Gellner's argument that nationalism is the outcome of industrial social organization corresponds to the historical experience of Europe and the Americas, but appears questionable as an explanation of nationalism in Asia and Africa. Anderson argued that the origins of nationalism in the Americas and Europe codified a collection of modular forms of "nation-ness" which were then selected and modified by nationalist movements in Asia and Africa. This, however, reduces nationalist movements in Asia and Africa to epiphenomena of Western imagination. Important research has been conducted on the relations in Asia and Africa between colonialism and nationalism. Partha Chatterjee argues that the basic pattern of anticolonial nationalism is a dual process of imitation of European economic, technological, and state forms and, simultaneously, of cultivating a cultural identity that is viewed as different from and superior to Europe.

Alon Confino

See also EUROCENTRISM; IMPERIALISM; MODERNIZATION THEORY; NATIONAL CHARACTER.

References

Anderson, Benedict. *Imagined Communities: Reflections on the Origins and Spread of Nationalism.* Revised ed. London, New York: Verso, 1991.

Gellner, Ernest. *Nations and Nationalism.* Oxford: Blackwell, 1983.

Hobsbawm, E.J. *Nations and Nationalism since 1780: Programme, Myth, Reality.* Cambridge, Eng.: Cambridge University Press, 1990.

Neale, Sir John Ernest (1890–1975)

British historian of Tudor England. After a difficult childhood during which he lost his father as a small boy and left school for a time at the age of fourteen, Neale completed an undergraduate degree at the University of Liverpool. From 1919 and for the rest of his career (save for a brief period at Manchester in 1925–1927), he was attached to University College, London, where he became the disciple and heir of the great Tudor historian A.F. Pollard; he succeeded Pollard as Astor professor of English history in 1927, a post he held until his retirement in 1956. He was knighted in 1955, and he continued to lead his Monday Seminar at the

Institute of Historical Research almost until his death. Neale's work put the reign of Elizabeth I in the forefront of Tudor studies. His biography of the queen became a bestseller, despite his detailed focus on her command of her councillors and genius for statecraft. These themes dominated his work on the Commons and the parliaments, and he was an early member of the board of the History of Parliament. Historians, including his most well-known doctoral student, Geoffrey Elton, have contested Neale's main points: the apotheosis of Elizabeth I, discounting of late medieval parliaments and lack of concern for the lords in the story, discovery of gentry pressure groups (the "Puritan Choir") who forced policy on government, and his emphasis on conflict rather than cooperation. But Neale's studies reshaped the field, although he died before the completion of the History of Parliament volumes on the Elizabethan Commons.

Arthur J. Slavin

Texts

Elizabeth I and Her Parliaments. 2 vols. London: Jonathan Cape, 1953–1957.
The Elizabethan House of Commons. London: Jonathan Cape, 1949.
Ed. *The House of Commons, 1558–1603.* 3 vols. London: History of Parliament Trust, 1981.
Queen Elizabeth. London: Jonathan Cape, 1934.

Nechkina, Militsa Vasilevna (1901–1985)

Russian historian. Nechkina was educated at Kazan University and then in the Institute of Red Professors under the supervision of M.N. Pokrovskii. She later taught at Moscow State University, became a full member of the All-Union Academy of Sciences (1958), and served as head of the Academy's Scholarly Council for the Study of the History of Historical Scholarship. Nechkina influenced Soviet historiography through her writings and as an "organizer of scholarship." Although not a member of the Communist Party, she served as one of the "conveyor belts" between the Party and historians. She sought to stem the upsurge of nationalism that marked Russian historical literature after 1934. After Stalin's death, Nechkina initiated a discussion of the "periodization of Soviet historical scholarship." This wide-ranging discussion stimulated conscience and thought and helped to launch the process that ultimately dissipated Marxist–Leninist ideology. She fostered the method of collective investigation. Nechkina's writings touched upon almost all questions of modern Russian history. She participated in discussions about the nature of the Russian historical process and about the revolutionary movement, with special emphasis on its theoretical aspects. She laid a firm foundation for the study of historical scholarship and set a high standard in her own writings.

George M. Enteen

Texts

Ed. *Ocherki istorii istoricheskoi nauki v SSSR* [An Outline of the History of Historical Studies in the USSR]. Vols. 2–5. Moscow: Nauka, 1960–1985.
Vasilii Osipovich Kliuchevskii. Moscow: Nauka, 1974.
Ed. *Vstrecha dvukh pokolenii (Iz istorii russkogo revoliutsionnogo dvizheniia kontsa 50–kh—nachala 60–kh godov XIX veka): Sbornik statei.* [The Meeting of Two Generations . . . a Collection of Articles]. Moscow: Nauka, 1980.

References

Vandalkovskoi, M.G., and V.A. Dunaevskogo. *Militsa Vasilevna Nechkina, 1901–1985.* Moscow: Nauka, 1987.

Needham, Noel Joseph Terence Montgomery (1900–1995)

Scientist and historian of Chinese Science. Needham spent half of his academic life researching in biochemistry, although his interest in the history of science is shown in his *History of Embriology* (1934). Needham's interest in China, which began in the 1930s, deepened greatly when he headed a scientific mission there in 1942. He returned to Cambridge in 1948 to devote the rest of his life to his monumental work, *Science and Civilization in China.* Initially, Needham was fortunate in attracting the assistance of several outstanding Chinese scholars, and later several other Western sinologists cooperated on the project. This work is encyclopedic in its treatment of a wide spectrum of sciences and pseudosciences, chemistry, alchemy, shipbuilding, agriculture, mathematics, astronomy, astrology, and clockmaking among others. To avoid being over–Sinocentric, it incorporates contrasting historical material on similar Western sciences. The work has already had a profound influence on sinological studies principally through Needham's concept of the nature of Chinese society and traditional Chinese mentality.

Carney T. Fisher

Texts

Ed. with Robert Pagel. *Background to Modern Science.* New York: Arno, 1975.

The Development of Iron and Steel Technology in China. Cambridge, Eng.: W. Heffer for Newcomen Society, 1964.

A History of Embryology. New York: Arno, 1975.

Science and Civilisation in China. 6 vols. in 15 parts. Cambridge, Eng.: Cambridge University Press, 1954–1988.

References

Li, Guohao, ed. *Explorations in the History of Science and Technology in China.* Shanghai: Chinese Classics Publishing House, 1982.

Teich, Mikulas, and Robert Young, eds. *Changing Perspectives in the History of Science: Essays in Honor of Joseph Needham.* London: Heinemann, 1973.

Neilson, Nellie (1873–1947)

Medieval economic historian. Born in Philadelphia, Neilson earned her graduate degrees at Bryn Mawr, studying with Charles McLean Andrews. At Cambridge and then Oxford she researched her dissertation topic with F.W. Maitland and Paul Vinogradoff. Chair of the history department at Mount Holyoke College from 1905 until her retirement, she was a fellow of the Royal Historical Society and the first woman president of the American Historical Association (1943) and of the Medieval Academy (1944). A leading authority on English manorialism, her articles appeared in a wide range of legal and historical journals. She coedited volume I of the *Cambridge Economic History of Europe* and contributed to the *Oxford Studies in Social and Legal History.* Her *Medieval Agrarian Economy* (1936) was reprinted into the 1970s. Interested in how agricultural settlement influenced the development of common law, Neilson's meticulous studies proved the diversity of manorial customs in England.

Elizabeth D. Schafer

Texts

The Cartulary and Terrier of Bilsington Priory. London: Oxford University Press, 1928.

Customary Rents. Oxford: Clarendon Press, 1910.

Economic Conditions on the Manors of Ramsey Abbey. Philadelphia: Press of Sherman, 1899.

A Terrier of Fleet (Lincolnshire). London: Oxford University Press, 1920.

References

Goggin, Jacqueline. "Challenging Sexual Discrimination in the Historical Profession: Women Historians and the American Historical Association, 1890–1940." *American Historical Review* 97 (1992): 769–802.

Grigg, David B. *The Dynamics of Agricultural Change: The Historical Experience.* London: Hutchinson, 1982.

Nennius (fl. 769)

Welsh antiquary and alleged author of *Historia Brittonum.* Nennius is the name appended by an eleventh-century prologue to an older anonymous Latin chronicle, the *Historia Brittonum* [History of the Britons], and as such has no historical value in answering the question of authorship. In this prologue, Nennius claims merely to "have made a heap of all that I have found." Nothing else is known about Nennius. A good deal more is known about the *Historia Brittonum,* a Latin chronicle of Welsh history, which was both very popular and suffered frequent revisions by medieval scribes. Written in Wales in 829/30, the *Historia* is a compilation of written and oral sources bearing on the Britons from their arrival in Britain to the last settlements of the Anglo-Saxons in the seventh century. It includes excerpts from a number of now lost sources; of particular note are a Kentish chronicle and a northern history covering obscure areas of Anglo-Saxon history. Its contents, however, vary considerably in historical value, ranging from Anglian genealogies to a list of the battles of the legendary Arthur (here no king but a war leader). It is unlike its contemporary chronicles in that its author attempted to arrange selections from many sources in a chronological order but did not construct a narrative to explain them. Despite its faults, the *Historia* remains one of the most important sources for British history for the period of the Anglo-Saxon settlements.

Bruce R. O'Brien

Texts

British History and the Welsh Annals. Ed. and trans. John Morris. London: Phillimore, 1980.

Chronica minora saec. IV. V. VI. VII [Minor Chronicles of the Fourth, Fifth, Sixth, and Seventh Centuries]. Vol 3. Ed. T. Mommsen. In *Monumenta Germaniae historica, Auctores antiquissimi,* vol. 13. Berlin: Weidmanns, 1898, 111–222.

The Historia Brittonum. Ed. David N. Dumville. 10 vols. Cambridge: D.S. Brewer, 1985– .

References

Dumville, David N. "The Historical Value of the *Historia Brittonum*." *Arthurian Literature* 6 (1986): 1–26.

———. "'Nennius' and the *Historia Brittonum*." *Studia celtica* 10–11 (1975–1976): 78–95.

Nepali Historiography

Traditional forms of history produced in the territory now comprising the kingdom of Nepal. Aside from brief references to their predecessors in the inscriptions of the Licchavi dynasty in the fifth to eighth centuries A.D., the earliest histories are the *vaṃśāvalīs* (literally "genealogies"), chronicles of events of religious or political significance, produced during the Malla period (A.D. 1200–1768). This is a genre also found in other parts of South Asia but particularly common in Nepal. The Malla *vaṃśāvalīs* were histories of "Nepal" in its original sense of the Kathmandu valley and its periphery, not the much larger modern kingdom established in the eighteenth century. The most important is the late-fourteenth-century *Gopālarājavaṃśāvalī*, beginning with the legendary Gopala kings and ending with the reign of Jayasthiti Malla under whom the history was completed. There are separate, overlapping narratives in Sanskrit and in Newari (the Tibeto-Burman vernacular of the valley), the Newari section being more detailed and precisely dated. When checked against the Licchavi inscriptions, the *Gopālarājavaṃśāvalī* generally gives authentic names but often out of order. In contrast, for recent events such as the Muslim incursion of 1349 the chronicler gives an eyewitness account. In the later Malla period (sixteenth–eighteenth centuries) the *vaṃśāvalī* form was continued but supplemented by *thyāsaphūs* ("folding books"), which are generally contemporary journals of court events.

After the Gorkha capture of Kathmandu in 1768, *vaṃśāvalīs* were normally written in Nepali, the language of the new rulers. Incorporating material from earlier chronicles but now generally with a clearly Buddhist or Hindu orientation, these still focused mainly on the Kathmandu valley. The examples published by Wright and Hasrat date from the early nineteenth century but *vaṃśāvalī* production continued until after 1900. Some of the later ones include an account by a companion of prime minister Jang Bahadur Rana's 1850 visit to Europe. The earlier Nepali-language chronicles are important sources for the Gorkha conquest but the treatment of the nineteenth century is valuable as an indicator of contemporary perceptions rather than a precise record of events.

There are also king-lists and chronicles for some of the pre-1768 hill states. Those concerning Gorkha itself are collectively known as the *Gorkhāvaṃśāvalī*. The most extensive version, the *Gorkhārājavaṃśāvalī*, now among the Hodgson Papers in the India Office Library, was prepared in 1837–1842. The Nepali text is available in Pant and a summary translation in Hasrat. These *vaṃśāvalīs* give few exact dates and the tradition may have been distorted to prove prominent families' long-standing association with the Shah dynasty.

In this century, Nepali historians have abandoned the *vaṃśāvalī* form in favor of systematic research on Western lines. Principal contributions are discussed by Adhikari and brief notices of English-language publications given in Whelpton (1990). Fuller attention has been given recently to the historical traditions (generally oral) of groups other than the dominant high-caste Nepali and Newari speakers, for example in a reconstruction of Gurung (Tamu) history by two Gurung scholars

John Whelpton

Texts

The Gopālarājavaṃśāvalī. Eds. Dhanavajra Vajracarya and Kamal Prakash Malla. Wiesbaden: Franz Steiner, 1985.

History of Nepal. Ed. Daniel Wright. New Delhi: Cosmo, 1986. (Reprint of 1877 edition.)

The History of Nepal As Told by Its Own and Contemporary Chroniclers. Ed. Bikram Jit Hasrat. Hoshiarpur: V.V. Research Institute, 1970.

Jang Bahadur in Europe. Ed. John Whelpton. Kathmandu: Sahayogi, 1983.

Pant, Dinesh Raj. *Gorkhāko Itihās* [History of Gorkha]. Vol. 4. Kathmandu: the author, 1994.

References

Adhikari, Krishna Kant. *A Brief Survey of Nepali Historiography*. Kathmandu: "Buku," 1980.

Tamu, Bhovar Palje, and Yarjung Kromchhe Tamu. "A Brief History of the Tamu Tribe." In *The Gurungs*, Bernard Pignède. English ed. Kathmandu, Ratna Pustak Bhandar, 1993.

Whelpton, John. *Nepal*. Oxford: Clio Press, 1990. World Bibliographical Series, no. 38.

Neshri, Mehemmed [Neṣri, Mehmed] (d. ca. 1520)

Ottoman Turkish historian and author of a six-part universal history titled the *Cihan-numa* or *Cosmorama* of which only the sixth and final part survives. The bulk of the work as it has been preserved is devoted to an account of the origins of the Ottoman dynasty and its history up to about A.D. 1485 (After Hegira [Islamic calendar] 890). Although Neshri recounts some of the events of Mehmed II's (r. 1451–1481) and the early part of Beyazid II's (r. 1481–1512) reigns from personal knowledge and observation, the chief value of his history lies in its preservation of earlier material from named as well as anonymous sources. His work, probably completed during the late 1480s or early 1490s, is in fact a skillful compilation drawing from a variety of sources. In addition to making use of folkloric and oral traditions dating from the first part of the fifteenth century and earlier, Neshri relied heavily on the work of his own contemporary, the historian Aşikpaşazade. The latter he used chiefly as a source of both fact and format but also sometimes as a foil. Biographical details concerning Neshri are remarkably sparse and neither his birthdate nor his date of death is known with any certainty. However as the "propagator" (lit., Neshri) of the early traditions of the Ottoman dynasty his work has unparalleled importance.

Rhoads Murphey

Texts

Gihannuma: Die altosmanische Chronik des Mevlana Mehmemmed Neschri. Ed. Th. Menzel and Fr. Taeschner. 2 vols. Leipzig: O. Harrassowitz, 1951–1955.

References

Menage, V.L. *Neshri's History of the Ottomans: The Sources and Development of the Text.* London and New York: Oxford University Press, 1964.

Nestor (ca. 1055–ca. 1115)

Medieval Russian hagiographer and chronicler. A monk at the Monastery of the Caves in Kiev, Nestor is considered the undisputed author of two major saints' lives: "Narrative of the Life, Death and Miracles of the Holy and Blessed Martyrs Boris and Gleb," and "The Life of the Venerable Theodosius." Throughout the nineteenth century, Nestor was also widely believed to have been the sole author of the *Russian Primary Chronicle,* the basic historical record of the Kievan state from its origins in the ninth century to the late eleventh century. Because of its traditional attribution, the *Primary Chronicle* has often been referred to in the historical literature as the "Chronicle of Nestor." Serious factual and stylistic inconsistencies between the chronicle and Nestor's two saints' lives, however,

have led many scholars to question his role. Perhaps the most important contribution to this debate was made around the turn of the century by the eminent Russian philologist, A.A. Shakhmatov. Through a painstaking comparison of surviving manuscripts, Shakhmatov showed that the *Primary Chronicle* was not a unified work of a single author, but rather a series of redactions produced throughout the eleventh and early twelfth centuries. Nestor, Shakhmatov suggested, was responsible for the redaction of 1111 in which earlier versions were compiled and supplemented to form the first comprehensive account of Kievan Rus'. Not all subsequent scholars, however, have been convinced by Shakhmatov's reconstruction. Given the extreme scarcity of sources, all attempts to establish the authorship of the *Primary Chronicle* are inevitably based on a fair amount of speculation. The true role of Nestor in the creation of the Russian chronicles will almost certainly remain obscure.

Nathaniel Knight

Texts

The Russian Primary Chronicle: Laurentian Text. Ed. and trans. Samuel Hazzard Cross and Olgerd P. Sherbowitz-Wetzor. Cambridge, MA: Medieval Academy of America, 1953.

Zenkovsky, Serge A. *Medieval Russia's Epics, Chronicles and Tales.* New York, E.P. Dutton, 1963.

References

Kuz'min, A.G. *Nachal'nye etapy drevnego russkogo letopisaniia* [The Beginning Stages of Ancient Russian Chronicle Writing]. Moscow: Izdatel'stvo moskovskogo universiteta, 1977.

Priselkov, M.D. *Nestor letopisets* [Nestor the Chronicler]. St. Petersburg [Leningrad]: Izdatel'stvo Brokgaus-Efron, 1923.

Shakhmatov, A.A. *Razyskaniia o drevneishikh russkikh letopisnykh svodakh* [Studies on Ancient Russian Chronicle Redactions]. St. Petersburg: n.p., 1908.

Vernadsky, George. *Kievan Russia.* New Haven, CT: Yale University Press, 1948.

Neugebauer, Otto (1899–1990)

Historian of ancient mathematics and astronomy. Neugebauer was born at Innsbruck, Austria, and raised at Graz. He served in an artillery unit on the Italian front in World War I, then studied at Graz University, Munich, and finally Göttingen, where he took a Ph.D. in the study of ancient Egyptian fractions. He was immediately hired into the university's mathematics department. After the establishment of the Nazi regime, Neugebauer left Germany in 1934, moving his family to Copenhagen, and after that to the United States (1939), where he took a post at Brown University in Providence, Rhode Island. There he remained and spent the rest of his professional life studying the history, origins, and the transmission of ancient mathematics and astronomy—Babylonian, Egyptian, and Greek. All of his work displays the highest standards of accuracy, rigor, and freedom from cant. The narrowest of specialists in one sense, in another he defined a broad subject indeed: the identification of a cultural area which, starting in Mesopotamia in the first millennium B.C., spread through the Mediterranean, then to Europe, and thence to the modern West, even traveling eastward into India. Modern calendars and clocks, with their sexagesimal numeration, attest to this filiation, the establishment of whose lines formed the lifework of Neugebauer, one of the greatest historians of science of the twentieth century.

Stuart O. Pierson

Texts

Astronomy and History. New York: Springer Verlag, 1983.
The Exact Sciences in Antiquity. Providence, RI: Brown University Press, 1957.
A History of Ancient Mathematical Astronomy. 3 vols. New York: Springer Verlag, 1975.

References

Pingree, David. "Éloge." *Isis* 82 (1991): 87–88.

Nevins, (Joseph) Allan (1890–1971)

American historian, journalist, and teacher. Nevins was born in Camp Point, Illinois. A graduate (1912) of the University of Illinois, he taught English there before beginning a fifteen-year career as a journalist on the staff of *The Nation* (1913–1928) and the *New York Evening Post* (1913–1924). In 1928, Nevins returned to teaching, accepting positions at Cornell and at Columbia University. He served with the Office of War Information during World War II. In 1948, he established Columbia's Oral History Project, which has subsequently served as a model for such programs. Nevins was a prolific and versatile historian who authored more than fifty full-length books and hundreds of articles. He was known for his exhaustive research and the literary grace of his narrative. Nevins's many biographies included *Grover Cleveland* (1932) and *Hamilton Fish* (1936), both of which won Pulitzer

prizes. The eight volumes published under the series title *The Ordeal of the Union* represent his most notable contribution to the field of history. He was once described by the historian C. Vann Woodward as "a one-man history book industry, a phenomenon of American productivity without parallel in the field." Nevins had an important influence on American historiography. A business history revisionist, he challenged the "robber baron" thesis and emphasized the positive attributes of the industrial leaders who created modern America. His Civil War volumes, in which he argued that the conflict was both inevitable and necessary, constituted a remarkable work of historical synthesis. In his *Gateway to History,* Nevins produced one of the finest introductions to the field of historiography.

Kevin J. O'Keefe

Texts

The Gateway to History. New York: Heath, 1938.
Grover Cleveland: A Study in Courage. New York: Dodd, Mead, 1932.
James Truslow Adams: Historian of the American Dream. Urbana: University of Illinois Press, 1968.
John D. Rockefeller: The Heroic Age of American Enterprise. New York: Scribner's, 1940.
The Ordeal of the Union. New York: Scribner's, 1947–1971.

New Historicism

Historically based form of literary criticism. New Historicism emerged in Renaissance studies of the late 1970s and was finally named by Stephen Greenblatt in a special issue of *Genre* in 1982. Its practitioners have been influenced by historical theorists such as Louis Althusser and Michel Foucault, but also by anthropologists such as Clifford Geertz, Marshall Sahlins, and Victor Turner. This combination of influences has led the New Historicists to break down the traditional boundaries of literary criticism and import the techniques and concerns of history, art, politics, economics, and anthropology and ultimately to set themselves up as self-conscious "cultural historians" concerned, primarily, with literary texts. In practice, this means that the New Historicists are (as the most articulate of the movement's theoreticians, Louis Montrose, has phrased it hyperaware of the historicity of texts and the textuality of history. They believe that literary and nonliterary texts circulate inseparably in a culture and that the expressive acts of any culture are intertwined with its material practices. Even privileged, putatively transcendent modes of discourse, say poetry, are complicit in the monetary and nonmonetary economies of exchange at work in that culture. At the same time, New Historicists are very resistant to overarching, hypothetical constructions and reluctant to acknowledge that any large-scale generalizations about a culture can be made. Here New Historicism intersects with the radical instability promulgated by postmodernist philosophy: no discourse is admitted as expressive of unchanging, universal truths; no literature represents an inalterable human nature; and no expressive act is free from the network of material practices that permeate its culture. New Historicist writing is often modeled upon the "thick description" of such anthropologists as Clifford Geertz: that is, a narrative in which the observer, whose subjectivity may be foregrounded by participation in the event being described, analyzes a specific cultural occurrence as an indicator of wider social meaning. The specific occurrence becomes a symbol, or perhaps metonym, for the culture as a whole. The New Historicists often use the radical juxtaposition of a well-known literary text and an obscure nonliterary text or historical event as the starting point for such a description. New Historicist writings, then, tend to favor surprising coincidences of history and text that draw the reader's attention to the messy interplay of social and cultural events. New Historicism has been roundly attacked by defenders of linear chronology and progressive history; it has been dismissed by many traditional literary theorists for its interdisciplinary drive and inconclusiveness; and it has upset political thinkers of both the Left and the Right. At its best, it is an accessible articulation of the new theoretical awareness of how history and culture define each other.

Paul Budra

Texts

Greenblatt, Stephen. *Shakespearean Negotiations.* Oxford: Clarendon Press, 1988.

Montrose, Louis. "Renaissance Literary Studies and the Subject of History." *English Literary Renaissance* 16, 1 (1986): 5–12.

References

Bradshaw, Graham. *Misrepresentations: Shakespeare and the Materialists.* Ithaca, NY: Cornell University Press, 1993.

Thomas, Brook. *The New Historicism: And Other Old-Fashioned Topics.* Princeton: Princeton University Press, 1991.

Veeser, H. Aram, ed. *The New Historicism.* New York: Routledge, 1989.

New History

In North American historiography, the term "New History" refers to a methodological revolt against the then dominant historical orthodoxy of "scientific history" during the first quarter of the twentieth century. The phrase appeared as early as an 1898 essay in the *American Historical Review,* and in 1900, Edward Eggleston urged the investigation of the "real history of men and women" in a presidential address to the American Historical Association entitled "The New History." It was, however, James Harvey Robinson who infused the term with broader meaning in his collection of essays, *The New History* (1912), and who generated support for his views among colleagues and students at Columbia University, most notably Charles Beard and Harry Elmer Barnes.

The New Historians sought to extend history beyond wars, politics, and governmental institutions and to embrace the total experience of humankind (though, in practice, they tended to emphasize intellectual, social, and economic history). The New Historians also looked to the social sciences, especially anthropology and social psychology, for insight into the causes of events; and despite their own considerable literary abilities, they scorned narrative history—especially about the premodern era—claiming that it lacked practical value.

Like the historians of the Enlightenment, the New Historians were historians "biased against the past." In the preface to their exceptionally successful textbook, *An Introduction to the History of Europe* (1907–1908), Robinson and Beard declared that they had "consistently subordinated the past to the present." Likewise, Robinson wrote in *The New History* of his desire for a history that would "turn on the past and exploit it in the interest of advance." New Historians hoped that history would become a genteel tool with which to advance a Progressive agenda while hastening the disappearance of traditional "superstitions." (Robinson's course on the intellectual history of Europe was known by his students as "The Downfall of Christianity.")

As has often been noted, the New History was hardly as original as its supporters argued. Voltaire, Macaulay, and J.R. Green, among others, had long since established the respectability of nonpolitical history; Frederick Jackson Turner had anticipated many of Robinson's themes by twenty years. Furthermore, although the New Historians were impressed by contemporary social science, they found it difficult to extract "lessons of history" from its hypotheses. Finally, the New Historians were unable to acknowledge, much less resolve, the tension inherent in a history that was supposed to be both factually objective and politically useful. During the 1930s the "New History" merged imperceptibly into Progressive history, the substantive side of the same "revolt against formalism."

John Austin Matzko

See also PROGRESSIVE HISTORY.

References

Breisach, Ernst. *Historiography: Ancient, Medieval, and Modern.* Chicago: University of Chicago Press, 1983.

Higham, John. *History: The Development of Historical Studies in the United States.* Baltimore, MD: Johns Hopkins University Press, 1989.

Novick, Peter. *That Noble Dream: The "Objectivity Question" and the American Historical Profession.* New York: Cambridge University Press, 1988.

New Testament, Views of History in
See CHRISTIANITY.

New Zealand Historiography

Historical writing about New Zealand, colonial period to present. New Zealand history was not an area of sustained academic study until the 1950s. Prior to this a considerable body of historical work had appeared, but it was largely produced outside academic walls. Descriptions of the country, its indigenous people and their culture, briefly penned on first European contact in 1642, were more extensively recorded by those on the late-eighteenth-century exploratory voyages of James Cook. Later visitors and newcomers—explorers, sealers, whalers, missionaries, travelers, and traders—also left descriptions. From 1840, when the country became a British colony, writers appeared from the ranks of colonial officials, the military, and settlers, and by 1900 this group included politicians, journalists, ethnographers, and natural scientists.

Apart from a handful of general studies, the work of these amateur historians falls broadly into two categories. The first and by far the largest portion—diaries and memoirs—comprises accounts of personal experiences, drawn from participants in the country's nineteenth-century events or from observers of its life. The second category encompasses those who wished to record the history, traditions, and culture of the Maori people

before this indigenous race became extinct, a fate widely believed to be both imminent and inevitable. Their study was assisted by the founding of the Polynesian Society in 1892 and facilitated by a small group of Maori who participated in collecting and recording traditional knowledge, usually in the Maori language.

Both categories maintained their following well into the twentieth century. Work in Maori history was furthered largely through those associated with museums and libraries, while the early diarists and memoirists developed into a still flourishing tradition of local, regional, institutional, and organizational histories. Most have been uneven in quality, but a good number by the 1980s were the product of capable practitioners.

Certain themes and interpretations have been evident in studies of New Zealand. Nineteenth-century work based its view implicitly, and often explicitly, on assumptions that colonization had brought civilization and progress and that the Wakefield "systematic" model, the basis for settlement in six regions, was to be praised for bringing in "superior stock" and creating the country's Englishness. Accounts rested within an imperial context of a colonial relationship between New Zealand and England. Where culture contact or conflict featured, the focus was on Western superiority and on Maori response.

When the colony was fifty years old, a new view of its history emerged as the 1890s Liberal government embarked on what was then seen as pioneering legislation. Incorporating some of the earlier perceptions, the politician-historian William Pember Reeves and foreign travelers presented New Zealand as a democratic, adventuresome society, to be celebrated as a social laboratory. Journalist-historians soon took up this theme and developed the notion that the country was a harmonious biracial society. Both interpretations persisted as a few academic historians began to study New Zealand history in the 1930s and 1940s, some stressing the significance of the British heritage, others—and in time more—giving greater weight to the role of local factors in shaping a national identity. Nevertheless it was within an imperial context that the country's history was portrayed in a celebratory burst of publication to mark its centenary in 1940. Some of the work, state-sponsored, evolved into official war history; in the 1980s it transformed itself again to enter the public history arena.

By the late 1950s a new generation of New Zealand–born academic historians was increasingly drawing New Zealand history out of its imperial context, questioning the long-standing interpretations and focusing on a New Zealand–centered experience. This became evident in two general academic histories—the first by Keith Sinclair (1959), the second by W.H. Oliver (1960)—and in case studies that critically reevaluated Wakefieldian settlement, Victorian humanitarianism, Maori–settler relations, and party politics.

From the 1960s the influence of Sinclair and Oliver (and to a lesser extent other academic historians and those in related areas) was seen in the work of their students. Against the background of the British empire's dissolution, one stream tended to reassess New Zealand's nineteenth-century experience: Maori contact with the Western world, missionary endeavor, government administration of Maori affairs, Maori social, religious, and political movements, and the 1860s wars—variously reevaluated as the Anglo-Maori wars, the land wars, and the New Zealand wars. Long presented as more or less a passive actor in events, Maori society was now studied more on its own terms. Another stream developed a strong social history orientation, initially focusing on the Liberal experience but branching into new fields. The results were incorporated by contributors into a new general history of the country, released in 1981 under Oliver's editorship.

Both streams evolved further, the one influenced by anthropology and current events in New Zealand, the other by sociology and general historiographical trends. Thus works in the 1980s moved into the history of medicine, labor and trade unions, sport, culture, the family, ethnic studies, defense and war studies, women's history and gender studies, and race relations. Historians' interests, long embedded in nineteenth century matters, have turned more to the twentieth century. University expansion into New Zealand history courses has produced a large body of serious scholars who, working within and outside academic walls in the 1980s and 1990s, continue to produce a flood of studies.

Although growth in social history has been remarkable, three other broad categories are notable: political history, historical biography, and Maori history. The first—a long-standing productive sector—was stimulated by the country's rapid political and economic changes from the 1970s. Interest in parties and politics generated monographs and prompted, within a decade, a revision of the 1981 general history.

Meanwhile historical biography received an enormous boost by the state-sponsored publication of a multivolume biographical dictionary, the first volume released to mark the country's 150th anniversary. Building on a tradition of historical biography, the dictionary is a continuing project that consciously explores underclasses and "outgroups" and encourages new evaluations of its subjects, including several hundred Maori.

Finally, reevaluation of the past, specifically the crown's dealings with the Maori since the Treaty of Waitangi in 1840, is at the core of the Waitangi Tribunal's work. Established by a 1975 statute, the tribunal has created a public consciousness that has stimulated a burst of writing on race relations and Maori history. Long-standing assumptions about the benign character of crown intervention, treaty-making, and administration have been overturned, although the place of the 1840 treaty between the Maori and the British crown, and implications for future action, are issues of continuing debate and interpretation. However, New Zealand history has not attracted a substantial body of Maori writers, although current interest and research into tribal and subtribal history is likely to herald change.

New Zealand historiography is young compared with that of older "new societies." Specialized monographs, collected essays, and journal articles still tend to be the main vehicles of expression. Historians have only begun to move away from chronicling specifics toward a broader conceptualizing and analysis. Miles Fairburn's venture into a reevaluation of the country's nineteenth-century society (seen as atomized and rootless rather than community-centered and progressive) has therefore stimulated a new debate.

Claudia Orange

See also AUSTRALIAN HISTORIOGRAPHY; PACIFIC ISLANDS HISTORIOGRAPHY.

References

Belich, J. *The New Zealand Wars and the Victorian Interpretation of Racial Conflict.* Auckland: Auckland University Press, 1986.

Binney, J., et al. *The People and the Land/Te tangata me te whenua: An Illustrated History of New Zealand 1820–1920.* Wellington: Allen & Unwin/Port Nicholson Press, 1990.

Brookes, B., et al., eds. *Women in History 2: Essays on Women in New Zealand.* Wellington: Bridget Williams Books, 1992.

Bryder, L. (ed.). *A Healthy Country: Essays on the Social History of Medicine in New Zealand.* Wellington: Bridget Williams Books, 1991.

Fairburn, M. *The Ideal Society and Its Enemies: The Foundations of Modern New Zealand Society 1850–1900.* Auckland: Auckland University Press, 1989.

McKinnon, M. *Independence and Foreign Policy: New Zealand Since 1935*. Auckland: Auckland University Press, 1993.

Orange, C. *The Treaty of Waitangi*. Wellington: Allen & Unwin/Port Nicholson Press, 1987.

Ward, A. *A Show of Justice: Racial "Amalgamation" in Nineteenth Century New Zealand*. Auckland: Auckland University Press; London: Oxford University Press, 1973.

Nicephorus [Nikephoros] Gregoras (1293/4–1359/60)

Byzantine scholar and historian. Nicephoras was born in Heracleia Pontice, the nephew of the city's bishop. He studied in Constantinople, was involved in the civil conflicts of the mid-fourteenth century, and was arrested in 1351, dying in disgrace in Constantinople. He ran a school at the Chora monastery, writing philosophical, hagiographical, theoretical, and astronomical as well as historical works, of which the most important is the *Rhomaike Historia* [Roman, i.e. Byzantine, History], in thirty-seven books, covering the period from 1204 to 1359, written in strict chronological order and emphasizing theological conflicts.

Stephen A. Stertz

Texts

Nicephori Gregorae Byzantina Historia [Byzantine History]. Ed. L. Schopen and I. Bekker. 3 vols. Bonn: Weber, 1829–1855.

References

Guilland, R. *Essai sur Nicephore Grégoras* [Essay on Nicephoras Gregoras]. Paris: P. Geuthner, 1926.

Moutsopoulos, E. "La notion de 'kairicité' historique chez Nicéphore Gregoras [The Notion of the Historical "Right Time" in Nicephorus Gregoras]." *Byzantina* 4 (1972): 205–213.

Niebuhr, Barthold Georg (1776–1831)

German historian. The son of Carsten Niebuhr, who had traveled widely in the Levant in the service of the king of Denmark, Niebuhr was born in Copenhagen, studied at Kiel, and in 1788-89 visited Great Britain. Returning home he rose to manage the Danish State Bank, and in 1806 he moved to Berlin to advise the government on Prussian finances, but resigned four years later and began to lecture at the University of Berlin.

Between 1816 and 1823 he served as Prussian ambassador to the Vatican and thereafter lectured at Bonn, where he died "of a chill." Niebuhr, the "Prussian Tacitus," made his name as a historian with the two-volume *Römische Geschichte* [History of Rome] (1811–1812), a landmark of historiography in general and of the study of regal and republican Rome in particular. Niebuhr contentiously postulated the oral transmission of early Roman history through poems. He also published an edition of Fronto (1816), jointly founded the periodical *Rheinisches Museum* (1827) and started the *Corpus Scriptorum Historiae Byzantinae* [Collection of Byzantine Histories], for which he produced the volume on Agathias (1829).

Richard Fowler

Texts

The History of Rome. Trans. Julius Charles Hare and Connop Thirlwall. New ed. 3 vols. London: Taylor, Walton and Maberly, 1851.

Lectures on Ancient History, from the Earliest Times to the Taking of Alexandria by Octavianus. Ed. M. Niebuhr; trans. Leonhard Schmitz. 3 vols. London: Taylor, Walton and Maberly, 1852.

References

Walther, G. *Niebuhrs Forschung* [Niebuhr's Research]. Stuttgart: Steiner Verlag, 1993.

———, ed. *Barthold Georg Niebuhr: Historiker und Staatsmann* [Barthold Georg Niebuhr: Historian and Statesman]. Bonn: Röhrscheid Verlag, 1984.

Witte, B.C. *Der preussische Tacitus* [The Prussian Tacitus]. Düsseldorf: Droste Verlag, 1979.

Nietzsche, Friedrich Wilhelm (1844–1900)

German philosopher. Trained as a classical philologist, Nietzsche was in effect a historian of Greek and Roman literature. His first book, *The Birth of Tragedy out of the Spirit of Music* (1871), attempted to explain the origins of the tragic sense. It was written under the influence of the philosophy of Arthur Schopenhauer and the music and personality of Richard Wagner; it also revealed Nietzsche's own remarkably speculative mind. The book veered so far from what was expected of a conscientious philologist that it appeared dishonest to many scholars. The negative scholarly reaction impelled Nietzsche into a career as a philosophical writer that entailed a critique of history as a discipline.

In the second of Nietzsche's *Untimely Meditations,* "On the Use and Disadvantage of History of Life" (1874), Nietzsche revenged himself upon the historical conscience of the nineteenth century. "There is a degree of insomnia, of rumination, of historical sense," he wrote, "which injures every living thing and finally destroys it." He argued that the century of great historians and historical philosophers suffered from a surfeit of history, destructive to life and creativity. This fundamental insight led Nietzsche to his caustic critique of the idea of progress, of science, and of the future of Western civilization. Long before World War I, Nietzsche rejected the optimistic notion that there was an intrinsic meaning to history, along with all of his century's attempts to divine that meaning, Hegelian, Marxist, and otherwise. For Nietzsche, the only meaning in history is the meaning imposed upon it by acts of will, in order to draw power from it.

Later writings such as *Beyond Good and Evil* (1886) and *On the Genealogy of Morals* (1887) display a novel method of understanding the history of human values by analyzing them in terms of their motives and consequences for life. It was a method so alien to the historical practice of his day that it was scarcely noticed and has only recently been recognized as the basis for an alternative historical practice. Since the publication of Michel Foucault's *The Order of Things* in 1966, however, Nietzsche's writings have been acknowledged to contain a powerful impetus to historical studies. Few historians of thought and ideas remain uninfluenced by Nietzsche in their methods.

Carl Pletsch

Texts

Beyond Good and Evil. Trans. Walter Kaufmann. New York: Random House, 1966.
The Birth of Tragedy. Trans. Walter Kaufmann. New York: Random House, 1967.
On the Advantage and Disadvantage of History for Life. Trans. Peter Preuss. Indianapolis, IN: Hackett, 1980.
On the Genealogy of Morals. Trans. R.J. Hollingdale. New York: Random House, 1967.

References:

Foucault, Michel. *The Order of Things.* New York: Random House, 1970.
Pletsch, Carl. *Young Nietzsche, Becoming a Genius.* New York: The Free Press, 1991.

Niida Noboru (1904–1966)

Japanese historian of China. Born in Sendai, Niida read law at the Tokyo Imperial University and joined its Institute of Oriental Culture, spending his entire career there. A pioneer in Chinese legal history, Niida left his mark on the study of wide-ranging areas of premodern Chinese law and society. His publications also include a number of edited texts of Chinese law codes and legal documents.

John Lee

Texts

Chūgoku hōseishi kenkyū [Studies in Chinese Legal History]. 4 vols. Tokyo: Tōkyō Daigaku Shuppan Kai, 1959–1964.
Tōrei shūi [Collected Fragments of the Tang Administrative Code]. Tokyo: Toho Bunka Gakuin Tokyo Kenkyujo, 1933.

Niketas Choniates (ca. 1155–ca. 1217)

Byzantine historian, official, and theologian. Niketas Choniates was born at Chonai in Phrygia, held provincial government posts, and was promoted to higher offices in Constantinople in the late twelfth century, culminating in the office of *logothetes ton sekreton* (official in charge of secret records). After the Latin capture of Constantinople in 1204, he fled to the court in exile at Nicaea, holding no major post and dying there in about 1217. His *Chronike diegesis* [Chronicle of Events] or *History,* written after 1206, is the leading source for events of the preceding eighty-eight years. He also wrote theological treatises.

Stephen A. Stertz

Texts

O City of Byzantium: Annals of Niketas Choniates. Trans. H.J. Magoulias. Detroit, MI: Wayne State University Press, 1984.

References

Kazhdan, A. "Der Körper im Geschichtswerk des Niketas Choniates. [The Human Body in the Historical Work of Niketes Choniates]." In *Fest und Alltag in Byzanz* [Festival and Daily Life in Byzantium], ed. G. Prinzing and D. Simon. Munich: C.H. Beck, 1990, 91–105.

Nipperdey, Thomas (1927–1992)

German historian. Nipperdey was born in Cologne and studied philosophy, history, and German philology at Göttingen, Cologne, and Cambridge, where he obtained a doctorate in philosophy in 1953. He became a "Privatdozent" and then a professor of history at Göttingen (1961–1963), Karlsruhe (1963–1967), Berlin (1967–1971), and Munich (1971–1992). Nipperdey's reputation as one of modern Germany's foremost historians of the nineteenth and early twentieth centuries rests on four major books and numerous articles on historical methodology. In his work on the German party system before 1918 (1961) he attempted to supplant the traditional ideological interpretation of the political parties of the German empire. He concentrated instead on the analysis of the institutional and sociopolitical framework in which the major parties were able to act and explained the structural conditions that prevented the development of a strong party system. His three voluminous texts on German history from 1800 to 1918 (published in 1983, 1990, and 1992) employ a pluralistic, multimethodological approach, which incorporates anthropological insights, and pay attention to historical structures. Like the French Annales historians, Nipperdey attempted an *histoire totale*. He wished to offer a more cautious and less ideological alternative to Hans Ulrich Wehler's dominant interpretation of the aims of "Historische Sozialwissenschaft." To some extent, he deemphasizes the traditional concentration on political and narrative history and consciously interprets historical processes from a present-day perspective. Nipperdey pursued an angle that did not concentrate on certainties but attempted to encompass all important perspectives because he wished to reveal the openness (that is, the noninevitability) of the historical process at any given point. He also tried to avoid passing judgments on historical events. In this respect Nipperdey can be regarded as a "neohistoricist"—a believer (with important qualifications) in Leopold von Ranke's dictum of the possibility of historical objectivity.

Klaus Larres

Texts

Deutsche Geschichte 1866–1918 [German History 1866–1918]. 2 vols. Munich: C.H. Beck, 1991–1993.

Germany: From Napoleon to Bismarck 1800–1866. 2 vols. Dublin: Gill and Macmillan, 1990.

Gesellschaft, Kultur, Theorie: Gesammelte Aufsätze zur Neueren Geschichte [Society, Culture, Theory: Collected Essays on Modern History]. Göttingen: Vandenhoeck and Ruprecht, 1976.

Die Organisation der politischen Parteien vor 1918 [The Organization of German Political Parties before 1918]. Düsseldorf: Droste, 1961.

Theorie und Erzählung in der Geschichte [Theory and Narrative in History]. Munich: Deutscher Taschenbuch Verlag, 1979.

References

Möller, H. "Bewahrung und Modernität. Zum historiographischen Werk von Thomas Nipperdey [Preservation and Modernity: The Historiographical Works of Thomas Nipperdey]." *Vierteljahrshefte für Zeitgeschichte* [Quarterly for Contemporary History] 40 (1992): 669–682.

Mommsen, W.J. "Die vielen Gesichter der Clio. Zum Tode Thomas Nipperdeys [The Many Faces of History at the Death of Thomas Nipperdey]." *Geschichte und Gesellschaft* [History and Society] 19 (1993): 408–423.

Nithard (ca. 800–ca. 845)

Frankish historian of Carolingian politics. The illegitimate son of Charlemagne's daughter, Bertha, and the court poet Angilbert, Nithard actively participated in the court and campaigns of Charles the Bald (d. 877). After 843, he became the lay abbot of Saint-Riquier near Amiens. He died fighting the Normans. One of the few early medieval lay historians, Nithard was commissioned by Charles the Bald in 841 to write the *Historiarum libri quattuor* [The Four Books of the Histories]. His relatively unsophisticated account, which favored his patron, chronicled the struggles between the sons of Louis the Pious from 817 to 843. In contrast, Nithard cast the reign of Lothar (d. 855) very negatively. His report of the oaths taken by Charles the Bald and Louis the German at Strasbourg in 842 represents the earliest written record of Old French. Only one ninth- or tenth-century copy from St. Médard, Soissons, survives, thus suggesting the obscurity of the text during the Middle Ages.

Bonnie Effros

Texts

Scholz, Bernhard Walter. *Carolingian Chronicles: Royal Frankish Annals and Nithard's Histories.* Ann Arbor: University of Michigan Press, 1970.

References

Nelson, Janet. "Public *Histories* and Private History in the Work of Nithard." *Speculum* 60 (1985): 251–293.

Sprigade, Klaus. "Zur Beurteilung Nithards als Historiker [On the Evaluation of Nithard as a Historian." *Heidelberger Jahrbücher* 16 (1972): 94–105.

Niẓām al-Dīn, Aḥmad ibn Muḥammad Mukīm al-Harawī (1549–1594)

Chief army commander and historian at the court of Akbar the Great. Niẓām al-Dīn came from a Persian family with a long record of service to the Mughal dynasty, and he joined Akbar's court at a young age. He served in various capacities and earned frequent promotions until he achieved the rank of Bakhshī of the empire, chief military commander. He finished his major work, the *Tabaḳāt-i-Akbarshāhī* [Regions of Akbar], in 1592–1593. This book is a study of the history of nine geographic regions that constituted the domain of Akbar. It is a straight political history arranged in the form of annals from the time the region had gained independence until it was conquered by Akbar. It ended with a description of the realm. Niẓām al-Dīn recounted events dispassionately offering very little analysis or judgment on individuals involved, and the result was a history devoid of controversy.

Mahmood Ibrahim

Texts

The Tabaqat-i-Akbari. Trans. B. De [*sic*]. 3 vols. Calcutta: The Asiatic Society, 1973.

References

Mukhia, Harbans. *Historians and Historiography during the Reign of Akbar*. New Delhi: Vikas Publishing House, 1976.

Nizami, Khaliq Ahmad. *On History and Historians of Medieval India*. New Delhi: Munshiram Manoharlal Publishers, 1983.

Rizvi, Sayyid Athar Abbas. *Religious and Intellectual History of the Muslims in Akbar's Reign*. New Delhi: Munshiram Manoharlal Publishers, 1975.

Norgate, Kate (1853–1935)

English historian. Norgate was born in London, the only child of Frederick Norgate, a bookseller, and his wife Fanny Athow, daughter of an established Norwich family. She was a pioneer among women historians of the later nineteenth century, venturing into the thitherto male-dominated field of medieval political history. Her first major work, *England under the Angevin Kings* was published in two volumes in 1887 and dedicated to the memory of her mentor, the English historian, John Richard Green. Green had encouraged and advised her in the development of a narrative strategy based upon research drawn from medieval chronicles and printed sources. Her work was heralded in the pages of the *English Historical Review* by Edward Augustus Freeman for "her firm grasp of facts and authorities." Norgate's work on the Angevin kings continued with the publication of *John Lackland* (1902) and *The Minority of Henry the Third* (1912). Her articles on "The Bull Laudabiliter" (1893) and "The Battle of Hastings" (1894) appeared in early volumes of *The English Historical Review*. Her expertise in medieval political history was recognized by her contemporaries; she contributed forty-four entries to the *Dictionary of National Biography*, edited by Leslie Stephen. She was elected an honorary fellow of Somerville College, Oxford, in 1929.

Ellen Jacobs

Texts

England under the Angevin Kings. London: Macmillan, 1887.

John Lackland. New York: AMS Press, 1970.

The Minority of Henry the Third. London: Macmillan, 1912.

Richard the Lion Heart. London: Macmillan, 1924.

References

Letters of John Richard Green. Ed. Leslie Stephen. New York: Macmillan, 1901.

Obituary. *The Times* [London], May 6, 1935.

Noro Eitarō (1900–1934)

Japanese economic historian. Noro was born in Hokkaidō and studied at Keiō Gijuku University in Tokyo, where he first became involved in radical politics. After graduation he worked for a labor research institute and began to publish widely on political and historical issues. In 1930 he joined the then illegal Japanese Communist Party and quickly became one of its leading activists and theoreticians. His *Nihon Shihonshugi Hattatsushi* [History of the Development of Japanese Capitalism] (1930), together with the jointly authored *Nihon Shihonshugi Hattatsushi Kōza* [Lectures on the Historical Development of Japanese Capitalism] (1932–1933), laid the foundations for the important branch of Japanese Marxist thought that became known as the *Kōza* school. Noro, like other *Kōza* school theorists believed that because Japanese capitalism had developed as the world entered the age of imperialism, and because of the feverish pace of Japanese industrialization, feudal and absolutist elements had been preserved and incorporated into Japanese capitalism. Noro based his approach particularly on an analysis of landholding and tenancy systems in preindustrial and industrial Japan, and his work provoked intense debates over the history of landlord–tenant relations in Japanese farming. In November 1934 Noro was arrested for his political activities, and three months later he died as a result of police torture at the age of 34.

Tessa Morris-Suzuki

Texts

Nihon Shihonshugi Hattatsushi. 2 vols. Tokyo: Iwanami Shoten, 1983.

Noro Eitarō Zenshū. 11 vols. Tokyo: Shin Nihon Shuppansha 1965.

References

Morris-Suzuki, Tessa. *A History of Japanese Economic Thought.* London and New York: Routledge, 1989.

Nosaka Sanzō et. al. *Noro Eitarō to Minshu Kakumei.* Tokyo, 1947.

Notestein, Wallace (1878–1969)

American historian of seventeenth-century England. A native of Wooster, Ohio, Notestein was educated at the College of Wooster and Yale University. He taught at the University of Kansas, the University of Minnesota, and Cornell University before becoming Sterling professor of English history at Yale University in 1928. At the end of World War I, he served in Paris as a member of the American Commission to Negotiate the Peace. Notestein's eminence as a research scholar derived principally from editing nine volumes of invaluable source materials on debates in the seventeenth-century English House of Commons. In 1924, he published *The Winning of the Initiative by the House of Commons* (1924), an extended essay that opened a new era in scholarship concerned with Parliament before the English Civil War. Notestein spent much of his long career researching records in the House of Commons, the British Museum, and parishes all over England. At the time of his death in 1969, he was completing work on a manuscript dealing with the development of the Common's independence during the early years of Stuart rule. In 1971, this work was published posthumously as *The House of Commons, 1604–1610.*

Kevin J. O'Keefe

Texts

The English People on the Eve of Colonization. New Haven, CT: Yale University Press, 1954.

The House of Commons, 1604–1610. New Haven, CT: Yale University Press, 1971.

The Scot in History. New Haven, CT: Yale University Press, 1946.

References

Richardson, R.C. *The Debate on the English Revolution Revisited.* London: Routledge, 1988.

Numismatics

The study of coins, medals, tokens, and paper money and their use as historical sources. Coins provide ruler lists for poorly documented societies, such as the Indo-Greek empire of Bactria; coins have also identified numerous anonymous antique portrait sculptures. Coins are essential for archaeologists. This is for two reasons: coins often bear dates or datable information (a portrait of a ruler, a renewal of tribunician power) and coins are mass production objects: every piece of sculpture is different, but a Trajan denarius is a Trajan denarius, and is simple to recognize and classify.

Numismatists use three basic techniques to study coins: style, die studies, and hoards. The doctrine of style was devised by the pioneer art historian Johann Joachim Winckelmann (1717–1768). Dating by style can lead to error, because numismatic design tends to be more conservative than art in general, although style is useful for mint attribution. The second technique is die studies. Most coins are struck from dies. Obverse and reverse dies wear at different rates; a mint will begin striking coins using obverse die 1 and reverse die A; then reverse die A will break, and the mint will begin using reverse die B; then obverse die 1 will break, and the mint will use obverse die 2; and so forth. It is thus possible to look for die links: coins sharing one die in common. One can assume that coins that are die-linked were struck at the same place and time. Pioneers of the use of die-linkage include Crosby's study on the cents of 1793 (1869, 1897); Imhoof-Blumer's study of the coins of Acarnania (1878); and Newell's reattribution of the mints of the Alexander coinage (1911). The third technique is the study of hoards. Before banks were common, people buried their money in the ground. Occasionally they never came back to recover it, and the hoards remained to be found by the plough or the metal detector. A hoard gives a snapshot of the coins in circulation in a particular area at a certain time. They are important for dating coins, particularly in the Greek period: if a coin is thought to be from the fourth century, yet it keeps on turning up in late-third-century hoards, we may have to redate by a century or so. The most extensive coin cabinet and the best numismatic library in the United

States are at the American Numismatic Society in New York City. The Society in New York also publishes a periodical bibliography, *Numismatic Literature,* which appears every six months.

John M. Kleeberg

Texts

Babelon, Ernest. *Traité des Monnaies Grecques et Romaines* [Treatise of Greek and Roman Coins]. Paris: Librairie Ernest Leroux, 1901–1932.

Breen, Walter. *Walter Breen's Complete Encyclopedia of U.S. and Colonial Coins.* New York: F.C.I. Press, 1988.

Crosby, Sylvester S. *The Early Coins of America.* Boston: Estes & Lauriat, 1878.

———. *The United States Coinage of 1793—Cents and Half Cents.* Boston: the author, 1897.

Imhoof-Blumer, Friedrich. *Die Münzen Akarnaniens* [The Coins of Acarnania]. Vienna: Manz'sche k.k. Hof-Verlags- und Universitäts-Buchhandlung, 1878.

Mommsen, Theodor. *Geschichte des Römischen Münzwesens* [The History of Roman Coinage]. Berlin: Weidmannsche Buchhandlung, 1860.

Mossman, Philip L. *Money of the American Colonies and Confederation: A Numismatic, Economic, and Historical Correlation.* New York: The American Numismatic Society, 1993.

Newell, Edward Theodore. "Reattribution of Certain Tetradrachms of Alexander the Great." *American Journal of Numismatics* 45 (1911): 1 ff.

Regling, Kurt. *Terina.* Berlin: Georg Reimer, 1906.

Svoronos, Joannes N., and Pick, Behrendt. *Les Monnaies d'Athènes* [The Coins of Athens]. Munich: F. Bruckmann, 1923–1926.

Thompson, Margaret, Mørkholm, Otto, and Kraay, Colin M. *An Inventory of Greek Coin Hoards.* New York: The American Numismatic Society, 1973.

References

Casey, P.J. *Understanding Ancient Coins.* Norman: University of Oklahoma Press, 1986.

Clain-Stefanelli, Elvira E. *Numismatic Bibliography.* Munich: Battenberg Verlag, 1984.

Grierson, Philip. *Numismatics.* Oxford: Oxford University Press, 1975.

Porteous, John. *Coins in History.* New York: G.P. Putnam's Sons, 1969.

N

O

Ō No Yasumaro (d. 723)

The chief compiler of the *Kojiki*. In 711 Ō No Yasumaro received an imperial order to write down two important oral histories. The resultant transcription formed the basis of the *Kojiki*, Japan's oldest extant chronicle. It records events from the mythological age of the gods until the reign of the Empress Suiko (A.D. 593–628). Unlike the *Nihon shoki*, the *Kojiki* was not an official history and was not written in classical Chinese but in a hybrid style that combined both Chinese and Japanese elements. The *Kojiki* was relatively neglected in the medieval period but in the Edo era renewed interest was shown in it by scholars of the "native learning" movement such as Kamo no Mabuchi and Motoori Norinaga. They regarded it as a more reliable source of information on indigenous traditions than the *Nihon shoki*. Since that time it has played an important role not only as a source of information about ancient Japan but also as a stimulus for the development of a sense of Japanese national identity.

Graham Squires

Texts

Kojiki. Ed. and trans. Donald L. Phillipi. Princeton, NJ, and Tokyo: Princeton University Press and the University of Tokyo Press, 1969.

References

Brownlee, John S. *Political Thought in Japanese Historical Writing: From Kojiki (712) to Tokushi Yoron (1712)*. Waterloo, Ont.: Wilfrid Laurier University Press, 1991.

Oakeshott, Michael Joseph (1901–1990)

English philosopher and political theorist. A political historian and idealist philosopher, Oakeshott counseled moderation over perfection. In histori-

ography, Oakeshott is best known for his book *Experience and Its Modes*, which has been an influential text in the philosophy of history. Its argument may be summarized as follows. We experience the world in many modes—historical, scientific, practical, and others. History is not a "practical" (or "Whiggish" or "moralistic" or "teleological") enterprise, nor does it seek scientific laws. The historical mode views the past as a fixed unity and lets the past speak for itself. History ought to be done for its own sake, in order to discover and describe this fixed unity in all its diverse particulars; its pieces should fall into place naturally without invoking scientific or teleological or religious explanations. By giving a complete, relational description of change, history renders human choice and behavior intelligible.

Charles Tandy

Texts

Experience and Its Modes. Cambridge, Eng.: Cambridge University Press, 1933.
On History and Other Essays. Oxford: Blackwell, 1983.

References

Franco, Paul. *The Political Philosophy of Michael Oakeshott*. New Haven, CT: Yale University Press, 1990.
Grant, Robert. *Oakeshott*. London: Claridge Press, 1990.
Norman, Jesse, ed. *The Achievement of Michael Oakeshott*. London: Duckworth, 1993.

Oberman, Heiko Augustinus (b. 1930)

Modern historian of late medieval and Reformation Europe. Born in Utrecht, Oberman studied at Utrecht and Oxford. In 1958, he began his teaching career as an instructor at Harvard University, where he became professor of church history in 1963. Oberman was called to a professorial chair at Tübingen in 1966. In 1984, he returned to the United States, taking up a professorship at the University of Arizona in Tucson. Oberman's first book, a study of the late medieval theologian Thomas Bradwardine (1957), established his reputation as a church historian; the stream of articles and books that followed made clear his broader historical orientation, a synthetic approach to the real-life origins and effects of the most crucial directions in Western thought that has been called the "social history of ideas." His *Harvest of Medieval Theology* (1963) and his *Werden und Wertung der Reformation* (1977; translated as *Masters of the Reformation* (1981) bracket twenty years of research into the continuity of late medieval and Reformation theology. The interim saw the publication of some thirteen books either written or edited by Oberman. His work demonstrates the impossibility of separating the later Middle Ages from the early modern period by such artificial boundaries as 1517 (Luther's posting of the 95 Theses) or 1492 (Columbus). His *Wurzeln des Antisemitismus* (1981, translated in 1984 as *The Roots of Antisemitism*) established him as a Christian scholar concerned with the perception and treatment of Jews in European society. Perhaps his best-known work, *Luther: Mensch zwischen Gott und Teufel* (1982, translated in 1989 as *Luther: Man between God and the Devil*), corrected the traditional Protestant portrayal of Luther as the "first modern man" by demonstrating that Luther remained, all through his life, a medieval man embedded in medieval experiences, ways of thinking, perceptions, and methods of reacting to the world and to God. Oberman's central contribution to history, to date, has been the programmatic demonstration of the unbreakable links between the later Middle Ages and the early modern period in theology, church, psychology, culture, and the everyday life of the mind.

Andrew Colin Gow

Texts

Archbishop Thomas Bradwardine, a Fourteenth Century Theologian: A Study of His Theology in Its Historical Context. Utrecht: Kemink and Zoon, 1957.
The Dawn of the Reformation: Essays in Late Medieval and Early Reformation Thought. Edinburgh: T. and T. Clark, 1986.
Forerunners of the Reformation: The Shape of Late

Medieval Thought. Trans. Paul L. Nylus. London: Lutterworth Press, 1967.
The Impact of the Reformation. Grand Rapids, MI: William B. Eerdmans, 1994.
Luther: Man between God and the Devil. New Haven, CT: Yale University Press, 1989.
Masters of the Reformation: The Emergence of a New Intellectual Climate in Europe. Trans. Dennis Martin. Cambridge, Eng.: Cambridge University Press, 1981.
The Roots of Anti-Semitism in the Age of Renaissance and Reformation. Trans. James I. Porter. Philadelphia: Fortress Press, 1984.

Ockley, Simon (1678–1720)

English orientalist and clergyman. Ockley was born in Exeter in 1678. In 1693, he entered Queen's College, Cambridge, and, on account of his flair for oriental languages, was appointed lecturer in Hebrew when he was only seventeen. He took holy orders and became curate at Swavesey in Cambridgeshire; in 1705 he was appointed vicar.

Ockley visited Oxford regularly, in order to examine Arabic manuscripts. He published several works, among the most important being *Introductio ad Lingus Orientalis* [Introduction to Oriental Language] (1706), an appeal for the study of oriental literature; *The Improvement of Human Reason, Exhibited in the Life of Hai eben Yokdhan* (1708), from the Arabic of Ibn Tufayl; and *The History of the Saracens,* of which volume 1, entitled *The Conquest of Syria, Persia and Egypt,* appeared in 1708. Volume 2 of the *History* appeared in 1718 and volume 3 in 1757. There were many reprints, and it was published in Leipzig in 1745 and France in 1748. Admitted a bachelor of divinity in Cambridge in 1710, a year later Ockley was appointed to the chair in Arabic. His later works include *Account of the Authority of the Arabic Mss in the Bodleian Library* (1712); *Account of South-west Barbary* (1713), an account by a Christian slave who had escaped in 1698; and *The Sentences of Ali* (1717), by the son-in-law of the Prophet. In 1717, Ockley was imprisoned in Cambridge Castle for debt. He died three years later and was buried in Swavesey.

Ockley's reputation rests upon *The History of the Saracens.* It was the first attempt to write a continuous account of the early Arab conquests in English, and would be used by Edward Gibbon. Based upon unpublished manuscripts, the first volume relates the lives of the Prophet's immediate successors and the second, the period from the Caliphate of Ali to the death of Abd al-Malik (A.D. 705). The third volume concerns the 'Abbāsid

Caliphate and is prefaced by a life of Muḥammad. Ockley's originality is shown by the sources he quotes, including a translation of "pseudo al-Waqidi's" *Futūḥ al-Shām* [Conquest of Syria], a work now regarded as unreliable; he used Archbishop William Laud's copy, dated 1458. Other works cited are the Koran, the historians Abu'l-Fida, Ibn al-Athīr, al-Ṭabarī, and al-Suyuti, and, for Persian sources, D'Herbelot's *Bibliothèque Orientale*. Ockley, like many, stigmatized the Prophet, yet he lauded the Arabs for their fine culture, language, and literature.

H. T. Norris

Texts

The History of Hayy Ibn Yaqzan. Ed. A.S. Fulton; trans. Ibn Yaqzan. London: Chapman and Hall, 1929.

The History of the Saracens. Second ed. 2 vols. London: R. Knaplock, 1708–1718.

The History of the Saracens. Third ed. London: A. Murray, 1870.

The Improvement of Human Reason, Exhibited in the Life of Hai eben Yokdhan. Trans. Ibn Tufayl. London: E. Powell, 1708.

Introductio ad Linguas Orientalis. Cambridge, Eng.: J. Owen, 1706.

References

Hamilton, Alistair. *Europe and the Arab World.* Dublin, Ireland: The Arcadian Group and Oxford University Press, 1994, 36–38.

Holt, P.M. *Studies in the History of the Near East.* London: F. Cass, 1973, 54–57; 62–63.

Wakefield, Colin. "Arabic Manuscripts in the Bodleian Library, the Seventeenth Century Collections." In *The "Arabick Interest" of the Natural Philosophers in Seventeenth-Century England,* ed. C.A. Russell. Leiden: E.J. Brill, 1994, 128–146.

O'Gorman, Edmundo (1906–1995)

Mexican historian. O'Gorman was born in Mexico City and received his law degree in 1928, thereafter practicing law for ten years. In 1948 he earned a master's degree in philosophy and was awarded a Ph.D. in history in 1951. Through much of this period (1938–1952) he was the historian for the Archivo General de la Nacion (National Archives), in which position he conducted primary research for several of his later works. He was also a professor and director of the seminar on historiography of the Facultad de Filosofia y Letras (Faculty of Philosophy and Letters).

The ideas of the Spanish philosopher José Ortega y Gasset influenced O'Gorman's perspective on history. Himself a neo-Orteguian historicist, O'Gorman's major intellectual preoccupation—developed in a series of books—is how Western civilization incorporated America through the idea of the discovery of America. It was necessary, in his view, for fifteenth- and sixteenth-century Europe to incorporate America not only politically and economically, but also philosophically. O'Gorman, who bases his speculations in such matters on solid documentary evidence, has written extensively on the history of ideas in Mexico and has also edited and translated several historical works.

Carlos Pérez

Texts

Fundamentos de la historia de América [Foundations of the History of America]. Mexico City: Imprenta Universitaria, 1942.

La idea del descubrimiento de América [The Idea of the Discovery of America]. Mexico City: Centro de Estudios Filosóficos, 1951.

The Invention of America. Bloomington: Indiana University Press, 1961.

"America." In *Major Trends in Mexican Philosophy.* Notre Dame, IN: University of Notre Dame Press, 1966.

References

La obra de Edmundo O'Gorman: Discursos y conferencias de homenaje en su 70 aniversario, 1976 [The Work of Edmundo O'Gorman: The 1976 Conference in Honor of His Seventieth Birthday]. Mexico City: Universidad Nacional Autonoma de Mexico, 1978.

Ortega y Medina, Juan A., ed. *Conciencia y autenticidad historicas: escritos en homenaje a Edmundo O'Gorman, emerito, aetatis anno LX dicata* [Consciousness and Historical Authenticity: Essays in Honor of Edmundo O'Gorman on his Sixtieth Birthday]. Mexico City: UNAM, 1968.

Torales Pacheco, Ma. Cristina. "Edmundo O'Gorman (1906–1995): Maestro y amigo [Edmundo O'Gorman (1906–1995): Teacher and Friend]." *Historia y Grafia* 5 (1995): 261–266.

Ogot, Bethwell Allan (b. 1929)

Kenyan historian. Ogot was born in Gem, in western Kenya. After receiving his undergraduate education at Makerere University College, he went to Britain to study first at St. Andrew's and then at the School of Oriental and African Studies (SOAS), University of London, where he earned his doctorate (1965). He has been professor and chair of history, dean of arts, and deputy vice-chancellor of Nairobi University. He chaired the UNESCO International Scientific Committee for the Drafting of a General History of Africa (1978–1983) and remains a commanding presence in African historiography. In the rehabilitation of the African world that Eurocentrism had labored to extirpate, Ogot has been a leading East African, and especially Kenyan, voice. "We demonstrated," he recalled in a 1979 essay ("Three Decades of Historical Studies in East Africa, 1949–1977") "that Mombassa, Kilwa, Lamu, Malindi, were not Arab cities—they were Swahili towns, and therefore African cities." The absence of written primary sources was once a major argument for the Eurocentric proposition of an ahistorical precolonial Africa. One forte of early Africanist historiography was thus the reinstatement of oral sources in historical methodology. Ogot has made an outstanding contribution in this regard, especially in the *History of the Southern Luo* (1967), his major work. Based largely on his collections of the people's traditions, the book examines the migrations, settlement, and evolution of the southern Luo, comprising the Padhola of eastern Uganda and the Luo of Kenya and Tanzania from the sixteenth century to the advent of European rule.

Ebere Nwaubani

Texts

Historical Dictionary of Kenya. Metuchen, NJ, and London: Scarecrow Press, 1981.

History of the Southern Luo: Migration and Settlement. Nairobi: East African Publishing House, 1967.

Kenya before 1900. Nairobi: East African Publishing House, 1976.

And F.B. Welbourne. *A Place to Feel at Home: A Study of Two Independent Churches in Western Kenya.* London and Nairobi: Oxford University Press, 1966.

Ed. *UNESCO General History of Africa. Volume 5, Africa from the Sixteenth to the Eighteenth Century.* Berkeley: University of California Press, 1992.

Ed. *War and Society in Africa.* London: Frank Cass, 1972.

Ed., with J.A. Kieran. *Zamani: A Survey of East African History.* Nairobi: East African Publishing House, 1968.

References

Africa Who's Who. London: Africa Books, 1991.
Wilson, E., ed. *Who's Who in East Africa 1967–68.* Nairobi: Marco Publishers, 1968, 128.

Oldmixon, John (1673–1742)

English historian and miscellaneous writer. Financially ruined by his father's premature death, Oldmixon cast his lot with the shady element in the London publishing world. The hack writer par excellence, he tried his hand at compiling, indexing, poetry, journalism, and history. Oldmixon's earliest significant historical work was *The British Empire in America* (1708), which made an economic case for empire. His spirited survey of English historiography, *The Critical History of England* (1724–1726), paved the way for his gargantuan *History of England* (1729–39), a patchwork of documents and partisan interpretation extolling Whig revolution principles and decrying Stuart kingship. During his career, Oldmixon gained notoriety for attacking the authenticity of the earl of Clarendon's royalist history of the English civil war and for writing various "secret histories" and scandalous biographies. Pilloried by the likes of Alexander Pope for a multitude of literary transgressions, Oldmixon was discredited in the polite society of his own day. Literary and historical scholars interested in British popular culture and empire may find, however, that Oldmixon warrants further study as one of the earliest historians of imperial Britain, whose audiences and genres ranged from commoner to nobleman, from Grub Street exposé to history in the grand manner.

Philip Hicks

Texts

The British Empire in America, Containing the History of the Discovery, Settlement, Progress and State of the British Colonies. Second ed. 2 vols. New York: A.M. Kelley, 1969.

References

Hicks, Philip. *Neoclassical History and English Culture: From Clarendon to Hume.* Basingstoke: Macmillan, 1996.

Rogers, Pat. *Grub Street: Studies in a Subculture.* London: Methuen, 1972.

Oliveira Lima, Manuel de (1867–1928)

Brazilian diplomat and amateur historian. Oliveira Lima was educated in Portugal and lived most of his life outside of Brazil. He chose voluntary exile in Washington, D.C., partly because of his pronounced monarchist sympathies, when he retired from the Brazilian diplomatic service in 1914. Until his death he taught international law at the Catholic University in Washington, to which he left his considerable library of more than forty thousand pieces. Oliveira's most influential work was a revisionist biography of João VI, who was responsible for moving the Portuguese court to Rio de Janeiro during the Napoleonic era—an act that heralded the end of Brazil's colonial status. Oliveira regarded Dom João as a critical figure in the creation of an independent Brazil. Based on original sources, Oliveira's work is considered a Brazilian masterpiece in three fields: history, biography, and literature. According to the historian Gilberto Freyre, it became a model for subsequent biographies on Brazilian monarchs. Oliveira believed that the historian should possess the gifts of both the scholar and the artist to insure that his "literary work proved suggestive and fruitful."

George L. Vásquez

Texts

Dom João VI no Brasil, 1808–1821 [Dom João VI in Brasil, 1808–1821]. 2 vols. Rio de Janeiro: Typ. do Jornal do Comercio, 1908.

References

Freyre, Gilberto. *Oliveira Lima, Don Quixote Gordo.* Recife, Brazil: Universidade Federal de Pernambuco, 1970.

Oliver, Roland Anthony (b. 1923)

British historian of Africa. Oliver was born in Kashmir and educated at Cambridge. At the School of Oriental and African Studies from 1948 until 1986, as founder of the *Journal of African History* in 1960, and as general editor of the eight-volume *Cambridge History of Africa* (1975–1986)—the latter two in collaboration with J.D. Fage—he guided the struggle to disprove the popular myth that Africa had no history. At the same time, he shaped the foundations of professional African historiography, combining archaeological, oral, and linguistic data to trace the development of technology, trade, and states. Oliver synthesized the fruits of this interdisciplinary approach in collaborative treatments of Africa's *Iron Age* (1975) and *Middle Ages* (1981), as well as in pioneering textbooks such as *A Short History of Africa* (1962), and in his deeply knowledgeable reflections on *The African Experience* (1991).

P.S. Zachernuk

Texts

The African Experience. London: Weidenfeld and Nicolson, 1991.

The Missionary Factor in East Africa. London: Longman and Green, 1952.

And B.M. Fagan. *Africa in the Iron Age.* Cambridge, Eng.: Cambridge University Press, 1975.

And A. Atmore. *The African Middle Ages.* Cambridge, Eng.: Cambridge University Press, 1981.

And J.D. Fage. *A Short History of Africa.* Sixth ed. Harmondsworth: Penguin, 1988.

References

Falola, Toyin, ed. *African Historiography: Essays in Honor of J.A. Ajayi.* Harlow: Longman, 1993.

Oral History

The activity of interviewing people of varying social backgrounds in order to record their memories as a historical source, or, alternatively, a type of historical writing based on such a source. Oral history is distinguished from "oral tradition," which is defined as information or stories about the past, handed down over several generations in oral form. Although the distinction has been challenged by some scholars, this article will deal primarily with the former.

Although oral history has achieved academic respectability only in the post–World War II period, and especially so since the rise of social history in the 1960s, the exploitation of oral sources as a means of getting at what happened in the relatively recent past is as old as historical writing itself. Herodotus (ca. 484–420 B.C.) relied on eyewitness accounts of events that he wrote down in his *Histories,* and other ancient historians similarly conversed with officials and travelers as a supplement to official documents and other sources. In the Middle Ages, meticulous and thorough monastic chroniclers such as Bede (672/73–735) and Orderic Vitalis (1075–1143) used similar oral techniques.

That none of these historians viewed oral and written sources as qualitatively different, nor as mutually exclusive, must have been in part a function of their having lived in societies in which writing was restricted to an elite minority and in which the absence of print limited the circulation of written documents. Yet even as late as the mid-nineteenth century, more than three centuries after the printing press had reoriented European mentalities in the direction of the written or printed word, historians continued to use oral

O

sources without much inhibition. Perhaps the best-known example of this is Jules Michelet (1798–1874), the distinguished French historian whose love of old documents was famous, yet who on many occasions laid down his papers to stroll among his countrymen and record their memories of the days of the Revolution and Napoleon. These interviews had a direct impact on his *History of the French Revolution*, and also on his essay on *The People*, a work that may be regarded as a direct ancestor of the kind of social history that today uses oral sources intensively.

It was ironically two of Michelet's countrymen, C.-V. Langlois (1863–1929) and Charles Seignobos (1854–1942), who together popularized the notion, implicit in German-influenced source criticism of the later nineteenth century, that all history must be based on the written record. Their widely read *Introduction to the Study of History* (first published in French in 1897 and translated into English in 1904) has since become a kind of byword for the worst naiveties of late-nineteenth-century historical positivism. In it, the authors decreed with confidence that "The historian works with documents; . . . no documents, no history." Within the context of late-nineteenth-century historiography, which was overwhelmingly political and legal in character, their strictures made some sense, as a kind of reaction against reliance on the faulty memories of officials, and as a way of pointing out the difficulty of reconstructing the more remote past—for instance, the medieval era in which Langlois specialized—without a written record. Langlois and Seignobos's book, although scarcely original, combined with the hegemony of Germanic *Quellenkritik* and British empiricism to marginalize oral sources for half a century, at least within the mainstream of the profession. A measure of the dominance of document-oriented historiography and of the explicit repudiation of oral sources can be found a few decades later, when the American historian James Westfall Thompson (1869–1941)—not coincidentally, a medievalist like C.-V. Langlois—wrote a posthumously published two-volume *History of Historical Writing* (1942), in which he apologized for the oral interviewing activities of Michelet as a kind of peculiar fetish to be overlooked in an otherwise reliable, document-driven scholar. In the United States, Homer C. Hockett claimed in his *The Critical Method in Historical Research and Writing* (1938; third ed. 1955), a kind of American Langlois and Seignobos, that history was strictly limited to "the written record of past or current events."

In spite of all this skepticism and even outright rejection, oral sources continued to be collected and studied, primarily in the context of investigating folklore and tracing dialects, or of recording "life stories," especially in a local setting. But it was not until the 1960s that oral history achieved academic status and professional respectability, while at the same time its practitioners began to work out a systematic set of practices and conventions. The reorientation of the historical discipline away from political, legal, and diplomatic history and toward social history, in particular "history from the bottom up," that occurred in the 1960s and early 1970s made the extended use of oral sources all but inevitable in the Industrialized Western nations, at the same time that Africanists were beginning to work out protocols for analyzing oral traditions within non- or semiliterate civilizations. Social history, precisely because it focuses on the previously neglected lives of ordinary people, eventually came to champion the value of oral sources, especially as a supplement to the kind of quantitative and aggregative kinds of demographic and economic history that for a time held the field, and which tended to present highly technical, numerical analyses of past life without much understanding of how those lives were experienced in reality—discussing the forests of bygone times with little sense of its individual trees. As Paul Thompson, Britain's leading exponent and practitioner of oral history has remarked in his indispensable survey of the subject, "Oral history is a history built around people. It thrusts life into history itself and it widens its scope."

The growth in the popularity of oral history since the 1960s has been assisted by technological developments, in particular advances in tape recording. Although it has always been possible to record oral testimony simply by transcribing it on the spot, as did Herodotus, it was and remains preferable to be able to have an accurate record of the testimony of a "subject" *as spoken*. The advent of small and inexpensive cassette recorders in the 1960s made the task of the interviewer that much easier. Instead of having to rely on his or her own memory of what was said (and thereby dangerously overlaying one set of past perceptions, those of the interviewee, with another, those of the interviewer), or alternatively spending much of the interview engaged in a manic shorthand scribbling, the interviewer armed with a recorder could concentrate on asking questions and listening carefully to the answers, relying on the tape to provide a full record of everything said, including gaps, hesitations, and nuances, a record that could then be transcribed into paper form at a later time.

The greatest successes of oral history have come in Scandinavia, Britain, and the United States, and only a few examples can be given here. In Finland and later in Sweden, archives for the systematic collection of oral historical sources were established in the mid-nineteenth century, albeit mainly in pursuit of dialect studies; it was the government-sponsored Swedish Institute for Folklore and Dialect Research that was first to make use of recording machines, as far back as the 1930s. In Britain, folklore and dialect pursuits, often with a nationalist tinge, similarly drove the use of oral sources in Ireland, Scotland, and Wales. In England, the nationalist aspect has been less prevalent, and although the study of dialect has not been ignored, it has long since ceased to be the primary, much less the only, reason for the use of oral history.

Two semipopular but widely respected collectors of oral evidence, George Ewart Evans and Ronald Blythe, exemplify different approaches to their material. Evans, in the pioneering rural study *Ask the Fellows Who Cut the Hay* (1956), in his later *Where Beards Wag All* (1970), and in many other works, tended to write directly from his record of what was spoken, leaving the language and the style of speech of his subjects in rough and unedited format—and thereby catching the flavor as well as the content of their memories, complete with dialects and odd turns of phrase. Blythe, in a celebrated investigation of Akenfield, a Suffolk village, employed a rather different approach, emphasizing individual life-stories rather than presenting, as had Evans, a picture of the entire community; Blythe also appears to have heavily edited his transcripts, removing the "ragged ends," as Thompson puts it, that almost certainly emerged from the original interview. The result is a more readable account of villagers' past lives that sacrifices the nuances and color of speech in the interest of clearly conveying the content of that speech. *Akenfield* probably did more to popularize oral history in Britain than any other single work, influencing a generation of local scholars and school-aged enthusiasts. It has also had its admirers abroad, such as the American oral historian, James Hoopes, who in 1979 declared Blythe's work to be "almost certainly the finest oral history ever published." Others, notably Thompson, have been somewhat less fulsome in its praise, noting a number of defects in the collection and rendition of the testimonies—Thompson plainly favoring Evans's warts-and-all approach—while nevertheless acknowledging the book's importance in promoting the practice of oral history.

A more scholarly approach to oral history developed in the 1970s as a greater number of university-based historians began to use oral sources in their research. Paul Thompson himself, working at the University of Essex and in collaboration with a number of associates, has done the most to promulgate standards for the collection and exploitation of oral evidence. His *Edwardians: The Remaking of British Society* (1975) provided a vivid portrait of British life in the first decade of the twentieth century, based on a wide variety of testimonies. These were drawn according to a "quota sample" system from a geographical and occupational cross-section of the country rather than from a particular locality, thereby permitting him to make broader generalizations than would be possible from the reconstruction of a particular community or from a more haphazard selection of interviewees.

In the United States and Canada, a number of first-rate examples of oral history exist, and the field is widening daily. In a pioneering postwar example, Allan Nevins (1890–1971) of Columbia University employed oral history to record the memoirs of certain important Americans. He later extended his approach and produced, with the help of collaborators, a multivolume investigation of Henry Ford's development of the mass-consumption automobile (1954; 1957–1963), effectively and critically using oral and written sources as supplements to, and correctives of, each other.

Nevins's top-down approach, which preceded the mushrooming of social history in the 1960s, influenced North American oral historiography in the direction of elite subjects for at least two decades, but the field has broadened considerably since then to take account of social history as a whole, and of its various related fields such as African-American history, Labor History, and Women's History. William L. Montell's *Saga of Coe Ridge: A Study in Oral History* (1970) provided an account, based heavily on oral evidence of both the traditional and more strictly "reminiscent" variety, of the development of a black community in southern Kentucky; at the same time, once again in the context of African-American historiography but this time within an urban setting, Paul Bullock provided a detailed analysis of *Watts: The Aftermath; An Inside View of the Ghetto, by the People of Watts* (1969), following the notorious riots; more recently, Sarah Flynn has provided a more general oral history of the civil rights movement beginning in the 1950s. In American labor history, the recording of individual autobiographies has remained an important undertaking, such as Alice and Staughton Lynd's collection, *Rank and File: Personal Histories by Working Class Organizers from America* (1973) and Peter Friedlander's exploration of the Detroit car industry in his *Emergence of a UAW Local, 1936–1939: A Study in Class and Culture* (1975). Studs Terkel's *Hard Times* (1970) and *Working* (1974) used extracts from a large collection of interviews to chronicle respectively the experiences of the unemployed during the Great Depression and of more than a hundred Americans employed in a variety of industries and occupations.

Outside Europe and North America, oral history has been used to good effect in cultures where literacy remains at a premium. In addition to the large numbers of studies of oral tradition in Africa, for instance, many historians of modern Africa take account of the testimonies of modern men and women about the relatively recent past, in order to shed light on such matters as tribalism, problems of development, gender roles, and the process of decolonization. Oral history has also been used to record memories and experiences of some of the century's most horrific or cataclysmic events, such as the Depression (as treated by Terkel or by Barry Broadfoot), the Russian Revolution and the Stalinist era, the Spanish Civil War, the treatment of and hardships encountered by minority groups and immigrant groups, especially in the United States, and, of course, both world wars; a few select examples are listed below under "Texts." Recent unrest in Latin America has provided fertile ground, as in Dianne Walta Hart's study of a Nicaraguan family. The Holocaust has proved a particularly important subject for oral historians, not least because of the great importance of recording the recollections of survivors before the wartime generation disappears: two recent examples are the collection of *Jewish Memories* by Lucette Valensi (1991) and Claude Lanzmann's published version of the various interviews that made up his monumental cinematic record, *Shoah*. Lanzmann's book was derived from a film, and it demonstrates well how oral history can be adapted to the film medium, allowing audiences, as it were, to see as well as hear testimony about the past from the perspective of the interviewer/filmmaker. Finally, in women's history oral sources have proved at least as valuable as in labor history, given the relative silence of documentary evidence about female life- and work-experience until relatively recently; the Black Women Oral History project is notable as an attempt to get at the memories of a group historically marginalized by both gender and race.

In addition to a great number of works that use oral history, and a good quantity of those written about different aspects of the subject or its practice, there are now various journals devoted to the collection, analysis, and dissemination of orally based historical scholarship. The Oral History Association in Britain publishes the periodical *Oral History;* in the United States, the *International Annual of Oral History* (formerly the *International Journal of Oral History*), *the Oral History Review,* and *Oral History Recorder* appear. This is to leave out of account the vast number of local history societies whose periodicals frequently publish oral historical materials.

Oral history has not been without its critics. In a recent (1992) theoretical study of orality and history (a work largely devoted to African traditions), Elizabeth Tonkin has challenged the formal distinction made by Jan Vansina and others between oral tradition and oral history; Tonkin also, however, points out some of the problems and complexities involved in the "social construction of oral history," paying close attention to questions of chronology and subjectivity. Tonkin, a defender of oral history, is undoubtedly correct that there remain a few scholars who continue to regard the phrase itself—"oral history"—as virtually an oxymoron. While most historians would no longer ascribe to the strict doctrine of "no documents, no history," it should be recognized that there are inescapable, if controllable, weaknesses in oral sources, as there are in written or archaeological ones. Problems of memory are among these: the further back one asks a subject to recall, the more likely are memories to be faulty, or to have become overlaid by present-day perceptions and indeed by the experiences of life: the problem with Thompson's Edwardians, it has been observed, is that in the intervening decades they also became Georgians and Elizabethans. Interviewees may not, also, recall the chronology of events accurately, as Nevins discovered in talking to Ford workers, and while the oral interview may be informative as to the perceptions of ordinary people, it is risky if such testimonies are the only source of information on the occurrence of a particular event. The best oral historians have addressed this problem by using documentary sources as a control for the inadequacies of memory.

Similar skepticism has been attached to the use of oral history for more traditional political topics—so-called elite oral history practiced by Nevins and the Columbia project that he established in the late 1940s. Anthony Seldon, one of its current British practitioners and defenders, has pointed out that elite interviewing continues to be regarded by many scholars as "the black sheep among the contemporary historian's sources." Here, the obvious defense of oral *social* history—that oral recollections of the inarticulate masses are the only kind one is likely to get, limitations and all—does not apply, since the political historian by definition has a wide array of official and private documents upon which to draw, and one might at first instance think the need for interviewing live subjects superfluous. A further concern is the almost inevitable tendency of retired politicians and civil servants to reconstruct events so as to place themselves, or their party, in a more favorable light—in the words of A.J.P. Taylor, who was deeply skeptical of the value of oral history, all that elite interviews can produce is "old men drooling about their youth." But advocates of this approach to political history, such Seldon and Joanna Pappworth, have fairly effectively answered these concerns, pointing out that an interview with a retired functionary is in some ways no less reliable than using that person's private or, *a fortiori,* published memoirs, which are subject to precisely the same sorts of distortion; and in at least one sense, the face-to-face interview is a preferable tool, since an interviewed subject, while guarded, is more likely to let slip spontaneous recollections and revealing anecdotal details on the spot than in a polished and self-censored memoir. Interviewers also have the ability, by sitting across the table and watching their subjects as well as listening to them, to pick up signs of hesitation, gesture, and body language that may provide a clue as to an interviewee's genuine, unspoken sense of events. It has also been observed that the very nature of official records, especially those generated by *in camera* meetings such as those of a cabinet (and as opposed to verbatim transcripts of parliamentary or congressional speeches), tend to record the end result of politics—motions passed, decisions taken, and so on—rather than the process of discussion and debate that led to the result. In short, every document has its own history; it is not a settled and definitive building block, as many historians have, and to some extent still do, argue. Oral interviews can fill in a picture that official papers leave only as a scant outline. Some of the best political histories and biographies, concerned with recent times, integrate interviews with participants in or witnesses to events with a thorough command of the documentary evidence: it would be hard to conceive of a mammoth work of political biography such as Martin Gilbert's of Winston Churchill, or the various recent biographies

of Lyndon Johnson, without oral evidence. A documents-only biography of such figures can all too easily be written, but it would scarcely be satisfactory. Anthony Seldon, at the Institute of Contemporary British History that he established with Peter Hennessy, has also pioneered various elite oral archives and "witness seminar" events in which key figures in various major episodes in the past meet together around the table for recorded and guided conversations.

The bibliography of works in and about oral history has multiplied at a furious rate in recent years, not least because of the popular appeal of oral sources. Whereas the study of many documents from the past (despite their open availability to the nonacademic researcher in "public" record offices) often requires a high degree of specialized training, virtually anyone armed with a tape recorder and notepad, from the secondary school student or undergraduate to the retired local citizen, can be his or her own oral historian, although naturally the results of such enterprises vary enormously in terms of ambition and quality. Given both its popularity and the existence of generally accepted standards for collection and transcription, combined, too, with a less naive faith in the truth of the written record than was the case a century ago, interest in oral history shows no sign of abating.

D.R. Woolf

See also AUTOBIOGRAPHY; MEMORY AND HISTORY; ORAL TRADITION; SOCIAL HISTORY; WOMEN'S HISTORY.

Texts
Blythe, Ronald. *Akenfield: Portrait of an English Village.* London: Penguin, 1969.
Dunar, Andrew J. *Building Hoover Dam: An Oral History of the Great Depression.* New York and Toronto: Maxwell Macmillan International, 1993.
Evans, George Ewart. *Ask the Fellows Who Cut the Hay.* London: Faber and Faber, 1956.
———. *The Crooked Scythe: An Anthology of Oral History.* Ed. David Gentleman. London: Faber and Faber, 1993.
———. *Where Beards Wag All: The Relevance of the Oral Tradition.* London: Faber, 1970.
Flynn, Sarah. *Voices of Freedom: An Oral History of the Civil Rights Movement from the 1950s through the 1980s.* New York: Bantam Books, 1990.
Fraser, Ronald. *Blood of Spain: An Oral History of the Spanish Civil War.* New York: Pantheon Books, 1986.

Hart, Dianne Walta. *Thanks to God and the Revolution: The Oral History of a Nicaraguan Family.* Madison: University of Wisconsin Press, 1990.

Lanzmann, Claude. *Shoah: An Oral History of the Holocaust: The Complete Text of the Film.* New York: Pantheon Books, 1985.

Lee, Joann Faung Jean. *Asian American Experiences in the United States: Oral Histories of First to Fourth Generation Americans from China, the Philippines, Japan, India, the Pacific Islands, Vietnam, and Cambodia.* New York: New Press, 1992.

Lourie, Richard. *Russia Speaks: An Oral History from the Revolution to the Present.* New York: HarperCollins, 1991.

Montell, William L. *The Saga of Coe Ridge: A Study in Oral History.* Knoxville: University of Tennessee Press, 1970.

Tamura, Linda. *The Hood River Issei: An Oral History of Japanese Settlers in Oregon's Hood River Valley.* Urbana: University of Illinois Press, 1993.

Thompson, Paul. *The Edwardians: The Remaking of British Society.* Second ed. London: New York: Routledge, 1992.

Valensi, Lucette. *Jewish Memories.* Berkeley: University of California Press, 1991.

References

Bogart, Barbara A., and William L. Montell. *Using Oral Sources in Local Historical Research.* Nashville, TN: American Association for State and Local History, 1981.

Gluck, Sherna B., and Daphne Patai, eds. *Women's Words: The Feminist Practice of Oral History.* New York: Routledge, 1991.

Grele, Ronald J. *Envelopes of Sound: The Art of Oral History.* Second ed. Chicago: Transaction Books, 1985.

Henige, David. *Oral Historiography.* London: Longman, 1982.

Hill, Ruth Edmonds, and Patricia Miller King, eds. *Guide to the Transcripts of the Black Women Oral History Project.* Westport, CT: Meckler, 1990.

Hoopes, James. *Oral History: An Introduction for Students.* Chapel Hill: University of North Carolina Press, 1979.

Lummis, Trevor. *Listening to History: The Authenticity of Oral Evidence.* London: Hutchinson, 1987.

The Oral History Collection of Columbia University. New York: Oral History Research Office, 1979.

Perks, Robert. *Oral History: An Annotated Bibliography.* London: British Library National Sound Archive, 1990.

Ritchie, Donald A. *Doing Oral History.* New York: Twayne, 1995.

Seldon, Anthony, and Joanna Pappworth. *By Word of Mouth: Elite Oral History.* London and New York: Methuen, 1983.

Sitton, Thad. *Oral History: A Guide for Teachers (and Others).* Austin: University of Texas Press, 1983.

Smith, Allen. *Directory of Oral History Collections.* Phoenix, AZ: Oryx Press, 1988.

Thompson, Paul. *The Voice of the Past: Oral History.* Second ed. Oxford and New York: Oxford University Press, 1988.

Tonkin, Elizabeth. *Narrating Our Pasts: The Social Construction of Oral History.* Cambridge: Cambridge University Press, 1992.

Yow, Valerie Raleigh. *Recording Oral History: A Practical Guide for Social Scientists.* Thousand Oaks, CA: Sage, 1994.

Oral Tradition

Information or stories about the past handed down from one generation to its successors in oral form. In oral, as in literate societies, there is a recognized need to preserve the present and recall the past. The body of material that accumulates over time as a result is most often called oral tradition, although other terms, such as oral history or oral testimony, are also used. In general, oral tradition can be defined as representing the sum of that which is recalled—or claimed to be recalled—about the past, but which has been committed to writing only at a later date or, in some cases, not at all.

Although oral tradition represents the sole possible means of intentionally preserving the memory of past events in societies without writing, it also exists in literate societies, paralleling and complementing the written record there, which is never so extensive as to encompass the historical experience of all elements of a society. Several recent studies on the role of orality in ancient and medieval societies—albeit necessarily viewed through the extant written sources—have illustrated the effects of this coexistence. The discussion here will concentrate on oral tradition as the principal form of historical evidence from and about nonliterate societies.

Oral tradition includes many of the kinds of historical materials found in written records, particularly written records of the more remote past, although their distribution is very different:

proverbs; praise songs; explicit and coded accounts of political events, although less often either social or economic information; accounts of group and subgroup origins; etiological explanations of the status quo; unusual astronomical events; droughts and famines; and so forth. Despite their occasionally unpromising appearance, all of these can be of value for the historian. Thus the accidental preservation of archaisms in sayings can provide hints about past linguistic and political affiliations; a reference to an unusual childhood of an early ruler can similarly be a covert reference to a change in political structure.

Oral traditions are seldom synthetic, though, and processes such as the adoption of agriculture, the development of a complex political system, territorial expansion, or population growth are usually attributed to a brief period of time, even a single moment, as with the so-called five "good" emperors of predynastic China. Nor does oral tradition very often preserve extended quantitative data.

Perhaps the most important characteristic of oral tradition for historians is that, unlike written evidence, it undergoes unrecorded changes at points of transmission due to faulty memories, social and political exigencies, even personality or group dynamic factors. Thus particular oral evidence collected from informants can be regarded only as the end-product of many transmissions, each susceptible in an unknown degree to change. This is also true for the transmission that takes place when an investigator collects oral data and reduces them to written form.

Because of these circumstances, distinct methods of acquiring and interpreting oral data have been developed. Although still continuing, the process began at least as early as the fifth century B.C., when Herodotus collected and processed oral information and told his readers how he had gone about it. Since then the exercise has recurred countless thousands of times, sometimes with the same awareness that Herodotus brought, sometimes not. Broadly speaking, two millennia of faith in an unusual capacity for recall in oral societies and in accurate transmission began to give way in the late nineteenth century to a more skeptical attitude, which has persisted fairly firmly ever since, though not without exceptions.

Perhaps the greatest of these exceptions was the credit given to oral evidence collected in the field throughout much of the formerly colonized world from the 1950s to the 1970s. The dawning independence of these vast areas brought with it the belief that their societies, many of which had been oral at the time of the onset of colonial rule, had retained extensive historical memories that had survived the impact of colonialism. These were at last committed to writing to serve as a backdrop and superstructure for the maneuvering that accompanied emerging nationhood.

From this conjuncture of opportunity and incentive came a flood of historical fieldwork that depended largely on collecting and interpreting oral data—data that had been preserved virtually untainted, or so it seemed, even while the societies in question were becoming increasingly literate. During these two decades such oral data were used, often unsupported, to establish chronologies, define origins and population movements, chart and explain state formation and growth, posit kinship relations, and the like—that is, much the kind of information that written histories had recorded and preserved in other societies.

After the decline of initial enthusiasm, it became clear that oral tradition, like written sources, is more complex than expected. For instance, it can encompass varying degrees of historical accuracy over a wide range of genres, sometimes combining several into a single tradition. Thus, in west Africa an enormous corpus of oral tradition has coalesced over time around the figure of Sunjata. The case illustrates several of the principal problems that face historians using such evidence: its achronicity (that is, its lack of reference to written calendars or to chronology), personalization, and anachronism. Although Sunjata was probably a historical figure from the thirteenth century, the traditions in which he now figures incorporate activities that occurred both before and since his time, lack a sense of historical context, and, by focusing on Sunjata, personalize what were actually large-scale and long-term developments.

A salient feature of oral tradition is its propensity to appropriate written materials without attribution, in much the same way as historians of the past ransacked other texts. This process, which is especially patent with regard to the creation and amplification of oral traditions under the stress of colonial rule in Africa, India, and southeast Asia (although also extending back at least to the Spanish conquests in the Americas) presumably has occurred beyond the historical record as well. When such features are identified in traditions, they could in some cases serve to corroborate the written record and thereby validate the traditions themselves. More often, they serve as a reminder of the vitality and resilience of the genre, and the opportunities that frequent transmission provides for absorbing new material and discarding old.

The concept of the "fixed text" was devised to compensate for these vagaries of transmission. By this interpretation many oral texts were regarded as immutable because societies imposed sanctions for deviations from the prescribed wording. However, recent studies on the performative aspects of oral transmission, for example, among griots of west Africa, have showed instead that transmitters of tradition prefer to emphasize the spontaneous and creative aspects of their craft and that their audiences often participate in this activity. Viewing oral tradition as influenced by considerations of performance adds a new, and not always comforting, dimension to its use as historical evidence.

As noted, an important feature that oral tradition does not share with written materials is the extent to which it is transmitted from one person to another and the difficulty in controlling or assessing the nature of these transmissions, which may reach the hundreds. The only transmission that is visible is that taking place between an informant and the individual(s) who eventually put(s) the tradition into written form. Studies of this process suggest that most often this exchange does not meet the prevailing rigorous requirements for the collection and preservation of knowledge about the past. This situation increases the complexity of collecting, preserving, and interpreting oral data since it involves a need to understand the circumstances of at least the final transmission, about which there is usually little concrete evidence.

In fact, direct access to undiluted oral testimony has always presented problems to historians. With few exceptions, even written accounts clearly based directly on oral data have not presented those data in their original form. As a problem this continues, since most of the information collected in the field during the past forty years remains unavailable, and its content and value must be inferred from the interpretations of it that have appeared in print.

For reasons that are not clear, some oral traditions fare much better than expected when compared to available external evidence. For instance, the chronology of traditions from the precolonial states of Senegambia relating to a period as early as the sixteenth century hold up well when tested against the numerous early eyewitness accounts of the region, even though there is no evidence that the traditions are in any way derivative of these accounts as, for instance, are traditions from the Guinea coast. More commonly, when such testing is possible, written sources either contradict oral traditions or speak to matters not recalled by oral tradition. This again illustrates the complexity and mixed character of oral tradition, whether used for cultural or historical purposes.

David Henige

See also AFRICAN HISTORIOGRAPHY; ORAL HISTORY.

References

Henige, David. *Oral Historiography.* London: Longman, 1982.

Tonkin, Elizabeth. *Narrating Our Pasts: The Social Construction of Oral History.* New York: Cambridge University Press, 1992.

Vansina, Jan. *Oral Tradition As History.* Madison: University of Wisconsin Press, 1985.

Orderic Vitalis (1075–1143)

Anglo-Norman historian. Born in Shropshire, England, of an English mother and a French priest, Orderic was sent at the age of ten to become a Benedictine monk in the Norman abbey of Saint-Evroult. An excellent calligrapher, Orderic was first introduced to the study of history by his work in the scriptorium and the teachings of John of Rheims. He would go on to produce the thirteen-volume *Ecclesiastical History,* a chronicle of the church from the nativity of Christ to his own day. The period immediately following the Norman invasion of England witnessed a flowering of monastic historical writing on both sides of the Channel, among which Orderic's work, modeled on Bede and Eusebius, stands apart. It carefully avoids the allegorical or apocalyptic in favor of moral interpretations. While Orderic made full use of the annals and histories he found in his own and other monastic libraries, the *Ecclesiastical History* is most valuable today for the insight it allows into the world of its writer. It provides a vivid, shrewd, and balanced picture of the families, habits, and personalities that dominated the Anglo-Norman world.

Krista Kesselring

Texts

The Ecclesiastical History of Orderic Vitalis. Trans. Marjorie Chibnall. 6 vols. Oxford: Oxford University Press, 1968–1980.

References

Chibnall, Marjorie. *The World of Orderic Vitalis.* Oxford: Oxford University Press, 1984.

Wolter, H. *Ordericus Vitalis.* Wiesbaden: Steiner, 1955.

Orientalism

Western historiography of the non-Western world. Originally referring to the European study of Asia, orientalism developed with western European commercial and political expansion to distant regions of the globe. Well-established from the seventeenth century, it flourished in the nineteenth and early twentieth centuries as European empire building in Asia stimulated European scholars to found numerous institutes of oriental studies. These examined the language, history, philosophy, religion, and politics of the cultures now intimately exposed to Europe.

However, after Edward Said's *Orientalism* (1978), the term now more commonly connotes a certain Western habit of mind about the study of the non-Western world. Adapting Michel Foucault's notion of discourse, Said used the case of European scholarship about the Arab world to argue that much European writing about foreign cultures constitutes an invention rooted not in actual knowledge, but in European preconceptions, images, and desires. Europe, in effect, defined itself against an "Orient" of its own invention, positing essential differences between itself and its oriental "other": the rational, moderate European was set against the fanatical, mystical Muslim. Moreover, this body of knowledge (especially in modern times) portrays the "Oriental" as necessarily inferior to the European, thus simultaneously justifying and facilitating imperial control over the former. Only the European—not the "Oriental"—can truly understand "Oriental" society and history, and thus only the European can control it. Historians have since applied Said's insights widely to Western scholarship about many parts of the non-Western world, examining in a large body of literature how Western material power and inherited stock ideas created a body of knowledge that obscured accurate understanding but aided ideologies of imperial control. Indian society, as a conspicuous example, was understood to be governed by unchanging caste relations, while dynamic forces cutting against caste were neglected. It therefore required European stimulation to liberate it from stagnation. Historians in the wake of Said have also highlighted how orientalist habits of mind were often inherited by non-Western intellectuals. Anticolonial nationalists, notably, inverted Western images of colonial societies to invent their own idyllic national histories and virtuous national traits, the better to highlight the destructive effects of European imperialism.

While some critiques of Western misperception have been overzealous, this deepening awareness of the orientalist qualities of Western scholarship has posed profound historiographical problems for those wishing to write histories of the non-Western world. It requires that existing literature be carefully reexamined for its Eurocentric perspectives, essentialist premises, and assumptions of difference. It also leads historians to ask if truly global histories can be written. These issues are now being addressed, for example by Gyan Prakash in "Writing Post-Orientalist Histories."

P.S. Zachernuk

See also EUROCENTRISM; HAMITIC HYPOTHESIS; IMPERIALISM.

References

Inden, Ronald. "Orientalist Constructions of India," *Modern Asian Studies* 20, 3 (1986): 401–446.

Mudimbe, V.Y. *The Idea of Africa.* Bloomington: Indiana University Press, 1994.

Prakash, Gyan. "Writing Post-Orientalist Histories of the Third World." In *Colonialism and Culture,* ed. N.B. Dirks. Ann Arbor: University of Michigan Press, 1992, 353–388.

Said, E.W. *Orientalism.* New York: Vintage, 1978.

Orosius, Paulus (fl. 390–420)

Medieval scholar and historian. Born on the Iberian peninsula, where he served for some time as a priest, Orosius moved to North Africa around A.D. 414. There he worked closely with St. Augustine. Orosius penned two antipagan theological works, and at Augustine's urging, began the work for which he is best known, the *Historiarum adversus paganus libri septum* [Seven Books against the Pagans]. A profane (that is to say, secular) history of the ancient world from a Christian viewpoint, this work used pagan histories in conjunction with the writings of Eusebius, the Scriptures, and the four-monarchy periodization derived from the Book of Daniel. It emphasized the importance of geography as a necessary background to any historical understanding. A universal history of the earthly city, roughly based on St. Augustine's philosophy of history, the *Seven Books* was widely read throughout the Middle Ages, with some two hundred manuscript copies surviving to the present day.

Krista Kesselring

Texts

The Seven Books of History against the Pagans. Trans. R.J. Deferrari. Washington, DC: Catholic University of America Press, 1964.

References

Lacroix, Bernard. *Orose et ses idées* [Orosius and His Ideas]. Montreal: Institut d'Études Medievales, 1965.

Smalley, Beryl. *Historians in the Middle Ages.* London: Thames and Hudson, 1974.

Sterns, Indrikes. *The Greater Medieval Historians: An Interpretation and a Bibliography.* Lanham, MD: University Press of America, 1980.

Osgood, Herbert Levi (1855–1918)

American colonial historian. Educated at Amherst College (1873–1877), the University of Berlin (1882–1883), and Columbia University (Ph.D., 1889), Osgood taught at Columbia from 1890 to 1918. He adhered rigidly to the Rankean notion of "scientific" objectivity and reliance on primary sources. Using an imperial framework and categorizing colonies by governmental type, not geographical economy, he traced the interaction of English institutions and evolving American conditions in a seven-volume political history. This project reflected his conviction that law and political institutions shaped social and economic forces. Osgood is often associated with Charles McLean Andrews and George Louis Beer in the "Imperial school" of American history.

Ross Evans Paulson

Texts

The American Colonies in the Eighteenth Century. New York: Columbia University Press, 1924.

The American Colonies in the Seventeenth Century. New York: Macmillan, 1904–1907.

References

Fox, Dixon Ryan. *Herbert Levi Osgood: An American Scholar.* New York: Columbia, 1924.

White, Philip L. "Herbert Levi Osgood: An Intellectual Tragedy." In *Perspectives on Early America History,* ed. Alden T. Vaughan and George A. Billias. New York: Harper & Row, 1973, 95–119.

Ostrogorsky, Georgije [George] (1902–1976)

Russian-born Yugoslav Byzantinist. Ostrogorsky was born in St. Petersburg but left Russia after the revolution of 1917. He studied first at Heidelberg (with Percy Schramm) and then (1924–1925) at Paris. He taught at the University of Breslau (now Wrocław), Poland, and, beginning in 1933, at Belgrade, where he assumed the chair of Byzantinology; in 1948 he founded and directed the Institute of Byzantine Studies of the Serbian Academy of Arts and Sciences. Ostrogorsky is principally known for three major achievements. His edition of the *Fontes Byzantini historiam populorum Jugoslaviae spectantes* [Byzantine Sources for the History of the Yugoslav Peoples] (1955–1971) was an important contribution to the history of then newly united Yugoslavia. Of wider interest were two monographs, a *History of the Byzantine State* published in Germany in 1940 and still in use; and his major study of the Byzantine *pronoia* or feudal institutions from the tenth to the twelfth centuries.

Stephen A. Stertz

Texts

"Agrarian Conditions in the Byzantine Empire in the Middle Ages." *Cambridge Economic History of Europe.* Second ed. Cambridge, Eng.: Cambridge University Press, 1966, vol. 1, 205–234, 774–779.

History of the Byzantine State. Trans. J.M. Hussey. Oxford: Blackwell, 1956.

Pour l'Histoire de la féodalité byzantine. Trans. Henri Grégoire (into French). Brussels: Institut de Philologie et d'Histoire Orientales et Slaves, 1954.

References

J. Ferluga, "Georg Ostrogorsky (1902–1976)." *Jahrbuch für Geschichte Osteuropas* [Yearbook for the History of Eastern Europe], new series 25 (1977): 632–636.

Ōtsuka Hisao (b. 1907)

Japanese economic and social historian. Ōtsuka studied at Tokyo University and later lectured in European economic history at Hōsei University, before returning to Tokyo University as a lecturer in 1939. Major influences on his work include Christian socialist thought, Marxism, and the ideas of Max Weber. Ōtsuka's writings are very wide-ranging, encompassing the economic history of western Europe and Japan, as well as the recent economic development of Southeast Asia. In his studies of western European industrialization, such as his *Kindai Ōshū Keizaishi Josetsu* [Introduction to the Modern Economic History of Europe] (1944), Ōtsuka particularly emphasized the role of small-scale rural and urban producers (as opposed to large-scale merchant capital) in the emergence of European industrial capitalism. His study *Shūkyō Kaikaku to Kindai Shakai* [The Reformation and Modern Society] (1948) also explored the ethical and ideological origins of modern Western society. In his postwar writings Ōtsuka was especially concerned with the nature of the precapitalist social community *(kyōdōtai)* and its influence in shaping the history of European and East Asian societies. During the 1960s and 1970s Ōtsuka applied his extensive knowledge of economic history to the contemporary problems of less developed countries, examining the factors underlying the "underdeveloped" or "monocultural" form of capitalism, which he saw as characteristic of postcolonial societies. Ōtsuka's broad historical vision and ability to synthesize material into clear theoretical frameworks helped to make the "Ōtsuka school" of history one of the most influential in post–World War II Japan.

Tessa Morris-Suzuki

Texts

Ōtsuka Hisao Chosakushū [Collected Works]. 10 vols. Tokyo: Iwanami Shoten, 1969–1970.
The Spirit of Capitalism: The Max Weber Thesis in an Economic Historical Perspective. Trans. M. Kondo. Tokyo: Institute of Developing Economies, 1976.

Otto of Freising (ca.1112–1158)

Chronicler and imperial biographer. Otto belonged to the highest echelon of German society and was himself the maternal uncle of Frederick Barbarossa. After pursuing advanced studies in Paris, Otto became a Cistercian monk and in 1138 was elected bishop of Freising. His main work, the *History of the Two Cities,* was dedicated to Barbarossa in 1157. Patterned after the universal chronicles of Eusebius, Jerome, and their medieval continuators, it traces history from Adam to 1146 in seven books and concludes with an eschatological eighth book. The work has few medieval peers as a contribution to the philosophy of history. While adopting St. Augustine's schema of "two cities," Otto broke with his model by tracing the shifting fortunes of the terrestrial city as well as the progress of its celestial counterpart. With the Investiture Contest, the peace of the church gave way to strife between popes and emperors, thus presaging the close of

history and the permanent separation of the two cities. Otto did not live to complete his second great work, *The Deeds of Frederick Barbarossa.* But in the two books of this that he did write, Otto dropped the tragic tone of the *History* and instead hailed Frederick as peacemaker. Otto's secretary, Rahewin, completed the work in two books covering the period from 1156 to 1160.

David F. Appleby

Texts

The Deeds of Frederick Barbarossa by Otto of Freising and His Continuator, Rahewin. Ed. and trans. Charles Christopher Mierow. New York: Norton: 1966.
The Two Cities: A Chronicle of Universal History to the Year 1146 A.D. by Otto, Bishop of Freising. Ed. and trans. Charles Christopher Mierow. New York: Columbia University Press, 1928.

References

Dahmus, Joseph. *Seven Medieval Historians.* Chicago: University of Chicago Press, 1982.
Goetz, Hans-Werner. *Das Geschichtsbild Ottos von Freising* [The Historical Outlook of Otto of Freising]. Beihefte zum Archiv für Kulturgeschichte, 19. Cologne: Böhlau, 1984.

Ouellet, Fernand (b. 1926)

French Canadian archivist and historian. Ouellet was born in Lac Bouchette, in the Lac St-Jean area of Quebec. He studied at Laval University in Quebec City, obtaining a Ph.D. in history there in 1966. He broadened his knowledge of the discipline by making a study of English-Canadian historians such as Donald Creighton and Harold Innis, as well as French specialists of socioeconomic history, particularly Ernest Labrousse and Pierre Chaunu. After working initially as an archivist, Ouellet has pursued a career as a history professor at Laval University, Carleton University, the University of Ottawa, and, finally, York University, from which he retired in 1995. In 1966, the publication of his work *Histoire économique et sociale du Québec, 1760–1850* [Economic and Social History of Quebec, 1760–1850] marked a revolution in Canadian historiography, whose object and methodology it redefined. Previously, the focus of French Canadian historiography had been the cultural survival of that society and the defense of its constitutional rights, as seen in the works of such historians as François-Xavier

Garneau and Lionel Groulx. Ouellet writes primarily socioeconomic history, although he does not neglect ideological and political analyses. In 1976 he published *Le Bas Canada 1791–1840: Changements structuraux et crise* [Lower Canada 1791–1840: Structural Changes and Crisis], which confirmed his theses. By virtue of its scope and originality, Ouellet's work is on the whole unique. It challenges the validity of interpretations developed by both traditional nationalists and neonationalists of Quebec. According to Ouellet, the explanation of French-Canadian economic inferiority lies not in the disruption of this society by the British conquest, but rather in the fact that French Canadians, ill-directed by their political and clerical elites and ill-served by their Old Regime mentality, were unable to adjust to modern capitalism. This theory has fueled debate and controversy among Quebec historians for decades. During the same period, through his quantitative approach focused on socioeconomic realities, Ouellet has not only redefined French Canadian historical approaches, but has also—thanks to the translation of his works into English—helped to enrich the substance and method of historiography in Canada as a whole.

Pierre Savard

Texts

Economic and Social History of Quebec, 1760–1850: Structures and Conjunctures. Toronto: Gage Publishing, 1980.

Economy, Class and Nation in Quebec: Interpretive Essays. Ed. and trans. Jacques A. Barbier. Toronto: Copp Clark Pitman, 1991.

Louis-Joseph Papineau: Un été divise. Ottawa: Societé historique du Canada, 1961.

Lower Canada, 1791–1860: Social Change and Nationalism. Toronto: McClelland and Stewart, 1980.

References

Gagnon, Serge. *Quebec and Its Historians. Vol II: The Twentieth Century.* Trans. Jane Brierley. Montreal: Harvest House, 1985.

Ovalle, Alonso de (1601–1651)

Chile's first important historian. Ovalle was born in Santiago; in 1618, he joined the Jesuit Order and then went to Argentina for eight years. On his return to Santiago, the Jesuits named him rector of the Convictorio de San Francisco Javier de Santiago. In 1640, the order sent him to Europe to recruit missionaries. Returning to South America from Europe, Ovalle contracted a fever that led to his death in Lima. During his visit to Europe, Ovalle was struck by the general ignorance about Chile and attempted to remedy this by writing the two-volume *Historica relación del Reyno de Chile y de las misiones y ministerios que ejercita en el la Compañia de Jesus* [Historical Relation of the Kingdom of Chile and Its Missions and Ministries Administered by the Company of Jesus], the first history of Chile. First published in Rome in 1646 (in both Castilian and Italian editions), this work presents not only a geographical, natural, social, and historical description of Chile, but also a detailed account of the Jesuits' missionary and educational activities. As a history, it is much more narrative and descriptive than analytical and critical, interweaving superstition with historical fact. As a primary source, however, it provides a window onto Chile's seventeenth-century colonial life and contains one of the first maps of Chile. The *Historica relación* idealized Ovalle's native land not only to demonstrate its equivalence with Europe, but also in order to attract missionaries.

Carlos Pérez

Texts

Historica Relación del Reino de Chile y de las misiones y ministerios que ejercita en el la Compañia de Jesus. Santiago de Chile: Instituto de Literatura Chilena, 1969.

References

Hanisch Espindola, Walter. *El historiador Alonso de Ovalle* [Alonso de Ovalle, Historian]. Caracas: Instituto de Investigaciones Historicas, Facultad de Humanidades y Educacion, Universidad Catolica "Andres Bello," 1976.

Oviedo y Baños, José de (1671–1728)

Colombian-born Venezuelan historian. Oviedo y Baños, Venezuela's first historian, was born in Santa Fe de Bogotá. After his father's death, the family moved to Lima, Peru. In 1685, José moved to Venezuela. José lived an active business, civic, religious, and family life before writing his memorable history of the conquest of Venezuela. During his years on the town council of Caracas, he explored its archives, writing a manuscript entitled "Treasury of Notices and General Index of the Most Remarkable Items Contained in the Capitular Books of the City of Caracas since Its Founding" that later provided the basis for his history. Besides archival material, he also used contemporary printed sources. The first part of the *Historia de la Conquista y poblacion de la provincia de Venezuela* covers the period from the discovery of the province to 1600. The second volume continued the history to the 1720s and contains many memorable episodes of these early colonial years. The book, first published at Madrid in 1723, has the honor of not only being the first book published by an American-born resident of Venezuela, but, in its second printing in 1824, it also became the first significant work to emerge from Venezuela's first printing press.

Carlos Pérez

Texts

The Conquest and Settlement of Venezuela. Trans. Jeannette Johnson Varner. Berkeley: University of California Press, 1987.

References

Morón, Guillermo. *Los cronistas y la historia* [The Chroniclers and History]. Caracas: Ministerio de Educación, Dirreción de Cultura y Bellas Artes, 1957.

———. *José de Oviedo y Baños, 1671–1783.* Caracas: Fundación Eugenio Mendoza, 1958.

O

P

Pachymeres, George (1242–1310)

Byzantine historian and ecclesiastical figure. Born in Nicaea, Pachymeres arrived in Constantinople following the expulsion of the Latins in 1261. Pachymeres held several high state and religious positions during his career. A prolific writer in a variety of genres, his most important work is a history entitled *Syngraphikai historiai* [Collected Histories], which continues the *Chronike syngraphe* (1203–1261) of George Akroplites for the period from 1261–1310. The work's two parts comprise the reign of Michael VII Palaeologus (1261–1282) in six books and part of the reign of Andronicus II (1282–1328) in seven books. Despite his pedantic indulgence in Homeric and archaic expressions, Pachymeres is an impartial eyewitness except in religious matters. The *Syngraphikai* is an indispensable source for the military history of the late thirteenth and early fourteenth centuries. It is important for the histories of the Balkans, the Mongols, the Fatimids, the Turkish expansion into Asia Minor, and the Catalan expedition of Roger de Flor.

Norman Tobias

Texts

De Michele et Andronice Paleologis [Concerning Michael and Andronicus Palaeologus]. Ed. Immanuel Bekker. 2 vols. Bonn: Ed. Weberi, 1835. (Books 1–6 only by Pachymeres.)

Relations historiques. Ed. A. Failler; trans. V. Laurent (into French). 2 vols. Paris: Belles Letttres, 1984.

References

Colonna, Maria E. *Gli storici bizantini dal IV al XV secolo: I Storici profani* [Byzantine Historians from the Fourth to the Fifteenth Century, I: Profane Historians]. Naples: Armanni, 1956.

Hunger, Hans. *Hochsprachliche profane Literatur der Byzantiner* [Byzantine Profane Literature]. 2 vols. Munich: C.H. Beck, 1978.

Krumbacher, Karl. *Geschichte der byzantinischen Litteratur* [History of Byzantine Literature]. Second ed. Munich: C.H. Beck, 1897.

Moravcsik, Gyula. *Byzantinoturicica.* Second ed. 2 vols. Berlin: Akademie-Verlag, 1958.

Pacific Islands Historiography

Pacific islands history did not develop a conscious academic identity until the 1950s. However, the modern discipline has a long-standing pedigree. The subject area was initially delineated by explorers from Europe who charted the islands from the early sixteenth to late eighteenth centuries. The region encompasses all the islands of the Pacific Ocean (including New Guinea) and is commonly divided into three areas labeled Melanesia, Micronesia, and Polynesia. The study of the islands, their indigenous cultures, and the arrival of Western newcomers, began with descriptions of explorers and those who followed them—missionaries, traders, travelers, ethnographers, and colonial officials. By 1900 virtually all of the islands had been formally incorporated into the respective empires of Britain, the United States, France, Holland, and Germany.

From the days of the European explorers to the end of World War II, accounts of the Pacific islands were set in an imperial context. With the partial exception of a relatively minor stream of ethnographic and anthropological enquiry, most studies of the Pacific islands were usually more concerned with the activities of Westerners as agents of empire, expanding Western commercial, religious, and administrative interests into the Pacific and in subsequent international rivalries and colonial rule. The islanders and their cultures were generally relegated to the background, as objects of Western initiatives, not subjects in their own right. Culture contact was often represented as a conflict between active, superior Westerners and passive, inferior islanders. The idea that Western contact had a "fatal impact" upon island societies became an unquestioned axiom of Pacific studies.

As colonial empires collapsed after World War II, historians began to decolonize history. Indigenous peoples were now deemed worthy subjects of serious academic research. The decolonization of Pacific islands history owes much to J.W. Davidson, foundation professor of the department of Pacific history at the Australian National University in the early 1950s. Davidson rejected the imperial historical agenda and argued for an island-centered perspective. Instead of studying colonial agents in their imperial context, island events were to be examined in an indigenous cultural context. Davidson established a research program that provided the foundation for modern Pacific islands history. It emphasized the necessity for more extensive archival collection and research, for a more interdisciplinary approach, and for fieldwork on the islands with close attention to indigenous accounts and traditions of the past. In general it involved investigating the nature and consequences of cultural interaction between island societies and increasing Western presence and influence. Islanders were encouraged to research and write their histories for a wider audience. The fruits of this research began to emerge from the late 1960s, and as graduates from Davidson's department established Pacific islands history in universities in Australia, New Zealand, the Pacific islands, and the United States, the 1970s saw a flood of specialized monographs and journal articles. Much consisted of detailed island case studies of culture contact. Since the mid-1980s a few attempts have been made to encompass such findings into general histories of Pacific islands history, but even today the published literature still consists largely of case studies. There has yet to develop any sustained regional or comparative treatment of the islands' past.

Certain themes and interpretations are predominant throughout the scholarship of the 1960s to the late 1980s. First, most concentrated on the period before 1900, that is, the islands' precolonial days. Pacific historians virtually ignored the twentieth century, probably because, unlike many other parts of the world, most Pacific islands had a very peaceful transition to constitutional independence from the 1960s to the 1980s. No obvious

contemporary political issues, such as revolutions or wars of national liberation, informed Pacific scholarship, whose territory for many remained steeped in Romantic notions of paradise. Furthermore, the rejection of the earlier imperial historical approach had been so vigorous that even the study of the period of colonial government was regarded as somewhat unfashionable.

Second, by shifting the focus from imperial activities to islander initiatives in the contact situation, it emphasized, at least for the period before formal colonial rule, how islanders were not passive and helpless when faced with Western presence and influence. On the contrary, it was argued, the course of events was frequently determined by the islanders' social, economic, religious, and political institutions and agenda. A wide range of initiatives was adopted, especially by leaders, to exploit new opportunities and cope with new challenges. Consequently, the long-standing assumptions about an inevitable fatal impact for these societies were substantially modified. Island societies were often depicted as highly resilient and adaptive.

Some significant historiographic shifts are now evident, in part because early optimistic expectations of many of the newly independent Pacific nation-states have not been realized, and because of increasing frustration in those islands that still have to regain political sovereignty. Political, social, economic, racial, cultural, military, and strategic tensions are now variously apparent in places like Fiji, New Guinea, French New Caledonia, and the former U.S. trust territories in Micronesia. Pacific islands do not feature among the world's major trouble spots, but many of them are less placid places than formerly. The historical agenda is now more informed by these current issues with a refocusing on events of the twentieth century and on the growth and consequences of colonial and postcolonial infrastructures. These perceptions are also being sharpened by the increasing numbers of Pacific islanders who participate in the academic discourse. Thus the island-centered perspective is being modified with the islands now viewed as part of both Pacific rim and global systems of investment, trade, and defense. In an ironic way, this shift represents a return to some of the concerns of the older, imperial history, although without embracing its former values.

Apart from these specific developments, Pacific islands history has in recent times been influenced by more general historiographic trends, such as an interest in gender studies and postmodern/postcolonial perspectives. In this later activity the usual historical sources are examined less for the information they ostensibly carry about some historical event, but as texts that illuminate the values of the recorders. Thus the study of Pacific islands history becomes essentially the study of those who have constructed this history.

K.R. Howe

References

Campbell, I.C. *A History of the Pacific Islands.* Christchurch: University of Canterbury Press, 1989.

Hanlon, David. *Upon a Stone Altar: A History of the Island of Pohnpei to 1890.* Honolulu, University of Hawaii Press, 1988.

Howe, K.R, Robert C. Kiste, and Brij V. Lal, eds. *Tides of History: The Pacific Islands in the Twentieth Century.* Honolulu: University of Hawaii Press, 1994.

Howe, K.R. *Where the Waves Fall. A New South Sea Islands History from First Settlement to Colonial Rule.* Honolulu: University of Hawaii Press, 1988.

Lal, Brij V. *Broken Waves: A History of the Fiji Islands in the Twentieth Century.* Honolulu, University of Hawaii Press, 1992.

Latukefu, Sione. *Church and State in Tonga.* Canberra: Australian National University Press, 1974.

Shineberg, Dorothy. *They Came for Sandalwood: A Study of the Sandalwood Trade in the South-West Pacific 1830–1865.* Melbourne: Melbourne University Press, 1967.

Paek Nam-un (1894–1979)

Korean Marxist historian and politician. Paek was introduced to Marxism while studying in Japan. He held academic positions in Korea, but was imprisoned for anti-Japanese activities. An active participant in politics after the independence of Korea, he became one of the highest members of the North Korean government. Paek pioneered Marxist history in Korea. In *Chosŏn Sawhoe Kyŏngjaesa* [Social and Economic History of Korea] (1933) he suggested four stages of the development of the Korean society: primitive communist, slavery, Asiatic feudal, and distorted capitalistic societies. To him, the society of Chosŏn had been in the early stages of capitalism, but Japanese colonialism had hindered the natural development of Korea into a communistic society. In this regard, only the country's independence could restart the natural evolution toward communism.

Minjae Kim

Texts

Chosŏn Sawhoe Kyŏngjaesa [Japanese spelling: *Chōō sen Shakai Keizaishi*]. Tokyo: Kaezōsha, 1933.

References

Cho Tong-gŏl et al., eds. *Han'gukŭi Yŏksa ga wa Yŏksahak* [Korean Historians and Their Works]. 2 vols. Seoul: Changjak gwa Pip'yŏngsa, 1994.

Paisiy of Hilendar (1722–1773)

Bulgarian historian and ideologist of the national liberation movement. Paisiy was born in Bansko in present-day Bulgarian Macedonia. At the age of twenty-three he entered the Hilendar monastery at Mount Athos. As an itinerant Orthodox monk, he toured Bulgaria and the Habsburg South Slavic provinces and collected information about Bulgarian history. In 1762, he completed his *Slavo-Bulgarian History,* which is considered the starting point of the Bulgarian national revival and of Bulgarian historiography. More than sixty handwritten copies of it have come down to us. Paisiy's narrative, containing a survey of Bulgarian history from Adam and Eve to the Ottoman invasion at the end of the fourteenth century, is highly patriotic and therefore focuses on the venerable exploits of czars and saints. It is mainly based on (the Russian translation of) the works of Mauro Orbini and Cesare Baronio on South Slavic and Slavic church history. In the introduction, Paisiy urges the Bulgarians to be proud of their nationhood and language and emphasizes the role of historiography in inciting patriotic feelings. He thus founded the "romantic" tradition in Bulgarian historiography, which was predominant until the 1870s.

R. Detrez

Texts

Raykov, Bozhidar. *Paisieviyat rukopis na "Istoriya slavyanobolgarskaya," 1762* [Paisiy's Manuscript of the "Slavo-Bulgarian History," 1762]. Sofia: Nauka i izkustvo, 1989.

References

Velchev, Velcho. *Paissi of Hilendar, Father of the Bulgarian Enlightenment.* Sofia: Sofia Press, 1981.

Pak Ŭn-sik (1859–1925)

Korean historian, journalist, and patriot. Exiled to Siberia and then to Shanghai when Japan annexed Korea, Pak Ŭn-sik became the prime minister and later the president of the provisional government of Korea at Shanghai and was generally regarded as a great spiritual leader for the independence movement. He wrote many books on the early history of Korea, on the history of the independence movement, and on Korean heroes and patriots. He brought a strongly held nationalism to his works, an attitude that would become a characteristic feature of many later historians of Korea. In *Han'guk T'ongsa* [The Tragic History of Korea] (1915), he condemned the Japanese aggression and openly favored the Korean independence movement. In *Han'guk Tongnip Undong chi Hyŏlsa* [The Bloody History of the Korean Independence Movement] (1920), he maintained that the Koreans, possessed as they were of a fierce nationalistic spirit, could never be assimilated into the Japanese, and that the independence movement of March 1, 1919, had been both populist in origin and an inevitable response to the Japanese colonial regime.

Minjae Kim

Texts

Han'guk Tongnip Undong chi Hyŏlsa. Ed. Nam Mansung. Seoul: Sŏmundang, 1975.
Han'guk T'ongsa. Ed. Yi Ch'ang-hŭi. 2 vols. Seoul: Pagyŏngsa, 1974–1975.

References

Hong Isŏp. "Pak Ŭn-sik, Han'guk T'ongsa wa Han'guk Tongnip Undong chi Hyŏlsa." *Saekyoyuk* [New Education] 101 (1963): 104–106.

Palacký, František (1798–1876)

Czech historian and leader of the Czech National Revival of the nineteenth century in the Habsburg Empire. Palacký was born in Hodslavice, Moravia. From 1812 to 1823 he studied at the prestigious Evangelical Lyceum at Pressburg in Hungary. He departed thence for Prague with an excellent education and a passionate commitment to the revival of national consciousness among the Czechs. In 1827, he was appointed historiographer of the Bohemian Estates and commissioned to write a scholarly history of Bohemia and Moravia. The latter became "the chief and ultimate end of all [his] endeavor" and a lifetime task. During the Revolution of 1848, Palacký also served as the chief Czech political spokesman, supporting, without success, the ideas of Austro-Slavism and the federalization of the Habsburg Monarchy. Palacký's leading role in the linguistic, cultural, and political reawakening of the Czechs would gain him the title of "Father of the Czech Nation." His classic history was published between 1836 and 1876, in five volumes and simultaneous German and Czech versions—the *Geschichte von Böhmen* [History of Bohemia] and the *Dějiny národu českého* [History of the Czech Nation]. It extended only to the year 1526 and focused on the Hussite Reformation. The product of critical, systematic historical method—vast archival research, pioneering work in the ancillary disciplines, and scores of detailed preliminary monographs of every variety—and written in an elegant literary style, the *Geschichte von Böhmen* established Palacký as the founder of modern Czech historiography. In it he also propounded an inspiring philosophy of Czech history, portraying the Czechs as predestined to be martyrs to the defense of democracy in church and state.

Joseph Frederick Zacek

Texts

Dějiny národu českého. Ed. Olga Svejkovská. 6 vols. Prague: Odeon, 1968–1973.
Spisy drobné [Miscellaneous Writings]. 3 vols. Prague: Bursík & Kohout, 1898–1902.
Würdigung der alten böhmischen Geschichtschreiber [An Evaluation of Old Bohemian Historians]. Prague: A. Borrosch, 1830.
Zur böhmischen Geschichtschreibung: Aktenmässige Aufschlüsse und Worte der Abwehr [On Bohemian Historical Writing: Documentary Conclusions and a Defense]. Prague: Friedrich Tempsky, 1871.

References

Morava, Georg J. *Franz Palacký.* Vienna: Österreichischer Bundesverlag, 1990.
Zacek, Joseph F. *Palacký: The Historian As Scholar and Nationalist.* The Hague: Mouton, 1970.

Paleography and Diplomatic

Two closely connected methods for the study of old documents that pay close attention to the hands used in writing the documents (paleography) and the forms the documents take (diplomatic). Paleography and diplomatic are ancillary historical "sciences" that rest on a high level of precision and rigorous attention to detail. Roughly speaking, they are the technical counterparts of epigraphy and papyrology (which apply to stone inscriptions and papyrus writings) and numismatics (which applies to the study of coins and medals). Paleography is the study of ancient handwriting, founded on a typology of styles of writing according to different systems, each system being made up of several "registers" (degrees of formality ranging from majuscule to cursive); dated examples of the specific types allows a dating to be inferred for the writing of manuscripts of the same type. Diplomatic involves the classification of documents—an approach most appropriate to formal documents, official acts, legal transactions, and so on—according to their form of words; the physical format, script, and means of authentication (seal, signature, etc.) are also relevant. Paleography and diplomatic may be used in close conjunction: for example, the identification of individual hands writing documents in a particular form may be crucial in determining the size of staff and volume of business of a specific chancery (the office in which the diplomatic affairs of a medieval or Renaissance state were conducted).

The development of paleography and diplomatic, along with many of the other ancillary sciences of history, derived in the first instance from problems of textual "tradition" (that is, the way in which ancient texts survived the Middle Ages to be rediscovered by later scholars) between antiquity and the Renaissance. The primary guardian of the writings of Western antiquity throughout the Middle Ages was the Christian church, and in particular the monastic orders. It was the task of Renaissance humanist scholars such as Petrarch and Poggio Bracciolini in Italy, or John Leland in England, to rescue these documents (mainly medieval copies rather than long-lost ancient originals) from destruction—for instance after Henry VIII's dissolution of the English monasteries in the 1530s—and to bring them to a wider world by editing them carefully and having them printed. Unfortunately, not every humanist scholar, even with the best of intentions, categorized documents in ways that we now find sensible. A notorious example is the early seventeenth-century English manuscript enthusiast Sir Robert Cotton, whose vast collections, much of them pillaged from the public records, formed the basis of the British Museum's collections of English manuscripts. Cotton performed a valuable function in saving many documents from probable destruction, but his lack of sensitivity to the order of original documents has resulted in the misarrangement of closely related ones and the removal of parts of complete manuscripts and their reclassification as parts of other manuscripts. Codicology, the study of how manuscript books are made, has an important role in correcting such mismanagement. Such problems as these are still detectable today, in varying degrees, with many of the collections made between ca. 1450 and 1700; the many French and Italian "virtuosi" who dabbled in manuscripts,

coins, and other artifacts more often than not lacked the skill to classify and identify their treasures. It was by way of dealing with these questions that paleography and diplomatic first arose between the mid-fifteenth and early eighteenth centuries.

Diplomatic, although often practiced in close relation to paleography, is used to determine the authenticity of individual copies of documents, by comparison with the forms of authentic originals; a diplomatic treatment of a given document or record will be able to authenticate it based on the precise forms of words used (which can vary considerably over both the short and long term), the proper style or title of officials such as kings and ambassadors mentioned therein, and the manner in which dates are recorded. Diplomatic therefore relies, like philology (the study of changes in language over time), on a keen sense of anachronism, the ability to discern the date of a copy, or even the existence of a forgery, from out-of-place terms or names or historically inaccurate means of dating. To give a simple example: a document allegedly issued by the king of England in the late fifteenth century and which referred to that ruler as also being "king" of Ireland would instantly be detected as a corrupt copy or even a forgery, since the royal chancery always styled the king "lord of Ireland" until 1540.

Many real cases, like modern clever replicas of a Rembrandt painting, are more subtle. The purpose of forgery in the Middle Ages was usually material advantage in legal claims or disputes, and many forgers were well acquainted with the appropriate forms for their purpose. Indeed, many of the most infamous of forgeries have been the work of skilled intellectuals nearly as gifted in the proper shape and content of documents as the official draftsmen whom they imitated, or the experts who later debunked their creations. Since it provides, together with reclassification and comparison of groups of documents, one of the ongoing problems for paleographers and diplomatists, the long history of forged documents and texts requires some discussion in this connection. The Middle Ages, for instance, produced the notorious Donation of Constantine. This was a document long taken to be a grant to the Papacy in perpetuity of sovereignty over western Europe, issued by the fourth-century Roman emperor Constantine. Various late medieval scholars had doubted its authenticity, but it took the philological skills of the humanist grammarian and rhetorician Lorenzo Valla (1407–1457) finally to expose it as an eighth-century forgery. The mythographer Annius of Viterbo or Giovanni Nanni similarly offered to

P

the world a set of bogus "histories," allegedly by authentic ancient authors, in his *Antiquitatum Variarum Volumina XVII* [Seventeen Volumes of Various Antiquities] (1498). These were decisively discredited as forgeries by the skillful French philologist Joseph Justus Scaliger (1540–1609) in the 1580s. Scaliger's younger contemporary, Isaac Casaubon (1559–1614), similarly debunked the myth of the "Hermetic texts," a set of occult writings that a century and a half of Renaissance scholars had taken as the authentic utterances of an ancient Egyptian sage. There are more modern instances, such as James Macpherson's eighteenth-century publication of the works of "Ossian," an entirely fictitious Celtic bard, and Thomas Chatterton, who invented forged poems and histories wholesale. Forgeries should be distinguished from counterfeits or fakes—bogus copies, usually dating from modern times, made for sale as pretended antiquities rather than for any legal force that may have attached to the document copied.

Routine exercises in diplomatic are often less spectacular and rely less on detecting inaccuracies in the language used (as in Valla's use of philology) than on the even more painstaking analysis of word forms and the shape of clauses in documents. The aims, however, are similar: to establish beyond reasonable doubt the authenticity of a document so that it may (or may not) be relied on as historical evidence of an event or past utterance. But problems other than verifying the form of the text or document exist, and this is where the work of the paleographer comes in.

Paleography is, clearly, closely related to diplomatic—not coincidentally, Jean Mabillon (1632–1707), a French Benedictine monk, is often regarded as the father of both, in his classic 1681 handbook *De re diplomatica Libri VI* [Six Books Regarding Diplomatic]. Paleography, however, is principally concerned with the actual physical drawing of letters and words (including the spacing between them). Its origins, as with philology (and, to a lesser extent, with diplomatic), go back to the Renaissance humanists, in particular Angelo Poliziano (1454–1494), and to French scholars of about two hundred years later such as Mabillon and his younger contemporary Bernard de Montfaucon (1655–1741), author in 1708 of *Palaeographica Graeca* [Greek Paleography]. The latter developed the first complete system for the authentication of medieval documents in the course of a dispute between Mabillon's Benedictine order and the Jesuit Daniel Papenbroeck over the veracity of certain documents from the seventh-century Merovingian Frankish kings. The work of

the Bollandists (a group of Belgian Jesuits) and Maurists (Mabillon and his French Benedictine associates) played a critical role in making paleography an indispensable historical tool. Mabillon's own classification of Latin book hands was refined significantly by the Italian nobleman and playwright Scipione Maffei (1675–1755), who was the first to explain the relation of various medieval and late antique hands to each other, attributing the existence of the various different hands to their descent, in the post-Roman world, from common late antique majuscule (upper case), minuscule (lower case), and cursive (a hand written with one letter joining the next to save a scribe time and effort). A little over a century later, a further advance was made by the German Ludwig Traube (1861–1907), who showed that medieval manuscripts can be used not only as the "vessels" for ancient texts, but also in their own right as primary sources for medieval thought and culture: a "bad" medieval text of Virgil may in fact be, if datable, a "good" source for medieval intellectual history.

It should be pointed out that paleography is often studied in two distinct but related ways, reflecting different usages of the term. In its elementary sense, students of history, comparative philology, literature, and related humanistic disciplines are often required as part of their advanced studies, to master the *reading* of old documents in unusual hands from different periods and cultures. Thus the paleographic skills required of a scholar working on the American civil war are different from those required of the seventeenth-century English civil war, or of sixteenth-century Italian notaries' records; these, in turn, are even more remote from those needed of a student of the medieval church or late Roman imperial administration. In the West alone, a wide range of standard hands has come and gone, such as the Merovingian cursive, the Carolingian minuscule (a famous medieval hand that provided the origins for Renaissance humanistic script and for many modern typefaces), the English chancery, court, and secretary hands, and the highly italicized letter-writing cursive commonplace in Europe and North America from the late seventeenth century on. The forms in which characters are written in many of these hands is quite different from the manner in which the same characters are written today, making decoding of, say, a document from the Spanish archives of the reign of Philip II, or of an administrative order by a medieval German bishop, quite a different and more challenging task than the reading of a manuscript letter by Abraham Lincoln or James Joyce (though of course many modern hands are also extremely difficult to master). Pedagogically, the teaching of paleography has come to center, at least in European universities, around giving students sufficient familiarity with a range of documents from their chosen period so as to allow them to recognize types of documents and to be able to read them with minimal difficulty.

This sort of paleographic study should therefore be distinguished from the second usage— what one might call "advanced paleography." This is generally practiced not by history students and scholars for whom the reading of a document is merely a necessary task to be undertaken so as to understand its contents, but by highly trained professional paleographers who have a wide range of experience with various types of hand from different periods, and with different but roughly contemporaneous hands, contained in the large manuscript collections on deposit at major treasuries like the Bibliothèque Nationale in Paris, the Vatican Library and Archives in Rome, the British Library in London, the Bodleian Library in Oxford, and numerous smaller collections around the world. For this type of paleographer, too, the reading of the document is but a preliminary to further study. The close dating of manuscripts written in a particular style is vital for the study of texts and their textual transmission, but it demands a minute familiarity with the changes over time that have affected that style of writing, a familiarity that comes only from the careful study of many examples. Consequently, the great paleographers of the past and present, from Mabillon and his near contemporary Charles du Fresne, Sieur Du Cange (1610–1688), to the great early eighteenth-century Anglo-Saxonist Humfrey Wanley (1672–1726), to the nineteenth-century German scholar Traube, to the early-twentieth-century medievalists of the École des Chartes in Paris, to Neil Ripley Ker (1908–1982), a brilliant Oxford manuscript expert of the mid-twentieth century, have had to develop an acute visual memory for hundreds of letter forms in thousands of manuscripts, allowing them accurately to pinpoint the features that allow a manuscript to be dated or its place of writing to be located. Taken with codicology these techniques allow the expert to study an ancient or medieval book as an object that can reveal more than meets the untrained eye.

In Britain, with a historical range of hands that existed often in resistance to the more dominant continental hands, paleography achieved its greatest rigor in the nineteenth and twentieth centuries through the work of scholars (often attached to the major repositories rather than to university posts), such as Sir Edward Maunde Thompson (1840–1929) and Montague Rhodes James (1862–1936). Maunde Thompson's 1912 *Manual of Greek and Latin Palaeography* is still in use today, while James's descriptive catalogs for many libaries remain the standard. Germany, with its strong tradition of classical philology dating back to the sixteenth century, has continued to contribute, especially in the areas of ancient and medieval manuscript culture, while the United States has also produced a variety of paleographically important works, such as Elias Avery Lowe's (1879–1969) *Codices Latini Antiquiores* [Ancient Latin Codexes].

D.R. Woolf

See also ARCHIVES; BIBLIOGRAPHY—HISTORICAL; BOLLANDISTS AND MAURISTS; EPIGRAPHY AND PAPYROLOGY; MUSEUMS; NUMISMATICS.

Texts

Jenkinson, Hilary, and Charles Johnson. *English Court Hand A.D. 1066 to 1500.* Oxford: Clarendon Press, 1915.

Lowe, E.A. *Codices Latini Antiquiores: A Palaeographical Guide to Latin Manuscripts Prior to the Ninth Century.* 12 vols. Oxford: Clarendon Press, 1934–1966.

Mabillon, Jean. *De re diplomatica Libri VI.* Rome: Bibliopola, 1965.

Maunde Thompson, Edward. *An Introduction to Greek and Latin Palaeography.* Oxford: Oxford University Press, 1912.

Osley, A.S., ed. and trans. *Scribes and Sources: Handbook of the Chancery Hand in the Sixteenth Century: Texts from the Writing-Masters.* London and Boston: Faber and Faber, 1980.

Traube, Ludwig. *Geschichte der Paläographie* [History of Paleography]. In *Vorlesungen und abhandlungen von Ludwig Traube* [Lectures and Treatises of Ludwig Traube], ed. Franz Boll. 3 vols. Munich: Beck, 1909–1920, vol. 1.

Wright, C.E. *English Vernacular Hands from the Twelfth to the Fifteenth Centuries.* Oxford: Clarendon Press, 1960.

References

Boyle, Leonard E. *Medieval Latin Palaeography: A Bibliographical Introduction.* Toronto: University of Toronto Press, 1984.

Grafton, Anthony. *Forgers and Critics: Creativity and Duplicity in Western Scholarship.* Princeton, NJ: Princeton University Press, 1990.

Greetham, D.C. *Textual Scholarship: An Introduction.* New York: Garland, 1992.

Knowles, David. *Great Historical Enterprises: Problems in Monastic History.* London and New York: Nelson, 1963.

Morison, Stanley. *Politics and Script: Aspects of Authority and Freedom in the Development of Graeco-Latin Script from the Sixth Century B.C. to the Twentieth Century A.D.* Oxford: Clarendon Press, 1972.

Myers, Robin, and Michael Harris, eds. *Fakes and Frauds: Varieties of Deception in Print and Manuscript.* Winchester, Eng. and Detroit, MI: St. Paul's Bibliographies and Omnigraphics Inc., 1989.

Nickell, Joe. *Pen, Ink, & Evidence.* Lexington: University of Kentucky Press, 1990.

Parkes, M.B., and A.G. Watson. *Medieval Scribes, Manuscripts & Libraries.* London: Scolar Press, 1978

Reynolds, L.D., and N.G. Wilson. *Scribes and Scholars: A Guide to the Transmission of Greek & Latin Literature.*

Tannenbaum, Samuel Aaron. *The Handwriting of the Renaissance.* New York: Columbia University Press, 1930.

Palmer, Robert Roswell (b. 1909)

American historian of eighteenth-century Europe. Palmer was born in Chicago and received his Ph.D. from Cornell (1934), where he studied with Carl Becker. He taught European history at Princeton, Washington University in St. Louis, and Yale. Palmer published several important works, and his translation of Georges Lefebvre's *Quatre-vingt-neuf* [The Coming of the French Revolution] (1947) introduced that author to the English-speaking world; but Palmer's principal historiographical contribution is his *Age of the Democratic Revolution.* Influenced by the political conditions of the post-1945 world, this study argues that eighteenth-century Europe and America experienced a common revolutionary struggle between liberal democrats and the aristocracies or oligarchies that controlled political power. While few historians were fully persuaded by the evidence supporting a universal Western revolution, Palmer's work provoked valuable debate and remains a masterful survey of politics in the late eighteenth century.

William S. Cormack

Texts

The Age of the Democratic Revolution: A Political History of Europe and America, 1760–1800.

2 vols. Princeton, NJ: Princeton University Press, 1959–1964.

Catholics and Unbelievers in Eighteenth Century France. Princeton, NJ: Princeton University Press, 1939.

Twelve Who Ruled: The Committee of Public Safety during the Terror. Princeton, NJ: Princeton University Press, 1941.

References

Amann, Peter, ed. *The Eighteenth-Century Revolution: French or Western?* Boston: D.C. Heath, 1963.

Palmieri, Matteo (1406–1475)

Florentine humanist. Initially an adherent of Leonardo Bruni's "civic humanism," Palmieri nevertheless served the Medici loyally in several public offices. Besides two philosophical works, Palmieri wrote *De captivitate Pisarum* [The Conquest of Pisa] (before 1450), an adaptation in humanist style of Neri Capponi's *Commentarii* (1420) on the same subject. Palmieri's chronologically organized *Annales* (1432–1474) covers the Florentine history of his days. His *Liber de temporibus* [The Times Passed] (1448) was a useful chronology of universal history from Christ to 1448. Palmieri copied his information largely from Sozomeno da Pistoia's *Chronicon* (1432–1458), but shortened it, and was most concerned about establishing precise dates ("distinctio temporum"), especially for the medieval period. The *Liber* was dedicated to Piero de' Medici, translated into Italian, widely copied in manuscript, and printed in several editions during the sixteenth century. This manual was one of the most consulted historical works of the Italian Renaissance.

Thomas Maissen

Texts

De captivitate Pisarum. Ed. Gino Scaramella. *Rerum Italicarum Scriptores,* new series, vol. 19:2. Città di Castello: S. Lapi, 1904.

Liber de temporibus: Annales. Ed. Gino Scaramella. *Rerum Italicarum Scriptores,* new series, vol. 26, part 1. Città di Castello: S. Lapi, 1906–1915.

References

Carpetto, George M. *The Humanism of Matteo Palmieri.* Rome: Bulzoni, 1984.

Cochrane, Eric. *Historians and Historiography in the Italian Renaissance.* Chicago: University of Chicago Press, 1981, 24–26; 146.

Finzi, Claudio. *Matteo Palmieri: Dalla 'vita civile' alla 'città di vita'* [Matteo Palmieri: From Civil Life to City of Life]. Varese: Giuffrè, 1984.

Shteppa, Konstantin F. *Russian Historians and the Soviet State.* New Brunswick, NJ: Rutgers University Press, 1962.

Pan Chao
See BAN ZHAO.

Pan Ku
See BAN GU.

Pankratova, Anna Mikhailovna (1897–1957)

Soviet historian. Pankratova graduated from Novorossiisk University in 1917 and the Institute of Red Professors in 1925. She studied under M.N. Pokrovskii and produced a major study on the socialization of industry in 1923 edited by him. At first defending her mentor, she later condemned Pokrovskii when he fell into disfavor under Stalin. Following the Stalinist line, she authored approximately two hundred works, largely on the history of the labor movement in Russia and on the history of diplomacy and, consequently, in the 1930s, came to be viewed as an official Soviet historian. She has been recognized widely in Russian-Soviet historiography as the epitome of the Stalinist historian. For her efforts, Pankratova was awarded a Stalin Prize in 1946; she was also made a member of the Academy of Sciences of the USSR and, in 1953, editor in chief of the journal *Voprosy istorii* [Problems of History]. In 1955, she edited a four-volume collection of *Dokumenti I Materiali* [Documents and Materials] on Russian labor for 1800–1891, and she collected and published information throughout the 1950s on Russian strikes. Pankratova's collection and good use of rare sources give many of her works a lasting significance.

Dennis Reinhartz

Texts
Dvadstat piat let istoricheskoi nauki v SSSR [Twenty-Five Years of Historical Scholarship in the USSR]. Moscow: Akademii nauk Soiuza, 1942.
A History of the USSR. 2 vols. Moscow: Foreign Languages Publishing House, 1947.

References
Barber, John. *Soviet Historians in Crisis, 1928–1932.* New York: Holmes and Meier, 1981.
Mazour, Anatole G. *The Writing of History in the Soviet Union.* Stanford, CA: Hoover Institution Press, 1971.

Pannikar, Kavalam Madhava (1894–1963)

Indian journalist, administrator, diplomat, and prolific writer. Born in Kerala, south India, Pannikar was educated in Madras, and at Christ Church, Oxford. He studied law at the Middle Temple, London, and taught at Aligarh Muslim University (1919–1922). In 1922 he left academia for successive careers in journalism (1922–1928), administrative service with the Indian princely states (1928–1948), and, after 1947, in diplomacy. Pannikar was a pioneer in the writing of both historical and contemporary affairs from the Asian point of view, but he did so, as in *Asia and Western Dominance* (1959), while also giving full consideration to the impact of the West. He believed that the independence of southeast Asian nations depended on the freedom of India first. In addition to over twenty books on history, diplomacy, and current affairs, he wrote four novels, two plays, and four volumes of poetry in his native south Indian language of Malayalam, and two volumes of memoirs.

Roger D. Long

Texts
Asia and Western Dominance. London: Allen and Unwin, 1959.
An Autobiography. Madras: Oxford University Press, 1977.
The Foundations of New India. London: Allen and Unwin, 1963.
The Future of South-East Asia, an Indian View. New York: Macmillan, 1943.
A Survey of Indian History. London: Meridian Books, 1947.

References
Banerjee, Tarasankar. *Sardar K.M. Pannikar: The Profile of a Historian.* Calcutta: Ratna Prakashan, 1977.

Panofsky, Erwin (1892–1968)

Art historian. Trained at Freiburg University, Panofsky became professor of art history at Hamburg, where he collaborated with Aby Warburg and his institute. Dismissed from his post by the Nazis, Panofsky moved to the United States and, after teaching at New York and Princeton universities, joined the Institute for Advanced Study at Princeton. His considerable publications ranged widely covering architecture, painting, and sculpture from the Middle Ages to the baroque in Italy and northern Europe. Panofsky's best-known works include *Idea: A Concept in Art Theory* (1924), examining relations between the intellect and the sensory experience of art, and *Gothic Architecture and Scholasticism* (1951), investigating theology and architecture. Panofsky sought to develop an interpretive methodology that would apply to the subject matter of all works of art; one, moreover, that was scientific. He articulated this method in a 1939 essay, "Iconography and Iconology: An Introduction to the Study of Renaissance Art." Panofsky proposed three levels of interpretation of works of art to extract their meaning: the first, "preiconographical," based on practical experience; the second, "iconographical," based on culturally specific learned convention (stories, allegories); the third "iconological" level, more complex and less verifiable, required what he called the "synthetic intuition" of "essential tendencies in the human mind." His comprehensive *Early Netherlandish Painting* (1953) and *Meaning in the Visual Arts* (1955), a collection of essays, further demonstrate this approach. Although postmodern scholars have questioned the assumptions of universality that inform these studies, Panofsky's influence on iconographical interpretation has been profound. Similarly his *Renaissance and Renascences in Western Art* (1960) has left its mark on notions of periodization across disciplines.

Sheila ffolliott

Texts

Early Netherlandish Painting. Cambridge, MA: Harvard University Press, 1953.

Meaning in the Visual Arts. Garden City, NY: Doubleday, 1955.

Renaissance and Renascences in Western Art. Stockholm: Almquist and Wiksell, 1960.

Studies in Iconology: Humanistic Themes in the Art of the Renaissance. New York: Oxford University Press, 1939.

References

Holly, Michael Ann. *Panofsky and the Foundations of Art History.* Ithaca, NY: Cornell University Press, 1984.

Lavin, Irving. *Meaning in the Visual Arts: Views from the Outside: A Centennial Commemoration of Erwin Panofsky (1892–1968).* Princeton, NJ: Institute for Advanced Study, 1995.

Paparrigopoulos, Constantinos (1815–1891)

Modern Greek historian. Paparrigopoulos was born in Constantinople, but took refuge with his family in Odessa in 1821, following the Turks' execution of his father along with senior Greek clergymen and notables in reprisal for the outbreak of the Greek war of independence. In 1830 he followed his family to Athens, where he spent the rest of his life. In 1843 he published his first monograph *Peri tis epoikiseos slavikon tinon phylon eis tin Peloponnison* [On the Settlement of Certain Slavic Tribes in the Peloponnese], in which he combated the views of Jacob Philipp Fallmerayer, while the following year he published *To teleftaion etos tis ellinikis eleftherias* [The Last Year of Greek freedom], which focused on ancient Greece's conquest by the Romans in 146 B.C. He was awarded a doctorate in absentia by the University of Munich in 1850 and in March 1851 he was appointed professor of history at the University of Athens. Besides his academic career he played an active part in the cultural and political life of the country through his frequent appearances in the press, his involvement in literary associations, and his role as an authoritative spokesman for Greek irredentist aspirations.

Paparrigopoulos's fame and his place in the Greek intellectual tradition rest on his *Istoria tou ellinikou ethnous* [History of the Greek Nation]. In 1853 he had produced under that title a short survey addressed to children, which, however, found a wide popular audience. In 1860 he began writing his large-scale history, which appeared successively in five volumes between 1862 and 1875, with a sixth volume entitled, *Epilogos eis tin Istorian tou Ellinikou ethnous* [Epilogue to the History of the Greek Nation] (1877). A French adaptation of the *Epilogue* appeared in Paris as *Histoire de la civilisation hellénique* (1878). The second definitive edition of the *History* appeared in 1885–1887.

The *Istoria* is the most imposing synthesis in Greek historiography. Its style is marked by magnificence and serenity and its intention is clearly to win over rather than overwhelm the reader with grandiloquent oratory. The major historiographical influences on Paparrigopoulos's work emanated not from earlier modern Greek historiography but from the writings of major contemporary European historians, notably George Grote, Thomas Babington Macaulay, Johann Gustav Droysen, and François Guizot. Paparrigopoulos's basic tenet is the continuity and unity of Greek history over three millenia. A collective historical agent, the Greek nation, primarily defined by its language and culture, is seen as marching through three historical phases, antiquity, the mediaeval Byzantine millenium, and the modern period from the fall of Constantinople in 1453 to the reconquest of Greek freedom in the nineteenth century, toward the accomplishment of its civilizing mission in Eastern Europe and the Near East. By means of this theory Paparrigopoulos responded to profound ideological and psychological cravings associated with nation building in nineteenth-century Greece and provided a basis for the elaboration of Greek identity. A century after his death his historical doctrine remains the dominant framework for the self-definition of contemporary Greece.

Paschalis M. Kitromilides

Texts

Istoria tou Ellinikou ethnous. 5 vols. Athens: Ekdotikos Oikos "Eleftheroudakis," 1925–1932.

References

Dimaras C.Th. *Constantinos Paparrigopoulos.* Athens: Cultural Foundation of the National Bank of Greece, 1986.

Kontos, Demosthenes. "Konstantinos Paparrigopoulos and the Emergence of the Idea of a Greek Nation." Ph.D. dissertation, University of Cincinnati, 1986.

Papyrology

See EPIGRAPHY AND PAPYROLOGY.

Pararaton

Title of a Javanese prose work. The name translates as "The Book of Kings." The connection with kings is essential, as it refers to the rulers of the Singhasari-Majapahit dynasty, which ruled in Java in the later Hindu-Javanese period. The names Singhasari and Majapahit refer to the places in East Java where the capital was located. The text of the *Pararaton* is known from a number of palm-leaf manuscripts from Bali, although it was probably compiled in Java in the course of the fifteenth century. The language is Middle Javanese. The story focuses on the founder of the line, Ken Angrok, who defeated the king of Kadiri and set up a new capital at Tumapel (Singhasari) in A.D. 1222. The supernatural signs of Ken Angrok's power feature here. Details are given of his successors, including an extensive account of the foundation of Majapahit in 1293 by Raden Wijaya, following an invasion by the Mongols and the

death of Kertanagara, last king of Singhasari. The final section of the text consists of concise notes on the Majapahit royal family down to the traditional end of the period in 1478. The data provided are not always consistent with information from other sources, as the text is of a legendary nature and probably based on oral traditions.

Stuart Robson

See also BABAD; *DESAWARNANA*.

Paret, Peter (b. 1924)

American cultural and military historian. Paret was born in Berlin and came to the United States in 1937. He was educated at the University of California, Berkeley, and at King's College, London, where he obtained his Ph.D. (1960). He has held appointments at Princeton, the University of California, Davis, and Stanford University and is currently professor emeritus in the School of Historical Studies at the Institute for Advanced Study in Princeton, New Jersey, having retired in 1997. For a time, Paret wrote primarily on the history of war. His most important works in this field are *Yorck and the Era of Prussian Reform* (1966), *Clausewitz and the State* (1976), and a collection of essays, *Understanding War* (1992). Basic to these writings is their author's interest in war as part of general history. While stressing the centrality of conflict and death in the history of war, he has blended its study with the history of society, ideas, institutions, and politics, an interdisciplinary and comparative approach that is revealed with particular clarity in his biography of Clausewitz. Since the late 1970s, Paret has turned increasingly to cultural history, producing *The Berlin Secession* (1980), a pioneering study of arts organizations in Central Europe, and *Art As History* (1988), which illuminates the rise and decline of German liberalism from the perspective of images and literary texts. More recently he has published essays on the interpretation of war in art, a subject treated in greater detail in *Imagined Battles: Reflections on War in European Art.*

Karl W. Schweizer

Texts

Art As History: Episodes in the Culture and Politics of Nineteenth-Century Germany. Princeton, NJ: Princeton University Press, 1988.

Clausewitz and the State. Oxford: Oxford University Press, 1976.

Imagined Battles: Reflections on War in European Art. Chapel Hill: University of North Carolina Press, 1997.

P

Understanding War: Essays on Clausewitz and the History of Military Power. Princeton, NJ: Princeton University Press, 1992.

Yorck and the Era of Prussian Reform, 1807–1815. Princeton, NJ: Princeton University Press, 1966.

Paris, Matthew (ca. 1200–1259)

English medieval monastic historian. Paris lived and wrote at St. Albans, the Benedictine abbey, a day's ride from Westminster, which provided for England the most authoritative contemporary and continuing chronicle from the twelfth century to the fifteenth. His main work was to revise and continue this history and its derivatives. Through his own travels and many contacts, including Henry III and his officials, Paris was well-informed and accurate, compiling a collection of documentary sources, his *Liber additamentorum.* He expressed his strong opinions in colorful Latin. Paris was proud of his abbey and order. He compiled a domestic chronicle as well as composing hagiographical verses about its patron and a prose account of the founder, Offa. He wrote three other hagiographies in Anglo-Norman verse, on Edward the Confessor and archbishops Becket and Edmund Rich, and brief Latin lives of Rich and his predecessor Stephen Langton. Several autograph manuscripts survive, embellished with Paris's drawings and maps.

C.M.D. Crowder

Texts

Matthaei Parisiensis, monachi sancti Albani, chronica majora. Ed. H.R. Luard. Rolls Series, 57. 7 vols. London: Longmans, 1872–1884.

Chronicles of Matthew Paris: Monastic Life in the Thirteenth Century. Ed. and trans. Richard Vaughan. Gloucester: Alan Sutton; New York: St. Martin's Press, 1984.

Flores historiarum. Ed. H.R. Luard. Rolls Series, 95. 3 vols. London: HMSO, 1890.

Gesta abbatum monasterii Sancti Albani. Ed. H.T. Riley. Rolls Series, 28, pt. iv. 3 vols. London: Longmans Green, 1867–1869.

Historia Anglorum, including *Abbreviatio chronicorum.* Ed. F. Madden. 3 vols. Nedeln, Liechtenstein: Kraus Reprint, 1964–1971.

The Illustrated Chronicles of Matthew Paris. Ed. and trans. Richard Vaughan. Cambridge, Eng.: Corpus Christi College, 1993.

References

Vaughan, Richard. *Matthew Paris.* Cambridge, Eng.: Cambridge University Press, 1958.

Lewis, Suzanne. *The Art of Matthew Paris in the Chronica Majora.* Berkeley: University of California Press, 1987.

Parkman, Francis (1823–1893)

Historian of North America. Born in Boston, Parkman graduated from Harvard in 1844. He obtained a law degree from Harvard in 1846, but never sought admission to the bar. Fascinated with history, he devoted his life to recounting the clash between the British, French, and Indians in the North American wilderness. Parkman's accomplishments were remarkable, considering that he was virtually blind and suffered nervous disorders that at times made it difficult for him to write more than six lines a day. Nevertheless, in preparation for *The California and Oregon Trail* (1849), he retraced the steps of Lewis and Clark, lived for a few weeks with a band of Sioux, and observed hunters, trappers, and half-breeds. The first volume of his masterpiece was *History of the Conspiracy of Pontiac* (1851), followed by *Pioneers of France in the New World* (1865), *The Jesuits in North America* (1867), *The Discovery of the Great West* (1849; better known by the title of its eleventh, 1879, edition, *LaSalle and the Discovery of the Great West), The Old Regime in Canada* (1874), *Count Frontenac and New France under Louis XIV* (1877), *Montcalm and Wolfe* (1884), and *A Half-Century of Conflict* (1892). Told against a backdrop of wilderness and Indian "savages," this superb literary history clearly preferred the democratic, Anglo-Saxon Protestants to the authoritarian, French Catholics.

John W. Storey

Texts

Complete Works of Francis Parkman. 10 vols. Boston: Little, Brown, 1890.

References

Pease, O.A. *Parkman's History: The Historian As Literary Artist.* New Haven, CT: Yale University Press, 1953.

Wade, Mason. *Francis Parkman: Heroic Historian.* New York: Viking, 1942.

Parrington, Vernon Louis (1871–1929)

Historian of American literature and culture. Raised in rural Kansas, Parrington spent most of his professional life in institutions such as the College of

Emporia, the University of Oklahoma, and the University of Washington, remote from major centers of American intellectual activity. Although he never received a Ph.D., his studies for a baccalaureate at Harvard and a trip to Europe in 1903–1904, confirmed his enthusiasm for Victorian critics of industrialism, such as John Ruskin and William Morris. At first, he taught composition and courses in British literature, but after 1900, his interests shifted permanently to American literature considered within its social and political contexts. Except for "The Puritan Divines, 1620–1720," which appeared in *The Cambridge History of American Literature* (1917), Parrington published little before his famous trilogy, *Main Currents in American Thought*. The first two volumes appeared in 1927 and gained Parrington the Pulitzer Prize. The third volume was published posthumously in 1930. Although Parrington's specific readings of particular authors no longer command a following, he pointed toward the New Literary History through his interdisciplinarity and his use of the concept of culture to link literary, intellectual, and social history.

Ellen Nore

Texts

Main Currents in American Thought. 3 vols. New York: Harcourt, Brace, 1927–1930.

References

Hall, H. Lark. *V.L. Parrington: Through the Avenue of Art*. Kent, OH, and London: Kent State University Press, 1994.

Paruta, Paolo (1540–1598)

Venetian statesman, political philosopher, and historian. Renaissance Venice appointed a series of eminent intellectuals to the post of official historian of the city; Paruta was chosen in 1580. In his *Historia vinetiana* [Venetian History] he covered the period 1513–1551, and he also left a *Historia della guerra di Cipro* [History of the War of Cyprus], covering the events of 1569–1573. These and other works were published posthumously. As a historian, Paruta modeled himself on Francesco Guicciardini but did not rise to the same level of independent judgment, psychological insight, and narrative portrayal of the complex webs of causality underlying events. He wrote the political and military history of the interstate conflicts of the sixteenth century with a Venetian slant, and like Machiavelli and Guicciardini, treated politics as morally autonomous, not subject to religious or ethical idealism.

William McCuaig

Texts

Historia della guerra di Cipro. In *Degli istorici delle cose Veneziane*. Venice: Lovisa, 1718.
Historia vinetiana. Venice: D. Nicolini, 1605; and as vols. 3–4 of the collection *Degli istorici delle cose Veneziane*. Venice: Lovisa, 1718.

References

Cochrane, Eric. *Historians and Historiography in the Italian Renaissance*. Chicago: University of Chicago Press, 1981, 234–235, 334.

Pârvan, Vasile (1882–1927)

Romanian archaeologist and historian. Pârvan was born in Perchiu, a Moldavian village in Romania. After completing his education first in Romania and then in Germany, he became, in 1908, a professor of ancient history at the University of Bucharest. Although he was only forty-five years old when he died, he had already achieved an international reputation, in particular for his contribution to the early development of archaeological studies in Romania. He promoted the first great efforts in excavation and was a director of the National Museum, as well as a member of the Romanian Academy. In addition, he was a founder of the Institute of South East European Studies and of the Romanian School in Rome.

Pârvan's first major work was his dissertation (1908), written under the supervision of Conrad Cichorius, which concerned the nationality of merchants in the Roman Empire; this was followed by a study of the Roman emperor Marcus Aurelius (1909). He then published a number of groundbreaking studies of early civilization in Romanian territory, including some epigraphical contributions on the history of Christianity (1911) and a summary of research on early Roman life in the same area (1923). Pârvan's major work is the *Getica* (1926), the first synthesis of Romanian prehistory, in which he underlined the importance of the early civilizations that had arisen in the Danubian region before the Roman era. In the same year, he developed another synthesis of ancient history in a series of lectures delivered at Cambridge and London, and published in 1928 under the title *Dacia*. Pârvan was not only an erudite scholar, but also one with a great interest in the literary art of writing history. He was also highly sensitive to the ethical problems of his time and to questions within the philosophy of history.

His lectures in this latter field, published in 1920 as *Idei și forme istorice* [Historical Thoughts and Forms], and in 1923 as *Memoriale* [Memorials], won him great prestige among his students.

S. Lemny

Texts

Contribuții epigrafice la istoria creștinismului daco-roman. Bucharest: Atelierele Grafice, 1911.

Dacia: An Outline of the Early Civilisations of the Carpatho-Danubian Countries. Cambridge, Eng.: Cambridge University Press, 1928.

Getica: O protoistorie a Daciei. Ed. Radu Florescu. Bucharest: Editura Meridiane, 1982.

Inceputurile vieții romane la gurile Dunării. Ed. Radu Vulpe. Bucharest: Editura științifică, 1974.

M. Aurelius Verus Caesar si L. Aurelius Commodus A.D.138–161. Bucharest: Minerva, 1909.

Die Nationalität der Kaufleute im römischen Kaiserreiche. Breslau: Buchdruckerei H. Fleischmann, 1908.

Scrieri [Writings]. Ed. Al. Zub. Bucharest: Editura științifică și enciclopedică, 1981.

References

Childe, V. Gordon. *The Danube in Prehistory.* Oxford: Oxford University Press, 1929, 385–398.

Zub, Alexandru. *Les dilemmes d'un historien: Vasile Pârvan (1882–1927)* [The Dilemma of a Historian: Vasile Pârvan]. Bucharest: Editura științifică și enciclopedică, 1985.

Pasquier, Etienne (1529–1615)

Parisian Parlementaire, *politique,* and encyclopedic historian. For half a century, amidst ongoing political and religious conflicts, Etienne Pasquier advocated an archival and legal base to historical studies in France. He was an inveterate foe of the Jesuits, loyal supporter of the monarchy and Gallicanism, and, while a persistent opponent of the Huguenots, he opposed forced conversions. He served in the Parlement of Paris from 1549 to 1603. His *Les Recherches de la France* [Researches of France] reflects his engagement in contemporary affairs, the influence of legal humanism, proficiency in Renaissance philological methods, and French patriotism. Started in 1560 and appearing posthumously in 1621 in its final version of ten books, the work includes broad historical surveys of French laws and institutions, the Church, antiquities, and the French language. All things are treated as subjects for historical study, but Pasquier insisted that the pleasing (and frequently erroneous) narrative, literary mode of writing history be distinguished from the difficult task of researching, interpreting, and recounting the true past. During his life, Pasquier was a central figure in French letters, an avid correspondent, and a friend of the leading intellectual figure and author, Michel de Montaigne.

Lawrence M. Bryant

Texts

Les Recherches de la France. Paris: Pierre Menard, 1643.

References

Huppert, George. *The Idea of Perfect History: Historical Erudition and Historical Philosophy in Renaissance France.* Urbana: University of Illinois Press, 1970.

Kelley, Donald R. *Foundations of Modern Historical Scholarship: Language, Law, and History in the French Renaissance.* New York: Columbia University Press, 1970.

Schiffman, Zachary Sayre. "An Anatomy of Historical Revolution in Renaissance France." *Renaissance Quarterly* 42 (1989): 507–633.

Thickett, D. *Bibliographie des Oeuvres d'Estienne Pasquier.* Geneva: Librairie Droz, 1956.

Thickett, D. *Estienne Pasquier (1529–1615).* London: Regency Press, 1979.

Patočka, Jan (1907–1977)

Modern Czech philosopher of history, student of Husserl, and author of Czechoslovakia's Charter 77 of human rights. In *Platon a Evropa* [Plato and Europe] (1973), which originated as private lectures from the early 1970s, Patočka argued that spiritual Europe had been born with Plato's "care for the soul" and "life in truth," the free pursuit of truth through Platonic dialogues in the freedom of the Polis. In *Heretical Essays in the Philosophy of History* first published in samizdat (1975), Patočka asked the question "what is the meaning of history," and answered that history has no meaning because people do not care for it. Modernity, in his view, had destroyed medieval care for the soul and its political ideal of united Europe, the *sacrum imperium.* Scientism had led to the division and self-destruction of Europe. The experience of sacrifice might still lead communities whose everyday existence was shaken, like dissidents, to reach transcendence. In *Was sind die Tschechen* [What Are the Czechs?], Patočka divided nations into grand, guided by a transcendental vision, and petty. It was the pettiness of the Czechs that led to their defeats in the twentieth century.

Aviezer Tucker

Texts

Heretical Essays in the Philosophy of History. Trans. Erazim Kohak. Peru, IL: Open Court, 1996.
Was sind die Tschechen: Kleiner Tatsachenbericht und Erklärungsversuch. Prague: Panorama, 1992.
Note: Patočka's works have been published in Czech since 1990, and some exist in French translation. A German collected edition is in progress.

References

Tucker, Aviezer. "Shipwrecked: Patočka's Philosophy of Czech History." History and Theory 35 (1996): 196–216.

Patriarchy

Term referring either to a pattern of government by male heads of households or to a generalized system of male dominance over women. Pastoral or preindustrial societies are the setting for patriarchy in the first sense; the second is not specific in time (or place). Although both deal with the exercise of male power, they emphasize different aspects. Thus men's domination over women in the household is implied in the first form of patriarchy, but it is not so important as the dominance of older over younger men; conversely, men's domination over each other is acknowledged in the second, but it is not seen as centrally related to men's power over women.

The second usage—male dominance created in gender inequalities—is the more recent. It is associated with feminist initiatives in the social sciences from the 1960s onward and carries forward a commitment to understanding and subverting the sources of male power. It has been a keynote of women's studies. With the rise of men's studies, moreover, the notion of men moving "beyond patriarchy" is current. Patriarchy used in this sense has significant counterhegemonic content. It serves an analytical purpose similar to racism or capitalism. Research addresses the connections between, and differences in, the three systems of inequality (racism, capitalism, and patriarchy) as they have affected women.

The use of patriarchy to identify a system of obedience to the senior male originated in the mid-nineteenth century and was part of evolutionary ideas. It was seen as a temporally limited phenomenon existing before the institutionalization of modern law. In the early twentieth century Weber identified patriarchy as a system of organized domination prior to state formation. Critics of the later definition of patriarchy suggest that the precision of its earlier use has been dissipated. While its advocates concede to a tendency to ahistoricism, universalism, and essentialism, they point to the transhistorical character of some of the relations that support male dominance (biological reproduction and heterosexuality, for example) and indicate a growing body of research concerned with identifying differences in patriarchy by place and time.

Patriarchy in the second sense is the only term available to historians to identify the totality of relationships that privilege men over women. Recent research has concentrated on this usage. Its major aspects are considered to be in the mode of production, more specifically in the exclusion from, or segregation of, women in paid work; the state's exclusion of women from access to resources and power; male violence and the intimidation of women; sexual relations and the social arrangements in which they are embodied; and the bias of cultural institutions, notably the church and media.

Valerie Burton

See also CAPITALISM; ESSENTIALISM; FEMINISM; GENDER; WOMEN'S HISTORY.

References

Beechey, Veronica. "On Patriarchy." *Feminist Review* 3 (1979): 66–82.
Connell, R.W. *Gender and Power.* Cambridge, Eng.: Polity, 1987.
Eisenstein, Zillah R., ed. *Capitalist Patriarchy.* New York: Monthly Review Press, 1979.
Hooks, Bell. *Feminist Theory: From Margin to Centre.* Boston: South End Press, 1984.
Lerner, Gerda. *The Creation of Patriarchy.* New York: Oxford University Press, 1986.
Middleton, Chris. "Peasants, Patriarchy and the Feudal Mode of Production in England." *Sociological Review* 29 (1981): 105–154.
Mies, Maria. *Patriarchy and Accumulation on a World Scale: Women in the International Division of Labour.* London: Zed Books, 1986.
Walby, Sylvia. *Women and Social Theory.* Oxford: Basil Blackwell, 1989.
Weber, Max. *Economy and Society.* Trans. and ed. Guenther Roth and Claus Wittich. Berkeley: University of California Press, 1987.
Michael Kauffman, ed. *Beyond Patriarchy: Essays by Men on Pleasure, Power and Change.* Oxford: Oxford University Press, 1987.

Patrizi, Francesco (1529–1597)

Renaissance Italian philosopher, historian, and man of letters. Patrizi was born in Cherso in Istria and educated at Ingolstadt and Padua. Subsequently he moved to Venice where he served as secretary to various nobles; his responsibilities took him to places throughout the Venetian empire (including Cyprus where he perfected his Greek) and elsewhere on the Continent. Duke Alfonso II brought Patrizi to Ferrara in 1578 as professor of Platonic philosophy. Fourteen years later he was summoned by Pope Clement VIII to teach Platonism in Rome, a position he held until his death. In addition to many other works on literature, military matters, and philosophy, Patrizi had printed in Venice in 1560 his *Della historia diece dialoghi* [Ten Dialogues on History], an early exercise in the philosophy and methodology of history in which he argued for history's status as science rather than literature. It proved one of the more influential examples of the late Renaissance genre of *Artes Historicae* [Arts of History].

Kenneth Bartlett

Texts

Della historia diece dialoghi. Venetia: A. Arrivabene, 1560.

References

Donazzolo, P. "Francesco Patrizi di Cherso, erudito del secolo decimosesto, 1529–1597" [Francesco Patrizi of Cherso, a Scholar of the Sixteenth Century]. *Atti e memorie della Societa` Istriana di Archeologia e Storia Patria* [Transactions of the Istrian Society for National Archaeology and History] 28 (1912): 1–147.

Kristeller, P.O. "Francesco Patrizi." In his *Eight Philosophers of the Italian Renaissance.* Stanford, CA: Stanford University Press, 1964, 110–126.

Paul the Deacon [Paulus Diaconus] (ca. 720–ca. 799)

Lombard historian and biographer. Of noble birth, Paul was educated at the Lombard royal capital of Pavia and later entered the monastery of Monte Cassino. In about A.D. 770 he presented a continuation of the *Breviary* of Eutropius to the Duchess of Benevento. The date of his Life of Pope Gregory I is unknown. Although derivative, these works reflect an effort to understand the momentous changes in Italy between the fourth and sixth centuries. In the early 780s, Paul spent several years in Francia seeking pardon for his brother, punished by Charlemagne after a rebellion against Frankish rule. For Bishop Angilram of Metz, he produced the *Deeds of the Bishops of Metz* highlighting the life of saintly Bishop Arnulf, a Carolingian ancestor. His greatest work, the *History of the Lombards,* dates from after his return to Italy and appears to have been unfinished at the time of his death. Despite its reliance on several earlier works, the *History of the Lombards* presents information not otherwise attested and reveals its author's interest in the continuity of ethnic history even in a period marked by the universalist aspirations of the Carolingians. It had a wide circulation during the Middle Ages.

David F. Appleby

Texts

History of the Lombards. Trans. William Dudley Foulke; ed. Edward Peters. Philadelphia: University of Pennsylvania Press, 1974.

Liber de episcopis Mettensibus [Deeds of the Bishops of Metz]. Ed. G.H. Pertz. *Monumenta Germaniae historica, Scriptorum tomus II.* Stuttgart: Anton Hiersemann, 1976, 260–270.

References

Bullough, Donald A. *Carolingian Renewal: Sources and Heritage.* Manchester and New York: Manchester University Press, 1991.

Goffart, Walter. *The Narrators of Barbarian History (A.D. 550–800): Jordanes, Gregory of Tours, Bede, and Paul the Deacon.* Princeton, NJ: Princeton University Press, 1988.

Peçevi İbrahim (1574–1650)

Ottoman historian. Peçevi was born in Pecs in southwestern Hungary (whence Peçevi, or Peçuylu) into a family with a long tradition of Ottoman military service, particularly on the empire's western border in Bosnia. Through his mother he was related to the influential Sokollu family of viziers. His own official career was principally as a local *defterdar* (treasurer) during the 1620s and 1630s in various provincial cities. Retiring in 1641, Peçevi spent his remaining years in Buda, Hungary, continuing to write his history. The *Tarih-i Peçevi* [Peçevi's history] is a chronicle of Ottoman history from the accession of Suleiman the Magnificent to the death of Murad IV (i.e., 1520–1640) and is especially valuable for the period 1590–1632, for which the author had firsthand knowledge. His work includes much unique reportage, particularly from personal experience of the Hungarian and Bosnian frontiers. His views, often expressed quite forcefully, can offer a different perspective from the majority of contemporary Istanbul-based Ottoman histories.

Christine Woodhead

Texts

Tarih-i Peçevi. 2 vols. Istanbul: n.p., 1864–1866.
Tarih-i Peçevi. Ed. F.Ç. Derin and V. Çabuk. Istanbul: Enderun Kitabevi, 1980.

References

Ahmed Refik [Altınay]. *Alimler ve sanatkarlar*. Istanbul: Orhaniye Matbaası, 1924, 129–150.
Derin, F.Ç. and V. Çabuk. "Introduction" to their edition of *Tarih-i Peçevi*.

Pei Songzhi [P'ei Sung-chih] (A.D. 372–451)

Commentator on Chen Shou's *Sanguo zhi* [Records of the Three Kingdoms]. *Sanguo zhi*, the history of the kingdoms of Wei, Shu, and Wu during the interregnum between the fall of the Han dynasty in 220 and the beginning of the Jin dynasty in 265, had frequently been criticized for its lack of detail and its author's occasional oversights. Pei Songzhi's commentary was written on the order of Emperor Wen of Liu-Song to address these specific flaws. Completed in 429, Pei's commentary was unique in that virtually all citations in it were quoted in full. Thus the commentary tripled the length of *Sanguo zhi* and preserved many self-contained passages from the 159 sources Pei cited, almost all of which have since been lost. In his commentary, Pei typically consulted a variety of sources to check the factual accuracy of *Sanguo zhi* as well as its author's interpretation and evaluation of the events and personages of the Three Kingdoms. He would also flesh out the important details concerning an event or fill gaps in the lives of individuals. Because of its critical and complementary nature, Pei's commentary became an integral part of *Sanguo zhi* and is always included in printed editions of that work.

Yuet Keung Lo

Texts

Chen Shou. *Sanguo zhi* [Records of Three Kingdoms]. Beijing: Zhonghua shuju, 1959.

References

Li Zongye. *Zhongguo Lishi yaoji jieshao* [Introduction to Major Works of Chinese History]. Shanghai: Shanghai Guji chubanshe, 1982.
Shen Yue. "Biography of Pei Songzhi." In *Songshu* [Song History]. 8 vols. Beijing: Zhonghua shuju, 1974, vol. 6, pp. 1698–1709.

Pekař, Josef (1870–1937)

Czech historian. Pekař can probably be called the best Czech historian of the twentieth century—and also the most controversial. Although he was not a conventional Catholic (and was shunned by some of his coreligionists), he sympathized with those who had tried to better the image of their church in Czech history and historiography and often helped them, when he felt that historical facts had warranted it. Yet Pekař believed that it was not religion or philosophical ideas, such as humanism, but the very destiny of the Czech people and nation—however they had been perceived at various times—that formed the chief content of Czech history and gave it its true meaning. This he argued with a particular passion in his essay, *Smysl českých dějin* [The Meaning of Czech History] (1929), which was composed originally in 1912 in opposition to the philosophy of Tomáš G. Masaryk and his adherents. The controversies that he stirred up in this and other works proved to be as beneficial, as they were forceful, for the maturing process of modern Czech historiography. Pekař was often maligned for his views, but many of his points are now gaining acceptance, as demonstrated by both later historiography and frequent reprints of his works.

Pekař paid his greatest attention to the periods of the Middle Ages and the early modern era. In his first great historiographical battle, he challenged the established picture of early Christianity in the Czech lands by confirming the tenth-century origins of the legend of St. Wenceslas, as written by a monk called Christian, and elevating this to the rank of a reliable chronicle in his *Nejstarší kronika česká* [The Oldest Czech Chronicle] (1903). On the basis of this and similar studies, published subsequently, he produced a composite image of the saintly duke in his *Svatý Václav* [Saint Wenceslas] (1929–1932), which found a wide acceptance. But he encountered a massive opposition to his largest work, *Žižka a jeho doba* [Žižka and His Time] (1927–1933), which presented a largely negative picture of the military leader of the Hussites, the man who had rallied to the cause of the martyred religious reformer, Jan Hus, in the 1420s. Although Pekař praised the rectitude and fortitude of Hus himself (to the chagrin of the Catholic Church), he depicted the Hussite wars as a fanatical, fundamentalist holy war, characteristic of other religious wars, in which horrendous and massive cruelties had been committed on both sides, and which were largely counterproductive with regard to their original intentions and final results. In contrast to this work, his picture and story of Albrecht Wallenstein, the supreme commander of the Habsburg Empire in the Thirty Years' War, who was assassinated on the emperor's orders when their relationship had soured, *Valdštejn, 1630–1634: Dějiny valdštejnského spiknutí* [Wallenstein, 1630–1634: The History of Wallenstein's Conspiracy] (1933–1934) met with little controversy either at home or abroad, where it also appeared in a German translation; this was a much revised and enlarged reedition of his earliest major work (1895). But his essay *Bílá Hora: Její příčiny a následky* [White Mountain: Its Causes and Consequences] (1921) once again aroused a large section of his profession and of the general public by arguing ardently that the Battle of White Mountain (1620), in which Habsburg armies had defeated an ill-conceived and mismanaged rebellion of the non-Catholic nobility of Bohemia, was the product of domestic divisions and decay, but proved to be an impulse for national renovation rather than the traditionally perceived *temno* or "age of darkness."

Pekař was also a pioneer of modern economic and social history. He produced a model work on Czech agrarian history in the seventeenth and eighteenth centuries, based on a detailed study of land registers, *České katastry, 1654–1789* [Czech Cadastres, 1654–1789] (1932). His account of life on one Bohemian estate in those times, *Kniha o Kosti* [A Book of Kost] (1935), is one of the most valued books of Czech historiography, both for its scholarly and literary qualities.

Through his historical works and his frequent commentaries on contemporary events Pekař became a truly national figure and twice, in 1927 and 1935, received some consideration among conservative circles as a potential candidate for the presidency of Czechoslovakia, which he resolutely rejected.

Josef Anderle

Texts

Bílá Hora: Její příčiny a následky. Prague: Vesmír, 1921.
České katastry, 1654–1789. Second ed. Prague: Historický klub, 1932.
Kniha o Kosti. Second ed. Prague: Melantrich, 1935.
Nejstarší kronika česká. Prague: Bursík & Kohout, 1903.
Smysl českých dějin. Second ed. Prague: Nákladem vlastním, 1929.
Svatý Václav. Second ed. Prague: Vlastním nákladem, 1932.
Valdštejn, 1630–1634: Dějiny valdštejnského spiknutí. Second ed. 2 vols. Prague: Melantrich, 1933–1934.
Žižka a jeho doba. 4 vols. Prague: Vesmír, 1927–1933.

References

Hanzal, Josef. *Josef Pekař.* Prague: Mladá fronta, 1992.
"Josef Pekař." In *Přehledné dějiny českého a slovenského dějepisectví* [General History of Czech and Slovak Historiography], František Kutnar. Prague: Státní pedagogické nakladatelství, 1977, vol. 2, 100–110, et passim.
Kalista, Zdeněk. *Josef Pekař.* Parts 1 and 2. Prague: Školní nakladatelství, 1941. Part 3. Prague: Torst, 1994.

Periodization, As Historical Problem

Controversies concerning subdivisions in the continuum of historical time. The Italian poet Petrarch [Francesco Petrarca] (1304–1374) originated the modern European scheme of historical periodization when he lamented that a "dark age" separated antiquity from modernity—by which he meant an age that had lost the light of classical Latin eloquence. This aesthetic judgment inspired the tripartite division of historical time into the "ancient," "medieval," and "modern" periods. As this secular scheme supplanted Christian conceptions of universal history, the periods came to be subdivided—ancient into Greek and Roman; medieval into the early, high, and late Middle Ages; modern into Renaissance, Reformation, Baroque, and Enlightenment. Controversies arose, however, over attempts to define the cultural unity of each age and explain how one age evolved into the next.

The German philosopher Georg W.F. Hegel (1770–1831) attributed the unity of each age to a "world historical spirit" that permeated every aspect of its culture, and he described how one age evolved into another as this "spirit" became increasingly conscious of itself as a historical entity. In reaction to this quasi-theological scheme, Karl Marx (1818–1883) argued that the cultural unity of each age derived from the conditions of material life—that each mode of economic production generated a social division of labor, manifesting itself in political structures that, in turn, supported cultural superstructures. An age was thus defined by its economic and social relations, and one age evolved into another as these relations changed, generating new political organizations and cultural ideals.

The Swiss art historian Jacob Burckhardt (1818–1897) rejected these totalizing schemes (especially the Hegelian one) and in so doing pioneered the modern study of cultural history. Instead of attempting to chart the entire course of historical evolution, Burckhardt contented himself with describing the cultures of certain selected ages, the unity of each of which he sought in the analysis of its distinctive historical circumstances and cultural products. His masterwork, *Die Kultur der Renaissance in Italien* [The Civilization of the Renaissance in Italy] (1860), shows how every aspect of Renaissance culture shared the same central characteristics, born of the distinctive political realities of Italian city-state life. Thus, despite his rejection of philosophical schemes and his close attention to historical sources, Burckhardt implicitly retained the Hegelian notion of a spirit characterizing an age.

Twentieth-century scholars have rejected this notion, questioning both Burckhardt's interpretation of the Renaissance and his method of cultural periodization. They have progressively undermined his conception of the unity of the Renaissance by showing that many aspects of life in Italy remained unchanged from medieval times. In the wake of this criticism, scholars have tended to abandon periodization entirely, referring not to the Renaissance (for example) but to fifteenth-century Italy, or lumping Renaissance, Reformation, Baroque, and Enlightenment together to form an "early modern" period, defined by chronological rather than cultural criteria.

Recently, however, a countervailing tendency has emerged, a tendency that gives greater weight to the evidence of cultural unity in any given period. There is, for example, more in common aesthetically between sixteenth-century literary works as a whole, regardless of the language in which they are written, than between sixteenth-century French poetry and its nineteenth-century French counterpart. The same aesthetic quality that characterizes all sixteenth-century literature can also be attributed to other cultural products of the period. One means of explaining this unity—and of defending the concept of periodization—is through an analysis of cultural transmission, whereby specific individuals (poets, painters, and philosophers, for example) share similar ideas and sentiments by virtue of living in overlapping social circles. They exchange ideas either directly, by residing in close proximity or by traveling, or indirectly, through the dissemination of their ideas via intermediaries or in written form. Recent studies in the transmission and diffusion of style thus explain aspects of cultural unity, while avoiding the Burckhardtian (and, ultimately, Hegelian) tendency to isolate a defining characteristic that pervades every dimension of life in an age.

Zachary S. Schiffman

See also DECLINE; *KULTURGESCHICHTE;* RENAISSANCE, HISTORIOGRAPHY DURING; *ZEITGEIST.*

References

Gombrich, E.H. *In Search of Cultural History.* Oxford: Oxford University Press, 1969.
Kerrigan, William, and Braden, Gordon. *The Idea of the Renaissance.* Baltimore, MD: Johns Hopkins University Press, 1989.
Mommsen, Theodor E. "Petrarch's Conception of the 'Dark Ages.'" *Speculum* 17 (1942): 226–242.

Persian Historiography

Historical writing by and about the Persian people, their culture, and their rulers; principally written in the territories constituting modern-day Iran. Pre-Islamic Persia had a rich tradition of epic poetry such as the *Gathas,* most of which were preserved by memory for several centuries before they were written down. Iranian epics include the *Shāhname* (book of kings), which was first written down in New Persian (the Arabic-alphabet version of the Persian language, commonly used from the tenth century A.D.) and is still recited in the twentieth century. This may reflect a period as early as the time of the appearance of the prophet Zoroaster (ca. 1000 B.C.), whose precise dates are unknown. The *Shāhname* contains a great deal of information about Parthian, Achaemenid, and ancient Aryan times, though it is difficult to work out a precise chronology from these sources. There has been considerable debate as to the degree to which Persian epics are a record of "secular" as opposed to religious (Zoroastrian) history. The epics, systematized into a legendary history under the Sassanians (third to seventh centuries A.D.), present the ancient myths as history, without real chronology. Although valuable information on the Persians can be found in the works of Greek historians (most notably Herodotus), it is only with the Islamization of Iran that a Persian historiographical tradition developed. Until the Mongol invasion, Arabic was the language of choice for historians of Persia. Thus works on the early centuries of Islam in Iran by such figures as al-Ṭabarī and al-Bīrūnī were written in Arabic and followed the Islamic prototype of sacred world histories. In later periods, however, a historiographical tradition in Persian developed as Persianized Turkic dynasties came to realize the value of Persian as the cultural language of Islamic Iran.

Turkish dynasties, established in eastern Iran, were rapidly Persianized and adopted Persian culture and language. Under their tutelage new historical works appeared. The Persian translation of al-Ṭabarī's history by Bal'ami, which differs in many ways from the original, was carried out under the sponsorship of the Samanid dynasty, which also revived pre-Islamic Persian civilization. The *Shāhnāmeh* of Firdawsī belongs to this era, as do the large number of "mirrors for princes" writings composed to instruct the kings in the art of governance.

Under the Safavids, historiography took a new form as the longevity of the dynasty allowed for the composition of official histories. The best known work of this genre is the *Tā'rīkh-i 'Ālam-ārā-yi 'Abbāsī* [History of Shah 'Abbās] of Iskandar Beg Munshī, the chief secretary at the court of Shah 'Abbās. At the same time, however, despite the bureaucratic nature of the Safavid state, very few of the official documents of the period have survived, the Safavid archives having been destroyed in the aftermath of the Afghan invasion of 1722.

Despite the very valuable material provided by the chroniclers about the events at the court, this class of works typically contains scant information about the lives of ordinary Persians. The little that we know about common people and their habits and customs prior to the late nineteenth century comes from the accounts provided by European travelers who began visiting the Iranian court as early as the fifteenth century, first to form alliances against the Ottomans and later to establish commercial relations. In the nineteenth century the ranks of European visitors was swelled by missionaries and diplomats. Whereas some limited their observations to their own personal experiences, others such as Lord Curzon engaged in more systematic studies of the Iranian political, social, and economic systems. In general the observations made by the European visitors are biased against Islam and Iran. At the same time, however, they do provide important glimpses into the Iranian society prior to the contemporary era.

For the nineteenth century, we are also fortunate to have accounts of travels by Iranians both in various parts of their own country and abroad. The works written in the earlier half of the century by Iranians who visited Europe, mainly England, are particularly useful in providing important information about the general worldview of the elite and their opinions on both the West and Iran. These works were frequently written with the explicit objective of encouraging reforms based on the European model in Iran. The easily accessible style of the travel accounts made them so popular with the reading public that when Iran's first novel appeared at the end of the nineteenth century it was written as a fictional travel account.

The nineteenth and early twentieth centuries also witnessed the emergence of modern historical writings about Iran as European historians, later joined by their Iranian counterparts, began analyzing both contemporary events such as the Constitutional Revolution (1906–1907) and earlier Persian history. In this category special mention should be made of the British orientalist Edward Granville Browne (1862–1926) and the Iranian historian Aḥmad Kasravi (1890–1946).

Twentieth-century Iran has been the subject of numerous studies by both Iranian and Western historians. In general, however, these scholars have focused intensely on the Constitutional Revolution and the period after the abdication of Reza Shah (1941), leaving the decade between 1930 and 1940 as one of the least studied eras in Iranian history. It is only recently, as some official documents and personal memoirs have become available, that scholars have begun reexamining this period.

The study of modern Iranian history assumed a new importance after the Islamic revolution of 1978–1979, as scholars began to look for the roots of the movement that brought Ayatollah Khomeini to power. The large body of works, in both Persian and western languages, that have appeared since the revolution rely heavily on other secondary sources in addition to official documents, newspapers, and, more recently, memoirs of former officials and participants in the movement. Although disagreements abound as to the nature of the revolution, its causes and preconditions, the role of ideology and culture, involvement of foreign powers, and so on, these works represent the wide array of approaches to the study of social movements common in the social sciences and have made important contributions to the study of middle-eastern social history in general.

Hootan Shambayati

See also ARABIC HISTORIOGRAPHY.

References

Aryanpur, Manoochehr, with Abbas Aryanpur Kashani. *A History of Persian Literature.* Tehran: College of Translation, 1973.

Browne, Edward Granville. *A History of Persian Literature in Modern Times* (A.D. 1500– 1924). Cambridge, Eng.: Cambridge University press, 1924.

———. *A History of Persian Literature under Tartar Dominion* (A.D. 1265–1502). Cambridge, Eng.: Cambridge University Press, 1920.

Faruqi, Nisar Ahmed. *Early Muslim Historiography: A Study of Early Transmitters of Arab History from the Rise of Islam up to the End of the Umayyad Period, 612–750 A.D.* Delhi: Idarah-i Adabiyat-i Delli, 1979.

Khalidi, Tarif. *Arabic Historical Thought in the Classical Period.* Cambridge, Eng.: Cambridge University Press, 1994.

Spuler, Bertold. "The Evolution of Persian Historiography." In *Historians of the Middle East,* ed. Bernard Lewis and P.M. Holt. London: Oxford University Press, 1962, 126–132.

Rosenthal, Franz. *A History of Muslim Historiography.* Leiden: E.J. Brill, 1968.

Waldman, Marilyn Robinson. *Toward a Theory of Historical Narrative: A Case Study in Perso-Islamicate Historiography.* Columbus: Ohio State University Press, 1980.

Pessen, Edward (1920–1992)

Historian of the United States. Born to a family of working-class Jewish immigrants in New York City, Pessen served in the army during World War II and completed his undergraduate education (1947) and his Ph.D. (1954) at Columbia University. He taught at a variety of universities, ending his career as distinguished professor of history at the graduate school of the City University of New York. One of the founders of the Society for Historians of the Early American Republic, he served as its president in 1985–1986. Pessen's scholarship questioned the positive view of the Age of Jackson found in works by Arthur M. Schlesinger Jr. and Robert Remini. His many publications included three notable books: *Most Uncommon Jacksonians: The Radical Leaders of the Early Labor Movement* (1967), *Jacksonian America: Society, Personality, and Politics* (1969); and *Riches, Class and Power before the Civil War* (1973). In these works, Pessen argued that Jacksonian politicians operated in a milieu of striking social inequality, human exploitation, and moral depravity. His posthumously published *Losing Our Souls* (1993) asked readers to judge policymakers by their deeds and not by their professed purposes.

Ellen Nore

Texts

"A Young Industrial Worker in Early World War II in New York City." *Labor History* 22 (1981): 269–281.

"History over the Years: To Continue or Not to Continue: A Cliophile's Early Crisis." *Organization of American Historians Newsletter* 16 (1988): 3–27.

Jacksonian America: Society, Personality, and Politics. Revised ed. Homewood, IL: Dorsey Press, 1978.

Losing Our Souls: The American Experience in the Cold War. Chicago: I.R. Dee, 1993.

Most Uncommon Jacksonians: The Radical Leaders of the Early Labor Movement. Albany: State University of New York Press, 1967.

Riches, Class and Power before the Civil War. Lexington, MA: D.C. Heath, 1973.

"Those Marvelous Depression Years: Reminiscences of the Big Apple." *New York History* 62 (1981): 188–200.

References

"The Egalitarian Myth: A Forum." *Social Science History* 5 (1981): 223–234; 6 (1982): 111–128; 6 (1982): 369–384; 6 (1982): 381–384.

"Forum: Social Structure and Politics in American History." *American Historical Review* 87 (1982): 1290–1341.

Kohl, Lawrence, and Johanna Shields. "Edward Pessen." *Journal of the Early Republic* 13 (1993): 76–78.

Petrarch [Francesco Petrarca] (1304–1374)

Italian lyric poet and first Renaissance humanist. Petrarch was born in Arezzo, grew up in Avignon (1311), and studied law at Montpellier and Bologna. In 1326, he joined the papal court in Avignon, taking minor orders. Petrarch traveled throughout Europe, and studied classical Latin, seeking proof for the links between classical culture and Christian teachings. Petrarch ventured in 1361 to Padua and then, in 1362, to Venice. He died in Arqua while working with a Virgil manuscript. Petrarch was noted for reviving an interesting classical learning producing a "rebirth," or renaissance, especially in writing poetry, which was to mark him as the father of Renaissance humanism. In 1340, he was offered the position of poet laureate in both Paris and Rome and accepted the Roman post in 1341. In addition to his vernacular *Canzoniere* (love poems dedicated to a woman named Laura, who died in the plague of 1348), Petrarch wrote a variety of works in a Latin closely modeled on ancient Roman stylists like Livy and Cicero. He wrote no history as such, but his *De Viris Illustribus* (lives of famous Romans completed after his death by a disciple Lombardo della Seta) would prove an influential model for later Renaissance biography; *Africa,* a posthumously published

P

epic poem retelling the Second Punic War was also a widely read treatment of a major episode in ancient history. His true influence on Renaissance historical thought, however, came in his realization of the gap that existed between his own time and antiquity, which had become separated by a *medium aevum* (middle age) marked by debased Latin. He endeavored in various ways to bridge this gap and restore ancient standards of literature; in *De Vita Solitaria* [On the Contemplative Life], completed in 1346, classical heroes mingle with churchly figures. It was this sense of period, and a related awareness of linguistic anachronism, that would influence later and more learned quattrocento humanists, such as Lorenzo Valla and Angelo Poliziano, to seek out original ancient manuscripts in the custody of the religious houses and to study ancient and patristic works with an acute attention to the problem of textual corruption, which occurred as medieval authors miscopied, either deliberately or unintentionally, their ancient sources.

Barbara Bennett Peterson

Texts

Africa. Ed. and trans. T.G. Bergin and Alice S. Wilson. New Haven, CT: Yale University Press, 1977.

De viris illustribus. Ed. Guido Martellotti. Florence: Sansoni, 1964.

De vita solitaria. Ed. Marco Noce. Milan: Mondadori, 1992.

Petrarch's Selected Sonnets, Odes and Letters. Ed. T.G. Bergin. New York: Appleton-Century-Crofts, 1966.

References

Cochrane, Eric. *Historians and Historiography in the Italian Renaissance.* Chicago: University of Chicago Press, 1981.

Kennedy, William J. *Authorizing Petrarch.* Ithaca, NY: Cornell University Press, 1994.

Tatham, E.H.R. *Francesco Petrarca: The First Modern Man of Letters.* London: Sheldon Press, 1925.

Petri, Olaus [Swedish: Olof Petersson] (1493–1552)

Reformation author and politician. After attending the University of Uppsala, Petri studied from 1516 to 1518 under Martin Luther in Wittenberg, then returned home to preach Lutheran reform. When Gustav Vasa became king in 1523, Petri became secretary to the city council of Stockholm, preacher in Stockholm cathedral, and, from 1531

to 1533, royal chancellor. A prolific writer, he translated Lutheran pamphlets, wrote hymns, contributed to the New Testament in Swedish, and produced Lutheran liturgical and homiletical works for the reformed Church of Sweden. His earthy, direct, and witty prose helped to shape the modern Swedish language. During the 1530s, he wrote a chronicle of Swedish history, *En Swensk Crönika,* in a blunt and critical vein. In contrast to his near contemporaries, Johannes and Olaus Magnus, Petri threw out the old legends of Gothic antiquity and Viking heroism to emphasize the slow growth of a Christian national culture. His refusal to write royal historical propaganda angered King Gustav. When his chronicle circulated in manuscript, Olaus Petri was sentenced to death but then was reprieved, fined, and eventually restored to favor.

J.R. Christianson

Texts

Olai Petri Svenskakronika. Ed. G.E. Klemming. Stockholm: H. Klemming, 1860.

References

Bergendoff, Conrad. *Olavus Petri and the Ecclesiastical Transformation in Sweden (1521–1552): A Study in the Swedish Reformation.* New York: Macmillan, 1928.

Johannesson, Kurt. *The Renaissance of the Goths in Sixteenth-Century Sweden: Johannes and Olaus Magnus As Politicians and Historians.* Ed. and trans. James Larson. Berkeley: University of California Press, 1991.

Philology

The science of textual criticism. Philology has a long history, originating in antiquity and culminating in the nineteenth century, when it attained its greatest precision. But the formative period in the development of this science was during the Renaissance, when philology established itself as an independent undertaking, after having served as the handmaiden of the humanist movement. Renaissance philology had profound consequences for the development of both modern historical consciousness and modern historical scholarship.

Humanists from Petrarch [Francesco Petrarca] (1304–1374) onward hoped to resurrect classical culture by restoring classical language and literature to their original purity. They thus expended great effort in searching for manuscripts of classical texts, comparing different copies of the same works in order to assemble more accurate classical editions, purged of scribal errors. In these editorial efforts, however, philology remained subordinate to the rhetorical goal of the humanist movement.

Lorenzo Valla (1407–1457) established philology's independence from rhetoric. He is best known for demonstrating that the "Donation of Constantine" was not a fourth-century text but a later forgery. He used internal and external modes of criticism, showing that the text was not written in fourth-century Latin and that its claims were controverted by historical evidence from the period. In Valla's hands, however, philology remained an art rather than a science, based more on inspired intuition than systematic technique.

Philology did not emerge as a science until the end of the fifteenth century, when the establishment of public libraries enabled scholars to consult manuscripts with ease, and when the spread of printing made it possible to secure each new advance in textual criticism. The first great figure in this science was Angelo Poliziano (1454–1494), who established a series of logical techniques for the explication and emendation of texts. These techniques were further elaborated in the sixteenth century by scholars like Guillaume Budé, Desiderius Erasmus, and Joseph Justus Scaliger.

These scholars anticipated some of the basic principles of later philological and historical scholarship. Regarding the internal criticism of a text, they inferred that its existing manuscripts descended from an archetype and that later manuscripts were less trustworthy than earlier ones. Regarding external criticism, they ranked corroborating documents according to their chronological proximity to the text under consideration. Their techniques of internal criticism laid the foundation for advances in nineteenth-century philology, which was able to establish the manuscript genealogy of a text with accuracy, from which the archetype could be reconstructed. And their techniques of external criticism heralded the distinction between primary and secondary sources, which is the hallmark of modern historical scholarship.

Renaissance philology undermined the goal of the humanist movement that had fostered it. Instead of facilitating the revival of classical culture, philology demonstrated that the ancient world was the product of unique historical circumstances. This perception of the historicity of antiquity is philology's greatest contribution to the development of modern historical consciousness. And this awareness is itself the byproduct of advances in scholarly techniques that helped establish the modern discipline of history.

Zachary S. Schiffman

See also ANACHRONISM; ANTIQUARIANISM; *MOS GALLICUS* AND *MOS ITALICUS;* PALEOGRAPHY AND DIPLOMATIC; RENAISSANCE, HISTORIOGRAPHY DURING.

References

Grafton, Anthony. *Joseph Scaliger.* Vol. 1. Oxford: Oxford University Press, 1983.

Kelley, Donald R. *Foundations of Modern Historical Scholarship.* New York: Columbia University Press, 1970.

Pfeiffer, Rudolf. *History of Classical Scholarship from the Beginning to the End of the Hellenistic Age.* Oxford: Clarendon Press, 1968.

———. *History of Classical Scholarship from 1300 to 1850.* Oxford: Clarendon Press, 1976.

Reynolds, L.D., and G.N. Wilson. *Scribes and Scholars.* Oxford: Oxford University Press, 1974.

Wilamovitz-Moellendorf, Ulrich von. *History of Classical Scholarship.* Trans. A. Harris. London: Duckworth, 1982.

Philosophy of History—Analytical

The metadisciplinary discussion of what can be known about history (past events) and what kind of knowledge is offered by historiography, the writings of historians *about* the past; in particular, an analysis of historiographic language and concepts such as objectivity, explanation, understanding, and causation. Until the late 1960s, the development of analytical philosophy of history had reflected developments in the philosophy of science, concentrating on formal analysis of historiographic language and concepts. One of the initial incentives for the development of analytical philosophy of historiography was the examination of the logical-positivist unified model of scientific knowledge. Historical writing seemed to pose the greatest challenge to this model. The clarification of the various similarities or differences between historiography, the social sciences, the natural sciences, and literature was the central task of analytical philosophy of history.

Analytical philosophies of history (in the sense of historiography rather than of "the past") can be classified according to their description and/or prescription of historiographic knowledge, how they envision the relation between historiographic knowledge and other kinds of knowledge, scientific, artistic, and so on, and the content they give to those similarities or dissimilarities. Traditionally, those holding that historiography is and should be a branch of the sciences are called *positivists.* Those upholding the descriptive and normative autonomy of historiography are variously called *humanists* or *idealists.* During "the golden age" of analytical philosophy of history from the 1930s to the 1960s, both positivists and humanists assumed in their arguments about objectivity and explanation the now defunct logical-positivist model of science.

Discussion of *objectivity* began with the naive conviction of the disciples of Ranke that historians can reach scientific standards of objectivity, when they can tell "just what happened," as this slogan (nearly always taken out of context) suggested. The humanists attempted to prove that historians cannot be "scientifically" objective because historians must make cultural or aesthetic value judgments, for example in selecting which events to mention in historiographic accounts and which to leave out. The humanists claimed that historians often make value judgments to distinguish conditions (that can be sufficient, necessary, or neither) of an event from its cause(s). Historiographic language, they argued, is imbued with value judgments. The positivists answered that all forms of enquiry including the scientific one are selective; there are "objective" criteria for distinguishing causes from conditions through conceptual analysis of the terms and comparison situations; value-imbued historiography can be translated into value-neutral language; and that the humanists themselves were bringing forward exceptional examples of bad historiography to support their claims.

The argument reached an impasse when each side was able to interpret the other side's evidence according to its thesis. Then, during the 1960s, philosophy of science discovered that the natural sciences themselves had been far less "objective" than was assumed by the positivists and the whole argument became obsolete. The humanists were right in their objection to positivist "objectivity." The positivists were right in claiming there is no clear line of demarcation between historiographic "subjectivity" and scientific "objectivity." The old dogma of empiricism that it is possible to differentiate "objective" observation from "subjective" evaluations passed away, and eventually took with it the analytical, as distinct from historiographic, argument about historiographic objectivity.

The argument about historiographic *explanation* began with Hempel's positivist formal model of universal explanation based on covering laws, applicable to all fields of knowledge, including historiography. Simply put, Hempel has claimed—with increasing sophistication since his

1942 essay "The Function of General Laws in History"—that if one event explains another, there must be some kind of covering law that connects them. Facing protests from historians, the positivists had to concede that historians are not conscious of any general laws of history. These laws may be trivial, learned from common sense; or probabilistic; or they may be simply statistical generalizations, leading to incomplete explanatory sketches. Historians rarely suggest sufficient causes. Usually, they propose necessary causes that are neither necessary nor sufficient. The hidden prescriptive element in the positivist account of explanation assumed that historians are bad scientists who should attempt to conform better to the one and only model of explanation.

The humanists objected to the covering law model of historiographic explanation. Most historical events are unique. *Unique* events cannot be subjected to generalizations or laws. So, either the positivist model of explanation is right, and historiographic explanation is impossible; or the positivist model is wrong. The humanists opted for the second and proposed alternative models of explanation. The positivists answered that in a sense all events are unique. Science treats unique events as complex combinations of repetitive elements governed by many laws. Accordingly, historians should explain unique complexes of repetitive events by referring to many laws. Some humanists suggested that at times historiography explained action by referring to its *rationality;* or by re-creating *emphatically* the thought process of the historical actors, as R.G. Collingwood suggested. To this the positivists replied that reasons are dispositions to action that explain actions in conjunction with covering laws and initial conditions.

The impasse in the argument ended with the demise of positivism and its model of explanation in the philosophy of science. Most postpositivist models of explanation hold that the structure of explanation is identical in all branches of knowledge. The difference lies in the degree of *confirmability* of these explanations. Since historiography does not have confirmed theories, it can neither explain scientifically, nor offer insights into the nature of explanation for philosophers of explanation. This led to a loss of interest in historiography on the part of analytical philosophers.

A related dispute arose between methodological individualism and holism. Should the units of historiographic analysis and explanation be groups or individuals? While this argument continues today vigorously in the philosophy of the social sciences, a consensus has emerged in philosophy of historiography, one which distinguishes metaphysical individualism (the reducibility of groups to individuals) from epistemic holism (the possibility of analyzing and explaining groups rather than individuals).

The last classical analytical enquiry is the study of historiography as a narrative. The narrativists (W.B. Gallie, Arthur Danto, Morton White, and Louis O. Mink) pointed out that histories are stories, with a beginning, a middle, and an end. In good narratives each part of the story leads to its end. Accordingly, historiographic selection of items and description of events refers to their future effects. Danto analyzed the language of historiography into *narrative sentences* that refer to at least two time-separated events but describe only the earlier event. For example, "the Velvet Revolution began with the student demonstrations in Prague on November 17, 1989." Historiographic narratives change with reinterpretation of the past in reference to events that happen later. Some claimed that a narrative by itself is a form of explanation, others pointed out that a narrative is a context for explaining why, of all the available alternatives, a historical actor chose one option. Critiques of narrative philosophy of historiography argued that historiographic accounts are not necessarily narratives and asked for clarification of the relation between historiographic narratives and the historical past, through historical evidence, raising the question of historical realism and truth. While analytical philosophers of historiography ran into increasing problems here, continental narrativists in a sense "bit the bullet" and disconnected historiography from history.

The analytical humanist narrativists hoped to defend the autonomy of historiography from both science and art. However, the continental nonanalytical philosophical tradition, closely affiliated with literary criticism, hermeneutics, structuralism, poststructuralism, and finally postmodernism, proved to be more fruitful and appropriate for the study of narratives. Contemporary discussion of historiographic narratives is now mostly rhetorical, seeing historiography as art.

Since the demise of logical-positivist philosophy of science in the 1960s, there has been a slow but steady decline in interest and research in analytical philosophy of history. The contents of the principal periodical devoted to critical philosophy of historiography, *History and Theory,* demonstrate the steady decline of analytical philosophy of history and its replacement by continental literary theories, represented in the work of Paul Ricoeur, Mink, and Hayden White. More recently, there have been attempts to apply the achievements of postpositivistic philosophy of science to the understanding of historiography. Historiography is as theoretical as science, although unlike science there are many coexisting, incommensurable, and unconfirmed historiographic paradigms, associated with "schools." Historiography thus shares its features with other disciplines whose theories are either too vague to be confirmable or have an insufficient unique positive confirming case. Whatever future analytical philosophy of historiography may have, it is likely to be based on applying the achievements of philosophy of science since the demise of logical positivism to the understanding of historiographic knowledge.

Aviezer Tucker

See also CAUSATION; COLLIGATION; CONTINGENCY; COUNTERFACTUALS; COVERING LAWS; DETERMINISM; DRAY, WILLIAM H.; FACT; PHILOSOPHY OF HISTORY—SUBSTANTIVE; SCIENTIFIC HISTORY.

Texts

Danto, Arthur C. *Narration and Knowledge.* New York: Columbia University Press, 1985.

Dray, William H., ed. *Philosophical Analysis and History.* New York: Harper and Row, 1966.

———. *Philosophy of History.* Englewood Cliffs, NJ: Prentice Hall, 1993.

Gardiner Patrick L. *Theories of History.* New York: Free Press, 1959.

History and Theory. (A scholarly journal devoted to philosophy of history, this has appeared since 1961, and includes periodic bibliographies of works in the philosophy of history.)

Mandelbaum, Maurice. *The Anatomy of Historical Knowledge.* Baltimore, MD: Johns Hopkins University Press, 1977.

Murphey, Murray. *Foundations of Historical Knowledge.* Albany, NY: SUNY Press, 1994.

———. *Our Knowledge of the Historical Past.* Indianapolis, IN: Bobbs-Merrill, 1973.

Tucker, Aviezer. "A Theory of Historiography As a Pre-Science." *Studies in History and Philosophy of Science* 23 (1993): 633–667.

White, Morton. *Foundations of Historical Knowledge.* Westport, CT: Greenwood Press, 1965.

Philosophy of History—Substantive

Insightful and inspired models of the whole of history. Substantive philosophy of history ideally has three defining characteristics: it presents a unifying descriptive model of what is assumed as the whole of significant history; that model explains historical change; and the model is projected into the future to suggest the meaning of history. Pure substantive philosophies of history, for example Karl Marx's, satisfy all three requirements. Take the Marxist statement "All history is the history of class struggle": Marxian substantive philosophy of history provides a unifying descriptive model of this history; the Marxian model attempts to explain all historical change as the evolution of class structures; and the model is projected into the future to predict the end of history in a classless society.

Ordinary historiography has none of these characteristics. Between the opposite poles of pure substantive philosophy of history and ordinary historiography there is a continuum of theories of history that satisfy to a greater or lesser degree the three conditions. For example, pure cyclical substantive philosophies of history lack meaning, although they offer a descriptive-explanatory model for the whole of history. Substantive philosophies of history are far more vague and general than ordinary historiography, and they consequently cannot be applied to concrete historical cases without interpretation. Had all historians been able to interpret a substantive philosophy of history identically and apply it successfully to, or deduce from it, the description, explanation, and prediction of the phenomena they study, that substantive philosophy of history would have become *the* scientific theory of history. Despite some hopes and expectations in this direction during the eighteenth and nineteenth centuries, there has never been such a scientific theory/substantive philosophy of history. Instead, ordinary historians who attempt to apply substantive philosophies of history must interpret them differently to fit their subject matter.

Similar in this respect to artistic insightful interpretations of the world, substantive philosophy of history does not have a corresponding relationship with history: it is either too vague to be confirmable or has insufficient positive instances for confirmation. Substantive philosophy of history is valuable in offering insightful answers to the quest for the meaning of history, unlike ordinary historiography. It is frequently asserted that substantive philosophy of history ended with Arnold Toynbee. Jan Patočka suggested in 1975 that history has no meaning because people have stopped looking for meaning in history. Yet the continuous interest in substantive philosophy of history and the introduction of new substantive philosophies of history in every generation, despite their methodological shortcomings, provides testimony to the continuous engagement of historical consciousness in the most seminal human questions: Where are we coming from? Where are we going to? What does it all mean?

By positing a teleological purpose to history, substantive philosophy of history provides a measure to gauge the meaning of historical events. If we know where we are going—the end of the historical narrative—then we can understand the meaning of the past and the present. Questions of historical destiny are most likely to be raised during periods of radical historical change. It is no coincidence that such changes tend to be accompanied by the introduction of new substantial philosophies of history that embody the ethos of the era. A few examples will illustrate this point: the decline of the Roman Empire and Augustine; the decline of the Arab empires and Ibn Khaldūn; the Enlightenment and Immanuel Kant; Romanticism and Johann Gottfried Herder; the French Revolution and the rise of nationalism and G.W.F. Hegel; the industrial revolution and Karl Marx; the advance of science and Auguste Comte, Herbert Spencer, and J.S. Mill; the post–World War I demise of the German empires, the crisis of modernity and cultural pessimism, and Oswald Spengler; the fall of the British Empire and Arnold Toynbee; the loss of U.S. world economic hegemony and Paul Kennedy; and the end of the cold war and Francis Fukuyama.

There are many possible classifications of substantive philosophies of history: religious versus secular; "scientific" versus metaphysical; "empirical" versus a priori; patterns versus laws versus trends; cyclical versus linear. The discussion of questions of common human destiny unfolding in time has religious roots. Most religious substantive philosophies of history combine a theodicy, a justification of God in history, and eschatology, assumption of the end of history. In the Old Testament book of Judges, history is presented as cyclical, with no eschatology. The tribes of Israel sin, and God sends a foreign oppressor; The Israelites repent and cry to God for salvation, and God sends them a judge or prophet who unites the tribes to fight the oppressor; the people are saved and live righteously for a time under the leadership of the judge; then they sin again, and so on. Later Judeo-Christian substantive philosophy of history has been linear, attributing to history definite stages from the creation of Adam and Eve to the kingdom of God. In the Old Testament, each stage, the creation, the fall, the flood, the divine choice of Abraham, the ten commandments, is accompanied by a testament, a treaty between God and a biblical protagonist, and is irreversible. Post-biblical Judaism added the messiah as the terminator of history through a series of apocalyptic wars and disasters, leading to the salvation of the righteous and the damnation of sinners and to a kingdom of God. Christianity interpreted Jesus as the messiah. Following the crucifixion and resurrection of Jesus, history will go on for a "millennium" until the second coming of Christ, Judgment Day, and the advent of the kingdom of God. Augustine (412–426) would further develop this scheme, dividing universal history into eight stages: from Adam to Noah, to Abraham, to king David, to the exile of Israel in Babylon, to the birth of Jesus. Following Augustine's own (sixth) age, a seventh "sabbatical" age lasting a millennium would be followed by the return of Jesus and the kingdom of God. Each stage prepares humanity for the next one, leading to the final readiness to accept the return of Jesus and the kingdom of God.

In Giambattista Vico's spiraling model of history (early eighteenth century), the cyclical *recourse* serves the linear *course* of history. To be receptive to Christianity, Roman civilization had to revert to barbarism. Arnold Toynbee (1934–1954) also posed a religious end as the purpose of a spiraling model of history, a universal religion. Some substantive philosophies of history include secularized versions of the religious schemes. Hegel's Reason is also God, and it justifies the course of history as leading to freedom and self-consciousness of the spirit. Marx, in turn, secularized the linear eschatological Judeo-Christian scheme of history. The fall became for him the appearance of private property, while Marx himself and the proletariat replaced the prophets and the chosen people, and the revolution and classless society supplanted Judgment Day and the kingdom of God. Most recently, Francis Fukuyama (1992) interpreted Hegel's linear eschatology as leading to liberal democracy as "the kingdom of God" and the "end of history."

While there has never actually been a scientific substantive philosophy of history, several substantive philosophies of history at least appeared to their proponents to be scientific. Auguste Comte developed an eschatology leading to the advent of positivism and sociology as a science of history. John Stuart Mill believed that the development of a science of history might parallel the development of physics, with initial empirical generalizations (paralleling Kepler) eventually being deduced from the general laws of human nature (paralleling Newton). Some Marxists conceived of Marx as that Newton of history. Oswald Spengler perceived himself as a biologist of cultures, while Toynbee was perceived as an "empiricist."

Substantive philosophies of history may be optimistic (progressive, evolutionary) or pessimistic (devolutionary), depending on the direction of history from the philosopher's point of view. Optimists include the Judeo-Christians, Augustine, Kant, Hegel, Marx, Toynbee, and Fukuyama. Among the pessimists are Ibn Khaldūn, Spengler (and his generation of European cultural pessimists), Martin Heidegger, Jan Patočka, and Paul Kennedy.

It is often difficult to classify substantive philosophies of history according to their historical determinism or indeterminism. As the analytical critics of substantive philosophy of history have pointed out, the very publication of historical predictions allows people to defy them. Still, it seems that most substantive philosophies of history are indeterminist, giving conditional predictions, based on artistic insights.

Aviezer Tucker

See also CHAOS THEORY AND HISTORY; CHRISTIANITY, VIEWS OF HISTORY IN; CONTINGENCY; DETERMINISM; PHILOSOPHY OF HISTORY—ANALYTICAL; SPENGLER, OSWALD; TIME; TOYNBEE, ARNOLD JOSEPH.

Texts

Augustine, Saint. *The City of God against the Pagans.* Trans. G.E. McCracken et al. Cambridge, MA: Harvard University Press, 1957.

Fukuyama, Francis. *The End of History and the Last Man.* New York: Free Press, 1992.

Hegel, Georg Wilhelm Friedrich. *The Philosophy of History.* Ed. J. Sibree; trans. C.J. Friedrich. Magnolia, MA: Peter Smith, 1970.

Ibn Khaldūn. *The Muqaddimah: An Introduction to History.* Ed. N.J. Dawood; trans. F. Rosenthal. Princeton, NJ: Princeton University Press, 1967.

Kant, Immanuel. *On History.* Ed. and trans. L.W. Beck et al. New York: Macmillan, 1963.

Kennedy, Paul M. *The Rise and Fall of the Great Powers: Economic Change and Military Conflict from 1500 to 2000.* London: Fontana Press, 1989.

Patočka, Jan. *Essais heretiques sur la philosophy de l'histoire* [Heretical Essays on the Philosophy of History]. Trans. E. Abrams (from Czech into French). Paris: Editions Verdier, 1981.

Spengler, Oswald. *The Decline of the West.* New York: Knopf, 1926.

Toynbee, Arnold J. *A Study of History.* Oxford: Oxford University Press, 1935–1961.

Vico, Giambattista. *The New Science of Giambattista Vico.* Trans. T.G. Bergin and M. Fisch. Ithaca, NY: Cornell University Press, 1984.

References

Fain, Haskel. *Between Philosophy and History: The Resurrection of Speculative Philosophy of History within the Analytic Tradition.* Princeton, NJ: Princeton University Press, 1970.

Mazlish, Bruce. *The Riddle of History: The Great Speculators from Vico to Freud.* New York: Harper and Row, 1966.

Photographs—Historical Analysis of

The use of photographs as historical evidence. Since its development in 1839, photography has produced a new and rapidly increasing information source for historians. These visual records are especially valuable for many historical issues and topics of the last one hundred years; historical photographs can be analyzed by a number of methods, most of which were initially developed by social scientists and have been adapted by historians.

Beginning in the days of the Crimean and U.S. civil wars, photographs increasingly became a popular medium; technological developments since 1888 greatly expanded the number of photographers and photographs. During the twentieth century, amateur and professional photographers have produced a prodigious visual record of the ordinary and extraordinary. While such traditional historical sources as diaries and personal letters declined in quantity during the twentieth century, photographs, snapshots, and family photograph albums became commonplace; these materials provide social historians interested in ordinary people with access to their lives and to the larger context for those lives. At the same time, in modern societies photographs increasingly came to reflect and to represent important cultural images and symbols.

Traditionally, historians have used photographs for illustrations only; Ralph Henry Gabriel's fifteen-volume *Pageant of America* (1926–1929) was one of the first works to use photographic illustrations extensively. There are also substantial literatures on the history of photography, on individual photographers, and on each photographic genre or type of photograph. These works provide important contextual information necessary to analyze photographs for content or meaning.

One approach to historical photoanalysis utilizes photographs to demonstrate historical changes. This rather straightforward method has been successfully applied by Harold Mayer and Richard Wade in *Chicago* (1969) and by Walter Rundell Jr. in *Early Texas Oil* (1977) to show respectively the changing urban landscape and the growth of an industry. In contrast, William Frassanito's *Antietam* (1978) used historical photographs to reconstruct accurately the sequence of events of this Civil War battle.

Other historians have applied social science methods to historical photographs in order to reveal the social history of ordinary people. These methods are especially valuable for identifying data on behavior, cultural patterns, and material culture from photographs; they can also help in the process of interviewing subjects for oral history. They can greatly aid studies of topics that have limited print sources but for which photographs are abundant. In a study of poor, rural African-American migrants in Washington, D.C., James Borchert overcame limited print sources by analyzing six hundred historical photographs taken by photojournalists, housing reformers, documentary photographers, and government agency photographers. With other data, the analysis documented the physical landscape and how it was used and shaped by its residents. In a social and cultural history of black San Francisco, Douglas Daniels found photographs more common than written material; he also reported improved oral histories when he interviewed with photographs. In both studies, photographs helped reveal African Americans as actors in history, not just as victims or subjects.

Another group of historians has drawn on social science insights for the study of myth and symbol. Michael Lesy used photographs from several large collections made by professional photographers to reveal the psychological state of residents in two communities; his alterations of photographs in the text remains highly controversial, however. In contrast, Alan Trachtenberg's *Reading American Photographs* (1989), identifies the political content in the work of such notable photographers as Mathew Brady, Lewis Hine, and Walker Evans. While using their work to define themselves and their art, those photographers also helped shape and define the nation's images.

Several caveats need mentioning here. As yet, few historians have used the massive numbers of "vernacular photographs" or snapshots taken by ordinary people during the last one hundred years, although social scientists have methods to analyze these materials. Photographs, as the photographers who take them, are influenced by a range of cultural factors; researchers need to take these as well as the technological possibilities and limitations of the medium into account. Finally, archives are only beginning to collect vernacular photographs; most still catalog them by photographer or collector rather than by subject.

James Borchert

See also ARCHIVES; ART AS HISTORICAL EVIDENCE; FILM AND HISTORY; MUSEUMS.

References

Borchert, James. *Alley Life in Washington.* Urbana: University of Illinois Press, 1980.
———. "Analysis of Historical Photographs." *Studies in Visual Communication* 7 (1981): 30–63.
———. "Historical Photo-Analysis." *Historical Methods* 15 (1982): 35–44.
Collier, John, Jr., and Malcolm Collier. *Visual Anthropology.* Albuquerque: University of New Mexico Press, 1986.
Daniels, Douglas. *Pioneer Urbanites.* Philadelphia: Temple University Press, 1980.
Frassanito, William. *Antietam.* New York: Charles Scribner's Sons, 1978.
Lesy, Michael. *Wisconsin Death Trip.* New York: Pantheon Books, 1973.
Lesy, Michael. *Real Life.* New York: Pantheon Books, 1976.
Mayer, Harold, and Richard Wade. *Chicago.* Chicago, University of Chicago Press, 1969.
Rundell, Walter, Jr. *Early Texas Oil.* College Station: Texas A & M University Press, 1977.
Trachtenberg, Alan. *Reading American Photographs.* New York: Hill and Wang, 1989.
Wagner, Jon, ed. *Images of Information.* Beverly Hills: Sage Publications, 1979.

Phrantzes, George (1401–1478)

Byzantine historian. Phrantzes (or Sphrantzes) pursued a distinguished political and diplomatic career at Constantinople and Mistra in the period of the last three Palaeologi. Following imprisonment, after the capture of Constantinople in 1453, Phrantzes escaped to Corfu, where he lived out his life as the monk Gregory. Phrantzes's autobiography, composed at Corfu, known as the *Chronicon Minus* to distinguish it from its expansion the *Chronicon Maius,* written by Makarios Melissenos, the metropolitan of Monembasia in the sixteenth century, provides an eyewitness account of the events of 1413 to 1477. Totally eschewing rhetoric and sophisticated digression, written in vernacular Greek, and providing factual and chronological accuracy, Phrantzes's work provides a fundamentally sound description of Byzantine court life—of its intrigues, foreign and domestic policy, internal dissension, and ultimate collapse. Marked, moreover, by exaggerated praise of the Palaeologi, hatred of political rivals and of the Ottomans, devotion to Orthodoxy and disdain for the Latins, it regards the Union of the Churches at Florence as a major diplomatic error and very definitely a factor in the fall of Byzantium.

Lionel J. Sanders

Texts

The Fall of the Byzantine Empire: A Chronicle by George Sphrantzes, 1401–77. Trans. Marios Philippides. Amherst: Massachusetts University Press, 1980.
Giorgi Sfranze Cronica. Trans. R. Maisano (into Italian). Rome: Accademia Nationale Lincei, 1990.

References

Carroll, Margaret G. *A Contemporary Greek Source for the Siege of Constantinople: The Sphrantzes Chronicle.* Amsterdam: A.M. Hakkert, 1985.

Piccolomini, Enea Silvio [Pope Pius II] (1405–1464)

Renaissance Italian humanist and pope. A humanist whose early support for the schismatic Council of Basel did not prevent his election as pope in 1458, Piccolomini was a member of a prominent Sienese family. He pursued the varied and peripatetic career typical of the early humanists, serving various ecclesiastical and political masters across Europe, including anti-Pope Felix V and Holy Roman emperor Frederick III (who crowned him poet laureate), before joining the papal curia in 1446. His historical works were largely polemical and include brief classically inspired biographical portraits of his contemporaries, the *De Viris Illustribus* [Concerning Famous Men] (1440–1450); a history of the Council of Basel; several extended histories oriented to winning Germans back to the papal party, the *Germania* (1457), *Historia Friderici III* (1458), *Historia Bohemica* (1458); and the wide-ranging, unfinished *Cosmographia,* which united geography with universal history. He is perhaps best known for his autobiography, the

Commentarii, first published in 1584, which he began after his elevation to the pontificate, and which contains a frank account of the politics that marked that election. Neither modest nor reserved, it aggressively promoted both its author and papal interests in Italian and European politics, and remains the only extant papal autobiography.

Nicholas Terpstra

Texts

Memoirs of a Renaissance Pope: The Commentaries of Pius II. Ed. L.C. Gabel; trans. F.A. Gragg. New York: Capricorn Books, 1962.
Opera Omnia [Complete Works]. Frankfurt: Minerva, 1967.

References

Cochrane, Eric. *Historians and Historiography in the Italian Renaissance.* Chicago: University of Chicago Press, 1981, 45–47.

Pieri, Piero (1893–1979)

Italian military historian. Pieri was born at Sondrio and studied under Gaetano Salvemini at the Scuola Normale Superiore di Pisa. During World War I he served as an officer in the Alpine Corps and was twice decorated with the Medal of Valor. His academic career began at the University of Naples (1922–1935) and ended at the University of Turin (1935–1963). A product of late-nineteenth- and early-twentieth-century Italian nationalism, Pieri had a comprehensive interest in the military history of Italy. He was influenced by the military writings of Machiavelli, Montecuccoli, Palmieri, and Carlo Pisacane. Over fifty years he produced a prolific flow of articles, monographs, and biographies of Italian military leaders, theorists of the art of war, and strategists covering the period from Roman history to the First World War. Pieri's most important writings are *Il Rinascimento e la crisi militare italiana* [The Renaissance and the Italian Military Crisis] (1952) and *A Military History of the Risorgimento: War and Insurrection* (1962). Both are regarded as classic studies of their respective periods. His *L'Italia nella Prima Guerra Mondiale* [Italy in World War I] (1965) remains one of the most important works on that subject. Pieri's interests in other periods of Italian military history and in great captains of Italian heritage are found throughout his long career, in books on subjects such as Julius Caesar, Augustus Caesar, Napoleon, and Garibaldi.

Norman Tobias

Texts

L'Italia nella Prima Guerra Mondiale. Turin: Einaudi, 1971.
Napoleone. Turin: Gherone, 1963.
Il Rinascimento e la crisi militare italiana. Turin: Einaudi, 1952.
Storia militare del Risorgimento: Guerre e insurrezioni. Turin: Einaudi, 1962.

References

Ropp, Theodore. *War in the Modern World.* Durham, NC: Duke University Press, 1959.
Salomone, A. William. "Italy." In *International Handbook of Historical Studies: Contemporary Research and Theory,* ed. Georg G. Iggers and H.T. Parker. Westport, CT: Greenwood Press, 1980, 233–251.

Pinto, Fernão Mendes (early sixteenth century–1583)

Portuguese soldier, diplomat, traveler, adventurer, and Jesuit. Pinto, a man of many facets, is a major figure in the sixteenth-century Portuguese expansion across the Asian seas. Born to a simple family in Montemor o Novo, he probably traveled to India in 1537. On reaching the Orient, he began travels in Asia, which took him from Ethiopia and Malacca to Sumatra, China, and Japan. His mainly factual account of the dizzying sequence of events and journeys he experienced is contained in the *Peregrinação* [Peregrination], written in Portugal, to which he returned in 1558 and where he died in 1583. Pinto's work, with its satirical, picaresque view of the motives which lay behind the official Portuguese expansion in the Orient, is regarded as unique in the field of Portuguese travel literature.

Jorge M. dos Santos Alves

Texts

The Travels of Fernão Mendes Pinto. Ed. and trans. Rebecca Catz. Chicago: University of Chicago Press, 1989.

References

Lach, Donald F. *Asia in the Making of Europe.* Vol. III, book I. Chicago: University of Chicago Press, 1993.
Correia, João David Pinto. *A Peregrinação de Fernão Mendes Pinto.* Lisbon: Seara Nova, 1983.

Pirenne, Henri (1862–1935)

Belgian medieval historian. Long associated with the University of Ghent where he taught, Pirenne was at first well known in his own country as a historian of Belgium, which had only recently won its independence from the Netherlands. He wrote a number of books on Belgian history, but it was his seven-volume *Histoire de la Belgique,* completed in 1932, that solidified his position as Belgium's finest historian. Historians of the Middle Ages, however, know Pirenne principally for the "Pirenne thesis," his revision of the early medieval period that described the process whereby Germanic and Islamic invaders replaced Roman authority in western Europe. First suggested in print in 1922, the "Pirenne thesis" reached thousands of undergraduates in his *Medieval Cities* (1925) and in the more specialized work completed just months before his death, *Mohammed and Charlemagne* (1937). Pirenne's thesis was that, contrary to the eighteenth-century historian Edward Gibbon, a magnificent Roman civilization had *not* been overthrown by barbarian invaders from Germany in the fourth and fifth centuries. The Germanic tribes perpetuated Roman culture, he argued, and it was the Islamic invasions of the seventh and eight centuries that finally brought about the end of the classical world. In perhaps the most oft-quoted passage from *Mohammed and Charlemagne,* Pirenne concluded that "it is therefore strictly correct to say that without Mohammed Charlemagne would have been inconceivable." The thesis been both criticized and defended ever since, yet any discussion of the boundaries between the ancient and medieval worlds must still begin with Pirenne.

Mack P. Holt

Texts

Belgian Democracy: Its Early History. Trans. James V. Saunders. London and New York: Longmans, Green and Co., 1915.

Economic and Social History of Medieval Europe. Trans. I.E. Clegg. New York: Harcourt, Brace, 1956.

History of Europe from the Invasions to the Sixteenth Century. Trans. Bernard Miall. New York: University Books, 1955.

Medieval Cities: Their Origins and the Revival of Trade. Trans. Frank D. Halsey. Princeton, NJ: Princeton University Press, 1974.

Mohammed and Charlemagne. Trans. Bernard Miall. New York: Norton, 1939.

References

Havighurst, Alfred E. *The Pirenne Thesis: Analysis, Criticism, and Revision.* Boston: D.C. Heath, 1958.

Hodges, Richard, and David Whitehouse. *Mohammed, Charlemegne and the Origins of Europe: Archaeology and the Pirenne Thesis.* Ithaca, NY: Cornell University Press, 1983.

Lyon, Bryce. *Henri Pirenne: A Biographical and Intellectual Study.* Ghent: E. Story-Scientia, 1964.

Platina [Sacchi], Bartolomeo (1421–1481)

Renaissance curial humanist. Born into a moderately prosperous family in Piadena near Cremona, Platina studied humanities in Mantua and Florence and went to Rome in 1461. A member of Pomponio Leto's Academy, Platina was imprisoned by Pope Paul II on the suspicion of republican conspiracy, but regained favor with Sixtus IV, who appointed him librarian of the Vatican Library. Besides some political treatises, Platina wrote a *Historia urbis Mantuae* [History of the City of Mantua] (1469). He became famous with his *Liber de vita Christi et omnium Pontificum* [Life of Christ and of All the Popes] (1475), a humanist elaboration of medieval sources, namely the *Liber Pontificalis,* Ptolemy of Lucca and Piccolomini's *Epitome* of Flavio Biondo's *Decades.* First printed in 1479, Platina's collection of biographies of the popes was often reprinted, abridged, and copied and was continued several times and translated into many languages. The frank narration and sometimes critical account (not only about Paul II) made church history for the first time a part of secular history. It was very popular throughout the sixteenth century and widely used by Protestant opponents of the curia too.

Thomas Maissen

Texts

Liber de vita Christi et omnium Pontificum. Ed. Giacinto Gaeda. *Rerum Italicarum Scriptores,* new series, vol. 3, part 1. Città di Castello: S. Lapi, 1913.

References

Campana, Augusto, and Paola Medioli Masotti, eds. *Bartolomeo Sacchi il Platina.* Padua: Antenore, 1986.

Platonov, Sergei Fedorovich (1860–1933)

Russian historian. Platonov was the most eminent historian of Russia between the death of V.O. Kliuchevskii in 1911 and the formation of orthodox Soviet historiography. Platonov combined the best features of the source-oriented St. Petersburg tradition with the breadth of vision of the Muscovite school of Russian history. The heart of his scholarly work was the era from 1598 to 1613, known as the "Time of Troubles," or *Smuta*. Platonov viewed it as a seminal period in Russian development. It was an extraordinarily chaotic era of civil unrest, foreign invasion, and political machinations, rendering lucid historical analysis extremely difficult. In his view, the *Smuta* was a threefold crisis composed of mutually reinforcing social, national, and dynastic dimensions. In its clarity, depth, flexibility, and national sensitivity, this interpretation was typical of Platonov's work as a whole. Characteristically, he also published several volumes of primary sources, related to the *Smuta*. As the leading historian of Russia in his day, and one blessed with a beautiful Russian style, Platonov was central to the creation of the next generation of Russian historians through his courses, textbooks, monographic studies, and handbooks. Unfortunately, his historical legacy suffered a severe rupture when he and a number of other prominent historians and social scientists were arrested on trumped up charges in October 1929. It is an ironic testimony to his prominence that the arrests are informally known as the "Platonov affair." These arrests and others that followed were part of the Stalinist campaign against all independent centers, in this case the professoriate and the Academy of Sciences. From a longer perspective, the affair can be seen as a traditional Muscovite assault on rival centers of Russian thought and interpreters of Russian history, especially in the northwest (Novgorod and St. Petersburg). Banished to Samrara, Platonov died of heart failure due to complications induced by the harsh conditions of his arrest and exile.

Unable to create their own historiographical tradition out of their thin cloth, the Stalinists turned perforce to the Russian prerevolutionary historical legacy. In 1937, the worst year of the purges, Platonov's four-volume history of the Time of Troubles was reissued. More telling still, the Communist Party's Higher School of Propagandists (later renamed the Higher Party School) printed a thousand copies of Platonov's manual of Russian history that same year. As archival material becomes available with the collapse of the Soviet Union, it will be worth investigating what direct influence Platonov's schema had on Soviet historians. However that may be, there is a strong similarity between his pragmatic, yet nationalist, positivism and the source-oriented, limited-range Marxist interpretive analyses of P.A. Zaionchkovskii and other Soviet historians of Russia. Even in death, Platonov continued to influence historical interpretation.

T. Sanders

Texts

History of Russia. Bloomington, IN: University Prints and Reprints, 1964.

Time of Troubles. Lawrence: University of Kansas, 1970.

References

Alexander, John T. "S.F. Platonov: Eminence and Obscurity." In *Boris Godunov, Tsar of Russia,* trans. L. Rex Pyles. Gulf Breeze, FL: Academic International Press, 1973, ix–xl.

Richard Hellie. "In Search of Ivan the Terrible." In *Ivan the Terrible.* Gulf Breeze, FL: Academic International Press, 1974.

———. "Sergei Fedorovich Platonov." In *Modern Encyclopedia of Russian and Soviet History,* ed. J.L. Wieczynski. 58 vols. Gulf Breeze, FL: Academic International Press, 1976–1994, vol. 28 (1982), 112–117.

Plekhanov, Georgii Valentinovich (1856–1918)

The "father of Russian Marxism" and Russian social historian. Plekhanov abandoned his studies at a mining institute in 1877 to work for a populist revolutionary group. Disappointed with the responses of peasants, he became a Marxist. He lived in Switzerland from 1880 to 1917. In 1883, he formed the Emancipation of Labor Group to spread Marxist ideas, and in 1898, he helped to found the Russian Social Democratic Labour Party. Eventually he broke with Lenin and the Bolsheviks. He interpreted Russia as being a kind of semi-oriental despotism, the result of economic backwardness and political insecurity, with a feeble urban and commercial life. His multivolume *History of Russian Social Thought* was never completed. He returned to Russia after the October Revolution, of which he disapproved, but he had virtually no influence on the events transpiring there.

Elizabeth V. Haigh

Texts

Art and Social Life. Ed. Andrew Rothstein. London: Lawrence & Wishart, 1953.

Fundamental Problems of Marxism [With an appendix of his essays: *The Materialist Conception of History; The Role of the*

Individual in History]. Trans. Julius Katzer; ed. V.A. Fomina. London: Lawrence & Wishart, 1969.

History of Russian Social Thought. Trans. B. Bekkar et al. New York: H. Fertig, 1967.

Selected Philosophical Works. Moscow: Foreign Languages Publishing House, 1961–.

Sochineniia [Collected Works]. 24 vols. Moscow: Gosudart stvennoe izdat el'stvo, 1923–1927.

References

Baron, Samuel H. *Plekhanov in Russian History and Soviet Historiography.* Pittsburgh, PA: University of Pittsburgh Press, 1995.

———. *Plekhanov: The Father of Russian Marxism.* Stanford, CA: Stanford University Press, 1963.

Plucknett, Theodore Frank Thomas (1897–1965)

English legal historian. Plucknett was educated at the University of London and Cambridge University. He began a long sojourn at Harvard in 1921, first as a student and later as a faculty member. He returned to England in 1931 to occupy the first position in legal history in England at the London School of Economics, where he remained for the rest of his academic career. He also served as the literary director of the Selden Society from 1937 to 1963 and as president of the Royal Historical Society from 1948 to 1952. Plucknett's goals in utilizing legal records were essentially historical: he sought to draw a sharp picture of medieval society based on its legal technicalities. With this goal in mind, he broke down the barriers between fields of legal history and the other specialties of the discipline, most noticeably economic and political history. Unlike F.W. Maitland, his great late Victorian predecessor, Plucknett saw historians, rather than lawyers, as those best equipped to do legal history. As he wrote in 1958, "to make legal history the preserve of professional lawyers is indeed to condemn it to extinction." His three most important works all bear witness to his historical focus. His *Concise History of the Common Law* (1929), which was dictated in a few weeks, remained for decades, and through five editions, the standard history for students and scholars. More significant for weighing Plucknett's importance are his *Legislation of Edward I* (1949) and *Early English Legal Literature* (1958). The first, originally his Ford lectures at Oxford, emphasizes through a close analysis of the earliest common law statutes that both disciplines, law and history, were required to

understand these peculiar acts of legislation. The second, also beginning its life as a series of lectures, examines the interplay of textbooks and the education of those involved in the law in the development of legal principles. Again, the concern is to understand not simply the text but the total context of legal sources. Plucknett had as significant an impact on historical studies through his work as an editor, editing or assisting completion of over twenty volumes for the Selden Society, usually without title-page credit. His vision of the immense value of these and all English legal records to historians continues to direct work on the history of the common law and so remains his legacy to the discipline.

Bruce R. O'Brien

Texts

A Concise History of the Common Law. Fifth ed. London: Butterworth, 1956.

Early English Legal Literature. Cambridge, Eng.: Cambridge University Press, 1958.

Edward I and the Criminal Law. Cambridge, Eng.: Cambridge University Press, 1960.

Legislation of Edward I. Oxford: Oxford University Press, 1949.

Studies in English Legal History. London: Hambledon Press, 1983.

References

Milsom, S.F.C. "T.F.T. Plucknett, 1897–1965." *Proceedings of the British Academy* 51 (1965): 505–519.

Plumb, Sir John Harold (b. 1911)

British historian of eighteenth-century England. Plumb was born in Leicester and educated at Cambridge, where his doctorate (1936) was supervised by G.M. Trevelyan. After war service as an intelligence analyst, Plumb rose from lecturer to professor of modern English history at Cambridge between 1946 and 1974 and was subsequently master of Christ's College, Cambridge, 1978 to 1982. Plumb also held visiting professorships at American universities. He was knighted in 1982. Specializing in eighteenth-century British political history, Plumb was both a serious researcher and a popularizer. His major scholarly works were *Sir Robert Walpole* (1956–1960) and *The Growth of Political Stability in England: 1675–1725* (1967). Plumb's textbook, *England in the Eighteenth Century* (1950), was frequently reprinted, and he wrote many popular and accessible books on subjects as far afield as the Italian Renaissance.

In his most controversial publication, *The Death of the Past* (1969), Plumb condemned the ideological use of history. He urged professional historians to write authoritative, unbiased works—not just for themselves but also for the educated public.

Don M. Cregier

Texts

The Death of the Past. Boston: Houghton Mifflin, 1969.

The Growth of Political Stability in England: 1675–1725. London: Macmillan, 1967.

Sir Robert Walpole. 2 vols. London: Cresset Press, 1956–1960.

References

Braddock, Robert C. "J.H. Plumb and the Whig Tradition." In *Recent Historians of Great Britain: Essays on the Post-1945 Generation,* ed. Walter L. Arnstein. Ames: Iowa State University, 1990, 101–120.

McKendrick, Neil. "J.H. Plumb: A Valedictory Tribute." In *Historical Perspectives: Studies in Thought and Society in Honour of J.H. Plumb,* ed. Neil McKendrick. London: Europa Publications, 1974, 1–18; 302–306.

Plutarch (ca. 45–ca. 123)

Greek biographer and essayist. Born at Chaeroneia and educated in Athens, Plutarch was a priest at Delphi and sometime ambassador and lecturer on philosophy at Rome. He became a Roman citizen early in life and was later honored by the emperor Trajan (98–117). Astonishingly erudite, if unoriginal, he composed more than a hundred works. Of these, *The Parallel Lives,* comparative biographies of important Greek and Roman political figures, are essential historical sources, although they must be consulted with care. Plutarch selected, arranged, and adapted his material to illustrate his subject's character and historical role, with historical accuracy only a secondary concern. Widely read in the Middle Ages and the Renaissance (in a famous French translation by Jacques Amyot that was in turn translated into English and other languages), his *Lives* proved an important model for biographical writing.

Thomas P. Hillman

Texts

Plutarch's Lives. 3 vols. London: Heinemann, 1967–1975.

References

Pelling, C.B.R. "Plutarch's Adaptation of His Source Material." *Journal of Hellenic Studies* 100 (1980): 127–140.

Stadter, Philip A. *A Commentary on Plutarch's Pericles.* Chapel Hill: University of North Carolina Press, 1989.

———. *Plutarch's Historical Methods: An Analysis of the Mulierum Virtutes.* Cambridge, MA: Harvard University Press, 1965.

Pocock, John Greville Agard (b. 1924)

Historian of political thought and discourse. Pocock was born in London but grew up in New Zealand. He received his B.A. in 1945 and his M.A. in 1946 from the University of New Zealand, his Ph.D. (under the direction of Herbert Butterfield and J.H. Plumb) at the University of Cambridge in 1952, and an honorary Litt.D. from Cambridge in 1972. He was professor of political science at the University of Canterbury (1959–1965); the William Eliot Smith professor of history, Washington University in St. Louis (1966–1974); and the Harry C. Black professor of history, Johns Hopkins University (1974–1994). In 1969, he helped found the Conference for the study of Political Thought and, in 1982, the Folger Institute Center for the History of British Political Thought. Pocock's histories of discursive traditions helped transform the history of political thought into the history of discourse, contributing to a general rethinking of intellectual history in the Anglo-American world. He studied paradigmatic language traditions that evolve, converge, and transform across centuries and continents. He exemplified his theoretical assumptions in a number of places, most cogently in the introduction to his collection of essays, *Virtue, Commerce and History,* and incorporated them into his two major historical works. In the first of these, *The Ancient Constitution and the Feudal Law,* Pocock examined the interplay between politics and history among seventeenth-century English common lawyers and antiquarians. He identified and established the significance of the "common law mind" and the language of custom that shaped both parliamentarian and royalist thought throughout the century. He also rescued from near obscurity, redefined, and demonstrated the importance of republican thinker James Harrington (whose political works he later edited) and elucidated the work of lesser-known authors such as Dr. Robert Brady. Pocock also pointed out John Locke's unique indifference to the most common language traditions of his time, historical argument and customary law, suggesting a reappraisal of Locke's constitutional legacy in the eighteenth century. In *The Machiavellian Moment,* Pocock described the evolution of the language of civic humanism in the early modern Western world. He charted the transformation of the republican ideal, with its participating, civic-minded citizens, from sixteenth-century Florence, where it was most radically articulated by Machiavelli, to pre-1660 England, where Harrington and others incorporated within it an agrarian ideal of private property. In the Augustan age, the civic humanist tradition was used to temper the most corrupting elements of the new commercial wealth. Across the Atlantic, Pocock asserted, this humanist republican legacy was as important to the founders of the American republic as Lockean constitutionalism.

Melinda Zook

Texts

The Ancient Constitution and the Feudal Law: A Study of English Historical Thought in the Seventeenth Century: A Reissue with a Retrospect. Cambridge, Eng.: Cambridge University Press, 1987.

The Machiavellian Moment: Florentine Political Thought and the Atlantic Republican Tradition. Princeton, NJ: Princeton University Press, 1975.

Ed. *The Political Works of James Harrington.* Cambridge, MA: Cambridge University Press, 1977.

Politics, Language and Time: Essays in Political Thought and History. New York: Atheneum, 1971.

Virtue, Commerce and History: Essays on Political Thought and History, Chiefly in the Eighteenth Century. Cambridge, Eng.: Cambridge University Press, 1985.

References

Hampsher-Monk, Iain. "Review Article: Political Languages in Time—the Work of J.G.A. Pocock." *British Journal of Political Science* 14 (1984): 89–116.

Harlan, David. "Intellectual History and the Return to Literature." *American Historical Review* 94 (1989): 581–609.

Hexter, J.H. "Review Essay: The Machiavellian Moment." *History and Theory* 16 (1977): 306–337.

Höpfl, Hans. "John Pocock's New History of Political Thought." *European Studies Review* 5 (1975): 193–206.

Pokrovskii, Mikhail Nikolaevich (1868–1932)

Russian historian. The leading Soviet Marxist historian of the 1920s and early 1930s, Pokrovskii studied at Moscow University under the supervision of P.G. Vinogradoff and V.O. Kliuchevskii. During the Revolution of 1905, he entered the Marxist camp and then spent most of the following decade in Paris composing his chief work, the five-volume *Istoria Rossii s drevnekh vremion* [History of Russia since Ancient Times]. In this he stated his major thesis, that Russian history manifested the same pattern of development as other European societies in that capitalism was a natural outcome of class conflict and not a foreign implant. Most of Pokrovskii's subsequent writings, which were numerous, reiterated this thesis and attacked non-Marxist historians who did not share it. After the October Revolution, Pokrovskii became the Party-designated leader of the "historical front," an array of pedagogical, scholarly, and propagandist institutions designed to establish the predominance of Marxist doctrine. Upon the Communist Party's takeover of the Russian Academy of Sciences in 1928, Pokrovskii was made a full member of that body. In the mid-1920s, he had devised policies and formulated a theory of cultural revolution that defended a measure of autonomy for non-Marxist scholars. As Stalin rose to power in the late 1920s, Pokrovskii, seeking renewal of his mandate, abandoned this moderate position and championed the campaign to silence non-Marxist scholars. In 1936 Stalin signaled a vituperative campaign against the memory of Pokrovskii and his ideas; he was branded as anti-Marxist and petty bourgeois, largely because his works were devoid of nationalist sentiment. Pokrovskii had thus helped to devise the instruments that were used against him posthumously.

George M. Enteen

Texts

Brief History of Russia. Trans. D.S. Mirsky. 2 vols. London: Martin Lawrence, 1933.

History of Russia from the Earliest Times to the Rise of Commercial Capitalism. Trans. J.D. Clarkson and M.R.M. Griffiths. Second ed. Bloomington: University Prints and Reprints, 1966.

Izbrannye proizvedeniia [Selected Works]. 4 vols. Moscow: Mysl', 1966–1967.

References

"Bibliografiia proizvodenii Akademika M.N. Pokrovskogo." *Arkhivno- Informatsionnyi Biulleten* [Archival Information Bulletin] 7 (1993): 6–72.

Chernobaev, A.A. *Professor s pikoi, ili Tri zhizni istorika M.N. Pokrovskogo* [Professor with a Pike, or the Three Lives of the Historian M.N. Pokrovskii]. Moscow: Politizdat, 1992.

George M. Enteen. *The Soviet Scholar-Bureaucrat: M.N. Pokrovskii and the Society of Marxist Historians.* University Park, PA: Penn State University Press, 1978.

Polish Historiography

Historical writing by and about the Polish people and nation. Among the earliest monuments of Polish historical writing are annals and chronicles. The former consisted of records kept on the margins of paschal (Easter) tables. The first annals, dating from the turn of the tenth century, were written in cathedral chapters and monasteries and recorded selected events such as the annals of the Cracow chapter, the old annals from the Holy Cross Mountains, and the Great Poland annals. In addition, monasteries also housed biographies of saints, catalogs of bishops, and books of deceased persons.

The chronicles were the highest achievement of medieval historiography. The earliest chronicle, known as *Kronika Anonima zwanego Gallem* [The Chronicle of the Anonymous called Gallus], dates from 1113 to 1117. It is an example of court historiography and is similar to the *gesta* of western Europe. It is marked by a lack of chronological precision (no dates are included) and is concerned with the picturesque and instructive description of the deeds of the ruler, intended to add splendor to his person and his dynasty. In the structure of his narrative the chronicler based himself, above all, on oral tradition. The *Kronika Mistrza Wincentego zwanego Kadłubkiem* [The Chronicle of Master Vincentius Called Kadłubek], dating from the early twelfth century, differs in character. Its books are recorded partly in the form of dialogue and partly as a continuous narrative, although Kadłubek, too, does not include dates. The greatest historical work dating from the Polish Middle Ages was the *Annales seu cronicae incliti Regni Poloniae* [Annales or Chronicles of the Glorious Kingdom of Poland], often referred to briefly as *The History of Poland,* written in twelve books by Jan Długosz (1415–1480), one of the most emi-nent historians of his day. His work, which records the history of Poland up to 1480, is similar to the annals in its association of text and yearly dates, and to the chronicles in its extended narrative. Długosz intended to describe the history of Poland critically, through the use of many sources, and his work thereby anticipates the methods of modern scholarly historiography.

Chroniclers of the early modern period were influenced by Długosz, whose work they copied or summarized. They found their models in the ancient rhetorical and pragmatic historiography of Rome, and they often mimicked the historio-graphical conventions of Sallust, Livy, and Tacitus. They also continued to write in Latin; it was only in the mid-sixteenth century that the Polish language came into use in historical writing. The most eminent representatives of historiography in that period included Maciej (or Matthew) Miechowita (ca. 1457–1523), Bernard Wapowski (ca. 1450–1535), Stanisław Orzechowski (1513–1566), Maciej (or Matthew) Stryjkowski (ca. 1514–before 1593), and Reinhold Heidenstein (1533–1620). Their chronicles, however, represented only fragments of the past. At the same time, attempts were made to create a new synthesis of Polish his-tory, especially in the works of Marcin Kromer (1512–1589). These included a description of Poland, *Polonia* [Poland] (1577), and the presen-tation of its history, *De origine et rebus gestis Polonorum libri XXX* [The Origin and Acts of the Poles in Thirty Books] (1557), in which Kromer included his conception of the Sarmatian origin of the Slavs. The first Polish endeavor to write a universal history was undertaken by Marcin Bielski (1495–1579) in his *Kronika wszystkiego świata* [Chronicle of the Whole World] (1551).

The seventeenth century marked the further development of Polish historiography, as religious disputes, combined with the growth of thought about the nature of the state, proved conducive to a more comprehensive and profound reflection upon the nation's past. The most prominent his-torians in this period included Szymon Starowolski (1588–1656), Paweł Piasecki (1579–1649), Albrycht Stanisław Radziwiłł (1595–1656), and Wawrzyniec Rudawski (1617–1690).

This type of erudite historiography continued to dominate the study of the past until well into the eighteenth century. Concurrently, however, an increasingly critical attitude to the sources devel-oped—this was the first great era of document editing in many parts of Europe— and many more Polish texts and records came to be published; mention should be made in particular of the

Volumina Legum, a collection of laws and resolutions adopted by the Polish Diet, whose publication started in 1732. Historical writing was, moreover, increasingly linked to the movement to reform the state. The need for a modern history of Poland that would give full attention to the role of the monarchy was fulfilled by the most eminent Polish historian of the period, Adam Naruszewicz (1733–1796), in his six-volume *Historia Narodu Polskiego* [A History of the Polish Nation] (1780–1824). His contemporary, Jędrzej Kitowicz (1728–1804) wrote the first history of Polish culture in the Sarmatian period, *Opis obyczajów za panowania Augusta III* [A Description of Manners under Augustus III].

In the nineteenth century, historiography was dominated by discussions of the causes of the partitions of Poland and the fall of the country. Historical theory, too, continued to evolve, promoting a still stronger form of source criticism, now thoroughly based on advances in the ancillary disciplines of history, such as paleography, diplomatic, and numismatics. The pursuit of historiography was also becoming professionalized, as it was elsewhere in Europe. An important role in this respect was played by the universities in Vilnius, Warsaw, Cracow, and Lvov. In spite of the partitions of the country, national historiography continued to develop as a surprisingly coherent whole, and it thereby in turn contributed to the development of a national historical consciousness. The pursuit of the past was now intended to ascertain the truth, but history at the same time retained an educational role. Rhetoric was not discarded. These ideas were reflected in the works of Joachim Lelewel (1786–1861), the most prominent Polish historian of the first half of the nineteenth century. His novel methodological conceptions were included in his *Historyka* [Theory of History] (1815). In his twenty-volume *Polska, dzieje i rzeczy jej* [Poland, Its History and Things Polish] (1856–1868), Lelewel's focus on the struggles of the peasant masses and his periodization of Polish history according to the progress of liberty, ensured that his influence on the spread of democracy would be immense and long-lasting.

The second half of the nineteenth century was marked by continued vigorous development in the study of history, due in large measure to the emergence of two rival historical schools, those of Cracow and Warsaw. Adherents of the former started from conservative assumptions and were loyal to the partition powers, leading them to a negative appraisal of Poland prior to the partitions. Among these authors, Józef Szujski (1845–1911), Walerian Kalinka (1826–1886), and Michał Bobrzyński (1849–1935) blamed the Poles themselves for the partitions. They were criticized by the Warsaw school, the politics of whose members were liberal and optimistic. Tadeusz Korzon (1839–1918) and Władysław Smoleński (1851–1926), for example, focused their research on the Enlightenment. They paid attention to the reforms carried out at that time and pointed to the emergence of a modern nation, capable of reviving the country. In contrast to the Cracow school, they blamed the partition powers for the collapse of the country.

Dreams of independence, reborn in the early twentieth century, are reflected in historiography. Research into the then recent history of Poland was combined with an emphasis on the tradition of the liberation movement, as for instance in the work of Szymon Askenazy (1866–1935) and Wacław Tokarz (1873–1937).

After Poland regained independence in 1918, conditions for historical writing improved significantly. This was owing to the livelier activity of the existing universities, and the advent of new ones, among them Poznan. New historical journals were launched, chairs of history were founded, and international contacts developed. Economic history emerged as a separate discipline thanks largely to Jan Rutkowski (1886–1949) and Franciszek Bujak (1875–1953). More traditional topics, such as the history of the state and of law, continued to be pursued, by, among others, Stanisław Kutrzeba (1874–1946) and Zygmunt Wojciechowski (1900–1955). Studies in the history of culture and education were undertaken by Stanisław Kot and Stanisław Łempicki, along with research into military history, by Tokarz and Marian Kukiel. Vigorous research took place into the political and social history of medieval Poland (conducted by, among others, Roman Grodecki, Władysław Semkowicz, and Kazimierz Tymieniecki). The modern period was covered by Bronisław Dembiński and Oskar Halecki, while Władysław Konopczyński (1880–1952) undertook the history of recent political and constitutional relations. Finally, some scholars began to pursue the relatively new areas of theory of history and the methodology of historical research.

World War II had a devastating effect, not least because of the considerable losses of historians. As far as was possible under the Nazi regime, many historians continued to conduct their research secretly; a clandestine university system even functioned under the Nazis. The parallels with other Nazi-occupied territories like Romania are striking. But, by the end of the war, the professional classes had been decimated, and many archives, libraries, and private collections of books had been destroyed. At the conclusion of hostilities only fifty professors of history remained to take up the reconstruction of academic life. Nevertheless, this took place quite rapidly, in part due to the organization of new universities (Toruń, Łódź, Lublin, Wrocław) and the foundation of specialized research institutes: the Polish Academy of Sciences came into being in 1952 and other new institutions included the Institute of History of Material Culture, the Army Institute of History, the Western Institute (which focused on the study of Polish–German relations), and the Jewish Historical Institute. Of the prewar generation of historians, those who continued their research into the late 1940s and 1950s included Rutkowski, Henryk Łowmiański, Stefan Kieniewicz, Henryk Wereszycki, Stanisław Hoszowski, and Marian Małowist. They were joined now by younger scholars, among them Aleksander Gieysztor, Witold Kula, and Gerard Labuda.

Many of these historians were divided in their attitudes toward the official Marxist doctrine promoted by the government. One group, which included the majority of prewar professors (such as Władysław Konopczyński and Kazimierz Górski) was opposed to Marxism. A smaller faction, including Rutkowski and Łowmiański, acknowledged some elements of historical materialism and availed themselves of its theoretical conceptions, while remaining opposed to its ideological implications. A third group (among them Celina Bobińska, Natalia Gąsiorowska, Żanna Kormanowa, Kula, Bogusław Leśnodorski, Stanisław Śreniowski) actively participated in the channeling of Polish historiography along Marxist lines. They disavowed most prewar historiography. The first two groups, persecuted by the authorities, deprived of academic chairs, and denied the opportunity of lecturing, were soon pushed to the margin of scholarly activity and some, most notably Halecki, went into exile. The departure of that generation abroad led to a split in Polish historical writing, between the historiography pursued by the émigrés (who continued the prewar tradition) and that pursued at home by scholars more or less burdened by the theory of historical materialism and by Marxist ideology, which underpinned the Communist regime. Polish historical institutes and societies (the Sikorski Institute in London and the Piłsudski Institute in New York) were established abroad as outlets for the émigrés.

Émigré historiography, also pursued by non-professional historians, focused on the problems of the struggle to regain independence, the reconstruction of Poland, and its history between 1914 and 1945, with special emphasis on the role of Józef Piłsudski. It also made no bones about the true relationship between Poland and the Soviet Union (exposing the Ribbentrop–Molotov pact and the murder of Polish officers in 1940 at Katyń) and the seizure of power by the Communists. Important synthetic studies on Polish history were published by Andrzej Albert, Stanisław Cat-Mackiewicz, and Paweł Zaremba (in the 1980s these were circulated in abridged version by piratical publishers in Poland). Further works were contributed by Jan Ciechanowski, Józef Garliński, Piotr S. Wandycz, and Tadeusz Zenczykowski. There were also many reprints of synthetic studies dating from the period between the world wars, among them the multivolume *Historia Polski 1864–1945* [History of Poland 1864–1945] by Władysław Pobóg-Malinowski and works by Wacław Jędrzejewicz, Marian Kukiel, and Stanisław Kutrzeba. Underground publications in Poland were produced by, among others, Władysław Bartoszewski, Marcin Król, Jan Józef Lipski, Jerzy Łojek, and Adam Michnik.

At home, during the first decade after the war, the authorities promoted studies in economic history, the history of material culture, the worker's movement, and class struggle. After 1956, marked by the comeback of Władysław Gomułka, there were some opportunities for livelier contact with Western historiographers. Polish contributions in that field were marked by Jan Baszkiewicz, Bronisław Geremek, Jerzy Kłoczowski, Marian Modzelewski, Henryk Samsonowicz, Maria Bogucka, Janusz Tazbir, and Józef Gierowski. Among the works of historians concerned with the controversial interwar period, the fate of Poles during World War II, and the postwar period were some that were strongly tendentious (for instance, Henryk Jabłoński, Włodzimierz T. Kowalski, and Tadeusz Walichnowski). Some of them exploited a wealth of sources and transmitted valuable data that were, however, rendered suspect by the Communist system. Still others tried to present the "truth" as far as the circumstances and censorship permitted; mention is due in particular of Andrzej Ajnenkiel, Henryk Batowski, Antoni Czubiński, Marian Marek Drozdowski, Eugeniusz Duraczyński, Andrzej Garlicki, Karol Grünberg, Jerzy Holzer, Tadeusz Jędruszczak, Piotr Łossowski, Czesław Łuczak, Czesław Madajczyk, Andrzej Micewski, and Jerzy Żarnowski. Studies continued in economic history (Maria Bogucka, Antonii Mączak, Henryk Samsonowicz, Jerzy Tomaszewski, Jerzy Topolski, and Andrzej Wyczański), in the theory of state and law (Stanisław Grodziski, Witold Maisel, Henryk Olszewski, Jan Wą´sicki, and Jerzy Wisłocki), and in military history (Stanisław Herbst, Bogdan Miśkiewicz, and Jan Wimmer). The history of Germany and Polish–German relations received attention (Antoni Czubiński, Jerzy Krasuski, Franciszek Ryszka, Stanisław Salmonowicz, Maria Wawrykowa, and Marian Wojciechowski) and Henryk Łowiański promoted the importance of investigating the history of Lithuania, Belorus, and Russia (Jerzy Ochmański). Studies on a synthesis of Polish history were initiated as were those into the history of historiography, mainly by Marian Serejski. (This work is being continued by Andrzej Feliks Grabski, Jerzy Maternicki, Jerzy Topolski, and Andrzej Wierzbicki.) Finally, an unorthodox interpretation of historical materialism, which originated in the 1960s and led to the study of the methodology and theory of history, was inspired and guided by Jerzy Topolski.

The political changes related to the Solidarity movement, with the resulting recovery by Poland of its autonomy after 1989, have opened new vistas for the reevaluation of the history of Poland, a task that Cezary Chlebowski, Krystyna Kersten, Jerzy Ślaski, Tomasz Strzembosz, Maria Turlejska, and Tadeusz Żenczykowski have undertaken. The abolition of censorship and access to archives and publications abroad now make it possible to fill "white gaps" (problems in Polish history, which for political reasons could not be publicly discussed) that obscure in particular Polish–Soviet relations and the history of post-1945 Poland. Polish historiography can again form a single stream. It is the task of the younger generation to rewrite it.

Ewa Domańska

See also BULGARIAN HISTORIOGRAPHY; HUNGARIAN HISTORIOGRAPHY; ROMANIAN HISTORIOGRAPHY; SOVIET HISTORIOGRAPHY.

Texts

Długosz, Jan. *Roczniki czyli Kroniki Sławnego Królestwa Polskiego* [History of Poland], 11 vols. Warsaw: PWN, 1964–1985.

Korzon, Tadeusz. *Wewnętrzne dzieje Polski za Stanisława Augusta (1764–1794)* [Home History of Poland in the Time of Stanislaus Augustus's Reign]. 6 vols. Cracow: L. Zwolinski, 1897–1898.

Łowmiański, Henryk. *Początki Polski* [The Origin of Poland]. 7 vols. Warsaw: PWN, 1963–1985.

Wandycz, Piotr S. *The Lands of Partitioned Poland, 1795–1918*. Seattle: University of Washington Press, 1974.

References

Dąbrowski, Jan. *Dawne dziejopisarstwo polskie (do roku 1480)* [Old Historiography in Poland up to 1480]. Wrocław: Zakład Narodowym. Ossolińskich, 1964.

Grabski, Andrzej Feliks. *Myśl historyczna polskiego Oświecenia* [Historical Thought of Polish Enlightenment]. Warsaw: PWN, 1976.

Serejski, Marian. *Zarys historii historiografii polskiej* [The Outline History of Polish Historiography]. 2 vols. Łódź: PWN, 1954.

Topolski, Jerzy. "Polish Historians and Marxism after World War II." *Studies in Soviet Thought* 48 (1992): 169–183.

Wandycz, Piotr S. "Historiography of the Countries of Eastern Europe: Poland." *American Historical Review* 97 (1992): 1011–1025.

Zybertowicz, Andrzej. *Między dogmatem a programem badawczym: Problemy stosowania materializmu historycznego we współczesnej historiografii polskiej* [Between the Dogma and a Research Program: Problems of Application of Historical Materialism in the Polish Contemporary Historical Writing]. Warsaw-Poznan: PWN, 1990.

Political Thought, History of

The history of political thought in the Anglo-American world was originally a subfield of political science rather than of history. To some degree, it remains so, especially in the United States; and its history is in good part the story of a series of struggles to define the subject between those who want to treat it as history like any other history and those who wish to see it as a way of reflecting upon political issues. Attempts to survey the literature of politics date back at least to the mid-nineteenth century (in, for example, Robert Blakey's *History of Political Literature* [1855]) and became established in such works as Paul Janet's *Histoire de la Science Politique* (1887), Sir Frederick Pollock's *Introduction to the History of the Science of Politics* (1980), and above all William Dunning's three-volume *History of Political Theories* (1902–1920). There were writers on the history of political thought who avoided such large-scale projects and wrote with greater historical precision (notably John Neville Figgis); and there were even some who managed to combine historical precision and the broad sweep. The best example of this may be Charles H. McIlwain's *Growth of Political Thought in the West* (1932), which like all of McIlwain's writings took strength from its author's care to examine carefully the language used in the texts he studied. But it was the work of Dunning and others that began the process, complete by the mid-twentieth century, of forming an agreed "canon" of political thinkers who formed a great tradition of political theorizing. The history of political thought was then written as the story of this great tradition, usually with individual attention being paid to each figure in the canon.

Undoubtedly, the most successful textbook embodiment of this approach was George Sabine's *History of Political Theory* (1937). Much more than his immediate predecessors, Sabine adopted explicitly relativistic beliefs, though in doing so he was merely revealing some of the inherent tensions within the German historical traditions on which the earlier writers had drawn. Sabine's "social relativism" led him to see that political theory was always, in part, a response to "whatever there may be in the historical and institutional setting that sets a problem to be solved." Thus his *History* was genuinely historical in its assumption that political theories must be understood in relation to their contemporary social *milieu*. Yet, he also saw political theory as part of philosophy, arguing that its history reflected attempts to use the best available tools to reflect on political problems of permanent interest and relevance. Sabine's relativism meant, however, that history was the best way of approaching political philosophy itself. Since no political philosophy (or statement of "values") was "true," then it was necessary to survey them all, taking from each what was most useful for the present. History thereby provided a way of doing political philosophy.

Sabine was more historically sophisticated than most, but he shared a number of general assumptions with others. The most obvious of these was the belief that the proper and most enlightening context within which to understand a great or classic political thinker was that made up of the other great thinkers in the canon. Usually, this meant that a thinker would be understood as reacting to, answering, or being influenced by his predecessors. History was a linear sequence of thinkers, each tending to be seen as one, at least, of the causes of the thought of his successor, with Plato being the ultimate cause of Locke.

But Locke could also be seen as participating in an enterprise *alongside* Plato, Aristotle, and the rest. This is a second assumption underlying the canon. All participants in it had to be understood as playing the same game. Thus the tradition of political thinking, the canon, came to be seen as held together by a shared set of concerns, or "perennial questions." All political thinkers were therefore expected to have addressed these perennial questions—the basis of and limits to political obligation, the nature of liberty or justice, and so on—and could, furthermore, be judged in terms of their relative success in tackling them, or the range of questions with which they were concerned. The subject "political theory" was taken, then, to have a timeless identity; the history of political thought went beyond describing individual contributions to this fixed subject, while also embracing a concern to judge and evaluate the contributions made to that subject.

This understanding of the history of political thought made it a discipline with an uncertain identity. The concentration on the "great thinkers," and the tendency to talk of political *theory* (rather than political thought) pushed it in the direction of being a branch of the history of philosophy; while the concern to judge and evaluate made it seem plausible to consider the history of political theory as simply a way of doing political theorizing or philosophizing of one's own, and of obvious contemporary relevance. If the issues had not changed, then we could learn as much about modern politics from Plato as we could from Marx. Some took this view to extremes, showing a hostility to any history that was not firmly subordinate to philosophy, most notably Leo Strauss, who stressed in *Natural Right and History* (1953) his hostility to "historicism" and to the value-free methods associated with Max Weber, as well as his belief that it was wrong to discuss the tradition of Western political thought without asking which thinkers were right and which wrong (a question answerable only philosophically and not historically). Any historians who attempted to avoid such judgment, or who adopted "relativist" assumptions of the sort that made thinkers incommensurable because of being products of different times and places, were ignoring the essential questions. Strauss's hostility to the "reductionism" inherent in historical approaches to political philosophy also led him to argue, in *Persecution and the Art of Writing* (1952), that all great writers communicated an esoteric as well as an exoteric teaching. This esoteric teaching could only be appreciated by an intelligent and painstaking "reading between the lines"; but it was nevertheless the teaching of permanent and timeless relevance. Strauss's faith in a great tradition of thinkers moved the history of political theory even closer to the history of philosophy (Strauss had little time for theorists who did not reach the level of philosophy), and this perspective was in broad terms shared by his fellow German-Jewish immigrants to the United States, Hannah Arendt and Eric Voegelin. Nevertheless, Strauss was to have the greatest influence on the discipline of political science (not on the discipline of history); and he has bequeathed to a large number of followers a curiously antihistoricist approach to the history of political thought.

While Strauss represented the pole at which history disappeared into philosophy, and Sabine the pole at which philosophy disappeared into a sort of history, there began to emerge by the 1960s two groups who rejected the assumptions upon which they both rested. Marxist historians, especially C.B. Macpherson in his *Political Theory of Possessive Individualism* (1962) challenged the idea that great political theorists could be understood largely in relation to one another. The central claim advanced by Macpherson was that the history of political thought needed to be located in a much broader context of economic and social change. Thus he attempted to show that seventeenth-century English political thought was generated by the emergence of a "market society" that altered men's basic assumptions about what was natural and normal in the world about them. Other Marxists went further than Macpherson in seeing political thought as a history of ideologies designed to legitimate and, by the process of hegemony, to obscure the realities concerning socioeconomic formations (especially, from the seventeenth century onward, capitalism).

Marxist approaches were quickly criticized by most historians of political thought who were suspicious of the tendency to reduce ideas to epiphenomena of social and economic realities. Such approaches still have appeal to those who wish to integrate the history of political (and other) ideas into a more general framework; but specialists in the field have probably been more affected by a second group of thinkers, sometimes known as "the Cambridge school": John Dunn, Quentin Skinner, and J.G.A. Pocock (the last of whom studied at Cambridge but has taught principally in the United States). The scholars of the Cambridge school did not spring out of nothing, and their work can broadly be interpreted as an attempt to apply a particular understanding of what *history* was about (one that built on the ideas of R.G. Collingwood, Herbert Butterfield—Pocock's mentor—and Michael Oakeshott) to the history of political thought, their approach to which was

importantly influenced by the Cambridge social historian and Lockean scholar, Peter Laslett. Furthermore, in a sense, these moves were the converse of the "behavioralism" of David Easton and others, which was so important in the discipline of political science in the 1950s. Easton believed that the history of political theory was a poor substitute for the creation of new political theory, and so essentially demanded that political scientists become properly scientific theorists rather than historians. There were those who said the same thing from the other side: that the history of political thought would benefit from being separated from the concerns of political scientists. Important groups, notably Strauss and his fellow émigrés, resisted the trend, but with only limited success. The key perception of the Cambridge school, that the history of political thought was practiced by Straussians and, indeed, by Marxists in ways that were deeply unhistorical, amounted to an attempt from the historians' side to separate history from political philosophy. Their goal (variously achieved) has been to suggest ways in which the usual rules of historical method could be applied to the history of political thought.

Primarily, this has involved a concern with three things: context, language, and intention. All political thought (or, as Pocock in particular would prefer, political *discourse*) is to be understood as a type of action that takes place within historically specific contexts. That action is to be understood in the first instance with reference to the intentions of the author. More precisely, political writing, like all writing, is an act of communication; so the intention that enables us to understand the action will be an intention to communicate a particular message or set of messages. Seeking the author's intention amounts, then, to asking what, for him or her, was the *point* of the writing. Putting the matter in this way, as Skinner has emphasized, enables us to see that in seeking to understand intentions we are not attempting to plumb the depths of an author's mind, but rather to capture an aspect of his or her text. This can be achieved by comparing the *language* (a term that extends beyond vocabulary and idiom to cover types of argument and even tone) used in the text with that of other similar writings of the same time and place. This will enable the historian to decide what the prevailing linguistic *conventions* were, and thus enable her or him to appreciate the conventions deployed in any particular text. Those conventions will reveal the message that the text must have been intended to communicate.

The criticisms of this approach have been numerous, coming particularly from Straussians and Marxists, but occasionally also from less easily labeled historians of political thought. There have also been criticisms based on poststructuralist literary theory and German hermeneutics. A number of themes run through this criticism, many of them seemingly applicable to any attempt at a genuinely historical understanding of political thought. Among the objections have been the claim that the approach ignores the contemporary relevance of political ideas, that it refuses to assess them or judge between ideas, that it belittles great thinkers by seeing them in a context built up from the writings of lesser minds, that its stress on linguistic context is no more than an anti-Marxist refusal to look at broader social and economic contexts, and so on. The charges, whatever their truth, reveal more than anything else the continuing gap between the concerns of political theorists and historians, both of whom still claim hegemony over the history of political thought. The division between historical (or, as critics would prefer, "historicist") approaches to political thought and approaches that permit direct engagement with past ideas (whether Straussian or the Gadamerian method of John Gunnell) remains deep, and often bitter, especially in the United States.

Glenn Burgess

References

Condren, Conal. *The Status and Appraisal of Classic Texts.* Princeton, NJ: Princeton University Press, 1985.

Gunnell, John G. *The Descent of Political Theory: The Genealogy of an American Vocation.* Chicago: University of Chicago Press, 1993.

———. *Political Theory: Tradition and Interpretation.* Cambridge, MA: Winthrop, 1979.

Pocock, J.G.A. *Politics, Language and Time.* New York: Atheneum, 1971.

Strauss, Leo. *What Is Political Philosophy? and Other Studies.* New York: The Free Press, 1959.

Tuck, Richard. "The History of Political Thought." In *New Perspectives on Historical Writing,* ed. Peter Burke. Cambridge, Eng.: Polity Press, 1991.

Tully, James ed. *Meaning and Context: Quentin Skinner and His Critics.* Cambridge, Eng.: Polity Press, 1988.

Pollard, Albert Frederick (1869–1948)

Tudor political and constitutional historian and professor of constitutional history at University College, London from 1903 to 1931. From his nonconformist and Gladstonian liberal background, Pollard derived his belief in parliament, constitutionalism, and the common law. His earliest work as assistant editor on the *Dictionary of National Biography* (1893–1902) stamped the character of much of his later work that, although showing an awareness of broader social and political focus, remained essentially biographical. He produced biographies of Protector Somerset, Henry VIII, Archbishop Cranmer, and Thomas Wolsey. An admirer of Henry VIII, he saw strong kingship and the achievement of undivided national sovereignty as essential to the establishment of the order that guaranteed liberty. Thus he integrated the "new monarchy" within the context of English parliamentary development, a thesis developed in his most controversial work, *The Evolution of Parliament* (1920). Pollard's work depended heavily on the teleological framework he inherited from his Whig predecessors, and he relied on printed calendars rather than consulting the original manuscripts. Although founding no "school" of history, his other main achievement was the development of a permanent center of postgraduate historical research at the University of London under the aegis of the Institute of Historical Research set up in 1921.

Ian W. Archer

Texts

The Evolution of Parliament. Second ed. London: Longmans, 1929.

Henry VIII. Introduction by J.E. Neale. London: Jonathan Cape, 1970.

Wolsey. Introduction by G.R. Elton. London: Fontana, 1965.

References

Blaas, P.B.M. *Continuity and Anachronism: Parliamentary and Constitutional Development in Whig Historiography and in the Anti-Whig Reaction between 1890 and 1930.* The Hague: Martinus Nijhoff, 1978, 274–344.

Hexter, J.H. *Reappraisals in History.* London: Longmans, 1961, chap. 3

Kenyon, J.P. *The History Men: The Historical Profession in England since the Renaissance.* London: Weidenfeld and Nicholson, 1983, 196–198; 202–206.

Polybius (ca. 200 B.C.–after 118 B.C.)

Greek statesman and historian. Polybius was born at Megalopolis in southern Greece. His father, a wealthy landowner, was an elected official of the Achaean League. Polybius also served the league as a diplomat and military officer. After Rome's victory in the Third Macedonian War, Polybius was among one thousand prominent Achaeans, suspected of pro-Macedonian sentiments, who were taken to Rome as hostages. He and the other detainees remained in Italy for about seventeen years. During this time Polybius was tutor to the sons of Aemilius Paullus, Rome's general in the Third Macedonian War; his friendship with Paullus and his family gave him access to the highest levels of Roman society. In about 150 B.C. Polybius and the other hostages were allowed to return to Greece. He did not remain long in Achaea, accompanying Scipio Aemilianus, his former pupil, on his campaign against Carthage in the Third Punic War. Polybius returned to Greece in 146 when war broke out between Rome and the Achaean League and helped to implement a peace agreement; he spent his later years traveling and writing.

Polybius wrote a history of Rome from the First Punic War in 264 to the destruction of Carthage and Corinth in 146 in forty books. Books 1 through 5 and part of book 7 have survived; the other books are fragmentary. His aim is to tell the story of Rome's rise to world power and the lessons to be learned from Rome's success. Polybius had an intimate knowledge of politics, diplomacy, and warfare, and his history is noted for its critical use of primary documents and oral sources as well as for its geographic and factual accuracy. Polybius's history also contained his vision of an *anakuklosis* (or *anacyclosis*), a political cycle of governments whereby each of Aristotle's "pure" forms of government (monarchy, aristocracy, polity) was succeeded by perverted counterpart (tyranny, oligarchy, mob-rule) and then, in turn by the next pure form—monarchy by tyranny, tyranny by aristocracy, aristocracy by oligarchy, and so on. This view would be widely influential on later political theorists such as Machiavelli after its rediscovery during the Renaissance, not least for Polybius's view that the Romans had established in their republic a proper balance or "mixed" government of all three types of regime. In addition to his history, Polybius also wrote a life of Philopoemen (a general of the Achaean League), a treatise on tactics, and a history of the Numantine War. None of these other works, however, is extant.

Ralph F. Gallucci

Texts

The Histories. Ed. and trans. W.R. Paton. 6 vols. New York: G.P. Putnam's Sons/ Loeb Classical Library, 1922–1927.

References

Eckstein, Arthur M. *Moral Vision in the Histories of Polybius.* Berkeley and Los Angeles: University of California Press, 1995.

Sacks, Kenneth W. *Polybius on the Writing of History.* Berkeley: University of California Press, 1981.

Walbank, F.W. *A Historical Commentary on Polybius.* Second ed. Oxford: Oxford University Press, 1967.

Pontano, Giovanni (1426/9–1503)

Neapolitan humanist. A native of Cerreto in southern Umbria and educated in Perugia, Pontano entered the service of the Aragonese Alfonso I of Naples in 1447. He served the king and his successor, Ferrante, in various diplomatic and political offices, finally as a prime minister, and was the head of the humanist Accademia called Pontaniana. Pontano retired only slowly from his official duties after the French invasion in 1495. Best known for his humanist poetry and moral essays, Pontano wrote a humanist account in six books about Ferrante's first war against the barons (*De bello neapolitano,* written in the 1490s). In June 1499 he finished a dialogue named *Actius,* the first humanist treatise on history. Comparing history to poetry, both of which promote the civic virtue of their readers, Pontano stressed the appropriate style (the classic criteria such as *brevitas* or *gravitas*) and the importance of orations; the model proposed in his treatise is that provided by the ancient Roman historian, Sallust.

Thomas Maissen

Texts

Actius. In *I Dialoghi* [Dialogues]. Ed. Carmelo Previtera. Florence: Sansoni, 1943.

De bello neapolitano. In *Thesaurus Antiquitatum et Historiarum Italiae* [Treasury of the Antiquities and History of Italy]. Ed. Joannes Georgius Graevius. 10 vols. Leiden: P. Van der Aa, 1704–1725, vol. 9, part 3.

References

Kidwell, Carol. *Pontano: Poet and Prime Minister.* London: Duckworth, 1991.

Portuguese Historiography

Historical writing in Portugal from the Middle Ages to the present. Portuguese historiography has a long tradition, Portugal having been an independent state since the twelfth century. Fernão Lopes (fl. fourteenth–fifteenth centuries) is usually considered the founder of Portuguese historiography. Somewhat later one finds the distinguished chronicle writers of the Discoveries and the Empire, such as Eanes de Zurara (1410/20–1473/4) or João de Barros (ca. 1496–1570), and the historians of the war of independence against the kingdom of Spain—to which Portugal was linked from 1580 to 1640—such as the Conde de Ericeira (1632–1690).

The emergence of modern historiography is principally associated with the name of Alexandre Herculano (1810–1877), but he himself came at the end of a series of historians and institutions without which his own contributions would have been impossible. The improvement of research methods, an attempt at a global approach (from a secular and social perspective), and objective writing are the features of the kind of historiography represented by Herculano, but one must give due credit to his predecessors, historians such as António Caetano de Sousa (1674–1759), Pascoal de Melo Freire (1738–1798), António Caetano do Amaral (1747–1819), João Pedro Ribeiro (1758–1839), and the Visconde of Santarém (1791–1856), all of whom were forerunners of Herculano. Institutions as well as individuals played an important part in this process, in particular the Royal Academy of History (founded in 1720), the University of Coimbra (especially since 1772 after the Enlightenment reforms), and the Royal Academy of Sciences (founded in 1779). Above all, however, one must pay close attention to the role played by liberalism (introduced to Portugal by the 1820 revolution and widely disseminated after 1834) through the debate about the secularization of society to which it gave rise. It is because of liberalism that the nineteenth century proved, in Portugal (and in other parts of Europe and America), a very important moment in the development of modern historiography. It was owing to the liberal influence that many historical works were produced while those essential tools of the historian, the archive and the dictionary, also began to appear. One can also detect in the same period the emergence of a "higher" journalism that assigned great significance to history, and the creation of further institutions for historical research, teaching, and the celebration of Portugal's historical heritage.

As this last point suggests, the nineteenth century was also marked by the increased production of such instruments of popular historical consciousness as commemorative statues and centenary celebrations, the social impact of which was considerable. In this context one must point to the "Curso Superior de Letras" [Advanced Course in the Arts], established in 1858–59, within which history was first taught as an autonomous subject, and to the "Sociedade de Geografia" (Geographical Society) whose foundation (1875) was closely connected with the exploration of Africa. Such institutions, serving both science and colonialism, were common in Europe at the end of the nineteenth century.

The connection between history and geography was also particularly strong at this time. The first faculty of arts was created at the University of Coimbra in 1911, in the early years of the First Republic; in Lisbon, a faculty of arts also emerged in the capital's recently created university, offering a degree in "Historical-Geographical Sciences." As for historiography itself, it would be correct to say that Herculano's tradition has endured throughout the nineteenth and twentieth centuries, continuing his studies of medieval history but also expanding them into the early modern period: as examples one may cite Rebelo da Silva (1822–1871), Gama Barros (1833–1925), and Costa Lobo (1840–1913).

Various "General Histories of Portugal" were also written in the nineteenth century, not all of them by Portuguese historians, and usually aimed at a wide nonspecialist audience, as for example, the works of the conservative liberal Pinheiro Chagas (1842–1895) or those of the socialist Oliveira Martins (1845–1894). Furthermore, one also begins to notice an increasing interest in contemporary history, an interest that reflects the great upheavals of the century and, above all, the prominence of historians of republican and even socialist tendencies. In this connection one should mention, in particular, names such as Latino Coelho (1825–1891), José de Arriaga (1848–1921), Teófilo Braga (1843–1924), and the already mentioned Oliveira Martins. Meanwhile, under the sponsorship and influence of the Geographical Society, the historiography of the Ultramarine Expansion and colonization was started (or at least restarted): here the outstanding name is that of the subfield's founder, Luciano Cordeiro (1844–1900). Also significant were the growing number of ethnological studies, written in conjunction with history and archaeology, the most important contributions to which were made by José Leite de Vasconcelos (1858–1941), founder of the journal *Arqueólogo Português* [Portuguese Archaeologist].

During the First Republic (1910–1926) a reaction set in to the philosophical and scientific positivism and anticlericalism that characterized the republican movement. Catholic and monarchical intellectuals, began to reject the rationalism of their predecessors and opted for a nationalist stance. Reflections of these tendencies in historiography and in the philosophy and methodology of history, can be seen in the works of several scholars: Fortunato de Almeida (1869–1933), the author of a *História da Igreja em Portugal* [History of the Church in Portugal] (1910–1922) and subsequently of a *História de Portugal* [History of Portugal] (1922–1929)]; Manuel Gonçalves Cerejeira (1888–1977), a professor of the Faculty of Arts of Coimbra, and later patriarch cardinal of Lisbon during the *Estado Novo* (New State) from 1932/33 to 1974; António de Vasconcelos (1860–1941), a priest who worked on the history of the university and various themes in religious and church history; the Jesuit Luís Gonzaga de Azevedo (1867–1930), author of a posthumously published *History of Portugal* (1944) that, however, covers only the Middle Ages; Fidelino de Figueiredo (1889–1967), a brilliant intellectual and founder of both the National Society of History and the *Revista de História* [Journal of History], which focused on the history of literature; and, finally, António Sardinha (1888–1925), a counterrevolutionary monarchist who tried to create a movement for the "revision" of the history of Portugal.

The most important historians of the first half of the twentieth century, Damião Peres (1889–1976) and Paulo Merêa (1889–1977), moved in these circles. Merêa was—along with Cabral Moncada (1888–1974), a confessed Germanophile; Marcello Caetano (1906–1980), Salazar's successor; and the catholic monarchist Guilherme Braga da Cruz (1916–1977)—among the greatest Portuguese historians of law. Peres, on the other hand, was primarily a scholar of the Middle Ages and of the Discoveries, and he was also the general editor of one of the most famous collaborative histories of Portugal, the *História de Portugal,* published by the Portucalence Editora, of Barcelos, from 1928 until 1937 (or until 1981, if we take into account the last of the supplements published in that year). The "História de Portugal de Barcelos," as it is widely known, had the merit of including historians of different schools and ideologies. Joaquim de Carvalho (1892–1958), one of the most important cultural historians, and a republican and a moderate opponent to the "New State," is a case in point. Nevertheless, this work still showed traces of the old nationalism, evident mainly in the initial

plan of the publication and in a few of the contributions, a tendency that was confirmed by the authorship of the last supplement, covering the "New State": this was written by Franco Nogueira, Salazar's minister of foreign affairs and his biographer.

We may say that during the "New State," at least until the 1960s, an "academic," erudite, and factual historiography reigned supreme. The medieval and early modern eras (in particular the Discoveries) were privileged, while contemporary history, which had been so important in the nineteenth century, now virtually disappeared. The work of the medieval scholars was, however, important, particularly that by the members of the "Coimbra School"—Damião Peres, Pierre David (1882–1955), Torcato de Sousa Soares (1903–1988), Salvador Arnaut (1913–1995), Avelino de Jesus Costa (b. 1908); so, too, were studies of political history, of which the works of Luís Ferrand de Almeida (b. 1922) are an example.

Also significant is the work done in the areas of economic history and history of the Discoveries, of which the stronger contributions have come from the "Lisbon school." Here the outstanding names are Virgínia Rau (1907–1973) and Jorge Borges de Macedo (b. 1921)—from a Marxist background—on economic history, and Joaquim Veríssimo Serrão (b.1925), on political and cultural history. But it is also worth mentioning that in the area of the history of the Discoveries some important work has been done by nonuniversity scholars of liberal tendencies (and thus not followers of the Salazar regime), who proposed other approaches, for example, Jaime Cortesão (1884–1960) and Duarte Leite (1864–1950). António Sérgio (1883–1969), an intellectual linked to one of the most representative and prestigious journals of the culture of opposition to the "New State," *Seara Nova,* was not strictly a historian in his methods, but he nevertheless wrote some of the most distinguished essays on Portuguese history. His approach, which falls into the tradition of Oliveira Martins, had great influence on historians who wished to deviate from the official line. João Ameal (1902–1982) and Caetano Beirão (1892–1968), monarchists who later became supporters of the "New State," were perhaps its most important essayists and apologists. There is no space in the present entry to discuss specific areas of historiography (some of which are covered more generally elsewhere in this volume), such as archaeology of the prehistoric and Roman past, classical studies, art history, literary history, the history of education, the history of science, and so on. But a few scholars, who represent significant developments in these areas, should at least be mentioned. António José Saraiva (b.1917), in mid-century and at the height of the Salazar regime, started writing a cultural-literary history of Marxist tendencies that he significantly rewrote after the revolution of April 1974. His collaborator, Óscar Lopes (b. 1917), has remained a more orthodox Marxist. Rodrigues Lapa (1897–1989), who was dismissed from the University of Lisbon under Salazar, is another significant literary historian of the Middle Ages. Another important literary and cultural historian was Hernâni Cidade (1887–1975). While in France during the 1960s, José Augusto França (b. 1922) began a history of art as a social phenomenon.

In general, one may say that Portuguese historiography, under the "New State," abandoned the great discussions that could have led to its further development and stuck to a rather narrow, positivist concept of accuracy, which privileged methodology and aligned historical writing as a whole more closely to the regime in power. As has been mentioned above, there were some exceptions, generally outside the university. On the other hand, in institutional terms the historical discipline flourished: there were degrees in history and philosophy after 1930, and in history in Coimbra and Lisbon after 1957, and in Oporto, 1962. In the universities and in the academies (the Academy of Science, the Geographical Society, and the Portuguese Academy of History, founded in 1936), historiography continued to be factual and explicitly nationalist. Further proof of this can be seen in the regularly produced and reproduced popular memory generated around the celebration of the great national events, such as the Foundation (1140), the Restoration (1640), or the Saga of the Discoveries (as in the celebration of the centenary of Prince Henry of Aviz, in 1960).

As we move from the 1950s to the 1960s, however, it is possible to see the beginning of a process of change that reflects the crisis in the governing regime and the colonial war. Outside the university community, and with connections to foreign scholars, particularly in France, a group of figures emerged who opposed the regime's interpretations. Vitorino Magalhães Godinho (b. 1918), a historian of the Discoveries and of economics, has been the most significant Portuguese practitioner of the "Histoire Nouvelle." Joel Serrão (b. 1919), a brilliant essayist, asserted himself as the coordinator of the first, and highly influential,

Dicionário de História de Portugal [Dictionary of Portuguese History] (1971). Other historians ventured again into contemporary history, starting with the nineteenth century in the first instance, and thereby breaking some new ground in historiography, albeit under the influence of the Left and Marxism. Two prominent examples of this approach are Vítor de Sá and Armando de Castro. Oliveira Marques, one of the most productive and varied historians, ranging thematically from the Middle Ages to the "New State," began teaching in the United States, at Columbia University, a Portuguese history on nonofficial lines. Later a synthesis of this was published: *História de Portugal* (1973).

Even within the universities one may notice symptoms of change. In the mid-1960s, Silva Dias (1916–1994) of the University of Coimbra, one of the most brilliant cultural historians of the century, began with his disciples to research and teach the history of the nineteenth century. António de Oliveira (b. 1931–) began research into socioeconomic history, using a demographic approach. Luís de Albuquerque (1917–1993) began work on historical cartography that has only recently been published. This work built upon earlier research by Jaime Cortesão and Armando Cortesão (1891–1977), whom Albuquerque was later to succeed as director of the Center for Cartographic Studies in the Faculty of Science, University of Coimbra, and on similar research by such as Gago Coutinho (1869–1959) and Teixeira da Mota (1920–1982), who had firsthand experience of naval techniques. The Social Investigations Group, directed by Sedas Nunes (d. 1991), and the journal *Análise Social* were important for the development of interdisciplinary studies, creating favorable conditions for the transformation of history into a true social science.

The passage on April 25, 1974, from an authoritarian, one-party regime to a democracy naturally completed this process of the transformation of the humanities and social sciences. After a phase of enthusiasm for Marxism and for the seductive "Histoire Nouvelle," historiography opened up to other influences, both in terms of approaches and themes. The French influence, dominant until that time, was increasingly challenged by the influence of other historiographies—southern European, Anglophone, and Germanic—the last, of course, had always been influential in legal history. If progress was especially marked in contemporary history, other areas also continued to grow. These included medieval history (where the name José Mattoso must be mentioned), the history of European expansion, colonization, and colonialism (some of which bore lingering traces of the historical approach of the celebration of Discoveries), and local and regional history (which has had a significant presence in Oporto, but also in Coimbra and in the Azores). In spite of some setbacks, such as the demotion of the teaching of history within the education system, it is undeniable that at the time of this writing, there is in Portugal a significant level of historiographic activity. This is apparent in the number of general histories of Portugal that have been published recently. Some are works of synthesis and reference, for example that of Oliveira Marques (new ed., 1995), or that of José Hermano Saraiva (latest enlarged ed., 1993). The latter is the most media-friendly and controversial of our historians, not least because he was a minister under both Salazar and Marcello Caetano. In addition, there are a number of more specialized and more wide-ranging collaborative efforts. These are the *História de Portugal* (1983), edited by Hermano Saraiva, with a large and heterogeneous team; the *História de Portugal* (1993–1994), with José Mattoso as the series editor but with each volume edited by a different historian; the *História de Portugal* (1993) edited by João Medina with a large team of scholars; and the *Nova História de Portugal,* edited by Joel Serrão and Oliveira Marques, of which a few volumes have already been published. Veríssimo Serrão's *História de Portugal* (1976–1990), although the work of a single author, also belongs in this company. Two recently published contemporary histories should also be mentioned: *História Contemporânea de Portugal* (1985–1990), edited by João Medina, and *Portugal Contemporâneo* (1989–1990), edited by António Reis.

Historical associations have also prospered. We may, as an example, point to the largest of these, the Association of the Teachers of History. Conferences and congresses of all kinds proliferate, the proceedings of which are usually published. The number of journals that publish historical material further demonstrate the development of research and interest in history. One need here mention only the ones that deal exclusively with history: *Revista Portuguesa de História,* the oldest journal of history published in Portugal, *Revista de História das Ideias, Conimbriga,* a journal of archaeology (all from Coimbra); *Revista de História,* (Oporto); *Cultura, Historia, Filosofia; Penélope, Ler História,* and *História* (Lisbon). Among these, *História* is aimed most explicitly at a general audience.

Luís Reis Torgal

Texts
Antologia da Historiografia Portuguesa. Ed. A.H. de Oliveira Marques. Lisbon: Europa-América, 1974–1975.

References
Bibliografia Anual da História de Portugal. Coimbra: Faculdade de Letras da Universidade de Coimbra, 1989.
Repertório Bibliográfico da Historiografia Portuguesa: (1974–1994) [Bibliographical Report on Portuguese Historiography, 1974–1994]. Coimbra: Faculdade de Letras da Universidade de Coimbra-Instituto Camões, 1995.
Serrão, Joaquim Veríssimo. *A Historiografia Portuguesa. Doutrina e Crítica* [Portuguese Historiography: Theory and Criticism]. 3 vols. Lisbon: Verbo, 1972–1974.
Torgal, Luís Reis, J.M. Amado Mendes, and Fernando Catroga. *História da História em Portugal (séculos XIX–XX)* [History of History in Portugal in the Nineteenth and Twentieth Centuries]. Lisbon: Círculo de Leitores, 1996.

Posidonius of Apamea (ca. 135–51 B.C.)

Greek polymath with wide philosophical, geographical, mathematical, scientific, and historiographical interests. A pupil of Panaetius, Posidonius headed the Stoic school at Rhodes and acted as Rhodian ambassador to Marius in 87–86 B.C. Distinguished in Roman literary circles, he was particularly close to Pompey and Cicero. Posidonius's *Historiai,* in fifty-two books continued Polybius's history and ran from 145 to 81 or possibly to 67 B.C. The work survives mainly through quotations in later writers, especially Strabo. Although as a Stoic, Posidonius appreciated Rome's role as a unifier of mankind, social unrest during the late Republic provoked Posidonius's jaundiced assessment of Roman cruelty.

Lionel J. Sanders

Texts
Posidonius. Ed. L. Edelstein and I.G. Kidd. Second ed. 2 vols. Cambridge, Eng.: Cambridge University Press, 1989.

References
Momigliano, Arnaldo D. *Alien Wisdom.* Cambridge, Eng.: Cambridge University Press, 1975, 32–39; 67–71.
Strasburger, H. "Posidonius on the Problem of the Roman Empire." *Journal of Roman Studies* 55 (1965): 40–53.

Postan, Sir Michael Moissey (1899–1981)

British émigré economic historian. Born in Tighina in the Ukraine (then part of Russia), Postan's early university training was disrupted by war and revolution. In 1919 and 1920 he eventually made his way to England and began studies at the London School of Economics in 1921. At this time he began first to study under and then to collaborate with the social historian Eileen Power, whom he married in 1937. In 1935 Postan became a fellow of Peterhouse, Cambridge, and he was elected to a professorship of economic history at the university in 1938. Postan was an expert in both medieval and twentieth-century economic history, but his primary focus was on the earlier period, where he specialized in the trade and rural society of the Middle Ages. Important publications here include his books *Medieval Trade and Finance* (1973), *The Medieval Economy and Society* (1973), major chapters in the first two volumes (1941 and 1952) of *The Cambridge Economic History of Europe* (second edition, 1966 and 1987), and a number of seminal articles and chapters (later collected in *Essays on Medieval Agriculture and General Problems of the Medieval Economy* (1973). His primary theoretical contribution was to apply the theories of Thomas Robert Malthus to economic development in the Middle Ages, a period in which the tension between population and agricultural resources was a primary determinant of the shape of economic development (especially as expressed in agricultural production). Postan's views also had a strong environmental element, where soil exhaustion became prevalent in times of increasing population and the expansion of arable farming into so-called marginal areas of poor soils (as most forcefully expressed in "Agrarian Society in Its Prime: Part 7, England" in the first volume of *The Cambridge Economic History of Europe*). The resulting deterioration of crop yields in such situations set in motion the cyclical pattern of rise and fall in agricultural production and hence population in primarily agrarian societies. Although recent work has modified Postan's theory, it still holds a major place in the study of medieval agrarian society.

John Langdon

Texts

Essays on Medieval Agriculture and General Problems of the Medieval Economy. Cambridge, Eng.: Cambridge University Press, 1973.

Fact and Relevance: Essays on Historical Method. Cambridge, Eng.: Cambridge University Press, 1971.

The Medieval Economy and Society. Berkeley: University of California Press, 1973.

Medieval Trade and Finance. Cambridge, Eng.: Cambridge University Press, 1973.

References

Bailey, Mark. *A Marginal Economy? East Anglian Breckland in the Later Middle Ages.* Cambridge: Cambridge University Press, 1989.

Campbell, B.M.S. "Agricultural Progress in Medieval England: Some Evidence from Eastern Norfolk." *Economic History Review,* second series 36 (1983): 26–46.

Postmodernism

Thought that rejects a universal or eternal structure or *logos.* Modernity implies faith in a *logos,* or a rational principle of Being, or the whole. It holds that true knowledge is grounded upon this *logos* and that such knowledge is, in principle, attainable. Such imperial philosophy and science rejects contingency and envisions the ultimate resolution of all "difference." It is found in all prominent modern doctrines: the materialist structuralism of Marxism, the *Aufhebung* of Hegelianism, the natural law of the *philosophes,* and the "clear and distinct" ideas of Descartes. Depending on how relentless one is, modernity can even be—as it is in Martin Heidegger and Jacques Derrida—traced back to Plato, Aristotle, and Parmenides. A "deconstruction" or rejection of "modern thought" could involve, therefore, the dismantling of the entire Western tradition.

It is such a deconstruction that postmodern thought proclaims: where moderns hid the abyss behind the grand structural narratives of natural law and historical dialectics, postmodern thought rejects all such metaphysical supports. An almost standard definition is Jean-Francois Lyotard's "I define *postmodern* as incredulit toward metanarratives." The use of the term "metanarrative" is, of course, meant to show that all metaphysical thought is constructed, a romance unconsciously put together by Western thought. For postmodernists, all so-called universal thought is, as Hans-Georg Gadamer calls it, local "prejudice." Postmodernism, does not, therefore, reject the possibility of knowledge; it simply gives it a different locus: where modern knowledge mandated transcending historical circumstances, postmodern thought maintains that all knowledge is a *product* of history and is hermeneutical.

In place of the old political "right" and "left," postmodernity establishes a new fault line: On one side are those comfortable without metanarratives—Lyotard, Foucault, Derrida, Hayden White, Dominick LaCapra, for example—and, on the other, those who—like Alasdair MacIntyre, Leo Strauss, Allan Bloom, and Francis Fukuyama—believe that metaphysical certainty is (for "the many" anyhow) essential and that postmodernism is simple Neronianism.

Glimpses of postmodern skepticism can be found earlier in ancient sophism, and in post-Renaissance authors such as Pascal, Donne, Cervantes, Montaigne, Velasquez, Bayle, Voltaire, Kierkegaard, and others. But the agreed-upon herald of postmodernism is Friedrich Nietzsche. It was he who dismantled not only the notion of the "author" (the "subject," the "ego," the *res cogitans*) as an "objective" self outside a historical context, but also the idea of "history" as an "objective" series of events apart from that constructed "self." The vision of the individual as a construct of history and history as the construct of the constructed individual highlights the postmodern vision of humanity as something tossed up from history and utterly dependent on contingency; and it demonstrates postmodern hostility to eternal universals like "human nature," "virtue," and "the good."

This problematized humanity was captured by the second great figure of postmodernism, Martin Heidegger. For Heidegger, humanity—*Dasein*—was "thrown" into history and all one's "knowledge" depended upon where one landed. Heidegger, therefore, sharpened the distinction between knowledge as hermeneutic interpretation from "within" history and objective understanding from "without." For Heidegger, the fact that knowledge was historical and local meant that it was the product of the historical "destiny" *(Geschick)* of a people. This "destiny" appears in language which is the signature of a particular people and the way they conceive of Being. It is the *Gestell* or sorting mechanism through which they sift what is and is not considered knowledge. Language is, therefore, the "house of Being." Because it necessarily particularizes the human race, language accounts for the multiple paradigms that exist in the world. According to Heidegger, one might *try* to bridge such local particularisms with artificially universal or scientific language; but this risks losing the local language and becoming alienated *(unheimlich)* in "objectivity" where local traditions and common sense are destroyed. Thus, postmodernism emphasizes the local, the cultural, the particular, the tribal basis of knowledge against the universality of modernity.

On the left, and among the vast numbers of intellectuals where a belief in progress and ultimate resolution substituted for metaphysical certainty, this crumbling of universality and historical "truth" at first had little effect. But then at Paris, in the student revolution of May 1968, the "Old Left" encountered and succumbed to postmodernism. Unable to accept or perhaps understand the demands of the students, French Marxism rejected the *soixante-huitards*. To the stunned students, this "betrayal" made Marxism indistinguishable from the rest of the "oppressive" metanarratives they abhorred. This demolition of the mental architecture of Marxism was a pivotal point. From it, postmodernism—with all its disorienting doubts—edged into the rest of secular humanism like a Trojan horse. Figures like Foucault turned on "humanism" the same fury Nietzsche had turned on Hegelianism; and neither Marxism nor secular humanism have ever been the same. According to Foucault, *all* humanistic knowledge is a mask for *power*. Scientific "knowledge"—with its universals, norms, truths, standards—inevitably marginalizes some group: women, minorities, gays, lesbians, and so on. Knowledge, Foucault taught postmodernists, was a *weapon (pouvoir/savoir)* laden with Nietzschean *ressentiment*.

Edmund E. Jacobitti

See also DERRIDA JACQUES; FEMINISM; FOUCAULT, MICHEL; GADAMER, HANS-GEORG; HEIDEGGER, MARTIN; MARXISM AND HISTORIOGRAPHY; NIETZSCHE.

Texts

Foucault, Michel. *Power/Knowledge.* Ed. Colin Gordon. New York: Pantheon Books, 1972.

Gadamer, Hans-Georg. *Truth and Method.* New York: Crossroad, 1984.

Heidegger, Martin. *Being and Time.* Trans. John Macquarrie and Edward Robinson. New York: Harper and Row, 1962.

Lyotard, Jean-Francois. *The Postmodern Condition.* Minneapolis: University of Minnesota Press, 1984.

References

Bruns, Gerald L. *Hermeneutics Ancient and Modern.* New Haven, CT: Yale University Press, 1992.

Norris, Christopher. *What's Wrong with Postmodernism.* Baltimore, MD: Johns Hopkins University Press, 1990.

Potter, David Morris (1910–1971)

American historian. A native of Augusta, Georgia, Potter graduated from Emory University in 1932 and pursued graduate study at Yale University. There he came under the influence of Ulrich B. Phillips, a leading historian of the South. His doctoral dissertation was an outstanding revisionist account of Abraham Lincoln and the secession crisis of 1860–1861. In 1942, he began nineteen years of teaching at Yale where he gained a reputation as a masterful scholar whose work was comprehensively researched and brilliantly interpretive. During the last decade of his life, he taught at Stanford University. At the time of his death, he was president of both the American Historical Association and the Organization of American Historians. Potter believed that historians would profit from combining the traditional methodology of their discipline with the conceptual approaches of the behavioral and social sciences. He attempted such a synthesis in *People of Plenty* (1954), a distinguished analysis of the entire American historical experience. The key to that experience, he argued, was to be found in economic abundance. After 1954, Potter's scholarship concentrated on the era of the American Civil War. At the time of his death he was close to completing *The Impending Crisis,* a superb analysis of the developments leading to sectional conflict. This volume, which challenged the notion that the conflict was inevitable, was finished by Don E. Fehrenbacher and received the Pulitzer Prize in 1977.

Kevin J. O'Keefe

Texts

The Impending Crisis, 1848–1861. New York: Harper and Row, 1976.

Lincoln and His Party in the Secession Crisis. New Haven, CT: Yale University Press, 1942.

People of Plenty: Economic Abundance and the American Character. Chicago: University of Chicago Press, 1954.

References

Cunliffe, Marcus, and Robin W. Winks. *Pastmasters: Some Essays on American Historians.* New York: Harper and Row, 1969.

Power, Eileen Edna le Poer (1889–1940)

Historian of medieval Britain. Power, a pioneer in the field of economic and social history, and one of the first to develop the study of women's history, was born in Altrincham, Cheshire. She studied at Girton College, Cambridge, the Sorbonne, the École des Chartes, and the London School of Economics. She served as director of history studies at Girton from 1913 until her move to the London School of Economics in 1921, where she was lecturer, reader, and professor (1931) at the university until her sudden death in 1940. Power's early research in medieval and social history resulted in her great monograph, *Medieval English Nunneries c. 1275 to 1535,* which appeared in 1922. This was the first in a series of publications by Power in which women figure prominently. They include her translation of *Le menagier de Paris,* as *The Goodman of Paris* (1928), her introduction to Johannes Herolt's *Miracles of the Blessed Virgin Mary* (1929), her essay on "The Position of Women," which appeared in *The Legacy of the Middle Ages* (1926), portraits of Chaucer's Prioress and the *menagier's* wife, which appear in her enormously popular and best-selling text, *Medieval People* (1924), and her essays on medieval women edited by M.M. Postan, *Medieval Women* (1975). Power's research into English rural life marked her attempt to turn the study of rural history away from traditional accounts of lord, serf, and manor to the study of "ordinary people," of social class, village life, agriculture, and trade. Her essays include, "The English Wool Trade in the Reign of Edward IV," which appeared in the *Cambridge Historical Journal* (1926); her study "Peasant Life and Rural Conditions," which appeared in the volume she coedited with M.M Postan, *Studies in English Trade in the Fifteenth Century.* The culmination of her research on the wool trade was evident in the Ford Lectures, delivered at Oxford in 1939 and published posthumously in 1941.

Ellen Jacobs

Texts

Medieval English Nunneries c. 1275 to 1535. Cambridge, Eng.: Cambridge University Press, 1922.

Medieval People. New York: Barnes and Noble, 1963.

Medieval Women. Ed. M.M. Postan. Cambridge, Eng.: Cambridge University Press, 1975.

The Wool Trade in English Medieval History. London: Oxford University Press, 1941.

References

Berg, Maxine. *A Woman in History: Eileen Power, 1889–1940.* Cambridge, Eng.: Cambridge University Press, 1996.

Clapham, J.H. "Eileen Power, 1889–1940." *Economica* 8 (1940): 351–359.

Webster, C.K. "Eileen Power (1889–1940)." *Economic Journal* 50 (1940): 561–572.

Prasad, Shiva (1823–1895)

Indian historian. Prasad, the author of some forty texts, was a government official who became an important figure in the education department. He was the author of *Itihasatimirnasaka* [The Illuminator of History] (1864), written in the Hindi language, and intended as a history textbook for schoolchildren. The book was reprinted several times and translated into English. The first part dealt with the Muslim period, the second part concerned British rule down to 1858, and the last part dealt with religion, society, and administration. He began part 1 by pointing out some of the errors of earlier historians, and he stated that his aim in the final part of the work was to demonstrate that India, in spite of its innate conservatism, had changed and would continue to change in the future, that India had always been badly governed, even during the Muslim period, and that the poor had always been miserable. He was, in fact, particularly harsh in his views of the Mughal empire. Loyal to the British government, he wrote about the benefits of British rule such as peace and security, the increase in trade, and social reform. His volumes have a place in the historiography of Hindi works and in the development of the Hindi language.

Roger D. Long

Texts

A History of Hindustan. Trans. Pandit Bhavanidat Joshi. Benares: Medical Hall Press, 1874.

References

Indian Education Commission Report of the Northwestern Provinces and Oudh Provincial Committee. Calcutta: Government Printing Press, 1884.

Prehistory, Ideas of and Study of

The scholarly recognition in western Europe of human existence predating the written word and subsequent interdisciplinary research in this field. Shortly before 700 B.C., the epic poet Hesiod in *Works and Days* proposed that there had been five eras of mankind: gold, silver, bronze, the age of heroes, and iron. Similarly, the Epicurean Lucretius (d. 55 B.C.) in *De rerum natura* [The Nature of Things] noted that primitive humans had used their nails and teeth before fashioning stone and metal to meet their needs. In Christian Europe, such concepts were superseded by biblical explanations for creation. As a result, it was not until after the discovery of indigenous peoples in the Americas that sixteenth-century scholars such as Pietro Martire d'Anghiera and Ferrante Imperato in *Dell'Historia Naturale* [Regarding Natural History] (1599) again questioned the nature of early human existence in Europe.

Following fortuitous discoveries of stone artifacts in Europe, Michele Mercati (d. 1593), superintendent of the Vatican botanical gardens and an avid antiquarian, suggested that early peoples had used these objects as weapons since they had no knowledge of metal. Likewise, William Dugdale in the *Antiquities of Warwickshire Illustrated* (1656) identified these stone artifacts as Briton armament. In *Musaeum Metallicum* (1648), however, Ulisse Aldrovandi proposed that stone tools resulted from a combination of thunder and lightning. None of these ideas was widely popular among scholars or the church; after Isaac de la Peyrère published his *Theological System upon that Pre-supposition That Men Were before Adam* (1655) the Inquisition seized and burned his work in Paris.

Instead, most scholars from the seventeenth to the nineteenth centuries interpreted antiquarian discoveries as physical evidence of societies previously identified in written sources. When Pierre Le Brasseur included a discussion of the megalithic tomb excavated at Cocherel in the north of France in his *Histoire civile et ecclésiastique du Comté d'Evreux* [Civil and Ecclesiastical History of the County of Evreux] (1685), the twenty human remains in the tomb were identified as Hunnic. Similarly, many scholars were wont to attribute megalithic remains to the Celts in France and Britain.

In 1734, both Nicolas Mahudel and Bernard de Montfaucon presented papers to the Académie des Inscriptions in Paris suggesting that humans had experienced three technological ages: stone, bronze, and iron. Contemporary Danish historians, such as Peter Frederik Suhm in his *Historien af Danmark, Norge og Holsten* [History of Denmark, Norway, and Holstein] (1776), likewise noted that primitive tools had been fashioned of stone before being manufactured of copper or, later, iron. In an effort to establish a similar framework in conjunction with funerary monuments, Pierre-Jean-Baptiste Legrand d'Aussy in his *Mémoire sur les anciennes sépultures nationales et les ornemens extérieurs* [Memoir of Ancient National Sepulchers and External Ornament] (1799), distinguished between six ages: fire, mounds, later mounds, pyres, individual sarcophagi, and mausoleums. In other words, he recognized the significance of establishing an absolute chronology, which included prehistoric material. In 1819, Christian

Jurgensen Thomsen thus organized the Danish National Museum's collections according to the ages of stone, bronze, and iron. This framework would ultimately be modified by John Lubbock in 1865 as the Paleolithic, Neolithic, Bronze, and Iron Ages.

Viewing modern society as a fusion of primitive, Christian, and classical elements, romantic scholars expressed heightened interest in national origins. Thus, the growing influence of the movement led to the foundation of institutions such as the Académie celtique in Paris in 1804. By 1814, however, in recognition of the problematic nature of Celtic history and archaeology, this organization became the Société royale des antiquaires de France. In pursuit of similar nationalist objectives, the German archaeologist Ludwig Lindenschmit in his *Handbuch der deutschen Alterthumskunde* [Handbook of German Antiquities] (1880) applied phrenological techniques in conjunction with literary evidence to identify exhumed human remains more precisely.

Among the obstacles to the development of a concept of prehistory in the nineteenth century were the widening divisions between the scholarly fields that contributed to its creation, including history, geology, archaeology, anthropology, and linguistics. Works critical to the establishment of prehistoric chronology, such as Charles Lyell's *Principles of Geology* (1830–1833), necessitated scholarly openmindedness to interdisciplinary research. Other factors lay in the inaccuracy and inadequacy of techniques for dating excavated materials. Arcisse de Caumont, whose *Cours d'antiquités monumentales* [Lesson in Monumental Antiquities] (1830–1841) assessed numismatic remains, sculpture, pottery, mosaics, and other diverse objects, contributed greatly to the formation of an improved chronological framework. Likewise, Wilhelm and Ludwig Lindenschmit in *Das germanische Todtenlager bei Selzen in der Provinz Rheinhessen* [The Germanic Burial Place Near Selzen in the Province of Rhine-Hessen] (1848), recognized the importance of refining an absolute chronology of archaeological finds. Such a methodological approach would enable the more accurate identification of human and other archaeological remains. Nonetheless, while antiquaries as early as the 1830s had ascertained the existence of human remains contemporary in age to those of extinct mammals, leading archaeologists such as Alfred Maury (d. 1892) continued to reject these hypotheses well into the 1860s.

In 1847, Jacques Boucher de Perthes proposed in the first volume of his *Antiquités celtiques et antédiluviennes* [Celtic and Antediluvian Antiquities] that humans had existed contemporary to mammals antedating the time of the flood. By observing shells, plant remains, and other formerly undocumented archaeological material, he demonstrated the importance of stratigraphy in dating early human remains. As these views gained scholarly acclaim, academic bodies such as the Congrès d'anthropologie et d'archéologie préhistorique were established to further this research (1866).

Thus, prehistorians of the late nineteenth and early twentieth century relied entirely upon retrieved artifacts for the reconstruction of remote eras. In his *Dawn of European Civilization* (1925), however, V. Gordon Childe (d. 1957) also recognized the need to supplement largely chronological descriptions of prehistoric humans with cultural methodology. Childe's work attempted to redefine the prehistoric communities through a recreation of their social system. The advantage of prehistoric archaeology lay in its ability to provide explanations for human activity over extremely long periods of time.

In the "new archaeology," as developed under Lewis R. Binford, prehistorical research has turned more to studying aspects of cultural systems than the artifacts themselves. More recently, Grahame Clark has effected collaboration with the environmental sciences. This ecological approach has allowed archaeologists to lessen their dependence on artifacts in the determination of ethnic groups. Glyn Daniel, in turn, has initiated the history of archaeology in works such as his *Idea of Prehistory* (1988), assessing the dominant influences in the development of an understanding of prehistory. Colin Renfrew has suggested that future research in this field will increasingly address the cognitive processes of prehistoric societies.

Bonnie Effros

See also ANTIQUARIANISM; ARCHAEOLOGY; MUSEUMS; NUMISMATICS.

Texts

Boucher de Perthes, Jacques. *Antiquités celtiques et antédiluviennes.* 3 vols. Paris: Treuttel et Wurtz, 1847–1864.

Cartailhac, Émile. *La France préhistorique d'après les sépultures et les monumens* [Prehistoric France According to Its Sepulchers and Monuments]. Second ed. Paris: F. Alcan, 1903.

Caumont, Arcisse de. *Cours d'antiquités monumentales.* 6 vols. Paris: Lange, 1830–1841.

Childe, V. Gordon. *The Dawn of European Civilization.* London: Kegan Paul, Trench and Trubner, 1925).

Lindenschmit, Wilhelm, and Ludwig. *Das germanische Todtenlager bei Selzen in der Provinz Rheinhessen.* Mainz: Verlag von Victor v. Zabern, 1848.

Lubbock, John. *Pre-historic Times.* Seventh ed. New York: H. Holt and Company, 1913.

Lyell, Charles. *Principles of Geology.* Eleventh ed. 2 vols. New York: D. Appleton & Co., 1892.

References

Binford, Sally R., and Lewis R. Binford, eds. *New Perspectives in Archeology.* Chicago: Aldine, 1968.

Clark, Grahame. "Prehistory since Childe." *Bulletin of the Institute of Archaeology, University of London* 13 (1976): 1–21.

Daniel, Glyn. "Stone, Bronze and Iron." In *To Illustrate the Monuments: Essays on Archaeology Presented to Stuart Piggott,* ed. J.V.S. Megaw. London: Thames and Hudson, 1976, 36–42.

Daniel, Glyn, and Colin Renfrew. *The Idea of Prehistory.* Edinburgh: Edinburgh University Press, 1988.

Laming-Emperaire, Annette. *Origines de l'archéologie préhistorique en France: Des superstitions médiévales à la découverte de l'homme fossile* [Origins of Prehistoric Archaeology in France: From Medieval Superstitions to the Discovery of Prehistoric Man]. Paris: Éditions A. et J. Picard et Cie., 1964.

Piggott, Stuart. *Approach to Archaeology.* Cambridge, MA: Harvard University Press, 1959.

Renfrew, Colin. *Towards an Archaeology of Mind.* Cambridge, Eng.: Cambridge University Press, 1982.

Sklenár, Karel. *Archaeology in Central Europe: The First 500 Years.* Trans. Iris Lewitová. Leicester, U.K., and New York: Leicester University Press and St. Martin's Press, 1983.

Prescott, William Hickling (1796–1859)

American historian. Trained as a lawyer, an accident left him partially blind and obliged him to seek an alternative career as a man of letters. Despite his handicap, Prescott became one of the most popular nineteenth-century American historians, and the first to achieve international recognition. His works on Spain and its empire include: *History of the Reign of Ferdinand and Isabella, the Catholic* (1837), *The History of the Conquest of Mexico* (1843), *History of the Conquest of Peru* (1847), and the three-volume *History of the Reign of Philip the Second, King of Spain* (1855–1858). Prescott was a romantic historian for whom history was a moral drama acted out by heroic protagonists. Influenced by Sir Walter Scott, his histories were characterized by the victory of civilization over barbarism. He was particularly drawn to national epics, whether the emergence of European nation-states or the conquest of indigenous empires. He disavowed the "Black Legend" and was the first U.S. historian to study the Spanish empire in a scholarly fashion, using original primary sources and bibliographical footnotes. Modern historians have faulted Prescott's lack of interpretation or analysis, his acceptance of Spanish primary sources at face value, his elitist perspective, his failure to consider economic and institutional factors, and his often patronizing treatment of the Aztec and Inca civilizations. Nevertheless, his achievements were considerable and his works remain highly readable.

George L. Vásquez

Texts

The History of the Conquest of Mexico. Abrid. and ed. C. Harvey Gardiner. Chicago: University of Chicago Press, 1966.

History of the Conquest of Peru. New York: Dutton, 1963.

History of the Reign of Ferdinand and Isabella, the Catholic. Ed. J.F. Kirk. 3 vols. Philadelphia: J.P. Lippincott, 1872.

History of the Reign of Ferdinand and Isabella, the Catholic. Ed. and abrid. by C. Harvey Gardiner. New York: Heritage Press, 1962.

History of the Reign of Philip the Second, King of Spain. Ed. J.F. Kirk. 3 vols. Philadelphia: J.B. Lippincott, 1882–1886.

References

Cockcroft, James D. "Prescott and His Sources: A Critical Appraisal." *Hispanic American Historical Review* 48 (1968): 61–74.

Humphreys, Robin A. "William Hickling Prescott: The Man and the Historian." *Hispanic American Historical Review* 39 (1959): 1–19.

Levin, David. *History As Romantic Art: Bancroft, Prescott, Motley, and Parkman.* Stanford: Stanford University Press, 1959.

Procopius (ca. 500–after 562?)

Byzantine official and historian. Born to a Greek-speaking family in Caesarae of Palestine, Procopius entered the imperial service in Constantinople, ultimately attaching himself to the emperor Justinian's (527–565) leading general, Belisarius. He accompanied the general on several campaigns, including the reconquest of Italy (536–540). Procopius, who possibly may be identified with the homonymous city prefect of 562, was thus well-placed to write a history of Justinian's reign and campaigns, and the first seven books of his *Histories of the Wars of Justinian* appeared about 550, with a final volume following a few years later. His *Buildings* (ca. 555) offered an account of Justinian's massive construction program. Although both of these works present a positive if not encomiastic picture of the emperor and Belisarius, Procopius is perhaps best known for his scandalous indictment of these two men and their wives known as the *Secret History.* This work, probably unpublished until Justinian's death but composed ca. 550, purports to tell the previously suppressed truth, adding color and detail to the first seven volumes of the *History,* although generally without contradicting the facts contained therein. Procopius's style was consciously classicizing, clearly influenced by the language of earlier historians, and he writes of Christians with a classical detachment based on stylistic rather than religious convictions.

Loren J. Samons II

Texts

Procopius. Trans. H.B. Dewing. 7 vols. Cambridge, MA: Loeb, 1914–1935.

The Secret History. Trans. G.A. Williamson. London: Penguin, 1966.

References

Cameron, Averil. *Procopius and the Sixth Century.* Berkeley: University of California Press, 1985.

Professionalization of History

Development of history as a discipline with associated scholarly refinements. A number of factors occurring in higher education in the region of Germany during the eighteenth and nineteenth centuries influenced a series of reforms and advances affecting the future discipline of history. Barthold Georg Niebuhr established historical research methods based on source criticism; associated initiatives in philology, hermeneutics, and exegesis of texts stimulated the climate of opinion for reform. At the new University of Berlin, founded in 1809, Leopold von Ranke formulated inductive research methodologies to be conducted among original sources and archival collections at appropriate sites such as the Papal Library in Rome, the diplomatic archives in Venice and Florence, and the national archives located in Paris, Vienna, and London. Ranke is also credited with the invention of the academic seminar, the primary vehicle for graduate training; he himself published dozens of historical works and vowed to re-create "the past as it actually happened," what he deemed at the time to be "scientific history." By "scientific," he meant a discipline guided by rigorous methodological assumptions. Other prominent German universities leading in the reform process were Göttingen, Heidelberg, Jena, and Tübingen.

These initiatives led to the separation of the discipline of history from the traditional medieval fields of law, medicine, and theology. Further developments contributed to the creation of other academic disciplines in higher education. What followed were specialization and professionalization, formal institutional organizations of universities into departments, an academic foundation for administration, the implementation of academic ranks for professors, a restructuring of academic degrees, and specific requirements for graduation at the various academic levels.

Features of reorganizing and restructuring of higher education in Germany, especially in the newly identified discipline of history, included development of courses of historical training and methodology, including the seminar, establishment of historical research techniques, publication of specialized historical periodicals and monographs, creation of historical institutes and professorial chairs at the universities, and renewal of emphasis on professional scholarship. Application of the process of critical analysis of sources in academic research and writing originated from basic historical research. Outside the universities, professional associations were founded that sponsored publications and provided opportunities for the advancement of careers in history. The American Historical Association, for example, was founded in 1884 by the very graduates of these German universities or their American models; two years later, Leopold von Ranke was made its first honorary member. The *American Historical Review,* which remains the preeminent journal of American historians, was founded in 1889.

During the late nineteenth century, many American historical scholars attended German universities, and in 1876, the Johns Hopkins University was founded in Baltimore, its history department explicitly structured on the German model. Harvard University and the other leading American, European, and Japanese universities soon reorganized, implementing the hierarchy of degrees including the doctor of philosophy (Ph.D.), graduate seminars, and scholarly research processes. The Ph.D. incorporated the dissertation, a unique contribution to the discipline in some ways comparable to the "masterpiece" of the medieval guild system. Since that time, historical monographs displaying in-depth research into and analysis of historical subjects have often been the product of this highest academic degree.

Eugene L. Rasor

References

Barzun, Jacques, and Graff, Henry F. *The Modern Researcher.* New York: Harcourt Brace, 1992.

Fitzsimons, Matthew A., Alfred G. Pundt, and Charles R. Nowell, eds. *The Development of Historiography.* Port Washington, NY: Kennikat, 1967.

Iggers, Georg G., and Harold T. Parker, eds. *International Handbook of Historical Studies: Contemporary Research and Theory.* Westport, CT: Greenwood, 1980.

Iggers, Georg G., and James M. Powell, eds. *Leopold von Ranke and the Shaping of the Historical Discipline.* Syracuse, NY: Syracuse University Press, 1990.

Novick, Peter. *That Noble Dream: The Objectivity Question and the American Historical Profession.* Cambridge, Eng., and New York: Cambridge University Press, 1988.

Progress, Idea of in Historical Writing

The belief that human history is developing in a positive, rather than negative, direction, as it has influenced historians and historical thinkers in the Western world from antiquity to the twentieth century.

History has generally been about change, both relative and absolute, and it has not always been seen as "progressive." Conversely, a belief in progress can be found at various times outside Western historical thought: perhaps the earliest historical thinkers to argue for a general progress in human affairs were Chinese philosophers such as Mo Di (fl. 479–438 B.C.), the founder of Mohism,

who believed that the past told a story of the advancement of civilization to greater order. But it is in the West, especially since the late eighteenth century, that the idea of progress has had its greatest impact, and modern non-Western histories owe a great deal to European theories built around types of progress, such as Marxism and positivism.

The idea of steady, positive change was not inherent in the earliest forms of history writing. The ancient Greeks gave relatively little thought to the course of "history" (here taken as meaning "the past") as a whole, which for many of them seemed a meaningless, or at best incomprehensible, congeries of random events. There is, for instance, not much sense of improvement, social or political, in either Herodotus or Thucydides, when weighed against the unfathomable intervention of the gods or of fate in human affairs. This began to change somewhat in the Hellenistic and Roman era. Polybius, although he subscribed to the view that all earthly governments rise and fall in a regular cycle, or *anakuklosis,* believed that the Romans whom he admired had hit on a constitution that could escape this pattern.

At the end of the republic and the beginning of the Augustan principate, Livy's account of Rome's rise from village to imperial power reveals a belief in progress, at least for individual states. The summary of Livy by L. Annaeus Florus, which was popular during the Middle Ages and Renaissance, later made Livy seem even more teleological (that is, written so as to lead naturally to an "end point") with its comparison of the early empire to the mature adulthood of a man. But Florus also saw the later empire as a period of senescence, making his work seem more cyclical than progressive. Outside the Greco-Roman world, the clearest sign of a progressive view of history comes from Jewish thought, with its sense of an unfolding covenant between God and his chosen people. Even so, social and political change as described in the Old Testament is not uniformly positive; the recurring cycle of favor and disfavor meted out to the Israelites over the centuries suggests that the characterization of Judaic thought as linear and progressive, and of Greco-Roman as cyclical and generally negative, has been greatly overstated.

During the Middle Ages, chroniclers and historians generally believed that the world of mutable, material objects and people was, and had been, in a prolonged period of decline. On the other hand, they also believed that God's divine plan for humanity was slowly being revealed; even if humans could not understand it, there *was* a clear pattern to history leading from the Creation and Fall through Christ's Incarnation and Cruci-fixion, to the eventual end of the world and Last Judgment. Hugh of St. Victor (d. 1141) envisaged a three-stage process (the number derived from the Trinity) whereby mankind proceeded toward a Time of Grace preceding the Judgment, in which all peoples enjoyed a "sacramental union" with God.

The profound influence of Saint Augustine, who had discouraged speculation on the future course of his "earthly city," impeded for several centuries the direct application of eschatology (the branch of theology concerned with "last things") to human history. Certain thinkers of millenarian views, however, departed from the Augustinian pattern and prophesied future developments in the history of Christendom. Thus Joachim of Fiore (ca. 1135–1202), a Calabrian monk, theorized that mankind was moving from an Age of the Father, through an Age of the Son, with an Age of the Holy Spirit to follow in his own lifetime. A rather more secular scheme was introduced by the imperial historian Otto of Freising (ca. 1112–1158), whose *Two Cities,* despite its debts to Augustine, offered a vision of history whereby world sovereignty had been transmitted over the ages to a succession of "Four Empires"; this idea would be taken up anew at the Reformation.

The Renaissance and Reformation eras did little to change perceived attitudes to history as a cycle of mainly negative change. Renaissance humanist historians such as the Florentine Leonardo Bruni (1370–1444) were capable, as Livy had been, of accounting of the rise to prosperity of their individual states; others, such as Machiavelli, were more pessimistic and continued to see the past as the playing field of a random and fickle Fortune rather than as the working out of a providential plan. The German chronicler Johannes Carion and his near contemporaries, the "Magdeburg Centuriators" both envisaged the Reformation as a sign of the imminent defeat of the Antichrist and the coming of a New Jerusalem, but also saw the medieval era, in common with most Protestant historiography of the time, as a period of pro-longed decline from early Christian values. By and large, then, the general vision of earthly af-fairs remained one of either steady decline or irra-tional and unpredictable change. Even those early apologists for recent accomplishments and inven-tions such as print, gunpowder, and the compass, such as the sixteenth-century Frenchman Louis Le Roy (1510–1577), saw even small steps forward, within individual civilizations, as part of an over-all pattern of mutability, rather than as a sign of an overall forward march of humanity. Francis

Bacon (1561–1626), who was influenced by Le Roy and by other sixteenth-century French *savants,* was somewhat firmer in his convictions of progress, arguing for man's successive emancipation, over the ages, from four "idols" of the mind (an assort-ment of misleading mental constructs and im-proper uses of language). Bacon also predicted a "Great Instauration" in which nature would be con-quered; but even though he has become famous as a kind of prophet of modern science, his various ex-perimental projects and occasional writings do not add up to a full-scale philosophy of history. In his one piece of extended historical writing, a 1622 bi-ography of study of the reign of England's Henry VII (r. 1485–1509), he remained tied to the con-ventional Renaissance notion that much of human destiny lay in the fickle hands of Fortune.

A full-blown idea of progress in the sense of a belief that *human* affairs were improving really only developed in the late seventeenth and early eighteenth centuries, in the aftermath of the early colonization of the New World, the virtual end of religious warfare (although not, of course, of war itself), and the achievements of the scientific revolution. It was no longer as easy to sustain a view of humanity as perpetually declining, and the long-standing debate over the relative merits of "ancients" (celebrated classical thinkers and writers in various disciplines) as compared to "moderns" (those living during and since the me-dieval period) was beginning to shift in favor of the latter. On the whole, the thought of the early Enlightenment continued to see human nature as a constant, unchanging essence and did not de-velop a notion of each age as unique and distinc-tive, the characteristic of the nineteenth-century Germanic movement known as Historicism. It did, however, concede that essential nature could be changed through education and a process of civilization independent of Christianization, and was thereby able to value certain non-Western cultures. Both Montesquieu (1689–1755) and Voltaire (1694–1778) would praise the achieve-ments of pagan cultures. In the case of the latter author, who saw the just-concluded age of Louis XIV as a kind of general cultural apogee in human affairs, the accomplishments of the Chinese, Indi-ans, and Muslims demonstrated the innate incli-nation of all peoples toward reason; the superior-ity of the West in his own time lay in its greater freedom from the grip of religion and custom.

Perhaps the deepest thinker on such matters was the Neapolitan philosopher and historian Giambattista Vico (1668–1744). In his most famous book, *Principi di una scienza nuova* [Principles of a New Science], first published in 1725, and expanded and reissued over the following two decades, Vico, echoing Bacon's "four idols" theory of a century earlier, theorized that human civilization had moved by stages through three ages: one of gods, a second of heroes, and a third (his own) of men. Each age was characterized by distinctive modes of speech, mentality, and culture, and although each age contained within it periods of rise and decline, a fully worked out belief in human progress, unfolding in a spiral rather than a straight line, emerges from his work.

Although Vico's work would have little direct influence until its rediscovery in the nineteenth century, one can see further thoughts on progress, although very different in flavor, in such later Enlightenment thinkers as Immanuel Kant (1724–1804), who may have been the first to coin the German term for progress in its modern sense *(Fortschritt),* in the sense of a future whose outcome could not be foretold merely by turning to the timeless essences of past experience. Kant's younger contemporary, Johann Gottfried Herder (1744–1803)—who identified the *Volk* or people as the great agent of change in history (thereby linking national history analogously to a human life cycle). A very different view from either of these, and in fact the first full-scale consideration of the notion of human progress itself, was propounded by Herder's French contemporary, the Marquis de Condorcet (1743–1794) in his *Sketch for a Historical Picture of the Progress of the Human Mind* (1793–1794). Condorcet thought his own time less the culmination of progress than a kind of jumping-off point for humanity, which, having freed itself from the tyranny of superstition and error, could now proceed full tilt toward a utopian conquest of nature and of social ills.

Condorcet's radicalism proved, for a time, the exception rather than the rule, particularly in the period of conservatism that set in after 1815. His younger contemporary Georg Wilhelm Friedrich Hegel (1770–1831) was an idealist philosopher who speculated on a pattern to history whereby a historical "idea" marched forward by stages in which progress was attained through a dialectical conflict wherein every successive "thesis" was matched by an "antithesis" and resolved in a "synthesis." This pattern, enacted in real events by certain "world historical figures" such as Napoleon, whom Hegel believed were the vehicles rather than the agents of change, would eventually culminate in the self-awareness of "reason," which in turn was embodied in the state and in the "freedom" that it conferred on its citizens.

As Hegel's politically loaded philosophy suggests, it would be a mistake to regard the idea of progress as the exclusive preserve of liberal thought; by 1800, the difference between liberalism or utopian radicalism lay less in the belief that human progress had, historically, been achieved, than in conflicting understandings of how this had come about, and, moreover, how far and how fast progress would unfold in the future. The romantics, especially the critics of the "age of revolutions" at the end of the eighteenth and beginning of the nineteenth century, did not assist in the spread of a progressive view of history, not least because the skepticism of thinkers like Edmund Burke (1729–1797) and François Auguste René de Chateaubriand (1768–1848) rejected sharp revolutionary change in favor of a more conservative emphasis on gradual progress through law and custom. On the other hand, romanticism also began to develop a sense of each age, even the long-criticized Middle Ages (largely dismissed by the Enlightenment thinkers as an era of superstition), as having an intrinsic worth. This idea would, in turn, be taken up by many of the great German historians of the century, notably Leopold von Ranke (1795–1886) who, despite his famous emphasis on telling the facts of the past "as it actually happened" remained a devout Lutheran committed to the idea that overall progress in human affairs—culminating in the post-Napoleonic nation-states of his own time—was reconcilable with a sympathetic understanding of the unique characteristics and contributions of each nation, past and present, toward universal history.

Aside from German historicism, the other major nineteenth-century contributions toward the idea of progress came from positivism and Marxism. The French thinker Auguste Comte (1798–1857), often credited as the founder of sociology, asserted the steady development of human thought from a theological and military orientation in the ancient world, through a metaphysical stage in the Middle Ages, and into a final period of "positive" scientific thought in the recent past and his own time. Although he discounted certain events (such as the French Revolution) as bumps along the road, he believed, not unlike Condorcet, that a kind of ideal society free of many of the social ills of his day lay at the end of this path.

Later in the century, Karl Marx and Friedrich Engels, who in terms of sheer numbers of modern followers were perhaps the most influential theorists on human history who ever lived, adapted Hegel's dialectical view of progress into

P

an explanation of past and future social change. Extrapolating from four prehistorical ages or modes of production (primitive Asiatic communism, oriental despotism, aristocratic feudalism, and bourgeois capitalism), each of which they decried for its faults while acknowledging its necessity as a stage of human development, they projected the eventual collapse of capitalism and the establishment of a communist society that would witness the disappearance of all social inequities, eventually permitting the state itself, after a transitional period, to "wither away." According to Marx, it would be only at this stage that history proper would begin.

A final, indirect influence on nineteenth-century historical thought was the adoption in biology of Darwin's principles of natural selection and the specific evolutionary theory of human development derived therefrom. It would be a mistake to regard Darwinian science, founded on close study of the natural development and extinction of species, as too closely analogous to Comtian positivism with its pronounced optimism, although Darwinians, such as Herbert Spencer (1820–1903), would apply evolutionary concepts directly to human history. Nevertheless, its worldwide influence on the popular historical outlook has made crude comparisons between natural "evolution" and human "progress" often difficult to resist.

Most of the grand theories of progress developed in the nineteenth century would have little immediate influence on actual historical writing, whatever their eventual implications for modern social thought. Comte himself did not much appeal to practicing historians; his imaginative leaps and generalizations proved difficult to square with the facts of history, which he himself had notoriously not studied. The only authors actually to write history in Comte's wake were themselves oddities: the Englishman Henry Thomas Buckle (1821–1862), whose *History of Civilisation in England* (1856–1861) urged his contemporaries to abandon political history and take up a study of the past following the canons of the natural sciences; and the antirevolutionary Frenchman, Hippolyte-Adolphe Taine (1828–1893), who borrowed the vocabulary of the sciences but eschewed any search for general laws in history. As for Marxism, the great era of its influence on historiography would await the practical application of Marx's ideas in Soviet Russia and later in the People's Republic of China, at which stage Western historians began seriously to incorporate Marxist and Marxian analysis into their work.

A somewhat more restrained optimism, neither reactionary nor revolutionary, can be found elsewhere in the nineteenth century, in the work of liberal historians in the Anglo-American tradition, such as John Robert Seeley (1834–1895), a defender of British imperial achievements. British historians celebrated their constitutional monarchy and system of relative religious tolerance as an apogee in civilized social arrangements, and it is this tendency in their thought that has been called the "Whig interpretation of history." It was a late Victorian historian of antiquity, John Bagnell Bury (1861–1927) of Cambridge, who wrote what amounted to an epitaph on European progress, just after World War I; his 1920 book *The Idea of Progress* is the first modern systematic study of the concept. It is Bury (significantly, an admirer of H.T. Buckle) who had pronounced history a science in the positivist mode during a famous address of 1903. The idea of progress in learning, law, manners, and especially science had by now influenced many historians' sense of their own profession; it had, moreover, convinced them of the need to train their students in "scientific" techniques for the collection and evaluation of evidence.

American historians, influenced both by eighteenth-century liberal economic thought and by ancient classical republicanism, began to conceive of their own national history, in Livy-like terms, as the fulfillment of a "manifest destiny" whereby the United States was fated to expand from frontier colonial settlements through independence toward conquest of the whole of the North American continent and even a major place on the world stage. George Bancroft (1800–1891), the greatest and most influential of nineteenth-century U.S. historians, epitomized this idea in his nationalistic ten-volume *History of the United States from the Discovery of the American Continent to the Present* (which despite its title ended in 1782), published between 1834 and 1874. Influenced by German historical methods (and praised in turn by Ranke), Bancroft's *History* celebrated the triumphant march of liberty and its embodiment in the new republic. This view of American history, taken up at the turn of the nineteenth century by progressives such as Frederick Jackson Turner (1861–1932), continues to be widely held today, although it is now most likely to appear in the writings of conservatives emphasizing the greatness of traditional American values, than of leftist critics of the inequities in social and economic arrangements: essentially, the former group holds that progress has already culminated and should be conserved; the latter believes that much work remains to be done. Two early examples of the latter view, from a non-Marxian perspective, are the American "New History" of the 1890s and early 1900s (including Turner and his contemporary James Harvey Robinson [1863–1936]) and the closely related "Progressive History" that followed just before and after World War I, whose representatives (Robinson, Charles Beard [1874–1948], Carl Becker [1873–1945], and Vernon L. Parrington [1871–1929]) emphasized the social function of historiography and urged that the historian actively work toward social progress.

There was already a hint of modernist gloom toward the fin de siècle in Friedrich Nietzche's (1844–1900) nihilism, but it would take the cataclysm of 1914 to 1918 to shake the firm grip that various competing notions of progress had now established on Western historiography. In the wake of World War I, the Great Depression, the excesses of totalitarianism, and World War II, twentieth-century historians have been wary of making broad philosophical generalizations about the past. Those that do often tend to subscribe more to cyclical patterns of successive cultures, each of which would inevitably fall into decadence (as in the case of Oswald Spengler's pessimistic *Decline of the West*) or a series of world civilizations (as in the example of Arnold J. Toynbee). European philosophers of history such as Benedetto Croce and Robin George Collingwood in turn repudiated the alliance between history and the natural sciences. And in the United States of the 1930s, former progressives like Beard and Becker abandoned any lingering illusions of history's capacity for sciencelike objectivity, adopting instead a relativism that permitted the individual historian to believe in linear progress (as did Beard) but made such views a matter of subjective faith rather than empirically demonstrable fact or absolute truth.

Against this pessimism, however, one stream in the popular understanding of human history continues to conceive of human social evolution as positive; this has been enhanced in recent years by the end of the Cold War (the euphoria of 1989 now dampened considerably by the horrors of Tiananmen, Rwanda, and Bosnia), the lowering of trade barriers, and the advent of the "Information Age." Despite the equally apparent reasons for despair at expanding population, the threat of environmental catastrophe, and new diseases such as AIDS, most readers prefer to take their history with an optimistic spin, prophesying still better things to come in the near future. This is demonstrated by the commercial success of world histories such as William H. McNeill's *Rise of the West,* with its progressive overtones, and particularly of the occasional nonacademic bestseller such as Francis Fukuyama's *End of History and the Last Man* (1992), the latter a conservative celebration of the collapse of communism and the dawn of a new world order of global peace and capitalist-driven prosperity.

D.R. Woolf

See also CHRISTIANITY, VIEWS OF HISTORY IN; DECLINE, IDEA OF; ENLIGHTENMENT HISTORIOGRAPHY; HISTORICISM; MARXISM AND HISTORIOGRAPHY; MILLENARIANISM; NEW HISTORY; PHILOSOPHY OF HISTORY—SUBSTANTIVE; PROGRESSIVE HISTORY; ROMANTICISM; SOCIOLOGY AND HISTORY; TIME; WHIG INTERPRETATION OF HISTORY.

Texts

Comte, Auguste. *Auguste Comte and Positivism: The Essential Writings.* Ed. Gertrud Lenzer. Chicago: University of Chicago Press, 1975.

Hegel, G.W.F. *Lectures on the Philosophy of World History, Introduction: Reason in History.* Ed. Johannes Hoffmeister; trans. H.B. Nisbet. Cambridge, Eng.: Cambridge University Press, 1975.

Herder, J.G. *J.G. Herder on Social and Political Culture.* Ed. F.M. Bernard. Cambridge, Eng.: Cambridge University Press, 1969.

McGinn, Bernard. *Visions of the End: Apocalyptic Traditions in the Middle Ages.* New York: Columbia University Press, 1979 (includes selections from Joachim of Fiore in translation).

Ranke, Leopold von. *The Secret of World History: Selected Writings on the Art and Science of History.* Ed. and trans. Roger Wines. New York: Fordham University Press, 1981.

Vico, Giambattista. *The New Science.* Trans. Thomas G. Bergin and Max Fisch. Revised ed. Ithaca, NY: Cornell University Press, 1984.

References

Berlin, Isaiah. *Vico and Herder.* London: Hogarth Press, 1976.

Breisach, Ernst. *Historiography: Ancient, Medieval, & Modern.* Second ed. Chicago: University of Chicago Press, 1994.

Bury, J.B. *The Idea of Progress: An Inquiry into Its Origin and Growth.* New York: Dover Publications, 1987.

Iggers, Georg G. *The German Conception of History: The National Tradition of Historical Thought from Herder to the Present.* Revised ed. Middletown, CT: Wesleyan University Press, 1983.

Koselleck, Reinhart. *Futures Past: On the Seman-tics of Historical Time.* Trans. Keith Tribe. Cambridge, MA: MIT Press, 1985.

Krieger, Leonard. *Ranke: The Meaning of History.* Chicago: University of Chicago Press, 1977.

Nisbet, Robert. *History of the Idea of Progress.* New Brunswick, NJ: Transaction Publishers, 1994.

Perkins, Robert L., ed. *History and System: Hegel's Philosophy of History.* Albany, NY: SUNY Press, 1984.

Progressive History

Historical movement embracing several U.S. historians who hoped to promote the broad reform movement, at its peak from about 1900 until World War I. During this period, often called the Progressive Age, many writers, politicians, and social scientists called for more governmental regulation of the economy, public services to benefit the working masses, an expansion of middle-class democracy, an end to political corruption, and the application of modern science to ameliorate social and industrial problems. Although influenced by European socialists, American progressives usually did not go so far as to advocate socialism, and most did not endorse the Marxist version of class conflict. The pragmatism and instrumentalism of William James and John Dewey provided an intellectual foundation for the movement. The progressive historians of the period did not constitute a single school, nor did they endorse a unified program; however, they generally believed progress was possible and favored a present-minded version of history that would promote left-of-center reforms.

The most prominent practitioners were James Harvey Robinson, Charles A. Beard, Vernon Parrington, Carl Becker, and Frederick Jackson Turner. Robinson's work concentrated upon the scientific and intellectual progress of humankind, with the idea that history should not just be a chronicle of the past, but rather a pragmatic weapon for explaining the present and controlling the future. Beard, at least in his early years, was associated with the left-leaning wing of progressivism, and his studies of the U.S. Constitution and the age of Jefferson emphasized class-based interests and economic motivations. Robinson and Beard became the main spokesmen for the "New History," a term that became almost synonymous with the progressive view of historiography. Parrington wrote a classic work of literary history, which interpreted American literature as a conflict between idealistic democrats and selfish reactionaries.

Becker was more detached than most progressives, but he cogently articulated the relativist view that history should constantly be revised from the perspective of contemporary concerns. Turner's views were at the right wing of the progressive movement. His progressivism was seen in his favorable version of Jacksonian democracy and in his advocacy of innovative methods, but his influential frontier thesis appeared to suggest limits of governmental control over social change. As a group, the progressive historians showed little interest in minorities of non-European ancestry, although individuals such as W.E.B. Du Bois were associated with the movement.

The goals and methods of the progressive historians were very similar to those of reform-minded social scientists who utilized history in the formation of theory, especially John Rogers Commons and Richard Ely. Likewise, progressive historians shared much in common with so-called muckrakers, the reforming journalists who attacked social injustices and corruption. Muckrakers such as Ida Tarbell, David Phillips, and Lincoln Steffins sometimes wrote popular versions of history as a means of furthering their agenda, the best example being Tarbell's *History of the Standard Oil Trust* (1904). After World War I, the reformist, present-minded perspective of progressive historiography was continued by the supporters of the New Deal/Great Society reforms, including Merle Curti, Harry Elmer Barnes, Henry Steele Commager, and Arthur Schlesinger Jr. Progressives of later periods usually showed more concern for minorities of non-European ancestry, but the adjective "progressive" increasingly was used as a protean label to refer to a variety of perspectives about the nature of progress.

Thomas T. Lewis

See also INTERDISCIPLINARY HISTORY; MARXISM AND HISTORIOGRAPHY; NEW HISTORY.

Texts

Beard, Charles A. *An Economic Interpretation of the Constitution.* New York: Macmillan, 1913.

Parrington, Vernon. *Main Currents in American Thought.* 3 vols. New York: Harcourt, Brace, 1927–1930.

Robinson, James Harvey. *The New History.* New York: Macmillan, 1912.

References

Breisach, Ernst. *American Progressive History: An Experiment in Modernization.* Chicago: University of Chicago Press, 1993.

Hofstadter, Richard. *The Progressive Historians: Turner, Beard, Parrington.* New York: Alfred Knopf, 1968.

Novick, Peter. *That Noble Dream: The "Objectivity Question" and the American Historical Profession.* New York: Cambridge University Press, 1988.

Skotheim, Robert. *American Intellectual Histories and Historians.* Princeton, NJ: Princeton University Press, 1966.

Prosopography

The detailed study of multiple biographies in order to solve historical problems. Modern usage of the word has been traced to 1743, and biographical compendia were popular in the nineteenth century, but prosopography was not adopted by professional historians as a tool until the early twentieth century. A pioneer was the American Charles A. Beard, in his *Economic Interpretation of the Constitution of the United States* (1913). Using somewhat tendentious data—an ongoing problem for prosopographers—Beard claimed that the framers of the U.S. Constitution were mainly influenced by economic class motives. Prosopography came into its own with the work of three historians working on very different periods, Sir Lewis Namier, Sir Ronald Syme, and R.K. Merton. In *The Structure of Politics at the Accession of George III* (1929), Namier revolutionized the study of British political history. Using biographical data exclusively, he constructed a group portrait of members of Parliament, revealing their interpersonal connections and shared socioeconomic interests. Syme's *The Roman Revolution* (1939) did much the same for politicians of the late Roman republic. Merton, an American sociologist, used prosopography in his *Science, Technology, and Society in Seventeenth Century England* (1938) to show a connection between Puritanism and a mental outlook sympathetic to natural science.

Namier and Syme, on the one hand, and Merton on the other, employed significantly different methods. The two British prosopographers used surviving documents and secondary biographical data to create scores of comparative case studies for analysis. Merton, in contrast, statistically correlated uniform variables about a relatively small sample group selected from the *Dictionary of National Biography*. These two approaches for several decades differentiated two schools of prosopography: the Namierite or elitist school, and the "multiple career-line analysis" or statistical school favored by social scientists and social historians attracted to quantification.

The perfection of computerized data processing in the 1960s and after, which enabled scholars to collate and analyze masses of information rapidly and accurately, greatly stimulated quantitative prosopography. It also discredited the impressionistic aspects of the Namierite school. Political prosopography—including its offshoot, psephology (the study of voting patterns)—continues to flourish in the computer age, but the major beneficiary has been social history. Quantitative prosopography utilizing the computer provided the basis for such elaborate studies as Theodore K. Rabb's *Enterprise and Empire: Merchant and Gentry Investment in the Expansion of England, 1575–1630* (1967); Lawrence Stone's *The Family, Sex and Marriage in England 1500–1800* (1977); Samuel Clark's *Social Origins of the Irish Land War* (1979); and Philip H. Burch's three-volume *Elites in American History* (1980–1981).

Prosopographers must beware of pitfalls, as Stone and other practitioners have conceded. These may include inadequate comparative data, especially for underprivileged social groups; inadvertent errors in classifying data; imperfect sampling techniques; and the difficulty or impossibility of factoring in abstractions such as ideas, ideologies, and prejudices. The methodology seems to work best when applied to well-defined groups within a fairly narrow time frame.

Don M. Cregier

See also BIOGRAPHY; INTERDISCIPLINARY HISTORY; SOCIAL HISTORY.

References
Beringer, Richard E. *Historical Analysis: Contemporary Approaches to Clio's Craft.* New York: John Wiley, 1978, 203–220.

Stone, Lawrence. *The Past and the Present Revisited.* London: Routledge and Kegan Paul, 1987, 45–73.

Psellus, Michael (1018–ca. 1082)

Byzantine scholar and historian. Psellus was born in Constantinople and held various public offices before 1054. Forced to retire to a monastery, he later returned to the capital as a court philosopher, dying some time after 1081. Psellus wrote numerous historical, philosophical, rhetorical, theological, and legal works as well as the *Chronography,* dealing with the 102 years before 1078; this emphasized (and probably exaggerated) his own political activities. Letters ascribed to him also survive.

Stephen A. Stertz

Texts

Fourteen Byzantine Rulers: The Chronographia.
Trans. E.R.A. Sewter. Revised ed. Baltimore,
MD: Penguin, 1953.

References

Chamberlain, C. "The Theory and Practice of
Imperial Panegyric in Michael Psellus."
Byzantion 56 (1986): 16–27.

Psychohistory

The integration of psychoanalysis and historical
scholarship. With its emphasis on unconscious
fantasies, the meaning of dreams, the defensive
functions of behavior and character, and the centrality of sexuality and aggression in human development, psychoanalysis concerns itself with matters
that are relevant to understanding historical actors.
Psychohistory has produced a wide range of psy-
choanalytically informed biographies of individuals and explored diverse collective phenomena.
Two events mark its beginnings. In December
1957 William Langer, a diplomatic historian, used
the occasion of his Presidential Address to the
American Historical Association to call on historians to familiarize themselves with depth psychology (i.e., psychoanalysis), and to integrate its findings into historical scholarship. The following year
the psychoanalyst Erik Erikson published *Young
Man Luther: A Study in Psychoanalysis and History.*

Langer cites Luther as an example of an individual who evoked a profound response in others because he expressed "the underlying, unconscious sentiments of large numbers of people and
[provided] them with an acceptable solution to
their religious problem." The depiction of Luther's
appeal is one of the major themes of *Young Man
Luther.* Erikson writes in the preface that Luther
provides an opportunity "to concentrate on the
powers of recovery inherent in the young ego." He
organizes his portrayal of Luther through the construct of identity. The essence of his interpretation was that in resolving his own identity crisis
Luther found a solution in Protestantism that had
widespread appeal.

These two early writers suggested that psychohistory could make a major contribution to
understanding the relationship between individual
historical experience and collective phenomena.
Since then, numerous articles and books have explored the interplay between psychoanalysis and
history, and the methodological similarities they
share. The role of empathy in each discipline has
received particular attention. The historian is a
part of the process he or she studies in the same
way that the clinician is part of the therapeutic encounter. This conception of history emphasizes
that in both history and psychoanalysis evidence
is always interpreted, and that facts are significant
only in a context of interpretation. At the same
time, both disciplines have developed methods
whose purpose is to insure that the personal factor is controlled and does not become a source
of distortion. Despite the similarities of their
methodologies, the use of psychoanalytic theory in
historical scholarship is controversial and has been
fiercely criticized as reductionist and irrelevant to
historical explanations. Its critics notwithstanding,
the relationship of psychoanalysis to history is a
powerful and compelling one.

The theoretical foundations of psychohistory
are difficult to characterize because the field does
not have a consensual or unified approach. Several
theoretical perspectives are evident within contemporary psychoanalysis itself. In addition, while
psychoanalytic concepts and theory openly inform
the arguments and interpretations in some studies, in others theory is not formally cited or is relegated to the footnotes.

The range of theoretical approaches available
includes ego psychology, object relations theory,
and self psychology. Each of these is a distinct
strand of contemporary psychoanalytic theory.
Ego psychology, as the name implies, approaches
the study of the individual through a focus on the
ego and its efforts to mediate between the demands
of the id and superego. Stress is placed on the ego's
capacity for adaptation as conflicts are successively
reworked and transformed as the individual ma-
tures. In his essay, "On the Uses of Psychology:
Conflict and Conciliation in Benjamin Franklin,"
Richard Bushman demonstrates how the delineation of adult psychological patterns casts light on
the style and content of an individual's work. He
links Franklin's technique as a diplomat and ne-
gotiator to a psychological pattern, revealed in
his *Autobiography,* whereby Franklin seeks to avoid
hostility, and endeavors to obtain gratification
without hurting others and by insuring mutual
benefit for both parties.

Self psychology holds that narcissism is an
essential feature of healthy development, and one
that follows its own developmental line. Disturbances in narcissistic development leave individuals with a weakened and fragmented sense of self.
They rely heavily on others for their sense of self-
worth and are vulnerable to rejection, to which
they react with rage and shame. Thomas Kohut's
Wilhelm II and the Germans: A Study in Leadership,

draws on self psychology to elucidate the historical significance of Wilhelm II's personality, his impact on the German people, and their influence on him.

Object relations theory emphasizes the preoedipal period. It conceptualizes psychic structure in terms of introjected "objects," which are the intrapsychic representations of significant figures in the infant's life. Repeated experiences of frustration and deprivation may result in objects being distorted. A stimulating application to historical analysis is Lewis Wurgaft's *Imperial Imagination: Magic and Myth in Kipling's India.* Wurgaft finds the notion of the intrapsychic object useful because culture and society, as represented by values, ideals, and myths, embody the individual's ultimate object world. He argues that the exploration of shared myths and ideals allows the historian to uncover the psychological concerns and fantasies that unite a group across several generations. His particular concern is with the British who served and lived in nineteenth-century India. He draws on the work of Rudyard Kipling to explore the many meanings that India held for the British. Wurgaft argues that in response to Indian demands for greater political recognition, the British became more rigid and controlling and developed a heroic mythology centered on their achievements, which idealized instinctual and social control. Political and psychological rigidity reinforced each other and resulted in defeat for the British and tragedy for India.

The application of psychoanalytic theory to the study of groups has also produced a diverse body of work. Among the most notable are Peter Loewenberg's "Psychohistorical Origins of the Nazi Youth Cohort" and John Demos's *Little Commonwealth* and *Entertaining Satan.* In their delineation of the particular unconscious fantasies that mobilize and bind groups these works make an important contribution to the study of groups. Nonetheless, psychohistorians tend to find psychoanalysis wanting when it comes to explaining group behavior. The argument that it does not provide an adequate theory of group dynamics may be symptomatic of the uncertainty many historians experience in trying to identify the mechanisms that connect individual experience to group behavior.

Nellie L. Thompson

References

Brugger, Robert J., ed. *Ourselves/Our Past: Psychological Approaches to American History.* Baltimore, MD: Johns Hopkins University Press, 1981.

Bushman, Richard. "On the Uses of Psychology: Conflict and Conciliation in Benjamin Franklin." *History and Theory* 5 (1966): 225–240.

Cocks, Geoffrey, and Travis Crosby, eds. *Psycho/History: Readings in the Method of Psychology, Psychoanalysis, and History.* New Haven, CT: Yale University Press, 1987.

Demos, John. *The Little Commonwealth: Family Life in Plymouth Colony.* New York: Oxford University Press, 1977.

Erikson, Erik. *Young Man Luther: A Study in Psychoanalysis and History.* New York: W.W. Norton and Co., 1958.

Kohut, Thomas. *Wilhelm II and the Germans: A Study in Leadership.* New York: Oxford University Press, 1991.

Loewenberg, Peter. *Decoding the Past: The Psychohistorical Approach.* New York: Alfred A. Knopf, 1983.

Mazlish, Bruce, ed. *Psychoanalysis and History.* New York: Grosset & Dunlap, 1971.

Stannard, David E. *Shrinking History: On Freud & the Failure of Psychohistory.* New York: Oxford University Press, 1980.

Wurgaft, Lewis D. *The Imperial Imagination: Magic and Myth in Kipling's India.* Middletown, CT: Wesleyan University Press, 1983.

Public History (United States)

A field of historical studies outside the university setting. In the United States, Robert Kelley (1925–1993) of the University of California at Santa Barbara is given credit for coining the term for the curriculum he developed there in 1976. According to Kelley, public history "refers to the employment . . . in government, private corporations, the media, historical societies and museums, even in private practice." Some areas of employment are newer and more controversial—for example, historians' contributions to public and corporate policy decisions.

Historians have practiced public history in the United States since the first stirring of an American historical consciousness. Local and state historical societies, the Library of Congress, the National Archives, and major private and university libraries are the primary repositories of the archives and memorabilia of the American people. Many archivists are historians. The early prime movers in historic preservation and collectors of American decorative arts could hardly be considered scholars in any modern sense. Giants like John Bach McMaster and James Ford Rhodes did not teach or have doctorates. They and others of their era wrote for a public avidly interested in history.

The American Historical Association (AHA) was founded in 1884 with the idea of balancing the membership between academic and amateur historians. For a period from 1904 to 1938 there was a section of the AHA called the Conference of State and Local Historical Societies, but interest in its sessions waned from the 1920s on. Historians outside the university were seen as antiquarians and dilettantes. In 1938 the executive secretary of the AHA asked leaders in the Local Historical Conference if they might in fact wish to disband. This suggestion was not greeted warmly, and by 1940 this group, consisting of directors of historical societies, archivists, museum curators, and historic preservationists, felt sufficiently disfranchised so that they proposed a new organization—the American Association of State and Local History (AASLH). Its mission was to help communities and local societies with their archives, their collections, their pageants and exhibits. The AASLH also intended to make historical scholarship accessible to the general public. In 1947 a small quarterly called *American Heritage: A Journal for Community History* was founded, and by 1954 it had expanded into a popular, illustrated magazine. Time-Life became interested and the historian Bruce Catton was hired as editor. By 1957 *American Heritage* had over 300,000 subscribers.

In recent times, the AASLH has been instrumental in providing technical help to small historical agencies in a multitude of areas from artifact conservation to the design and interpretation of exhibits. The association has also contributed significantly to professionalization within smaller agencies.

Arguably some of the most exciting developments in American history during the 1920s and 1930s happened outside the university. In the 1920s, both Colonial Williamsburg and Greenfield Village were founded by John D. Rockefeller and Henry Ford, respectively. Henry Francis Dupont began his collection of Americana, to be housed at Winterthur outside Wilmington. The American wing of the Metropolitan Museum of Art in New York opened in 1924. Since the founding of the Society for the Preservation of New England Antiquities in 1910, interest in historic preservation had been growing. The Historic American Building Survey and the National Park Service both thrived during the 1930s. Although academic historians initially paid little attention, these activities and institutions became very popular with the general public.

In the past three decades, public history has been fueled by developments in social history with an interest in ordinary people, their behavior, and institutions. These historians pursue such topics as community history, ethnic history, women's history, and folklore and its relation to written and/or oral history. "History from the bottom up," was the clarion call for this group of scholars. Along with the interest in ordinary people came a corresponding interest in the structures of communities, turning historians once again to the study of local history and its sources.

Another essential ingredient for the development of public history was the academic job crisis of the 1970s, which made university appointments scarce and made it possible for historical agencies to upgrade their programs by hiring staff with more and better graduate degrees. Historians within the university were forced by declining enrollments to encourage their students to look for work in business and in government. To be sure, some trained historians *chose* to work outside of the university, but many opted for such a career because there were no other positions to be found. The old-timers who had worked in the historical agencies resented the newcomers, but by now, twenty years later, these new public historians have proven their value. Local historical exhibits are no longer chauvinistic displays, but are more likely to address social issues and bring to the public new and sophisticated interpretations of the past. These new historians changed the focus of the public institutions in which they found employment and at the same time proved themselves worthy custodians of the public's heritage.

In this environment there arose within the university the notion of public or applied history. Social scientists had for some time taken positions on public and private policy, but historians had traditionally refrained from such involvement. Now, according to the leading exponents of public history—Robert Kelley, Wesley Johnson, Joel Tarr, and Peter Stearns—a major function of the trained public historian is to be a team player in the determination of policy. These policies concern war and peace, expansion and contraction of business, conservation of resources: the range of social, political, and economic experience.

Having gained a place in the university, public history programs now face the problem of defining their curricula. While there is some agreement that courses in traditional research methods and historiography are necessary, consensus begins to break down after that. The problem is the need for specialization within the field. Corporate historians, archivists, preservationists, museum directors, and curators need different skills and require a complex of interdisciplinary instruction. This array of needs is best addressed by a customized program designed to match student interests with courses providing preprofessional training for these various occupations.

Elizabeth Hitz

See also ARCHIVES; MUSEUMS.

References

Blatti, Jo, ed. *Past Meets Present: Essays about Historic Interpretation and Public Audiences.* Washington, DC: Smithsonian Institution Press, 1987.

Frisch, Michael. *A Shared Authority: Essays on the Craft and Meaning of Oral and Public History.* Albany, NY: SUNY Press, 1990.

Howe, Barbara J., and Emory L. Kent. *Public History: An Introduction.* Malabar, FL: Krieger, 1986.

Leffler, Phyllis K., and Joseph Brent, eds. *Public History Readings.* Malabar, FL: Krieger, 1992.

Public/Private, Historical Division of

Dualistic concept used by historians to distinguish between activities primarily associated with men (work, politics, war) and women (domestic and family life). More than just a concept, some argue that the public/private dichotomy is central to the organization of Western, capitalist society. A third perspective regards the public/private split as a prescribed ideal for gender relations in certain historical periods and places, such as classical Athens and Victorian England and North America. In the sixteenth and seventeenth centuries, public activities and politics were increasingly defined as male. Protestant reformers and writers attacked female rulers, quoting Scripture and citing "nature" in arguing that women could not be rulers since they belonged under the authority of a man. Several authors countered that queens could rule over subjects and still be subject to husbands in their private lives. By the late eighteenth century debates over the meaning of citizenship in the era of revolution suggested the possibility, only realized later, of reconceptualizing women as political beings, as citizens. Women's roles as wives and mothers were reinforced in the late eighteenth, and into the nineteenth, century. Termed "separate spheres," the division between public/private was associated most strongly with the formation of the middle class. At a more general level, Friedrich Engels viewed the public/private split as central to the development of industrial capitalist society— so long as woman was restricted to private domestic labor and shut out of socially productive work, she would never be equal to man, he argued.

Historians of North American and European women since the 1960s have debated the merits of the public/private dichotomy in helping to understand the historical experiences of women (and men). Some have used it as an analytical tool to explain women's subordination and victimization, arguing that women's restriction to the private sphere effectively ruled out participation in economic, legal, and political affairs. By the mid-1970s, some historians began to reinterpret the private sphere as an arena for a distinctive women's culture, especially among middle-class women, arguing that female networks based on close kinship and friendship ties sustained women in their daily lives and gave them a sense of power and status denied them in male-dominated society. In the 1980s, this approach was heavily criticized as imprecise and misleading because it confused prescribed ideals with behavior. Some historians also made distinctions between the historiographical concept and its qualities as an ideal or a practice. Linda Kerber, for example, discussed the separation between public/private as a rhetorical construction or metaphor. Others pointed out that the concept obscured the links between the spheres, such as the important claim to citizenship made by feminists, based on their roles within the domestic and family realm. Critics also noted that the public/private dichotomy was largely irrelevant to nonwhite women and women from other classes and non-European cultures. Despite these interventions, some recent historical work has argued that the concept remains useful and relevant because of the power it has had and continues to have in shaping the roles of women and men.

European historians, in fact, continue to explore the significance of and to define the boundaries between public and private. Their investigations, unlike those in the United States, arose in response to the work of the sociologist Jürgen Habermas and his book *The Structural Transformation of the Public Sphere.* He argued that a new "public sphere" emerged in eighteenth-century Europe, a place of "free" and open discourse across classes and political hierarchies, presaging new, more democratic relationships between subjects and rulers. Feminist historians of Europe have been critical of this analysis. Because women were essentially excluded from this dialogue, women's historians question the use of words like "free" and "democratic" in describing this public sphere. Despite this criticism these conceptions of the public and the private (the "particular" as it is identified in France) have led to many valuable works of European social history, many from a gendered perspective that differentiates between and describes both women's and men's roles and activities.

Linda Kealey

See also FEMINISM; GENDER; PATRIARCHY; WOMEN'S HISTORY, NORTH AMERICAN.

References

Ariès, Philippe, and Georges Duby, eds. *A History of Private Life.* 5 vols. Cambridge, MA: Harvard University Press, 1987–1991.

Davidoff, Leonore, and C. Hall. *Family Fortunes: Men and Women of the English Middle Class.* Chicago: University of Chicago Press, 1987.

Fraser, Nancy. "Rethinking the Public Sphere: A Contribution to the Critique of Actually Existing Democracy." In *Habermas and the Public Sphere,* ed. Craig Calhoun. Cambridge, MA: MIT Press, 1992, 109–142.

Guildford, Janet, and Suzanne Morton, eds. *Separate Spheres: Women's Worlds in the 19th-Century Maritimes.* Fredericton, Canada: Acadiensis Press, 1994.

Habermas, Jürgen. *The Structural Transformation of the Public Sphere: An Inquiry into a Category of Bourgeois Society.* Trans. Thomas Burger in association with Frederick Lawrence. Cambridge, MA: MIT Press, 1989.

Kerber, Linda. "Separate Spheres, Female Worlds, Woman's Place: The Rhetoric of Women's History." *Journal of American History* 75 (1988): 9–39.

Landes, Joan. *Women and the Public Sphere in the Age of the French Revolution.* Ithaca, NY: Cornell University Press, 1988.

Reverby, Susan M., and D.O. Helly, eds. *Gendered Domains: Rethinking Public and Private in Women's History: Essays from the Seventh Berkshire Conference on the History of Women.* Ithaca, NY: Cornell University Press, 1992.

Wiesner, Merry E. *Women and Gender in Early Modern Europe.* Cambridge, Eng.: Cambridge University Press, 1993.

Q

Qi Xia [Ch'i Hsia] (b. 1923)

Chinese historian. Born in Juye in Shandong province, Qi attended National Southwest United University in 1944 and graduated in 1948 with his B.A. from Beijing University, where he also undertook his graduate studies. For more than forty years Qi has been engaged in studying Song history. He established his leadership in the field with publication of *Songdai jingjishi* [Economic History of the Song Dynasty] (1987–1988), which is recognized as the first work to present Chinese economic history from the perspective of dynastic history—a systematic and thoroughgoing Marxist exploration of the Chinese economy during the Song period. In addition, he has presented many original ideas on such issues as the internal periodization of Chinese traditional society, the underlying theories of Chinese peasant wars, and the status of the Song economy within the longer course of Chinese economic history. He also has done considerable research in the histories of the Qin and Han dynasties. That a specialist in Song history could also publish notable pieces in these other spheres is regarded as a considerable accomplishment among contemporary Chinese historians.

Shao Dongfang

Texts

Qin Han nongmin zhanzhengshi [A History of Peasant Wars during the Qin-Han Period]. Beijing: Sanlian shudian, 1962.

Qiushi ji [Seeking the Truth]. Tianjin: Tianjin renmin chubanshe, 1982.

Songdai jingjishi. Shanghai: Shanghai renmin chubanshe, 1987–1988.

Wang Anshi bianfa [The Wang Anshi's Reform]. Shanghai: Shanghai renmin chubanshe, 1959.

References

Feuerwerker, Albert, ed. *History in Communist China.* Cambridge, MA: M.I.T. Press, 1968.

Feuerwerker, Albert, and S. Cheng. *Chinese Communist Studies of Modern Chinese History.* Cambridge, MA: Harvard University Press, 1961.

Yang Weisheng. "A Brief Survey of Song Dynasty Studies in China over the Past Decade." *The Bulletin of Sung Yuan Studies* 20 (1988): 1–17.

Qian Daxin [Ch'ien Ta-sin] (1728–1804)

Chinese historian, scholar, and poet. Qian Daxin was born in Jiading (today's Shanghai area). Since childhood his reputation for keen learning had been widespread. In 1754 he obtained the highest civil-service degree and then served in the Hanlin Academy for about twenty years. After his father's death in 1775, he retired from office. From 1778 on he taught in several academies in Nanjing, Songjiang, and Suzhou until his own death. Qian devoted most of his energy to historical studies, although his learning in the Confucian classics was also profound. Qian's scholarship was notable for its precision and breadth. He excelled most other historians of his time not only in applying evidential-research methodology, already highly developed in classical studies, to historiography, but also in using a wide knowledge of such subjects as mathematics, astronomy, and calendars in his historical enquiries. Moreover, he extended his research to the histories of non-Chinese dynasties such as Liao (907–1125), Jin (1115–1234), and especially the Yuan (1271–1368). Qian's most representative works are the *Nianershi kaoyi* [An Enquiry into Discrepancies among the Twenty-Two Standard Histories] (1780), *Shijiazhai yanxinlu*

[Record of Cultivating New Knowledge in the Shijia Study] (1804–1806), and *Qianyantang wenji* [Collected Essays from the Qianyan Hall] (1806). Therein he delved into various aspects of the histories and classics; he also undertook textual criticism and topical research and made occasional moral judgments.

Shoucheng Yan

Texts

Bu Yuanshi yiwenzhi [Supplementary Treatise of Bibliography on the *Yuan History*]. In *Nianwushi bubian*. Beijing: Zhonghua shuju, 1955.

Nianereshi kaoyi. In *Congshu jicheng chubian*. Shanghai: Shangwu yinshuguan, 1935–1937.

Qianyantang ji [Collected Works from the Qianyan Hall]. Shanghai: Shanghai guji chubanshe, 1989.

Shijiazhai yanxinlu. In *Sibu beiyao*. Shanghai: Zhonghua shuju, 1936.

Yuanshi shizubiao [Tables of Clans and Families in the *Yuan History*]. In *Nianwushi bubian*. Beijing: Zhonghua shuju, 1955.

References

Chai Degeng. *Shixue congkao* [Miscellaneous Studies in Historiography]. Beijing: Zhonghua shuju, 1982.

Chen Qingquan et al., eds. *Zhongguo shixuejia pingzhuan* [Critical Biographies of Chinese Historians], vol. 2. Zhengzhou: Zhongzhou guji chubanshe, 1985.

Qian Mu [Ch'ien Mu] (1895–1990)

Chinese cultural historian. Born to a poor family in Jiangsu province, Qian received no further formal education after high school but was able to teach himself classical languages and history while teaching in an elementary school. Qian achieved recognition as an authority on ancient history with two publications, *Liu Xiang, Xin fu zi nianpu* [Chronological Record of Liu Xiang and Xin, Father and Son] (1930) and *Xianqin zhuzi xinian* [Chronological Studies of the pre-Qin thinkers] (1935). He moved to Hong Kong in 1949 and founded the New Asia Academy. For more than five decades, Qian used his historical writing to urge his countrymen to the quest to revitalize China: to look to Chinese roots for inspiration rather than to the West. In his *Guoshi dagang* [Outline History of the Nation] (1940), Qian Mu described the vitality of Chinese culture and the rationale of Chinese institutions. In his *Zhuzi xin xuean* [New Intellectual Biography of Zhu Xi] (1971), Qian Mu demonstrated, through the example of the Neo-Confucian scholar Zhu Xi [Chu Hsi] (1130–1200), how old learning could continue to give rise to new thought.

Tze-ki Hon

Texts

Guoshi dagang. Taibei: Shangwu yinshu guan, 1982.

Qian Han shi. Hong Kong: Da Zhongguo yinshua chang, 1966.

Zhuzi xin xuean. Chengdu: Bashu shushe, 1986.

References

Dennerline, Jerry. *Qian Mu and the World of Seven Mansions*. New Haven, CT: Yale University Press, 1988.

Quan Zuwang [Ch'üan Tsu-wang] (1705–1755)

Chinese historian and Neo-Confucian scholar. Quan was born in the Yin district, Zhejiang. Soon after obtaining the highest civil-service degree in 1736, he left Beijing and returned south. There he dedicated his life to writing and teaching until his death in poverty. Quan's interest in historiography focused on three fields: loyalists in the transition from Ming-dyansty to Qing-dynasty rule, early Qing Confucian scholars, and local literati of eastern Zhejiang. His many biographical writings—collected in the *Jieqiting ji* [Works from the Jiqi Pavilion] (1804)—record the activities, feelings, and circumstances of these groups. Quan also engaged in serious studies of the Confucian classics and ancient histories, his representative works in this area being the *Jingshi wenda* [Questions and Answers on the Classics and Histories] (1765) and *Hanshu dilizhi jiyi* [An Enquiry into Doubtful Points in the Geographical Treatise of the History of the Former Han] (ca. 1804). As a follower of Huang Zongxi's Eastern Zhejiang school of historiography, Quan completed and expanded Huang's unfinished *Song Yuan xuean* [Records of Sung and Yuan Confucian Scholars] (1846). Unlike Huang, he paid more attention to historical details and methodology than to the philosophical meanings of events.

Shoucheng Yan

Texts

Hanshu dilizhi jiyi. In *Siming congshu* [Collection of Works from Simin (i.e., modern Ningbo)]. Ed. Zhang Shouyong. Part 1. Ningbo: Zhang Shouyong's Yueyuan, 1932.

Jieqiting ji. In *Sibu congkan chubian.* Shanghai: Shangwu yinshuguan, 1919–1922.
Jinshi wenda. Included in *Jieqiting ji.*
Song Yuan xuean. Beijing: Zhonghua shuju, 1986.

References

Jia Kai. *Shixue tonglun* [Introduction to Historiography]. Taibei: Xuesheng shuju, 1985.
Jiang Tianshu. *Quan Xieshan nianpu* [Chronological Biography of Quan Zuwang]. Shanghai: Shangwu yinshuguan, 1933.

Quantitative History

See CLIOMETRICS; SERIAL HISTORY.

Québécois Historiography

Indigenous historical writing of the Québécois or French-Canadian people from the mid-nineteenth century to the present. Most scholars trace the origins of French-Canadian historiography to the works of François-Xavier Garneau, whose *Histoire du Canada* appeared in 1844. Garneau wrote during a period of great disillusionment when French Canadians saw their language and culture officially repressed by a British policy of cultural assimilation. Garneau sought by his history to foster a sense of national pride in his compatriots. Critical of clerical influence and governmental paternalism during the French regime, Garneau placed blame for the British conquest of 1760 and the failure of French colonization squarely on the shoulders of clerical and royal authority. While Garneau's *Histoire* was extremely popular, he was severely condemned by the church and was forced to revise subsequent editions of his work.

The clerical reaction to Garneau was an indication of things to come. In the 1860s the abbé Ferland published his *Cours d'histoire du Canada,* which advanced an interpretation more to the liking of clerical authorities. To him, the French Canadians were distinguished by their spiritual nature and their rejection of materialism, which he saw as the downfall of other North American peoples. With minor alterations Ferland's interpretation dominated French-Canadian historiography for the next sixty years. While the clerical interpretation did evolve, it was mostly in the interpretation of the post-conquest period. Following the providential interpretation of French-Canadian history, some clerics came to see the conquest itself as a sign of divine intervention. Conquest by Britain had at least spared French Canada from the abuses of the French Revolution.

The First World War was a watershed for the evolution of French-Canadian nationalism and consequently for that of French-Canadian historiography. The war was marked by intense ethnic conflict in domestic politics, the most serious coming over the issue of conscription for overseas service. As a result of these tensions the French-Canadian nationalism of the 1920s became more aggressive and more centered on protecting the cultural survival and political autonomy of French Canadians living in the province of Quebec. The leading exponent of this new ideology would also come to dominate French-Canadian historiography into the 1950s. The abbé Lionel Groulx's view of New France reproduced many of the features of the traditional clerical interpretation; his portrayal of French Canada after the conquest was that of a small nation struggling heroically to preserve its distinctiveness in the face of repeated attempts at assimilation. Like many historians of his time Groulx emphasized the unique characteristics of the French Canadians as a *race,* and in his more polemical tracts he condemned apostasy and intermarriage as threats to racial purity and at times was openly anti-Semitic.

By the time of World War II, Quebec had become a predominantly urban and industrial society. The war itself, marked by political conflicts similar to those of the first war over the same issue of conscription, hastened a change in mentalities, which was reflected in the work of postwar historians. Grouped around the Université de Montréal, the neonationalist school of French-Canadian historiography retained Groulx's essential emphasis on history as national struggle while adding a social dimension that took the place of race as a means of explaining the unique historical evolution of the French Canadians as a people. Three men dominated this school: Maurice Séguin, Michel Brunet, and Guy Frégault. Brunet's conquest theory, which held that the British occupation had decapitated French-Canadian society by forcing its business class into exile and ensuring the dominance of the clerical elite, was widely publicized as an explanation for contemporary French-Canadian economic inferiority. Guy Frégault lent credence to the decapitation hypothesis by a more detailed study of "New France" on the eve of the conquest. Frégault's work sought to demonstrate that "New France" was a "normal" colony of a mercantilist power, whose growth into a nation had been abruptly altered by the conquest.

The emphasis on social development which appeared in the neonationalist writings was echoed in the works of another school of historians emerging from the province's other major institution of higher learning, the Université Laval in Quebec City. Their most significant contribution came in the area of demographic and economic history, where they adapted techniques borrowed from the French Annales school. Marcel Trudel, the dean of this group, studied the evolution of the seigneurial system of land tenure in "New France." Fernand Ouellet's *Histoire économique et sociale du Québec 1760–1850,* published in 1966, became one of the most important books in the evolution of French-Canadian historiography. Directly inspired by the Annalistes, Ouellet painstakingly reconstructed the development of Quebec's economy and the social changes that grew out of that development. Ouellet emphasized the failure of French-Canadian elites to adapt to the advent of capitalism, a result of the persistence of *Ancien régime* social structures and the *mentalités* that grew out of them.

Although Ouellet's indictment of traditional elites met with resistance from nationalist circles, his methodological innovations transformed French-Canadian historiography. Coinciding as it did with the expansion of graduate studies in the province, this change in emphasis has created a rich social history tradition. In the history of "New France," for example, the myth of the pious nature of early settlement was shattered by Louise Dechêne's *Habitants et Marchands* which chronicled the evolution of seventeenth-century Montreal from missionary outpost to the thriving hub of "New France's" economy. For the early nineteenth century the work of Jean-Pierre Wallot and Gilles Paquet challenged Ouellet's hypothesis of an agricultural crisis through the use of cliometrics and studies of local economies.

In the past twenty years French-Canadian historiography has broadened both in scope and subject matter. Most of the new work deals with the late nineteenth and twentieth centuries from a variety of approaches including women's history, labor history, and urban history. The uniqueness of current French-Canadian historiography lies in the continued influence of French scholarship. This is demonstrated in the popularity of demographic studies and the adoption of French methods in sociocultural history, which have inspired numerous studies of social attitudes toward disease, insanity and criminality, and *histoire du livre*. This tendency toward subjects of an interdisciplinary nature has in turn stimulated the development of several research centers grouping together scholars from various disciplines in the social sciences. The most impressive collaborative projects are devoted to the study of demographic history and historical geography. Most notable among these centers is the Institut interuniversitaire de recherches sur les populations, under the direction of the prominent demographic historian Gérard Bouchard.

Louis-Georges Harvey

See also CANADIAN HISTORIOGRAPHY.

Texts

Brunet, Michel. *Canadians et Canadiens: Études sur l'histoire et la pensée des deux Canadas.* Montreal: Fides, 1954.

Dechêne, Louise. *Habitants and Merchants in Seventeenth-Century Montreal.* Trans. Liana Vardi. Montreal: McGill-Queens University Press, 1992.

Ferland, Jean-Baptiste-Antoine. *Cours d'histoire du Canada.* Quebec: A. Coté, 1861–1865.

Garneau, François-Xavier. *Histoire du Canada depuis sa découverte jusqu'à nos jours* [History of Canada from the Discovery to Our Own Times]. Quebec: N. Aubin, 1845–1852.

Groulx, Lionel. *Histoire du Canada français depuis la découverte* [History of French Canada since the Discovery]. Montreal: Action nationale, 1951.

Ouellet, Fernand. *Economic and Social History of Quebec, 1760–1850: Structures and Conjunctures.* Ottawa: Gage Publishing, 1980.

References

Gagnon, Serge. *Quebec and Its Historians, 1840–1920.* Trans. Yves Brunelle. Montreal: Harvest House, 1982.

Gagnon, Serge. *Quebec and Its Historians: The Twentieth Century.* Trans. Jane Brierley. Montreal: Harvest House, 1985.

Quinet, Edgar (1803–1875)

French historian, political philosopher, and poet. Born in Bourg, Quinet was exposed to military life by his father, commissioner of war under the Republic, while at the same time being given a strict Protestant education under the careful scrutiny of his mother. In 1841 he accepted a professorship at the Collège de France in Paris. Influenced by his reading of Rousseau and Herder, he conceived of ideas as causative agents that were organically expressed in religion, individuals, and nations; in *Le Génie des Religions* [The Spirit of Religions] (1842) he placed religion at the core of national history. By 1845, in *Le Christianisme et la Révolution française* [Christianity and the French Revolution],

Quinet proclaimed that there should be a total separation of church and state. Although the Catholic Church was outmoded for the modern world, only Protestantism, successful in the English and American revolutions, offered some help. In his greatest work, *La Révolution* (1865), Quinet wrote a history of liberty, and searched for the original genius of the French Revolution, a genius that had failed to find success in 1789, 1830, or 1848.

John B. Roney

Texts

Le christianisme et la révolution française. Paris: Fayard, 1984.

France et Allemagne. Ed. C. Cestre. Oxford: Clarendon Press, 1908.

Le Génie des Religions. Paris: Chamerot, 1851.

The Religious Revolution of the Nineteenth Century. London: Trubner, 1881.

The Roman Church and Modern Society. New York: Gates and Stedman, 1845.

References

Aeschimann, Willy. *La pensée d'Edgar Quinet: Étude sur la formation de ses idées* [The Thought of Edgar Quinet: A Study in the Formation of His Ideas]. Paris: Anthropos, 1986.

Crossley, Ceri. *Edgar Quinet (1803–1875): A Study in Romantic Thought.* Lexington, KY: French Forum, 1983.

Powers, R.H. *Edgar Quinet: A Study in French Patriotism.* Dallas: Southern Methodist University Press, 1957.

Q

R

Radical History (United States)

History written in the United States by left-wing scholars, principally in the 1960s. In protest to the war in Vietnam, poverty and racism at home, and the traditional pattern of education and earning one's bread, a new radicalism in social thought emerged in the 1960s. Although often identified as the new revolt of the young, it was both less and more than that, for while nearly fourteen million souls swelled the ranks of the youth population in the 1960s, only a minority of them participated directly in or expressed sympathy for political dissent and the search for a new lifestyle. But as is often the case among intellectuals in relation to the whole society from which they were estranged, the young radicals, whose motto was "You can't trust anyone over thirty," had an influence out of all proportion to their numbers.

The New Radicalism, or New Left as it was sometimes called, was a pluralistic, amorphous grouping, embracing among others the Free Speech movement, the Students for a Democratic Society, and the various antiwar organizations composed mainly of white middle-class youth. Furthermore, the New Radicalism operated essentially on three levels. On the political level, it was an antiestablishment protest against all the obvious inequities of American life; on a more complex level it was a moral revulsion against a society that was perceived as being increasingly corrupt; and on the last level it was an existential revolt against remote impersonal forces that were not responsive to human needs. For many, this meant figuratively reaching out and grabbing their university administrations by the throat, forcing the termination of such practices as CIA recruitment on campuses, curtailment of Pentagon-related research on campus, and the introduction of a more "relevant" curriculum. The result was turmoil and violence at universities from California to New York, culminating with the shooting deaths of four students on the campus of Kent State University by National Guardsmen in May 1970. By the end of the decade, "the movement" was gone.

Their favorite philosophers ranged from Herbert Marcuse, whose *One Dimensional Man* helped them locate totalitarianism in the government and society of the United States, to Jean Paul Sartre, whose *No Exit* said it all; their favorite musicians were Joan Baez and Bob Dylan; their favorite films, *The Graduate* and *Easy Rider;* and their favorite turn-ons, marijuana, or grass, and LSD, or lysergic acid diethylamide. Their favorite historians included William Appleman Williams, Staughton Lynd, Noam Chomsky, Gabriel Kolko, and Howard Zinn, all of whom found themselves pitted against the imputed political conservatism of the profession as well as in search of a "usable past." Williams's contribution was the general thesis, in his words, that "empire is as American as apple pie." Through his frontier-expansionistic theory of causation, which assumed that U.S. foreign policy derived rationally and logically (if routinely) from an inherently expansionist capitalist political economy, Williams revived and updated an earlier economic revisionism, subsumed and moved beyond the "realist" critique of his own generation, and called for the reconstruction of American national life along democratic socialist lines—economically self-sufficient and politically free from overseas entanglements. Kolko, who upheld the extreme left of the political spectrum, was unrelenting in his criticism of American diplomacy, especially in Vietnam.

Lynd, Chomsky, and Zinn supplied the conscience of the new radicalism. Lynd argued that one of the main tasks of the historian was to project an alternative future on the basis of the richness of the American past, while Chomsky argued that it was "the responsibility of intellectuals to speak the truth and to expose lies." For his part, Zinn posed the challenge "that the special qualities of control possessed by the modern liberal system demanded a long revolutionary process of struggle and example."

Joseph M. Siracusa

See also AMERICAN HISTORIOGRAPHY; CLASS; HISTORY WORKSHOP; LABOR HISTORY; MARXISM AND HISTORIOGRAPHY.

References

Bernstein, Barton J., ed. *Towards a New Past: Dissenting Essays in American History.* New York: Pantheon Books, 1968.

Newfield, Jack. *The Prophetic Minority.* New York: New American Library, 1966.

Novick, Peter. *That Noble Dream: The "Objectivity Question" and the American Historical Profession.* Cambridge: Cambridge University Press, 1988.

Roszak, Theodore, ed. *The Dissenting Academy.* New York: Pantheon Books, 1967.

Siracusa, Joseph M. *New Left Diplomatic Histories and Historians: The American Revisionists.* Second ed. Claremont, CA: Regina Books, 1993.

Skotheim, Robert A. *Totalitarianism and American Social Thought.* New York: Rhinehart and Winston, 1971.

Zinn, Howard. *Postwar America: 1945–1971.* Indianapolis, IN: Bobbs-Merrill Co., 1973.

Raemond, Florimond de (1540–1601)

French politician and historian. Raemond was a member of the Parlement of Bordeaux and defended Catholicism against Protestants. He continually expanded his exposé of "Pope Joan" (1587). Raemond's first edition of Blaise de Monluc's memoirs (1592) was creditable. His vernacular *History of Heresy* (published posthumously in 1605), was his best-known work, describing Lutheranism's entrance into France via Strasbourg. Calvinism he thought worse than Lutheranism. His account of Anabaptism, which attracted artisans and women, amounted to an early instance of the history of *mentalités.* His title predicted Protestantism's decline nearly a century before the abolition of the Edict of Nantes. Popular despite (or because of) his prejudices, he influenced the Catholic historians Louis Maimbourg and Bishop Bossuet. Although

he was ignored in the Enlightenment, Raemond was rediscovered in the nineteenth century, and many modern scholars view him as anthropologically astute.

Barbara Sher Tinsley

Texts

L'Anti-Christ. Paris: Abel L'Angelier, 1599.

L'Anti-papesse ou, erreur populaire de la papesse Jane [Popular Error of the Pope Joan]. Lyon: Benoist Rigaud, 1595.

L'Histoire de la naissance, progrez et decadence de l'heresie de ce siècle [History of the Birth, Progress and Decline of Heresy in This Century]. Paris: Guillaume de la Nove, 1605.

References

Dubois, Claude-Gilbert. *La Conception de l'histoire en France au XVIᵉ Siècle* [The Idea of History in Sixteenth Century France]. Paris: A.-G. Nizet, 1977.

Giono, Jean. "Preface" to Blaise de Monluc, *Commentaires* [Commentaries]. Ed. Paul Courteault. Paris: Éditions Gallimard, 1964.

Tinsley, Barbara Sher. *History and Polemics in the French Reformation: Florimond de Raemond Defender of the Church.* Selinsgrove, PA: Susquehanna University Press; London and Toronto, Associated University Presses, 1992.

Raffles, Sir Thomas Stamford (1781–1826)

Colonial administrator and orientalist. Raffles left school at the age of fourteen to work as a clerk with the East India Company in London. Self-taught in the sciences and languages he was appointed assistant to the chief secretary of Penang in 1805. Raffles and his wife lived in Penang until 1811 when Britain arranged with French-occupied Holland to administer temporarily Dutch East Indian possessions. He was then appointed lieutenant-general of Java for four and a half years, during which he strove to replace the Dutch mercantilist monopoly with a free market, abolish forced labor, introduce land-based direct taxation, and reform the police and judiciary. Despite Raffles's wishes to the contrary, Java was restored to the Dutch shortly after he was recalled to London in 1816. Ill and recently widowed he wrote his major work, the *History of Java* in six months. Published in two volumes in 1817, it describes the languages, geography, anthropology, literature, and botany of Java and details the benefits of his reforms. Its anti-Dutch polemic includes statistics showing a declining population under Dutch rule and estimates that under British rule Java would become the populous hub of a trading empire stretching from China to Australia.

Mary C. Quilty

Texts

The History of Java. London: Oxford University Press, 1965.
Memoir of the Life and Public Service of Sir Thomas Stamford Raffles. London: John Murray, 1830.

References

Bastin, John. "English Sources for the Modern Period of Indonesian History." In *An Introduction to Indonesian Historiography,* ed. Soedjatmoko et al. Ithaca, NY: Cornell University Press, 1965, 252–271.
Collis, M. *Raffles.* London: Faber and Faber, 1966.
Quilty, Mary. "Textual Empires: A Reading of Early British Histories of Southeast Asia." Ph.D. thesis, University of Melbourne, 1992.
Wurtzburg, C. *Raffles of the Eastern Isles.* Singapore: Oxford University Press, 1986.

Ragionieri, Ernesto (1926–1975)

Italian intellectual historian. In a career that spanned four decades, Ragionieri was associated with the University of Florence, and his relationship with the city mirrored that of Benedetto Croce with his beloved Naples. Although an avowed Communist from his youth at the university, Ragionieri insisted that the historian employ "scientific reflection" at all times. His first work, an elaboration of his thesis, was *La polemica sulla Weltgeschichte* [A Polemic on World History] (1951), in which he began a lifelong study of German history and culture. His *Un comune socialista, Sesto Fiorentino* [A Socialist Commune] (1953) became a model for the genre of local history. In *Socialdemocrazia tedesca e socialisti italiani* (1961), Ragionieri examined the relationship between German social democracy and Italian socialism; and in 1968 there appeared his *Il marxismo e l'Internazionale.* Before his untimely death, he began the monumental task of editing and publishing the writings of Palmiro Togliatti (1893–1964), who had been a colleague of Gramsci in establishing the Communist Party in Italy. Ragioneri's *La Terza Internazionale e il Partito comunista italiano* [The Third International and the Italian Communist Party] was published posthumously in 1978.

Stanislao G. Pugliese

Texts

Un comune socialista, Sesto Fiorentino. Rome: Riuniti, 1976.
Il movimento socialista in Italia (1850–1922) [The Socialist Movement in Italy, 1850–1922]. Milan: Teti, 1976.
La Terza Internazionale e il partito comunista italiano. Turin: Einaudi, 1978.

References

Bibliografia delli scritti di Ernesto Ragionieri [Bibliography of the Writings of Ernesto Ragionieri]. Florence: Olschki, 1980.
Garin, Eugenio. "Ernesto Ragionieri." *Belfagor* 33 (1978): 297–320.

Rai Sanyō (1780–1832)

Japanese historian. Born in Osaka to a family in the service of the lord of Hiroshima, Rai encountered trouble frequently in his youth owing to his restless spirit. Disowned by the family in 1804, he earned his living subsequently through teaching and writing. His fame as a historian rests chiefly on two posthumous works: *Nihon gaishi* [An Unofficial History of Japan] and *Nichon seiki* [Political Records of Japan]. Completed in 1829 and first published in 1844, the former is a history of warrior rule in Japan, from its origins in the twelfth century to Rai's own time; the latter, published a year later, is a history of Japanese sovereigns, from the mythical beginning to the Emperor Go Yōzei (r. 1586–1610). Written in Chinese, both works represent what is essentially a Confucian interpretation of Japanese history.

John Lee

Texts

Rai Sanyō Nihon gaishi [The Unofficial History of Japan by Rai Sanyō]. Ed. Andō Hideo. Tokyo: Kondō Shuppan Sha, 1982.
Rai Sanyō shoga daibatsu hyoshaku [Selections from Rai Sanyō]. Ed. Chojirō Taketani. Tokyo: Meiji Shoin, 1983.

References

Beasley, W.G., and Carmen Blacker. "Japanese Historical Writing in the Tokugawa Period (1603–1868)." In *Historians of China and Japan,* ed. W.G. Beasley and E.G. Pulleyblank. London: Oxford University Press, 1961, 245–263.

Rajabangsavatar Brah Sisowath Monivong, Brah Norodom Sihanouk [Royal Chronicle of King Sisowath Monivong and King Norodom Sihanouk]

Cambodian chronicle manuscript, consisting of 934 pages of lightly ruled foolscap, in at least two hands, copied from earlier texts and assembled in 1949. The manuscript, never published, deals cursorily with events in the reign of King Sisowath Monivong (1927–1941) and in far more detail with the early years of the reign of Norodom Sihanouk (r. 1941–1955; 1993–); no chronicle texts from the later years of Sihanouk's reign have survived, and a chronicle for this period may never have been compiled. Both texts spring from a venerable tradition, stretching back to Angkorean times (ca. A.D. 802–ca. 1431), whereby accounts of a king's activities became part of his successor's regalia. Both texts are royal in focus. Monivong's is fragmentary, and seems to represent a need to compose some kind of document rather than an accurate or detailed description of the reign. The Sihanouk portion, covering more than eight hundred pages, contains extracts from speeches, newspapers, and official correspondence, but no effort is made to organize the material thematically or to comment on it. There is no evidence that either king read or edited the texts.

David Chandler

References

Chandler, David. "Cambodian Palace Chronicles (rajabangsavatar) 1927–1949: Kingship and Historiography at the End of the Colonial Era." In *Perceptions of the Past in Southeast Asia,* ed. David Marr and Anthony Reid. Singapore: Heinemann Educational Books, 1979, 207–218.

Ralegh, Sir Walter (1552–1618)

English courtier and historian. Born in Devon, England, Ralegh served Elizabeth I but was imprisoned in 1604 by her successor, James I. He was executed in 1618, a martyr many believed, to that king's pro-Spanish policy. During his years as a prisoner, Ralegh had composed the *History of the World* (1614) to persuade James's heir-apparent, Prince Henry, that, among other things, Spain remained a menace. Universalist in conception, the *History* began with the creation, consisted of five books, and ended in the second century B.C. Adopting a providential scheme, Ralegh avowed that a divine order rules human affairs and shapes national destinies, suggesting that the English were now God's favored people as well as the heirs to imperial Rome. He also used Machiavellian insights for political analysis and invoked skeptical ideas, especially in his pessimistic preface and poignant conclusion. Though unfinished according to its original plan, the *History* was well received, and was widely read during the following century, inspiring Oliver Cromwell's anti-Spanish policy of the 1650s.

Adriana A.N. McCrea

Texts

Ralegh, Sir Walter. *The History of the World.* Ed. C.A. Patrides. London: MacMillan, 1971.

References

Greenblatt, Stephen. *Sir Walter Ralegh: The Renaissance Man and His Roles.* New Haven, CT: Yale University Press, 1973.

Woolf, D.R. *The Idea of History in Early Stuart England: Erudition, Ideology and "The Light of Truth" from the Accession of James I to the Civil War.* Toronto: University of Toronto Press, 1990.

Ranger, Terence Osborn (b. 1929)

British historian of southern and eastern Africa. After receiving his doctorate from Oxford in 1958 for a thesis on seventeenth-century Irish history, Ranger lectured at the University College of Rhodesia and Nyasaland until the rise of Ian Smith's white supremacist government in 1963 prompted him to move to the University College of Dar es Salaam in newly independent Tanzania. More recently, he has held professorships at the University of California, Los Angeles (1969–1974) and the University of Manchester (1974–1987) and currently holds the chair of African history at Oxford.

Amid the political climate of decolonization in the 1960s, Ranger soon changed his field of interest from Ireland to Africa and became a founding member of the nationalist school of African history. This represented a departure from the previous racist, Eurocentric colonial histories. His seminal works glorified the precolonial past and claimed that African resistance to colonial conquest at the turn of the nineteenth and twentieth centuries had direct connections to modern mass nationalism. His most well-known book, *Revolt in Southern Rhodesia,* described the Ndebele and Shona revolt against British rule in 1896–1897 as an attempt by an emerging religious leadership to enlarge the scale of resistance and create a protonationalist movement. Although the subsequent research of Julian Cobbing and David Beach has demonstrated the inaccuracy of Ranger's interpretation, it must be understood that he wrote this book at a time when the African liberation movement in Rhodesia (now Zimbabwe) was bitterly divided and in need of historical inspiration. Consequently, Ranger's version of the 1896 uprising is still dominant in the Zimbabwean school system and many academic texts. In 1968 Ranger adapted the thesis in his book into a Pan-African conceptualization of the history of African resistance, published originally as two articles in the *Journal of African History* and subsequently as a chapter in the anthology *Colonialism in Africa*. This conceptualization, positing specific stages of African resistance, each following the other in defined forms as primary resistance, secondary revolt, tertiary millennial movements, elite nationalism, and modern mass nationalism, had enormous influence on subsequent research on case studies of African resistance and nationalism.

Timothy J. Stapleton

Texts

"African Reactions to the Imposition of Colonial Rule in East and Central Africa." In *Colonialism in Africa, 1870–1960.* Vol. 1, *The History and Politics of Colonialism, 1870–1914,* ed. L.H. Gann and Peter Duignan. Cambridge, Eng.: Cambridge University Press, 1969, 293–324.

The African Voice in Southern Rhodesia. New York: Heinemann, 1970.

Are We Not Also Men? The Samkange Family and African Politics in Zimbabwe 1920–1964. London: James Currey, 1995.

"Connections between 'Primary Resistance' Movements and Modern Mass Nationalism in East and Central Africa." *Journal of African History* 9 (1968): 3–4.

Dance and Society in Eastern Africa 1890–1940. New York: Heinemann, 1975.

Peasant Consciousness and Guerrilla War: A Comparative Study. London: James Currey, 1985.

Revolt in Southern Rhodesia, 1896–97. New York: Heinemann, 1967.

References

Beach, D. "Chimurenga: The Shona Rising of 1896–1897." *Journal of African History* 20 (1979): 395–420.

Cobbing, J. "The Absent Priesthood: Another Look at the Rhodesian Risings of 1896–1897." *Journal of African History* 18 (1977): 61–84.

Ranke, Leopold von (1795–1886)

R

German historian. Ranke was born in the small Thuringian town of Wiehe, which in 1815 became Prussian, into an intensely Lutheran family whose male forebears, with the exception of his father who was a lawyer, had for many generations been Lutheran pastors. Ranke has often been considered as the most important founder of modern historical science, as the scholar who together with Barthold Georg Niebuhr contributed most to the development of critical methods of historical research. Yet despite his fame, he occupied a relatively solitary role in German historical scholarship. Far from breaking with Enlightenment traditions of historiography, as has often been asserted, he in many ways preserved the values and attitudes of pre-1789 Europe in a postrevolutionary and post-Napoleonic era. In an age of nationalism, he acknowledged the central role of nationality after the French Revolution but maintained a broadly European view for which the great established monarchies—Prussia, Austria, Russia, England, and France—were more important than ethnic units. He thus devoted himself to the history of the papacy, France, and England as well as of Germany, and in his old age he sought to complete his work with a history of the world.

A great deal of his inspiration came from his Lutheran religiosity as well as from his reading of the German Idealist philosophers, foremost among them Johann Gottlieb Fichte. At the famous secondary school of Schulpforta, which had been attended by many of the great minds of the time, he obtained a firm grounding in Protestant religion and in the Greek and Roman classics. As a student at the University of Leipzig (1814–1818), where he originally enrolled in theology, he received solid training in critical philological methods from the classicist Gottfried Hermann. His doctoral dissertation, now lost, dealt with Thucydides. From 1818 to 1825 he taught classics and ancient history at the Gymnasium in Frankfurt/Oder. His first book, *The Histories of the Latin and Germanic Peoples from 1494 to 1514* (1824–1825), set the parameters of his later work. He proceeded from the conception of a European community based, as the title suggested, on the merger of Germanic and Latin culture but excluding the Greek and Russian Orthodox world. For him the rise of the centralized monarchical state and of Protestantism was central to the emergence of the modern world. The most influential part of the book was, however, its appendix in which he judged previous literature on the basis of the critical analysis of primary sources on which, for him, scholarly history rested. Proceeding from what he considered inconsistencies and inaccuracies in the classical treatments by Francesco Guicciardini and Paolo Giovio of the period of the early-sixteenth-century Italian wars, which he treated in his own book, he insisted that the historian must base his account exclusively on primary sources. He himself used the reports of the Venetian ambassadors, which he found in manuscript form in Berlin, as the basis for his narration. As he wrote in the now famous preface, the historian should refrain from making judgments and "merely show how it really [eigentlich] was." This, however, by no means meant, as American and French admirers later erroneously assumed, that the historian should restrict himself to the firmly established facts as they revealed themselves in the sources. Rather, Ranke, in the tradition of Lutheran pietism and of German idealistic philosophy, was convinced in all his work that there was meaning and coherence in history and that the established political institutions embodied moral forces. The proximity to Hegel is striking, although Ranke emphatically rejects the latter's reduction of history to a grand scheme. The historian for Ranke must proceed from the particular or individual to the general, not the reverse, but the particular opens the path to a perception of the great moral forces manifest in history. Thus, while rejecting the idea of progress, Ranke nevertheless, like Hegel, saw in Protestant Europe the apex of history and at the same time opposed the liberal and democratic heritage of the French Revolution. For Ranke, as for Hegel, world history is the history of Europe. And despite his call for "impartiality" (Unpartheylichkeit) and objectivity, he was convinced of the solidity and beneficence of the established order as it had grown historically and thus projected a conservative bias into his conception of the past.

In the works that followed, Ranke traced the emergence of the modern European state system as he understood it. Political and religious history were closely intertwined. Those works included *The Roman Popes in the Last Four Centuries* (1834–1837); *German History in the Time of the Reformation* (1839–1847); *Nine Books of Prussian History* (1847–1848); *French History Especially in the 16th and 17th Centuries* (1852–1861); *English History in the Sixteenth and Seventeenth Centuries* (1859–1867); and the uncompleted *World History* (1880–1888).

With his seminar method, Ranke set a model for the training of historians in systematic, critical research methods, which was copied throughout the world as history became a professional discipline.

Many of the great historians of the nineteenth century, for example Georg Waitz, Wilhelm von Giesebrecht, Heinrich von Sybel, and Jacob Burckhardt, were his students. Paradoxically, his influence was greater in medieval than in modern studies, the period which interested him most. The historians of the Prussian school, such as Sybel, Johann Gustav Droysen, and Heinrich Treitschke, took over his emphasis on working with primary sources, particularly documents of state, but repudiated his purported value neutrality and his concentration on foreign affairs and the balance of power, and openly espoused a history that championed nationalistic aims. It was this approach to history, not Ranke's, that dominated the German historical profession well into the second third of the twentieth century.

Georg G. Iggers

Texts

The Secret of World History: Selected Writings on the Art and Science of History. Ed. and trans. Roger Wines. New York: Fordham University Press, 1981.

The Theory and Practice of History. Ed. Georg G. Iggers and Konrad Von Moltke. Indianapolis, IN: Bobbs-Merrill, 1973.

References

Gilbert, Felix. *History: Politics or Culture? Ranke and Burckhardt.* Princeton, NJ: Princeton University Press, 1990.

Iggers, Georg G., and James H. Powell. *Leopold von Ranke and the Shaping of the Historical Discipline.* Syracuse, NY: Syracuse University Press, 1990.

Krieger, Leonard. *Ranke: The Meaning of History.* Chicago: University of Chicago Press, 1977.

Von Laue, Theodore H. *Leopold von Ranke: The Formative Years.* Princeton, NJ: Princeton University Press, 1950.

Rapant, Daniel (1897–1988)

Slovak historian, archivist, and university professor. Rapant's schooling in Skalica was interrupted by military service in Italy during World War I, after which he studied at the university in Bratislava (1918–1922), at the College of Archives in Prague (1919–1921), and at the Sorbonne (1922–1923). While working as an archivist in Bratislava (1924–1933) he also taught at Comenius University. He became professor of Slovak history in 1933 and, in 1945, was named rector. Expelled from his professorship by the Communists in 1950, from 1952 until 1958 he worked at the University Library in Bratislava. The most significant modern Slovak historian, his works argued that the Slovaks had a distinct history within a central European context and also contributed to shaping modern Slovak historiography. His early works, such as *Národ a dejiny* [Nation and History] (1924), argued that the Slovaks had their own specific history prior to the formation of the Czechoslovak state in 1918, and he documented the attempts by the Magyars to force the assimilation of the Slovaks in *K počiatkom mad'arizácie 1–2* [On the Beginnings of Magyarization] (1927). He investigated the ancient and medieval periods of Slovak history but devoted special attention to the period of the national revival (1790–1848) in thirteen volumes, which documented the history of the Slovak national uprising of 1848–1849.

David P. Daniel

Texts

Ilegálna mad'arizácia 1790–1840 [Illegal Magyarization, 1790–1840]. Martin: Matica slovenská, 1947.

K počiatkom mad'arizácie 1–2 [Beginning of Magyarization 1–2]. Bratislava: Zemedelské Museum, 1927–1931.

"K pokusom o novú historicko-filozofickú koncepciu slovenského národného obrodenia [Towards an Attempt at a New Historical-Philosophical Conception of the Slovak National Revival]." *Slovenska literatúra* 12 (1965): 437–457.

Národ a dejiny. Prúdy 8 (1924): 470–477.

Sedliacke povstanie na východnom Slovensku roku 1831, 1–2 [Peasant Uprising in eastern Slovakia in 1831, 1–2]. Bratislava: Slovak Academy of Sciences, 1953.

"Slovak Politics in 1848–1849." *The Slavonic Review* 68 (1948–1949): 67–90; 381–413.

Slovenské povstanie roku 1848–49, 1–5 [The Slovak Uprising of 1848–49]. Vol. 1, Martin: Matica slovenská, 1937; vol. 2, Martin: Neografia, 1947–1950; vols. 3–4, Bratislava: Akadémia, 1937–1972.

References

Mannová, Elena, and David Paul Daniel, ed. *A Guide to Historiography in Slovakia.* Studia Historica Slovaca XX. Bratislava: Slovak Academy of Sciences, 1995.

"Nekrológy [Obituary]." *Historický časopis* 36 (1988): 822–824.

Rapin-Thoyras, Paul de (1661–1725)

Huguenot historian of England. Rapin, a member of a family of Languedoc lawyers, left France after the Revocation of the Edict of Nantes in 1685 and, hero worshiping, joined William of Orange three years later in his descent on England. Rewarded for his loyalty and gaining access to the fringes of the English patronage system, Rapin was for thirteen years tutor to the young son of the Earl of Portland and began working on his projected *History of England* in 1705. Encouraged by the appearance of Thomas Rymer's *Foedera* and by the political consequences of the Hanoverian succession, Rapin persevered with his project and eight volumes appeared in 1727; a posthumously published English translation edited by N. Tindal guaranteed the text a wider audience. Much admired, Rapin's *History* went through six printings of the French edition and five of the English by the middle of the eighteenth century. Rapin's was the first systematic Whig history of England, depicting a clear linear development from the Anglo Saxons to the Whig patriots of the Glorious Revolution. But it did not survive the devastating assault launched on it by David Hume, nor—under Macaulay in the nineteenth century—was the Whig interpretation revived in this form.

R.C. Richardson

Texts

The History of England. Ed. N. Tindal. Third ed. 4 vols. London: J. and P. Knapton, 1743–1747.

References

Trevor-Roper, H.R. "A Huguenot Historian: Paul Rapin." In *Huguenots in Britain and Their French Background 1550–1800,* ed. Irene Scouloudi. London: Routledge, 1987, 3– 19.

Rashīd al-Dīn Ṭabīb [Rašîd ad-Dîn] (1247–1318)

Persian chronicler of the Mongol empire and world historian. Born in Hamadan, Rashīd al-Dīn converted from Judaism to Islam and entered the service of Persia's Mongol rulers as a physician. Under Ghazan Khan (1295–1304), Rashīd al-Dīn rose to high position and, under Ghazan's successor Öldjeytü (1304–1316), became a fabulously wealthy *wazīr* (vizier). After Öldjeytü's death, Rashīd was dismissed and then executed, together with his son, in 1318. The first volume of Rashīd's *Djami' 'al-tawārīkh* [Collection of Chronicles], written under Ghazan Khan's patronage, contains invaluable material on the Mongols from their tribal origins to the break-up of the empire. The second volume, commissioned by Öldjeytü and covering Eurasia from China to Europe, is perhaps the first genuine world history. In his plainly written but monumentally conceived work, Rashīd relied heavily on native informants about more distant realms and rejected any need to evaluate their accounts in terms of his own Islamic beliefs.

Christopher Pratt Atwood

Texts

Die Chinageschichte des Rašîd ad-Dîn [The Chinese History of Rashid al-Din]. Trans. Karl Jahn. Vienna: Kommissionverlag H. Böhlaus, 1971.

Successors of Genghis Khan. Trans. John Andrew Boyle. New York: Columbia University Press, 1971.

References

Jahn, Karl. *Rashid al-Din's History of India.* The Hague: Mouton, 1965.

Ratkoš, Peter (1921–1987)

Slovak historian. Ratkoš studied history and Slovak in the Faculty of Arts of Comenius University (1941–1945) where he subsequently worked as an instructor in the historical seminar. From 1950 until 1986 he was a researcher in the Institute of Historical Sciences of the Slovak Academy of Sciences. His area of interest was the early history of Slovakia from the period of the Great Moravian empire until the beginning of the sixteenth century, and his numerous articles presented the results of his investigations of the work of Cyril and Methodius in Slovakia, the ethnogenesis of the Slovaks, medieval settlement patterns, the history of towns, the history of mining, the influence of the radical reformation in Slovakia, and the Turkish occupation of Slovakia. His study of the revolt of the miners of the mining cities of central Slovakia in 1526 and of the genesis of feudalism and serfdom in Hungary reflected his Marxist interpretative approach. He prepared editions of documents concerning Great Moravia and the revolt of the miners, and contributed to synthetic works on Slovak and Czechoslovak history.

David P. Daniel

Texts

Povstanie baníkov na Slovensku 1525–26 [The Uprising of the Miners in Slovakia, 1525–26]. Bratislava: Slovak Academy of Sciences, 1963.

Pramene k dejinám Veľkej Moravy [Sources on the History of the Great Moravian Empire]. Bratislava: Slovak Academy of Sciences, 1964–1968.

Príspevok k dejinám banského práva a baníctva na Slovakia [Contribution to the History of Mining Law and Mining in Slovakia]. Bratislava: Slovak Academy of Sciences, 1951.

Slovensko v dobe veľkomoravske [Slovakia in the Era of the Great Moravian Empire]. Košice: Východoslovenské vydavateľstvo, 1988.

References

Mannová, Elena, and David Paul Daniel, eds. *A Guide to Historiography in Slovakia. Studia Historica Slovaca XX.* Bratislava: Slovak Academy of Sciences, 1995.

Ray [Bengali: Raya], Nihar-ranjan (1903–1981)

Indian historian. Ray was born in what is now Bangladesh, but was educated in Calcutta and Leiden. He was trained as a historian of ancient India. His dissertation on "The Political History of Ancient India from c. 600 A.D.–c. 900 A.D." earned the Mrinalini Gold Medal from the University of Calcutta in 1926. In his early works Ray was interested in the dynasties of ancient India and in Indian iconography. Although he employed traditional positivist methods of historical research, he was a scholar of diverse interests who wrote on literature, the Bengali writer Tagore, nationalism, Sikhism, and the arts. He was profoundly influenced by nationalism (especially the Bengali Brahmo version of it), Tagore, and Marxism. From 1945, his works showed a marked shift away from purely political and religious history toward cultural and social history. His *Maurya and Sunga Art* (1945) and *An Introduction to the Study of Theravada Buddhism* (1946) illustrate the extent of his new interests.

Ray's most important book, however, was his *Bangalir Itihas-Adiparva* [History of the Bengali People, Early period] (1949). It was an outstanding work both in quality and in size, running to 1,300 pages. The work, which marks the culmination of a process of research and writing in Bengal that began around 1800, was a summary of the scholarship done by other scholars over the preceding century and a half and, at the same time, an original interpretation of history that demonstrated the capacity of the Bengali language to express complex historical themes. A "total history," *Bangalir Itihas-Adiparva* weaves together religion, topography and land-use patterns, social structures, cultural and religious history, economic activities, and political history. Its interpretation of the land grants in early Bengal was a particularly significant and pioneering venture, in which Ray became the first modern scholar to draw economic and social information from these religious copperplate inscriptions.

S.N. Mukherjee

Texts

An Approach to Indian Art. Chandigarh: Publication Bureau, Panjab University, 1974.

Bangalira itihasa: Adi parba. Third ed. 2 vols. Calcutta: Pascimabanga Niraksharata Durikarana Samiti, 1980; translated as *History of the Bengali people: Ancient Period.* Trans. John W. Wood. Calcutta: Orient Longman, 1994.

An Introduction to the Study of Theravada Buddhism in Burma. Calcutta: University of Calcutta, 1946.

Maurya and Sunga Art. Calcutta: University of Calcutta, 1945.

Sanskrit Buddhism in Burma. Calcutta: University of Calcutta, 1936.

References

Chattopadhyaya, Debiprasad, ed. *History and Society: Essays in Honour of Professor Niharranjan Ray.* Calcutta: K.P. Bagchi, 1978.

Ray, Amita, H. Sanyal, and S.C. Ray, eds. *Indian Studies: Essays Presented in Memory of Prof. Niharranjan Ray.* Delhi: Caxton, 1984.

Raychaudhuri, Hemchandra C. (1892–1957)

Indian historian. Raychaudhuri was professor of history at the University of Calcutta. His *Political History of Ancient India* (1923) was a groundbreaking work, which competed with, and mostly replaced, Vincent Smith's *Early History of India* (1904) in schools and colleges. The first part of the work, which as its title suggests was mainly concerned with political history, aimed to trace the history of India from before 600 B.C. through the examination of an array of Vedic, Puranic, Buddhist, Jaina, and other sources. The second part covered more familiar ground, taking India's story up to the fifth century A.D. Raychaudhuri was interested in discovering the "truth," rather than in presenting theory, and many find his mass of data dry and uninviting, but he presented his analysis and chronology in a manner that was widely welcomed at the time among scholars of early India and considered a major advance. Raychaudhuri

believed that various kings in Indian history, such as the renowned king Ashoka, had been too idealistic and pacific, and therefore disastrous for India, as had division among Indians, which allowed India to be invaded numerous times during its history.

Roger D. Long

Texts

With R.C. Majumdar and Kalikinkar Datta. *An Advanced History of India.* London: Macmillan, 1946.

Materials for the Study of the Early History of the Vaishnava Sect. Calcutta: University of Calcutta Press, 1920.

Political History of Ancient India: From the Accession of Parikshit to the Extinction of the Gupta Dynasty. Sixth Ed. Calcutta: University of Calcutta Press, 1953.

References

Bhagowalia, Urmila. *Vaisnavism and Society in Northern India 700–1200.* New Delhi: Intellectual Book Center, 1980.

Reading, History of

See BOOK, HISTORY OF THE.

Rekishi Monogatari

Historical tales written in Japanese prose from the late eleventh to the fourteenth centuries, together covering the history of the imperial court until 1333. Distinguishing them from earlier literary works, such as *Ise Monogatari* [Tales of Ise] and *Genji Monogatari* [Tales of Genji], and later military tales such as *Taiheiki* [Chronicle of Great Peace], modern historians placed about six works in this category. The earliest is *Eiga Monogatari* [A Tale of Flowering Fortunes], celebrating the lives and careers of Fujiwara Michinaga (966–1028) and his successors. Clearly influenced by diaries and narrative court romances, the unknown authoress departs radically from the language, form, and content of official, Chinese-style histories and focuses on the private emotional and aesthetic experience of aristocratic life. *Ōkagami* [Great Mirror] is a shorter, more unified work with some Chinese historiographic elements, using the voice of an ancient narrator. This form is also adopted in *Imakagami* [Mirror of the Present] and *Masukagami* [Clear Mirror]. All told, the tales significantly altered Japanese conceptions of the nature and content of history.

Rosemary Gray Trott

Texts

Ōkagami: The Great Mirror. Trans. Helen Craig McCullough. Princeton, NJ: Princeton University Press, 1980.

A Tale of Flowering Fortunes. Trans. William H. and Helen Craig McCullough. Stanford, CA: Stanford University Press, 1980.

References

Brownlee, John S. *Political Thought in Japanese Historical Writing from Kojiki (712) to Tokushi Yoron (1712).* Waterloo: Wilfrid Laurier University Press, 1991.

Konishi Jin'ichi. *A History of Japanese Literature, Volume Three: The High Middle Ages.* Trans. Aileen Gatten and Mark Harbison; ed. Earl Miner. Princeton, NJ: Princeton University Press, 1991.

Relativism

The notion that truths in history are relative, not absolute. Relativism is indeed a tricky concept, about which clouds of obfuscation had already begun to form when it was still in swaddling clothes. Frequent assertions to the contrary notwithstanding, the notion of relativism has little if anything to do with Einstein's theory of relativity, in either its general or special form. Yet it is at least a distant cousin to certain currents of scientific thought extant in the West at the beginning of the twentieth century.

One can make a distinction between epistemological, or cognitive, relativism, which emphasizes the limitations of human knowledge, and ethical, or moral, relativism, which holds at a minimum that standards of morality are neither universal nor immutable. Historical relativism—the notion that historical truths are relative to time and place—can best be viewed as a subspecies of cognitive relativism, but it has also been tagged (and condemned as) a variant of moral relativism.

In the American context, historical relativism first reared its head in the wake of World War I. Until that time virtually all historians in the United States held fast to the dictum of the eminent German historian Leopold von Ranke that the aim of historical writing was to relate past events as they actually happened. The true historian, in short, was objective, and did not allow preconceived notions to get in the way of the cold, hard facts. During the Progressive Era the so-called New Historians shook things up a bit by repudiating such naive inductivism and declaring that history should ingest more than politics, law, and diplomacy into its maw. Their (selectively applied) environmental approach to ideas and their present-day political concerns seemed to threaten the ideal of objectivity on one level. But their zealous commitment to making the historians' craft more scientific was anything but relativist in nature.

The devastation wrought by World War I led historians of all stripes to call into question the idea of progress, the very linchpin of "scientific" history. Professional and popular historians alike found themselves caught up in an acrimonious dispute over the origins of the war. In a climate of opinion marked by disillusionment and doubt, that indigenous American philosophy of pragmatism, which set great store on the mutability of truth, became all the more appealing. Simultaneously many anthropologists were arguing that ethical beliefs were the product of particular cultures, while a small but vocal group of legal scholars came to the conclusion that even judges—the paragon of impartiality—were strongly influenced by personal prejudices and subconscious feelings. Warm winds of philosophical relativism were also blowing in from across the Atlantic.

By the mid-1930s, and in the thick of a worldwide depression, historical relativism had come into its own. Throughout that decade Carl Becker and Charles Beard, two proponents of Progressive History, waged a running battle against their fellow historians. Beard and Becker insisted that the historian is a part of the historical process and that the social milieu and motivation of the individual historian usually mattered more than the evidence in formulating historical interpretations. As Beard put it, written history, in the final analysis, was an act of faith. Becker and Beard were never entirely comfortable with the relativist label. Yet it stuck to them like flypaper.

Beard and Becker faced no shortage of critics, virtually all of whom accused the two historians of pouring cold water on the "noble dream," as Beard had ironically termed it, of disinterested scholarship. Antirelativists generally focused their attacks upon the practical implications of relativism, and in doing so conflated cognitive and ethical relativism. To many antirelativists, with one eye cocked on European totalitarianism, the logical culmination of relativism was fascism. Calmer scholars who still saw relativism as the devil's handiwork insistently raised a simple question. How could the West render a judgment on totalitarianism of any kind if certain truths were not absolute, or at least treated as if they were?

In the face of Hitler, many anthropologists, legal scholars, and historians shed their relativist vestments. Many did not, however, positing a close connection between absolutist creeds and authoritarian deeds and maintaining that America itself rested upon a relativist foundation. Moreover, they pointed to the inescapable fact that relativists were no less hostile to Hitler than antirelativists. In fact, isolationists and interventionists were to be found in both philosophical camps. Nonetheless the belief persisted that relativism left the West unprepared for the forces of fascism (and evidence for this conviction could be found in the staunch isolationism of Beard). Consequently the relativist star lost a good deal of its luster. Yet relativist arguments continued to be made throughout the late 1940s and 1950s, even though they were often given a conservative twist.

The 1960s was a curious decade, in historiography as much as in society at large. Not a few traditional historians put the relativist millstone around the neck of the New Left revisionists, perhaps confusing occasional shrillness and present-mindedness with the doctrine of relativism. Most New Leftists, however, clung tenaciously to the notion that all they were doing was pursuing the truth, irrespective of the consequences. Ranke, it seemed, was alive and well, after all. A peculiar form of relativism did emerge, however, among some of the younger African-American historians. In their view, objectivity was a white shibboleth and only black scholars should write about black history. A similar kind of plea was entered by many feminist historians, for whom objective history was a pernicious male construct. Few of these historians actually called themselves relativists. Interestingly, Becker and Beard had never carried their relativism that far.

A more recognizable and less overtly political form of relativism also manifested itself during and after that turbulent decade, beginning with the physicist Thomas Kuhn, who argued in his now classic *Structure of Scientific Revolutions* (1962) that evidence and logic counted for comparatively little in establishing, maintaining and even overturning what he called "paradigms," overarching frameworks of interpretation that governed "normal" research in the natural sciences. Although directed at historians of science, Kuhn's work was tremendously influential in both the social sciences and humanities as a whole.

Since Kuhn's time, toilers in those vineyards would soon sound even more relativistic notes. Literary theorist Stanley Fish took great pains to emphasize the indeterminate meaning of literary texts. Law professor Sanford Levinson, a fellow traveler of the Critical Legal Studies movement, went further and declared there were as many possible interpretations of the Constitution as there were of *Hamlet*. On the historiographical front, Hayden White went so far as to call those who believed in studying the past for its own sake cultural necrophiliacs. Not unlike Carl Becker, he argued that history is best understood as a branch of literature. White wore the relativist label unabashedly, and it was clear by the mid-1970s that the postmodern moment had come.

Some final observations are in order. Opponents of relativism, while undoubtedly acting in good faith, have too often resorted to hyperbole. It was not uncommon for Beard and Becker's adversaries consistently to caricature their views. Neither historian had actually denied the knowability of truth, or given the back of his hand to the scientific method; Beard, in fact, was quite emphatic in making the point that just because we cannot know *everything* does not mean that we can't know *anything*. None of their writings was remotely relativistic when it came to the natural sciences. (In this they resemble their postmodern relatives very little.) Even Karl Mannheim, the German sociologist of knowledge whose ideas Beard drew upon so promiscuously, was not the extreme relativist that his rivals painted.

Those uneasy about some of the newer branches on the relativist tree have often been off the mark, too. The narrative historians who embrace objectivity have on occasion castigated quantitative historians as relativists, even though cliometrics is resolutely positivist in methodology. Many critics of the postmodern "linguistic turn," seeing the specter of political correctness virtually everywhere, suggest a tight relationship between relativism and leftism. Certainly Thomas Kuhn's writings cannot be understood in this light. Actually, many on the Left have assailed the new relativism precisely because of its potentially conservative implications.

Yet the critics cannot simply be dismissed. They are on target when they hold that far too often relativists have failed to make the necessary distinction between the psychology of historical interpretation, on the one hand, and its logic, on the other. One can also easily understand—and appreciate—the ethical dimension to their insistence that there is a "there" there. We can be certain of one thing, though. The "truth" will continue to be contested terrain, which means that relativism—of one sort or another—is here to stay.

Barry Riccio

See also DETERMINISM; NEW HISTORY; PHILOSO-
PHY OF HISTORY—ANALYTICAL; POSTMODERNISM;
PROGRESSIVE HISTORY; SCIENTIFIC HISTORY.

Texts

Beard, Charles A. "That Noble Dream." In *The
Varieties of History: From Voltaire to the
Present,* ed. Fritz Stern. Revised ed. New
York: Vintage Books, 1972, 314–328.
———. "Written History As an Act of Faith."
In *The Philosophy of History in Our Time,*
ed. Hans Meyerhoff. Garden City, NY:
Doubleday Anchor Books, 1959, 138–151.
Becker, Carl. "What Are Historical Facts?" In
The Philosophy of History in Our Time, ed.
Hans Meyerhoff. Garden City, NY:
Doubleday Anchor Books, 1959, 119–137.

References

Brecht, Arnold. *Political Theory: The Foundations
of Twentieth-Century Political Thought.*
Princeton, NJ: Princeton University Press,
1959.
Novick, Peter. *That Noble Dream: The "Objectiv-
ity Question" and the American Historical
Profession.* Cambridge, Eng.: Cambridge
University Press, 1988.
Purcell, Edward A. *The Crisis of Democratic
Theory: Scientific Naturalism and the Prob-
lem of Value.* Lexington: University Press of
Kentucky, 1973.

Religions, History of

Historical study of human activities, experiences,
structures, and meanings insofar as these disclose
and relate to what people take to be ultimate in
reality. Two sets of academic traditions organize
and define the way religions are studied historically. One set includes the historiographies of particular religions, like Islamic history, church history, and the history of Australian religions or
African religions. In these, historians give their
attention to a particular religion, resulting in
works that present or explain each religion historically. The other set embraces various approaches to
the academic study of religion, known in German
as *Religionswissenschaft,* but translated into English
as "history of religions." Here historians undertake
the comparative study of more than one religion
and tend toward the construction of theories,
typologies, and analogies, with the aim of understanding the character of religion as a phenomenon
in life. Students and scholars in each group and
subgroup have little communication with each

other, yet they all make different, and important, contributions to the historical study of
religions which, if combined, would benefit the
study as a whole.

The social organization of the history of religions enforces this intellectual fragmentation by
dispersing the enterprise across many academic
institutions, curricula, journals, and publishing
divisions. The aims of the study vary accordingly.
History departments in colleges and universities
touch upon the history of religions when the religions interconnect with something else, like politics, states, wars, social movements, and the lives
of leaders. Departments of religious studies, which
seek to understand religion and religious traditions, link the historical study of religions with
other methods, such as sociological, psychological, anthropological, and philosophical approaches to religions. They examine particular
religious traditions, like Judaism and Hinduism,
by combining historical study with systematic
analysis, social studies, and experiential encounters.
Departments of regional studies, like Middle Eastern studies, South Asian studies, Ibero-American
studies, and the classics usually include the history
of the religions of the area under consideration.
Anthropology departments cover whatever historical study of aboriginal religions is possible
within their analysis of primal societies. Theological schools and philosophical institutions devoted
to the training of religious leadership and the exposition of a particular religious tradition, like the
Christian and Jewish, make historical study of their
own tradition a significant part of the curriculum.
The approach to the study and the content depend
upon the academic neighborhood in which the
historical study of religions takes place.

An immense ambiguity about the meaning of
religion dominates the history of religions. The
academic study of religious history treats religion
both as a phenomenon separate from other types
of things and as an inseparable and integral dimension of all of life. The specific view of religion,
developed in Europe and carried throughout the
world via Western-style universities and publishing houses, reflects the secularization of a Christian dualism, which divides reality into spiritual
and temporal realms. On this view, the history of
religion treats specifically religious things, like
churches and temples, rituals and worship, priests
and shamans, and doctrines and creeds. By contrast, the integral view of religion, in keeping with
the orthodox teachings of virtually all the religions,
mirrors the testimony of devotees who experience
religion as a way of life. On this view, religious

history includes the representation of the ultimate and moral dimension of anything whatsoever that is shaped by a religion's touch—Islamic society, Chinese dynasties, the land of native peoples, the plays of Shakespeare, Christian impulses for and against capitalism, the castes of India, social initiation among the Akan of Ghana.

Traditional histories of a particular religion, whether written or spoken, are invariably the work of the devout. No barrier intervenes between the enunciation of the religion and presentation of the history of the religion. Divine and demonic agency coexist and interact with human agency and natural events. Spirits cohabit with people. Traditions as diverse as the books of the Kings and the Chronicles in ancient Hebrew historiography, the *Vishnu Purāṇa* in classical Hindu historiography, the life of the Prophet in Islamic historiography, and oral histories of African peoples have in common that the topics treated and the explanations offered freely intermingle the divine, the demonic, the human, and the natural. Even Leopold von Ranke, widely claimed in North America as a progenitor of Western secular historiography, understood human history as the divine education of humanity and said so in his historical writings.

In recent times, the historical study of religions has bifurcated into two types. One kind includes theologies of history, religious philosophies of history, and histories in which the historians freely reveal their own religious orientation and continue to intermingle the divine and the human. Among those who represent the histories of their religions in this way are Buddhist and Hindu philosophers and historians, Christian, Jewish, and Islamic historians and theologians, and native spiritual leaders. Some examples are: R.C. Majumdar, a Hindu historian, in his shorter writings on Hinduism and history; Arnold Toynbee, for a time writing from within the Anglican religion, in his universal history, *A Study of History;* Enrique Dussel, a Latin American historian working within liberation theology, in *History and the Theology of Liberation,* and Mircea Eliade, who believed that all religions reflected something of ultimate reality, as a preeminent practitioner of the comparative history of religions.

The other type removes all explicit references to the divine from the history books. The common feature of these histories is that they treat the history of religions as a study of things human. The explanations provided are cast entirely in human and natural terms. Many authors of such histories have no wish to deny the reality of the divine in history even though, for the sake of discerning the human and natural factors at play, they leave it out. In works such as Majumdar's monumental *History and Culture of the Indian People* and any of Herbert Butterfield's histories, readers may readily detect the religious orientation of the author once they are attuned to it and can go to the author's parallel writings to see how the divine is included therein. Some authors reduce the history of religion to the human, claiming that religion is nothing other than a human phenomenon. E.P. Thompson's interpretation of Methodism in *The Making of the English Working Class* is an example. Others reduce religion still farther, denying the reality of human religious experience and explaining the history of religions entirely by reference to political, economic, social, linguistic, or psychological factors. Mircea Eliade combats both types of reductionism in *Patterns in Comparative Religion,* as do most of the contributors to the multivolume *Encyclopedia of Religion,* which Eliade edited. Those who affirm the reality of human religious experience and reject reductionism divide over how they explain the history of religious phenomena, whether by reference chiefly to religious factors or to a multiplicity of factors, religious and nonreligious.

All these issues are perennial and compel historians of religions to make decisions about their work, especially their own commitments about religion: whether they deal only with particulars and specific religions or with comparisons, typologies, and analogues; whether they resort to theory of religion or not; what connections they seek among the historians of religion in different fields; what they take religion to mean; what they do about the divine and the demonic; what range of things they include in their topics; what they incorporate in their explanations. Other issues surface as well. It is not self-evident that historians can really understand religion with the evidential methods of historical study. Devotees repeatedly testify that much about religious experience is ineffable, and much is utterly interior. When devotees tell about their experience, historians cannot be sure that they are receiving an authentic report. It is not certain that historians who study a religion whose way they do not follow can really understand the religion. At the same time, it does seem that outsiders to a religion can see things that insiders overlook. When historians study the religions as human phenomena, it is not clear that they grasp everything that is happening. Apparently devotees of all the religions claim that things happen that have nothing to do with human agency and natural events. It is one thing for historians to say that devotees believe that God

R

did something beyond anything humans did, and quite another to account for those happenings attributed to God for which there is no obvious human explanation. Historians provide historical explanations, and not religious explanations, of the history of religions.

The historical study of religion has been more controversial than most other kinds of historical study. Linkages between a historian's convictions and the historical study of religion seem to hold even when the historian claims that there are no linkages. It seems that all religions tie their self-understanding to their history in some way, and not just those, like Christianity, Judaism, and Islam, whose teachings are saturated with historical interpretation. When historians probe the complexities of the history of any religion, they frequently find things or present things that disturb either the devotees of the religion or the outsiders to the religion. Moreover, it is noteworthy that when a religion is in decline, the study of the religion seems to decline, but when the religion is in renewal, the study of the religion seems to revive as well.

C. T. McIntire

See also CHRISTIANITY VIEWS OF HISTORY IN; ECCLESIASTICAL HISTORY.

References

Bianchi, Ugo. *The History of Religions*. Leiden: E.J. Brill, 1975.

Eliade, Mircea, and J.M. Kitagawa, eds. *The History of Religions: Essays in Methodology*. Chicago: University of Chicago Press, 1959.

Sharpe, Eric J. *Comparative Religion: A History*. Second ed. LaSalle: Open Court, 1986.

Renaissance, Historiography during the

The forms of historical writing in western Europe between about 1300 and about 1700. During the Renaissance previous traditions (among them chronicles, annals, and various kinds of biography) blended with rediscovered classical models and new social and economic demands to produce modification but not radical transformation in both consciousness of the past and how that consciousness was represented. The degree of continuity between the Middle Ages and the Renaissance is perhaps clearest on the score of conceptions of time. While it is often said that Christian time already in the Middle Ages presupposed a linear, forward-moving scale—in fact, progress toward the end of time—the goal of Christian history demanded a return to the beginning, and

thus produced a constant cyclical movement, as in Augustine's theory of the two cities. Nothing changed on this score in the Renaissance, as the difficulties Renaissance historians experienced in detecting the difference between themselves and the past immediately makes manifest. For some, like Petrarch (1304–1374) who could not live in his own time but knew perfectly well that he could not escape to classical antiquity, either, the solution was to live only after death by creating a reputation for the future, or in some unstable time in which both he and his classical heroes could coexist. Petrarch, as one of the first to wrestle with the problem, produced a complicated solution. More usually, Renaissance historians' insistence on the power of classical examples and their fondness for the explicitly cyclical schemes of classical historiography (perhaps especially of Polybius) produced a simple collapse of present into past time, which made the development of a sense of anachronism virtually impossible. True, Renaissance men and women may not have regarded all periods as virtually identical, as medieval people may have done, but by the same token they did not separate their era from its models. Even Lorenzo Valla's (1407–1457) famous exposure of the Donation of Constantine as a forgery because it contained words from the eighth century A.D., although allegedly written in the fourth, did not reflect a full sense of anachronism, since Valla also regarded the Latin of imperial Rome as normative for his time. Similarly, Renaissance historians continued to believe until the very end of the seventeenth century that the ancients were far superior to the moderns.

As in the Middle Ages, in formal and often substantive terms history continued to be structured mainly as moral commentary, cast especially in the form of exemplary lives or *exempla* of any kind (examples, technically a literary form all to itself) designed to illustrate the virtues. The way any real lives or examples had to be edited in order to make them serve a didactic purpose went unnoticed until Pierre Bayle (1647–1706) excoriated nearly all preceding historians on that score, only to fill his work with his very own new examples. Like Bayle, most of his predecessors also claimed to introduce a more realistic treatment of the world, especially in the matter of causes, but like many such claims, this one was more rhetorical than substantive. That is, Renaissance historians less analyzed things "the way they were" than represented them in sometimes new ways. Where medieval historiography had been obviously typological, finding the sense of events in their replication of some overarching pattern, this was less clearly the case in the Renaissance, with its superficially much greater concern with details and individuals. But both were in their turn as much creations as inventions.

Changes in Florentine historiography in the course of the fifteenth and sixteenth centuries illustrate the point. Early on, Leonardo Bruni (1370–1444), adapting the classical form of the *laudatio urbis* (praise of a city) produced a polemical version of Florentine history designed to defend the increasingly beleaguered republic. Early in the sixteenth century, Niccolò Machiavelli (1469–1527) took a more complicated line in his *History of Florence,* but that work was still essentially designed to create his version of the city, including, through the invention of speeches, a perfectly respectable classical, rhetorical technique; and its object remained to point a moral, however much Machiavelli may have played with the traditional virtue of prudence. Thus neither Bruni nor Machiavelli saw things "the way they were," but at the same time they were no longer writing a chronicle of events organized in some fairly simple kind of time sequence. In formal and rhetorical terms (not to mention political, one of the most important determinants of both form and content in Renaissance historiography), history had indeed changed. The distance between Bruni and Machiavelli, however, captures another major dynamic of Renaissance historiography. Bruni wrote in Latin, while Machiavelli chose Italian; the interplay between the two languages helped further to loosen formal and linguistic constraints and produce experimentation in forms and perceptions, especially as persons with less formal education tried their hand. Paradoxically, the Renaissance also saw the development of the profession of historian and the admission of history as an independent form of knowing, no longer another branch of literature. New subdisciplines quickly followed, among them art history, invented almost single-handedly by Giorgio Vasari (1511–1574).

While exemplarity—the heart of the relation between literature and history in the Renaissance—remained perhaps the central dynamic, it was encapsulated in a variety of new forms, often, but not exclusively, modeled on classical precedents. Thus, for example, Paolo Giovio (1486–1552) attempted to write a universal history, probably drawing on Polybius's precedent; he had many followers in the seventeenth century. The antithesis of universal history, national history, followed in the civic footsteps of Bruni and Machiavelli. Lawyers especially wrote a good deal of history, and not just those who practiced historical jurisprudence (the *mos gallicus,* or French mode of jurisprudence). Antiquarians, many of them lawyers and long left out of consideration, manifested new notions of the kinds of things that counted as past, even as their encyclopedic curiosity threatened to burst the bounds of any formal conception of history, and they existed in an uneasy relation to writers of historical narrative (even when the antiquarian and the historian were one and the same). Similarly, a more general impulse to collecting in many of the same people led among other things to the creation of the first museums, yet another new form of historiography and of organizing the world. Finally, natural history, which began—especially in Italy—as at least as credulous a discipline as hagiography, had by the end of the seventeenth century begun to develop standards for the criticism of its sources in tandem with the scientific revolution, which reciprocally owed a great deal to antiquarians of nature.

As in the case of natural history, so more generally: the Renaissance created important new methods of treating historical sources, undoubtedly its most important contribution, and one in which antiquarians played a major role. Some of the impetus came from the same humanist concern with antiquity, which gave grammarians like Valla their professional concern with language. Yet polemical warfare, forcing various camps to defend their heroes, was the chief force behind both humanists and antiquaries. Thus the most sustained attention to the problem of source criticism came in the sixteenth century and after in the domain of ecclesiastical history, where the fracture between Catholics and Protestants drove the warring parties to work hard to establish their truth claims. The Magdeburg Centuriators in the middle of the century produced a Protestant canon of church history, Catholic historians like Cesare Baronio (1538–1607) rejoindered, and that conflict led on in the next century to major new tools of historical criticism, especially as developed by the Bollandists and by Jean Mabillon (1632–1707), Benedictine monks who revolutionized the treatment of hagiography. The treatment of the Council of Trent in Protestant and Catholic historiography, above all by Paolo Sarpi (1552–1623) and Sforza Pallavicino (1607–1667), both of whom jammed their narratives with circumstantial detail (and Pallavicino combed the Vatican Library and Archives—including those of the Inquisition—for sources), also played a major role. A very similar process occurred in England, where the civil war made increasingly urgent the critical evaluation of party claims.

Thomas F. Mayer

R

See also ANACHRONISM; ANTIQUARIANISM; *ARS HISTORICA;* BIOGRAPHY; ECCLESIASTICAL HISTORY; HAGIOGRAPHY; *HISTORIA;* LAW AND HISTORY; LITERATURE AND HISTORY; MAGDEBURG CENTURIATORS; MARTYROLOGY; *MOS GALLICUS* AND *MOS ITALICUS;* MUSEUMS; PHILOLOGY.

Texts
Kelley, Donald R., ed. *Versions of History from Antiquity to the Enlightenment.* New Haven, CT, and London: Yale University Press, 1991.
Niccolò Machiavelli. *The History of Florence.* Trans. Laura F. Banfield and Harvey C. Mansfield. Princeton, NJ: Princeton University Press, 1988.

References
Cochrane, Eric. *Historians and Historiography in the Italian Renaissance.* Chicago: University of Chicago Press, 1981.
Findlen, Paula. *Possessing Nature: Museums, Collecting, and Scientific Culture in Early Modern Italy.* Berkeley and London: University of California Press, 1994.
Huppert, George. *The Idea of Perfect History.* Urbana: University of Illinois Press, 1970.
Kelley, Donald R. *Foundations of Modern Historical Scholarship: Language, Law, and History in the French Renaissance.* New York: Columbia University Press, 1970.
Levine, Joseph M. *Humanism and History: Origins of Modern English Historiography.* Ithaca, NY: Cornell University Press, 1987.
Struever, Nancy S. *The Language of History in the Renaissance: Rhetoric and Historical Consciousness in Florentine Humanism.* Princeton, NJ: Princeton University Press, 1970.
Woolf, D.R. *The Idea of History in Early Stuart England: Erudition, Ideology, and the Light of Truth from the Accession of James I to the Civil War.* Toronto: University of Toronto Press, 1990.

Renan, (Joseph-) Ernest (1823–1892)
French historian of religion and man of letters. Ernest Renan was raised in a poor family in Brittany, and after studying for the priesthood in several seminaries, he became skeptical about historical Christianity and left the Catholic Church in 1845. A Hebrew scholar, he wrote his doctoral thesis on Averroës, and in 1860 he participated in an archaeological mission to the Middle East. Elected as a professor of Hebrew at the Collège de France in 1862, he was suspended because of the uproar about his rejection of the divine origins of Christianity, but he returned as director of the Collège thirty years later. His most famous book, *Vie de Jésus* [Life of Jesus], was the first volume of *Histoire des origines du christianisme* [History of the Origins of Christianity] (1863–1883). His voluminous writings included *Histoire du peuple d'Israël* [History of the People of Israel] (1887–1893). Elected to the French Academy in 1878, Renan is remembered for his subtle irony and elegant style as well as for his scholarship.

Thomas T. Lewis

Texts
Oeuvres complètes [Complete Works]. Ed. Henriette Psichari. 10 vols. Paris: Calmann-Levy, 1947–1961.

References
Chadbourne, Richard. *Ernest Renan.* New York: Twayne, 1968.
Wardman, Harold. *Ernest Renan: A Critical Biography.* London: Athlone Press, 1964.

Revolution, As Historical Concept
The ways in which the idea of revolution has been conceptualized by historians. Revolution is generally defined as an attempt to make radical change in the system of government generally involving some type of force and violence, although in earlier periods the word often meant quite the opposite: during the Renaissance, it was used to denote a conservative *return* to established principles and institutions and the repudiation of innovation. It seems to have acquired its modern association with innovation and change by the early eighteenth century.

War has often acted as a stimulant to theories of revolution. Historians in the West have, in recent times, tended to stress political factors over others such as social, economic, and cultural. In the twentieth century, the concept has expanded to a global basis. Modern historians have been influenced by classic treatments of revolution: Edmund Burke and Thomas Paine carried on a debate over the significance and contributions of the French Revolution during the early 1790s, Burke as an alarmed critic from the perspective of the Right, and Paine as an enthusiastic supporter and later participant from the Left. (The format of the political spectrum, Right, Center, and Left, itself originated from seating practices of the National Assembly during the early years of the French Revolution: Right for conservative and authoritarian, Center for moderate and liberal, and Left for radical and socialist.)

Burke, a prominent Parliamentarian, had been sympathetic to the cause of the American Revolution of the 1770s. To him, King George III had exceeded his power when he taxed the colonists. The case of the French Revolution was opposite: all that was good was being ruthlessly swept away with the bad. Burke greatly feared such anarchy would spread to his beloved England. Thomas Paine, incredibly a participant in both the American and French revolutions and a well-known dissident in England, systematically repudiated in his *Rights of Man* the attacks of Burke on the revolution and revolutionaries in France.

Later contributions, from the far Left, came from Karl Marx and Friedrich Engels, who formulated influential concepts of revolution in a series of joint writings in the middle and later decades of the nineteenth century, most notably in *The Communist Manifesto,* written by Marx and Engels just before the revolutions of 1848. Among the ideas of Marx and Engels were dialectic materialism, determinism, and the theory of permanent revolution. Lenin, Joseph Stalin, and Mao Zedong elaborated variously on these concepts, in writing and in practice in Russia and China. Leon Trotsky, a leading participant in the Russian revolutions of 1905 and 1917, also wrote voluminously on revolution.

In *Revolutions and Revolutionists: A Comprehensive Guide to the Literature* (1982), Robert Blackey collected more than 6,200 entries, up from 2,400 in an edition of 1976, and noted that prior to the mid-1960s, revolution was not a subject of academic or popular appeal. Chalmers Johnson formulated a typology, a total of six types of revolution, for example, including millenarian and anarchistic rebellions, Jacobin and Bolshevik revolutions, and militarized mass insurrections such as guerrilla warfare.

Comparative approaches to revolution in the Western sense can be traced to Crane Brinton's classic study, *The Anatomy of Revolution* (1938; revised edition 1965). Brinton selected the four modern successful Western revolutions, the English of the 1640s and 1680s, the American of the 1770s, the French of the 1790s and 1800s, and the Russian of the 1910s and 1920s, and systematically subjected them to comparative analysis, including following what he called the full cycle of revolution. Brinton generally concluded that each began with the center of gravity of political power strongly on the Right, each then shifted across the spectrum to the Left, and, then, each returned to the Right. There were 220 entries in his bibliography.

Another comparative approach incorporates a series of Right-Center-Left charts to demonstrate shifts that occur in specific revolutions, including Western and non-Western ones: in chronological order, the Czech "Hussite," the English "Puritan," the French "Bourgeois," the Russian "Bolshevik," the Turkish "National," and the Chinese "Communist" revolutions. This series of morphological patterns has been formulated by Jaroslav Krejci in *Great Revolutions Compared* (1983).

Seeing the various national revolutions of the late eighteenth and early nineteenth century as a single, collective "Atlantic Revolution," Robert R. Palmer presented the thesis that an international democratic revolutionary movement incorporating common characteristics, and including, of course, the American and French revolutions, spread during the last four decades of the eighteenth century to most states and throughout the continents contiguous to the Atlantic ocean. Meanwhile, in the first book of a trilogy on the history of the "long nineteenth century," 1789–1914, the Marxist historian Eric J. Hobsbawm has written of the age of revolutions, reviewing events in Greece, the Ottoman empire, Spain, Naples, South America, France, Belgium, Poland, and Ireland. Hobsbawm effectively incorporates economic, social, and even cultural factors, in addition to political.

Social theorists have also contributed to the conceptualization of revolution. Hannah Arendt's *On Revolution* (1963), is a grandiose study of the phenomenon of revolution, emphasizing only a few legitimate and great ones, the American, French, and Russian. Theda Skocpol, in *States and Social Revolutions,* selects three social revolutions, the French, Russian, and Chinese. Each of these states faced wars with more advanced capitalist enemies and each suffered from structural weaknesses.

Classic studies of comparative revolution tended to focus exclusively on modern times and in the West. In contrast, Jack Goldstone has pushed back the dates to the early modern period, 1500–1850, and expanded the geography to a global perspective, including political disasters in the Middle East and the collapse of the Ming dynasty in China. Goldstone formulates causal models of early revolutions and rebellions, emphasizing primarily the role of demography and its consequences. For example, he elaborates on a general crisis of the seventeenth century, with extreme population and price increases. States were unable to cope with these changes.

George Rudé, a British-educated historian who taught in Australia and Canada, conducted innovative and intensive research in police records and accounts of popular disturbances, producing,

R

among other, broader works, *The Crowd in the French Revolution* (1967). Through a combination of political and social approaches, Rudé corrected myths and stereotypes about participation in riots and revolutionary disturbances. For example, he demonstrated that rioters in the early years of the French Revolution were respectable, employed, solid citizens with no criminal records.

Most recently, a new category of modern revolution has emerged that does not fit into the classic Western models: revolutions in nonindustrialized, or Third World, countries, such as those in Central America, Iran, and the Sudan. Interpretations are varied and expansive, and the term has often been overworked: for example, by Abbie Hoffman of the "New Left" movement in the United States in the 1960s, in his *Revolution for the Hell of It* (1968), and more recently in a 1994 book that deals primarily with free markets and deregulation, *A Conservative Revolution: The Thatcher–Reagan Decade in Perspective.*

Eugene L. Rasor

See also FRENCH REVOLUTION.

Texts

Arendt, Hannah. *On Revolution.* New York: Viking, 1982.
Brinton, Crane. *The Anatomy of Revolution.* New York: Random House, 1965.
Burke, Edmund. *Reflections on the Revolution in France.* Indianapolis, IN: Bobbs-Merrill, 1955.
Marx, Karl, and Friedrich Engels. *The Communist Manifesto.* New York: Kerr, 1978.
Palmer, Robert R. *The Age of the Democratic Revolution: A Political History of Europe and America.* 2 vols. Princeton, NJ: Princeton University Press, 1959–1963.

References

Blackey, Robert. *Revolutions and Revolutionists: A Comprehensive Guide to the Literature.* Santa Barbara, CA: ABC-Clio, 1982.
Dunn, John M. *Modern Revolutions: An Introduction to the Analysis of a Political Phenomenon.* Cambridge, Eng.: Cambridge University Press, 1989.
Goldstone, Jack A. *Revolution and Rebellion in the Early Modern World.* Berkeley: University of California Press, 1991.
Johnson, Chalmers. *Revolution and the Social System.* Stanford, CA: Stanford University Press, 1964.
Paynton, Clifford T., and Robert Blackey, eds. *Why Revolution: Theories and Analysis.* Cambridge: Schenkman, 1971.

Skocpol, Theda. *States and Social Revolutions: A Comparative Analysis of France, Russia, and China.* Cambridge, Eng.: Cambridge University Press, 1988.

Rhenanus, Beatus (1485–1547)

German humanist historian. Born in Alsace, Rhenanus received the M.A. at Paris in 1505. Rhenanus associated with scholars seeking reform of church and society, who thereby challenged scholastic philosopher-theologians. Under the influence of Desiderius Erasmus (a close friend who would name Rhenanus in his will as editor of his works), Rhenanus shunned allegorical interpretations of Scripture in favor of philological-historical studies. Initially a supporter of Luther against ecclesiastical corruption, he in the end rejected the Reformation. While in the employ of Johannes Froben, the Basel printer, Rhenanus had edited works by Seneca, Pliny, Tacitus, and Livy, and he won acclaim in his time chiefly through these editorial achievements. His own writings, however, are also impressive and include biographies of Erasmus and Geiler of Kaisersberg, as well as shorter biographical sketches of various of the authors whose works he edited. Rhenanus was an ardent admirer of the fifteenth-century Italian antiquary and topographer, Flavio Biondo, whose standards of research he applied in his own *Rerum Germanicarum libri tres* [Three Books on German History] (1531). In this work Rhenanus dismissed unfounded traditions, especially that of the supposed Trojan origins of the Germanic peoples. His research confirmed Paolo Emili's contention that the French derived their origins from Germanic, rather than Trojan, ancestry—a highly contentious issue in the historical writing of the sixteenth century.

James Edward McGoldrick

Texts

Beati Rhenani Selestadiensis rerum Germanicarum libri tres. Strasbourg: Lazarus Zetzner, 1610.
"Life of Erasmus." In *Christian Humanism and the Reformation,* ed. John C. Olin. Second ed. New York: Fordham University Press, 1988.
Ed. *T. Livii Patavini historiae principis Decades tres cum dimidia.* Venice: Giunti, 1541.

References

D'Amico, John F. *Theory and Practice in Renaissance Textual Criticism: Beatus Rhenanus between Conjecture and History.* Berkeley: University of California Press, 1988.

Rhetoric and Historical Writing

The nodal point of the conflicted relationship between history and literature in western European historiography. The relationship has its origins in classical culture, in which since the time of Gorgias (ca. 480 B.C.–ca. 399 B.C.) the role of rhetoric—understood here as the use of language for persuasion (the narrower question of the value of technical rhetoric to historians has almost always been decided in the negative)—in serious speaking and writing was frequently in question. Plato's (ca. 429 B.C.–347 B.C.) strongly negative reaction to Gorgias's emphasis on the power of speech established the other of the two poles between which attitudes to history and rhetoric have stretched ever since. Historians insisted on the related distinction between history and poetry, among them the Greek Thucydides (ca. 471 B.C.–400 B.C.), who roundly attacked what he called his predecessor Herodotus's poetic myth-making, but Thucydides' own propensity for invented speeches neatly illustrates how difficult it was for historians to do without rhetoric.

The Romans regarded history and rhetoric as branches of literature, and thought that all three had a serious, moral purpose. As Cicero (106 B.C.–43 B.C.), the consummate rhetorician, politician, and orator, put it, history was "the mistress of life," and both it and rhetoric more generally were about finding and inculcating truth, unlike poetry. Rhetoric was the means to induce readers to imitate the examples of which history consisted, and make it useful. Much early Christian historiography agreed that pleasure and utility had to be combined in history writing until Augustine (A.D. 354–430), who had been a practicing rhetorician, converted to Christianity and decided that history was no more than a record of important events in the past. Utility had excluded pleasure.

In the Middle Ages, history continued to be a branch of the quadrivium, the educational scheme essentially derived from Roman rhetoric, and its patron saint continued to be Cicero, although the balance between utility and pleasure tipped in Augustine's direction. In the fourteenth century, the revival of more purely classical (and pagan) rhetorical techniques raised again the issue of the legitimacy of persuasion in historical writing. For the humanists, beginning with Petrarch (1304–1374), there was no doubt that persuasion lay at the heart of what they did; they differed only in their ultimate objects and the precise kinds of technical rhetoric they preferred. They tried to make history fully pleasing and useful again. Thus Petrarch tried to write Ciceronian Latin with the object of establishing his own identity. Most of his successors agreed with his choice of Cicero as model, but more often than not put it to broader ends, especially the so-called civic humanist or nationalist historians, who wrote from a political perspective.

Occasional mutterings about the evils of rhetoric sometimes led to full-blown skepticism about the possibility of historical knowledge, most clearly in the case of the German writer Heinrich Cornelius Agrippa von Nettesheim (1486–1535), who started from the premise that history was rhetoric and then proceeded to demonstrate how its persuasive end almost always distorted the way it was actually written. Yet history remained a rhetorical enterprise during and after the Reformation. The objects again differed, but Catholic and Protestant historians continued to believe firmly that their job was moral suasion and the best means to that end was rhetoric.

History and rhetoric remained firmly joined until some time in the eighteenth century. Thomas Hobbes (1588–1679), for example, still practiced fully rhetorical historical criticism, whatever the new scientific ends to which he may have put it. And David Hume (1711–1776) singled historians out relative to philosophers and poets as the only "true friends of virtue" because they kept to an essentially Ciceronian view of their office: it demanded adherence to truth, but the result still had to move its readers. But the balance was already tipping toward the side of utility (the facts) at the expense of the pleasant, as the first glimmerings of scientific history made their appearance. With the rise of the German historical school at Göttingen and then the virtually complete triumph of other kinds of scientific history in the nineteenth century, one of the greatest ruptures in western European historiography was completed. History took an explicitly antirhetorical stance. The search for truth and moral education became separated and truth was left as the only legitimate historical end. Harold Temperley's approving observation about one of the most prominent of English scientific historians, J.B. Bury (1861–1927), that for him "the first step forward was to cut history loose from rhetoric," well marks this development.

Until late in the twentieth century this attitude prevailed virtually everywhere in the West. Beginning about 1970, however, a few historians, especially in the United States, began to turn back to history's roots in rhetoric, usually by means of drawing inspiration from current literary criticism, which had remained much closer to classical rhetoric despite efforts similar to those in history to escape its clutches. Perhaps the most important of these historians is Dominic LaCapra, but he is only one of a number, some of them also major figures (like Donald McCloskey and Allan Megill) in the move to transcend present disciplinary boundaries, as for example in the Project on the Rhetoric of Inquiry at the University of Iowa and other such programs elsewhere. Similarly, historians like Nancy Struever have been very active in efforts both to revive the language of history and to restore its moral purpose.

Thomas F. Mayer

See also GREEK HISTORIOGRAPHY; POSTMODERNISM.

Texts
Kelley, Donald R., ed. *Versions of History from Antiquity to the Enlightenment.* New Haven, CT, and London: Yale University Press, 1991.

References
Kennedy, George A. *Classical Rhetoric and Its Christian and Secular Tradition from Ancient to Modern Times.* Chapel Hill: University of North Carolina Press, 1980.
LaCapra, Dominic. *Soundings in Critical Theory.* Ithaca, NY: Cornell University Press, 1990.
Struever, Nancy S. *Theory As Practice: Ethical Inquiry in the Renaissance.* Chicago and London: University of Chicago Press, 1992.
Woodman, A.J. *Rhetoric in Classical Historiography: Four Studies.* London: Croom Helm, 1988.

Rhodes, James Ford (1848–1927)
American businessman and historian. Rhodes made a comfortable fortune at his family's iron and coal business in Cleveland before retiring in 1885 to write the *History of the United States from the Compromise of 1850* (1892–1928), in nine volumes. Although virtually unknown in 1893, Rhodes quickly rose to prominence in his adopted Boston and was elected president of the American Historical Association in 1898. Rhodes's history of the Civil War, on which his reputation rests, was praised by his contemporaries for its comparative fair-mindedness and literary clarity and because its nationalistic, evolutionary, and racist premises reflected the era of its publication. Rhodes's reputation declined rapidly after 1920. His *Historical Essays* (1909) reveals the intellectual presuppositions and working habits of one of the last of the "gentlemen amateurs."

John Austin Matzko

Texts
Historical Essays. New York: Macmillan, 1909.
History of the Civil War, 1861–1865. Ed. E.B. Long. New York: Ungar, 1961.
History of the United States from the Compromise of 1850. 9 vols. New York: Harper & Bros., 1893–1928.

References
Cruden, Robert. *James Ford Rhodes: The Man, the Historian, and His Work.* Cleveland, OH: Cleveland Press of Western Reserve University, 1961.
Grant, Robert. *Commemorative Tribute to James Ford Rhodes.* New York: American Academy of Arts and Letters, 1928.

Richer of St. Remi (ca. 945–ca. 998)
Frankish monk and chronicler. Born into a west Frankish aristocratic family, Richer entered the monastery of St. Remi, Rheims, where he studied the classics under Gerbert (later Pope Sylvester II) at the cathedral school. Later in life he probably studied medicine in Chartres for a time. His knowledge of both the classics and medicine is clearly evident in the *Historiae* written, between 991 and 998, at the suggestion of his former master. The *Historiae,* which records the history of France from 888 to 995, consists of four books and begins where Hincmar's *Annales* finishes. For the period before 966, Richer's most important source was Flodoard of Rheims's *Historia Remensis Ecclesiae* [History of the Church of Rheims] (upon which he studiously tried to improve), but the later part of his work rests on original research. In Rheims he was ideally situated to observe political developments and, although an apologist for the Capetians, Richer is an important witness for the era during which they succeeded the Carolingians.

G.H. Gerrits

Texts
Richer: Histoire de son temps [A History of His Times]. Trans. J. Guadet. 2 vols. New York: Johnson Reprint, 1968.

References
Manitius, Max. *Geschichte der lateinischen Literatur des Mittelalters* [History of the Latin Literature of the Middle Ages]. Vol. 2. Munich: C.H. Beck, 1964.
Smalley, Beryl. *Historians in the Middle Ages.* London: Thames and Hudson, 1974.

Rickert, Heinrich (1863–1936)

German philosopher of history. Rickert developed Wilhelm Windelband's axiological philosophy of history. Rickert influenced many social scientists, including Max Weber. The first complete edition of his *Die Grenzen der naturwissenschaftliche Begriffsbildung* [The Limits of Concept Formation in Natural Science] appeared in 1902. In this work, Rickert sought to replace Auguste Comte's skeptical empiricism and Hegel's speculative rationalism with his own quasi-Kantian synthesis, which may be summarized as follows. Positivism naively denies the realm of values, while idealism is overly certain of axiological details. Nomothetic methodology abstracts from reality to find universal (value-free) laws. Ideographic methodology sees unique (valuable) individuals (whether planets or humans). History requires a world neither all structure nor completely structureless. Both methodologies work together to advance scientific knowledge, whereas, in Rickert's view, Wilhelm Dilthey's subjective approach to history lacks scientific rigor. Ideographic methodology is rooted in the cultural values of the professional researcher: selective representation of the unique individual, specifically including the relevant cultural/axiological context (not reproduction of the complete manifold), is valuable. In practice we must assume the reality of existence and of values even when sure knowledge of "is" and "ought" is lacking. Only with valid values, realized perhaps in a future universal culture, may we perfectly understand the course of history, thus synthesizing "is" and "ought."

Charles Tandy

Texts

The Limits of Concept Formation in Natural Science. Trans. and abrid. Guy Oakes. Cambridge, Eng.: Cambridge University Press, 1986.
Science and History. Trans. George Reisman; ed. Arthur Goddard. Princeton, NJ: Van Nostrand, 1962.

References

Oakes, Guy. *Weber and Rickert.* Cambridge, MA: MIT Press, 1988.

Ridolfi, Roberto (b. 1899)

Florentine archivist and historian. Born to an old noble family, after World War I Ridolfi immersed himself in the Archivio di Stato in Florence. He thought of himself as "a discoverer of paper," and published many important texts he found, including much of the national edition of Savonarola's works. Ridolfi's most important work appeared before 1960, including twelve books (counting editions) and an autobiography. His central historical work consisted of three biographies: *Girolamo Savonarola* (1950); *Niccolò Machiavelli* (1952); and *Francesco Guicciardini* (1958). The major theme of his work was the gap between humans and the reality they inhabit. The lives of Savonarola and Machiavelli, his most famous books, highlight the way in which their visions attempted to overcome that breach.

Thomas F. Mayer

Texts

Note: All of these works exist in numerous revised editions in Italian. All English translations are by Cecil Grayson.
The Life of Francesco Guicciardini. London: Routledge and Kegan Paul, 1967.
———. *The Life of Girolamo Savonarola.* London: Routledge and Kegan Paul, 1953.
———. *The Life of Niccolò Machiavelli.* London: Routledge and Kegan Paul, 1963.

References

Martelli, Mario. *L'opera di Roberto Ridolfi* [The Work of Roberto Ridolfi]. Florence: Leo S. Olschki, 1962.

Ritter, Gerhard (1889–1967)

German historian. Ritter was an eminent representative of traditional historical thought in Germany. As the holder of a chair at the University of Freiburg im Breisgau from 1925 to 1956, Ritter engaged in most of the political and historical debates of his time. During World War II he joined the conservative resistance movement against the Nazi regime. After the war Ritter played an important role in the reconstruction of West German historical scholarship. Ritter believed that German history had followed a separate road from the rest of Europe, and advocated the rejection of western European political and intellectual traditions. He always remained committed to the traditional emphasis on national power as the central theme in historical writing. In *Machtstaat und Utopie* [State Power and Utopia] (1940) he examined the ambiguous relationship between power politics and morality. In *Europa und die deutsche Frage* [Europe and the German Question] (1948) he argued that national socialism had been the heir of mass politics and a totalitarian version of democracy, rather than the offspring of authoritarianism. After the war he generally sought to underline the fundamental discontinuity between the legacy of Prussian–German traditions and the Nazi dictatorship. This view was crucial to his interpretation of the German resistance against Hitler in *Carl Goerdeler und die deutsche Widerstandsbewegung* [Carl Goerdeler and the German Resistance Movement] (1954). In *Staatskunst und Kriegshandwerk: das Problem des "Militarismus" in Deutschland* [Statecraft and the Art of War: The Problem of "Militarism" in Germany] (1954–1968) he investigated the interrelationship between state politics and the military apparatus. In later life Ritter became an outspoken opponent of the conclusions in Fritz Fischer's book on German war aims in World War I, *Griff nach der Weltmacht* [The Grasp for World Power].

Georgi Verbeeck

Texts

Carl Goerdeler und die deutsche Widerstandsbewegung: Europa und die deutsche Frage. Munich: Münchner Verlag, 1948.

Machtstaat und Utopie. Munich: R. Oldenbourg, 1943.

Staatskunst und Kriegshandwerk: Das Problem des "Militarismus" in Deutschland. 4 vols. Munich, R. Oldenbourg, 1954–1968.

References

Iggers, Georg G. *The German Conception of History: The National Tradition of Historical Thought from Herder to the Present.* Second ed. Middletown, CT: Wesleyan University Press, 1983.

———, ed. *The Social History of Politics: Critical Perspectives in West German Historical Writing since 1945.* Leamington Spa and Heidelberg: Berg Publishers, 1985.

Maehl, William Harvey. "Gerhard Ritter." In *Historians of Modern Europe,* ed. Hans A. Schmitt. Baton Rouge: Louisiana State University Press, 1971, 152–205.

Schwabe, Klaus, and Rolf Reichardt, eds. *Gerhard Ritter.* Boppard am Rhein: Boldt, 1984.

Riva-Agüero, José de la (1885–1944)

Peruvian historian, literary critic, teacher, political figure, and apologist for the Roman Catholic Church. Riva-Agüero, great-grandson of Peru's first president, was the leader of the "Generation of 1900," those Peruvian intellectuals who reached maturity at the turn of the century and who opposed *caudillismo* (strong-man rule), favored a modicum of democratic reform, and were guided by the example of France. Riva-Agüero's undergraduate thesis, *Carácter de la literatura del Perú independiente* [The Character of the Literature of Independent Peru] (1905), was the first attempt to provide an outline of Peruvian literature. His doctoral dissertation, *La historia en el Perú* [History in Peru] (1910), is a history of Peruvian historiography, the earliest work of its kind to be written in Latin America. Riva-Agüero's masterpiece, *Paisajes peruanos* [Peruvian Landscapes], which was written in 1916, is an essay in Peruvian nationalism that has been compared to Domingo Faustino Sarmiento's *Facundo* [Barbarism and Civilization] and Euclides da Cunha's *Os Sertoes Campanha de Canudos* [Rebellion in the Backlands]. Riva-Agüero wrote on all phases of Peruvian history and not simply on colonial Peru, as many of his detractors have claimed. Particularly significant was his conviction that "Peruvianism" meant the triumph of *mestizaje* (the half-caste descendants of European and Indian intermarriage)—thus his eloquent defense of the Inca Garcilaso de la Vega. Although he believed that one could not escape the importance of environmental, ethnic, and economic factors in history, he regarded "the collective psychology" of the people as paramount, as it was the cement that held history together.

George L. Vásquez

Texts

Obras Completas de José de la Riva-Agüero [Complete Works]. 12 vols. to date. Lima: Pontificia Universidad Católica del Perú, 1962– .

Paisajes Peruanos. Lima: Instituto Riva-Agüero de la Pontificia Universidad Católica del Perú, 1995.

References

Bonner, Fred. "José de la Riva-Agüero (1885–1944), Peruvian Historian." *Hispanic American Historical Review* 36 (1956): 490–502.

Porras Barrenechea, Raúl. "Estudio Preliminar [Preliminary Study]." In *Obras Completas de José de la Riva-Agüero.* Lima: Pontificia Universidad Católica del Perú, 1962, vol. 9, xi–clxxxviii.

Robert, Louise Felicité Guinement de Kéralio (1758–1821)

French author, activist, editor, and novelist. Codirector of the *Mercure National* with her conventioneer husband, François, she edited the *Journal d'Etat et du Citoyen* [State and Citizens' Newspaper]. As a member of a learned academy and patriotic club, Louise advocated public debate. Jules Michelet would later admire her republicanism. During the Revolution, the Roberts helped to bring about the Girondins' downfall. Having survived the Terror and its aftermath, the couple then engaged in the Belgian wine trade. As a historian, Robert was the author of a popular documentary *Histoire d'Elizabeth, reine d'Angleterre* [History of Elizabeth I] (1786–1789), which led Mallet du Pan to hail her "new authorial identity, the woman historian." This identity, and her republicanism, failed to translate into any kind of advocacy of female equality, and in *Les Crimes des Reines de France* [The Crimes of French Queens] (1791), Robert wrote that women were born to obey, not legislate. Of her proposed forty-volume edition of women's works, she published fourteen tomes (1786–1789).

Barbara Sher Tinsley

Texts

Les Crimes des Reines de France. Paris: Bureau des Revolutions de Paris, 1791.
Histoire d'Elizabeth, reine d'Angleterre. Paris: the author, 1786–1789.

References

Antheunis, L. *Le Conventionnel Belge François Robert (1763–1826) et sa Femme Louise de Kéralio* [The Conventioneer François Robert and His Wife, Louise de Keralio]. Wetteren: Éditions Bracke, 1955.
Brive, Marie-France, ed. *Les Femmes et la Revolution Française* [Women and the French Revolution]. Toulouse: Presses Universitaires de Mirail, 1989, vol. 2 (see essays by E. Colwill, B. Slama, and N. Pellegrin).
Censer, Jack R. *Prelude to Power.* Baltimore, MD: Johns Hopkins University Press, 1976.
Diefendorf, Barbara, and Carla Hesse, eds. *Culture and Identity in Early Modern Europe.* Ann Arbor: University of Michigan Press, 1993.
Smith, Bonnie. "The Contribution of Women to Modern Historiography in Great Britain, France, and the United States, 1750–1940." *American Historical Review* 89 (1984): 709–732.

Robertson, William (1721–1793)

Scottish historian and clergyman. William Robertson was born in Borthwick, Midlothian, and, like his father, became a minister. He attended Dalkeith Grammar School and Edinburgh University, to which he returned as principal in 1762, having become the leader of the Moderates in the Church of Scotland. Shortly thereafter he sat as the moderator of the general assembly of the church and was appointed historiographer royal. He died in Edinburgh. His success as a historian came with his first work, the *History of Scotland* (1759), which analyzed Scottish feudalism; in its wake came his *History of the Reign of Charles V* (1769), a survey of German history (the first volume of which contains a sweeping and brilliant summary of medieval history), and his *History of America* (1777), a comparative native history. These histories drew praise from contemporary historians for their judgment, research, and eloquence. Robertson made his mark through his careful sifting of evidence to reveal both the broad patterns of European civilization and the material and environmental factors shaping it. He felt that research was a continuing process and, although he seldom left the vicinity of Edinburgh, he took pride in his efforts to obtain documentary evidence and meticulously cited exact references so as to allow others to continue his work.

David R. Schweitzer

Texts

The History of America. Revised ed. 2 vols. New York: Samuel Campbell, 1798.
The History of Scotland during the Reign of Queen Mary and of King James VI. Millwood, NY: Kraus Reprint, 1976.
The History of the Reign of the Emperor Charles V. 3 vols. Philadelphia: Robert Bell, 1770–1771.
The Progress of Society in Europe. Ed. Felix Gilbert. Chicago: University of Chicago Press, 1972.
The Works of William Robertson. 6 vols. London: J.F. Dove, 1826.

References

Humphreys, R.A. "William Robertson and His 'History of America.'" In his *Tradition and Revolt in Latin America and Other Essays.* London: Weidenfeld & Nicolson, 1969.
Meek, R.L. *Social Science and the Ignoble Savage.* Cambridge, Eng.: Cambridge University Press, 1976.

Robinson, James Harvey (1863–1936)

American historian. Robinson was born in Bloomington, Illinois. He pursued his undergraduate studies at Harvard University and completed a master's degree in history there in 1888. He then studied at the University of Freiburg, where he worked under the German historian, Herman E. von Holst, and earned his Ph.D. in 1890.

A year later he accepted a teaching position in European history at the University of Pennsylvania and in 1895, he began a long and noteworthy career at Columbia University. At both Pennsylvania and Columbia, Robinson was a leader in the transformation of history into a modern academic discipline. He emphasized the methods and techniques that he had learned in Germany: extensive research in original sources; detached and unbiased judgments and a determination to see the history of each age in its own terms. These ideas were reflected in his *Introduction to the History of Western Europe* (1902), the first great European history textbook published in the United States. Later in his career, Robinson championed the "New History," calling for an expansion of the scope of the discipline to include social, intellectual, and economic history. Urging historians to utilize the newly established social sciences, he emphasized the study of the past as useful primarily for understanding the present and for achieving social progress. "The present has hitherto been the willing victim of the past," he wrote, "the time has come when it should turn on the past and exploit it in the interest of advance." Robinson became the leader at Columbia of a group of "New Historians," which included James Shotwell, Lynn Thorndike, and Charles Beard.

Kevin J. O'Keefe

Texts

The Humanizing of Knowledge. New York: Doran, 1923.

An Introduction to the History of Western Europe. Boston and London: Ginn, 1902.

The Mind in the Making. New York and London: Harper, 1921.

The New History: Essays Illustrating the Modern Historical Outlook. New York: Macmillan, 1912.

References

Hendricks, Luther V. *James Harvey Robinson: Teacher of History.* New York: King's Crown Press, 1946.

Novick, Peter. *That Noble Dream: The "Objectivity Question" and the American Historical Profession.* Cambridge, Eng.: Cambridge University Press, 1988.

Rodrigues, João de (ca. 1561–1634)

Jesuit grammarian and historian of Japan. Rodrigues was born in Sernancelhe in Portugal. He entered the Society of Jesus in 1580, three years after his arrival in Japan. He remained in Japan for almost all of the next thirty-six years, until the persecution of Japanese Christians and foreign priests caused his withdrawal to Macao. Although he lived mainly in Nagasaki, Rodrigues traveled extensively and visited different parts of Japan. Noted for his fluency in Japanese, he acted as interpreter in negotiations with Toyotomi Hideyoshi and later Tokugawa Ieyasu in regard to Portuguese trade and Jesuit mission affairs. In 1608, he published in Nagasaki his pioneering Japanese grammar, *Arte da Lingoa de Iapan,* which also contained considerable information concerning Japanese history, poetry, pronunciation, and etiquette. It is for this work, and subsequent editions of it produced in Macao, that he is chiefly remembered.

A. Hamish Ion

Texts

This Island of Japan: João Rodrigues' Account of 16th-Century Japan. Trans. and ed. Michael Cooper, S.J. Tokyo and New York: Kodansha International, 1973.

References

Cooper, Michael, S.J. *Rodrigues the Interpreter: An Early Jesuit in Japan and China.* New York and Tokyo: Weatherhill, 1974.

Roger de Hoveden [Roger of Howden] (fl. 1171–1201/1202)

English chronicler, parson, crusader, and royal justice. His father arranged his succession to the parsonage of Howden in the mid-1170s. A northern circuit justice in the late 1180s, Roger can be placed by a charter at the 1190–1191 siege of Acre, during which period he chronicled in detail the events of the Crusade between August 1190 and late August 1191, at which latter time he accompanied Philip Augustus to France. During the last decade before his 1201/2 death he lived in his inherited parsonage. No documents explicitly link the justice, crusader, and parson, but the historian's disputed professional affiliations fit well chronologically and explain the often tedious bureaucratic style and preoccupations with matters of the court evinced in Roger's only signed work, the *Chronica,* which he composed in retirement. The *Chronica* reuses Roger's earlier history (once erroneously attributed to Benedict of Peterborough but now firmly established as the work of Roger) the *Gesta Regis Henrici Secundi,* an unpolished and unsigned account composed nearly annually from 1172 to 1193; the

Chronica corrects several of the *Gesta*'s mistaken suppositions while adding further information. Both works are crucial sources for later accounts of the courts of Henry II and Richard I.

Georges Whalen

Texts

The Annals of Roger de Hoveden. Trans. H.T. Riley. 2 vols. London: H.G. Bohn, 1853.

Chronica magistri Rogeri de Houedene. Ed. William Stubbs. 4 vols. Rolls Series, 51. London: Longman, 1868–1871.

Gesta Regis Henrici Secundi Benedicti Abbatis. Ed. William Stubbs. Rolls Series, 49. 2 vols. London: Longmans, Green, Reader, and Dyer, 1867.

References

Corner, David. "The *Gesta Regis Henrici Secundi* and *Chronica* of Roger, Parson of Howden." *Bulletin of the Institute of Historical Research* 56 (1983): 126–144.

Gillingham, John "Roger of Howden on Crusade." In *Medieval Historical Writing in the Christian and Islamic Worlds,* ed. D.O. Morgan. London: SOAS, 1982, 60–75.

Stenton, Doris. "Roger of Howden and Benedict." *English Historical Review* 68 (1953): 574–582.

Roger of Wendover (fl. 1200–1236)

English monk of St. Albans, chronicler, and founder of the three-century-long St. Albans's tradition of historical writing. Although relatively little is known of Roger's life, his great successor, Matthew Paris, mentions his 1219 demotion from the position of Prior at Belvoir, Lincolnshire, for wasting the abbey's resources. Matthew Paris probably worked with Wendover from 1217 until the latter's death. A broad and thorough source compilation, his *Flores historiarum* became a principal historical resource much used and expanded by subsequent medieval historians. The observations in his *Chronica* reflect, with relatively uncritical neutrality, the conventions and information in a good number of his sources until the late twelfth century. The work's importance increases at the year 1201, at which point cease the contributions of Roger Howden (or Hoveden) and Ralph Diceto, but it remains error-prone up to the death of King John in 1216. Wendover was perhaps the first to testify in writing to John's already legendary reputation as a bad king. His interest in Henry III's minority, while Wendover headed the St. Albans scriptorium (1219–1236), helped to create an ideal of limited monarchy that later historians such as William Stubbs took as foreshadowing ideas of constitutional rule.

Georges Whalen

Texts

Rogeri de Wendover Chronica, sive, Flores Historiarum. Ed. Henry O. Coxe. 4 vols. London: English Historical Society Publications, 1841–1842.

Roger of Wendover's Flowers of History. Trans. J.A. Giles. 2 vols. Felinfach, Wales: Llanerch, 1993.

References

Galbraith, Viven Hunter. *Roger Wendover and Matthew Paris.* Glasgow: University of Glasgow, 1970.

Gransden, Antonia. *Historical Writing in England, c. 550–c. 1307.* Ithaca, NY: Cornell University Press, 1974.

Schnith, Karl. *England in einer sich wandelnden Welt (1189–1250)* [England in a Changing World]. Stuttgart: Anton Hersemann, 1974.

Rogers, James Edwin Thorold (1823–1890)

English clergyman, member of parliament, political economist, and historian. Rogers was born in West Meon, Hampshire, and was educated in Southampton and King's College, London and received his M.A. at Oxford in 1849 shortly before being ordained. He was active in the tractarian movement, but lost sympathy with it and resigned his order in 1870. Rogers studied political economy during his leisure and was elected the first Tooke professor of statistics and economic science at King's College, London, in 1859, whereupon he began his researches into the history of agriculture and prices. He taught political economics at Oxford from 1862 until 1867 while his friendship with Richard Cobden encouraged his involvement in agitation for political reform. He later served as Liberal member of Parliament for the borough of Southwark from 1880 until 1885, and then Bermondsey until 1886. His lecturing activities resumed in 1883 at Oxford until his death there seven years later. Rogers is remembered as an economic historian principally through his *History of Agriculture and Prices* (1866–1902), a minute and scholarly investigation, which remains a standard work, and *Six Centuries of Work and*

Wages (1884), now largely outdated. His writings generally advanced the claims that industrialization impoverished the working man and that political action could result in social change.

David R. Schweitzer

Texts

History of Agriculture and Prices in England. 7 vols. in 8. Oxford: Clarendon Press, 1866–1902.

Six Centuries of Work and Wages: The History of English Labour. New ed. London: G. Allen and Unwin, 1949.

References

Harvie, C. *Lights of Liberalism.* London: Allen Lane, 1976.

Roman Historiography, Ancient (ca. 200 B.C.–ca. A.D. 500)

Roman historical writing, generally in Latin, and usually in an annalistic format. Since the Romans adopted the writing of history from their Greek neighbors, Roman historiography cannot be separated from the wider Hellenic and Hellenistic forms of the genre. In fact, the fundamental impetus behind Roman history writing can be divided into two constitutive elements: Greek historiography and the need of Romans to explain their own history to themselves and their Greek neighbors; and the ancient Roman practice of maintaining annual lists of portents, disasters, religious festivals, and magistrates, known as the tables of the pontiffs *(tabulae pontificum),* later codified as the *Annales Maximi* [Great Annals]. The precise origins of these annals, and the lists of magistrates such as the consuls, is a subject of great controversy, but we can state with some assurance that by the time of the Gallic sack of Rome (390 or 387 B.C.) records of this type were regularly kept. In the subsequent period Romans must have become aware of Greek historians, whose works often touched on Italian affairs and were occasionally devoted to the history of Hellenes in Italy and Sicily. This contact culminated in the first attempts by Romans to write their own history, significantly choosing Greek as the language for this endeavor. The Roman senator Fabius Pictor apparently composed the first such work (ca. 200 B.C.), but his annals (now lost) were quickly followed by others. Perhaps the greatest historian of Rome in the Greek language was not a Roman at all, but the Greek aristocrat Polybius, who was brought to Italy as a nominal hostage after the victory of Lucius Aemilius Paullus in 168. Polybius wrote an authoritative work covering the period between the first and third Punic Wars (264–146) that focused on Rome's rise to supremacy through the struggles with Carthage and relations with the Greek east. His importance for Latin authors is best seen in his use by Livy in the first century B.C., who based much of his own account of the Second Punic War and the invasion of Hannibal (218–201) on this source.

Marcus Porcius Cato is generally thought to have written Roman history in the native Latin tongue first, but his *Origines* (ca. 150) is lost except for a few fragments. From the mid-second century B.C. a series of Romans writing in Latin composed the history of their city-empire, usually adopting an annalistic format, which viewed the world from a Roman center. Roman historiography is thus in some ways connected to a branch of Greek historiography sometimes called "horography" (from Greek *horos,* "year"), a kind of annalistic local history. Roman "horography," however, was always painted on a wider canvas, since the Romans already possessed an empire when they began to write their history. Moreover, in subject matter the Roman authors looked to the "memorable deeds of men" identified by Herodotus and Thucydides as the proper subject of historical enquiry. This, for the ancients, invariably meant war and politics. Nonetheless, Roman historians also adopted the historiographical techniques used by the Greeks to augment their narratives, including the ethnographical or geographical digression, mimetic and synoptic presentation of events, and especially the use of direct speech. In the last case the Romans perhaps held less closely to the standard of Thucydides and Polybius, who maintained that speeches should (at least ideally) represent what was actually said (to what degree they held to their own standards is a matter of continuing controversy). The Roman love of rhetoric and oratory, and the important role this played in Roman politics provided some Roman historians with an opportunity to develop the speech into a form of commentary and literary device of immense import and flexibility. Moreover, it was established by authors like Fabius Pictor and Cato that Roman historiography would generally be composed by men of affairs—politicians who had themselves commanded armies and addressed the senate. The academic historian was a relative rarity, Livy providing the most famous exception. Sallust, Asinius Pollio, and Tacitus are among the more famous Roman statesmen-historians.

Roman politicians also began to compose commentaries, or memoirs, on their own lives, political careers, and campaigns sometime around 100 B.C., a development which Cato, who preferred not even to name the particular generals in his own work, would have undoubtedly decried. These works, while not technically histories, served as extremely valuable sources for historians and biographers. Although most of these works, such as those of Publius Rutilius Rufus and Lucius Sulla, are lost (apart from fragments), those of Caesar remain among the great literary achievements of antiquity. Similarly, the development of biography in the Hellenistic world, adopted by Romans such as Cornelius Nepos (first century B.C.), and Suetonius (early second century A.D.), cannot be wholly separated from historiography proper, which it both influenced and in some ways emulated. The biographical element in Roman historians becomes evident and important by the time Sallust composed his monographs (ca. 44–35 B.C.) on the war with Jugurtha (107–104) and the Catilinarian conspiracy (63 B.C.), and it pervades Tacitus's *Annals* (ca. A.D. 110), who nonetheless maintained the traditional annalistic format.

It would not be illegitimate to connect this movement toward the personal and biographical in Roman historiography with changes in Roman politics. Rome in the last century B.C. became very much an empire of great men vying for personal supremacy until Caesar defeated or pardoned his enemies and made himself dictator. His adopted son, Augustus, completed the process, founding an imperial dynasty that preserved many of the forms of the republic while transferring the actual reins of power into the hands of one man (and his faction). Roman historiography in its imperial incarnation likewise maintained the forms of republican history, with annual magistrates noted assiduously even after they ceased to hold anything more than ceremonial significance. Tacitus strikes the pose of an archrepublican senator, even praising the radical reformer Sulla, while nonetheless recognizing that a good emperor was the best government *he* could expect. Historiography thus became focused on the deeds and misdeeds of individuals, with the reigns of emperors generally supplying the real organizational structure.

Historians of the Roman Empire continued in both Latin and Greek in the middle and later empire, while the subject of historiography itself received a special treatise by Lucian in the second century. While the writing of full-dress history in the annalistic style apparently became somewhat less popular after Tacitus, biography, epitome, and the simple chronicle were frequently composed. As the political center of the empire moved eastward, the Hellenic historian reasserted himself in the person of Dio Cassius, a Greek general and consul of the third century, who composed a history in eighty books (much of which is extant) that combined the annalistic, Rome-centered tradition with a classicizing Attic style reminiscent of Thucydides. It is perhaps not surprising that Ammianus Marcellinus, who has been called the last historian of antiquity, and who wrote in a stylistically self-conscious Latin, was himself a Greek. However, Roman historiography in its Latin form survived the split of the empire into halves and the invasion of the western division by barbarian forces in the fifth century A.D. Increasingly the historian became a denizen of the monastery, and Latin history on the Roman model was composed throughout the Middle Ages into the modern era.

Loren J. Samons II

See also ANTIQUARIANISM; BIOGRAPHY; GREEK HISTORIOGRAPHY—ANCIENT.

References

Dorey, T.A., ed. *The Latin Historians.* New York: Basic Books, 1966.

Fornara, C. *The Nature of History in Ancient Greece and Rome.* Berkeley: University of California Press, 1983.

Frier, B. *Libri Annales Pontificorum Maximorum: The Origins of the Annalistic Tradition.* Rome: American Academy in Rome, 1979.

Goffart, W. *The Narrators of Barbarian History.* Princeton, NJ: Princeton University Press, 1988.

Laistner, M.W. *The Greater Roman Historians.* Berkeley: University of California Press, 1947.

Peter, H. *Historicorum Romanorum Reliquiae* [Relics of the Roman Historians]. 2 vols. Stuttgart: Teubner, 1967.

Syme, R. *Tacitus.* 2 vols. Oxford: Oxford University Press, 1958.

Romanian Historiography

The writing of history in Romania, about the Romanian people. The chronicles from the fifteenth and sixteenth centuries are typical of the first age of Romanian historiography. Written in Slavonic, which was the liturgical language, these mentioned the most important events of Romanian princes' reigns. Their authors did this in a laconic manner, without the intention of analyzing these events or understanding their historical significance.

During the seventeenth century, the Romanian aristocracy consolidated its political leadership and expressed a taste for historical writing. This coincided with the end of an "official" historiography, written at the court of the princes, and the beginning of a new one, reflecting the interests of the aristocrats. Grigore Ureche, for example, wrote a chronicle from the foundation of Moldavia in 1359 up to 1594. More important was Miron Costin, an educated boyar who was killed by the prince of Moldavia because of his political conspiracies. Costin wrote a chronicle that follows Ureche's (relating Moldavia's history between 1594 and 1661), as well as an outline of Romanian origins and other historical writings. The Romanian language took the place of Slavonic. The historical outlook of each author is more distinctive, although they remain steeped in a medieval mentality.

At the end of the seventeenth century, this type of historical writing reached its apogee and the first signs of a modern conception of historiography appear in the works of two prominent personalities. The first of these was the prince of Moldavia, Dimitrie Cantemir. The other was Constantin Cantacuzino, a great aristocrat from Wallachia, who wrote a history of his country (although the authorship of this has been contested).

The eighteenth century brought a crisis in Romanian historiography. This was only one consequence of the tightening of Ottoman rule in Moldavia and Wallachia, and of Austrian rule in Transylvania. While the historical writings of this period are less significant, interest in history continued to grow, involving readers from a wider social background. A major renovation took place only at the end of the century, when some Romanian scholars from Transylvania combined their efforts to defend the political rights of their nation. This cultural and political movement, called "the Transylvanian school," was representative of the age of Enlightenment. History was the most useful tool employed by the movement's members. Several scholars, of modest social origin and belonging to the Greco-Catholic clergy, made a noticeable contribution: Samuil Micu finished his *Istoria și lucrurile și întîmplările românilor* in 1805, although he did not see it published; Gheorghe Șincai, author of *Hronica românilor și a mai multor neamuri,* published his work only in fragments in 1808–1809; and especially Petru Maior, who published the *Istoria pentru începutul românilor în Dachia* [History of the Origins of the Romanians in Dacia] in 1812. The studies that they completed at Rome and Vienna helped them to enlarge their information considerably and to use new methods

derived from western European historical writing. They offered a critical analysis, but, at the same time, they remained sensitive to national ideology in speaking of the putative Roman origin, and of the historical continuity and unity of the Romanian people.

Nineteenth-century historiography nourished itself from this contribution. Some of the leaders of the 1848 revolution were at the same time historians who laid the foundations of modern historical writing in Romania. These include Nicolae Bălcescu, who wrote a history of prince Michael the Brave (a symbol of Romanian unity), and particularly Mihail Kogălniceanu, who made the most significant contributions to the renovation of national history. They considered history as "the fundamental book of a nation." The historiography of this period contains all the features of romanticism: the affirmation of national feeling; a resurgence of interest in the Middle Ages; and a renewed taste for narrative as a mode of historical writing.

After the great events in the construction of modern Romania (the Union of Moldavia and Wallachia in 1859, and the united country's independence in 1877), historiography affirmed itself as a separate field. It acquired an important place in education and was taught in the newly created universities at Iași and Bucharest. The recently founded Romanian Academy, the country's highest scientific institution, appointed several leading historians to its department of history: these included Bogdan Petriceicu Hasdeu, Alexandru Odobescu (known also as a literary writer), Grigore Tocilescu, and Dimitrie A. Sturdza. The historical section of *Analele Academiei Române* [Romanian Academy Annals] became the most famous journal of historical studies. But in spite of the increasing number of studies, many remained uncritical of their sources.

It would take a new generation, educated both in Romania and abroad (especially in Germany and France) to give historiography the rigor of nineteenth-century positivism. The fellowship *Junimea literară* [the Literary Youth] at Iași had a major role in the diffusion of a critical sense throughout Romanian culture. One of the first to give to Romanian historiography a Europeanwide prestige was Alexandru D. Xenopol, a member of *Junimea literară* who dedicated himself to historical studies.

A further step was taken at the end of the nineteenth century by the Școala critică (critical school), which brought together some young historians, who had been raised in the German tradition of positivism, such as Ioan Bogdan, Dumitru

Onciul, and Nicolae Iorga. These men denounced dilettantism in history, demanding a critical analysis of documents. This was also the time when a massive publication of Romanian and foreign documents began, together with the rise of ancillary fields of history like epigraphy, numismatics, and paleography. Some historians gained their reputations through a deeper analysis of special fields. Vasile Pârvan turned to archaeology and ancient history; Ioan Bogdan and D. Onciul became experts on the Middle Ages. Only Iorga, through his extraordinary creativity and interest in all of history, ventured beyond the boundaries of the critical school.

This school's influence continued after World War I, when Romania achieved national unity. While Iorga remained the preeminent historian, Romanian historiography, as a whole, grew richer between the two world wars. The influence of the critical school on university education increased, while the number of professors grew, together with the number of universities within Romania's new boundaries. Within the universities were founded the first institutes of historical research: the Institutes of National History at Cluj and Iasi, and, at Bucharest, the Institute for Byzantine Studies, the Institute for South-east European Studies, and the Institute of World History. The museums and the Public Archives were given a new organization that allowed them to cooperate more fully in historical research. While *Analele Academiei Române* maintained its high reputation, it was soon joined by newer journals: *Revista istorică* [Historical Journal], edited under Iorga's direction; *Arhivele Basarabiei* [Bassarabia Archives]; *Cercetări istorice* [Historical Researches]; *Revue historique du Sud-Est Européen* [Historical Review of South-Eastern Europe]; and others. The most important historical innovations, however, emerged from the *Revista istorică romînă* [Romanian Historical Journal], under the direction of some of Iorga's students, including Gheorghe I. Brătianu, Constantin C. Giurescu, and Petru P. Panaitescu. This provided a fresh impetus to historical research. Furthermore, the publication of this journal signified a direct, and some senses personal, challenge to Iorga's thitherto undisputed authority in historiography.

On the eve of World War II, Romanian historiography was thus fully fledged, as may be seen in the contributions of Romanian historians to European historical journals on history, in their presence at conferences and symposia around the world, and in their lectures at several European and American universities. This rapid development was interrupted by the war and then by Romania's Communist system. Under these conditions, some of the great historians died (Iorga was assassinated by the Romanian far Right in 1940; Brătianu died in a Communist prison in 1953). Under the Communists, history was regarded as a tool of ideology, with priority given almost exclusively to economic and social history, and in particular to the history of the working class and of the Communist Party itself. The government instituted by Ceauşescu initially allowed a brief relaxation of this regime, which explains the honors bestowed by it upon some old historians like Giurescu or Panaitescu. This was not to last, however, for Ceauşescu soon imposed his own dictatorship and a renewed censorship. Even in these circumstances, serious research was not abandoned by some historians, among whom David Prodan is perhaps the most important. The government contributed to this in some degree by developing the research system and granting financial aid for the publication of historical journals and of great sets of public records such as *Documenta Romaniae Historica*.

The end of Communism opened a new age for Romanian historiography. Ideological censorship no longer exists. The connections with foreign centers of research are growing. Even if some historians continue to complain about difficulties in the publication of their journals and books, there are strong reasons to believe that Romanian historiography will continue to develop.

S. Lemny

References

Hitchins, Keith. "Historiography of the Countries of Eastern Europe: Romania." *American Historical Review* 97 (1992): 1064–1083.

Kellogg, Frederick. *A History of Romanian Historical Writing.* Bakersfield, CA: Charles Schlacks Publishers, 1990.

Michelson, Paul E. "The Master of Synthesis: Constantin C. Giurescu and the Coming of the Age of Romanian Historiography, 1919–1947." In *Romania between East and West: Historical Essays in Memory of Constantin C. Giurescu,* ed. Stephen Fischer-Galati, Radu R. Florescu, and George R. Ursul. New York: Columbia University Press, 1982.

Stefănescu, Ştefan, ed. *Enciclopedia istoriografiei româneşti* [Encyclopedia of Romanian Historical Writing]. Bucharest: Editura ştiinţifică şi Enciclopedică, 1978.

Zub, Al. *De la istoria critică la criticism* [From Critical History to Critical Excess]. Bucharest: Editura Academiei, 1985.

R

———. *Istorie si istorici în România interbelică* [History and Historians in Romania between the Two World Wars]. Iaşi: Editura Junimea, 1989.

———. *A scrie si a face istorie: Istoriografia română postpaşoptistă* [Writing and Making History: Romanian Historiography after 1848]. Iaşi: Editura Junimea, 1981.

Romanticism

Broad cultural movement in Europe that found its greatest expression in historical writing of the early nineteenth century. Romantic historical writing gained momentum in the legal studies of Karl Friedrich Eichhorn and Friedrich Karl von Savigny, and later Jacob Grimm, who argued for a long development and evolution of law in conformity with national culture and the people *(Volk)*. Their historical writing attempted to show the inner genius of traditional institutions that had continually developed at a natural rate; revolution as rapid change was against nature and against the spirit of institutions.

The central principle of romanticism was a resacralization of nature. At the foundation of reality was a belief in the existence of the *Spirit* in history—for Georg Wilhelm Friedrich Hegel the "Idea," for Friedrich Wilhelm Schelling the "World Spirit," and for Johann Gottlieb Fichte the "Ego principle"—as another expression of divine providence. Romantics believed that classical rationalists had limited access to the spirit, and that their imposition of order through solely established scientific laws was untenable. This mechanism and skepticism did not satisfy romantics; the true reflection of the spirit could only be seen by access to the inner, sensuous human dimensions. In France, Jean-Jacques Rousseau had developed similar tastes in literature and thought and offered a more realistic picture of human behavior, rather than the prescriptive conventions of classicism. His novel *La nouvelle Héloïse* (1761) became very popular throughout western Europe. Romanticism found its way into philosophy (in the form of idealism), literature, art, religion, and historical studies, although each of these fields developed in different ways in the countries wherein romanticism acquired exponents.

In historical writing, the expression of romanticism became particularly compelling during the French Revolution and Napoleonic wars that greatly disrupted the developing nation-states. Conservatives, such as Edmund Burke, used a romantic vision to condemn revolutionary political ideas and practices. Others, such as François-Auguste-René, Vicomte de Chateaubriand, found romanticism particularly useful in defending the Catholic Church against Enlightenment rationalism. The ordered world of the Enlightenment thinkers was torn apart by social upheavals. Germaine de Staël, especially in her *L'Allemagne* [Germany] (1810), proved an important influence on a future generation of historians by encouraging a more pan-European movement of history, literature, and Christianity. The period of the Bourbon Restoration and July Monarchy, from 1815 to 1848, produced the greatest number of romantic historical writings. Liberals and democratic republicans began to employ romantic categories to support the later revolutionary movements, and romanticism became a weapon in a war of words. Rejecting the official view of French history, they rediscovered the richness and diversity of an obscured past that gave meaning and purpose to the present. Bourgeois and liberal support for revolution came from historians such as François Guizot and Adolphe Thiers who used romantic categories to show that an underlying unity had always existed in France. The spirit of liberty was manifest through constitutional monarchies and mediated through the talent of its best-educated statesman. The more radical and populist theories of Jules Michelet and Edgar Quinet, by contrast, used romanticism to point to the rights of individuals and the common people. In all of these cases, romanticism supported the vigorous growth of nationalism, which eventually led to the *Risorgimento* in Italy and the unification of Germany. The American historian John Lothrop Motley wrote passionately about the triumph of liberty in the revolt of the Dutch against the Spanish. It offered a framework to account for the process of development over time whereby an original people *(Volk, peuple)* could be recovered. No longer did national identity find its only expression in king and noble. The apparent diversity of people in any nation had an internal unity of culture and language.

Romantic histories employed a narrative form that often highlighted the role of heroes and heroines. They became the embodiment of the sage who, aware of his own inner genius, and with a Promethean desire, stood up to the seemingly overpowering forces of nature. The successes or failures of the hero, often flawed and hence more realistic, became important lessons for the reader who could identify with the outcome; or, in the case of Friedrich Schiller's William Tell, the hero symbolized and unified the nation. Romantics appealed to the individual conscience, which alone could have direct access to the forces of nature and the immanent activity of the divine in the world.

There was a strong connection between the numerous historical novels and the plethora of national histories written in the nineteenth century. In Britain, Sir Walter Scott inspired several generations of historians to pay close attention to the writing of history in a manner that enabled the readers to feel as if they had actually met the actors, through a concentration on details and descriptions. Scott was also partially responsible for the revival of interest in the mystery and chivalry of the medieval world. History to the romantics was not merely a chronology of facts legitimized by an authoritative institution, whether church or king. Historical writing became the expression of the drama of life in all its feelings, richness of depiction, speeches, and living color. The historical portraits of Thomas Carlyle remain an example of the ability of historians to capture individual human characters in a rich text.

There are a number of common elements in romantic historical writing. If the spirit was manifest in time, the historian's task was to record and analyze these particular phenomena. History was a revelation, and the historian became the new priest. Johann Gottfried von Herder and Johann Wolfgang Goethe had conceived of an organicism in nature, whereby all creation shares in the same substance throughout time. The symbol of the seed growing into the mature tree became a commonplace trope through which broader questions of human history and tradition could be addressed. For the romantic, every minute element, every particular, partakes in a universal reality. History meant change and development, and hence diversity. Humans are able to have a consciousness of the inner unity, however, through a sensibility of elements of the past that are persevered in time, not a mechanistic, rational argument. The problem of duality between material reality and spirit, a seemingly unbridgeable gap, could be crossed by means of new poetic and religious expressions. Poetry, consequently, also became a powerful medium to express this inner reality, and thus span the distance between the two worlds, past and present, which remained otherwise forever distinct. Romantic language created intermediary images that could become immediately perceived by the "eyes of the soul." These intellectuals did much to promote a study of the human mind and moral struggles, and strove to understand the extent of human self-consciousness. There had never been such an emphasis on the individual and a recognition of an inner personal life. The structure of national and universal history often became closely linked to the historian's own life experience.

One way to describe the romantic historical text is through the metaphor of taxonomy. Prosper de Barante animated his narrative with vivid colors that gave the sense that the past, as it was received, was in a moment truly revived. The reader felt the presence of historical actors and actresses, as if it were possible to reach out and touch them; above all, such writing allowed the imagination to soar. Primary texts, the sources of history that time had preserved, needed to become reanimated so that their original authors could indeed speak once more. Just as the historian pointed to manifestations of the "spirit" at a particular time, the inner dimensions of history, the contemporary reader could experience this once again, as it must have originally appeared. By contrast, after 1850, historians in the Rankean era began to search for a depersonalized and dispassionate history based on archival sources alone. Romantics wanted to avoid the abstraction of the particular into the universal by the use of local color, a common feature in contemporary painting. In contrast to the detached objectivity of later nineteenth-century positivism, more romantic renderings of primary texts (Carlyle's edition of the letters and speeches of Oliver Cromwell, for example) intended the reader to confront the otherness and uniqueness of the original source in its actual color, not an approximate reconstruction. Romantic historians thus faced the tension between an unassailable past and an uncertain future with histories that accounted for both diversity and unity in history, and catered to a generation of readers hungry to understand their own unique experience while living in a vast and plural world.

John B. Roney

See also ENLIGHTENMENT HISTORIOGRAPHY; GERMAN HISTORICAL THOUGHT; *KULTURGESCHICHTE*; *VOLK*.

Texts

Larry H. Peer, ed. *The Romantic Manifesto: An Anthology.* New York: Peter Lang, 1988.

References

Allen, James Smith. *Popular French Romanticism: Authors, Readers, and Books in the Nineteenth Century.* Syracuse, NY: Syracuse University Press, 1981.

Bann, Stephen. *The Clothing of Clio: A Study of the Representation of History in Nineteenth-Century Britain and France*. Cambridge, Eng.: Cambridge University Press, 1984.

———. *Romanticism and the Rise of History.* New York: Maxwell Macmillan, 1995.

Cranston, Maurice. *The Romantic Movement.* Oxford: Basil Blackwell, 1994.

Furst, Lillian. *Romanticism in Perspective: A Comparative Study of Aspects of the Romantic Movements in England, France, and Germany.* New York: St. Martin's Press, 1969.

Gooch, G.P. *History and Historians in the Nineteenth Century.* Boston: Beacon Press, 1959.

Menhennet, Alan. *The Romantic Movement.* London: Croom Helm, 1981.

Milner, Max. *Le Romantisme, I, 1820–1843.* Paris: B. Arthaud, 1973.

Orr, Linda. *Headless History: Nineteenth-Century French Historiography of the Revolution.* Ithaca, NY: Cornell University Press, 1990.

Trevor-Roper, Hugh. *The Romantic Movement and the Study of History.* London: The Athlone Press, 1969.

Texts

Erflaters van onze beschaving: Nederlandse gestalten uit zes eeuwen [Testators of Our Civilization: Dutch Figures from Six Centuries]. Amsterdam: Querido, 1979.

De Lage Landen bij de Zee: Een geschiedenis van het Nederlandse volk [The Low Countries near the Sea: A History of the Dutch People]. Amsterdam: Querido, 1979.

The Watershed of Two Eras. Europe in 1900. Trans. A.J. Pomerans. Middletown, CT: Wesleyan University Press, 1978.

References

Hageraats, B., ed. *"Geloof niet wat geschiedschrijvers zeggen . . ." Honderd jaar Jan Romein 1893–1993* ["Don't Believe What Historians Say . . ." A Centenary of Jan Romein 1893–1993]. Amsterdam: International Institute of Social History, 1995.

Tollebeek, J. *De toga van Fruin: Denken over geschiedenis in Nederland sinds 1860* [Fruin's Gown: Thinking about History in the Netherlands since 1860]. Amsterdam: Wereldbibliotheek, 1996.

Romein, Jan Marius (1893–1962)

Dutch historian. Romein was born in Rotterdam. Already engaged in the Communist movement while a student, he initially carried out secretarial and editorial work for the Party. In addition, he worked as a freelance journalist and historian. In 1939, he was appointed associate professor of Dutch history at the Municipal University of Amsterdam. After World War II, this was converted into a full professorship of modern history. Romein died in Amsterdam. In spite of his internationally oriented Marxist views, Romein became chiefly known before World War II for two surveys of national history, written together with his wife, Annie Verschoor: *De Lage Landen bij de Zee* [The Low Countries near the Sea] (1934) and its biographical complement, the *Erflaters van onze beschaving* [Testators of Our Civilization] (1938–1940). After the war, he focused his attention on the philosophy of history (inspired by Arnold Toynbee) and on the anti-Eurocentric study of colonial history. Meanwhile, he worked on his *Op het breukvlak van twee eeuwen* [The Watershed of Two Eras] (published posthumously in 1967), an unfinished general history of the political, social, economic, and cultural changes that had taken place in Europe around 1900.

Jo Tollebeek

Romeo, Rosario (1924–1987)

Italian historian. Born in Giarre (Sicily), Romeo was a pupil of Gioacchino Volpe, Nino Valeri, and Federico Chabod, at the Istituto Italiano per gli Studi Storici in Naples until 1956. He then became a professor, first at the University of Messina (Sicily) and later in Rome, where he taught modern history until the end of his career. His books and his numerous essays, which began to appear in the 1950s, expatiate on the origins of the Italian nation and on Italian history from the Risorgimento to the advent of fascism. In *Risorgimento e capitalismo* (two influential essays published separately in 1956 and 1958, but best known in their one-volume edition of 1959) he established an interpretation of the political and economic process of Italian unification based on the critique of the Marxist Antonio Gramsci and of the nationalist Gioacchino Volpe. His view of Italian modern history is founded on the idea that, although in the *Mezzogiorno* the progressive forces set in motion during the Risorgimento were not capable, in the long run, of permanently modifying a backwards socioeconomical structure (*Risorgimento in Sicilia* [1950]), in other parts of the country the unification—as pushed forward by the Piedmontese Prime Minister Cavour (*Cavour e il suo tempo* [1969–1984])—played a fundamental role in the building of a new nation, in creating a distinctively Italian liberal consciousness, and in laying the foundations of Italy's economic modernization.

Guido Abbattista

Texts

Breve storia della grande industria in Italia [A Brief History of Big Industry in Italy]. Bologna: Zanichelli, 1961.

Cavour e il suo tempo [Cavour and His Times]. 3 vols. Bari: Laterza, 1969–1984.

L'Italia moderna tra storia e storiografia [Modern Italy in History and Historiography]. Florence: Le Monnier, 1977.

L'Italia unita e la prima guerra mondiale [Italian Unity and the First World War]. Bari: Laterza, 1978.

Risorgimento e capitalismo [The Risorgimento and Capitalism]. Bari: Laterza, 1959.

Risorgimento in Sicilia [The Risorgimento in Sicily]. Bari: Laterza, 1982.

References

Pescosolido, Guido. *Rosario Romeo*. Bari: Laterza, 1990.

Rosenberg, Hans (1904–1988)

German-born émigré historian. Born in Hanover, Rosenberg studied at the universities of Cologne, Freiburg im Breisgau, and Berlin. He received his scholarly education from Friedrich Meinecke and Johannes Ziekursch. Rosenberg left Germany in 1933 for Great Britain, and finally emigrated to the United States in 1935, where he started his academic career, initially at Brooklyn College, New York, and later at the University of California, Berkeley. In 1976 he returned to Germany to hold an honorary position at Freiburg. Rosenberg's work concentrated on the social, economic, and political history of modern Germany. In his major works *Bureaucracy, Aristocracy, and Autocracy: The Prussian Experience, 1660–1815* (1958) and *Grosse Depression und Bismarckzeit* (1967) he elaborated the thesis of a German *Sonderweg* (unique development or "special path"), stressing persistent illiberal traditions within Germany's national history that had culminated in the rise of national socialism. In his later work Rosenberg contributed to a new interpretation of Germany's social and economic development, showing the growing importance of bureaucratic rule in German history. He sought to transform traditional intellectual history into a social history of political ideas. As a leading representative of German scholarship in exile, Rosenberg made an important contribution to the study of German history in the United States. He also inspired the critical reexamination of nineteenth- and twentieth-century German history by a younger postwar generation of historians in Germany.

Georgi Verbeeck

Texts

Bureaucracy, Aristocracy, and Autocracy: The Prussian Experience, 1660–1815. Cambridge, MA: Harvard University Press, 1958.

Grosse Depression und Bismarckzeit [The Great Depression and the Era of Bismarck]. Berlin: Walter de Gruyter, 1967.

Politische Denkströmungen im deutschen Vormärz [Currents of German Political Thought before 1848]. Göttingen: Vandenhoeck & Ruprecht, 1972.

References

Epstein, Catherine. *A Past Renewed: A Catalog of German-Speaking Refugee Historians in the United States after 1933*. Cambridge, Eng.: Cambridge University Press, 1993.

Lehmann, Hartmut, and James J. Sheehan, eds. *An Interrupted Past: German-Speaking Refugee Historians in the United States after 1933*. Cambridge, Eng.: Cambridge University Press, 1991.

Ritter, Gerhard A. "Hans Rosenberg 1904–1988." *Geschichte und Gesellschaft* [History and Society] 15 (1989): 282–302.

Rostovtzeff, Michael Ivanovitch (1870–1952)

Russian-American historian. Rostovtzeff was born near Kiev in 1870, studied at Kiev and St. Petersburg, held a professorship in the latter city, and began publishing on agricultural life in antiquity, *Studien zur Geschichte des römischen Kolonates* [Studies in the History of the Roman Colonate] appearing in 1910. During the Russian revolution, Rostovtzeff emigrated first to England and then to the United States, where he taught at the University of Wisconsin and Yale. His major later publications include *The Social and Economic History of the Roman Empire* (1926), *A History of the Ancient World* (1926–1927), and *The Social and Economic History of the Hellenistic World* (1941). His research was marked by the integration of narrative sources and less traditional historical materials found in epigraphy, papyrology, numismatics, and archaeology.

Stephen A. Stertz

Texts

Ed. *The Excavations of Dura-Europos . . . Preliminary Reports.* New Haven, CT: Yale University Press, 1929–1952.

A History of the Ancient World. Trans. J.D. Duff. 2 vols. Oxford: Clarendon Press, 1926–1927.

A Large Estate in Egypt in the Third Century B.C. Madison: University of Wisconsin Press, 1922.

The Social and Economic History of the Hellenistic World. 3 vols. Oxford: Clarendon Press, 1941.

The Social and Economic History of the Roman Empire. Second ed. 2 vols. Oxford: Clarendon Press, 1957.

References

Christ, K. *Von Gibbon zu Rostovzeff.* Darmstadt: Wissenschaftliche Buchgesellschaft, 1972, 334–349.

Roth, Cecil (1899–1970)

English historian, journalist, and lecturer. Roth was born in London, obtained the B.A., M.A., B. Litt., and D. Phil. from Oxford University and served in the British army during World War I. He worked as a journalist, freelance writer, and lecturer until 1939, when he went to Oxford as reader in Jewish Studies. He remained there until retirement in 1964. He began research in Italy while preparing a doctoral thesis that was published as *The Last Florentine Republic* in 1925. Roth's study of Renaissance Italy led him to primary materials about Jewish life in the Middle Ages, and the history of his own people thereafter became the focus of his interest and of his prolific writings. An orthodox Jew, Roth was well informed about secular scholarship and enjoyed wide acclaim as a renowned authority in his field. He is most widely recognized for two books on English Jewry: *A History of the Jews in England* (1941) and *The Jews of Medieval Oxford* (1951). He died in Jerusalem.

James Edward McGoldrick

Texts

A Bird's Eye View of Jewish History. Cincinnati, OH: Union of American Hebrew Congregations, 1934.

The History of the Jews in England. Third ed. Oxford: Clarendon Press, 1978.

The History of the Jews in Italy. Philadelphia: Jewish Publication Society, 1946.

The Jewish Contribution to Civilization. Cincinnati, OH: Union of American Hebrew Congregations, 1940.

The Jewish People: Four Thousand Years of Survival. London: Thames & Hudson, 1966.

The Jews in the Renaissance. Philadelphia: Jewish Publication Society, 1959.

The Jews of Medieval Oxford. Oxford: Clarendon Press, 1951.

References

Roth, Irene. *Cecil Roth, Historian without Tears: A Memoir.* New York: Sepher-Hermon Press, 1982.

Shaftesley, John M., ed. *Remember the Days: Essays on Anglo-Jewish History Presented to Cecil Roth by Members of the Council of the Jewish Historical Society of England.* London: Jewish Historical Society of England, 1966.

Round, John Horace (1854–1928)

Medieval historian and controversialist. Round graduated from Balliol College, Oxford, where he obtained a first-class degree in modern history in 1878. Conservative in politics, he energetically pursued a variety of genealogical studies, most notably *Studies in Peerage and Family History* (1901). His attack on Edward Augustus Freeman's account of the Norman conquest was not published until after Freeman's death, but other scholars entered the lists of controversy and a dispute ensued. In such debates Round was dogged to the point of eccentricity, but he was also capable of lasting achievement. His *Feudal England* (1895) suggested that the key to understanding the massive Norman land survey contained in Domesday Book lay in the assessment of Danegeld. Round also asserted that knight-service was an innovation introduced by William the Conqueror and not a gradual development as contemporary historians had believed. It is with Round's work that the modern study of Domesday Book may be said to begin.

Myron C. Noonkester

Texts

Family Origins and Other Studies. Ed. William Page. London: Constable, 1930.

Feudal England. Westport, CT: Greenwood Press, 1979.

Geoffrey de Mandeville. Loneon: Longmans, Green, 1892.

Studies in Peerage and Family History. London: Constable, 1901.

References

Kenyon, J.P. *The History Men.* Second ed. London: Weidenfeld and Nicolson, 1993.

Rowbotham, Sheila (b. 1943)

British feminist historian. Rowbotham was born at Leeds, England, and earned a B.A. from Oxford University in 1966. She taught for the Workers Educational Association and was a staff writer for the socialist paper *Black Dwarf* and the feminist journal *Red Day*, occasionally using the pseudonym Sheila Turner. Considered a "socialist feminist," she has been active in the English women's movement since it began in the late 1960s. Rowbotham desired to correct the omission of women in history books especially by giving voice to the "emerging woman" of the feminist movement. Her books, *Women, Resistance, and Revolution* (1972) and *Hidden from History* (1973), have been considered foundations for feminist history. Reviewer Mica Foot stated that Rowbotham had created "history out of silence," crediting women for being responsible individuals. Rowbotham's other works examine women's issues, especially social conditions, child care, and employment.

Elizabeth D. Schafer

Texts

Ed., with Swasti Mitter. *Dignity and Daily Bread: New Forms of Economic Organising among Poor Women in the Third World and the First.* London: Routledge, 1994.

Dreams and Dilemmas: Collected Writings. London: Virago, 1983.

Hidden from History: Rediscovering Women in History from the Seventeenth Century to the Present. New York: Vintage, 1976.

The Past Is Before Us: Feminism in Action since the 1960s. London and Boston: Pandora, 1989.

Women in Movement: Feminism and Social Action. New York: Routledge, 1992.

Women, Resistance, and Revolution: A History of Women and Revolution in the Modern World. New York: Pantheon, 1972.

References

"Interview with Sheila Rowbotham." In *Visions of History,* ed. Marho: Radical Historians' Organization. New York: Pantheon, 1983.

Offen, Karen, Ruth Roach Pierson, and Jane Rendall, eds. *Writing Women's History: International Perspectives.* Bloomington: Indiana University Press, 1991.

Rudé, George (1910–1993)

British social historian and pioneer of "history from below." Born in Oslo, Norway, Rudé received his B.A. in languages at Cambridge University in 1931, and while working as a schoolmaster, decided to study history at the University of London. In 1950 he completed his Ph.D. thesis under the supervision of Alfred Cobban, on Parisian workers during the French Revolution. Since the climate of the cold war made it impossible for Rudé, supporter of Communist causes, to find a position in a British university, he accepted professorships in Australia and then at Concordia University in Montreal, Canada. Writing from an "open" Marxist perspective, he emphasized class conflict and sympathized with laborers, especially those who rebelled, but he rejected determinist or reductionist approaches. The author of fifteen books, Rudé has been widely admired for his exhaustive and innovative research in the history of revolutionary "crowds" identifying many of the faces in the crowd.

Thomas T. Lewis

See also MARXISM AND HISTORIOGRAPHY; SOCIAL HISTORY; SOCIOLOGY AND HISTORY.

Texts

And Eric Hobsbawm. *Captain Swing.* London: Pimlico, 1993.

"The Changing Face of the Crowd." In *The Historian's Workshop: Original Essays by Sixteen Historians,* ed. Lewis Curtis Jr. New York: Alfred Knopf, 1970, 187–203.

The Crowd in History. Revised ed. London: Lawrence and Wishart, 1981.

The Crowd in the French Revolution. Oxford: Clarendon Press, 1959.

Ideology and Popular Protest. Ed. Harvey J. Kaye. Chapel Hill: University of North Carolina Press, 1995.

Paris and London in the Eighteenth Century: Studies in Popular Protest. London: Collins, 1970.

Robespierre: Portrait of a Revolutionary Democrat. London: Collins, 1975.

Wilkes and Liberty. London: Lawrence and Wishart, 1973.

References

Krantz, Frederick, ed. *"History from Below": Studies in Popular Protest and Popular Ideology in Honour of George Rudé.* Montreal: Concordia University Press, 1985.

Runciman, Sir James Cochran Stevenson (b. 1903)

British historian of Byzantium. Steven Runciman, as he is known, was born in Northumberland and studied at Eton and Trinity College, Cambridge.

He taught at Cambridge until World War II, during which he held diplomatic posts and taught at the University of Istanbul. Afterward he held numerous temporary lectureships, but no permanent university position. He was knighted in 1958 and made a companion of honour in 1984. Runciman is the author of a number of important works on Byzantium, including his magisterial three-volume *History of the Crusades*.

Stephen A. Stertz

Texts

Byzantine Civilization. London: Arnold, 1955.

The Eastern Schism. Oxford: Clarendon Press, 1955.

The Emperor Romanus Lecapenus and His Reign. Cambridge, Eng.: Cambridge University Press, 1929.

A History of the Crusades. 3 vols. Cambridge, Eng.: Cambridge University Press, 1951–1954.

References

Byzantine and Modern Greek Studies 4 (1978) [a festschrift in honor of Runciman].

Connell, J. *The House by Herod's Gate.* London: S. Low, 1947.

Rural History

Historical writing dealing with the countryside, including works categorized as agricultural history, agrarian history, and peasant studies. Ironically, there has been an inverse correlation between the vitality of rural life and the writing of rural history: in the twentieth century, the field has grown in North America and Europe in the context of declining numbers of farmers and rural dwellers.

In North America and Europe alike, rural history has long been a field of significant scholarly activity. Frederick Jackson Turner and Walter Prescott Webb's studies of the relationship between the physical realities of life on the North American frontier and the nature of the societies that developed there date from the first third of the twentieth century. So, too, do the detailed agricultural histories of the eastern United States written by Percy Bidwell, John Falconer, and L.C. Gray. When Marc Bloch published *Les Caractères Originaux de l'Histoire Rural Française* (later translated as *French Rural History*) in 1931, a book which in many ways pioneered the rural history of today, he was engaged in a debate with yet older traditions of rural history, acknowledging his debts and disagreements with scholars such as his senior contemporary, Henri Sée, and the great nineteenth-century scholar Fustel de Coulanges.

Rural history's development from these early beginnings has, however, been uneven. Until recently, North American scholars working in the field have decried the lack of attention given to their subject. In North America, interest in rural history declined in the middle decades of the century and continued to languish in the late 1960s and 1970s as a new social history began to emerge. Those who pioneered the study of labor history, women's history, family history, and social structure and mobility in a North American context tended to pursue their subjects within an urban environment, which entailed a very different perspective on their subjects. It is only in the last two decades that this has changed significantly. The shift, however, has been quite substantial. In the 1980s and 1990s, rural history has become a flourishing field in North America, and it has happened in large part because a new generation of social historians has chosen to pursue its interests in rural settings. The history of the relationship between social history and rural history on the other side of the Atlantic is quite different and the fruitful relationship between the two much older. The Annales movement provides a particularly striking contrast. In the French context, rural history, such as that written by Georges Lefebvre, Marc Bloch, and, more recently, Pierre Goubert, was at the cutting edge of the emergence of a new social history. Rather than deflecting attention away from the countryside, social history found its métier in the study of rural subjects.

Although the patterns of development have varied from place to place, there are broad trends uniting the study of rural history. On both sides of the Atlantic, there has been a shift away from a rural history that focused on agricultural techniques, land use, the marketing of agricultural goods, and the formal legal frameworks that governed these. Rural history continues to include the study of these issues, but it has come to encompass a much broader range of topics. Moreover, in broadening its scope, the subject of rural history has also become much more interdisciplinary. It has, in short, become more ambitious. Rural historians have increasingly come to see the whole of the experience of life as it was lived on the land as their purview. Furthermore, they have concerned themselves with using rural mentalities to explain broader historical shifts.

This concern to capture the whole of the rural experience has involved rural historians in a wide variety of pursuits. The study of rural fertility patterns and inheritance strategies has been one of these. Rural studies probing these issues, such as Pierre Goubert's analysis of peasant life in the Beauvaisis (1960), and Emmanuel Le Roy Ladurie's examination of long-term trends in Languedoc (second edition, 1966) have come to form a core component of the growth of demographic history as a distinct subdiscipline of history. Family life and household organization have received a good deal of attention from rural historians as well. Others have attempted to explore the psychological universe of country people, probing, in one fashion or another, the mentality of rural residents. Works in this area, such as Carlo Ginzburg's *I Benandanti* (1974; translated 1983 as *The Night Battles: Witchcraft and Agrarian Cults in the Sixteenth and Seventeenth Centuries), Le Roy Ladurie's *Montaillou: The Promised Land of Error* (1975), and Eugen Weber's *Peasants Into Frenchmen: The Modernization of Rural France, 1870–1914* (1976), draw from a variety of approaches, integrating the traditional tools of the historian's craft with techniques and understandings drawn from other disciplines such as anthropology, folklore, and psychology.

The nature of interhousehold social relations in the countryside has been a topic that has received extensive consideration as well. Historians working in this area have probed issues such as rural stratification, cooperation, and competition in the countryside and the extent of rural solidarity. Such studies have often been closely linked with examinations of the complexities of rural economic life and the relationship between rural labor and rural production, on the one hand, and urban labor and urban production on the other. Studies of these aspects of rural life, such as those by Rudolf Braun, Franklin Mendels, and Jean Quataert, have pointed to fundamental difficulties in compartmentalizing rural history, as the lines between rural and urban production and rural and urban labor have, when subjected to close scrutiny, become increasingly blurred. They also highlight the limitations of one of the central approaches rural historians have used in their endeavors to grasp the whole of rural life: the community study.

As we learn more about the extent of rural trade and migration patterns, the pitfalls of attempting to understand rural lives by focusing on the occurrences in a single geographic locality become increasingly apparent for many periods and places. Rural politics and rural protest are yet another area of rural life that has received much attention. Research on these subjects has unfolded in the context of a century in which rural unrest has remained a central aspect of global history. As with many of the other foci of the new rural history, the study of rural protest has been enriched by interdisciplinary work and by comparative approaches. Scholars studying rural protest in New England and colonial British North America have drawn from understandings emerging from scholarship on peasant protest in France and Britain, those studying rural protest in the British Isles from the experiences of peasant life in Europe and elsewhere. One of the central features of the new rural history that has taken shape over the last quarter of a century, whether it be focused on politics, or inheritance strategies, or migratory labor, has been this interest in placing the particularities of regional rural histories in a comparative context and understanding them in terms of broader patterns.

Yet another of the general features of much of the new rural history has been a concern to integrate rural history into broader histories in a way that will highlight the extent to which rural dwellers were agents in shaping big historical changes. Rural history has come, increasingly, to address issues such as the role of rural workers in industrialization and in the formation of working classes, the significance of country people in the shaping of national politics, and the fit between the character of economic and social relations in the countryside and the development of capitalism.

Rusty Bittermann

See also ANNALES SCHOOL; DEMOGRAPHY—HISTORICAL; FAMILY HISTORY (COMPARATIVE); LABOR HISTORY; LOCAL HISTORY; SOCIAL HISTORY; URBAN HISTORY; WOMEN'S HISTORY.

Texts

Forster, Robert, and Orest Ranum, eds. *Rural Society in France: Selections from the Annales: Economies, Sociétés, Civilisations.* Trans. Elborg Forster and Patricia M. Ranum. Baltimore, MD: Johns Hopkins University Press, 1977.

Hahn, Steven, and Jonathan Prude, eds. *The Countryside in the Age of Capitalist Transformation: Essays in the Social History of Rural America.* Chapel Hill: University of North Carolina Press, 1985.

References

Herr, Richard, ed. *Themes in Rural History of the Western World.* Ames: Iowa State University Press, 1993.

Swierenga, Robert. "Agriculture and Rural Life: The New Rural History." In *Ordinary People and Everyday Life: Perspectives on the New Social History,* ed. James B. Gardner and George Rollie Adams. Nashville, TN: The American Association for State and Local History, 1983, 90–113.

R

Thompson, John. "Writing about Rural Life and Agriculture." In *Writing about Canada: A Handbook for Modern Canadian History,* ed. John Schultz. Scarborough: Prentice-Hall, 1990, 97–119.

Rusden, George William (1819–1903)

Anglo-Australian historian, educationist, and civil servant, Rusden was born in England and emigrated to Australia in 1834. From 1840 he owned and managed wool growing properties until he became an agent for the National Schools, in 1849. From 1851 to 1856 he was a civil servant, clerk of the Legislative Council and clerk of both houses of parliament, in Victoria. He continued in public life until 1882 when he retired to England. For health reasons he returned to Melbourne in 1893, where he lived until his death. Rusden's major historical writings comprised a *History of New Zealand* and a *History of Australia*—the most substantial political histories published about both countries, only surpassed (in the Australian case) by Manning Clark's work in the twentieth century. More novel was the centrality Rusden placed on relations between "first peoples" and invading colonials in both countries; and the credence Rusden gave to Maori and Aboriginal testimony. These features influenced the development of New Zealand race relations historiography from the late 1950s and provided a countervailing perspective to Social Darwinist explanations for the dispossession of Aborigines in Australia. Rusden's work also foreshadowed the development of imperial history in Britain from the 1880s.

William Thorpe

Texts

Ed. *Aureretanga: Groans of the Maoris.* London: William Ridgway, 1888.

Discovery, Survey and Settlement of Port Phillip. London: Williams and Northgate, 1872.

History of Australia. 3 vols. London: Chapman and Hall, 1883.

History of New Zealand. 3 vols. London: Chapman and Hall, 1883.

References

Blainey, A., and M. Lazarus. "Rusden, George William." In *Australian Dictionary of Biography, volume 6: 1851–1890,* ed. G. Serle and R. Ward. Carlton: Melbourne University Press, 72–74.

Davidson, J.W. "New Zealand 1820–1870: An Essay in Re-interpretation." *Historical Studies Australia and New Zealand* 5 (1953): 349–360.

Olssen, E. "Where to from Here? Reflections on the Twentieth-Century Historiography of Nineteenth-Century New Zealand." *New Zealand Journal of History* 26 (1992): 54–77.

Reynolds, H., ed. *Aborigines and Settlers.* Stanmore: Cassell, 1972.

Trainor, L. "Historians As Imperialists: Some Roots of British Imperial History 1880–1900." *New Zealand Journal of History* 15 (1981): 39–48.

Russian Historiography (to 1917)

Russian historical writing in its earliest stages grew out of the tradition of monastic chronicles. The result of a series of compilations in the eleventh and early twelfth century, the *Povest' vremennykh let* [Tale of Bygone Years], tells the story of the origins of the Eastern Slavs and their unification into the state of Kievan Rus' by the Riurik dynasty. The *Tale,* commonly referred to as the *Primary Chronicle,* served as the introduction to a variety of local chronicles that flourished in the thirteenth through the fifteenth centuries as Kievan Rus' splintered into a collection of feuding principalities. With the growth of the powerful Muscovite state in the fifteenth and sixteenth centuries, chronicle writing began once again to reflect events on a broader scale. To enhance the power and prestige of the dynasty, chroniclers began to place Muscovy in the context of world history propagating the notion of Moscow as the Third Rome and tracing the origins of the ruling dynasty to Prus, the mythological brother of Augustus Caesar. The so-called *Stepennaia kniga* [Book of Degrees], a detailed genealogical record of the ruling dynasty produced in the reign of Ivan the Terrible, and the *Khronograf* [Chronograph], a compendium of world historical events drawing heavily on Byzantine sources, are among the most significant historical works from this era. The turbulent events of the late sixteenth and early seventeenth centuries gave rise to a genre of partisan historical narratives often written on the basis of personal recollection. Andrei Mikhailovich Kniaz Kurbskii's (1528–1583) *Istoriia o velikom kniaze Moskovskim* [History of the Muscovite Grand Prince], assumed to have been written in the 1560s, is perhaps the first and best-known example of this genre.

The integration of Ukraine into the Russian empire in the mid-seventeenth century brought new sources and more sophisticated techniques of narrative and criticism. One important example is Innokentii Gizel's (d. 1683) *Synopsis* (1674), a brief overview emphasizing the theme of solidarity between Russia and Ukraine. The *Synopsis* is noteworthy for its variety of sources and rudimentary methods of textual criticism. Written in an accessible literary style, Gizel's *Synopsis* enjoyed broad popularity and was reprinted numerous times throughout the eighteenth century.

The reforms of Peter the Great in the early eighteenth century, in opening Russia to the influence of Western ideas, brought an awareness of the need to create a new account of Russia's past, one in which human reason and will, rather than divine providence, would stand as the primary force driving the progression of historical events. As they set to their task, Russian historians were faced with two distinct challenges, which would continue to engage their attention for well over a century. First, sources neglected for centuries in monastic libraries and state chanceries needed to be collected, restored, analyzed, edited, and published. Secondly, these newly uncovered sources had to be crafted into a comprehensive historical narrative that would be acceptable both from a literary and a scholarly perspective. Vasilii Nikitich Tatishchev (1686–1750) was among the first to take up these challenges. Tatishchev's major work, *Istoriia Rossiiskaia s samikh drevneishikh vremen* [Russian History from the Most Ancient Times], was largely a compilation of chronicles accompanied by critical annotations, but the work also included unfinished "notes" in which he employed methods of comparative textual analysis to construct a historical synthesis. Although Tatishchev's history was not published during his lifetime, the manuscript was an indispensable source for subsequent historians and was eventually published in the 1770s.

Tatishchev's legacy in the collection and publication of sources was continued by the German émigrés Gerhard Friedrich Müller (1705–1783) and August Ludwig Schlözer (1735–1809). A resident of Russia from the age of twenty, Müller spent his formative years as a scholar, from 1733 to 1743, searching the far reaches of the empire for historical materials as part of the Academy of Science's Great Siberian Expedition. Müller's two major works, *Opisanie Sibirskogo tsarstva* [A Description of the Kingdom of Siberia] (1750) and *Opyt novoi istorii Rossii* [Essay on Recent Russian History] (1760) were based primarily on documents collected during his travels. Müller is also known for his advocacy of the so-called Norman theory, which traces the origins of the ruling dynasty of Kievan Rus' back to a Scandinavian tribe known as the Varangians. By supporting the seemingly unpatriotic notion that the Kievan state had Germanic origins, Müller earned the disfavor of many of his Russian colleagues both during his lifetime and in posterity.

A talented linguist, trained in textual criticism and comparative philology, Schlözer, who came to Russia in 1761 at Müller's invitation, devoted his energies primarily to the study of the early Russian chronicles. He was the first to undertake the arduous tasks of textual and linguistic analysis necessary to produce a definitive rendition of the ancient chronicles and reconstruct the history of their creation. Even after his return to Göttingen University in 1769, Schlözer continued his studies in Russian history and in the first decade of the nineteenth century published his most important work—an authoritative annotated edition of the *Primary Chronicle.*

The body of sources available to historians was augmented substantially in the late eighteenth and early nineteenth century by the activities of wealthy collectors of books, manuscripts, and artifacts, such as Count Aleksei Ivanovich Musin-Pushkin (1744–1817) and, especially, Count Nikolai Petrovich Rumiantsev (1754–1826). Inspired by the growing upsurge in national sentiment, Rumiantsev dedicated his wealth to the study of Russian antiquity, funding an extensive series of "archeographic" expeditions in which historians combed through provincial archives and monastic libraries searching for ancient manuscripts. By the 1830s these activities had attracted government support with the funding of a six-year-long official expedition, led by P.M. Stroev, and the establishment of a permanent archeographic commission with branches in all the provincial capitals of European Russia.

The problem of creating a comprehensive and accessible narrative of Russian history was first addressed by Mikhail Vasil'evich Lomonosov (1711–1765) who, in 1751, received a commission from Empress Elizabeth to write a complete history of Russia. Lomonosov's *Drevniaia rossiiskaia istoriia* [Ancient Russian History] (1766) covered only the earliest period, however, and is notable for its limited sources and primitive methodology. A more successful synthesis was produced by Prince Mikhail Mikhailovich Shcherbatov (1733–1790), whose seven-volume *Istoriia rossiiskaia ot drevneishikh vremen* [Russian History from Ancient

Times] (1770–1791) featured a wide range of sources marshaled in support of the author's views on the rights and privileges of the nobility. Shcherbatov's contemporary, Ivan Nikitich Boltin (1735–1792) is known for his critical articles, which stand out as early attempts to construct an overarching conception of Russia's historical development.

Eighteenth-century Russian historiography reached its culmination in the work of Nikolai Mikhailovich Karamzin (1766–1826). Making broad use of newly available sources and critical methods, Karamzin provided the long-awaited comprehensive narrative in his twelve-volume *Istoriia gosudarstva rossiiskogo* [History of the Russian State] (1818–1829). Centered around the theme of *edinovlastie,* strong unified state power, Karamzin's history featured highly stylized literary descriptions of the exploits and achievements of Russia's rulers flavored with frequent didactic interludes. The main body of the text was accompanied by extensive notes containing critical analysis and excerpts from the sources. Karamzin's history was received very favorably at the time of publication and remains to this day a classic text. But not all of Karamzin's contemporaries were satisfied with his achievement. Nikolai Alekseevich Polevoi (1796–1846) disliked Karamzin's exclusive focus on Russia's rulers and called for a truly national history encompassing the entire population. Polevoi's own *Istorii russkogo naroda* [History of the Russian People] in four volumes (1829–1833) failed, however, to live up to its ambitious title, largely due to the lack of appropriate sources and methodology. Another contemporary, Mikhail Kachenovskii (1775–1842), influenced by B.G. Niebuhr's study of ancient Rome, questioned the authenticity of many of the Karamzin's sources including the *Primary Chronicle.* While Kachenovskii and his followers—the so-called skeptical school—stimulated the development of textual criticism, their doubts were generally not shared by later historians, and they were unable to offer any positive alternatives to Karamzin.

The emergence of the so-called state school of Russian history in the 1840s brought forth a fundamentally new set of problems, decisively surpassing in the process the achievements of Karamzin. Deeply influenced by Hegelian philosophy, the state school historians sought to present Russian history as the gradual and inexorable unfolding of a single historical process. The key to this process lay in the evolution of forms of social organization from a society based on kinship ties in which the individual is subjugated to the collective of a modern state in which the rights of the individual are guaranteed by law. Konstantin Dmitrievich Kavelin (1818–1886), in his article *Vzgliad na iuridicheskii byt drevnei Rossii* [A Perspective on Ancient Russian Juridical Folkways] (1847), provided a succinct and eloquent explanation of the historical dynamic underlying the work of the state school. Kavelin's colleague, Sergei Mikhailovich Solov'ev (1820–1879), made it his life's work to elaborate this scheme in a seamless account of Russia's historical development presented in twenty-nine meticulously researched volumes. The publication of Solov'ev's *Istoriia Rossii s drevneishikh vremen* [History of Russia from Ancient Times] (1851–1879) was a colossal event in the development of Russian historiography, bringing to light a mass of previously unknown historical material within the framework of a masterful analytical scheme.

While the conceptions of the state school historians remained dominant throughout most of the nineteenth century, some contemporaries took issue with its overwhelming focus on the centralized state and began to stress the unique contributions and experiences of Russia's regions. Closely connected with the radical movement of the 1860s, Afanasii Prokof'evich Shchapov (1830–1876) advanced an approach to Russian history based on the principle of regionalism and the dynamic role of the masses. Nikolai Ivanovich Kostomarov (1820–1885), a prolific popularizer best known for his work on Ukrainian history, emphasized the role of federalism in ancient Russia and put forth the notion of national spirit as a force driving historical change.

The period from the 1870s up to the February Revolution of 1917 saw a vast outpouring of historical literature. Specialized journals such as *Russkaia starina* [Russian Antiquity], *Istoricheskii arkhiv* [Historical Archive], and *Golos minuvshchego* [Voice of the Past] published enormous quantities of memoirs and archival documents, while studies by respected historians were a constant feature in Russia's most influential periodicals. Amid this prolific output, two distinct schools can be distinguished. Based respectively in Moscow and St. Petersburg, each of them embodied, in different ways, then prevalent methods and approaches. Dominated in the early years by Konstantin Nikolaevich Bestuzhev-Riumin (1829–1897), the Petersburg school was distinguished by its meticulous and cautious methodology. Avoiding broad schematic generalizations, its members produced tightly woven historical narratives that never strayed far from the sources. The Petersburg school was particularly influential in its development and application of the ancillary historical disciplines such as paleography, epigraphy, and numismatics. Outstanding works produced by the Petersburg school include Sergei Fedorovich Platonov's (1860–1933) magisterial study of the seventeenth century "Time of Troubles," Aleksei Aleksandrovich Shakhmatov's (1864–1920) groundbreaking work on the early Russian chronicles, and Aleksandr Evgenevich Presniakov's (1870–1929) reconstruction of the formation of the Muscovite state.

The Moscow historical school was centered around the formidable figure of Vasilii Osipovich Kliuchevskii (1841–1911). Gifted with a unique combination of insight and artistry, Kliuchevskii crafted in his lectures and monographs some of the most vivid and penetrating images in Russian historical literature. Taking as his starting point the model of the state school, as laid out by his teachers Sergei Solov'ev and Boris Chicherin, Kliuchevskii broadened its scope devoting greater attention to the role of social and, particularly, economic factors. At the same time, the steady inexorable pace of historical change, characteristic of Solov'ev's writing, was replaced in Kliuchevskii's work by a succession of holistic systems separated by periods of cataclysmic change. Kliuchevskii's thought is best represented in his *Kurs russkoi istorii* [Course of Russian History], a survey published toward the end of his life on the basis of his university lectures. Kliuchevskii's students shared with their teacher an attraction toward broad interpretive scenarios and a multidimensional historical approach in which political structures and processes were placed within broader social and economic contexts. Foremost among Kliuchevskii's pupils was Pavel Nikolaevich Miliukov (1859–1943) who, in addition to his contributions as a historian, was also an important figure in Russian politics. Miliukov's major historical works, most notably his *Gosudarstvennoe khoziaistvo Rossii v pervoi chetverti XVIII stoletiia i reforma Petra Velikogo* [The State Economy in Russia in the First Quarter of the Eighteenth Century and the Reforms of Peter the Great] (1891) and *Ocherki istorii russkoi kul'tury* [Outlines of the History of Russian Culture] (1895–1896), are characterized by masterful handling of sources, vast erudition, and a need to account for Russia's historical alienation from the West and show a dynamic leading toward a rapprochement. Other important historians of the Moscow school include Mikhail Mikhailovich Bogoslovskii (1870–1925), known for his work on Peter the Great, Matvei Liubarskii (1860–1936), a specialist on the Grand Duchy of Lithuania, Aleksandr Aleksandrovich Kizevetter (1866–1933), and Iurii Vladimirovich Got'e (1873–1943).

From the 1890s onward, Russian historians came to be more and more influenced by the prevalent trend of economic materialism. Visible to a limited extent in the work of Kliuchevskii and Miliukov, this tendency found its fullest expression in the writings of the so-called Legal Marxists, most notably Petr Berngardovich Struve's (1870–1944) study of the economy of serfdom and Mikhail Ivanovich Tugan-Baranovskii's (1865–1919) history of Russian industry. Another influential development from this period was Nikolai Pavlovich Pavlov-Sil'vanskii's (1869–1907) elaboration of a theory of feudalism in Russia.

The first attempt to construct a comprehensive Marxist interpretation of Russian history was undertaken by Mikhail Nikolaevich Pokrovskii (1868–1932), a student of Kliuchevskii who would later go on to play a central role in the development of the Soviet historical profession in the 1920s. Vowing to purge Russian history of all traces of idealist thinking, Pokrovskii, in his three-volume *Russkaia istoriia s drevneishikh vremen* [Russian History from Ancient Times] (1913), tried to present economic interest as the sole causal agent in history. But ultimately, Pokrovskii, having rejected the need to undertake independent archival research, was unable to transcend the underlying assumptions and organizational schemes of his predecessors, on whom he relied for his factual data.

Despite the radical transformations brought about by the 1917 revolution and subsequent civil war, the historiographical tradition of prerevolutionary Russia proved to be quite enduring. Subject to widespread harassment and repression, particularly during the ascendancy of Pokrovskii in the 1920s and early 1930s, many of the younger historians who had come of age before the revolution, such as Boris Dmitrievich Grekov (1882–1953), Stepan Borisovich Veselovskii (1876–1952), and Evgenii Viktorovich Tarle (1874–1955), continued nonetheless to produce important works throughout the Stalin era. Historians forced into exile by the revolution faced a no less difficult path. Hampered in the first decades of exile by inadequate scholarly resources and material hardship, few were able to produce substantial innovative works, and only the best known such as Miliukov and Kizevetter gained the recognition of their European colleagues. But with the upsurge of interest in Russia in the aftermath of World War II, particularly in the United States, émigré historians such as Michael Karpovich (1888–1959) and George Vernadsky (1887–1973) were able to attain university positions and were instrumental in training the first generations of Anglo-American specialists in Russian history.

Nathaniel Knight

See also SOVIET HISTORIOGRAPHY; UKRAINIAN HISTORIOGRAPHY.

References

Mazour, Anatole G. *Modern Russian Historiography.* Revised ed. Westport, CT: Greenwood, 1975.

Miliukov, P.N. *Glavnye techeniia russkoi istoricheskoi mysli* [Main Currents of Russian Historical Thought]. Third ed. St. Petersburg: Aver'ianov, 1913.

Ocherki istorii istoricheskoi nauki v SSSR [Outlines of the History of Historical Science in the USSR]. 3 vols. Moscow: Nauka, 1955–1963.

Rubinshtein, N.L. *Russkaia istoriografiia* [Russian Historiography]. Moscow: OGIZ-Gospolitizdat, 1941.

Shapiro, A.L. *Istoriografiia s drevneishikh vremen do 1917 goda* [Historiography from Ancient Times to 1917]. St. Petersburg: Assotsiatsiia "Rossiia"—Izdatel'stvo "Kul'tura," 1993.

Rutkowski, Jan (1886–1949)

Polish economic historian. Rutkowski was born in Warsaw and studied in Paris under Henri Seé in the École Pratique des Haute Etudes (1910–1911). He obtained his *venia legendi* on the strength of his *Étude sur la répartition et l'organisation de la propriété foncière en Bretagne au XVIIIᵉ siècle* [Studies in the Distribution and Organization of Landed Wealth in Eighteenth-Century Britain] (1912). He became a professor at the University of Poznan in 1919 and died there thirty years later. In 1931, jointly with Franciszek Bujak, he founded the journal *Roczniki Dziejów Społecznych i Gospodarczych* [Annals of Social and Economic History]. In cooperation with Bujak, Rutkowski succeeded in establishing economic history as a discipline separate from history. He himself was mainly concerned with economic history in early modern times; in theoretical terms, he was an adherent of historical materialism. Availing himself of a wide range of sources, he was also able to apply statistical methods to his subject and thereby helped to lay the foundations of the economic history of the feudal system. His conception of the distribution of incomes was one of the most important theoretical achievements in Polish historiography in the first half of the twentieth century. In 1923,

Rutkowski published the first Polish synthesis of the economic history of Poland prior to the partitions of the country, reissued in an enlarged version as *Historia Gopodarcza Polski* [The Economic History of Poland] (1947–1950).

Ewa Domańska

Texts

The Distribution of Incomes in a Feudal System. Ed. Jerzy Topolski. Warsaw and Cracow: Ossolineum, 1991.

Histoire économique de la Pologne avant les partages. Paris: Champion, 1927.

References

Topolski, Jerzy. *O nowy model historii: Jan Rutkowski (1886–1949)* [Toward a New Model of History: Jan Rutkowski, 1886–1949]. Warsaw: PIW, 1986.

Ruvarac, Ilarion (1832–1905)

Serbian historian. Ruvarac was born in Sremska Mitrovica (Vojvodina). He studied law in Vienna and became professor of theology in Sremski Karlovci. Ruvarac introduced critical methods into Serbian historiography. He broke with the traditional forms of historical writing that had merely used, with little critical sense, chronicles and old songs glorifying the Serbian past. Ruvarac's own skepticism was directed toward four major questions: the role of Vuk Branković, the Kossovo battle, the murder of King Vukašin on Czar Uroš, the immigration of the Serbs to Vojvodina, and the autonomy of Montenegro during Turkish rule. Sometimes, his criticism was overdone, as in the case of Count Djordje Branković; Ruvarac's work also tended to show a slight bias in favor of Austria-Hungary.

Robert Stallaerts

Texts

Pejović, Božidar, ed. *Stojan Novaković i filološka kritika: Izabrani kritiški radovi Stojana Novakovića, Ilariona Ruvarca, Jovana živanovića* et al. [Stojan Novaković and Philological Criticism: Selected Critical Studies of Stojan Novaković, Ilarion Ruvarac, Jovan Živanović et al.]. Novi Sad: Matica sprska; Belgrade: Institut za književnost i umetnost, 1975.

References

Milutinović, Kosta. "Franjo Rački i Ilarion Ruvarac" [Franjo Rački and Ilarion Ruvarac]. *Zbornik za Istoriju* 21 (1980): 159–170.

Rymer, Thomas (1641–1713)

English antiquary. Rymer was born in North Yorkshire and educated in Northallerton and at Sidney Sussex College, Cambridge. There is a startling juxtaposition in the facts that his father was executed for treason in the early part of the reign of Charles II and that Rymer himself—after a false start as a drama critic—was appointed historiographer royal in 1693 at a salary of £200 per annum. Commissioned to assemble a printed collection of source material relating to treatises and alliances, Rymer was to do for England what Goldast, Chifflet, and Leibniz had already done for other countries in Europe. His multivolume *Foedera* was the result and is generally regarded as one of the great scholarly achievements of early-eighteenth-century historiography. The strict isolation of diplomatic material, however, proved more difficult to achieve than Rymer's original commission might have suggested; he ran short of money, at times he paid insufficient attention to differing versions of the same texts, and a secretary—Robert Sanderson—was needed to complete the project after Rymer's death. In its finished state, *Foedera,* the great reference work, extends chronologically from the reign of Henry I to the accession of Charles I in 1625 and provided an ample quarry for later historians to plunder.

R.C. Richardson

Texts

Foedera. Second ed. 20 vols. London: J. Tonson, 1726–1735.

References

Douglas, D.C. *English Scholars 1660–1730.* London: Eyre and Spottiswoode, 1951.

R

S

al-Sa'dī, 'Abd al-Raḥmān (fl. 1596–1656)

Arab historian, author of the *Ta'rīkh al-Sūdān*, an Arabic chronicle of the Muslim kingdoms of West Africa. Al-Sa'dī was born in Timbuktu of Arab ancestry, although the family had been settled there for several generations. Little is known of his early life, but in his maturity he worked in the service of the Bāshalik of Timbuktu. His chronicle in thirty-five chapters has at its core the history of the Songhay empire between the mid-fifteenth century, when it came into being, and 1591, when it was conquered by troops of the Sa'dian sultan of Morocco, al-Manṣūr. The first half of this work also incorporates material on the earlier empire of Mali and several chapters of collective biography of the scholars and holy men of Timbuktu and Jenne. The second half of the work is a detailed history of the Middle Niger region under the Bāshas, originally appointed by the Moroccan sultans but soon largely independent. Much of this is based on al-Sa'dī's personal knowledge of events, while the earlier part depends mainly on the oral testimony of Timbuktu scholars and notables and the biographical dictionary *Kifāyat al-muḥtāj* of Aḥmad Bābā of Timbuktu (d. 1627). A notable feature of the second half of the work is the interspersed chapters of obituaries and important events arranged chronologically, a form that became popular in the region. Stylistically it is drab and sometimes obscure, owing to al-Sa'dī's poor command of Arabic, although its *histoire événementielle* (event-oriented) approach is sometimes relieved by dialogic dramatization reminiscent of oral history. It is, nevertheless, a valuable complement to the only other chronicle of the period, the *Ta'rīkh al-fattāsh*.

John O. Hunwick

Texts

Tarikh es-Soudân. Trans. O. Houdas and E. Bénoist (into French). Paris: Leroux, 1898–1900. Reprint: Paris: Adrien-Maisonneuve, 1964.

Sa'dūddin Bin Hasan Can (1535–1599)

Ottoman historian, poet, and statesman. Sa'dūddin, also known as Hoca Efendi, was born in Istanbul, where he trained and worked as a Muslim religious scholar. In 1573, he was appointed *Hoca* (tutor) to Prince Murad. When Murad became sultan in 1595, Sa'dūddin became active in the political life of the empire, advising his student on a wide variety of domestic and foreign issues, from appointments of high officials to military campaigns against the Austro-Hungarian empire. He held a number of high positions during the reigns of Murad III and his successor, Mehmed III (r. 1595–1603), and mentored several prominent poets and historians. A prolific writer, his most famous work, *Tāc al-Tevārīkh* [The Crown of Histories], chronicles the history of the Ottoman dynasty from its origins to the death of Sultan Selim I in 1520. This carefully researched and eloquent chronicle, based on earlier Persian and Arabic chronicles as well as Sa'dūddin's own observations and research, served as the basis of several works written by later Ottoman historians.

Corinne Blake

Texts

Tāc al-Tevārīkh. Ed. I. Parmaksizŏglu. Ankara: Kültür Bakanliği, 1992.

The Capture of Constantinople. Ed. and trans. E.J.W. Gibb. London, 1879 (a partial translation only).

References

Refik, Ahmed. *Hoca Sa'deddin.* Istanbul: Kanaat Kütüphanesi, 1933.

Sagas

Term borrowed from Old Norse *saga* to identify epic narratives in a broad sense. Found in the most ancient forms of Old Norse literature, and rooted in the word *segja* (say or tell), *saga* corroborates both the oral origins of history and current, postmodern concerns about the primacy of language as the constitutive agent of human consciousness for creating social meaning. Since the late ninth century, Norwegian settlers in Iceland reported in oral prose the events they considered memorable (*sǫguligr*, sagalike), thereby manifesting the historian's imperative to choose. Implying both language and its articulation in story form, *saga* thereby has a double meaning, identifying both the event and its telling. The word can be employed for historical and fictional events alike, and since the re-creation of a past event is possible only through the mental absorption of the story told (or read) later, it transgresses the boundary between history and literature and exemplifies the permeability of conceptualizing society.

Beginning in the early twelfth century, Norse authors collected and sifted information about their society and its rulers, fashioning their work into sober vernacular histories. In the second half of the century the previously oral *saga* was written down, resulting in less mediated narratives in which shorter stories (*sǫgur*) were incorporated into the larger *saga*. During the next two hundred years the saga form became the preferred literary medium regardless of subject, subsuming all previous genres and creating a need for further, more precise, classification.

Privileged in the earlier histories, Norwegian monarchs also became the first subjects of written sagas. From the 1150s to the early 1300s the so-called kings' sagas (*konungasǫgur*) treat Norwegian monarchs from mythic times to the end of the thirteenth century. They include brief synoptic accounts of several kings, biographies of individual monarchs in different versions, and major compendia. Better known, and justly considered the pride of Icelandic literature, are the sagas of Icelanders (*Íslendingasǫgur*). Some fifty of these extant sagas and short stories were written during the thirteenth century and describe with realism and verisimilitude the Norwegian immigrants' origins, their travels abroad, and final settlement in Iceland. They focus on the century following the establishment of the General Assembly in 930, the so-called saga age. In contrast, the contemporary sagas (*samtíðarsǫgur*) treating Icelandic lay and clerical aristocracy, identify narratives in which a relatively short time intervenes between the authors and the time described.

After Icelandic authors had covered the obvious historical subjects but not yet exhausted their historical curiosity, they turned to the mythical past in narratives that remained popular until the nineteenth century. This branch is normally divided into two groups, the legendary or heroic sagas (*fornaldarsǫgur*) and the chivalric sagas (*riddarasǫgur*)—each containing some thirty narratives, the former staged in the north and the latter in European or global settings. The voracity of the new form is suggested by its ability to transform the disparate genres of Eddic poetry and Chrétien de Troyes's romances into saga prose.

Jenny Jochens

See also SCANDINAVIAN HISTORIOGRAPHY.

Texts

Andersson, Theodore M., and William Ian Miller. *Law and Literature in Medieval Iceland: "Ljósvstninga saga" and "Valla-Ljóts saga."* Stanford, CA: Stanford University Press, 1989.

Njal's Saga. Trans. Magnus Magnusson and Hermann Pálsson. London: Penguin, 1960.

Orkneyinga saga: The History of the Earls of Orkney. Trans. Hermann Pálsson and Paul Edwards. New York: Penguin, 1981.

Seven Viking Romances. Trans. Hermann Pálsson and Paul Edwards. New York: Penguin, 1985.

Sturlunga Saga. Trans. Julia H. McGrew and R. George Thomas. 2 vols. New York: Twayne, 1970–1974.

References

Clover, Carol J., and John Lindow, eds. *Old Norse-Icelandic Literature: A Critical Guide.* Ithaca, NY: Cornell University Press, 1985.

Einarsson, Stefán. *A History of Icelandic Literature.* Baltimore, MD: Johns Hopkins University Press, 1957.

Sørensen, Preben Meulengracht. *Saga and Society.* Trans. John Tucker. Odense: Odense University Press, 1993.

Sahlins, Marshall (b. 1930)

American cultural and historical anthropologist of the Pacific islands. Sahlins received his Ph.D. from Columbia University and has taught at the universities of Michigan and Chicago. His early writings concerned cultural evolution and hunter-gatherer economies. The early history of Western contact with Hawaii has been the focus of his historical anthropology. Drawing on French structuralism, he argues for a dialectic between culture and history. Culture provides structures that give meaning to historical events; it selects from and organizes complex realities, especially in encounters with the unfamiliar. Thus, for example, the arrival of Captain Cook in Hawaii was interpreted by native islanders in relation to their preexisting culture. Concrete historical events, however, put given cultural meanings at risk and often transform them. Culture thus organizes a particular historical event and the event in turn transforms culture.

Renato Rosaldo

Texts

Anahulu: The Anthropology of History in the Kingdom of Hawaii. Vol. 1, *Historical Anthropology.* Chicago: University of Chicago Press, 1992.

Historical Metaphors and Mythical Realities: Structure in the Early History of the Sandwich Islands Kingdom. Ann Arbor: University of Michigan Press, 1981.

How "Natives" Think: About Captain Cook, for Example. Chicago: University of Chicago Press, 1995.

Islands of History. Chicago: University of Chicago Press, 1985.

References

Burke, Peter. *History and Social Theory.* Cambridge, Eng.: Polity, 1992.

Saigusa Hiroto (1892–1963)

Philosopher and historian of Japanese science and technology. Born in Yamagata district, in Hiroshima prefecture, Saigusa was one of the principal organizers, in 1932, of the "Yuibutsuron Kenkyūkai [Society for the Study of Materialism]." In 1934, he published the important *Nihon ni okeru tetsugakuteki kannenron no hattatsushi* [History of the Development of Philosophical Idealism in Japan], one of the first major works to trace the history of modern Japanese philosophy and to evaluate it critically. His *Gijutsu shi* [The History of Technology] (1940) is an often-cited text. Saigusa compiled multivolume series of books such as *Nihon kagaku koten zensho* [Classics of Japanese Science] (1942). In the early 1960s, he helped organize the massive twenty-five-volume project *Nihon kagaku gijutsu shi taikei* [Outline of the History of Japanese Science and Technology]. The thirteen-volume *Saigusa Hiroto chosaku shū* [The Collected Works of Saigusa Hiroto] was published posthumously in 1977 by Chūō Kōronsha.

Morris F. Low

Texts

Gijutsu shi [The History of Technology]. Tokyo: Tōyō Keizai Shinpōsha, 1940.

Nihon ni okeru tetsugakuteki kannenron no hattatsushi [History of the Development of Philosophical Idealism in Japan]. Tokyo: Kōbundō, 1969.

Saigusa Hiroto chosaku shū [Collected Works]. 12 vols. plus supplement. Tokyo: Chūō Kōronsha, 1972–1977.

References

Itō Shuntarō et al., eds. *Kagakushi gijutsushi jiten* [Dictionary of the History of Science and Technology]. Tokyo: Kōbundō, 1983.

Sainte-Beuve, Charles Augustin (1804–1869)

French literary historian and critic. Born at Boulogne-sur-Mer, Sainte-Beuve studied medicine in Paris, but abandoned that profession to write literary articles for *Le Globe.* During the 1830s, he lectured at Lausanne on Port Royal and contributed literary portraits to the *Revue des deux mondes.* In 1849, Sainte-Beuve became a literary critic for *Le Constitutionnel,* where he continued writing for the next twenty years. He was appointed to the chair of Latin poetry at the Collège de France in 1854 and the École Normale in 1857. He died in Paris. Sainte-Beuve's greatest works were *Port Royal (1840–1859),* followed by *Causeries du Lundi* (1857–1862) and *Nouveaux Lundis* (1865–1870). Based on primary texts, Port Royal is a history of the spiritual and social aspects of the monastery and of Jansenism. The *Causeries* are accounts of the lives of leading French figures from antiquity to the eighteenth century. Sainte-Beuve was a pioneer of the modern biographical method. He sought to correlate the writings of an individual author with the forces of environment and heredity. He remained skeptical of historical methodology and endeavored to write "a natural history of minds." His works remain important because of their historical accuracy and attention to detail.

Leigh Whaley

Texts

Causeries du lundi. 16 vols. Paris: Garnier, 1944–1949.

Nouveaux lundis. 13 vols. Paris: Michel Lévy Frères, 1867–1972.

Port-Royal, édition documentaire. Ed. René Louis Doyon et Charles Marchesné. 10 vols. Paris: La Connaissance, 1926–1932.

References

Lehmann, Andrew George. *Sainte-Beuve: Portrait of the Critic 1804–1842*. Oxford: Clarendon Press, 1962.

Nicolson, Harold George. *Sainte-Beuve*. London: Constable, 1957.

Sainte-Palaye, Jean-Baptiste de la Curne de (1697–1781)

French medievalist and lexicographer. Born in Auxerre to a noble family, Sainte-Palaye was educated at the Oratorian Collège de Juilly and then studied law at the University of Paris. After a brief, unsuccessful public career, he turned to scholarship and in 1724 was elected to the Académie des Inscriptions. His most influential work was the *Memoirs on Ancient Chivalry* (1746–1750). Although later criticized for its sentimentality and anachronism, the *Memoirs* was a masterpiece of cultural history. In Sainte-Palaye's view, chivalry must be understood in light of the language, literature, and customs of its medieval participants. For this reason, he spent decades studying the development of the French language and editing medieval romances. His glossary of Old French adopted the same historical approach to the vernacular sources of medieval history that Charles du Fresne, Sieur du Cange, had earlier taken to the Latin and Greek sources. In 1758, the glossary project earned him a seat in the Académie Française. Sainte-Palaye also wrote a massive dictionary of French antiquities intended as a guide to French history between the thirteenth and seventeenth centuries. While neither the glossary nor the dictionary appeared before his death, Sainte-Palaye did see the publication of his three-volume *Histoire littéraire des troubadours* [Literary History of the Troubadours] (1774).

David F. Appleby

Texts

Histoire littéraire des troubadours. 3 vols. Paris: Durand neveu, 1774; reprint, 3 vols. in 1. Geneva: Slatkine Reprints, 1967.

Mémoires sur l'ancienne chevalerie considérée comme un établissement politique et militaire [Memoirs of Ancient Chivalry Viewed As a Political and Military Institution]. Second ed. 3 vols. Paris: La Veuve Duchesne, 1781.

References

Gossman, Lionel. *Medievalism and the Ideologies of the Enlightenment: The World and Work of La Curne de Sainte-Palaye*. Baltimore, MD: Johns Hopkins University Press, 1968.

Sallust [Gaius Sallustius Crispus] (86 B.C.–35 B.C.)

Roman politician and historian. Sallust's first political act of note was his opposition to Cicero and Milo as tribune in 52. He was expelled from the Senate in 50 and then allied himself with Julius Caesar. He briefly governed in North Africa in 46 and 45 before returning to Rome. After narrowly escaping extortion charges he retired from public life and began his writings. His first work, *Bellum Catilinae* [The Conspiracy of Cataline], chronicled Catiline's conspiracy and treated both Caesar and Cato as heroes. *Bellum Iurgurthium* [The War of Jurgurtha], his second work, concerned Rome's activities in Numidia in the late second century. His final work, *Historiae* [The Histories], was never completed; its annals cover the years 78–67 B.C., and it unfortunately survives only in fragmentary form. Sallust took Thucydides as his model; his goal was to develop a style of Roman history worthy of its Greek predecessors, full of polished phrases and archaic vocabulary. His analysis was generally pessimistic about human motivations and linked political instability directly to the character failings of his subjects. Sallust defined a new era in Roman historiography; Tacitus in particular was heavily influenced by Sallust's style and cynicism. He remained popular into the Christian era and later in the Renaissance.

Ruth McClelland-Nugent

Texts

Catalina, Iurgurtha, Historiarum fragmenta selecta C. Sallusti Crispi [Cataline, Jugurtha: Selected Fragments]. Ed. L.D. Reynolds. Oxford: Clarendon Press, 1991.

The Jugurthine War: The Conspiracy of Catiline. Trans. S.A. Handford. Baltimore, MD: Penguin, 1963.

Sallust: The Histories. Ed. and trans. Patrick McGushin. Oxford: Clarendon Press, 1992.

References

Scanlon, Thomas R. *The Influence of Thucydides on Sallust*. Heidelberg: Winter, 1980.

Williams, Ann Thomas. *Villain or Hero? Sallust's Portrayal of Catiline*. New York: P. Lang, 1994.

Woodman, A.J. *Rhetoric in Classical Historiography: Four Studies*. London: Croom Helm, 1988.

Salmon, Lucy Maynard (1853–1927)

American historian and educator. Salmon was born and raised in Fulton, New York. She attended the University of Michigan, completing both an A.B. (1876) and an A.M. (1883) degree. She returned to graduate study as a fellow in history at Bryn Mawr College (1886–1887) working under Woodrow Wilson. In 1887, she went to Vassar College where she remained as a professor of history until her death. In an era when few women achieved academic prominence in history, Salmon's greatest influence was as an educator. In her teaching she introduced the project method, intensive student use of the library and of primary historical materials to further the independent study of history. Salmon's interest in the materials of everyday living as significant for the interpretation of the past led to her most substantial works. Two volumes, *The Newspaper and the Historian* and *The Newspaper and Authority* (1923), study the newspaper as important historical material and remain the works by which her scholarship is measured. At her death, she left an unfinished work on the history of the fan. Although contemporaries, who privileged political history above all else, criticized Salmon for her interest—passed on to students at her Vassar seminar—in "mundane" objects of everyday life, her interest in this area represents an important early attempt by a woman historian to broaden the scope of historical study to cover domestic life and material culture.

Laurie J. Gagnier

Texts
Domestic Service. New York: Macmillan, 1897.
The Newspaper and Authority. New York: Octagon Books, 1923.
The Newspaper and the Historian. New York: Octagon Books, 1923.
Progress in the Household. New York: Houghton, Mifflin, 1906.
Why Is History Rewritten? Ed. E.P. Cheyney. New York: Oxford University Press, 1929.

References
Brown, Louise Fargo. *Apostle of Democracy: The Life of Lucy Maynard Salmon.* New York and London: Harper and Brothers, 1943.
Smith, Bonnie G. "The Contribution of Women to Modern Historiography in Great Britain, France, and the United States, 1750–1940." *American Historical Review* 89 (1984): 709–732.
Zinsser, Judith P. *History and Feminism: A Glass Half Full.* Boston: Twayne, 1993.

Salvador, Frei Vicente do (1564–1636/39)

Brazilian historian. Salvador was both the first Brazilian-born historian and the first to write a general history of Brazil, the *História Geral,* covering the period from 1500 to 1627. Divided into five books it is not only a subjective description of the Portuguese colony, but also a full-scale work of humanist historiography following the Ciceronian and Renaissance dictum that history should be a "light of truth and mistress of life." The first two books present an enthusiastic general description of the colony and a highly critical analysis of Portuguese colonization from the perspective of a "Brazilian." According to Salvador, the Portuguese were only "usufructuaries of the land, not landlords." The second book finishes with an account of the fate of the "capitanias hereditárias," the first attempt by the Portuguese government to organize and explore the colony. Books 3, 4, and 5 summarize events from 1539 to 1626, including the installation of the first general government up to Diogo Luís de Oliveira. Salvador's later commentators agree that his sources were principally personal observation and a number of books about various aspects of Brazil, rather than official documentation of the sort that would be employed by later Brazilian historians.

Nilo Odalia

Texts
Historia do Brazil [History of Brazil]. Belo Horizonte: Itatiaia, 1982.

Salvatorelli, Luigi (1886–1974)

Italian historian, journalist, and antifascist. In 1915 Salvatorelli was appointed professor of church history at the University of Naples. After military service, he became a journalist and coeditor of *La Stampa,* Turin's largest newspaper and one of the most respected and influential in Italy. After five years, the fascist regime forced him to turn over the directorship of the newspaper to party functionaries and Salvatorelli returned to research on ecclesiastical history, which eventually resulted in several major works: *From Locke to Reitzenstein: The Historical Investigation of the Origins of Christianity* was published in English and Italian in 1929; *Storia della letteratura latina cristiana dalle origini alla meta del VI secolo* [The History of Latin Christian Literature from Its Origins to the End of the Sixth Century] (1936); *La politica della Santa Sede dopo la guerra* [The Politics of the Holy See after the War] (1937); and *Pio XI e la sua eredita'* [Pius XI and His Inheritance] (1939). Later works included *L'Italia medievale dalle invasioni barbariche agli inizi del secolo XI* [History of Medieval Italy from the Barbarian Invasions to the Beginning of the Eleventh Century] (1937) and a history of medieval communes, *L'Italia comunale dal secolo XI alla meta' del secolo XIV* [The Communes of Italy from the Eleventh Century to the Middle of the Fourteenth Century] (1940). His interests eventually widened to include the Risorgimento and the fascist era, resulting in *Il pensiero politico italiano dal 1700 al 1870* [Italian Political Thought, 1700–1870] (1935, 1940) and *Pensiero e azione del Risorgimento* (1943), which was translated as *The Risorgimento: Thought and Action* (1943). On a larger canvas he wrote about the twentieth century in *Storia del Novecento* [History of the Nineteenth Century] (1957) and Europe in *Storia d'Europa* [History of Europe] (1961). He is perhaps best known for his highly regarded collaboration with Giovanni Mira, *Storia d'Italia nel periodo fascista* [History of Italy in the Fascist Period] which first appeared in 1952. His major work on historiography, published in 1964, is *Miti e storia* [Myth and History].

Stanislao G. Pugliese

Texts

Concise History of Italy from Prehistoric Times to Our Own Day. New York: AMS Press, 1977.

Miti e storia. Turin: Einaudi, 1964.

The Risorgimento: Thought and Action. Trans. Mario Domandi. New York: Harper and Row, 1970.

Storia d'Italia nel periodo fascista. Third ed. 2 vols. Turin: Einaudi, 1972.

References

"Omaggio a Luigi Salvatorelli." *Rivista storica italiana* 78 (1966): 469–543.

Saitta, Armando. "Luigi Salvatorelli." *Critica storica* 14 (1977): 91–148.

Salvemini, Gaetano (1873–1957)

Italian historian and committed antifascist exile. Salvemini devoted his life to impassioned teaching, scholarly research, and improving the social and economic conditions of the impoverished peasants of the Italian south. In 1908 an earthquake killed his wife and five children. He himself was professor of history at the universities of Messina, Pisa, and Florence, and he later taught at Harvard after fleeing fascist Italy. His important early work, *Magnati e popolani in Firenze dal 1280 al 1295* [Nobles and Commoners in Florence,

1280–1295] (1899) utilized Marxist conceptions of class struggle in describing the conflict between groups in medieval Florence. His subsequent research departed from the Marxist framework; although remaining within the democratic socialist tradition, Salvemini often went his own way. His next major projects were on the French Revolution, *La Rivoluzione Francese* (1905) and *Giuseppe Mazzini* (1905). His historical work is known for its character of *concretismo,* an inductive method based on pragmatism. His label of contempt for Prime Minister Giolitti—"il ministro della malavita" (minister of the underworld)—struck a chord in Italy. With the advent of fascism, he began a twenty-year period of activism, leading some of the most important of the younger antifascist intellectuals, first in Florence, later in Paris and the United States, where he founded the Mazzini Society. His experience of exile is recounted in *Memorie di un fuoruscito* [Memoirs of a Political Exile] (1960). In 1943, he coauthored with Giorgio La Piana, *What to Do with Italy,* a blueprint for postwar Italian society without a monarchy, fascism, or the Catholic Church. His most important work on historiography was *Historian and Scientist: An Essay on the Nature of History and the Social Sciences* (1939).

Stanislao G. Pugliese

Texts

The French Revolution. New York: Holt, 1954.

Mazzini. Trans. I.M. Rawson. New York: Collier, 1962.

Opere. Milan: Feltrinelli, 1961– .

The Origins of Fascism in Italy. Ed. Roberto Vivarelli. New York: Harper & Row, 1973.

Socialismo, riformismo, democrazia: Antologia di scritti di Gaetano Salvemini [Socialism, Reform, and Democracy: An Anthology of the Writings of Gaetano Salvemini]. Ed. Enzo Tagliacozzo and Sergio Bucchi. Rome: Laterza, 1990.

Under the Axe of Fascism. New York: Citadel, 1971.

References

Cantarella, Michele. *Bibliografia Salveminiana, 1892–1984* [Salvemini Bibliography]. Rome: Bonacci Editore, 1986.

Salvadori, Massimo L. *Gaetano Salvemini.* Turin: Einaudi, 1963.

Sestan, Ernesto, ed. *Atti del convegno su Gaetano Salvemini: Firenze, 8–10 novembre 1975* [Proceedings of the Conference on Gaetano Salvemini Held in Florence, 8–10 November 1975]. Milan: Il saggiatore, 1977.

Sansom, Sir George Bailey (1883–1965)

English historian of Japan. Sansom was born and educated in England but also studied in France and Germany. He joined the British consular service and was sent to Japan in 1903 where he stayed until 1940. After a brief stay in Singapore in 1941 he became the minister concerned with Far Eastern Affairs in the British Embassy in Washington. After the end of the Pacific War Sansom taught at Columbia University and became the first director of the newly established Far Eastern Institute. Sansom wrote a number of detailed general survey–style books on Japan in which he self-consciously tried to make Japanese history understandable for a Western audience. Before the outbreak of the Pacific War, he was effectively the only Western expert on Japanese history, and even after the war his books have continued to be widely read and to have a broad influence especially as university texts.

Graham Squires

Texts

A History of Japan. 3 vols. Stanford, CA: Stanford University Press, 1958–1964.
Japan: A Short Cultural History. London: The Cresset Press, 1931.
The Western World and Japan: A Study of the Interaction of European and Asiatic Cultures. New York: Knopf, 1950.

Sapori, Armando (1892–1975)

Italian Medieval and Renaissance economic historian. Sapori was born in Siena and completed his doctorate in law there in 1919. An eleven-year stint as an archivist in the state archive at Florence led eventually to a university career, with chairs at Ferrara and Florence. It was in the latter city that he spent the greater part of his career and, in a typically Sienese-Florentine manner, found no difficulty in melding an academic calling with an active urban and political life, even serving a term in the Italian Senate (1948–1953). He died in Milan, leaving scholarship the legacy of an immense bibliography of his publications. Especially significant are studies from archival sources of the great Tuscan mercantile families such as the Medici, Bardi, Peruzzi, Frescobaldi, and others. Unfortunately, most of his work remains untranslated and in regular use only by economic history specialists. Happily, besides Gladys Elliott's translation, *Merchants and Companies in Ancient Florence* (1955), there is a little book originally published in French as *Le Marchand italien au moyen*

âge (1952), which, translated as *The Italian Merchant in the Middle Ages* (1970), remains a polished gem and an "undergraduate's delight."

Kerry E. Spiers

Texts

The Italian Merchant in the Middle Ages. Trans. Patricia A. Kennen. New York: Norton, 1970.
Le Mercatura Medievale. Florence: Sansoni, 1972.
Merchants and Companies in Ancient Florence. Trans. G. Elliott. Florence: n.p., 1955.

References

[Various authors]. *Studi in onore di Armando Sapori* [Studies in Honor of Armando Sapori]. 2 vols. Milan: Istituto editoriale cisalpino, 1957.

Sarkar, Sir Jadunath (1870–1958)

Historian of medieval and Mughal India. Born in North Bengal, Sarkar completed his arts degrees in English literature at Presidency College, Calcutta, graduating in 1892. Appointed to the Provincial Educational Service in 1898 and promoted to the Indian Educational Service in 1918, he held chairs of English and history at a variety of esteemed institutions, including Banaras Hindu University. Upon his retirement in 1925, he was appointed vice-chancellor-designate of the University of Calcutta. After two years, he moved to Darjeeling because of ill health, but returned to South Calcutta in 1940, remaining there until his death. Throughout his life, Sarkar received innumerable honours, notably the Campbell Gold Medal of the Royal Asiatic Society, an honorary D.Litt., and a knighthood. As a result of his reliance on original sources and objective approach to history, Sarkar is hailed as the first of the scientific historiographers in India. His most renowned work, the five-volume *History of Aurangzib,* completed in 1924, provides a chronological account of history and an accurate depiction of characters. A highly prolific writer, Sarkar published books and articles on a wide range of subjects, including Mughal politics, Bengali saints, and medieval Maharashtra.

Siobhan Lambert Hurley

Texts

Trans. *Anecdotes of Aurangzib.* Third ed. London: Sangam, 1988.
Bihar and Orissa during the fall of the Mughal Empire. Patna: Patna University, 1932.

Fall of the Mughal Empire. Fourth ed. 4 vols. London: Sangam, 1988–1992.

History of Aurangzib. 5 vols. Bombay: Orient Longman, 1972–1974.

House of Shivaji. Second ed. Calcutta: M.C. Sarkar, 1948.

The Mughal Administration: Six Lectures. Patna: Patna University, 1920.

Short History of Aurangzib. Calcutta: M.C. Sarkar, 1930.

Studies in Mughal India. Second ed. Calcutta: M.C. Sarkar, 1919.

References

Gupta, H.R. *Life and Letters of Sir Jadunath Sarkar.* Hoshiarpur: Panjab University, 1957.

Khobrekar, V.G., gen. ed., and S.R. Titekar, ed. *The Making of a Princely Historian: Letters of Sir J.N. Sarkar to Dr. Raghubir Sinh of Sitaman.* Bombay: Maharashtra State Board for Archives and Archaeology, 1975.

Sarpi, Paolo (1552–1623)

Venetian priest, heterodox thinker, and historian of the Council of Trent. The son of an unsuccessful merchant and a Venetian woman of respectable family, he entered the Servite Order at the age of fourteen. Appointed prior of the Venetian province of his order in 1568, he soon established himself as a reform-minded cleric, while already revealing intellectual tendencies that his most recent student, David Wootton, deems "agnostic." Over the ensuing years, as official business took him outside Venice (and in particular to Rome) he developed a broad international network of friends and correspondents, including a number of French Protestants and moderate or *politique* Catholics. Several early brushes with the Inquisition over his friendships further encouraged his reformist and skeptical proclivities. He was appointed state theologian in 1606, at a time when Venice was under papal Interdict (1606–1607). He remained active in the aftermath of this crisis, corresponding with Protestants in England and French Gallicans, who shared his antipathy to papal autocracy.

Sarpi was the author of a variety of works in religion, philosophy, jurisprudence, and history, although many were not published in his own time, in large measure owing to their heterodox views. As a historian, Sarpi wrote several minor and one major book. The minor books include the *History of Benefices* (a historical overview of the origins and growth of ecclesiastical wealth from a hostile perspective), a history of the Inquisition commissioned by the Venetian Senate, and the *Istoria dell' Interdetto* [History of the Interdict], the latter intended for inclusion in the French historian Jacques-Auguste de Thou's *History of His Own Times* (too "hot" to smuggle to Paris, it remained in manuscript like the *History of Benefices*). He also wrote a supplement to Minuccio Minucci's *Historia degli Uscochi* [History of the Uskoks], an official defense of the Venetian war against the Habsburgs over the Uskok pirates who had attacked Venetian shipping.

Sarpi is best known for the *Istoria del Concilio tridentino,* completed in 1616 and first published in England in 1619 under the pseudonym Pietro Soave Polano; this was translated into English as *The History of the Council of Trent* in the following year. Profoundly critical of the council—the mid-sixteenth-century body that had repudiated internal reform and launched Roman Catholicism on the road to aggressive Counter Reformation—Sarpi raised serious questions about the authority of the church and revealed the council as a series of meetings torn by internecine politics and deeply divided on many issues. The work was widely read by Protestants and moderate Catholics elsewhere in Europe throughout the seventeenth century; Sarpi himself correctly anticipated its appeal, calling his work "the Iliad of our times." As a piece of late humanist historiography, influenced by earlier Italian historians (most notably Francesco Guicciardini) it is regarded as an exemplary distillation of a variety of sources into a work that, far from being a straight narrative of events, rather approaches its material as holding the answers to a number of historical problems, such as the failure of reform, that needed explanation in Sarpi's own day. Scholars have disagreed as to the *History's* accuracy, although most would now concede that it is, if by no means impartial, at least methodical and intellectually honest in its selection and representation of evidence, albeit from an openly antipapal perspective.

D.R. Woolf

Texts

The Historie of the Councel of Trent. Trans. Nathaniel Brent. London: Robert Baker and John Bill, 1620.

"History of Benefices" and Selections from "History of the Council of Trent." Ed. Peter Burke. New York: Washington Square Press (Simon and Schuster), 1967.

Istoria dell' Interdetto e altri scritti edite e inediti.
Ed. M.D. Busnelli and G. Gambarin.
3 vols. Bari: G. Laterza, 1940.
Opere. Ed. Gaetano and Luisa Cozzi. Milan and
Naples: R. Ricciardi, 1969.

References
Cochrane, Eric. *Historians and Historiography in
the Italian Renaissance.* Chicago: University
of Chicago Press, 1981, 472–478.
Cozzi, Gaetano. *Paolo Sarpi tra Venezia e
l'Europa* [Paolo Sarpi between Venice and
Europe]. Turin: G. Einaudi, 1978.
Getto, Giovanni. *Paolo Sarpi.* Florence: L.S.
Olschki, 1967.
Vivanti, Corrado. "Una fone del *Istoria del
Concilio Tridentino* di Paolo Sarpi [A
Source for the History of the Council of
Trent by Paolo Sarpi]. *Rivista storica
italiana* 83 (1971): 608–632.
Wootton, David. *Paolo Sarpi: Between Renais-
sance and Enlightenment.* Cambridge, Eng.:
Cambridge University Press, 1983.

Sars, Ernst (1835–1917)

Norwegian historian. The son of a zoology professor, Sars became Norway's greatest historian of the
nineteenth century. As an archivist from 1860 to
1874, he mastered the primary sources of Norwegian history. *Norge under Foreningen med Danmark*
[Norway in Union with Denmark] appeared serially from 1858 to 1865. During the 1860s, Sars
read Comte, Darwin, Spencer, and Mill, and developed a radically positivistic view of history as a
science of human behavior. This approach shaped
Udsigt over den norske historie [Survey of Norwegian History] (1873), which aroused storms of
protest but gained him a professorship at the University of Oslo. His view of history emphasized
gradual, organic structural changes through conflict over long periods of time. He believed that
the land-owning peasant class shaped the fundamental character of Norway, while urban and
official classes gradually emerged as bearers of an
active national awareness. Sars played a key role in
radicalizing prominent Norwegian figures like
Bjørnstjerne Bjørnson, Arne Garborg, and Jonas
Lie. He helped to shape the national consciousness
of late-nineteenth-century Norway, and Halvdan
Koht (1873–1965) made him the patron saint of
Marxist historians who dominated twentieth-
century Norwegian historical writing.

J.R. Christianson

Texts
Norges politiske historie, 1815–1885 [Norway's
Political History 1815–1885]. Christiania:
O. Andersens, 1904.
Udsigt over den norske historie. Second ed. 2 vols.
Christiania: A. Cammermeyer, 1877–1893.

References
Dahl, Ottar. *Norsk historieforskning i 19. og 20.
århundre* [Norwegian Historical Writing in
the Nineteenth and Twentieth Centuries].
Oslo: Universitetsforlaget, 1970.
Stokker, Kathleen Marie. *NYT NORSK
TIDSSKRIFT and J.E. Sars: Their Influence
on the Modern Breakthrough in Norway.*
Ph.D. thesis, University of Wisconsin–
Madison, 1979.

Sarton, George (1884–1956)

Historian of science and editor. Sarton was born at
Ghent, Belgium, the only child in a civil servant's
family. He studied chemistry, crystallography, and
mathematics at Ghent University, but, as he discovered early on through his reading of Auguste
Comte, Pierre Duhem, Paul Tannery, and Henri
Poincaré, his true vocation was the positivist mission to make history of science a rallying point for
the history of civilization as a narrative of endless
progress. He brought to this project a missionary's
zeal. In 1912 Sarton founded what is still the premier journal in the field, *Isis,* with its inexpressibly
valuable annual bibliography; in 1936 he founded
a companion journal, *Osiris,* to absorb the over-
flow. As the titles suggest, there was a masonic side
to Sarton's mind. In 1915 Sarton emigrated to the
United States. The Carnegie Institution in Washington, D.C., appointed him to a research post,
and Harvard University gave him an office and a
course to teach. From these positions Sarton successfully promoted the history of science.

Stuart O. Pierson

Texts
Ancient Science and Modern Civilization. London:
Arnold, 1954.
*The Appreciation of Ancient and Medieval Science
during the Renaissance (1450–1600).* Philadel-
phia: University of Pennsylvania Press, 1955.
Galen of Pergamon. Lawrence: University of
Kansas Press, 1965.
A History of Science. 2 vols. Cambridge, MA:
Harvard University Press, 1952–1959.
The History of Science and the New Humanism.
Third ed. New York: Braziller, 1956.

Introduction to the History of Science. 3 vols. in
5 parts. Baltimore, MD: Williams and
Wilkins, 1953.
The Study of the History of Science. Cambridge,
MA: Harvard University, 1936.

References

Merton, Robert. "George Sarton." *Isis* 76
(1985): 470–486.
*Studies and Essays in the History of Science and
Learning Offered in Homage to George
Sarton on the Occasion of His Sixtieth Birth-
day.* Ed. M.F. Ashley Montagu. New York:
Schuman, 1946.
Thackray, Arnold, and Robert Merton. "Sarton."
Dictionary of Scientific Biography, 12, 107–114.

Savigny, Friedrich Karl von (1779–1861)

German jurist and historian. Savigny was educated
at the universities of Göttingen and Marburg,
taught in Marburg (1800–1804), and became a
professor in Landshut (1808–1810) before accepting Wilhelm von Humboldt's invitation to hold a
chair at the new University of Berlin (1810–1842).
Having been active since 1810 as a member of the
commission charged with revising Prussia's civil
code, he served as Prussian justice minister from
1842 until his retirement in 1848. Savigny was the
most influential German jurist of the nineteenth
century. He established his reputation with *The
Ius Possessionis of the Civil Law* (1803), a work
that founded the modern systematic approach to
jurisprudence. Subsequently, Savigny became
the founder of the so-called Historical School of
Jurisprudence, a group of scholars who held that
all existing legislation derived from the spirit,
customs, and traditions of a people. According to
this school, it was not possible to discover the
meaning and content of any legislation without
careful historical investigation; nor could laws be
imposed or codified by outside forces (for example, a government or state) that ignored the
peculiar characteristics of a people. In his quar-
rel with A.F.J. Thibaut (a Heidelberg law professor inspired by awakening German nationalism),
Savigny rejected his opponent's call for a unified
German civil code in the pamphlet "Of the Vocation of Our Age for Legislation and Jurisprudence" (1814), which made Savigny world famous. Together with K.F. Eichhorn he founded
the highly influential *Zeitschrift für geschichtliche
Rechtswissenschaft* [Journal of the Historical Science of Law] in 1815.

Klaus Larres

Texts

History of Roman Law during the Middle Ages.
Trans. E. Cathcart. Westport, CT:
Hyperion, 1979.
System of the Modern Roman Law. Trans.
W. Holloway. Madras: J. Higginbotham,
1867.

References

Gmür, R. *Savigny und die Entwicklung der
Rechtswissenschaft* [Savigny and the De-
velopment of Legal Studies]. Münster:
Aschendorff, 1962.
Hattenhauer, H. *Thibaut und Savigny: Ihre
programmatischen Schriften* [Thibaut and
Savigny: Their Programmatic Writings].
Munich: Franz Vahlen, 1973.
Thieme, H. "Savigny und das deutsche Recht
[Savigny and German Law]." *Zeitschrift
der Savigny-Stiftung für Rechtsgeschichte.
Germanistische Abteilung* [Journal of the
Savigny Foundation for Legal History,
Germanic Branch] 80 (1963): 1–26.

Saxo Grammaticus (fl. 1185–1210)

Danish historian. Very little is known about
Saxo, except that he was born into a well-known
warrior family, studied in France, and served
archbishops Absalon and Andreas of Lund, where
he may have been a canon. Archbishop Absalon
commissioned the *Gesta Danorum* [Deeds of the
Danes] on which Saxo's fame as a historian and
Denmark's most important medieval writer rests.
The work consists of sixteen books, the first nine
of which deal with the pre-Christian period and
the remaining seven with the Christian era. For
the first nine books Saxo drew heavily on Scandinavian mythology and sagas, while for the historical era he relied on both written and oral
sources. The *Gesta* is written in a remarkably correct late-classical Latin, which marks Saxo as a
leading representative of the twelfth-century renaissance. His view of history was also a classical
one, and the *Gesta* belongs to the genre of "national
histories," which aimed at providing the barbarian
kingdoms with a recorded, and hence respectable,
past such as the classical civilizations had. However, as a work of history the *Gesta* is, for the most
part, inaccurate and unreliable. The most trustworthy, and therefore valuable as a historical
source, are the last three books, which concentrate
on the first half of the Waldemar era in Danish
history (1157–1202).

G.H. Gerrits

Texts

The History of the Danes. 2 vols. Trans. Peter
    Fisher; ed. Hilda Ellis Davidson. Cam-
    bridge, Eng.: Brewer, Rowland and
    Littlefield, 1979–1980.

References

Friis-Jensen, Karsten, ed. *Saxo Grammaticus:*
    A Medieval Author between Norse and Latin
    Culture. Copenhagen: Museum
    Tusculanum Press, 1981.

Scandinavian Historiography

The writing of history in Denmark, Norway, and
Sweden, medieval era to present. Native Scandinavian
historiography began with the twelfth century and
developed simultaneously with the consolidation of
the medieval kingdoms in Denmark, Norway, and
Sweden and the conversion to Christianity. The
earliest works, based on blendings of fact and fiction, were intended to praise kings or church leaders, provide moral examples, and entertain. For
Denmark they include *AElnoths Krönike* [AElnoth's
Chronicle], (ca.1120); Sven Aggesen's *Brevis historia*
regum [Brief History of Kings] (ca. 1185); and Saxo
Grammaticus's sixteen-volume *Gesta Danorum*
[Deeds of the Danes], from the early thirteenth century. For Norway, there is Theodoricus's *Historia*
de Antiquitate Regum Norwagensium [History of
Norwegian Kings], ca. 1180, and Snorri Sturluson's
(1178/79–1241) masterpiece, *Heimskringla,* a compendium of Norwegian kings' sagas beginning with
Odin and ending with Magnus Erlingsson and
dating from early-thirteenth-century Iceland. The
earliest histories of Sweden include several thirteenth-
century kings' lists and three rhymed royal chronicles; *Erik's Chronicle* from the early fourteenth
century, *Karl's Chronicle* from the mid-fifteenth
century, and *Sture's Chronicle* from the late fifteenth
century. Providing a churchman's views for the same
period is Ericus Olai's *Chronica regni gothorum*
[Chronicle of the Gothic Kingdoms] (1470s).

As was the case throughout Europe in the
early modern period (1500–1800), Nordic history
was a tool of the state, more a literary form used
to justify and glorify the state than an intellectual
discipline. In Denmark, this can be seen in the
repeated efforts by royal historiographers, beginning with Hans Svaning, to produce a definitive *Latin* history of the Danish kingdom.
In 1575, Anders Sörensen Vedel published a Danish-
language version of Saxo Grammaticus, and nine
years later began work on what he planned to be
a twenty-two-volume history. The project, now

titled *Danmarks Riges Krönike* [Chronicle of
the Danish Kingdom], was taken over by Arild
Huitfeldt, and nine volumes were published between 1596 and 1605. This work, highly praised
by later historians, was the standard Danish history
for over a century. The most important works in
Danish history for the seventeenth century were
largely antiquarian in nature and included Peder
Hansen Resen's *Dansk Atlas,* Arne Magnusson's
collection of Norse saga manuscripts, and Ole
Worm's [Olaus Wormius] study of Danish runic
inscriptions, *Monumenta Danica.* Ludwig Holberg's
three-volume *Dannemarks Riges Historie* [History
of the Danish Kingdom] from the 1730s was the
standard work for over a century.

Norway gradually lost its political autonomy
after 1319 and with this also lost an independent
historiography. There were no court historiographers, nor was there a university with faculty to
carry on the medieval cultural traditions or write
history. Norwegian history was included in Danish history until the late eighteenth century, when
a national reawakening began to develop. In this
context, Gerhard Schöning's *Norges Riiges Historie*
[History of the Norwegian Kingdom] from 1771
to 1773 was a breakthrough.

In Sweden, the development of history parallels the growth of the Vasa dynasty from 1523
and then the rise and fall of Sweden as a great
power in the North. Olaus Petri's [Swedish: Olof
Petersson] *En Swensk Crönika* [Swedish Chronicle]
from the late 1530s was intended to be a standard
work, but it was condemned by King Gustav I for
what he interpreted as criticism and was not published until 1818. Exiles actually produced the
best histories for Sweden in the sixteenth century.
Johannes Magnus's strongly anti-Vasa *Historia de*
omnibus Gothorum Sueonumque [History of the
Gothic Kingdom of Sweden] was published in Rome
in 1554. His brother, Olaus Magnus (Gothus), published his *Historia om de Nordiska Folken* [History
of the Nordic People], also in Rome, a year later.
The most important work of the seventeenth century was Olof Rudbeck's *Atlantica* (1679–1698), in
which it was argued that Atlantis was Sweden, that
this region was the first settled after the biblical
flood, and that civilization was spread to the world
by the Goths (that is, the Swedes). Rudbeck's work
marked the highpoint of Gothicism, an interpretative view that reached back nearly two centuries
and illustrated the role of history as a tool in state
building. As remarkable as were the conclusions
Rudbeck reached, his careful use of the emerging
scientific method and the elaborate arguments he
constructed in defense of his views are even more so.

Two major histories dominate the eighteenth century in Sweden. Olof Dalin's three-volume *Svea rikes historia* [History of the Swedish Kingdom], commissioned by the parliament, broke with the seventeenth century's preoccupation with the historical greatness of Sweden and challenged, in the spirit of the Enlightenment, many of the old myths. Sven Lagerbring's four-volume *Sweas rikes historia* [History of the Swedish Kingdom] (1769–1783) was important for its critical scholarship. Lagerbring worked to separate literary sources from historical and believed that finding the truth was an essential obligation of the historian.

The nineteenth century witnessed the increasing professionalization of the discipline, specialization, and a number of methodological and interpretive developments, which paralleled those taking place in Europe and America.

In Denmark, Kristian Erslev and his friend Marcus Rubin were two of the leading figures. National and political studies remained central, and a patriotic interpretative skew prevailed, especially during the period of conflict over the duchies of Schleswig and Holstein. At the same time, source collection and criticism became established as the bases of sound historical research.

Given Norway's disappearance as an independent state for almost four hundred years, it is hardly surprising that the country's history in the nineteenth and twentieth centuries was more strongly influenced by nationalist currents than was the case in Denmark or Sweden. After 1814 a "Norwegian historical school" developed, centered at the new university in Christiania/Oslo and led by Rudolf Keyser, Peder Andreas Munch, Christian Lange, and Carl Anger. Together they established an interpretive base founded on a Norwegian-centered view of the nation's history. Among the central elements of this school were a thesis that the Norwegians belonged to a unique ethnic stock that had migrated into Norway from the north, rather than from the south; an interpretation that what was traditionally viewed as Scandinavian medieval culture was almost entirely Norwegian and Icelandic; a denial of a Scandinavian cultural unity; and a strongly anti-Danish perspective. In addition to publishing texts for all educational levels, articles, monographs, and edited texts, members of the school were important for copying or recovering important primary sources of Norwegian history that were housed abroad.

Although critical methods and competing interpretative views have gained acceptance, this national school continues to be influential. The great moments in Norway's past—the Viking Age, the thirteenth century, 1814, the struggle for independence, and the experiences of World War II—remain popular and occupy central places in many studies.

Sweden's international relations and political situation during the nineteenth century created fewer pressures to push national/patriotic views of the past—although the differences between Swedish history and Danish or Norwegian are but matters of degree. The same breakthrough of critical historical scholarship occurred. Of primary importance were careful critique of sources and equally careful consideration of the contexts in which the sources were produced. Erik Gustaf Geijer dominates the first half of nineteenth-century Swedish historiography, Harald Hjärne the latter half. Geijer was strongly influenced by national romanticism and is best known for his three-volume *Svenska folkets historia* [A History of the Swedish People] (1832–1836). Geijer and his contemporary, A.M. Strinnholm, were also important for publishing collections of primary sources. A contradictory pattern developed that was reflected in narrow national (and largely political) studies and more international and comparative studies, such as those of Hjärne, who was also important in transplanting the German seminar method to the teaching of history to Sweden.

Scandinavian historians in the twentieth century have become increasingly diverse in their specializations, methodologies, and interpretations. The growth of higher education and the accompanying increase in the number of universities have been important factors in these changes. The interpretive dominance of Copenhagen, Oslo, Uppsala, and Lund has waned. At the same time, the seminar has become very important as a format for teaching history and research, and this has led to a number of significant long-term, thematic "projects" in the Nordic countries such as those in Sweden on internal and overseas migration, the family, and World War II. Some of these have also been Scandinavian in focus and participation, for instance a cross-national study of agrarian contraction in the Middle Ages.

Each of the Nordic countries has its historical journals. *Historisk Tidsskrift,* Denmark's primary history journal, was established in 1840 and was published until 1845; it was succeeded by *Nyt Historisk Tidsskrift* (1846–1857), and then by the journal that continues to publish today, again entitled *Historisk Tidsskrift.* Norway's oldest historical periodicals date from the 1830s, and the foremost, *Historisk Tidsskrift,* was established in 1871. Sweden's *Historisk Tidsskrift,* founded in

1881, long remained the mouthpiece of the conservative school. Lauritz and Curt Weibull, leading historians at Lund and Gothenburg, respectively, outspoken critics of their conservative colleagues, and advocates of a highly critical, comparative, and nonnationalist approach to Nordic history, established a second major journal, *Scandia* (1928–1986). In 1979, the historical societies in the Nordic countries began to publish *The Scandinavian Journal of History*, which was intended to present the work of Scandinavian historians to an international audience.

Scandinavia has also long been the focus of scholars from outside the region. The oldest reference to the region is usually ascribed to Pliny the Elder from ca. A.D. 79. Other works of the classical period include those of Tacitus (A.D. 98) and Ptolemy (ca. A.D. 150). References in Irish, Anglo-Saxon, and Frankish chronicles, as well as several Islamic works, provide information about the Viking period. Rimbert's life of Saint Ansgar and Adam of Bremen's history of the Archbishopric of Hamburg-Bremen are important medieval sources. Voltaire's biography of Sweden's Charles XII, although highly idiosyncratic, remains a useful study. In the twentieth century a number of historians from the United Kingdom and North America have concentrated on Scandinavia including Michael Roberts, Stewart P. Oakley, Thomas Munck, Franklin Scott, and H. Arnold Barton. In addition to producing many important monographs, these historians have helped to support English-language journals dedicated to Nordic history and related topics including *The Scandinavian Economic History Review* (1953–), *Scandinavica* (1962–), and *Scandinavian Studies* (1917–).

Byron J. Nordstrom

See also ESTONIAN HISTORIOGRAPHY; FINNISH HISTORIOGRAPHY; LATVIAN HISTORIOGRAPHY; LITHUANIAN HISTORIOGRAPHY; SAGAS.

Texts

Geijer, E.G. *Svenska folkets historia.* 3 vols. Örebro: N.M. Lindh, 1832–1836.

Gothus, Olaus Magnus. *Historia om de nordiska folken.* Ed. John Granlund. Stockholm: Gidlund, 1976.

Hjärne, Harald. *Svenska/ryska forhandlingar, 1564–1572.* Uppsala: Almqvist & Wiksell, 1897.

Keyser, R. *Norges historia.* Christiania/Oslo: P.T. Malling, 1866–1870.

Lagerbring, Sven. *Skrifter och brev.* Compiled by L. Weibull. Lund: Berlingska, 1907.

———. *Swea rikes historia.* Stockholm: C. Stolpe, 1769–1783.

Lange, Christian. *De norske klosters historie i middelalderen.* Christiania/Oslo: Tonsberg, 1856.

Magnes, Johannes. *Historia de omnibus Gothorum Svenonumque regibus.* Rome: n.p., 1554.

Petri, Olaus. *Svenska krönike.* Stockholm: G.E. Klemming, 1860.

Saxo Grammaticus. *History of the Danes.* Ed. Hilda Ellis-Davidson; trans. Peter Fisher. 2 vols. Cambridge, Eng., and Totowa, NJ: Rowman and Littlefield, 1979–1980.

Schöning, Gerhard. *Domkirken i Trondhjem.* Trondheim: Foreningen Facsimilia Nidrosiensia, 1959.

———. *Norges riiges historie.* Copenhagen. Mumme og Faber, 1771–1781.

References

Barton, H.A. *Scandinavia in the Revolutionary Era.* Minneapolis: University of Minnesota Press, 1986.

Cornell, J., ed. "Vad är historia." In *Den svenska historien,* vol. 1. Stockholm: Bonniers, 1977– .

Danstrup, J. et al., eds. *Kulturhistorisk Leksikon for Nordisk Middelalder,* vol. 6. Copenhagen: Rosenskilde og Bagger, 1956–1978.

Eriksson, G. "Science and Learning in the Baroque Era." In *The Age of New Sweden,* ed. Arne Losman, Agneta Lündström, and Margareta Revera. Stockholm: Livrustkammaren: The Royal Armoury, 1988.

Falnes, O.J. *National Romanticism in Norway.* New York: AMS Press, 1968.

Sawyer, B., and P. Sawyer. *Medieval Scandinavia.* Minneapolis: University of Minnesota Press, 1993.

Scott, F. *Sweden: The Nation's History.* Second ed. Carbondale: Southern Illinois University Press, 1988.

Schlesinger, Arthur Meier, Sr. (1888–1965)

American historian and educator. Born in Xenia, Ohio, Schlesinger was educated at Ohio State University, where he later taught history from 1912 to 1919, and Columbia University, from which he obtained a doctorate (1918). After teaching at the State University of Iowa from 1919 to 1924, he joined the history faculty at Harvard, where he stayed until his retirement in 1954. A distinguished teacher and a prolific author, Schlesinger's most significant contribution was to American colonial history. In *The Colonial Merchants and the*

S

American Revolution, 1763–1776 (1918), he examined how American merchants, whose welfare and prosperity depended upon friendly relations with Great Britain, were lured by the tea question into an alliance with and subsequently outmaneuvered by a small but determined body of patriots. A later work, *Prelude to Independence: The Newspaper War on Britain, 1764–1776* (1957), explored how American journalists nourished the cause of the patriots. Schlesinger's other notable works were *New Viewpoints in American History* (1922); *The Rise of the City, 1878–1898* (1933), a pioneering study in urban history; *The American As Reformer* (1950), whose thesis was that Americans were natural rebels against the status quo because of their immigrant roots and lack of excessive traditional baggage; and *In Retrospect: The History of a Historian* (1963), an autobiographical statement. With Dixon R. Fox, Schlesinger was also the general editor of *A History of American Life* (1928–1943), a thirteen-volume series that focused on social history. Such works made Schlesinger one of the more influential historians of the first half of the twentieth century.

John W. Storey

Texts

The American As Reformer. Cambridge, MA: Harvard University Press, 1950.
Colonial Merchants and the American Revolution. New York: Columbia University Press, 1918.
The Rise of the City, 1878–1898. New York: Macmillan, 1933.

References

Schlesinger, Arthur M., Sr. *In Retrospect: The History of a Historian.* New York: Harcourt, Brace, and World, 1963.
Schlesinger, Arthur M., Jr. *Nothing Stands Still: Essays.* Cambridge, MA: Belknap Press, 1969.

Schlözer, August Ludwig von (1735–1809)

German historian, editor, and statistician. Schlözer was born in the principality of Kirchenberg (Franconia), the son of a Lutheran pastor. He studied at the universities of Wittenberg and Göttingen and in 1755 took up a post as tutor in Stockholm. In 1761, he went to St. Petersburg with Gerhard Friedrich Müller, the royal historiographer, as Müller's literary assistant. Schlözer left Russia in 1767, returning to the University of Göttingen, which had offered him a professorship. He retired from teaching in 1805 and died four years later. Schlözer is often considered the father of modern Russian historical writing, owing chiefly to his monumental collections of primary sources, his pioneering use of population statistics, and his definitive edition (1802–1805) of the Russian *Primary Chronicle,* attributed to Nestor, which marked an important advance in the development of Russian historiography. Schlözer also helped lay the foundation of statistical science in several of his books, and he stimulated widespread interest in what was then called "universal history" in his *Weltgeschichte* (1785), an innovative work that viewed world history as both an account of mankind and a means of revealing a universal unity, linking wide-ranging consequences with their causes. In setting new critical standards and establishing history as a serious form of scholarship, Schlözer left a legacy that helped to shape the evolution of German historiography during the nineteenth century.

Karl W. Schweizer

Texts

Allgemeines Statsrecht und Statsverfassungslehre [General Laws of States and Constitutions]. Göttingen: Vandenhoeck & Ruprecht, 1793.
Kritische Sammlungen zur Geschichte der Deutschen in Siebenburgen [Critical Articles on the History of the Germans in Siebenburgen]. Ed. Harald Zimmermann. Cologne: Bohlau, 1979.
Ed. *Nestor.* 3 vols. St. Petersburg: Imperatorskaia Tipografiia, 1809–1819.
Neuverändertes Russland, oder, Leben Catharinae der Zweyten. [Newly Changing Russia, or the Life of Catherine the Second]. 2 vols. Riga: J.F. Hartknock, 1767.
Theorie der Statistik: Nebst Ideen über das Studium der Politik überhaupt [Statistical Theory, as Well as Ideas about the Study of History in General]. Göttingen: Vandenhoeck & Ruprecht, 1804.
Weltgeschichte nach ihren Hauptheilen im Auszug und Zusammenhange [Key Aspects of World History: Summary and Context]. Göttingen: Vandenhoek & Ruprecht, 1792–1801.

References

Bond, M.A. "A.L. von Schlözer: A German Political Journalist." *European Studies* 6 (1976): 61–72.
Butterfield, Herbert. *Man on His Past.* Cambridge, Eng.: Cambridge University Press, 1955.
Rogger, H. *National Consciousness in Eighteenth Century Russia.* Cambridge, MA: Harvard University Press, 1960.

Schmoller, Gustav von (1838–1917)

German economist and historian. Schmoller (von Schmoller after 1908) studied politics at the University of Tübingen and earned his doctorate in 1860 with an award-winning study of economic thought during the Reformation. In 1864 he became professor extraordinarius in Halle, moving in 1872 to Strasbourg. In 1882 he was appointed to a chair in Berlin. Beginning in 1884 he was a member of the Prussian Council of State and in 1887 was appointed the official historian of Brandenburg. From 1881 he edited the *Jahrbuch für Gesetzgebung, Verwaltung und Volkswirtschaft* [Yearbook for Legislation, Administration, and Economy] better known as the *Schmoller-Jahrbuch*. In 1899 Schmoller became a member of the Prussian Upper House, representing the University of Berlin. Schmoller, founder and leader of the younger generation of the historical school of economics, repudiated alike the political economy of Adam Smith and David Ricardo, the abstract rationalism of the Austrian school, and the neo-Hegelianism of Karl Marx. In opposition to these writers he wanted to place economic man within the historical development of cultures; accordingly, he proposed a study of civilization that was in turn grounded in both history and economics. Schmoller's most important historical writing is the *Geschichte der deutschen Kleingewerbe* [History of German Small Business] (1870), an evaluation of regional statistics of trades. In the book *Die Strassburger Tucher- und Weberzunft* [The Cloth and Weavers' Guild of Strasbourg] (1879) he dealt with problems of urban constitutional and economic life through an examination of a single craft guild. Schmoller believed that mercantilism had contributed constitutionally to the modern Prussian state, and his academic and political influence declined after the disappearance of the Historical School from the universities. After this he attempted to influence state social policy through the *Verein für Sozialpolitik* (Association for Social Politics), which he had founded in 1872 and led after 1890, in accordance with the principals of the "Pulpit Socialists" *(Kathedersozialisten)*.

Thomas Fuchs

Texts

The Economics of Gustav Schmoller, As Revealed in His Grundriss der allgemeinen Volkswirtschaftslehre [Outline of General Economic Teaching]. Trans. W. Abraham and H. Weingast. New York: Brooklyn College, 1942.
The Mercantile System and Its Historical Significance. New York: Kelley, 1967.
Die Strassburger Tucher- und Weberzunft. Urkunden und Darstellungen nebst Regesten und Glossar [The Cloth and Weavers' Guild of Strasbourg: Documents and Accounts as Well as Registers and Glossaries]. Strasbourg: Karl J. Trübner, 1879.
Zur Geschichte der deutschen Kleingewerbe im 19. Jahrhundert: Statistische und nationalökonomische Untersuchungen [History of German Small Business in the Nineteenth Century: Statistical and Economic Studies]. Halle: Verlag der Buchhandlung des Waisenhauses, 1870.

References

Anderson, P.R. "Gustav von Schmoller." In *Some Historians of Modern Europe. Essays in Historiography by Former Students of the Department of History of the University of Chicago,* ed. B.E. Schmitt. Chicago: The University of Chicago Press, 1942, 415–443.
Balabkin, N.W. *Not by Theory Alone: The Economics of Gustav von Schmoller and Its Legacy to America.* Berlin: Duncker & Humblot, 1988.

Schramm, Percy Ernst (1894–1970)

German historian of the medieval and modern eras. Born into the bourgeois, Protestant elite of Hamburg, Schramm studied history there and in Munich after military service in World War I. He wrote his dissertation (1922) and "Habilitation" (1924) in Heidelberg and was appointed in 1929 as professor of medieval and modern history in Göttingen, where he became one of that university's, and his country's, most prominent historians. His numerous and voluminous books center around three main subjects. The first was the history of medieval European emperors, monarchs, and popes. Schramm frequently focused on the influence of antiquity on medieval political ideas and often used pictorial source materials to analyze the symbolic dimension of political leadership. The second was the history of the upper classes of Hamburg from the seventeenth century onward, in which connection he used the history of his own family as an example of the German bourgeoisie. The third area was the history of World War II. On this subject he was able to put to good use his own life history, since he had been attached as a Wehrmacht major to the army's headquarters, where he kept its diary. In the editing of this diary he collaborated with Andreas Hillgruber, Walther Hubatsch, and Hans-Adolf

Jacobsen. Although Schramm did not lead any "school," he was one of the most productive and—as one of the editors of the *Historische Zeitschrift* from 1931 onward—among the most influential German historians of his generation.

Chris F.G. Lorenz

Texts

Die deutschen Kaiser und Könige in Bildern ihrer Zeit (751–1190) [German Emperors and Kings in Pictures of Their Time]. Munich: Prestel, 1983.

Geschichte des englischen Königstum im Lichte der Krönung [The History of English Kingship As Reflected in the Coronation Ceremony]. Cologne: Böhlau, 1970.

Hamburg, Deutschland und die Welt [Hamburg, Germany and the World]. Munich: Callwey, 1943.

Herrschaftszeichen und Staatssymbolik [Symbols of Power and State Symbolism]. 3 vols. Stuttgart: Hiersemann, 1954–1956.

Hitlers Tischgespräche im Führerhauptquartier 1941–1942 [Hitler's Table-Talk in the Führer's Headquarters, 1941–1942]. Stuttgart: Seewald Verlag 1965.

Kaiser, Rom und Renovatio [The Emperor, Rome, and Renovation]. 2 vols. Darmstadt: Wissenschaftliche Buchgesellschaft, 1957.

Der König von Frankreich [The King of France]. 2 vols. Darmstadt: Wissenschaftliche Buchgesellschaft, 1960.

Kriegstagebuch des Oberkommandos der Wehrmacht 1940–1945 [War Diary of the German Army High Command, 1940–1945]. Munich: Deutscher Taschenbuch Verlag, 1962.

References

Claessen, P., and P. Schreibert, eds. *Festschrift für Percy Ernst Schramm*. Wiesbaden: Franz Steiner Verlag, 1964.

Heimpel, Hermann. "Königstum, Wandel der Welt, Bürgertum: Nachruf auf P.E. Schramm" [Monarchy, World Change, Bourgeoisie: An Obituary of P.E. Schramm]. *Historische Zeitschrift* 214 (1972): 96–108.

Science, History of

Historical writing, mainly from the nineteenth century onward, about science in the past: its changing contents, the social and cultural contexts in which science has been pursued, and the impact of science upon its material and intellectual environment over time. Just as in the history of historiography at large a broad two-stage division can be maintained, with the development of professional standards in the course of the nineteenth century marking the turning point, the historiography of science has undergone a similar transition. But there are also significant differences between what happened in historiography at large and in the historiography of science. These differences stem mainly from the fact that the latter specialism used to be (as it still largely is) the domain of scholars with a background in the sciences and/or philosophy, rather than in "general" history.

A trickle of historical writing has accompanied the advance of science from early times onward. Certain scientists (for instance, Aristotle, Bernardino Baldi, and Johannes Kepler) made occasional observations on the performance of forerunners of their own scientific endeavors. In the eighteenth century the trickle turned into a stream, with a number of mostly French "érudits" chronicling in considerable detail and with often considerable sophistication the history of the mathematical sciences, in particular. In the middle of the nineteenth century these efforts culminated in William Whewell's *History of the Inductive Sciences,* which covered the nonmathematical sciences as well. All this work may broadly be termed "internal" in the sense of tracing successions of scientific ideas, practices, triumphs, and (on occasion) failures.

Whereas Whewell's work exemplifies a philosopher's principal interest in the history of science—with an urge to distill from the past of science a generalized pattern of scientific advance—the bulk of work during the nineteenth and early twentieth centuries was produced by scientists who, at the end of a creative career in science, decided to look back. Almost inevitably, such looking back consisted of tracing down the centuries the "primitive" roots of one or another modern scientific conception. Much valuable historical information could be, and was, gained this way, in a process reinforced considerably by the start, on the grand scale, of the publication of source materials, such as the *Edizione Nazionale* of Galileo's works, notes, and letters around the turn of the twentieth century by Antonio Favaro. Still, neither the search for overall patterns of scientific advance, nor topical tracing back, nor publication of source materials add up to a sympathetic understanding of the past in its own right.

A search for ways and means to achieve such understanding began in the early twentieth century. The person who started it—rather inadvertently—was the scientist/philosopher Pierre Duhem (1861–1916). His extraordinary thesis was that the birth of modern science had taken place not in the period of Copernicus to Newton, but rather in fourteenth-century Paris. This thesis occasioned a debate which, as one important byproduct, ushered in the establishment of such approaches to, and criteria for, a truly historical understanding of a given segment of the past, as obtained already in other subdivisions of the historical discipline. Between the 1920s and the 1940s, a whole range of authors with an education in (most often) science and/or (on occasion) in philosophy, and writing with a variety of motives, came to formulate and to practice professional aims and methods for the historiography of science. These aims and methods turned out to be broadly the same as those practiced by the historian at large; still, they were not adopted from history at large so much as reinvented.

There are at least two reasons why things happened this way. The first is that historians used (as most of them still do) to abstain from the domain of the history of science altogether, both out of a reasonable concern over lack of scientific proficiency and out of a customary yet quite misplaced feeling that somehow the history of science does not belong to history at large. The other reason is that the temptations of finalism are even harder to withstand for the historian of science than for historians otherwise specialized. After all, science is different from other domains of human endeavor in that scientists are in the habit of claiming for it a methodical attainment of the truth (or at least something closely approaching truth) about nature. Judgments that in other domains come down to matters of subjective preference are, in the scientific domain, taken to be rather a matter of objective validity. Hence, it has always been a particularly tough challenge to treat a past scientist, busily engaged as he or she was with conceptions we now know to be wrong or at least not sufficiently true, with all seriousness required for sympathetic, historical understanding.

One radical way to meet that challenge has been to deny the claim to truth so often made for science. The element of unhistorical triumphalism that may easily creep into the historiography of science can be countervened by taking science to be a body of insights in which subjective elements (be it in the way discoveries are made or in how they gain recognition) reign more or less supreme. The relativist current that has, since the 1960s, swept over philosophy and sociology of science has deeply influenced trends in the historiography of science too. The moderately relativist, philosophical views of Thomas Kuhn have not as such

very significantly altered the direction of research in the history of science (in particular, his intricate pattern of paradigms and puzzle-solving and crises and revolutions has only rarely been applied). But two related, more radical varieties of relativism have successively had a considerable impact on much history of science writing. One is the "Hermeticist" current, which deeply occupied the discipline in the 1960s and 1970s. The recognition of the contemporary vitality of pre-eighteenth-century magical notions besides, and often intermingled with, the cultivation of allegedly "pure" science had evident roots in the "counterculture" movement of the 1960s, with its often scathing condemnation of the scientific enterprise as such. Similarly, views of nature as being nothing but a human convention or a social construction, which were worked out in the late 1970s and 1980s by certain sociologists of science, are now in process of refocusing substantial portions of history of science writing. Still, while it is in general true to say that changing conceptions of science have accordingly shaped views of the past of science, too, this is not to say that the tradition—stemming, as noted, from the 1920s and 1930s—of sympathetically examining scientific ideas of the past in their own right and as part of an ongoing, intrinsic logic of scientific advance has ceased to exist or to flourish. Despite the ideological overtones that are noticeable in debates inside the profession, coexistence—whether more or less peaceful— of a range of approaches and conceptions is what meets the eye of the present-day observer of the discipline. The principal common theme appears to be the search for an ever deeper "historization" of the history of science, in the sense of getting rid of ever more distortions of the picture of the past that may arise from our standpoint in the present.

The search has affected different periods and loci of the history of science in different ways. Thus, there is the study of non-Western traditions in science. On the whole, the amount of factual knowledge available is as yet several orders of magnitude smaller than is true of the Western tradition. Meanwhile, pioneers like Otto Neugebauer for Egyptian and Babylonian science, or Joseph Needham for Chinese science, have deeply altered earlier preconceptions about the allegedly unique (as distinguished from singular) place of Western science in history. As one result, the road toward a cross-culturally comparative historiography of science seems now to lie open.

The history of Western science is customarily broken down into ancient science (the Greco-Roman tradition), medieval science, Renaissance science, early modern science, and modern science—it is with increasing rarity that historians investigate topics in more than one of these periods. The birth of early modern science in the seventeenth century has for a long time been at the center of the field, and it is still the locus where novel approaches are tried out and most hotly debated. Here Alexandre Koyré's idea that what he conceptualized as the "scientific revolution" signified an overall change in worldview has deeply molded historiography in the "internalist" mode since the 1940s. Almost equally influential in exemplifying a variety of "externalist" conceptions of how science is embedded in culture and society have been studies in a Marxist vein, but also books by Robert K. Merton (1938) and by Steven Shapin and Simon Schaffer (1985).

Efforts at the synthetic treatment of periods up to modern science—once quite frequent—are still at times being undertaken. There is no overview of the whole of Western science that meets present-day standards. Existing efforts, while courageous, have tended to turn into either popular heroics or factual chronicles or somewhat spotty selections from the point onward where the scientific revolution is left behind. After all, science after Newton has become ever more detailed and complex. Here the bulk of historical analysis is nowadays being located, spread out as it inevitably is over a proliferating number of scientists and of scientific disciplines and subdisciplines. Here, too, the amount of technical proficiency required to master the contents of science involved increases accordingly.

The historian of science must bring many tools to the trade, stemming in part from scientific and in part from humanist traditions; hence, he or she has been apt to be a rather versatile person. This versatility has had important consequences.

One is the striking variety of university departments in which (besides science museums and archives) these people are located—one finds them in history departments, science departments, philosophy departments, social studies of science departments, and so on. This was true when historians of science were lonely mavericks; it has been no less true since chairs and groups began to be set up in earnest. In the aftermath of World War II the center moved from the European continent to the English-speaking world, and in particular to the United States. There, in the 1920s and 1930s, George Sarton had prepared institutional opportunities enthusiastically grabbed by the first generation of professionals, who were riding on the crest of the wave favoring history of science as a possible bridge between the world of science and the world of the humanities. But the professional cultivation of the history of science also established itself in the United Kingdom, in Canada, in a range of countries on the European continent, and in smaller measure in Latin America, Japan, and several other countries with a scientific tradition of their own.

The versatility of the history of science finds expression on other levels as well. There has been a huge variety of scientific disciplines, ranging from pure mathematics to, for example, plant taxonomy; there is also a huge range of historical topics connected in one way or another with science. There once were even historians of science who, like R. Hooykaas (1906–1994), were still capable of shifting freely from Renaissance alchemy to nineteenth-century uniformitarianism in geology; from the impact of the Voyages of Discovery on Portuguese science and letters to the relations between science and religion in the age of the Reformation; from Renaissance views on art and nature to the origins of crystallography.

History of science is no less versatile in sharing, so to speak, open boundaries with a good number of related disciplines. Among these, history of technology, history of medicine, philosophy of science, and sociology of science bear the brunt of the interstate traffic. But science has been so narrowly bound up over the centuries with matters of world view that the history of religion and the history of philosophy are hardly less close neighbors, as multitudes of studies covering these domains can testify. It is nonetheless striking how rarely efforts have been made to integrate the history of science into history at large, just as it is striking how rarely "general" historians have contributed insights of their own to an understanding of the past of science, whether by itself or in its social and its cultural contexts. A big gap has been yawning here, which the present entry may just possibly help bridge in some small measure. For despite the remoteness, to the "general" historian, of the object of prime concern to the historian of science, science has become a constituent of our culture that "general" historians may ignore only at considerable intellectual costs.

H. Floris Cohen

References

Cohen, H. Floris. *The Scientific Revolution: A Historiographical Inquiry.* Chicago and London: University of Chicago Press, 1994.

Kragh, Helge. *An Introduction to the Historiography of Science.* Cambridge, Eng.: Cambridge University Press, 1987.

Olby, R.C. et al., eds. *Companion to the History of Modern Science*. London: Routledge, 1990.

Thackray, Arnold. "History of Science." In *A Guide to the Culture of Science, Technology, and Medicine*, ed. P. Durbin. New York: Free Press, 1980, 3–69.

Scientific History

(1) Historiography that uses a methodology similar to that of the natural sciences. (2) In the German sense of *Wissenschaft*, historiography as a rigorous, critical, inquiry.

In regard to the first definition, nineteenth-century positivists expressed optimism about the prospects for the creation of a science of history, scientific historiography. Auguste Comte predicted the creation of a science of society in sociology. J.S. Mill predicted in *A System of Logic* that empirical historiographic generalizations would be deducible from the laws of human nature, as Kepler's laws were deduced from Newton's. The positivists assumed that all the fields of knowledge, from the most simple and remote from man (astronomy) to the most complex and nearest to man (human history), would follow the stages of development of physics, culminating in the creation of determinist science. On the other hand, neo-Kantians such as Wilhelm Windelband, Heinrich Rickert, and Wilhelm Dilthey attempted to defend the methodological autonomy of historiography on *normative* grounds. Whether or not scientific historiography is possible, they held it would be a boring and thankless task to oversee the essence of historiography as a humane "science" providing *verstehen* (understanding) of history, by its very nature concrete, unique, and value-laden. Windelband, Rickert, Dilthey, Benedetto Croce, R.G. Collingwood, Karl Popper, Michael Oakeshott, and others differed in their characterization of the essence and specific methodologies of nonscientific historiography and the kind of understanding it provides, holding that understanding in historiography is variously rational (Popper), intentional (the phenomenologists), empathetic understanding from "within" of human action (Collingwood), communicative (Frankfurt school hermeneuticists such as Karl Otto Apel), or a kind of textual interpretation (hermeneutics as employed by Paul Ricoeur).

In the twentieth century, Karl Marx was believed by some of his followers to have discovered the laws of history. Partly as a reaction against Marxist claims, philosophers such as Popper, Isaiah Berlin, and W.H. Walsh, attempted to prove on *epistemological* grounds that if not impossible, scientific history is highly improbable. Since their image of science was positivist, many of their arguments were raised against historiography conceived of as a positivist science, deterministic, mechanistic, prognostic, and deduced from other sciences (psychology and/or the social sciences). Three *metaphysical* issues influence the probability of scientific historiography in the post-positivist sense of science: the uniqueness, chaos, and complexity of history. If historical events are unique, nonrepetitive, and irreducible to more basic elements, it is then impossible to confirm or test generalizing scientific theories about them. History may also be too complex and chaotic for testing even stochastic and nonprognostic theories. Conflicting metaphysical speculations about the uniqueness, chaos, and complexity of history abound.

In regard to the second definition, consistent historiographic rigorous critical examination of, and search for, evidence started in Germany in the second half of the nineteenth century with Leopold von Ranke. This new disciplinary methodology deserved the German title *Wissenschaft*, which translated into English as either "critical history" or "scientific history." It was used, in this sense, by J.B. Bury, in his famous declaration that "History is a science, nothing more and nothing less." Since in English "science" is more closely associated with the methodology of the natural sciences, "critical historiography" is probably a more accurate term to describe definition 2.

Aviezer Tucker

See also CHAOS THEORY AND HISTORY; DETERMINISM; PHILOSOPHY OF HISTORY—ANALYTICAL.

References
Berlin, Isaiah. "The Concept of Scientific History." In *Philosophical Analysis and History*, ed. William H. Dray. New York: Harper and Row, 1966, 5–53.

Walsh, W.H. "The Limits of Scientific History." Also in Dray, 54–74.

Scottish Historiography

Historical writing in Scotland, medieval to modern. The first systematic history of Scotland emerged in the fourteenth century as a patriotic response to the assertions of England's Plantagenet monarchs that they possessed a suzerainty over Scotland. Edward I's attempt to realize his claim had, from the 1290s, ushered in a bitter and prolonged struggle between the kingdoms, which in turn catalyzed an emerging sense of Scottish nationhood. In furtherance of his case, Edward I had exploited Geoffrey of Monmouth's legendary history of the origins of Britain, and the leaders of the Scottish nation were forced to contrive an answer rebutting the myth found in the twelfth-century *Historia Regum Britanniae*, according to which the eldest son of Brutus, the first King of Britain, had succeeded to England, while Scotland had been the portion of a younger son. In its stead, Scottish jurists and chroniclers began to mould an alternative account of the originally and continuously independent history of the Scots kingdom and nation. Elements of this patriotic story can be traced in Scottish pleadings at the papal curia around 1300 and in the Declaration of Arbroath (1320), the patriotic manifesto that celebrated the conclusion of the most critical phase of Anglo-Scottish warfare. However, the myth's full realization as a major piece of historical writing came only in the chronicle of John of Fordun (ca. 1320–ca. 1384) and its continuation by Walter Bower (ca. 1385–1449). At the heart of the Scottish historical tradition founded by Fordun, which continued to dominate the expression of national identity until the early eighteenth century, was the myth of the ancient foundation of the independent Scottish kingdom in 330 B.C. under the legendary Fergus MacFerquhard. This patriotic history depended on a spurious lineage of about forty early kings, and the defense of this ancient line against the efforts of antiquaries from other parts of the British Isles to demolish it was to become one of the principal constituents of Scottish historiography.

In the sixteenth century, two prominent humanists, Hector Boece (ca. 1465–1536) and George Buchanan (1506–1582), rendered the myth of Scottish antiquity into an immaculate Latinity and presented it in the idiom of Livian civic virtue. Boece's history of Scotland, published in 1527, was popularized in a Scots vernacular translation by John Bellenden (ca. 1490–ca. 1550). It traced the history of the Scots nation from its mythical ancient origins and couched the political history of the kingdom in the form of a *speculum principis* [mirror of princes], whose narrative content was to recur in Buchanan's works as the evidential basis for an antimonarchical ideology. Of necessity, Buchanan's humanism had evolved differently from Boece's. Buchanan began his scholarly career an adherent of Erasmian philology, but as the prospects for humanist reform within the

Catholic Church declined, became a champion of Protestantism, and thus ended up espousing a fully fledged Calvinist resistance theory. Buchanan's *Rerum Scoticarum Historia* (1582) incorporates some of his wider philological interests, but should be read in tandem with his political tract *De Iure Regni Apud Scotos* [Concerning the Law of Kingship among the Scots] (1579), which interprets the Scottish monarchy as limited, accountable and, in cases of tyranny, liable to the ultimate sanction of deposition by an ill-defined body of the nation, a thesis that legitimated the imposition of the Reformation upon, and then overthrow of, Mary, Queen of Scots.

The main exception to the patriotic tradition established by Fordun was the work of John Mair, or Major (1467–1550), a late scholastic who authored the punningly titled history of Great Britain, *Britanniae Majoris Historia* (1521). This was a sophisticated work that criticized the chauvinistic origin legends of both England and Scotland, an exercise presumably linked to Major's overall strategy of promoting Anglo-Scottish reconciliation. However, Major's unfortunate combination of skepticism and British aspirations proved less influential within Scottish historiography than the patriotic tradition he had set out to revise. Although the presence of Scots in Scotland before the fifth century A.D. was contested by antiquarians in other parts of the British Isles, such as Humphrey Llwyd of Wales in his *Breviary of Britayne* (Latin edition 1568; English translation 1572), it remained a shibboleth of Scottish identity, shaping the agenda of seventeenth-century polemical antiquarianism. Despite the continuing defense of Scotland's origin myths, early modern Scottish historiography was receptive to a variety of intellectual influences—humanism, stoicism, providentialism—which, it has been argued, were to nourish the sophisticated historical writing associated with Scotland's celebrated eighteenth-century Enlightenment.

The Scottish Reformation stimulated a vigorous tradition of ecclesiastical historiography pioneered by the founding father of Scottish Protestantism, John Knox (ca. 1514–1572), in his *History of the Reformation in Scotland*. The ambiguous legacy of Scottish Reformed principles in the sphere of church government was to lead to a hardening of divisions between rival Episcopalian and Presbyterian camps, each with its own historical champion, respectively, Archbishop John Spottiswoode (1565–1637) and David Calderwood (1575–1650). A resilient antiquarian tradition began in the seventeenth century with Sir James

Balfour of Denmilne (ca. 1598–1657). Balfour's magpie zeal for the collection of historical documents was followed by the polymathic antiquarianism of Sir Robert Sibbald (1641–1722), a distinguished geographer and naturalist. Sibbald investigated national and local antiquities in several monographs and unpublished manuscripts, and he contributed Scottish material to the edition of William Camden's *Britannia* produced in 1695 under the auspices of Edmund Gibson. The antiquarian tradition continued to flower in the eighteenth century, but was eclipsed by the decidedly unantiquarian style of historiography associated with the Scottish Enlightenment. Nevertheless Father Thomas Innes (1662–1744), an émigré priest associated with the Scots College in Paris, exploded the national myth of a line of Scottish kings stretching back to Fergus MacFerquhard in 330 B.C. A disciple of the art of diplomatic pioneered by Mabillon, Innes identified the canonical line of the first forty monarchs as spurious accretions of later medieval forgeries that had duped the credulous patriot Hector Boece, who had believed them to be authentic regnal lists of a much earlier provenance. Other antiquaries such as James Anderson (1662–1728); the Jacobite scholar, publisher, and librarian Thomas Ruddiman (1674–1757); and Sir David Dalrymple, Lord Hailes (1726–1792) also made important contributions in other areas.

Some historians have argued that the Union of 1707, which incorporated England and Scotland within the united kingdom of Great Britain, provoked a crisis of identity that found expression in patriotic historiography, for example *The Martial Atchievements of the Scots Nation* (1711–1715) by the Jacobite (that is, supporter of the ousted Stuart dynasty) antiquarian Patrick Abercromby (1656–1716?). Nevertheless, partisan identities were also a marked feature of historical writing in this period. There was considerable jousting between Whig Presbyterian and Jacobite Episcopalian schools of interpretation. The most celebrated product of this culture of historical contestation was the Presbyterian classic by the Reverend Robert Wodrow, *The History of the Sufferings of the Church of Scotland* (1721–1722), which dealt with the experience of the persecuted Covenanters during the Episcopalian regime of the Restoration era.

The Scottish Enlightenment of the mid-eighteenth century was in some respects the golden age of Scottish historiography, though history thrived less as a discipline in its own right than as a branch of a broadly conceived moral philosophy embracing ethics, jurisprudence, and the nascent social sciences. Figures such as David Hume (1711–1776), Henry Home, Lord Kames (1696–1782), William Robertson (1721–1793), John Millar (1735–1801), and Adam Smith (1723–1790), in the lectures he delivered on jurisprudence, all made notable advances in historical method. Hume was a harsh critic of vulgar philosophical errors in history, such as theories of ancient-constitutional prescription that ignored the vast gulf in institutional forms between antiquity and the present. Kames elaborated a theory of conjectural back-projection that would enable historians to construct plausible hypotheses as a means both of filling lacunae in the historical record and of reconstructing the society of preliterate primitive man. One of the hallmarks of the Scottish Enlightenment was stadialism, a conjectural account of the progress of mankind through three or four stages of economic, social, and cultural development from the savagery of the hunter-gatherer state to the refinement of commercial modernity. Yet the achievement of the Scottish Enlightenment was not an unqualified success. Philosophical history and a pioneering historical sociology flourished at the expense of antiquarian values. The likes of Hume and Robertson were cavalier in their approach to archival research, while the antiquarian tradition represented by Hailes was desiccated because unfertilized by the new theoretical insights. Another major question mark over the contribution of the Scottish Enlightenment to a Scottish historical discipline arises from its general disregard for the importance of the Scottish past as a worthy subject of the new history. Although Robertson completed a *History of Scotland* (1759), Millar treated the history of Scotland as a subsection of his *Historical View of the English Government* (1787), Hume having already pointedly transformed a project begun as *The History of Great Britain* into *The History of England*.

It fell to Sir Walter Scott (1771–1832) to unite the antiquarian and philosophical traditions, and to renew interest in Scotland's own distinctive past. The Scottish sequence within Scott's *Waverley Novels,* including *Waverley* itself, *The Antiquary* and *Old Mortality,* explained to contemporary Scots in vivid terms the transformation of their fractious, martial, and crisis-ridden nation of the early modern period into a refined and commercial civil society. Scott's novels not only had a tremendous impact on the development of the historical novel throughout Europe and North America, but also stimulated historians such as Thomas Babington Macaulay to a greater interest

S

in the uses of folklore as a source for the writing of social history, and in a novelistic pacing and presentation of narrative history. Scott was also actively involved in the establishment of the Bannatyne Club (1823), which started a fashion for the creation of historical clubs dedicated to the publication of the records and texts of Scottish history. However, this successful trend imploded into sectarian sniping with the establishment of the Wodrow Society (1841) and the Spottiswoode Society (1843), sponsoring, respectively, rival Presbyterian and Episcopalian publications. Although Patrick Fraser Tytler (1791–1849) and John Hill Burton (1809–1881) produced monumental multivolume national histories, the Scottish past had lost political significance. Scottish history became a scene of romantic escapism and local color, fenced off from a Whig saga of state formation and constitutional evolution in which the wider experience of the British peoples was collapsed into the history of England.

The advent of professionalization and an anti-Whig revisionism has rejuvenated Scottish historiography, especially in the late twentieth century. There have been considerable successes in the medieval field, associated in particular with Geoffrey Barrow (b. 1924) and Archibald Duncan (b. 1926); for the Reformation period Gordon Donaldson (1913–1993) was magisterial. In the modern era, the main focus has been on social and economic history, where Christopher Smout (b. 1933) has produced the most significant achievement of modern Scottish historiography— a two-volume history of the Scottish people between the sixteenth and twentieth centuries. The Union of 1707 is at the heart of many current controversies. Were the causes of the union political or economic, and was the Scots parliament won over by bribery? Were the economic and cultural successes of Scotland in the age of Enlightenment a product of union, or of deeper indigenous trends? Indeed, the legacy of the parliamentary union has distorted the basic contours of Scottish historiography. Energies have been diverted from the political history of the period since 1707, an area that remains underdeveloped.

Colin Kidd

See also ENGLISH HISTORIOGRAPHY; IRISH HISTORIOGRAPHY.

References

Allan, D. *Virtue, Learning and the Scottish Enlightenment.* Edinburgh: Edinburgh University Press, 1993.

Ash, M. *The Strange Death of Scottish History.* Edinburgh: Ramsay Head Press, 1980.
Forbes, Duncan. *Hume's Philosophical Politics.* Cambridge, Eng.: Cambridge University Press, 1975.
Kidd, Colin. *Subverting Scotland's Past.* Cambridge, Eng.: Cambridge University Press, 1993.
McFarlane, I.D. *Buchanan.* London: Duckworth, 1980.
Mason, R.A. "Scotching the Brut." In *Scotland and England 1286–1815,* ed. R.A. Mason. Edinburgh: John Donald, 1987.
Scots Antiquaries and Historians. Dundee: Abertay Historical Society, 1972.

Sée, Henri (1864–1936)

French historian of economy, society, and ideas. Sée was born near Paris and educated at the Sorbonne. He joined the faculty of the University of Rennes in 1893 and remained there until ill health forced him to give up teaching in 1920. A remarkably productive retirement followed: he published twenty books and dozens of articles in the years 1920–1935. Although he was trained as a medievalist, Sée was especially interested in collectivities and institutions in France from the sixteenth century to the nineteenth. He wrote on rural classes and agrarian life, the history of commerce and industry, urbanism and capitalism, and political ideas of the Ancien Régime and also published philosophical and methodological articles. Despite his focus on economic subjects, he rejected strict historical materialism as well as social history based on legal classifications.

Bruce L. Venarde

Texts

Economic and Social Conditions in France during the Eighteenth Century. Trans. Edwin H. Zeydel. New York: Knopf, 1927.
The Economic Interpretation of History. Trans. Melvin M. Knight. New York: Adelphi Company, 1929.
Modern Capitalism, Its Origins and Evolution. Trans. Homer B. Vanderblue and Georges F. Doriot. New York: Adelphi Company, 1928.

References

Rébillon, Armand. *Henri Sée (1864–1936), sa vie et ses travaux* [Henri Sée (1864–1936): His Life and Works]. Rennes: Imprimerie Oberthur, 1936.

Seebohm, Frederic (1833–1912)

English historian and businessman. Born in Bradford as the son of a wool merchant, Frederic Seebohm had a busy life as a banker and a prominent public figure, as well as writing voluminously on history. His first historical interest was in Christianity, for which he wrote *The Oxford Reformers* (1867), *The Era of Protestant Revolution* (1874), and *The Christian Hypothesis* (1876). But the works for which Seebohm is most well known focused on early British society and agriculture, particularly *The English Village Community* (1883), *The Tribal System in Wales* (1895), and *Tribal Custom in Anglo-Saxon Law* (1902). Of these, *The English Village Community* was his most important book. Its main thesis was that the manorial system in medieval England had, in fact, been introduced to Britain in Roman times, reacting against the then commonly held view that it was primarily a Germanic importation during the early Anglo-Saxon period. Although this conclusion was soon to be overturned by P. Vinogradoff, F.W. Maitland, and others, Seebohm's synthetic and broadly comparative approach, mixing topographical analysis with the examination of documentary and other evidence drawn from England, Wales, and Germany, continued to command great respect long after his death. Always grounded in solid common sense, Seebohm's views on such subjects as the evolution of the medieval plough team and the essential precondition of serfdom for the development of manorialism still remain relevant for historians today.

John Langdon

Texts

The English Village Community. Cambridge, Eng.: Cambridge University Press, 1926.
The Oxford Reformers. London: Longmans, Green, 1896.
Tribal Custom in Anglo-Saxon Law. London: Longmans, Green, 1902.
The Tribal System in Wales. London and New York: Longmans, Green, 1895.

References

Stenton, F.M. "Frederic Seebohm." In *Preparatory to Anglo-Saxon England,* ed. F.M. Stenton and D. Stenton. Oxford: Clarendon Press, 1970.

Seeley, Sir John Robert (1834–1895)

English historian of imperialism. Born in London, Seeley studied classics at Christ's College, Cambridge before assuming the chair of Latin at University College, London. He returned to Cambridge in 1869 as Regius professor of modern history. He influenced the policy that, for the first time, accorded to the professional historian a full-fledged academic status in England. A Christian Socialist and a whig positivist, Seeley authored a controversial essay on Christian morality, *Ecce Homo* (1865), designed as a biography of Jesus as a man. His best historical work, *The Life and Times of Stein* (1878) extolled Prussian nationalism while deploring Napoleon's universal monarchy. Although renowned worldwide as the ideologue of British imperialism, Seeley, in his highly influential *Expansion of England* (1883) justified imperialism but refrained from espousing further conquests. Great Britain, according to him, had acquired the colonies in a state of absence of mind, and needed to preserve and consolidate its empire as an imperial confederation. Predominantly interested in political history, Seeley was a strong exponent of the study of history as a didactic science of state and statesmanship.

Pradip Bhaumik

Texts

The Expansion of England. Chicago: University of Chicago Press, 1971.
The Growth of British Policy. 2 vols. Cambridge, Eng.: Cambridge University Press, 1922.
The Life and Times of Stein. 3 vols. New York: Greenwood Press, 1968.

References

Kenyon, J.P. *The History Men.* Second ed. London: Weidenfeld and Nicolson, 1993.
Rein, Gustav A. *Sir John Robert Seeley: A Study of the Historian.* Trans. John L. Herkless. Wolfeboro, NH: Longwood Academic, 1987.
Wormell, Deborah. *Sir John Seeley and the Uses of History.* Cambridge, Eng.: Cambridge University Press, 1980.

Seignobos, Charles (1854–1942)

French historian. Seignobos trained at the École Normale under the tutelage of the educational reformer and historian Ernest Lavisse. In 1877 he toured a number of Rhenish universities. He was impressed by the rigor of German source criticism, but appalled by what he deemed the myopic vision of German historiography. In 1890 Seignobos began a long and prestigious career at the Sorbonne. In collaboration with the medievalist Charles-Victor Langlois, he taught an innovative and influential historiography class. The two exhorted their students to eschew the rhetorical tradition of French historiography in favor of the new methodology that is now often called "positivist." According to Seignobos, history ought to be "a science of reasoning," in which the scholar takes the facts that he has gleaned from texts and synthesizes them in order to form generalizations. He set out these principles in a pair of textbooks. In 1898 he coauthored with Langlois an *Introduction aux études historiques* [Introduction to Historical Studies]; then, in 1901 he authored by himself *La Méthode historique appliquée aux sciences sociales* [The Historical Method Applied to the Social Sciences], a work influenced by Durkheimian sociology. Although he wrote numerous books of history, Seignobos is remembered primarily as a pedagogue. He endeavored to imbue in his students the liberal values of the Third Republic. Emblematic of this liberalism were the apologia that he penned in defense of the beleaguered Captain Alfred Dreyfus. His political stance riled Catholic conservatives, who stormed his classes and accused him, a nonpracticing Protestant, of corrupting his students with radical ideas. By the early 1930s, Seignobos was considered to be anything but radical. Led by Lucien Febvre, the Annalistes assailed both his bourgeois values and what they believed to be his narrow, fact-oriented, methodology.

Edward Michalik

Texts

L'éducation de la démocratie: Leçons professées à l'école des hautes études sociales [The Education of the Democracy: Lessons Taught at the School of Advanced Social Studies]. Paris: F. Alcan, 1903.

The Evolution of the French People. Trans. Catherine Philips. New York: A.A. Knopf, 1932.

With Charles-Victor Langlois. *Introduction to the Study of History.* Trans. G.G. Berry. New York: Henry Holt and Company, 1925.

References

Keylor, William. *Academy and Community: The Foundation of the French Historical Profession.* Cambridge, MA: Harvard University Press, 1975.

Moody, Joseph. "The Third Republic and the Church: A Case History of Three French Historians." *The Catholic Historical Review* 66 (1980): 1–15.

Noiriel, Gérard. "Une Histoire sociale du politique est-elle possible? [A Social History of Politics: Is It Possible?]." *Vingtième siècle* 24 (1989): 81–96.

Selden, John (1584–1654)

English antiquary, jurist, and politician. Born in Sussex, according to one account the son of a local musician, Selden was educated at Hart Hall, Oxford, where he developed an interest in English and European antiquities. He subsequently attended the Inner Temple and was called to the bar in 1612. A longtime steward to Henry Grey, earl of Kent (and perhaps, later, the lover of the earl's widow), Selden served in several parliaments of the early seventeenth century, his command of foreign languages and of English legal archives proving indispensable to parliamentarians in search of precedents in their disputes with James I and Charles I. He was briefly imprisoned for his parliamentary activities in 1621 and again in 1629. Although no puritan, he remained in London as a supporter of the Long Parliament during the English civil wars, but his moderate, erastian views on religion caused his influence on events to wane. Selden's earliest writings, such as *Jani Anglorum* [The English Janus], concerned the development of English laws and government from ancient times through the Norman Conquest and presented a more sophisticated version of England's "ancient constitution" than that articulated by another common lawyer, Sir Edward Coke (1552–1634). He broadened his views in a magisterial survey of European ranks, *Titles of Honor* (1614; expanded edition 1632) and various works on parliamentary privilege. Later in life, he began to move away from the study of English legal antiquities to broader issues of natural law. He became engaged in a debate with the Dutch scholar Hugo Grotius, against whom he defended (in his *Mare Clausum*, written about 1618 and first published in 1635) the Stuart kings' right to treat the English channel as a British possession rather than a "free sea." But perhaps Selden's most significant historical achievement was *The History of Tithes*. This work, which appeared in print in 1618, was based on an enormous range of documentary material, in addition to old chronicles, and in several languages. It traced the history of tithing practices from biblical times to his own day and challenged the notion (although Selden denied doing any such thing) that the right of clergy to tithes had always existed. This embroiled him in a controversy with several opponents, lay and clerical, and in which he was ordered to refrain from defending himself. The work is significant not just for its sources, but for its very title: Selden was the first English historian to conceive of his subject—which previously would have been considered proper material for an antiquary rather than a historian—as history; conversely, this allowed him to redefine history, in the manner of French sixteenth-century scholars who had influenced his thought, as embracing the past *in toto,* not just the history of kings and wars. Still a useful source on its subject after four centuries, it was a potent influence on English historical thought in the seventeenth century.

D.R. Woolf

Texts

Ad Fletam dissertatio. Ed. David Ogg. New York: Hein and Co., 1980.
The Historie of Tithes. London: n.p., 1618.
Titles of Honor. Second ed. London: R. Whitaker, 1632.

References

Berkowitz, David S. *Young John Selden's Formative Years: Politics and Society in Early Seventeenth-Century England.* Washington, DC: Folger Shakespeare Library, 1988.
Christianson, Paul. *Discourse on History, Law, and Governance in the Public Career of John Selden, 1610–1635.* Toronto: University of Toronto Press, 1996.
———. "Young John Selden and the Ancient Constitution, 1610–1618." *Proceedings of the American Philosophical Society* 128 (1984): 271–315.
Woolf, D.R. *The Idea of History in Early Stuart England.* Toronto: University of Toronto Press, 1990, 200–242.

Serbian Historiography

Historical writing by and about the Serbian people, principally since 1800. Serbian historiography, which implicitly acknowledges the existence of the Serbs as a separate people, has been closely connected to the political evolution of the Serbian and Yugoslav states, but it also reveals the autonomous development of a scientific and professional tradition. Four main stages can be discerned in the development of Serbian historiography: traditional historiography; the critical school of Ilarion Ruvarac and his followers; the Communist–Marxist legacy; and the renewed Serbian nationalist movement.

Serbian historiography before 1800 heavily leaned upon the tradition of folk songs and the chronicles of its own saints and kings. It was enriched by the Chronicles of Count Branković, the main source of historical knowledge of the Serbs until the appearance of Jovan Rajić's *Istorija* (1794–1795), which in turn provided the spiritual inspiration for the Serbian revolution of 1804. During the nineteenth century the traditional historical school, the major representatives of which were the Belgrade professor and academician P. Srećković and the historian Č. Mijatović, continued to build upon this heritage. Challenging in particular the opinions of Srećković, Ilarion Ruvarac (1832–1905) developed his own critical method of historic enquiry. Carefully checking all available sources and rejecting mythological and purely patriotic elements, Ruvarac shed new light on several questions of Serbian national historiography, such as the role of Vuk Branković in the battle of Kosovo, the murder by Vukašin on Czar Uroš, the immigration of the Serbs to Vojvodina, and the autonomy of Montenegro during Turkish rule. He also inspired his followers in the period until the outbreak of World War I, to put Serbian historiography on a higher level. One of these followers was Stanoje Stanojević, author of the *Istorija sprskog naroda* [History of the Serbs] (1908), and in the same period, the Czech K. Jireček made a significant contribution to Serbian historiography with his broad but analytical *Geschichte der Serben* [History of the Serbs] (1918), in which he confirmed a number of Ruvarac's theses. The interwar period brought further progress with contributions by various historians, such as Slobodan Jovanović, and in 1933, V. Ćorović published his authoritatively and very popular *Istorija Jugoslavije* [History of Yugoslavia]. On the other hand, Serbian historiography regained its nationalistic ethos in the writings of J. Cvijić and V. Ćubrilović.

Historiography was given a new direction after World War II by the introduction of the Marxist paradigm at the installation of the Tito regime. Political and diplomatic history was supplemented by analytical studies of the economic and social development of Yugoslavia, for example in two multiauthored works, the two-volume *Istorija naroda Jugoslavije,* edited by Mihailo Dinić (1953–1959), and *Istorija Jugoslavije,* edited by Ivan Božić (1972). But Marxist historiography quickly showed its limitations in the rigidly orthodox manner in which it interpreted political and social movements (especially in recent history), and in its utter neglect of certain taboo themes. The axiom of unity and brotherhood likewise excluded the treatment of sensitive issues of nationalism. After the death of Tito and with the gradual decline of the federal Communist Party, these previously forbidden historical themes were presented to the public, and not always in a way that respected the canons of high professional work. An early step in this direction was the attack on Tito by his earlier official biographer Vladimir Dedijer, in a work entitled *Novi Prilozi za Biografiju Josipa Broza Tita* [New Contributions to the Biography of Josip Broz Tito]. An outspoken and openly political piece of work was the *Memorandum* produced by the Serbian Academy of Arts and Sciences of 1986, as was Vojislav Koštunica's study of the historical role of the Communists in the elimination of the multiparty system. Just as it had during the heyday of communism, Serbian historiography in recent years has assumed a highly polemical role. Under the constant pressure of Serbian nationalism and continuing war, it does not seem likely at present that historiography will soon establish for itself an autonomous space of the sort it enjoyed in the days of Ruvarac.

Robert Stallaerts

See also CROATIAN HISTORIOGRAPHY.

References

Banac, Ivo. "Historiography of the Countries of Eastern Europe: Yugoslavia." *American Historical Review* 97 (1992): 1084–1104.

Božić, Ivan, et al. eds. *Istorija Jugoslavije.* Belgrade: Prosveta, 1972.

Dedijer, Vladimir et al. *History of Yugoslavia.* Trans. Kordija Kveder. New York: McGraw-Hill, 1974.

———. *Novi Prilozi za Biografiju Josipa Broza Tita.* 3 vols. Zagreb: Mladost, 1980–1984.

Dix Années d'Historiographie Yougoslave [Ten Years of Yugoslav Historiography]. Belgrade: Savez Istorijskih Društava Jugoslavije [League of Historical Societies], 1955.

Janković, Dragoslav, ed. *The Historiography of Yugoslavia 1965–1975.* Belgrade: The Association of Yugoslav Historical Societies, 1975.

Jiriček, K. *Istorija Srba* [History of the Serbs]. Trans. Jovan Radonić. Belgrade: Naučna Knjiga, 1952.

Koštunica, Vojislav, and Kosta Čavoški. *Party Pluralism or Monism: Social Movements and the Political System in Yugoslavia, 1944–1949.* East European Monographs, Social Science Monographs, no. 189. New York: Columbia University Press, n.d.

Tadić, Jorgo. *Historiographie Yougoslave. 1955–65.* [Historiography of Yugoslavia, 1955–1965.] Belgrade: Savez Istorijskih Društava Jugoslavije, 1965.

Serial History

Form of historical writing based on quantitative analysis of statistical series, pioneered in France in the 1930s and popular internationally into the 1980s. Serial history, which was influenced by the work of the economist François Simiand, was first practiced by French economic historians. In its earliest form, it entailed elaborating statistical series for such variables as prices, wages, profits, production, and trade, with a view toward identifying long- and short-term fluctuations in the economy. Seminal works in this genre include Ernest Labrousse, *Esquisse du mouvement des prix et des revenus en France au XVIIIe siècle* [Sketch of the Movement of Prices and Incomes in Eighteenth-Century France] (1933) and Pierre and Huguette Chaunu, *Séville et l'Atlantique, 1540–1650* [Seville and the Atlantic] (1955–1959).

In subsequent decades, serial history was extended to other fields of endeavor, notably demographic, social, and cultural history, and began to be practiced outside of France. In the demographic sphere, historians used parish registers and census records to establish series of births, marriages, and deaths, which enabled them to discuss average ages at marriage and death, rates of fecundity and illegitimacy, and other aspects of family structure. Owing to the slowness of family reconstitution, even when computer-assisted, investigators often focused on individual communities. Examples of such local studies are Étienne Gautier and Louis Henry, *La Population de Crulai, paroisse normande* [The Population of Crulai, a Norman Parish] (1958) and Kenneth Lockridge, *A New England Town: The First Hundred Years, Dedham, Massachusetts, 1636–1737* (1970). Other, more ambitious monographs dealt with entire regions, and combined serial analysis of both economics and demography. Classic works of this type include Pierre Goubert, *Beauvais et le Beauvaisis de 1600 à 1730* [Beauvais and the Beauvaisis from 1600 to 1730] (1960), Emmanuel Le Roy Ladurie, *Les Paysans de Languedoc* [The Peasants of Languedoc] (1966), and David Herlihy and Christiane Klapisch-Zuber, *Les Toscans et leurs familles* [Tuscans and Their Families] (1978). Also combining economics and demography, but paying particular attention to patterns of migration, is Jean-Pierre Poussou, *Bordeaux et le Sud-Ouest au XVIIIe siècle* [Bordeaux and the Southwest in the Eighteenth Century] (1983). A general work based on serial demography is Peter Laslett, *The World We Have Lost* (1965).

In the area of social history, serial analysis of tax rolls, probate records, marriage contracts, and voter lists was used to define social categories, for example, the nineteenth-century French bourgeoisie, in terms of economic position, legal status, and professional activity. Collective behavior could also be examined serially, as shown by Michelle Perrot in *Les Ouvriers en Grève, France 1871–1890* [Workers on Strike] (1974). In the 1970s, historians began to employ serial documents to help construct a history of attitudes, or *mentalités*. Michel Vovelle, for example, was able to describe changing patterns of religious observance in eighteenth-century Provence based on quantification of a series of wills.

Leslie Choquette

See also ANNALES SCHOOL; CLIOMETRICS; DEMOGRAPHY—HISTORICAL; ECONOMIC HISTORY; FAMILY HISTORY (COMPARATIVE); FAMILY RECONSTITUTION.

Texts

Chaunu, Pierre, and Huguette Chaunu. *Séville et l'Amérique aux XVIᵉ et XVIIᵉ siècles*. Paris: Flammarion, 1977.

Daumard, Adeline. *Les Bourgeois et la bourgeoisie en France depuis 1815*. Paris: Aubier, 1987.

Gautier, Étienne, and Louis Henry. *La Population de Crulai, paroisse normande: Étude historique*. Paris: Presses universitaires de France, 1958.

Goubert, Pierre. *Beauvais et le Beauvaisis de 1600 à 1730*. Paris: SEVPEN, 1960.

Herlihy, David, and Christiane Klapisch-Zuber. *Tuscans and Their Families: A Study of the Florentine Catasto of 1427*. New Haven, CT: Yale University Press, 1985.

Labrousse, Ernest. *Esquisse du mouvement des prix et des revenus en France au XVIIIᵉ siècle*. 2 vols. Paris: Editions des archives contemporaines, 1984.

Laslett, Peter. *The World We Have Lost: Further Explored*. Third ed. London: Methuen, 1983.

Le Roy Ladurie, Emmanuel. *The Peasants of Languedoc*. Trans. John Day. Urbana: University of Illinois Press, 1974.

Lockridge, Kenneth. *A New England Town: The First Hundred Years, Dedham, Massachusetts, 1636–1737*. Second ed. New York: Norton, 1985.

Perrot, Michelle. *Workers on Strike: France, 1871–1890*. Trans. Chris Turner. New Haven, CT: Yale University Press, 1987.

Poussou, Jean-Pierre. *Bordeaux et le Sud-Ouest au XVIIIᵉ siècle*. Paris: J. Touzot, 1983.

Vovelle, Michel. *Piété baroque et déchristianisation en Provence au XVIIIᵉ siècle*. Paris: Plon, 1973.

References

Chaunu, Pierre. *Histoire quantitative, histoire sérielle*. Paris: Armand Colin, 1978.

Le Roy Ladurie, Emmanuel. *The Territory of the Historian*. Trans. Ben and Siân Reynolds. Chicago: University of Chicago Press, 1979.

Seton-Watson, Robert William (1879–1951)

Scottish historian. Born in Perthshire to a well-known family, he graduated with distinction from New College. Eventually renowned for his expertise in European history, his early impact was as a publicist. Essays in the *Spectator,* writing as "Scotus Viator," foreshadowed his impact on central Europe and contretemps with the Magyars. During the "Great War" he worked at Crewe House (Department of Propaganda in Enemy Countries), an appendage of the Department of Information Intelligence Bureau. His governmental assignment, scholarly interests, and work with the Serbian Relief Fund, provided ample background for veiled consultations at the Paris Peace Conference; he is considered by many as the single individual most responsible for the demise of the Habsburg monarchy. From 1922 until 1945 he served as Masaryk professor at the University of London, where he coedited *Slavonic and East European Studies*. Then, at Oxford, until his retirement in 1949, he lectured as professor in Czechoslovak studies. As expert on British foreign policy as on the ethnic complexities of eastern Europe, he published widely and with distinction.

William O. Oldson

Texts

Britain in Europe, 1789–1914. New York: Macmillan, 1937.

Disraeli, Gladstone and the Eastern Question. London: F. Cass, 1971.

A History of the Czechs and Slovaks. Hamden, CT: Archon, 1965.

A History of the Roumanians. New York: Anchor, 1963.

Racial Problems in Hungary. London: Constable, 1908.

The Rise of Nationality in the Balkans. New York: H. Fertig, 1966.

References

Obituaries from the Times. Reading: Newspaper Archive Developments, 1979.

Sexuality

By any measure the body of historical writings on sexuality is both recent and enormous in volume. In the early 1950s when Gordon Rattray Taylor began his book *Sex in History* (1954), not even the "full assistance" of the authorities in the British Museum reading room could produce for him a single reliable history of sexuality on which he could base his own research. By the canons of the professional historiography of his day, Taylor was more or less correct in his appraisal, though there were abundant published materials available that were not, strictly speaking, historical in nature. Still, the flood of work, especially since the mid-1970s, on every aspect of the history of sexuality has been impressive. There are now journals and book series devoted solely to the history of sexuality and widespread interest in the subject among historians and scholars in related disciplines.

Taylor also complained of the tendentiousness, inclining either toward the "scandalous or the moralistic," inherent in earlier writings on sexuality, but his efforts to write an objective history of sexuality were marked by his own bias against the last vestiges of Victorian culture, still intent on repressing publicity about sexuality or spiritualizing it to achieve more civilized standards of behavior. The issues are at present different, but the temptations of advocacy are no less strong for contemporary scholars. This may be an occupational hazard for students of sexuality in any discipline.

Although he did not acknowledge it, Taylor was himself the heir of late-nineteenth-century medical and anthropological specialists on sexuality who were interested in sex as a natural phenomenon, and who often used historical materials as raw material or illustrations for their work. Richard von Krafft-Ebing, Havelock Ellis, Magnus Hirschfeld, Sigmund Freud, Paolo Mantegazza and the other pioneers of modern sexology relied, more or less uncritically, on accounts of sexuality outside the modern European experience to undergird their essentially enlightened views on the natural variations of sex in nature and society. Although they replaced history with the oral interview or with laboratory methods, Alfred Kinsey, Virginia Johnson, and William Masters fit nicely into this scientific tradition, as pointed out by Vern Bullough.

Freud and his generation were thus the first to name and identify the sexual perversions—masochism, sadism, fetishism, homosexuality, and others—making it possible to conceive of people as masochists, sadists, homosexuals, and the like.

The reformist aim of the experts who "medicalized" sexuality in the 1880s and 1890s was to identify individuals who were sick and to propose cures rather than punishments for their condition. However, a number of repressive laws were drafted in this era in Austria, Germany, Great Britain, and the United States aimed at both public and private sexuality that were heavily dependent on descriptions of the new sexual perversions, so that by 1900 or so unconventional sexual behavior was scrutinized, punished, and treated more aggressively than ever before. Despite their own progressive agendas, it has been impossible, in the end, for modern historians of sexuality to eschew this medicalized terminology, and thus avoid indirectly endorsing the ideological implications that flow from it.

The task of the first scholarly histories of sexuality was to subject Victorian intolerance and repressiveness to intensive criticism. In *The Other Victorians* (1964), Steven Marcus painted an account of Victorian sexuality that emphasized the rigidity of its code of sexual respectability. For Marcus, pornography, prostitution, and perversion were the necessary dialectical opposites of this "official" respectability, the wages of its hypocrisy. The history of prostitution particularly thrived on the exposure of the double standard that consigned some women to "madonna" and others to "magdalene" status, while permitting men to choose unconstrainedly between the two. The best of these histories, by Judith Walkowitz and Alain Corbin, have revealed the extent of medical complicity in the construction of a regulated regime of prostitution designed to ensure clients and respectable society a certain degree of protection.

Another driving force in the earliest modern writings was the effort to portray the history of homosexuality and lesbianism as tragically marked by the efforts of orthodox heterosexual culture to segregate these sexual minorities medically and legally (see, for instance, the books by Carroll Smith-Rosenberg and Jeffrey Weeks). Sexologists and purity crusaders have been the villains in these accounts, and pioneer sex reformers and sexual martyrs the heroes and heroines. Almost from the beginning, the history of homosexuality has been dominated by the split in contemporary sexual politics between the "essentialists" and the "social constructionists," usefully summed up in a famous essay by the late John Boswell published in the 1989 anthology *Hidden from History.* The question whether homosexuals are born or constructed has thus exercised a certain tyranny over the whole of the history of sexuality and has even constituted much of the research agenda of specialists in human sexuality. Most authors have learned to treat this issue in a nuanced way, but the pressure of contemporary politics ensures no one can avoid it.

The single most important methodological and epistemological contribution to the field was made in 1976 by the French philosopher Michel Foucault in the first volume of his *History of Sexuality*. Foucault challenged the interpretation of the Victorian sexual order as self-consciously repressive, arguing instead that it was the Victorians' obsession with sexuality that generated the voluminous literature both on the perversions and on "normal" heterosexual, reproductive sex. This insight has been unusually fruitful for the most recent generation of historians. Many historians, such as David F. Greenberg, David Halperin, and Robert Nye, have attempted to complete Foucault's unfulfilled agenda by revealing how medically constructed sexual identities have provided ready-made sociocognitive models that constrained, in their respective ways, the sexual freedom of individuals. Foucault was discounting the idea common in the 1970s that the emancipation from orthodox sexual norms and the dismantling of the legal apparatus of sexual regulation was equivalent to full, personal sexual emancipation. He thus effectively undermined the enlightened aspirations of the previous generation of historians bent on exposing the evils of the legal regulation of sexuality.

The history of sexuality after Foucault has largely incorporated his insights while avoiding his extreme linguistic determinism. Past sexual identities are now usually portrayed as historically constructed but "real," and, in a development that perhaps signals the normalization of the field, social history has begun to replace the intellectual and ideological emphases of the 1970s. As a consequence, there is now greater weight placed on "sexualities" than on a single hegemonic code or ideal of sexuality, and this classificational pluralism has also come to include "homosexualities," "masculinities," and "femininities" (see for instance the works listed below by Mason, D'Emilio and Freedman, and Connell). Class, nationality, ethnicity, religion, and region are now recognized as important influences on sexual norms and behavior: notable examples are the contributions to the 1992 collection edited by Andrew Parker, and George Chauncey's 1995 study of *Gay New York*. Social history has also provided us a greater appreciation of the subtle influences on sexuality that occur on cultural borders, such as those that have occurred in the imperial domains of numerous European powers.

The rich detail of social history also permits us to appreciate the entire spectrum of human sexuality that has perhaps always flourished between the essentially ideological boundaries of asceticism and sexual license, male and female. Sexual passion, as Peter Gay has noted, flourished at the height of Victorian prudery, or within the religious orders of the medieval and early modern church (as in the case study by Judith Brown of Benedetta Carlini, a seventeenth-century Italian abbess); and George Mosse has shown that powerful homosexual impulses have emerged at the very heart of wholly masculine enterprises. Scholars such as Thomas Laqueur have also told us in convincing detail that bodies are essentially ambiguous things whose sexed and gendered identities have changed over time, or, occasionally, within the lifetimes of willful individuals like the Chevalier D'Eon (the subject of a study by Gary Kates) who, although a man, dressed as a woman during the last half of his life.

Finally, historians of sexuality have fruitfully demonstrated the powerful role that sexual metaphors have played in social, political, and cultural history. Lynn Hunt and Sara Maza, for instance, have shown in their respective books that individuals and sometimes entire regimes are crippled or empowered through their popular association with particular sexual narratives and imagery. Research by other scholars (Joel Schwartz on Rousseau and Dorinda Outram on the body in the French Revolution, to cite but two examples) has also revealed the extent to which sexual metaphors and assumptions about sexuality have constituted much of the history of political and social theory in the West.

Robert A. Nye

See also FEMINISM; GENDER; PATRIARCHY; PUBLIC/PRIVATE, HISTORICAL DIVISION OF; SOCIAL HISTORY; WOMEN'S HISTORY.

References

Brown, Judith. *Immodest Acts: The Life of a Lesbian Nun in Renaissance Italy*. New York: Oxford University Press, 1991.

Bullough, Vern. *Science in the Bedroom: A History of Sex Research*. New York: Basic books, 1994.

Chauncey, George. *Gay New York*. New York: Basic Books, 1995.

Connell, R.W. *Masculinities*. London: Polity Press, 1995.

Corbin, Alain. *Women for Hire. Prostitution and Sexuality in France after 1850*. Cambridge, MA: Harvard University Press, 1990.

D'Emilio, John and Freedman, Estelle. *Intimate Matters: A History of Sexuality in America.* New York: Harper and Row, 1988.

Duberman, Martin, et al. *Hidden from History: Reclaiming the Gay and Lesbian Past.* New York: NAL, 1989.

Foucault, Michel. *The History of Sexuality,* vol 1. Trans. Robert Hurley. New York: Random House, 1978.

Gay, Peter. *The Bourgeois Experience.* 2 vols. New York: Oxford University Press, 1984–1986.

Greenberg, David F. *The Construction of Homosexuality.* Chicago: University of Chicago Press, 1988.

Halperin, David. *One Hundred Years of Homosexuality.* New York: Routledge, 1990.

Hunt, Lynn. *The Family Romance of the French Revolution.* Berkeley: University of California Press, 1994.

Kates, Gary. *Monsieur D'Eon Is a Woman.* New York: Basic Books, 1995.

Laqueur, Thomas. *Making Sex: Body and Gender from the Greeks to Freud.* Cambridge, MA: Harvard University Press, 1990.

Mason, Michael. *The Making of Victorian Sexuality.* New York: Oxford University Press, 1994.

Maza, Sara. *Public Lives, Private Affairs.* Berkeley: University of California Press, 1993.

Mosse, George. *Nationalism and Sexuality.* New York: Fertig, 1985.

Nye, Robert. *Masculinity and Male Codes of Honor in Modern France.* New York: Oxford University Press, 1993.

Outram, Dorinda. *The Body and the French Revolution.* New Haven, CT: Yale University Press, 1989.

Parker, Andrew, et. al. *Nationalisms and Sexualities.* New York: Routledge, 1992.

Schwartz, Joel. *The Sexual Politics of Jean-Jacques Rousseau.* Chicago: University of Chicago Press, 1984.

Smith-Rosenberg, Carroll. *Disorderly Conduct: Visions of Gender in Victorian America.* New York: Oxford University Press, 1886.

Walkowitz, Judith. *Prostitution and Victorian Society: Women, Class, and the State.* Cambridge, Eng.: Cambridge University Press, 1980.

Weeks, Jeffrey. *Sex, Politics and Society.* London: Longmans, 1989.

Shakespeare, William (1564–1616)

English playwright and poet. Shakespeare was born in Stratford-upon-Avon. By 1592 he was active in the London theatre as an actor, playwright, and eventually theater investor. Over the course of twenty years he produced some thirty-eight plays, ten of which deal with English history. *Henry VI,* parts 1, 2, and 3, together with *Richard III,* compose the First Tetralogy and cover the period from the Wars of the Roses to the beginning of the Tudor dynasty. *Richard II, Henry IV,* parts 1 and 2, and *Henry V* form the Second Tetralogy or "Henriad" and cover the period from the end of Richard II's reign to the marriage of Henry V. Two other plays, *King John* and *Henry VIII* stand alone as studies of the reigns of these monarchs. Shakespeare drew heavily from Raphael Holinshed's *Chronicles* (1587) as well as from Robert Fabyan, John Stow, Richard Grafton, Edward Hall, and John Foxe for source material. Although Shakespeare did not invent the Tudor history play, he did popularize it through innovations in form and scope. While some chronicle history lent itself to traditional dramatic forms—*Richard II* is a tragedy—much of the material did not, and therefore Shakespeare's plays are formally experimental hybrids. While history plays before Shakespeare focused almost exclusively upon political rulers, Shakespeare also represented the effect of historical processes upon the underclasses. Finally, Shakespeare's history plays cannot be considered simple Tudor propaganda. Rather, they are both a celebration of the events leading to the reign of Elizabeth I and a questioning of established Tudor history, the nature of monarchy, and the role of personality and ideology in history. Although Shakespeare was no historian, his plays had a profound influence on the ways in which the English have envisaged their own past.

Paul Budra

Texts
The Complete Works of Shakespeare. Ed. David Bevington. New York: HarperCollins, 1992.

References
Ribner, Irving. *The English History Play in the Age of Shakespeare.* Revised ed. New York: Barnes & Noble, 1965.

Saccio, Peter. *Shakespeare's English Kings: History, Chronicle, and Drama.* London: Oxford University Press, 1977.

Shang Yue [Shang Yüeh] (1902–1982)

Chinese Marxist historian and publicist. Shang Yue was born in Luoshan, Henan province. After completing middle school in Kaifeng, in 1921 he enrolled in the English language department of Peking University (Beida). In 1926, without graduating, Shang left Beida to engage in revolutionary work. He joined the Communist Party in 1927 and until 1939 worked as an organizer and editor of a succession of radical periodicals. From 1940, he turned principally to the study and teaching of history, becoming in 1950 a professor of history and department head at the newly established People's University in Beijing. Shang was the leading author of a new textbook widely used in the People's Republic of China: *Zhongguo lishi gangyao* [Outline of Chinese History] (1954). In the antirightist hysteria of the late 1950s, this text together with Shang's *Zhongguo zibenzhuyi guanxi fasheng ji yanbian di chubu yanjiu* [Preliminary investigations of the origin and development of capitalist economic relations in China] (1956) occasioned fierce attacks for asserting the presence of "capitalist sprouts" in Ming and Qing China. This allegedly contradicted Mao Zedong's directive that it was only "in the middle of the nineteenth century that great internal changes took place in China as a result of the penetration of foreign capitalism," and supposedly called into question the necessity of the revolution led by the Communist Party. Shang remained in eclipse until the death of Mao in 1976, doing as much historical writing as he could.

Albert Feuerwerker

Texts

Shang Yue shixue lunwen xuanji [Selected Historical Essays by Shang Yue]. Beijing: Renmin, 1984. (This includes a chronological list of his writings.)

References

Feuerwerker, Albert, and S. Cheng, eds. *Chinese Communist Studies of Modern Chinese History.* Cambridge, MA: Harvard University Press, 1961.

Shen Bingzhen [Shen Ping-chen] (1679–1738)

Chinese historian, scholar, and poet. Shen Bingzhen was a native of Guian, Zhejiang. After failing eight times in the provincial examinations, he occupied himself with studying the classics and histories. In 1735 he and his younger brother were recommended as competitors for a special, imperially sponsored examination in "broad learning and elegant writing." Although he was not successful in that examination, his learning was admired by prominent scholars. Shen's reputation as a historian rests on the *Xin-Jiu Tangshu hechao* (first published in 1813), a careful comparative study of the

older and newer standard histories of the Tang dynasty. In 1739, when the Qing government sponsored a reediting of the Twenty-One Dynastic Histories, much of this work was incorporated in the editorial notes. Shen also compiled a valuable reference work, the *Nianyishi sipu.* It consists of four chronological tables (reign years, recipients of noble titles, names of chief ministers, and awards of posthumous titles) for the Twenty-One Dynastic Histories (actually including twenty-two histories). Shen's philological work, the *Jiujing bianzi dumeng* [An Analysis of Words and Phrases in the Nine Classics], was included in the Qing imperial collection of *Siku quanshu* [Complete Library in Four Treasuries]. An outgrowth of his interest in poetry was the *Tangshi jinfen* [An Anthology of Phrases from Tang Poetry].

Shoucheng Yan

Texts

Nianyishi sipu [Four Chronological Tables for the Twenty-One Standard Histories]. Taibei: Yiwen yinshuguan, 1964.
Xin-Jiu Tangshu hechao [A Comparative Study of the Old and New Tang Histories]. Hangzhou: Wu'shi Qinglaitang, 1871.

References

Li Huan, ed. *Guochao qixian leizheng chubian* [Classified Biographies of the Personages of the Qing Dynasty]. Taibei: Wenhai chubanshe, 1966.

Shen Chia-pen

See SHEN JIABEN.

Shen Jiaben [Shen Chia-pen] (1840–1913)

Chinese scholar and proponent of legal reform during the late Qing period. A native of Wuxing, Zhejiang province, Shen Jiaben was a member of a prominent family of scholar-officials and obtained the *jinshi* degree in 1883. For many years he was an official of the Board of Punishments, spending much of his time studying Chinese legal history and compiling books on law. His main work on the history of criminal law is collected in *Lidai xingfa kao* [A Historical Study of Chinese Criminal Law], included in his posthumous *Shen Jiyi xiansheng yishu* [Collected Works] (1929).

Shen's experience as a provincial-level official from 1893, in the middle of conflicts between the local population and foreign missionaries, made him aware of the inadequacies of the Qing legal code. When the Qing court undertook reforms after the Boxer Uprising in 1900, Shen was appointed vice president of the Board of Punishments [Ministry of Justice from 1905] and charged with responsibility for revising the Qing code with the aim of securing the abolition of extraterritoriality. His efforts, based on drafts by Japanese advisers that sharply distinguished procedure in criminal and civil cases and separated legal and ethical matters, were blocked by more conservative officials. In 1910 Shen was able, however, to obtain imperial approval of a new criminal code that departed less from the Chinese legal tradition than had the earlier drafts. This code, *Qinding da Qing xin lu,* remained in force until 1929.

Albert Feuerwerker

Texts

Lidai xingfa kao. 4 vols. Beijing: Zhonghua, 1985.

References

Reynolds, Douglas R. *China, 1898–1912: The Xinzheng Revolution and Japan.* Cambridge, MA: Harvard University Press, 1993.

Shen Ping-chen

See SHEN BINGZHEN.

Shen Yue [Shen Yüeh] (441–513)

Chinese historian, and compiler of *Songshu* [Song History]. A devoted Buddhist layman and Taoist recluse notwithstanding, Shen was actively engaged in court politics and his official career spanned the three dynasties of Song, Qi, and Liang. Known for his erudition, Shen claimed that he had begun to write history at the age of twenty. During his lifetime he compiled over four hundred scrolls of writing. Most of these were historical works and have long been lost. *Songshu,* which covers the history the Liu-Song dynasty from 405 to 479, is the most well known work among those still extant. It was written by imperial order and was completed in fourteen months. Such unprecedented efficiency was owed to the existence of several good histories of the Liu-Song that were incorporated into Shen's own history. The original *Songshu* had one hundred chapters, but many of them were no longer extant by the tenth century. The missing parts were filled in by the corresponding accounts from Li Yanshou's *Nanshi* [History of the Southern Dynasties].

Yuet Keung Lo

Texts

Songshu. 8 vols. Beijing: Zhonghua shuju, 1974.

References

Mather, Richard B. *The Poet Shen Yüeh (441–513): The Reticent Marquis.* Princeton, NJ: Princeton University Press, 1988.

Yao Silian. "Biography of Shen Yue." In *Liangshu* [Liang History]. 3 vols. Beijing: Zhonghua shuju, 1973.

Shigeno Yasutugu (1827–1910)

Japanese historian. A founder of modern academic history in Japan, Shigeno combined traditional scholarship with Western scientific history. In 1875 he joined the new Bureau of Historiography to compile a history of Japan, using traditional methods. In 1888 he was concurrently appointed professor at Bunka College, later Tokyo Imperial University. The Japanese were greatly influenced by Ludwig Riess (1861–1928), who came to their country in 1887 and introduced Rankean scientific method. A learned society was established, and *Shigaku Zasshi* [Journal of Historical Scholarship] began in 1889; it remains Japan's leading historical journal. With his colleagues, Shigeno at the age of sixty attacked traditional beliefs about history so vigorously that he was called "Dr. Massacre." He inflamed public opinion in 1890 by claiming that Kojima Takanori, a fourteenth-century loyalist hero, never existed. Widely criticized and challenged to duels, Shigneno claimed the correctness of his method and defended his position until his death.

John S. Brownlee

Texts

Shigeno Hakushi Shigaku Ronbun Shū [Collected Historical Essays of Dr. Shigeno]. Ed. Ōkubo Toshiaki. 4 vols. Tokyo: Meisho Fūkyū Kai, 1989.

References

Numata Jirō "Shigeno Yasutsugu and the Modern Tokyo Tradition of Historical Writing." In *Historians of China and Japan,* ed. W.G. Beasley and E.G. Pulleyblank. Oxford: Oxford University Press, 1961, 264–287.

Shihabi, Haydar Aḥmad (1761–1835)

Lebanese historian, prince, and statesman. Shihabi was born in the town of Dayr al-Qamar, Mount Lebanon. His family belonged to the Shihabi dynasty, which presided over the affairs of Mount

Lebanon, on behalf of the Ottoman Sultan, between 1697 and 1841. Educated privately in the traditional manner of an Arab prince, he gradually gained the confidence of his relative Amir Bashir II (1789–1840), the governor of Mount Lebanon, becoming a member of his inner circle. It was this position that enabled Shihabi to write a political history of Mount Lebanon based on a selection of official documents. At the time of his death he was still pursuing his activities as a keen chronicler of his times.

Shihabi's reputation rests on his chronicle entitled *al-Ghurar al-hisan fi akhbar abna' al-zaman* [The Most Illustrious Aspects of the Narratives of the Times]. Written in the traditional style of medieval Muslim historians, it opens with the rise of Islam and carries the narrative down to 1832. While its non-Lebanese sections are drawn from secondary sources, its treatment of the dynastic history of Mount Lebanon is based on primary sources. More importantly, Shihabi was perhaps the first Arab historian to dwell at length on the eruption of the French Revolution and its consequences, as well as the career and reforms of Napoleon Bonaparte. Most of his chronicle was in fact the result of a workshop composed of well-known Syro-Lebanese writers, such as the brothers Tannus al-Shidyaq (1794–1861) and Faris al-Shidyaq (1804–1887).

Y.M. Choueiri

Texts
Lubnan fi 'ahd al-umara' al-shihabiyyin [Lebanon in the Reign of the Shihabi Princes]. Ed. Asad Rustum and F.E. al-Bustani. 3 vols. (including parts II and III of *Kitab al-ghurar al-hisan fi akhbar abna' al-zaman*). Beirut: Lebanese University Publications, 1969.

References
Hourani, A.H. "Historians of Lebanon." In *Historians of the Middle East,* ed. Bernard Lewis and P.M. Holt. London: Oxford University Press, 1962, 226–245.

Sigebert of Gembloux [Sigebertus Gemblacensis] (ca. 1030–1112)
Medieval hagiographer, chronicler, and polemicist. Nothing is known of Sigebert's origins and family. While very young, he became an oblate at the monastery of Gembloux (diocese of Liège). He spent his early adult years as a teacher at the monastery of St. Vincent in Metz, during which time he composed his first works. He returned to Gembloux between 1070 and 1075, where he remained for the rest of his life, a famous and respected hagiographer and chronicler. The major focus of his work was biography. Sigebert composed at least seven saints' lives, narrated the deeds of the abbots of Gembloux *(Gesta abbatum Gemblaciensium),* and compiled a *Libellus de illustribus viris* [Little Book of Famous Men] (1111/12), all of which betrayed a keen interest in his forefathers at Metz and Gembloux. He was also a chronicler who compiled one of the most influential of medieval world chronicles, the *Chronica Sigeberti.* This commenced in A.D. 381, the point at which St. Jerome had finished his continuation of Eusebius, and continued to 1111. In the chronicle and his book on chronology, the *Liber decennalis* (1092), Sigebert showed an unusual interest in the accurate dating of events, a combination of historical and chronographical interests not seen so arrayed since Bede in the eighth century. Sigebert was also a polemicist in the Investiture Controversy, composing letters and tractates on the side of the *regnum.* Ironically, given his reputation as a historian, Sigebert was also a forger; he appears to have forged charters and letters that were inserted into his biographies and chronicles. Since this discovery, the broader credibility of the *Chronica, Gesta,* and some saints' lives has been called into question. Nevertheless, Sigebert had a great influence on his contemporaries and on succeeding generations of writers in two ways; he was the first medieval author to revive the ancient genre of the catalog of authors, by which a number of otherwise unknown writers and their works have been saved from oblivion, and he was the first medieval chronicler to revive Eusebius and Jerome's annalistic-synchronistic scheme of history by attempting to impose order on universal, rather than local or royal, history. His chronicle is undoubtedly the most important world chronicle before the work of Otto of Freising in the twelfth century.

Bruce R. O'Brien

Texts
Liber decennalis. Ed. Joachim Wiesenbach. Weimar: H. Bohlau, 1986, 9–15.
Patrologia latina. Ed. J.-P. Migne. Paris, 1880, vol. 160.

References
Von den Brincken, Anna-Dorothee. "*Contemporalitas Regnorum:* Beobachtungen zum Versuch des Sigebert von Gembloux, die Chronik des Hieronymus fortzusetzen." In *Historiographia medievalis: Studien zur*

Geschichtsschreibung und Quellenkunde des Mittelalters [Medieval Historiography: Studies on History Writing and Source Publication in the Middle Ages], ed. Dieter Berg and Hans-Werner Goetz. Darmstadt: Wissenschaftliche Buchgesellschaft, 1988, 201–205 (a list of Sigebert's works with their most recent editions).

de Waha, M. "Sigebert de Gembloux faussaire? Le chroniqueur et les *sources anciennes* de son abbaye [Sigebert the Forger? The Chronicler and the Ancient Sources of his Abbey]." *Revue belge de philologie et d'histoire* 55 (1977): 989–1036.

Sigonio, Carlo (ca. 1523–1584)

Historian of the ancient Roman republic, of late antiquity, and of medieval Italy; university professor of humanities (ancient, language, and literature) in Venice, Padua, and Bologna. Sigonio was born in Modena to a family of middling social status, and studied arts and medicine at the University of Bologna without taking a degree. He began his teaching career as municipal lecturer in humanities in Modena, and held a similar, though much more eminent, post in the Scuola di San Marco in Venice from 1552 to 1560, then taught in the University of Padua from 1560 to 1563 before moving to the University of Bologna in 1563. He was one of the most highly paid and popular professors in that university at the time of his sudden death. Sigonio's fundamental works on Roman history, including his edition of and commentary on Livy, were published in the years 1555–1574. Although he studied the institutions of the Roman republic synchronically, he nevertheless gave a much richer idea of its diachronic development than any previous scholar. Sigonio turned to annalistic narrative in writing the history of late antiquity in *Historiarum de Occidentali Imperio libri XX* [History of the Western Roman Empire in Twenty Books] (1578) and medieval Italy in *Historiarum de Regno Italiae libri XV* [History of the Kingdom of Italy in Fifteen Books] (1574; 1580). Together they give an account of the period 284–1200. These works are massively researched, and exemplify the sixteenth-century growth of historical criticism in the comparison and selection of sources and the establishment of chronology. Sigonio's history of medieval Italy is a monument of national historiography, but like his other works it was reprinted north of the Alps rather than in Italy in the later sixteenth and early seventeenth centuries, for it did not conform to the canons of Counter-Reformation culture and undermined many ecclesiastical and municipal legends. Sigonio was the author of works on other subjects, including Hebrew history in the Old Testament period. His heirs were Theodor Mommsen, in Roman studies, and Ludovico Antonio Muratori, in medieval studies.

William McCuaig

Texts
Opera omnia [Collected Works]. Milan, n.p., 1732–1737.

References
McCuaig, William. *Carlo Sigonio.* Princeton, NJ: Princeton University Press, 1989.

Sima Guang [Ssu-ma Kuang] (1019–1086)

Chinese statesman, historian, and essayist. Sima Guang was born in Henan province and attained the rank of chief minister in a long and distinguished political career. He was a conservative Neo-Confucian who opposed the regime of Wang Anshi, whose radical socialist reforms directed toward a prosperous state and a strong military threatened the existing power structure and various social groups. The hostility between the two factions led to Sima Guang's exile in Luoyang, where he and his coauthors Liu Bin, Fan Zuyu, among others, completed a general history of China—*Zizhi tongjian* [Comprehensive Mirror As an Aid to Government] in 1085. This chronological narrative covers the period from 403 B.C. to A.D. 959 and dwells on the rise and fall of dynasties. Where sources disagree, they are evaluated or listed in an appendix, the *Kaoyi* [Examination of Discrepancies]. Sima Guang sought positive evidence from the sources and Confucian morality to strengthen the didactic import of his work to improve the government of his day and the future. His historical criticism and methodology deeply influenced premodern Vietnamese, Korean, and Japanese historiographical traditions. A prolific writer, Sima Guang's extant works of historical value include *Jigu Lu* [Survey of Records Past] and *Wenguo wenzheng Sima Gong wenji* [Collected Writings of Sima Guang].

Jennifer W. Jay

Texts
The Chronicle of the Three Kingdoms (220–265). Trans. Achilles Fang. 2 vols. Cambridge, MA: Harvard University Press, 1952–1965, chapters 69–78.

The Last of the Han. Trans. Rafe de Crespigny. Canberra: Australian National University, 1969, chapters 58–68.

Sima wengong wenji [Collected Writings of Sima Guang]. Beijing: Zhonghua shuju, 1985.

Zizhi tongjian. Hu Sanxing annot. Taibei: Guoxue jiben congshu, 1971.

References

Bol, Peter K. "Government, Society, and State: On the Political Visions of Ssu-ma Kuang and Wang An-shih." In *Ordering the World,* ed. Robert P. Hymes and Conrad Schirokauer. Berkeley: University of California Press, 1993, 128–192.

Pulleyblank, E.G. "Chinese Historical Criticism: Liu Chih-chi and Ssu-ma Kuang." In *Historians of China and Japan,* ed. W.G. Beasley and E.G. Pulleyblank. London: Oxford University Press, 1961, 135–166.

Sima Qian [Ssu-ma Ch'ien] (145–85 B.C.)

Chinese historian and author of *Shiji* [Records of the Historian]. The Sima family in ancient times had been court chroniclers, and Sima Qian's father, Sima Tan, served as grand historian at the court of Emperor Wu (r. 140–88) of the Former Han dynasty. Sima Qian himself succeeded to his father's post in 108 B.C. and continued to write the *Shiji,* a project his father had initiated, covering the period from the mythical past, through the establishment of the Han, down to the reign of Emperor Wu. Before its completion, Sima Qian was condemned to castration when he offended the emperor by speaking in public defense of a general who had failed in a campaign against the Xiongnu barbarians of the north and had been forced to surrender. Sima Qian underwent the disgraceful punishment in order to finish his history rather than committing suicide, as was customary in such circumstances, hoping that his history would redeem his name in later ages. It took him twenty years to finish the *Shiji,* the first comprehensive history of what was then known about their past by the Chinese. Undergirding his historical narrative was Sima Qian's inclination both to teach moral lessons and to articulate his own philosophy of history. He considered the human will to be the locomotive of history, and he was able to integrate the event-oriented tradition of *Shangshu* [Book of Documents] and the annalistic tradition represented by *Chunqiu* [Spring and Autumn Annals] by organizing historical events around the lives of clusters of individuals. Divided into five sections in 130 chapters—twelve Basic Annals, ten Chronological Tables, eight Treatises, thirty Noble Houses, and seventy Biographies—the *Shiji* marked the beginning of the annals-and-biographies tradition in China, which became the model for all dynastic histories of later times.

Yuet Keung Lo

Texts

Ssu-ma Ch'ien: Grand Historian of China. Ed. Burton Watson. New York: Columbia University Press, 1958.

References

Beasley, W.G., and E.G. Pulleyblank. *Historians of China and Japan.* London: Oxford University Press, 1961.

Butterfield, Herbert. *The Origins of History.* London: Eyre Methuen, 1981, 221–230.

Gardner, Charles S. *Chinese Traditional Historiography.* Cambridge, MA: Harvard University Press, 1938.

Hardy, Grant R. "Objectivity and Interpretation in the *Shih-chi.*" Ph.D. thesis, Yale University, 1988.

Simiand, François (1873–1935)

French economist. Simiand was born in Gières, studied philosophy at the École Normale Supérieure, and became an economist after being inspired by Émile Durkheim. He served as librarian for the ministries of commerce and labor, and participated in economic policymaking during and after World War I. A professor at the École Pratique des Hautes Études, the Conservatoire National des Arts et Métiers, and the Collège de France, he died in Saint-Raphaël. Simiand championed the inductive method in economics, or the analysis of statistical series. He viewed economic development as the result of a long-term cycle, in which monetary depressions (B phases) alternated with periods of inflation and expansion (A phases). His major work, *Le Salaire, l'évolution sociale et la monnaie: essai de théorie expérimentale du salaire* [Wages, Social Evolution and Currency: Toward an Experimental Theory of Wages] (1932), influenced two generations of French social and economic historians, including Georges Lefebvre and the Annalistes.

Leslie Choquette

Texts

Le Salaire, l'évolution sociale et la monnaie: Essai de théorie expérimentale du salaire. 3 vols. Paris: F. Alcan, 1932.

Méthode historique et sciences sociales. Ed. Marina
   Cedronio Paris: Editions des archives
   contemporaines, 1987.

References

Damalas, Basile. *L'Oeuvre scientifique de François
   Simiand.* Paris: PUF, 1943.

Simmel, Georg (1858–1918)

German philosopher and a founder of sociology.
A major figure in the neo-Kantian tradition,
Simmel influenced many social scientists, including Max Weber. Simmel's completely revised 1905
edition of *Die Probleme der Geschichtsphilosophie*
[Problems in the Philosophy of History] articu-
lates historiography's epistemology as follows:
Historians are like artists in that they do not
"photographically" reproduce an object except
perhaps as part of their larger mission of selective representation; unlike artists, they seek to
represent sequences of nonfictional "objects." The
historian translates and synthesizes rather than
reproduces, and selects based on style, purpose,
and axiological (that is, those pertaining to values)
criteria. A human mind constructs the categories
"physical"/"mental," thus outlining the boundaries of nature/history. The numerous mental
categories are hierarchical and fluid, varying
from one discipline, culture, or person to another. These mental forms structure not only
cognitions, but the nonconscious and our feelings
and volitions as well. Historical realism (the "photograph" theory) is not the way of historiographic
knowledge. For Simmel, this modified Kantian
epistemology permitted free agency and made
history possible.

Charles Tandy

Texts

Conflict in Modern Culture and Other Essays.
   London: Collier-Macmillan. 1964.
Essays in Interpretation in Social Science. Ed. and
   trans. Guy Oakes. Totowa, NJ: Rowman
   and Littlefield, 1980.
The Problems of the Philosophy of History. Trans.
   Guy Oakes. New York: Free Press, 1977.

References

Kaern, Michael, et al., eds. *Georg Simmel and
   Contemporary Sociology.* Dordrecht: Kluwer
   Academic, 1990.
Lawrence, P.A. *Georg Simmel: Sociologist and
   European.* Sunbury-on-Thames, Eng.:
   Nelson, 1976.

Sin Ch'ae-ho (1880–1936)

Korean historian, journalist, and patriot. Sin Ch'ae-
ho was a leading journalist who criticized the annexation of Korea by Japan and called for popular
armed revolt. A committed anarchist, he was arrested by the Japanese government and died in
prison. In *Toksa Sinnon* [Correct Readings in Korean History] (1908), Sin superimposed his strong
nationalism on the interpretation of Korean history. In his view, the Korean people rather than the
country's kings had contributed most to the making of Korean history; and the principal pedagogical purpose of the study of history was to bring
people to awareness of the importance of self-determination in the development of Korean society. He
envisaged the broader process of global history as an
unfolding spiritual struggle between "self" and
"non-self," a view contained in his two major historical works *Chosŏn Sanggo Sa* [The History of
Ancient Korea] (1924) and *Chosŏnsa Yŏn'gu ch'o*
[Exploratory Studies in Korean History] (1930).

Minjae Kim

Texts

Chosŏn Sanggo Sa. 2 vols. Seoul: Samsŏng
   Munhwa Chaedan, 1977.
Chosŏnsa Yŏn'gu ch'o. Seoul: Uryu Munhwasa, 1974.
Toksa Sinnon. In *Taehan Maeil Sinbo,* 27 Aug.–
   13 Dec. 1908.

References

Yi Man-yŏl. *Tanjae Sin Ch'ae-ho Yŏksahak Yŏn-gu*
   [A Study on the Historical Works of Sin Ch'ae-
   ho]. Seoul: Munhak gwa Chisŏngsa, 1990.

Sinhalese Historiography

Chronicles of the Sinhalese people. The most important work of Sinhalese historiography is the
Mahâvmsa and its continuation the *Cūlavamsa,*
both written in Pali language. This chronicle narrates the history of the island of Sri Lanka from the
third century B.C. to the end of the thirteenth century A.D. The chronicle actually continues its narrative until the late eighteenth century A.D., but
its importance as a historical record declines.
The *Mahâvmsa,* which describes events until the
beginning of the fourth century A.D., was composed in the sixth century. The *Cūlavamsa* is in
three parts, which were composed, respectively, in
the late twelfth century A.D., in the early fourteenth
century A.D., and in the mid-eighteenth century
A.D. There is a supplementary chapter narrating
events that occurred from 1780 to 1815, composed in the early years of the twentieth century.

This major chronicle superseded all previous works both in the depth and breadth of the subject matter and in its polished poetical form, which at times resembles a Sanskrit *kâvya*. The chronicle is a work by Buddhist monks of the *mahâvihâra* [great temple] fraternity who kept the records of major political events in the island and occurrences within the Buddhist church under individual rulers, whose meritorious deeds to the Buddhist church were an essential facet of the records. The entire chronicle is a remarkable achievement, as it provides a continuous account of major events of the life of a people over two thousand years. Political and religious events are usually dealt with in great detail, while the socioeconomic life of the people is relegated to the background. Its authors did not pretend to cover all events or to represent all points of view, but they make no effort to draw moral lessons from history. The value of the chronicle as a historical record has been confirmed by reference to contemporary inscriptions and literary works. Those sections of the chronicle that conform to the ideals of *kâvya* literature are centered around rulers who were great benefactors of the Buddhist order and also key political figures in the history of the island. The chronicle as a whole has served as a source of inspiration for the Sinhalese, and as such has exercised great influence on their views and ideals. This is not surprising, for most Sinhalese are Buddhists, and the chronicle emphasizes the close affinity between the people and their religion.

Other important writings in early Sinhalese historiography include the last two chapters of *Pûjâvalia* (late thirteenth century), *Nikâyasangrahaya* (late fourteenth century), and *Râjâvaliya* (fourteenth–nineteenth centuries). The first two works are representative of compilations based on the records kept by lesser Buddhist monasteries, which sometimes differed from the main chronicle in minor details or opinions. The last work, *Râjâvaliya,* is a hybrid account of important events in the history of the island, composed by different writers over a long period. There are literary works too, dating from the thirteenth century onward, which contain contemporary historical matter, conceived in a more accessible form than the main chronicle. These minor works are useful in filling gaps in the history of the island as recorded in the main chronicle which becomes increasingly silent on important events and even one-sided when recording the events which were disadvantageous to the Sinhalese in their dealings with European powers.

M.R. Fernando

References

Perera, L.S. "The Pali Chronicles of Ceylon." In *Historians of India, Pakistan and Ceylon,* ed. C.H. Philips. London: Oxford University Press, 1967, 29–43.

Godakumbura, C.E. "Historical Writings in Sinhalese." Also in Philips, 72–86.

Sismondi, Jean-Charles-Leonard Simonde de (1773–1842)

Historian and economist. Born in Geneva, Sismondi traveled to France to train for a career in banking. During the Revolution he returned to Geneva, where he was imprisoned briefly as an aristocrat before taking refuge in England and then Italy. Sismondi began publishing his sixteen-volume *Histoire des républiques italiennes du moyen âge* as well as economic treatises in the first years of the nineteenth century. He became a French citizen and a member of the intellectual circle surrounding Mme. de Staël and Benjamin Constant. At the time of the Second Restoration, Sismondi returned to Geneva, where he died in 1842.

In his own lifetime, Sismondi was best known as a historian, a reputation that rested on his history of medieval Italy and, especially, on the *Histoire des français,* a project that had reached twenty-nine volumes when he died, leaving it incomplete. Since his death, however, Sismondi's economic treatises have achieved greater prominence. Although in his earlier work Sismondi advocated laissez-faire economics (*Traité de la richesse commericale,* 1803), he later revised his views and became one of the earliest critics of classical political economy (*Nouveaux principes d'économie politique,* 1819, and *Études sur l'économie politique,* 1837–1838).

Carol E. Harrison

Texts

Histoire des français [History of the French]. 29 vols. Paris: Chez Treuttel et Wurtz, 1821–1842.

Histoire des républiques italiennes du moyen âge [History of the Medieval Italian Republics]. 16 vols. Paris: Chez H. Nicolle, 1807–1818.

A History of the Italian Republics, Being a View of the Origin, Progress and Fall of Italian Freedom (translation in one volume). London: Longman, Brown, Green and Longmans, 1851.

New Principles of Political Economy: Of Wealth in Its Relation to Population. Trans. R. Hyse. New Brunswick, NJ: Transaction Publishers, 1991.

Traité de la richesse commerciale [Treatise on
Commercial Wealth]. 2 vols. Geneva:
J.J. Paschoud, 1803.

References

Coleman, William. *Death Is a Social Disease:
Public Health and Political Economy in Early
Industrial France.* Madison: University of
Wisconsin Press, 1982.
Waeber, Paul. *Sismondi: Une biographie.* Geneva:
Slatkine, 1991.

Skepticism

Skepticism about the possibility of historical
knowledge has been expressed by philosophers
and others in the West from antiquity onward.
However, it was only in the seventeenth and
eighteenth centuries that we find a sustained
debate on the problem. The case for the doubt or
"pyrrhonism," summarized in a brief passage in
Descartes's *Discourse on Method* (1638), was made
more fully in two notorious and provocative texts,
both French: François La Mothe Le Vayer's *Du peu
de certitude qu'il y a dans l'histoire* [On the Lack of
Certainty in History] (second, enl. ed., 1668) and
Pierre Bayle's *Critique générale de l'histoire de
Calvinisme de M. Maimbourg* [A General Critique of the Maimbourg's History of Calvinism]
(1682). Both texts emphasize the problem of bias.
La Mothe asked what our view of the Punic
War would be if we had access to an account
from the Carthaginian side, while Bayle contrasted
the views of Catholics and Protestants. At a more
precise level, early-eighteenth-century scholars became more and more doubtful of the received account of the early history of Rome, dismissing the
story of Romulus and Remus, for instance, as myth
rather than history.

At least equally worrying to historians as the
problems of bias and hearsay was the problem of
forgery. From the Renaissance onward, scholars
denied the authenticity of one famous document
after another; the Donation of Constantine, the
histories of the Trojan War by Dares and Dictys, the
decretals of Isidore, the letters of Phalaris the
tyrant of Sicily, the charters of the Merovingian
kings, and even parts of the Bible. However, the
prize for skepticism surely goes to the Jesuit scholar
Jean Hardouin, who claimed that most of the writings of the fathers of the church, and almost all
classical literature, had been forged in the fourteenth century by a group of men he called "the
faction." Hardouin is an extreme and possibly
paranoid case, but one that reveals the breadth

and depth of what might be called the "crisis" of
historical knowledge at the end of the seventeenth century, in the course of which some writers described history as nothing but fiction.

This crisis was resolved, in the sense that arguments against the skeptics were put forward
and became a new orthodoxy. For example, the
Benedictine Jean Mabillon defended the authenticity of Merovingian charters and formulated a
number of rules of source criticism in his monumental study *De re diplomatica* (1681). Other
scholars, including Hardouin himself, emphasized
the reliability of the evidence of material culture,
notably inscriptions, coins, and medals. Refuta-
tions of skepticism began to appear in the early eighteenth century. The German professor F.G. Bierling,
for example, in *De pyrrhonismo historico* [On Historical Pyrrhonism] (1724), distinguished three
levels of probability in history, from the maximum
(that Julius Caesar existed, for example) through
the medium (the reasons for the abdication of the
emperor Charles V) to the minimum (the complicity of Mary Queen of Scots in the murder of
Darnley). Thus the challenge of the skeptics had the
beneficial result of compelling historians to reexamine both their assumptions and their methods.

In the age of Ranke, the pendulum swung the
other way, and historians, having developed a
methodical critique of sources, felt confident that
they were able to discover "the facts" on the basis
of "the documents." Only in the late twentieth
century have we seen a swing back to skepticism
and the revival of the comparison between history
and fiction, based this time on the idea that both
works of history and the documents on which
they are based are literary artifacts. It remains to
be seen who will be the new Bierling, and whether
the second crisis will be resolved as easily and as
productively as the first.

Peter Burke

See also BOLLANDISTS AND MAURISTS; ENLIGHTEN-
MENT HISTORIOGRAPHY; POSTMODERNISM.

Texts

Bayle, P. *Critique générale de l'histoire du
Calvinisme de M. Maimbourg.* Second ed.
"A Villefranche": Pierre Le Blanc, 1683.
La Mothe Le Vayer, F. *Du peu de certitude qu'il y
a dans l'histoire.* Paris, 1668.

References

Borghero, Carlo. *La certezza e la storia:
Cartesiansimo, pirronismo e conoscenza
storica* [Certainty and History:

Cartesianism, Pyrrhonism and Historical Knowledge]. Milan: F. Angeli, 1983.

Popkin, Richard H. "Scepticism and the Study of History." In *David Hume, Philosophical Historian*, ed. David F. Norton and R.H. Popkin. Indianapolis, IN: Bobbs-Merrill, 1965, ix–xxxi.

Skinner, Quentin Robert Duthie (b. 1940)

Historian of political thought and philosopher of history and politics. Skinner was educated at the University of Cambridge, and from 1978 to 1996 was professor of political science at Cambridge; in 1996 he was appointed the successor to Patrick Collinson (the distinguished historian of English Puritanism) as Regius professor of modern history at Cambridge. Skinner has exerted wide influence through his writings on the methodology of intellectual history and the history of political thought. In a series of articles published during the 1960s and 1970s (most reprinted in the 1988 volume *Meaning and Context*), Skinner advanced a view of the history of ideas (especially political ideas) that insisted on the need to view the act of writing as an *action* like any other, to be understood primarily with reference to the *intentions* of the actor/ author. He further stressed that those intentions could only be accurately recovered when a text was read in the light of the relevant linguistic and intellectual conventions contemporary to it. These arguments were clinched (and in part prefigured) in a dazzling series of articles that demonstrated their application to Thomas Hobbes.

Skinner's major two-volume historical work, *The Foundations of Modern Political Thought* (1978), applied the methods that he had advocated on a broader front, analyzing the various genres of Renaissance and Reformation political writing, and placing within the framework thus constructed the "classic" thinkers, in this way revealing their engagement with the debates current among their contemporaries. This work was followed by a short study of *Machiavelli* (1981). Critics of Skinner's approach to the history of political thought often condemned it for what they perceived to be its sterile antiquarianism. However, in a body of work published mostly in the 1980s on the history of the concept of liberty, Skinner has (mostly implicitly) replied to that criticism by showing how the attempt to understand past ideas as they actually were can free us from the parochial and limited perspectives fashionable in our own time. In particular, he has exposed the severe limitations of the sharp distinction commonly made by contemporary political philosophers between "negative" and "positive" liberty by showing that Renaissance republican thinkers had an understanding of liberty that was able to combine elements of both. In his most recent work Skinner has returned to Hobbes, and is exploring the influence on his ethical theory of the rhetorical traditions of Renaissance humanism. This most recent work, then, remains committed to the exploration of new contexts as a way of illuminating the intentions of classic thinkers.

Glenn Burgess

Texts

Foundations of Modern Political Thought. 2 vols. Cambridge, Eng.: Cambridge University Press, 1978.

Machiavelli. New York: Hill and Wang (Past Masters Series), 1981.

Reason and Rhetoric in the Philosophy of Hobbes. Cambridge, Eng.: Cambridge University Press, 1996.

Ed. *The Return of Grand Theory in the Human Sciences.* Cambridge, Eng., and New York: Cambridge University Press, 1985.

References

Tully, James, ed. *Meaning and Context: Quentin Skinner and His Critics.* Cambridge, Eng.: Polity Press, 1988.

Slavery (American), Historiography of

Historical writing from the nineteenth century to the present day concerned with slavery in the pre–Civil War United States. A system of forced labor and racial oppression that took shape in the latter half of the seventeenth century in the British North American colonies, American slavery flourished in the southern states after independence until it was abruptly terminated by constitutional amendment in 1865 following the Civil War. Slavery's powerful and complex role in provoking the sectional crisis, shaping the character and identity of the South, promoting white racism, and determining the contours of African-American historical experience insured that it would receive extensive scholarly attention and excite no small degree of controversy.

In its time slavery lacked neither defenders nor critics, though detached scholars were in short supply. Fugitive slave narratives written by or for escaped slaves, such as the justly famous *My Bondage and My Freedom* (1855) by Frederick Douglass, made no attempt to be objective: indeed, often published to advance the antislavery cause, fugitive narratives nonetheless contain information and cogent insights about daily life from the slaves' points of view. Itinerant writers, most notably Frederick Law Olmsted in *The Cotton Kingdom: A Traveller's Observations on Cotton and Slavery in the American Slave States* (1861), viewed slavery from the altogether different vantage point of the relatively disinterested outside observer. In *The Impending Crisis of the South* (1859), Southerner Hinton Rowan Helper used census data to demonstrate that economic development in his region lagged badly behind areas in the North with fewer natural advantages because it had embraced racial slavery, an inefficient, unproductive system in his judgment. Proslavery writers like George Fitzhugh in *Cannibals All! or, Slaves Without Masters* (1857) defended rather than studied slavery: their defenses ranged from racism, to traditional scriptural and philosophical arguments favoring the enslavement of lesser peoples, to biting critiques of free labor capitalist society. Their depictions of plantation slavery bore little resemblance to the system poignantly described in the many fugitive slave narratives.

After the Civil War, writers critical of slavery on moral, economic, and political grounds and hostile to the slaveholding South's drive for independence held the upper hand, a not surprising development in light of the Union victory and the abolition of slavery. James Ford Rhodes, in the first volume (1893) of his *History of the United States from the Compromise of 1850,* expressed the major interpretations of slavery then prevailing outside the former Confederacy: that slavery was inefficient and the Southern economy based on it moribund by the late antebellum period, that slaves were poor workers and badly used, and that the planter class was arrogant and reactionary. By the turn of the century, most white historians of slavery shared the then common assumption of black inferiority, which colored their judgments about the profitability of slavery, the quality of slave life and the nature of the master–slave relationship, the wisdom or folly of emancipation, and the effects of enslavement on African Americans. A small band of black scholars, including Carter G. Woodson and W.E.B. DuBois, reconstructed chapters of the African-American historical experience without the racial outlook of most of their professional colleagues, but they were little heeded.

Modern historical analysis of the institution of slavery began with Ulrich B. Phillips's book *American Negro Slavery: A Survey of the Supply, Employment and Control of Negro Labor As De-*

termined by the Plantation Regime (1918). For his time, Phillips was an unusually thorough researcher in primary archival materials. He placed the large plantation at the center of Southern life and regarded it as the font of an admirable Southern civilization. The organization of the economy around plantations was not inherently unproductive, Phillips argued, but its marriage to racial slavery eventually made it all but impossible for most planters to turn a profit. Once economically necessary and beneficial, slavery by the late antebellum period had become an albatross on the Southern economy but equally an essential instrument of race control. The planter class, as civilized and honorable as any American elite, had governed slaves kindly and firmly, much to the benefit of a race that Phillips considered inferior to his own.

Major elements of Phillips's analysis, particularly its economic analysis of slavery and its exclusive focus on large plantations, drew critical fire before mid-century, but the core of it remained viable until Kenneth M. Stampp published *The Peculiar Institution: Slavery in the Ante-Bellum South* in 1956. Matching Phillips point by point, Stampp argued that slavery was generally a profitable enterprise, that slave owners in particular and white society generally demeaned, abused, and persecuted black slaves, that slaves were badly fed and clothed as well as overworked, and that slaves resisted their oppressors sometimes openly and more frequently covertly. Stampp rejected Phillips's racism and interpreted slave behavior such as malingering and dissembling as elements of a consciously fashioned culture of resistance rather than proof of inherent black laziness or dishonesty. Stanley M. Elkins pushed the theme of slave mistreatment much further in *Slavery: A Problem in American Institutional and Intellectual Life* (1959). Accepting the view presented by Frank Tannenbaum in *Slave and Citizen: The Negro in the Americas* (1946) among others that slavery was more extreme and race relations more rigid in the United States than elsewhere in the hemisphere, Elkins argued that American slavery was unusually harsh and especially devastating to slaves. With no premodern slave code to guide them nor centralized authority of crown or church to limit them, American slaveholders came closest to practicing the logic of slavery, the reduction of person to thing. American slavery, like the modern concentration camp, demolished its inmates' personalities and produced mass slave infantilization. Although little of Elkins's thesis survived critical challenge, it energized the study of American slavery and directed attention to the treatment slaves received and how they accommodated themselves to or resisted bondage.

The 1960s and 1970s saw a huge outpouring of scholarly work on slavery, much of it focused on the slaves themselves. John W. Blassingame's *The Slave Community: Plantation Life in the Ante-Bellum South* (1972) did not minimize the power of masters in slaves' lives, but its exploration of largely black sources for clues about slave life, culture, personality, and resistance strategies led to conclusions radically different from those made by Elkins. In *The Black Family in Slavery and in Freedom, 1750–1925* (1976), Herbert G. Gutman based his claim that the black family survived the travails of slavery on slave family genealogies reconstructed from plantation account books and the testimonies of thousands of freshly emancipated slaves about their marital history and status. Itself a reflection of distinctive African-American values and the product of black creative responses to harsh conditions, the family, in Gutman's view, had enabled slaves and free blacks to re-create and bequeath their own values and identities from one generation to the next. Their largely oral folk culture, richly expressed in tales of animal tricksters and in spirituals as Lawrence Levine showed in his *Black Culture and Black Consciousness: Afro-American Folk Thought from Slavery to Freedom* (1977). This culture exhibited a subtle humor, sense of self-worth, friendship with Jesus, expectation of heavenly reward, identity with the Israelites of the Old Testament, and desire for justice far beyond the imagining of an abjectly victimized servile population.

Perhaps the most ambitious modern study of American slavery is *Roll, Jordan, Roll: The World the Slaves Made* (1974) by the Marxist historian Eugene D. Genovese. Exercising hegemonic control over Southern whites, planters developed a paternalistic relationship with their slaves from which they derived an ethical defense of slaveholding. For their part, slaves accepted elements of planter paternalism and within its confines created for themselves as much cultural autonomy and material comfort as possible. Their most enduring and vital creation was a religion of joy, hope, personal affirmation, and national identity that was at once spiritually uplifting and politically unrevolutionary. Genovese writes movingly about the functions and predicaments of slave drivers, mammies, household servants, and preachers who straddled the distinctive worlds of master and slaves and brought aspects of each to the other. Slavery may have been profitable; it set the terms under which whites and blacks developed relationships of great variety and complexity with one another; and the manner in which it functioned for slaves as well as whites can best be understood, Genovese insists, as a variant of traditional paternalism.

Whether slavery was profitable and whether it benefited or damaged the Southern economy are questions of long standing. From the 1930s onward, the old orthodoxy of unprofitability and ruin progressively lost ground. In 1958 two economists, Alfred H. Conrad and John R. Meyer, argued in an essay on "The Economics of Slavery in the Ante Bellum South" that slavery was both profitable as a business and beneficial to the regional economy. The most forceful expansion of those points appeared in *Time on the Cross: the Economics of American Negro Slavery* (1974) by cliometric historians Robert W. Fogel and Stanley L. Engerman. Not at all modest about their methodologies, models, and exhaustive exploitation of databases, the authors demonstrated to a largely accepting readership that slavery was profitable, that planters behaved rationally by investing in slaves and land, and that the South's slave-based economy was among the most efficient and prosperous in the world. Other claims—for example, that slaves were good and efficient workers with a strong work ethic and that they were not whipped as frequently, treated as badly, exploited as radically, or sexually abused as systematically as neo-abolitionist historians like Kenneth Stampp had contended—provoked controversy every bit as intense as the one that had swirled around Elkins's *Slavery*. Among the earliest counterattacks was *Reckoning with Slavery* (1976) by Paul A. David and four other scholars. Fogel has recently returned to many of the themes set forth in *Time on the Cross* in a masterful work that also analyzes the success of the antislavery and abolition movements entitled *Without Consent or Contract* (1989).

The influence of slavery on an array of political and ideological developments in America has been the subject of an enormous number of books and articles. Particularly stimulating are: Edmund S. Morgan's *American Slavery, American Freedom: the Ordeal of Colonial Virginia* (1975), an exploration of the interplay between the simultaneous evolutions of racial slavery and representative government in that plantation colony and *The Road to Disunion: Secessionists at Bay, 1776–1854* (1990), in which William H. Freehling examines the importance of slavery to the development of Southern nationalism and the effects slave-owning had on the character and outlook of the South's political elites.

The historical relationship between slavery and American racism has intrigued many scholars. Into a chicken-and-egg contention involving slavery and racism, Winthrop Jordan's *White Over Black* (1968) brought a sophisticated analysis of western European cultural attitudes toward race and color; Jordan suggested that English colonials in the early seventeenth century were predisposed to view black Africans and tawney Indians as different from and less than themselves, and that this was important but by no means determinative in their decision to enslave other races. George Frederickson's *The Black Image in the White Mind* extends the study of racism and its relationship to both slavery and democratic egalitarianism into the nineteenth century.

Much has been learned about American slavery from comparative studies. Philip Curtin's *The Atlantic Slave Trade: A Census* (1969) highlighted one indisputably unique feature of American slavery: the reproductive success of the American slave population, a finding that invited rethinking of the claims made earlier by Tannenbaum, Elkins, and others. Continuing his study of American racial attitudes, George Frederickson compared the American South and South Africa in *White Supremacy* (1981). He found that the two societies differed in fundamental ways, black South Africans being a majority living on their traditional lands while African Americans were a minority in a country to which they were involuntarily exiled; in both instances, however, the construction of slave systems based on racial distinctions created institutions and ideologies of white supremacy that were able to maintain their dominance long after slavery was abolished. Peter Kolchin's *Unfree Labor: American Slavery and Russian Serfdom* (1987) compares systems of bondage sharing a number of interesting similarities, but also differing in key respects, such as the American version having been based on race and the Russian not so-based. The comparison led Kolchin to caution against interpretations of American slavery that claim for slaves wide cultural autonomy and adequate material support. The broadly historical intellectual and ideological context for the American debate over slavery can be found in three impressive monographs by David Brion Davis: *The Problem of Slavery in Western Culture* (1966), *The Problem of Slavery in the Age of Revolution, 1770–1823* (1975), and *Slavery and Human Progress* (1984). That American slavery shared certain essential elements with all slave systems, modern and ancient, those based on race and those not, emerges from the expansive work of historical sociologist Orlando Patterson in *Slavery and Social Death* (1982).

The best recent study of the institution is *American Slavery, 1619–1877* (1993) by Peter Kolchin, a work informed by comparative studies and strengthened by a thorough understanding of the historiography of American slavery. Peter J. Parish's *Slavery: History and Historians* (1989) is a reliable historiographical survey concentrating on American slavery. The most important scholarly journals in the field are *The Journal of Negro History*, *The Journal of Southern History*, and *Slavery and Abolition: A Journal of Comparative Studies*.

John T. O'Brien

See also AMERICAN HISTORIOGRAPHY; CLIOMETRICS.

Texts

Elkins, Stanley M. *Slavery: A Problem in American Institutional and Intellectual Life*. Third ed., revised. Chicago: University of Chicago Press, 1976.

Fogel Robert W., and Stanley M. Engerman. *Time on the Cross: The Economics of American Negro Slavery*. Boston: Little, Brown, 1974.

Genovese, Eugene E. *Roll, Jordan, Roll: The World the Slaves Made*. New York: Pantheon, 1974.

Kolchin, Peter. *American Slavery: 1619–1877*. New York: Hill and Wang, 1993.

Phillips, Ulrich B. *American Negro Slavery: A Survey of the Supply, Employment and Control of Negro Labor As Determined by the Plantation Regime*. New York: Appleton, 1918.

Rawick, George P., ed. *The American Slave: A Composite Biography*. 39 vols. Westport, CT: Greenwood Press, 1972–1979.

Rhodes, James Ford. *History of the United States from the Compromise of 1850*. 9 vols. New York: Macmillan, 1893–1928 (vol. 1 of this work covers slavery).

Stampp, Kenneth M. *The Peculiar Institution: Slavery in the Ante-Bellum South*. New York: Knopf, 1956.

References

Kolchin, Peter. "Re-evaluating the Antebellum Slave Community: A Comparative Perspective." *Journal of American History* 70 (1983): 579–601.

Miller, Joseph. *Slavery: A Worldwide Bibliography*. White Plains, NY: Kraus International, 1985, updated annually in the journal *Slavery and Abolition*.

Parish, Peter J. *Slavery: History and Historians*. New York: Harper & Row, 1989.

Sleidanus [Philippson], Johannes (1506–1556)

Lutheran historian. Born in Schleiden (whence his name), Sleidanus was educated in Belgium and France. He became secretary to Guillaume and Jean du Bellay, and served as the French observer of the Hagenau and Regensburg colloquies. Allying himself with Protestantism after reading Calvin, Sleidanus moved to Strasbourg and in 1545 was a representative of the Schmalkaldic (German Protestant) League in England. He returned to the service of Strasbourg in 1551 by becoming that city's representative at the Council of Trent. Sleidanus's works reflect political activity and interest. *Zwei Reden an Kaiser und Reich* [Two Orations to the Emperor and the Empire] (1544) is meant to undermine both papacy and empire. His 1545 *De Statu Religionis et Reipublicae Carolo Quinto Caesare Commentarii* [Commentaries on the State of Religion and the Empire under Emperor Charles V] is the first Reformation history, one based on information from Reformers and diplomatic documents. The result is a history that combines religious and political aspects, but also one in which the success of Protestantism is due to secular powers. Finally, Sleidanus wrote a three-part *Chronicle of World Empires;* in this he uses the sequence of kingdoms in the Book of Daniel to depict the course of European history. His works were widely read across Protestant Europe in the sixteenth and seventeenth centuries.

Ralph Keen

Texts

De Statu Religionis et Reipublicae Carolo Quinto Caesare Commentarii. 3 vols. Osnabrück: Zeller, 1968.

Zwei Reden an Kaiser und Reich. Ed. E. Böhmer. Tübingen: Litterarischer Verein in Stuttgart, 1879.

References

Friedensburg, Walter. *Johannes Sleidanus.* Leipzig: M. Heinsius, 1935.

Vogelstein, Ingeborg B. *Johann Sleidan's Commentaries.* Lanham, MD: University Press of America, 1986.

Smith, Preserved (1880–1941)

American historian of early modern Europe. The son of a noted Old Testament scholar, Smith was also greatly influenced by his mentor at Columbia University, James Harvey Robinson. Shy and handicapped by fragile health, Smith devoted himself almost entirely to study, teaching (at Cornell University), and writing. Like other major "New Historians," Smith possessed a felicitous style that enabled him to reach a comparatively wide readership with his rationalist and humanist histories, notably biographies of Martin Luther (1911) and Erasmus (1923), a history of the Reformation (1920), and an incomplete *History of Modern Culture* (1930, 1934). In 1913, Smith became, in all probability, the first American historian to attempt an application of Freudian theory to history—although this experiment had little influence on his own later writings.

John Austin Matzko

Texts

The Age of the Reformation. New York: H. Holt, 1920.

Erasmus: A Study of His Life, Ideals, and Place in History. New York and London: Harper Brothers, 1923.

A History of Modern Culture. New York: H. Holt, 1930.

The Life and Letters of Martin Luther. Boston and New York: Houghton Mifflin, 1911.

References

Gilbert, William. "The Work of Preserved Smith." *Journal of Modern History* 23 (1951): 354–365.

Smith, Vincent Arthur (1848–1920)

Irish historian of India. Smith was born in Dublin and educated there at Trinity College before joining the Indian Civil Service in 1869, rising to Commissioner in 1898. Smith's father was a prominent doctor and amateur numismatist and archaeologist, and Smith published several works on those subjects as well as history before his retirement in 1900 to take up the position of reader in Indian history and Hindustani at the University of Dublin. He wrote several volumes of history, including the renowned *Early History of India* (1904), mostly a political history, and *The Oxford History of India* (1918). This became the standard work on Indian history, being adopted by Indian schools and colleges, and was still in print at the end of the twentieth century. Smith had a pragmatic conception of history, believing the past should illuminate the present and be a guide for current and future action. A hero-worshipper of many early Indian rulers, he reserved his greatest praise for Alexander the Great.

Roger D. Long

Texts

Akbar: The Great Mogul, 1542–1605. Oxford: Clarendon Press, 1917.

Asoka: The Buddhist Emperor of India. Oxford: Clarendon Press, 1901.

The Early History of India. Oxford: Clarendon Press, 1904.

A History of the Fine Art in India and Ceylon. Oxford: Clarendon Press, 1911.

The Oxford History of India. Fourth ed. Ed. Percival Spear. Delhi: Oxford University Press, 1958.

References

Metcalf, Thomas R. *Ideologies of the Raj.* Cambridge, Eng.: Cambridge University Press, 1994.

Snorri Sturluson (1178/79–1241)

Icelandic leader, historian, and poet. One of the greatest authors of medieval Europe, Snorri was the son of an Icelandic chieftain. Good connections and political skill brought him power, and Snorri became lawspeaker of the Icelandic parliament from 1215 to 1218. He also composed skaldic poetry, wrote the *Prose Edda,* a handbook for skalds, and probably also the saga of his tenth-century ancestor, *Egil Skalagrimsson.* Snorri then spent the years 1218–1220 at the Norwegian court and returned with a commission to bring Iceland under Norwegian overlordship. He was soon engaged in a bloody feud with his own powerful kinsmen, while also writing the saga of St. Olaf of Norway, which eventually became a major part of his historical masterpiece, *Heimskringla,* the saga of the kings of Norway from legendary times until the year 1177. As a historian, Snorri evaluated his Latin, vernacular, and oral sources critically, established a clear chronology and causal linkages, then wove a tightly unified story emphasizing clashes between individuals as its driving force, demonstrating masterly psychological insight.

J.R. Christianson

Texts

Heimskringla: History of the Kings of Norway. Ed. and trans. Lee M. Hollander. Austin: University of Texas Press, 1964.

King Harald's Saga. Ed. and trans. Magnus Magnusson and Hermann Pálsson. New York: Penguin, 1966.

References

Bagge, Sverre. *Society and Politics in Snorri Sturluson's Heimskringla.* Berkeley: University of California Press, 1991.

Ciklamini, Marlene. *Snorri Sturluson.* Boston: Twayne, 1978.

Soboul, Albert (1914–1982)

French historian. Although born in rural Algeria, Soboul was educated at Nîmes and Paris. By 1939 he had committed himself to a career teaching history and joined the Communist Party. After serving briefly in World War II, he entered the teaching profession, then, after the liberation, completed his doctoral dissertation. His thesis, which examined the Parisian laboring classes during the Terror, brought him a university post. From 1967 until his death, Soboul taught at the Sorbonne. Soboul's numerous publications examined history "from below." Following the lead of his mentor, Georges Lefebvre, he considered the period 1789–1799 as a bourgeois revolution that abolished feudalism and aristocratic privilege. But he also emphasized the simultaneous popular revolutions that the restless urban workers and peasants waged to secure political and social equality.

James Friguglietti

Texts

The French Revolution, 1789–1799: From the Storming of the Bastille to Napoleon. Trans. Alan Forrest and Colin Jones. New York: Random House, 1975.

The Parisian Sans-culottes and the French Revolution, 1793–4. Trans. Gwynne Lewis. Oxford: Clarendon Press, 1964.

References

Friguglietti, James. "The French Revolution Seen from the Left: Albert Soboul As a Historian." In *Proceedings of the Twelfth Annual Meeting of the Western Society for French History,* ed. John F. Sweets. Lawrence: University of Kansas, 1985, 100–107.

Social History

Major branch of historical writing, concerned with society, its structure and components, and with aspects of human behavior, in past times. Social history, defined as an effort to analyze broad characteristics of a society in past time, is as old as the study of history itself. Herodotus, for example, included consideration of all sorts of popular customs and beliefs in his historical work, as did Ibn Khaldūn in the glory years of Islam, and Voltaire in the European Enlightenment. Good histories have always encompassed more than a single institution, even the state, in considering a variety of groups and patterns. The efforts of recent social historians to highlight and formalize this wider compass, though often heralded as novel, clearly build on important past precedent.

At the same time, contemporary social history is new, constructed in France since the late 1920s, in the United States, England, and Germany since the 1960s. Its novelty reflects not just an openness to broad perspectives on societies past, but an interest in specific topics, like leisure or social mobility, long ignored in serious historical scholarship. Its novelty reflects also a concern for looking at all groups in society as serious actors in shaping the historical experience, and not as peripheral elements, involved significantly only in cases of popular insurrections, or as members of the undifferentiated masses. The new social history, in sum, has developed a dizzying range of topics that are to varying degrees remote from the staples of standard political and intellectual history. It has put groups of ordinary people—women, African Americans, workers, peasants—into central historical roles, examining their past experiences as primary subjects of enquiry and assuming a causal force for their interactions with other groups and institutions. The new social history has also, in exploring histories of ordinary people and diverse facets of social behavior, experimented with a variety of methodologies, including quantification, and with unusual interdisciplinary connections with sociology and, more recently, cultural anthropology. Social history is not wedded, it must be emphasized, to any single methodology; it is just as eclectic in this regard as history in general. But there has been rather more methodological and analytical focus in social history than in the wider discipline, if only to establish the parameters of a novel historical endeavor.

In between the commitment of magisterial histories to broad comments on social patterns, and the rise of the new social history in the later twentieth century, came the increasing commitment of professional historians to national political agendas, from the late nineteenth century onward. Historical research and history textbooks, in western Europe and the United States, concentrated increasingly on political and diplomatic developments, rather narrowly construed. Despite some important exceptions (the famous Turner thesis, in American historiography, was a comment on social outlets, for example), history seemed to consist primarily of kings, presidents, constitutions, wars, and alliances. Economic history balanced this to an extent, to be sure, but it focused heavily on rather impersonal trends such as trade flows and technologies. The rise of intellectual history was a further leaven, and did help open the way for social history. But formal intellectual history focused so intensely on the causal power of great minds and great ideas that it either isolated its subject matter—one great thought leads to another, with relatively little opening to broader social forces—or generalized grandiosely about the characteristics of an age, as if formal philosophy determined all else. The narrowness of national political histories was modified, but not really reversed.

In this context the social history that persisted was, for the most part, antiquarian and unacknowledged. Much of it consisted of amateur descriptions of "how people lived" in the past, with attention focused on costumes, eating utensils, and housing design. The purpose of this research was to add some human touches to the drier stuff of academic history, without, however, challenging the latter or pretending a connection with the larger processes of politics or culture. Characteristic titles, in the United States, included such works by Alice Morse Earle as *Curious Punishments of Bygone Days* (1896) and *Costumes of Colonial Times* (1911). This was a type of history rejected by later social historians as "pots and pans" history, although in very recent times it has made a comeback in the form of highly sophisticated and often quantitative studies of "material culture." Closely related to this antiquarian, often nostalgic definition of social history was a larger tendency to define social history topically as "history with the politics left out," a 1940s phrase of the English scholar G.M. Trevelyan. While the phrase captured some impulses in social history resolutely to pursue subjects outside a formal political orbit, it also reflected social history's increasing marginality until the great forward thrust of the past generation of scholarship. As late as 1968, an essay on social history in the *International Encyclopedia of the Social Sciences* noted the lack of vigor in social history in the United States and the "fact" that no one seemed to care. Developments in Europe seemed alone worthy of note, as the field, itself narrowly defined, had almost faded from view in the United States.

The surge of social history since the late 1960s, with important prior precedent in France, has been one of the most dramatic developments in modern social science scholarship, greatly expanding the range and definition of what historians can achieve. Along with the geographical extension of historians' interests, itself often imbued with sociohistorical content, the rise of social history has transformed what history covers and how it is defined. And while social history is in a sense more renewed than new, as it revives earlier interests in developments beyond the levels of political and intellectual leadership, the reaction to its prior decline has greatly enlarged and sharpened its claims. The focus on a wide range of social groups, and on a similarly expansive range of facets of the human experience, mark the novelty. Growing subfields, such as the history of illness and insanity or the history of emotions, simply find no precedent in social histories past. Claims for the active agency of key subgroups, like ethnic minorities in the United States or peasantry around the world, also recast the process of historical explanation.

Three related factors explain the rise of the new forms of social history over the past generation or more of historical scholarship. First, many practitioners simply grew impatient with the limitations of nationalist political history. They found certain topics played out, others inadequately analyzed because of the narrow range of explanations possible. The excitement of new topics was frequently enhanced by the discovery of new kinds of archival materials, detailing the meaning and significance of popular festivals or family forms.

Political inspiration undoubtedly guided many of the early social historians in places like France, England, and the United States, although it is vital to emphasize that this cause alone does not explain either the rise or the content of social history. Many social historians were political radicals—and the unusual commitment of French intellectuals to the political Left helps explain the early hold of social history in France. Social history easily responded to a concern for the conditions of ordinary people, with catchy but revealing slogans like "history from the bottom up." Initial interest, on the part of social historians, in peasants, workers, immigrants, and slaves clearly followed from a desire to use history to create better understanding of current social issues and greater sympathy for currently dispossessed groups. It was no accident that social history gained ground in Britain and the United States during the 1960s, as a scholarly conveyance of many of the political issues of that decade; or that it has been sustained subsequently by causes such as feminism. Political inspiration, which has not inhibited serious, diverse scholarship in dealing with ordinary people, has led to interesting tensions in social history. Some practitioners have emphasized the powerlessness of ordinary people, highlighting the exploitation to which they have been subjected. More, however, have stressed agency, the capacity of groups even as brutally subordinated as slaves or people labeled insane to affect their environment and to interact with the forces that impinge upon them, and not through outright protest alone.

The third force that inspired the rise of social history involved a growing interest in interdisciplinary contacts, as a source of valid historical topics and of methods and models that could fruitfully be applied to the past. The growing influence of sociology brought many historians to realize the significance of subjects like the family or social mobility, while also highlighting the extent to which serious historical perspective needed to be applied to permit full understanding. Fundamental interpretive issues required historical data. Only social history, for example, could allow scholars to assess the causation of popular protest, testing theories that argued deprivation as a cause against theories that put forth the impact of rising expectations. Generalizations about the family and its interaction with developments such as industrialization also linked sociological concerns with those of social history. Social science contacts not only extended history's topical range. They also brought methods that were not commonly used by historians. Quantification was the first beneficiary, in the early interaction with sociology. More recently, as social history's outreach has extended to cultural anthropology and even literary-cultural studies, such method-borrowing has included anthropological "thick description," ethnography and oral history, and discourse analysis. Finally, the contacts with various social sciences encouraged many social historians to identify their particular craft with a high level of analysis. Merely recording data was insufficient; the data must be given meaning, explained, even related to larger models such as modernization or family disintegration. To be sure, some social history remains descriptive, particularly certain of the hymns to exploited groups, but the analytical and explanatory impulse is strong.

Spurred by a quest for new excitement, political relevance, and social science contacts, early efforts in social history inevitably furthered subsequent work. Growing awareness of the redefinitions of history developed by the interwar Annales school in France, for example, helped support the development of the "new social history" of the 1960s and 1970s in the United States. E.P. Thompson's neo-Marxist interpretation of the English working class, designed to rescue this class from "the enormous condescension of posterity," inspired a whole generation of "new labor historians" in the United States, eager to see labor history not as the machinations of institutional trade unionism alone, but as a portrait of the goals and behaviors of workers themselves.

Fed by these several factors, social history moved from a challenge to the disciplinary establishment to a mainstream subdiscipline, within about twenty years. Revealingly the "new" tag began to decline, as sociohistorical contours became familiar and acceptable. The successes of social history can be measured in many ways. By 1990, 35 percent of all practicing historians in the United States called themselves social historians, an amazing increase given the fact that social history fields only began to be admitted to American graduate training in the early 1960s. More important than numbers, however, a host of social history topics, including family history, the history of crime, the history of sexuality, as well as more politically potent staples like women's history, had become firmly established, many with their own journals, all with their own sets of practitioners and a rich historiography. Social history's rise had influenced the wider reaches of social science and history. Historical sociology had become one of the leading fields in a discipline seeking clearer directions. Work in specific social science areas, such as drinking, or death rituals, or emotions, increasingly included contributions from social historians. Key subfields in history, such as urban, labor, and even intellectual history, had been considerably redefined on the basis of sociohistorical concerns for ordinary people and a wider array of topics. Social history had virtually taken over the academic (as opposed to amateur) history of medicine, while influencing the larger history of science and strongly redirecting research in military history. History teaching and textbooks, although not fully transformed by social history, had been widely affected. By the 1970s the U.S. College Board increased the social history content of its Advanced Placement tests. Textbooks most readily picked up coverage of key groups, like African Americans and women, but some of social history's new topical range also informed the genre, particularly at the college level.

Social historians themselves continued to evolve. Some early topical staples, like the study of American social mobility, receded in importance, while subjects like the history of adolescence or of old age gained new ground. New contemporary interests inevitably provoked explorations of topics such as homosexuality, often with exciting results. Early fascination with quantification definitely declined, in favor of qualitative methods and a greater mixture of sources. By the 1980s, partly inspired by the increasing linkage with anthropology, examination of deeply held beliefs (for a time labeled mentalities) commanded a growing amount of research. Many social historians became fascinated with cultural constructionism, that is, the power of cultures to shape basic ideas and behaviors in such areas as gender, sexuality, or disease. Changes in social history spurred some discontent, as some older practitioners objected to newer fads. On the whole, however, the changes preserved social history's vitality and its capacity to expand the range of topics open to serious historical inquiry.

The rise and evolution of social history inevitably presented some new problems and challenges, for social historians themselves and for the wider historical discipline. The issue of sources, agonizing in the early years, proved largely addressable: social historians were adept at uncovering new materials and new uses for old. More troubling in the long run was the sheer proliferation of topics in social history, which caused some to question the field's coherence. Was social history mainly negatively defined, in terms of unconventional topics, or did it have more positive consistency? Appeals for greater synthesis resonated through the 1980s. More self-conscious emphasis on delineating the basic causes of shifts in social patterns—what one sociologist/historian called the "big changes" that shape a host of specific social behaviors in any given period—gradually reduced some of the concern for social history's randomness, but some questions persisted.

In the United States, conservatives, both historians and others, mounted a counterattack against social history in the 1980s, arguing that decreasing attention to the staples of historical enquiry had weakened history's educational role. In this rendering, the purpose of history is to provide a common fund of knowledge about the basic institutions and values of our civilization, and to offer students heroic examples for emulation. Social history had diluted coverage of the basic institutions and values by talking about subcultures, protests, and simply a wider variety of topics. It had downgraded biography in favor of other, less personal historical foci. And so it had opened the educational gates to a new level of ignorance and immorality. These charges were not proved. They did not take into account social history's ability to appeal to students on the basis of recognizable groups and topics and social history's active contention that people are not simply prey to forces beyond their control, given their active agency. Social history continued to gain ground curricularly, but the debate with the conservative purists was by no means fully resolved by the mid-1990s.

Predictably, social history also faced challenges from new sets of innovators who felt that their keys to the historical kingdom fit better than those of the social historians. Psychohistory, once a potential alternative to social history, had never rivaled the latter's achievement. But in the 1990s some self-defined "new" cultural historians began to attack social history's dominance. Variously, they challenged the truth claims of any historians, which antagonized many social historians who believed that sheer relativism was unnecessary. They began to argue more for dense reading of limited texts than for tests of representativeness, and they often argued that culture shaped the whole historical reality. These claims, although related to the growing importance of cultural analysis within social history, set up potential contestations for the future.

The most important issues, implicit since the rise of the field as a discretely defined research area, involved the implications of social history's topical status. The readiest definition of the field, as involving attention to various social groups and an expanded range of social behaviors, labeled social history as a set of subjects different from those of economic, intellectual, or political history. This categorization was accurate enough as far as it went. But many social historians argued that their topics, collectively, were so substantial as to require some wider recastings of the ways history was presented; and many contended that ultimately social history would have to be reintegrated with history's other topics not mechanically, but in ways that would reflect the ways sociohistorical research had reshaped an understanding of the past.

What, for example, is the appropriate basis for historical periodization? Many social historians initially used established periods for their new topics, simply as conveniences. Hence a variety of social trends were presented as if they tidily ended in 1914. This was a stopgap at best. Unless one assumed that the causes of social phenomena emanated disproportionately from the state, conventional periodization was often inappropriate. In modern European history, developments in the eighteenth century, some of them grouped around the new social history concept of protoindustrialization, began to loom much larger than standard periodization would allow. In contrast, the Renaissance as a social history category,

although not entirely dislodged, declined in significance. Classic subperiods in American history, revolving around presidencies or political movements, were similarly recast in social histories of leisure, or gender, or sexuality.

How should history be presented? Many social historians eschewed conventional narratives, although this was not uniformly the case and was widely debated. While social historians utilized chronology, some attempted to convey change and continuities by focusing on processes, rather than events that had clear story lines. A case in point: the advent of new levels of birth control, occurring in the nineteenth century in Europe and the United States, is a vital development in modern social history. It summed up a myriad of individual events—decisions to change the number of children desired, and the methods and goals of sexuality. But, aside from the possibility of a few case studies derived from autobiographies, this was not exactly a story in the more conventional historical sense. It invited presentations of quantitative data and analyses of motivations and results for which standard narrative was inappropriate. Social history did not put forth a definitive alternative to event-based narrative, but it definitely issued some challenges. Certainly, social historians routinely downplayed biographies as a subset of narrative history, although individual studies might be used to illustrate some of the groups and processes that really commanded attention in the field.

How should the topics of social history be linked back to concerns about politics and great ideas? An initial impulse, never uniform in any event, to bypass the state in defining characteristic social history topics, led to an urgent plea, by the early 1980s, to "put the state back in." But the political developments that meshed best with social history had less to do with detailed maneuverings of individual politicians, less even to do with constitutional structures, than with the relationship between various groups and the state and the effective functions the state maintained to influence social activity. Basic changes in state functions, or shifts in access to political power, were not entirely novel topics, but they called for a more selective and analytical approach to political data than conventional history had offered. The result could be fruitful, but it required some soul searching by social and political historians alike. And the fact remained that social historians continued to resist any insistence that every significant historical topic have a clear political referent; the field's range remained wider than the state alone, and its practitioners, some exceptions aside, did not see their primary role as contributing new vision to hoary staples such as the Civil War or the Progressive Era.

The new social history, by its very success and by its distinctive claims as an overall orientation to the past and not simply as a discrete set of topics, inevitably raised fundamental issues. It was not always clear, even as the field moved into its second generation, how or whether some of these issues would be resolved. At the same time, the field continued to be vital. Its impact not only on historical research but also on research in kindred social sciences was increasing by the 1990s. Initially a pioneering venture, claiming far more than traditional social historians had presumed, the new social history had become a central approach in the discipline as a whole in most parts of the world and concerning all major time periods. At its best it had expanded not only the definition, but also the relevance and excitement of the past in the process.

Peter N. Stearns

See also ANTHROPOLOGY AND HISTORY; DEMOGRAPHY—HISTORICAL; FAMILY HISTORY (COMPARATIVE); GENEALOGY; LABOR HISTORY; SOCIOLOGY AND HISTORY; WOMEN'S HISTORY.

References

Stearns, Peter N., ed. *Expanding the Past: A Reader in Social History.* New York: New York University Press, 1988.

Zunz, Olivier, ed. *Reliving the Past: The Worlds of Social History.* Chapel Hill: University of North Carolina Press, 1985.

Sociology and History

The application of sociological principles to historical subjects, carried out by both historians and sociologists; including but not limited to "historical sociology." Since their establishment, the relations between history and sociology have given rise to an unfinished but fruitful discussion of the strengths and weaknesses (usually misrepresented), and differences and similarities between the only two disciplines that make periodic claims to be *the* science of human society as a whole and to take as their subject matter the whole range of human behavior. The "dialogue of the deaf," as Peter Burke has called it, is still not concluded today. Three main answers have been given to the question of the relationship between sociology and history: (1) there is (or should be) no difference between history and sociology; (2) there are differences of a substantial character between history and sociology; or (3) there are differences between history and sociology but they are of an insubstantial nature.

A preliminary question raised by these different approaches is whether we should really speak of two different disciplines rather than of one social science, or of a single articulation of all the particular social sciences under the aegis of either sociology or history. The idea that sociology is *the* social science par excellence, or at least the federating science of particular social sciences, including history, has tended to be supported by most sociologists. Both the practitioners of what by the end of the eighteenth century was already being called "social science," and the French philosopher Auguste Comte, who shortly after coined the term "sociology," envisaged the creation of a "unified social science" whose aim would be to study human societies with the same methods that had been so successfully employed in the natural sciences to *explain* them through laws. Both Karl Marx and Emile Durkheim, who adopted Comte's conception of sociology, agreed that it was necessary to follow this path.

Nothing could be more opposed to the point of view of historians who, at the beginning of the nineteenth century, had seen the conversion of their own discipline into a "science," initiated by Ranke and the German historical school; starting with the advent of historicism, historians had also seen their proper subject as the science of human beings and peoples. To understand individuality and the individual evolution of both collective and individual entities became the aim of professional historians, now newly armed with the Rankean critical method. Despite what is usually written on the subject, nineteenth-century historians did not adopt a narrower perspective than their enlightened predecessors, even though those who had the greatest influence on public opinion, following Ranke, certainly practiced traditional political history based on archival sources, examined according to the rules of critical philology.

At the end of the nineteenth century the Rankean paradigm, together with its privileging of political history and its idealizing historicism, were thrown into doubt. In the "Lamprechtstreit," German historiographical practices defeated what a posteriori can be called a social scientific approach. The most important result of this controversy was to enable Otto Hintze and especially Max Weber to find ways in which to study the social world from the tradition of historicist hermeneutics. It is often repeated by textbooks that Weber was one of the founders of sociology, yet he always described himself not as a sociologist but as a political economist or a comparative historian.

This sort of problem barely arose in Britain, where the legacy of the German historical school was received very late and only in part, and where it built on an indigenous tradition of antitheoretical empiricism. In the United States, however, James Harvey Robinson's "New History," and the work of "progressive" historians such as Carl Becker and Harry Elmer Barnes, was influenced by social evolutionism and pragmatism and by the thought of iconoclastic Europeans like Karl Lamprecht. These American historians were consequently the first to develop what would later be called "total history" (usually associated with the French Annales school) on a large scale, while at the same time, a profoundly ahistorical sociology reached its first high point in America. Finally, the problem was raised also by young French historians who were attracted by the global vision of Durkheim's sociological approach but who, like the philosopher Henri Berr, were also increasingly convinced that the synthesis of scientific knowledge of human societies was properly the task of history rather than sociology. Although pursuing conflicting institutional goals, there were more points of agreement than disagreement between Durkheim and his followers, on the one hand, and, on the other, the Berr-influenced historians Lucien Febvre and Marc Bloch, who founded the *Annales d'histoire économique et sociale,* and with it the Annales school, in 1929. The common aim of both these groups was to study social phenomena scientifically, but the *Annalistes* soon achieved dominance over the sociologists and in France history, not sociology, became the disciplinary nucleus of the social sciences.

An outcome of these changes in social thought in the period roughly speaking between 1890 and 1930 was the laying of the foundations of a "historiographical revolution" that, after 1945, led to the rapid development of social history. This, in turn, provided the core of total history, the social science of the human societies of the past. From then on, a significant number of historians began to understood history as a social science that should establish relations with the rest of the sciences, beginning with sociology.

By the 1950s, the work of Lucien Febvre and Fernand Braudel in France had come to the forefront, but in Britain and Germany "traditional" historiography maintained its dominance at least until the 1960s. In the United States, "social science history" met with greater resistance than in France, while, paradoxically, sociology developed at a rate unequaled in any other country of the world.

In the last two decades only two of the three answers given to the question of the relationship between sociology and history listed above have been maintained. Many historians and sociologists now think that, if there are differences between both disciplines, these are not substantial. Some such differences can be summarized as follows: (a) the old distinction between sociology as a "nomothetic" (law-giving) discipline and history as an "ideographic" one, concerned with individuals, should no longer be understood as a difference of principle but rather of emphasis; (b) history studies the past through incomplete fragments while sociology, in addition to working "in the past" can also generate present "evidence"; (c) the differences between them are themselves of an institutional nature and concern the apprenticeship and practice of both disciplines; (d) the mode of reasoning employed in each is distinct, sociological argumentation being not only historical but also experimental; (e) much more frequently than the historian, the sociologist assumes the right to isolate a specific macrosocial phenomenon from within the historical flux in order to explain it; and (f) a characteristic trait of sociology, compared to history, is its systematic aspiration to generalization through the search for general or evolutionary laws or structural models.

In addition, there is an influential minority in favor of the first of the three answers suggested above. Giddens's theory of "structuration" (according to which with the recovery of temporality as integral to social theory history and sociology become methodologically indistinguishable) influenced Philip Abrams, among others. Abrams suggested the reconstitution of history and sociology as historical sociology, while Christopher Lloyd has advocated "a threefold division of labour, within a unified science of society (which should properly be called 'sociology') between social theory, structural history and action history." (317)

Over the last twenty-five years the English-speaking world in particular has seen what Dennis Smith has called "the rise of historical sociology," which Abrams had proposed, although not always from the same premises. In the 1960s, which also witnessed the establishment of social history, young historical sociologists rebelled against what C. Wright Mills called general orthodoxies such as the "grand theory" and "abstracted empiricism," and especially against the Durkheimian theory of modernization and the functionalism associated with Talcott Parsons. This meant the reintroduction of variety, conflict, and the processes of specific histories in macroscopic presentations of social change and the search for techniques sensitive to temporal processes.

Despite the complementary character of social history and historical sociology, and their common aims, historical sociologists such as Theda Skocpol argue that history and sociology will never be able to converge entirely and achieve the eagerly desired reality of a "unified historical social science." This point of view may be naïve. It is not clear what the epistemological basis is that allows us to speak of "historical sociology." One of the shortest definitions most often used by its practitioners is that "historical sociology" is simply "historically grounded sociology." However, aside from the question of different emphasis and the diversity of research subjects, it may be asked whether it is possible to have a sociology which is *not* "historically grounded." In any case, the rise of "historical sociology" shows the depth of the *rapprochement* between sociology and history since the 1960s.

Ignacio Olábarri

See also ANNALES SCHOOL; ANTHROPOLOGY AND HISTORY; CULTURAL HISTORY; PROGRESSIVE HISTORY; SOCIAL HISTORY.

References

Abbott, Andrew. "History and Sociology: The Lost Synthesis." *Social Science History* 15 (1991): 201–238.

Abrams, Philip. *Historical Sociology*. Ithaca, NY: Cornell University Press, 1982.

Burke, Peter. *History and Social Theory*. Cambridge, Eng.: Polity, 1992.

Giddens, Anthony. *The Constitution of Society*. Cambridge, Eng.: Polity, 1984.

Hill, Stephen, and Paul Rock, eds. "'The Uses of History in Society': A Debate." *British Journal of Sociology* 45 (1994): 1–77.

Lloyd, Christopher. *Explanation in Social History*. Oxford: Blackwell, 1986.

Moulin, Raymond, ed. *Historiens et sociologues aujourd'hui* [Historians and Sociology Today]. Paris: C.N.R.S., 1986.

Skocpol, Theda, ed. *Vision and Method in Historical Sociology*. New York: Cambridge University Press, 1984.

Smith, Dennis. *The Rise of Historical Sociology*. Cambridge, Eng.: Polity, 1991.

Solov'ev, Sergei Mikhailovich (1820–1879)

Russian historian and historiographer. A graduate of Moscow University, he became a professor there and served as rector between 1871 and 1877. A Russian nationalist with Slavophile tendencies, he raised the university's historical scholarship to a professional level. He had a profound belief in history as a process and was founder of what was dubbed the "organic" school. He argued that the process of Russia's evolution from a primitive, family-based society to a monarchic state was organic, rational, and progressive. There was a very sharp break between Kievan Rus' and Muscovy, but thereafter, the chronological thread was the Russian autocracy. He emphasized the significance of geography for Russian history and stressed the importance of Moscow's location for the expansion of the Muscovite state. His masterpiece was the twenty-nine-volume *Istoriia Rossii s drevneishikh vremen* [History of Russia from Earliest Times]. He also wrote widely on Russian historiography.

Elizabeth V. Haigh

Texts

Istoriia Rossii s drevneishikh vremen. 15 vols. Moscow: Sotsial' no-ekonomicheskaia lit-ra, 1959–1966.

History of Russia [translation of *Istoriia*]. Ed. and trans. Hugh F. Graham. Gulf Breeze, FL: Academic International Press, 1976.

References

Black, J.L. "The 'State School' Interpretation of Russian History: A Re-Appraisal of Its Genetic Origins." *Jahrbücher für Geschichte osteuropas* N.F. 31 (1973): 509–530.

Grothusen, Klaus-Detlev. "S.M. Solov'ev's Stellung in der russischen Historiographie" [Solov'ev's Position in Russian Historiography]." *Forschungen zur Osteuropaischen Geschichte* [Research on East European History] 4 (1956): 7–102.

Somesvara III (r. ca. 1124–1138)

Indian king of the Chalukya dynasty of Kalyani, historian, and social commentator. He was the author of *Manasollasa,* also known as the *Abhilasitarthachintamani,* an encyclopedic and voluminous work written in Sanskrit and an important source on the cultural conditions of medieval India. He also wrote the incomplete historical manuscript, *Vikramankabhyudayam,* which recounts the life of his father, and other works.

Manasollasa is divided into five parts and one hundred chapters, each chapter with a separate theme, and was intended to instruct members of royal families into their duties and customs. It is a "book which teaches the world" on myriad topics, including what qualities a king would need to extend his dominions, how to secure his throne, how to ensure the loyalty of subjects, the role of state officers, tax rates, alchemy, and medicine. Somesvara was a powerful ruler but almost nothing is known about his personal life from the few inscriptions of his time.

Roger D. Long

Texts

Kirtikaumundi: A Life of Vastupala. Ed. Abaji Vishnu Kathavate. Bombay: Government Central Book Depot, 1883.
Manasollasa of King Bhulokamalla Somesvara. Ed. G.K. Shrigondekar. Baroda: Oriental Institute, 1967.
Ramasatakam of Somesvara. Ed. Punyavijaya and Bhogilal Jayachandbhai Sandesara. Baroda: Oriental Institute, 1965.
Vikramankabhyudayam: A Historical Sanskrit Campu. Ed. Murari Lal Nagar. Baroda: Oriental Institute, 1966.

References

Warder, A.K. *An Introduction to Indian Historiography.* Bombay: Popular Prakashan, 1972.

Sorel, Albert (1842–1906)

French diplomatic historian. Born in Harfleur in 1842, Sorel initially pursued a legal and civil service career, joining the Ministry of Foreign Affairs shortly before the Franco-Prussian War (1870). In 1872, however, he became professor of diplomatic history at the École des Sciences Politiques. Sorel's most important work, the eight-volume *L'Europe et la Révolution française* [Europe and the French Revolution], was published between 1885 and 1904. In this study, Sorel insisted upon the basic continuities of French foreign policy, linking old regime, revolution, and Napoleon. In particular, he argued that it was the historic pursuit of the "natural frontiers" that had set revolutionary and Napoleonic France at odds with the rest of Europe. Sorel's sympathetic interpretation of Napoleonic foreign policy was quite influential, although it has been criticized for being excessively deterministic.

Ian Germani

Texts

Essais d'histoire et de critique [Essays on History and Criticism]. Paris: Plon, 1883.
L'Europe et la Révolution française. 8 vols. Paris: Plon, 1885–1904.
Lectures historiques [Historical Lectures]. Paris: Plon-Nourrit, 1894.
Nouveaux essais d'histoire et de critique [New Essays on History and Criticism]. Paris: Plon-Nourrit, 1898.

References

Geyl, Pieter. *Napoleon, For and Against.* Trans. Olive Renier. Harmondsworth: Penguin, 1965.

South African Historiography

Historical writing on South Africa since the late nineteenth century. Before the arrival of Europeans, the indigenous people of South Africa, whose languages lacked a written script, recorded their history through oral tradition, which is still practiced today. However, the first historians to write about South Africa were whites who sought to chronicle the settlement of the country and justify European dominance over blacks. Through the turn of the nineteenth and twentieth centuries, George M. Theal, widely recognized as the founder of this settler school, produced numerous volumes on South African history and also edited collections of related colonial documents for publication. Unconcerned with analysis, Theal's eleven-volume *History of South Africa* celebrated the progress of white "civilization" and relegated blacks to a subordinate role in the country's past. Succeeding Theal as the leading settler historian, George Cory, a chemistry professor at Rhodes University in Grahamstown, wrote the *Rise of South Africa* in the 1920s, which established a tradition of procolonial and antiblack historical writing that would remain influential for many generations.

With the rise of Afrikaner nationalism leading up to the Anglo-Boer War of 1899–1902 and their political dominance in the Union of South Africa after 1910, Afrikaner historians began to glorify their own past. This was intensified after the election of the Afrikaner National party in 1948 and the institutionalization of racist, apartheid policies. Fundamental to this school was the romanticization of the Great Trek of the 1830s as a nationalist movement of Afrikaners escaping oppressive British rule at the cape by migrating inland to an empty land that had been depopulated by brutal tribal warfare. Africans were portrayed as irrationally violent and inherently duplicitous savages who, as the biblical children of Ham, were put on earth to serve whites. By the 1960s and 1970s F.A. Van Jaarsveld had become the leading figure in this genre, which came to dominate history texts used in the South African school system.

White South African liberals reacted against both the settler and Afrikaner schools of thought. In the 1930s and 1940s, William M. Macmillan, C.W. De Kiewiet, and Eric Walker wrote histories that claimed that the racially based problems in the country could be traced back to settler dispossession of African people in the early nineteenth century. These historians were the first to bring analysis into South African history and attempted, albeit with a touch of white paternalism, to be sympathetic to blacks. Interestingly, the early liberals were the first to see economic factors as critical to South African history.

With the decolonization of tropical Africa in the 1960s, Africanist historians glorified precolonial history in order to give a sense of historical pride to the newly independent states. In turn, some South African historians, mostly English-speaking white liberals, attempted to emulate these developments. In 1966, John Omer-Cooper, a South African who taught at universities in both Nigeria and Zambia, became the first historian to describe the rise of Shaka's Zulu Kingdom in the 1820s as a positive example of African nation building. Three years later, Monica Wilson and Leonard Thompson published the *Oxford History of South Africa*, which would come to define this new liberal Africanist school. These historians saw the problems of their time as rooted primarily in anachronistic Afrikanerdom. Since Dutch settlers had first arrived at the Cape in 1652, their descendants lacked the liberal attitudes developed during the eighteenth-century European Enlightenment. According to the liberal Africanist school, institutionalized racism was economically irrational and would eventually deteriorate because of the natural integrative tendencies of free enterprise. However, economics was assigned an almost insignificant role in the Anglo-Boer war of 1899–1902, which liberals portrayed as a struggle between Afrikaner self-determination and British strategic necessity to control the sea route to India.

Frustrated by the further institutionalization of apartheid through a homeland policy that stripped South African blacks of citizenship in their own country and influenced by the radicalism of the late 1960s and early 1970s, Marxist historians quickly attacked the liberal Africanist school for ignoring economics and class. They claimed that capitalism constituted the very foundation of apartheid and that the only way to destroy it was through a Marxist revolution. While F.A. Johnstone was the first to publish a book in this emerging radical school, the mostly unpublished work of Martin Legassick was vital in its development. As the production of gold in South Africa was more expensive than in other parts of the world, the radicals claimed that the government's racist policies were aimed primarily at cutting costs by providing European mine owners with a constant and extremely cheap supply of African labor. Pushed into tiny reserves by various land acts and the inadequacies of underfunded black education, Africans had little choice but to become migrant laborers who were kept in low-paying jobs by a color bar that reserved higher-paying positions for whites. Anthony Atmore and Shula Marks maintained that the Anglo-Boer War had been a struggle over who would control the capitalist development of South Africa. Radicals also criticized liberals for portraying Africans as an undifferentiated mass. Consequently, a series of studies appeared that concentrated on the material contradictions of various African societies in South Africa and how this affected their response to colonial intrusion.

In a critique of South African historiography, Harrison Wright suggested that both liberals and radicals were too concerned with "the burden of the present" and accused the latter of misapplying Western class analysis to non-Western societies. In turn, many radicals were forced to admit that they had gone too far in dismissing such salient, non-economic factors as Afrikaner nationalism.

Timothy J. Stapleton

See also AFRICAN HISTORIOGRAPHY, SUB-SAHARAN.

References

Cory, G.E. *The Rise of South Africa.* 5 vols. London: Longmans, Green and Company, 1910–1930.

De Kiewiet, C.W. *The Imperial Factor in South Africa.* Cambridge, Eng.: Cambridge University Press, 1837.

Johnstone, F.R. *Class, Race and Gold: A Study of Class Relations and Racial Discrimination in South Africa.* London: Routledge and Kegan Paul, 1976.

Macmillan, W.M. *Bantu, Boer and Briton.* London: Faber and Guyer, 1929.

———. *The Cape Colour Question.* London: Faber and Guyer, 1927.

Omer-Cooper, J.D. *The Zulu Aftermath.* London: Longmans, 1966.

Theal, G.M. *History of South Africa*. 11 vols. London: Fisher Unwin, 1892–1919.

Van Jaarsveld, F.A. *The Afrikaner's Interpretation of South African History*. Cape Town: Simondium Publishers, 1964.

Walker, E. *A History of South Africa*. London: Longmans, 1928.

Wilson, M., and Thompson, L., eds. *The Oxford History of South Africa*. 2 vols. Oxford: Oxford University Press, 1969–1971.

Wright, H.M. *The Burden of the Present: Liberal-Radical Controversy over Southern African History*. Cape Town: David Philip, 1977.

Southern, Richard William (b. 1912)

English historian of medieval Europe. Southern was born in Newcastle upon Tyne February 8, 1912. He took first-class honors in modern history at Balliol College, Oxford, in 1932. After four years as a junior fellow at Exeter College, Oxford (during which period he also studied at Paris and Munich), he returned to Balliol College as fellow and tutor. After service in World War II, Southern returned to academic life and held various positions at Oxford and Cambridge before becoming Chichele professor of modern history at Oxford (1961–1969). He served as president of the Royal Historical Society (1968–1972) and of the Selden Society (1973–1976). After retiring from the Chichele chair, he became president of St. John's College, Oxford, from 1969 to 1981. He was knighted in 1974. Southern's interests were wide, ranging from the intellectual and cultural foundations of medieval Europe (his classic first book, *The Making of the Middle Ages*, has been translated into numerous foreign languages), the career and thought of St. Anselm, the life of Robert Grosseteste, and medieval historiography. Throughout his writings, Southern has continued the work of his teachers, V.H. Galbraith and F.M. Powicke, and complements the work of his fellow student, Dom David Knowles, but in all his unique ability to synthesize and make vivid has given him preeminence among English historians of the medieval church.

Kerry E. Spiers

Texts

Ed. and trans. *The Life of St. Anselm of Canterbury by Eadmer*. London and New York: Nelson Medieval Texts, 1962.

The Making of the Middle Ages. London: Hutchinson, 1953.

Medieval Humanism and Other Studies. Oxford: Clarendon Press, 1970.

Robert Grosseteste. Oxford: Oxford University Press, 1986.

St. Anselm and His Biographer: A Study of Monastic Life and Thought. Cambridge, Eng.: Cambridge University Press, 1963.

Western Society and the Church in the Middle Ages. Harmondsworth: Penguin, 1970.

Western Views of Islam in the Middle Ages. Cambridge, MA: Harvard University Press, 1962.

Soviet Historiography

The historical profession in the Soviet Union was marked by both intellectual achievement and intellectual compromise. Considering it to be "the most political of sciences," the ideological oversight agencies of the Communist Party and the Soviet state carefully scrutinized historical practice. From the late 1920s until the very collapse of the Communist system, an orthodox historiographical position defined the limits of the acceptable in historical interpretation. In general, the more closely connected with contemporary political problems, the more likely that a historiographical topic would be distorted by ideological concerns voiced from on high. In addition, the overtly instrumental approach to history and to all the social sciences—based on the Marxist–Leninist concept that there is no such thing as science for science's sake and that every interpretive position serves political ends—denied the historical profession the autonomous realm for intellectual inquiry necessary to a truly vibrant discipline. Hence, professional history as the legitimate interpreter of the nation's past experience was marginalized in the Soviet period, meaning that novelists, filmmakers, and other nonprofessional historians would serve as the integrators of past experience into synthetic visions once the Gorbachev leadership group allowed more open investigation of such issues.

Despite its flaws, the historical profession in the USSR attracted individuals of enormous learning and insight, generated work on previously understudied topics, and witnessed significant development in related disciplines, such as archaeology and source study. In terms of problematics, Soviet historians expanded the list of legitimate topics and produced important work in the history of revolutions and "revolutionary situations," the history of the working class and "social" history (in Soviet terms any history of the lower classes), the history of non-Russian Soviet nationalities, not to mention the history of the Communist Party, the Russian civil war, and World War II.

Owing to the political limitations on interpretive enquiry, many historians devoted themselves to *Quellenforschungen,* resulting in a vast array of documentary publications and a rich mining of archival holdings. Moreover, their analyses in certain areas influenced Western historical practice, as, for example, in the debate over the particularities *(osobennosti)* of Russian absolutism.

Instructive of the historical approach adopted by effective Soviet historians in this era is the work of Petr Zaionchkovskii, the late dean of Russian political history in the last decades of the nineteenth century. Zaionchkovskii not only produced a number of monographic studies dealing with significant developments in the era, but he also oversaw the preparation and publication of a multivolume guide to memoirs, diaries, and other historical sources. His interpretative approach was a form of what might be termed "Marxist–Leninist Positivism." That is to say, within certain loosely defined, but real, limits regarding interpretation, methodology, and problematics, historians were free to pursue an essentially positivist historical practice. In this, they were returning to the historiographical traditions and practices of late imperial Russian history, the only viable intellectual current at their disposal. If they examined peasant wars, serf emancipations, and "revolutionary situations" as opposed to state finances, local self-government, or czarist foreign policy, they nonetheless applied the same encyclopedic coverage of available sources, rigorous analysis of materials, and careful exposition of findings. Mandatory citations of Lenin and other externals, represented in many cases an ideological gloss having little impact on the core material. The best examples of this genre, for example Zaionchkovskii's oeuvre, compare quite favorably with the work of late imperial Russian historians and represent genuine additions to historical knowledge.

In broad evolutionary terms, Soviet historiography had three significant "moments." The first, formative, and fatal moment was the purge of historians that began in the late 1920s. Even before the purges, state influence over the historical profession was pronounced by Western standards. Since czarist Russia had had practically no tradition of private universities, professors had always been state employees, reinforcing state control over academic life. The Communists continued the practice of state domination, establishing control over universities and historical institutes soon after the seizure of power in 1917. Through most of the 1920s, that control took the shape of administrative oversight, alterations in the history curriculum

in the direction of Marxism and social science (as opposed to traditional political history), some weeding out of the faculty, control of most journals, and the creation of competitive centers such as the Communist Academy. Moreover, the dean of the new Soviet historical community, Mikhail Pokrovskii (a sort of renegade student of V.O. Kliuchevskii) had articulated a new "Communist" historical scheme emphasizing the role of merchant capital and taking a very critical view of the Russian autocracy. This interpretation was promoted in an increasingly exclusive manner. Thus, state and party control over the historical profession was already quite strong by 1929.

Late in that year there occurred a turn to the use of physical coercion that marked a quantum change in the culture and corpus of Soviet historiography. Beginning with the outrageously false accusations of the so-called Platonov affair, state security agencies used terror, public and private denunciations, arrest, exile, and execution to cow the historical profession. At the same time, Pokrovskii's interpretative scheme was debunked, having proved too abstract for mass consumption, too critical for use in the triumphal constructionism of the first Five-Year Plans, and of no direct political use to Stalin. The purge of the historians and the intellectual elite—even though some, such as Evgenii Tarle and Iurii Got'e, returned from the camps to provide years of service—set the stage for the gross falsification and reinterpretation of the past of the Stalinist era. The signal event here was the publication of the infamous *History of the Communist Party of the Soviet Union (Bolsheviks), Short Course,* a history of the Communist Party that is generally known simply as the *Short Course.* The Platonov affair and its aftermaths left no doubt that intellectual life, including historical practice, would have any kind of independent existence. Combined with the Soviet social transformation to a mass-based society dominated by a badly educated and anti-intellectual Communist elite, the Platonov affair left Soviet historiography a crippled remnant of its former self.

The second significant "moment" came in the form of the Burdzhalov affair in 1956, in which the historian Eduard Burdzhalov attempted to publish a revisionist interpretation of the February Revolution of 1917. Responding to the post-Stalinist "thaw" and the more open cultural environment that existed after Khrushchev's partial denunciation of Stalin (in his so-called Secret Speech delivered at the Twentieth Party Congress), Burdzhalov essayed an expansion of the intellectual and interpretive boundaries of Soviet historiography. The leadership of the Communist Party was still working out the nature and extent of the de-Stalinization program, however, and Burdzhalov's frontal assault failed.

Still, historical practice never returned completely to its distorted Stalinist form. While the instrumental approach to historical study never completely disappeared, the worst features of Soviet historical practice ended with the death of Stalin in 1953. The egregious falsifications and distortions of the past were now limited to the most overtly political questions, and whole sections of the Russian and Soviet past were quietly opened up for a certain type of serious historical analysis. It was this stage in particular that witnessed the re-emergence of the positivist tradition, transmitted both by holdovers from the pre-Soviet era, such as Got'e and Tarle, and in extant works. It is a matter of bitter irony that many of the classics produced in the golden age of czarist Russian historiography (works by eminent historians, such as Kliuchevskii, Got'e, and Platonov) were republished in the second half of the 1930s. One thousand copies of Platonov's general textbook treatment of Russian history were even reproduced for use in the Higher Party School. While such influences reentered Soviet historical practice, especially after Stalin's death, they always remained muted and undemonstrative. There is a Russian proverb, "Walk quietly and you will go a lot further." In the wake of the Burdzhalov affair, many Soviet historians did just that.

The final significant shift came with Gorbachev's decision to champion *glasnost'* in historical study. Unfortunately, Gorbachev's conversion to "openness" and to the study of all the "blank spots" in Soviet historical analysis was as instrumental in its own way as had been the approach to history of previous Communist leaders. He preached "openness" only when it became clear that he needed public opinion to counter the bunkered-in resistance of the Communist Party *apparat;* and this openness extended only to the degree needed to rehabilitate the Soviet past in a non-Stalinist sense, leaving untouched many sensitive areas (for example, the Katyn forest massacre during the "Great Patriotic War"). Whatever its long-term impact would have been, Gorbachev's call for *glasnost'* came too close to the end of the Communist experiment to have had a significant impact on Soviet historical practice.

The main lines of Soviet historiography remained unchanged by the brief interlude of *glasnost':* to wit, some expansion of the historical problematic, yeoman work in archives and with documents, combined with serious study of limited and politically sensitive topics. Yet, when one considers the enormous state funding allocated in the USSR for professional history at both the federal and the republic levels and the growth and development of historiography in other developed countries over the same period, then one cannot help feeling that much of Soviet historiography was both a tragedy and a waste.

T. Sanders

See also MARXISM AND HISTORIOGRAPHY; RUSSIAN HISTORIOGRAPHY (TO 1917).

Texts

History of the Communist Party of the Soviet Union (Bolsheviks), Short Course. Toronto: Francis White Publishers, 1939.

History of the Communist Party of the Soviet Union. Ed. B.N. Ponomarev; trans. Andrew Rothstein. Moscow: Foreign Language Publishing, 1960.

References

Baron, Samuel H., and Nancy W. Heer. "The Soviet Union: Historiography Since Stalin." In *International Handbook of Historical Studies: Contemporary Research and Theory,* ed. Georg G. Iggers and Harold T. Parker. Westport, CT: Greenwood Press, 1979.

Black, C.E., ed. *Rewriting Russian History: Soviet Interpretations of Russia's Past.* New York: Frederick A. Praeger, 1956.

Burdzhalov, E.N. *Russia's Second Revolution: The February 1917 Uprising in Petrograd.* Ed. and trans. Donald J. Raleigh. Bloomington: Indiana University Press, 1978.

Davies, R.W. *Soviet History in the Gorbachev Revolution.* Bloomington: Indiana University Press, 1989.

Enteen, G.M. *The Soviet Scholar-Bureaucrat; M.N. Pokrovskii and the Society of Marxist Historians.* University Park: Pennsylvania State University Press, 1978.

Heer, Nancy Whittier. *Politics and History in the Soviet Union.* Cambridge, MA: MIT Press, 1971.

Keep, J., and L. Brisby, eds. *Contemporary History in the Soviet Mirror.* New York: Praeger, 1964.

Mazour, Anatole. *The Writing of History in the Soviet Union.* Stanford, CA: Hoover Institution Press, 1971.

Nekrick, Aleksandr. *Forsake Fear: Memoirs of an Historian.* Trans. Donald Lineburgh. Armonk, NY: M.E. Sharpe, Inc., 1989.

Wieczynki, Joseph L., and George N. Rhyne, eds. *Modern Encyclopedia of Russian and Soviet History.* 55 vols. Gulf Breeze, FL: Academic International Press, 1976–1993.

Spanish Historiography

Historical works written on the Iberian peninsula by subjects of the governments that, from the Roman Empire up to our time, have come to make up present-day Spain. During the long period of Romanization, "Hispania" acquired a cultural as well as a geographical personality (the Iberian peninsula), recognized in the work of the Hispano-Roman historian, Orosius. In the sixth century, the Visigoth kingdom of Toledo achieved a notable degree of religious and social unity in a territory that coincided practically in its entirety with the limits of the peninsula. The collective consciousness of its inhabitants bore little resemblance, however, to modern, Spanish national sentiment. In the sixth century, Saint Isidore of Seville (ca. 570–636) wrote both a *Chronicon* [Chronicle], an account of God's providential and universal plans, and a history of the Gothic, Vandal, and Suevic kings.

The Muslim invasion at the beginning of the eighth century was quickly faced by various groups of resistance in the northern mountains where, running from west to east, several sovereign kingdoms lay: Asturias (later Asturias and Leon from which Portugal—an independent kingdom from 1139—and Castile broke away); Navarre; and Aragon and Catalonia, where, united in the person of their sovereigns from 1137, the same formula of personal union and conservation of their own institutions in their respective territories was maintained and later applied in the reconquered kingdoms of Majorca (1229) and Valencia (1238) and the territories acquired in the expansion into the western Mediterranean (Sicily, 1282; Naples, 1443).

In the Asturian-Leonese area (definitively united with Castile in 1230), the Isidorian tradition was maintained for five centuries through a series of chronicles composed in Latin by clerics, at the same time that the kings revealed their aim of becoming the heirs to the Visigoth monarchy. Beginning with the early chronicles of Albelda and Alfonso III, this tradition reached its full maturity in the thirteenth century with the two works commissioned by Alfonso X the Wise (1252–1284), a *History of the World* and a *History of Spain* in which the kingdom of Castile and Leon is the main protagonist.

The historiographical production of the other kingdoms (including the Muslim kingdoms of Al-Andalus) shows to what extent Alfonso X's history and its successors evinced a particular vision of Spain, favored by the consciousness of a geographical and cultural reality known as Hispania. The Crown of Aragon composed its own history in a general chronicle written in Latin and Catalan; several other works of the thirteenth and fourteenth centuries mark the high point of medieval Catalan historiography.

The Crown of Aragon's economic and dynastic crisis, unsolved by the accession to the Aragon throne in 1412 of the Trastamara family, already reigning in Castile, did not extinguish the area's diverse political, cultural, and historiographical traditions. Interest now shifted to the kingdom of Aragon where the group of humanists associated with Cardinal Margarit (1421–1484), who dreamt of the reunification of the former Roman Hispania, coexisted with the hymn of praise to the virtues and heroic deeds of the Aragonese nation of Gualberto Fabricio de Vagad's *Cronica de Aragon* (1499). The first chronicles of the kingdom of Navarre were also composed in the fifteenth century. In the later Middle Ages the ethnic consciousness of Spain lay, then, in a relatively dormant state.

In the later Middle Ages, nobles in the various Hispanic kingdoms, as in the rest of Europe, showed a growing interest in history as well as an increasingly better knowledge of the classics, accompanied by a partial return to the use of Latin, and the range of historiographical genres was extended. Dynastic conflicts and the struggles between the Castilian monarchs and nobility provide the background to the *Chronicles* of Chancellor López de Ayala (1332–1407), an exceptionally talented writer with an excellent background in the classics. The clerics García de Santamaría (d. 1456) and Sánchez de Arévalo (1404–1470) used Latin in their defense of the crown and its mission to govern the whole of Spain.

Chivalrous historiographical works in the manner of Froissart are, however, uncommon in the Hispanic kingdoms, perhaps the most notable exception being Rodríguez de Lena's meticulous description of a famous joust of 1434. Chronicles of cities are also rare, in comparison with Germany or Italy, while biographies or collections of biographical portraits (Fernán Pérez de Guzmán [1376–1460] and Hernando del Pulgar [ca. 1425–ca. 1494]), travel books, and memoirs can all be found.

The unity of the crowns of Aragon and Castile in 1474, in the persons of their sovereigns (first the Catholic kings Ferdinand and Isabella; then, the Habsburgs), without detriment to the ancient institutions of each kingdom, revived, nevertheless, the "unitarist" tradition of the Astur-Leonese chroniclers of the ninth century. This was accentuated by the fact that the American enterprise was fundamentally Castilian and that the weight of the foreign policy of the Catholic monarchy from the sixteenth to the seventeenth century was mainly borne by the kingdom of Castile. The Italian humanists brought to Spain by the Catholic kings worked in this tradition. Antonio de Nebrija (1444–1522) is one example, as is the Jesuit, Juan de Mariana (1536–1623), whose general history of Spain continued to be read up until the nineteenth century.

Castilian dominance was also reflected in historians of the New World, in the theory of history (Melchor Cano [1509–1560]) and in humanist historiography as represented by Diego Hurtado de Mendoza (1503–1575). The decline that began in the seventeenth century affected all the areas mentioned, even though external and internal armed conflicts produced some first-rate work, such as that of the Portuguese writer, Francisco Manuel de Melo (1611–1676), and the Catalan, Francisco de Moncada (1586–1635). More generally, the crisis of the Spanish monarchy in the mid-seventeenth century favored the outlying kingdoms. Aragon produced the finest Hispanic historian of the sixteenth century in Jerónimo de Zurita y Castro (1512–1580), whose *Annals* are an authentic peninsular history written from the Aragonese perspective. The Aragonese continued this work in the seventeenth century through the appointment of official chroniclers, such as Bartolomé Leonardo de Argensola (1562–1631), Juan Francisco Andrés de Uztarroz (1606–1653), and Diego José Dormer (ca. 1650–1705). The general estates of the kingdom of Navarre also for the first time appointed a chronicler, the Jesuit José de Moret (1615–1687), author of Navarre's *Annals*. The specific and politically motivated historiography of the Basque provinces began in the sixteenth century.

The Hispanic world came very late to the study of "antiquities": we must wait until the end of the seventeenth century and for two writers more linked to the Italian than the Spanish culture, Nicolás Antonio (1617–1684) and Gaspar Ibáñez de Segovia Peralta y Mendoza, marquis of Mondéjar (1628–1708). The development of documentary collections, the auxiliary sciences, criticism of historical falsifications, and the achievement of the new goal of a universal history that did not unjustly neglect Spain's contribution, occurred during the eighteenth century. During this period, too, the foundations of Arabic studies were laid, American studies were strengthened, and economic history, legal history, literary history, and church history were all developed. Useful general histories of Spain were written, especially Juan Francisco Masdeu's (1744–1817), "unattached," as Diego Catalán has put it, "to Castilian messianism."

While a new Spanish nationalism can be said to have appeared toward the end of the eighteenth century among the enlightened intellectuals, the same is true of the old "cultural nations" that made up the Catholic monarchy and in some cases it was even more accentuated, in nostalgia for the charters lost by Catalonia, Aragon, Valencia, and Majorca in the war of the Spanish Succession (1701–1714), and in the continuity of national histories, in open conflict with the central power, in Navarre and the Basque provinces where local charters had been maintained.

This tension between competing "Spanish historiographies" was expressed in dialectical form between Spanish nationalism and peripheral nationalisms throughout the nineteenth and twentieth centuries. In the meantime, the gap between Spain and the advanced nations of Europe and America grew ever wider as a result of the various crises that afflicted the country during the first half of the nineteenth century: the Peninsular War, the loss of the colonies, Spain's descent to third-power status, the civil wars between liberals and traditionalists, which only ceased in 1876, although moderate liberals had controlled central government from 1833. Their effort up to 1931 to reconcile the monarchy, religion, and civil liberties, within a system that was neither absolutist nor democratic, combined with what has been described as "retrospective nationalism," made history one of the main supports of the new Spain, and Modesto Lafuente's (1806–1866) *Historia general de España* (29 vols., 1850–1866) the most widely read historiographical expression of these new principles.

In terms of the process of institutionalization of the new science, in the development of new documentary collections and of the auxiliary sciences, the chief influence on Spanish historiography during the nineteenth century was French. German influence was particularly notable in the first part of the twentieth century. The authority of the "positivist" school dominated practically the entire historiographical spectrum from 1875 onward. German historicism—which José Ortega y Gasset (1883–1955) wished to renew—was not, however, received in Spain, and neither was Comtian positivism nor Marxism. It was only well into the nineteenth century that Marcelino Menéndez Pelayo (1856–1912) came to identify the core of the Spanish *Volksgeist* with Catholicism. At the same time, a first generation of self-taught scholars, such as Eduardo de Hinojosa (1852–1919), Fidal Fita (1835–1917), and Francisco Codera (1836–1917), made it possible for history finally to take shape as a science in the first thirty years of the twentieth century, and a new generation of professional scholars soon followed: Ramón Menéndez Pidal (1869–1968), Rafael Altamira (1866–1951), Julián Ribera (1858–1934), and Miguel Asín Palacios (1871–1944) are proof also of the extent to which professional historians had opened up new fields of study, an achievement that the civil war placed in grave danger, but did not entirely obliterate.

The dialectic between Spanish nationalism and the nationalisms of the outlying regions/nations partly accounts for the historians' obsession with romantic issues. The trauma of the civil war and the unresolved conflicts that lay behind it explain why the historians of the 1940s and 1950s, both those in exile and those still in Spain, turned once more to questions such as the definition of the essence of Spain, the study of Spain's formation as a historical reality, and of course, the weighing-up of the importance of the elements of unity and plurality in the course of the history of the Iberian peninsula; these fundamental issues involved Spanish historians in complex controversies, the most important of which was that between Claudio Sánchez Albornoz (1893–1984) and Américo Castro (1885–1972).

In spite of the trauma caused by the civil war and postwar period, from the 1950s onward Spanish historians carried on with the task of the renewal of historical studies begun in the first part of the century. They were strongly influenced by the French Annales movement (represented by the work of the Catalan Jaime Vicens Vives [1910–1960]) and by Marxism (through the French historian Pierre Vilar [b. 1906]). The British school of Raymond Carr (b. 1919), various American trends, and, finally, the "Bielefeld school," have all influenced recent Spanish historiography, an outshoot today, as two hundred years ago, of that of the leading Western countries. In recent years outstanding work has undoubtedly been done by Spanish historians but, even in these cases, their slowness in incorporating new ways of understanding history has limited their influence outside Spain.

Ignacio Olábarri

See also BASQUE HISTORIOGRAPHY; CATALAN HISTORIOGRAPHY; PORTUGUESE HISTORIOGRAPHY.

References

Catalán, Diego. "España en su historiografía: De objeto a sujeto de la historia [Spain in Her Historiography: From Object to Subject of History]." Introductory essay to R. Menéndez Pidal, *Los españoles en su historia* [1947]. Madrid: Espasa-Calpe, 1982, 9–67.

Morales Moya, Antonio. "Historia de la historiografía española [History of Spanish Historiography]." In *Enciclopedia de Historia de España* [Encyclopedia of the History of Spain], ed. M. Artola. Vol. VII. Madrid: Alianza, 1993, 583–684.

Olábarri, Ignacio. "Un conflicto entre nacionalismos: La 'cuestion regional' en España, 1808–1939 [A Clash between Nationalisms: The 'Regional Question' in Spain, 1808–1939]." In *La España de las Autonomías* [The Autonomist Spain], ed. F. Fernández. Madrid: Instituto de Estudios de Administración Local, 1985, 69–147.

Sánchez Alonso, Benito. *Historia de la Historiografía española* [History of Spanish Historiography]. 3 vols. Madrid: CSIC, 1944–1950.

Spear, Thomas George Percival (1901–1982)

British historian of India. In the course of a long academic career, leavened by wartime employment in the government of India's information service, Spear wrote eight books on modern Indian history. He was born in Bath, Somerset, and educated at Monkton School and St. Catharine's College, Cambridge, where he read both parts of the History Tripos and undertook doctoral studies. In 1924, he became a lecturer at St. Stephen's College, Delhi, and subsequently a reader at Delhi University. He held a Leverhulme research fellowship in England from 1937 to 1939. In 1945, he became fellow and bursar of Selwyn College, Cambridge, and in 1963, a University lecturer in South Asian history. His first book was *The Nabobs: A Study of the Social Life of the English in Eighteenth Century India* (1932, reprinted 1963). His four later general histories of modern India were widely read: *India, Pakistan and the West* (1949); Part 3 of *The Oxford History of India* (1958; republished as a separate volume in 1965); *India, a Modern History* (1961); and Volume 2 of Pelican's *History of India* (1965). Perhaps his most important scholarship concerned the premutiny century of Mughal decline and British expansion, best exemplified in *The Twilight of the Mughuls: Studies in Late Mughul India* (1951). In retirement Spear published a biography of Robert Clive (1975). His last book, *India Remembered* (1981), was jointly authored with his wife, Margaret. As Owen Chadwick, Master of Selwyn College, said in his funeral address: "No one of our age did more to foster and extend the knowledge of the history of India in this country."

Robin J. Moore

Texts

A History of India. 2 vols. Baltimore, MD: Penguin, 1965–1966 (vol. 2 only).

India, a Modern History. New ed. Ann Arbor: University of Michigan Press, 1972.

India, Pakistan and the West. London: Oxford University Press, 1949.

The Nabobs: A Study of the Social Life of the English in Eighteenth Century India. London: Oxford University Press, 1963.

The Oxford History of India. Part 3. Oxford: Oxford University Press, 1958.

The Twilight of the Mughuls: Studies in Late Mughul India. Oxford: Oxford University Press, 1980.

Spelman, Sir Henry (ca. 1564–1641)

English historian and antiquary. Spelman was probably born in 1564. After graduating from Cambridge in 1583, he studied at Furnival's Inn and later at Lincoln's Inn, two London schools of the common law. In about 1586 Spelman became a founding member of the Elizabethan Society of Antiquaries, a group that he was to attempt unsuccessfully to revive in 1614. Spelman was intermittently involved in both central and local politics, sitting in the 1597 and 1625 parliaments, and acting as High Sheriff of Norfolk in 1604, the year in which he was knighted. He sat at various times on several royal commissions, concerned with Irish and colonial affairs; and served as a justice of the peace for Norfolk. But the bulk of his life was devoted initially to the management of his Norfolk estates and then, especially after his move to London in 1612, to antiquarian scholarship. Sir Henry Spelman died in London during October 1641. He is chiefly remembered as being, along with John Selden, a pioneer in the rediscovery of England's feudal past. In his dictionary of barbaric and obsolete terms to be found in medieval historical records, the *Archaeologus* (vol. 1, 1626; published posthumously in a complete edition, 1664), Spelman argued that feudal law and feudal knight-service were introduced to England in fully developed form only by the Norman Conquest. He thus broke down the prevailing assumption among legal scholars that English law had developed from Anglo-Saxon times without interruption or external influence. His understanding of feudal law, further developed in his *Treatise of Feuds and Tenures by Knight-Service in England* (written 1639), enabled Spelman to suggest that the English parliament was largely of post-Conquest origin. It grew out of the king's feudal court, to which his

barons (who held land directly from the king) only were initially summoned. Representatives of the commons were a later addition, not called regularly until the reign of Henry III, when feudal relationships had begun to decay. Spelman's ideas on the history of parliament were to enter political debate only when taken up by Robert Brady in the 1680s. Spelman was also deeply interested in ecclesiastical history and was a zealous defender of the church's rights. In addition to works defending historically the church's right to tithes, he produced a remarkable *History and Fate of Sacrilege* (first printed 1698), which detailed the suffering that had befallen those who acquired church property as a result of the Reformation.

Glenn Burgess

Texts

Concilia, decreta, leges, constitutiones, in re ecclesiarum orbis Britanici [Councils, Decretals, Laws, and Constitutions of the British churches]. Ed. J. Stephens. London: P. Stephens and C. Meredith, 1639.

Glossarium Archaiologicum. London: Alice Warren, 1664.

The History and Fate of Sacrilege. London: John Hartley, 1698.

References

Pocock, J.G.A. *The Ancient Constitution and the Feudal Law: A Study of English Historical Thought in the Seventeenth Century.* Second ed. Cambridge, Eng.: Cambridge University Press, 1987.

Powicke, F.M. "Sir Henry Spelman and the *Concilia.*" *Proceedings of the British Academy* 16 (1931): 1–37.

Woolf, D.R. *The Idea of History in Early Stuart England.* Toronto: University of Toronto Press, 1990.

Spengler, Oswald (1880–1936)

German substantive philosopher of history. Spengler belonged to the post–World War I generation of German "conservative-revolutionaries." Like Martin Heidegger, Friedrich Jünger, Ludwig Klages, and Carl Schmitt, Spengler combined impressive erudition and brilliant originality with a distrust of liberal democracy and its values. Spengler differentiated between mathematical mechanistic understanding, which was appropriate to inanimate things, and analogical organic understanding, appropriate to living things. Spengler called his methodology "morphology," studying the stages of cultural development and finding intercultural analogies. Despite their morphological similarities, different cultures cannot understand each other—for example, Westerners cannot comprehend the Indian concepts of zero and nirvana. Consequently there cannot be intercultural influences. Spengler's own brilliant interpretations of other cultures in fact suggest the opposite.

In his celebrated study of *The Decline of the West* (1918–1922), Spengler identified eight distinct cultures: Egyptian, Chinese, ancient Semitic, Indian, Mexican, Apollonian (Greco-Roman), Magic (Jewish, Arab, ancient Christian, and late Roman), and Faustian (European). He then ingeniously demonstrated the connections between these cultures' spacial perceptions, art, architecture, geometry, mathematics, politics, economics, social structures, and symbolism. All cultures go through an organic cycle of birth, maturation, decline, and death, civilization being the last stage in the development of culture. The civilized decline of the Apollonian world began with the Hellenic world, and its Faustian counterpart commenced in the nineteenth century. Signs of civilization include imperialism and territorial expansion. On this account, Spengler saw World War I as only the first in a series of wars and America as the new Rome; from his vantage point, the age of great art, music, and philosophy was over, and all that lay ahead was moral decline, intellectual fossilization, and philosophical skepticism and relativism.

Aviezer Tucker

Texts

The Decline of the West. Trans. Charles Francis Atkinson. New York: Knopf, 1926.

References

Fischer, Klaus P. *History and Prophecy: Oswald Spengler and the Decline of the West.* New York: Peter Lang, 1989.

Goddard, E.H., and P.A. Gibbons. *Civilisation or Civilisations: An Essay in the Spenglerian Philosophy of History.* London: Constable, 1926.

Hale, William Harlan. *Challenge to Defeat: Modern Man in Goethe's World and Spengler's Century.* New York: Harcourt, Brace, 1932.

Hughes, H. Stuart. *Oswald Spengler, a Critical Estimate.* Revised ed. New York: Scribner, 1962.

Spruill, Julia Cherry (1899–1986)

U.S. women's historian. Spruill graduated from the North Carolina College for Women in the 1920s and earned an M.A. in history from the University of North Carolina. Drawing almost entirely on contemporary primary sources including wills, inventories, legal records, housekeeping manuals, diaries, and letters, Spruill was among the first historians to outline such aspects of female domestic and public life as childbearing practices, meal preparation, education and reading habits, courtship and marriage patterns, and rituals. Her work was published in 1938 as *Women's Life and Work in the Southern Colonies.* Reflecting the times in which it was written the book concentrates almost exclusively on the upper classes, and there is no effort to deal with black experience on its own terms. Even so, richly anecdotal sections still bear reading and identify Spruill as a pioneer in U.S. social and women's history.

Barbara A. McGowan

Texts

Women's Life and Work in the Southern Colonies. Chapel Hill: University of North Carolina Press, 1938.

References

Scott, Anne F., ed. *Unheard Voices: The First Historians of Southern Women.* Charlottesville: University Press of Virginia, 1993.

Srbik, Heinrich Ritter von (1878–1951)

Austrian historian. Srbik studied history in Vienna and obtained his doctorate in 1902. He became a professor of history in Graz (1912–1922) and Vienna (1922–1945). He was minister of education in 1929/30 and served as a member of the Reichstag in Berlin and president of the Academy of Sciences in Vienna from 1938 to 1945. Having declined an offer to serve in the government of K. Schuschnigg, who attempted to prevent the "Anschluss" of Austria to Germany in 1938, Srbik joined the Nazi Party in the same year. His scholarly work was strongly inspired by political events in inter-war Europe. Srbik gradually came to see history from a pan-German perspective. Above all, he wished to overcome the traditional division of German intellectual life into the strongly opposed beliefs that either a "smaller" or a "larger" Germany (*Kleindeutschland* or *Grossdeutschland*) would be most beneficial for the further development of "Greater Germany" and Europe as a whole. The precision and scholarship of most of Srbik's historical work are generally well respected. His biography of Metternich won acclaim for its innovative treatment of its subject against the spiritual, political, social, and psychological background of his times. Srbik's later historical writings and his political convictions, which were sympathetic to Nazi ideology, combined with his latent anti-Semitism, have, however, undermined his reputation.

Klaus Larres

Texts

Deutsche Einheit: Idee und Wirklichkeit vom heiligen Reich bis Königgrätz [German Unity: Its Idea and Reality from the Holy Roman Empire to the Battle of Königgrätz]. 4 vols. Munich: F. Bruckmann, 1935–1942.

Geist und Geschichte vom deutschen Humanismus bis zur Gegenwart [The Spirit and History of German Humanism up to the Present]. 2 vols. Munich: F. Bruckmann, 1950–1951.

Metternich: Der Staatsmann und der Mensch [Metternich: The Statesman and the Man]. 3 vols. Graz: Akademischer Druck, 1979–1984.

Wallensteins Ende: Ursachen, Verlauf und Ende der Katastrophe [Wallenstein's Death: Causes, Course, and Conclusion of a Catastrophe]. Vienna: L.W. Seidel, 1920.

References

Agnelli, A. *Heinrich Ritter von Srbik.* Naples: Guida, 1975.

Kämmerer, J., ed. *Die wissenschaftliche Korrespondenz des Historikers 1912–45* [The Scholarly Correspondence of Historians, 1912–45]. Boppard: H. Boldt, 1988.

Reinalter, H. "Heinrich Ritter von Srbik." In *Deutsche Historiker,* vol. 8., ed. H.U. Wehler. Göttingen: Vandenhoeck & Ruprecht, 1982, 78–95.

Rumpler, H. "Felix Schwarzenberg und das 'Dritte Deutschland': Überlegungen zu Heinrich von Srbiks Interpretation der deutschen Politik Österreichs [Felix Schwarzenberg and the "Third Germany": Thoughts on Heinrich von Srbik's Interpretation of Austria's German Policy]." In *Beiträge zur neueren Geschichte Österreichs* [Contributions to Recent Austrian History], ed. H. Fichtenau and E. Zöllner. Vienna: Veroffentlichungen des Instituts für osterreichische Geschichtsforschung, 1974, 371–382.

Sweet, P.R. "The Historical Writing of Heinrich Ritter von Srbik." *History and Theory* 10 (1970): 37–58.

Ssu-ma Ch'ien

See SIMA QIAN.

Ssu-ma Kuang

See SIMA GUANG.

Stein, Lorenz von (1815–1890)

German historian, sociologist, and jurist. Stein was born in Schleswig, studied in Kiel, Jena, Berlin, and Paris, and was a professor of political studies at Kiel and Vienna. Stein developed an influential historical sociology based on insights into the dynamic expansion of equality since the French Revolution. His study of socialism and communism in France (1842) argued that the eighteenth-century movement for political equality had been superseded by the working-class movement for social equality. Ironically, although it was intended to warn against an impending social revolution, the book popularized French socialist doctrines in Germany. His other major works, the three-volume *Geschichte der socialen Bewegung in Frankreich von 1789 bis auf unsere Tage* [The History of the Social Movement in France from 1789 to Our Day] (1850–1855) and *System der Staatswissenschaft* [System of Political Science] (1852–1856), analyzed the socioeconomic conditions of class conflict. Deeply influenced by Hegel's political philosophy, Stein advocated the idea of a "social monarchy" that would remain above society and regulate social conflict through enlightened reform. Stein's theories contributed to the creation of an authoritarian social welfare state in Germany in the 1880s.

Warren Breckman

Texts

The History of the Social Movement in France, 1789–1850. Ed. and trans. Kaethe Mengelberg. Totowa, NJ: Bedminster Press, 1964.

Der Socialismus und Communismus des heutigen Frankreichs [Socialism and Communism in Contemporary France]. Leipzig: Wigand, 1842.

System der Staatswissenschaft. 2 vols. Osnabruck: O. Zeller, 1964.

References

Blasius, Dirk, and Eckart Pankoke. *Lorenz von Stein.* Darmstadt: Wissenschaftliche Buchgesellschaft, 1977.

Stenton, Doris Mary [née Parsons] (1894–1971)

English historian. Stenton was educated at Reading Abbey School and Reading University College. In 1916, Frank Merry Stenton, her professor (whom she married three years later), set her to work on Lincoln records. She became assistant lecturer in history at Reading from 1917 and was promoted to lecturer in 1919 and senior lecturer in 1952. From 1956 to her retirement in 1959 she held the position of reader. She was awarded honorary doctorates by Reading (1948) and Oxford (1968). As honorary secretary of the Pipe Roll Society and general editor of the society's publications after its refounding in 1923–1924, she helped to provide the necessary tools for succeeding generations of historians of medieval England. Stenton established new standards for the editing of English legal documents (for instance, in her several Selden Society editions of Assize Rolls and Eyres), and she also oversaw editions of the pipe rolls of Richard I and John. She continued to promote the publication of primary sources while serving on the executive committees of the Royal Historical and Selden societies, mainly during the 1950s. Stenton's interest in the economic and social contexts that had produced legal documents led her to write, among other works, *The English Woman in History.* After her husband's death in 1967, she completed revised editions of his works.

Georges Whalen

Texts

English Justice between the Norman Conquest and the Great Charter, 1066–1215. Philadelphia: American Philosophical Society, 1964.
English Society in the Early Middle Ages. Fourth ed. Harmondsworth: Penguin, 1965.
The English Woman in History. London: Allen and Unwin, 1957.

References

Liber Memoralis Doris Mary Stenton. Pipe Roll Society, new series 41 (1976): 1–32.
Major, Kathleen. "Doris Mary Stenton 1894–1971." *Proceedings of the British Academy* 58 (1972): 525–535.

Stenton, Sir Frank Merry (1880–1967)

English historian. Stenton was educated in Southwell, before spending two years studying music at the Reading Extension College (later Reading University). In 1899 he took up a scholarship in history at Keble College, Oxford. He wrote his first articles while a history schoolmaster at Llandovery from 1904–1908. He returned to Reading in 1908 as research fellow and, from 1912, as the university's first professor of modern history. In 1919 he married his former student, Doris Parsons (a distinguished scholar in her own right), and he became vice-chancellor of the university four years prior to his retirement in 1950. Twice president of the Royal Historical Society, he was awarded a number of honorary doctorates and was knighted in 1948. His involvement in the British Academy and Lincoln Records Society source publications series led him to cofound the English Place-Name Society in 1924 and to revive the Pipe Roll Society in 1925. Stenton's principal work, *Anglo-Saxon England* (1943), is a comprehensive treatment of its subject, drawing on a wide variety of disciplines to illuminate English society in the period from 400 to 1087. It was the first full-scale history of the period to make full use of modern critical scholarship. Incorporating information from Latin Danelaw documents into a study informed by diplomatics, archaeology, numismatics, and onomastics, *Anglo-Saxon England* also integrates economic, social, and political history. Its wealth of detail has helped to promote research on more restricted topics by providing a magisterially drawn context for specialists' studies.

Georges Whalen

Texts

Anglo-Saxon England. Third ed. Ed. Doris Stenton and Dorothy Whitelock. Oxford: Oxford University Press, 1971.
The First Century of English Feudalism, 1066–1166. Second ed. Oxford: Oxford University Press, 1961.
Preparatory to Anglo-Saxon England: Being the Collected Papers of Frank Merry Stenton. Ed. Doris M. Stenton. Oxford: Oxford University Press, 1970.

References

Stenton, Doris Mary. "Frank Merry Stenton 1880–1967." *Proceedings of the British Academy* 54 (1968): 315–423.

Stern, Daniel [pseudonym for Marie Catherine Sophie de Flavigny, Comtesse d'Agoult] (1805–1876)

Novelist and historian of the French Revolution of 1848. Marie d'Agoult was born into the French aristocracy and in 1827 married the comte Charles d'Agoult, member of a prominent noble family.

D'Agoult was initially famed for abandoning her family in 1833 to live with the pianist Franz Liszt. She began her career as a woman of letters by maintaining a Parisian salon (occasionally in cooperation with George Sand). Most of her published work dates from after 1839 when she ended her relationship with Liszt, settled in Paris, and adopted the pen-name Daniel Stern.

Stern is best known for her *Histoire de la Révolution de 1848* [History of the Revolution of 1848], published in three volumes from 1850 to 1853. She explained the revolution as a spontaneous union of the bourgeoisie and the Parisian popular classes; it was both the final act of Catholic absolutism and the introduction of a modern, rational, republican state. Stern's *Histoire* emphasized that the transformations wrought by 1848 were not simply political, but also social. Her narrative includes vivid portraits of the principal actors of the revolution, both political figures, such as Louis-Philippe and Lamartine, and the Parisian crowd that Stern saw, sympathetically, as the guiding force behind revolutionary events.

Carol E. Harrison

Texts

Esquisses morales et politiques [Political and Moral Sketches]. Paris: Pagnerre, 1849.
Histoire de la Révolution de 1848. 3 vols. Paris: G. Sandre, 1850–1853.
Mes souvenirs, 1806–1833 [Memoirs]. Paris: Levy, 1877.

References

Desanti, Dominique. *Daniel, ou le visage secret d'une comtesse romantique, Marie d'Agoult* [Daniel, or the Secret Face of a Romantic Countess]. Paris: Stock, 1980.
Walton, Whitney. "Writing the 1848 Revolution: Politics, Gender, and Feminism in the Works of French Women of Letters." *French Historical Studies* 18 (1994): 1001–1024.

Stone, Lawrence (b. 1919)

Anglo-American historian. Stone's education at Christ Church, Oxford, which began in 1938, was not completed until 1946 because of his wartime naval service. (Even this interruption, however, bore historical fruit since it resulted in 1944 in Stone's first published article, on the Armada campaign of 1588.) After 1947 Stone taught in Oxford, first at University College (1947–1950) and then at Wadham College (1950–1963).

Increasingly disillusioned with the insularity of the Oxford syllabus and its narrow and conservative approach to historical studies and worn down by the constant round of undergraduate teaching, Stone quit England for the United States in 1963. He became Dodge professor of history at Princeton in that year and soon after took American citizenship. On his initiative the Shelby Cullom Davis Center for Historical Studies was set up at Princeton in 1968. He retired from Princeton in 1989. Stone's greatest intellectual debt—frequently acknowledged—was to R.H. Tawney, and it was on Tawney's side that Stone intervened in 1948 with a key article in the "Gentry Controversy." Savaged by a well-aimed but brutal assault by H.R. Trevor-Roper, it took years for Stone to recover fully and to publish a weighty rejoinder, *The Crisis of the Aristocracy 1558–1641* (1965). Stone has subsequently produced two further quantitative contributions to this field—*Family and Fortune: Studies in Aristocratic Finance in the Sixteenth and Seventeenth Centuries* (1973) and, most recently, a computer-aided study, *An Open Elite? England 1540–1880* (1984). Taken together these three volumes extend to more than two thousand pages of print. But Stone has authored eight other books, edited four more, and contributed almost fifty essays to books and periodicals. Of the books the most notable are his trilogy on English marriage—*The Road to Divorce: England 1530–1987* (1990); *Marriage in England, 1660–1753* (1992); and *Broken Lives: Separation and Divorce in England, 1660–1857* (1993). A firm believer in the value of linking history and the social sciences, Stone, in *The Causes of the English Revolution* (1972, second ed., 1985), controversially offered a conceptual model that owed much to political scientists and sociologists. Many of Stone's essays of a pronounced theoretical and methodological kind were collected together as *The Past and the Present* (1981, second enl. ed., 1987).

R.C. Richardson

Texts

The Causes of the English Revolution. Second ed. New York: Routledge and Kegan Paul/Methuen, 1986.
The Crisis of the Aristocracy 1558–1641. Oxford: Clarendon Press, 1965.
Family and Fortune: Studies in Aristocratic Finance in the Sixteenth and Seventeenth Centuries. Oxford: Clarendon Press, 1973.
The Family, Sex and Marriage in England, 1500–1800. New York: Harper and Row, 1977.

And Jeanne C. Fawtier Stone. *An Open Elite? England 1540–1880.* Oxford: Clarendon Press, 1984.

The Past and the Present Revisited. London: Routledge and Kegan Paul, 1987.

The Road to Divorce: England 1530–1987. Oxford, Eng.: Oxford University Press, 1990.

References

Beier, A.L., D. Cannadine, and J.M. Rosenheim, eds. *The First Modern Society: Essays in Honour of Lawrence Stone.* Cambridge, Eng.: Cambridge University Press, 1989.

Berlatsky, J. "Lawrence Stone: Social Science and History." In *Recent Historians of Great Britain: Essays on the Post 1945 Generation,* ed. W.L. Arnstein. Ames: Iowa University Press, 1990, 75–100.

Hexter, J.H. *On Historians.* London: Collins, 1979.

Stopes, Charlotte Carmichael (1841–1929)

British scholar and supporter of the vote for women. Born in Edinburgh, Charlotte Stopes enrolled in Women's University Classes conducted by friendly professors before the opening of Scotch universities to women in 1892. She received the highest certificates then possible and a first-class honours diploma. She married Henry Stopes, an architect, civil engineer, and anthropologist, in 1879. After settling in Norwood, Stopes became known for her research and publication on women's issues. Her works, *British Freewomen: Their Historical Privileges* (1894), *Women's Protest* (1896), and *The Sphere of "Man" in Relation to That of "Women" in the Constitution* (1908), all protest against women's political, legal, and economic subjugation by men. Arguing for a homogeneous system of law, Stopes attacked the nonvoting status of women as unconstitutional, placing much of the blame on the jurist Sir Edward Coke's reinterpretation of women's legal position in the seventeenth century.

Laurie J. Gagnier

Texts

British Freewomen: Their Historical Privileges. London: S. Sonnenchein, 1894.

The Life of Henry Third Earl of Southampton, Shakespeare's Patron. New York: AMS Press, 1920.

The Sphere of "Man" in Relation to That of "Women" in the Constitution. London: T. Fisher Unwin, 1908.

Stow, John (ca. 1525–1605)

English chronicler and antiquarian. Stow was born in London, the son of a tallow chandler. Little is known of his early life, and there is no evidence that he attended any type of school. He was admitted to the freedom of the Merchant Taylors' company in 1547, but spent the bulk of his time collecting historical records and writing. His first publication was an edition of the works of Chaucer (1561). Beginning in 1565 Stow published a series of chronicles that culminated in the quarto *Annales of England* (1605), which recounted the history of England through the accession of James I; the *Annales* were subsequently reprinted and revised by Edmund Howes (1615, 1632). Stow also produced smaller, abridged chronicles or "Summaries" that made history accessible to a wider public. Associated with William Camden and with the members of the Elizabethan Society of Antiquaries, his most enduring work was *A Survey of London* (1598; rev. ed. 1603), the classic topographical account of the city during the sixteenth century. Among the most prolific of Elizabethan historians, Stow is important not only for his published works and collection of manuscripts, but also for his unique perspective as a citizen historian. Unlike most early modern historical writers, he lacked the formal education and social status required to be ranked as a gentleman and consequently wrote history that reflected the interests and values of the common people of his day.

Barrett L. Beer

Texts

The Annales of England. London: G. Bishop and T. Adams, 1605.

A Survey of London by John Stow Reprinted from the Text of 1603, with Introduction and Notes. Ed. Charles L. Kingsford. 2 vols. Oxford: Clarendon Press, 1908.

References

Beer, Barrett L. "John Stow and Tudor Rebellions, 1549–1569." *Journal of British Studies* 27 (1988): 352–374.

Levy, F.J. *Tudor Historical Thought.* San Marino, CA: Huntington Library, 1967.

McKisack, May. *Medieval History in the Tudor Age.* Oxford: Clarendon Press, 1971.

Strickland, Agnes (1796–1874)

English historian. Strickland and her eight siblings were educated by their father, Thomas Strickland, who evidently encouraged them in literary ambitions: six of his children became published authors.

The financial pressures felt by the family after his death in 1818 stimulated Agnes and her sister Elizabeth in their pursuit of literary careers. They began by publishing essays and children's books, mostly on historical topics. Their first major success, *Lives of the Queens of England* (1840–1848), was jointly authored but appeared, at Elizabeth's desire, under Agnes's name only. The twelve-volume series was widely praised for its accessible style and its abundant use of contemporary letters and documents; almost as widely, it was criticized for its perceived partiality and its disregard for conventional standards of historical significance. The sisters collaborated on numerous further projects, including *Lives of the Queens of Scotland and English Princesses* (1850–1859) and *Lives of the Bachelor Kings of England* (1861). Agnes also published several historical and fictional works on her own, including an edition of the letters of Mary Queen of Scots (1843). Strickland's histories are often overtly didactic: she emphasizes women's potential for benevolent moral and spiritual influence, a potential she finds exemplified by most of her historical subjects. Despite their tendentiousness in this respect, her volumes remain valuable resources because of her extensive original research.

Rohan Maitzen

Texts

Ed. *Letters of Mary Queen of Scots.* 3 vols. London: M. Colburn, 1842–1843.

Lives of the Bachelor Kings of England. London: Simpkin, Marshall, 1861.

Lives of the Queens of England. 12 vols. London: H. Colburn, 1840–1848.

Lives of the Queens of Scotland and English Princesses Connected with the Royal Succession of Great Britain. 8 vols. Edinburgh and London: Wm. Blackwood & Sons, 1850–1859.

References

Maitzen, Rohan. "'This Feminine Preserve': Historical Biographies by Victorian Women." *Victorian Studies* 38 (1995): 371–393.

Mitchell, Rosemary. "Separate Spheres and Early Women's History." In her "Approaches to English History in Text and Image in Britain, c. 1830–1870." D.Phil. dissertation, Oxford University, 1993, chap. 5, 131–175.

Pope-Hennessy, Una. *Agnes Strickland: Biographer of the Queens of England, 1796–1874.* London: Chatto & Windus, 1940.

Strickland, Jane Margaret. *Life of Agnes Strickland.* Edinburgh and London: Wm. Blackwood & Sons, 1887.

Structuralism

An intellectual movement of the 1950s and 1960s identified with the research of the French anthropologist Claude Lévi-Strauss into the deep structure of symbolic language. Lévi-Strauss argued for the existence of a common framework of symbolic forms underpinning the use of language in all cultures. His intent was to reveal the integral coherence of cultural systems in all times and places, however different they might appear to be from one another, and so to challenge the ethnocentrism of Western historiography for privileging the values and achievements of Western culture as a unique creation.

The structuralist anthropology stemming from Lévi-Strauss's work has enriched both the subject matter and the methods of contemporary historiography. It has also exposed the limitations of the narrative history upon which so much of Western historiography had hitherto been based, with its focus on the historicity of particular events and personalities. Still, some historians had taken up similar methods long before the term "structuralism" had acquired intellectual currency. As early as the eighteenth century, Giambattista Vico, in his *New Science* (1744), had argued for the historical development of a universal poetics of language (a "common mental dictionary") that prepared the way for reflective thought. There are also structuralist notions implicit in the theories of Karl Marx and Sigmund Freud in their search for hermeneutic keys to hidden patterns of history.

More directly germane to the preoccupations of structural anthropology was the work of the French historians associated with the Annales school of historiography, notably that of Fernand Braudel. In a famous debate launched in 1958, Braudel took issue with Lévi-Strauss for his atemporal model of the deep structures of culture and offered an alternative modulated by long-term historical change. Like Lévi-Strauss, Braudel worked with a conception of binary oppositions as the building blocks of cultural systems, whose dynamics he explained in terms of the antinomy between forces retarding and forces promoting historical change. Even the most stable cultural structures, Braudel contended, were not immune to modifications over long periods of time. The issue, he proposed, is not timeful versus timeless structures, but the way in which different kinds of structures are situated within historical time. Historical time, he taught, is relative to the nature of the phenomena under investigation. Changes in geological processes are glacially slow, but nonetheless real. Social processes are characterized by a quicker tempo, but one still too slow to be noticed within the span of living memory. Changes in political processes, by contrast, are easily observed, and so have come to constitute the backbone of historical chronology, even though they convey a misleading impression of history's rapid movement.

The Annales historians sought to compensate for the deficiencies of narrative political history by expanding the scope of their enterprise to encompass a range of topics that lent themselves to structuralist analysis. Research into demographic, ethnographic, social, and economic processes called for a kind of analysis that placed vast quantities of data in serial patterns so as to highlight common practices or long-range trends and thereby to minimize the importance of particular personalities or unique events. Vis-à-vis conventional historiography, one effect of such scholarship was to underscore the inertial power of the past by redirecting attention to historical problems that could be interpreted only in terms of long-range processes.

Even for the dramatic change attending revolutions and other crises or catastrophes, the Annalistes discounted the causal role of singular personalities and events, and proposed instead the significance of encounters among clashing cultural systems that were themselves products of long-range structural change. Herein historians sympathetic to Marxism learned from and joined forces with them. Historians of revolutionary movements in France (for example, Ernest Labrousse and Georges Lefebvre) redirected attention from the force of immediate personalities and events to the "revolution from below," the crises precipitated by the "conjunctures" of discordant structural processes that had been in the making, often unnoticed, for long periods of time: for example, the growing obsolescence of rigid legal and political institutions, the impact of long-term economic cycles, emerging popular protest over grievances of long standing, and the subversive effects of new forms of political discourse or new technologies of communication.

Structuralist methods also underpinned the history of collective mentalities, an interest of the early pioneers of Annales scholarship renewed in the 1960s as an alternative to the more elitist history of ideas. As early as 1929, Lucien Febvre had called for an inventory of the "mental equipment" of the past—the web of habits, customs, and tacit understandings that provides the sinews of tradition. Such studies of early modern France (Pierre Goubert, Robert Mandrou) underscored the tenacious power of traditional mores as obstacles to innovation. Others paid more attention to the emergence of structures of thought identified with the coming of the modern age—Philippe Ariès's interpretation of the historical elaboration of the stages of life reconceived as a developmental process, for example, or Norbert Elias's rendering of the historical construction of a code of manners common to Western culture by the eighteenth century. The quest for individual opportunity and personal growth characteristic of modern culture, they suggested, was ironically made possible by the self-discipline fostered by more elaborate codes of conduct.

Here the work of Michel Foucault is germane, preparing the way for poststructuralism. What interested Foucault was the structuring process itself, which, he argued, favors not the perpetuation of traditions but rather their ongoing and sometimes dramatic disruption ("epistemic breaks"). He studied the process by which new discursive practices were created or old ones redeployed to justify expanding systems for managing social behavior in modern Western society. Discourse tends to incite more discourse, he argued, and so complicates and accelerates the structuring process. His method of analyzing the forms of culture apart from the values they were intended to publicize points to the fragility of the ideological justifications underpinning modern cultural systems and evinces his own waning faith in their power.

Perhaps the most enduring impact of structuralism upon historiography has been the development of global history of the sort written by the American historian William McNeill. He traces the dynamics of world history in terms of the encounters among civilizations, by which military and political balances are upset, new forms of commerce are introduced, and alien technologies and values are exchanged. Through such encounters the equilibria of previously self-contained cultures are disturbed, but over time new, often larger cultural systems are established, culminating in the structure of global connections that give form to contemporary civilization.

Patrick H. Hutton

See also ANNALES SCHOOL; BRAUDEL, FERNAND; DERRIDA, JACQUES; FOUCAULT, MICHEL; HISTORICISM; MENTALITIES; POSTMODERNISM; SERIAL HISTORY; VICO, GIAMBATTISTA; WHITE, HAYDEN.

Texts

Braudel, Fernand. *On History*. Trans. Sarah Matthews. Chicago: University of Chicago Press, 1980.

Foucault, Michel. *The Archaeology of Knowledge*. Trans. A.M. Sheridan Smith. New York: Harper and Row, 1972.

Lévi-Strauss, Claude. *Structural Anthropology*. Trans. Claire Jacobson. New York: Basic Books, 1963.

McNeill, William. *Mythistory and Other Essays*. Chicago: University of Chicago Press, 1986.

References

Bourdé, Guy, and Hervé Martin. *Les Écoles historiques* [Historical Schools]. Paris: Seuil, 1983.

Burguière, André, ed. "Histoire et structure." Special issue of *Annales: Economies, sociétés, civilisations*, 26/3 and 4 (May–August 1971).

Hutton, Patrick. "The History of Mentalities." *History and Theory* 20 (1981): 237–259.

Le Goff, Jacques, Roger Chartier, and Jacques Revel, eds. *La Nouvelle Histoire* [The New History]. Paris: Retz-C.E.P.L., 1978.

Megill, Allan. *Prophets of Extremity*. Berkeley: University of California, 1985.

Stubbs, William (1825–1901)

English historian, bishop, and academic. William Stubbs was born in Yorksire in 1825 and attended the Ripon School prior to matriculating at Oxford. Ordained to the Anglican priesthood (1850) Stubbs focused his academic and clerical life in Oxford. He served as librarian of Lambeth Palace (1862), Regius professor of history at Oxford (1866–1884), bishop of Chester (1884–88), and bishop of Oxford (1888–1901). During the period from 1858 to 1889 Stubbs was absorbed in English medieval history and formulated a new analysis of medieval English constitutional history. Stubbs's most popular publication was the three-volume *Constitutional History of England in Its Origin and Development* (1873–1878). In this work Stubbs demonstrated a mastery of sources and, despite his own firm Tory allegiances, advanced what amounted to a version of the "Whig" interpretation of history—in the sense that it was teleological, and focused on the evolution of the constitution of his own time. This interpretation has long since been abandoned by medieval historians. More enduring as historical works are the nineteen volumes of medieval chronicles and other materials that he edited in the Rolls Series; from the *Chronicle Memorials of Richard I* (1864), through his two-volume edition of the works of William of Malmesbury, Stubbs provided quality tools for generations of historians. The introductions that he wrote to these editions were published together in a separate volume and became an influential guide to medieval historical sources. As a scholar, he provided an important link between English historiography and the newer legal and historical scholarship developing in nineteenth-century Germany.

William T. Walker

Texts

The Constitutional History of England in Its Origin and Development. 3 vols. Buffalo, NY: Hein and Co., 1987.

Ed. with A.W. Haddan. *Councils and Ecclesiastical Documents of the Anglo-Saxon Church*. Oxford: Clarendon Press, 1869–1878.

Historical Introductions to the Rolls Series. Ed. A. Hassall. London and New York: Longmans, Green, 1902.

Lectures on European History. Ed. A. Hassall. London: Longmans, Green, 1904.

Letters of William Stubbs, Bishop of Oxford, 1825–1901. Ed. W.H. Hutton. London: Constable, 1904.

Select Charters and Other Documents Illustrative of English History. Ninth ed. Ed. H.W.C. Davis. Littleton, CO: F.B. Rothman, 1985.

References

Burrow, J.W. *A Liberal Descent: Victorian Historians and the English Past*. Cambridge, Eng.: Cambridge University Press, 1981, 126–151.

Williams, Neville. "Stubbs' Appointment As Regius Professor, 1866." *Bulletin of the Institute of Historical Research* 33 (1960): 121–125.

Stukeley, William (1687–1765)

English antiquarian and cleric. William Stukeley was born in Lincolnshire and attended Corpus Christi College, Cambridge, before embarking on a clerical career, during which he served successively as rector of All Saints, Stamford (1729–1747), and of St. George-the-Martyr, London (1747–1765). He died in London. Stukeley was a cofounder of the Society of Antiquaries (1718) and a prolific author on archaeological topics. His most enduring works were *Stonehenge, a Temple Restored to the British Druids* (1740) and *Abury* [Avebury], *a Temple of the British Druids* (1743), in which he argued that the Druids had advanced a patriarchal religion. His other works included *Itinerarium Curiosum* (1724) and the regrettable publication of the fraudulent *Account of Richard of Cirencester* (1757) which was based on Charles Bertram's *De Situ Britanniae*. Although later in life Stukeley's obsession with Stonehenge tarnished his reputation, much of his earlier archaeological work was sound, and he did much to promote the systematic study of antiquarian artifacts and ancient structures.

William T. Walker

Texts

Abury [Avebury], a Temple of the British Druids. London: W. Innys et al., 1743.
Itinerarium Curiosum. London: for the author, 1724.
Stonehenge, a Temple Restored to the British Druids. Ed. R.D. Richardson, Jr. New York: Garland, 1984.

References

Piggott, S. *William Stukeley: An Eighteenth-Century Antiquary.* Revised ed. London: Thames and Hudson, 1985.

Suetonius Tranquillus, Gaius (ca. 70–ca. 122)

Roman official and biographer. Suetonius came from an equestrian (knightly) background, perhaps from North Africa. His father was a military tribune under the emperor Otho. Suetonius followed an administrative career, reaching several prestigious posts while composing his works. Knowledge of his life comes chiefly from internal references and from Pliny. While the biographer also composed lives of famous writers (grammarians, poets, historians, and so on), some of which survive, his most famous contribution is the *De Vita Caesarum* [Lives of the Caesars], which treated leaders of the Roman state from Julius Caesar to Domitian. Characterized by attention to personal lives, this work is an important source, and useful contrast to Tacitus, for the early principate. Suetonius's approach had a great impact on the genre of biography up to Einhard.

R.M. Frakes

Texts

Suetonius. Ed. J.C. Rolfe. Cambridge, MA: Harvard University Press/Loeb Classical Library, 1920.
The Twelve Caesars. Trans. Robert Graves. New York: Penguin, 1979.

References

Baldwin, Barry. *Suetonius.* Amsterdam: A.M. Hakkert, 1983.
Wallace-Hadrill, Andrew. *Suetonius: The Scholar and His Caesars.* London: Duckworth, 1983.

Suger of St. Denis (1081–1151)

French monk, royal adviser, architectural innovator, and chronicler. Of humble birth, Suger entered the royal abbey of St. Denis at an early age and was elected its abbot in 1122. Today, his abbacy is best known for the reconstruction of the abbey church in the innovative Gothic architectural style. Suger was also a leading adviser to Kings Louis VI (with whom he had been educated) and Louis VII. During the latter's two-year absence (1147–1149) from France, Suger served as regent. He wrote laudatory chronicles of the reigns in which he himself played such a prominent role: *The Life of Louis (VI) the Fat,* completed in 1144, and *The History of King Louis VII* on which he was working at the time of his death. These were the first in a series of royal biographies written at St. Denis, and became part of the *Grandes Chroniques de France* [Great Chronicles of France] compiled and written at the abbey between 1274 and 1461.

G.H. Gerrits

Texts

Oeuvres complètes de Suger [Complete Works]. Ed. A. Lecoy de la Marche. Paris: J. Renouard, 1867.

References

Aubert, Marcel. *Suger.* Paris: Fontenelle, 1950.
Spiegel, Gabrielle M. *The Chronicle Tradition of Saint-Denis: A Survey.* Brookline, MA: Classical Folia Editions, 1978.

Sun Yirang [Sun I-jang] (1848–1908)

Chinese classical scholar, epigrapher, and educational reformer. Sun Yirang's father was a Qing official from a scholarly Wenzhou family. After helping Zeng Guofan fight the Taipings, he took up teaching at the Ziyang Academy in Hangzhou. While assisting Zeng in scholarly endeavors there, the young Sun Yirang imbibed the learning of the *kaozheng* (practical studies) tradition and became interested in stone and bronze inscriptions. In 1867 he passed the provincial *(juren)* examinations. Disturbed by the destruction of libraries during the Taiping uprising, he then compiled systematic bibliographies and assembled a collection of rare

S

scholarly works. During the 1870s, 1880s, and 1890s he immersed himself in critical studies of three of these texts, the *Shujing,* the *Zhouli,* and the *Mozi.* He had these studies printed in the 1890s, together with his critical edition of the *Mozi.* Despite links with the 1898 reformers, he was not harmed when they were toppled. Following the facsimile publication of Shang dynasty oracle bones in 1903, Sun's philological training, classical knowledge, and rare epigraphic skills enabled him to recognize the bones' significance and carry out pioneering studies, printed in 1917, that contributed fundamentally to putting the understanding of ancient Chinese history on a new footing in the era of the May Fourth movement.

G.R. Blue

Texts

Zhou li Zhengyi [Ethical Principles of the Book of Rites]. 6 vols. Taibei: Taiwan shangwu yinshuguan, 1967.
Zhayi [Transcriptions from Antiquity]. Jinan: Ji lu shushe, 1989.

References

Elman, Benjamin A. *From Philosophy to Philology: Intellectual and Social Aspects of Change in Late Imperial China.* Cambridge, MA, and London: Council on East Asian Studies, Harvard University, 1984, 254–256.
Rankin, Mary Backus. "Local Reform Movements in Chekiang before 1900." In *Reform in Nineteenth-Century China,* ed. P.A. Cohen and J.K. Fairbank. Cambridge, MA, and London: East Asian Research Center, Harvard University, 1976, 221–230.
Tu Lien-chê. "Sun I-jang." In *Eminent Chinese of the Ch'ing Period (1644–1912),* ed. A.W. Hummel. Washington, DC: Government Printing Office, 1943, 677–679.
Zhu Fangpu. *Sun Yirang nianpu* [Chronological Biography of Sun Yirang]. Shanghai: Shangwu yinshuguan, 1935.

Sutherland, Dame Lucy Stuart (1903–1980)

British historian and educator. Sutherland was born in Geelong, Australia, the daughter of a mining engineer. She was educated in South Africa after her family emigrated there, and subsequently took a first-class B.A. in history at Oxford University in 1927. From 1927 to 1941, she was a fellow and tutor of Somerville College, Oxford. She was principal of Lady Margaret Hall, Oxford, from 1945 to 1971. Between 1946 and 1969, Sutherland served on many government committees and commissions. She became a Dame of the British Empire in 1969. Sutherland wrote prolifically on eighteenth-century British political, imperial, economic, and institutional history. Her major work was *The East India Company in Eighteenth Century Politics* (1952). She edited the second volume of *The Correspondence of Edmund Burke* (1960) and contributed to *The House of Commons, 1754–1790* (1964), edited by Sir Lewis Namier. Sutherland was noted for her rigorous scholarly standards, which she passed on to the young historians whom she guided.

Don M. Cregier

Texts

The East India Company in Eighteenth Century Politics. Oxford: Clarendon Press, 1952.
Politics and Finance in the Eighteenth Century. Ed. Aubrey Newman. London: Hambledon Press, 1984.

References

Obituary, *Times* [London], August 21, 1980, p. 12.
Whiteman, Anne, J.S. Bromley, and P.G.M. Dickson, eds. *Statesmen, Scholars and Merchants: Essays in Eighteenth Century History Presented to Dame Lucy Sutherland.* Oxford: Clarendon Press, 1973, vii–xv; 351–359.

Sybel, Heinrich von (1817–1895)

German historian. Sybel was educated at the University of Berlin and became professor of history successively at Bonn (1844–1846), Marburg (1846–1856), Munich (1856–1861), and again at Bonn (1861–1895). From 1875 he also served as director of the Prussian State Archives in Berlin. He founded the *Historische Zeitschrift* (1859), which remains today the leading German historical journal, and initiated several other lasting scholarly projects. He was a member of the Prussian Parliament (1862–1864, 1874–1880), and of the North German Parliament (1867), and also sat in the Frankfurt National Assembly (1848) and in the Erfurt Assembly (1860). Like his teacher, Leopold von Ranke, Sybel had wide-ranging interests and conducted meticulous research in primary sources. He rejected, however, Ranke's dictum of a historian's detachment from his work. Instead, Sybel believed that it was not possible to exclude contemporary influences from a historian's writing. He was a positivist who believed that his practical political experience as a liberal-conservative Prussian nationalist benefited his scholarly work by enabling him to employ a more realistic perspective on the past. Sybel was also convinced that history was subject to inherent laws of causality and that these laws could be discovered through systematic research. In later life he tended to personalize historical events, and having gained Bismarck's permission to use Prussian documents, wrote in an apologetic way about the reign of Wilhelm I. He is remembered particularly for the many political and historical controversies in which he was involved. For example, in his dispute with J. von Ficker, a representative of the movement for the creation of a larger Germany (Grossdeutschland), Sybel, who believed in a smaller Germany (Kleindeutschland), was highly critical of the universalism of the medieval German emperors.

Klaus Larres

Texts

The Founding of the German Empire by Wilhelm I. Trans. M.L. Perrin and G. Bradford Jr. 7 vols. New York: Crowell, 1890–1898.

The History and Literature of the Crusades. London: Chapman and Hall, 1861.

History of the French Revolution. Trans. Walter C. Perry. 4 vols. London: J. Murray, 1867–1869.

Kleine Historische Schriften [Shorter Historical Writings]. 3 vols. Munich: Literarisch-Artistische Anstalt der J.G. Cotta'schen Buchhandlung, 1863.

Vorträge und Abhandlungen von Heinrich von Sybel [Lectures and Articles]. Ed. C. Varrentrapp. Leipzig: R. Oldenbourg, 1897.

Vorträge und Aufsätze [Lectures and Essays]. Berlin: A. Hofmann, 1874.

References

Dotterweich, V. *Heinrich von Sybel: Geschichtswissenschaft in politischer Absicht (1817–1861)* [Historical Science with a Political Purpose]. Göttingen: Vandenhoeck and Rupprecht, 1978.

Flaig, H. "The Historian As Pedagogue of the Nation." *History* 59 (1974): 18–32.

Iggers, Georg G. *The German Conception of History.* Second ed. Middletown, CT: Wesleyan University Press, 1983, chapters 4–5.

Seier, H. "Heinrich von Sybel." In *Deutsche Historiker* [German Historians], vol. 5, ed. Hans-Ulrich Wehler. Göttingen: Vandenhoeck and Rupprecht, 1973, 132–146.

Seier, H. *Die Staatsidee Heinrich von Sybels in den Wandlungen der Reichsgründungszeit 1862–71* [Heinrich von Sybel's Idea of the State during the Transformation of the Reich]. Lübeck: Matthieson, 1961.

Southard, Robert. *Droysen and the Prussian School of History.* Lexington: University of Kentucky Press, 1995.

Sykes, Percy Molesworth (1867–1945)

British administrator, soldier, and historian. Sykes was born in Canterbury, England, into a religious family that had close connections with the British armed forces. Educated at Rugby School and the Royal Military College, Sandhurst, he went on to join the Dragoon Guards in 1888. In 1893 he served with his regiment in India, becoming, a year later, the British Consul for Kerman and Persian Baluchistan. He was promoted to captain in 1897. After serving in the Boer War as an intelligence officer, he transferred to the Indian army in 1902 and became lieutenant-colonel in 1914. He was also a keen traveler, particularly in Iran and Afghanistan, where he undertook expeditions extending over several years. During World War I he served as brigadier-general at the head of a strong Persian police force. In 1920, he retired from the army and dedicated the rest of his life to historical and geographical pursuits.

Sykes's reputation as a historian rests on his two books, *A History of Persia* (1916) and *A History of Afghanistan* (1940). Each history was composed of two volumes with maps and illustrations. Whereas his work on Persia enjoyed great success, his second book on Afghanistan does not seem to have commanded much attention. However, both books were conceived along similar lines whereby the history of each country is treated from the dawn of history down to the author's own time. Being a soldier and an administrator, Sykes tended to concentrate on military and political events, paying scant attention to social and economic developments. Although his books were distinguished for their accuracy and flowing style, their thrust was an undisguised admiration for royalty and dynastic rule.

Y.M. Choueiri

Texts

A History of Afghanistan. 2 vols. London: Macmillan, 1940.

A History of Persia. Third ed. 2 vols. London: Macmillan, 1963.

Syme, Sir Ronald (1903–1989)

Historian of ancient Rome. Born in New Zealand, Syme studied classics at Oxford University and taught there from 1929. After wartime diplomatic service in then Yugoslavia and Turkey, he became

Camden professor of ancient history at Oxford in 1949, holding the post until his retirement in 1970. He was knighted in 1959. In *The Roman Revolution* (1939), Syme charted the factional politics behind the transition from Roman republic to principate. His *Tacitus* (1958) extended the study of Roman elite networks and ideologies into a later period. *The Augustan Aristocracy* (1986) returns to the analysis of a ruling class "unique in duration and predominance," to conclude with a measured defense of the early principate as a form of discipline without despotism. Syme's work as a historian is marked by careful attention to the literary and epigraphic sources for individual careers and social groupings, sensitivity to the ideals and vocabulary of political life, and a strong sense of the cultural implications of regional difference.

M. Vessey

Texts

Ammianus and the Historia Augusta. Oxford: Clarendon Press, 1968.
Anatolica: Studies in Strabo. Ed. A.R. Birley. Oxford: Oxford University Press, 1995.
The Augustan Aristocracy. Oxford: Clarendon Press, 1986.
Emperors and Biography: Studies in the Historia Augusta. Oxford: Clarendon Press, 1971.
History in Ovid. Oxford: Clarendon Press, 1978.
Roman Papers. Ed. E. Badian and A.R. Birley. 7 vols. Oxford: Clarendon Press, 1979–1991.
The Roman Revolution. Oxford: Clarendon Press, 1939.
Sallust. Berkeley: University of California Press, 1964.
Tacitus. 2 vols. Oxford: Clarendon Press, 1958.

References

Alföldy, Géza. *Two Princeps [sic]: Augustus and Sir Ronald Syme.* Pavia: Amministrazione di Athenaeum, Università di Pavia, 1993.

Symonds, John Addington (1840–1893)

English poet, literary critic, and historian. Born in Bristol, he studied at Harrow and Balliol College, Oxford, under Benjamin Jowett. In 1862 he became a fellow of Magdalen College. His best-known historical work, *The Renaissance in Italy* (1875–1886), is a seven-volume study of the development of Italian culture. It presented the history of the Renaissance as an example of progress and a break from the church's efforts to restrain human nature. Once freedom of human nature was attained, political freedom could follow. Symond's sympathy for the Re-naissance was in part an expression of his unusually open attitude to his homosexuality, which was also expressed in more tortured form in his translation of Michelangelo's sonnets (1878).

Thomas F. Mayer

Texts

The Renaissance in Italy. 7 vols. London: John Murray, 1914.
Trans. *The Sonnets of Michael Angelo and Tommaso Campanella.* London: Smith, Elder, 1878.

References

Dale, Peter Allan. "Beyond Humanism: J.A. Symonds and the Replotting of the Renaissance." *Clio* 17 (1988): 109–137.
Grosskurth, Phyllis. *The Woeful Victorian: A Biography of John Addington Symonds.* New York: Holt, Rinehart and Winston, 1965.

Szalay, Låszlö (1813–1864)

Hungarian historian. Szalay studied philosophy and law in Pest. Prior to 1848 he acquired a reputation as a prestigious legal scholar, liberal politician, and journalist and became a leading personality of the "centralist" group that attempted to establish centralized state institutions in an effort to harmonize conflicting social interests. During the 1848 revolution he served on the staff of the Ministry of Justice, and then as a diplomatic representative of his government in Frankfurt, Paris, and London. Following the Hungarian defeat in the war of independence against the Habsburgs and Czarist Russia, he lived in exile in Switzerland, where he remained until 1855, during which period he worked on his comprehensive history of Hungary. Following his return to Hungary, he represented the town of Pest in the Hungarian Parliament in 1861, and served from 1861 to 1864 as general secretary of the Hungarian Academy of Sciences. Szalay's unfinished six-volume *Magyarország története* [History of Hungary], a survey of Hungarian history from its beginnings to 1707, was the first attempt at a historical synthesis of his country's history to be based on the principles of modern source-criticism and was written in the spirit of liberal nationalism. In it he concentrated on political and legal history and foreign policy; economic, social, and cultural historical developments lay beyond the range of his interests. Szalay's most important works, other than this, deal with the political history of Hungary in the second half of the sixteenth century.

Attila Pók

Texts

Adalékok a magyar nemzet történetéhez a XVI. században [Contributions to the History of the Hungarian Nation in the Sixteenth Century]. Pest: Lauffer, 1859.

Erdély és a Porta (1567–1578) [Transylvania and the Porte, 1567–1578]. Pest: Lauffer, 1860.

Magyarország története [History of Hungary]. 6 vols. Leipzig and Pest: Geibel Karolý Tulajdona, 1852–1859.

References

Pamlényi, Ervin: "Szalay László Magyarország története [László Szalay's History of Hungary]." *A Magyar Tudományos Akadémia Társadalmi Történeti Tudományok Osztályának Közleményei* [Communications of the Section for Social-Historical Sciences of the Hungarian Academy of Sciences] 14 (1965): 29–39.

Szekfű, Gyula (1883–1955)

Hungarian historian. One of the most prestigious of modern Hungarian historians, Szekfű was a major figure of the *Geistesgeschichte* (intellectual history) school in Hungary. Having studied in Budapest, he joined the staff of the Hungarian National Museum in 1904 and was subsequently appointed to a position at the National Archives. He was sent to Vienna as a Hungarian representative to the *Hofkammerarchiv* (1908–1910) and the *Haus-, Hof-, und Staatsarchiv* (1910–1925). Returning to Hungary in 1925 he took up the post of professor of modern Hungarian history at Péter Pázmány University in Budapest. After World War II he served from 1946 to 1948 as Hungarian envoy in Moscow, and sat from 1953 to 1955 as a member of the Hungarian parliament. Szekfű's earliest works deal with medieval Hungarian social history. His book on the leader of the early-eighteenth-century anti-Habsburg Hungarian insurrection, Ferenc Rákóczi II, placed Szekfű at the center of heated political debates in 1913–1915, largely because of his alleged Habsburg sympathies. His most influential historical work of the interwar period, the *Három nemzedék,* (1920) blamed "rootless" Hungarian liberalism for the decline of modern Hungarian society, concluding with the post–World War I collapse of the Hungarian state. Szekfű coauthored (with Bálint Hóman) a multivolume synthesis of Hungarian history that has not been rivaled to this day, contributing the sections covering the period from 1458 to 1914. Both in his scholarly works and in his extensive journalistic and political publications, he championed the necessity of conservative reforms based on deeply entrenched national traditions. On the other hand, his open antifascism and his critical evaluation of the political role of the traditional Hungarian middle classes made possible his adjustment to the conditions of intellectual life imposed on Hungary once it fell into the Soviet sphere of influence after World War II.

Attila Pók

Texts

Három nemzedék [Three Generations]. Budapest: Élet nyomda, 1920.

A magyar állam életrajza [The Biography of the Hungarian State]. Budapest: M. Dick, 1917.

Magyar történet [Hungarian History]. Vols. 4–7 only. 8 vols. Budapest: Királyi magyar egyetemi nyomda, 1928–1934.

Serviensek és familiárisok [Servientes and Familiares]. Budapest: Magyar Tudományos Akadémia 1912.

A számûzött Rákóczi [The Exiled Rákóczi]. Budapest: Királyi magyar egyetemi nyomda, 1913.

References

Glatz, Ferenc. *Történetiró és politika: Szekfü, Steier, Thim és Miskolczy nemzetröl és államról* [Historians and Politics: Szekfü, Steier, Thim and Miskolczy on Nation and State]. Budapest: Akadémiai Kiadó, 1980, 89–248.

Szűcs, Jenő (1928–1988)

Hungarian historian. Szűcs studied in Budapest and worked from 1952 to 1960 as an archivist at the Hungarian National Archives. From 1960 until his death he was a member of the Institute of History in the Hungarian Academy of Sciences. In the early phase of his career he dealt with the history of medieval Hungarian towns; after 1960, however, his interests shifted toward the origins of national identities. Szűcs analyzed medieval interpretations of the concept of *natio* (tribe or race) and under the impact of politically motivated contemporary discussions about the regional divisions of Europe, he prepared one of the most original works of twentieth-century Hungarian historical scholarship. His outline of the three historical regions of Europe, which covers social, economic, political, and cultural questions, supplies a great deal of historical evidence to support his thesis of the existence of a distinctive east-central Europe (located between Russia and Germany); in Szűcs's judgment, this region was and remained strikingly different from eastern Europe and historically had followed western patterns of development, albeit belatedly and in a somewhat disorted manner.

Attila Pók

Texts

Nation und Geschichte [Nation and History]. Cologne: Bohlau, 1981.

A nemzet historikuma és a történetszemlélet nemzeti látószöge (Hozzászólás egy vitához) [The History of the Nation and the National Approach to History: Contribution to a Debate]. Budapest: Akadémiai Kiadó, 1970.

"The Three Historical Regions of Europe." *Acta Historica Academiae Hungariae Scientarium* [Historical Transactions of the Hungarian Academy of Sciences] 29 (1983): 131–184.

Les trois Europes [The Three Europes]. Ed. Fernand Braudel; trans. Veronique Charaire, Gábor Klaniczay, and Philippe Thureau-Dangin (into French). Paris: Editions l'Harmattan, 1985.

Az utolsó Árpádok [The last Árpáds]. Budapest: História-MTA Történettudományi Intézete, 1993.

Városok és kézmûvesség a XV. századi Magyarországon [Towns and the Handicraft Industry in Fifteenth-Century Hungary]. Budapest: Mûvelt Nép, 1955.

References

Engel, Pál. "Szűcs, Jenő." *Történelmi Szemle* [Historical Review] 32 (1989): 3–4.

T

al-Ṭabarī, Abu Djafar Muḥammad bin Djarir (838/839–923)

Muslim historian. Al-Ṭabarī was born in the city of Amul in the province of Tabaristan in present-day Iran. After finishing his early studies in his native town, he traveled to Baghdad to study with the famous jurist Ahmad bin Hanbal, but arrived there shortly after the latter's death. After spending some time in Baghdad he left for Syria and Egypt, eventually returning to Baghdad where he remained until his death. Al-Ṭabarī's best-known work is *Ta'rīkh al-rasul wa al-muluk* [History of Prophets and Kings], a multivolume history of the world. It begins with a general discussion of the early prophets and kings and follows with the history of the Sassanid dynasty in Iran. The next section covers the period of the prophet Muḥammad and the first four caliphs followed by detailed discussions of the Umayyad and the 'Abbāsid dynasties, ending in 915. *Ta'rīkh al-rasul wa al-Muluk* is one of the most important primary sources for the study of the early Islamic period and is in the process of being translated into English under the title *History of al-Ṭabarī*.

Hootan Shambayati

Texts

The History of al-Ṭabarī. Albany: State University of New York Press, 1985–.
Ikhtilaf al-fuqaha. [Disagreements among Jurists.] Miṣr, Egypt: al-Mawsuat, 1902.
Selection from the Annals of Tabari. Ed. and trans. M.J. de Goeje. Leiden: E.J. Brill, 1902.

References

Duri, A.A. *The Rise of Historical Writing among the Arabs*. Ed. and trans. Lawrence I. Conrad. Princeton, NJ: Princeton University Press, 1983.

Khalidi, Tarif. *Arabic Historical Thought in the Classical Period*. Cambridge, Eng.: Cambridge University Press, 1994.
Rosenthal, Franz. *A History of Muslim Historiography*. Second ed. Leiden: E.J. Brill, 1968.

Tacitus, Publius (?) Cornelius (ca. 56–ca. 120)

Roman historian, senator, and governor. Cornelius Tacitus (whose *praenomen* is uncertain) arose from a relatively obscure family of provincial origin, beginning his official career under the emperor Vespasian (69–79) and apparently achieving notability as an orator. In 77 he married the daughter of Agricola, the future governor of Britain. He advanced under the reign of Domitian (81–96) to the praetorship (88) and became consul under the emperor Nerva (96–98) in 97. Some time later he served as proconsular governor in Asia (ca. 112). He died a few years later, perhaps early in the reign of Hadrian (117–138). Among Tacitus's works are three short monographs: *Agricola* (98) is a biography of his father-in-law; the *Dialogus* (of uncertain date) treats the decline of Roman oratory; and the *Germania* (98) consists of an ethnographical treatise on the people and customs of that region. But Tacitus's reputation as the greatest Roman historian rests on his two major works, neither of which has survived antiquity intact. Together they covered Roman history from the death of Augustus in A.D. 14 to the assassination of Domitian in 96. Of the *Histories,* which treated the period after 68, only a portion recounting the tumultuous year after Nero's demise survives. More of the *Annals* is extant, including long sections describing the reigns of Tiberius, Claudius, and Nero.

Tacitus attached himself conspicuously to the tradition of annalistic historiography in Rome, often striking the pose of an archconservative

Republican senator. His major works, however, expand on the court life that in fact dominated the Roman Empire of his day, and Tacitus clearly distinguished between the oppression of Nero or Tiberius and the relative freedom of speech under Nerva or Trajan. Tacitus wrote in a severe, constricted, and epigrammatic style, which recalls the conscious archaism of Sallust but is ultimately original. He eschewed the long and florid sentences of Livy, preferring a critical style of vigor and rapidity rarely equaled. His influence has been perhaps greater in the modern than in the ancient world, although Ammianus Marcellinus chose to begin his work where Tacitus's ended. Both Gibbon in the eighteenth century and Ronald Syme in the twentieth adopted Tacitus's critical view of Augustus, and Syme ends his massive study with the remark "Men and dynasties pass, but style abides."

Loren J. Samons II

Texts

The Annals of Imperial Rome. Trans. M. Grant. London: Penguin, 1989.
The Histories. Trans. K. Wellesley. London: Penguin, 1964.
The Agricola and the Germania. Trans. H. Mattingly. London: Penguin, 1948.
Works. Trans. C.H. Moore, J. Jackson, W. Peterson, and M. Hutton. 5 vols. Cambridge, MA: Loeb, 1914–1937.

References

Martin, Ronald H. *Tacitus.* Berkeley: University of California Press, 1981.
Mellor, Ronald. *Tacitus.* New York: Routledge, 1983.
Syme, Ronald. *Tacitus.* 2 vols. Oxford: Oxford University Press, 1958.

Taguchi Ukichi (1855–1905)

Historian and economist of Meiji Japan, who was a leading intellectual figure in the 1880s. The most important issue of the early Meiji era was how to change traditional Japan into a modern society comparable to Europe and America: what was then known as *Bunmei–kaika* (westernization). As a believer in the economic doctrines of Adam Smith, Taguchi criticized the government's trade policy as protective and proposed free trade. Although he was not a professional scholar, he contributed much to economics and history through the publishing of such writings and journals. His most famous work on history is *Nippon Kaika Shōshi* [The Historical Process of Westernization in Japan]

(1877–1882). He is also well known for his founding of *Tokyo Keizai Zasshi* [The Tokyo Economic Journal] in 1879, the first journal of economics in Japan, which was published until 1920. In addition, he also published a journal on history called *Shikai* [The Great Sea of History].

Takashi Fujii

Texts

Teiken Taguchi Ukichi Zenshū [Complete Works]. Tokyo: Yoshikawakōbunkan, 1989.

References

Sugihara, S. *Seiyō Keizaigaku to Kindai Nippon* [Western Economics and the Modernization of Japan]. Tokyo: Miraisha, 1972.

Taine, Hippolyte-Adolphe (1828–1893)

French philosopher, critic, and historian. Born at Vouziers and educated in Paris at the École Normale, he taught philosophy at several colleges before obtaining a doctorate for his study of *La Fontaine et ses fables* (1853), published in 1860. In 1864, he became professor of art history at the École des Beaux Arts, a position he held for over twenty years. He died in Paris. In 1858 Taine published his *Essai de critique et d'histoire* [Essay on Criticism and History], in which he stipulated that history was a science. His *History of English Literature* (1863) represents Taine's attempt at psychological and deterministic history. He strove to write a critical history of humanity rather than a narration of historical events. Taine's most significant contribution to history was his monumental *Origines de la France contemporaine* [Origins of Modern France] (1876–1893), which strove to explain to contemporaries the growth of the modern centralized and authoritarian state. Pessimistic and critical of both the old regime and the French Revolution, Taine's was the first antirevolutionary history written. It remained at the center of historiographical controversy for over half a century. This controversy reached a climax with Alphonse Aulard, a republican historian, who wrote a detailed criticism of the *Origines*. Taine's *Origines* influenced the development of the French conservative school including the works of Bourget, Maurras, and Barrès.

Leigh Whaley

Texts

The Ancient Regime. New York: Holt, 1885.
Essai de critique et d'histoire. Fourteenth ed. Paris: Hachette, 1923.

The French Revolution. Trans. John Durand. 3 vols. New York: Holt, 1878–1885.

History of English Literature. Fourth ed. 4 vols. Trans. H. Van Laun. London: Chatto, 1920.

La Régime Moderne [The Modern Regime]. 2 vols. Paris: Librairie Hachette, 1891–1894.

References

Léger, François. *Monsieur Taine.* Paris: Criterion, 1993.

Lombardo, Patrizia. "Hippolyte Taine between Art and Science." *Yale French Studies* 77 (1990): 117–133.

Weinstein, Leo. *Hippolyte Taine.* New York: Twayne, 1972.

Tawney, Richard Henry (1880–1962)

English social and economic historian and political theorist. Tawney was born in Calcutta and educated at Rugby School and Balliol College, Oxford. His deep-seated Christian Socialism prompted him toward a lifelong commitment to the Workers' Educational Association, and to put his very considerable talents at the disposal of the Labour Party. Although he stood unsuccessfully as a Parliamentary candidate for the Labour Party in 1918, 1922, and 1924, he was the principal author of the Labour Party's education policy—*Secondary Education for All* (1922). His hard-hitting *Acquisitive Society* (1921) and *Equality* (1931) became tracts for the times. It was characteristic of Tawney that in World War I he enlisted in the ranks and declined a commission. Later on it was no less in keeping with this essentially unassuming man that he twice refused offers of a peerage from Labour prime ministers MacDonald and Attlee. Tawney's academic career was at the London School of Economics (1920–1949) where he was promoted first to the position of reader (1923) and then to professor (1931). He was a founding editor of the *Economic History Review* (1927–1934) and was elected fellow of the British Academy in 1935. Tawney's keen interest in the problems and injustices of the present mingled readily with his concern for the social and economic past. In this very real sense his study of *Land and Labour in China* (1932) was not an aberration. His main field of interest—"Tawney's century," as it became known—extended from 1540 to 1640. His principal contributions to this subject were *The Agrarian Problem in the Sixteenth Century* (1912), *Tudor Economic Documents* (coedited with Eileen Power, 1924), *Religion and the Rise of Capitalism* (1926), and *Business and Politics under James I* (1958), to-

gether with controversial key articles on "The Rise of the Gentry" and on "Harrington's Interpretation of His Age" (1941). Although too self-effacing and idiosyncratic to found a "school," Tawney's influence reverberated for years after his death.

R.C. Richardson

Texts

The Agrarian Problem in the Sixteenth Century. London and New York: Longmans, Green, 1912.

Business and Politics under James I: Lionel Cranfield As Merchant and Minister. Cambridge: Cambridge University Press, 1958.

History and Society: Essays by R.H. Tawney. Ed. J.M. Winter. London: Routledge and Kegan Paul, 1978.

Religion and the Rise of Capitalism. London: Murray, 1926.

Ed., with Eileen Power. *Tudor Economic Documents.* 3 vols. London: Longmans, 1924.

References

Richardson, R.C. *The Debate on the English Revolution Revisited.* London: Routledge, 1988.

Terrill, R. *R.H. Tawney and His Times: Socialism As Fellowship.* London: Deutsch, 1974.

Wright, A. *R.H. Tawney.* Manchester: Manchester University Press, 1987.

Taylor, Alan John Percivale (1906–1990)

English historian. Taylor attended Bootham School, York, and Oriel College, Oxford (1924–1927). He became a lecturer in modern history at Manchester University (1932–1938), a fellow of Magdalen College, Oxford (1938–1976), and special lecturer in international history at Oxford University (1953–1963). From the 1950s onward he also pursued a successful career as a journalist and as a panel member of a television news magazine. In the 1970s he delivered the first-ever televised series of historical lectures, three of which were subsequently published as books. Taylor was one of the most outstanding but also one of the most controversial and nonconformist historians of his generation; thus Oxford University never saw fit to offer him a professorial chair. Taylor's reputation as a scholar rests on his voluminous work regarding the international relations between the great European powers since the French Revolution, often concentrating on German and Austrian history. He produced numerous articles and books including *The Habsburg Monarchy, 1815–1918* (1941); *The Course of German History* (1945); *The Struggle for Mastery in Europe,*

1848–1918 (1954); *Bismarck: The Man and the Statesman* (1955); *The Trouble-Makers: Dissent over Foreign Policy, 1792–1939* (1956); and *The First World War* (1963). The study of war and "pure" diplomatic history on the basis of archival and, since the 1950s, increasingly, printed documents and secondary sources, led him to concentrate on traditional high politics while neglecting social movements and economic and cultural factors. Although quite orthodox in his methodology and aim his approach was also critical and even irreverent; emphasizing chance and accident in history it thus often belittled the emperors and politicians of the day. His insistence on questioning long-held historical assumptions made him write many revisionist works, the most controversial of which was *The Origins of the Second World War* (1961). While certainly not showing any sympathies toward the Nazis, Taylor reopened this issue by arguing that Hitler was merely the agent of the German people, a conventional politician who stumbled into war. Miscalculation and the German national character in general, rather than the pursuit of a grand design, had led to the outbreak of war. From the early 1960s Taylor began to concentrate increasingly on the history of his own country producing above all the respected work *English History, 1914–1945* (1965), as well as several other books.

Klaus Larres

Texts

The Course of German History. London: Methuen, 1961.

English History, 1914–1945. New York: Oxford University Press, 1985.

The First World War. Harmondsworth: Penguin Books, 1963.

The Origins of the Second World War. London: Hamilton, 1961.

The Struggle for Mastery in Europe, 1848–1918. Oxford: Clarendon Press, 1954.

The Trouble-Makers: Dissent over Foreign Policy, 1792–1939. Bloomington: Indiana University Press, 1958.

References

Cole, R. *A.J.P. Taylor: Traitor within the Gates.* London: Macmillan, 1993.

Sisman, A. *A.J.P. Taylor: A Biography.* London: Sinclair-Stevenson, 1994.

Taylor, A.J.P. *Letters to Eva 1969–83.* Ed. Eva H. Taylor. London: Century, 1991.

———. *A Personal History.* London: Hamilton, 1983.

Wrigley, C. "A.J.P. Taylor: A Nonconforming Radical Historian of Europe." *Contemporary European History* 3 (1994): 73–86.

———. "Alan John Percivale Taylor 1906–1990." *Proceedings of the British Academy* 82 (1993): 493–524.

———. Ed. *A.J.P. Taylor: A Complete Annotated Bibliography and Guide to His Historical Writing.* Brighton: Harvester Press, 1980.

Temperley, Harold William Vazeille (1879–1939)

Diplomatic historian and Liberal politician. Temperley was born and died in Cambridge, England, where his father was an official of the university. He studied history at King's College, Cambridge. Temperley was greatly influenced by Lord Acton, Regius professor of modern history at Cambridge; he himself was, in turn, the mentor of a younger historian, Herbert Butterfield (both Temperley and Butterfield would occupy the position of master of Peterhouse, Cambridge). Temperley was active in the Liberal party during the early decades of the twentieth century but withdrew from national politics as the party declined during the 1920s. He was a member of the British delegation to the Paris Peace Conference of 1919. Temperley's interests lay in British diplomatic history, wherein his contribution concerned George Canning and the early nineteenth century. He founded the *Cambridge Historical Journal* (now the *Historical Journal*) and served as its editor for twelve years. With George P. Gooch, he edited the official publication of British diplomatic documents on the origins of World War I and stimulated developments in international cooperation in historical research. Among other works, he was the author of a standard textbook on nineteenth- and twentieth-century Europe, originally published in 1927, and still in print.

Eugene L. Rasor

Texts

Ed., with G.P. Gooch. *British Documents on the Origins of the War, 1898–1914.* 11 vols. in 13 parts. London: HMSO, 1926–1938.

And A.J. Grant. *Europe in the Nineteenth and Twentieth Centuries.* Ed. Agatha Ramm. 2 vols. London: Longman, 1984.

The Foreign Policy of Canning, 1822–1827: England, the Neo-holy Alliance, and the New World. Second ed. Hamden, CT: Archon Books, 1966.

Frederic the Great and Kaiser Joseph: An Episode of
   War and Diplomacy in the Eighteenth Cen-
   tury. Second ed. London, Cass, 1968.
Ed. A History of the Peace Conference of Paris.
   6 vols. London and New York, Oxford
   University Press, 1969.

References

Fair, John D. Harold Temperley: A Scholar and
   Romantic in the Public Realm. Newark:
   University of Delaware Press, 1992.

Thai Historiography—Chronicles (including *tamnan*, stories or legends, and *phongsawadan*, annals or dynastic histories)

Premodern form of historical writing of the various peoples (Thai, Yuan, Lao, Shan, Lue, and others) speaking Tai languages of Thailand, Laos,
Burma, southwest China, and northeast India. The
earliest Tai historical writings probably originated as memorized king-lists and recitations of
important events that began to be written in the
fifteenth and sixteenth centuries. Then they came
to be inspired by the examples provided by the
historiography of Buddhism, especially from Sri
Lanka (Ceylon). "Phongsawadan," the dynastic
chronicles of the Kingdom of Ayudhya (Siam),
are peculiar to what is now central Thailand and
differ little from the chronicles that elsewhere in
the Tai-speaking world are referred to as *tamnan*
or *phün*. Modern writing distinguishes scientific
prawattisat (history) from premodern *tamnan* and
phongsawadan so pretentiously that the distinction
is meaningless.

The earliest *tamnan* are best represented by
the Khun Burom (or Borom) legends of Laos,
which relate the origins of human society from
people who emerged from a gourd and invited a
god to descend from the heavens to be their king.
Similar stories appear in the earliest historical writings of Tai peoples elsewhere, including such texts
as the *Ahom Buranji* of northeast India, early Tai
Lue chronicles of southwest Yunnan (China); and
the earliest texts from what is now extreme northern Thailand, such as the *Tamnan Suwanna Khom
Kham*, the *Tamnan Suwanna Kham Daeng*, and the
Tamnan Müang Ngoen Yang Chiang Saen, all translated into French by Notton.

The oldest historical legends were constantly
updated and expanded and acquired more detail
and relatively accurate dates from about the eleventh century and especially from the thirteenth
century. The most important of these is commonly

thought to be the lengthy story of Khun Cüang,
the legendary king who is said to have conquered
much of interior mainland Southeast Asia in the
eleventh century.

As the various Tai peoples founded major
states and were exposed to newly invigorated
Theravada Buddhism from Sri Lanka in the thirteenth and fourteenth centuries, they were exposed
to the historical writings of South Asian Buddhism, including particularly the Pali language
Mahavamsa and the *Dipavamsa*, which inspired a
great flourishing of historical writing throughout
the region in the fifteenth and sixteenth centuries.
The earliest such texts probably were written by
Buddhist monks in both Pali and Thai, and were
concerned with placing ancient kings like Khun
Cüang into a Buddhist context (the *Vamsamalini*)
or chronicling the coming of Buddhism to the
region like the *Mulasasana*. The best of these emanated from Chiang Mai, the capital of the old
Kingdom of Lan Na, in the sixteenth century, and
included the authoritative *Jinakalamali* by the
Venerable Ratanapañña. All was placed within a
Buddhist cyclical conception of time, which anticipated a five-thousand-year lifetime for the Buddhist religion, beginning with the death of the
Buddha (traditionally 543 B.C.).

Increasingly secular historical writing built
upon both historical legends and this Buddhist
background, taking as their temporal framework
the lifespan of a kingdom. In Siam (Thailand),
such histories were written by the early seventeenth
century, surviving only in a version compiled by
the visiting Dutch merchant Jeremias Van Vliet
(1640). Dynastic chronicles, *phongsawadan*, soon
followed, including especially the *Luang Prasoet
Chronicle*, named like other Ayudhya chronicles
from the name of the manuscript owner, which
was composed in 1680.

The main spurt of chronicle writing, however, is associated especially with the terrible period
of war and devastation that lasted from 1760 to
1828, when numerous Tai struggled to understand
the calamities that had befallen them. In Siam, the
earliest such chronicle was the *Phan* Canthanumat
version (1795), which is a carefully dated and detailed chronicle of Ayudhya which is especially full
in its coverage from the late sixteenth century onward.
It is especially concerned with dynastic succession
and with warfare with Burma and Cambodia. The
Phan Canthanumat version is closely followed by
two undated versions, of the Reverend Phonnarat
and *Phra* Cakkraphatdiphong, and by the British
Museum version (1807), so named because it was
there that the manuscript was found in the 1950s.

These were checked and compared, and an authoritative version was compiled around 1855 on the order of King Mongkut (r. 1851–1868), now called the Royal Autograph Edition. These, however, were concerned almost exclusively with the history of the old Kingdom of Ayutthaya (1351–1767) and the succeeding reign of King Taksin (r. 1767–1782). To fill in the history since that time, King Mongkut had one of his ministers, *Caophraya* Thiphakorawong (Kham Bunnag), compile histories of the first four reigns (1782–1868) of the Chakri dynasty of Bangkok; and the chronicles of the Second Reign were subsequently revised by Mongkut's son Prince Damrong Rajanubhab (1861–1943).

In the northern regions of what is now Thailand, there was a similar spurt of history writing especially in the 1820s, motivated by very much the same causes—the desire to learn from, and avoid a repetition of, the calamities of the preceding half-century. Of these, the best are the Nan Chronicle of *Saenluang* Ratchasomphan and the anonymous Chiang Mai Chronicle. Both are based on a careful and critical reading of older texts, which they partially incorporate. Nearly every locality in north Thailand has its own such chronicle. In what is now Laos, similar chronicles were written for the old principalities of Luang Prabang, Vientiane, and Champassak, as well as for the Shan, Khoen, and Lue principalities of Burma and southwestern China.

Almost all Tai chronicles are anonymous, for premodern local cultures discounted individual authorship even of the region's great literary masterpieces. Chronicles were usually written either on thick bark-paper, or incised onto palm-leaves, both of which can last for hundreds of years even in a damp climate where insects can be expected to eat such materials.

The Tai chronicles are very fully dated throughout the period from the thirteenth century (and sometimes earlier). They usually use the *Culasakarat* era (C.S. + 638 = A.D.), and add the animal names of years like the Chinese. Important dates are specified not only by weekday and phase of the moon but also, in the northern regions, by planetary positions.

David K. Wyatt

See also THAI HISTORIOGRAPHY: MODERN (FROM 1900).

Texts

"The Abridged Royal Chronicle of Ayudhya of Prince Paramanuchitchinorot." Trans. David K. Wyatt. *Journal of the Siam Society* 61 (1973): 25–50.

Annales du Siam. Trans. Camille Notton. 4 vols. Paris and Bangkok: C. Lavauzelle, 1926–1939.

Archaimbault, Charles. "Les annales de l'ancien royaume de S'ieng Khwang [Annals of the Ancient Realm of S'ieng Khwang." *Bulletin de l'Ecole Française d'Extrême-Orient* 53 (1967): 557–674.

Archaimbault, Charles. "L'histoire de Campasak." *Journal asiatique* 249 (1961): 519–595.

Archaimbault, Charles. *Contribution a l'étude d'un cycle de legendes lau.* Paris: Publications École Française d'Extrême-Orient no. 119, 1980.

The Chiang Mai Chronicle. Trans. David K. Wyatt and Aroonrut Wichienkeeo. 3 vols. Chiang Mai: Silkworm Books, 1995.

The Crystal Sands: The Chronicles of Nagara Sri Dharrmaraja. Ed. David K. Wyatt. Ithaca, NY: Cornell University Southeast Asia Program, 1975.

Frankfurter, Oscar. "Translation of 'Events in Ayudhya from Chulasakaraj 686–966.'" *Journal of the Siam Society* 6 (1909): 1–21; reprinted in *Selected Articles from the Siam Society Journal,* I. Bangkok: Siam Society, 1954, 36–62.

Kingdom of Laos. Ed. René de Berval. Saigon: France-Asie, 1959.

"Mulasasana Wat Pa Daeng: The Chronicle of the Founding of Buddhism of the Wat Pa Daeng Tradition." Trans. Sommai Premchit and Donald K. Swearer. *Journal of the Siam Society* 65 (1977): 73–110.

The Padaeng Chronicle and the Jengtung State Chronicle Translated. Trans. Sao Saimong Mangrai. Ann Arbor: University of Michigan Center for South and Southeast Asian Studies, 1981.

Ratanapañña Thera. *The Sheaf of Garlands of the Epochs of the Conqueror.* Trans. N.A. Jayawickrama. London: Pali Text Society, 1968.

Ratchasomphan, Saenluang. *The Nan Chronicle.* Trans. David K. Wyatt. Ithaca, NY: Cornell University Southeast Asia Program, 1994.

The Royal Chronicles of Ayutthaya. Trans. Richard D. Cushman. Bangkok: Siam Society, forthcoming.

Saveng Phinith. *Contribution à l'histoire du royaume de Luang Prabang* [Contribution to the History of the Realm of Luang Prabang]. Paris: Publications EFEO, no. 141, 1987.

Thiphakorawong, Caophraya. *The Dynastic Chronicles, Bangkok Era, the First Reign.* Trans. E. Thadeus Flood and Chadin Flood. 2 vols. Tokyo: Center for East Asian Cultural Studies, 1978.

Thiphakorawong, Caophraya. *The Dynastic Chronicles, Bangkok Era, the Fourth Reign.* trans. E. Thadeus Flood and Chadin Flood. 5 vols. Tokyo: Center for East Asian Cultural Studies, 1965–1979.

Van Vliet, Jeremias. *The Short History of the Kings of Siam, by Jeremias van Vliet [1640].* Ed. David K. Wyatt; trans. Leonard Andaya. Bangkok: Siam Society, 1975.

Vickery, Michael. "The '2/k 125 fragment': A Lost Chronicle of Ayutthaya." *Journal of the Siam Society* 65 (1977): 1–80.

References

Wyatt, David K. "Chronicle Traditions in Thai Historiography." In *Southeast Asian History and Historiography: Essays Presented to D.G.E. Hall,* ed. C.D. Cowan and O.W. Wolters. Ithaca, NY: Cornell University Press, 1976, 107–122; reprinted in David K. Wyatt, *Studies in Thai History: Collected Articles.* Chiang Mai: Silkworm Books, 1994, 1–21.

Thai Historiography—Modern (from 1900)

Modern Thai historiography can be broadly classified into four major schools: royalist, nationalist, socialist, and critical humanist. The respective contexts that gave rise to these historiographies are (1) formation of Thai absolutist territorial state during the reign of King Chulalongkorn (1868–1910), (2) propagation of nationalism during the two world wars, (3) ideological struggle under the cold war atmosphere, and (4) planned economic development systematically since 1961.

Siam (Thailand since 1939) prior to the mid-nineteenth century was a loosely organized empire. Perceptions of the past of the ruling minority in the urban centers were greatly different in both form and content from those of the vast populace. Having survived the colonization period as an independent kingdom with fixed boundaries, Siam in the early twentieth century needed a new historiography for use in the nationwide compulsory education of its subjects. The founder of this required historiography was Prince Damrong (1862–1943), who, since as early as 1930, has been revered as "the Father of Thai History." Damrong's historiography possessed the following characteristics. First, it

urged as prerequisites for doing history both a critical attitude toward sources and the practice of the various tools of historical criticism. Second, its scope was, more or less, limited to those of dynastic activities and a unilinear succession of kingdoms: Sukhothai, Ayutthaya, Thonburi, and Bangkok. Finally, it conveyed a conservative overtone, deriving from the aristocratic and paternalistic viewpoint of its author. For its contemporaries, this royalist historiography provided an impression of comfort, continuity, unity, and hierarchy and order in the age of crisis of the monarchy that still suffered form foreign extraterritorial rights and some domestic revolts. The prince's historiographical style also helped to ensure that his works have continued to be well-regarded—the cool, comforting, and solemn "classic stuff" of modern Thai literary creation.

The most influential protagonist of Thai nationalist historiography was Luang Wichit Wathakan (1898–1962). He was the first historian to praise Damrong as the founder of Thai historical writing, and he accepted the prince's framework almost in its entirety. What Wichit Wathakan added to Thai historiography was mainly to inject a strong nationalism into the perception of the Thai past, through the hundreds of nationalistic songs and historical plays he composed as a source of legitimization for the new regime that supplanted the absolute monarchy following the bloodless "revolution" of 1932. In this schema, the abstract conception was created of the "Thai people," whose patriotism was the driving force for their historical destination. Moreover, in his twelve-volume *Prawattisat Sakon* [World History] (1929–1931), he ranked Siam among the leading civilized and independent countries of the eastern hemisphere.

The most popular figure in Thai socialist historiography is Jit Phumisak (1930–1966). Jit graduated in 1957 from the Faculty of Arts of Chulalongkorn University. From 1958 to 1964 he was imprisoned by the military government. After being released, he fled into the jungle to join a guerrilla movement and was eventually killed by a police patrol in May 1966. *Chomna Sakdina Thai* [The Real Face of Thai Feudalism Today] (1957) was an attempt to apply Marxist historical materialism to Thai history. In portraying the Thai past as a tragic episode of exploitation of man by man, Jit thereby called for a revolutionary change of the social system of his own day, seeking to demonstrate its historical necessity in a rather mechanistic method of argument. His text was banned because it refused to use suitable language to refer to royalty, instead recasting the king as a "comittee chairman" who safeguarded the profits of the feudalist ruling class.

Thai historiography since the 1960s has gradually moved at first to a negation of its political and pedagogic precursors, then to an apparently value-free academic enterprise, and most recently to a milder, more sophisticated form of discursive practice that takes into account contemporary relations of power and knowledge. This historiography of the 1980s and since has thus promoted a kind of pluralism. The principal message it conveys is that any single claim to an ontologically "true" account of the Thai collective past must be questioned, if not rejected out of hand. No school can now claim to rule the field of contemporary Thai historiography with a single methodological tool or theoretical strait-jacket. As the most prominent Thai historian of today, Nidhi Aeusrivongse, of Chiangmai University, has recently declared: "May it be that no government has the power to determine what the correct version of history is; then we can use our own wisdom to choose how we are going to deal with the past ourselves." For a history that is open-ended, it is a fruitful suggestion that one should be critical about the sources of information and power, and guided by human dignity.

Somkiat Wanthana

See also DAMRONG RAJANUBHAB, PRINCE; THAI HISTORIOGRAPHY: CHRONICLES; WICHIT WATHAKAN.

References

Anderson, Benedict. "Studies of the Thai State: The State of Thai Studies." In *The Study of Thailand,* ed. Eliezer B. Ayal. Athens: Ohio University Center for International Studies, 1978.

Reynolds, Craig J. *Thai Radical Discourse: The Real Face of Thai Feudalism Today.* Ithaca, NY: Cornell University Southeast Asia Program, 1987.

Wanthana, Somkiat. "The Politics of Modern Thai Historiography." Ph.D. thesis, Monash University, 1986.

Theal, George McCall (1837–1919)

South African historian, archivist, and settler. Theal was born in Saint John, New Brunswick, Canada, and decided to stay in South Africa while visiting the Cape Colony on his way to Australia in 1861. While Theal was initially employed as a teacher and newspaper reporter, he worked as a colonial agent during the last war of dispossession against the Xhosa (1877–1878) and eventually became a government archival researcher who traveled to London and The Hague to copy documents relating to South Africa. He died in Cape Town. Founding the "settler school" of South African history, Theal wrote about the progress and positive impact of European colonization. Although his work condemned Africans as uncivilized savages, he collected (but unfortunately did not record) oral traditions from many elderly blacks and devoted a considerable portion of his writing to precolonial history. Theal's writing lacks analysis and follows a strictly narrative pattern. However, because his books and collections of documents formed the basis of most subsequent histories he is widely recognized as the father of South African history as an academic discipline.

Timothy J. Stapleton

Texts

Basutoland Records. 3 vols. Cape Town: W.A. Richards and Sons, 1883.

History of South Africa. 11 vols. London: Fisher Unwin, 1892–1919.

Records of the Cape Colony. 36 vols. London: Public Records Office, 1897–1905.

References

Babrow, M. "A Critical Assessment of George McCall Theal." MA thesis, University of Cape Town, 1962.

Bosman, Izak Daniel. *Dr. George McCall Theal as die geskiedskrywer van Suid-Afrika* [Dr George McCall Theal As Historian of South Africa]. Amsterdam: Swets en Zeitlinger, 1931.

Immelman, R.F.M. *George McCall Theal: A Biographical Sketch.* Cape Town: Struik, 1964.

Theopompus (ca. 379–ca. 320 B.C.)

Chian (Greek) historian and orator, generally grouped with the school of the rhetorician Isocrates. Theopompus wrote rhetorical pieces including attack(s) on Plato; an *Epitome of Herodotus;* a *Greek History (Hellenica)* in twelve books that continued Thucydides' account to 394 B.C.; and his famous *Philippica* in fifty-eight books, which covered the period of Philip's career from 360/59 to 336 B.C. His works are lost but were influential in antiquity, particularly the *Philippica.* Citations in later literature (fragments) and comments *(testimonia)* give clues to the style and content of his work. His style was famous; his moral severity, notorious. Ambivalent toward Demosthenes, he excessively vilified Philip, Alexander's father. His *On the Treasures* involved detailed historical research.

Gordon Shrimpton

Texts

Jacoby, F., ed. *Die Fragmente der Griechischen Historiker*. Vol. 2B. Leiden: E.J. Brill, 1962.

References

Connor, W.R. *Theopompus and Fifth-Century Athens*. Cambridge, MA: Harvard University Press, 1968.

Shrimpton, G.S. *Theopompus the Historian*. Montreal and Buffalo: McGill-Queen's University Press, 1991.

Thierry, Augustin (1795–1856)

French Romantic historian. Born in Blois, Thierry attended the École Normale Supérieure before becoming secretary to Henri de Saint-Simon. Subsequently, he turned to journalism, writing first for the *Censeur européen* and then for the *Courrier français*. Although blind by the time he was thirty, he continued his historical work through the aid of secretaries. Inspired by romanticism and by liberalism, Thierry's articles (published collectively in 1834 and 1827) called for a new history, one that would, instead of recounting the exploits of the ruling classes, evoke the traditions of the people, as well as their struggle to preserve and extend their liberty. Thierry's concern to bring to life this struggle inspired a famous essay on "Jacques Bonhomme" in which the French people were represented as an individual struggling against successive servitudes imposed since Roman times (1820). The same theme was pursued in his history of the Norman Conquest of England (1825), which sympathized with the defeated Saxons, and his *Essai sur le Tiers Etat* [Essay on the Third Estate] (1850). Critical of the works of Mézeray, Anquetil, and Velly for their anachronistic portrayal of French history, Thierry demanded that historians return to the sources of contemporary chroniclers, and provide an authentic re-creation of the variety of France's historical experience. The distinctive history of each province, town, or period should be recognized. Thierry's own historical works, although widely read, were perhaps less influential than his historical criticism.

Ian Germani

Texts

Dix ans d'études historiques [Ten Years of Historical Studies]. Fourth ed. Paris: J. Tessier, 1842.

The Formation and Progress of the Tiers Etat, or Third Estate in France. Trans. F.B. Wells. 2 vols. London: H.G. Bohn, 1859.

History of the Conquest of England by the Normans. Ed. J.A. Price. 2 vols. London: J.M. Dent, 1907.

Lettres sur l'histoire de France [Letters on the History of France]. New ed. Paris: Garnier, 1866.

Tales of the Early Franks. Trans. M.F.O. Jenkins. University: University of Alabama Press, 1977.

References

Engel-Janosi, Friedrich. *Four Studies in French Romantic Historical Writing*. Baltimore, MD: Johns Hopkins University Press, 1955.

Gossman, L. *Augustin Thierry and Liberal Historiography*. Middletown, CT: Wesleyan University Press, 1976.

Mellon, Stanley. *The Political Uses of History*. Stanford, CA: Stanford University Press, 1958.

Rearick, Charles. *Beyond the Enlightenment*. Bloomington: Indiana University Press, 1974.

Thiers, Adolphe (1797–1877)

French historian and politician. The remarkable political career of Thiers, which spanned more than forty years under very different governments, points to the power that his historical writing had to nurture political ideas. He never held an academic post, and although many of his works were less analytical than those of others, he wrote with greater detachment than many historians of his day. His popular histories captured the reality of political life and outlined the inevitable and necessary course of history, without moral judgments. Thiers's *Histoire de la révolution française* [History of the French Revolution] (1823–1827), was one of the earliest studies of the Revolution and set the stage for numerous interpretations that followed. His narrative was based on eyewitness accounts and numerous details, especially financial and military aspects. Although he was fearful of the passion of the masses in this mainly political tract, he was supportive of the general course of the Revolution, which had allowed men of talent, such as himself, new opportunities. Napoleon became the embodiment of the new, resilient French nation that emerged from the Revolution, though as a politician Thiers actively supported the English model of constitutional monarchy.

John B. Roney

Texts

The History of the Consulate and the Empire of France under Napoleon. Trans. P. Forbes Campbell. 20 vols. London: Henry Colburn, 1845–1862.
The History of the French Revolution. Trans. F. Shoberl. 5 vols. Philadelphia: J.B. Lippincott, 1894.

References

Albrecht-Carrié, René. *Adolphe Thiers, or The Triumph of the Bourgeoisie.* Boston: Twayne, 1977.
Bury, J.P.T., and R.P. Tombs. *Thiers, 1797–1877: A Political Life.* London: Allen and Unwin, 1986.
Guiral, Pierre. *Adolphe Thiers.* Paris: Fayard, 1986.

Thietmar of Merseburg (975–1018)

German bishop and historian. The son of the Count of Waldeck in Saxony, Thietmar was educated in monasteries at Quedlinburg and Magdeburg. Ordained in 1004, he was appointed bishop of Merseburg five years later. Between 1012 and his death in 1018, he wrote the *Chronicle* on which his fame as a historian rests. Begun simply as a history of the bishopric of Merseburg, Thietmar soon expanded his work into a history of early imperial Germany. The first four books of the *Chronicle* deal with the time from Henry I to Otto III and the last four with the reign of Henry II. For the first part of his work, Thietmar relied above all on Widukind's *Saxon History* and the *Quedlinburg Annals,* as well as on documentary sources. For the history of the reign of Henry II he drew primarily on first-hand knowledge and, consequently, his work is an important historical source for that period. What Thietmar's *Chronicle* lacks in style, it makes up for in the historical information it provides; the insights it offers into contemporary conditions and elite mentalities; and its presentation of frank judgments regarding conditions, individuals, and events.

G.H. Gerrits

Texts

Thietmar von Merseburg: Die Chronik [Chronicle]. Trans. W. Trillmich (into German). Darmstadt: Wissenschaftliche Buchgesellschaft, 1957.

References

Langosch, Karl. "Thietmar von Merseburg." In *Die deutsche Literatur des Mittelalters: Verfasserslexikon* [German Literature of the Middle Ages: A Biographical Dictionary] 4 (1953): 433–442.
Manitius, Max. *Geschichte der lateinischen Literatur des Mittelalters* [History of Latin Literature of the Middle Ages]. Vol. 2. Munich: C.H. Beck, 1964.

Thiphakorawong, Chaophraya (1813–1870)

Thai chronicler. Thiphakorawong was a senior member of the powerful Bunnag family and held some of the highest posts in the royal administration during the reigns of king Rama III, Rama IV, and Rama V.

Thiphakorawong is best known for his dynastic chronicles of the first four reigns of the Chakri dynasty, written in 1869 at the request of Rama V, the fifth Chakri monarch. Modeled on the dynastic chronicles of the kingdom of Ayuthaya, Thiphakorawong's chronicles were the last in this historiographical genre before it was abandoned by the Thai court as an inadequate form of historical representation. Because sources for this period (1782–1867) are few Thiphakorawong's chronicles have assumed great importance in Thai historiography. Questions have recently been raised as to what changes were made to the original manuscripts when they were edited and published by Prince Damrong in the early twentieth century.

Patrick Jory

Texts

The Dynastic Chronicles, Bangkok Era, the First Reign. Revised for publication by Kromluang Damrongrachanuphap, Chaophraya Thiphakorawong ed. Trans. and ed. Thadeus and Chadin Flood. 2 vols. Tokyo: Centre for East Asian Cultural Studies, 1978–1990.
The Dynastic Chronicles, Bangkok Era, the Fourth Reign. BE 2394–2411 (A.D. 1851–1868). Trans. Chadin Flood. 5 vols. Tokyo: Centre for East Asian Cultural Studies, 1965–1974.

References

Phirotthirarach, Somjai. "The Historical Writings of Chaophraya Thipakorawong." Ph.D. dissertation, Northern Illinois University, 1983.

Reynolds, Craig J. "Buddhist Cosmography in Thai History, with Special Reference to Nineteenth-Century Cultural Change." *Journal of Asian Studies* 35 (1976): 203–220.

Thiroux d'Arconville, Marie Geneviève Charlotte [née Darlus] (1720–1805)

French historian. At the age of fifteen, she married Louis Thiroux d'Arconville, later president of the Parlement of Paris, by whom she would have three sons. A semireclusive Jansenist, she was devoted to learning from an early age. After smallpox disfigured her at the age of twenty-three, she abandoned all interests except her family and her studies, which included anatomy, history, physics, chemistry, geology, and medicine; at the age of fifty she would undertake scientific experiments. Thiroux knew Voltaire, Turgot, Malesherbes, Lavoisier, Condorcet, and other savants. In addition to her Paris mansion, she frequently resided at Meudon, where she established a free hospice and from which base she was able to order books from Parisian libraries without leaving home. She translated George Savile, marquis of Halifax's *Advice to His Son* (1756), Alexander Monro's *Osteology* (1759), the Rev. Kenneth Macaulay's *History of Saint Kilda* (1765), and Hervey's *Memoirs*. Her own writings included original treatises on putrefaction and the passions. Natalie Zemon Davis has called Thiroux's *Marie de Médicis* (1774), which was based on manuscript sources, "a device" for writing seventeenth-century history in an era when women did not generally write full-scale histories. In this work, she underscored Marie's feminine faults, arguing that Marie had lacked the masculine virtues required for governance; consideration of gender entered her work only to this extent. Her *Vie de Cardinal d'Ossat* [Life of Cardinal Arnaud d'Ossat] (1771) was well done, but the *Histoire de François II* [History of Francis II] (1783) contained errors. After the French Revolution, which claimed one of her sons and her fortune, she stopped publishing her work, but thirteen volumes of manuscripts survived her death.

Barbara Sher Tinsley

Texts

Histoire de François II. Paris: Belin, 1783.
Vie de Cardinal d'Ossat. Paris: Herissant, 1771.
Vie de Marie de Médicis. Paris: Ruault, 1774.

References

Brive, Marie-France, ed. *Les Femmes et la Revolution Française* [Women and the French Revolution]. Toulouse: Presses Universitaires du Mirail, 1991, vol. 2.

Davis, Natalie Zemon. "Gender and Genre: Women As Historical Writers, 1400–1820." In *Beyond Their Sex: Learned Women of the European Past,* ed. Patricia Labalme. New York and London: New York University Press, 1980, 153–182.

Smith, Bonnie G. "The Contribution of Women to Modern Historiography in Great Britain, France, and the United States, 1750–1940." *American Historical Review.* 89 (1984): 709–732.

Thirsk, (Irene) Joan (b. 1922)

English agrarian historian. Born in London and educated at Westfield College and the London School of Economics (where R.H. Tawney supervised her postgraduate research), Thirsk's academic career was spent at the University of Leicester (1951–1965) and at Oxford (1965–1983) where she succeeded W.G. Hoskins as reader in economic history. Her earliest published articles stemmed from her doctoral research on interregnum land transfers and the Restoration land settlement. Thereafter its principal landmarks have been *English Peasant Farming* (1957), volumes IV and V of the *Agrarian History of England and Wales* (1967 and 1984–1985), covering the period 1500–1750; *Seventeenth-Century Economic Documents* (1972); and *Economic Policy and Projects: The Development of a Consumer Society in Early Modern England* (1978). For thirty-five years after 1957 she served on the editorial board of the journal *Past & Present,* was editor of the *Agricultural History Review* from 1964 to 1972, and in 1974 succeeded H.P.R. Finberg as general editor of the *Agrarian History of England and Wales*. A considerable linguist, Thirsk has been well placed to develop comparative perspectives in her research (on land tenures and inheritance, for instance), and her versatility embraces subjects as diverse as horses, fashion, rural industries, the diffusion of innovation, and the history of women. Working very much within the best traditions of the Leicester school of English local history, Thirsk has made creative use of previously neglected sources such as probate records to define agricultural regions and farm types and to explore the development of agricultural and other specialisms. Her collected essays—*The Rural Economy of England* (1984)—

bear witness to the breadth of her historical interests, to her logical, problem-solving approach, and to a social conscience in some ways akin to Tawney's. Further essays have appeared since then, enough to fill another volume. Thirsk was elected fellow of the British Academy in 1974 and was awarded the Order of the British Empire in 1993.

R.C. Richardson

Texts

Ed. *The Agrarian History of England and Wales.* Volume 4: Cambridge, Eng.: Cambridge University Press, 1967; Volume 5: Cambridge, Eng.: Cambridge University Press, 1984–1985.

Economic Policy and Projects: The Development of a Consumer Society in Early Modern England. Oxford: Oxford University Press, 1978.

English Peasant Farming: The Agrarian History of Lincolnshire from Tudor to Recent Times. London: Routledge and Kegan Paul, 1957.

The Rural Economy of England: Collected Essays. London: Hambledon Press, 1984.

Ed., with J.P. Cooper. *Seventeenth-Century Economic Documents.* Oxford: Clarendon Press, 1972.

References

Chartres, John, and David Hey, eds. *English Rural Society 1500–1800: Essays in Honour of Joan Thirsk.* Cambridge, Eng.: Cambridge University Press, 1990.

Thomas, Sir Keith Vivian (b. 1933)

British social and cultural historian of the early modern period. Born in Wales and educated at Balliol College, Oxford, he was for much of his working life tutor in history at St John's College, Oxford. Since 1985 he has been president of Corpus Christi College, Oxford. He has been a leading and early advocate of an interdisciplinary approach to historical study, the fruits of which were manifest in his *Religion and the Decline of Magic* (1971). This work drew on the findings of anthropologists to explore the significance of hitherto marginalized phenomena such as witchcraft, wizardry, and astrology, all of which provided Tudor and Stuart English people with means of understanding their world and coping with the misfortunes of daily life. The book made a pioneering contribution to the debate about the relationship between popular and elite cultures by arguing for a gradual withdrawal of educated elite opinion from a shared system of beliefs. A second book,

Man and the Natural World (1983), showed how anthropocentric attitudes toward the natural world were gradually displaced by social change, advances in science, and the secularization of thought. A series of articles on topics as diverse as Thomas Hobbes, the uses of the past, school discipline, cleanliness, literacy, numeracy, jokes, age as a principle of order, and late-twentieth-century Oxford college life, testify to the broadening of the range of historical enquiry of which he has been a leading advocate. He has eschewed quantitative methods in favor of an eclectic use of qualitative materials, which is always sensitive to the plurality of contemporary responses to the phenomenon under discussion.

Ian W. Archer

Texts

Man and the Natural World: Changing Attitudes in England, 1500–1800. London: Allen Lane, 1983.

Religion and the Decline of Magic: Studies in Popular Beliefs in Sixteenth and Seventeenth Century England. London: Weidenfeld and Nicholson, 1971.

References

Geertz, H., and K. Thomas. "An Anthropology of Religion and Magic." *Journal of Interdisciplinary History* 6 (1975): 71–109.

Thompson, Edward Palmer (1924–1993)

English historian, activist, theorist, and teacher. After service in Italy during World War II, Thompson attended Cambridge University, where he joined the Communist Party of Great Britain. After the Soviet invasion of Hungary in 1956 he left the Party, devoting his energies to *The New Reasoner* and later the *New Left Review,* founded in 1960. Upon finding his socialist-humanist philosophy at odds with the structuralist abstractions and Althusserian reasoning of some of his colleagues, Thompson quit the *Review,* joining Raymond Williams and Dorothy Thompson in a clarion call for a new democratic socialism. As an extramural tutor with the University of Leeds, and subsequently as an instructor in the Centre for Social History at the University of Warwick, Thompson established a reputation as a great teacher, in particular as one who valued direct experience in the workplace, and theory linked to action. After resigning from Warwick in 1971, he turned to fulltime writing and to serving as a speaker, writer, and organizer in support of European nuclear disarmament.

Thompson sought to restore a role to individual agency in Marxist historiography. In *The Making of the English Working Class* (1963) he took issue with structural models of class, which depicted class as a thing or object, arguing instead that class was neither a structure nor a category, but rather "something which in fact happens (and can be shown to have happened) in human relationships." English workers, according to Thompson, were intricately involved in the creation of their own class consciousness. In the *Making*, as well as in his many important essays (most of them collected in a volume entitled *Customs in Common*), Thompson wrote powerfully and eloquently about the moral economy, plebeian religion, and the vitality of popular culture as manifested in such customs as the charivari and wife sale. Although focusing upon English history, Thompson's work has attracted attention around the world, largely because of his rejection of crude determinism, his defense of a narrative style, his insistence upon the dignity of human labor, and his celebration of ordinary people as the fundamental makers of history.

Ian Dyck

Texts

Customs in Common. London: Merlin, 1991.
The Making of the English Working Class. London: Victor Gollancz, 1963.
The Poverty of Theory and Other Essays. London: Merlin, 1978.
Whigs and Hunters: The Origins of the Black Acts. London: Allen Lane, 1975.
William Morris: Romantic to Revolutionary. London: Lawrence and Wishart, 1955.
Witness against the Beast: William Blake and the Moral Law. Cambridge, Eng.: Cambridge University Press, 1993.

References

Kaye, Harvey, and Keith McClelland, eds. *E.P. Thompson: Critical Perspectives*. Oxford: Polity, 1990.
Palmer, Bryan. *Objections and Oppositions: The Histories and Politics of E.P. Thompson*. London: Verso, 1994.
Rule, J., and R. Malcolmson, eds. *Protest and Survival: Essays for E.P. Thompson*. London: Merlin, 1993.

Thompson, Leonard Monteath (b. 1916)

South African historian. Born in England, educated in South Africa and then at Oxford, Thompson began teaching at the University of Cape Town in 1946. At UCLA through the 1960s, then at Yale from 1968, he introduced concerns that animated other African historians in the 1960s, such as T.O. Ranger, into South African historiography. The *Oxford History* (1969–1971), *African Societies* (1969), and *Survival in Two Worlds* (1975) employ anthropology and oral history to explore the dynamics and developments within African societies, displacing Europeans from the central position previously awarded them. South African historians in the 1970s, exemplified by Shula Marks, criticized Thompson for focusing on the problem of racial cooperation while ignoring the ways racial groups and racism had been shaped by capitalism. Thompson's *Political Mythology of Apartheid* (1985) illustrates a further interest in historiography and the relation between myths and material forces in history.

P.S. Zachernuk

Texts

Ed. *African Societies in Southern Africa*. London: Heinemann, 1969.
A History of South Africa. New Haven, CT: Yale University Press, 1990.
And Monica Wilson, eds. *Oxford History of South Africa*. 2 vols. Oxford: Oxford University Press, 1969–1971.
The Political Mythology of Apartheid. New Haven, CT: Yale University Press, 1985.
Survival in Two Worlds. Oxford: Oxford University Press, 1975.
The Unification of South Africa, 1902–1910. Oxford: Clarendon, 1960.

References

Falola, Toyin, ed. *African Historiography: Essays in Honor of J.A. Ajayi*. Harlow: Longman, 1993.

Thorndike, (Everett) Lynn (1882–1965)

American medievalist and historian of science. Thorndike was born at Lynn, Massachusetts. He received his B.A. from Connecticut's Wesleyan University and his Ph.D. from Columbia University (1905) where he later became a professor; his 1905 dissertation, "The Place of Magic in the Intellectual History of Europe," foreshadowed his academic specialty. Thorndike founded the History of Science Society and was a fellow of the Medieval Academy of America and president of the American Historical Association. His most significant scholarly work focused on medieval scientific history as discussed in his monumental *History of Magic and Experimental Science* (1923–1958).

Influenced by James Harvey Robinson's intellectual history, Thorndike examined the relationship of magic and science by consulting obscure manuscripts. He defended alchemists and astrologers as prescientists, looking for "a reasoned explanation of natural phenomena." His work altered traditional interpretations that these men were merely wizards and charlatans and suggested that their experimentation formed the basis of modern science. He has also been praised for his pioneering textbooks, *The History of Medieval Europe* (1917) and *A Short History of Civilization* (1926).

Elizabeth D. Schafer

Texts

And Pearl Kibre, eds. *A Catalogue of Incipits of Mediaeval Scientific Writings in Latin.* Revised ed. London: Medieval Academy of America, 1963.
A History of Magical and Experimental Science. 8 vols. New York: Macmillan, 1923–1958.
Latin Treatises on Comets between 1238 and 1386 A.D. Chicago: University of Chicago Press, 1950.

References

Garroglou, Kostas, Jean Christianidis, and E. Nicolaidis. *Trends in the Historiography of Science.* Dordrecht: Kluwer Academic, 1993.
Kibre, Pearl. "A Bibliography of the Published Writings of Lynn Thorndike, 1905–1952." *Osiris* 19 (1954): 5–22.

Thucydides (ca. 460–400 B.C.)

Greek historian. Thucydides was born in Athens, into a prominent family. He began writing his *History of the Peloponnesian War* (between Athens and Sparta) in 431 B.C., the year in which it began, because he felt it would be the greatest war of all time. His book breaks off in mid-sentence while describing the year 411, although references to the outcome of the war show that he was still writing in 404. We know of no other writings. He caught the plague which broke out in Athens in 430 but recovered, and in 424 he was elected as a general and sent to relieve Amphipolis. He arrived too late, and the Athenians exiled him for his failure. He was a great admirer of Pericles, but a critic of Athenian democracy. He suggested that in Pericles' time, Athens was democratic in name but was in fact ruled by its first citizen; whereas after Pericles' death from the plague in 429, more equally balanced politicians tore Athens apart by pandering to the wishes of the people. He blamed these men for Athens's defeat.

Thucydides saw himself as more scientific than Herodotus, whom he implicitly criticized as a mere "storyteller." Thucydides insisted that no one could know what had happened in the distant past, and that even when investigating contemporary events, most people were naive. He insisted that only rigorous and extensive cross-examination of eyewitnesses could lead to the truth. In this, he was very much part of an intellectual revolution going on at Athens in the late fifth century. He claimed that he was not writing to win the attention of an immediate audience. He coined many new words, and wrote exceedingly dense prose. He knew that his book was hard work to read, just as it had been hard work to write; but for those fit to understand it, it would be a possession for all time.

He did not, however, cut all links with earlier writers. Like Herodotus, he put his key passages into direct speeches by protagonists. But unlike Herodotus, he felt a need to justify this. He explained that he himself had been present when many of the speeches had been delivered and had interviewed people who had been present at others. He admitted that he could not always remember the exact words used, but nevertheless claimed to reproduce the general sense of the speech and what the speaker ought to have said. Historians have argued ever since over how far Thucydides' speeches are genuine accounts and how far they are his own editorializing.

Thucydides saw expediency as the only law of interstate politics. His tone was deadpan but implicitly moralistic. He seems to have been genuinely horrified by the implications of his own views, and saw the Peloponnesian War as corrupting decent human relations of honor, piety, and affection. The starkness of his moral vision accounts for much of the book's success, although most later ancient historians ignored his severe methodological strictures.

Ian Morris

See also GREEK HISTORIOGRAPHY—ANCIENT; HERODOTUS.

Texts

History of the Peloponnesian War. Trans. Rex Warner. Second ed. New York: Penguin, 1972.

References

Connor, W.R. *Thucydides.* Princeton, NJ: Princeton University Press, 1984.
Gomme, Arnold W., Antony Andrewes, and Kenneth J. Dover. *An Historical Commentary on Thucydides.* 4 vols. Oxford: Clarendon Press, 1945–1981.

Thurmair, Johann

See AVENTINUS.

Thuróczi, János

See JOHN OF THURÓCZ.

Tibenský, Ján (b. 1923)

Slovak historian. Born in Budmerice, Tibenský studied at Comenius University and in 1951 became a member of the Institute of Historical Studies of the Slovak Academy of Sciences where he also served as the director of the department of history of science and technology (1960–1978). He was also the external director of the Encyclopaedic Institute of the Academy (1970–1972). His particular interests were the era of the Slovak national revival and the history of technology in Slovakia, which he investigated and interpreted according to Marxist principles of historiography. He was a coauthor of the first Marxist synthesis of Czechoslovak history, and he published studies of George Fandly (1950), J. Papánek and J. Sklenár (1948), Adam František Kollár (1983), and Matthias Bél (1987). Tibenský also directed the preparation of the *Priekopníci prírodných vied a techniky na Slovensku, 1–2* [Pioneers of the Natural, Medical and Technological Sciences in Slovakia], compiled the *Bibliografia prírodných, lekárskych a technických vied na Slovensku do roku 1850, 1–2* [Bibliography of Natural, Medical and Technological Sciences in Slovakia to 1850] (1976), and participated in the production of other synthetic historical works.

David P. Daniel

Texts

Bibliografia prírodných, lekárskych a technických vied na Slovensku do roku 1850, 1–2. Martin: Matica slovenská, 1976.

Dejiny Slovenska slovom a obrazom [History of Slovakia in Word and Picture]. Martin: Osveta, 1973.

Dejiny vied a techniky na Slovensku [History of Science and Technology in Slovakia]. Martin: Osveta, 1979.

J. Papánek-J. Sklenár: Obrancovia slovenskej národnostnosti v 18. storoèia [Revivalists of Slovak Nationality in the Eighteenth Century]. Martin: Osveta, 1958.

Ed. *Matej Bel: Doba-život-dielo* [Matej Bel: Time, Life, Work]. Bratislava: Veda, 1987.

Prhled československých dějin I [Overview of Czechoslovak History, I]. Prague, 1958.

Gen. ed. *Priekopníci prírodných vied a techniky na Slovensku, 1–2.* Bratislava: Obzor, 1986–1988.

"Slovak Historiography in the Period of the Beginnings of the Slovak National Revival 1780–1830." *Studia Historica Slovaca* 13 (1984): 107–135.

Slovenský Sokrates: Život a dielo Adama Františka Kollára [Slovak Socrates: Life and Work of Adam František Kollar]. Bratislava: Tatran, 1983.

References

Mannová, Elena, and David Paul Daniel, eds. *A Guide to Historiography in Slovakia*: Studia Historica Slovaca XX. Bratislava: Slovak Academy of Sciences, 1995.

Tillemont, Louis Sébastien Le Nain de (1637–1698)

French historian of Christian imperial Rome and medieval hagiography. Tillemont was born to a Parisian parlementary family. Following studies in Greek, Latin, antiquities, and theology, he pursued research in ecclesiastical history. Ordained in 1676, Tillemont spent three years in Paris at the Jansenist abbey of Port-Royal-des-Champs before its dissolution. He thereafter worked at his private library, maintaining contact with Maurists such as Jean Mabillon. Tillemont focused on the critical analysis and verification of ecclesiastical sources, reflecting the Jansenist defense of Catholic fidelity to primitive Church custom. Jansenist works traditionally integrated theology, history, and translations of Scripture, which were necessary to the education of priests. Among Tillemont's translations was the unpublished *Histoire de Saint-Louis* [History of St. Louis] (1688). Two later works, *L'histoire des Empereurs et des autres Princes qui ont régné durant les six premier siècles de l'Église* [The History of Emperors and Other Princes Who Reigned during the First Six Centuries of the Church] (1690–1738) and *Mémoires pour servir à l'Histoire ecclésiastique des six premiers siècles* [Memoirs of the First Six Centuries of Ecclesiastical History] (1693–1712), both received wide acclaim despite the latter's poor reception among theological censors.

Bonnie Effros

Texts

Ecclesiastical Memoirs of the Six First Centuries. Trans. Thomas Deacon. 2 vols. London: J. Wilford and W. Clayton, 1731–1735.

L'histoire des Empereurs. 6 vols. Venice: F. Pitteri, 1732–1739.

La Vie de Sainte-Geneviève, vierge, patronne de Paris [Life of St. Genevieve, Virgin, Patron Saint of Paris]. 6 vols. New York: Johnson Reprint, 1965.

La Vie de Saint-Louis, roi de France [Life of St. Louis, King of France]. 6 vols. Paris: J. Renouard, 1847–1851.

References

Neveu, Bruno. *Un historien à l'école de Port-Royal: Sébastien le Nain de Tillemont 1637–1698* [A Historian of the School of Port-Royal: Sébastien le Nain de Tillemont 1637–1698]. Archives internationales d'histoire des idées, vol. 15. The Hague: Martinus Nijhoff, 1966.

———. "Sébastien Le Nain de Tillemont (1637–1698) et l'érudition ecclésiastique de son temps [Sébastien Le Nain de Tillemont (1637–1698) and Ecclesiastical Learning in His Time]." In *Religion, érudition et critique à la fin du XVIIe siècle et au début du XVIIIe* [Religion, Erudition and Criticism in the Late Seventeenth and Early Eighteenth Century]. Paris: Presses Universitaires de France, 1967, 21–32.

Time

The feature of all that exists whereby phenomena of every kind occur and recur according to relations of earlier and later, and present, past, and future; an element of historical understanding which an inquiry must include in order to study anything historically. Historians invariably make time relations central to their studies and their definitions of history. Whatever the field of inquiry, time is a sine qua non of historical perspective. Historians from any culture and epoch are specialists in time relations. They first of all arrange the things they wish to study so that earlier things precede later ones, whether individually or in time series. Wherever possible they date things, if not precisely, then within a range of time. This permits them to designate which things are older and which are younger. They commonly group things by periods of time (ancient, medieval, and modern, the Káli age, the Depression) as determined by beginnings and endings of significant features of phenomena. This leads to the suggestion of phases and stages within the existence of something, estimated by reference to sequences observed in previous, but similar kinds of things (stages of learning, infancy to old age, decline).

Historians encounter a multiplicity of times and time perspectives coexisting within any topic. Every interacting social group or person brings different times into the events. There are more modes of time involved than the astronomic time registered by calendars and clocks, and more temporal subtleties than those covered by centuries and decades: internal biological time, aging, psychological time, wages, business cycles, *la longue durée,* liturgical and sacred time, musical rhythm, dream time, the right time to fall in love, fictional time, computer time.

Time words and time indicators appear in every sentence historians write or speak. Histories written in Indo-European languages carry time in the verb tenses present, past, and future. Some languages in which people write or tell histories, like many African languages, have verb tenses of only two types, one for events that continue to influence the present and another for those that do not. Other languages, like Hopi and Burmese, possess no verb tenses, but, as apparently in every known language, other words or sounds serve to indicate time relations. For instance, to utter "seed" anticipates future grain, and "harvest" recalls past planting. Time present, past, and future layer and interweave with untold complexity. Time past remains in everything still existing, within memories, structures, words, traditions, customs, habits, phobias, regrets, scars, rock strata, DNA, and hydrogen molecules. Time future emerges with every new act, every birth of a calf, every earthquake, in hopes, plans, expectations, visions, intentions, projects, and plans. Time present is now, when things exist, when things happen, when people act. Any time, throughout the ages and in any culture, was once a time present. Whether in people's experiences or in historians' inquiries, when time present changes, so do times past and future, shifting in more ways than we can number. History is thus not about the past alone, but about times present, past, and future. Historians deal with past history, current history, and future history.

Historians depend on being able to reckon time. People count time in relation to any cyclical phenomenon. The association of time with counting and measurement in historical study is so pervasive that generations of students in North America and Europe have disliked history at school and university because they have to learn too many dates. Aristotle construed time as the "number of motion in respect of before and after." Classical Hindu traditions name time Kála, from the root for "calculate," and in medieval Hindu historiography the *Vishnu Purāṇa* discloses Kála as a form of divine Vishnu: "Hear now how Kála is applied to measure the duration of Brahmá, and of all other sentient beings, as well as of those which are unconscious, as the mountains, oceans, and the like." Apparently every culture reckons time by the day and night cycle, the monthly cycle of the moon, and the annual rotation of the earth around the sun. Other modes of counting add on to these: seasons (rainy and dry, the four seasons), the agricultural and cattle cycles, reigns of rulers and dynasties (Roman emperors, Chinese dynasties), professors' sabbaticals, generations, the rhythmic vibrations of quartz crystals. Seconds, minutes, and hours as standard units are numerical abstractions, as are decades, centuries, and millennia. People learned to count the sequences of annual cycles by designating a constant starting time: the creation of the world for Jews, the founding of Rome, the Mayan "Long Count," or Muḥammad's Hejira. By virtue of the domination of the world by European and North American cultures, both the Christian reckoning of time from the birth of Jesus Christ, A.D. *(anno domini)* and B.C. (before Christ), and the temporal abstractions of the clock have enveloped the globe and encompassed all human cultures. With the help of historian-like geologists, evolutionary biologists, paleontographers, and astronomers, they have driven universal history back to the possible origin of our earth (ca. 5 billion years) and the universe as a whole (ca. 10–20 billion years).

When they wish to indicate what they mean by time, historians, along with philosophers and theologians, usually contrast or pair time with something else, and employ metaphors. In classical Greek and many Christian traditions, time refers to the changing, moving, imperfect, and the human and natural, while eternity signifies the unchanging, stable, perfect, and God. In Hindu traditions, time contrasts with timelessness, which is Brahman, and in Buddhist traditions with nothingness. In modern secular thought, time is paired with space as one of two dimensions of the universe, or joined to three spatial dimensions as the fourth dimension. Many voices speak of time as unreal in contrast with what they regard as real: the eternal forms (Platonists), the All (Hindu historians), thought (R.G. Collingwood), perceptions (perceptual psychology), discourse (Michel Foucault), historians' histories (E.H. Carr). The metaphors for time in historical writings are endless: time is a line, a wheel, a course, a stream, an arrow, a passage, a destroyer, an avenger, a judge, a theater, a drama, a form of Vishnu, a deity; time counts, extends, unrolls, flows, moves, runs out,

grows, deceives, ravages, heals. Even the most precisely worded concepts of time are metaphor laden: time is the "moving image of eternity" (Plato); "Absolute, true and mathematical time, of itself, and by its own nature, flows uniformly on, without regard to anything external" (Isaac Newton); time is "lived duration" (Henri Bergson). Historians used to claim that Western cultures lived by linear time, while Eastern cultures followed cyclic time. It seems more likely that all cultures embrace both linear and cyclic understandings of time, symbolizing in different ways that things occur and recur, and that phenomena are both unique and similar to others of the same kind.

C.T. McIntire

See also CHRISTIANITY, VIEWS OF HISTORY IN; PERIODIZATION, AS HISTORICAL PROBLEM.

Texts

Fraser, J.T., ed. *The Voices of Time: A Cooperative Survey of Man's Views of Time As Expressed by the Sciences and the Humanities.* Second ed. Amherst, MA: University of Massachusetts Press, 1981.

Sherover, Charles M., ed. *The Human Experience of Time: The Development of Its Philosophical Meaning.* New York: New York University Press, 1975.

References

Breisach, Ernst. *Historiography: Ancient, Medieval, and Modern.* Second ed. Chicago: University of Chicago Press, 1994.

McIntire, C.T. "Historical Study and the Historical Dimension of Our World." In *History and Historical Understanding,* ed. C.T. McIntire and Ronald A. Wells. Grand Rapids, MI: W.B. Eerdmans, 1984.

Whitrow, G.J. *Time in History: Views of Time from Prehistory to the Present Day.* Oxford: Oxford University Press, 1989.

Tiounn Chronicle

A Khmer-language Cambodian historical text commenced under the supervision of the palace minister of Cambodia, Tiounn, in 1928 and completed in 1934. The text drew on a range of earlier chronicles, including those of Prince Nupparot (1878) and the so-called Nong chronicle (1818). It covers events in Cambodian history, from a king's perspective, between mythical times and the accession of King Sisowath Monivong (1927) under whose reign it was compiled. The text offers no interpretations, and neither benefits nor suffers from exposure to European historical methods. Because it formed part of the king's regalia and because few books were printed in Cambodia in the colonial era, the text was not published in Khmer until the waning years of the monarchy. The printed version omits material from the reign of King Sisowath (1904–1927) included in the 1934 text.

Michael Vickery has argued that Cambodian chronicles, including this one, that treat events earlier than 1550 cannot be verified, and were often copied with little alteration from Thai chronicles about Thailand. For later periods, however, the *Tiounn Chronicle* can be read alongside other sources. The sections about the sixteenth and seventeenth centuries, translated into French by Khin Sok and Mak Phoeun, are lively, detailed, and of considerable interest. The sketchier portions treating the nineteenth century are useful to scholars wishing to construct a chronological framework. In sum, the *Tiounn Chronicle*, focused on royal behavior, is a thorough and often reliable indigenous synthesis of several Cambodian chronicle traditions.

David Chandler

See also CAMBODIAN HISTORIOGRAPHY.

Texts

Chroniques royales du Cambodge (de 1594 à 1677). Trans. Mak Phoeun. Paris: EFEO, 1987.
Sok, Khin, trans. *Chroniques royales du Cambodge (de 1417 à 1595).* Trans. Khin Sok. Paris: EFEO, 1988.
Sut, Eng. *Akkasar mahaboros khmer* [Documents about Cambodian Heroes]. Ed. Eng Sut. Phnom Penh: Ly Sa, 1969.

References

Chandler, David P. "Duties of the Corps of Royal Scribes: An Undated Khmer Manuscript from the Colonial Era." *Journal of the Siam Society* 63 (1975): 343–348.
Coedès, George. "Essai du classification des documents historiques cambodgiens conservés à la bibliothèque de l'École Française d'Extreme Orient [Essay on the Classification of Cambodian Historical Documents Preserved in the Library of the French School of the Far East]." *Bulletin de l'École Française d'Extreme Orient (BEFEO)* 18 (1918): 1–19.
Vickery, Michael. *Cambodia after Angkor: The Chronicular Evidence for the Fourteenth to the Sixteenth Century.* Ann Arbor, MI: University Microfilms, 1979.

———. "The Composition and Transmission of the Ayudhya and Cambodian Chronicles." In *Perceptions of the Past in Southeast Asia,* ed. Anthony Reid and David Marr. Singapore: Heinemann Educational Books, 1979, 130–154.

Tiraboschi, Girolamo (1731–1794)

Italian antiquary, librarian, and historian. Born in Bergamo, he joined the Jesuit order and secured the chair in rhetoric at the principal Jesuit college of Milan in 1755. His three-volume history of the twelfth-century order of the Umiliati, the *Vetera umiliatorum monumenta* (1766–1768), was a contribution to the growing field of medieval history established in Italy by Ludovico Antonio Muratori; it led to his appointment in 1770 to the prestigious librarianship of the Este dukes in Modena, a position he held until his death. His many projects during this period included a six-volume dictionary of Modenese writers entitled *Biblioteca modenese* (1781–1786), a *Dizionario topografico-storico degli Stati estensi* on the antiquities of the area, published posthumously, and the *Nuovo giornale de' letterati* literary journal, which he directed from 1773 to 1790. But his masterwork was the *Storia della letteratura*. Still consulted as the first comprehensive literary history of Italy, this work aims to combine accuracy of detail, knowledge of the documents, and cultural historiography in the broad sense understood by contemporaries like Voltaire, whose interpretative stance, however, he utterly rejected. After the first edition of 1772–1782, he had time to revise the entire work for a second edition in 1787–1794.

B. Dooley

Texts

Biblioteca modenese, o, notizie delle vite e delle opere degli scrittori nati negli stati del . . . duca di Modena [The Modenese Library, or, Notes on the Lives and Works of the Writers Born in the Duchy of Modena]. 6 vols. Anastatic reprint. Bologna: Forni, 1971.
Dizionario topografico-storico degli stati estensi [Topographical-Historical Dictionary of the Este states]. Anastatic reprint. Bologna: Forni, 1979.

References

Getto, Giovanni. *Storia delle storie letterarie.* Milan: V. Bompiani, 1942.

Tocqueville, Alexis de (1805–1859)

French statesman, political scientist, and historian. Tocqueville was born in Verneuil-sur-Seine to an aristocratic family. He began his career as a magistrate and was influenced by the liberalism of historian François Guizot. In 1831 and 1832, he traveled throughout the United States, investigating the workings of American democracy. He was elected to the French Chamber of Deputies in 1839 and came to prominence during the Revolution of 1848, serving briefly as minister of foreign affairs. He was forced to retire from politics after Louis-Napoléon's coup d'état, and died in Cannes in 1859. Tocqueville's best-known work is *De la démocratie en Amérique* [Democracy in America] (1835–1840), which explores the advantages and pitfalls of a political system based on civil equality. Tocqueville believed that democracy was historically inevitable, but needed to be reconciled with political liberty. Tocqueville's *Souvenirs* [Recollections] (1851), which analyze the failure of the Revolution of 1848, were never intended for publication. They illustrate Tocqueville's rejection of socialism and his critique of France's revolutionary tradition. *L'Ancien Régime et la révolution* [The Ancien Regime and the Revolution] (1856) was intended as the first part of a larger study that was never completed. It stresses the continuities between the absolute monarchy and the revolutionary regimes that followed, particularly in terms of political centralization. In recent years, it has inspired revisionist interpretations of the French Revolution by such non-Marxist scholars as François Furet.

Leslie Choquette

Texts

The Ancien Regime. Trans. John Bonner. London: Dent, 1988.
Democracy in America. Trans. Henry Reeve et al. 2 vols. New York: Vintage, 1990.
Recollections: The French Revolution of 1848. Ed. J.P. Mayer and A.P. Kerr; trans. George Lawrence. New Brunswick, NJ: Transaction Books, 1987.

References

Jardin, André. *Tocqueville: A Biography.* Trans. Lydia Davis with Robert Hemenway. New York: Farrar, Straus & Giroux, 1988.
White, Hayden. *Metahistory: The Historical Imagination in Nineteenth Century Europe.* Baltimore, MD: Johns Hopkins University Press, 1973.

Tokutomi Sohō [Iichirō] (1863–1957)

Japanese journalist and founding member of the *Minyusha* publishing group. Tokutomi was born in Kumamoto. He studied at the Kumamoto Yōgakkō and later at the Dōshisha School in Kyoto, where he was baptized a Christian by JōNiijma. In 1882 Tokutomi opened a private school, the Ōe Gijuku, in Kumamoto and also began to write. Moving to Tokyo in 1886, he published his most famous book, *Shorai no Nihon* [The Future Japan] (1886). Tokutomi, in this national bestseller, supported Western-style parliamentary government, pacifism, and internationalism. Following the book's success, Tokutomi was able to start an influential weekly journal, *Kokumin no tomo* [The People's Friend], published between 1887 and 1898, and also, from 1890, the daily newspaper *Kokumin Shinbun*. Among the contributors to these publications were Yamaji Aizan, Tokutomi Roka, and Takekoshi Yosaburō. After the turn of the century, Tokutomi become more conservative in his political views.

A. Hamish Ion

Texts

The Future Japan. Trans. and ed. Sinh Vinh with Hiroaki Matsuzawa and Nicholas Wickenden. Edmonton: University of Alberta Press, 1989.

References

Pierson, John D. *Tokutomi, Sohō 1863–1957: A Journalist for Modern Japan.* Princeton, NJ: Princeton University Press, 1980.

Toneri, Prince (677–735)

Japanese historian. Prince Toneri is credited with compiling the *Nihon shoki* (Chronicle of Japan), the first of the six official histories of Japan written in the eighth and ninth centuries. The work, in thirty volumes (plus an additional volume of genealogical charts), was completed in 720 and gives an account of Japanese history from the mythical age of the gods up to the reign of the Empress Jitō (686–697). Unlike the earlier *Kojiki,* which emphasized ancient myths, the *Nihon shoki* stressed recent events and showed a greater awareness of Japan's relations with foreign countries. After its completion, the *Nihon shoki* was widely read in educated circles and has subsequently been the subject of innumerable commentaries. Its significance lies not only in the information it provides about ancient Japan but also in the role it has played in the development of Japan's sense of national identity.

Graham Squires

Texts

Nihongi: Chronicles of Japan from the Earliest Times to A.D. *697.* Trans. W.G. Aston. London: George Allen and Unwin, 1956.

References

Sakamoto, T. *The Six National Histories of Japan.* Trans. John S. Brownlee. Vancouver and Tokyo: UBC Press and the University of Tokyo Press, 1991.

Topolski, Jerzy (b. 1928)

Polish historian and philosopher of history. Topolski was born in Poznan. Since 1959 he has been associated with the University of Poznan. Topolski is a full member of the Polish Academy of Sciences and a member of the editorial boards, among others, of the influential journals *History and Theory* and *Storia della Storiografia.* A cofounder of the so-called Poznan School of Methodology, which combined nonorthodox interpretations of Marxism with the philosophy of science, Topolski has concentrated his research in the history of Europe from the sixteenth to the eighteenth centuries, publishing works such as *La nascitá del capitalismo in Europa: Crisi economica e accumulazione originaria fra il XIVe ed il XVIe secolo* [The Birth of Capitalism in Europe] (1979). Editor and coauthor of *Dzieje Polski* [History of Poland] (1981) and many synthetic studies of various regions of Poland. He also initiated the publication of a six-volume synthetic study: *Polska: Dzieje narodu i kultury* [Poland: the History of the Nation and Its Culture], of which he is the author of the second volume: *Polska XVI–XVII wieku* [Poland from XVIth to XVIIIth Century] (1994). His most important works include: *Metodologia historii* [Methodology of History] (1968), *Rozumienie historii* [Understanding History] (1978), and *Teoria wiedzy historycznej* [The Theory of Historical Knowledge] (1983).

Ewa Domańska

Texts

Historia Polski od czasów najdawniejszych do 1990 roku [History of Poland to 1990]. Warsaw and Cracow: Polczek, 1992.

The Manorial Economy in Early-Modern East-Central Europe: Origins, Development and Consequences. London: Variorum, 1994.

Methodology of History. Trans. Olgierd Wojtasiewicz. Warsaw: PWN, 1976.

References

Drozdowski, Marian, et al. "Jerzy Topolski—for a New Shape of the Historical Science." In *Między Historią a Teorią* [Between History and Theory], ed. Marian Drozdowski. Warsaw-Poznan: PWN, 1988, 50–65.

Toulmin Smith, Lucy (1838–1911)

British medievalist and textual editor. The daughter of the antiquarian and publicist Joshua Toulmin Smith, she was born in Boston, Massachusetts, but moved with her family to London in 1842. Educated by her parents, Toulmin Smith for many years was her father's research and editorial assistant. Following Joshua's death in 1869, his daughter continued the medieval studies into which he had initiated her. Between 1870 and 1910, Lucy Toulmin Smith edited, individually or with other scholars, many important medieval texts. From 1894 until her death, Toulmin Smith was librarian of Manchester College, Oxford. Toulmin Smith's major scholarly contributions were editions of the *York Mystery Plays* (1885); *Expeditions to Prussia and the Holy Land by Henry, Earl of Derby* (1894); and John Leland's *Itineraries* (1906–1910). In 1886 Toulmin Smith compiled a historical manual of English grammar, and in 1889 she translated into English Jules Jusserand's *English Wayfaring Life in the Middle Ages.* A modest, retiring woman, Toulmin Smith was described by an obituary writer as having contributed "service to English scholarship . . . altogether out of proportion to her notoriety."

Don M. Cregier

Texts

Trans. *English Wayfaring Life in the Middle Ages.* Eighth ed. London: T.F. Unwin, 1896.

Ed. *Expeditions to Prussia and the Holy Land Made by Henry, Earl of Derby (afterwards Henry IV) in the Years 1390–1 and 1392–3.* London: Camden Society, new series, 52 (1894).

Ed. *The Itinerary of John Leland in or about the Years 1535–1543.* 5 vols. Carbondale: Southern Illinois University Press, 1964.

References

Obituary. *Times* [London], December 21, 1911, p. 11.

Graves, Edgar B., ed. *A Bibliography of English History to 1485.* London: Oxford University Press, 1975.

Tout, Thomas Frederick (1855–1929)

English historian of medieval administration, and founder of "Manchester School" of history. Tout was educated at Balliol College, Oxford, and began his teaching career at St. David's College, Lampeter, in 1881. He joined the faculty of Owens College, Manchester (now the University of Manchester), in 1890, remaining there until his retirement in 1925. Immediately thereafter, he was honored by election to the presidency of the Royal Historical Society. Tout was most influenced by William Stubbs, his tutor at Balliol, and by Continental scholars such as Eugène Deprez and Henri Pirenne, whose combining of institutional history with the study of diplomatic Tout thought a model for English historians. Ironically, the bulk of Tout's work was in the field of textbooks and biography; he wrote a number of history surveys and was perhaps the most frequent contributor to the *Dictionary of National Biography*. Tout also wrote what has been referred to as "pot-boiling" history. His methodology, however, is seen in the more mature and elaborate works of his Manchester years. In the Continental scholarship of his day, Tout found his own raison d'être, turning from political narrative as Stubbs had written to studies of administration, the people behind the scenes who implemented policy. He brought to Manchester the Continental focus on archival records and the concomitant training in diplomatic and paleography that raised the preparation of historians in England to the level of their French and German contemporaries. This was the achievement of the Manchester School of history. Tout's greatest influence, as an administrative historian, can be seen developing in some of his earliest serious work, from his edition of the *State Trials of the Reign of Edward I* (with Hilda Johnstone, 1906) to his *Place of the Reign of Edward II in English History* (1914). The latter is a revisionist work that eschews narrative, presenting instead a history of Edward II's administrators, whose place in the governance of the realm had, Tout thought, been overlooked. His *magnum opus* is his *Chapters in the Administrative History of Mediaeval England* (1920–1933), which reveals the power of Tout's imagination. More resembling the antiquarian scholarship of seventeenth-century scholars such as Thomas Madox than the work by his own contemporaries, these studies attempt to describe comprehensively the relationship of administration and policy. *Chapters* has been called one of the outstanding achievements of English historical learning. Like most of Tout's work, it is a reaction against the centrality given to Parliament in constitutional histories written during the nineteenth century. Tout was in England one of the progenitors of nonnarrative analytical history that was to dominate much twentieth-century historical writing.

Bruce R. O'Brien

Texts

Chapters in the Administrative History of Mediaeval England: The Wardrobe, the Chamber, and the Small Seals. 6 vols. Manchester: Manchester University Press, 1920–1933.

The Collected Papers of Thomas Frederick Tout with a Memoir and Bibliography. 3 vols. Manchester: Manchester University Press, 1932–1934.

The Place of the Reign of Edward II in English History. Ed. Hilda Johnstone. Revised ed. Westport, CT: Greenwood Press, 1976.

References

Blaas, P.B.M. *Continuity and Anachronism: Parliamentary and Constitutional Development in Whig Historiography and the Anti-Whig Reaction between 1890 and 1930.* The Hague: Martinus Nijhoff, 1978.

Powicke, F.M. "Thomas Frederick Tout, 1855–1929." *Proceedings of the British Academy* 15 (1930): 491–518.

Toynbee Arnold Joseph (1889–1975)

Historian of classical Greece and Rome, and theorist of the comparative study of world history. Over a span of fifty years (1921–1972) Toynbee worked on and published in stages the most comprehensive and audacious universal history ever written. Born in London, England, he received a traditional education in the Greek and Latin classics, first at Winchester College residential school, then at Balliol College, Oxford (B.A. 1911). He taught briefly at Balliol and at the University of London. From 1924 until 1955 he was director of studies and research scholar at the Royal Institute of International Affairs in Chatham House, London.

As a historian, Toynbee published in three areas. In ancient Greek and Roman history, his works included *Greek Historical Thought* (1924), *Hellenism* (1959), and *Hannibal's Legacy* (1965). In contemporary history, he wrote or directed the *Survey of International Affairs* for the years 1925–1938, an exhaustive annual review of world politics. In the comparative study of the history of civilizations, he published, among other works, *An Historian's Approach to Religion* (1956), *Mankind and Mother Earth* (1976), and *A Study of History*

(1934–1961, 1972), his enormous universal history, and the achievement for which he is generally remembered.

Toynbee rejected nations and politics as the primary historical categories and worked instead with civilizations on the horizon of world history. His remarkably flexible theory of history proposed theories of both recurrence and progress. He sought to examine and explain in a nondeterministic way the cycle of genesis, growth, breakdown, and disintegration of every civilization past and present. The primal dynamic was the interaction of challenge and response. Initially (1934) he identified twenty-one civilizations in world history, contrasted with some 650 primitive societies, later changing the number to 23 (1961), and 31 (1972). All but Western civilization were either gone or in disintegration, and this last was experiencing its own time of troubles. At first (1934) he understood progress as a general movement from primitive societies to civilizations, with the religions serving as chrysalis. Later (1940, 1954), reflecting a Christian view of history, he perceived progress as the spiritual fulfillment of humanity, with the civilizations functioning as wheels bearing humanity onward to the higher religions.

C.T. McIntire

Texts

Mankind and Mother Earth: A Narrative History of the World. New York: Oxford University Press, 1976.

Some Problems of Greek History. London: Oxford University Press, 1969.

A Study of History. 12 vols. Oxford: Oxford University Press, 1934–1961.

A Study of History (abrid. ed.): (1) Ed. D.C. Somervell. 2 vols. London: Oxford University Press, 1946–1957; (2) one-volume ed. rev. and abrid. by Toynbee and Jane Caplan. London and New York: Oxford University Press, 1972.

References

McIntire, C.T., and Marvin Perry, eds. *Toynbee: Reappraisals.* Toronto: University of Toronto Press, 1989.

McNeill, William H. *Toynbee: A Life.* Oxford: Oxford University Press, 1989.

Trân Trọng Kim (1882–1953)

Vietnamese educationalist, author, and conservative politician. From an intellectual family, Kim was educated at two metropolitan French colleges before being appointed inspector of primary education in colonial Tonkin. In 1945, he turned to politics as prime minister in the Japanese-endorsed government swept away by the August Revolution. His most influential works were the 1928 two-volume *Việt-Nam Su'- Lu'ọ'c* [An Outline History of Vietnam] and *Nho Giáo* (1930–1933), a history of Confucianism. Both circulated widely in Vietnam. The *Outline History* wedded cultural conservatism and political elitism to a Western methodology that regarded history as the factual reporting of the past. As the first "modern" history, Kim's unrevised account remained a standard text in the Republic of Vietnam until 1975. It is still in print but has not been translated.

N.J. Cooke

Texts

Nho Giáo. Saigon: Tan Viet, n.d.
Việt-Nam Su'-Lu'ọ'c. 2 vols. Saigon: Bo Giao-duc, 1971.

References

Marr, David G. *Vietnamese Tradition on Trial 1920–1945.* Berkeley: University of California Press, 1981.

Treitschke, Heinrich von (1834–1896)

German historian and political thinker. Treitschke studied politics, history, and economics at the universities of Bonn, Leipzig, Heidelberg, Tübingen, and Freiburg, earning his doctorate at Freiburg in 1854. After his habilitation in 1859 he became professor of politics in Freiburg. Chairs in history followed at Kiel (1866), Heidelberg (1876), and Berlin (1874), where he succeeded Leopold von Ranke. He also followed Ranke as historian of the Prussian State in 1886. From that year on, Treitschke served as editor of the *Preussische Jahrbücher.* From 1871 to 1879 he sat with the National Liberals as a member of the Reichstag; he continued to sit from 1879 to 1884, although as an independent. In 1895 he became an editor of the leading German historical journal, the *Historische Zeitschrift.* In his political thinking Treitschke first sympathized with the National Liberals, but in the course of the empire's unification gradually became a supporter of the autocratic monarchy. He fought against Social Democracy and opposed the reforming ideas of Gustav von Schmoller. As he grew older, Treitschke increasingly loaded his journalistic writings with chauvinistic, antidemocratic, and anti-Semitic slogans and thereby helped to nurture feelings of resentment in the German middle classes. He also advocated a violently expansionist foreign policy and urged an aggressive rearming in defense against Britain. Treitschke was one of the most widely read historians of the Wilhelmian epoch and had considerable influence on the ruling elites. He saw himself as both a historian and a political scientist. Refusing to submit to the demands of strict historical criticism and objectivity, his work consistently promoted the political goal of national unification under Prussian leadership. As early as his postdoctoral thesis, Treitschke had proclaimed the primacy of the political state over society, and proclaimed the social sciences as superfluous; in his view, the state possesses its own existence, distinct from the society over which it rules. His major historical work was the five-volume *Deutsche Geschichte im 19. Jahrhundert* [History of Germany in the Nineteenth Century] (1879–1894), which in fact stopped in 1848. In this work he considered German history from the Prussian standpoint, for which he was attacked by Hermann Baumgarten.

Thomas Fuchs

Texts

Historische und Politische Aufsätze [Historical and Political Essays]. Eighth ed. 2 vols. Leipzig: S. Hirzel, 1921.
Treitschke's History of Germany in the Nineteenth Century. Trans. E. and C. Paul. 7 vols. London: Jarrold & Sons, 1915–1919.
What We Demand from France. London: Macmillan, 1870.

References

Dorpalen, A. *Heinrich von Treitschke.* New Haven, CT: Yale University Press, 1957.
Iggers, Georg G. *The German Conception of History: The National Tradition of Historical Thought from Herder to the Present.* Revised ed. Middletown, CT: Wesleyan University Press, 1983.

Trevelyan, George Macaulay (1876–1962)

English historian. The son of Sir George Otto Trevelyan, who was himself the nephew and biographer of Thomas Babington Macaulay, Trevelyan was born in Stratford-on-Avon into a traditional Whig family. He attended Harrow school and Trinity College, Cambridge, where he was elected a fellow in 1896. Finding the Cambridge atmosphere oppressive (it was there that the historian J.R. Seeley had called Trevelyan's great-uncle Macaulay a charlatan) and his teaching duties a distraction from writing, he left for London in 1903. He completed his *England under the Stuarts* in 1904; it proved an enormous success and is still being reprinted. Trevelyan subsequently produced a vast output of historical studies: *Lord Grey and the Reform Bill* (1920) and *Manin and the Venetian Revolution* (1923) met with limited success, but his *British History in the Nineteenth Century* (1922) and his *History of England* (1926) were bestsellers. He returned to Cambridge as Regius professor of modern history (1927–1940), subsequently becoming master of Trinity College, Cambridge (1940–1951). Although branded as a Whig historian, he received numerous honors and became chancellor of Durham University in 1950. The last of his major works was his *English Social History* (1944); despite being criticized for its lack of analysis (and for its now notorious definition of social history as "history with the politics left out"), this caught the attention of the general reader and sold in vast numbers, confirming Trevelyan in his reputation as a learned yet highly readable historian.

David R. Schweitzer

Texts

An Autobiography and Other Essays. London: Longmans, Green, 1949.
British History in the Nineteenth Century. London: Longmans Green, 1937.
Clio, a Muse, and Other Essays. Freeport, NY: Books for Libraries Press, 1968.
England in the Age of Wycliffe. London: Longmans, 1972.
England under Queen Anne. 3 vols. London: Longmans, Green, 1936.
England under the Stuarts. Revised ed. London: Methuen; New York: Barnes and Noble, 1965.
English Social History: A Survey of Six Centuries. London: Longman, 1961.
History of England. Ed. Asa Briggs. London: Longman, 1973.

References

Cannadine, David. *G.M. Trevelyan: A Life in History.* New York: Norton, 1993.
Moorman, Mary Trevelyan. *George Macaulay Trevelyan: A Memoir.* London: Hamish Hamilton, 1980.
Plumb, John Harold. *G.M. Trevelyan.* London: Longmans, Green, 1951.

Trevor-Roper, Hugh Redwald [Baron Dacre of Glanton] (b. 1914)

British historian and iconoclastic and witty essayist. Appropriately for the son-in-law of Field Marshal Earl Haig, Trevor-Roper has strong Conservative Party connections. He owed his controversial appointment (1957–1980) as Regius professor of modern history, Oxford, to Prime Minister Harold Macmillan. From 1974 to 1988, he served as a director of the (London) *Times* newspaper, and in 1979 he was created a life peer by the new prime minister Margaret Thatcher. Following his retirement from Oxford, he served from 1980 to 1987 as master of Peterhouse, Cambridge. Trevor-Roper is not identified with a magnum opus, although his first book, a biography of seventeenth-century English Archbishop William Laud (1940) remains useful. Instead, he is renowned as an outstanding essayist, distinguished for his versatility, lucid style, and dislike of fanatics and ideologues. His popular reputation was established with a book on Nazi Germany, *The Last Days of Hitler* (1947), a by-product of his wartime service in British intelligence that had reached its seventh edition by 1995. The majority of his writings, in contrast, deal with elites in sixteenth- and seventeenth-century England and Europe. A short monograph, *The Gentry, 1540–1640* (1953), which refuted the arguments of R.H. Tawney and Lawrence Stone, initiated the historical controversy often known as the "Storm over the Gentry." In *The Gentry,* Trevor-Roper attacked the identification of political and religious radicalism with prosperous "rising" gentry landlords. Most of his subsequent books are collections of his many essays and reviews.

David M. Fahey

Texts

Archbishop Laud, 1573–1645. London: Macmillan, 1940.

Catholics, Anglicans, and Puritans: Seventeenth-Century Essays. Chicago: University of Chicago Press, 1988.

The European Witch-Craze of the Sixteenth and Seventeenth Centuries: And Other Essays. New York: Harper & Row, 1969.

The Gentry, 1540–1640: The Economic History Review. Supplement 1. London: Cambridge University Press for the Economic History Society, 1953.

The Last Days of Hitler. Seventh ed. London: Papermac, 1995.

References

Mehta, Ved. *Fly and the Fly-Bottle: Encounters with British Intellectuals.* Boston: Little, Brown, 1962.

Rowse, A.L. *Historians I Have Known.* London: Duckworth, 1995.

Stone, Lawrence. "The Undaunted Whig: Hugh Trevor-Roper and the Art of the Historical Essay." *Times Literary Supplement* 5 (June 1992): 3–5.

Trivet [or Trevet], Nicholas (1258–1328/1334)

English historian. Trivet was one of a small number of Oxford educated Dominicans responsible for encouraging the revival of classical studies in fourteenth-century England. His works range from expositions on Livy and Seneca the Younger, then little known, to biblical and nonbiblical commentaries. His three main historical works were the *Annales sex regum Angliae* [Annals of Six Kings of England], a history of the kings of England from Stephen to Edward I; the *Historia,* a universal chronicle from creation to the birth of Christ; and the Anglo-Norman Chronicles, another universal history culminating in the 1330s. Although different in style, all three demonstrate Trivet's profound and unusual knowledge of classical historiography and the critical methods employed by ancient writers. His works circulated widely on the Continent, where they were read by such luminaries as Petrarch, and he is acknowledged as having made a significant contribution to the beginnings, later in the fourteenth century, of a genuinely humanist approach to classical literature and history.

Cynthia J. Neville

Texts

Annales sex regum Angliae. Ed. T. Hog. London: English Historical Society Publications, vol. 10, 1845.

References

Dean, R.J. "Nicholas Trevet, Historian." In *Medieval Learning and Literature: Essays Presented to Richard William Hunt,* ed. J.J.G. Alexander and M.T. Gibson. Oxford: Clarendon Press, 1976, 328–352.

Smalley, Beryl. *English Friars and Antiquity in the Early Fourteenth Century.* New York: Barnes and Noble, 1960.

Troels-Lund, Troels Frederik (1840–1921)

Danish historian. Troels-Lund was born and raised in Copenhagen. He grew up a romantic, strongly influenced by his parents' warmth, passion, and love of nature. Later, he rejected both romanticism and the intense Christianity of his uncle, Sören Kierkegaard, for more rationalist ideals. His early studies were in theology, but from the 1870s he turned his attention to history. For the next thirty years his scholarship, which followed rationalist, source critical, and historicist lines, centered on early modern Danish history, the role of leading individuals in shaping that history, and the history of the kingdom's people. In the last years of his life his work became more introspective and philosophical. Among his more important works are *Mogens Heineson* (1877), *Dagligt Liv i Norden* (fourteen volumes, 1879–1901), and *Peder Oxe* (1906).

Byron J. Nordstrom

Texts

Dagligt liv i Norden i det sekstends århundrede [Everyday Life in Norden in the Sixteenth Century]. Sixth ed. Copenhagen: Gyldendal, 1968.

Peder Oxe: et historisk billed [Peder Oxe: A Historical Portrait]. Copenhagen: Schubothe, 1906.

De tre nordiske brodrefolk [The Brotherhood of the Nordic Peoples]. Copenhagen: Schubotheske Forlag, 1906.

Troels-Lund: Et liv, barndom og ungdom [Troels-Lund: A Life, Childhood and Youth]. Copenhagen: H. Hagerup, 1924.

References

Bach, Erik. *Danske Historieskrivare* [Danish Historical Writing]. Copenhagen: J.H. Schultz, 1942.

Jorgensen, Ellen. *Danske Historikere fra Saxo til Kr. Erslev* [Danish Historians from Saxo to Kristian Erslev]. Copenhagen: Gyldendsal, 1923.

———. *Historiens studium i Danmark i det 19. aarhundrede, udg. af den Danske historiske förening paa Carlsbergfondets bekostning* [Historical Studies in Denmark during the Nineteenth Century]. Copenhagen: B. Lunos bogtrykkeri, 1943.

Troeltsch, Ernst (1865–1923)

German theologian, philosopher, and historian of religion. From 1884 to 1888 Troeltsch studied theology in Erlangen, Berlin, and Göttingen. After the First Theological Examination he completed his curacy in 1888/1889 in Munich. In 1891 he did his licentiate at Göttingen with a study about *Vernunft und Offenbarung bei Gerhard und Melanchthon* [Reason and Revelation in Gerhard and Melanchthon], with which book he also habilitated. In 1892 Troeltsch became professor extraordinarius at Göttingen, and in 1894 he was appointed to a chair in theology at the University of Heidelberg. In 1915 he attained a chair in philosophy at the University of Berlin. Troeltsch's political thought, like his historical ideas, was similar to that of Max Weber, with whom he shared a house in Heidelberg. He participated in the "Evangelisch-sozialer Kongress," generally siding with the Liberals, and also represented the University of Heidelberg in the Upper House of the legislature in Baden. He saw World War I as a cultural conflict and, while expressing approval for German nationalism, spoke out against the annexationists and national-conservatives. He supported the Weimar Republic without reservation and in 1919–1921 served as an Undersecretary of State in the Prussian Ministry of Culture. In the *Spektatorbriefe* (1918–1922) he used a journalistic medium to publish his opinions on political events.

Troeltsch is regarded, along with Adolf von Harnack, as the most important modern German liberal theologian. As a historian, his work had little influence in his own time, but has since been recognized as significant. His most important historical writings are the *Soziallehren der christlichen Kirchen und Gruppen* [The Social Teachings of the Christian Churches and Groups] (1912) and the *Bedeutung des Protestantismus für die Entstehung der modernen Welt* [The Significance of Protestantism for the Rise of the Modern World] (1906). In those works Troeltsch described the sects of the European Reformation as an early form of religious community building; following the Weber thesis on the relation between Protestantism and capitalism, Troeltsch attributed to them a major role in the formation of modern society. On the other hand, he also argued that it was with the Enlightenment rather than with the Reformation that the modern world finally asserted itself. In his book *Der Historismus und seine Probleme* [Historicism and Its Problems] Troeltsch dealt with questions of the logic of history, explaining German historicism as a by-product of modern scientific thinking.

Thomas Fuchs

Texts

Gesammelte Schriften [Complete Writings]. Ed.
H. Baron. 4 vols. Tübingen: J.C.B. Mohr
(Paul Siebeck), 1912–1924.

The Social Teaching of the Christian Churches.
Trans. O. Wyon. Fourth ed. 2 vols. London:
George Allen & Unwin, 1956.

*Spektator-Briefe: Aufsätze über die deutsche
Revolution und die Weltpolitik 1918/20*
[Spectator Letters: Essays on the Ger-
man Revolution and World Affairs]. Ed.
H. Baron. Tübingen: J.C.B. Mohr (Paul
Siebeck), 1924.

Writings on Theology and Religion. Ed. R. Morgan
and M. Pye. London: Duckworth, 1977.

References

Drescher, H.-G. *Ernst Troeltsch: His Life and
Work.* Trans. J. Bowden. London: SCM
Press, 1992.

Iggers, Georg G. *The German Conception of
History: The National Tradition of Histori-
cal Thought from Herder to the Present.*
Revised ed. Middletown, CT: Wesleyan
University Press, 1983.

Rubanowice, R.J. *Crisis in Consciousness: The
Thought of Ernst Troeltsch.* Tallahassee:
University Press of Florida, 1982.

Trotsky, Leon [Lev Davidovich Bronstein] (1879–1940)

Bolshevik revolutionary, Marxist historian, and
analyst of the USSR's Stalinist regime. He became
a Marxist as a young man but joined the Bolsheviks
only in July 1917, just in time to provide the strategy for the November coup d'état. Appointed the
peoples' commissar for war and chairman of the
Supreme War Council, he organized the Red Army
into a fighting force that won the civil war. He is
known for his theory of permanent revolution and
his criticism of Stalin's theory of socialism in one
country. He was expelled from the Communist
Party in 1927 and assassinated near Mexico City by
order of Stalin. Trotsky's writing was polemical and
his analyses were based on economics and class. He
alleged that the only truly proletarian party was the
Bolsheviks, that World War I was "bourgeois imperialist," and that the Provisional Government was
"imperialist." His *Russische Revolution*, published in
German in 1908, is an important source for the
origin of the 1905 revolution, and *Revolution Betrayed* of 1937 is one of the first Marxist analyses of
the nature of Stalinism.

Elizabeth V. Haigh

Texts

The History of the Russian Revolution. Trans. M.
Eastman. 3 vols. New York: Simon and
Schuster, 1932–1933.

Writings of Leon Trotsky. 14 vols. New York:
Pathfinder, 1991.

References

Deutscher, Isaac. *The Prophet Armed, Trotsky:
1879–1921.* London: Vintage Books,
1954.

———. *The Prophet Outcast, Trotsky: 1929–
1940.* London: Vintage Books, 1963.

———. *The Prophet Unarmed, Trotsky: 1921–
29.* London: Vintage Books, 1959.

Tru'o'ng Vĩnh Ký (1837–1898).

Vietnamese Catholic intellectual, educationalist,
and advocate of romanized Vietnamese script in
the early colonial period. Born in southern Vietnam, Ký was educated in Chinese classics and
several European languages. He joined the colonial administration early, in 1860, and later traveled to France. In 1862 he helped edit the first
Vietnamese newspaper, *Gia tinh Báo,* and later
taught probationary French administrators. In
all, Ký wrote more than one hundred books in
Vietnamese and French. The most influential was
the school history text, *Cours d'histoire annamite,*
which combined oral and written sources in the
first Western-style narrative of Vietnam from its
legendary beginnings onward. Ký's reputation ensured that many later colonial writers uncritically
accepted his account as an authoritative source
for precolonial history.

N.J. Cooke

Texts

Cours d'histoire annamite. 2 vols. Saigon:
Imprimerie du gouvernement, 1875–
1877.

References

Osborne, M.E. *The French Presence in
Cochinchina and Cambodia.* Ithaca, NY:
Cornell University Press, 1969.

Ts'ai Mei-piao

See CAI MEIBIAO.

Ts'en Chung-mien

See CEN ZHONGMIAN.

Tso Ch'iu-ming
See ZUO QIUMING.

Tsuchiya Takao (1896–1988)
Marxist-influenced Japanese economic historian. After graduating from Tokyo University in 1921, he worked for his alma mater, except for the period when Marxism became politically unacceptable during World War II. He was born in Tokyo, but raised in Akita and Sendai following his father's death. After an unhappy childhood, he became one of the earliest Marxists in Japan. After graduation, he devoted himself to the study of Japanese economic history. His main interest lay in the birth of Japanese capitalism, since he believed that it was capitalism that lay behind poverty. He was especially interested in the significance of the Meiji Restoration. His first publication was *Hōken Shakai Hōkai Katei no Kenkyū* [A Study of the Breakdown of Japanese Feudalism] (1927). After World War II, he explored the field of Japanese business history. One of his notable works was a study of Eiichi Shibusawa, a famous businessman of the Meiji era, in whose life and thought Tsuchiya tried to explore the spirit of Japanese capitalism.

Takashi Fujii

Texts
Nippon Keizaishi Gaiyō [Outline of Japanese Economic History]. Tokyo: Iwanamishoten, 1953.
Nippon Shihonshugi no Keieishiteki Kenkyū [A Study of Japanese Business History]. Tokyo: Misuzushobō, 1954.

References
Nagahara, K., and M. Kano. *Nippon no Rekishi–ka* [Japanese historians]. Tokyo: Nipponhyōronsha, 1976.

Tsuda Sōkichi (1873–1961)
The most liberal among prewar Japanese historians, whose method became the basis for postwar scholarship. A graduate of Tokyo Senmon Gakkō (later Waseda University), Tsuda was not trained in the narrow documentary method practiced at Tokyo Imperial University. Appointed to Waseda in 1918, he retired in 1940. As a professor at a private university, he was not obliged to subscribe to and uphold official "truths" like professors at the state universities. From 1913 Tsuda questioned such received doctrines as the Age of the Gods and the early emperors, which were based on *Kojiki* (712) and *Nihongi* (720). Tsuda held that these myths had been concocted by eighth-century intelligentsia. Found guilty of lese majesty in 1942, he was sentenced to two years imprisonment but was freed on a technicality. Tsuda remained controversial after 1945 not for attacking the imperial state as a victim of prosecution, but rather for his affirmation of it; he blamed individuals rather than the system itself for his prosecution. Despite their disappointment in his stance, postwar scholars continued to follow his methods, thereby dismissing the myths as the starting point of Japanese history.

John S. Brownlee

Texts
Tsuda Sōkichi Zenshū [Complete Works of Tsuda Sōkichi]. 27 vols. Tokyo: Iwanami Shoten, 1965. Revised ed. 12 of 35 projected vols., 1986– .

References
Yun-tai Tam. "Rationalism Versus Nationalism: Tsuda Sōkichi (1873–1961)." In *History in the Service of the Japanese Nation,* ed. John S. Brownlee. Toronto: University of Toronto–York University Joint Centre on Modern East Asia, 1983.

Tu Chi
See TU JI.

Tu Ji [Tu Chi] (1856–1921)
Chinese historian, specialist in frontier historical geography and Mongolian history. Although not a formal member of the New Text School, Tu Ji's scholarship was imbued with the late Qing spirit of statecraft, which stressed the practical application of learning. His earlier works, such as *Guangdong yuditu* [Atlas of Guangdong] (1890) and *Heilongjiang yuditushuo* [Annotated Atlas of Heilongjiang] (1899), were written at a time when China was rethinking its frontier defense in the face of the intrusion of the West. His *magnum opus* was *Mengwu'er shiji* [History of the Mongols], on which he allegedly commenced work as early as 1895. Often hailed as China's first ethnic history, *Mengwu'er shiji* was written with the conviction that Mongolian history should be studied in its own right, whereas scholars had hitherto shown little interest beyond the span of the Yuan dynasty (1279–1368). The first installment of this monu-

mental work was published in 1911, when the question of Mongolian independence became a heated issue. The book was completed in final form in 1934 by his son, who took up the project after Tu Ji's untimely death in 1921.

W.K. Cheng

Texts

Mengwu'er shiji. In *Yuanshi erzhong.* Shanghai: Guji chubanshe, 1989.

References

Qui Zunyi and Yuan Yingguang. *Zhongguo jindai shixue shi* [Modern Chinese Historiography]. 2 vols. Jiangsu: Guji chubanshe, 1989.

Tuchman, Barbara Wertheim (1912–1989)

American historian. Tuchman was born in New York City and educated at Radcliffe (B.A., 1933). In the late 1930s she was a reporter for the *Nation.* After World War II she settled with her physician husband in Connecticut, where she raised a family and later began to write history. Her lack of academic status gave her, she believed, a fresh point of view. Her works are both thoroughly professional and popular; well written, some of her books were bestsellers. Several deal with World War I and the period just before its outbreak. *The Guns of August* (1962), which won the Pulitzer Prize, discusses the beginning of the war and was the basis for a film of the same name (1964). Tuchman's *Proud Tower* (1966) is a treatment of selected topics in European history just before the war. She also wrote about other topics, including China in *Stilwell and the American Experience in China* (1971), for which she again received the Pulitzer Prize; fourteenth-century Europe in *A Distant Mirror* (1978); historical mistakes in *The March of Folly* (1984); and the American Revolution in her final book, *The First Salute* (1988).

Walter A. Sutton

Texts

A Distant Mirror: The Calamitous Fourteenth Century. New York: Knopf, 1978.
The Guns of August. New York: Macmillan, 1962.
The March of Folly from Troy to Vietnam. New York: Knopf, 1984.
Practicing History. New York: Knopf, 1981.
Stilwell and the American Experience in China, 1911–45. New York: Macmillan, 1970.

Turner, Frederick Jackson (1861–1932)

American historian. Turner was born in the small village of Portage, Wisconsin, itself not long removed from the frontier experience that so fascinated him in later years. Educated at the University of Wisconsin and the new doctoral program at the Johns Hopkins University, his academic career was spent first at Wisconsin, where he developed an outstanding graduate program in American history, and after 1910 at Harvard. He died in Pasadena, California, where in retirement he had held a research appointment at the Huntington Library.

Turner is best known for his 1893 address arguing that the frontier experience was a central element in the shaping of American institutions and national character. Over the next decade or so the frontier thesis gradually came to dominate American historiography, making Turner's 1893 paper arguably the most influential article ever written by an American historian. A related interest of Turner in later years was the importance of sectional conflict and regionalism in the development of the United States, but his major scholarly work on this subject remained unfinished at his death.

There were only a few dissenters to the widespread acceptance of the frontier thesis during Turner's lifetime, but the attacks have mounted in scope and intensity ever since. Critics complained about Turner's shifting and imprecise use of "frontier" and his overbroad claims of its significance. Was the frontier primarily a process, a transitional geographic area, or a state of mind? Skeptics also rejected Turner's emphasis on the importance of sectional conflict because of his inability to provide precise definitions of the sections and their subregions over time, let alone to determine their significance on various issues. Even Turner found the definitional problems insurmountable, although he remained convinced of the value of the effort.

Although Turner is chiefly remembered for his pioneering insights about the significance of the frontier and sectionalism, it is a mistake to limit his historiographic contributions to these two broad but controversial themes. His study of history was omnivorous and all-encompassing, his approach that of a relativist who believed in multiple causation. He sought to understand everything contributing to the development of the American nation, in the process incorporating the methodologies and findings of other related disciplines. Turner was always more concerned with exploring the sources—broadly defined—and in raising fresh and provocative questions than in producing definitive answers. For him research was never ending.

In keeping with this expansive outlook, he was easily diverted from the task of fleshing out and testing his ideas. For this he has been justly criticized by later historians. By concentrating on Turner's failure to subject his provocative ideas to rigorous definition and scholarly analysis and by focusing especially on his more extravagant popular rhetoric, however, his critics largely overlook his many other contributions to American historiography. Early in his career, for example, Turner forever broadened the study of diplomatic history by exploring French, British, and Spanish archives and demonstrating the complexity of the forces influencing European relations with the New World. Likewise he preached the significance of immigration history, and although he did little work on it himself, two of his students, George M. Stephenson and Marcus Lee Hansen, would pioneer the field. He stressed the importance of social and intellectual history a generation before his last student, Merle Curti, and others began to develop it. It was Turner who conceived the Carnegie Institution project that resulted in Charles O. Paullin's massive *Atlas of the Historical Geography of the United States* (1932). He also played the leading role in proposing and raising funds for the multivolume *Dictionary of American Biography.* Turner thus should be remembered not for the inadequacies of some of his theories but as a remarkably creative stimulating force, who profoundly influenced the profession as have few American historians before or since.

E. David Cronon

Texts

The Early Writings of Frederick Jackson Turner. Ed. Everett E. Edwards. Madison: State Historical Society of Wisconsin, 1938.

The Frontier in American History. New York: Holt, 1920.

The Significance of Sections in American History. New York: Holt, 1932.

References

Billington, Ray A. *Frederick Jackson Turner: Historian, Scholar, Teacher.* New York: Oxford University Press, 1973.

Jacobs, Wilbur R. *On Turner's Trail: 100 Years of Writing Western History.* Lawrence: University of Kansas Press, 1994.

Tyrrell, James (1642–1717)

English Whig polemicist, historian, and antiquary. Tyrrell was born in Middlesex and was the grandson of James Ussher (1581–1656), the celebrated archbishop of Armagh. Tyrrell studied law in London and received an M.A. at Oxford. He retired to his Buckinghamshire estate in the 1680s, although he remained in contact with London Whigs, including John Locke—a close friend—and William Petyt. In 1681, Tyrrell published *Patriarcha non Monarcha,* a long, complicated response to the royalist Sir Robert Filmer's *Patriarcha.* Between 1691 and 1694, Tyrrell published a series of political dialogues, ultimately collected together in 1718 as *Bibiliotheca Politica,* which presented a synthesis of Whig ideology, incorporating the ideas of Locke, Petyt, and others. The remainder of his life was spent working on his *General History of England,* although he published only three volumes. Tyrrell's central purpose was to refute royalist claims, particularly those of Dr. Robert Brady, that the Norman Conquest had dramatically reshaped England, destroying its so-called ancient constitution.

Melinda Zook

Texts

Bibliotheca Politica: An Enquiry into the Ancient Constitution . . . in Thirteen Dialogues. London: R. Baldwin, 1694.

A Brief Enquiry into the Ancient Constitution and Government of England. London: R. Baldwin, 1695.

The General History of England, Both Ecclesiastical and Civil . . . to the Reign of William III. 3 vols. London: W. Rogers et al., 1698–1704.

Patriarcha non Monarcha: The Patriarch Unmonarch'd. London: R. Janeway, 1681.

References

Earl, D.W.L. "Procrustean Feudalism: An Interpretative Dilemma in English Historical Narrative, 1700–1725." *Historical Journal* 19 (1976): 33–51.

Gough, J.W. "James Tyrrell, Whig Historian and Friend of John Locke." *Historical Journal* 19 (1976): 581–610.

Pocock, J.G.A. *The Ancient Constitution and the Feudal Law.* Second ed. Cambridge, Eng.: Cambridge University Press, 1987.

Zook, Melinda S. "The Propagators of Revolution: Conspiratorial Politics and Radical Whig Culture in Late Stuart England." Ph.D. thesis, Georgetown University, 1993.

U

Ukrainian Historiography

The writing of history in Ukraine, medieval times to present. Early in the eleventh century, shortly after the official christianization of the Rus', monks began to compose annual records or chronicles consisting of current events, stories, legends, and biographies. The most notable example of such medieval Ukrainian historiography is the *Primary Chronicle* attributed to Nestor of the Kievan cave monastery, which begins with an account of early slavic migrations. It served as a model for other such compilations into the fifteenth century. Another noteworthy example is the Galician Volhynian Chronicle of 1200. A new category of chronicle was developed in the late seventeenth and early eighteenth centuries by recorders of Cossack affairs. These remain important sources for study of the Cossack-Hetman state of the seventeenth and eighteenth centuries.

The rise of national Ukrainian consciousness in the nineteenth century was accompanied by the development of historical scholarship. Much attention was focused on the formation of the Cossack state, historians treating it as part of a continuum extending back to Kievan Rus', the medieval state destroyed by Tatar invaders in the thirteenth century. One of the first formal scholars was Mykola Kostomarov (1817–1885), a lecturer at the universities of Kiev (now Kyiv) and St. Petersburg. He is known as the founder of the populist trend in Ukrainian history. His investigation of the life of the common people and his studies of Hetman Ukraine led him to argue for the national distinctiveness of the Ukrainian people based on their unique historical development. Another member of the school, Oleksander Lazarevsky (1834–1902) concentrated on left bank Ukraine in the seventeenth and eighteenth centuries, especially on the relationship between the peasantry and the Cossack starshyna (elders).

While virtually all Ukrainian historians and intellectuals favored cultural autonomy for Ukraine, they differed about the degree of independent statehood that was desirable. Pantelemon Kulish (1819–1897), for example, who wrote a *History of the Reunification of Rus* and *Secession of Left Bank Ukraine from Poland,* was alienated from most other scholars because he advocated the development of Ukrainian high culture within a Russian empire. A more popular position was that of Mykhailo Drahomanov (1841–1895), a historian of ancient Rus' and a collector of Ukrainian folklore who favored an autonomous Ukrainian state within federalist Russia and Austria-Hungary. Even so, he was dismissed from Kiev University for his nationalistic tendencies.

One of the strongest representatives of the populist school of historiography was Volodymyr Antonovych (1834–1908), who studied the socio-economy of right bank Ukraine in the sixteenth to the eighteenth centuries. A professor at Kiev University, he founded a Kievan school of history, which laid the foundations of modern Ukrainian historiography. Members of his school included Dmytro Bahalii (1857–1932), who held the chair of Ukrainian studies at Kharkiv University, organized its historical archives, and made contributions to the history of Left Bank and southern Ukraine; Ivan Lynnychenko (1857–1926) who studied Kievan Rus' and Galicia in the fourteenth and fifteenth centuries, albeit from a Russian imperial viewpoint; and Mitrofan Dovnar-Zapolskii (1867–1934) who concentrated on the economics and ethnography of medieval Belorus.

The preeminent member of the Kievan School was Mykhailo Hrushevsky (1866–1934). His *History of Ukrainian Rus,* which appeared in ten volumes between 1898 and 1937, introduced the first scholarly scheme for the history of the Ukrainian people in all their territories. He addressed both social and political issues. He founded a school of history in Lvov, then moved to Kiev after the 1905 revolution where he established a center of historical research in the Ukrainian Scientific Society. He was briefly the president of the Ukrainian Rada established after the abdication of Emperor Nicholas II.

Since then, many representatives of a "statist" school of historiography have demonstrated the political-historical evolution of the Ukrainian people from medieval Kievan Rus' through the hetman state to the Ukrainian state of 1917–1920. Among them were Vyacheslav Lypynsky (1882–1931), Stepan Tomashevsky (1845–1930), and Dmytro Doroshenko (1882–1951). In the 1920s, research flourished in Ukrainian lands, much of it rooted in Hrushevsky's scheme. Dmytro Baali (1857–1932) and Mykhailo Slabchenko (1882–1952) created centers of historical studies in Kharkiv and Odessa, respectively. In the 1930s, however, authorities in the USSR prohibited independent Ukrainian studies and many scholars were purged. Slabchenko, for example, was arrested in 1929 and died in obscurity.

Scholarship continued to be done in Galicia, often by Hrushevsky's former students, until World War II. For example, Myron Korduba (1876–1947), a professor at Warsaw and Lvov Universities, wrote on medieval Ukraine, on Khmelnitsky, and on Ukrainian historiography. Ivan Krypiakevych (1886–1967), a professor in Lviv, studied the socioeconomy and culture of sixteenth- and seventeenth-century Galicia. When western Ukraine was annexed to the USSR, the interpretation of Ukrainian history was subsumed into Russian studies. In 1954, Krypiakevych produced a large monograph extolling Bohdan Khmelnitsky's role in the "reunification" of Russia and Ukraine.

As scholarship was stifled in Ukraine however, it developed in the West, some of it initiated by émigrés. Important work has been done at many centers for slavic studies and most particularly at the Institutes of Ukrainian Studies at Harvard University, the University of Toronto, and the University of Alberta. As contacts grow between scholars in Ukraine and elsewhere, and as new material becomes available, the field will grow in importance.

Elizabeth V. Haigh

Texts

Doroshenko, Dmytro. *History of the Ukraine.* Trans. and abrid. Hanna Chikalenko-Keller; ed. G.W. Simpson. Edmonton, Alberta: Institute Press, 1939.

Hrushevsky, Mykhailo. *A History of Ukraine.* Ed. O.J. Frederiksen. New Haven, CT: Yale University Press, 1941.

Kostomarov, Nikolai Ivanovich. *Book of the Genesis of the Ukrainian People.* Ed. with commentary by B. Yanivsky. New York: Research Program on the USSR, 1954.

Nestor. *The Russian Primary Chronicle: Laurentian Text.* Ed. and trans. Samuel Hazzard Cross and Olgard P. Sherbowitz. Cambridge, MA: Medieval Academy of America, 1953.

References

Pidhainy, O. *Ukrainian Historiography and the Great East-European Revolution.* Toronto and New York: New Review Books 1968.

Ullmann, Walter (1910–1983)

Austrian émigré medievalist. Ullmann was a lawyer who emigrated to the United Kingdom after the 1938 German annexation of Austria. After holding a variety of posts in England, he settled at Cambridge University, lecturing to large numbers of undergraduates and supervising many graduate students from 1949 to 1978. Part of a Germanophone émigré wave, he helped introduce Anglophone historians to contemporary continental European historiography, including the use of liturgy and theology as sources for politics. In particular, Ullmann was known for a distinctive emphasis on jurisprudential issues and legal sources, treated within a broad chronological sweep. Through the legal lens, he studied "the medieval Church perceived as an organization of government." In his vision, medieval politico-religious organization shifted from descending to ascending sources of authority; paradoxically, he simultaneously argued from the idealist assumption that the medieval papacy was a stable "idea" that slowly "realized itself" in institutional form. Through more than four hundred repeatedly translated and reprinted publications, he influenced historians at every level from undergraduate to professional; most of his works are now out of print, but his former students remain active.

Felice Lifshitz

Texts

The Growth of Papal Government in the Middle Ages. London: Methuen, 1955.

A History of Political Thought: The Middle Ages. Harmondsworth: Penguin, 1965.

Medieval Papalism: The Political Theories of the Medieval Canonists. London: Methuen, 1949.

Principles of Government and Politics in the
    Middle Ages. London: Methuen, 1961.
A Short History of the Papacy in the Middle Ages.
    London: Methuen, 1972.

References

Garnett, George. "Biography" and "Supplementary Bibliography." In Ullmann, *Law and Jurisdiction in the Middle Ages,* ed. George Garnett. London: Variorum Reprints, 1988, ix–xviii.

Linehan, Peter. "Bibliography of Walter Ullmann's Writings." In *Authority and Power: Studies on Medieval Law and Government Presented to Walter Ullmann on his Seventieth Birthday,* ed. B. Tierney and P. Linehan. Cambridge, Eng.: Cambridge University Press, 1980, 255–274.

United States

See AMERICAN HISTORIOGRAPHY; IMPERIAL SCHOOL OF AMERICAN HISTORY; NEW HISTORY; PROGRESSIVE HISTORY; RADICAL HISTORY (UNITED STATES).

Unwin, George (1870–1925)

British economic historian. Unwin was born in Stockport, the eldest of six children of a railway employee. During the 1890s he attended University College, Cardiff, and Lincoln College, Oxford, where he studied literature and classics. He later studied economics at the University of Berlin (1898). After returning to England he lectured on economic history at the London School of Economics and at Edinburgh University, before he finally settled in the chair of economic history at the University of Manchester. Unwin's major academic interest lay in the field of economic history. He is credited with having substantially altered the perspective of economic history from political to sociological and with injecting impersonal and international factors into his works. His most important contributions were *The Gilds and Companies of London* (1908) and *Finance and Trade under Edward III* (1918). The latter consisted of essays from the history school of the University of Manchester. Included are his own articles on the wool trade and the Black Death, focusing on fourteenth-century Europe. Though always in ill health that led to his premature death, he was also respected for the assistance he provided to students and other historians; his admirers included even those, such as R.H. Tawney, who disagreed with many of his views.

Eugene L. Rasor

Texts

Finance and Trade under Edward III. New York: Kelley, 1962.
The Gilds and Companies of London. London: Frank Cass, 1963.
Industrial Organisation in the Sixteenth and Seventeenth Centuries. Oxford: Clarendon Press, 1904.
Studies in Economic History: The Collected Papers of George Unwin. Ed. R.H. Tawney. London: Frank Cass, 1958.

References

Tawney, R.H. "Introduction." In *Studies in Economic History: The Collected Papers of George Unwin,* ed. Tawney.

Urban History

Specialized subfield of historical research and writing that has somewhat different origins and development patterns in different countries. Urban history is especially visible in the United States, Canada, Australia, and the United Kingdom, but it also has practitioners in most European nations, Latin America, India, Japan, and China.

In the United States, where the field is most fully developed, urban history emerged in the 1960s as part of the broader movement toward a new social history. A few historians in the years before 1950 did write about cities—Carl Bridenbaugh on American colonial cities, Arthur M. Schlesinger Sr. on the social history of the industrial city, Bessie Pierce on Chicago, Blake McKelvey on Rochester, and Bayrd Still on Milwaukee were early pioneers in American urban history. These early studies were essentially descriptive and narrative rather than analytical, often taking the form of the "urban biography." Noteworthy analytical studies during the formative period of urban history were Oscar Handlin's *Boston's Immigrants* (1941) and Richard C. Wade's *Urban Frontier* (1959). The early band of urban historians established an Urban History Group within the American Historical Association in 1954 and began publishing a modest *Urban History Group Newsletter* (1954–1975).

The 1960s brought dramatic change to the American historical profession. The mainstream consensus history of previous years—an elitist history focused mostly on national political events—began to fragment under the pressure of the social strains and political conflicts of the decade. A new social history emerged, as scholars began to examine such subjects as race, ethnicity, class, and gender; a bottom-up approach challenged the earlier top-down history. The computer revolution of the 1960s also made possible a more exact social science history, with its emphasis on quantification and analytical rigor. These shifts in historiographical tradition coincided with the ghetto riots and the "urban crisis" of the 1960s. It is not surprising, then, that some of the new social historians turned to the city, seeking to illuminate the historical background of the nation's contemporary urban problems.

Urban history in the United States was energized by the convergence of changing social patterns and historiographical trends in the 1960s. The ferment of academic debate pushed urban history in several different directions by the early 1960s. Sam Bass Warner Jr., in *Streetcar Suburbs* (1962), suggested an ecological approach to urban history research. A study of population redistribution in late-nineteenth-century Boston, Warner's book linked new transportation innovations with suburban building patterns and the class dimensions of new neighborhood formation. Warner built upon earlier suggestions of Eric E. Lampard, who in numerous articles urged urban historians to study urbanization as a "societal process" that required examination of such "interacting elements as population, topography, economy, social organization, political process, civic leadership and urban imagery." Warner's later book *The Private City* (1968), reflected an early effort to provide an analytical framework for conceptualizing the process of urbanization. Samuel P. Hays and Roy Lubove also published studies in the 1960s that pioneered an ecological approach to urban history research.

The work of Stephan Thernstrom staked out a second new path in American urban history in the 1960s. In *Poverty and Progress: Social Mobility in a Nineteenth-Century City* (1964) and in a later book, *The Other Bostonians* (1973), Thernstrom pioneered in the use of manuscript census sources and quantitative analysis in probing the conception of nineteenth-century America as a land of opportunity. Although narrowly focused on the question of social mobility and ignoring larger issues such as the process of urbanization or city building, Thernstrom's approach was widely imitated, as younger historians began replicating his work for other cities. By the early 1970s, the term "new" urban history had been taken over by the quantifiers in the Thernstrom tradition who were mostly studying mobility and related issues. Thus, the new urban history came to be perceived as a special sort of quantitative history.

The new urban history faded rather quickly in the 1970s, as urban historians came to realize the narrowness of the methodology and the wide range of research questions that could not be addressed quantitatively. Warner's ecological approach has had more longevity among practitioners of urban history. Thus, after a false start in the 1960s, when some urbanists were diverted by the presumed advantages of quantification, American urban history as a research field blossomed in the 1970s and after. Symptomatic of new initiatives was the founding of the *Journal of Urban History* in 1974. Open to diverse methodologies and approaches, the *JUH* has provided a barometer of urban history for over twenty years.

Since the early 1970s, American urban historians have pursued a multitude of subjects in their exploration of cities and urban life. Many studies continue to use the case study approach, focusing on specific urban problems of national import within the historic context of a single city. Typical of this approach are Arnold R. Hirsch's *Making the Second Ghetto* (1983), a study of Chicago, and Olivier Zunz's *The Changing Face of Inequality* (1982), a study of Detroit. Other urban historians have pursued a comparative framework in exploring urban dimensions in several cities. Richard C. Wade's *Slavery in the Cities* (1964) and Gary B. Nash's *The Urban Crucible* (1979) adopted this methodology. Still other historians have analyzed urban developments on a national scale: Sam Bass Warner Jr., *The Urban Wilderness* (1972); Mark I. Gelfand, *A Nation of Cities* (1975); and Kenneth T. Jackson, *Crabgrass Frontier* (1985); among others.

American urban history has never been a static field, and since the 1980s some significant shifts of focus have taken place. The scholarly output of the 1960s and 1970s was heavily weighted toward the nineteenth century, with some attention to the progressive era, 1900 to 1920. This scholarship offered a heavy dose of urban political history, with many books on political bosses and urban reformers, with a secondary area of interest in the history of urban infrastructure and services such as transit, public health, social welfare, policing, schooling, and housing. This work was also strongly slanted toward cities and urban development in the Northeast and Midwest. The urban history written since about 1980 has shifted dramatically to twentieth-century topics and to the unexplored urban dimensions of the South and West. Modern urban historians especially placed their sights on the post–World War II sunbelt cities. Carl Abbott's *New Urban America* (1981) and David R. Goldfield's *Cotton Fields and Skyscrapers* (1982) led the historical charge into the sunbelt regions.

In addition, the subject matter for urban historians has moved away from city politics and services to such topics as race and ethnicity, sports and leisure, culture and consumerism, technology and planning, gender and class structure. Outstanding works from these genres of urban history include Perry R. Duis, *The Saloon* (1983); John Bodnar, *The Transplanted* (1985); Kathy Peiss, *Cheap Amusements* (1986); Timothy J. Gilfoyle, *City of Eros* (1992); Roy Rosenzweig, *Eight Hours for What We Will* (1983); Steven A. Riess, *City Games* (1989); Stuart M. Blumin, *The Emergence of the Middle Class* (1989); James R. Grossman, *Land of Hope* (1989); and Harold L. Platt, *The Electric City* (1991). In African-American urban history, a new interpretive thrust has placed the agency of black people at the center of the story. Building on the insights of E.P. Thompson and Herbert G. Gutman, scholars studying urban workers and immigrants have found that the powerless did indeed have some control over their own lives. Pursuing a regional approach more common in Canada, Australia, and Latin America, William Cronon's *Nature's Metropolis* (1991) demonstrated the workings of an economic "ecosystem" that linked Chicago with a vast rural hinterland. A newer urban political history has also appeared, reflected in Philip J. Ethington's important book, *The Public City* (1994), which deals with the political construction of urban life in late-nineteenth-century San Francisco.

This newer urban history in the United States reveals a startling degree of diversity and creativity. Reflecting this new scholarly energy, an Urban History Association (UHA) was established in 1988. Along with a revived *Urban History Newsletter* (since 1989), the UHA now provides a central forum for debate and discussion for a sprawling field that has resisted the imposition of rigid methodological or theoretical boundaries.

In Great Britain, urban history is also a post–World War II development. In the early 1960s, an older tradition of local history seemingly merged with social and economic history (usually a separate department in British universities) to produce a British urban history. The merger was first evident at the University of Leicester, where in 1962 H.J. Dyos presided over an ad hoc meeting of scholars with urban interests. Subsequently, Dyos provided the organizational energy for the formation of an Urban History Group within the Economic History Society and edited a British *Urban History Newsletter* (1963–1974); the *Newsletter* evolved into a more elaborate *Urban History Yearbook* (1974–1991) and then a journal, *Urban*

History (since 1992). Dyos's edited collection, *The Study of Urban History* (1968), heavily methodological, served as a springboard for urban history scholars as the field was finding definition. Dyos almost single-handedly built urban history in Britain, or at least helped urban-oriented scholars develop a consciousness about their work as urban history. He convened conferences, edited a book series, established a research agenda for the field, and published some important works of his own: *Victorian Suburb* (1961); *British Transport* (1969), with D.H. Aldcroft; *The Victorian City* (1973), with Michael Wolff; and *Exploring the Urban Past* (1982).

Following the Dyos agenda, British urban history tended to focus on the process of urbanization, on linking the social structure and the physical structure, and on the interconnections between urban population, technology, values, and the environment. This research strategy found expression in a number of outstanding works in British urban history by Asa Briggs, Anthony Sutcliffe, Gareth Stedman Jones, George Rudé, Martin Daunton, Derek Fraser, Anthony S. Wohl, Geoffrey Crossick, Penelope Corfield, John Patten, Richard Rodger, and Robert J. Morris. Most of this work focuses on the physical growth of the Victorian city, on slums and suburbs, and on nineteenth-century urbanization. Little has been done on the twentieth-century British city, and the recent cultural turn reflected in U.S. urban history has yet to be imitated in Britain. Planning historians comprise a thriving sector of British urban history, and the Planning History Association and its journal, *Planning Perspectives* (published since 1986), edited by Gordon Cherry and Anthony Sutcliffe, have become an integral component of the urban history apparatus in Great Britain. Dyos died in 1978, but his legacy can be found in a final set of conference proceedings, *The Pursuit of Urban History* (1983), edited by Derek Fraser and Anthony Sutcliffe.

Urban history in Australia represents an amalgam of American and British patterns. Traditionally, Australian historians were entranced by the "Australian legend," the powerful rural mythology surrounding the role of the "bush" or outback in the nation's history. Despite the fact that Australia is one of the most urbanized of nations, with over 90 percent of the population living in eight capital cities and their suburbs, urban history did not emerge as a self-conscious field until the mid-1960s. An early push beyond traditional local history came with the work of the economic historian Noel G. Butlin, whose *Investment in Australian Economic Development, 1861–1901* (1964) first demonstrated the economic importance of urbanization in late-nineteenth-century Australia.

As in the United States and the United Kingdom, much of the early work in Australian urban history has taken the form of case studies of patterns of urbanization, urban social structure, urban policymaking, urban economic development, immigration and housing, the growth of suburbs, and the relationship of city and region. These studies have been heavily influenced by the wave of social history that had earlier begun to reshape American and British urban history. This work focuses primarily on the nineteenth century, but a few important studies have moved into the twentieth century. Significant Australian urban histories include: Ronald Lawson, *Brisbane in the 1890s* (1973); John Hirst, *Adelaide and the Country* (1973); Graeme Davison, *The Rise and Fall of Marvellous Melbourne* (1978); Weston Bate, *Lucky City* (1978) and *Life After Gold* (1993); Peter Spearitt, *Sydney since the Twenties* (1978); C.T. Stannage, *The People of Perth* (1979); Shirley Fitzgerald, *Rising Damp: Sydney, 1870–90* (1987); Alan Mayne, *Representing the Slum* (1990); and John Lack, *A History of Footscray* (1991). Few Australian urban historians have moved beyond the case study approach, although Sean Glynn's brief monograph, *Urbanization in Australian History, 1788–1900* (1975), suggested the possibilities of synthesis. David Hamer in *New Towns in the New World* (1990) and Lionel Frost in *The New Urban Frontier* (1991) place Australian urbanization in a larger comparative framework. The work of some social scientists, especially Max Neutze, I.H. Burnley, Patrick Troy, Frank Stilwell, and Leonie Sandercock, provides additional perspectives on Australian urbanization and urban life. A special issue of the *Journal of Urban History* on "Cities Down Under" (November 1995) provides a good introduction to current methods and interpretations in Australian urban history.

In Canada, where urban history emerged in the early 1970s, American and British scholarship also had an important influence on methodology and interpretation. Urban history as a "city-building" process (promoted by Dyos, Lampard, and Warner) was pursued by some Canadian scholars, while others adopted the social scientific techniques of the American quantifiers, and still others used the insights of the Chicago school of sociology in researching urban communities and social groups. But Canada also had a home-grown interpretive framework built upon the concept of "metropolitanism." The economic historian J.M.S.

Careless first advanced this thesis in 1954, later elaborated in his book *Frontier and Metropolis* (1989), which conceptualized a hierarchical system of cities of differing size and importance, and posited the mutual interdependence of cities and their regional hinterlands. These varied approaches assured that Canadian urban history would be marked by the same scholarly diversity that prevailed in the United States, United Kingdom, and Australia.

The first signs of institutionalization of Canadian urban history came in 1971, when a small group of historians with urban interests formed a standing committee of the Canadian Historical Association and began sponsoring meetings. Within a year, these organizational efforts blossomed in the creation of the *Urban History Review* (since 1972), which began to provide a central forum for work in Canadian urban history. The chief promoters of the field in Canada were Alan Artibise and Gilbert Stelter, an indefatigable team of advocates and organizers. Together, Artibise and Stelter organized urban history conferences and published a stream of edited volumes that gathered the best of Canada's fledgling urban history: *The Canadian City* (1977, new edition 1984); *The Usable Urban Past* (1979); *Town and City* (1981); *Shaping the Urban Landscape* (1982); *Power and Place* (1986); *Cities and Urbanization* (1990); and *Canada's Urban Past* (1981), a bibliography that listed more than seven thousand entries on Canadian urban history. As elsewhere, much of the published scholarship uses the case study approach and deals with nineteenth-century Canadian cities. Major works in the field include Peter Goheen, *Victorian Toronto* (1970); Michael B. Katz, *The People of Hamilton, Canada West* (1975); Alan Artibise, *Winnipeg: A Social History of Urban Growth* (1975); John C. Weaver, *Shaping the Canadian City* (1977); Paul-André Linteau, *Maisonneuve* (1981); Norbert MacDonald, *Distant Neighbors* (1987); and Richard Harris, *Unplanned Suburbs* (1996). As in the other English-speaking nations, urban history in Canada has developed no single defining methodology, although the topics studied and the research models utilized are generally those common elsewhere.

Urban history in Europe has several different origins and the published research has taken varied forms. Every European nation has a long tradition of local or community history, but an analytical urban history using the city as a conceptual framework is a very recent development. The Belgian historian Henri Pirenne, in *Medieval Cities* (1925), gave a scholarly impetus to the study of European towns and cities. Lewis Mumford's *Culture of Cities* (1938) and *The City in History* (1961) also influenced thinking about the historical role of European cities. More recently, European urban history has been synthesized in excellent fashion: Paul M. Hohenberg and Lynn H. Lees, *The Making of Urban Europe, 1000–1994* (1995); Josef W. Konvitz, *The Urban Millenium: The City-building Process from the Early Middle Ages to the Present* (1985); Jan de Vries, *European Urbanization, 1500–1800* (1984); and Christopher R. Friedrichs, *The Early Modern City, 1450–1750* (1995). Generally, British and North American research models supplied much of the impetus for an emerging but still weakly developed European urban history. In France, the historiographical traditions of the Annales school promoted consideration of town and city life as a powerful moving force in history. In his most famous works—*The Mediterranean* (1949), *The Identity of France* (1986), and *Civilization and Capitalism* (1979)—for instance, Fernand Braudel incorporated lengthy sections on urban life and functions. But while social history found new dimensions in France, urban history has not developed as a conceptual category among French historians. Actually, British and American scholars have written more explicit French urban histories: Norma Evenson on Parisian architectural history, Anthony Sutcliffe and David H. Pinkney on planning in Paris, Charles Tilly and George Rudé on crowds and revolutionaries, Richard Cobb on Paris and its hinterland, John Merriman on nineteenth-century French cities, Lenard R. Berlanstein and Ann-Louise Shapiro on Parisian workers and the poor, Josef W. Konvitz on French seaports, William H. Sewell on Marseille. The evolution of French urban history is discussed in Daniel Roche's article, "Urban History in France," in the *Urban History Yearbook* (1980).

The same problem of definition appeared in Italy, where a form of "microhistory" has emerged, a localized social history best exemplified in the work of Carlo Ginzburg. "Storia urbana" is a very recent development in Italy, although two journals on the subject date from the mid-1970s: *Storia della Città* (since 1976) and *Storia Urbana* (since 1977). American scholars who have written productively on Italian cities include Richard A. Goldthwaite, David Herlihy, Gene A. Brucker, Eric Cochrane, Samuel K. Cohn, Frederic C. Lane, Richard C. Trexler, and Robert C. Davis. Some Italian scholars have written on American urban history, notably Giorgio Ciucci, et al., *The American City* (1973, trans. 1979).

In Germany, local or town history traditionally has been enormously popular; even small towns have their own local history museum, while those of larger cities such as Hamburg and Munich are munificent. Partially influenced by the American "new" urban history, German historians have moved toward a more systematic social history in recent decades, especially toward the "history of everyday life," or *alltagsgeschichte,* which to some extent has focused on town and city life. Nevertheless, a clearly defined subfield of German urban history has been slow to develop. Some organizational efforts did emerge in the 1970s with the creation of an Institute for Comparative Urban History Research at the University of Munster, and with the organization of a Study Group for Urban History Research, which holds annual conferences and publishes an urban history journal, *Die alte Stadt* (since 1978). Historical geographers in Germany have also provided new interdisciplinary perspectives, as suggested in the essays in Dietrich Denecke's and Gareth Shaw's edited volume, *Urban Historical Geography* (1988). Yet, as in other European nations, urban history remains an ambiguous conceptual framework for most historians. A good historiographical summary of German urban history can be found in the *Urban History Yearbook* (1981).

In Sweden, a long tradition of local and community history reflected a society where only 10 percent of the population was urbanized as late as 1900 and where the industrial revolution occurred much later than in other parts of Europe. An Institute for Urban History was founded in 1919, monographic literature on towns and cities began appearing in the 1920s, and Stockholm University insituted a chair in urban history in 1950. However, a more conceptualized, analytical urban history began only in the 1960s. Using research models derived from North American scholars, some Swedish historians pursued a newer form of social history focused on questions of demographic change, industrialization, migration, class structure, social policy, city planning, and the built environment. Few unifying patterns are apparent in Swedish urban history, but *Growth and Transformation of the Modern City* (1979), edited by Ingrid Hammarstrom and Thomas Hall suggests the diversity of approaches. A series of atlases of historic Scandinavian cities has been supported by the Institute for Urban History in Stockholm and the Danish Committee for Urban History. Hammarstrom's "Urban History in Scandinavia," *Urban History Yearbook* (1978), provides a good introduction to urban history in Sweden and neighboring Denmark, Norway, and Finland.

The diversity and the ambiguity of urban history in France, Italy, Germany, and Sweden seems characteristic elsewhere, as well. In the former

Eastern Bloc nations, Marxist approaches typified urban scholarship, especially on such economic subjects as the decline of feudalism, the rise of capitalism, the industrial revolution, and urban class structure. Western scholars writing on Russian cities include Michael F. Hamm, Gilbert Rozman, James S. Bater, Thomas Fedor, J. Michael Hittle, Robert E. Johnson, Joseph Bradley, Daniel Brower, and Diane Koenker. Historiographical articles on Russian urban history in the *Journal of Urban History* by Michael F. Hamm (November 1977) and Lawrence N. Langer (February 1979) provide good introductions to the subject. The early development of urban history in Poland is discussed in Edward D. Wynot's article, "Urban History in Poland," *Journal of Urban History* (November 1979). On southeast Europe, begin with Nikolai Todorov, *The Balkan City* (1983). As elsewhere, analytical urban history in Europe is mostly a late-twentieth-century development, usually building on strong local history traditions but heavily influenced in recent years by new social history models in Britain and the United States.

Urban history has developed a strong tradition among Latin Americanists, both in Latin American countries and in the United States. In the precolonial era, Central and South American Indians developed advanced urban civilizations, especially in Mexico and Peru. Jorge E. Hardoy's *Pre-Columbian Cities* (1964, trans. 1973) provides an exhaustive exploration of this early urban history. In the colonial era, building on their city-oriented Iberian and Mediterranean traditions, the Spaniards and the Portuguese built new metropolitan-centered colonies. A colonial urban system developed in which cities, often built on the remains of Indian cities, came to dominate the economic life of a vast hinterland (similar in some ways to the Australian and Canadian experience). A good survey of the historiography can be found in Susan Socolow and Lyman Johnson, "Urbanization in Colonial Latin America," *Journal of Urban History* (November 1981). In the nineteenth and twentieth centuries, the tendency toward urban concentration intensified dramatically, and the impact of the metropolitan-hinterland complex spread over greater distances. Significant studies of modern Latin American urbanization have been written by Richard M. Morse, James R. Scobie, Warren Dean, Walter D. Harris, Mary C. Karasch, June E. Hahner, Elizabeth Anne Kuznesof, John E. Kicza, Jeffrey D. Needell, and Mark D. Szuchman, among others. The major journals in Latin American history—*Hispanic American Historical Review, Latin American Research Review,* and *Journal of Latin American Studies*—have all devoted considerable attention to the urban dimension of Latin American history.

In India, despite the vast multitudes who have crowded the cities of the Indian subcontinent, urban history is remarkably undeveloped. Howard Spodek, whose article "Studying the History of Urbanization in India," *Journal of Urban History* (May 1980) provided an early survey of the historiography, noted only a handful of Western-style urban histories. Western scholars who have written important work on Indian urban history include Howard Spodek, Frank P. Conlon, Kenneth Gillion, Susan J. Lewandowski, Veena T. Oldenburg, Diana L. Eck, Robert Grant Irving, Christine Dobbin, Christopher Bayly, Morris D. Morris, and Anthony King. Among Indian scholars, the work of Ashish Bose, S.N. Mukherjee, K.N. Chaudhuri, and Narayani Gupta stands out. Some of this urban history is modeled on Western studies of the city and deals with such subjects as migration, urban elites, merchant communities, urban government, planning, religion, interethnic relations, and the impact of the caste system on urban life. These studies are mostly focused on single cities. Another historiographic tradition—the "network-and-center model"—builds on the conception of a larger national urban system, with cities of varying size serving as economic, political, and cultural nodes linked to surrounding hinterlands. Urban history in India is the subject of Narayani Gupta's historiographical article in the *Urban History Yearbook* (1981). The Urban History Association of India was established in 1978.

In the premodern era, Chinese cities were the largest in the world, yet the scholarly study of Chinese urban history is only in its earliest stages. In the postwar era, when urban history emerged as part of a systematic social history in the Western world, Chinese communist revolutionaries shut off independent academic inquiry. Orthodox political ideology in China, wrote David D. Buck, demanded "emphasis on the role of the peasantry as a creative force in Chinese history." Consequently, Chinese historians focused on peasant uprisings and class struggles, but ignored the important economic, political, and cultural role of cities. After the Cultural Revolution ended in 1976, a new educational emphasis was placed on local history, essentially to celebrate the achievements of communist rule. Only in the last decade has a social scientific urban history, borrowed from Western research models, made a modest beginning. However, some Western scholars have contributed to a growing bibliography on urban China.

For the ancient period, one must begin with Paul Wheatley's magisterial *Pivot of the Four Quarters* (1971). More recent works on Chinese cities and urbanization have been written by G. William Skinner, Mark Elvin, Emily Honig, William T. Rowe, Christopher Howe, David D. Buck, Susan Mann, R.J.R. Kirkby, David Strand, Elizabeth J. Perry, Frederic E. Wakeman, and Linda C. Johnson. David D. Buck's historiographical article on Chinese urban history in the *Urban History Yearbook* (1987) provides an excellent introduction to the subject. In 1995, a Chinese urban history newsletter, *Wall and Market,* published in the United States, made its first appearance.

Japan, too, had a tradition of ancient cities that evolved by the seventeenth century into a system of "castletowns" serving administrative, economic, and defensive functions. New port cities arose after the opening to the West in the 1850s, as did new industrial cities. A considerable urban history has been written in Japan since the 1960s, some urban biographies and other studies dealing with urban politics, demographic and social structure, planning and housing, and urban economics and transit. Takeo Yazaki, *Social Change and the City in Japan* (trans. 1968), offers a good overview. Paralleling developments among Western scholars, an urban study group was formed at St. Paul's University in Tokyo in 1971, followed by an academic journal, *Comparative Urban History Review* (published since 1982). Japanese scholars have also pursued planning history, as reported in Shunichi Watanabe's article, "Planning History in Japan," in *Urban History Yearbook* (1980). The first important Western study of Japanese urban life was Ronald P. Dore, *City Life in Japan* (1958), a sociological study of a Tokyo neighborhood. More recent studies in English have been written by Gary D. Allison, David Kornhauser, John W. Hall, Kurt Steiner, Terry MacDougall, and Theodore Bestor. Jeffrey E. Hanes has written of the Japanese "megalopolis" in the *Journal of Urban History* (February, 1993). Gilbert Rozman has written an excellent comparative urban study of Japan and China: *Urban Networks in Ch'ing China and Tokugawa Japan* (1974).

As this historiographical survey has demonstrated, urban history has its advocates throughout the modern world. Most countries had an earlier tradition of local history, but only in the postwar epoch did an analytical and systematic social science approach to city and community begin to supplant the often more amateurish local history tradition. In retrospect, the timing of modern urban history's emergence seems predictable: it begins first in the United States and Great Britain,

shaped by the new wave of social history that affected the entire profession. Subsequently, Canadian and Australian historians modeled their urban histories on those newly current in the United States and the United Kingdom. Even in Europe, where separate "new" schools of history, such as the French Annales, had emerged, American and British social science history had an important impact, although an explicit urban history still remains elusive in France, Italy, and Germany. In the non-Western world—in Latin America, India, China, and Japan—a modern urban history evolved more slowly and somewhat later, in the 1970s and 1980s, but Western research models were significant in shaping scholarly agendas. Similar patterns emerged in the historiography of urbanization in Israel and the Middle East, the Caribbean, and South Africa. A growing scholarship in comparative urban history also has become discernible since the 1970s, typified by Brian J.L. Berry's *Comparative Urbanization* (rev. ed. 1981) or Donald J. Olsen's *The City As a Work of Art* (1986). Marked by scholarly energy and diversity, urban history at the end of the twentieth century appears to be a field with a promising future. Urban historians can build not only on several decades of creative scholarship, but on the intrinsic interest that most people have in community life.

Raymond A. Mohl

See also LOCAL HISTORY; RURAL HISTORY; SOCIAL HISTORY.

References

Buenker, John D., et al., eds. *Urban History: A Guide to Information Sources.* Detroit: Gale Research Company, 1981.

Dyos, H.J., ed. *The Study of Urban History.* London: Edward Arnold, 1968.

Engeli, Christian, and Horst Matzerath, eds. *Modern Urban History in Europe, USA and Japan.* Oxford: Berg, 1989.

Fraser, Derek, and Anthony Sutcliffe, eds. *The Pursuit of Urban History.* London: Edward Arnold, 1983.

Goldfield, David R., and Blaine A. Brownell. *Urban America: A History.* Second ed. Boston: Houghton Mifflin, 1990.

Hohenberg, Paul M., and Lynn Hollen Lees. *The Making of Urban Europe, 1000–1994.* Cambridge, MA: Harvard University Press, 1995.

Stave, Bruce M. *The Making of Urban History: Historiography through Oral History.* Beverly Hills, CA: Sage Publications, Inc., 1977.

U

Stelter, Gilbert A., and Alan F.J. Artibise, eds. *The Canadian City: Essays in Urban and Social History.* Revised ed. Ottawa: Carleton University Press, 1984.

Sutcliffe, Anthony, ed. *Metropolis, 1890–1940.* London: Mansell, 1984.

Thernstrom, Stephan, and Richard Sennett, eds. *Nineteenth-Century Cities: Essays in the New Urban History.* New Haven, CT: Yale University Press, 1969.

Warner, Sam Bass Jr. *The Urban Wilderness: A History of the American City.* New York: Harper and Row, 1972.

V

Valentijn, François (1666–1727)

Dutch encyclopedist of Indonesia. Valentijn studied philosophy and theology at Utrecht and Leiden and served the Dutch East Indies Company as minister of religion in Java and the Moluccas from 1685 to 1695 and 1706 to 1713. On his return to the Netherlands, he assembled *Oud en Nieuw Oost-Indien* [The Old and New East Indies], a five-volume compendium on Asia compiled from a wide variety of sources, including personal observation, the papers of the scientist Rumphius (ca. 1628–1702), and official records such as the minutes of church council meetings. The Indonesian archipelago received most attention, but the collection covered virtually all coastal states and regions from the Cape of Good Hope to Japan. A large number of maps and plates is included. The structure of the work is haphazard and uneven, and Valentijn shows relatively little knowledge of or interest in indigenous Asian societies. Nonetheless, the detail he provides on trade, geography, and the living conditions of Europeans in the Indies makes his work a valuable source for the seventeenth and early eighteenth centuries in Indonesia.

Robert Cribb

Texts

Oud en Nieuw Oost-Indien. 5 vols. in 8 parts. Dordrecht & Amsterdam: Van Braam and Onder de Linden, 1724–1726.

References

Hall, D.G.E., ed. *Historians of South East Asia.* London: Oxford University Press, 1961.

Valla, Lorenzo (1407–1457)

Italian humanist and historian. Valla is most famous for his critical debunking of the Donation of Constantine, written while in the service of Alfonso I, king of Naples (Alfonso V of Aragon). Born in Rome, Valla became a pupil of Vittorino da Feltre. He held the chair of rhetoric at Pavia from 1431–1433, where he engaged in a polemic with the legal faculty. After his time in Naples, Valla returned to Rome as secretary to Pope Nicholas V in 1450. His work is mainly philological and philosophical, but he is important to historiography as one of the first scholars to approach a modern sense of anachronism. This is evident from his proof, written in 1440, that the Donation was a forgery because it contained a number of words not in use during the fourth century A.D. when it was allegedly written.

Thomas F. Mayer

Texts

Valla, Lorenzo. *The Profession of the Religious and the Principal Arguments from the Falsely-Believed and Forged Donation of Constantine.* Ed. and trans. O.Z. Pugliese. Toronto: Centre for Reformation and Renaissance Studies, 1985.

References

Kelley, Donald. *Foundations of Modern Historical Scholarship: Language, Law, and History in the French Renaissance.* New York: Columbia University Press, 1970, 19–50.

Vansina, Jan (b. 1929)

Historian and anthropologist of central Africa. Born in Antwerp, Belgium, Vansina received a Ph.D. from the University of Leuven in 1957 and was appointed to the University of Wisconsin at Madison in 1960 where he eventually became Vilas research professor of history in 1976. In 1981, he became vice president of the UNESCO committee for writing a general history of Africa. Beginning in the 1950s, he has continued to conduct extensive fieldwork in Zaire, Rwanda, Burundi, Congo, and Libya. While Vansina has become one of the leading advocates of the use of oral tradition as evidence for reconstructing the precolonial past, he has also been diligent in recognizing the limitations and abuses of these sources. In fact, Vansina's influence in this area has spread well beyond African studies to the point where no general discussion of oral culture would be complete without mentioning his work. Employing oral sources, Vansina has produced detailed histories of the Tio and Kuba societies of central Africa. In additional, he has contributed significantly to the complex, multidisciplinary debate over the origins and expansion of Bantu languages throughout central, eastern, and southern Africa.

Timothy J. Stapleton

Texts

Art and History in Africa. London: Longman, 1983.
Children of Woot: A History of the Kuba People. Madison: University of Wisconsin Press, 1978.
Kingdoms of the Savana. Madison: University of Wisconsin Press, 1966.
"New Linguistic Evidence and the 'Bantu Expansion.'" *Journal of African History* 36 (1995): 173–195.
Oral Tradition. London: Routledge and Kegan Paul, 1965.
Oral Tradition As History. London: James Currey, 1985.
Paths in the Rainforest. Madison: University of Wisconsin Press, 1990.
The Tio Kingdom of Middle Congo. Oxford: Oxford University Press, 1973.
"Western Bantu Expansion." *Journal of African History* 25 (1984): 131–149.

References

Henige, David. *Oral Historiography.* London: Longman, 1982.

Varchi, Benedetto (1503–1565)

Florentine historian and poet. Varchi was a student of the neo-Platonist Francisco Diacceto. Despite long-standing Medici patronage toward the Florentine neo-Platonists, Varchi himself was an opponent of the family and a supporter of the last Florentine republic. Thereafter he moved in the circle of Pietro Bembo and was one of the founders of the Academy of the Infiammati. In 1542 he reconciled with Duke Cosimo I and returned to Florence, where he became one of the arbiters of Medici cultural policy. Late in life he consummated a drift toward evangelical religion by becoming a priest. Varchi was best known as a commentator on Dante and as a proponent of Italian over Latin. His *Storia fiorentina* [Florentine History] is one of the most typical works of sixteenth-century Florentine historiography. Unlike histories by most of his contemporaries, Varchi's lacks an overriding political theme and instead has a noncausal, concrete character.

Thomas F. Mayer

Texts

Varchi, Benedetto. *Storia fiorentina,* in his *Opere.* Trieste: Lloyd Adriatico, 1858.

References

Montevecchi, Alessandro. *Storici di Firenze: Studi su Nardi, Nerli e Varchi* [Historians of Florence: Studies on Nardi, Nerli and Varchi]. Bologna: Patron, 1989.
Pirotti, Umberto. *Benedetto Varchi e la cultura del suo tempo* [Benedetto Varchi and the Culture of His Time]. Florence: Leo S. Olschki, 1971.

Varga, Lucie (1904–1941)

Austrian émigré historian. Varga studied history and art history at the University of Vienna, graduating in 1931. After teaching for a few years, she married the writer Franz Borkenau and emigrated with him to France, but the marriage ended in 1935. Between 1934 and 1937 she collaborated with the distinguished French historian Lucien Febvre and may have been his mistress. Having lost her job with a news agency following the French military defeat in 1940, she died of diabetic shock the next year, in impoverished circumstances. In her dissertation, written under the supervision of Alfons Dopsch, Varga traced the metaphor of the "Dark Ages" up to the Enlightenment. Febvre engaged her as a research assistant in part because of his respect for Dopsch, but soon entrusted her with not only writing book summaries for his research, but also with reviews and independent projects. Between 1934 and 1939 she published several studies in *Annales, Revue de Synthèse,* and *Revue d'histoire des religions.* These writings undertook two major tasks on two very different eras, medieval and modern: the first was a historical and anthropological analysis of mentalities in Germany and the Alps during the early Nazi period; the second consisted of a close reading and analysis of the historical sources concerning the medieval heresy of Catharism.

James P. Niessen

Texts

Les autorités invisibles [Invisible Authorities]. Ed. Peter Schöttler. Paris: Les Editions du Cerf, 1991.

Das Schlagwort vom "Finsteren Mittelalter" [The Phrase "Dark Ages"]. Aalen: Scientia Verlag, 1978.

References

Davis, Natalie Zemon. "Women and the World of the Annales." *History Workshop* 33 (1992): 121–137.

Schöttler, Peter. Introduction to *Les autorités invisibles.*

———. "Lucie Varga: A Central European Refugee in the Circle of the French 'Annales,' 1934–1941." *History Workshop* 33 (1992): 100–120.

Varnhagen, Francisco Adolfo de (1816–1878)

Brazilian historian and diplomat. Varnhagen studied in Portugal and Brazil, fought in the Portuguese civil wars in the 1820s, and served in various diplomatic posts. He was Brazil's first prominent historian in the national period and is known principally for two works: the two-volume *História geral do Brasil* [General History of Brazil] (1854–1857), and the *História da independência do Brasil* [History of Brasilian Independence], which was published posthumously in 1917. The first of these was the only nineteenth-century attempt to deal with the entire scope of Brazilian history, from the discovery to the declaration of independence. Varnhagen's distinguishing characteristic was his use of new source materials, especially diplomatic correspondence, held in European archives. João Capistrano de Abreu, the great turn-of-the century Brazilian historian, faulted Varnhagen for his pedestrian style, his uncongenial temperament, and his failure to provide an adequate periodization of Brazilian history. Nevertheless, he viewed Varnhagen as both "the teacher and the guide" of future Brazilian historians because he had examined areas of the past previously ignored, such as the relations between the colonists and indigenous population, the reasons for exploring the backlands, and the importance of geo-

graphic determinism. More recently, however, Stanley Stein has concluded that Varnhagen was too uncritical of the Brazilian monarchy and "neglected social and economic history."

George L. Vásquez

Texts

História da independência do Brasil. Rio de Janeiro: Impresa Nacional, 1917.

História das Lutas com os Holandeses no Brasil [History of the Struggles against the Dutch in Brazil]. Vienna: C. Finsterbeck, 1871.

História geral do Brasil, antes da sua separação e independência de Portugal. Ninth ed. Ed. João Capistrano de Abreu and Rodolfo Garcia. 5 vols. in 3 parts. Sao Paulo: Edições Melhoramentos, 1978.

References

Capistrano de Abreu, João. "A Critique of Francisco Adolfo de Varnhagen." In *Perspectives on Brazilian History,* ed. E. Bradford Burns. New York: Columbia University Press, 1967, 143–155.

Schwartz, S.B. "Francisco Adolfo de Varnhagen: Diplomat, Patriot, Historian." *Hispanic American Historical Review* 47 (1967): 185–202.

Varsik, Branislav (1904–1994)

Slovak archivist and historian. Varsik studied at Comenius University in Bratislava, where he was active in the Union of Slovak Students (1925–1928) and also studied in Prague, Vienna, and Paris. He worked in the Regional Archives in Bratislava (1929–1939) and from 1933 also lectured on early modern Slovak history at Comenius University in Bratislava He became an adjunct (1938) and then full professor (1940) of history at the university. At the same time he served as the inspector of archives and libraries (1939–1951) and as the editor in chief of *Historica Slovaca* (1941–1949). After World War II he worked on identifying the cultural and archival monuments that Hungary should return to Slovakia. He served as head of the department of general history and archives of Comenius University and edited the journal *Historica* from 1958 until his retirement in 1974. He initially investigated Czech and Slovak contacts during the Hussite and Reformation eras but later turned to investigate the ethnogenesis of the Slovaks, Hungarian–Slovak relations, the history of the medieval settlement of Slovakia, and the origin of the oldest place-names in Slovakia. His works sought to demonstrate that the Slovaks had an independent identity and history that began before the entry of the Magyars into the middle Danubian basin.

David P. Daniel

Texts

Die Bedeutung der Ansiedlungsforschung der Ostslowakei für die Frage der Entstehung und Entwicklung der slowakischen Nationalität [The Significance of the Research of the Settlement of Eastern Slovakia for the Question of the Origin and Development of the Slovak Nationality]. Historica, Zborník Filozofickej Fakulty Univerzity Komenského 12–13 (1961–1962): 191–214.

Husiti and reformácia na Slovensku do Žilinskej synody [Hussites and the Reformation in Slovakia until the Synod of Žilina]. Zborník Filozofickej Faculty Univerzity Komenského VIII (1932).

Husitské revolučné hnutie a slovensko [The Hussite Revolutionary Movement and Slovakia]. Bratislava: Slovak Academy of Sciences, 1965.

Národnostný problém trnavskej univerzity [The National Problem of Trnava University]. Bratislava: Nakladem Učene společnosť Safaríkova, 1938.

Osídlenie Košickej kotliny I–III [Settlement of the Košice Basin]. Bratislava: Slovak Academy of Sciences, 1964–1977.

Otázky vzniku a vývinu slovenského zemianstva [Questions about the Origin and Development of the Slovak Yeomanry]. Bratislava: Veda, 1988.

Slováci na praskej univerzite do konca stredoveku [Slovaks at the University of Prague until the End of the Middle Ages]. Zborník Filozofickej Fakulty Univerzity Komenského IV, 1926.

Z osídlenia západného a stredného Slovenska [From the Settlement of Western and Central Slovakia]. Bratislava: Veda, 1984.

References

Mannová Elena, and David Paul Daniel, eds. *A Guide to Historiography in Slovakia:* Studia Historica Slovaca XX. Bratislava: Slovak Academy of Sciences, 1995.

Varsik, Branislav. *O čom mlčia archivy* [About That on Which the Archives Are Silent]. Bratislava: Slovenský Spisovateľ, 1987.

Vasari, Giorgio (1511–1574)

Artist and art historian. Born in Arezzo, Vasari went to nearby Florence in 1524 to study painting. His subsequent career combined artistic commissions and service to the Medici, history painting, and history writing. The historian Paolo Giovio advised him in both kinds of historical representation. Vasari's reputation rests primarily on his literary work, *Le vite de più eccellenti pittori scultori et architettori* [The Lives of the Most Eminent Painters, Sculptors, and Architects] (1550; greatly expanded in 1568). Inspired by Pliny, Plutarch, and Boccaccio, as well as by hagiography, rhetoric, and humanist notions of exemplarity, Vasari composed individual artists' biographies. What distinguishes his work—the first systematic history of art—is his arranging these lives into three distinct periods, each introduced by a preface articulating his method and biases. Vasari placed art along a line of progress: rising from a postantique low to perfection achieved by Michelangelo. His biographical approach, emphasizing individual genius, remains fundamental to art history practice.

Sheila ffolliott

Texts

Lives of the Most Eminent Painters, Sculptors and Architects by Giorgio Vasari. Ed. and trans. Gaston de Vere. 10 vols. London: Macmillan, 1912–1914.

References

Boase, T.S.R. *Giorgio Vasari: The Man and the Book*. Princeton, NJ: Princeton University Press, 1979.

Rubin, Patricia Lee. *Giorgio Vasari: Art and History*. New Haven, CT, and London: Yale University Press, 1995.

Velasco, Juan de (1727–1792)

Ecuadoran historian. Velasco, Ecuador's first historian, was born in Riobamba, Ecuador, and joined the Society of Jesus at the age of seventeen. Besides teaching, he visited all of the territories of the Real Audiencia of Quito as a missionary. In 1767, the Spanish monarchy banished the Jesuits from its empire, and Velasco went into exile in Italy. He died in Faenza. At the request of the Spanish government, Velasco wrote his *Historia del Reino de Quito* [History of the Kingdom of Quito], which is composed of three volumes dealing, respectively, with natural history, ancient history, and modern history. The first volume is an exposition of the vegetable and animal kingdoms, including the human element; the second traces Ecuador's history from the first populations to the Spanish conquest and subsequent civil wars in 1550; and the third, on modern history, recounts events from 1551 to 1557 with a historical, geographic, political, and ecclesiastical description of the provinces. Velasco's unpublished *Historia Moderna y Cronica de la Compañia de Jesus* [Modern History and Chronicle of the Company of Jesus] relates the hardships experienced by the exiled Jesuits. He also wrote an unpublished collection of poetry, *Colección de poesías varias, hecha por un ocioso en la ciudad de Faenza* [Collection of Various Poems Composed by a Wanderer in the City of Faenza], and a grammar, *Vocabulario de la lengua peruano-quitense* [A Vocabulary of the Peruvian-Quito Language].

Carlos Pérez

Texts

Historia del reino de Quito en la America Meridional [History of the South American Kingdom of Quito]. Quito: Editorial Casa de la Cultura Ecuatoriana, 1977.

References

Astudillo Espinosa, Celin. *Juan de Velasco: historiador, biologo y naturalista: Biografia* [Juan de Velasco: Historian, Biologist, and Naturalist: A Biography]. Quito: Editorial Casa de la Cultura Ecuatoriana, 1978.

Larrea, Carlos Manuel. *Tres historiadores: Velasco, Gonzalez Suarez, Jijon y Caamano* [Three Historians: Velasco, Gonzalez Suarez, Jijon y Caamano]. Quito: Casa de la Cultura Ecuatoriana "Benjamin Carrion," 1988.

Venturi, Franco (1914–1994)

Italian historian of the Enlightenment and of Russia. Professor of modern history at the University of Turin, Venturi was the foremost authority on the Enlightenment in Italy. In addition, his works on Russian history have established him as one of the most wide-ranging of modern historians. He was editor of the *Rivista Storica Italiana,* the foremost historical journal in Italy. Venturi began his study of the Enlightenment with Diderot and the *Encyclopédie,* and continued with a multivolume study of the eighteenth century's major thinkers, entitled *Settecento riformatore.* Venturi was concerned with the evolution and diffusion of Enlightenment thought throughout Italian and European society. Consequently, his work often focused on journalism and the ideal of cosmopolitanism as

developed by the eighteenth-century philosophes. His 1969 Trevelyan lectures at Cambridge have been translated into English as *Utopia and Reform in the Enlightenment* (1971) as have a collection of essays entitled *Italy and the Enlightenment* (1972). His work on Russia includes a study of the populist and socialist movements in the nineteenth century, and a collection of essays; both works have been translated into English. Venturi's study on historiography, *L'Italia fuori d'Italia,* an examination of how non-Italian scholars have dealt with the history of Italy, is the third volume in the *Storia d'Italia* (Turin: Einaudi, 1973) series.

Stanislao G. Pugliese

Texts

The End of the Old Regime in Europe, 1768–1776. Trans. R. Burr Litchfield. 2 vols. Princeton, NJ: Princeton University Press, 1989–1991.

Italy and the Enlightenment: Studies in a Cosmopolitan Century. Ed. Stuart J. Woolf; trans. Susan Corsi. New York: New York University Press, 1972.

Roots of Revolution: A History of the Populist and Socialist Movements in Nineteenth Century Russia. Trans. Francis Haskell. Chicago: University of Chicago Press, 1983.

Settecento riformatore [Eighteenth-Century Reformers]. 4 vols. Turin: Einaudi, 1969–1984.

Studies in Free Russia. Chicago: University of Chicago Press, 1982.

Utopia and Reform in the Enlightenment. Cambridge, Eng.: Cambridge University Press, 1971.

References

L'età dei lumi: Studi storici sul settecento Europeo in onore di Franco Venturi [The Age of Enlightenment: Historical Studies on Eighteenth-century Europe in Honor of Franco Venturi]. 2 vols. Naples: Jovene, 1985.

Vergil, Polydore (ca. 1470–1555)

Renaissance Italian churchman and historian. Vergil was born in Urbino, Italy. After study at Padua and Bologna, he took priest's orders and served as a secretary to the duke of Urbino. In 1502 Vergil went to England as subcollector of Peter's Pence through the influence of the Collector, his relation, Adriano Castelli, Bishop of Hereford. Vergil quickly accumulated ecclesiastical livings, and was naturalized in 1510. In 1515 he was imprisoned for his failure to secure a cardinal's hat for Thomas Wolsey, but was released soon after Wolsey's elevation to the Sacred College. Vergil remained in England during the Reformation, accepting the Act of Supremacy and other religious changes. Old and sick, he returned to Italy in 1553, dying in 1555 at his native Urbino. In addition to such popular works as his *Proverbiorum Libellus* [Book of Proverbs] (1498) and *De inventoribus rerum* [Of the Inventors of Things] (1499), Vergil's major works were historical: an edition of Gildas (1525) and the *Anglica Historia* [English History], first published at Basel in 1534. This is often regarded as the first full-length humanist history of England. Although heavily dependent on earlier work, Vergil not only used primary materials but also introduced the most advanced Italian historiographical methods. Still, his desire to praise the Tudor dynasty, and his hatred of Wolsey were also important elements in his treatment of events. No full translation of the work exists; different sections were edited by Henry Ellis in the nineteenth century (using a Tudor translation) and by Denys Hay in 1950.

Kenneth Bartlett

Texts

Anglica Historia, A.D. *1485–1537*. Trans. Denys Hay. Camden Society, Third series, 74 (1950).
Polydore Vergil's English History. Ed. H. Ellis. Camden Society, Original series, 36 (1846).
Three Books of Polydore Vergil's English History, Comprising the Reigns of Henry VI, Edward IV, and Richard III. Ed. H. Ellis. Camden Society, Original series, 29 (1844).

References

Hay, Denis. *Polydore Vergil, Renaissance Historian and Man of Letters*. Oxford: Oxford University Press, 1952.
Levy, F.J. *Tudor Historical Thought*. San Marino, CA: Huntington Library, 1967.

Vernadsky, George (1887–1973)

Russian historian of Ukrainian descent and representative of the "Eurasian school" of Russian history. The son of an eminent scientist, George Vernadsky studied in Moscow and St. Petersburg. An opponent of Bolshevism, he left Russia at the end of the Civil War. After a time in Prague, he accepted a teaching position at Yale University and developed its Slavic holdings. Because of his Ukrainian ancestry, Vernadsky was interested in the "Ukrainian question" both historically and in relation to contemporary affairs. He drew a clear contrast between Kievan Rus' and Muscovy, arguing that the Mongol invasion decisively affected the psychology of the Rus' and the subsequent development of Russia. He found Mongol roots for some Russian words, for the evolution of military forces and tactics, and for certain Muscovite social practices. He argued that the state of Muscovy and its autocratic czardom were successors to the Mongol Khan and the Golden Horde. The institutions, legal norms, and psychology of Muscovite Russia were their legacy. This remains a controversial thesis.

Elizabeth V. Haigh

Texts

Bohdan, Hetman of Ukraine. New Haven, CT: Yale University Press, 1941.
A History of Russia. 5 vols. New Haven, CT: Yale University Press, 1943–1967.
The Mongols and Russia. New Haven, CT: Yale University Press, 1953.

References

Ferguson, Alan D., ed. *Essays in Russian History*. Hamden, CT: Archon Books, 1964.

Veyne, Paul (b. 1930)

French historian of antiquity. Veyne was born in Provence and studied at the École Normale Supérieure in Paris and the French School at Rome, becoming professor at the University of Aix-en-Provence and, from 1976, at the Collège de France. Veyne has made his reputation with works addressing both particular themes from the ancient world and general theoretical questions. His *Comment on écrit l'histoire* (1971), later translated into English as *Writing History*, effectively denies the value of theories of history while advocating an approach "without frontiers," using methodologies from all the humanities. The influence of Michel Foucault on Veyne's thinking is acknowledged in *Foucault révolutionne l'histoire* [Foucault Revolutionizes History] (1978). Veyne's *Le pain et le cirque* [Bread and Circuses] (1976) investigates "euergetism," or elite benefaction, in the ancient world from the Greek city-states to the Roman Empire. The brief *Les Grecs ont-ils cru à leurs mythes?* [Did the Greeks Believe in Their Myths?] (1983) is especially interesting on Hellenistic and Second Sophistic Greek authors. *La société romaine* [Roman Society] (1991) is a collection of nine of Veyne's articles.

Richard Fowler

Texts

Bread and Circuses. Trans. B. Pearce; and abrid. by O. Murray. London: Allen Lane, 1990.

Did the Greeks Believe in Their Myths? Trans. P. Wissing. Chicago: Chicago University Press, 1988.

Writing History. Trans. M. Moore-Rinvolucri. Manchester: Manchester University Press, 1984.

Vianna, Francisco José de Oliveira (1883–1951)

Brazilian historian. An influential theorist of Brazilian conservativism, Vianna was primarily concerned with the foundations and the organization of the Brazilian nation—the fundamental problem confronting Brazilian intellectuals of the nineteenth century. During Vargas's period of dictatorship (1930–1945), he was an influential adviser. Beginning with his first published book, the two-volume *Populações Meridionais do Brasil,* Vianna's chief concern was to construct a reading of Brazilian history capable of sustaining a social and political reorganization of Brazil along modern lines, as a powerful corporate state that could minimize its inherited historical problems. These problems included the immensity of the country's space, and in Vianna's view the colonial conquest of territory had actually meant the creation of numerous empty spaces, scattered indiscriminately and occupied by isolated families with little relation to their neighbors and less to urban life. The secondary problems of social insolidarity and a strong sense of individuality were born of this isolation, as people developed attachments only to their immediate family groups, thereby making the definition of traditional social classes (and, by implication, class struggle) impossible. This in turn made difficulty the construction of a "typical" Brazilian rather than a citizen defined exclusively in terms of regional ethnic, cultural, and social characteristics. Vianna saw education and a strong, centralized state as the means toward an integrated society.

Nilo Odalia

Texts

Evolucão do povo brasileiro. Fourth ed. Rio de Janeiro: J. Olympio, 1956.

O occaso do Imperio. Third ed. Rio de Janeiro: J. Olympio, 1959.

Populacões meridionais do Brasil: Historia, organizacão, psicologia. Third ed. 2 vols. Belo Horizonte: Itatiaia, 1987.

References

Tavares, José Nilo. *Autoritarismo e dependencia: Oliveira Vianna e Alberto Torres* [Authoritarianism and Dependency: Oliveira Vianna and Alberto Torres]. Rio de Janeiro: Achiame, 1979.

Vicens Vives, Jaime (1910–1960)

Catalan historian and teacher who was responsible for the historical renewal in post–civil war Spain. Vicens held the chair of modern European history at the University of Barcelona, where he also taught economic history. He began his career questioning the traditional interpretation of the fifteenth century in his doctoral thesis, *Ferran II i la Ciutat de Barcelona, 1476–1516* [Ferdinand II and the City of Barcelona, 1479–1516] (1936–1937). After coming into contact with the French historian (and founder of the journal *Annales*) Lucien Febvre in 1950, Vicens became the champion of the *Annales* interpretation of history in Spain. He was also influenced by Fernand Braudel's analysis of space and time as well as Braudel's concept of mentalities. The last decade of Vicens's life witnessed a phenomenal output: he started two important journals; he oversaw a general history of Catalonia while contributing two volumes himself; together with Juan Nadal, he wrote the first synthesis of Spanish economic history; he authored a textbook on modern European history; and he directed the first social, economic, and cultural history of Spain and the Hispanic world. Vicens's disciples and collaborators included some of the best historians of contemporary Spain.

George L. Vásquez

Texts

Approaches to the History of Spain. Ed. and trans. Joan Connelly Ullman. Berkeley: University of California Press, 1967.

An Economic History of Spain. Trans. Frances M. López-Morillas. Princeton, NJ: Princeton University Press, 1969.

Ferran II i la Ciutat de Barcelona, 1476–1516. 3 vols. Barcelona: Tipográfia Emporium, 1936–1937.

References

Mercader Riba, Juan. "Jaime Vicens Vives: Su obra histórica [Jaime Vicens Vives: His Historical Works]." *Arbor* 66 (1967): 37–56.

Vico, Giambattista (1668–1744)

Italian philosopher, scholar, and historian. "Philosopher of history" is perhaps the least inaccurate brief description of Vico, although the phrase had not yet been coined in his day. Born in Naples, the son of a bookseller, and trained in rhetoric, of which he was professor at the University of Naples, and in Roman law (a chair of law was his great but unfulfilled ambition), Vico made a few substantive contributions to historical studies. These included a paper on ancient Roman feasts; the *Principum neapolitanorum coniurationis anni MDCCI historia* (1702), a narrative of an unsuccessful anti-Spanish conspiracy at Naples; and *De rebus gestis Antonii Caraphaei* (1716), a biography of a local aristocrat, Antonio Caraffa. But his major claim to fame—a fame denied him until the nineteenth century—was his *Principi di una scienza nuova* [Principles of a New Science], first published in 1725, and revised and enlarged over the next twenty years. The book was a study not only of history (including what the author called "history of ideas") but also of law, poetry, philosophy, and theology. Although he made a sharp distinction between two kinds of knowledge, knowledge of nature and knowledge of humanity, Vico viewed himself as the Galileo or the Newton of history, and so described his book as an attempt to provide the principles of a "new science." His great discovery was that of three ages of human history, which he called the age of gods, the age of heroes, and the age of men, distinguished by different kinds of law, language, and mentality. These ages recurred from time to time—Vico tried to reconcile a Christian view of providence with the cyclical view of history dominant in the ancient world. Although his book includes fascinating brief discussions of the Middle Ages and of ancient China, Japan, Mexico, and Ethiopia, Vico's theories were based primarily on his meditations on ancient Greek and Roman history. His most profound and original observations concerned the first age and its "poetic mode of thought," concrete and metaphorical like the thought of children. In a section of his book entitled "the discovery of the true Homer," Vico presented the *Iliad* and the *Odyssey* (like the Greek myths) as histories of ancient Greek customs, precious evidence of what would later be described as "primitive" thought.

Peter Burke

Texts

The New Science. Trans. Thomas G. Bergin and Max Fisch (from the third ed., 1744). Revised ed. Ithaca, NY: Cornell University Press, 1984.

On the Most Ancient Wisdom of the Italians: Unearthed from the Origins of the Latin Language: Including the Disputation with The Giornale De' Letterati D'italia. Ed. and trans. L.M. Palmer. Ithaca, NY: Cornell University Press, 1988.

On the Study Methods of Our Time. Trans. Elio Gianturco. Ithaca, NY: Cornell University Press, 1990.

References

Burke, Peter. *Vico.* Oxford: Oxford University Press, 1985.

Lilla, Mark. *G.B. Vico: The Making of an Anti-Modern.* Cambridge, MA: Harvard University Press, 1993.

Mali, Joseph. *The Rehabilitation of Myth: Vico's New Science.* Cambridge, Eng.: Cambridge University Press, 1992.

Vietnamese Historiography

Vietnamese historiography dates from the mid-tenth century, when the earliest known historical material written by Vietnamese appears. Since that time, the writing of Vietnamese history has shown stunning changes. We can divide Vietnam's historiography into three broad phases: an independent period after Chinese rule (939–ca. 1884); the period of French colonial rule (ca. 1884–1954); and the postcolonial independence period (1954–present).

Vietnamese Historiography, 939–1884

Many of the arguments over Vietnamese history from the tenth through nineteenth centuries have centered on Confucianism's impact on Vietnam. But scholars have sometimes confused the use of Chinese Confucian sources and forms with the adoption of Confucianism in toto. The impact of Confucianism has ebbed and flowed during Vietnamese history, and other currents of thought (like beliefs in Buddhism and in the spirit world) have influenced Vietnamese historical thinking. It was not until the fifteenth century that Confucianism became the state orthodoxy, one that was not uniformly followed in the centuries that followed.

The earliest surviving court history based on Vietnamese sources is the *Viet su luoc* [Historical Annals of Viet], completed in the late fourteenth century. It is probably an abridged version of the *Dai Viet Su ky* [Historical Records of Great Viet] that Le Van Huu presented to the Tran dynasty court in 1272. The most important early history, however, is Ngo Si Lien's *Dai Viet su ky toan thu* [Complete Historical Annals of Great

Viet], presented to the Tran court in 1479. This work adopts the chronicle form of history and uses the events of the past to draw moral lessons for future generations.

Ngo Si Lien's 1479 work incorporates Le Van Huu's history from 1272, the *Dai Viêt su ky*, into the text. Le Van Huu's work had exhibited Vietnamese particularities: for example, unlike Chinese historians, Le Van Huu showed little interest in the Confucian virtue of filial piety. In contrast, Ngo Si Lien's *Dai Viêt su ky toan thu* is quite Confucian, as shown by the comments that Ngo Si Lien inserted in the text when he came across incidents that struck him as of dubious moral value.

Vietnamese also compiled collections of folk tales and supernatural beliefs. Notable are the *Viêt dien u linh tap* [Compilation of the Departed Spirits of the Viet Realm], compiled by Ly Te Xuyen in 1329, and the *Linh Nam chich quai* [Wonder Plucked from the Dust of Linh Nam], compiled by Tran The Phap in the fourteenth century. These tales fall squarely within the Vietnamese historiographical tradition.

Among the greatest historians of Vietnam is the scholar Le Quy Don (ca. 1726–1784), author of such works as *Van dai loai ngu* [The Classified Discourse of the Library] and the *Kien van tieu luc* [Small Chronicle of Things Seen and Heard]. These works exhibit his encyclopedic interest in everything from conceptions of human change to Confucian morality to geography and politics.

Compared to earlier periods in Vietnamese history, many historical sources survive from the Nguyen dynasty (1802–1945). The major history produced in the nineteenth century was the *Kham dinh viet su thong giam cuong muc* [Imperially Ordered Text and Commentary Completely Reflecting the History of Viet]. It followed the Vietnamese historiographical tradition inaugurated in the thirteenth century. This chronicle, published in 1884, covers Vietnamese history up to 1789. Another major resource for historians is the 538 volume *Dai Nam thuc luc* [Veritable records of the Great South].

The Nguyen dynasty came from the south, whereas earlier rulers had come from the north. The dynasty's sources thus provide a different regional perspective on the past as well as giving a nineteenth-century view of events covered in earlier chronicles.

The Colonial Period (ca. 1884–1954)

The colonial period inaugurated new approaches to the writing of history. French scholars like Georges Coedès, Louis Finot, Albert Maybon, and Henri Maspero excelled in the study of precolonial history and archaeology. Scholarly writing on the French colonial impact, however, was of uneven quality. Both French and Vietnamese authors tended, often mistakenly, to interpret all of Vietnamese history as a variation on the Chinese model. Nonetheless, historians from this period left a great legacy: they introduced new ways of thinking about the past. It is in this period, for example, that nationalism and Marxism began to take root among the Vietnamese intelligentsia and eventually revolutionized their writing of history.

During the colonial period, the Vietnamese wrote few outstanding works of history. Hampered by strict censorship and often enamored of Western learning, they muted their viewpoints and often disparaged the Vietnamese past. The most influential works included two works by Trân Trọng Kim: *Viet Nam su luoc* [Outline History of Vietnam] (1929–1930), a work that developed a five stage version of Vietnamese history, and *Nhogiao* [Confucianism]. Dao Duy Anh contributed *Viet Nam van hoa su cuong* [Short History of Vietnamese Culture] (1938), which examined the Vietnamese past through a vaguely Marxist framework. Dao Duy Anh moved beyond the study of a high culture based on texts to understand culture as common cultural practices and beliefs. Other well-known historians writing in the colonial period include Phan Boi Chau, Nguyen Van To, Hoang Thuc Tram (Hoa Bang), Ngo Tat To, and Tran Van Giap.

Postcolonial Period (1954–present)

Historians writing since independence have distanced themselves from their colonial predecessors. Nationalism and Marxism, existing in an uneasy tension, have strongly marked their writings. We see the nationalist impact in one of the great themes of the historiography of this period: the need to center Vietnamese history on Vietnam, and not to see it as a passive reaction to foreign influences. Historians have also attempted, with limited success, to incorporate the histories of non-Vietnamese ethnic groups into the historiography of the country.

Marxism has influenced northern historians markedly, both in terms of the broad subjects chosen (such as economic history, peasant and worker struggles) and in specific methodological approaches (for instance class analysis, the Asiatic Mode of Production, stage theories of historical evolution). But Vietnamese historians have often appropriated Marxism critically; furthermore, they have sometimes explored topics like heroism, resistance, nationalism, and the nature of Vietnamese identity in a decidedly un-Marxist manner. It is also true that modern Vietnamese historians, like their precolonial predecessors, have accorded more importance to the study of literature than a strict Marxist–Leninist would allow.

Among the leading historians in Vietnam of the past fifty years are Tran Huy Lieu, Dinh Xuan Lam, Tran Van Giau, Phan Huy Le, Tran Quoc Vuong, Ha Va Tan, and Phan Dai Doan. They have pioneered writings in everything from the Mongol invasion of Vietnam in the thirteenth century to studies of feudalism, land tenure, Buddhist history, and resistance to the French. To these historians, we must also add the names of a few authors who are known in several fields. For example, Dao Duy Anh and Hoang Thuc Tram (penname: Hoa Bang) have contributed important studies on literature, translated important texts from the Chinese, and written historical studies. Leading historians from the south are few, although one could mention Ta Chi Dai Truong, who has written on a range of issues from tenth-century Vietnam to the Tay Son rebellion of the eighteenth century. Finally, the scholars Hoang Xuan Han and Nguyen The Anh have contributed significantly to Vietnamese historical debates both when in Vietnam and when living in France.

Shawn McHale

References

Pelley, Patricia. "Writing Revolution: The New History in Post-Colonial Vietnam." Ph.D. dissertation, Cornell University, 1993.

Reid, Anthony, and David Marr, eds. *Perceptions of the Past in Southeast Asia*. Singapore: Heinemann, 1979.

Smith, Ralph B. "Sino-Vietnamese Sources for the Nguyên Period: An Introduction." *Bulletin of the School of Oriental and African Studies* 30 pt. 3 (1967): 600–621.

Taylor, Keith Weller. "Appendix O: Sources for Early Vietnamese History." In his *Birth of Vietnam*. Berkeley and Los Angeles: University of California Press, 1983.

Villani, Giovanni (ca. 1276–1348)

Florentine chronicler. Villani was a Florentine banker. After representing his firm abroad, he returned to Florence in 1307 to marry and to hold civic offices. When his bank failed in 1338, he was imprisoned for debt and retired from public life. In 1300 Villani conceived the idea of writing a history of Florence from its origins to his own time. He began to keep a diary of events in about 1322 and wrote most of it from 1333 to 1341. His *Chronicle* included biblical stories, fantastic legends, and omens as facts. But when he reached his own time, Villani sought statistical information about Florence: the city's population and revenues, the number of doctors and lawyers, the daily consumption of wine and bread, and how many children attended school. Some of the statistics are erroneous, others fairly accurate. Villani's *Chronicle* combined a medieval belief in legends, omens, and astrology, with the merchant's passion for accurate information. His *Chronicle* is an example of medieval historiography that is still used by historians today.

Paul F. Grendler

Texts

Cronica. Ed. F.G. Dragomanni. 4 vols. Florence: Sansone Coen, 1844–1845.

Villani's Chronicle: Being Selections from the First Nine Books of the Croniche Fiorentine. Trans. R.E. Selfe and P.H. Wicksteed. Second revised ed. London: Constable, 1906.

References

Green, Louis. *Chronicle into History*. Cambridge, Eng.: Cambridge University Press, 1972.

Villari, Pasquale (1827–1917)

Italian historian, journalist and senator from Naples. Villari was professor of history at the University of Pisa (1859–1865) and in Florence (1865–1913). His first major historical work was *Introduzione alla storia d'Italia dal cominciamento delle Repubbliche del Medioevo alla Riforma di Savonarola* [Introduction to the History of Italy from the Beginning of the Medieval Republics to the Reform of Savonarola] (1849), which led to his noted biographies of Savonarola (1860) and Machiavelli (1877–1882). For Villari, Savonarola and Machiavelli represented the dual nature of the Italian Renaissance; he admired the former but was ambivalent toward the latter. Villari's interest in the question whether history was an "art" or a "science" led to the publication of his *L'origine e il progresso della filosofia della storia* [Origins and Progress of the Philosophy of History] in 1859. Although he advocated the use of positivism as an analytical tool in historical research, Villari never abandoned the Neapolitan tradition of historiography initiated by Giambattista Vico and sided with Leopold von Ranke in believing that history was both science and art.

Stanislao G. Pugliese

Texts

Life and Times of Girolamo Savonarola. Trans. Linda Villari. New York: Charles Scribner's Sons, 1899.

Life and Times of Niccolò Machiavelli. Trans. Linda Villari. New York: Greenwood Press, 1968.

The Two First Centuries of Florentine History. Trans. Linda Villari. New York: AMS Press, 1975.

References

Cicalese, Marialuisa. *Note per un profilo di Pasquale Villari.* Rome: Istituto storico italiano per l'età moderna e contemporanea, 1979.

Villehardouin, Geoffrey of (ca. 1150–ca. 1213)

Marshal of Champagne and Romania (the Latin empire of Constantinople), crusader, and crusade historian. Villehardouin's *La Conquête de Constantinople* [The Conquest of Constantinople] is the most comprehensive account of the Fourth Crusade and, along with Robert of Clari's history of the Fourth Crusade, is the earliest surviving work of history in French prose. As Villehardouin tells the story, a series of unforeseen circumstances drove the crusaders to Constantinople and impelled them to capture the city in April, 1204.

Modern historians divide sharply on the reliability of Villehardouin's memoirs. Searchers after conspiracies point to Villehardouin's position in the second rank of the crusade's leadership and conclude that his account is biased to the point of gross distortion and outright falsehood. Historians who accept the broad outlines of Villehardouin's "theory of accidents" view his history as the memoirs of an unintrospective but well-informed military man who attempted to tell the truth as he perceived it.

Villehardouin undoubtedly reported and interpreted events from the perspectives of his class, culture, and position and clearly failed to report certain disquieting facts that could place the crusaders, and especially the crusade's leaders, in a bad light. Notwithstanding these limitations, his story appears to be essentially reliable, albeit incomplete. He displays a fine eye for military and political details, many of which are confirmable by independent records, and his numerous dates, numbers, and similar data have the ring of authenticity.

Alfred J. Andrea

Texts

The Conquest of Constantinople. In *Chronicles of the Crusades,* trans. M.R.B. Shaw. Harmondsworth: Penguin, 1963.

La Conquête de Constantinople. Ed. and trans. Edmond Faral (into modern French). Revised ed. 2 vols. Paris: Société d'Édition "Les Belles Lettres," 1961.

References

Beer, Jeannette M.A. *Villehardouin: Epic Historian.* Geneva: Librairie Droz, 1968

Queller, Donald E. *The Fourth Crusade: The Conquest of Constantinople, 1201–1204.* Philadelphia: University of Pennsylvania Press, 1977.

Vincent of Beauvais (ca. 1190–ca. 1264)

Dominican encyclopedist. One of the first Dominicans in Paris, Vincent was educational adviser to King Louis IX, who financed some of his researches. In addition to treatises on education, government, and theology, Vincent produced a massive compilation of excerpts from more than four hundred classical, Christian, and Arabic authors, the greatest encyclopedia between Isidore of Seville and Diderot. The second of its three parts, *Speculum historiale* [The Mirror of History], presents a Christian version of history from Adam to Louis IX's crusade in 3,794 chapters, 1,334 closely printed folio pages totaling over 1.2 million words in its most recent edition. The most popular part of the encyclopedia, it was translated into French by 1328, subsequently appearing in Dutch, Spanish, and German versions, and was used by many Renaissance historians. Vincent used his sources critically, ranking various categories of materials in order of preference by their credibility, indicating when he was uncertain as to the truth of a statement and disagreeing with even his favorite authors.

Joseph M. McCarthy

Texts

Speculum historiale in *Bibliotheca mundi Vincentii Burgundi.* 4 vols. Douai, 1624. Reprint ed., New York: Kraus, 1964.

References

Smalley, Beryl. *Historians in the Middle Ages.* London: Thames and Hudson, 1974.

Weber, Richard K. *Vincent of Beauvais: A Study in Medieval Historiography.* Kalamazoo, MI: UMI, 1965.

Vinogradoff, Sir Paul Gavrilovitch (1854–1925)

British social and legal historian. Born in Kostroma, Russia, Vinogradoff led a distinguished academic life that spanned a continent. Receiving his university training in Germany (where he studied with the ancient historian Theodor Mommsen) and Russia, he became professor of history at the University of Moscow in 1887. Growing repression by the Russian government eventually forced him to resign his position in 1901 and move to England. In 1903 he was elected to the chair of jurisprudence at Oxford, which position he held until his death. During his career, Vinogradoff produced a massive quantity of work on medieval history and comparative law. He is chiefly known for his studies of the legal and social context of rural society in medieval England, and in particular for three major works: *Villeinage in England* (originally published in Russian in 1892), *The Growth of the Manor* (1904), and *English Society in the Eleventh Century* (1908). *Villeinage in England,* often hailed as Vinogradoff's best work, was an immensely sensitive and learned exploration of the legal framework within which medieval peasants lived. Its method of fusing medieval legal and social development set a model for subsequent work by F.W. Maitland, F.M. Stenton, and others. Following John Horace Round, Vinogradoff also felt strongly that the Norman Conquest instituted a critical change in the development of English society and law (an idea most forcefully expressed in his *English Society in the Eleventh Century*). Altogether, Vinogradoff inaugurated the strong Russian/Soviet impact upon medieval English studies that would be continued by M.M. Postan and E.A. Kosminskii.

John Langdon

Texts

English Society in the Eleventh Century. Oxford: Clarendon Press, 1908.

The Growth of the Manor. New York: Macmillan, 1905.

Outlines of Historical Jurisprudence. Holmes Beach, FL: Gaunt, 1994.

Villeinage in England. Oxford: Clarendon Press, 1892.

References

Fisher, H.A.L. "Paul Vinogradoff: A Memoir." In *Collected Papers of Paul Vinogradoff.* 2 vols. London: Wildy, 1963, vol. 1.

Vitezović, Pavao Ritter (1652–1713)

Croatian librarian, printer, and historian. Vitezović was born in Senj. He traveled a great deal and was self-taught. He became skilled in engraving while at the court of Janez Weikhard Valvasor. In 1861, he was elected Senj's representative to the Sopron Diet and later became a representative of the Ban and the Sabor at the Viennese court. He also managed a library and an official printing office in Zagreb. His most significant achievement is related to his work as representative of the Sabor in a commission that was established to determine the frontier line after the 1699 Peace of Sremski Karlovci [Carlowitz]. In his book *Croatia rediviva* [Croatia Revived] (1700) he fixed the frontiers of all Croatia *(limites totius Croatiae).* Vitezović used the term "Croatian" as a synonym for "Illyrian" and so extended the meaning of "Croatian" to all Slavs. In this way, he was the forerunner of the idea of the unity of the South Slavs, and of the Illyrianist movement of Ljudevit Gaj. Vitezović's other historical work includes a chronicle partly based on the previous work of Antun Vramec, *Kronika aliti szpomen vszega szieta vikov* [Chronicle, or a Remembrance of All the Ages of the World] (1696), his *Anagrammaton, Sive Laurus auxiliatoribus Ungariae liber secundus* [The Second Book of Anagrams, or a Laurel Wreath to the Helpers of Hungary, 1869], and a history of Bosnia, *Bosna captiva* [Bosnia Occupied] (1712). He also produced a heraldic manual, *Stemmatographia, sive Armorum Illyricorum delineatio, descriptio et restitutio* [The Arms of the Illyrians Delineated, Described and Restored] (1701), that was later adapted into a Serbian version by Hristofor Žefarović. Of Vitezović's unpublished manuscripts, the most interesting is the Latin *Serbiae illustratae libri octo* [History of Serbia in Eight Books].

Robert Stallaerts

Texts

Gortan, Veljko "Pavao Ritter Vitezović—Paulus Ritter (1652–1713)." In *Hrvatski Latinisti– Croatici Auctores qui latine scripserunt. II. Pisci 17–19. Stoljeća - Auctores Saec. XVII–XIX.* [Croatian Latinists: Croatian Authors who Wrote in Latin. II. Writers of the Seventeenth to Nineteenth Centuries], ed. Veljko Gortan and Vladimir Vratović. Zagreb: Matica Hrvatska Zora, 1970, 123–165.

Vramac, Antun. *Kronika, aliti szpomenek vszega szveta vekov.* Zagreb: Ivan Weitz, 1744.

References

Banac, Ivo. "The Revived Croatia of Pavao Ritter Vitezović." *Harvard Ukrainian Studies* 10 (1986): 492–507.

Volk

German term for a group (derived from the Old German root words *folk, folc,* or *volc*), that is value-neutral, with the exception of the social-hierarchical meaning of "common folk." In opposition to the Cartesian deductive approach and, then, to the French Enlightenment, the concept of *Volk* moved into historiographical focus, particularly through the works of Johann Gottfried Herder and Justus Möser. There the *Volk,* as a group shaped by a common culture, was seen as the proper foundation of the state, being anterior and superior to it. Whether conceived as an organism or as a *Gestalt,* the *Volk* constituted a unit by virtue of shared customs and a language, which served as the depository and transmitter of the heritage of the *Volk.* Literature and music were expressions of the soul of the *Volk,* making possible the genetic tracing of a *Volk's* development. All of history was *Völkergeschichte* in which states and empires figured as constructs of power, destructive if they expanded beyond the area of the *Volk.* The universality of history was not vouchsafed by progress toward a uniformly rational stage but by the equality of all *Völker* in the divine plan. The subsequent context of the Napoleonic wars stressed the element of differentiation from other people, inherent in *Volk.* The accentuation of uniqueness gave much support to emerging nineteenth century nationalism. In the latter's historiography the advocacy of the nation-state (a state based on the commonality of the *Volk*) overshadowed eighteenth-century universalism and the cautionary note on the state. In the theory of history the *Volk* (with its *Volksseele,* deprived of its romantic connotations) played a key role in Karl Lamprecht's historical new cultural history. After 1918, the disappointments and disorientation of the period led to *völkisch* historical writings that affirmed the identity of the German *Volk* by the negation of all that was considered "outside" the *Volk.* That facilitated the linking of the term *Volk* with race (particularly anti-Semitism) and a *Blut und Boden* [Blood and Soil] perspective. However, in Hitler's Germany the *völkische* interpretation of German history, with its horrible consequences in life, remained theoretically a fragment. After 1945, responsible strains of *Volksgeschichte,* be they early attempts at cultural history (by, for instance, Werner Conze and Otto Brunner) or *Landesgeschichte* (regional history), would not link up with ease with the striving for a life-encompassing history in Western historiography. When, after the 1950s, German structural social history began to flourish it found a *volksgeschichtliche* basis of limited usefulness, because of its institutional isolation in *Landesgeschichte,* insufficient focus on modernity, aversion to large-scale generalizations, and limited openness to some of the social sciences. Yet, elements of the more *völkisch*-oriented German *Strukturgeschichte* did survive in subsequent historiographical theory.

Ernst Breisach

See also ENLIGHTENMENT HISTORIOGRAPHY; GERMAN HISTORICAL THOUGHT; HISTORICISM; *KULTURGESCHICHTE.*

References

Oberkrome, Willi. *Volksgeschichte: Methodische Inventionen und völkische Ideologisierung in der deutschen Geschichtswissenschaft 1918–1945* [People's History: Methodological Inventions and Racial Ideology in German Historical Study, 1918–1945]. Göttingen: Vandenhoeck & Ruprecht: 1993.

Volpe, Gioacchino (1876–1971)

Italian historian. Volpe, who began his career by focusing on the history of the medieval communes and heretical sects, was the most important Italian historian to support fascism. He was professor of modern history at the University of Milan (1905–1924) and then at the University of Rome (1924–1940), where he headed the Institute of Modern and Contemporary History. He was the founder of the Istituto Fascista di Cultura, a member of the Italian Academy and director of the *Rivista Storica Italiana.* Volpe advanced the concept of an "economic-juridical" perspective for historical research, which stressed that changes in society and its institutions were the results of the complex interrelationship between economics and class. The rise of medieval heretical sects, in this analysis, reflected social upheaval and economic distress. This interpretive framework, embodied in his work *Il Medioevo* [The Middle Ages] (1927) influenced medieval historiography for several decades. In the same year he published *L'Italia in cammino* [Italy's Journey], which, along with his *Storia del movimento fascista* [History of the Fascist Movement] (1939), gained him status as the official historian of fascism. His last major work was the three-volume *L'Italia Moderna* [Modern Italy] (1943–1952).

Stanislao G. Pugliese

V

Texts

L'Italia in cammino. Rome: Editori Laterza, 1991.

Il Medioevo. Florence: Sansoni, 1966.

References

Cervelli, Innocenzo. *Gioacchino Volpe.* Naples: Guida, 1977.

Tannenbaum, Edward R. "Gioacchino Volpe." In *Historians of Modern Europe,* ed. Hans A. Schmitt. Baton Rouge: Louisiana State University Press, 1971.

Voltaire (1694–1778)

Pseudonym of François Marie Arouet, French philosophe, poet, dramatist, and historian. Born into a bourgeois Parisian family, Voltaire first achieved notoriety in his twenties as a playwright. The political indiscretions of Voltaire's early works led to a short exile in England, following which he published *The Philosophical Letters on the English* (1734). Voltaire extended the social criticism of the *Philosophical Letters* with *Candide* (1759) and a series of pamphlets demanding religious toleration in connection with incidents of official persecution. At his death in 1778, Voltaire left an enormously varied literary output and an unrivaled reputation as the leading figure of the French Enlightenment.

Voltaire's best-known works of history are *The Age of Louis XIV* (1752) and the *Essay on the Customs and the Spirit of Nations* (1756). In *Louis XIV* Voltaire attempted to characterize France's classical period, not merely to write an account of the life of the king or of the diplomatic and military events of his reign. Voltaire abandoned chronological narrative and emphasized achievement in the arts and sciences. The *Essay on Customs* was an effort to describe the progress of civilization in a genuinely universal context. Rejecting the traditional biblical and Christian frame, the *Essay's* first chapters concern China and India rather than Christian Europe.

Carol E. Harrison

Texts

Voltaire: The Age of Louis XIV and Other Selected Writings. Ed. and trans. J.H. Brumfitt. New York: Twayne Publishers, 1963.

Les oeuvres complètes de Voltaire [The Complete Works of Voltaire]. Ed. T. Besterman, later W.H. Barber and U. Kölving. Geneva: Institut et Musée Voltaire and Toronto: University of Toronto Press, 1968– .

References

Brumfitt, J.H. "Introduction." In *Les oeuvres complètes de Voltaire,* vol. 59, 1969.

Gay, Peter. *Voltaire's Politics.* Second ed. New Haven, CT: Yale University Press, 1988.

Wace (ca. 1100–ca. 1174)

Anglo-Norman chronicler and narrative poet. Wace was born on the Isle of Jersey, grandson of the chamberlain of Robert I, Duke of Normandy. Educated in France, he presented his *Roman de Brut* (the basis for Layamon's later work) to Eleanor of Aquitaine in 1155. In 1160 Henry II commissioned Wace to write a chronicle of the Dukes of Normandy. This, the *Roman de Rou,* is the basis of Wace's reputation as a historian. A prologue in Alexandrine meter, the *Chronique ascendante,* traces back from Henry II to Rou. The work's main body, in descending order, divides into two parts; the first in Alexandrine from Rou to Richard the Fearless, the remainder in couplets of eight syllables. This work is of value in preserving oral traditional accounts of the Norman Conquest.

Kerry E. Spiers

Texts

Le Roman de Rou de Wace. Ed. A.J. Holden. 2 vols. Paris: Editions A. & J. Picard, 1970–1973.

References

Gransden, Antonia. *Historical Writing in England, I: c. 550 to c. 1307.* Ithaca, NY: Cornell University Press, 1974.

Wagenaar, Jan (1709–1773)

Dutch merchant, publicist, and historian. Born in Amsterdam and trained as a tradesman, Wagenaar initially ran a lumber business until, in 1758, he was appointed Amsterdam's historiographer. Two years later, he also became first clerk of the Town Clerk's Office, a position which he held until his death, in Amsterdam. Wagenaar's fame as a historian is based on two works. His *Vaderlandsche historie* [National History] (1749–1759) is an extensive survey of Dutch history, largely centered on the province of Holland, preeminently republican, and conceived as a history of freedom and encroachments upon it. It remained authoritative until well into the nineteenth century. For his *Amsterdam* (1760–1767), a thematically broadly conceived town history, Wagenaar, thanks to his position, was able to use restricted records. Before the publication of these two works, which were repeatedly adapted, reissued, and continued, he also wrote on the contemporary history of the republic.

Jo Tollebeek

Texts

Amsterdam: in zyne opkomst, aanwas, geschiedenissen, voorregten, koophandel, gebouwen, kerkenstaat, schoolen, schutterye, gilden en regeeringe [Amsterdam: Its Rise, Growth, Histories, Privileges, Commerce, Buildings, Churches, Schools, Militias, Guilds and Governments]. 13 vols. Amsterdam: Is. Tirion & Yntema & Tieboel, 1760–1768.

Vaderlandsche historie, vervattende de geschiedenissen der nu Vereenigde Nederlanden, inzonderheid die van Holland, van de vroegste tyden af [National History, Containing the Histories of the Now United Netherlands, Especially That of Holland, since the Earliest Days]. 21 vols. Amsterdam: J. Allart, 1790–1796.

References

Castendijk, R.J. *Jan Wagenaar en zijn "Vaderlandsche historie"* [Jan Wagenaar and His "National History"]. Schiedam: Wijchers, 1927.

Wessels, L.H.M. "Jan Wagenaar (1709–1773): Bijdrage tot een herwaardering [Jan Wagenaar (1709–1773): A Contribution to a Revaluation]." In *Geschiedschrijving in Nederland* [Historical Writing in the Netherlands], ed. P.A.M. Geurts and A.E.M. Janssen. The Hague: Martinus Nijhoff, 1981, vol. 1, 116–140.

Waitz, Georg (1813–1886)

German historian. Waitz was educated at the universities of Kiel and Berlin. He moved to Hanover in 1836 to assist with the publication of the *Monumenta Germaniae Historica,* the huge project of collecting, editing, and publishing medieval German documents. He became a professor of history at Kiel (1842–1846), Berlin (1846–1849), and Göttingen (from 1849) and was appointed editor of the *Monumenta* in 1875, whereupon he immediately began to modernize the enterprise. He also continued F.C. Dahlmann's bibliography of German History, producing the third, fourth, and fifth editions (1869–1883) of the work, which since then has been known as "Dahlmann-Waitz." In the course of his career Waitz, a convinced nationalist, became involved in politics. While at Kiel he represented his university in the provincial parliament and worked to prevent the incorporation of Schleswig-Holstein into Denmark; he also sat as a representative in the Frankfurt National Parliament in 1848–1849 and played a part in drafting the liberal constitution that this abortive assembly produced. Waitz, who was strongly influenced by his teacher Leopold von Ranke, was one of the foremost historians of his generation, and himself an influential teacher; he established Göttingen University as a world-renowned center for historical studies. Waitz concentrated on the Middle Ages and on institutional and constitutional history; unlike his mentor, Ranke, he was less a narrative historian than a formidable analyst and organizer of historical sources. His magnum opus was the meticulously researched, clear, and insightful eight-volume work *Deutsche Verfassungsgeschichte* [German Constitutional History] (1844–1878), a study of German institutions from the Frankish kingdoms to the end of the twelfth century.

Klaus Larres

Texts

Deutsche Verfassungsgeschichte. 8 vols. in 10 parts. Kiel: Homann, 1874–1885.
Jahrbücher des Deutschen Reiches unter König Heinrich I [Yearbooks of the German Empire under King Henry I]. Darmstadt: Wissenschaftliche Buchgesellschaft, 1963.
Quellenkunde der deutschen Geschichte [Sources on German History, or "Dahlmann-Waitz"]. 2 vols. Leipzig: Köhler, 1931–1932.

References

Bresslau, H. *Geschichte der Monumenta Germaniae Historica.* Hanover: Hahnsche Buchhandlung, 1921.
Grundmann, Herbert. *Monumenta Germaniae Historica, 1819–1969.* Munich: Monumenta Germaniae Historica; Cologne: Böhlau, 1969.

Walsingham, Thomas (ca. 1345–ca. 1422)

English monk and chronicler. Born, most likely, in Walsingham, Norfolk, he entered St. Albans Abbey around 1364. He lived there until his death, except from 1394 to 1396 when he was prior of Wymondham, Norfolk. Around 1380, Walsingham revived the historiographical tradition at St. Albans of which Matthew Paris had been the most prominent representative. Perhaps also the author of the continuation to Ranulf Higden's *Polychronicon,* Walsingham's major work is his extension of Paris's *Chronica Majora,* a history of England. For the period 1272–1377, Walsingham relied on older chronicles, but for the years 1377–1392 his work is original. He also continued Paris's history of St. Albans, the *Gesta Abbatum Monasterii Sancti Albani* [Deeds of the Abbots of the Monastery of St. Albans] to 1393. While at Wymondham, Walsingham produced a condensed version of the *Chronica Majora,* entitled *Historia Anglicana.* Around 1400, he resumed work on the *Chronica Majora,* and brought it to 1420. He also continued the *Historia Anglicana* [English History], bringing it to 1422 before his death. Five other historical works written by Walsingham are deemed less significant than the ones mentioned. Sometimes regarded as the last of the great medieval chroniclers, Walsingham helped St. Albans become once again the leading center of historical writing in England.

G.H. Gerrits

Texts

Chronicon Angliae ab Anno Domini 1328 usque ad Annum 1388 [Chronicle of England from 1328–1388]. Ed. E.M. Thompson. Rolls Series, 54. London: Longman, 1874.
Gesta Abbatum monasterii Sancti Albani. Ed. H.T. Riley. Rolls Series, 28, pt. iv. 3 vols. London: Longmans, 1867–1869.

The St. Albans Chronicle, 1406–1420. Ed. V.H. Galbraith. Oxford: Clarendon Press, 1937.

Thomae Walsingham, quondam monachi S. Albani, historia anglicana. Ed. H.T. Riley. Rolls Series, 28, pt. i. 2 vols. London: Longman, 1863–1864.

References
Gransden, Antonia. *Historical Writing in England, ii: c. 1307 to the Early Sixteenth Century.* London and Ithaca, NY: Routledge and Kegan Paul and Cornell University Press, 1982.

Taylor, John. *English Historical Literature in the Fourteenth Century.* Oxford: Clarendon Press, 1987.

Wan Sitong [Wan Ssu-t'ung] (1638–1702)

Chinese historian and scholar of the Confucian classics. A native of Yin district, Zhejiang, Wan was a student of Huang Zongxi and thus accepted the emphasis of Huang's teacher, Liu Zongzhou, on studying ritual and bringing the classics to bear on contemporary problems. In 1678 Wan helped Xu Qianxue (1631–1694) to compile the *Duli tongkao* [Complete Study of (Mourning) Rites]. Thereafter Wan went to Peking (now Beijing) to assist in compiling the Standard History of his fallen dynasty. Refusing to accept office under the Qing dynasty, he worked privately in the History Office, as de facto editor in chief of the *Standard History of the Ming,* for thirteen years. Wan's approach to writing a general history of the Ming was to use the Veritable Records (although he acknowledged their shortcomings) as framework for collating information from all other kinds of sources, especially those on individual lives and local events. Regarding chronological tables as indispensable for long history works, Wan produced eighty such tables in order to arrange important events schematically for all of the Standard Histories. His keen interest in loyalists during times of dynastic change led him to write such works as the *Songji zhongyi lu* [Account of the Loyal and Righteous at the End of the Song]. His scholarship and moral principles are most evident in the *Qunshu yibian,* a collection of essays on the classics and histories.

Shoucheng Yan

Texts
Bu lidai shibiao [Supplementary Chronological Tables for Successive Dynasties]. In *Siming congshu* [Collection of Works from Simin (i.e., modern Ningbo)]. Ed. Zhang Shouyong. Part 7. Ningbo: Zhang Shouyong's Yueyan, 1940.

Lidai jiyuan huikao [A Comprehensive Study of Regnal Years of Successive Dynasties]. In *Siming congshu.* Ed. Zhang Shouyong. Part 4. Shanghai: Shangwu yinshuguan, 1936.

Lidai shibiao [Chronological Tables for Successive Dynasties]. In *Sibu beiyao.* Shanghai: Zhonghua shuju, 1936.

Qunshu yibian [Judgments on Doubtful Points in Various Classics and Histories]. Taibei: Guangwen shuju, 1972.

Rulin zongpai [Confucian Schools and Their Branches]. In *Siming congshu,* ed. Zhang Shouyong. Part 3. Ningbo: Zhang Shouyong's Yueyuan, 1935.

Songji zhongyi lu. In *Siming congshu,* ed. Zhang Shouyong. Part 2. Ningbo: Zhang Shouyong's Yueyuan, 1934.

References
Chen Xunci and Fang Zuyou. *Wan Sitong nianpu* [Chronological Biography of Wan Sitong]. Hong Kong: Chinese University Press, 1991.

Struve, Lynn A. "The Early Ch'ing Legacy of Huang Tsung-hsi: A Reexamination." *Asia Major,* third series 1 (1988): 83–122.

Wan Ssu-t'ung

See WAN SITONG.

Wang Fu Chih

See WANG FUZHI.

Wang Fuzhi [Wang Fu Chih] (1619–1692)

Chinese historian during late Ming and early Qing periods. A versatile scholar in poetry, philosophy, history, astronomy, medicine, and military art, Wang produced seventy-three works on various subjects during his life. Wang was also a political activist; committed to reviving the Ming dynasty in 1639–1640 at the age of twenty, he remained embroiled in factional politics until he was forced to retire from court eleven years later. He spent the rest of his life writing while fleeing from the persecution of the Manchus. Using Sima Guang's *Zizhi tongjian* [Comprehensive Mirror As an Aid to Government] as a springboard, he articulated his historical and political thinking in *Du Tongjian lun* [On the Comprehensive Mirror]. His historical analysis typically focuses on the origin, the causes, the background and context, the evolution, and the influence and repercussions of the subject matter under scrutiny. In Wang's view, the vicissitudes in Chinese history were historically determined and rises and falls inevitably followed each other in a cycle.

Yuet Keung Lo

Texts

Du Tongjian lun. Beijing: Zhonghua shuju, 1975.

Notes on Poetry from the Ginger Studio. Ed. and trans. Siu-Kit Wong. Hong Kong: Chinese University Press, 1987.

References

Hummel, Arthur W., ed. *Eminent Chinese of the Ch'ing Period (1644–1912).* New York: Paragon Book Gallery, 1970, 817–819.

McMorran, Ian C. "Wang Fu-chih and His Political Thought." D.Phil. dissertation, Oxford University, 1968.

Wang Guowei [Wang Kuo-wei] (1877–1927)

Chinese historian. A prolific scholar of German philosophy, Chinese lyric poetry and literature, Song and Yuan plays, ancient China, and Chinese frontier history, Wang was born in Haining, Zhejiang province. He went to Shanghai in 1898 where he met Luo Zhenyu, the famous scholar and collector of Shang oracle bones, thereby beginning a lifelong mentor–protégé relationship that ended only with Wang's tragic suicide in 1927. Wang was said to have abandoned his earlier interests in philosophy and literary history for the ancient Chinese past at Luo's urging following the end of the Qing dynasty in 1912. Wang was among the first in China to utilize archaeological artifacts extensively together with received texts from ancient times in approaching and resolving historical problems. His works on the predynastic lords of the Shang, for example, based on his mentor's rich collection of oracle bones, is legendary. His scholarly achievements too wide and numerous to cite individually, Wang's celebrated "antiquarian" scholarship was nevertheless motivated by a cultural conservativism to restore the reliability and credibility of the received traditions of the Chinese past in the face of the rising tide of historical skepticism among his contemporaries.

W.K. Cheng

Texts

Wang Guowei xiansheng quanji [The Complete Works of Wang Guowei]. 25 vols. Taibei: Datong shuju, 1976.

References

Bonner, Joey. *Wang Kuo-Wei: An Intellectual Biography.* Cambridge, MA: Harvard University Press, 1986.

Xu Guansan. *Xin shixue jiushi nian* [Ninety Years of New History]. Hong Kong: Chinese University of Hong Kong Press, 1986.

Wang Hsien-ch'ien

See WANG XIANQIAN.

Wang Kaiyun [Wang K'ei-yün] (1833–1916)

Chinese classicist and historian of local and military history. A native of Xiangtan, Hunan province, Wang made his career mainly in teaching. He had been employed as tutor by several high officials who included the governor-general of Shandong and the imperial prince, Su Shun. After serving briefly on the staff of the famous Hun official Zeng Guofan, he returned to teaching in several renowned academies in Sichuan, Hunan, and Jiangxi. He was appointed to head the Historiographical Office for the Compilation of Qing History in the early Republic. Perhaps best remembered for his identification of Moses as the ancient Chinese philosopher Mozi (Mo Di), thus proving, according to him, the Chinese origin of Western learning, Wang's reputation as a historian was first built on his work on several *fangzhi* or local gazetteers. His most famous historical work, however, was *Xiangjun zhi* [History of the Hunan Army] (1887). When it was commissioned by Zen Jize in 1875, it was intended to be essentially a hagiographical account of Zeng Guofan (Zeng Jize's father) and his Hunan army in their suppression of the Taiping Rebellion. *Xiangjun zhi,* however, turned out to be less laudatory than expected and thus invited the chagrin of many powerful Hunan veterans who campaigned for its destruction. It survived thanks to a Sichuan edition.

W.K. Cheng

Texts

Xiangjun zhi. Changsha, Hunan: Yuelu shushe, 1983.

References

Gui Zunyi, and Yan Yingguang. *Zhongguo jindai shixue shi* [Modern Chinese Historiography]. Jiangsu: Guji chubanshe, 1989.

Wang K'ei-yün

See WANG KAIYUN.

Wang Kuo-wei
See WANG GUOWEI.

Wang Mingsheng [Wang Ming-sheng] (1722–1798)

Chinese historian, scholar, and poet. Wang Mingsheng was born in Jiading (today's Shanghai area). In 1754 Wang obtained the highest civil-service degree, together with his brother-in-law, the famous historian Qian Daxin, and became a compiler in the Hanlin Academy. He retired from office when his mother died in 1763. Subsequently he moved to Suzhou and engaged in studying and writing for the remainder of his life. Wang's reputation among his contemporaries mainly rested on his scholarship in the Confucian classics. Influenced by Hui Dong of the Suzhou school who emphasized learning from Han-dynasty scholarship, Wang firmly defended the legacy of the Later Han Confucian master Zheng Xuan (127–200), as was manifest in his *Shangshu houan* [Concluding Judgments on the *Book of Documents*] (1780). Later in life Wang applied the research methods he had developed in classical studies to historiography. His most outstanding work in this vein is the *Shiqishi shangque* [Deliberations on the Seventeen Standard Histories] (1787), which forms a trio in Qing-period evidential-research historiography with Zhao Yi's *Nianershi zhaji* [Notes on the Twenty-Two Standard Histories] and Qian Daxin's *Nianershi kaoyi* [An enquiry into Discrepancies among the Twenty-Two Standard Histories]. It includes textual criticism, research on institutions and geography, comments on historical figures and events, discussion of research methods, and evaluation of the various histories. In the *Yishu bian* [On the Gradual Development of Learning] (1842), which addresses a wide range of topics, Wang summarized and supplemented his lifelong scholarship.

Shoucheng Yan

Texts

Shangshu houan. In *Huang Qing jingjie*. Taibei: Yiwen yinshuguan, 1965.
Shiqishi shangque. In *Congshu jicheng chubian*. Shanghai: Shangwu yinshuguan, 1935–1937.
Xizhuang shicun gao [Anthology of Wang Mingsheng's Early Works]. Privately published, 1766.
Yishu bian. Ed. Ze Heshou. Published by Shen Maode's Shikaitang, 1842.

References

Chai Degeng. *Shixue congkao* [Miscellaneous Studies in Historiography]. Beijing: Zhonghua shuju, 1982.
Chen Qingquan, et al., eds. *Zhongguo shixuejia pingzhuan* [Critical Biographies of Chinese Historians], vol. 2. Zhengzhou: Zhongzhou guji chubanshe, 1985.

Wang Xianqian [Wang Hsien-ch'ien] (1842–1917)

Chinese classicist and specialist in Han dynasty history. Born in Changsha, Hunan province, Wang retired to his native province in 1890 after a long career in the Qing civil service that included a posting at the Imperial Historiographical Office. A renowned classicist, he compiled *Huang Qing jingjie xubian* [Supplement to the Qing Exegesis of the Classics] (1886–1888) and served as chancellor of two of the most renowned academies in Hunan, becoming the intellectual leader of a local conservative gentry elite that was vehemently opposed to the radical reformers then active in the province. Although not unsympathetic to limited reform, Wang nevertheless found heretical any attempt to alter China's dynastic institutions and traditional order, as advocated by Kang Youwei and Li Qichao. His *Riben yuanliu kao* [On the Origins of Japan] (1901), although somewhat untimely (it was published after the breakdown of the Kang-Liang reform movement in 1898), attributed the success of Meiji Japan's reforms to the Japanese people's staunch adherence to imperial sanctity. Less politically expedient and more reputable in scholarly terms were Wang's works in Han historiography. His *Hanshu buzhu* [Supplementary Annotation of the History of the Former Han] was recognized as a major contribution in its field. But his *Hou Hanshu jijie* [Collected Annotations of the History of the Later Han], partially published in 1915, remained incomplete at Wang's death.

W.K. Cheng

Texts

Hanshu buzhu. Beijing: Zhonghua shuju, 1983.
Hou Hanshu jijie. Beijing: Zhonghua shuju, 1984.

References

Gui Zunyi and Yuan Yingguang. *Zhongguo jindai shixue she* [Modern Chinese Historiography]. 2 vols. Jiangsu: Guji chubanshe, 1989.

Warburg, Aby (1866–1929) and the Warburg School

German art historian and library founder. The oldest child of a Hamburg banking family, Warburg resisted tradition and studied art history at the University of Bonn. At that time, art history emphasized the form of artworks, especially the evolution of artistic style. Beginning with his dissertation on Botticelli's mythologies, Warburg's analytical method differed: it concerned individual works of art and historical situations. He regarded visual motifs and images as records of human experience; like written texts, both were part of the raw material of cultural history; and, while German scholarship emphasized the rationality of antiquity, Warburg, influenced by Nietzsche's characterization, considered the irrational side significant as well. Warburg's publications were not numerous, nor have they been sufficiently translated. His major contribution to cultural history is the library that he assembled in his house (Kulturwissenschaftliche Bibliotek Warburg). Warburg envisaged a library broad enough to encompass any aspect of human endeavor that might provide a context for works of art. Convinced that normal classification systems inhibited serendipitous discovery, he concerned himself, moreover, with the ideal arrangement for the library: this, rather than anything he wrote, is his magnum opus. Unaffiliated with any academic institution, Warburg's library, under the direction of Fritz Saxl, nevertheless spawned an institute and a distinguished series of publications. In 1933, because of the German political situation, the library moved to London, eventually being incorporated into University of London as the Warburg Institute.

Warburg, although shunning official university positions, attracted students and colleagues to his Hamburg home who shared his interests in and approach to the classical tradition. This group, sometimes referred to as the Warburg school, included Warburg's close associates: his assistant Gertrud Bing (1892–1964), who later edited his publications, and the institute's first director, Fritz Saxl (1890–1948), who shared Warburg's interest in Renaissance astrology. Art historians such as Erwin Panofsky (1892–1968) and Edgar Wind (1900–1971), the first editor of the institute's publications and later the occupant of the first chair in art history at Oxford, were also early associates. Sir E.H. (Ernst) Gombrich (b. 1909) became the institute's director in London.

Sheila ffolliott

Texts

Aby Warburg: Ausgewälte Schriften und Würdigungen [Aby Warburg: Selected Publications and Evaluations of His Work]. Ed. Dieter Wuttke. Baden-Baden: V. Koerner, 1980.
Gesammelte Schriften [Collected Works]. 2 vols. Leipzig-Berlin: B.G. Teubner, 1932.

References

Bredekamp, Horst, Michael Diers, and Charlotte Schoell-Glass. *Aby Warburg: Akten des internationale Symposiums Hamburg 1990* [Aby Warburg: Proceedings of the International Symposium in Hamburg]. Weinheim: VCH, 1991.
Gombrich, E.H. *Aby Warburg: An Intellectual Biography.* London: The Warburg Institute, 1970.
Podro, Michael. *The Critical Historians of Art.* New Haven, CT, and London: Yale University Press, 1982.

Warren, Mercy Otis (1728–1814)

American historian, poet, playwright, and patriot. Warren was born in Barnstable, Massachusetts, the sister of the firebrand James Otis. She married James Warren, the Massachusetts political leader, in 1754, and eventually came to know most of the leaders of the American Revolution. Her intensely patriotic writings give an insider's view of events and personalities. For instance, while one of her satirical plays, *The Adulateur* (1773), poked fun at Governor Thomas Hutchinson of Massachusetts and hinted that revolution was imminent, another, *The Group* (1775), speculated on the possible consequences of the cancellation of the Massachusetts charter by King George III. A collection of her poetry, *Poems Dramatic and Miscellaneous (1790),* also disclosed her obvious partisanship. Warren is perhaps best known for her three-volume *History of the Rise, Progress, and Termination of the American Revolution* (1805). Beginning with the Stamp Act and concentrating largely on military matters, this account is of value for its observations about key personalities, such as Hutchinson and George and Martha Washington.

John W. Storey

Texts

Adams, John. *Correspondence between John Adams and Mercy Warren.* Ed. C.F. Adams. New York: Arno Press, 1972.
History of the Rise, Progress, and Termination of the American Revolution. Ed. Lester H. Cohen. 2 vols. Indianapolis, IN: Liberty Classics, 1988.

References

Brown, Alice. *Mercy Warren*. New York: Scribner, 1903.

Laska, Vera. *"Remember the Ladies": Outstanding Women of the American Revolution*. Boston: Bicentennial Commission, 1976.

Watsuji Tetsurō (1889–1960)

Japanese philosopher and cultural historian. The son of a doctor, Watsuji studied philosophy at Tokyo University and later lectured at Kyoto University (1925–1934) and at Tokyo University (1934–1949). Watsuji was strongly influenced by the ideas of Friedrich Nietzsche and Martin Heidegger. In the 1920s he became increasingly involved in research on the history of Japanese art and thought, and his writings on this subject— including *Nihon Seishinshi Kenkyū* [Studies in the History of the Japanese Spirit] (1926) and *Genshi Bukkyō no Jissen Tetsugaku* [The Practical Philosophy of Primitive Buddhism] (1927)—contributed to an upsurge of interest in the history of Japanese culture. Perhaps the most enduringly influential of his works, however, was *Fūdo* (1935; translated into English as *A Climate* in 1961), in which he sought to trace the impact of the natural environment on society and history. A central argument of this work was that the distinctive Japanese climate, with its mixture of monsoons and cold winters, had played a formative role in shaping the development of social institutions such as the family and the emperor-centered state. Watsuji's postwar writings reflected the somber mood induced by Japan's defeat in World War II. Most notable of these was *Sakoku* [The Closed Country] (1950), in which Watsuji attributed Japan's weak position in the modern world to its failure to absorb the scientific spirit of the European Renaissance.

Tessa Morris-Suzuki

Texts

Climate and Culture: A Philosophical Study. Trans. G. Bownas. Revised ed. New York: Greenwood, 1988.

Watsuji Tetsurō Zenshū. 27 vols. Tokyo: Iwanami Shoten, 1961–1992.

References

Najita, T., and H.D. Harootunian. "Japanese Revolt against the West: Political and Cultural Criticism in the Twentieth Century." In *The Cambridge History of Modern Japan*, vol. 6. Cambridge, Eng.: Cambridge University Press, 1988.

Yuasa, Y. *Watsuji Tetsurō*. Tokyo: Sanichi Shobo, 1973.

Wavrin, Jean de (ca. 1400–1474)

Burgundian soldier, courtier, bibliophile, and chronicler. Jean de Wavrin spent the first half of his life, until 1437, fighting in the Hundred Years' War on behalf of the Anglo-Burgundian alliance. He was at Agincourt, where his father and half-brother were killed, and he fought in the 1420 crusade against Bohemian Hussites. In retirement in 1445, he began a six-volume history of England, to 1471, in Anglo-Norman prose, entitled the *Recueil des Croniques et Anchiennes Istories de la Grant Bretaigne, a present nomme Engleterre* [A Collection of Chronicles and Ancient Histories of Great Britain, Now Called England]. Wavrin's chief contribution lies in his many details of the final chapters of the Hundred Years' War from the Anglo-Burgundian perspective, complementing the French perspectives of Jean Froissart and Enguerrand de Monstrelet.

Christopher M. Bellitto

Texts

A Collection of the Chronicles and Ancient Histories of Great Britain, Now Called England. Trans. William Hardy and Edward L.C.P. Hardy. 3 vols. Rolls Series, vol. 40. London: Longman, 1864.

References

Naber, Antoinette. "Jean de Wavrin, un bibliophile du quinzième siècle" [Jean de Wavrin, a Fifteenth Century Bibliophile]. *Revue du Nord* 69 (1987): 281–293.

———. "Les manuscrits d'un bibliophile bourguignon du XVᵉ siècle, Jean de Wavrin" [The Manuscripts of a Fifteenth-Century Burgundian Bibliophile, Jean de Wavrin]. *Revue du Nord* 72 (1990): 23–48.

Webb, Sidney (1859–1947) and Beatrice (1858–1943)

English social reformers and historians. Married in 1892 and sharing collectivist ideals, the Webbs became pioneers in British social and administrative history. After founding the London School of Economics and Political Science in 1895, the Webbs published their *History of Trade Unionism* (1894), followed by *Industrial Democracy* (1897), which continue to influence scholars with the breadth of original research. The largest of the Webbs' works was their nine-volume *English Local Government from the Revolution to the Municipal Corporations Act* (1906–1929), which remains one of the couple's greatest personal and intellectual achievements. As members of the Fabian Society, the Webbs believed, as their works reflect, that the extension of political democracy was inevitable and would result in continued social and economic change, although not by revolutionary means. Instead, the Webbs subscribed to the "inevitability of gradualness." They held that the attainment of socialism would result from a demand for taxation to finance social services on a greatly expanded scale. This understanding of a political and economic evolution for socialism allowed the Webbs to forge ties with the British Labour Party. The Webbs' involvement with the Labour Party also led to the injection of Fabian ideas of a minimum national standard into party policy. This belief would later become the foundation of the welfare state.

Laurie J. Gagnier

Texts

A Constitution for the Socialist Commonwealth of Great Britain. London: London School of Economics and Political Science, 1920.

English Local Government from the Revolution to the Municipal Corporations Act. 9 vols. London: Longmans, Green, 1906–1929.

History of Trade Unionism. London: Printed by the authors for the Trade Unionists of the United Kingdom, 1894.

Industrial Democracy. London: Longmans, Green, 1897.

References

Radice, Lisanne. *Beatrice and Sidney Webb: Fabian Socialists.* London: Macmillan, 1984.

Webb, Beatrice. *The Diary of Beatrice Webb.* Ed. N. and J. Mackenzie. 4 vols. London: Virago, 1982–1985.

———. *My Apprenticeship.* London: Longmans, Green, 1926.

———. *Our Partnership.* Ed. B. Drake and M.I. Cole, Cambridge, Eng: Cambridge University Press, 1975.

Weber, Marianne (1870–1954)

German feminist, sociologist, and biographer. Weber served as the chairperson in 1919–1920 of the "League of German Women's Organizations," the organizing body of the moderate middle-class women's movement. She was active in centrist-democratic politics during the Weimar Republic. In essays and books, Weber investigated contemporary feminist issues as well as the history of women. Her major work *Ehefrau und Mutter in der Rechtsentwicklung* [Wife and Mother in Legal Development] (1907) united legal and cultural history to discuss the practical effects of legal structures upon women's lives from antiquity to the present. She believed that modern divorce law and women's growing economic independence had removed the coercive basis for marriage, but she insisted on the ethical and spiritual value of marriage and the primacy of familial over vocational roles in women's lives. Weber crucially influenced the reception of the work of her husband, the sociologist Max Weber, after his death in 1920. She wrote a biography of Max Weber that remains a key reference work, and she edited numerous posthumous volumes of his writings.

Warren Breckman

Texts

Ehefrau und Mutter in der Rechtsentwicklung. Tübingen: J.C.B. Mohr, 1907.

Die Frauen und die Liebe [Women and Love]. Leipzig: Karl Rober Langewiesche Verlag, 1935.

Die Idee der Ehe und die Ehescheidung [The Ideas of Marriage and Divorce]. Frankfurt: Frankfurter Societäts-druckerei, 1929.

Max Weber: A Biography. Trans. Harry Zohn. New York: John Wiley & Sons, 1975.

References

Weber, Marianne. *Lebenserrinerungen* [Memoirs]. Bremen: J. Storm, 1948.

Weber, Max (1864–1920)

German founder of modern sociology, and a major influence on twentieth-century historical thought. Weber was born in Erfurt, Thuringia, and studied in Berlin, Heidelberg, and Göttingen. In 1896 he accepted a chair in political economy at Heidelberg, where he remained until his death.

In his best-known study, *The Protestant Ethic and the Spirit of Capitalism* (1904–1905), Weber argued that any understanding of the origins of modern capitalism in western Europe and northern America must not neglect the important causal influence of a "modern economic ethic." The roots of this "spirit of capitalism," which implied an unusually methodical orientation toward work and the accumulation of profit, could not be located alone in economic forces, nor in human greed or the general evolution of history. Rather, according to Weber, the Methodist, Pietist, Baptist, and Calvinist "ascetic Protestant" sects and churches of the seventeenth and eighteenth centuries in England, Germany, and the United States constituted its major sources.

As a result of this influential and controversial classic, Weber is often viewed, in contrast to Marx, as a sociologist who exclusively emphasized the power of "ideas" in history. However, he examined *both* "ideas" and "interests" in a variety of other studies. On the one hand, he sought in his three-volume "Economic Ethics of the World Religions" (all published in 1920) to assess whether the economic ethics of Confucianism, Taoism, Hinduism, Buddhism, Jainism, or ancient Judaism influenced the economic activity of believers in a manner comparable to ascetic Protestantism and, as well, to ascertain whether, in particular, political, legal, and economic constellations in China, India, and ancient Israel could be said to be comparable to the political, legal, and economic constellations of modernizing Europe and North America. On the other hand, Weber argued in *Economy and Society* (1921) that societies as such can be best understood by reference, primarily, to a number of fundamental "orders of life" *(Lebensordnungen),* each of which potentially develop according to its indigenous dynamic: the economy, religion, law, rulership *(Herrschaft),* status groups, and family orders. In this systematic sociological treatise, he again attempted, as also in his *Agrarian Sociology of Ancient Civilizations* (1924) and *General Economic History* (1923) and now on a much broader scale than in *The Protestant Ethic,* to isolate the uniqueness of the modern West. As a result of rigorous comparisons to a variety of civilizations, Weber charted the extent to which "formal rationality"—an orientation of activity toward impersonal rules, prescriptions, laws, and economic transactions—had become widespread in modern Western societies in the economy, law, and rulership domains. He was concerned that such orientations, now unrestrained by the "substantive rationalities" rooted in values that had emanated in the past largely from the domain of religion, would lead to an overabundance of "means–end rational" *(zweckrationales Handeln)* action in our daily lives. As a consequence, all value-based action, and especially ethical action, would be, he feared, weakened.

Although more apparent in *The Protestant Ethic* study, Weber's methodology, which he took great pains to articulate, was that of the *verstehende* sociologist: he sought to understand the *subjective*

meaningfulness of actions by referring to the context of values, traditions, and interests within which they occurred. Moreover, he is commonly viewed as the founder of the notion—today widely misunderstood—that modern social scientists must strenuously practice an ethos of "objectivity" in conducting their research (1922).

Stephen Kalberg

Texts

The Agrarian Sociology of Ancient Civilizations. Trans. R.I. Frank. London: NLB, 1976.

Ancient Judaism. Ed. and trans. Hans H. Gerth and Don Martindale. New York: Free Press, 1952.

Economy and Society. Ed. Guenther Roth and Claus Wittich. New York: Bedminster, 1968.

General Economic History. Trans. Frank H. Knight. Glencoe, IL: Free Press, 1927.

The Methodology of the Social Sciences. Ed. and trans. Edward A. Shils and Henry A. Finch. New York: Free Press, 1949.

The Protestant Ethic and the Spirit of Capitalism. Trans. Talcott Parsons. New York: Scribner's, 1930.

The Religion of China. Ed. and trans. Hans H. Gerth. New York: Free Press, 1951.

The Religion of India. Ed. and trans. Hans H. Gerth and Don Martindale. New York: Free Press, 1958.

References

Bendix, Reinhard. *Max Weber: An Intellectual Portrait.* Berkeley: University of California Press, 1960.

Kalberg, Stephen. *Max Weber's Comparative-Historical Sociology.* Chicago: University of Chicago Press, 1994.

Wedgwood, Cicely Veronica (b. 1910)

English historian and biographer. Born in Northumberland, Wedgwood inherited a love for writing from her mother, an author of historical and topographical books. After extensive European travel and study at the universities of Bonn and Paris, she earned her B.A. from Oxford, where A.L. Rowse was her mentor. Rowse and G.M. Trevelyan became her stylistic models. Her major interest is the seventeenth century, about which she has written extensively in generally narrative, rather than analytic, style. Because of her skill as a communicator, her books have enjoyed acclaim from general readers as well as from other scholars. *The Thirty*

Years War (1938), *Oliver Cromwell* (1939), *William the Silent* (1944), and *Richelieu and the French Monarchy* (1962) are among her most celebrated works. Although praised by reviewers, Wedgwood has often incurred criticism for her preference for narrative writing. Some scholars hold that she gives inadequate attention to causes and consequences. She has contended in response that intelligent readers are able to discern such matters themselves. Despite some criticisms, she has received numerous awards and honorary degrees, the British Order of Merit among them.

James Edward McGoldrick

Texts

A Coffin for King Charles. New York: Macmillan Company, 1964.

Edward Gibbon. London: Longmans, Green, 1955.

The Great Rebellion: The King's Peace, 1637–1641. London: Collins, 1955.

The Great Rebellion: The King's War, 1641–1647. London: Collins, 1958.

Truth and Opinion: Historical Essays. New York: Macmillan Company, 1960.

References

Ollard, R., and P. Tudor-Craig, eds. *For Veronica Wedgwood These: Studies in Seventeenth Century History.* London: Collins, 1986.

Richardson, R.C. *The Debate on the English Revolution.* London: Methuen, 1977.

Wei Cheng

See WEI ZHENG.

Wei Yuan [Wei Yüan] (1794–1856)

Chinese historian and geographer. Born into a Hunanese gentry family, Wei Yuan was educated in the Confucian tradition. Although he favored the New Text school, he was syncretic in his approach to classical scholarship. Living in a period of dynastic decline, he advocated statecraft reformism for the renovation of the country. His experience as editor of an encyclopedia on statecraft (1826) further increased his interest in public affairs. Throughout his career, he helped formulate many programs aiming at solving critical issues such as river conservancy and salt administration. His concern for the decay of the dynasty motivated him to write the *Shengwu ji* [Records of Imperial Exploits], which described Qing (1644–1911) military achievements up to the Daoguang [Tao-

kuang] (1821–1850) period. A few months after China's defeat in the Opium War (1839–1842), he edited the *Haiguo tuzhi* [Illustrated Treatises of the Sea Kingdoms] to remind the Chinese of the importance of world geography and coastal defense. His last work, the *Yuanshi xinbian* [A Revised History of the Yuan Dynasty, 1279–1368], was published posthumously in 1905.

Henry Y.S. Chan

Texts

Shengwu ji. Yangzhou, 1846.

References

Leonard, Jane Kate. *Wei Yuan and China's Rediscovery of the Maritime World.* Cambridge, MA: Harvard University Press, 1984.

Wei Zheng [Wei Cheng] (580–643)

Chinese historian, chief minister, and poet. Wei Zheng was born in Shandong province and was orphaned at a young age. A Daoist monk with literary skills before assuming a distinguished political career, he first served the crown prince before joining the staff of his employer's rival, the later Emperor Taizong. A trusted minister who also conducted two military expeditions, Wei argued against the enfeoffment of high ministers and members of the imperial family and contributed crucially to the strength of Taizong's reign, the Zhenguan (True Vision) period. When Wei died after seventeen years of service, the emperor equated his blunt criticism and moral guidance with the function of a mirror pointing out flaws for correction. As a historian, Wei Zheng's major accomplishment is the Standard History of the Sui dynasty—*Suishu* [History of the Sui]—compiled in 629–636. The Sui dynasty (581–617) was a short-lived but significant period in which Wei Zheng lived before holding office in the Tang dynasty. Chiefly noted for accuracy and conciseness in his historiography, he also supervised the writing of the histories of the Northern Dynasties. Wei's large corpus of works also includes poetry and essays.

Jennifer W. Jay

Texts

Le Traité Economique de "Souei-chou." Trans. Etienne Balazs (into French). Leiden: E.J. Brill, 1953.

Le Traité Juridique du "Souei-chou." Trans. Etienne Balazs (into French). Leiden: E.J. Brill, 1954.

Sui shu [History of the Sui Dynasty]. Beijing: Zhonghua shuju, 1973.

Wei Zhenggong gong shiji, wenji [Collected Prose and Poetry of Wei Zheng]. Shanghai: Congshu jicheng editions, 1937.

References
Weschler, Howard J. *Mirror to the Son of Heaven: Wei Cheng at the Court of T'ang T'ai-tsung.* New Haven, CT: Yale University Press, 1974.

Weil, Gustav (1808–1889)
Austrian-born historian of the Arab Caliphs. Born in Salzburg, Weil entered the University of Heidelberg in 1828 to study philosophy and history. He complemented his formal studies by learning the Arabic language. In 1830 he accompanied the French military expedition to Algiers as a reporter for *Augsburger Allgemeine Zeitung.* In January 1831, he traveled to Cairo where he was employed as a French instructor in the medical school. In Cairo, he continued his studies by learning Persian and Turkish and attending the lectures of Egyptian philologists. In 1835 Weil returned to Europe after a brief stay in Istanbul. With some difficulty he was able to secure a position at the University of Heidelberg first as a librarian and after 1861 as a professor. Weil's best-known work is *Geschichte der Chalifen* [History of the Caliphs] published in five volumes between 1846 and 1862. It includes the history of the four early caliphs, the Umayyad and 'Abbāssid dynasties, and the Egyptian and Spanish caliphates. One of the earliest undertakings of its kind, the work continues Weil's earlier publication on the life of Muḥammad (1843) and draws heavily on the works of Muslim historians.

Hootan Shambayati

Texts
The Bible, the Koran, and the Talmud; or, Biblical Legends of the Mussulmans. London: Brown, Green, and Longmans, 1846.

Geschichte der islamitischen Volker von Mohammed bis zur Zeit des sultan Selim ubersichtlich dargestellt [History of the Islamic Peoples from the Time of Muḥammad to That of Sultan Selim Presented Clearly]. Stuttgart: Riegerm, 1866.

A History of the Islamic Peoples. Trans. S. Khuda Bakhsh. Lahore: Accurate Printers, 1978.

Mohammed der Prophet, sein Leben und seine Lehre [Muḥammad the Prophet, His Life and Teachings]. Stuttgart: Metzler'schen Buchhandlung, 1843.

References
Dunlop, D.M. "Some Remarks on Weil's History of the Caliphs." In *Historians of the Middle East,* ed. Bernard Lewis and P.M. Holt. London: Oxford University Press, 1962, 315–329.

Wells, Herbert George (1866–1946)
English novelist, sociologist, and popular historian. Wells was born in Bromley, Kent. In his youth he held a number of jobs before turning to writing. His first works were science fiction, including his best known *The Time Machine* (1895) and *The War of the Worlds* (1898). These and other novels demonstrate that he was both a utopian and a socialist. World War I convinced Wells that he had to help shape the evolution of mankind through popular education, and one result of this belief was his two historical works: *The Outline of History* (1919–1920) and *A Short History of the World* (1922). These sold many copies in the 1920s and 1930s and had considerable influence on their readers. Wells was not a professional historian and relied on secondary works and encyclopedias for his information. Despite the global scope implied in their titles, the histories deal mainly with Europe, but they are clearly written and interesting and continue to be read a half century after his death. Wells's writings reflect his desire that the Great War would lead mankind to put an end to war and that the future would be one of peace. He died disillusioned, having witnessed the renewed carnage of World War II.

Walter A. Sutton

Texts
Experiment in Autobiography. New York: Macmillan, 1934.

The Outline of History: Being a Plain History of Life and Mankind. Revised ed. Garden City, NY: Doubleday, 1971.

A Short History of the World. New York: Macmillan, 1922.

References
MacKenzie, Norman I., and Jeanne MacKenzie. *H.G. Wells: A Biography.* New York: Simon and Schuster, 1973.

Murray, Brian. *H.G. Wells.* New York: Continuum, 1990.

West, Anthony. *H.G. Wells: Aspects of a Life.* New York: Random House, 1984.

Wen Daya [Wen Ta-ya] (fl. sixth–seventh centuries A.D.)

Chinese historian during the early Tang dynasty. The author of *Da Tang chuangye qijuzhu* [Court Diary of the Founding of the Great Tang] (621–626), Wen Daya was on Li Yuan's staff in charge of records when the latter revolted against the Sui dynasty in 617. His three-chapter work was a first-hand account of the 357 days of insurrection that culminated in the founding of the Tang dynasty in 618. Its importance lies not only in Wen's privilege as an eyewitness chronicler, but also in the fact that his work was written before the Tang government began to influence the writing of the past by creating the Historiographical Office in 629 under the great Taizong emperor, Li Shimin. The only court diary extant from pre-Qing times, it is now generally considered a reliable source on early Tang history, about which its account differs from the Standard Histories on some crucial issues. For instance, in Wen the decision to revolt was attributed to Li Yuan, whereas traditionally it was credited to the machinations of his second son, Li Shimin. Wan was also considerably more sympathetic to Li Yuan's eldest son, Li Jancheng, who would be murdered in 626 by none other than Li Shimin in the latter's campaign to become the next emperor.

W.K. Cheng

Texts

Da Tang chuangye qijuzhu. Beijing: Zhonghua shuju, 1985.

References

Bingham, Woodbridge. "Wen Ta-ya: The First Recorder of T'ang Dynasty." *Journal of the American Oriental Society* 57 (1937): 368–374.

Tang Changru, ed. *Sui Tang Wudai shi* [History of the Sui, Tang, and Five Dynasties]. Beijing and Shanghai: Zhongguo da baike quanshu chubanshe, 1988.

Twitchett, Denis. *The Writing of Official History under the T'ang.* Cambridge, Eng.: Cambridge University Press, 1992.

Wen Ta-ya

See WEN DAYA.

Wheeler, James Talboys (1824–1897)

British historian of India. Wheeler began his career as a publisher and bookseller before traveling to India in 1858 to become editor of the Madras *Spectator.* He was then appointed professor at Madras Presidency College and employed to examine old Madras records, producing *Annals of the Madras Presidency* (1861) and over ten other books on contemporary Indian affairs and history. He was assistant secretary in the Foreign Department, the Government of India (1862–1870), and secretary to the chief commissioner of British Burma (1870–1873). Wheeler's work was important for the gathering of early data, for the recording of contemporary events, and for his historical works which, although written in the years after the revolt of 1857, and unsympathetic to every epoch of Indian history before the arrival of the British, are an important record of nineteenth-century imperial attitudes.

Roger D. Long

Texts

Annals of the Madras Presidency. 3 vols. Madras: J. Higginbotham, 1861.

Early Records of British India. London: N. Trubner, 1878.

The History of India from the Earliest Ages. 4 vols. London: N. Trubner, 1867–1881.

Madras in the Olden Time, 1639–1748. Madras: J. Higginbotham, 1882.

Memorandum on the Records of the Foreign Department. Calcutta: Foreign Department Press, 1865.

Memorandum on the Records of the Home Department. Calcutta: Home Secretariat Press, 1868.

Summary of Affairs of the Mahratta States, 1627 to 1856. Calcutta: Government Printing Press, 1878.

Wheeler, Sir [Robert Eric] Mortimer (1890–1976)

British archaeologist. A University of London D.Litt., (Brigadier) Mortimer Wheeler served the Royal Field Artillery in both world wars. Between the wars he led excavations of Roman sites in Wales, England (Lydney in Gloucestershire, Verulamium in Hertfordshire, and Maiden Castle in Dorset), and France (Brittany and Normandy). Wheeler devised the grid method of excavation by which a network of cellular squares was employed for intensive digging of complex sites. Later, he reorganized the Archaeological Survey of India and trained an entire cadre of professional archaeologists in the decolonized subcontinent. Wheeler's excavations at Harappa and Mohenjodaro established a new chronology for the Indus valley civilization and determined definitively the identity of several of its principal ruins. His findings of synchronous artifacts at Arikamedu and Brahmagiri confirmed the dates of the megaliths of southern India. Wheeler was remarkable for his extraordinary energy, meticulousness, and diligence in his profession.

Pradip Bhaumik

Texts

Archaeology from the Earth. Baltimore, MD: Penguin, 1966.

Civilizations of the Indus Valley and Beyond. London: Thames and Hudson, 1966.

Early India and Pakistan: To Ashoka. Revised ed. New York: Praeger, 1968.

The Indus Civilization. Third ed. Cambridge, Eng.: Cambridge University Press, 1968.

Rome beyond the Imperial Frontiers. London: Bell, 1954.

References

Clark, Ronald W. *Sir Mortimer Wheeler.* New York: Roy Publishers, 1960.

Hawkes, Jacquetta. *Mortimer Wheeler: Adventurer in Archaeology.* London: Weidenfeld & Nicolson, 1982.

Whig Interpretation of History

Primarily the view that lauds Britain's constitutional development and the emergence of religious and civic liberty; now applied in a more general sense, and derogatively, to any form of anachronistic or present-minded history. The Whig interpretation, in its primary and narrower sense, took shape around 1700 partially as a justification for the Glorious Revolution of 1688. Early Whig historians defended seventeenth-century parliamentary heroes and martyrs and the antiquity of the House of Commons. Narratives by James Tyrrell (1696–1704) and John Oldmixon (1724) suggested how England's foundations of liberty had been protected against power and priestcraft. Paul de Rapin-Thoyras, a French Huguenot, informed foreigners (in a narrative translated into English, 1725–1731) how the maintenance of an old and free Germanic constitution permitted England's rapid rise to world power since 1688. Even though Robert Brady had already unmasked the mythology of constitutional continuity, this Whig interpretation dominated English historiography through the mid-eighteenth century and, through Rapin-Thoyras and anglophile philosophes, influenced continental historiography as well.

The Whig tradition shifted from early vulgar Whiggism, through the skeptical Whiggism of David Hume, to the scientific Whiggism of Thomas Babington Macaulay. Hume's *History of England* (1754–1761) displaced Rapin-Thoyras's in the mid-eighteenth century and remained the dominant narrative for nearly a century. Whigs excoriated Hume for debunking their heroes and the mythical ancient constitution. But although a Tory in sympathies, Hume replaced these elements with his own Whiggish belief in progress. Between 1848 and 1879, Macaulay, Edward Augustus Freeman, and William Stubbs powerfully restated the Whig interpretation. These Victorian Whigs maintained the basic narrative: England had held on more securely to primitive Germanic institutions than had continental Europe; the Glorious Revolution vindicated ancient rights. But they now argued that a free constitution arose slowly only between Magna Carta and 1688. And they emphasized local institutions and long-range social processes rather than parliamentary heroes and individual acts or providence. Macaulay supplanted Hume by wedding Hume's stadial view of material progress to Edmund Burke's praise of England's continuity with its past even in the midst of change. Consensual politicians and moderate public discussion through the Reform Act of 1832 allowed toleration, responsible government, the two-party system, and constitutional monarchy to flourish.

The Whig narrative of liberal development retreated in the 1880s. Historicism, archival research, source-criticism, and professionalization discredited narrative set pieces such as Anglo-Saxon democracy or baronial liberalism under King John. World War I further eroded liberal certainties, and, between the wars, historians began to criticize the Whig interpretation in both its narrow and its generic senses. The most influential critique was a thin volume by Herbert Butterfield, entitled *The Whig Interpretation of History,* which censured the teleological focus on victorious Protestants and Whigs. Butterfield also decried the subordination of the past to the present and the stress on only the origins of contemporary institutions (whether from necessary selection and organization or from a disregard to changing context). Yet, while Butterfield criticized Whig progressivism in 1931, he would come to laud Whig traditionalism in *The Englishman and His History* in 1944 (a paradox explicable by recalling the various strands of Whiggism).

Whig spotting continues. The term is often used to attack historians who: emphasize inevitability (whether because of teleology, anachronism, or a penchant for the new and emerging); who reify developing liberal institutions; or who elevate personal battles to conflicts of principles. But Marxist and social historians have been similarly criticized for projecting onto the past their own ideas of what is important. Perhaps too, the narrative mode of historical writing favored by Whigs necessarily emphasizes continuity and community.

Newton E. Key

References

Blaas, P.B.M. *Continuity and Anachronism.* The Hague and Boston: Nijhoff, 1978.

Burrow, J.W. *A Liberal Descent: Victorian Historians and the English Past.* Cambridge, Eng.: Cambridge University Press, 1981.

Butterfield, Herbert. *The Englishman and His History.* Cambridge, Eng.: Cambridge University Press, 1944.

———. *The Whig Interpretation of History.* London: G. Bell and Sons, 1931.

Pocock, J.G.A. "The Varieties of Whiggism from Exclusion to Reform: A History of Ideology and Discourse." In his *Virtue, Commerce, and History: Essays on Political Thought and History, Chiefly in the Eighteenth Century.* Cambridge, Eng.: Cambridge University Press, 1985, 215–310.

White, Hayden (b. 1928)

American scholar of European historiography and cultural critic. As professor of the history of consciousness at the University of California at Santa Cruz, White has played a leading role since the 1970s in acquainting students of history in the United States with the rhetorical groundwork of historical writing. At a time when most of the efforts of theorists of history have been directed toward establishing history's credentials as a science, White has reexamined and reaffirmed its ancient standing as an art. In this respect, he has carried on the project of the English historicist R.G. Collingwood to explain history as a special kind of science, and so has refuted those analytical philosophers who chide historians for having failed to establish general laws of historical explanation. White contends that the natural sciences committed themselves in the seventeenth century to a particular model of employing scientific understanding. Historians never reached a corresponding consensus, in part because of the variety of rhetorical modes in which great works of history have been written. Historical understanding in its inception, White argues, is an imaginative act, akin to that of poets and novelists.

White's first major work, *Metahistory* (1973), was a comprehensive study of the diverse rhetorical strategies employed by the great nineteenth-century European historians (Jules Michelet, Leopold von Ranke, Alexis de Tocqueville, Jacob Burckhardt) and philosophers of history (G.W.F. Hegel, Karl Marx, Friedrich Nietzsche, Benedetto Croce). He has since elaborated on his thesis in wide-ranging surveys of current issues in contemporary historiography, notably in *The Tropics of Discourse* (1978) and *The Content of the Form* (1987). White's theory of the "deep structure" of historical narrative is very much his own, although he acknowledges an intellectual debt to the literary theorists Northrop Frye and Kenneth Burke and to a lesser extent the French structuralists Roland Barthes, Jacques Derrida, and Michel Foucault.

Probably the most profound influence on his thinking has been the early-eighteenth-century Italian philosopher-historian, Giambattista Vico, whose theory of tropes provides the framework around which White composed *Metahistory.* For Vico, all thought has its sources in the logic of poetry's historically elaborated deep structures, the figures of speech (metaphor, metonymy, synecdoche, irony) that give form to all verbal expression. Following Vico, White argues that a historical work, like any imaginative endeavor, is in its inception a creative act, and that the poetic logic of the trope underpinning its narrative provides the key to its metahistorical identity. In *Metahistory* he types historians according to the tropological mode in which they employ their narrative. Herein he does not wish to reduce history to its rhetoric, or to discredit the importance of research. His point is that historians of necessity adopt models that prefigure the shape of their interpretation. The measure of a great work of history lies not merely in the data presented but in its rhetorical capacity to produce significant meaning.

White amplified his theory in arguing that these metahistorical models mobilize the rhetorical resources with which historians craft their interpretations. He presents these under three classifications: strategies for seeking truth (formism, mechanism, organicism, contextualism); story archetypes (romance, tragedy, comedy, satire); and justifying ideologies (anarchist, conservative, liberal, radical). The combination chosen from among this repertoire of possibilities defines a historian's historiographical style. The writing of a work of history, therefore, involves a dialectical move between imaginative prefiguration and a more reflective configuration of rhetorical possibilities.

For White, history is a highly structured literary form, but one that gives historians the freedom to fashion their own arguments and so to produce their own meanings. There is no right or wrong interpretation, he contends, provided a historian's research is honest. Rather, the quality of their interpretations resides in the depth of meaning their imaginative constructs allow. That is why classics in historical scholarship have been created throughout history, not just with advances in the latest techniques or findings in research. Historical meanings, he explains, are ultimately allegorical; they are of value for what they can tell us about life. For that reason, White concludes, history continues to share with literature a grounding in the poetics of ancient mythology.

Patrick Hutton

Texts

The Content of the Form. Baltimore, MD: Johns Hopkins University Press, 1987.
Metahistory: The Historical Imagination in Nineteenth-Century Europe. Baltimore, MD: Johns Hopkins University Press, 1973.
Tropics of Discourse: Essays in Cultural Criticism. Baltimore, MD: Johns Hopkins University Press, 1978.

References

"*Metahistory:* Six Critiques." *History and Theory* 19 (1980): Beiheft 19.
Jenkins, Keith. *On "What Is History?:" From Carr abd Elton to Roly and White.* London: Routledge, 1995.

Whitelock, Dorothy (1901–1982)

English medievalist. Whitelock was born in Leeds and studied at Cambridge, where she was trained in an interdisciplinary approach that placed the highest value on primary sources. Whitelock went on to become the foremost editor of Anglo-Saxon texts of her generation. Early publications include editions of *Anglo-Saxon Wills* (1930) and Wulfstan's *Sermo Lupi ad Anglos* (1939, rev. ed. 1963). The volume she edited for the series *English Historical Documents, Vol. 1 c. 500–1042* (rev. ed., 1979) is magisterial. Other authoritative editions that constitute her legacy include *Councils and Synods with Other Documents Relating to the English Church, 1, Part 1:871–1066* (1981), a revision of the texts of *Sweet's Anglo-Saxon Reader* (1967), and a translation of the *Anglo-Saxon Chronicle* (1961) that remains standard today. Her work, however, was by no means restricted to texts and translations. Studies and syntheses encompass *The Audience of Beowulf* (1951), *The Beginnings of English Society* (1952), *From Bede to Alfred* (1980), and *History, Law and Literature in 10th–11th Century England* (1981). Whitelock was selected for Cambridge's prestigious Elrington and Bosworth Professorship in 1957; she retired from that chair in 1969 but continued her productive research with little pause until limited by a stroke two years before her death.

Kerry E. Spiers

Texts

Ed. and trans. *The Anglo-Saxon Chronicle.* London: Eyre and Spottiswoode, 1961.
The Audience of Beowulf. Oxford: Clarendon Press, 1951.
The Beginnings of English Society. Harmondsworth: Penguin, 1952.
From Bede to Alfred. London: Variorum Reprints, 1980.
History, Law and Literature in 10th–11th Century England. London: Variorum Reprints, 1981.

Wichit Wathakan [Vichitr Vadhakan] (1898–1962)

Thai historian, author, and politician. Wichit was born into humble circumstances in Uthai Thani province, central Thailand, and educated in Bangkok. As director of the department of fine arts during the 1930s, Wichit produced a series of influential nationalist musical plays, the best known *Lu'at suphan* [The Blood of Suphan] (1936). He was a prominent figure in the military government of Phibun Songkram (1938–1944) and also served as Thailand's ambassador to Japan during World War II. In the immediate postwar period, Wichit left the bureaucracy and pursued a successful career as a novelist and short-story writer. He subsequently returned to government service, where he held a variety of official positions including that of senior personal adviser to Prime Minister Sarit Thanarat. Wichit died in Bangkok in 1962. He is best known as a popular historian and playright; his most famous historical work, the twelve-volume *Prawatisat sakon* [Universal History] was published in 1930.

Scot Barmé

Texts

Thailand's Case. Bangkok: Thai Commercial Press, 1941.

References

Barmé, Scot. *Luang Wichit Wathakan and the Creation of a Thai Identity.* Singapore: Institute of Southeast Asian Studies, 1993.

Thak Chaloemtiarana. *Thailand: The Politics of Despotic Paternalism.* Bangkok: Social Science Association of Thailand, Thai Khadi Institute, Thammasat University, 1979.

Widukind of Corvey (ca. 925–after 973)

German chronicler. The facts of Widukind's life are obscure other than the probability that he became a Benedictine in 940. His Saxon history, completed 967–968, and dedicated to Mathilde, the daughter of Otto the Great, remains the prime source for the reigns of Henry I and Otto I. Especially significant are his descriptions of Otto's coronation and the Battle of Lechfeld (955).

Kerry E. Spiers

Texts

The Three Books of the Deeds of the Saxons. Trans. R. Wood. Ann Arbor, MI: University Microfilms, 1949.

Widukindi monachi Corbeiensis Rerum gestarum Saxonicarum Libri tres. Ed. G. Waitz et al. Fifth ed. *Monumenta Germanicae Historicae, Scriptores.* Hanover: Hahn, 1935.

References

Beumann, Helmut. *Widukind von Korvei.* Weimar: Hermann Böhlaus Nachfolger, 1950.

Brundage, James. "Widukind of Corvey and the Non-Roman Imperial Idea." *Mediaeval Studies* 21 (1960): 15–26.

William of Malmesbury (ca. 1095–1143)

Anglo-Norman monk, librarian, and historian. Born in Wiltshire of Anglo-Saxon and Norman parentage, he entered the abbey of Malmesbury while very young and remained there, excluding intervals of travel, for the remainder of his life. William traveled widely throughout England under the sponsorship of Queen Mathilda in 1115, and later of Robert, earl of Gloucester. On these journeys he collected books and other materials for his abbey's library that were to prove essential sources for his histories of England's ecclesiastical and secular rulers. Unusual among contemporaries for his emphasis on what are now called primary sources, he assembled the comprehensive *Polyhistor,* a collection of documents for students. Both his histories, the *Gesta Regum Anglorum* [Deeds of the Kings of England] and the *Gesta Pontificum Anglorum* [Deeds of the Prelates of England], began to circulate to other monasteries in 1125, although he continued to polish and update them. He also wrote hagiographic accounts and a history of his house, the *Antiquities of Glastonbury.* His activities made Malmesbury's library a major English intellectual center, allowing him to decline the office of abbot in 1140. By 1200 his major histories were among the best-known English histories and as influential as the quasifictitious works of Geoffrey of Monmouth. His sober attention to detail and provision of verifiable source details have ensured an enduring historiographic popularity since the early nineteenth century.

Georges Whalen

Texts

Antiquities of Glastonbury. Ed. and trans. J. Scott. Woodbridge, Suffolk: Boydell and Brewer, 1981.

Historia Novella. Ed. and trans. K.R. Potter. London: Nelson, 1955.

Willelmi Malmesbiriensis monachi De gestis pontificum Anglorum libri quinque. Ed. N.E.S.A. Hamilton. London: Rolls Series, vol. 52, 1870.

Willelmi Malmesbiriensis monachi De gestis regum Anglorum libri quinque; historiae novellae libri tres. Ed. William Stubbs. 2 vols. London: Rolls Series, vol. 90, 1887–1889.

References

Gransden, Antonia. *Historical Writing in England c. 550 to c. 1307.* Ithaca, NY: Cornell University Press, 1974.

Thomson, Rodney M. *William of Malmesbury.* Woodbridge, Eng.: Boydell and Brewer, 1987.

William of Poitiers (fl. 1050–1077)

Norman knight, later ducal chaplain, archdeacon of Lisieux, and historian. The fact that his sister was abbess of the nunnery of Saint-Léger de Préaux suggests that William was of noble origins. The chronicler Orderic Vitalis writes that William attended Poitiers's philosophical schools in the 1040s, after participation in several ducal campaigns. His belated clerical vocation ensured his use of military accounts from the broad range of court contacts accessible to ducal chaplains. In 1073–74, William completed an account of the Norman Conquest of England, presenting the newly ensconced King William I as its hero. The incomplete text, covering the years 1035 to 1067 only, is preserved in a 1619 edition based on a unique manuscript that has itself since been lost, although the history is known to have begun earlier and covered the period up to 1071. He was unable to take the work further although he probably lived into the 1090s, dying before 1101. The influence of William's style and attitudes is recognizable in Orderic's account of the years 1067 to 1072, through close comparison of the texts. William's depiction of events is chronologically closest to that contained in the Bayeux Tapestry.

Georges Whalen

Texts

Histoire de Guillaume le conquérant [History of William the Conqueror]. Ed. and trans. Raymonde Foreville. Paris: Les Belles Lettres, 1952.

References

Dorey, T.A. "William of Poitiers: 'Gesta Gullielmi Ducis.'" In *Latin Historians,* ed. T.A. Dorey. London: Routledge and Kegan Paul, 1966, 139–155.

Foreville, Raymonde. "Aux origines de la renaissance juridique [On the Origins of the Judicial Renaissance]." *Le Moyen Age* 58 (1952): 43–83.

William of Tyre (ca. 1130–ca. 1184)

Cleric, statesman, and historian. William, the son of French or Italian parents, was born in Jerusalem. Little is known of his childhood. When he was about sixteen years old he went to Europe to complete his education for the priesthood, studying the liberal arts, theology, and civil law at the universities of Paris, Orleans, and Bologna. After twenty years he returned to the Crusader Kingdom of Jerusalem, serving as tutor to the future King Baldwin IV and as a diplomat under Baldwin's father, King Amaury. Within a year of Amaury's death in 1174, William was elected archbishop of Tyre and then appointed royal chancellor. He wrote three works: the first two, an account of the Third Lateran Council and a history of the Muslim East from the time of Muḥammad until ca. 1180, are lost. William's surviving work is his *Historia rerum in partibus transmarinis gestarum* [A History of Deeds Done beyond the Sea]. The first eight books of this work are a history of the First Crusade; thereafter he treats the major events in the reigns of each succeeding king of Jerusalem down to 1184. His history draws on a wide range of earlier writers as well as documents and oral tradition and is noted for its critical approach and even-handed treatment of the Muslim world.

Ralph F. Gallucci

Texts

A History of Deeds Done beyond the Sea. Ed. and trans. E.A. Babcock and A.C. Krey. 2 vols. New York: Columbia University Press, 1943.

References

Edbury, Peter W., and John Gordon Rowe. *William of Tyre: Historian of the Latin East.* Cambridge, Eng.: Cambridge University Press, 1988.

Vessey, D.W.T.C. "William of Tyre and the Art of Historiography." *Mediaeval Studies* 35 (1973): 433–455.

Williams, Raymond (1921–1988)

Welsh polymath, known for his studies of modern culture. A humanist Marxist and a committed socialist, Williams emerged from humble origins to become a leading intellectual figure in the New Left in Britain during the 1950s and 1960s. At once a professor, critic, journalist, essayist, dramatist, and novelist, he published some thirty books and hundreds of articles. A veteran of World War II (1941–1945), Williams was educated at Cambridge University (1939–1941, 1945–1946). For many years he taught literature and current affairs in an adult education program sponsored by Oxford University (1946–1961) before returning to Cambridge as a professor of drama (1961–1983). Briefly a member of the Communist Party before the war and later active in the Labour Party (1961–1966), he maintained a lifelong sympathy for Marx's aesthetic vision of an egalitarian society. In his quest to apply Marxist principles to the cultural sphere, he exemplifies the turn of many Marxist intellectuals in western Europe in the mid-twentieth century from economic toward cultural concerns. At the same time, he remained engaged with a tradition of British authors (Matthew Arnold, John Ruskin, Thomas Carlyle, D.H. Lawrence, F.R. Leavis, George Orwell) who like himself envisioned a nobler ideal of what modern, industrial society might be.

Williams's perspective on the history of modern culture is most directly appreciated in two works of his prime: *Culture and Society* (1958) and *The Long Revolution* (1961). In the former, he traced modifications in the use of several "keywords" (industry, democracy, class, art, and culture) as indices of the changing structure of modern industrial society. His interest in the linguistic building blocks of cultural structures and his sensitivity to social "structures of feeling" suggest affinities with the structuralist notions of the French historians of mentalities. Williams posed his conception of culture as a community's entire way of life as an alternative to its traditional identification with intellectual or artistic elites. The culture that he envisaged and worked actively to promote was one based on common participation and mutual responsibility. In the latter, he outlined the "long revolution" through which he believed such a society was being fashioned. Emerging historically on parallel democratic, industrial, and cultural planes, it had been underway in Britain since the eighteenth century, although even there it was far from completion and in many parts of the world barely begun. Herein he was particularly interested in the expansion of public access to education, the media, and the arts in ways that would open the possibility for creative self-realization to all.

Williams's long-range historical perspective on the making of the good society reveals how diffuse the Marxist vision of history had become by the mid-twentieth century. Still, he remained true to Marx in his belief that such a society is worth creating and that in seeking to do so we become aware of our capacity to shape our own destiny.

Patrick Hutton

Texts

Culture and Society, 1780–1950. New York: Columbia University Press, 1958.

The Long Revolution. London: Penguin, 1961.

Marxism and Literature. Oxford: Oxford University Press, 1977.

References

Eagleton, Terry, ed. *Raymond Williams: Critical Perspectives.* Cambridge, Eng.: Polity Press, 1989.

Morgan, W. John, and Peter Preston, eds. *Raymond Williams: Politics, Education, Letters.* New York: St. Martin's Press, 1993.

O'Conner, Alan. *Raymond Williams: Writings, Culture, Politics.* Oxford: Blackwell, 1989.

Williams, William Appleman (1921–1992)

American historian. Williams was born in Atlantic, Iowa, in 1921 and educated at the United States Naval Academy at Annapolis; on leaving the navy he attended the University of Wisconsin, where he received his Ph.D. in 1950 and taught for many years. Williams, who served in 1981 as president of the Organization of American Historians, was the reluctant leader of the so-called Wisconsin school of diplomatic history. While at Wisconsin, he laid the groundwork for a small but influential number of revisionist historians who came to maturity in the 1960s and 1970s. Following his lead, these historians conceived a critique of the United States' external relations as a legitimate vehicle in urging, they hoped, the nonviolent replacement of America's imperial or empire-minded expansionist political economy with a democratic socialism that was economically self-sufficient and politically free from international entanglements such as Vietnam. According to Williams himself, the *Weltanschauung* of the great majority of Americans throughout their history consisted of "having defined everything good in terms of a surplus of property [a belief which originally derived from an earlier abundance of, and relatively easy access to, western lands], the problem . . . [being] one of developing techniques for securing good things from a succession of new frontiers." From the beginning of the republic the seemingly limitless frontier was generally regarded as the principal source of national strength, in that Americans believed "representative government, economic prosperity, and personal happiness . . . depend[ed] on expansion westward." This view of the world, however, contained the seeds of its own weakness and ultimately its own destruction. In regarding the expansion of the frontier as a necessary function and absolute prerequisite both of democracy and capitalism, Americans came to judge "a surplus of property as a substitute for thought about society." The pursuit of such an illusion resulted in the "Great Evasion."

Joseph M. Siracusa

Texts

The Great Evasion. Chicago: Quadrangle Books, 1964.

Empire As a Way of Life. New York: Oxford University Press, 1980.

The Tragedy of American Diplomacy. Revised and expanded ed. New York: Dell, 1962.

References

Abelove, Henry, et al., eds. *Visions of History.* New York: Pantheon, 1976.

Siracusa, Joseph M. *New Left Diplomatic Histories and Historians: The American Revisionists.* Second ed. Claremont, CA: Regina Books, 1993.

Winckelmann, Johann Joachim (1717–1768)

Art historian. The son of a shoemaker, Winckelmann was born in the town of Stendal in Prussia. His teachers recognized his intelligence, and he was encouraged to study theology. His passion, however, was for Greek and Roman antiquity, and he left his theological studies to become a librarian near the Saxon capital of Dresden. His most important and influential work, *Geschichte der Kunst des Altertums* [History of Ancient Art] (1764), revolutionized art history by emphasizing the work of art itself, rather than the artist. Instead of biographies of artists and enumerations of their work (as in the tradition of Renaissance writers such as Georgio Vasari), Winckelmann stressed the evolution of styles and periodization, and how they reflected the social and cultural contexts in which they developed. His work not only defined the discipline of art history but also initiated the revival of the cult of antiquity and neoclassicism. He was a harsh critic of the domination of baroque and rococo styles in Germany and advocated a return to the classical Greek conception of beauty and the ideal, pure form.

John R. Hinde

Texts

The History of Ancient Art. Trans. G.H. Lodge. 4 vols. Boston: J.R. Osgood, 1873.
Writings on Art. Ed. David Irwin. London: Phaidon, 1972.

References

Leppmann, Wolfgang. *Winckelmann.* New York: Alfred Knopf, 1970.

Windelband, Wilhelm (1848–1915)

German philosopher and historian of philosophy. Born in Potsdam, Windelband graduated from the Potsdam gymnasium before attending the universities of Jena, Berlin, and Göttingen, completing his doctorate in 1870 at the latter university under Rudolf Hermann Lotze, one of the first German thinkers of his generation to voice the slogan: "Back to Kant!" This expressed a desire to subject the foundations of knowledge to rational criticism as well as to abandon the metaphysical orientation of earlier idealists. Windelband would pursue that project in the domain of historical epistemology. After service in the Franco-Prussian War, he returned to Göttingen, later holding positions at Zurich, Freiburg im Breisgau, Strasbourg, and Heidelberg. At Heidelberg Windelband and his student, Heinrich Rickert, formed the Baden or Southwestern school of Neo-Kantian philosophy. He was a major participant in the theoretical disputes of his time over the intellectual status of history. Windelband and his Neo-Kantian colleagues came out strongly against positivism, which to them meant the inappropriate intrusion of science into human studies. His 1894 rectorial address at Strasbourg, "History and Natural Science," was an early shot in the later "Battle of Methods." Windelband's position was summed up in his famous distinction between the ideographic (descriptive) and nomothetic (generalizing) treatment of phenomena. Humanistic disciplines like history describe individual events in their particularity. Science, in contrast, seeks general laws for which individual events are particular instances. History differs from science also in assigning values or meaning to events through the operation of our normative or value-giving consciousness. Windelband's transcendental normative consciousness was his answer to the problem of relativism raised by historicism.

Thomas E. Willey

Texts

A History of Philosophy. Trans. James Tufts. 2 vols. New York: Harper and Brothers, 1958.
"History and Natural Science: Rectorial Address, Strasbourg, 1894." Trans. Guy Oakes. *History and Theory* 19 (1980): 165–185.
Theories in Logic. Trans. James Tufts. New York: Philosophical Library, 1961.

References

Willey, Thomas E. *Back to Kant: The Revival of Kantianism in German Social and Historical Thought, 1860–1914.* Detroit: Wayne State University Press, 1978.

Wipo of Burgundy (990/1000–after 1046)

Court chaplain, poet, and biographer. All that is known of Wipo derives from his own writings. He was born in the German-speaking area of Burgundy and received a relatively good education in the pagan and Christian classics. He came to Germany under Emperor Henry II and was present at the election of Emperor Conrad II (r. 1024–1039). His official post was that of court chaplain to Conrad, but he claims that poor health often prevented him from officiating. He accompanied the emperor on his expedition against Burgundy in the winter of 1033 and on his campaign against the Slavs in 1035. Wipo may have served as tutor to

Henry III and was present at Henry's imperial coronation in 1046. His only surviving prose work is his *Gesta Chuonradi II Imperatoris* [Deeds of the Emperor Conrad II], composed probably in 1045–1046 and covering the reigns of Conrad and Henry to that time. It is a generally reliable account and one of the best of the few early medieval biographies of laymen. Although Wipo praises Conrad's piety, he is not afraid to disagree with the emperor on ecclesiastical matters. Wipo was also the author of four extant poems, including the "Proverbia" (1028) dedicated to Henry III, a lament for the death of Conrad appended to the *Gesta*, and the hymn *Victimae paschali laudes* [Praises of the paschal victim], which became part of the Easter liturgy.

Monica Sandor

Texts

Imperial Lives and Letters of the Eleventh Century. Trans. T.E. Mommsen and K.F. Morrison. New York: Columbia University Press, 1962.

Wiponis Opera. Ed. Harry Bresslau. *Monumenta Germaniae Historica: Scriptores rerum Germanicarum,* new series, 61. Hanover and Leipzig: Hahnsche Buchhandlung, 1915.

References

Pertz, G.H. *Über Wipos Leben und Schriften* [Wipo's Life and Works]. Berlin: Abhandlungen der Berliner Akademie, 1851.

Smalley, Beryl. *Historians in the Middle Ages.* London: Thames and Hudson, 1974.

Witt, Henriette Elizabeth Guizot de (1829–1908)

French historian. De Witt, the eldest daughter of the French historian and politician François Guizot, was born in Paris. Her mother, Élisa Dillon, who had penned a French history for children, died when Henriette was very young, and her father and grandmother educated her with historical readings. Henriette grew up in Paris where her father held office during the reign of Louis Philippe and accompanied her father when he was exiled to England during the 1848 revolution. She married Conrad de Witt and wrote several novels before her death. Historiographically, de Witt is best known for finishing her father's work. She edited volumes six through eight of Guizot's *L'histoire de France depuis 1789 jusqu'en 1848* [The History of France from 1789 to 1848]

(1872–1883) and documented the family's history in *Monsieur Guizot in Private Life, 1787–1874* (1882). She completed the work to correct misconceptions of her father's motives and to provide insight into his private persona. De Witt hoped that her historical "lessons will not be without fruit for the new generation[s]." She also aided the advancement of women's history with *Les Femmes dans l'histoire* [Women in History] (1889), a work that emphasized the importance of women's roles in civilization, and compiled several collections of letters and memoirs of interest to French historians.

Elizabeth D. Schafer

Texts

Les bourgeois de Calais. Paris: May et Motteroz, 1890.

Les Femmes dans l'histoire. Paris: Hachette, 1888.

L'histoire de France depuis 1789 jusqu'en 1848. Paris: Hachette, 1875–1876.

Ed. François Guizot. *L'histoire de France depuis 1789 jusqu'en 1848, racontée à mes petits-enfants* [History of France from 1789 to 1848, As Told to My Grandchildren]. 2 vols. Paris: Hachette, 1880.

Ed. *Lettres de M. Guizot à sa famille et à ses amis* [Monsieur Guizot's Letters to His Family and Friends]. Paris: Hachette, 1884.

Monsieur Guizot in Private Life, 1787–1874. Trans. M.C.M. Simpson. London: Hurst and Blackett, 1880.

Motherless; or, A Parisian Family. New York: Harper & Brothers, 1871.

References

Johnson, Douglas. *Guizot: Aspects of French History 1787–1874.* Toronto and London: University of Toronto Press, 1963.

Wittfogel, Karl (1896–1988)

German social historian. Born in Germany, Wittfogel earned his doctorate from the University of Frankfurt. After time in a concentration camp as a communist critic of Hitler, he undertook research in the United States. A controversial scholar, Wittfogel is best known for elaborating Karl Marx's concept of an Asiatic mode of production in terms of dependence on large-scale hydraulic engineering. Wittfogel sought a universal "scientific" explanation of the relations between the natural environment, society, and the means of production, which would adequately account for Asiatic social formation. His groundbreaking early work on China (1931) set out his concept of despotic power, wielded through a centralized ruling bureaucracy that managed, but did not own, the means of production. Later, taking a strongly antitotalitarian stance, he applied these themes to other non-European traditional societies, in *Oriental Despotism,* and then to modern communist industrial states. Other scholars have argued that in many despotic hydraulic societies, particularly on the Indian subcontinent, social structure was fragmented rather than centralized and the nature of power more charismatic than bureaucratic. Wittfogel's characterization of Chinese society as "hydraulic" has also been contested.

Rosemary Gray Trott

Texts

With Fen Chiasheng et. al. *History of Chinese Society: Liao (907–1125).* New York: American Philosophical Society, 1949.

Oriental Despotism. New Haven, CT: Yale University Press, 1957.

Wirtschaft und Gesellschaft Chinas [Economy and Society of China]. Leipzig: C.L. Hirschfeld, 1931.

References

O'Leary, Brendan. *The Asiatic Mode of Production: Oriental Despotism, Historical Materialism and Indian History.* Oxford: Blackwell, 1989.

Ulmen, G.L. *The Science of Society: Towards an Understanding of the Life and Work of Karl August Wittfogel.* The Hague: Mouton, 1978.

Wolf, Friedrich August [Christian Wilhelm Friedrich August] (1759–1824)

German classical scholar. Wolf was born at Hainrode, south of the Harz, and matriculated at the University of Göttingen in 1777, where he insisted on entering himself as a "student of philology." In 1783 he became professor of philosophy and Pädagogik at the University of Halle, where he started a philological seminar to train classical teachers and lectured until the closure of the university in 1806. Thereafter he lived in Berlin, jointly founding the periodical *Museum der Altertumswissenschaft.* He died at Marseilles. Wolf's unified conception of classical studies was expressed by his coinage, *Altertumswissenschaft*

[Knowledge of Antiquity]. His most famous work, the enormously influential *Prolegomena ad Homerum* (1795), was originally intended to introduce a revision of his edition of Homer (1784–1785). In fact, it set in motion the so-called Homeric question. Wolf contended that the Homeric poems were composed orally, by many authors, and only combined much later: reconstructing an original text was thus impossible. Many of the ideas were not new, but the rigor of the argumentation was revolutionary. Wolf also published editions of various classical texts, including Plato's *Symposium* (1782), Hesiod's *Theogony* (1783), and Herodian (1792).

Richard Fowler

Texts

Prolegomena to Homer, 1795. Trans. A. Grafton, G.W. Most, and J.E.G. Zetzel. Princeton, NJ: Princeton University Press, 1985.

References

Pfeiffer, R. *History of Classical Scholarship from 1300 to 1850.* Oxford: Clarendon Press, 1976, 173–177.

Wölfflin, Heinrich (1864–1945)

Swiss art historian. Wölfflin was born in Winterthur, lived in Germany from 1875 to 1882, and returned to Switzerland to study at the University of Basel under Jacob Burckhardt. In 1893, he succeeded Burckhart as professor of art history. He also taught in Berlin (1901–1912), Munich (1912–1924), and Zurich (1924–1934), where he died. He became one of the founders of modern art history with *Renaissance und Barock* (1888) and *Die klassische Kunst* [Classic Art] (1899), which prepared the ground for his most influential work, *Kunstgeschichtliche Grundbegriffe: Das Problem der Stilentwicklung in der Neueren Kunst* (1915) [Principles of Art History]. Influenced by Burckhardt's belief that art has its own life and history, Wölfflin formulated a method of classifying art according to five principles of comparison: linear versus painterly qualities; plane versus recession; closed versus open form; multiplicity versus unity; and clearness versus unclearness. With this method of formal analysis of the creative process Wölfflin explained the historical evolution of styles from one period to the next. Wölfflin also wrote on subjects such as Albrecht Dürer and Michelangelo. His *Kleine Schriften (1885–1933)* [Short Writings] was published in 1946.

Elvy Setterqvist O'Brien

Texts

Classic Art. Trans. Peter and Linda Murray. Fifth ed. London: Phaidon, 1994.

Principles of Art History: The Problem of the Development of Style in Later Art. Trans. M.D. Hottinger. New York: Dover Publications, 1932.

Renaissance and Baroque. Trans. Kathrin Simon. London: Collins, 1964.

References

Kultermann, Udo. *The History of Art History.* Pleasantville, NY: Abaris Books, 1993.

Lurz, Meinhold. *Heinrich Wölfflin: Biographie einer Kunsttheorie.* Worms: Werner, 1981.

Wolpert, Stanley Albert (b. 1927)

American historian of India. Born in New York, Wolpert studied marine engineering before sailing to India, which he saw for the first time just after Gandhi's assassination. Falling under the spell of Indian civilization, he returned to the United States to study its history, receiving his Ph.D. from the University of Pennsylvania in 1959. Among his other activities, Wolpert has been a novelist. As a historian, he has made a number of contributions to Indian historiography. His *Tilak and Gokhale* (1962) became a classic of the early nationalist movement, and he followed that with over a dozen other books, including the renowned *Nine Hours to Rama* (1962), *Jinnah of Pakistan* (1984), and *Zulfi Bhutto of Pakistan* (1993). In his biographies he looks at his subjects from a variety of perspectives, including the psychological. His *New History of India,* a comprehensive history of the subcontinent written in the tradition of J. Talboys Wheeler and Vincent Smith, is the most widely used survey of the history of India.

Roger D. Long

Texts

Jinnah of Pakistan. New York: Oxford University Press, 1984.

Morley and India 1906–1910. Berkeley: University of California Press, 1967.

A New History of India. Fourth ed. New York: Oxford University Press, 1993.

Tilak and Gokhale: Revolution and Reform in the Making of Modern India. Berkeley: University of California Press, 1962.

Zulfi Bhutto of Pakistan: His Life and Times. New York: Oxford University Press, 1993.

Women's History—African

Subfield of African history and women's studies beginning in the 1970s. African women's history grew out of the resurgence of Western feminism in conjunction with the U.S. civil rights movement of the 1960s and the establishment of African history as a field focused upon the history of Africans (rather than of European imperial history) in the 1960s, combined with the explosion of interest in social and economic history in the 1970s. Until that point scholarly interest in African women was confined mainly to anthropological works in which their roles were embedded in descriptions of marriage customs, fertility rituals, witchcraft, and domestic labor. Male dominance and/or exclusivity was assumed, along with housewifery as women's chief occupation. In the 1960s, however, a scattering of works appeared by such authors as Suzanne Comhaire-Sylvain, H.J. Simons, and Mary Smith. More concentrated attention to African women's history developed in the 1970s, arising partly from Ester Boserup's, *Woman's Role in Economic Development* (1970), which critiqued the impact of colonialism on African women and the introduction of more sophisticated technology, while pointing out the importance of their agricultural activities as producers of most of Africa's food crops. Some of the first systematic attempts to develop African women's history found expression in two collections edited by Nancy Hafkin and Edna Bay in 1975–1976. The contributors emphasized the interplay of economics and social organization as they discussed changes in women's roles in politics, religion, marriage, and other realms, especially in response to colonialism.

Since 1976 more than a hundred articles and more than sixty monographs have appeared on the subject of women in Africa, many of which are explicitly historical and most of which have historical implications. The field has assumed prominence within African history as one of its most innovative areas, garnering four African Studies Association Herskovits Book Awards since 1979, an unusually high representation from one field within African studies as a whole. Most of the work is strongly interdisciplinary with extensive cross-fertilization from social, economic, and symbolic anthropology, linguistics, sociology, political science, and, more recently, literature, and literary criticism. As women's studies has developed as a discipline in the 1970s and 1980s and African women themselves have become more involved in scholarly activities, there has been more interaction through conferences to create an international feminist agenda that has had an impact on African women's history, which remains *histoire engagée* committed to improving the situation of African women and therefore less abstract than some contemporary strains of feminism. There are strong links to the rapidly expanding field of women in development (WID).

Following Boserup and Hafkin and Bay, the dominant trend in African women's history in the 1970s and 1980s involved economizing relationships. In contrast to the earlier structural–functionalist view that stressed the complementarity of women's and men's roles in "traditional" African societies, historians of African women stressed advantages and disadvantages for women and men deriving from socioeconomic structure, effectively disaggregating the household. Unlike historians and anthropologists of Western women who divided the world into the public and the private and claimed that women's disabilities in terms of power and authority as well as law derived from confinement to the private sphere, historians of African women found little distinction between private and public spheres in most African societies. They broadened the areas of study into politics and the state, as well as the economy. Popular subjects included the important roles of African women in slavery as owners and as slaves, the effects of colonialism and absorption into the world capitalist economy, the relationship between women's productive and reproductive labor, the effects on women, and participation of women in, changing modes of production, gender stratification in relation to class formation before, during, and after colonialism, and the mutability of colonial legal forms as they affected women. In studies of changing marriage forms scholars discovered the fallacy of assuming that Africans had adopted Western forms without making critical modifications. Political perspectives included a focus on dual-sex political systems and women's activism. In the best work the tension between views of women as victims of male manipulations and as determiners of their own fate is evident. Some questioned the simple equation of male dominance with female exploitation and suggested complexities in the relationship of gender to class formation by looking critically at female hierarchies within family structure, trade, and slavery.

The influence of international feminism and the perspectives of African women themselves are evident in the 1980s in the greater attention given to women's agency and to issues such as genital mutilation of women (clitoridectomy and infibulation practiced widely in Sudan, Egypt, and Somalia, and among certain societies elsewhere).

The focus on women's agency has meant emphasis on women's solidarity, embodied in such works as Margaret Strobel's *Muslim Women in Mombasa, 1890–1975* (1979), Claire Robertson's *Sharing the Same Bowl* (1984), Luise White's *Comforts of Home* (1990), and Megan Vaughan and Henrietta L. Moore's *Cutting Down Trees* (1994), whose diversity in terms of topics (religion, dance groups, trade, prostitution, agriculture, and environment) conveys the richness of women's experiences. A focus on genital mutilation of women relates to a feminist concern about women's control over their own bodies. Scholars have explained its origins, its societal contexts, and its role in affirming female solidarity and hierarchy as well as patriarchal values, and agreed on the desirability of its abolition. African women scholars have been concerned about both widespread exaggeration of its incidence and cultural imperialism by Westerners, and the popularization and misrepresentation of the issue in writings and film by Alice Walker and Fran Hosken, which have strongly influenced U.S. feminist views. Africa's precolonial and colonial past continues to influence present perspectives on both sides of the ocean. Because of the vastness and diversity of Africa as a continent, scholars are wary of generalization and many key works consist of collections of topically akin articles. The awareness of diversity in turn gave many African, African American, and Africanist scholars a strong role in furthering and broadening concepts of multicultural education.

Contemporary trends include an increased influence of symbolic anthropology and of postmodernism, in which particular attention is paid to the construction of gender, presaged by Francille Wilson's 1984 article, "Reinventing the Past and Circumscribing the Future: *Authenticité* and the Negative Image of Women's Work in Zaire." Changes in the construction of gender in Africa are becoming of interest. The disaggregation of the household and the state with gender in mind is a trend. So also is material culture, especially as it relates to women's roles in environmental catastrophe and renewal, and agricultural history. The state as a gendered institution is receiving continual attention. The strong concern of historians with promoting women's empowerment and economic well-being continues in works aimed not only at establishing the past in terms of women's experiences but also at improving the present. African women's history has been influenced by its origins and goals, and has led the way in innovations in African history.

Claire C. Robertson

See also AFRICAN HISTORIOGRAPHY; WOMEN'S HISTORY—EAST ASIAN AND SOUTHEAST ASIAN, ETC.

References

Afonja, Simi. "Changing Modes of Production and the Sexual Division of Labor among the Yoruba." *Signs* 7 (1981): 299–313.

Aidoo, Agnes A. "Asante Queen Mothers in Government and Politics in the Nineteenth Century." In *The Black Woman Cross-Culturally,* ed. F.C. Steady. Cambridge, MA: Schenkman, 1982, 65–77.

Bay, Edna, ed. *Women and Work in Africa.* Boulder, CO: Westview, 1982.

Berger, Iris. *Threads of Solidarity: Women in South African Industry, 1900–1980.* Bloomington: Indiana University Press, 1992.

Hay, Margaret J., and Marcia Wright, eds. *African Women and the Law: Historical Perspectives.* Boston: Boston University African Studies Center, 1982.

Johnson-Odim, Cheryl. "Women in Anti-Colonial Activity in Southwestern Nigeria." *African Studies Review* 25 (1982): 137–158.

Manikom, Linzi. "Ruling Relations: Rethinking State and Gender in South African History." *Journal of African History* 33 (1992): 441–465.

Mann, Kristin. *Marrying Well: Marriage, Status and Social Change among the Educated Elite in Colonial Lagos.* Cambridge, Eng.: Cambridge University Press, 1985.

Marks, Shula. *Nursing and the Construction of Apartheid: Black Women in White.* New York: St. Martin's Press, 1994.

Muntemba, Maud. "Women and Agricultural Change in the Railway Region of Zambia: Dispossession and Counterstrategies, 1930–1970." In *Women and Work in Africa,* ed. Bay. Boulder, CO: Westview, 1982, 83–104.

Newbury, Catherine. "Ebutumwa Bw'emiogo, The Tyranny of Cassava: A Tax Revolt in Zaire." *Canadian Journal of African Studies* 18 (1984): 35–54.

Parpart, Jane L., and Kathleen Staudt, eds. *Women and the State in Africa.* Boulder: Lynn Rienner, 1989.

Robertson, Claire C., and Iris Berger, eds. *Women and Class in Africa.* New York: Africana, 1986.

————, and Martin A. Klein, eds. *Women and Slavery in Africa.* Madison: University of Wisconsin Press, 1983.

Schmidt, Elizabeth. *Peasants, Traders and Wives. Shona Women in the History of Zimbabwe, 1870–1939.* Portsmouth, NH: Heinemann, 1992.

Wilson, Francille. "Reinventing the Past and Circumscribing the Future: *Authenticité* and the Negative Image of Women's Work in Zaire." In *Women and Work in Africa,* ed. Bay. Boulder, CO: Westview, 1982, 153–170.

Women's History—East Asian and Southeast Asian

Historiography with women and women's roles in society as its subject, with specific focus on China, Japan, Korea, Hong Kong, and Taiwan (for East Asia), and Indonesia, Malaysia, the Philippines, Singapore, Thailand, Vietnam, and so forth (for Southeast Asia). Much of the scholarship in this field is concentrated on the nineteenth and twentieth centuries. Asian women's history emerged as a research field over the last twenty to thirty years and is generally informed by feminist theory in method and approach. The historiography of women in east Asia and Southeast Asia is a rethinking of the social, political, and cultural histories of these regions in terms of asymmetries between men and women and, more fundamentally, the relation between gender and sociocultural norms and practices. There tends to be a critical focus on patriarchal society, commonly elaborated through an examination of various inequalities encountered by women in the indigenous sociocultural context and as a result of collusion between Western colonizing powers and indigenous governments.

For periods preceding the nineteenth century, the historiographical corpus is largely confined to China and Japan. The focus here is on Confucian patriarchy and the impact of its ideology, reified as law and orthodoxy, on the lives of women in medieval and late imperial China and Japan. (The Confucian ideal of women, as prescribed by the Confucian orthodoxies of both traditional China and Japan, was one of complete obedience and submission to men.) Such scholarship thus analyzes the social, political, and economic disempowerment of women in Asian patriarchal societies and reexamines, in this context, the problem of women's relative insignificance in existing historical representations of these societies. Thus, this mode of historiography seeks less to create a separate "women's history" or to "fill the historiographical gap" on women than to deal with the fundamental question of women's subordination. Very little is available on women's history predating the nineteenth century for southeast Asia.

Women's history of the nineteenth and twentieth centuries dominates this form of historiography, particularly in relation to the issues of nationalism, women's emancipation, women's rights and identity politics. The political domination and colonization of much of Asia by Western imperialist powers over the last 150 years was accompanied by the spread of modern Western thought and the influence of Western metropolitan cultures. By the 1920s, the emancipation of women was already being publicized by many Asian (male) political leaders as a key reform issue in an "oppressive and backward" traditional Asia. Women's subordination was also a common theme in the then emergent literatures of resistance and nationalism and was viewed, in many instances, as a symbolic representation of the political powerlessness of the colonized in relation to their Western colonizers.

It was in the struggles for national independence across Southeast Asia and east Asia that the first Asian women's movements were established. Remarkable women such as Raden Adjeng Kartini (1879–1904) of Indonesia, Qiu Jin (1875–1907) of China, and Kanno Suga (1881–1911) of Japan spoke out against the discrimination and subordination of women and initiated movements aimed at freeing women from restrictions imposed by traditional Asian laws and customs. It is important to note that these prominent historical individuals tended to be members of the local elite in their communities. The idea of democratic rights, for instance, a woman's right to be educated, could have been sustained only within these Westernized and/or Western-educated circles. Thus, histories of modern Asian women have tended on the whole to focus on the biographies of elite women and their political and cultural activities. Archival and other historical documents on Asian women in this early modern period tend also to reflect this bias.

In recent years, this imbalance has been addressed through a critique of the essentializing of "woman" at the expense of individual women's lives, lived plurally. Much of this new critical direction has come from south Asian women's history, where groundbreaking theoretical work has been done on women's history in the Third World and/or postcolonial context. Overall, however, it is still the work of feminist scholars of Western women's history that has exercised the greatest influence on recent publication in east Asian and Southeast Asian women's histories.

Gloria Davies

See also FEMINISM; GENDER; PATRIARCHY; WOMEN'S HISTORY—AFRICAN, EASTERN EUROPEAN, INDIAN AND PAKISTANI, LATIN AMERICAN, NORTH AMERICAN, WESTERN EUROPEAN.

Texts

Allison, Encarnacion. *The Filipino Woman, Her Social Economic and Political Status 1565–1933.* Manila: University of the Philippines Press, 1934.

Bernstein, Gail Lee, ed. *Recreating Japanese Women 1600–1945.* Berkeley: University of California Press, 1991.

Gilmartin, Christina K., et al., eds. *Engendering China: Women, Culture and the State.* Cambridge, MA: Harvard University Press, 1994.

Jayawardena, Kumari. *Feminism and Nationalism in the Third World.* London: Zed Books, 1986.

Johnson-Odim, Cheryl, and Margaret Strobel, eds. *Expanding the Boundaries of Women's History: Essays on Women in the Third World.* Bloomington: Indiana University Press, 1992.

Kartini, Raden Adjeng. *Letters of a Javanese Princess.* Ed. Hildred Geertz and trans. Agnes Lousie Symmers. New York: W.W. Norton, 1964.

Kumar, Nita, ed. *Women As Subjects: South Asian Histories.* Charlottesville, VA: University Press of Virginia, 1994.

Offen, Karen, Ruth Roach Pierson, and Jane Rendall, eds. *Writing Women's History: International Perspectives.* London: Macmillan, 1991.

Vreede-de Stuers, Cora. *The Indonesian Woman: Struggles and Achievements.* The Hague: Mouton, 1960.

Watson, Rubie S., and Patricia Buckley Ebrey, eds. *Marriage and Inequality in Chinese Society.* Berkeley: University of California Press, 1991.

Women's History—Eastern European

Historical works about women in Eastern Europe, Russia, and the former Soviet Union. While autobiographies, biographies, and literary works by women have been common in this area, monographs in significant number are relatively recent. The largest number of works have been about Russian women. Most of these books and articles have been written about women in the period from the emancipation of the serfs in 1861 to the end of the 1920s. Among those that have contributed to our understanding of women's lives, the following are especially helpful: Linda Edmondson's book and articles about feminism in Russia; Richard Stites's articles and comprehensive survey of all branches of the women's liberation movement; Rose Glickman's accounts of female factory workers and peasant women healers; David Ransel's studies of the family and foundling care in Imperial Russia; biographies of the scientist and writer Sofia Kovalevskaia by Ann Hibner Koblitz, of the Bolshevik activist Alexandra Kollontai by Barbara Evans Clements, Beatrice Farnsworth, and Cathy Porter, and of Inessa Armand by R.C. Elwood; Laura Engelstein's portrait of turn-of-the-century images of sexuality; Wendy Goldman's and Elizabeth Woods's surveys of the theory and practice of the Bolshevik sexual revolution; and Elizabeth Waters's work on images of women in the Soviet and post-Soviet periods. Barbara Alpern Engel is noteworthy for the range of her work on women revolutionaries, members of the intelligentsia, mothers and daughters, and peasants and working women, and also for her attempts to develop a theory of women's activism in this period. Although the worlds of history and literature have too often been separate, Vera Dunham and Barbara Heldt have been successful in bridging the gap: Dunham in her study of Stalinist images of women, and Heldt in her groundbreaking *Terrible Perfection,* especially in her analysis of women's memoir literature.

On the later Soviet period, Gail Warshofsky Lapidus's survey *Women in Soviet Society;* the studies of women's economic position by Alistair McAuley, Joel Moses, and Michael Paul Sacks; the work of Susan Bridger on women and agriculture; Mary Buckley on Soviet politics; Laura Attwood on sex roles; and Tatyana Mamonova on Soviet feminism have been notable.

The medieval and early modern periods in Russia have been less studied. Significant work has been done by Eve Levin with her study of sex and society in medieval Russia and by Ann Kleimola, Dan Kaiser, and Nancy Kollmann concerning medieval law and society. The role of religion in women's lives has received even less attention, though Brenda Meehan, known for her innovative article comparing Russian and Western attitudes toward female rulers at the time of Catherine the Great, has also contributed pioneering studies of prominent religious women in *Holy Women of Russia,* and Joanna Hubbs has pointed to the strength of the pagan tradition in mother Russia.

Non-Russian women in the former Soviet Union have received far less attention than have their Russian counterparts. Martha Bohachevsky-Chomiak's *Feminists Despite Themselves: Women in Ukrainian Community Life, 1884–1939* is a comprehensive survey of the topic with a good deal of general information about Ukrainian women in that period. Christine Worobec's work includes studies of both Russian and Ukrainian peasant women. Stephania Halychyn sheds some light on the neglected subjects of Ukrainian women in the labor camps and during the 1930s famine. Rosalind Marsh's collection of papers from the Harrogate conference about Ukrainian women will add to the slim literature in this field. R. Aminova and Gregory Massell have contributed valuable studies of central Asian women as a "surrogate proletariat" and of Bolshevik efforts to emancipate them. Valentina Bodrova and Richard Anker compare fertility data in most of eastern Europe, Uzbekistan, and Cuba. Studies of women in the Caucasus, however, remain to be written.

The literature on women in the other parts of eastern Europe is also thin, and consists primarily of memoirs and political histories. Sharon Wolchik and Alfred G. Meyer's *Women, State and Party in Eastern Europe* is a good survey for the Communist and pre-Communist periods. On Romanian women, Mary Ellen Fischer has surveyed political developments and Gail Kligman has studied peasant rituals and traditions in Transylvania. On women in the former Czechoslovakia, Alena Heitlinger, Karen Johnson Freeze, Hilda Scott, and Sharon Wolchik have contributed important work. Memoir literature includes Heda Margolius Kovaly's chronicle of her survival through the Holocaust and Communist purges, Eva Kanturkova's account of her detention in a Czech prison, and Rosemary Kavan's description of her life in Prague. For women in the former Yugoslavia, Mary Reed has studied Croatian women in the interwar period, and Susan Woodward, Vida Tomsic, and Silva Meznaric have each studied women in the Communist period; Slavenka Draculic has written her memoirs about this period. Ivan and Nancy Volgyes have contributed to the study of women in Hungary as have Robert McIntyre's analyses of the Communist government's population policies, and Zsuzsa Ferge's observations about Hungarian attempts at social engineering in relation to work and the family. Studies of Polish women include work by Aleksandra Jasinska and Renata Siemienska on the "socialist personality," and by Barbara Wolfe Jancar on dissident women.

Jews were a significant minority in all the countries of pre-Holocaust Eastern Europe. Jewish women were often prominent in social movements, both secular and sectarian, particularly from the late nineteenth century to World War II. Memoirs and monographs chronicle the lives of such activists as Eva Broido, Lidia Dan, Esther Frumkin, Gesia Gelfman, Anna Kuliscioff, and Rosa Luxemburg. Noteworthy in this regard is Naomi Shepherd's *Price below Rubies: Jewish Women As Rebels and Radicals* (1993). Women's Holocaust memoirs are appearing in increasing numbers, as survivors near the end of their lives and wish to leave a testament to the horrors they witnessed. Autobiographies and biographies of partisans and fighters such as Chaika Grossman, Vladka Meed, and Hannah Senesh; of those who passed as Aryans, like Bianca Rosenberg; of camp survivors such as Gerda Weissmann Klein; and testimony collected by Jehoshua and Anna Eibeshitz and Vera Laska are all part of this growing literature. More attention is now being paid to the Yiddish-speaking culture that flourished before the Holocaust. *Found Treasures,* a recent anthology of writing by Yiddish women writers, is the most complete to date. *Life Is with People* is still the most comprehensive description of a Jewish small town/village *(shtetl).*

For the most part these books and articles have served to make the lives and accomplishments of women visible; more of this important work needs to be done before any meaningful theoretical constructs can be developed.

Rochelle Goldberg Ruthchild

See also FEMINISM; GENDER; PATRIARCHY; WOMEN'S HISTORY—AFRICAN, EAST AND SOUTHEAST ASIAN, INDIAN AND PAKISTANI, LATIN AMERICAN, NORTH AMERICAN, WESTERN EUROPEAN.

References

Atkinson, D., A. Dallin, and G.W. Lapidus, eds. *Women in Russia.* Stanford, CA: Stanford University Press, 1977.

Bohachevsky-Chomiak, Martha. *Feminists Despite Themselves: Women in Ukrainian Community Life, 1884–1939.* Edmonton: Canadian Institute of Ukrainian Studies, University of Alberta, 1988.

Edmondson, Linda H. *Feminism in Russia, 1900–17.* London and Exeter, NH: Heinemann Educational, 1984.

———. ed. *Women and Society in Russia and the Soviet Union.* Cambridge, Eng., and New York: Cambridge University Press, 1992.

Lapidus, Gail Warshofsky. *Women in Soviet Society: Equality, Development, and Social Change.* Berkeley: University of California Press, 1978.

Nelson, Barbara J., and Nadjma Chowdhury, eds. *Women and Politics Worldwide.* New Haven, CT: Yale University Press, 1994.

Stites, Richard. *The Women's Liberation Movement in Russia: Feminism, Nihilism, and Bolshevism, 1860–1930.* Revised ed. Princeton, NJ: Princeton University Press, 1991.

Wolchik, Sharon, and Alfred G. Meyer. *Women, State, and Party in Eastern Europe.* Durham, NC: Duke University Press, 1985.

Yedlin, Tova. *Women in Eastern Europe and the Soviet Union.* New York: Praeger, 1980.

Women's History—Indian and Pakistani

Form of history with women as specific subjects rather than discussed incidentally, developed as a coherent field in south Asia since the 1970s. Studies of the role and status of women in India and Pakistan have until recently been fragmentary; although contributions to scholarship have been published since the last century, they were never perceived as forming a coherent theme in historiography and were not integrated into general histories. However, this has been increasingly remedied in writing inspired particularly by the report of the Indian National Committee on the Status of Women (1974) and Indian feminism more generally. The emergence of women's history is also part of the general shift in Indian history from a preoccupation with political and economic themes to much greater emphasis on social and cultural questions.

Accounts such as A.S. Altekar's basic study have linked women of the ancient past with the contemporary present. Sanskrit literature and epic mythology have long attracted attention, focusing especially on representation of women in early texts. There are also numerous detailed works on the religious traditions and their development in regard to conceptions of womanhood. The work of Susan Wadley and Prabhati Mukherjee illustrates the power of "normative models" and the notions of female divinity in Hindu beliefs, while Gail Minault and Hanna Papanek's analysis of seclusion among south Asian Muslims demonstrates the cultural construction of gender, and the very circumscribed worlds, rather than spheres, of Muslim women.

For the period from the thirteenth to the eighteenth century, there is a relative dearth of historical scholarship, due principally to lack of sources. There is much debate over methodology and research techniques, but as Veena Talwar Oldenberg's article shows, oral history can be effectively integrated with more traditional sources. Yet, women's voices are still too rarely heard despite exceptions such as Rosalind O'Hanlon's translation and republication of Tarabai Shinde's text on the disabilities of widowhood.

Traditional writing on the social reform debates of the nineteenth century over the issues of widow remarriage, *sati* (widow burning), child marriage, age of consent, and female education all failed to make women the direct subject of enquiry. Recent studies, for example Lata Mani's article in the anthology *Recasting Women* have, however, effectively overturned the liberal interpretation of this era, and elucidated the methods by which patriarchal society, both indigenous and colonial, controlled women as symbols of its tradition.

The late colonial period now receives a great deal of attention, and the imbalance of historical scholarship is being redressed. A number of important edited collections by J. Krishnamurty, Kumkum Sangari and Sudesh Vaid, and Nita Kumar tackle a very wide range of topics. In regional monographs, Bengal (and its emergent middle class) has received attention in the work of Meredith Borthwick and Malavika Karlekar, and gender relations in Haryana are now the subject of a substantial study by Prem Chowdhry.

For the nationalist period, there are a number of important works, of which Manmohan Kaur's study is now in its third edition. The neglected roles of women in peasant and other social movements are the subject of D.K. Singha Roy's work; while some accounts relate to the nineteenth century, much is relatively contemporary. Since independence, the women's movement has generated interest in women's status in all strata of society, which is reflected in the great number of publications in the field of women's studies.

The upsurge of interest in South Asian women's history has provided an opportunity to rethink the categories and paradigms of Indian history generally, and yet a great deal of research remains to be done.

Emma C. Alexander

See also IMPERIALISM; INDIAN HISTORIOGRAPHY; PATRIARCHY; WOMEN'S HISTORY—AFRICAN, EAST AND SOUTHEAST ASIAN.

Texts

Altekar, Anant Sadashiv. *Position of Women in Hindu Civilisation: From Prehistoric Times to the Present Day.* Delhi: Motilal Banarsidass, 1962.

Basu, Aparna. "Women's History in India." In *Writing Women's History: International Perspectives,* ed. Karen Offen, Ruth Roach Pierson, and Jane Rendall. London, Macmillan, 1991, 181–209.

Borthwick, Meredith. *The Changing Role of Women in Bengal, 1849–1905.* Princeton, NJ: Princeton University Press, 1986.

Chowdhry, Prem. *The Veiled Women: Shifting Gender Equations in Rural Haryana 1880–1990.* Delhi and New York: Oxford University Press, 1994.

Karlekar, Malavika. *Voices from Within: Early Personal Narratives of Bengali Women.* Delhi: Oxford University Press, 1991.

Kaur, Manmohan. *Women in India's Freedom Struggle.* New Delhi: Sterling, 1985.

Krishnamurty, J., ed. *Women in Colonial India: Essays on Survival, Work and the State.* Delhi and New York: Oxford University Press, 1989.

Kumar, Nita, ed. *Women As Subjects: South Asian Histories.* Charlottesville: University of Virginia Press, 1994.

Mukherjee, Prabhati. *Hindu Women: Normative Models.* Calcutta: Orient Longman, 1978.

O'Hanlon, Rosalind. *A Comparison between Women and Men: Tarabai Shinde and the Critique of Gender Relations in Colonial India.* Madras: Oxford University Press, 1994.

Oldenburg, Veena Talwar. "Lifestyle As Resistance: The Case of the Courtesans of Lucknow." In *Contesting Power: Resistance and Everyday Social Relations in South Asia,* ed. Gyan Prakash and Douglas Haynes. Delhi: Oxford University Press, 1991, 23–61.

Papanek, Hanna, and Gail Minault, eds. *Separate Worlds: Studies of Purdah in South Asia.* Columbia, MO.: South Asia Books, 1982.

Roy, Debal K. Singha. *Women in Peasant Movements: Tebhaga and After.* Delhi: Manohar, 1992.

Sangari, Kumkum, and Sudesh Vaid, eds. *Recasting Women: Essays in Indian Colonial History.* New Brunswick, NJ: Rutgers University Press, 1990.

Wadley, Susan. "Women and the Hindu Tradition." *Signs* 3 (1978): 113–125.

Women's History—Islamic

Women's history is a relatively underdeveloped field in Middle East and Islamic history. Some serious research on women's history has been done using the older approaches of women worthies and compensatory political history as well as newer methods in social history and the study of dominant and contesting gender discourse.

The history of notable women, women who have played a visible (although often neglected in history-writing) role in public activities in Middle Eastern society has usually taken the form of biographical studies of famous women, or the retelling of well-known historical events with new recognition of the part played by individual women. This is still the most common approach to women's history in the Middle East and one with a long indigenous tradition. The biographies of the Prophet's wives and other notable women of the early Muslim community was a hagiographic genre aimed at providing models of behavior for later Muslims. It also constituted a genre that perhaps unwittingly attested to the importance of women, as public political actors and sources of spiritual inspiration, in the early Muslim community. Women also figured in the *ṭabaqāt* (biographical dictionaries) which were produced over the course of the Islamic centuries. These dictionaries featured biographies of important, usually in the sense of religious learning or local prominence, persons of the time. Some of these dictionaries included significant numbers of women, particularly in the pre-Ottoman years.

These biographical studies allow historians to research the part famous women played as, for example, in the retelling of the events of early Islam with attention to the role of women in Leila Ahmed's *Women and Gender in Islam* or a review of Islamic history focusing on elite women who wielded real political power in Fatima Mernissi's *Forgotten Queens of Islam*. The study of these notable women has also led to a total reassessment of the exercise of power in at least one case: Leslie Pierce's *Imperial Harem,* a study of the elite women of the Ottoman sultan's harem, contests the standard version of the exercise of power in the empire. The importance of the household institution and the mothers (in particular) but also the wives, daughters, and concubines of the reigning monarch in the making of policy at the highest levels of the empire changed the way we must think about Ottoman politics and contributed to present debates on the position of the indigenous tradition on women's roles in public politics and public space. Above all, these studies have made the point

that women are as fully capable of wielding power and exercising authority as men. The feminist critics of the women worthies genre focus on its elite bias and the dangers of glorifying the past activities of an elite in a time when a more democratic and egalitarian vision of society is seen as critical to any social progress.

A second approach focuses on writing the histories of women's political movements and activities, whether they were feminist (i.e., focused on the achievement of women's rights) or nationalist. Feminist movements are very much part of the modern history of the region and often integrally linked to the history of nationalist struggle. The history of feminism is most developed in Egypt, particularly in the form of histories of the Egyptian Feminist Union by Huda Sha'rawi and Margot Badran. Although it is usually written in an institutional history style that reconstructs the events, leaders, and activities of the organization, movement narratives have been very important for a present sense of continuity, as well as for exploring ongoing feminist issues such as that of the troubled relationship between Western feminism and Arab feminism. The early Egyptian movement, for example, tended to model itself and its goals on European feminism with all the resultant problems of class bias and the difficulties of dealing with the relationship between gender oppression and national oppression.

The political and institutional approach also looks at women's activities in movements that were not ostensibly feminist. Most important has been the participation of women in the nationalist movements so central to modern history of the region. This is, perhaps, the most developed approach in Palestinian history: there are a number of studies of women and Palestinian nationalism and important ongoing projects of the reconstruction of women's roles in the modern struggle for Palestine being undertaken in the region.

The most controversial issue that arises in the realm of political history concerns the relationship between feminism and nationalism or, put differently, the complex relation of gender, nation, class, and race. The problematic ways in which some Western feminists have approached this issue is still a topic of debate. No single clear answer has emerged to suggest how to order these layers or to put an end to the feminist/nationalist tension; we have, instead, a multiplicity of voices and experiences.

Social historians have easily moved, in their study of the social and economic life of the people, be they peasants, workers, merchants, or slaves, to

W

include the women who formed the majority of past populations. The social history approach in the Middle East, good examples of which can be found in Nikki R. Keddie and Beth Baron's anthology *Women in Middle Eastern History,* has looked at women as economic actors, and as members of communities, families, and classes. By constituting history as including the life patterns, thoughts, and activities of the ordinary person, social history opened up a world of new dimensions far from the arenas of traditional political history.

In the context of Islamic history, this work can be revolutionary insofar as it shatters the myth of the Muslim woman's passivity and isolation in some kind of secluded, unchanging traditional world. When historians study specific times and places (for instance peasant and urban working women in nineteenth-century Egypt, or nineteenth-century Aleppan women), they discover that women were well integrated into the economy of the time. They find a good deal of specialization by gender, but women were very much part of the economic life of their communities and therefore very much affected by the changes resulting from European penetration. At this point, however, we do not have enough material on the social history of women and men alike to make generalizations. This is perhaps the most under-researched area of Islamic or Arab history although there is a wealth of documents, particularly for the Ottoman period for which we have the rich resources of the Islamic court records, available for research on most major Arab and Turkish towns.

The field of social history is not particularly prone to controversies; we see widespread agreement on the inclusion of women among historians who do social history. The only major question concerns the import of that inclusion: is there a new awareness of the many ways in which society is gendered as a result of such inclusion? The answer varies widely depending on the historian.

There is strong current interest in one final approach, that of the study of gender discourse, perhaps the fastest evolving field in women's history in the region. The study of discourse on gender attends to the ways in which the dominant culture in a particular place and time has defined maleness and femaleness as points of opposition, of difference, with the male in a position of power and domination. There is clear resonance in the Middle East: women's historians want to understand how the male-privileging "Islamic" discourse on male and female has evolved. They also must pay attention to the subversive discourses, that is, to the ways in which people attempt to undermine and contest the discourse of power.

There is a sense of immediacy in the context of much of the Middle East today where an "Islamist" or "Muslim fundamentalist" discourse is evoked to define women's roles and power in ways that are often confining and restrictive. We find an intriguing intersection of the present Islamist discourse on a monolithic and immutable Islam that dictates certain gender roles with an Orientalist discourse that also stresses the unchanging and, in its version, oppressive gender system imposed by Islamic law and thought. Fatima Mernissi, in her book *The Veil and the Male Elite,* raised a call several years ago for feminist scholars to engage in serious study of the Islamic tradition, not to leave the representation and interpretation of this tradition entirely in the hands of those who would emphasize its more conservative and even anti-feminist side. Fadwa Malti-Douglas, in *Woman's Body, Woman's Word,* explored the complexities of Arabo-Islamic writing on gender. Both authors question Islamist claims of continuity and immutability. Research in Islamic history allowed them to contest current discourses with a voice of authority, and construct subversive discourses based on a clarity of historical vision.

Not all Middle East feminists agree that this is a research priority. Some argue that to engage with the "Islamic" discourse on gender is a mistake: we are dealing here with a gender system that cannot be rehabilitated, and feminist historians risk wasting their time and effort, as well as the integrity of their vision, if they pursue the strategy of debating the Islamist interpretation of gender in Islam. They are also doomed to lose the argument in the sense that the conservative Islamic scholar will always have the last say on topics construed as religious.

Judith E. Tucker

See also BIOGRAPHY; FEMINISM; GENDER; PUBLIC/ PRIVATE, HISTORICAL DIVISION; WOMEN'S HISTORY—AFRICAN, ETC.

Texts

Amīn, Qāsim. *al-a'mal al-kamila li Qāsim Amīn* [The Complete Works of Qāsim Amīn]. Ed. Muḥammad 'Amara. 2 vols. Beirut: al-mu'assa al-'arabiyya lil-dirasat wa'l nashr, 1976.

Badran, Margot, and Miriam Cooke, eds. *Opening the Gates: A Century of Arab Feminist Writing.* Bloomington: Indiana University Press, 1990.

Sha'rawi, Huda. *Harem Years: The Memoirs of an Egyptian Feminist.* Trans. Margot Badran. New York: The Feminist Press, 1987.

References

Ahmed, Leila. *Women and Gender in Islam: Historical Roots of a Modern Debate.* New Haven, CT: Yale University Press, 1992.

Badran, Margot. *Feminists, Islam, and Nation: Gender and the Making of Modern Egypt.* Princeton, NJ: Princeton University Press, 1995.

Baron, Beth. *The Women's Awakening in Egypt. Culture, Society, and the Press.* New Haven, CT: Yale University Press, 1994.

Graham-Brown, Sarah. *Images of Women: The Portrayal of Women in Photography of the Middle East, 1860–1950.* New York: Columbia University Press, 1988.

Kandiyoti, Deniz, ed. *Women, Islam, and the State.* London: Macmillan, 1991.

Keddie, Nikki R., and Beth Baron, eds. *Women in Middle Eastern History.* New Haven, CT: Yale University Press, 1991.

Malti-Douglas, Fadwa. *Woman's Body, Woman's Word: Gender and Discourse in Arabo-Islamic Writing.* Princeton, NJ: Princeton University Press, 1991.

Mernissi, Fatima. *The Forgotten Queens of Islam.* Trans. Mary Jo Lakeland. Minneapolis: University of Minnesota Press, 1993.

———. *The Veil and the Male Elite.* Trans. Mary Jo Lakeland. Reading, MA: Addison-Wesley, 1991.

Peirce, Leslie. *The Imperial Harem: Women and Sovereignty in the Ottoman Empire.* New York: Oxford University Press, 1993.

Tucker, Judith. *Women in Nineteenth Century Egypt.* Cambridge, Eng.: Cambridge University Press, 1985.

Women's History—Latin American

Long ago only a handful of Latin American women were ever identifiable beyond the region. Perhaps best known is Eva Perón, the object of adoration among working and middle classes in Argentina both before and after her death in 1952. Known in the English-speaking world largely through Andrew Lloyd Webber's musical *Evita*, Eva Duarte was born poor. While a struggling cabaret singer, she married a young military officer named Juan Domingo Perón who later became president of Argentina. Eva's enormous personal popularity stemmed from her style of dispensing social justice to the Argentine poor, from which she herself had come, and contributed handsomely to her husband's popularity, which, coincidentally, waned after her death.

The second best known woman from Latin America is Sor Juana Inés de la Cruz (1651–1695), the talented and prolific Mexican poet whose writing soon became part of the canon of Spanish literature, rendering her familiar to countless generations of students of literature. Scores of biographies have been written, most recently by the gifted modern Mexican poet, Octavio Paz.

Next on the list comes the woman known as La Malinche (d. 1521), the Nahua noblewoman who accompanied Hernán Cortés as his translator during his conquest of Mexico, warning him of ambushes and surprise retaliations that might well have cost his and his follower's lives. Yet opinion of La Malinche in Mexico is divided between those who see her as a traitor/collaborator and those who see her as a female victim of Spanish sexual domination. Still others, more recently—such as Frances Karttunen (*Between Worlds: Interpreters, Guides, and Survivors,* 1995), see her as a woman rejected by her own people as a child, exiled to live among the Maya, and who simply chose another form of exile or life-in-between for herself.

The final, perhaps least well known woman was Saint Rose of Lima (1586–1617), the first person (male or female) born in the Western Hemisphere to have been canonized by the Roman Catholic Church. Born to a wealthy Spanish family, Rose adopted a life of mystical contemplation, demonstrating that spiritual purity could coexist in the rough-and-tumble environment of the viceroyalty of Peru.

Aside from these and a few other notable women, little sustained scholarship on women appeared before the 1970s. Since then significant advances have been made in two arenas—economic and family history.

Prior to the conquest of Latin America, women's roles have been explored in relation to their very distinctive place in cosmology, especially within the large Inca and Aztec empires (see Irene Silverblatt's *Moon, Sun and Witches,* 1987). While some cosmological feminine images have continued, most have had to reinvent themselves in Spanish forms. However, under both Spanish and Portuguese law introduced during the sixteenth century, women held considerable economic rights. To sell property that a wife inherited or received as a gift from her parents before marriage, her husband had to have her explicit permission. If widowed, a woman automatically owned half of her husband's estate and could exercise both fiduciary and legal guardianship over her minor children, relishing an economic authority rarely permitted her counterpart in the English-speaking Americas.

Finally, and most unlike the English-speaking world, both sons and daughters inherited equally. While parents could make a special bequest to one of their offspring, all acknowledged children, legitimate and illegitimate alike, received an equal share with other siblings. Wealthy parents sometimes favored daughters in this process as they did, for example, in seventeenth-century São Paulo, as noted by Muriel Nazzari in the *Disappearance of the Dowry* (1991). During the eighteenth and later centuries, the trend to favoring daughters was reversed.

In the arena of family relations, a large number of stereotypes about Latin American women were felled by scholarship this century. Marriage turned out to be far less common than had previously been imagined, among both wealthy and poorer families. Whether church law during the colonial period created fear of a rapidly regretted decision, or whether the partners shared a reluctance to lose the leverage they maintained in informal relationships, marriage occurred relatively infrequently, contributing to the exceptionally high level of illegitimate births, a trend that has continued to the present day.

Next there is the well-known romanticism of Latin American courtships. Choice of a marriage partner and the expectations of courtship have also turned out to be somewhat different than anticipated. Unlike Mediterranean societies such as Greece, where courtship was virtually unheard of until the present generation, arranged marriages seem to have been more the exception than the rule, and a rather more romantic view of marriage prevailed with parental authority exercised discretely (see Patricia Seed, *To Love, Honor, and Obey in Colonial Mexico,* 1987). Courtship itself often involved a fully indulged display of high emotional drama in which men's and women's roles reversed, leaving women in control and men displaying characteristically "feminine" emotional vulnerability.

Recently historians have called attention to what Linda Lewin calls "*de facto* polygamous families" whereby men maintain more than one family circle, sometimes marrying more than once, but more often simply maintaining second families. Some of these new arrangements resulted from flight. During the colonial era, Spaniards fled across the ocean apparently for economic improvement, leaving wives and families behind, while contemporary young men sometimes abandon homes to cross the border into the United States, acquiring new families or relationships in the new land.

Other de facto polygamous families in both Spanish- and Portuguese-speaking Americas have appeared when men having sufficient economic resources began to support two or more separate households, leaving men with more limited incomes at a disadvantage. This phenomenon is the most culturally distinctive Latin American patriarchal practice.

Partly because of relatively low rates of marriage and the economic and legal advantages of widowhood, population censuses have historically found (and continue to encounter) large numbers of women who describe themselves as "widows." Some are indeed surviving spouses, but others are single mothers, and still others have an absent or runaway spouse, divorced in fact through physical separation but not in law. Often women simply remove any appearance of dishonor by adopting the acceptable legal and economic independence of a "widow," while the man has gone on to more lucrative or advantageous relationships or who maintains other households.

Patricia Seed

See also FAMILY HISTORY (COMPARATIVE); GENDER; LATIN AMERICAN HISTORIOGRAPHY; MEXICAN HISTORIOGRAPHY; PATRIARCHY; WOMEN'S HISTORY—AFRICAN.

References

Arrom, Silvia M. *The Women of Mexico City, 1790–1857.* Stanford, CA: Stanford University Press, 1985.

Boyer, Richard E. *Lives of the Bigamists: Marriage, Family and Community in Colonial Mexico.* Albuquerque: University of New Mexico Press, 1995.

Gonzalbo Aizpuru, Pilar, ed. *Las mujeres en la Nueva España: Educacción y vida cotidiana* [Women in New Spain: Education and Daily Life]. Mexico City: El Colegio de Mexico, 1987.

Karttunen, Frances. *Between Worlds: Interpreters, Guides, and Survivors.* New Brunswick, NJ: Rutgers University Press, 1995.

Kuznesof, Elizabeth Anne. *Household Economy and Urban Development: São Paulo, 1765–1836.* Boulder, CO: Westview Press, 1986.

Lavrin, Asuncion. *Women, Feminism, and Social Change in Argentina, Chile, and Uruguay, 1890–1940.* Lincoln: University of Nebraska Press, 1995.

———, ed. *Sexuality and Marriage in Colonial Latin America.* Lincoln: University of Nebraska Press, 1989.

Lewin, Linda. *Politics and Parental in Paraiba: A Case Study of Family-Based Oligarchy in Brazil.* Princeton, NJ: Princeton University Press, 1987.

Nazzari, Muriel. *Disappearance of the Dowry: Women, Families and Social Change in São Paulo, Brazil (1600–1900).* Stanford, CA: Stanford University Press, 1991.

Paz, Octavio. *Sor Juana, or The Traps of Faith.* Trans. Margaret Sayres Peden. Cambridge, MA: Harvard University Press, 1988.

Pescatello, Ann, ed. *Female and Male in Latin America.* Pittsburgh, PA: University of Pittsburgh Press, 1973.

Seed, Patricia. *To Love, Honor, and Obey in Colonial Mexico: Conflicts over Marriage Choice.* Stanford, CA: Stanford University Press, 1987.

Silverblatt, Irene M. *Moon, Sun and Witches: Gender Ideologies and Class in Inca and Colonial Peru.* Princeton, NJ: Princeton University Press, 1987.

Taylor, Julie M. *Eva Perón, the Myths of a Woman.* Chicago: University of Chicago Press, 1979.

Women's History—North American

A distinctive field rooted in the "new" social history of the 1960s and 1970s as well as the second wave of feminism. Preceding those decades, feminists of the late nineteenth and early twentieth centuries also contributed to historical studies focused on women, often in the form of investigative reporting in such areas as women's employment or the legal status of women. A few, like Mary Beard, wrote overarching interpretations; she argued in 1946 that women's experience of subordination was greatly exaggerated and that women also played key roles in shaping history.

"Women's history" is a term that implies women can be studied historically and distinctly as a separate group within society. The emergence of social history in North America challenged older traditions of studying elites and offered the potential for research on ordinary people, particularly oppressed groups such as blacks, workers, immigrants, and women. The cross-fertilization of history and the social sciences in the post–World War II period and related interests in liberation struggles in the Third World and at home (Vietnam war, civil rights movement, feminism, and the student movement) marked the beginnings of a strong interest in new approaches and methods in history.

The specific roots of the "new women's history" are to be found in two areas: radical social movements such as the Women's Liberation Movement; and in a scholarly interest among historians in social movements such as nineteenth-century reform and suffrage campaigns. The latter led historians such as Barbara Welter to ask questions about women's experiences, particularly those middle-class women that Welter discussed in 1966 in "The Cult of True Womanhood." Welter's focus on the middle class and her acceptance of a rigid separation between male and female spheres was challenged three years later in Gerda Lerner's "The Lady and the Mill Girl," which distinguished working-class women's experiences from those of the middle class and insisted on the centrality of class in studying women's history.

The late 1960s and early 1970s witnessed the growth of the grassroots Women's Liberation Movement, within which numerous small study or consciousness-raising groups began to question the absence of women from serious academic studies, including history. Small groups conducted their own reading and research, committed to making women's history available to a wide audience in popular formats. Questions of race and class difference were debated in this early, transitional phase of women's history.

In Canada, women's history emerged in the early 1970s in similar circumstances. While Veronica Strong-Boag was one of the first to explore the history of a middle-class women's group in her thesis on the National Council of Women of Canada, women's movement activists and historians in Toronto gathered together a collection of articles focused on women's work with an explicit class and gender framework, thus providing an alternative approach to women's history that remained influential in the development of the field.

Women's history in the 1970s was also influenced by developments in other disciplines, including sociology and anthropology. Michelle Rosaldo's reformulation of the public/private dichotomy in the mid-1970s provided a theoretical framework that fit well with historians' attempts to explain women's subordination and oppression in the private sphere. Middle-class women's experiences in particular seemed to fit this framework and the latter encouraged historians to move away from the earlier concentration on oppression toward an understanding of those areas closest to female experience—family, housework, children. By the mid-1970s, historians began to develop a positive view of women's sphere as providing an arena for the emergence of "women's culture." As a concept, "women's culture" remained popular from 1975 to the early 1980s. By revaluing what women did, this concept opened the door to viewing women as agents rather than victims. At the same time, this approach marked a retreat from politics to culture, a trend reflected in some parts of the contemporary women's movement. Critics of the homogenizing perspective of a universal women's culture argued that this approach romanticized and depoliticized women's history by leaving class, race, and other differences out. In Canada, women's history developed with close links to labor history in the 1970s and 1980s and the women's culture model was less prominent. In both Canada and the United States, however, women's historians returned to related questions concerning the links between public and private.

By the 1980s, the women's culture model was increasingly challenged by the re-emergence of debates on differences among women—racial or ethnic difference, sexual preference, as well as class difference. In this decade, African-American women's history flourished, as did Chicana, Asian-American, and other histories of minority women. In Canada, ethnic and immigrant women's history achieved more prominence and challenged a predominantly white, Anglo-Saxon focus; African-Canadian women's history has only appeared in recent years.

The 1980s also witnessed a challenge from poststructural theorists intent on exposing perceived limits of previous approaches, such as that of social history with its emphasis on class analysis and its claims to understand historical "experience." Poststructuralists suggested that gender ought to be treated as a category of analysis and rejected simplistic use of gender as a substitute for "women." Challenging the idea that historical experience could be readily understood, post-structuralists instead advocated the exploration and deconstruction of apparently natural categories, such as "women," to reveal how they are socially constructed through language, texts, cultural symbols, and structures of power. In the works of historians like Joan W. Scott, gender analysis reveals the socially constructed differences between the sexes that are expressed through binary oppositions (such as male/female or public/private). Gender serves, then, as a primary organizing field through which power is constituted and thus the deconstruction of language provides an important method of understanding and dismantling unequal power relationships.

While poststructuralism has been rejected by some, it clearly has left its mark on the field. While some scholars pinpoint its tendency to depoliticize women's history, or view it as more useful for studying elite groups, others have applied post-structural analysis to rethink concepts such as class. U.S. historian Ava Baron has pointed out that labor history has associated "class" with the workplace and male workers, thus isolating women workers' history from the rest of labor history. Like the Canadian historian Bettina Bradbury, Baron suggested that a gender-sensitive working-class history opens up new studies of masculinity and femininity. As Bradbury herself noted, men are not just workers but also family members, thereby breaking down the opposition between work/home and public/private. Such a perspective allows for a framework that takes into account multiple identities—class, gender, race and ethnicity, among others.

These debates continue in the 1990s with social historians contesting the views of post-structuralists who have, according to the former, rewritten the historiography as a triumphalist narrative of increasing theoretical sophistication. As social historians continue to insist, the earlier women's history of the 1970s and 1980s was never merely descriptive, nor was it unaware of diversity and differences among women. While social historians have incorporated some of the useful insights generated by post-structuralism, they have also firmly retained their grounding in gender, race-ethnicity, and class analysis.

Linda Kealey

See also FEMINISM; GENDER; PATRIARCHY; PUBLIC/ PRIVATE, HISTORICAL DIVISION OF; WOMEN'S HISTORY—WESTERN EUROPEAN.

References

Acton, Janice, et al., eds. *Women at Work: Ontario, 1850–1930.* Toronto: Canadian Women's Educational Press, 1974.

Baron, Ava. "On Looking at Men: Masculinity and the Making of a Gendered Working-Class History." In *Feminists Revision History,* ed. Anne-Louise Shapiro. New Brunswick, NJ: Rutgers University Press, 1994, 146–171.

Beard, Mary. *Woman As Force in History.* New York: Macmillan, 1946.

Bradbury, Bettina. *Working Families.* Toronto: McClelland and Stewart, 1993.

Burnet, Jean, ed. *Looking into My Sister's Eyes: An Exploration in Women's History.* Toronto: Multicultural History Society of Ontario, 1986.

DuBois, Ellen, et al. "Politics and Culture in Women's History: A Symposium." *Feminist Studies* 6 (1980): 26–64.

Hoff, Joan. "Gender As a Postmodern Category of Paralysis." *Women's History Review* 3 (1994): 149–168.

Jones, Jacqueline. *Labor of Love, Labor of Sorrow: Black Women, Work and the Family from Slavery to the Present.* New York: Basic Books, 1985.

Kerber, Linda K. "Separate Spheres, Female Worlds, Woman's Place: The Rhetoric of Women's History." *Journal of American History* 75 (1988): 9–39.

Lerner, Gerda. *The Majority Finds Its Past: Placing Women in History.* New York: Oxford University Press, 1979.

Parr, Joy. *The Gender of Breadwinners: Women, Men and Change in Two Industrial Towns, 1880–1950.* Toronto: University of Toronto Press, 1990.

Rosaldo, Michelle, and Louise Lamphere, eds. *Woman, Culture and Society.* Stanford, CA: Stanford University Press, 1974.

Scott, Joan W. "Gender: A Useful Category of Historical Analysis." In her *Gender and the Politics of History.* New York: Columbia University Press, 1988.

Smith-Rosenberg, Carroll. "Hearing Women's Words: A Feminist Reconstruction of History." In her *Disorderly Conduct: Visions of Gender in Victorian America.* New York: Knopf/Random House, 1985.

Vogel, Lise. "Telling Tales: Historians of Our Own Lives." *Journal of Women's History* 2 (1991): 89–101.

Welter, Barbara. "The Cult of True Womanhood, 1800–60." In her *Dimity Convictions.* Athens: Ohio University Press, 1976, 21–41.

Women's History—Western European

The historiography of women in western Europe dates back to the heroines depicted in the fourteenth- and early-fifteenth-century writings of Boccaccio and Christine de Pizan. Both produced treatises on the accomplishments and virtues of notable women. The trope of women's worthiness became a major feature in women's history in the works of such authors as Louise Keralio Robert in France in the eighteenth century, the Strickland sisters in nineteenth-century Britain, or the Dutch historian Johanna Naber writing between 1887 and 1941. Until the 1960s these tens of thousands of books depicting queens, regents, aristocrats,

learned women, warriors, travelers, and salonnières formed a counterpoint to the heroic history of men and served to constitute a political imagination on which feminists could draw in building their campaigns for women's rights.

Simultaneously throughout these centuries the broader social and cultural history of western European women took shape in the many memoirs by salon hostesses such as the Countesse de Boigne; the studies of court customs and everyday life by amateur historians such as Stephanie de Genlis, Mary Berry, Lucy Aikin, and Sarah Taylor Austin; and the histories of patronnesses and practitioners of the arts by writers such as Julia Cartwright and Janet Ross. When women entered the university and learned the practices of scientific history, they produced professional studies in these areas. Mary Bateson's work on the double convent, Eileen Power's study of nunneries, and Alice Clark's investigation of working women in the seventeenth century served as classics until the 1970s.

Across the nineteenth century and into the twentieth, feminist historians (both amateur and professional) explored the legal, political, and constitutional position of women, mostly from the medieval era on, casting their studies in terms of the status of women's rights. A few of these reform-minded investigators like Clarisse Bader and Olympe Audouard looked to the classical period, ancient Egypt and the near East, and the history of women in other regions of the world to assess the position of western European women across time. Liberal and imperial historical theories derived from men's history in the modern period had maintained that women's position in society had drastically improved with the rise of Christianity, the development of constitutional government, and the triumph of a specifically "Western" set of values. Since at least the time of Mary Wortley Montagu into the early twentieth century, the findings of historians of women and travelers often disputed that claim. (Joan Kelly's essay "Did Women Have a Renaissance" was among the first widely circulated feminist critiques of these assumptions in the late twentieth century.)

In many respects the rise of professionalization provided an ambiguous context for the writing of women's history in twentieth-century western Europe. On the one hand the admission of women to universities to receive professional training provided them with new skills and often (but not always) gained them access to libraries and repositories of historical material. On the other, professional history devalued writing about everyday life, the household, and other institutions with large numbers of women and children. In the early twentieth century, as social and cultural history began to gain some stature in the profession, these too were mostly articulated as men's history: male organizations like guilds or great male cultural figures. As the profession itself used gender hierarchies even to imagine what it did, writings by women and about women's past were devalued. As a result, the production of women's history in and about western Europe experienced the same decline as it did in other countries of the West until the late 1960s.

The reemergence of a mass feminist movement in western Europe and the United States fostered new enthusiasm for historical investigations of women's lives. The ground was also being prepared by a scholarly wave of quantitative, social, and demographic history investigating class, fertility, work, the family, and other areas from which information about women might be gleaned. In addition the expansion of anthropology as a discipline provided new justifications for studying more than traditional political and economic elites and important methods for historians who wanted to look at women and everyday life. But it was the feminist movement that pointed to the inadequacies of both the new social and demographic history and anthropology because neither of these approaches actually studied women as distinct historical subjects. Instead women were only incidentally included in their accounts. It remained for feminist historians to synthesize subject, disciplinary approaches, and methodology.

In 1971 Natalie Zemon Davis, then of the University of Toronto, circulated a mimeographed bibliography of works on women in early modern history. Davis's burgeoning study of women in early modern France added anthropological methods to historical ones in studies of widows, youth and the control of sexuality, and women in urban and familial roles. Statistical methods, the focus on class, and sociological ideas of life-cycles influenced such works as *Women, Work and Family,* a comparative study of English and French working-class women's lives by Louise Tilly and Joan Scott. Christiane Klapisch-Zuber used statistical methods to investigate Italian Renaissance family strategies and women's power within them. Mary Hartman's *Victorian Murderesses* (British and French) was among the first to study women's relationship to criminality and deviancy. Although this new scholarship on working-class women was most prominent, studies of women suffragists and middle-class worthies continued to be popular. This more traditional women's history gained in sophistication with use of these new methodologies. The works and lives of such pioneers as Mary Wollstonecraft, Christine de Pizan, and Simone de Beauvoir were the object of intense interest in the 1970s and 1980s.

From the 1980s on historical journals that took western European women's lives as at least one of their foci appeared: these included *Penelope, Gender and History, The Journal of Women's History, Clio, Frontiers, Jahrboek voor Vrouwengeschiedenis, Lover, Literatuuroverzicht voor de vrouwenbewegung, Signs,* and *Feminist Studies.* The publication of monographs allowed the development of more synthetic works and edited collections such as Renate Bridenthal and Claudia Koonz (eds.), *Becoming Visible;* Marilyn Boxer and Jean Quataert, *Connecting Spheres;* Merry Wiesner, *Women and Gender in Early Modern Europe;* Ute Frevert, *Women in German History;* Mary Nash, *Mujer, familia y trahajo en Espana* [Women, Family and Work in Spain]; Georges Duby and Michelle Perrot (eds.), *Storia delle donne in occidente* [History of Women] (5 vols.); and Annette Kuhn's series "Frauen in der Geschichte [Women in History]." Publications of documents and the opening of women's archives and women's studies centers throughout Europe and North America also contributed to expanding research opportunities. Although established presses published histories of women, a new group of women's presses such as the Feminist Press, Virago, Pandora, Editions des femmes, and others focused on scholarship about women. The widening area of topics, however, was crucial to continuing vitality. The lives of Jewish women and women of varying ethnicities within the western European context provoked heated debate over the nature of women's participation in the Third Reich and about the ways to consider the history of women who were not necessarily part of the great power structure. Lively research, such as that on women in the Spanish civil war and anarchist movements, on Scandinavian women, and on participation in resistance movements also pushed the boundaries of scholarship.

In 1986 Joan Scott published "Gender: A Useful Category of Historical Analysis," a theoretical pronouncement challenging historians to drop the search for women's historical agency and to adopt instead the study of gender. For Scott, as in fact for some of the "new social historians" such as Lawrence Stone, women could not be studied apart from men. The difference between the old family history, however, was that Scott was influenced by postmodern and structuralist theorists such as Jacques Derrrida and Michel Foucault. In fact, Foucault had already strongly influenced such works as Alain Corbin's *Les filles de noce* and the scholarship of Arlette Farge, as well as theories of "sex roles" or "sexual difference" in the humanities. Scott made these theories accessible and important to historians. The result was such notable works as Catherine Hall's and Leonore Davidoff's *Family Fortunes,* a study of the men and women of the English middle class.

Other imperatives reshaped western European women's history in these years, foremost among them the emergence of a broadly defined field of inquiry called cultural studies. Cultural studies gave impetus to rethinking western European women's history in terms of imperialism and colonization, the body, sexual orientation, consumer culture, the social construction of knowledge, and the relationship of women and gender to language and power. Some of the major works exploring women's and gender history from these analytical perspectives are: Martin Duberman, Martha Vicinus, and George Chauncey (eds.), *Hidden from History: Reclaiming the Gay and Lesbian Past;* Barbara Duden, *Woman beneath the Skin: Nineteenth-Century German Medicine;* Londa Schiebinger, *Nature's Body* and *The Mind Has No Sex?;* Lisa Tichner, *Spectacle of Women: Representations of the English Women's Suffrage Movement;* and Antoinette Burton, *Burdens of History: Gender and the Imperial Experience.* Attacks on the welfare state provoked studies such as Gisela Bock and Pat Thane (eds.), *Maternity and Gender Politics,* and Jane Lewis, *Women and Social Policies in Europe.* New attention to women as citizens appeared in such works as Gisela Bock and Susan James (eds.), *Beyond Equality and Difference,* while other historians such as Geneviève Fraisse, Joan Landes, Carole Pateman, and Lynn Hunt explored the gendering of the state. Finally, as the tradition matured scholarly interest developed in the historiography of women's history and the development of women's role in historical institutions. As in so many other areas of women's history Natalie Zemon Davis had pioneered this branch of inquiry with several articles that appeared in the 1970s as well as in her American Historical Association presidential address, "History's Two Bodies," which considered the interaction of men and women as historical writers and researchers.

Bonnie G. Smith

References

Anderson, Bonnie S., and Judith P. Zinsser. *A History of Their Own: Women in Europe from Pre-history to the Present.* New York: Harper and Row, 1988.

Boxer, Marilyn, and Jean Quataert, eds. *Connecting Spheres: Women in the Western World, 1500 to the Present.* New York: Oxford University Press, 1987.

Bridenthal, Renate, and Claudia Koonz. *Becoming Visible: Women in European History.* Boston: Houghton Mifflin, 1978.

Davis, Natalie Zemon. "Gender and Genre: Women As Historical Writers, 1400–1820." In *Beyond Their Sex: Learned Women of the European Past,* ed. Patricia Labalme. New York: New York University Press, 1980.

Duby, Georges, and Michelle Perrot, eds. *A History of Women in the West.* Cambridge, MA: Harvard University Press, 1994.

Frevert, Ute. *Women in German History.* New York: Berg, 1989.

Offen, Karen, Ruth R. Pierson, and Jane Rendall, eds. *Writing Women's History: International Perspectives.* Bloomington: Indiana University Press, 1991.

Scott Joan. *Gender and the Politics of History.* New York: Columbia University Press, 1988.

Smith, Bonnie G. *Changing Lives: Women in European History since 1700.* Lexington: D.C. Heath, 1989.

———. "Women's Contribution to Modern Historiography in Great Britain, France, and the United States, 1750–1940." *American Historical Review* 89 (1984): 709–732.

Wiesner, Merry. *Women and Gender in Early Modern Europe.* Cambridge, Eng.: Cambridge University Press, 1993.

Zinsser, Judith P. *History and Feminism: A Glass Half Full.* New York: Twayne, 1993.

Wood, Anthony (1631–1695)

English antiquary. Wood was educated at Merton College, Oxford, and thereafter lived a reclusive and frequently cantankerous life opposite his old college, devoting himself to collecting books and manuscripts about the university that had reared him. He profited greatly form his connection with William Fulman, Fellow of Corpus Christi College, who gained access for Wood to that college's extensive archives and who commented on and corrected his antiquarian writings. At various times in his life he also enjoyed the friendship or patronage of Dr. John Fell, dean of Christ Church,

John Aubrey, and White Kennett, later bishop of Peterborough. Wood's chief publications were the *History and Antiquities of the University of Oxford* (1674) and *Athenae Oxonienses* (1691–1692), a collection of biographies of Oxford-educated writers, principally of his own and recent times.

R.C. Richardson

Texts

Athenae Oxonienses. An Exact History of All the Writers and Bishops Who Have Had Their Education in the University of Oxford. Ed. P. Bliss. 4 vols. London: F.C. and J. Rivington, 1813–1820.

Life and Times of Anthony Wood. Ed. A. Clark. 5 vols. Oxford: Oxford Historical Society, 1891–1895.

Survey of the Antiquities of the City of Oxford. Ed. A. Clark. 3 vols. Oxford: Oxford Historical Society, 1889–1899.

References

Douglas, D.C. *English Scholars, 1660–1730.* Second ed. London: Eyre and Spottiswoode, 1951.

Wood, George Arnold (1865–1928)

Australian historian. Born in Lancashire, England, and educated at Balliol College, Oxford, Wood became in 1891 the first professor of history appointed in the Australian colonies. As a student, he had been inspired by the medievalist, William Stubbs, to introduce precepts of academic, "scientific" historical research upon accepting the new Challis chair of history at the University of Sydney. History to Wood was a principled unfolding of high moral purpose, and during the Boer War (1899–1902), he adopted a parallel public course against British military "injustice," forming the Australian Anti-War League and courting considerable press antagonism and a university senate censure in the process. During World War I, however, he became a voluble supporter of Britain's military mission. As an inspiring lecturer, heavily committed to teaching, he was less a prolifically publishing historian than an inspiration for future generations of scholars. He did much, in particular, to encourage the research and teaching of Australian history for which he developed considerable passion. In 1922, he published *The Discovery of Australia,* advancing British primacy in European Pacific exploration, and an influential article, exonerating the character of Australia's convict forbears. This was followed in 1925 by a history for Australian children, *The Voyage of the Endeavour.* In addition, he presided from 1913 as literary editor over thirty-two volumes of the prestigious *Historical Records of Australia.* He was preparing a chapter on Pacific exploration for the *Cambridge History of the British Empire* when, plagued by severe ill-health and acute depression, he committed suicide.

Raymond Evans

Texts

The Discovery of Australia. Ed. J.C. Beaglehole. Rev. ed. Melbourne: Macmillan, 1969.

The Voyage of the Endeavour. Melbourne: Macmillan, 1944.

References

Crawford, R.M. *"A Bit of a Rebel": The Life and Work of George Arnold Wood.* Sydney: Sydney University Press, 1975.

Fletcher, B.H. "George Arnold Wood and Imperial History at Sydney University." *Journal of the Royal Australian Historical Society* 79 (1993): 54–71.

Moses, J.A. *Prussian-German Militarism 1914–18 in Australian Perspective: The Thought of George Arnold Wood.* Berne: Peter Lang, 1991.

Woodson, Carter Godwin (1875–1950)

American historian and educator. The son of former slaves, Woodson was born in New Canton, Virginia. Largely self-taught until the age of seventeen, he moved in 1892 to Huntington, West Virginia, where he worked in the mines and attended school. His first degree was from Berea College in Kentucky (1903). After teaching in the Philippines and traveling abroad, he earned a B.A. and an M.A. from the University of Chicago and a Ph.D. from Harvard (1912). From 1909 to 1922 he taught high school in Washington, D.C., and briefly served as a dean at Howard College and West Virginia State College. Often called the father of black history, Woodson devoted his academic life to the advancement of African-American studies. He organized the Association for the Study of Negro Life and History, which has published the *Journal of Negro History* since 1916. In 1926 he introduced Negro History Week. Later, also seeking to reach a more popular audience, he wrote *The Negro in Our History* and started the *Negro History Bulletin.* His scholarly works included *The Education of the Negro Prior to 1861* (1915), *A Century of Negro Migration* (1918), *The History of the Negro Church* (1921), and several volumes of source materials on African-American life.

John W. Storey

Texts

A Century of Negro Migration. New York: Russell and Russell, 1969.

The Education of the Negro Prior to 1861. New York: Arno Press, 1968.

The History of the Negro Church. Washington, DC: Associated Publishers, 1921.

References

Logan, Rayford W. "Carter G. Woodson: Mirror and Molder of His Time, 1875–1950." *Journal of Negro History* 58 (1973): 1–17.

Thorpe, Earl E. *Black Historians: A Critique.* New York: Morrow, 1971.

Woodward, Comer Vann (b. 1908)

American historian and educator. Woodward was born in Vanndale, Arkansas. After earning degrees from Emory and Columbia universities, he completed his doctorate in history at the University of North Carolina in 1937. Woodward joined the faculty of Johns Hopkins University following wartime naval service (1943–1946) and later completed his teaching career with Yale University (1961–1977). During his tenure in New Haven, he was elected president of the American Historical Association and also of the Organization of American Historians in the same year (1969). Woodward used the opportunity to espouse his concern over the increasing specialization and Eurocentric emphasis within the profession. With *Tom Watson, Agrarian Rebel* (1938), Woodward set the stage for a reinterpretation of the history of the postbellum American South. Such revisionism burst upon the scene with *Origins of the New South* (1951), a volume that won the Bancroft Prize and remains a vanguard study in the field. Woodward's decades of penetrating analysis have debunked formerly prevailing myths concerning the "Solid South," the role of the Redeemers, and the "Negro question," among many others, as unfounded post-Reconstruction white supremacist demagoguery. Equally important, Woodward has throughout his career been a moralist who has sought to demonstrate the relevance of Southern history to contemporary national issues, especially race relations. Hence, *The Strange Career of Jim Crow* (1955) gained support for a then burgeoning civil rights movement. The capstone of Woodward's passion for the human element in history, however, is his Pulitzer Prize–winning edition of the diary of a Southern woman during the Civil War, *Mary Chesnut's Civil War* (1981). Having never truly retired, Woodward remains the quintessential Southern Renaissance man.

William E. Fischer Jr.

Texts

The Burden of Southern History. Third ed. Baton Rouge: Louisiana State University Press, 1993.

Origins of the New South, 1877–1913. Revised ed. Baton Rouge: Louisiana State University Press, 1971 (vol. 9 of *A History of the South.* Ed. by W.H. Stephenson and E.M. Coulter).

The Strange Career of Jim Crow. Third ed. New York: Oxford University Press, 1974.

Thinking Back: The Perils of Writing History. Baton Rouge: Louisiana State University Press, 1986.

Tom Watson, Agrarian Rebel. Second ed. Savannah, GA: Beehive Press, 1973.

References

King, Richard H. *A Southern Renaissance: The Cultural Awakening of the American South, 1930–1955.* New York: Oxford University Press, 1980.

Masur, Louis P. "The Published Writings of C. Vann Woodward: A Bibliography." In *Region, Race, and Reconstruction: Essays in Honor of C. Vann Woodward,* ed. J. Morgan Kousser and James M. McPherson. New York: Oxford University Press, 1982.

Worcester [or Botoner], William (1415–1482)

Antiquary, topographer, secretary, and physician. Sometimes surnamed Botoner after his mother's family, William Worcester was born in Bristol, the son of an important burgess. By 1432 he was attending Oxford and in 1438 entered the service of the soldier/courtier Sir John Fastolf. Fastolf's death in 1459 plunged Worcester into a series of legal battles with the Paston family over their deceased master's will. Freed of those problems by 1477, Worcester devoted himself to the study of English antiquity and topography until his death in 1482. Worcester's earlier historical works, the lost *Acta Domini Johannis Fastolf* and *The Boke of Noblesse* (begun in 1451 and finalized in 1474) glorified chivalry and war with France. His other works, such as the lost *De agri Norfolciensis familiis antiquis* [On the Ancient Families of Norfolk], were more antiquarian in nature. The *Itinerary* is his most famous work and is a notebook of his antiquarian and topographical travels around England. Its manuscript includes a full description of Bristol, which anticipated John Stow's *Survey of London* a century later. Worcester provided a model for later antiquarians even though his broad curiosity was frequently marred by his complete credulity.

Ronald H. Fritze

Texts

The Boke of Noblesse. Ed. J.G. Nichols. London: Roxburgh Club, 1860.

William Worcestre Itineraries. Ed. and trans. J.H. Harvey. Oxford: Oxford University Press, 1969.

References

Gransden, Antonia. *Historical Writing in England: II, c.1307 to the Early Sixteenth Century.* Ithaca, NY: Cornell University Press, 1982.

World History

Analysis of the past from a global point of view. History emerged as a professional discipline during the nineteenth century, an age of intense state building activity in Europe. In light of this political context, it is not surprising that scholars concentrated their attention on national states, their constitutions, institutions, and relations with other states. From the emergence of their discipline to the present day, professional historians have mostly viewed the past from the perspective of national states. In many ways, the predominantly national focus of historical scholarship has enabled historians to explain the past in persuasive fashion. National states rank among the most dynamic of all human institutions, after all, and their policies have been crucially important for the development of modern world history.

During the twentieth century, however, historians have become increasingly aware that adequate treatment of many historical problems requires an analytical framework larger than those offered by national communities. Many historical processes do not recognize national boundary lines, but work their effects on a regional, continental, or even global scale. These processes include population movements, economic fluctuations, climatic changes, transfers of technology, biological exchanges, imperial expansion, long-distance trade, and the spread of religious faiths, ideas, and ideals. In analyzing these processes, scholars have given shape to the field of world history—historical scholarship undertaken not from the viewpoint of national states, but rather from the perspective of the global community.

To many people, the term "world history" brings to mind the works of philosophers of history such as Oswald Spengler, Arnold J. Toynbee, and others who sought to distill some particular meaning or derive some philosophical significance from the past. Toynbee in particular enjoyed a wide following among the general public, presumably because he outlined straightforward and ostensibly commonsensical principles that purported to explain large processes such as the rise and fall of civilizations. Yet professional historians have mostly found fault with Toynbee and the other philosophers of history, who misunderstood many of the world's peoples and misrepresented their experiences while seeking to draw lessons from the past.

Apart from the philosophers of history, world historians have concentrated their efforts on the analysis of historical processes rather than speculation about the meaning of the world's past. In practice, world historians generally undertake large-scale comparative and cross-cultural analyses, and they have elaborated several distinctive ways of approaching the past from a global point of view.

One school of analysis studies processes that have guided the development of the modern world, from 1500 C.E. to the present, and draws inspiration from the work of the sociologist Max Weber. Often known as modernization analysts, members of this school seek to understand the means by which rural, agricultural societies became urban and industrial. In *The Dynamics of Modernization: A Study in Comparative History,* for example, Cyril E. Black envisaged a large-scale process by which "traditional" societies became "modern." The process, which Black believed to be universally applicable, involved several distinct transformations by which societies relied on science and technology instead of inherited cultural traditions, mobilized human resources through mass education and modern communications, invested in industrialization, concentrated their population in cities, and generated an ethic of individualism and competition. Critics have noted that the modernization school assumes the experience of western Europe and North America as a norm and thus distorts the experiences of other lands. More recent work by E.L. Jones, however, suggests that modernization analysis inspired by Weber does not necessarily entail a Eurocentric interpretation. In *Growth Recurring: Economic Change in World History,* Jones examined the cases of Song China, Tokugawa Japan, and modern Europe, all of which independently experienced significant, per capita, economic growth. Indeed, Jones held that in the absence of confiscatory regimes, economic growth is quite natural and is likely to characterize any society at any time.

Sharply opposed to the Weberian school of modernization analysis is the world-system school, which draws inspiration from the work of Karl Marx. World-system analysts hold that most of the world cannot reasonably expect to experience the transformations that Black saw as leading to modernity or the economic growth that Jones saw as a natural condition of human society. As represented by Immanuel Wallerstein's multivolume study of *The Modern World-System,* the world-system school views imperialism and colonialism as the key features of modern world history. From the sixteenth through the early twentieth century, according to the world-system analysts, Western nations established their hegemony in the world and subjected its various regions to the demands of the capitalist world economy. Imperial and colonial powers then ruthlessly extracted surplus wealth, which they used to finance their own economic development, while thwarting development in subject lands. Only in the context of this capitalist world system is it possible to understand political economy.

Since the 1970s, world-system analysis has deeply influenced historical studies and suggested new interpretations of modern world history. In *Europe and the People Without History,* for example, the anthropologist Eric Wolf argued that capitalist techniques of economic organization and exploitation brought about thoroughgoing changes in the political, social, and economic orders of Asia, Africa, and the Americas. Meanwhile, the world-system perspective has also suggested fresh insights into premodern times. In *Before European Hegemony: The World System, A.D. 1250–1350,* Janet L. Abu-Lughod argued persuasively that only a systemwide analysis will lead to adequate understanding of trade and economic development in the eastern hemisphere during the era of the Mongol empires.

While sociologists, anthropologists, economists, and political scientists have been most active in the development of the modernization and world-system schools of analysis, professional historians have also contributed to the emergence of world history as a field of study. One school of historians has focused attention on the phenomenon of cultural and technological diffusion and its effects on the societies touched by diffusion. Thus William H. McNeill offered a broad-based analysis of diffusion in *The Rise of the West: A History of the Human Community.* McNeill held that interaction between peoples of different societies was one of the principal agents of change in world history, since skills and technologies have always flowed readily between peoples, bringing about constantly changing configurations of power and social organization. Recognizing the large role played by technology in the modern world, Daniel R. Headrick examined the problem of technological diffusion in *The Tentacles of Progress: Technology Transfer in the Age of Imperialism, 1850–1940.* In Headrick's view, technological diffusion was a very complicated process during the imperial era, as Europeans sought to protect and preserve the technological advantages that they enjoyed over other peoples. Nevertheless, like McNeill, Headrick viewed the development, implementation, and diffusion of advanced technology as a crucial theme in modern world history.

Another school of professional historians has analyzed large-scale patterns in the world's economic and social history. Their studies have dealt mostly with the themes of long-distance trade and the economic integration of large regions, such as the world's major ocean basins. In *Cross-Cultural Trade in World History,* for example, Philip D. Curtin examined patterns of long-distance trade from ancient times to the present. He concentrated attention on the phenomenon of the trade diaspora—communities of merchants, agents, brokers, and others who crossed cultural boundary lines in the interests of commerce—in order to shed light on the structures of long-distance trade and the role of merchants as cross-cultural brokers. In a complementary vein, K.N. Chaudhuri studied the remarkable effects of trade in the Indian Ocean. In *Asia before Europe: Economy and Civilisation of the Indian Ocean from the Rise of Islam to 1750,* Chaudhuri argued that well-articulated trade networks began to push the Indian Ocean basin toward economic integration long before modern times. Thus, Curtin, Chaudhuri, and others of this school have thrown light on the structures and dynamics of economic history that have shaped the world's experience over the long term.

Yet another school of world historians has concentrated attention on environmental, ecological, and biological processes that have worked their effects on a global scale. In *Plagues and Peoples,* William H. McNeill studied the effects of infectious and contagious diseases when they crossed biological boundary lines. In *Ecological Imperialism: The Biological Expansion of Europe, 900–1900,* Alfred W. Crosby undertook an even larger task, as he sought to explain on biological grounds why European plants, animals, and human communities have successfully established themselves in many different and widely scattered parts of the world. He argued that exotic and devastating diseases opened niches for European peoples, who then introduced plants and animals that faced no natural predators. In combination, then, European species disrupted the environments that they entered and established themselves securely throughout much of the world's temperate zones. The works of McNeill, Crosby, and other environmental historians have thus shown that biological processes working on a global scale have decisively influenced the world's development.

Although not yet developed to the point that they merit recognition as distinctive schools of analysis, it is possible that two additional approaches to world history are currently emerging, as scholars attempt to understand the significance of cross-cultural encounters and of cross-cultural gender relations for the world's past. In *Prophets of Rebellion: Millenarian Protest Movements against the European Colonial Order,* Michael P. Adas examined cases of spirited resistance against European colonial intrusion based on cultural and religious traditions of long standing. In *Old World Encounters: Cross-Cultural Contacts and Exchanges in Pre-Modern Times,* Jerry H. Bentley studied cross-cultural interaction as a global process that helped to define several patterns of cross-cultural conversion, conflict, and compromise even in the premodern world. Meanwhile, the cross-cultural gender analysis of Margaret Strobel's *European Women and the Second British Empire* throws important light on the experiences of all parties to imperial relationships.

World history is still emerging as a field of study, and it seems likely that analyses of cross-cultural encounters and of gender relations will develop into major concerns of world historians. In any case, even as a young field, world history has generated important and useful insights into the world's past, and it is certain that historical analysis from a global point of view will continue to develop as a field of historical scholarship.

Jerry H. Bentley

See also ATLASES—HISTORICAL; ENVIRONMENTAL HISTORY—WORLD; GEOGRAPHY—HISTORICAL; MODERNIZATION THEORY; WORLD-SYSTEMS THEORY/ DEPENDENCY THEORY.

Texts

Abu-Lughod, Janet L. *Before European Hegemony: The World System, A.D. 1250–1350.* New York: Oxford University Press, 1989.

Adas, Michael P. *Prophets of Rebellion: Millenarian Protest Movements against the European Colonial Order.* New York: Cambridge University Press, 1987.

Bentley, Jerry H. *Old World Encounters: Cross-Cultural Contacts and Exchanges in Pre-Modern Times.* New York: Oxford University Press, 1993.

Black, Cyril E. *The Dynamics of Modernization: A Study in Comparative History.* New York: Harper and Row, 1966.

Chaudhuri, K.N. *Asia before Europe: Economy and Civilisation of the Indian Ocean from the Rise of Islam to 1750.* Cambridge, Eng.: Cambridge University Press, 1990.

Crosby, Alfred W. *Ecological Imperialism: The Biological Expansion of Europe, 900–1900.* New York: Cambridge University Press, 1986.

Curtin, Philip D. *Cross-Cultural Trade in World History.* New York: Cambridge University Press, 1984.

Headrick, Daniel R. *The Tentacles of Progress: Technology Transfer in the Age of Imperialism, 1850–1940.* New York: Oxford University Press, 1988.

Jones, E.L. *Growth Recurring: Economic Change in World History.* Oxford: Oxford University Press, 1988.

McNeill, William H. *Plagues and Peoples.* Garden City, N.Y.: Anchor, 1976.

———. *The Rise of the West: A History of the Human Community.* Chicago: University of Chicago Press, 1963.

Spengler, Oswald. *The Decline of the West.* 2 vols. Trans. by C.F. Atkinson. New York: Knopf, 1934.

Strobel, Margaret. *European Women and the Second British Empire.* Bloomington: Indiana University Press, 1991.

Toynbee, Arnold J. *A Study of History.* 12 vols. Oxford: Oxford University Press, 1934–1961.

Wallerstein, Immanuel. *The Modern World-System.* 3 vols. to date. New York: Academic Press, 1974– .

Wolf, Eric. *Europe and the People without History.* Berkeley: University of California Press, 1982.

References

Bentley, Jerry H. *Shapes of World History in Twentieth-Century Scholarship.* Washington: American Historical Association, 1996.

Costello, Paul. *World Historians and Their Goals: Twentieth-Century Answers to Modernism.* DeKalb: Northern Illinois University Press, 1993.

Lockard, Craig A. "Global History, Modernization, and the World-System Approach: A Critique." *The History Teacher* 14 (1981): 489–515.

So, Alvin Y. *Social Change and Development: Modernization, Dependency, and World-System Theories*. Newbury Park, CA: Sage, 1990.

World-Systems Theory/ Dependency Theory

World-systems theory is not really a theory, but rather a project that attempts to develop a historical social science freed from a number of biases, particularly evolutionism, reductionism, Eurocentrism, statecentrism, and compartmentalism. The proponents of this project call for a new approach, one that looks at the world as a system. Only then, they argue, will we be able to establish a historical social science free of the above failings. This is a collective project. Immanuel Wallerstein is one of its most prolific authors, but many others join him.

The world-systems project has its origins in dependency theory, which flourished in the 1960s and 1970s. This theory, or set of ideas, was spearheaded by economists and other social scientists in Latin America especially, who sought to explore the reasons for the continuing unequal relationships between the peoples of the industrialized (developed) North and the underdeveloped South. Drawing on the thinking of Marx and Lenin, these scholars rejected the liberal assumption central to the modernization approach, that underdevelopment was due to inadequate national policies and insufficient understanding of Western technology in the South. They argued instead that underdevelopment was largely the result of unequal and exploitative economic relations between the dominant powers in the North (metropole) and their client states in the South (periphery). Examining patterns of trade and exchange between developing and industrialized countries, these scholars concluded that economic underdevelopment is created by a persistent outflow of money and goods from the South to the North, that prospects for development in any one country are determined by its position in the international economy, and that the position of each country in the international economy is historically determined. Moreover, they believe underdeveloped (developing) countries cannot expect to pass through the same phases of economic development as advanced capitalist countries because their internal conditions are different and that the industrially advanced countries at various stages of development have been able to use underdeveloped economies as sources of cheap raw materials and as markets for their goods and surplus capital. Scholars writing in this tradition argue that these unequal relations are perpetuated and managed by a clientele class in the South that collaborates with the dominant capitalist class in the North. Markets and technology transfers are thus structured in ways that maintain and perpetuate underdevelopment in the South and the domination of the North. To overcome this, dependency theorists called for the overthrow of this clientele class, an end to links with the North, and a focus on self-reliant development. This perspective and its prescriptions attracted many intellectuals (and some policymakers) in the South, who saw in it both an explanation for their underdevelopment and a means to overcome that legacy.

The world-systems project has drawn on this perspective, along with that of the Annales school of history, with its rejection of positivist mainstream history and its insistence on a holistic approach to historical analysis, and on the realist tradition in international relations theory, particularly its interpretation of nation-state behavior. The world systems approach argues that a capitalist world economy has been in existence since the sixteenth century. From then on, according to world-systems scholars, the capitalist system has incorporated a growing number of previously more or less isolated and self-sufficient societies into a complex system based on functional relationships. The process of expansion has occurred at the level of geography and socioeconomic change. As a result, a small number of core states have transformed a huge external arena into a periphery. Between these core states and the periphery, the world-systems theorists believe semiperipheries have had a key role in the functioning of the system. The core states have taken the role of industrial producers while the periphery produce agricultural goods. However, this division is not seen as the result of two different and incompatible systems of capitalism, as dependency theorists argue. Rather, the world is seen as a whole system, in which economic and political cycles continually occur, but where the economic rather than the political forces have preeminence. This interpretation avoids the dependency theorists' tendency to divide the world into two distinct warring camps—the developed and the underdeveloped worlds. Rather, Wallerstein and his colleagues believe the incorporation of peripheral areas into the world system will be completed in the next fifty years, when the Marxist model of the world capitalist system will correspond to empirical reality. They predict the eventual weakening of the core states as the semiperiphery takes on an increasingly important role. Development will have to come through movement toward semiperipheral status, an option available to comparatively few countries.

Most liberals and neoclassical economists reject the world systems and dependency perspectives outright. Some Marxists have raised questions as well, pointing out that dependency theorists have simply turned modernization on its head, arguing against capitalism and technology transfers rather than for them. These critics do not see capitalism as the cause of underdevelopment; rather they believe classes and contradictions within Third World nations and their impact on relations with the North must be understood if one is properly to evaluate Third World development (or underdevelopment). World-systems theory is criticized for its preoccupation with circulation rather than production, its tendency to ignore the role of class and class struggle, and its rather premature assumption that we can identify a world bourgeoisie and a world proletariat. However, adherents of this perspective, while recognizing the need to respond to some of these criticisms, maintain their loyalty to the approach and continue to develop their analysis within the world-systems framework.

Jane L. Parpart

See also IMPERIALISM; MODERNIZATION THEORY; WORLD HISTORY.

References

Amin, S., G. Arrighi, A.G. Frank, and I. Wallerstein. *Dynamics of Global Crisis.* New York: Monthly Review Press, 1982.

Frank, A.G. *Reflections on the World Economic Crisis.* New York: Monthly Review Press, 1981.

Hettne, Bjorn. *Development Theory and the Three Worlds.* Second ed. London: Longman Scientific and Technical, 1995.

Wallerstein, I. *The Capitalist World Economy.* Cambridge, Eng.: Cambridge University Press, 1979.

Wu Ching

See WU JING.

Wu Feng (b. 1926)

Chinese historian. Born in Xingcheng in Manchuria, Wu graduated from Northeast University in 1951. He taught there until his retirement in 1992. Wu's major research interests focus on the histories of the Sui and Tang dynasties (581–907) and historical literature. His book *Sui Tang Wuda shi* [Histories of the Sui, Tang, and Five Dynasties] (1984) marks Wu's important contribution to the field of Chinese medieval history. On the basis of his rich knowledge, he published *Sui Tang lishi wenxian jishi* [An Examination of Historical Literature in the Sui and Tang Dynasties] (1987), a work that presents evidence of his vigor, industry, and breadth of vision and adds in significant measure to understanding of Sui and Tang historical literature. Wu has also edited several important history reference books, including *Jianming zhongguo guji cidian* [Concise Dictionary of Chinese Ancient Books], *Zhonghua sixiang baoku* [Treasury of Chinese Thought], and *Zhonghua ruxue tongdian* [Encyclopedia of Chinese Confucianism], which are indispensable to modern students of Chinese history and thought.

Shao Dongfang

Texts

Sui Tang lishi wenxian jishi. Zhengzhou: Zhongzhou guji chubanshe, 1987.

Sui Tang Wudai shi. Shenyang: Liaoning renmin chubanshe, 1984.

References

Feuerwerker, Albert, ed. *History in Communist China.* Cambridge, MA: M.I.T. Press, 1968.

Wu Han (1909–1969)

Pioneering modern Chinese historian of the Ming period and political activist. Born into a poor landowning family, Wu attended Qinghua University in Beijing. Under the influence of his mentors, Hu Shi, Jiang Tingfu, and Gu Jiegang, he began his study of Ming (1368–1644) history. In the 1930s, his studies of society and politics from a non-Marxist historical materialist viewpoint laid the foundation for modern Ming historiography. Wu supplemented critical textual research with other sources such as archaeological findings and Ming fiction and incorporated economic and social factors in his analyses. The four versions of his biography of the Ming founder, Zhu Yuanzhang, published from 1944 to 1965, brought together his research on the early Ming and exemplified his evolution toward Marxism. In the 1940s Wu's opposition to the Nationalist government led him into political activity in the Democratic League in the United Front. After the founding of the People's Republic in 1949, he served as vice mayor of Beijing until 1966. In 1957, Wu joined the Communist Party. A newspaper article in 1965, backed by Mao Zedong, accused him of writing the opera, "The Dismissal of Hai Rui," to attack Mao and the Communist Party. This is recognized as the beginning of the Great Cultural Revolution. Wu died in prison (1969), labeled a traitor. In 1979, his reputation was restored, and he was honored by Deng Xiaoping's regime.

Mary G. Mazur

Texts

Hai Jui Dismissed from Office. Trans. C.C. Huang. Honolulu: University Press of Hawaii, 1972.

Wu Han shixue lunzhu xuanji [Selected Historical Works by Wu Han]. Ed. Beijing shi lishi xuehui. Beijing: Renmin chubanshe, 1984.

Wu Han wenji [Collected Works by Wu Han]. Ed. Li Hua, Yang Zhao, and Zhang Xikong. 4 vols. Beijing: Beijing chubanshe, 1988.

Wu Han zawen xuan [Selected *zawen* (essays) by Wu Han]. Beijing: Renmin wenxue chubanshe, 1979.

Wu Nanxing (Collective penname for Deng Tuo, Liao Mosha, and Wu Han). *Sanjiacun zhaji* [Notes from Three Villages]. Beijing: Renmin wenxue chubanshe, 1979.

References

Mazur, Mary Gale. "A Man of His Times, Wu Han the Historian." Ph.D. dissertation, University of Chicago, 1993.

Pusey, James R. *Wu Han Attacking the Present through the Past.* Harvard East Asian Monograph Series, vol. 33. Cambridge, MA: Harvard University Press, 1969.

Wu Jing [Wu Ching] (670–749)

Chinese historian and official. Born in Kaifeng, Henan province, Wu Jing had a long career in office, finishing up as tutor to the crown prince. History writing was his lifelong passion, and he spent many years in the History Office, where he worked together with the more eminent historiographer Liu Zhiji. Wu Jing was charged with the responsibilities of compiling a national history of the Tang *(Tangshu),* and in addition initiated two private projects in this regard, one annalistic and the other dynastic. He also wrote the veritable records for the reigns of Empress Wu and emperors Zhongzong and Ruizong. Wu Jing was known as a perfectionist and was inclined toward brevity and conciseness; his compulsion to revise left many projects unfinished. The *Zhenguan zhengyao* [Essentials of the Government of the True Vision Period] is his only extant work. It is an anthology of the discussions Emperor Taizong held with his ministers during his firm and forceful reign, Zhenguan (626–649). Regarded as a model for frank discourse between a strong emperor and worthy ministers, this work was widely circulated in Japan, Korea, and Vietnam; it was also translated into the Tangut, Khitan, Jurchen, Mongolian, and Manchu languages.

Jennifer W. Jay

Texts

Jogan seiyo [Essentials of the Government of the True Vision Period]. Trans. Taneshige Harada (into Japanese). Tokyo: Meiji shoin, 1986.

Zhenguan zhengyao. Shanghai Shanghai guji chuban she, 1978.

References

Twitchett, Denis. *The Writing of Official History under the T'ang.* Cambridge, Eng.: Cambridge University Press, 1992.

Wu Jung-kuang

See WU RONGGUANG.

Wu Rongguang [Wu Jung-kuang] (1773–1843)

Chinese traditional historian. Wu passed the *jinshi* examinations in 1799 and was immediately recruited into the Hanlin Academy, beginning a successful bureaucratic career that culminated in his becoming governor of Hunan in 1831. He retired in 1840 to his native Canton to devote himself to scholarship. His major work, the *Lidai mingren nianpu,* contains the dates and posthumous titles for major historical figures from the beginnings of the Han dynasty in 202 B.C. to 1843. His comments on the Qing dynasty ritual system are found in his *Wu xue lu chubian.*

Carney T. Fisher

Texts

Hsin chou hsiao hsia chi. 5 vols. China: n.p., 1905.

Lidai mingren nianpu. Shanghai: Shanghai shudian, 1989.

X

Xenophon (ca. 430–354 B.C.)

Athenian writer and acquaintance of Socrates. A member of the younger Cyrus's expedition against Artaxerxes II of Persia, Xenophon, after Cyrus's death at Cynaxa, played a key role in extricating the Greek mercenaries from Asia. Exiled from Athens in 398 B.C. probably for pro-Spartan and pro-Persian sympathies, Xenophon served in Sparta's militia and after 394 B.C. retired to an estate granted him by Sparta at Scillus near Elis. Ousted from Scillus following Sparta's defeat at Leuctra in 371 B.C., Xenophon spent his last years at Corinth and Athens, which now readmitted him. A prolific writer, Xenophon composed autobiography, political biography, philosophical biography, and biographical fiction, as well as works on Spartan constitutional history, monarchical theory, estate management, horsemanship, and cavalry command. The *Hellenica,* Xenophon's only purely historiographical work, covered Greek history from 411 to 362 B.C., and continued Thucydides' history. It is characterized by a biographical and moral thrust, a superstitious slant, and a lack of political focus and sophistication. Others of his works, notably the *Cyropaedia,* became influential in later years as models for didactic biography.

Lionel J. Sanders

Texts

The Education of Cyrus. Trans. H.G. Dakyns. London: J.M. Dent, 1914.

Hellenica. Ed. and trans. C.L. Brownson. London: Heinemann, 1918.

References

Gray, Vivienne. *The Character of Xenophon's Hellenica.* Baltimore, MD: Johns Hopkins University Press, 1989.

Momigliano, Arnaldo D. *The Development of Greek Biography.* Second ed. Cambridge, MA: Harvard University Press, 1993, 46–58.

Xenopol, Alexandru Dimitrie (1847–1920)

Romanian historian and philosopher of history. Xenopol was born in Iaşi in Moldavia. After studying law, philosophy, and history in Germany (1867–1871) and then spending a brief period as a magistrate, he became a professor of Romanian history at the University of Iaşi. He was a member of the Romanian Academy and also of the Académie des Sciences Morales et Politiques in Paris; he delivered several lectures at the Sorbonne and the Collège de France. A frequent contributor to Gabriel Monod's *Revue historique,* Xenopol also participated in a number of international conferences and became his generation's outstanding "ambassador" for Romanian historiography in the West, as Nicolae Iorga, his most famous student, would remark. He died in Bucharest. Xenopol's first historical contributions were a study of the Russo-Turkish wars, published in 1880, and a polemical work on the origins and the continuity of Romanian people (1884). But his most representative work is a six-volume general history of Romania, the *Istoria românilor din Dacia traiană* [Romanian History from Trajan Dacia] (1888–1893). This was the first complete synthesis of Romanian history (in comparison, Xenopol's most important predecessor, Mihail Kogălniceanu, had published only a single volume), and both in substance and style represented a major achievement in the writing of his country's national history. In addition to the *Istoria,* Xenopol published in 1902 the two- volume *Domnia lui Cuza Vodă* [The Reign of Prince Cuza]. His historiographical reputation rests, however, on his work in the philosophy and methodology of history. In *Les Principes fondamentaux de l'histoire* [Basic Principles of History] (1899), Xenopol attempted, in his own words "to invent a science of history," bringing to his experience as a practicing historian insights and reflections drawn from related fields such as philosophy, sociology, economics, and ethnology. In this work he became one of the earliest historians to speak of "serial laws in history." The work was subsequently thoroughly revised and published in 1908 as *La Théorie de l'histoire* [The Theory of History]. Although they are not widely read today, both of these works were much discussed and analyzed by some of the greatest historians and philosophers of the day, including Henri Berr, Emile Boutroux, Benedetto Croce, Paul Lacombe, Gabriel Monod, and Charles Seignobos.

S. Lemny

Texts

Domnia lui Cuza Vodă. 2 vols. Iaşi: Editor "Dacia," 1903.

Une énigme historique: Les Roumains au moyen-âge. Paris: E. Leroux, 1885.

Etudes historiques sur le peuple roumain [Historical Studies on the Romanian People]. Jassy: Saraga, 1887.

Histoire des Roumains de la Dacie Trajane depuis les origines jusqu'à l'Union des Principautés [Romanian History from Trajan Dacia to the Origins of the Union of the Kingdoms]. 2 vols. Paris: E. Leroux, 1896.

Istoria partidelor politice în România [A History of Political Parties in Romania]. 2 vols. Bucharest: A. Baer, 1910.

Les Principes fondamentaux de l'histoire. Paris: E. Leroux, 1899.

La Théorie de l'histoire. Paris: E. Leroux, 1908.

References

Hiemstra, Paul A. *Alexandru D. Xenopol and the Development of Romanian Historiography.* New York: Garland, 1987.

Zub, Al. *L'historiographie roumaine à l'âge de la synthèse: A.D. Xenopol* [Romanian Historiography in the Age of Synthesis: A.D. Xenopol]. Bucharest: Editura ştiinţifică şi Enciclopedică, 1983.

Xiao Gongquan [Hsiao Kung-ch'üan] (1897–1981)

Chinese political scientist and historian. Xiao attended a modern middle school in Shanghai and later entered Qinghua Academy in Beijing, where he took part in the May Fourth movement (1919). After graduating in 1920, he went to the United States, where he briefly studied journalism and later philosophy. Following his return to China (1926), Xiao taught as professor of political science at Yanjing and Qinghua universities and at Beijing Law Academy. In 1948, as the civil war worsened, he left for Taiwan before moving to the United States to teach at the University of Washington. At home in Western thought, Xiao's most important works, on various aspects of political history, were either written in English or have been translated into English.

Mary G. Mazur

Texts

Compromise in Imperial China. Seattle: School of International Studies, University of Washington, 1979.

A History of Chinese Political Thought, vol. 1. Trans. F.W. Mote. Princeton, NJ: Princeton University Press, 1979.

A Modern China and a New World: K'ang Yu-wei, Reformer and Utopian, 1858–1927. Seattle: University of Washington Press, 1975.

Rural China, Imperial Control in the Nineteenth Century. Seattle: University of Washington Press, 1960.

References

Buxbaum, David C., and Frederick W. Mote, eds. *Transition and Permanence, Chinese History and Culture: A Festschrift in Honor of Dr. Hsiao Kung-ch'üan.* Hong Kong: Cathay Press, 1972.

Xiao Yishan [Hsiao I-shan] (1902–1978)

Chinese historian whose pioneering work in the 1920s became the foundation for later research in Qing dynasty (1648–1911) history. Xiao had finished two volumes of his *Qing tongshi* [General History of the Qing Dynasty] by the time he graduated from Beijing University. His historical analysis emphasized social development and national revolution. After teaching at Qinghua and Nanjing Central universities he went to study in Europe. While at Cambridge University he collected materials on the Taiping Heavenly Kingdom, unavailable in China because of the Qing suppression of information on the rebellion. Xiao held numerous academic positions and became an active supporter of the Nationalists in the late 1940s civil war. After the Nationalist defeat

(1948), he went to Taiwan and taught at Taiwan University. Later he chaired the editorial committee for the official *Qing History* for the Republic of China.

Mary G. Mazur

Texts
Qing tongshi [General History of the Qing]. 5 vols. Taibei: Taiwan Commercial Press, 1962–1963.

Xiao Zixian [Hsiao Tzu-hsien] (489–537)
Chinese historian. Xiao Zixian was a grandson of the founder of the Qi dynasty (479–502) and served the succeeding Liang (502–557) dynasty as minister of personnel. Xiao is known to have composed a number of histories, such as works variously entitled *History of the Later Han, Draft History of the Jin*, and *Account of the Northern Expedition under the Putong Reign*. But all have been lost except the *Nan Qi shu* [History of the Southern Qi; originally called History of the Qi], which he wrote privately and presented to the Liang court. This history originally consisted of sixty *juan* (chapters), but one *juan* (probably the prefatory notes) has long been lost. Although Xiao has been criticized for writing too favorably about his ancestors in the Qi ruling house, his firsthand knowledge and privileged access to source materials are considered strong points of the *Nan Qi shu*. Xiao is noted for his concise style, especially the method of "analogical description," whereby a group of similar figures or related events are incorporated into a certain figure's biography. He also is praised for the topical studies in the *Nan Qi shu*, especially the "Treatise on the Official System," which gives a clear picture of the complicated official organization and titles characteristic of the Southern Dynasties.

Shoucheng Yan

Texts
Nan-Qi shu. Beijing: Zhonghua shuju, 1983.

References
Chai Degeng. *Shiji juyao* [Introduction to Important History Works]. Beijing: Beijing chubanshe, 1982.

Chen Qingquan, et al., eds. *Zhongguo shixuejia pingzhuan* [Critical Biographies of Chinese Historians]. Vol. 1. Zhengzhou: Zhongzhou guji chubanshe, 1985.

Xun Yue [Hsun Yüeh] (148–209)
Chinese historian and philosopher. Born into an intellectual literati family at Yingchuan, in Honan, Xun Yue lived in obscurity for forty-seven years as a result of the political upheavals in the last decades of the Later Han (25–220). When Cao Cao [Ts'ao Ts'ao] (155–220) and his followers temporarily restored the Han court at Xuchang, Honan in 196, Xun Yue was invited to join the imperial government. As custodian of the Secret Archives, he produced two major works in thirteen years. The *Hanji* [Chronicles of the Han], compiled under imperial commission, traces the rise and fall of the Former Han (206 B.C.–A.D. 9). The *Shenjian* [Extended Reflections] is a philosophical work on the political and social issues of his time. His writings, although highly praised by scholars from the third to eighth centuries, have been criticized by the Neo-Confucianists since the Song (960–1279). Today, Xun Yue is mainly known as a pioneer among dynastic chroniclers. His *Hanji* remains a valuable source for the study of Han history.

Henry Y.S. Chan

Texts
Hsun Yueh and the Mind of Late Han China: A Translation of the Shen-chien. Trans. Ch'en Ch'i-yun. Princeton, NJ: Princeton University Press, 1980.

References
Ch'en Ch'i-yun. *Hsun Yueh: The Life and Reflections of an Early Medieval Confucian.* Cambridge, Eng.: Cambridge University Press, 1975.

Y

Yamagata Bantō [Masuya Kouemon] (1748–1821)

Japanese merchant scholar. Born into a prosperous peasant family, the Hasegawa, near Osaka, he moved into Osaka in 1760 when adopted into the Masuya merchant enterprise run by an uncle. Contemporarily known as Masuya Kouemon, he is remembered in history by his nom de plume, Yamagata Bantō. In the 1790s he was active, with great success, in the reorganization of the fiscal structures of several domains, with a focus on reforming the rice exchange systems. He was an active member of the Kaitokudō, an Osaka merchant academy that promoted practical managerial skills integrated with Confucian philosophical ideals. He was a student of Dutch learning, a proponent of the heliocentric theory, an early economic theorist, and a critic of ancient lore, such as found in the creation myths, and of Buddhism. He is perhaps best remembered as author of the twelve-volume *Yume no shiro* [In Place of Dreams], written between 1802 and 1807. This work critiques the "dreams" of religion, superstition, and other escapes into fantasy, and champions scientific reasoning, especially astronomy. He considered science as the basis for a new view of knowledge and action based upon a critical skepticism toward received history and a strong emphasis upon the actual workings of political economy.

James Edward Ketelaar

Texts

Yume no shiro. In Nihon keizai sōsho, vol. 25. Tokyo: Keimeisha, 1925.

References

Najita, Tetsuo. *Visions of Virtue in Tokugawa Japan: The Kaitokudō Merchant Academy of Osaka.* Chicago: University of Chicago Press, 1987.

Yamaji Aizan (1864–1917)

Japanese socialist, Christian, and journalist. Born in Edo (Tokyo) to a family closely associated with the Tokugawa government; his father fought on the Tokugawa side in the war of 1868 and thus Aizan began his life from the losing side of the political world. Yamaji began studying English at age eleven and became a primary school instructor at sixteen. He became a Christian and joined a Methodist academy at age twenty-five. At twenty-eight he began the Christian journal *Gokyō* [Preservation of the Teaching]; at twenty-nine he joined Tokutomi Soho's *Minyusha* (People's Party) and worked as a journalist for the *Kokumin shimbun* [Citizen's Newspaper], focusing on history. Heavily influenced by Social Darwinism and Unitarian theology, he tried to champion individual rights and freedoms within the framework of a national political structure. To this end, he saw Tokugawa peasants as the precursors of the modern common citizen in their shared struggles for individual rights. He was also very active in the formation of the Japanese National Socialist Party and in protests against the imperial system. In 1909 he published a book on Ashikaga Takauji, a fourteenth-century warrior, that was strongly critical of imperial claims to national rule. Calling the court's actions "unmitigated violence and a travesty of justice" he also asserted that subsequent claims of imperial divinity were a mere "farce." His writings were banned and he was placed under censure.

James Edward Ketelaar

Texts

Yamaji Aizan shū [Selected Works of Yamaji Aizan]. Ed. Oka Toshiro. Tokyo: Sanichishóbo, 1983.

References

Kimura Tokio. *Nihon nashanorizumu shiron* [History of Japanese Nationalism]. Tokyo: Waseda Daigaku, 1973.

Yamin, Muhammad (1903–1962)

Indonesian politician and historian. Born in West Sumatra and trained as a lawyer in Batavia, Yamin was involved in Indonesian nationalist politics, in and out of parliament, from the late 1920s until his death. He was generally aligned with the radical, noncommunist Left, and became one of the leading ideologists of Sukarno's Guided Democracy in the early 1960s. Yamin was among the first to use history to support the Indonesian nationalist program. Many of his literary works had a historical setting and from 1945 he published a series of historical works whose main aim was to show the antiquity of the idea of Indonesia in the archipelago and to celebrate the memory of those historical figures whom he saw as pioneers of Indonesian unity. He was especially enthusiastic about the contribution of the fourteenth-century Javanese empire of Majapahit and its prime minister Gadjah Mada.

Robert Cribb

Texts

Gadjah Mada: Pahlawan Persatuan Nusantara. Fourth ed. Jakarta: Balai Pustaka, 1953.

References

Noer, Deliar. "Yamin and Hamka: Two Routes to an Indonesian Identity." In *Perceptions of the Past in Southeast Asia,* ed. Anthony Reid and David Marr. Singapore: Heinemann, 1979, 249–262.

Yan Shigu [Yen Shih-ku] (581–645)

Chinese historian and commentator on *Hanshu* [Han History]. *Hanshu,* the first dynastic history in China, written by Ban Gu and his sister Ban Zhao in the first century, attracted over twenty commentaries in the subsequent four centuries. One reason for such a phenomenon was that *Hanshu* contains a great number of Han-dynasty interpretations of Confucian classics. Transmitted through various intellectual lineages from pre-Han times, these interpretations themselves required a commentary to unravel them. *Hanshu*'s popularity and importance, and the plethora of piecemeal commentaries on the text, called for a more systematic commentary in the seventh century. In 637 Yan Shigu was ordered by Prince Chengqian to write a critical commentary on *Hanshu.* He critiqued, disentangled, and improved on the previous commentaries. His commentary is best known for its clarity and attention to details, and it has always been highly regarded as the standard commentary on *Hanshu.* Yan's uncle, Youqin, had also written a commentary on *Hanshu,* and it was fully incorporated into Yan's commentary without explicit acknowledgment. Some scholars have accused Yan of plagiarism while others have defended him by arguing that he was only following conventional practice in integrating within his commentary the familial tradition of scholarship on *Hanshu.*

Yuet Keung Lo

Texts

Ban Gu. *Hanshu* [Han History]. 8 vols. Beijing: Zhonghua shuju, 1962.

References

Jin Yüfu. *Zhongguo shixue shi* [History of Chinese Historiography]. Shanghai: Commercial Press, 1957.
Liu Xu. "Biography of Yan Shigu." In *Jiu Tangshu* [Old Tang History]. 16 vols. Beijing: Zhonghua, 1975.

Yan Yan [Yen Yen] (1575–1645)

Chinese historian. Yan Yan was a native of Jiading (today's Shanghai area) and obtained a licentiate-level civil-service degree during the reign of Wanli (1573–1619) in the late Ming dynasty. In 1645, when troops of the conquering Qing dynasty attacked Jiading, Yan fled to the nearby countryside and died there.

Unlike most literati in his native district, Yan was not absorbed in belles-lettres but showed a great interest in history. At the age of forty, Yan began to study Sima Guang's *Comprehensive Mirror for Aid in Governance.* After thirty years of persistent effort, and with the assistance of his student Tan Yunhou, Yan completed the supplement to that work, the *Zizhi tongjian bu,* which is regarded as second only to Hu Sanxing's commentary among great feats of scholarship on the *Comprehensive Mirror.* In Yan's view, Sima Guang had done well in treating prominent figures and political affairs, but had neglected local events and the lives of the less prominent. So Yan added to the *Comprehensive Mirror* a great deal of material (mainly from the Standard Histories) about recluses, men of letters, Buddhist and Taoist priests, women, and others. This voluminous work was not published until the early 1850s. Another historical work by Yan Yan, the *Song-Yuan xubian* [Supplement to the Comprehensive Mirror for the Song and Yuan] has not survived.

Shoucheng Yan

Texts
Tongjian buzheng lue [Outline of the Notes and Additions to the Comprehensive Mirror]. Shanghai: Shangwu yinshuguan, 1935.
Zizhi tongjian bu [Notes and Additions to the Comprehensive Mirror for Aid in Governance]. China: Sheng Kang's Sibulou, 1876.

References
Liu Naihe, and Song Yanshen, eds. *Zizhi tongjian conglun* [Collected Studies of the Comprehensive Mirror for Aid in Governance]. Zhengzhou: Henan renmin chubanshe, 1985.

Yanagita Kunio (1875–1962)

Japanese historian and folklorist. Yanagita was born in a rural district of Hyogo prefecture and studied at Tokyo University. After graduating in 1900, he worked first at the Ministry of Agriculture and Commerce and was then employed as a counselor in the Cabinet Legislation Bureau, and as the chief secretary of the House of Peers. On his retirement from public service in 1920, he became active as a professional folklorist, specializing in the problem of peasant poverty. He authored a number of historical works such as *Toshi to Nōson* [Large Cities Vs. Villages] (1929) and *Meiji Taishō shi Sesō–hen* [A History of the Meiji and Taishō Eras] (1931). According to these studies, Japanese industry was remarkably well-developed in the early twentieth century, but agriculture remained relatively backward. Consequently, peasants became poorer than workers. Yanagita found that the cause of their poverty stemmed from precapitalistic modes of management, and he advocated the movement of agricultural policy toward more capitalistic methods. He proposed regionalism as a solution to this problem; although usually considered folklore rather than history, his work offered profound insights into the mentality of the Japanese peasantry.

Takashi Fujii

Texts
Yanagita Kunio Zenshū [The Complete Works of Yanagita Kunio]. Tokyo: Chikumashobó, 1989–1991.

References
Takashi Fujii. *Yanagita Kunio—Keiseisaimin no gaku* [Yanagita Kunio: His Social Policy]. Nagoya: Nagoya University Press, 1995.

al-Ya'qūbī, Aḥmad ibn Abi Ya'qūb (d. ca. 897)

Arabic-Islamic historian and geographer. Al-Ya'qubi was in all probability the first world cultural historian of Islamic civilization, the first to attempt to place his own Islamic culture in the context of previous universal cultures. Little is known of his life except that he was born in Baghdad, traveled extensively in his youth, and worked in Egypt as a state bureaucrat. The *Ta'rīkh* [History] of al-Ya'qūbī is divided into two parts, the first devoted to ancient nations and the second to Islamic history. In the first part, the achievements of each nation in the arts and sciences are recorded. In the second, al-Ya'qūbī treats Islamic history dynastically. Among the more unusual features of this work are the accurate and often extensive citations of ancient sources and the use of astronomy to establish exact dates. Al-Ya'qūbī employs a continuous narrative style, dispensing with the more cumbersome citation of the chain of transmitters *(isnad)* of each historical report, thus helping to establish a new historiographic style more in tune with literary tastes than with the methodology of the religious sciences. Al-Ya'qūbī also wrote a short but important treatise entitled *Mushākalat al-Nās li zamānihim* [The Affinity of People with Their Own Times], in which he attempted to show how people tend to imitate the manners and conduct of their rulers.

Tarif Khalidi

Texts
Ta'rīkh. Ed. M.T. Houtsma. Leiden: E.J. Brill, 1883.
Mushakalat al-Nas li zamanihim. Ed. W. Millward. Beirut: Dar al-Kitab al-Jadid, 1962.

References
Duri, A.A. *The Rise of Historical Writing among the Arabs*. Ed. and trans. Lawrence I. Conrad. Princeton, NJ: Princeton University Press, 1983.
Khalidi, Tarif. *Arabic Historical Thought in the Classical Period*. Cambridge, Eng.: Cambridge University Press, 1994.

Yates, Dame Frances Amelia, (1899–1981)

British historian of the Renaissance. After studying French at the University of London, from which she received her M.A. in 1926 (with an honorary doctorate of Letters following in 1965), Yates began her career as a private scholar. In 1941, however, she established an affiliation with the Warburg Institute (itself connected to the University of London), an association that lasted the remainder of her long life; indeed, despite her retirement from teaching in 1967, she was editor of the *Journal of the Warburg and Courtauld Institutes* from 1943 until 1981. In 1977 Yates was named a Dame of the British Empire. Although she wrote a number of earlier books on subjects such as the Italian scholar in Jacobean England, *John Florio* (1934), and on *The French Academies of the Sixteenth Century* (1947), her reputation is built primarily on those published in the 1960s and 1970s. In these compelling works, which were both stylishly written and exhaustively researched, Yates focused her attention on the growth of the Hermetic and Rosicrucian movements in the Renaissance and on the leading role that she believed they played in the development of early modern science. Yates insisted upon the survival, and even preeminence, of mysticism and magical or psychic beliefs throughout a period that other historians believed had witnessed the birth of "rational" science. Although she has been criticized for her willingness to push her theories to the extreme, often on the basis of ambiguous evidence, her pioneering work convinced modern researchers to evaluate more fully the historical context of the scientific revolution, taking into account even those widespread contemporary opinions that seem in retrospect unscientific.

Kathryn M. Brammall

Texts

The Art of Memory. Chicago: University of Chicago Press, 1966.

Astraea: The Imperial Theme in the Sixteenth Century. London: Routledge & Kegan Paul, 1975.

Collected Essays. 3 Vols. London: Routledge & Kegan Paul, 1982–1984.

The French Academies of The Sixteenth Century. London: Routledge, 1988.

Giordano Bruno and the Hermetic Tradition. Chicago: University of Chicago Press, 1964.

John Florio: The Life of an Italian in Shakespeare's England. Cambridge, Eng.: Cambridge University Press, 1934.

The Rosicrucian Enlightenment. London: Routledge & Kegan Paul, 1972.

References

Cohen, H. Floris. *The Scientific Revolution: A Historiographical Inquiry.* Chicago: University of Chicago Press, 1994.

Vickers, Brian. "Frances Yates and the Writing of History." *Journal of Modern History* 51 (1979): 287–316.

Yen Yen

See YAN YAN.

Yi Ik (1681–1763)

Korean scholar. Yi Ik lived in an age of factional struggle and gave up a political career to turn to a life of study. Although he did not write a historical work proper, he discussed methodologies of studying Korean history in great depth and with penetrating insight. He paved a way to establish *sirhak* (the branch of knowledge concerned with "practical learning") and tried to amalgamate traditional Confucian ideas with newly introduced Western scholarship. A prominent progressive scholar in Korean history, he also suggested profound reforms of his government and society. In his encyclopedic *Sŏngho Sasŏl* (ca. 1760) and in other influential works he was probably the first to advocate the study of Korean history in its own right, and to call for an open-minded approach to neighboring countries, including Japan. His inclusion of Manchuria and northeastern China in the boundaries of early Korean kingdoms left great impact to later nationalistic historians. Yi Ik emphasized the accidental nature of history and warned against historical interpretations based on hindsight and written exclusively from the point of view of the victors; in this he was an early opponent of what Western historians two centuries later would call the "Whig interpretation" of history. He also proclaimed the need for historical criticism of documents in the search for objectivity in history.

Minjae Kim

Texts

Kukyŏk Sŏngho Sasŏl [Miscellaneous Discussions of Yi Ik]. Ed. Minjok Munhwa Ch'ujinhoe 10 vols. Seoul, 1977–1978.

References

Han U-gŭn. *Sŏngho Yi Ik Yŏn'gu* [Studies on Yi Ik]. Seoul: Seoul National University Press, 1980.

Yi Nŭng-hwa (1869–1943)

Korean historian and scholar. Yi, who collected an enormous number of historical documents during his lifetime, was one of the authors of *Chosŏnsa,* the official *History of Korea,* which was commissioned by the Japanese government. He wrote histories of all the major religions in Korea, including Buddhism, Confucianism, and Christianity. Among his many other interests were Korean shamanism, mythology, medicine, love and sex, the family, marriage, women, costumes, education, language, poetry, and social history. Yi was probably the most versatile historian of modern Korea. Many of his books pioneered new fields of study, for example women's history, which he treated in his *Chosŏn Yŏsok-ko* [History of Women in Korea].

Minjae Kim

Texts

Chosŏn Musokko [History of Shamanism in Korea]. Ed. Yi Jae-gon. Seoul: Tongmunsŏn, 1991.
Chosŏn Pulgyo T'ongsa [History of Buddhism in Korea]. Ed. Yun Jae-yong. 3 vols. Seoul: Pagyŏngsa, 1980.

References

Kim Sutae. "Yi Nŭng-hwa wa Kŭŭi Sahak [Yi Nŭng-hwa and His Historical Views]." *Tong'a Yŏn'gu* [East Asian Studies] 4 (1984): 95–124.

Yuan Hong [Yüan Hung] (328–376)

Chinese historian. A native of Henan, Yuan Hong served on the staff of Huan Wen (312–373), a powerful minister of the Eastern Jin (317–420). Yuan's interest in history concerned mainly the recent past. His major achievement was the *Hou Han ji* [Annals of the Later Han], a chronicle of Chinese history under the Later Han (25–220). Rich in detail, it incorporated a number of earlier works and served as a major source for the Standard History of that dynasty, the *Hou Hanshu* [History of the Later Han]. Much of the value of Yuan's own work was subsequently superseded by the latter, but it is still consulted for information not found elsewhere.

John Lee

Texts

Hou Han ji. Taibei: Commercial Press, 1976.

References

Han Yu-shan. *Elements of Chinese Historiography.* Hollywood, CA: W.M. Hawley, 1955, 162.

Yuan Shu [Yüan Shu] (1131–1205)

Chinese historian. A native of Fujian, Yuan Shu passed the civil service examination in 1163, but subsequently led an undistinguished career. His fame rests rather on a major new innovation that he helped introduce to Chinese historiography. Written with the aim of making the *Zizhi tongjian (Tzu-chih t'ung-chien)* [Comprehensive Mirror in Aid of Government] of Sima Guang [Ssu-ma Kuang] (1019–1086) easier to use, his *Tongjian jishi benmuo (T'ung-chien chi-shih pen-mo)* [Beginnings and Ends of the Events in the Comprehensive Mirror] rearranged its content on the basis of 239 major events between 403 B.C. and A.D. 959. The narrative for each event was arranged chronologically. Published in 1174, it was widely admired by his contemporaries and ultimately gave rise to a new style of event-based historiography, referred to generally as the *jishi benmuo* style or *benmuo* style.

John Lee

Texts

Tongjian jishi benmuo [Beginnings and Ends of the Events in the Comprehensive Mirror]. Shanghai: Shanghai kuchih chubanshe, 1994.

References

W.G. Beasley and E.G. Pulleyblank, eds. *Historians of China and Japan.* London: Oxford University Press, 1961, 158–159.
Han Yu-shan. *Elements of Chinese Historiography.* Hollywood, CA: W.M. Hawley, 1955.

Yugoslav Historiography

See CROATIAN HISTORIOGRAPHY; SERBIAN HISTORIOGRAPHY.

Z

Zavala, Silvio A. (b. 1909)

Mexican historian. Zavala was born in Mérida, Yucatán, and studied in Mexico before attending the Universidad Central de Madrid. Here he studied under Rafael Altamira and received his degree in 1931. His thesis, which dealt with the Spanish conquest of Mexico, was published soon after and determined the direction of his subsequent career. Zavala taught at the Colegio de México, served as the secretary and director of many organizations, and was the founder and editor of *Revista de Historia de América* [Review of the History of America]. The scope of Zavala's interests has reached well beyond the confines of Mexico. He studied both Latin American history and the Americas over extended periods. In particular, he pioneered the history of the indigenous peoples of Latin America, stressing the role of the conquest and the encounter, and developed the study of the encomienda and of Indian slavery. He also studied the early historian of the Conquest, Bartolomé de Las Casas. Within Latin America, he was one of the few historians to see the value of a hemispheric approach and stressed the history of the Americas as a wider region. He wrote *The Colonial Period in the History of the New World* (1962) and the monumental, two-volume *El mundo americano en la época colonial* [The American World in the Colonial Epoch] (1967).

Russell M. Magnaghi

Texts

The Defence of Human Rights in Latin America, Sixteenth to Eighteenth Centuries. Paris: UNESCO, 1964.

La encomienda indiana [The Indian Encomienda]. Madrid: Imprenta helénica, 1935.

De encomiendas y propiedad territorial en algunas regiones de la América española [Encomiendas and Territorial Property in Some Regions of Spanish America]. México City: Antigua librería Robredo, de J. Porrúa e hijos, 1940.

Los esclavos indios en Nueva España [Indian Slavery in New Spain]. México City: Colegio Nacional, 1967.

La Filosofía política en la conquista de América [Philosophy of the Conquest of America]. México City: Fondo de Cultura Económica, 1947, 1984.

References

Bakewell, Peter. "An Interview with Silvio Zavala." *Hispanic American Historical Review* 62 (1982): 553–568.

Chevalier, François. "Silvio Zavala, primer historiador de la América hispano-indígena: El caso del trabajo de la tierra [Silvio Zavala, First Historian of Spanish Native America: The Case of the Labor of the Land]." *Historia Mexicana* 39 (1989): 21–31.

Zaydān, Jurjī [Zaidan, Gurgi] (1861–1914)

Lebanese-Egyptian journalist, historian, and historical novelist. Born into a Greek Orthodox family in Beirut, Zaydān enrolled at the Syrian Protestant College (now the American University of Beirut) as a medical student in 1881, but left the college a year later. In 1883, he arrived in Cairo and soon decided upon a career in journalism and history. In 1884 he accompanied the British expedition to Khartoum as a translator. In the summer of 1886, he visited London, to familiarize himself with Islamic manuscripts at British institutions. After his return to Cairo in the winter of 1886, he emerged as one of the leading advocates of Arab nationalism. Zaydān's single most important contribution to the Arab cause was the publication of *Al-hilāl*, a journal devoted to Arab and Islamic heritage. Founded in 1892, *Al-hilāl* became an overnight success and is still in publication today. Zaydān is one of the founders of the genre of historical novels in Arabic literature. He used his twenty-one novels as a medium for popularizing Arab civilization and history. His works in history and linguistics are also devoted to the same cause. His five-volume *Ta'rīkh al-tamaddun al-Islami* [History of Islamic Civilization] (1902–1906) is principally a history of Arab contributions to Islamic culture. His advocacy of Arab nationalism also led him to a strong interest in linguistics. Unlike his Muslim compatriots, who saw Islam as the principal basis of Arab nationalism, for Zaydān it was common language and heritage that united the Arabs.

Hootan Shambayati

Texts

Muallafat Jirji Zaydān al-kamilah [Collected Works]. 21 vols. Beirut: Dar al-Jil, 1981–1983.
Ta'rīkh al-tamaddun al-Islami. 5 vols. Cairo: Matba'at al-Hilal, 1902–1906.
Umayyads and Abbasids: Being the Fourth Part of Jurji Zaydan's History of Islamic Civilization. Trans. D.S. Margoliouth. Westport, CT: Hyperion Press, 1980.

References

The Autobiography of Jurji Zaidan: Including Four Letters to His Son. Ed. and trans. Thomas Philipp. Washington, DC: Three Continents Press, 1990.
Ayalon, Ami. *The Press in the Arab Middle East.* New York: Oxford University Press, 1995.
Philipp, Thomas. *Gurgi Zaidan: His Life and Thought.* Beirut: F. Steiner, 1979.

Zeitgeist

German term referring to the dominant spirit of a historical period, the "climate of opinion" or the "spirit of the age." The concept presupposes that history consists of a series of discrete eras and that a single pervasive belief system or worldview determines the intellectual, social, and political life of each era as a whole. These assumptions first appeared in eighteenth-century philosophers' awareness of their century's epochal uniqueness, reflected in Voltaire's enquiries into the "spirit of the times" or Kant's description of the modern "critical age." Hegel expressed the Romantic and Idealist understanding of *Zeitgeist* as the identity of human history and the divine. According to Hegel, the level of human intellectual development *and* the unfolding presence within human history of Spirit, or God, determine the character of every epoch. Hegel's philosophy sought to apprehend the intellectual content of each epoch, while maintaining that no form of human knowledge, including philosophy, may transcend the spirit of its own epoch. Although historicists like Leopold von Ranke and Jacob Burckhardt rejected Hegel's belief that the *Zeitgeiste* of individual epochs are stages in the universal history of the *Geist der Zeit* (spirit of the time), the assumption that knowledge and values are time-bound remains fundamental to all forms of Historicism and historical relativism. In the twentieth century, the *Zeitgeist* concept has been particularly influential in some forms of intellectual history, like the German *Geistesgeschichte* (intellectual history) or A.O. Lovejoy's "history of ideas." It has also influenced modern thinking about historical periodization, causation, and meaning. Nonetheless, the idealist presuppositions of the concept have produced many critics. Marx's analysis of ideology, the Annales school's *"histoire des mentalités,"* Mannheim's "sociology of knowledge," Kuhn's "paradigm," or Foucault's *"épistème"* are all related to the *Zeitgeist* concept, but they represent attempts to anchor the historical formation of knowledge, beliefs, and values in social, political, or economic relations, or the specific practices of institutions and scientific disciplines.

Warren Breckman

See also HISTORICISM; IDEAS, HISTORY OF; *KULTURGESCHICHTE;* MENTALITIES; ROMANTICISM.

References

Baur, Karl. *Zeitgeist und Geschichte* [Zeitgeist and History]. Munich: Callwey, 1978.
Collingwood, R.G. *The Idea of History.* Revised ed. New York: Oxford University Press, 1993.
Löwith, Karl. *From Hegel to Nietzsche.* Trans. D.E. Green. New York: Holt, Rinehart and Winston, 1964.

Zhang Binglin [Chang Ping-lin] (1869–1936)

Chinese revolutionary intellectual and historian. A native of Zhejiang, Zhang Binglin spent his youth studying privately and became involved in the anti-Manchu revolutionary movement. Persecuted by the authorities, he fled in exile to Japan three times between 1898 and 1906 and was imprisoned between 1903 and 1906. Beginning with the *Qiushu (Ch'iu-shu)* [Book of Persecutions], published in 1901, Zhang wrote eclectically on Chinese culture and history, presenting a uniquely ethnocentric reinterpretation. He was also influenced by Buddhist philosophy and showed an inclination toward nihilism and anarchism.

John Lee

Texts

Zhang Shi congshu [Collected Works of Zhang Binglin]. Hangzhou: Zhejiang Library, 1919.

Zhang Taiyan xuanji [Selected Works of Zhang Binglin]. Shanghai: Renmin Chubanshe, 1981.

References

Chang, Hao. *Chinese Intellectuals in Crisis: Search for Order and Meaning (1890–1911)*. Berkeley and Los Angeles: University of California Press, 1987, 104–145.

Shimada, Kenji. *Pioneer of the Chinese Revolution: Zhang Binglin and Confucianism*. Trans. Joshua A. Fogel. Stanford, CA: Stanford University Press, 1990.

Zhang Xuecheng [Chang Hsueh-ch'eng] (1738–1801)

Chinese historian and writer. Zhang was born into a gentry family in Zhejiang province; his father, who had obtained his *jinshi* degree, taught in a few academies but never held a high post in the government. Zhang himself achieved his *jinshi* degree only in 1778, after a number of failed attempts, when he was already forty-one years old. But his success in the examination did not assist him in securing a governmental post, owing in part to his shy and eccentric personality. Consequently, Zhang was obliged to take several successive teaching positions to support his family. On some other occasions, he was commissioned to edit a few gazeteers *(Fangzhi),* in which he put into practice his own theories of gazeteer writing. He believed that the gazeteers should use local sources and eyewitness material and have an accent on recent events instead of remote ones.

Zhang's major contribution to Chinese historiography is his *Wenshi tongyi* [General Meaning of Literature and History], most of which he completed in the face of constant and severe economic difficulties. Zhang stated that all knowledge, including history, should serve practical statesmanship. He opposed the tendency of the prevailing *Kaozheng* (evidential research) school, which encouraged scholars to focus only on the details. He likewise preferred the writing of general history to that of dynastic histories, on the grounds that the former enables one to see the long-term outcomes of human action. Zhang brought a broad and inclusive outlook to historical sources. According to him, all the records of the past—including epitaphs, stone and bronze inscriptions, local gazeteers, genealogies, proverbs, and even songs—were potential sources for historical study. He also argued that the classics were indeed past histories. But these original ideas failed to be noticed in Zhang's time. It was left to modern scholars such as Hu Shi (1891–1962) to resuscitate people's interest in Zhang and his achievement in historiography.

Q. Edward Wang

Texts

Jiaochou Tongyi tongjie [A Complete Exegesis of the General Meaning of Bibliography]. Shanghai: Shanghai guji chubanshe, 1987.

Wenshi Tongyi xinbian [A New Edition of the General Meaning of Literature and History]. Ed. Cang Xiuliang. Shanghai: Shanghai guji chubanshe, 1993.

Zhang Xuecheng yishu [Zhang Xuecheng's Bequeathed Works]. Beijing: Wenwu chubanshe, 1985.

References

Cang Xiuliang. *Zhang Xuecheng he Wenshi Tongyi* [Zhang Xuecheng and the General Meaning of Literature and History]. Beijing: Zhonghua shuju, 1984.

Demieville, P. "Chang Hsueh-ch'eng and His Historiography." In *Historians of China and Japan,* ed. W.G. Beasley and E.G. Pulleyblank. London: Oxford University Press, 1961, 167–186.

Hu Shi. *Zhang Shizhai* [Zhang's penname] *nianpu* [A Chronological Biography of Zhang Xuecheng]. Shanghai: Shangwu yinshuguan, 1929.

Nivison, David S. *The Life and Thought of Chang Hsueh-cheng (1738–1801)*. Stanford, CA: Stanford University Press, 1966.

Zhao Yi [Chao I] (1727–1814)

Chinese historian and poet of the Qing period. After passing the civil service examinations and becoming the *juren* at twenty-four, Zhao was recruited into the Historiographical Office at court, working on the *Comprehensive Mirror as an Aid to Government.* Later he became the *jinshi* and took other posts in the court, such as that of secretary to the Grand Council, and in the local governments of southeast China. He retired to his hometown Wujin in Jiangsu province in his forties, where he spent the remainder of his life on scholarly activities. Zhao, along with Qian Daxin and Wang Mingsheng, was one of the three highly acclaimed historians in the late Qing dynasty, well known for his evidential research on ancient historical texts. But, unlike Qian and Wang, who concentrated on giving exegeses to the ancient texts, Zhao attempted historical synthesis, using inductive method to collect and compare various contemporary and later records. He therefore noticed and attempted to shed light on general trends in history. *Nianer shi zhaji* [Miscellaneous Notes on the Twenty-Two Dynastic Histories], completed in 1796 and first published in 1799, was Zhao's most representative work and embodies his historical methodology. In his own time, however, Zhao was better known as a poet than a historian. It was late Qing scholars like Liang Qichao and the Canadian historian E.G. Pulleyblank who discovered Zhao's outstanding contribution to the development of historical methodology in China.

Q. Edward Wang

Texts

Nianer shi zhaiji [Miscellaneous Notes on the Twenty-Two Dynastic Histories]. Ed. Wang Shumin. 2 vols. Beijing: Zhonghua shuju, 1984.

References

Du Weiyun [Tu Wei-yun]. *Zhao Yi zhuan* [A Biography of Zhao Yi]. Taibei: Shibao wenhua chuban shiye youxian gongsi, 1983.

Elman, Benjamin A. *From Philosophy to Philology: Intellectual and Social Aspects of Change in Late Imperial China.* Cambridge, MA: Harvard University Council on East Asian Studies, 1984.

Liang Qichao [Liang Ch'i-ch'ao]. *Intellectual Trends in the Ch'ing Period.* Trans. Immanuel C.Y. Hsu. Cambridge, MA: Harvard University Press, 1959.

Zheng Qiao [Cheng Chiao] (1104–1162)

Chinese historian and bibliographer. Zheng Qiao was born in Putian, Fujian, and spent most of his life studying and writing in the Jiaji Mountains of his home district. In A.D. 1149 manuscripts of certain of his works, which he carried to the capital on foot, were accepted for inclusion in the Imperial Library. Zheng was ordered in 1162 to present his major work, the *Tongzhi* [Comprehensive Historical Record], to the throne, but died shortly thereafter. Zheng was noted for his critical spirit and his idea of *huitong* (unity and wholeness) in writing history. His wide ranging studies included paleography, philology, phonetics, astronomy, mathematics, and geography. Unlike most scholars of his time, Zheng sought experiential knowledge of natural objects such as plants and insects. His critical attitude was manifest in his challenge to the authenticity of prefaces to the *Book of the Odes.* Zheng's aim was to compile a comprehensive history that incorporated all knowledge of culture and nature and ran through dynastic divisions. To that end he compiled the *Tongzhi,* which he hoped would make all other histories obsolete. Zheng's originality lay mainly in the work's "Twenty Treatises," especially those on families and clans, philology, phonetics, the collation and classification of books, charts and tables, metal and stone inscriptions, natural calamities and blessings, and plants and insects.

Shoucheng Yan

Texts

Erya zhu [Commentary on the *Erya*]. In *Xuejin taoyuan.* Reprinted in *Baibu congshu jicheng.* Taibei: Yiwen yinshuguan, 1965.

Jiaji yigao [Collected Works of Zheng Qiao]. In *Congshu jicheng chubian.* Shanghai: Shangwu yinshuguan, 1935–1937.

Tongzhi. Shanghai: Shangwu yinshuguan, 1935.

References

Liu Jie. *Zhongguo shixueshi gao* [Draft History of Chinese Historiography]. Zhengzhou: Zhongzhou shuhuashe, 1982.

Zhang Xu. *Tongzhi zhongxu jian* [Commentary on the "General Introduction" to the *Tongzhi*]. Shanghai: Shangwu yinshuguan, 1924.

Zhu Xi [Chu Hsi] (1130–1200)

Chinese philosopher and historian. Zhu Xi dominated Chinese thought for seven hundred years from the Southern Song, through the Yuan, Ming, and Qing dynasties. He wrote about and commented on historical and contemporary people and events. He critically examined historical sources with a view to determining their authorship and authenticity, employing scientific methods such as collation, emendation, and phonetics. He doubted not only the authorship but also the accuracy of the contents of revered Confucian classics and, while collating different editions of the various works, looked for corruptions that had occurred during transmission. One of the important works he produced was the *Tong jian gang mu,* an abridgment of Sima Guang's monumental and voluminous work *Zi zhi tong jian* [Comprehensive Mirror as an Aid to Government], published in 1084. The size, chronological approach, and scattered nature of the *Comprehensive Mirror* made it difficult to get a complete picture on a topic, from beginning to end. Zhu Xi condensed the *Comprehensive Mirror* from its original 294 to 59 chapters, rearranging thematic material in order to make information on particular topics more accessible. His work enjoyed high esteem and influence during the Ming and Qing dynasties, especially after the Kang Xi emperor of the Qing dynasty designated it as the work to be used by candidates in preparing to take the civil service examinations.

Tao Tien-yi

Texts
Zhu zi da chuan [Complete Collection of the Literary Works of Master Zhu]. Si Bu Bei Yao ed. Shanghai: Zhonghua shuju, 1929.
Zhu zi wen ji [Collection of Literary Works of Master Zhu]. Shanghai: Shang wu yin shu guan, 1936.

References
Chan Wing-tsit. *Chu Hsi, Life and Thought.* Hong Kong: The Chinese University Press, 1987.
Qian Mu. *Zhu zi xin xue an* [New Study of Master Zhu's Thought]. Taibei: San min shu ju, 1971.

Zlatarski, Vasil (1866–1935)
Bulgarian historian. Born in Tûrnovo, Zlatarski studied history in Saint-Petersburg and archaeology in Berlin. From 1906 until his death he was a professor of Bulgarian and Balkan history at the University of Sofia. Zlatarski's main field of research was the period from the formation of the first Bulgarian Empire (681–1018) until the collapse of the second (1186–1393) as a result of the Ottoman conquest (with nearly two centuries of Byzantine dominance in between). It was he who introduced this periodization, which is still generally accepted. Zlatarski was particularly interested

in the development of the state institutions and the cultural aspects of Bulgarian medieval history and paid due attention to the proto-Bulgarian founders of the Bulgarian state. As an archaeologist, Zlatarski initiated the excavations in the inner city of the old Bulgarian capital of Preslav. He synthesized his more than two hundred publications in the monumental but unfinished *History of the Bulgarian State During the Middle Ages* (1918–1940).

R. Detrez

Texts
Istoriya na bûlgarskata dûrzhava prez srednite vekove [History of the Bulgarian State during the Middle Ages]. 3 vols. Sofia: Nauka i izkustvo, 1970–1972.
Izbrani proizvedeniya [Selected works]. Ed. Petŭr Petrov. Sofia: Nauka i izkustvo, 1971.

Zosimus [Zosimos] (fl. 500)
Byzantine official and historian. Zosimus held the honorific title of *comes* (count) and was a lawyer in the imperial treasury. Nothing else is known about his life, although it is evident from his work that he was a pagan. His *New History,* written about 501, deals with Roman history to A.D. 410. It generally blames the fall of Rome on Christianity and emphasizes events in Constantinople, giving us information not elsewhere available about aspects of late antiquity, particularly the third century and the last years of the fourth.

Stephen A. Stertz

Texts
Historia Nova. Ed. L. Mendelssohn. Leipzig: B.G. Teubner, 1887.
New History. Trans. R.T. Ridley. Sydney: Australian Association for Byzantine Studies, 1982.

References
Condurachi, E. "Les idées politiques de Zosime [Political Ideas of Zosimus]." In *Rivista classica.* Bucharest: Faculté des Lettres, 1941–1942, 115–127.
Green, T.M. "Zosimus, Orosius and Their Traditions: Comparative Studies in Pagan and Christian Historiography." Ph.D. dissertation, New York University, 1974.
Paschoud, François. *Cinq études sur Zosime* [Five Studies on Zosimus]. Paris: Presses universitaires de France, 1975.

Z

Zuo Qiuming [Tso Ch'iu-ming]

Chinese historian, traditionally accepted as author of the *Zuozhuan* (fl. fourth century B.C.?). The Zuo Qiuming who is praised by Confucius in the *Analects,* is traditionally taken as the author of the *Zuozhuan* commentary on the *Chunqiu* [Spring and Autumn Annals] and the *Guoyo* [Discourses on State]. The sinologist Bernhard Karlgren maintains that the textual evidence suggests that both books are not by the same author. Modern scholars deny Zuo's authorship of either work, claiming that the *Zuozhuan* was composed by an anonymous author early in the Warring States period between 468 and 300 B.C. Citing oral transmission of historical texts, they hold that both books are the product of "blind" history storytellers, the *Zuozhuan* having been written finally by an anonymous scholar from the state of Wei, who used the *Guoyu* and several other historical sources as the basis for his narrative. He is said to have been of the school of oral transmission that took Zuo Qiuming as its founder and most prestigious exponent.

Carney T. Fisher

Texts

The Tso Chuan: Selections from China's Oldest Narrative History. Trans. Burton Watson. New York: Columbia University Press, 1989.

References

Cheng, Anne. "Ch'un ch'iu, Kung yang, Ku liang and Tso chuan." In *Early Chinese Texts: A Bibliographic Guide,* ed. Michael Lowe. Berkeley: Institute of East Asian Studies, University of California, 1993, 67–77.
Karlgren, Bernhard. *On the Authenticity and Nature of the Tso Chuan.* Goteborg, Sweden: Elanders boktryckeri aktiebolag, 1926.
Zhongshu Xu. "*Zuozhuan* de zuoche ji qi chengshu niandai [The Authorship and Date of the *Zuozhuan*]." In *Zhuongguo shixue shi lunji,* ed. Wu Ze. Shanghai: Renmin chubanshe, 1980, 60–86.

Zurara, Gomes Eanes de (1410/20–1473/4)

Portuguese historian. Born in Ribatejo, he was educated as a prótegé of King Afonso V. He was head and curator of the Royal Library from 1451 to 1454 and head of the Archives of the Realm *(Torre do Tombo)* from then until his death. The first chronicler of the Portuguese discoveries, Zurara remained firmly rooted in the tradition of medieval historical writing that viewed the commencement of the Portuguese expansion as a service to Christianity by the kings of Portugal and Prince Henry the Navigator; a national version of the Crusades against the Muslims in North Africa. These historiographical parameters are seen particularly clearly in the two most significant among the four chronicles that he wrote: *Crónica da Tomada de Ceuta por El Rei D. João I* [Chronicle of the Conquest of Ceuta by King John the First] (1644) and *Crónica dos Feitos da Guiné* [Chronicle of the Deeds of Guinea] (1841).

Jorge M. dos Santos Alves

Texts

The Chronicle of the Discovery and Conquest of Guinea. Trans. C.R. Beazley and E. Prestage. 2 vols. London: Hakluyt Society, vols. 95 and 100, 1896–1899.
Conquests and Discoveries of Henry the Navigator: Being the Chronicles of Azurara. Ed. Virginia de Castro e Almeida; trans. B. Miall. London: G. Allen and Unwin, 1936.
Crónica da Tomada de Ceuta. Ed. F.M. Esteves Pereira. Lisbon: Academia das Sciencias de Lisboa, 1915.
Crónica do Conde D. Duarte de Meneses [Chronicle of Count D. Duarte de Meneses]. Ed. Larry King. Lisbon: Univ. Nova/Faculdade de Ciências Socialis e Humanas, 1978.
Crónica do Conde D. Pedro de Meneses [Chronicle of Count D. Pedro de Meneses]. Ed. J.A. de Freitas Carvalho. Oporto: n.p.; Braga: Barbosa and Xavier, 1988.
Crónica dos Feitos da Guiné. Ed. Torquato de Sousa Soares. 2 vols. Lisbon: Academia Portuguesa da História, 1978–1981.

References

Barreto, Luís Filipe. *Descobrimentos e Renascimento: Formas de Ser e Pensar nos séculos XV e XVI* [Discoveries and Renaissance: Ways of Being and Thinking in the Fifteenth and Sixteenth Centuries]. Lisbon: Imprensa Nacional-Casa da Moeda, 1982.

Zurita y Castro, Jerónimo de (1512–1580)

Spanish humanist historian. Born in 1512 in Zaragoza into an illustrious family, Zurita's father was the court physician to King Ferdinand II. In 1548, Zurita was named the royal chronicler and, at the same time, the secretary to the Holy Office of the Inquisition, in which latter office he succeeded his father-in-law. Zurita traveled to the Netherlands, Sicily, Naples, and Rome in order to gather materials with which to explain and illustrate his historical studies. At the end of thirty years of research, he had completed his work. The last volume of his best-known book, *Anales,* was published in the year of Zurita's death. (This volume, entitled *Historia de don Fernando Católico,* is considered by some to be a separate work.) *Anales de la Corona de Aragón* [Annals of the Crown of Aragon] begins with the Muslim invasion of the Iberian peninsula and ends with the reign of Ferdinand II. Zurita's aim was to write an unbiased account of his subject; he rejected previously written histories and instead based his book on archival sources and documents. The *Anales* is organized chronologically, in the fashion of most Renaissance histories, but also includes verbatim transcriptions of many of the documents he used. His efforts to be completely objective and to present only the material found in original documents—a mark of his humanism—resulted in a dispassionate style in which the presentation of various documents and sources is broken up only by comments inserted by Zurita. The work is invaluable not least because Zurita included many archival documents that have since been lost and for which the *Anales* remains the sole source. Zurita left a number of works at his death that still remain unpublished.

His other major contribution, written in Latin was the *Indices rerum ab Aragoniae regibus gestarum* [Witnesses to the Deeds of the Aragonese Kings]. In addition, he produced critical editions of a number of texts, such as Pedro López Ayala's chronicles of Peter I, Henry II, John I, and Henry III.

Damon L. Woods

Texts

Anales de la Corona de Aragon, compuestos por Jeronimo Zurita. Ed. Angel Canellas Lopez. 9 vols. Zaragoza, Institución Fernando el Catolico, 1967–1985.

Indices de la gestas de los reyes de Aragon, desde comienzos del reinado al año 1410. Ed. Angel Canellas. Zaragoza: Institución Fernando el Catolico, 1984.

Text and concordances of the Abreviacion del Halconero. Ed. James B. Larkin. Madison, WI: Hispanic Seminary of Medieval Studies, 1989.

References

Canellas, Angel. "El Historiador Jeronimo Zurita." In *Jeronimo Zurita: Su Epoca y Su Escuela* [Conference Proceedings]. Institución "Fernando el Católico," 1986.

Z

Index

The principal purpose of this index is to aid the reader in finding material on a specific historian or historiographical subject elsewhere in the volume than under an alphabetized entry. Incidental references to subjects such as national history are not indexed, for instance a casual reference in a biographical entry to an author's interest in the history of Korea; more substantive references to such subjects, for instance an author's formulation of a major thesis or a significant contribution to a debate, are indexed. Because the index is designed to facilitate reference to specific articles under broad topics, index headings are often different than precise alphabetical entries. Thus *See* and *See also* references in the index are to index headings rather than to articles. Bold face signifies that there is an article specifically about the subject or person listed.

Names of historians mentioned only in Texts and References are not indexed. Names of monarchs or other rulers are indexed where they are specifically related to a historiographical matter but not where only mentioned incidentally to establish period. Country and place names are not indexed except where a historical work cited specifically deals with them. Universities (*e.g.,* Heidelberg; Oxford), institutes or "schools" that figure prominently in historiography or theory (*e.g.,* Frankfurt School; Ecole Pratique des Hautes Etudes) are indexed where they played a significant role, but are not indexed if mentioned only as a place where a historian earned a degree or taught. Individual works by cited authors are not indexed though anonymous or collected works by multiple authors are. Select major periodicals are indexed by title; more specialized journals are not separately indexed. Finally, cross-references given in the text are not normally repeated in the index.

Anderson, Philip 153
Andreades, Andreas 380
Andreano, Ralph 185
Andrés de Rocha, Diego 536
Andrés de Uztarroz, Juan Francisco 858
Andrews, Charles McLean 21, 450–51, 653, 680
Angelov, Dimitûr 117
Anger, Carl 812
Angkorean period, Cambodia 134–35, 189, 760
Anglo-Saxon Chronicle 177
Angyal, Dávid 432
Anker, Richard 954
Ankersmit, F.R. 202
Annales d'histoire économique et sociale 31, 93, 310, 333, 496, 850
Annales: économies, sociétés, civilisations 31, 36, 105, 289, 334, 341, 496, 548, 916
Annales School 10, 11, 22, 23, 28, **31–33**, 84, 88, 92, 104, 108, 146, 193, 214, 266, 288, 333–34, 356, 357, 473, 507, 529, 540, 544, 549, 569, 615, 638, 648, 662, 754, 792, 824, 835, 850, 859, 866–67, 911, 913, 921, 971, 986
Annals and annalistic writing 73, 176–77, 237, 272, 273, 317, 440, 483–84, 512, 587, 642, 720, 782, 783, 875; *see also* Chronicles
Annuaire de l'Afrique du Nord 10
Anquetil, Louis-Pierre 330, 883
Ansbert 212
Anselm, Saint 854
Anthropology or anthropologists 27, 44, 101, 233, 299, 350, 462, 469, 612, 651, 656, 659, 736, 793, 802–803, 845, 866, 886, 950–51
and history **33–36**, 214, 297–98, 378, 463–64, 470, 657, 964; *see also* Ethnohistory
Antiquarianism **36–39**, 45, 136, 274–75, 277, 280, 331, 353, 401, 413, 472, 530, 553, 569, 581, 591, 632, 639–40, 646, 689, 698, 718, 735–36, 771, 799, 811, 820–21, 824, 860, 865, 868–69, 892, 894, 895, 932, 965–66
pejorative sense of 39, 317, 430, 607, 839, 845, 967
Antonio, Nicolás 858
Antonovych, Volodymyr 905
Anysas, Martynas Senprusiu 565
Apel, Karl Otto 819
Apes or Apess, William **39**
Appadurai, Arjun 462
Appleby, Joyce Oldham 233
Applewhite, Harriet **336**
Appian **40**, 619–20

Aquinas, Saint Thomas 368
Arabic Historiography **40–42**, 189, 426, 435–42, 503, 521–22, 555–56, 577, 604, 620, 668–69, 679, 801, 832–33, 875, 939, 957–59, 981
Arai Hakuseki **42–43**, 484
Arana, Sabino 77
Arató, Endre 433
Arbaleste du Plessis-Mornay, Charlotte d' **43**
Arbousse-Bastide, Paul 108
Archaeology 37, **43–45**, 84, 168, 248, 276, 324, 382, 446, 517, 574, 697, 728, 843, 868–69, 932, 940–41, 989; *see also* Prehistory
archaeological evidence 215, 327, 539, 671, 789
New Archaeology 736
Prehistoric Archaeology 43–44, 735–36
Processual and post-Processual 44
Archdeacon, Thomas J. 447
Architecture, and history **45–46**, 51, 453, 569, 638, 640
Archives, Archivists and Record Offices 18, **46–48**, 83, 115, 149–50, 246, 253, 280, 286, 329, 353, 355, 432, 533, 539, 544, 557, 558, 569, 573, 578, 590, 618, 669, 686, 698, 722, 723, 747–49, 762, 771, 777, 795, 818, 849, 856, 873, 895, 917, 977, 990
Oral archives 673
Arendt, Hannah 422, 724, 773
Arguedas, Alcides 543
Ariès, Philippe **48–49**, 867
Aristotle 3, 37, 201, 250, 291, 301, 329, 562, 640, 724, 732, 816
Armstrong, John 296
Arnaudov, Mihail 117
Argenson, René-Louis de Voyer, marquis d' 331
Argentine historiography 555, 556, 626–27; *see also* Latin America
Arnaudov, Mihail 117
Arnaut, Salvador 729
Arnold, David 460, 461
Arnold, Matthew 945
Aron, Raymond 202
Arriaga, José de 728
Arrian **49**, 376, 619
Ars Historica and *trattatisti* **49–50**, 475, 562, 647–48, 700
Art, as Historical Evidence **50–52**
Art History 50–52, 143, 221, 321, 326, 371, 401, 480, 589, 693–94, 695, 771, 918, 934, 935, 947, 949
Arthur, legendary king of Britain 136, 273, 410, 653

Old Testament, or Hebrew Bible 230, 324,
374, 399, 497, 710, 739, 769, 841
Bibliography, Historical **88–89**, 168, 246, 489,
496, 532–33, 809, 869, 910, 930,
988; *see also* Book, History of the
Bičanić, R. 209
Bichurin, Nikita Iakovlevich **89–90**
Bickerman, Elias Joseph **90**
Bidwell, Percy 792
Bielefeld School, Germany 203, 859
Bielinski, Josef 564
Bielski, Marcin 720
Bierling, F.G. 838
Biji. See Chinese Historiography
Bilderdijk, Willem 252
Bilhaṇa 456
Bilsky, Lester 289, 290
Binford, Lewis Roberts 44
Bing, Gertrud 934
Biography and biographers 53, 81, **90–92**, 110,
147–48, 171, 175, 177, 212–13, 216,
255, 271 264, 272, 328, 330, 363,
376, 378, 403, 439, 441, 456–58,
475, 476, 477, 479, 493, 554, 591,
592–93, 606, 607, 621, 622, 627,
628, 647, 652, 670, 681, 696, 700,
713, 718, 726, 746–47, 752, 783,
802, 803, 833, 843, 847, 848, 859,
861, 898, 936, 947–48, 950, 953,
954, 959, 972, 975, 977; *see also* Autobiography; Prosopography
collective biography 91, 98, 195, 281, 474,
566, 608, 659, 715, 745, 857, 866,
869, 918, 966
historical biography 90, 369–70, 392,
433–34, 659
ṭabaqāt (Islamic biographical dictionaries)
436, 441, 442, 801, 957
Biondo, Flavio 37, **92**, 369, 562, 569, 582,
715, 774
al-Bīrūnī, Abu'l-Rayḥān Muḥammad **92–93**,
703
Bismarck, Otto von 362, 593, 637
Bizzarri, Pietro **93**
Black, Cyril E. 968, 969
Black History. *See* African-American Historiography
Black Legend, the 534, 538, 539, 737
Blainey, Geoffrey 58
Blake, William 236
Blakey, Robert 723
Blassingame, John W. 26, 841
bled al-makhzen vs *bled es-siba,* historical category
9, 10
Blind Harry (Scots writer) 71

Bliss, Michael 138
Bloch, Gustave 93
Bloch, Joseph 598
Bloch, Marc 23, 31, 32, 87, 88, **93–94**, 105, 193,
247, 251, 310, 333, 334, 356, 357, 373,
469, 547, 551, 611, 792, 850
Blok, Petrus Johannes 253
Bloom, Allan 733
Blumin, Stuart M. 909
Bluntschli, Johann 5
Blyden, Edward W. 396
Blythe, Ronald 673
Boahen, Albert Adu **94**
Boas, Franz 464
Boas, George 443, 444
Bobbio, Norberto 477
Bobińska, Celina 722
Bobrzyński, Michał **95**, 721
Boccaccio, Giovanni 591, 918, 963
Bock, Gisela **95**, 965
Bodin, Jean 50, 64, 91, **96**, 226, 293, 295,
325, 329, 413, 547
Bodnar, John 447, 909
Bodrova, Valentina 954
Boece, Hector **96**, 820, 821
Boehme, Jakob 236
Boethius, Anicius Manlius Torquatus Severinus
96–97, 201, 323, 580
Bofarull y Mascaró, Próspero de 145
Bogdan, Ioan 784, 785
Bogoslovskii, Mikhail Mikhailovich 797
Bogucka, Maria 722, 723
Bogue, Alan 261
Bohachevsky-Chomiak, Martha 954
Bohannan, Paul 15
Bohr, Niels 443
Bois, Guy 600
Bolingbroke, Henry St. John, Henry, Viscount
38, **97**, 294
Bolland, Jean 83, 97, 392
Bollandists and Maurists **97–98**, 330, 392,
578, 690, 771, 889
Boltin, Ivan Nikitich 796
Bolton, Geoffrey 58
Bolton, Herbert Eugene **99**, 539
Bonacich, Edna 447
Bonaparte, Napoleon 74, 131, 319, 621, 714,
741, 823, 833, 852, 884
Bonfini, Antonio 431
Boniecki, Adam 564
Bonwick, James 56
Book, History of the **99–101**, 222, 265
French *histoire du livre* 100–101, 754
Boorstin, Daniel 24, 25, **101–102**, 401
Bor, Pieter Christiaenzoon 252

Burdzhalov Eduard 855–56
  Burdzhalov affair 855–56
Burgin, Miron 544
Burke, Edmund **119**, 154, 361, 550, 579, 581,
    741, 772–73, 941
Burke, Kenneth 942
Burke, Peter 849
Burkholder, Mark A. 540
Burmese Historiography **119–22**, 342, 417–
    18, 880
Burmov, Aleksandûr 117
Burnet, Gilbert **123**, 274, 275
Burnet, Thomas **123**
Burnley, I.H. 910
Burns, E. Bradford 420
Burns, Ken 27
Burstyn, Joan 263
Burton, Antoinette 965
Burton, John Hill 822
Burtt, Edwin Arthur **123–24**
Bury, John Bagnell **124**, 201, 280, 742, 775,
    819
Business and Economic History (journal) 125
Business History **124–26**, 188, 526, 901
Business History (journal) 125
Business History Review 125
Bushman, Richard 746
Bustamente, Carlos María de 613
Butlin, Noel G. 909
Butterfield, Sir Herbert 30, **126–27**, 725, 769,
    941
Butzer, Karl 289
Byzantinium and Byzantine Empire 116, 124,
    127–29, 133, 152, 178, 277, 380,
    394, 531, 641, 680, 738, 791, 989
  Historical writing in **127–29**, 138, 378,
    620, 660, 661, 685, 712, 737, 745,
    989

C
Cabral, Amilcar 453
Cadière, Léopold **131**
Cadwallader, legendary British king 355
Caesar, Augustus 239, 256, 714, 783, 794, 875
Caesar, Gaius (or Caius) Julius **131–32**, 273,
    276, 323, 619, 714, 783, 804
Caetani, Leone **132**
Caetano, Marcello 729, 731
Caffaro of Genoa **132**
Cahen, Claude **133**
Cai Meibiao [Ts'ai Mei-piao] **133–34**
Caillet-Bois, R.R. 544
Cain, Louis 186
Cain, P.J. 449

Calamy, Edmund 276
Calancha y Benavides, Antonio de la 536
Calderwood, David 820
Calendars 174
Callaway, Helen 449
Callcott, George 19
Callender, John 18
Cam, Helen Maud **134**
Cambodian Historiography **134–36**, 189, 760,
    891–92
Cambridge Ancient History 327
Cambridge Economic History 391, 469
Cambridge Group for the History of Population
    and Social Structure 195, 231, 283,
    308, 353, 615
Cambridge History of Africa 12
Cambridge History of China 306
Cambridge History of the British Empire 448, 966
Cambridge Medieval History 77
Cambridge Modern History 4, 77, 279, 280
Cambridge "School" of Political Thought 725
Cambridge, University of 279, 289, 460
Camden, William 37, 38, **136**, 149, 259, 274,
    275, 280, 530, 569, 821, 865
Caminer, Domenico 379
Campión, Arturo 77
Canadian Historiography, English **136–38**,
    262, 681, 910, 961–62; *see also*
    Québécois Historiography
Candeloro, Giorgio 477
Cano, Melchor 858
Cantacuzenos (Kantakouzenos), John VI, Byz-
    antine emperor and memorialist 128,
    138–39, 620
Cantacuzino, Constantin 784
Cantemir, Dimitrie **139**, 784
Cantimori, Delio 102, **139–40**, 369, 477
Cantù, Cesare 476
Capgrave, John **140**
Capistrano de Abreu, João 107, **140–41**, 917
Capitalism 32, 53, 58, 125–26, **141–42**, 169,
    182, 187, 193, 205, 241, 270, 311,
    335, 398, 402, 411, 451, 452, 486,
    518, 521, 554, 598, 599–600, 627,
    633, 663, 681, 699, 741, 749, 769,
    793, 822, 899, 901, 912, 936–37,
    946, 971–72
Capmany, Antonio de 145
Capponi, Gino 476
Capponi, Neri 692
Cardim, Fernão 107
Cardozo, E. 544
Careless, J.M.S. 137, 910
Caresmar, Jaime 145
Carion [Nägelin], Johann **142**, 740

Carlyle, Thomas 91, **142–43**, 338, 787, 945
Carr, David 648
Carr, Edward Hallett **143**, 191, 235, 891
Carr, Raymond 859
Carson, Rachel 287
Cartwright, Julia 7, **143–44**, 963
Carus, Friedrich August 442
Carus-Wilson, Eleanora N. 282
Carvalho, Joaquim de 729
Casaubon, Isaac 73, 330, 414, 690
Cassiodorus **144**, 494
Cassirer, Ernst 443
Castiglioni, Branda 76
Castro, Américo **144–45**, 443, 859
Castro, Armando de 730
Cat-Mackiewicz, Stanisław 722
Catalan Historiography **145–46**, 857, 859, 921
Catalán, Diego 858
Catholicism. *See* Roman Catholicism
Cattaneo, Carlo 476
Cattley, S.R. 326
Cato, Marcus Porcius 782, 783
Catton, Bruce 27, 748
Caumont, Arcisse de 736
Causation, in history 128, **146–47**, 201, 206,
        234, 359, 360, 632, 647, 708
Cavalcanti, Giovanni 474
Cavendish, George 91
Cavendish, Margaret, duchess of Newcastle
        147–48, 318, 434
Caxton, William 272
Celalzade, Mustafa Çelebi **148**
Çelebi, Katib 645
Cellini, Benvenuto 360
Celtic Revival 472
Celtis, Conrad 37, 61, 358
Cen Zhongmian [Tsen Chung-mien] **148–49**
Censorship and persecution of historians or
        historical works 24, 38, 93, 104,
        149–50, 168, 169, 170, 210, 226,
        248, 274, 330, 347, 398, 403, 421,
        444, 476, 484, 485–86, 500, 505,
        508, 521, 533, 535, 553, 558, 559,
        592, 594, 663, 706, 716, 719, 723,
        753, 762–63, 772, 811, 834, 835,
        855, 881–82, 901, 906, 973, 979, 987
    Freedom of Information Acts 149–50
Central Asian Historiography **150–51**; *see also*
        Mongolian history and culture
*Centre de Recherches et d'Etudes sur les Sociétés
        Méditerranéennes* 10
Centre national de la recherche scientifique
        (CNRS) 155
Cerejeira, Manuel Gonçalves 729
Cervantes, Miguel de 144, 733

Cevallos, P.F. 542
Chaadaev, P.I. 623
Chabod, Federico **151–52**, 477
Chadwick, Owen 859
Chagas, Manuel Pinheiro 728
Chaikovsky, Yuri 290
Chakrabarty, Dipesh 461, 462
Chakravarty, Ranabir 290
Chalkokondyles, Laonikos 128, **152**, 378, 620
Chaloupecky, Václav 219
Chamorro, Pedro Joaquin **152**
Chance in history. *See* Contingency; Fortune
Chandieu, Antoine de la Roche 596
Chandler, Alfred D., Jr. 125, 126, 261
Chandran, Subash 290
Change, Ideas concerning historical 158, 605,
        739–43, 787
Chaos Theory **153**
Charlemagne 53, 264, 328, 700
Charles I, King of England, Scotland and Ireland
        180, 259, 274, 388, 579, 799
Charles V, Emperor 192, 583
Charles of Belsunce, Viscount 77
Charles the Bold, Duke of Burgundy 328
Chartier, Roger 100, 214, 334
Chartism 183
Chastellain, Georges **154**
Chastenay-Lanty, Louise-Marie-Victorine,
        Comtesse de **154**
Chateaubriand, François Auguste René, vicomte
        de **154–55**, 332, 741, 786
Chatterjee, Bankim Chandra 389
Chatterjee, Partha 461, 651
Chatterton, Thomas 690
Chaudhuri, K.N. 912, 969
Chaudhuri, Sashi Bhusan **155**
Chauncey, George 829, 965
Chaunu, Huguette 155, 826
Chaunu, Pierre 32, **155–56**, 333, 681, 826
Chen Bangzhan [Ch'en Pang-chan] 171
Chen Shou [Ch'en Shou] **156**, 701
Chen Yinke [Chen Yin Ko] **156**
Chen Yuan [Chen Yüan] **156–57**
Cheng, Lucie 447
Cherniss, Harold 443
Cherry, Gordon 909
Chevalier, François 613
Cheyney, Edward Potts **157**
Chiang Mai Chronicle 880
Chicherin, Boris 797
Ch'ien Mu. *See* Qian Mu
Ch'ien Ta-sin. *See* Qian Daxin
Chifflet, Jean Jacques 799
Child, Lydia Maria Francis **158**
Childe, Vere Gordon 57, 736

Macpherson, James 690
Mączak, Antonii 723
Madajczyk, Czesław 722
Madox, Thomas 275, 581–82, 895
Maeda Naonori 487
Maffei, Raffaele **582**
Maffei, Scipione 690
Magdeburg Centuries and Magdeburg
    Centuriators (German Reformation)
    73, 209, 257, **582–83**, 740, 771
Maghreb, region 8–11, 440
Magnus, Johannes 583, 811
Magnus, Olaus **583**, 811
Magnusson, Arne 811
Mahan, Alfred Thayer **583–84**, 622
Mahudel, Nicolas 735
Maier, Charles S. 203
Maiguashca, Juan 538
Maimbourg, Louis 758
Maina wa Kinyatti 150
Maior, Petru 139, **584**, 784
Mair or Major, John 820
Maisel, Witold 723
Maitland, Frederic William 77, 134, 279, 281,
    548, 551, **584–85**, 653, 717, 823,
    926
Majumdar, Ramesh Chandra 155, 416, 769
Mak Phoeun 135, 892
Maksimeiko, Nikolai A. 564
Malalas, John 128
Malaxos, Manuel 378
Malay historical writing **585–89**
Mâle, Emile 321, **589**
Malin, James 287
Malinovskii, Joannikii A. 564
Malinowski, Bronislaw 34, 464
Malone, Dumas 91, 443
Małowist, Marian 32, **589**, 722
Malthus, Thomas Robert and Malthusianism
    232, 391, 600, 732
Malti-Douglas, Fadwa 958
Mályusz, Elemér 432, 433, **590**
Mamlūks and Mamlūk period 41, 61, 235–36,
    240, 435, 440, 442, 500
Mamonova, Tatyana 954
Manchester School, Economics 53
Manchester School, History 895
Manchu language historical writing. *See* Chinese
    Historiography
Mandelbaum, Maurice 146–47, 234, 414
Mandrou, Robert Louis Réné 333, **590–91**,
    867
Manetho 378, **591**
Manetti, Giannozzo 72, **591**
Mani, Lata 462, 956

Mann, Susan 913
Mannheim, Karl 24, 266, 415, 767, 986
Mansergh, Nicholas 448
Mansi, Giovanni Domenico **592**
Manski, Ernst-Eberhard 290
al-Mansūr, sultan of Morocco 801
Manzoni, Alessandro 476
Mantegazza, Paolo 828
Mantoux, Paul 260
Mao Zedong [Mao Tse-tung] 169, 308, 487,
    557, **592**, 773, 831, 973
Maori history and tradition 658–59
Maps. *See* Atlases
al-Maqrīzī, Takī al-Dīn 61, 437, 442
Marāthā Historiography 249, **592–93**
Marcks, Erich 362, **593**
Marcus, George E. 35, 464
Marcus, Steven 828
Marcuse, Herbert 363, 757
Marczali, Henrik 432, **593–94**
Margadant, Jo Burr 263
Margarit, Cardinal 857
Mariana, Juan de 529, 858
Marianus Scotus **594**
Marion, Michel 100
Marks, Shula 853, 887
Marques, Oliveira 730, 731
Marsden, William **594–95**
Marsh, George Perkins 288
Marsh, Rosalind 954
Marshall, Alfred 216, 260
Marshall, Thomas 99
Martène, Edmond 98
Martin, Henri-Jean 100, 310
Martín, Luis 540
Martini, Martino **595**
Martire d'Anghiera, Pietro 735
Martius, Karl Friedrich Philip von 107
Martyrology 257, 273, 326, 392, 434, 497,
    595–97
Marure A. 542
Maruyama Masao 487, **597**
Marx, Karl 34, 86, 141, 182, 193, 214, 233,
    236, 255, 270, 296, 313, 361–62,
    404, 461, 467, 469, 502, 525, 526,
    528, 548, 551, 592, **597–98**, 600,
    604, 607, 648, 702, 710, 711, 724,
    741–42, 773, 815, 819, 849, 866,
    937, 942, 945, 948, 968, 971, 986
Marxism and Marxist historians 9, 11, 12–13,
    23, 26, 34, 52, 57, 87, 108, 117, 125,
    133, 135, 143, 146, 151, 168–70, 182,
    187, 193, 202, 205, 209, 211, 214,
    219, 222, 235, 236, 253, 294, 296,
    308, 309, 317, 326, 333, 334–36,

Political Thought, History of 82, 502, 580–81, 608, 718–19, **723–26**, 839
Poliziano, Angelo 690, 706, 707
Pollard, Albert Frederick 280, 651, **726**
Pollio, Asinius 782
Pollock, Sir Frederick 723
Polo, Marco 439
Polybius 40, 50, 111, 127, 136, 291, 323, 352, 369, 376, 377, 412, 580, 619, 620, **727**, 731, 739, 770, 771, 782
Pomponazzi, Pietro 301
Pomponius (Roman lawyer) 547
Poni, Carlo 616
Pontano, Giovanni 49, **727**
Pontanus, Johannes Isacius 252
Ponting, Clive 289
Poole, Reginald Lane 77, 279, 280
Pope, Alexander 670
Popper, Sir Karl R. 203, 207, 234, 235, 414, 415, 819
Popular culture 224, 369
Popular movements. *See* History from Below
Population. *See* Demography, Historical; Immigration
Porras Barrenechea, Raul 541, 544
Porshnev, Boris 638
Porter, Cathy 954
Porthan, Henrik Gabriel 317
Portuguese Historiography **300**, 370, 407, 572, **714**, **728–31**, 990; *see also* European Expansion
Portus, C.V. 57
Posidonius of Apamea 376, 378, **731**
Positivism and Positivist Historiography 20, 28, 190, 193, 207, 247, 250, 253, 371, 389, 432, 476, 532, 539, 543, 593, 648, 672, 708, 729, 739, 741, 742, 784, 809, 819, 855, 858, 870, 924, 947, 971
Postan, Sir Michael Moissey 391, 600, **732**, 734, 926
Posthumus, Nicolaas Wilhelmus 253
Postmodernism 13, 23, 59, 86, 182, 296, 311, 316, 415, 461, 551, 560–61, 603, 609–10, 617, 625, 686, 694, **732–33**, 767, 802
Poststructuralism and Deconstruction 59, 182, 323–24, 352, 357, 462, 560–61, 603, 648, 709, 726, 962
Potter, David Morris 25, 26, 28, 650
Pouget, Antoine 632
Pounds, Norman 356, 357
Poussou, Jean-Pierre 826
Power, Eileen 282, 732, **734**, 963
Powicke, F.M. 854

Poza, Andrés de 76
Prado Júnior, Caio 108
Prado y Ugarteche, Javier 539, 543
Prakash, Gyan 462, 679
Prasad, Shiva **735**
Pratt, J.W. 453
Pray, György 431
Prediction, in history 414–15
Prehistory 44, 298, 697, **735–37**
Prendergast, J.P. 472
Prentice, Alison 262
Prescott, William Hickling 19, 539, 540, 562, **737**
Presniakov, Aleksandr Evgenevich 797
Prices, history of 259, 395, 528–29
Prigogine, Ilya 153
Primat of St. Denis 328
Printing and print culture, history of 265, 310; *see also* Book, History of
Priskos of Panion 127
Private Life. *See* Public and Private
Procacci, Giuliano 477
Prochaska, Antoni 564
Procopius (Greek: Prokopios) 111, 127, 178, 582, 620, **738**
Prodan, David 785
Professionalization of history 5, 57, 83, 108, 218, 253, 279, 285, 294, 424, 432, 466, 485, 495, 496, 544, 637, **738–39**, 762, 771, 812, 822, 963–64
Progress 19, 22, 24, 46, 55, 57, 124, 168, 200, 258, 296, 408, 426, 491, 548, 579, 625, 661, 721, **739–43**, 821, 896, 918, 927, 928, 941
   Stadialism 624, 821, 941
Progressive History, in United States 21, 22–25, 137, 245, 657–58, **744–45**, 766, 850
Propaganda, panegyric or polemic 149, 248, 370, 596, 706, 830, 869; *see also* Censorship
Prosopography 91, 195, 281, **745**; *see also* Biography
Protestantism 257, 258, 338, 471–72, 530, 596–97, 625, 755, 761, 775, 808, 843, 899, 937; *see also* Catholicism; Reformation, Protestant
Providence or Providentialism 18, 25, 126, 128, 212, 285, 293, 323, 324–25, 330, 387, 388, 434, 562, 625–26, 632, 647, 739–40, 753, 760, 820, 857, 941
Prucha, Francis Paul 464
Prudentius 392
Prussian School of historians, Germany 365
Prynne, William 47

Song Dynasty, China 160–61, 164, 171, 396, 557, 567, 751, 988
Song Qi 160
Soom, Arnold 295
Sorel, Albert **852**
Source criticism (German: *Quellenkritik*) 98, 241, 252, 279, 300, 318, 319, 329, 331, 358, 417, 474, 548, 553, 559, 582, 672, 761–62, 771, 796, 823, 838, 872, 982; *see also* Philology
  Editing and Publication of sources/document collections 56, 68, 71, 77, 98, 157, 189, 221, 229, 242, 246, 264, 275, 278, 279, 310, 318, 330, 332, 346, 347, 348, 380, 381, 384, 387, 400, 412, 431, 432, 455, 475, 509, 558, 560, 563–65, 574, 617–18, 629, 639–40, 660, 661, 664, 717, 720–21, 764, 777, 785, 787, 795, 796, 799, 804, 814, 815, 816, 822, 855, 863, 865, 866, 868, 878, 894, 930, 943, 964, 966, 989, 991
Sousa, António Caetano de 728
South African Historiography **852–54**, 882, 887
Southern Historical Association 21
Southern History (U.S.) 21, 327, 734, 967
Southern Liang Dynasty, China 164
Southern, Richard William **854**
Soviet Union 51–52, 295, 565, 599
  collapse of 13, 190
  Historiography in 554, 693, 716, **854–56**
Sozomeno da Pistoia 692
Sozomenus (Greek: Sozomenos) 128
Spalding, Karen 540
Spanheim, Ezechiel 285
Spanish-American War 17, 453
Spanish Civil War 611
Spanish Historiography 144, 206, 322, 529, 533, 610, 611, **857–59**, 990–91; *see also* Basque Historiography; Catalan Historiography; Latin America
Sparks, Jared 18
Spaull, Andrew 263
Spaventa, Bertrando 476
Spear, Margaret 859
Spear, Thomas George Percival **859**
Spearitt, Peter 910
Speeches, invented, included by historians 375, 377, 580–81, 782, 888; *see also* Rhetoric
Spelman, Sir Henry 275, 547, **860**
Spencer, Herbert 247, 340, 519, 543, 710, 742, 809
Spengler, Oswald 193, 227, 521, 711, 743, **860–61**, 968
Speroni, Sperone 475

Sphrantzes, George. *See* Phrantzes
Spinoza, Baruch or Benedict de 498
Spiridon, Fr. Ieroskhimonakh 116
Spitzer, Leo 443
Spivak, Gayatri Chakravorty 461–62
Spodek, Howard 912
Spottiswoode, Archbishop John 820
Sprengel, Kurt 607
Spruill, Julia Cherry **861**
Spruner, Karl von 54
Sraffa, Piero 241
Srbik, Heinrich Ritter von **861–62**
Srećković, P. 825
Śreniowski, Stanisław 722
Sri Lanka 457–58, 586
Stadialism. *See under* Progress
Stadnicki, Kazimierz 564
Staël, Anne Louise Germaine de 332, 786, 837
Stageiritis, A. 379
Stakauskas, Juozas 564–65
Stalin, Joseph 143, 149, 235, 295, 503, 719, 773, 855, 900
  Stalinism 24, 219, 236, 415, 599, 601, 674, 693, 716, 797, 855–56, 900, 954
Stampp, Kenneth M. 26, 185, 840, 841
Stannage, C.T. 910
Stannard, David 292
Stanojević, Stanoje 825
Stapel, Frederik Wilhelm 465
Staples thesis 137, 208, 468
Starobinski, Jean 443
Starowolski, Szymon 720
Statistical analysis programs 196
Stearns, Peter 749
Stedman Jones, Gareth. *See* Jones, Gareth Stedman
Steffins, Lincoln 744
Stein, Lorenz von **862**
Stein, Stanley 917
Steiner, Kurt 913
Stelter, Gilbert 910
Stengers, Jean 84
Stenton, Doris Mary **863**
Stenton, Sir Frank Merry **863**, 926
Stephen, Leslie 91, 114, 280, 663
Stephens, John 44
Stephenson, George M. 903
Stern, Daniel **863–64**
Stern, Fritz 520
Stern, Steve J. 540
Stewart, Dugald 623
Stewart, John 136
Stichter, Sharon 528
Stijl, Simon 252
Still, Bayrd 907

Umayyad Dynasty 40, 604, 875, 939
Unanue, José Hipolito 537
Uncertainty principle 23
Underhill, Frank 137
Undzhiev, Ivan 117
UNESCO *General History of Africa* 12, 94, 670
Universities, and history 25, 57, 108, 137, 177,
    258, 260, 278–79, 294–95, 380, 486,
    495, 544, 564, 641, 721–22, 728,
    730, 738–39, 747–49, 785, 797, 812,
    818, 963; *see also* under select university
    names or locations, e.g. Heidelburg,
    Oxford, etc.
Unwin, George 259, 282, **907**
Urban, William 565
Urban History 27, 28, 286, 382, 447, 530,
    638–39, **907–14**
    Urban History (periodical) 909
    Urban History Association 909
Ureche, Grigore 784
Usque, Samuel 489
Ussher, James, archbishop and chronologer 903
USSR. *See* Soviet Union
Usuard 596

V

Vagad, Gualberto Fabricio de 857
Vahtre, Sulev 295
Vaid, Sudesh 956
Vākpatirāja 456
Valancius, Bishop Motiejus 564
Valcárcel, Carlos Daniel 541
Valcárcel, Luis E. 541
Valensi, Lucette 674
Valentijn, François **915**
Valeri, Nino 477
Valiani, Leo 477
Valla, Lorenzo 145, 257, 413, 689–90, 706,
    707, 770, 771, **915**
Vallenilla Lanz, Laureano 543
Valls i Taberner, Ferrán 145
Vaṃśāvalis 457, 654
Van Creveld, Martin L. 622
Van de Ven, G. 290
van de Walle, Etienne 470
Van den Brink, Reinier Cornelis Bakhuizen 253
Van der Veer, Peter 462
Van der Wee, Herman 84
Van der Windt H.J. 290
Van Jaarsveld, F.A. 853
Van Kirk, Sylvia 138
Vansina, Jan 12, 84, **915–16**
Varchi, Benedetto **916**
Varga, Lucie **916–17**

Varnhagen, Francisco Adolfo de 107, **917**
Varro, Marcus Terentius 37
Varsik, Branislav **917–18**
Vasari, Giorgio 45, 91, 475, 771, **918**, 947
Vasconcelos, António de 729
Vasconcelos, José Leite de 613, 728
Vauban, Sébastien le Prestre de 621
Vaughan, Megan 951
Vázquez-Machicado, Humberto 544
Vecoli, Rudolph J. 447
Vedel, Anders Sörensen 811
Vegetius 620, 621
Velasco, Juan de **918–19**
Vendotis, Georgios 379
Venelin, Yuriy 116
Venezuelan Historiography 537, 539, 682
Venturi, Franco 443, **919**
Venturi, Lionello 443
Vergil, Polydore 273, 274, 305, 356, 394, 642,
    919–20
Verissimo, José 107
Veríssimo Serrão, Joaquim 729, 731
Verlinden, Charles 32
Vernadsky, George 797, **920**
Verri, Alessandro 475
Verri, Pietro 475
Verschoor, Annie 788
Verstehen 146, 190, 214, 238, 243, 361, 937
Vertot, René-Aubert de 331
Veselovskii, Stepan Borisovich 797
Vespasiano da Bisticci 474
Veyne, Paul **920–21**
Veysey, Lawrence 262
Vianna, Francisco José de Oliveira 107, **921**
Vicens Vives, Jaime 146, 540, 859, **921**
Vicente do Salvador, Frei 107
Vicinus, Martha 965
Vickery, Michael 135, 892
Vico, Giambattista 22, 45, 87, 211, 227, 284,
    314–15, 332, 415, 442, 475, 476,
    551, 611, 615, 642, 711, 740–41,
    866, **922**, 924, 942
Victoria History of the Counties of England (or
    "Victoria County History") 38,
    280, 569
Vicuña Mackenna, Benjamin 543
Vidal de la Blache, Paul 32, 333, 356
Vierkandt, Alfred 393
Vietnam 131, 134, 135, 757, 946, 961
    Vietnamese Historiography 222, 549, 834,
        896, 900, **922–24**
*Vierteljahrsschrift für Wirtschafts- und
    Sozialgeschichte*
Vilar, Pierre 146, 859
Villani, Giovanni **924**